AN INTRODUCTION TO

Management Science

Quantitative Approaches to Decision Making

SEVENTH EDITION

AN INTRODUCTION TO
Management Science

Quantitative Approaches to Decision Making

SEVENTH EDITION

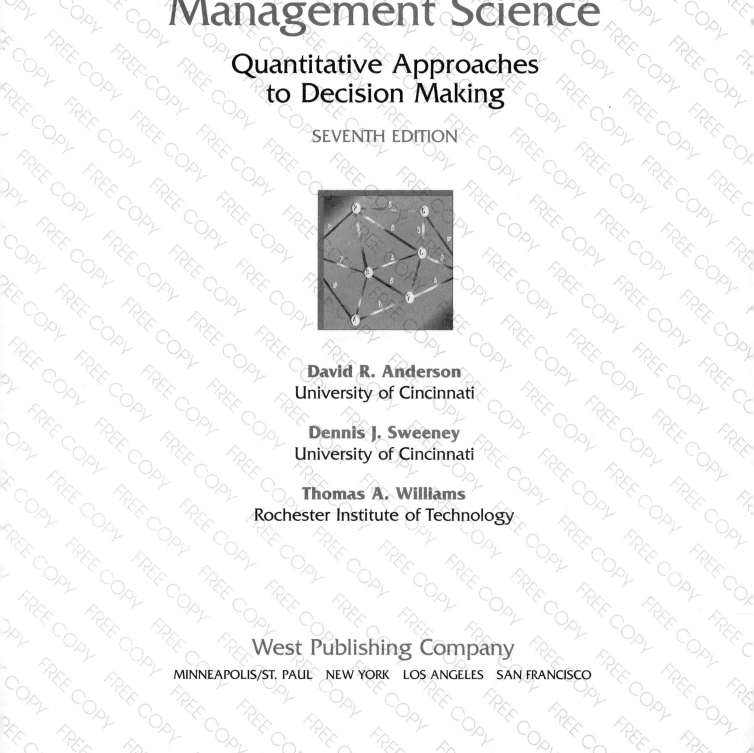

David R. Anderson
University of Cincinnati

Dennis J. Sweeney
University of Cincinnati

Thomas A. Williams
Rochester Institute of Technology

West Publishing Company

MINNEAPOLIS/ST. PAUL   NEW YORK   LOS ANGELES   SAN FRANCISCO

To Our Parents

Design   John Rokusek
Copyediting   Luana Richards
Composition   Carlisle Communications
Proofreading   Lynn Reichel
Artwork   Rolin Graphics
Cover Image   John Rokusek
Indexing   Sandi Schroeder
Production, Printing, and Prepress by West Publishing Company

West's Commitment to the Environment

In 1906, West Publishing Company began recycling materials left over from the production of books. This began a tradition of efficient and responsible use of resources. Today, up to 95 percent of our legal books and 70 percent of our college and school texts are printed on recycled, acid-free stock. West also recycles nearly 22 million pounds of scrap paper annually—the equivalent of 181,717 trees. Since the 1960s, West has devised ways to capture and recycle waste inks, solvents, oils, and vapors created in the printing process. We also recycle plastics of all kinds, wood, glass, corrugated cardboard, and batteries, and have eliminated the use of styrofoam book packaging. We at West are proud of the longevity and the scope of our commitment to the environment.

 PRINTED ON 10% POST CONSUMER RECYCLED PAPER

New Annotated Instructor's Edition

The new **Annotated Instructor's Edition** of *Management Science* includes margin notes that help instructors make better use of the text and its ancillary package. These notes tie the textbook and package together as illustrated below; these annotations are just a sampling of the kinds of aids provided in the AIE.

❖ **Teaching Notes** point out common pitfalls for students and ways to avoid them. This note can be found in Chapter 5.

> Artificial variables can be dropped from the tableau once they leave the basis. Leaving them in will not lead to the wrong solution, but it will cause more work.

Since a_4 is an artificial variable that was added simply to obtain an initial basic feasible solution, we can now drop its associated column from the simplex tableau. Indeed, whenever artificial variables are used, they can be dropped from the simplex tableau as soon as they have been eliminated from the basic feasible solution.

When artificial variables are required to obtain an initial basic feasible solution, the iterations . . . (continues)

❖ **Historical Background** is provided in notes like this one, found in Chapter 1.

> In the early 1950s George Dantzig taught the first formal courses in linear programming at the Department of Agriculture Graduate School in Washington, D.C.

Probably the most significant development was the discovery by George Dantzig, in 1947, of the simplex method for solving linear programming problems. Many more methodological developments followed, and in 1957 the first book on operations research was published by Churchman, Ackoff, and Arnoff.[1]

Concurrently with these methodological developments, there was a virtual explosion in computing power made available through digital computers . . . (continues)

❖ **End-of-chapter problems** are labeled by topic, making it easier to know which problems to assign for practice. You can find this note in Chapter 8.

> 19. Branch-and-bound solution, 0-1 variables.

19. The integer programming formulation of the Ice-Cold Refrigerator Company capital budgeting problem is presented below.

   Max $\quad 90x_1 + 40x_2 + 10x_3 + 37x_4$

   s.t.

   $\quad\quad 15x_1 + 10x_2 + 10x_3 + 15x_4 \leq 40$

   (continues)

❖ **Self-help annotations** appear in both the AIE and student editions and give instructors and students an idea of what students should be able to accomplish at a particular point in the chapter. This annotation is from Chapter 14.

> You should be able to develop a decision recommendation using the optimistic, conservative and minimax regret approaches. Try Problem 1(b).

Note that the three approaches discussed in this section have provided different recommendations. This is not in itself bad. It simply reflects the difference in decision-making philosophies that underlie the various approaches. Ultimately, the decision maker will have to choose the most appropriate approach and then make the final decision accordingly. The major criticism of the approaches discussed in this section is that . . . (continues)

Supplements Available with This Edition

❖ The TEST BANK by Constance McLaren (Indiana State University) includes multiple-choice and true/false questions, short answer and computational problems for each chapter. Page and topic references for each question are provided and keyed to the answer.

❖ The STUDY GUIDE by John Loucks (St. Edward's University-Texas) and John Lawrence and Barry Pasternack (both of Cal State-Fullerton) helps students organize text material for review. Each chapter includes a point-by-point summary, a review of definitions, true/false questions, illustrated problems with solutions, problem-solving tips, flow charts for algorithms and procedures, and more.

❖ The FULLY WORKED DEMONSTRATION PROBLEMS by the authors are included on approximately 270 transparency masters. Problems parallel examples and end-of-chapter problems in the text.

❖ ASTOUND™ PRESENTATION SOFTWARE contains major graphics from the text and study guide, including learning objectives, flow charts and demonstration problems. ASTOUND allows instructors to manipulate preloaded transparency material. Instructors can also create their own transparencies using animated text, sounds, graphs, icons and more.

❖ A SOLUTIONS MANUAL by the authors includes solutions for all textbook problems including case problems and Management Science in Practice questions.

❖ MANAGEMENT SCIENTIST™ SOFTWARE VERSION 3.0 provides computer modules for working through all quantitative problems in the course, and also solves bigger linear programming, assignment and transportation problems. Management Scientist is class-tested to run with little or no supervision from the instructor. The software is accompanied by approximately 120 pages of documentation including examples of how to use the module on actual problems. Improvements to version 3.0 include revisions of the LP and IP modules to improve both the computational speed and accuracy of the software, and the addition of a problem solution menu. Management Scientist software is IBM-compatible and available in 5 ¼″ or 3 ½″ disks. The package is available free to adopters as a site license; students may purchase the software shrinkwrapped with the text for a small additional charge.

❖ WESTEST™ allows instructors to create, edit, store and print exams. Users can randomly or selectively choose questions, import graphs, add new or edit existing questions, view summaries of the exam, and more.

❖ LINDO LP SOFTWARE is an easy-to-use yet powerful LP and IP optimizer used in examples throughout the text. Educational versions of LINDO and LINDO Mac (including documentation) are available on 5 ¼″ or 3 ½″ disks and can be shrinkwrapped with the text.

❖ LOTUS® 1-2-3® MBA SUPER-SHEETS by Owen Carrol and Jeffrey Kahn are templates set up to solve problems from the text. A copyable master disk and 100⁺ pages of documentation are available free to adopters, or the package is available for sale to students.

Contents

CHAPTER 4   Linear Programming Applications, 130

CHAPTER 5   Linear Programming: The Simplex Method, 188

CHAPTER 6	Simplex-Based Sensitivity Analysis and Duality, 240

CHAPTER 7	Transportation, Assignment, and Transshipment Problems, 272

CHAPTER 8

Integer Linear Programming, 343

CHAPTER 9

Network Models, 380

CHAPTER 10   Project Scheduling: PERT/CPM, 412

CHAPTER 11   Inventory Models, 463

CHAPTER 12   Waiting Line Models, 519

CHAPTER 16

Forecasting,   686

Preface

Approximately 20 years ago, the three of us were assistant professors in the Department of Quantitative Analysis at the University of Cincinnati. Our graduate educations and experiences had convinced us of the valuable potential for management science and operations research techniques in business administration and related fields. We were committed to the challenge of writing a textbook that would help make the mathematical and technical concepts of management science understandable and useful to nonmathematicians. Judging from the responses from our teaching colleagues and thousands of students, we have successfully met that challenge. Thus, 20 years later, assisted by the helpful comments and suggestions of many users, we are pleased to offer the seventh edition of *An Introduction to Management Science.*

Our purpose continues to be to provide students with a sound conceptual understanding of the role that management science plays in the decision-making process. Written with the needs of the nonmathematician in mind, the text is applications oriented. As each new concept is introduced, a problem scenario or application is presented that helps motivate the topic; we then illustrate how management science assists in solving the problem. Using this style throughout the text, we describe the many quantitative methods that have been developed over the years, explain how they work, and show how they can be applied and interpreted. We have found that this approach helps to motivate the student by demonstrating not only how the procedure works, but also how it can contribute to the decision-making process.

Changes in the Seventh Edition

In preparing the seventh edition, we have been careful to maintain the overall format and approach of the previous editions. However, based on our own classroom experience and suggestions from users of previous editions, a number of changes have been made to enhance the content, managerial orientation, and readability of the text.

New Management Science in Practice Applications End-of-chapter application sections provided by practitioners continue to be a feature of the text. We are pleased to be able to add recent management science applications from Eastman Kodak (Chapter 3), Electronic Data Systems (Chapter 9), and the Upjohn Company (Chapter 13) to the seventh edition. These applications provide information about the company, the role of management science within the company, and an overview of a management science application that relates to the material the student has covered in the chapter. A total of 15 management science in practice applications now appear in the text.

Linear Programming   Some significant changes have been made to the material on linear programming in Chapters 2–6. Graphical sensitivity analysis has been moved to Chapter 2 so that this chapter provides a complete treatment of graphical solution and interpretation. Guidelines for linear programming model formulation have been expanded and are now presented in Chapter 3. This chapter includes additional examples of model formulation and provides an improved discussion of the interpretation of computer solutions to linear programming models. Both LINDO and The Management Scientist software packages are discussed.

Chapter 4, which continues to emphasize the broad range of linear programming applications, includes a new production management model on cross-training and work force allocation to departments. A significant revision of the presentation on duality now appears in Chapter 6. Finally, the problems at the end of the linear programming chapters have been reorganized to more closely follow the order of the material presented in the chapter. Generally, basic concepts are treated in the initial problems with the more challenging problems appearing at the end of the problem set.

Transshipment Problem Expanded   The treatment of the transportation, assignment, and transshipment problems were unified around the notion of a network flow model in the previous edition. In the new edition, the material on the transshipment model has been expanded to include the more complex situation where shipments occur between warehouses and between customers, as well as directly from plants to customers.

New Case Problems   Case problems appear at the end of most chapters. In general, the case problems expose the student to larger problems that require more judgment and some user flexibility in both approach and analysis. A managerial report is required for each case problem. New case problems on truck-leasing strategy (Chapter 3), investment asset allocation (Chapter 4), and distribution system design (Chapter 7) have been added to this edition.

Self-Test Problems   New to the edition are self test problems for the students. As students progress through each chapter, marginal notes will refer the students to specific end-of-chapter problems they should be able to solve at that point. Worked-out solutions to the self test problems are provided in Appendix H of the text so that each student may immediately evaluate his or her ability to handle the material. We recommend that instructors assign all self-test problems for the material covered in the course. There are an ample number of end-of-chapter problems available for additional homework assignments.

Other Changes   A variety of other changes have been made throughout the text. All of the changes cannot be listed here, but examples include the statement of assumptions for the economic order quantity model accompanied by annotations that state how other inventory models in the chapter are based on variations of the EOQ model. In addition, the example computer simulation program in Chapter 13 has been modernized. The BASIC language variable names should enable the student to easily follow the programming logic used to simulate the system under study.

Prerequisite   The mathematical prerequisite for this text is a course in algebra. An introductory knowledge of probability and statistics would be desirable, but not necessary, for Chapters 10–14, 16, and 17. Only Chapter 19, which discusses calculus-based solution procedures and which we consider optional, requires a knowledge of differential calculus.

Throughout the text, we have utilized generally accepted notation for the topic being covered. Thus, students who pursue study beyond the level of this text should find the difficulties of reading more advanced material minimized. To assist in further study, a bibliography is included in the backmatter of the book.

Course Outline Flexibility

The text has been designed to enhance the instructor's flexibility in selecting topics to meet specific course needs. The single-quarter and single-semester outlines that follow are a sampling of the many options available.

A one-quarter outline stressing linear programming, model development, and applications:

- Introduction (Chapter 1)
- Introduction to Linear Programming and Computer Solution (Chapters 2 and 3)
- Linear Programming Applications (selected portions of Chapters 4 and 7)
- Project Management: PERT/CPM (Chapter 10)
- Waiting Lines (Chapter 12)
- Computer Simulation (Chapter 13)
- Decision Analysis (Chapter 14)

The instructor in a one-semester course who wants to focus on model development and other applications could either spend more time on the applications in Chapter 4 or cover additional topics. One possible outline, stressing linear programming, model development, and applications, would be

- Introduction (Chapter 1)
- Introduction to Linear Programming (Chapters 2 and 3)
- Linear Programming Applications (Chapter 4)
- Simplex Method (Chapters 5 and 6)
- Transportation, Assignment, and Transshipment Models (Chapter 7)
- Integer Programming (Chapter 8)
- Project Management: PERT/CPM (Chapter 10)
- Inventory Models (Chapter 11)
- Waiting Lines (Chapter 12)
- Computer Simulation (Chapter 13)
- Decision Analysis (Chapter 14)
- Multicriteria Decision Making (Chapter 15)

Acknowledgments

We owe a debt to many of our colleagues and friends for their helpful comments and suggestions during the development of this and previous editions. Among these are Robert L. Armacost, E. Leonard Arnoff, John W. Auer, Uttarayan Bagchi, Edward Baker, Norman Baker, James Bartos, Richard Beckwith, Oded Berman, Stanley Brooking, Jeffrey Camm, Thomas Case, John Eatman, Ron Ebert, Don Edwards, Peter Ellis, Lawrence Ettkin, Jim Evans, Terri Friel, Robert Garfinkel, Damodar Golhar, Stephen Goodman, Jack Goodwin, Richard Gunther, Nicholas G. Hall, Michael E. Hanna, David Hott, Raymond Jackson, Muhannad Khawaja, Bharat Kolluri, Robert Landeros, Darlene Lanier, John Lawrence, Jr., Phillip Lowery, Prem Mann, William G. Marchal, Kamlesh Mathur, Joseph Mazzola, Cynthia S. McCahon, Richard McCready, Patrick McKeown, Constance McLaren, Edward Minieka, Richard C. Morey, Alan Neebe, Brian F. O'Neil,

David Pentico, Gary Pickett, B. Madhusudan Rao, Handanhal V. Ravinder, Douglas V. Rippy, Donna Retzlaff-Roberts, Richard Rosenthal, Sam H. Roy, Antoinette Somers, Carol Stamm, Christopher S. Tang, Willban Terpening, William Truscott, James Vigen, Ed Winkofsky, Bruce Woodworth, M. Zafer Yakin, and Cathleen Zucco.

Our associates from organizations who supplied the Management Science in Practice applications made a major contribution to the text. These individuals are cited in a credit line on the first page of each application.

We are also indebted to our editor, Mary Schiller, production editor, Tom Hilt, promotion manager John Tuvey, and others at West Publishing Company for their editorial counsel and support during the preparation of this text.

David R. Anderson
Dennis J. Sweeney
Thomas A. Williams

CHAPTER 1

Introduction

Management science (MS), an approach to managerial decision making that is based on the scientific method, makes extensive use of quantitative analysis. A variety of names exists for the body of knowledge involving quantitative approaches to decision making; in addition to management science, another widely known and accepted name is *operations research* (OR). Today, many use the terms *operations research* and *management science* interchangeably. We shall treat them as synonyms throughout the text.

The scientific management revolution of the early 1900s, initiated by Frederic W. Taylor, provided the foundation for MS/OR. But modern management science/operations research is generally considered to have originated during the World War II period, when operations research teams were formed to deal with strategic and tactical problems faced by the military. These teams, which often consisted of people with diverse specialties (e.g., mathematicians, engineers, and behavioral scientists), were joined together to solve a common problem through the utilization of the scientific method. After the war, many of these team members continued their research on quantitative approaches to decision making.

Two developments that occurred during the post–World War II period led to the growth and use of management science in nonmilitary applications. First, continued research on quantitative approaches to decision making resulted in numerous methodological developments. Probably the most significant development was the discovery by George Dantzig, in 1947, of the simplex method for solving linear programming problems. Many more methodological developments followed, and in 1957 the first book on operations research was published by Churchman, Ackoff, and Arnoff.[1]

Concurrently with these methodological developments, there was a virtual explosion in computing power made available through digital computers. Computers enabled practitioners to use the methodological advances to successfully solve a large variety of industrial problems. The computer technology explosion continues; microcomputers are

In the early 1950s George Dantzig taught the first formal courses in linear programming at the Department of Agriculture Graduate School in Washington, D.C.

---

[1] C. W. Churchman, R. L. Ackoff, and E. L. Arnoff, *Introduction to Operations Research* (New York: Wiley, 1957).

now more powerful than the mainframe computers of the 1970s. Today, variants of the post–World War II methodological developments are being used on microcomputers to solve problems larger than those solved on mainframe computers in the 1980s.

1.1 Problem Solving and Decision Making

In 1910 John Dewey, the originator of the Dewey decimal system, is credited as being the first to describe the stages of problem solving. He described them as (1) What is the problem? (2) What are the alternatives? and (3) Which alternative is best?

Problem solving can be defined as the process of identifying a difference between some actual and some desired state of affairs and then taking action to resolve the difference. For problems important enough to justify the time and effort of careful analysis, the problem-solving process involves the following seven steps:

1. Identify and define the problem.
2. Determine the set of alternative solutions.
3. Determine the criterion or criteria that will be used to evaluate the alternatives.
4. Evaluate the alternatives.
5. Choose an alternative.
6. Implement the selected alternative.
7. Evaluate the results, and determine if a satisfactory solution has been obtained.

Decision making is the term generally associated with the first five steps of the problem-solving process. Thus, the first step of decision making is to identify and define the problem. Decision making ends with the choosing of an alternative, which is the act of making the decision.

Let us consider the following example of a decision-making process. For the moment assume that you will be graduating from college in the next few months, that you have completed the interviewing process, and that you have been lucky enough to receive job offers from four companies. Your problem is that you are currently unemployed and that you would like a position that will lead to a satisfying career.

Once the problem of obtaining a position that will lead to a satisfying career has been defined, the next step in the decision-making process is to identify the set of alternatives available. Assume that the alternatives available to you are these four job offers: one from a company located in Rochester, New York; one from a company located in Dallas, Texas; one from a company located in Greensboro, North Carolina; and one from a company located in Pittsburgh, Pennsylvania. Thus, the alternatives for your decision problem can be stated as follows:

1. Accept the position offered by the company located in Rochester, New York.
2. Accept the position offered by the company located in Dallas, Texas.
3. Accept the position offered by the company located in Greensboro, North Carolina.
4. Accept the position offered by the company located in Pittsburgh, Pennsylvania.

The next step of the problem-solving process involves determining the criterion or criteria that will be used to evaluate the four alternatives. Obviously, the starting salary is going to be a factor of some importance. If this were the only criterion of importance to you, the alternative selected as "best" would be the one with the highest starting salary. Problems in which the objective is to find the best solution with respect to one criterion are referred to as *single-criterion* decision problems.

For the current problem, suppose that you have also concluded that the potential for advancement and the location of the job are two other criteria of major importance. Thus, the three criteria in your decision problem are starting salary, potential for advancement, and location. Problems that involve more than one criterion are referred to as *multicriteria* decision problems.

The next step of the decision-making process is to evaluate each of the alternatives with respect to each criterion. For example, evaluating each alternative relative to the starting salary criterion is done simply by recording the starting salary for each job alternative. Evaluating each alternative with respect to the potential for advancement and the location of the job is more difficult to do, however, since these evaluations are based primarily on subjective factors that are often difficult to quantify. Assume for now that you have decided to measure potential for advancement and job location by rating each of these criteria as poor, fair, average, good, or excellent. The data that you have compiled are shown in Table 1.1.

You are now ready to make a choice from the available alternatives. What makes this choice phase so difficult is that the criteria are probably not all equally important, and no one alternative is "best" with regard to all criteria. Although we will present a method for dealing with situations like this later in the text, for now let us suppose that after a careful evaluation of the data in Table 1.1, you have decided to select alternative 3; alternative 3 is thus referred to as the *decision.*

At this point in time, the decision-making process is complete. In summary, we see that this process involves five steps:

1. Define the problem.
2. Identify the alternatives.
3. Determine the criteria.
4. Evaluate the alternatives.
5. Choose an alternative.

Note that missing from this list are the last two steps in the problem-solving process: implementing the selected alternative and evaluating the results to determine whether a satisfactory solution has been obtained. This is not meant to diminish the importance of each of these activities, but to emphasize the more limited scope of the term *decision making* as compared to the term *problem solving.* Figure 1.1 summarizes the relationship between these two concepts.

Experts in decision making, such as Herbert Simon, indicate that "to understand what is involved in decision making that term has to be interpreted broadly—so broadly as to become almost synonymous with managing."[2] As we begin to look more carefully at the role of management science in decision making, we will concentrate our attention on problems that practicing managers might encounter in their roles as decision makers.

---

[2]H. A. Simon, *The New Science of Decision Making,* rev. ed. (Englewood Cliffs, N.J.: Prentice-Hall, 1977), p. 39.

Table 1.1	Alternative	Starting Salary	Potential for Advancement	Job Location
Data for the Job Evaluation Decision-Making Problem	Rochester	$28,500	Average	Fair
	Dallas	$26,000	Excellent	Average
	Greensboro	$26,000	Good	Excellent
	Pittsburgh	$27,000	Average	Good

Figure 1.1
The Relationship Between
Problem Solving and Decision
Making

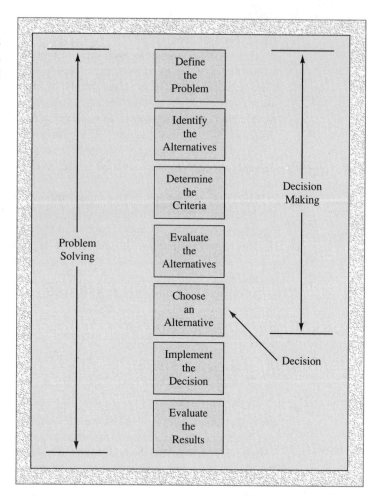

1.2 Quantitative Analysis and Decision-Making

Consider the flowchart presented in Figure 1.2. Note that we have combined the first three steps of the decision-making process under the heading of "Structuring the Problem" and the latter two steps under the heading "Analyzing the Problem." Let us now consider in more detail how to carry out the set of activities that make up the decision-making process.

Figure 1.3 shows that the analysis phase of the decision-making process may take on two basic forms: qualitative and quantitative. Qualitative analysis is based primarily on the manager's judgment and experience; it includes the manager's intuitive "feel" for the problem and is more an art than a science. If the manager has had experience with similar problems, or if the problem is relatively simple, heavy emphasis may be placed upon a qualitative analysis. However, if the manager has had little experience with similar problems, or if the problem is sufficiently complex, then a quantitative analysis of the problem can be a very important consideration in the manager's final decision.

When using the quantitative approach, an analyst will concentrate on the quantitative facts or data associated with the problem and develop mathematical expressions that describe the objectives, constraints, and other relationships that exist in the problem. Then, by using one or more quantitative methods, the analyst will make a recommendation based on the quantitative aspects of the problem.

One meaning of the Greek word from which the word *analysis* is derived is "to resolve into its elements." Thus, quantitative or qualitative analysis can be viewed as a way of thinking about a problem in which we follow a principle of breaking down the problem into its component parts.

Quantitative methods are especially helpful with large, complex problems. For example, in the coordination of the thousands of tasks associated with landing the Apollo 11 safely on the moon, quantitative techniques helped to ensure that over 300,000 pieces of work performed by over 400,000 people were integrated smoothly.

While skills in the qualitative approach are inherent in the manager and usually increase with experience, the skills of the quantitative approach can be learned only by studying the assumptions and methods of management science. A manager can increase decision-making effectiveness by learning more about quantitative methodology and by better understanding its contribution to the decision-making process. The manager who is knowledgeable in quantitative decision-making procedures is in a much better position to compare and evaluate the qualitative and quantitative sources of recommendations and ultimately to combine the two sources in order to make the best possible decision.

The box in Figure 1.3 entitled "Quantitative Analysis" encompasses most of the subject matter of this text. We will consider a managerial problem, introduce the appropriate quantitative methodology, and then develop the recommended decision.

In closing this section, let us briefly state some of the reasons why a quantitative approach might be used in the decision-making process:

You should understand why quantitative approaches might be needed in a particular problem. Try Problem 4.

1. The problem is complex, and the manager cannot develop a good solution without the aid of quantitative analysis.
2. The problem is very important (e.g., a great deal of money is involved), and the manager desires a thorough analysis before attempting to make a decision.

Figure 1.2
An Alternate Classification of the Decision-Making Process

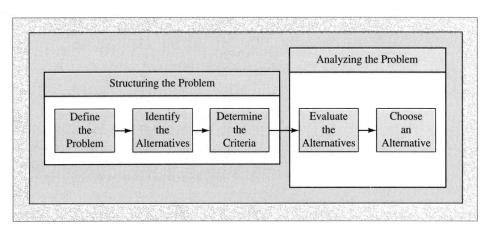

Figure 1.3
The Role of Qualitative and Quantitative Analysis

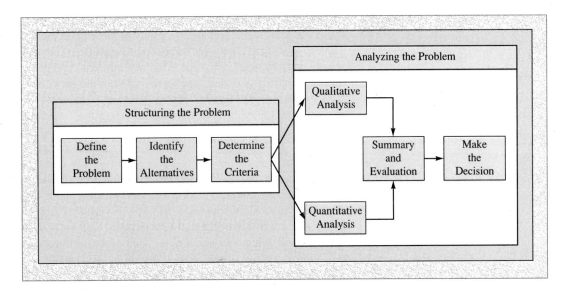

3. The problem is new, and the manager has no previous experience to draw on.
4. The problem is repetitive, and the manager saves time and effort by relying on quantitative procedures to make routine decision recommendations.

1.3 Quantitative Analysis

The problem definition step of the decision-making process is the most critical component in determining the success or failure of any quantitative approach to decision making. It usually takes imagination, teamwork, and considerable effort to transform a rather general problem description into a well-defined problem that can be approached quantitatively. For example, a broadly described excessive inventory problem must be clearly defined in terms of specific objectives and operating constraints before an analyst can begin the quantitative analysis process.

To successfully apply quantitative analysis to decision making, the management scientist must work closely with the manager or user of the results. When both the management scientist and the manager agree that the problem has been adequately defined, the management scientist will begin work on developing a model that can be used to represent the problem mathematically. Solution procedures can then be developed for the model in order to select the decision that "best" solves the problem.

Model Development

Models are representations of real objects or situations. These representations, or models, can be presented in various forms. For example, a scale model of an airplane is a representation of a real airplane. Similarly, a child's toy truck is a model of a real truck. The model airplane and toy truck are examples of models that are physical replicas of real objects. In modeling terminology, physical replicas are referred to as *iconic* models.

A second classification of models includes those that are physical in form but do not have the same physical appearance as the object being modeled. Such models are referred to as *analog* models. The speedometer of an automobile is an analog model; the position of the needle on the dial represents the speed of the automobile. A thermometer is another analog model representing temperature.

A third classification of models—the type we will primarily be studying—includes those that represent a problem by a system of symbols and mathematical relationships or expressions. Such models are referred to as *mathematical* models and are a critical part of any quantitative approach to decision making. For example, the total profit from the sale of a product can be determined by multiplying the profit per unit by the quantity sold. If we let x represent the number of units sold and P the total profit, then, with a profit of $10 per unit, the following mathematical model defines the total profit earned by selling x units:

$$P = 10x \tag{1.1}$$

The purpose, or value, of any model is that it enables us to make inferences about the real situation by studying and analyzing the model. For example, an airplane designer might test an iconic model of a new airplane in a wind tunnel to learn about the potential flying characteristics of the full-size airplane. Similarly, a mathematical model may be used to make inferences about how much profit will be earned if a specified quantity of a particular product is sold. According to the mathematical model of equation (1.1), we would expect to obtain a $30 profit by selling three units of the product.

In general, experimenting with models requires less time and is less expensive than experimenting with the real object or situation. A model airplane is certainly quicker and less expensive to build and study than the full-size airplane. Similarly, the above mathematical model allows a quick identification of profit expectations without actually requiring the manager to produce and sell x units. Models also have the advantage of reducing the risk associated with experimenting with the real situation. In particular, bad designs or bad decisions that cause the model airplane to crash or a mathematical model to project a $10,000 loss can be avoided in the real situation.

The value of model-based conclusions and decisions is dependent on how well the model represents the real situation. The more closely the scale model represents the real airplane, the more accurate the conclusions and predictions will be. Similarly, the more closely the mathematical model represents the company's true profit–volume relationship, the more accurate the profit projections will be.

Since this text deals with quantitative analysis based on mathematical models, let us look more closely at the mathematical modeling process. When initially considering a managerial problem, we usually find that the problem definition phase leads to a specific objective, such as maximization of profit or minimization of cost, and possibly a set of restrictions or *constraints,* such as production capacities. The success of the mathematical model and quantitative approach will depend heavily on how accurately the objective and constraints can be expressed in terms of mathematical equations or relationships.

A mathematical expression that describes the problem's objective is referred to as the *objective function.* For example, the profit equation $P = 10x$ would be an objective function for a firm attempting to maximize profit. A production capacity constraint would be necessary if, for instance, 5 hours are required to produce each unit and there are only 40 hours available per week. Let x indicate the number of units produced each week. The production time constraint is given by

$$5x \leq 40 \tag{1.2}$$

The value of $5x$ is the total time required to produce x units; the symbol $\leq$ indicates that the production time required must be less than or equal to the 40 hours available.

The decision problem or question is the following: How many units of the product should be scheduled each week to maximize profit? A complete mathematical model for this simple production problem is

$$\text{Maximize} \quad P = 10x \quad \text{objective function}$$
subject to (s.t.)

$$\left. \begin{array}{r} 5x \leq 40 \\ x \geq 0 \end{array} \right\} \text{constraints}$$

The $x \geq 0$ constraint requires the production quantity x to be greater than or equal to zero, which simply recognizes the fact that it is not possible to manufacture a negative number of units. The optimal solution to this model can be easily calculated and is given by $x = 8$, with an associated profit of $80. This model is an example of a linear programming model. In subsequent chapters we will discuss more complicated mathematical models and learn how to solve them in situations where the answers are not nearly so obvious.

In the above mathematical model, the profit per unit ($10), the production time per unit (5 hours), and the production capacity (40 hours) are environmental factors that are not under the control of the manager or decision maker. Such environmental factors, which can affect both the objective function and the constraints, are referred to as *uncontrollable inputs* to the model. Inputs that are controlled or determined by the decision maker are referred to as *controllable inputs* to the model. In the above example, the production

Herbert A. Simon, a Nobel prize winner in economics and an expert in decision making, has said that a mathematical model does not have to be exact; it just has to be close enough to provide better results than can be obtained by common sense.

quantity x is the controllable input to the model. Controllable inputs are the decision alternatives specified by the manager and thus are also referred to as the *decision variables* of the model.

Once all controllable and uncontrollable inputs are specified, the objective function and constraints can be evaluated, and the output of the model determined. In this sense, the output of the model is simply the projection of what would happen if those particular environmental factors and decisions occurred in the real situation. A flowchart of how controllable and uncontrollable inputs are transformed by the mathematical model into output is shown in Figure 1.4. A similar flowchart showing the specific details of the production model is shown in Figure 1.5.

As stated earlier, the uncontrollable inputs are those the decision maker cannot influence. The specific controllable and uncontrollable inputs of a model depend on the particular problem or decision-making situation. In the production problem, the production time available (40), is an uncontrollable input. However, if it were possible to hire more employees or use overtime, the number of hours of production time would become a controllable input and therefore a decision variable in the model.

Uncontrollable inputs can either be known exactly or be uncertain and subject to variation. If all uncontrollable inputs to a model are known and cannot vary, the model is referred to as a *deterministic* model. Corporate income tax rates are not under the influence of the manager and thus constitute an uncontrollable input in many decision models. Since these rates are known and fixed (at least in the short run), a mathematical model with corporate income tax rates as the only uncontrollable input would be a deterministic model. The distinguishing feature of a deterministic model is that the uncontrollable input values are known in advance.

Uncontrollable inputs are "givens" in a mathematical model. In a deterministic model, they are constants; in a stochastic model, they are described by probability distributions.

If any of the uncontrollable inputs are uncertain and subject to variation, the model is referred to as a *stochastic* or *probabilistic* model. An uncontrollable input to many production planning models is demand for the product. Since future demand may be any of a range of values, a mathematical model that treats demand with uncertainty would be called a stochastic model. In the production model, the number of hours of production time required per unit, the total hours available, and the unit profit were all uncontrollable inputs. Since the uncontrollable inputs were all known to take on fixed values, the model was deterministic. If, however, the number of hours of production time per unit could vary from 3 to 6 hours depending on the quality of the raw material, the model would be stochastic. The distinguishing feature of a stochastic model is that the value of the output cannot be determined even if the value of the controllable input is known because the

Figure 1.4
Flowchart of the Process of Transforming Model Inputs into Output

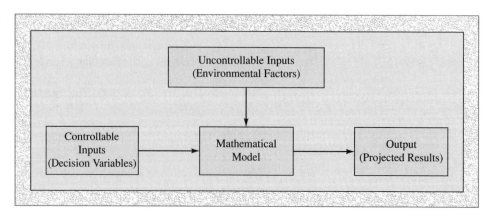

Figure 1.5
Flowchart for the Production
Model

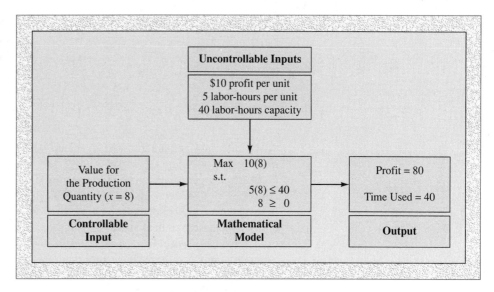

specific values of the uncontrollable inputs are unknown. In this respect, stochastic models are often more difficult to analyze.

Data Preparation

Another step in the quantitative analysis of a problem is the preparation of the data required by the model. Data in this sense refer to the values of the uncontrollable inputs to the model. All uncontrollable inputs or data must be specified before we can analyze the model and recommend a decision or solution for the problem.

In the production model, the values of the uncontrollable inputs or data were $10 per unit for profit, 5 hours per unit for production time, and 40 hours for production capacity. In the development of the model, these data values were known and incorporated into the model as it was being developed. If the model is relatively small and the uncontrollable input values or data required are few, the quantitative analyst will probably combine model development and data preparation into one step. That is, in these situations the data values are inserted as the equations of the mathematical model are developed.

However, in many mathematical modeling situations, the data or uncontrollable input values are not readily available. In these situations the management scientist may know that the model will need profit per unit, production time, and production capacity data, but the values will not be known until the accounting, production, and engineering departments can be consulted. Rather than attempting to collect the required data as the model is being developed, the analyst will usually adopt a general notation for the model development step and then a separate data preparation step will be performed to obtain the uncontrollable input values required by the model.

Using the general notation

$$c = \text{profit per unit}$$
$$a = \text{production time in hours per unit}$$
$$b = \text{production capacity in hours}$$

the model development step of the production problem would result in the following general model:

$$\text{Max} \quad cx$$
$$\text{s.t.}$$
$$ax \leq b$$
$$x \geq 0$$

A separate data preparation step to identify the values for *c, a,* and *b* would then be necessary to complete the model.

Many inexperienced quantitative analysts assume that once the problem has been defined and a general model developed, the problem is essentially solved. These individuals tend to believe that data preparation is a trivial step in the process and can be easily handled by clerical staff. Actually, this assumption could not be farther from the truth, especially with large-scale models that have numerous data input values. For example, a moderate-size linear programming model with 50 decision variables and 25 constraints could have over 1300 data elements that must be identified in the data preparation step. The time required to prepare these data and the possibility of data collection errors will make the data preparation step a critical part of the quantitative analysis process. Often, a fairly large data base is needed to support a mathematical model, and information systems specialists also become involved in the data preparation step.

Model Solution

Once the model development and data preparation steps have been completed, we can proceed to the model solution step. In this step, the analyst will attempt to identify the values of the decision variables that provide the "best" output for the model. The specific decision-variable value or values providing the "best" output will be referred to as the *optimal solution* for the model. For the production problem, the model solution step involves finding the value of the production quantity decision variable *x* that maximizes profit while not causing a violation of the production capacity constraint.

One procedure that might be used in the model solution step involves a trial-and-error approach, where the model is used to test and evaluate various decision alternatives. In the production model, this would mean testing and evaluating the model under various production quantities or values of *x.* Referring to Figure 1.5, note that we could input trial values for *x* and check the corresponding output for projected profit and satisfaction of the production capacity constraint. If a particular decision alternative does not satisfy one or more of the model constraints, the decision alternative is rejected as being *infeasible,* regardless of the objective function value. If all constraints are satisfied, the decision alternative is *feasible* and a candidate for the "best" solution or recommended decision. Through this trial-and-error process of evaluating selected decision alternatives, a decision maker can identify a good—and possibly the best—feasible solution to the problem. This solution would then be the recommended decision for the problem.

Table 1.2 shows the results of a trial-and-error approach to solving the production model of Figure 1.5. The recommended decision is a production quantity of 8 since the feasible solution with the highest projected profit occurs at *x* = 8.

While the trial-and-error solution process is often acceptable and can provide valuable information for the manager, it has the drawbacks of not necessarily providing the best solution and of being inefficient in terms of requiring numerous calculations if many decision alternatives are tried. Thus, quantitative analysts have developed special solution

Table 1.2 Trial-and-Error Solution for the Production Model of Figure 1.5	Decision Alternative (Production Quantity) x	Projected Profit	Total Hours of Production	Feasible Solution? (capacity = 40)
	0	0	0	Yes
	2	20	10	Yes
	4	40	20	Yes
	6	60	30	Yes
	8	80	40	Yes
	10	100	50	No
	12	120	60	No

procedures for many models that are much more efficient than the trial-and-error approach. Throughout this text, you will be introduced to solution procedures that are applicable to the specific mathematical models that will be formulated. While some relatively small models or problems can be solved by hand computations, most practical applications require the use of a computer.

In building a mathematical model, it is usually impossible to account for all factors in the problem; thus, you must simplify. An important consideration is the extent to which you are willing to trade off realism in the model for ease of model development and solution.

It is important to realize that the model development and model solution steps are not completely separable. While an analyst will want to develop an accurate model or representation of the actual problem situation, the analyst will also want to be able to find a solution to the model. If we approach the model development step by attempting to find the most accurate and realistic mathematical model, we may find the model so large and complex that it is impossible to obtain a solution. In this case, a simpler and perhaps more easily understood model with a readily available solution procedure is preferred even if the recommended solution is only a rough approximation of the best decision. As you learn more about quantitative solution procedures, you will have a better idea of the types of mathematical models that can be developed and solved.

You should now understand the concept of a mathematical model and what is referred to as the optimal solution to the model. Try Problem 8.

After a model solution has been obtained, both the management scientist and the manager will be interested in determining how good the solution really is. While the analyst has undoubtedly taken many precautions to develop a realistic model, often the goodness or accuracy of the model cannot be assessed until model solutions are generated. Model testing and validation are frequently conducted with relatively small "test" problems that have known or at least expected solutions. If the model generates the expected solutions, and if other output information appears correct, the go-ahead may be given to use the model on the full-scale problem. However, if the model test and validation identify potential problems or inaccuracies inherent in the model, corrective action, such as model modification and/or collection of more accurate input data, may be taken. Whatever the corrective action, the model solution will not be used in practice until the model has satisfactorily passed testing and validation.

Report Generation

An important part of the quantitative analysis process is the preparation of managerial reports based on the model's solution. Referring to Figure 1.3, we see that the solution based on the quantitative analysis of a problem is one of the inputs that is considered by the manager before making a final decision. Thus, it is essential that the results of the model appear in a managerial report that can be easily understood by the decision maker. The report should include the recommended decision and other pertinent information about the model results that may be helpful to the decision maker.

A Note Regarding Implementation

As discussed in Section 1.2, it is the responsibility of the manager to integrate the quantitative solution with qualitative considerations in order to make the best possible decision. After doing this, the manager must oversee the implementation and follow-up evaluation of the decision. During the implementation and follow-up, the manager should continue to monitor the contribution of the model. At times, this process may lead to requests for model expansion or refinement that will cause the management scientist to return to one of the earlier steps of the quantitative analysis process.

Successful implementation of results is of critical importance to the management scientist as well as the manager. If the results of the quantitative analysis process are not correctly implemented, the entire effort may be of no value. It doesn't take too many unsuccessful implementations before the management scientist is out of work. Because implementation often requires people to do things differently (and more effectively, one hopes), it often meets with resistance. People want to know, "What's wrong with the way I've been doing it?" and so on. One of the most effective ways to ensure a successful implementation is to secure as much user involvement as possible throughout the modeling process. If the user feels he/she has been involved in identifying the problem and developing the solutions, he/she is much more likely to enthusiastically implement the results. The success rate for implementing the results of a management science project is much greater for those projects in which there has been extensive user involvement.

1.4 Models of Cost, Revenue, and Profit

Some of the most basic quantitative models arising in business and economic applications are those involving the relationship between a volume variable—such as production volume or sales volume—and cost, revenue, or profit. Through the use of these models, a manager can determine the projected cost, revenue, and/or profit associated with an established production quantity or a forecasted sales volume. Financial planning, production planning, sales quotas, and other areas of decision making can benefit from such cost, revenue, and profit models.

Cost and Volume Models

The cost of manufacturing or producing a particular product is a function of the volume produced. This cost can usually be defined as a sum of two costs: fixed cost and variable cost. *Fixed cost* is the portion of the total cost that does not depend on the production volume; this cost remains the same no matter how much is produced. *Variable cost,* on the other hand, is the portion of the total cost that is dependent on and varies with the production volume. For example, suppose that the setup cost for a production line is $3000. This is a fixed cost that is incurred regardless of the number of units eventually produced. In addition, suppose that variable labor and material costs are $2 for each unit produced. The cost–volume model for producing x units would be written as

$$C(x) = 3000 + 2x \qquad (1.3)$$

where

$$x = \text{production volume in units}$$
$$C(x) = \text{total cost of producing } x \text{ units}$$

Use of the model in equation (1.3) will determine the total production cost once the production volume is established. For example, a production volume of $x = 1200$ units would result in a total cost of $C(1200) = 3000 + 2(1200) = \$5400$.

Marginal cost is defined as the rate of change of the total cost with respect to volume. That is, it is the cost increase associated with a one-unit increase in the production volume. In the cost model of equation (1.3), we see that the total cost $C(x)$ will increase by \$2 for each unit increase in the production volume. Thus, the marginal cost is \$2. With more complex total cost models, marginal cost may depend on the production volume. In such cases, we could have marginal cost increasing or decreasing with the production volume x.

Revenue and Volume Models

A manager will also want information on the projected revenue associated with selling a specified number of units. Thus, a model of the relationship between revenue and volume is also needed. Suppose that the product referred to above sells for \$5 per unit. The model for total revenue can be written as

$$R(x) = 5x \tag{1.4}$$

where

$$x = \text{sales volume in units}$$
$$R(x) = \text{total revenue associated with selling } x \text{ units}$$

Marginal revenue is defined as the rate of change of total revenue with respect to sales volume. That is, it is the increase in total revenue resulting from a one-unit increase in sales volume. In the model of equation (1.4), we see that the marginal revenue is \$5. In this case, marginal revenue is constant and does not vary with the sales volume. With more complex models, we may find that marginal revenue increases or decreases as the sales volume x increases.

Profit and Volume Models

One of the most important criteria for managerial decision making is profit. Managers need to be able to know the profit implications of their decisions. If we assume that we will only produce what can be sold, the production volume and sales volume will be equal. We can combine equations (1.3) and (1.4) to develop a profit–volume model that will determine profit associated with a specified production–sales volume. Since total profit is total revenue minus total cost, the following model provides the profit associated with producing and selling x units:

$$P(x) = R(x) - C(x)$$
$$= 5x - (3000 + 2x) = -3000 + 3x \tag{1.5}$$

Thus, the model for profit $P(x)$ can be derived from the models of the revenue–volume and cost–volume relationships.

Break-even Analysis

Using equation (1.5), we can now determine the profit associated with any production volume x. For example, suppose a demand forecast indicates that 500 units of the product can be sold. The decision to produce and sell the 500 units results in a projected profit of

$$P(500) = -3000 + 3(500) = -1500$$

In other words, a loss of $1500 is predicted. If sales are expected to be 500 units, the manager may decide against producing the product. However, a demand forecast of 1800 units would show a projected profit of

$$P(1800) = -3000 + 3(1800) = 2400$$

This profit may be enough to justify proceeding with the production and sale of the product.

We see that a volume of 500 units will yield a loss, whereas a volume of 1800 provides a profit. The volume that results in total revenue equaling total cost (providing $0 profit) is called the *break-even point*. If the break-even point is known, a manager can quickly infer that a volume above the break-even point will result in a profit, while a volume below the break-even point will result in a loss. Thus, the break-even point for a product provides valuable information for a manager who must make a yes/no decision concerning production of the product.

Let us now return to the example above and show how the profit model in equation (1.5) can be used to compute the break-even point. The break-even point can be found by setting the profit expression equal to zero and solving for the production volume. Using equation (1.5), we have

$$P(x) = -3000 + 3x = 0$$

$$3x = 3000$$

$$x = 1000$$

You should now be able to determine the break-even point for a quantitative model. Try Problem 15.

With this information, we know that production and sales of the product must be at least 1000 units before a profit can be expected. The graph of the total cost model, the total revenue model, and the location of the break-even point is shown in Figure 1.6.

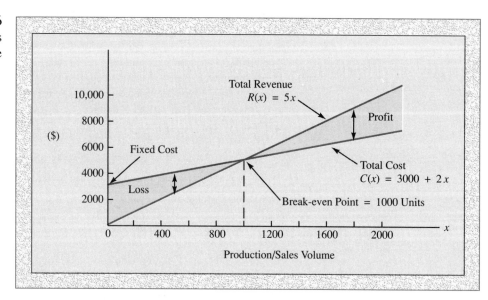

Figure 1.6
Graph of the Break-even Analysis for the Production Example

1.5 Management Science in Practice

In this section we present a brief overview of the management science techniques covered in this text. We will then present the results of surveys that show which techniques have been used most frequently in practice and what needs to be done to enable you to successfully utilize quantitative approaches throughout your career.

Management Science Techniques

The following management science techniques are covered in this text.

Linear Programming. Linear programming is a problem-solving approach that has been developed for situations involving maximizing or minimizing a linear function subject to linear constraints that limit the degree to which the objective can be pursued. The production model developed in the previous section (see Figure 1.5) is an example of a simple linear programming model.

Integer Linear Programming. Integer linear programming is an approach used for problems that can be set up as linear programs with the additional requirement that some or all of the decision recommendations be integer values.

Network Models. A network is a graphical description of a problem consisting of circles called nodes that are interconnected by lines called arcs. Specialized solution procedures exist for these types of problems, enabling us to quickly solve many managerial problems in such areas as transportation system design, information system design, and project scheduling.

Project Management: PERT/CPM. In many situations, managers are responsible for planning, scheduling, and controlling projects that consist of numerous separate jobs or tasks performed by a variety of departments, individuals, and so forth. The PERT (Program Evaluation and Review Technique) and CPM (Critical Path Method) techniques help managers carry out their project scheduling responsibilities.

Inventory Models. Inventory models are used by managers faced with the dual problems of maintaining sufficient inventories to meet demand for goods and, at the same time, incurring the lowest possible inventory holding costs.

Waiting-Line or Queueing Models. Waiting-line or queueing models have been developed to help managers understand and make better decisions concerning the operation of systems involving waiting lines.

Computer Simulation. Computer simulation is a technique used to model the operation of a system over time. This technique employs a computer program to model the operation and perform simulation computations.

Decision Analysis. Decision analysis can be used to determine optimal strategies in situations involving several decision alternatives and an uncertain or risk-filled pattern of events.

Goal Programming. Goal programming is a technique for solving multicriteria decision problems, usually within the framework of linear programming.

Analytic Hierarchy Process. A multicriteria decision-making technique that permits the inclusion of subjective factors in arriving at a recommended decision.

Forecasting. Forecasting methods are techniques that can be used to predict future aspects of a business operation.

Markov-Process Models. Markov-process models are useful in studying the evolution of certain systems over repeated trials. For example, Markov processes have been used to describe the probability that a machine that is functioning in one period will continue to function or break down in another period.

Dynamic Programming. Dynamic programming is an approach that allows us to break up a large problem in such a fashion that once all the smaller problems have been solved, we are left with an optimal solution to the large problem.

Calculus-Based Procedures. Calculus-based procedures are used to solve problems that involve a nonlinear objective function and/or constraints involving nonlinear functions of the decision variables.

Methods Used Most Frequently

A survey of corporate executives conducted by Forgionne[3] indicated how often a variety of management science techniques are used. As Table 1.3 shows, the most frequently used techniques are statistical methods, computer simulation, PERT/CPM, linear programming, and queueing theory. A survey by Ledbetter and Cox[4] lends further support to these findings by ranking regression (statistical analysis), linear programming, simulation, network models (PERT/CPM), queueing, dynamic programming, and game theory in order of usage.

---

[3]G. A. Forgionne, "Corporate Management Science Activities," *Interfaces* 13, n. 3 (1983):20–23.

[4]W. Ledbetter and J. Cox, "Are OR Techniques Being Used?" *Industrial Engineering* 9, no. 2 (1977):19–21.

Table 1.3
The Utilization of Management Science and Operations Research Methodologies

Methodology	Frequency of Use (% of respondents)		
	Never	Moderate	Frequent
Statistical	1.6	38.7	59.7
Computer simulation	12.9	53.2	33.9
PERT/CPM	25.8	53.2	21.0
Linear programming	25.8	59.7	14.5
Queueing theory	40.3	50.0	9.7
Nonlinear programming	53.2	38.7	8.1
Dynamic programming	61.3	33.9	4.8
Game theory	69.4	27.4	3.2

A survey by Thomas and DaCosta[5] showed that 88% of all large corporations use forecasting and over 50% use quantitative approaches to production scheduling, inventory control, capital budgeting, and transportation. A study conducted by Gaither[6] of the applications of management science in manufacturing firms also supports the high frequency of utilization for statistical analysis, simulation, and linear programming. However, PERT/CPM is identified as the method most frequently used in the manufacturing firms surveyed. The manufacturing firms also report a higher than average usage of queueing theory, nonlinear programming, and integer programming.

As part of a survey of practitioners in government, industry, and academia, Shannon, Long, and Buckles[7] asked practitioners to indicate whether they were familiar with the various quantitative methods and whether they had actually used the methods in specific applications. The results, which are shown in Table 1.4, provide further support that linear programming, simulation, network analysis, and queueing theory are perhaps the most frequently known and utilized management science techniques.

Implications for the Use of Management Science

"A valuable OR person is a person who perceives their job as solving a problem, not as developing an algorithm. Once you make that transition, you're going to be a valuable part of any company."
Stephan Regulinski, Vice President—Financial Planning and Analysis, United Airlines.

Recently, Morgan[8] reviewed 12 company surveys and 3 practitioner surveys that have been conducted in the last 30 years, including each of the studies referred to above. Her analysis provided further support that PERT/CPM, linear programming, and simulation are among the most frequently used methods. More importantly, however, after critical examination of all the survey results, she concluded that (1) any firm just beginning to use management science techniques should locate analysts in functional areas, not in centralized units; (2) the initial use of management science should focus on the more frequently used and more useful techniques; and (3) the barriers to the use of management

[5]G. Thomas and J. DaCosta, "A Sample Survey of Corporate Operations Research," *Interfaces* 9, no. 4 (1979):102–11.

[6]N. Gaither, "The Adoption of Operations Research Techniques by Manufacturing Organizations," *Decision Sciences* 6, no. 4 (1975):797–813.

[7]R. E. Shannon, S. S. Long, and B. P. Buckles, "Operations Research Methodologies in Industrial Engineering: A Survey," *AIIE Transactions* 12, no. 4 (1980):364–67.

[8]C. L. Morgan, "A Survey of MS/OR Surveys," *Interfaces* 19, no. 6 (1989):95–103.

Table 1.4
Familiarity with and Use of Various Quantitative Methods by Management Science Practitioners

Method	Familiarity Rank	Usage (%)
Linear programming	1	83.8
Simulation	2	80.3
Network analysis	3	58.1
Queueing theory	4	54.7
Decision trees	5	54.7
Integer programming	6	38.5
Dynamic programming	7	32.5
Nonlinear programming	8	30.7
Markov processes	9	31.6
Replacement analysis	10	38.5
Game theory	11	13.7
Goal programming	12	20.5

science can best be removed by increasing the manager's understanding of management science techniques. Furthermore, to gain the confidence and support of top management, MS/OR analysts must learn to sell their approaches and solutions, with particular emphasis placed on improving communications with managers.

Helping to bridge the gap between the manager and the MS/OR analyst is a major focus of this text. As authors and MS/OR practitioners, we want to help develop an understanding of what the management science techniques are, how they are used, and, most importantly, how they can assist managers throughout their careers in making better decisions.

NOTES & COMMENTS

1. Operations research analyst is listed by the Bureau of Labor Statistics as one of the fastest growing occupations for careers requiring a bachelor's degree; they predict a growth from 57,000 jobs in 1990 to 100,000 jobs in 2005, an increase of 73%.

2. The Operations Research Society of America (ORSA), The Institute of Management Sciences (TIMS), and The Decision Sciences Institute (DSI) are three professional societies that publish journals and newsletters dealing with current research and applications of quantitative methods.

1.6 A Microcomputer Software Package

As stated earlier, developments in computer technology have been a major factor in making quantitative methods available to decision makers. Currently, microcomputer software packages of quantitative methods are making many techniques easier to use. A software package called *The Management Scientist* has been prepared to accompany this text. It can be used to solve problems in this text as well as small-scale problems encountered in practice. Working with this software package will give you an understanding of the role of the computer in applying quantitative methods to decision problems.

The Management Scientist software package contains modules, or programs, that will enable you to solve problems in the following chapters and topical areas:

Chapters 2–6	Linear programming
Chapter 7	Transportation and assignment problems
Chapter 8	Integer linear programming
Chapter 9	Shortest route and minimal spanning tree
Chapter 10	PERT/CPM
Chapter 11	Inventory models
Chapter 12	Waiting-line models
Chapter 14	Decision analysis
Chapter 16	Forecasting
Chapter 17	Markov processes

Use of The Management Scientist with this text is optional. Occasionally, we will insert a figure in the text that will show the output The Management Scientist would have provided for the problem being solved. But, familiarity with the software is not necessary to understand the figure. If you decide to use The Management Scientist software package, it will come with directions for installing the package on your microcomputer. The remainder of this section provides an introduction to the use of this software package.

Top Level Menu

After installing and starting to run The Management Scientist software, you will encounter the Top Level Menu shown in Figure 1.7. The choices on the menu provide access to the corresponding modules, or programs. Simply enter the number of your selection, press "Return," and the requested module will be loaded into the computer's memory. When you have obtained the solution information from the module selected, you may return to the Top Level Menu. At this point, you may select another module or menu choice 13, which will let you exit the package.

All of the programs in The Management Scientist are menu-driven. At various steps of all modules, menus will appear on the screen. By entering the number corresponding to your choice, you will be able to proceed as desired with the analysis and solution.

Problem Selection Menu

After you select a module from the Top Level Menu, the module will load into the computer's memory and a title screen for the module will be displayed. The title screen contains a brief description of the types of problems the module can be used to solve.

After the title screen appears, you may press "Return," to obtain the problem selection menu, such as the one shown in Figure 1.8. From the problem selection menu, you may choose to create a new problem, retrieve a previously saved problem from a data disk, continue with the current problem, delete a previously saved problem on a data disk, or exit the module by returning to the Top Level Menu.

Data Input

Anytime a problem is being considered for the first time, you must select the option to create a new problem from the problem selection menu (see Figure 1.8). The module will

Figure 1.7
Top Level Menu of The Management Scientist Software Package

```
              THE MANAGEMENT SCIENTIST

                   Top Level Menu

   1  Linear Programming          7  PERT/CPM

   2  Transportation              8  Inventory Models

   3  Assignment                  9  Waiting Lines

   4  Integer Linear Programming 10  Decision Analysis

   5  Shortest Route             11  Forecasting

   6  Minimal Spanning Tree      12  Markov Processes

              13  EXIT PROGRAM
```

Figure 1.8
Problem Selection Menu for The
Management Scientist Software
Package

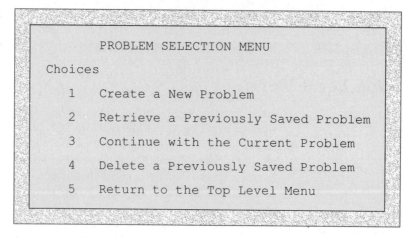

```
              PROBLEM SELECTION MENU

     Choices

          1    Create a New Problem

          2    Retrieve a Previously Saved Problem

          3    Continue with the Current Problem

          4    Delete a Previously Saved Problem

          5    Return to the Top Level Menu
```

then guide you through the data input process by displaying prompts that indicate the information or data to be entered. By first studying the quantitative method in the text, you should easily understand the information or data prompts displayed by the module.

Problem Disposition Menu

Once a problem has been created, The Management Scientist will display the problem disposition menu. From this menu you may choose to solve the problem, display/edit the problem, or return to the problem selection menu. If you choose to solve the problem, The Management Scientist will solve the problem and display the solution on the screen.

Solution and Output Information

The type of information provided and its interpretation varies with the module selected. By reading the corresponding chapter in the text, you should be able to interpret the output information. After the solution and other output information have been displayed on the screen, you will be provided with the option of deciding whether or not to send the information to the printer. If you choose to obtain printed output, input data as well as the solution information will be printed.

Data Editing

Occasionally during the data input process you may strike the wrong key or numerical value and then press "Return." This will enter the incorrect value into the program. However, by selecting the display/edit option from the problem disposition menu, you will be given the opportunity to modify or change any of the original input data.

Saving, Retrieving, and/or Deleting Problems

The Management Scientist allows you to save problems for future use on a data disk. You will be given the opportunity to specify the disk drive to be used for problem saving when you initially start up the software package. Thereafter, the problem-saving option on the problem disposition menu can be used to save a problem on the selected disk drive. If this option is selected, you will be provided with instructions for naming the problem. The problem will be saved automatically, using the name specified.

When reentering the module at a later date, the Retrieve option from the problem selection menu will let you recall a previously saved problem. Simply enter the name of the saved problem, and it will be loaded and become active in the module. When you no longer need access to a particular problem, the Delete option from the problem selection menu can be used to erase the problem from your data disk.

Further Advice About Data Input

When using The Management Scientist, you may find the following data input suggestions helpful.

1. Do not enter commas (,) with your input data. For example, to enter the numerical value of 104,000, simply type the six digits 104000.
2. Do not enter the dollar sign ($) for profit or cost data. For example, a cost of $20.00 should be entered as 20.
3. Do not enter the percent sign (%) if percentage input is requested. For a percentage of 25%, simply enter 25. Do not enter 25% or .25.
4. If the computer did not interpret your input correctly (e.g., you tried to input a comma), the message "Redo from start" may appear. This message refers to the input question or prompt you are currently responding to, and it means to respond to the same question or prompt again.
5. For data values containing the digit zero, be sure to enter the numeric 0 rather than the letter O.
6. Occasionally, a quantitative model will be formulated with fractional values such as $\frac{1}{4}$, $\frac{2}{3}$, $\frac{5}{6}$, and so on. The data input for the computer must be in decimal form. The fraction of $\frac{1}{4}$ can be entered as .25. However, the fractions $\frac{2}{3}$ and $\frac{5}{6}$ have repeating decimal forms. In cases such as these, we recommend the convention of rounding to five places. Thus, the corresponding decimal values of .66667 and .83333 should be entered.
7. Finally, we recommend that in general you attempt to scale extremely large input data so that smaller numbers may be input and operated on by the computer. For example, a cost of $2,500,000 may be scaled to 2.5 with the understanding that the data used in the problem reflect millions of dollars.

Summary

This is a book about how management science may be used to help managers make better decisions. The focus of this text is on the decision-making process and on the role of management science in that process. We have discussed the problem orientation of this process and in an overview have shown how mathematical models can be used in this type of analysis.

The difference between the model and the situation or managerial problem it represents is an important point. Mathematical models are abstractions of real-world situations and, as such, cannot capture all the aspects of the real situation. However, if a model can capture the major relevant aspects of the problem and can then provide a solution recommendation, it can be a valuable aid to decision making.

One of the characteristics of management science that will become increasingly apparent as we proceed through the text is the search for a best solution to the problem. In carrying out the quantitative analysis, we shall be attempting to develop procedures for finding the "best" or optimal solution.

Glossary

We suggest that students form their own glossary as they read the text. They should try, as much as possible, to express each term in their own words. Our experience is that students who follow this suggestion have a much better understanding of the material in the chapter and perform better on exams.

Problem solving The process of identifying a difference between some actual and some desired state of affairs and then taking action to resolve the difference.

Decision making The process of defining the problem, identifying the alternatives, determining the criteria, evaluating the alternatives, and choosing an alternative.

Single-criterion decision problem A problem in which the objective is to find the "best" solution with respect to just one criterion.

Multicriteria decision problem A problem that involves more than one criterion; the objective is to find the "best" solution, taking into account all the criteria.

Decision The alternative selected.

Model A representation of a real object or situation.

Iconic model A physical replica or representation of a real object.

Analog model While physical in form, an analog model does not have a physical appearance similar to the real object or situation it represents.

Mathematical model Mathematical symbols and expressions used to represent a real situation.

Constraints Restrictions or limitations imposed on a problem.

Objective function A mathematical expression used to represent the criterion for evaluating solutions to a problem.

Controllable input The decision alternatives or inputs that can be specified by the decision maker.

Decision variable Another term for controllable input.

Uncontrollable input The environmental factors or inputs that cannot be controlled by the decision maker.

Deterministic model A model in which all uncontrollable inputs are known and cannot vary.

Stochastic model A model in which at least one uncontrollable input is uncertain and subject to variation; stochastic models are also referred to as **probabilistic models.**

Optimal solution The specific decision variable value or values that provide the "best" output for the model.

Feasible solution A decision alternative or solution that satisfies all constraints.

Infeasible solution A decision alternative or solution that violates one or more constraints.

Fixed cost The portion of the total cost that does not depend on the production volume; this cost remains the same no matter how much is produced.

Variable cost The portion of the total cost that is dependent on and varies with the production volume.

Marginal cost The rate of change of the total cost with respect to volume.

Marginal revenue The rate of change of total revenue with respect to sales volume.

Break-even point The volume that results in total revenue equaling total cost.

Problems

1. Terminology

2. Reasons for growth

3. Quantitative versus qualitative approaches

1. Define the terms *management science* and *operations research.*

2. Describe the major reasons for the growth in the use of management science since World War II.

3. Discuss the different roles played by the qualitative and quantitative approaches to managerial decision making. Why is it important for a manager or decision maker to have a good understanding of both of these approaches to decision making?

4. A firm has just completed a new plant that will produce over 500 different products, using over 50 different production lines and machines. The production scheduling decisions are critical in that sales will be lost if customer demands are not met on time. If no individual in the firm has had experience with this production operation, and if new production schedules must be generated each week, why should the firm consider a quantitative approach to the production scheduling problem?

5. List and discuss the steps of the decision making process.

6. Give an example of each of the three types of models discussed in this chapter: iconic, analog, and mathematical.

7. What are the advantages of analyzing and experimenting with a model as opposed to a real object or situation?

8. Recall the production model from Figure 1.5:

$$\text{Max} \quad 10x$$
$$\text{s.t.}$$
$$5x \leq 40$$
$$x \geq 0$$

Suppose the firm in this example considers a second product that has a unit profit of $5 and requires 2 hours for each unit produced. Use y as the number of units of product 2 produced.
  a. Show the mathematical model when both products are considered simultaneously.
  b. Identify the controllable and uncontrollable inputs for this model.
  c. Draw the flowchart of the input–output process for this model (see Figure 1.5).
  d. What are the optimal solution values of x and y?

9. Is the model developed in Problem 8 a deterministic or a stochastic model? Explain.

10. Suppose we modify the model in Figure 1.5 to obtain the following mathematical model:

$$\text{Max} \quad 10x$$
$$\text{s.t.}$$
$$ax \leq 40$$
$$x \geq 0$$

where a is the number of hours required for each unit produced. With $a = 5$, the optimal solution is $x = 8$. If we have a stochastic model with $a = 3$, $a = 4$, $a = 5$, or $a = 6$ as the possible values for the number of hours required per unit, what is the optimal value for x? What problems does this stochastic model cause?

11. A retail store in Des Moines, Iowa, receives shipments of a particular product from Kansas City and Minneapolis. Let

$$x = \text{units of product received from Kansas City}$$
$$y = \text{units of product received from Minneapolis}$$

  a. Write an expression for the total units of product received by the retail store in Des Moines.
  b. Shipments from Kansas City cost $0.20 per unit, and shipments from Minneapolis cost $0.25 per unit. Develop an objective function representing the total cost of shipments to Des Moines.
  c. Assuming the monthly demand at the retail store is 5000 units, develop a constraint that requires 5000 units to be shipped to Des Moines.
  d. No more than 4000 units can be shipped from Kansas City, and no more than 3000 units can be shipped from Minneapolis in a month. Develop constraints to model this situation.

e. Of course, negative amounts cannot be shipped. Combine the objective function and constraints developed to state a mathematical model for satisfying the demand at the Des Moines retail store at minimum cost.

12. Suppose you are going on a weekend trip to a city that is d miles away. Develop a model that determines your round-trip gasoline costs. What assumptions or approximations do you have to make to treat this model as a deterministic model? Are these assumptions or approximations acceptable to you?

13. For most products, higher prices result in a decreased demand, whereas lower product prices result in an increased demand. Let

$$d = \text{annual demand for a product in units}$$
$$p = \text{price per unit}$$

Assume that a firm accepts the following price–demand relationship as being realistic:

$$d = 800 - 10p$$

where the price p must be between $20 and $70.
a. How many units can the firm sell at the $20 per-unit price? At the $70 per-unit price?
b. Show the mathematical model for the total revenue (TR), which is the annual demand multiplied by the unit price.
c. Based on other considerations, the firm's management will only consider price alternatives of $30, $40, and $50. Use your model from part (b) to determine the price alternative that will maximize the total revenue.
d. What are the expected annual demand and the total revenue according to your recommended price?

14. Suppose that a manager has a choice between the following two mathematical models of a given situation: (a) a relatively simple model that is a reasonable approximation of the real situation and (b) a thorough and complex model that is the most accurate mathematical representation of the real situation possible. Why might the model described in part (a) be preferred by the manager?

15. The O'Neill Shoe Manufacturing Company will produce a special-style shoe if the order size is large enough to provide a reasonable profit. For each special-style order, the company incurs a fixed cost of $1000 for the production setup. The variable cost is $30 per pair, and each pair sells for $40.
a. Let x indicate the number of pairs of shoes produced. Develop a mathematical model for the total cost of producing x pairs of shoes.
b. Let P indicate the total profit. Develop a mathematical model for the total profit realized from an order for x pairs of shoes.
c. How large must the shoe order be before O'Neill will break even?

16. Financial Analysts, Inc., is an investment firm that manages stock portfolios for a number of clients. A new client has just requested that the firm handle an $80,000 portfolio. As an initial investment strategy, the client would like to restrict the portfolio to a mix of the following two stocks:

Stock	Price/ Share	Estimated Annual Return/Share	Maximum Possible Investment
Oil Alaska	$50	$6	$50,000
Southwest Petroleum	$30	$4	$45,000

Let

$$x = \text{number of shares of Oil Alaska}$$
$$y = \text{number of shares of Southwest Petroleum}$$

a.

Develop the objective function, assuming that the client desires to maximize the total annual return.

b. Show the mathematical expression for each of the following three constraints:
(1) Total investment funds available are $80,000.
(2) Maximum Oil Alaska investment is $50,000.
(3) Maximum Southwest Petroleum investment is $45,000.

Note: Adding the $x \geq 0$ and $y \geq 0$ constraints provides a linear programming model for the investment problem. A solution procedure for this model will be discussed in Chapter 2.

17. A somewhat more complex relationship. Relates to the production scheduling model in Chapter 4.

17. Models of inventory systems frequently consider the relationships among a beginning inventory, a production quantity, a demand or sales, and an ending inventory. For a given production period j, let

$$s_{j-1} = \text{ending inventory from the previous period}$$
$$\text{(beginning inventory for period } j)$$

$$x_j = \text{production quantity in period } j$$

$$d_j = \text{demand in period } j$$

$$s_j = \text{ending inventory for period } j$$

a. Write the mathematical relationship or model that describes how the above four variables are related.

b. What constraint should be added if production capacity for period j is given by C_j?

c. What constraint should be added if safety stock requirements for period j mandate an ending inventory of at least I_j?

Management Science In Practice Feature

Management Science in Practice write-ups prepared by practitioners are presented at the end of 15 chapters. We feel these provide a meaningful extension to the text material. The purpose of these application write-ups is to provide the reader with a better appreciation for the types of companies that use management science and the types of problems these companies are able to solve.

Each Management Science in Practice write-up begins with a description of the company involved and continues with a discussion of the areas where the company has successfully applied quantitative methods. The remainder of the write-up deals with an application that is closely related to the preceding chapter and/or part of the book. An effort has been made to avoid unnecessary technical detail and to focus on the managerial aspects and the value of the results to the company.

Since Chapter 1 is designed to provide an introduction to management science, we have not emphasized any particular solution methodology. Thus, we have placed the Mead Corporation write-up at the end of this first chapter because it provides an overview of several areas in which management science can be used effectively. It is evidence of the impact quantitative approaches to decision making are having at some companies.

MANAGEMENT SCIENCE IN PRACTICE

Mead Corporation*

Dayton, Ohio

Mead is a major producer of papers for premium periodicals, books, commercial printing, and business forms, with special expertise in coating technologies. The company and its affiliates also produce pulp and lumber, a variety of specialty papers, and converted wood and paper products. Mead is a leader in the design and manufacture of multiple packaging and packaging systems for beverage and other consumable markets. The company is a world leader in the production of coated board, and manufactures shipping containers and corrugating medium. Mead is a major manufacturer of paper-based school and office products, and operates a nationwide network of distribution centers for paper, packaging and supplies. Mead is a pioneer in computer-assisted information retrieval and an important publisher of legal information. Its on-line services are used throughout the world by professionals in a wide range of disciplines.

Management Science at Mead Corporation

Management science applications at Mead are developed and implemented by the company's Decision Analysis (DA) Department. The DA Department provides timely, efficient internal consulting services to the operating groups and corporate staff in the functional areas of operations, finance, marketing, and human resources. The department assists decision makers by providing them with analytical tools of management science as well as personal analysis and recommendations. Through conversations and observations, the department recognizes needs where management science techniques are applicable, and it then recommends appropriate projects. In addition, the department provides a resource reservoir for information and assistance on quantitative methodology and assumes responsibility for keeping current in management science techniques that could produce efficiencies at Mead. This charter results in a variety of projects and applications that span the corporation. Four examples of management science applications at Mead are described below.

A Corporate Planning System

The DA Department built and maintains a corporate planning system. This system allows business units to create and evaluate their five-year plans in an interactive computer environment.

Once the individual business units have finished their planning, the system consolidates the information at a group level. The assumptions of the units and the group are evaluated and reconciled. The use of this computer model facilitates this process by ensuring uniformity of calculations and reporting by all the planning units. Ultimately, the information is consolidated and evaluated at a corporate level.

A Timberland Financing Model

Another example of a management science application involves the development of a timberland financing model. Working directly with financial management, analysts assisted in the creation of a deterministic model that considered the major factors in a timberland financing arrangement. The model was used to examine the liability and profitability of timberland acquisition under various assumptions concerning forest growth rates, the inflation rate, and other financial considerations. By using the model, management was able to examine fully the acquisition and modify the financial arrangement as operating conditions warranted. The model is currently operated and modified by financial management and is considered a major tool in the examination of timberland financing.

Inventory Analysis

Inventory analysis is an area in which more sophisticated tools of management science have been used. Simulation models have been used to describe the major factors (e.g., demand or usage rates, lead times, and production rates) in an inventory system. Typically, an inventory model includes purchase, storage, ordering, stockout, and degradation costs. The simulation model is used to evaluate reorder points, safety stocks, customer service levels, review periods, and the response time of the inventory system to extraordinary events.

Once developed and in place, the model can be updated as economic and operating conditions change. Thus, the model can be used by management to evaluate its inventory system on an ongoing basis and to ensure that it is operating in a cost-efficient manner. These inventory simulation models are user friendly and can be operated and maintained by management with little formal computer training.

A Timber Harvesting Model

Mead has also used models to assist with the long-range management of the company's timberland. Through the use of large-scale linear programs, timber harvesting plans have been developed to cover a substantial time horizon. These models consider wood market conditions, mill pulpwood requirements, harvesting capacities, and general forest management principles.

—Continued on next page

*The authors are indebted to Dr. Edward P. Winkofsky, Mead Corporation, Dayton, Ohio, for providing this application.

—Continued from previous page

Within these constraints, the model develops an optimal harvesting and purchasing schedule based on discounted cash flow. Alternative schedules are developed to reflect various assumptions concerning forest growth, wood availability, and general economic conditions.

Quantitative methods are also used in the development of the inputs for the linear programming models described above. Timber prices and supplies as well as mill requirements must be forecast over the time horizon. Advanced sampling techniques are used to evaluate land holdings and to project forest growth. The harvest schedule is developed through the use of a number of management science techniques.

Summary

The applications briefly described above—although only a few of the many management science projects at Mead—convey the breadth of the activities currently in use within the company. The management scientist at Mead must be able to work in a number of different environments and be proficient in a wide range of quantitative methods. In addition, the analyst must possess exceptional oral and written communication skills. Only with this background will the analyst be able to achieve the major objective of management science at Mead—the development and implementation of user-friendly quantitative models that will support and enhance management decision making throughout the organization.

Questions

1. Which techniques listed in Table 1.3 are being used in the four management science applications described at the Mead Corporation?
2. Which of the Mead applications use a deterministic model, and which use a stochastic model? What conditions in the applications indicate a stochastic model is necessary?
3. Discuss how the quantitative analysis process described in Section 1.3 occurs in Mead's inventory analysis application.
4. Discuss the benefits associated with the management science applications at Mead.

CHAPTER 2

Linear Programming:
The Graphical Method

Linear programming was initially referred to as "programming in a linear structure." In 1948 Tjalling Koopmans suggested to George Dantzig that the name was much too long; Koopman's suggestion was to shorten it to linear programming. George Dantzig agreed, and the field we now know as linear programming was named.

Linear programming is a problem-solving approach that has been developed to help managers make decisions. Some typical applications of linear programming are described below:

1. A manufacturer wants to develop a production schedule and an inventory policy that will satisfy sales demand in future periods. Ideally, the schedule and policy will enable the company to satisfy demand and at the same time *minimize* the total production and inventory costs.

2. A financial analyst must select an investment portfolio from a variety of stock and bond investment alternatives. The analyst would like to establish the portfolio that *maximizes* the return on investment.

3. A marketing manager wants to determine how best to allocate a fixed advertising budget among alternative advertising media such as radio, television, newspapers, and magazines. The manager would like to determine the media mix that *maximizes* the advertising effectiveness.

4. A company has warehouses in a number of locations throughout the United States. Given a set of customer demands for its products, the company would like to determine which warehouse should ship how much product to which customers so that the total transportation costs are *minimized*.

These are only a few examples of situations where linear programming has been used successfully, but they illustrate the diversity of linear programming applications. A close scrutiny reveals one basic property that all of them have in common. In each example, we were concerned with *maximizing* or *minimizing* some quantity. We wanted to minimize costs in example 1, we wanted to maximize return on investment in example 2, we wanted to maximize advertising effectiveness in example 3, and we wanted to minimize total transportation costs in example 4. *In all linear programming problems, the maximization or minimization of some quantity is the objective.*

A second property of all linear programming problems is that there are restrictions or *constraints* that limit the degree to which the objective can be pursued. In example 1 the

28

manufacturer is restricted by constraints requiring product demand to be satisfied and by the constraints limiting production capacity. The financial analyst's portfolio problem is constrained by the total amount of investment funds available and the maximum amounts that can be invested in each stock or bond. The marketing manager's media selection decision is constrained by a fixed advertising budget and the availability of the various media. In the transportation problem, the minimum-cost shipping schedule is constrained by the supply of product available at each warehouse. *Thus, constraints are another general feature of every linear programming problem.*

2.1   A Simple Maximization Problem

The RMC, Inc., problem situation (see Problems 21, 50, and 51) provides a good classroom illustration of the material covered in this chapter.

Par, Inc., is a small manufacturer of golf equipment and supplies whose management has decided to move into the market for medium- and high-priced golf bags. Par's distributor is enthusiastic about the new product line and has agreed to buy all the golf bags Par produces over the next 3 months.

After a thorough investigation of the steps involved in manufacturing a golf bag, management has determined that each golf bag produced will require the following operations:

1. Cutting and dyeing the material
2. Sewing
3. Finishing (inserting umbrella holder, club separators, etc.)
4. Inspection and packaging

The director of manufacturing has analyzed each of the operations and concluded that if the company produces a medium-priced standard model, each bag will require $7/10$ hour in the cutting and dyeing department, $1/2$ hour in the sewing department, 1 hour in the finishing department, and $1/10$ hour in the inspection and packaging department. The more expensive deluxe model will require 1 hour for cutting and dyeing, $5/6$ hour for sewing, $2/3$ hour for finishing, and $1/4$ hour for inspection and packaging. This production information is summarized in Table 2.1.

The accounting department has analyzed these production figures, assigned all relevant variable costs, and arrived at prices for both bags that will result in a profit contribution[1] of $10 for every standard bag and $9 for every deluxe bag produced.

The student should understand that we are maximizing profit contribution, not profit. Overhead and other shared costs must be deducted before arriving at a profit figure.

In addition, after studying departmental work load projections, the director of manufacturing estimates that 630 hours for cutting and dyeing, 600 hours for sewing, 708 hours for finishing, and 135 hours for inspection and packaging will be available for the production of golf bags during the next 3 months.

---

[1]From an accounting perspective, this is more correctly described as the contribution margin per bag; for example, overhead and other shared costs have not been allocated.

Table 2.1
Production Requirements per Golf Bag

	Production Time (hours)			
Product	Cutting and Dyeing	Sewing	Finishing	Inspection and Packaging
Standard bag	$7/10$	$1/2$	1	$1/10$
Deluxe bag	1	$5/6$	$2/3$	$1/4$

You may find it useful to break a small class into teams of three or four students. Let them attempt to obtain a solution for the problem you use in your lecture. After 20 minutes, ask a team leader from each group to briefly summarize their solution and problem-solving approach. This exercise provides a good basis for discussing the graphical solution method and forces the student to think about the subject matter from a problem-solving perspective.

The company's problem is to determine how many standard and deluxe bags it should produce to maximize the total profit contribution. If you were in charge of production scheduling for Par, Inc., what decision would you make? That is, how many standard and how many deluxe bags would you produce in the next 3 months? Write your decision below. Later you can check and see how well you did.

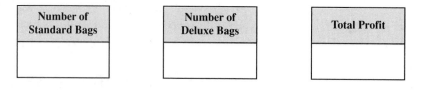

Number of Standard Bags	Number of Deluxe Bags	Total Profit

2.2 The Objective Function

As pointed out earlier, every linear programming problem has a maximization or minimization objective. For the Par problem, the objective is to maximize the total profit contribution. We can write this objective in mathematical form with the introduction of some simple notation. Let

x_1 = number of standard bags Par, Inc., produces
x_2 = number of deluxe bags Par, Inc., produces

Par's profit contribution will come from two sources: (1) the profit contribution made by producing x_1 standard bags and (2) the profit contribution made by producing x_2 deluxe bags. Since Par makes $10 for every standard bag produced, the company will make $10x_1$ if x_1 standard bags are produced. Also, since Par makes $9 for every deluxe bag produced, the company will make $9x_2$ if x_2 deluxe bags are produced. Denoting the total profit contribution by z, we have

$$\text{Total profit contribution} = z = \$10x_1 + \$9x_2$$

From now on we will assume that the profit contribution is measured in dollars and write the total profit contribution expression without the dollar signs. That is,

$$\text{Total profit contribution} = z = 10x_1 + 9x_2 \tag{2.1}$$

Par's problem can now be stated as one of choosing values for the variables x_1 and x_2 that will yield the highest possible value of z. In linear programming terminology, we refer to x_1 and x_2 as the *decision variables*. Since the objective—maximize total profit contribution—is a function of these decision variables, we refer to $10x_1 + 9x_2$ as the *objective function*. Using max as an abbreviation for maximize, Par's objective is written as follows:

$$\max z = \max 10x_1 + 9x_2 \tag{2.2}$$

In this problem, any particular production combination of standard and deluxe bags is referred to as a *solution* to the problem. However, only those solutions that satisfy *all* the constraints are referred to as *feasible solutions*. The particular feasible production combination (feasible solution) that results in the largest profit contribution will be referred to as the *optimal* production combination or, equivalently, as the *optimal solution.* At this point, however, we have no idea what the optimal solution will be. Indeed, we have not even developed a procedure for identifying feasible solutions. The procedure for determining feasible solutions requires us first to identify all the constraints of the problem.

2.3 The Constraints

Every standard and deluxe bag produced must go through four manufacturing operations. Since there is a limited amount of production time available for each of these operations, we can expect that four constraints will limit the total number of golf bags Par can produce.

From the production information (see Table 2.1), we know that every standard bag Par manufactures will use $7/10$ hour for cutting and dyeing. Hence, the total number of hours of cutting and dyeing time used in the manufacture of x_1 standard bags will be $7/10\,x_1$. On the other hand, every deluxe bag Par produces will use 1 hour for cutting and dyeing; thus, x_2 deluxe bags will use $1x_2$ hours of cutting and dyeing time. The total cutting and dyeing time required for the production of x_1 standard bags and x_2 deluxe bags is given by

$$\text{Total cutting and dyeing time required} = 7/10\,x_1 + 1x_2$$

Since the director of manufacturing has stated that Par has at most 630 hours of cutting and dyeing time available, it follows that the product combination we select must satisfy the requirement

$$7/10\,x_1 + 1x_2 \le 630 \tag{2.3}$$

Students should check to see that the units of measurement on the left-hand side of the constraint match the units of measurement on the right-hand side.

where the symbol $\le$ means *less than or equal to.* Relationship (2.3) is referred to as an inequality and denotes the fact that the total number of hours used for the cutting and dyeing operation in the production of x_1 standard bags and x_2 deluxe bags must be less than or equal to the maximum amount of cutting and dyeing time the company has available.

From Table 2.1 we also see that every standard bag manufactured will require $1/2$ hour for sewing and every deluxe bag will require $5/6$ hour for sewing. Since there are 600 hours of sewing time available, it follows that

$$1/2\,x_1 + 5/6\,x_2 \le 600 \tag{2.4}$$

is the mathematical representation of the sewing constraint. Verify for yourself that the constraint for the finishing time available is

$$1x_1 + 2/3\,x_2 \le 708 \tag{2.5}$$

and that the constraint for the inspection and packaging time available is

$$1/10\,x_1 + 1/4\,x_2 \le 135 \tag{2.6}$$

We now have specified the mathematical relationships for the constraints associated with the four production operations. Are there any other constraints we have forgotten? Can Par produce a negative number of standard or deluxe bags? Clearly, the answer is no. Thus, to prevent the decision variables x_1 and x_2 from having negative values, two constraints

$$x_1 \ge 0 \quad \text{and} \quad x_2 \ge 0 \tag{2.7}$$

must be added. The symbol $\geq$ means *greater than or equal to.* These constraints ensure that the solution to the problem will contain nonnegative values for the decision variables and are thus referred to as the *nonnegativity constraints.* Nonnegativity constraints are a general feature of all linear programming problems and will be written in the following abbreviated form:

$$x_1, x_2 \geq 0$$

2.4 Mathematical Statement of the Par, Inc., Problem

You should be able to formulate a mathematical model for a maximization linear programming problem with less-than-or-equal-to constraints. Try Problem 22(a).

The mathematical statement or mathematical formulation of the Par, Inc., problem is now complete. We have succeeded in translating the objective and constraints of the "real-world" problem into a set of mathematical relationships referred to as a *mathematical model.* The complete mathematical model for the Par problem is as follows:

$$\text{Max} \quad 10x_1 + 9x_2$$

subject to (s.t.)

$$\tfrac{7}{10}x_1 + 1x_2 \leq 630 \quad \text{Cutting and dyeing}$$

$$\tfrac{1}{2}x_1 + \tfrac{5}{6}x_2 \leq 600 \quad \text{Sewing}$$

$$1x_1 + \tfrac{2}{3}x_2 \leq 708 \quad \text{Finishing}$$

$$\tfrac{1}{10}x_1 + \tfrac{1}{4}x_2 \leq 135 \quad \text{Inspection and packaging}$$

$$x_1, x_2 \geq 0$$

Our job now is to find the product mix (i.e., the combination of x_1 and x_2) that satisfies all the constraints and, at the same time, yields a value for the objective function that is greater than or equal to the value given by any other feasible solution. Once this is done, we will have found the optimal solution to the problem.

The above mathematical model of the Par problem is a *linear program.* The problem has the objective and constraints that, as we said earlier, are common properties of all linear programs. But what is the special feature of this mathematical model that makes it a linear program? The special feature that makes it a linear program is that the objective function and all constraint functions (the left-hand sides of the constraint inequalities) are linear functions of the decision variables.

Mathematical functions in which each variable appears in a separate term and is raised to the first power are called *linear functions.* The objective function $(10x_1 + 9x_2)$ is linear since each decision variable appears in a separate term and has an exponent of 1. If the objective function had appeared as $10x_1^2 + 9\sqrt{x_2}$, it would not have been a linear function, and we would not have a linear program. The amount of production time required in the cutting and dyeing department $(\tfrac{7}{10}x_1 + 1x_2)$ is also a linear function of the decision variables for the same reason. Similarly, the functions of the left-hand side of all the constraint inequalities (the constraint functions) are linear functions. Thus, the mathematical formulation of this problem is referred to as a linear program.

You should now be able to recognize the types of mathematical relationships that can be found in a linear program. Try Problem 1.

We can now note that linear *programming* has nothing to do with computer programming. The use of the word *programming* here means "choosing a course of action." Linear programming involves choosing a course of action when the mathematical model of the problem contains only linear functions.

2.5 Graphical Solution

A linear programming problem involving only two decision variables can be solved using a graphical solution procedure. Let us begin the graphical solution procedure by developing a graph that displays the possible solutions (x_1 and x_2 values) for the Par problem. The graph (Figure 2.1) will have values of x_1 on the horizontal axis and values of x_2 on the vertical axis. Any point on the graph can be identified by the x_1 and x_2 values, which indicate the position of the point along the x_1 and x_2 axes, respectively. Since every point (x_1, x_2) corresponds to a possible solution, every point on the graph is called a *solution point.* The solution point where $x_1 = 0$ and $x_2 = 0$ is referred to as the origin.

The next step is to determine which of the solution points corresponds to feasible solutions for the linear program. Both x_1 and x_2 are required to be nonnegative, so we need only consider that portion of the graph where $x_1 \geq 0$ and $x_2 \geq 0$. In Figure 2.2 the arrows point to the portion of the solution region where these nonnegativity requirements are satisfied. Since linear programming decision variables are always required to be nonnegative, all future graphs will show only the portion of the solution region corresponding to nonnegative values for the decision variables.

Earlier, we saw that the inequality representing the cutting and dyeing constraint is

$$\tfrac{7}{10} x_1 + 1 x_2 \leq 630$$

To show all solution points that satisfy this relationship, we start by graphing the solution points satisfying the constraint as an equality. That is, the points where $\tfrac{7}{10} x_1 + 1 x_2 = 630$. Since the graph of this equation is a line, it can be obtained by identifying two points that satisfy the equation and then drawing a line through the points. Setting $x_1 = 0$ and solving for x_2, we see that the point $(x_1 = 0, x_2 = 630)$ satisfies the above equation. To find a second point satisfying this equation, we set $x_2 = 0$ and solve for x_1. By doing this, we obtain $\tfrac{7}{10} x_1 + 1(0) = 630$, or $x_1 = 900$. Thus, a second point

Figure 2.1
Solution Points for the
Two-Variable Par, Inc., Problem

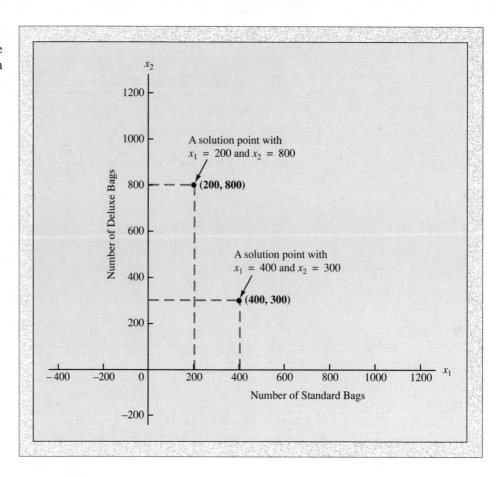

Figure 2.2
The Nonnegativity Constraints

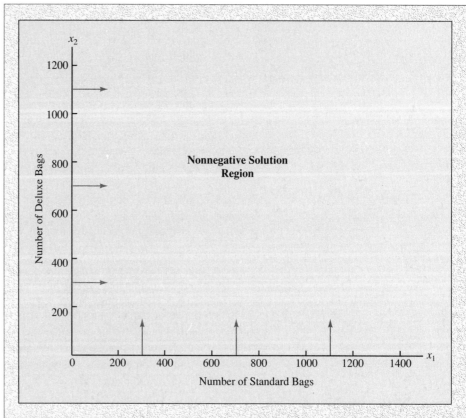

satisfying the equation is ($x_1 = 900$, $x_2 = 0$). Given these two points, we can now graph the line corresponding to the equation

$$\tfrac{7}{10} x_1 + 1 x_2 = 630$$

This line, which will be called the cutting and dyeing *constraint line,* is shown in Figure 2.3. We have labeled this line "C & D" to indicate that it represents the cutting and dyeing constraint line.

Recall that the inequality representing the cutting and dyeing constraint is

$$\tfrac{7}{10} x_1 + 1 x_2 \le 630$$

Can you identify all of the solution points that satisfy this constraint? Since all points on the line satisfy $\tfrac{7}{10} x_1 + 1 x_2 = 630$, we know any point on this line must satisfy the constraint. But where are the solution points satisfying $\tfrac{7}{10} x_1 + 1 x_2 < 630$? Consider two solution points: ($x_1 = 200$, $x_2 = 200$) and ($x_1 = 600$, $x_2 = 500$). You can see from Figure 2.3 that the first solution point is below the constraint line and the second is above the constraint line. Which of these solutions will satisfy the cutting and dyeing constraint? For the point ($x_1 = 200$, $x_2 = 200$), we see that

$$\tfrac{7}{10} x_1 + 1 x_2 = \tfrac{7}{10}(200) + 1(200) = 340$$

Figure 2.3
The Cutting and Dyeing
Constraint Line

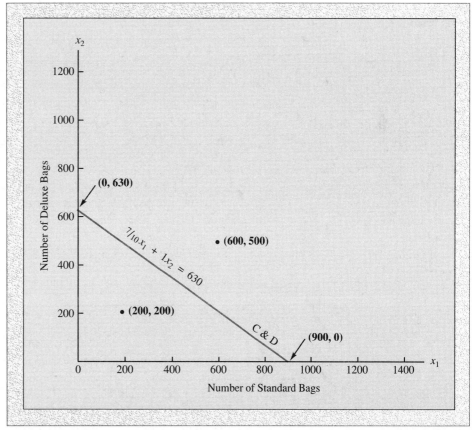

Figure 2.4
Feasible Solutions for the Cutting
and Dyeing Constraint Are
Represented by the Shaded Region

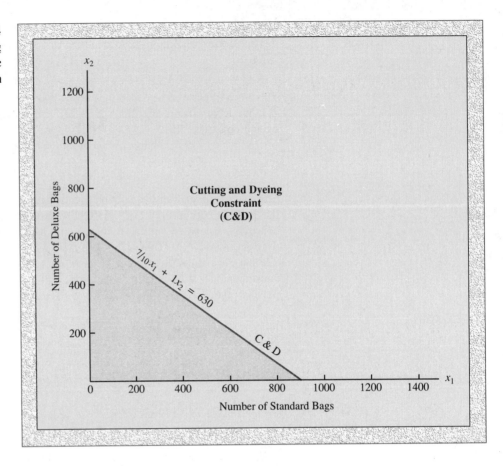

Since the 340 hours is less than the 630 hours available, the $(x_1 = 200,\ x_2 = 200)$ production combination, or solution point, satisfies the constraint. For the point $(x_1 = 600,\ x_2 = 500)$, we have

$$\tfrac{7}{10}x_1 + 1x_2 = \tfrac{7}{10}(600) + 1(500) = 920$$

The 920 hours is greater than the 630 hours available, so the $(x_1 = 600,\ x_2 = 500)$ solution point does not satisfy the constraint and is thus not feasible.

It turns out that if a solution point is not feasible for a particular constraint, then all other solution points on the same side of that constraint line are not feasible. If a solution point is feasible for a particular constraint, then all other solution points on the same side of the constraint line are feasible for that constraint. Thus, one needs to evaluate the constraint function for only one solution point to determine which side of a constraint line is feasible. In Figure 2.4 we indicate all points satisfying the cutting and dyeing constraint by the shaded region.

We continue by identifying the solution points satisfying each of the other three constraints. The solutions that are feasible for each of these constraints are shown in Figure 2.5.

We now have four separate graphs showing the feasible solution points for each of the four constraints. In a linear programming problem, we need to identify the solution points that satisfy *all* the constraints *simultaneously*. To find these solution points, we can draw all four constraints on one graph and observe the region containing the points that do in fact satisfy all the constraints simultaneously.

You should now be able to graph a constraint line and find the solution points that are feasible. Try Problem 2.

Figure 2.5   Feasible Solutions for the Sewing, Finishing, and Inspection and Packaging Constraints Are Represented by the Shaded Regions

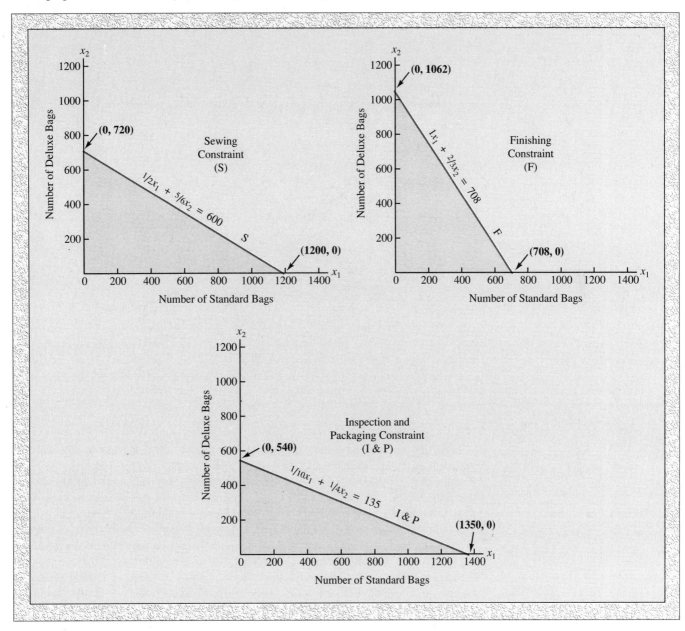

You should now be able to find the feasible region given several constraints. Try Problem 7.

The graphs in Figures 2.4 and 2.5 can be superimposed to obtain one graph with all four constraints. This combined-constraint graph is shown in Figure 2.6. The shaded region in this figure includes every solution point that satisfies all the constraints simultaneously. Since solutions that satisfy all the constraints are termed *feasible solutions,* the shaded region is called the feasible solution region, or simply the *feasible region.* Any point on the boundary of the feasible region or within the feasible region is a *feasible solution point.*

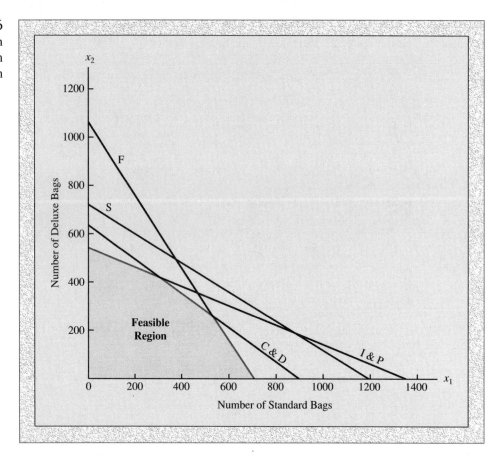

Now that we have identified the feasible region, we are ready to proceed with the graphical solution procedure and find the optimal solution to the Par, Inc., problem. Recall that the optimal solution for a linear programming problem is the feasible solution that provides the best possible value of the objective function. Let us start the optimizing step of the graphical solution procedure by redrawing the feasible region on a separate graph. The graph is shown in Figure 2.7.

One approach to finding the optimal solution would be to evaluate the objective function for each feasible solution; the optimal solution would then be the one yielding the largest value. The difficulty with this approach is that there are an infinite number of feasible solutions; thus, since it is not possible to evaluate an infinity of feasible solutions, this trial-and-error procedure cannot be used to identify the optimal solution.

Rather than trying to compute the profit contribution for each feasible solution, we select an arbitrary value for profit contribution and identify all the feasible solutions (x_1, x_2) that yield the selected value. For example, what feasible solutions provide a profit contribution of $1800? These solutions are given by the values of x_1 and x_2 in the feasible region that will make the objective function

$$10x_1 + 9x_2 = 1800$$

Can you graph the profit line for a linear program? Try Problem 5.

The above expression is simply the equation of a line. Thus, all feasible solution points (x_1, x_2) yielding a profit contribution of $1800 must be on the line. We learned earlier in

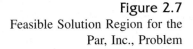

Figure 2.7
Feasible Solution Region for the
Par, Inc., Problem

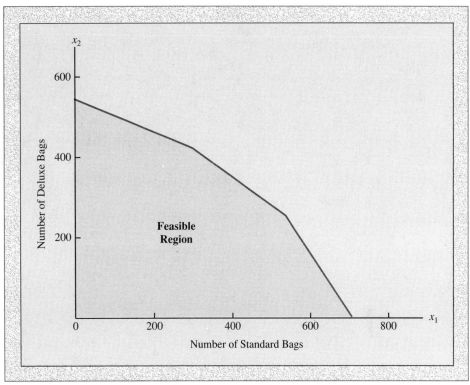

this section how to graph a constraint line. The procedure for graphing the profit or objective function line is the same. Letting $x_1 = 0$, we see that x_2 must be 200; thus, the solution point ($x_1 = 0$, $x_2 = 200$) is on the line. Similarly, by letting $x_2 = 0$, we see that the solution point ($x_1 = 180$, $x_2 = 0$) is also on the line. Drawing the line through these two points identifies all the solutions that have a profit contribution of $1800. A graph of this profit line is presented in Figure 2.8.

Since the objective is to find the feasible solution yielding the largest profit contribution, let us proceed by selecting higher profit contributions and finding the solutions yielding the selected values. For instance, let us find all solutions yielding profit contributions of $3600 and $5400. To do so, we must find the x_1 and x_2 values that are on the following lines:

$$10x_1 + 9x_2 = 3600$$

and

$$10x_1 + 9x_2 = 5400$$

Using the previous procedure for graphing profit and constraint lines, we have drawn the $3600 and $5400 profit lines on the graph in Figure 2.9. While not all solution points on the $5400 profit line are in the feasible region, at least some points on the line are, and it is therefore possible to obtain a feasible solution that provides a $5400 profit contribution.

Can we find a feasible solution yielding an even higher profit contribution? Look at Figure 2.9, and see what general observations you can make about the profit lines already

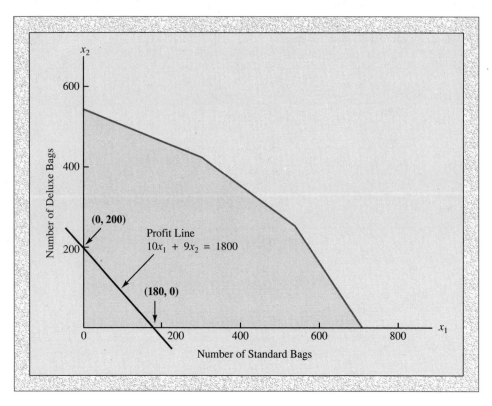

Figure 2.8
$1800 Profit Line for the Par, Inc., Problem

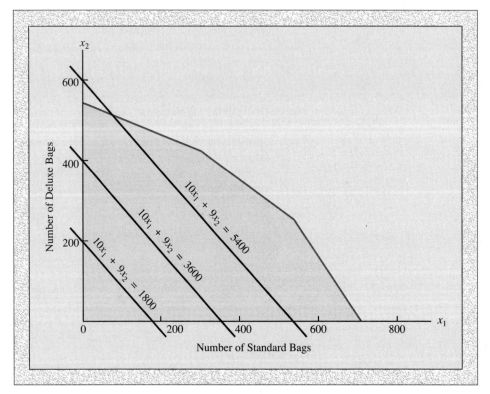

Figure 2.9
Selected Profit Lines for the Par, Inc., Problem

drawn. Note the following: (1) the profit lines are *parallel* to each other, and (2) higher profit lines are obtained as we move farther from the origin. This can also be seen algebraically. Let z represent total profit. The objective function is

$$z = 10x_1 + 9x_2$$

Solving for x_2 in terms of x_1 and z, we obtain

$$9x_2 = -10x_1 + z$$

$$x_2 = -\tfrac{10}{9}x_1 + \tfrac{1}{9}z \qquad (2.8)$$

Equation (2.8) is the *slope–intercept form* of the linear equation relating x_1 and x_2. The coefficient of x_1, $-\tfrac{10}{9}$, is the slope of the line, and the term $\tfrac{1}{9}z$ is the x_2 intercept (i.e., the value of x_2 where the graph of equation (2.8) crosses the x_2 axis). Substituting the profit contributions of $z = 1800$, $z = 3600$, and $z = 5400$ into equation (2.8) yields the following slope–intercept equations for the profit lines shown in Figure 2.9:
For $z = 1800$,

$$x_2 = -\tfrac{10}{9}x_1 + 200$$

For $z = 3600$,

$$x_2 = -\tfrac{10}{9}x_1 + 400$$

For $z = 5400$,

$$x_2 = -\tfrac{10}{9}x_1 + 600$$

The slope ($-\tfrac{10}{9}$) is the same for each profit line since the profit lines are parallel. Further, we see that the x_2 intercept increases with larger profit contributions. Thus, higher profit lines are farther from the origin.

Because the profit lines are parallel and higher profit lines are farther from the origin, we can obtain solutions that yield increasingly larger values for the objective function by continuing to move the profit line farther from the origin in such a fashion that it remains parallel to the other profit lines. However, at some point we will find that any further outward movement will place the profit line completely outside the feasible region. Since solutions outside the feasible region are unacceptable, the point in the feasible region that lies on the highest profit line is the optimal solution to the linear program.

You should now be able to identify the optimal solution point for this problem. Use a ruler or the edge of a piece of paper, and move the profit line as far from the origin as you can. What is the last point in the feasible region that you reach? This point, which is the optimal solution, is shown graphically in Figure 2.10.

The optimal values of the decision variables are the x_1 and x_2 values at the optimal solution. Depending on the accuracy of the graph, you may or may not be able to determine the *exact* x_1 and x_2 values. Referring to the graph in Figure 2.10, the best we can do is conclude that the optimal production combination consists of approximately 550 standard bags (x_1) and approximately 250 deluxe bags (x_2).

A closer inspection of Figures 2.6 and 2.10 shows that the optimal solution point is at the intersection of the cutting and dyeing and the finishing constraint lines. That is, the optimal solution point is on both the cutting and dyeing constraint line

$$\tfrac{7}{10}x_1 + 1x_2 = 630 \qquad (2.9)$$

Figure 2.10
Optimal Solution for the Par, Inc.,
Problem

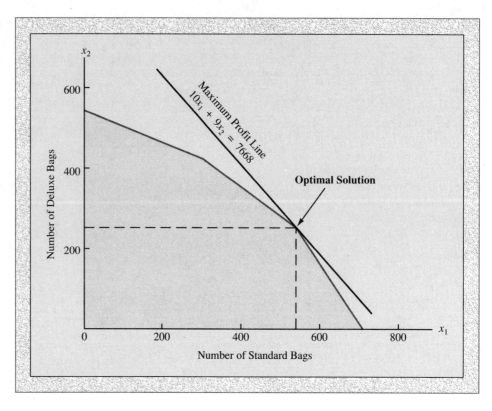

and the finishing constraint line

$$1x_1 + \tfrac{2}{3}x_2 = 708 \tag{2.10}$$

Thus, the optimal values of the decision variables x_1 and x_2 must satisfy both equations (2.9) and (2.10) simultaneously. Using equation (2.9) and solving for x_1 gives

$$\tfrac{7}{10}x_1 = 630 - 1x_2$$

or

$$x_1 = 900 - \tfrac{10}{7}x_2 \tag{2.11}$$

Substituting this expression for x_1 into equation (2.10) and solving for x_2 provide the following:

$$1(900 - \tfrac{10}{7}x_2) + \tfrac{2}{3}x_2 = 708$$

$$900 - \tfrac{10}{7}x_2 + \tfrac{2}{3}x_2 = 708$$

$$900 - \tfrac{30}{21}x_2 + \tfrac{14}{21}x_2 = 708$$

$$-\tfrac{16}{21}x_2 = -192$$

$$x_2 = \frac{192}{\tfrac{16}{21}} = 252$$

Although the optimal solution to the Par, Inc., problem consists of integer values for the decision variables, students should understand that this will not always be the case.

Using $x_2 = 252$ in equation (2.11) and solving for x_1, we obtain

$$x_1 = 900 - {}^{10}\!/_7(252)$$

$$= 900 - 360 = 540$$

The exact location of the optimal solution point is $x_1 = 540$ and $x_2 = 252$. Hence, the optimal production quantities for Par, Inc., are 540 standard bags and 252 deluxe bags, with a resulting profit contribution of $10(540) + 9(252) = \$7668$.

You should now be able to use the graphical solution procedure to identify the optimal solution and find the exact values of the decision variables at the optimal solution. Try Problem 11.

For a linear programming problem with two decision variables, the exact values of the decision variables can be determined by first using the graphical solution procedure to identify the optimal solution point and then solving the two simultaneous constraint equations associated with it.

A Note on Graphing Lines

As can be seen from the graphical solution of the Par, Inc., problem, an important aspect of the graphical method is the ability to graph lines showing the constraints and the objective function of the linear program. The procedure we have used for graphing the equation of a line is to find any two points satisfying the equation and then draw the line through the two points. For the Par, Inc., constraints, the two points were easily found by first setting $x_1 = 0$ and solving the constraint equation for x_2. Then we set $x_2 = 0$ and solved for x_1. For the cutting and dyeing constraint line

$$\tfrac{7}{10}x_1 + 1x_2 = 630$$

this procedure identified the two points ($x_1 = 0$, $x_2 = 630$) and ($x_1 = 900$, $x_2 = 0$). The cutting and dyeing constraint line was then graphed by drawing a line through these two points.

All constraint and objective function lines in two-variable linear programs can be graphed if two points on the line can be identified. However, finding the two points on the line is not always as easy as shown in the Par, Inc., problem. For example, consider the following constraint:

$$2x_1 - 1x_2 \leq 100$$

Using the equality form and setting $x_1 = 0$, we find the point ($x_1 = 0$, $x_2 = -100$) is on the constraint line. Setting $x_2 = 0$, we find a second point ($x_1 = 50$, $x_2 = 0$) on the constraint line. If we have drawn only the nonnegative ($x_1 \geq 0$, $x_2 \geq 0$) portion of the graph, the first point ($x_1 = 0$, $x_2 = -100$) cannot be plotted because $x_2 = -100$ is not on the graph. Whenever we have two points on the line, but one or both of the points cannot be plotted in the nonnegative portion of the graph, the simplest approach is to enlarge the graph to include the negative x_1 and/or x_2 axes. In this example, the point ($x_1 = 0$, $x_2 = -100$) can be plotted by extending the graph to include the negative x_2 axis. Once both points satisfying the constraint equation have been located, the line can be drawn. The constraint line and the feasible solutions for the constraint $2x_1 - 1x_2 \leq 100$ are shown in Figure 2.11.

As another example, let us consider a constraint of the form

$$1x_1 - 1x_2 \geq 0$$

Figure 2.11
Feasible Solutions for the
Constraint $2x_1 - 1x_2 \leq 100$

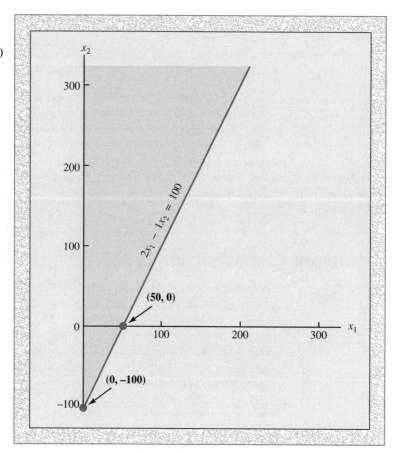

To find all solutions satisfying the constraint as an equality, we first set $x_1 = 0$ and solve for x_2. This shows that the origin ($x_1 = 0$, $x_2 = 0$) is on the constraint line. Setting $x_2 = 0$ and solving for x_1 provides the same point. However, we can obtain a second point on the line by setting x_2 equal to any value other than zero and then solving for x_1. For instance, setting $x_2 = 100$ and solving for x_1, we find that the point ($x_1 = 100$, $x_2 = 100$) is on the line. With the two points ($x_1 = 0$, $x_2 = 0$) and ($x_1 = 100$, $x_2 = 100$), the constraint line $1x_1 - 1x_2 = 0$ and the feasible solutions for $1x_1 - 1x_2 \geq 0$ can be plotted as shown in Figure 2.12.

Summary of the Graphical Solution Procedure for Maximization Problems

As additional practice in using the graphical solution procedure, try Problem 22(b), 22(c), and 22(d).

As we have seen, the graphical solution procedure is a method for solving two-variable linear programming problems such as the Par, Inc., problem. The steps of the graphical solution procedure for a maximization problem are summarized below.

1. Prepare a graph of the feasible solution points for each of the constraints.
2. Determine the feasible region by identifying the solution points that satisfy all the constraints simultaneously.
3. Draw an objective function line showing the values of the x_1 and x_2 variables that yield a specified value of the objective function.

Figure 2.12
Feasible Solutions for the
Constraint $1x_1 - 1x_2 \geq 0$

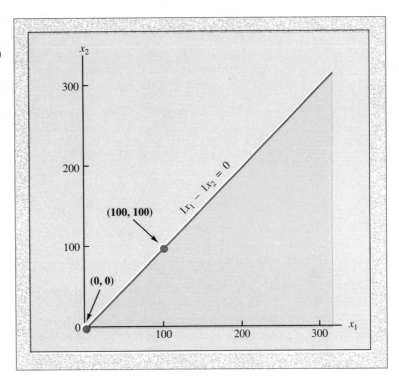

4. Move parallel objective function lines toward larger objective function values until further movement would take the line completely outside the feasible region.

5. A feasible solution point on the objective function line with the largest value is the optimal solution.

Slack Variables

In addition to the optimal solution of $x_1 = 540$ standard bags and $x_2 = 252$ deluxe bags and the expected profit of $7668, Par's management will probably want information about the production time requirements for each production operation. We can obtain this information by substituting the optimal x_1 and x_2 values into the constraint functions for the linear program. For the Par, Inc., problem, the production time requirements are as follows:

$$\tfrac{7}{10}(540) + 1(252) = 630 \text{ hours of cutting and dyeing time}$$

$$\tfrac{1}{2}(540) + \tfrac{5}{6}(252) = 480 \text{ hours of sewing time}$$

$$1(540) + \tfrac{2}{3}(252) = 708 \text{ hours of finishing time}$$

$$\tfrac{1}{10}(540) + \tfrac{1}{4}(252) = 117 \text{ hours of inspection and packaging time}$$

The above results show management that the production of 540 standard bags and 252 deluxe bags will require all available cutting and dyeing time (630 hours) and all available finishing time (708 hours), while 120 hours of sewing time (600 − 480) and 18 hours of inspection and packaging time (135 − 117) will remain idle. The 120 hours of unused sewing time and 18 hours of unused inspection and packaging time are referred to as *slack* for the two departments. In linear programming terminology, any unused or idle capacity for a ≤ constraint is referred to as the *slack* associated with the constraint.

Can you identify the slack associated with a constraint? Try Problem 22(e).

Variables are often added to the formulation of a linear programming problem to represent the slack, or idle capacity. Such variables are called *slack variables*, and since the unused capacity makes no contribution to profit, they have coefficients of zero in the objective function. After the addition of slack variables to the mathematical statement of the Par, Inc., problem, the mathematical model appears as follows:

$$\text{Max} \quad 10x_1 + 9x_2 + 0s_1 + 0s_2 + 0s_3 + 0s_4$$

s.t.

$$\frac{7}{10}x_1 + 1x_2 + 1s_1 \qquad\qquad\qquad = 630$$

$$\frac{1}{2}x_1 + \frac{5}{6}x_2 \qquad + 1s_2 \qquad\qquad = 600$$

$$1x_1 + \frac{2}{3}x_2 \qquad\qquad + 1s_3 \qquad = 708$$

$$\frac{1}{10}x_1 + \frac{1}{4}x_2 \qquad\qquad\qquad + 1s_4 = 135$$

$$x_1, x_2, s_1, s_2, s_3, s_4 \geq 0$$

Whenever a linear program is written in a form with all constraints expressed as equalities, it is said to be written in *standard form*.

Can you write a linear program in standard form? Try Problem 18.

At the optimal solution of $x_1 = 540$ and $x_2 = 252$, the values for the slack variables are as follows:

Constraint	Value of Slack Variable
Cutting and dyeing	$s_1 = 0$
Sewing	$s_2 = 120$
Finishing	$s_3 = 0$
Inspection and packaging	$s_4 = 18$

Could we have used the graphical solution to provide some of this information? The answer is yes. By finding the optimal solution point on Figure 2.6, we can see that the cutting and dyeing and the finishing constraints restrict, or *bind*, the feasible region at this point. Thus, this solution requires the use of all available time for these two operations. In other words, the graph shows us that the cutting and dyeing and the finishing departments will have zero slack. On the other hand, since the sewing and the inspection and packaging constraints are not binding the feasible region at the optimal solution, we can expect some unused time or slack for these two operations.

As a final comment on the graphical analysis of this problem, we call your attention to the sewing capacity constraint as shown in Figure 2.6. Note, in particular, that this constraint did not affect the feasible region. That is, the feasible region would be the same whether the sewing capacity constraint were included or not. This tells us that there is enough sewing time available to accommodate any production level that can be achieved by the other three departments. Since the sewing constraint does not affect the feasible region and thus cannot affect the optimal solution, it is called a *redundant constraint*.

It is easy to recognize redundant constraints using the graphical solution method. In problems with more than two decision variables, however, redundant constraints will usually not be apparent.

NOTES & COMMENTS

1. In the standard-form representation of a linear programming model, the objective function coefficients for slack variables are zero. This implies that slack variables do not affect the value of the objective function. However, in some applications, unused resources can be sold and thereby contribute to profit. In such cases, the ordinary slack variable becomes a decision variable representing the amount of resources to be sold. A nonzero coefficient in the objective function would reflect the profit associated with selling a unit of the resource.

2. Redundant constraints do not affect the feasible region and as a result can be removed from a linear programming model without affecting the optimal solution. However, if the linear programming model is to be resolved later, changes in some of the data might make a previously redundant constraint into a critical binding constraint. Thus, we recommend keeping all constraints in the linear programming model even though at some point in time one or more of the constraints may be redundant.

2.6   Extreme Points and the Optimal Solution

Suppose that the profit contribution for Par's standard golf bag is reduced from \$10 to \$5 per bag, while the profit contribution for the deluxe golf bag and all the constraints remain unchanged. The complete linear programming model of this new problem is identical to the mathematical model in Section 2.4, except for the revised objective function:

$$\text{Max } z = 5x_1 + 9x_2$$

How does this change in the objective function affect the optimal solution to the Par, Inc., problem? Figure 2.13 shows the graphical solution of this new problem with the revised objective function. Note that since the constraints have not changed, the feasible region has not changed. However, the profit lines have been altered to reflect the new objective function.

By moving the profit line in a parallel manner toward higher profit values, we find the optimal solution as shown in Figure 2.13. The values of the decision variables at this point are $x_1 = 300$ and $x_2 = 420$. The reduced profit contribution for the standard bag has caused a change in the optimal solution. In fact, as you may have suspected, we are cutting back the production of the lower-profit standard bags and increasing the production of the higher-profit deluxe bags.

What have you noticed about the location of the optimal solutions in the two linear programming problems that we have solved thus far? Look closely at the graphical solutions in Figures 2.10 and 2.13. An important observation that you should be able to make is that the optimal solutions occur at one of the vertices or "corners" of the feasible region. In linear programming terminology, these vertices are referred to as the *extreme points* of the feasible region. The Par, Inc., problem has five vertices, or five extreme points, for its feasible region (see Figure 2.14). We can now formally state our observation about the location of optimal solutions as follows:[2]

---

[2]We will see in Section 2.8 that there are two special cases (infeasibility and unboundedness) in linear programming where there is no optimal solution, and the above statement does not apply.

Figure 2.13
Optimal Solution for the Par, Inc.,
Problem with an Objective
Function of $5x_1 + 9x_2$

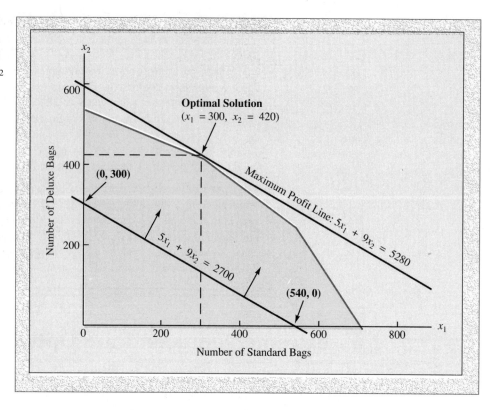

Figure 2.14
The Five Extreme Points of the
Feasible Region for the Par, Inc.,
Problem

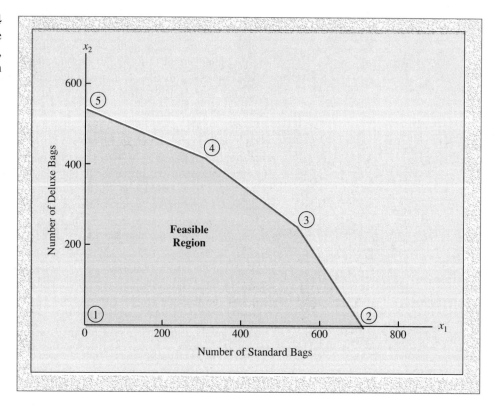

> An optimal solution to a linear programming problem can be found at an extreme point of the feasible region for the problem.

You should be able to identify the extreme points of the feasible region and determine the optimal solution by computing and comparing the objective function value at each extreme point. Try Problem 14.

This property means that if you are looking for the optimal solution to a linear programming problem, you do not have to evaluate all feasible solution points. In fact, you have to consider *only* the feasible solutions that occur at the extreme points of the feasible region. Thus, for the Par, Inc., problem, instead of computing and comparing the profit contributions for all feasible solutions, we can find the optimal solution by evaluating the five extreme-point solutions and selecting the one that provides the largest profit contribution. Actually, the graphical solution procedure is nothing more than a convenient way of identifying an optimal extreme point for two-variable problems.

2.7 A Simple Minimization Problem

The Par, Inc., problem involved maximization; however, many linear programming problems involve minimization. For example, consider the case of M&D Chemicals. M&D Chemicals produces two products that are sold as raw materials to companies manufacturing bath soaps and laundry detergents.

Based on an analysis of current inventory levels and potential demand for the coming month, M&D's management has specified that the combined production for products 1 and 2 must total at least 350 gallons. Separately, a major customer's order for 125 gallons of product 1 must also be satisfied. Product 1 requires 2 hours of processing time per gallon while product 2 requires 1 hour of processing time per gallon, and for the coming month, 600 hours of processing time are available. M&D's objective is to satisfy the above requirements at a minimum total production cost. Production costs are $2 per gallon for product 1 and $3 per gallon for product 2.

To find the minimum-cost production schedule, let us write the M&D Chemicals problem as a linear program. Following a procedure similar to the one used for Par, Inc., we first define the decision variables and the objective function for the problem. Let

$$x_1 = \text{number of gallons of product 1 produced}$$
$$x_2 = \text{number of gallons of product 2 produced}$$

Since the production costs are $2 per gallon for product 1 and $3 per gallon for product 2, the objective function which corresponds to the minimization of the total production cost can be written as

$$\text{Min } 2x_1 + 3x_2$$

Next consider the constraints placed on the M&D Chemicals problem. To satisfy the major customer's demand for 125 gallons of product 1, we know x_1 must be at least 125. Thus, we write the constraint

$$1x_1 \geq 125$$

Since the combined production for both products must total at least 350 gallons, we can write the constraint

$$1x_1 + 1x_2 \geq 350$$

Finally, since the limitation on available processing time is 600 hours, we add the constraint

$$2x_1 + 1x_2 \leq 600$$

After adding the nonnegativity constraints $(x_1, x_2 \geq 0)$, we have the following linear program for the M&D Chemicals problem:

Min $2x_1 + 3x_2$

s.t.

$1x_1 \qquad \geq 125$ Demand for product 1

$1x_1 + 1x_2 \geq 350$ Total production

$2x_1 + 1x_2 \leq 600$ Processing time

$x_1, x_2 \geq 0$

Since the linear programming model has only two decision variables, the graphical solution procedure can be used to find the optimal production quantities. The graphical method for this problem, just as in the Par problem, requires us to first graph the constraint lines to find the feasible region. By graphing each constraint line separately and then checking points on either side of the constraint line, the feasible solutions for each constraint can be identified. By combining the feasible solutions for each constraint on the same graph, we obtain the feasible region shown in Figure 2.15.

Figure 2.15
The Feasible Region for the M&D Chemicals Problem

Figure 2.16
Graphical Solution for the M&D
Chemicals Problem

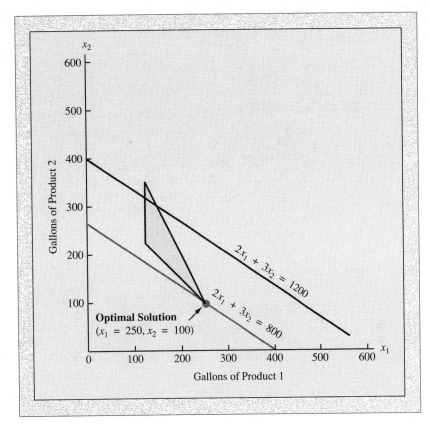

To find the minimum-cost solution, we now draw the objective function line corresponding to a particular total cost value. For example, we might start by drawing the line $2x_1 + 3x_2 = 1200$. This line is shown in Figure 2.16. Clearly there are points in the feasible region that would provide a total cost of $1200. To find the values of x_1 and x_2 that provide smaller total cost values, we move the objective function line in a lower left direction until, if we moved it any farther, it would be entirely outside the feasible region. Note that the objective function line $2x_1 + 3x_2 = 800$ intersects the feasible region at the extreme point $x_1 = 250$ and $x_2 = 100$. This extreme point provides the minimum-cost solution with an objective function value of 800. From Figures 2.15 and 2.16, we can see that the total production constraint and the processing time constraint are binding. Just as in every linear programming problem, the optimal solution occurs at an extreme point of the feasible region.

Summary of the Graphical Solution Procedure
for Minimization Problems

Can you use the graphical solution procedure to determine the optimal solution for a minimization problem? Try Problem 29.

The steps of the graphical solution procedure for a minimization problem are summarized below:

1. Prepare a graph of the feasible solution points for each of the constraints.
2. Determine the feasible region by identifying the solution points that satisfy all the constraints simultaneously.
3. Draw an objective function line showing the values of the x_1 and x_2 variables that yield a specified value of the objective function.

4. Move parallel objective function lines toward smaller objective function values until further movement would take the line completely outside the feasible region.
5. A feasible solution point on the objective function line with the smallest value is the optimal solution.

Surplus Variables

A complete analysis of the minimum-cost solution to the M&D Chemicals problem shows that the desired total production of $1x_1 + 1x_2 = 350$ gallons has been achieved by using all available processing time of $2x_1 + 1x_2 = 2(250) + 1(100) = 600$ hours. In addition, note that the constraint requiring that product 1 demand be met has been satisfied with $x_1 = 250$ gallons. In fact, the production of product 1 exceeds its minimum level by $250 - 125 = 125$ gallons. This excess production for product 1 is referred to as *surplus*. In linear programming terminology, any excess quantity corresponding to a $\geq$ constraint is referred to as surplus.

Recall that with a $\leq$ constraint, a slack variable can be added to the left-hand side of the inequality to convert the constraint to equality form. With a $\geq$ constraint, a *surplus variable* can be subtracted from the left-hand side of the inequality to convert the constraint to equality form. Just as with slack variables, surplus variables are given a coefficient of zero in the objective function because they have no effect on its value. After including two surplus variables for the $\geq$ constraints and one slack variable for the $\leq$ constraint, the linear programming model of the M&D Chemicals problem appears as follows:

$$\text{Min} \quad 2x_1 + 3x_2 + 0s_1 + 0s_2 + 0s_3$$

s.t.

$$
\begin{array}{rcl}
1x_1 \qquad\quad - 1s_1 \qquad\qquad\quad & = & 125 \\
1x_1 + 1x_2 \qquad\quad - 1s_2 \qquad\quad & = & 350 \\
2x_1 + 1x_2 \qquad\qquad\quad + 1s_3 & = & 600
\end{array}
$$

$$x_1, x_2, s_1, s_2, s_3 \geq 0$$

You should now be able to use slack and surplus variables to write a linear program in standard form. Try Problem 33.

All the constraints are now equalities. Hence, the above formulation is the standard-form representation of the M&D Chemicals problem. At the optimal solution of $x_1 = 250$ and $x_2 = 100$, the values of the surplus and slack variables are as follows:

Constraint	Value of Surplus or Slack Variables
Demand for product 1	$s_1 = 125$
Total production	$s_2 = 0$
Processing time	$s_3 = 0$

Refer to Figures 2.15 and 2.16. Note that the zero surplus and slack variables are associated with the constraints that are binding at the optimal solution—that is, the total production and processing time constraints. The surplus of 125 units is associated with the nonbinding constraint on the demand for product 1.

Note that in the Par, Inc., problem, all the constraints were of the $\leq$ type and that in the M&D Chemicals problem, the constraints were a mixture of $\geq$ and $\leq$ types. The number and types of constraints encountered in a particular linear programming problem will depend on the specific conditions existing in the problem. Linear programming problems may have some $\leq$ constraints, some $\geq$ constraints, and some $=$ constraints. For an equality constraint, feasible solutions must lie directly on the constraint line.

An example of a linear program with all three constraint forms is given below:

$$\text{Min} \quad 2x_1 + 2x_2$$

s.t.

$$1x_1 + 3x_2 \leq 12$$

$$3x_1 + 1x_2 \geq 13$$

$$1x_1 - 1x_2 = 3$$

$$x_1, x_2 \geq 0$$

The standard-form representation of this problem is

$$\text{Min} \quad 2x_1 + 2x_2 + 0s_1 + 0s_2$$

s.t.

$$1x_1 + 3x_2 + 1s_1 \qquad = 12$$

$$3x_1 + 1x_2 \qquad - 1s_2 = 13$$

$$1x_1 - 1x_2 \qquad = 3$$

$$x_1, x_2, s_1, s_2 \geq 0$$

This formulation requires a slack variable for the $\leq$ constraint and a surplus variable for the $\geq$ constraint. However, neither a slack nor a surplus variable is required for the third constraint since it is already in equality form.

The graphical solution procedure is a convenient way to find optimal extreme-point solutions for two-variable linear programming problems. When solving linear programs graphically, it is not necessary to write the problem in its standard form. Nevertheless, we should be able to compute the values of the slack and surplus variables and understand what they mean. In Chapter 3 we shall see that the values of slack and surplus variables are included in the computer solution of linear programs. In Chapter 5 we will introduce an algebraic solution procedure, the simplex method, which can be used to find optimal extreme-point solutions for linear programming problems with as many as several thousand decision variables. The mathematical steps of the simplex method involve solving simultaneous equations that represent the constraints of the linear program. Thus, in setting up a linear program for solution by the simplex method, we must have one linear equation for each constraint in the problem; therefore, the problem must be in its standard form.

As a final point, it is important to realize that the standard form of the linear programming problem is equivalent to the original formulation of the problem. That is, the optimal solution to any linear programming problem is the same as the optimal

Try Problem 32 to practice solving a linear program with all three constraint forms.

solution to the standard form of the problem. The standard form has not changed the basic problem; it has only changed how we write the constraints for the problem.

2.8 Special Cases

In this section we discuss three special situations that can arise when we attempt to solve linear programming problems.

Alternative Optimal Solutions

From our discussion of the graphical solution procedure, we know that optimal solutions can be found at the extreme points of the feasible region. Now let us consider the special case where the optimal objective function line coincides with one of the binding constraint lines on the boundary of the feasible region. We will see that this can lead to the case of *alternative optimal solutions;* in such cases, more than one solution provides the optimal value for the objective function.

As an example of the case of alternative optimal solutions, let us return to the Par, Inc., problem with the four constraints and feasible region as previously defined. However, let us assume that the profit for the standard golf bag (x_1) has been decreased to \$6.30. The revised objective function becomes $6.3x_1 + 9x_2$. The graphical solution of this problem is shown in Figure 2.17. Note that the optimal solution still occurs at an extreme point. In fact, it occurs at two extreme points: extreme point ④ ($x_1 = 300$, $x_2 = 420$) and extreme point ③ ($x_1 = 540$, $x_2 = 252$).

The objective function values at these two extreme points are identical; that is,

$$6.3x_1 + 9x_2 = 6.3(300) + 9(420) = 5670$$

and

$$6.3x_1 + 9x_2 = 6.3(540) + 9(252) = 5670$$

Furthermore, any point on the line connecting the two optimal extreme points also provides an optimal solution. For example, the solution point ($x_1 = 420$, $x_2 = 336$), which is halfway between the two extreme points, also provides the optimal objective function value of

$$6.3x_1 + 9x_2 = 6.3(420) + 9(336) = 5670$$

A linear programming problem with alternative optimal solutions is generally a good situation for the manager or decision maker. It means that several combinations of the decision variables are optimal and that the manager can select the specific optimal solution that is most desirable.

Infeasibility

Problems with no feasible solution do arise in practice. Most often it's because management's expectations are too high or because too many restrictions have been placed on the problem.

Infeasibility occurs when no solution to the linear programming problem satisfies all the constraints, including the nonnegativity conditions $x_1, x_2 \geq 0$. Graphically, infeasibility means that a feasible region does not exist; that is, there are no points that satisfy all the constraints and the nonnegativity conditions simultaneously. To illustrate this situation, let us look again at the problem faced by Par, Inc.

Suppose that management had specified that at least 500 of the standard bags and at least 360 of the deluxe bags must be manufactured. The graph of the solution region may

Figure 2.17
Par, Inc., Problem with an
Objective Function of $6.3x_1 + 9x_2$
(Alternative Optimal Solutions)

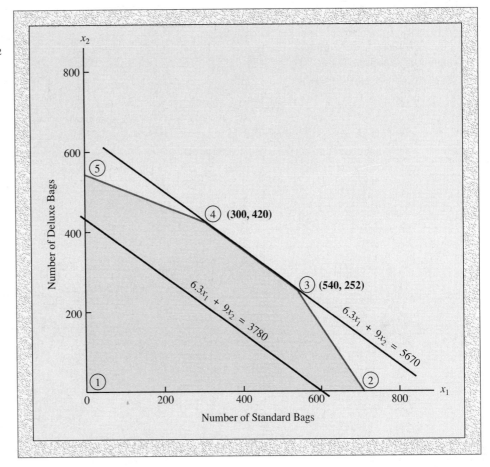

Figure 2.17
Par, Inc., Problem with an
Objective Function of $6.3x_1 + 9x_2$
(Alternative Optimal Solutions)

now be constructed to reflect these new requirements (see Figure 2.18). The shaded area in the lower left-hand portion of the graph depicts those points satisfying the departmental constraints on the availability of time. The shaded area in the upper right-hand portion depicts those points satisfying the minimum production requirements of 500 standard and 360 deluxe bags. But there are no points satisfying both sets of constraints. Thus, we see that if management imposes these minimum production requirements, there will be no feasible solution to the linear programming model.

How should we interpret infeasibility in terms of this current problem? First, we should tell management that given the resources available (i.e., production time for cutting and dyeing, sewing, finishing, and inspection and packaging), it is not possible to make 500 standard bags and 360 deluxe bags. Moreover, we can tell management exactly how much of each resource must be expended to make it possible to manufacture 500 standard and 360 deluxe bags. Table 2.2 shows the minimum amounts of resources that must be available, the amounts currently available, and additional amounts that would be required to accomplish this. Thus, we need 80 more hours for cutting and dyeing, 32 more hours for finishing, and 5 more hours for inspection and packaging to meet management's minimum production requirements.

If, after seeing the above information, management still wants to manufacture 500 standard and 360 deluxe bags, additional resources must be provided. Perhaps this will mean hiring another person to work in the cutting and dyeing department, transferring a person from elsewhere in the plant to work part-time in the finishing department, or

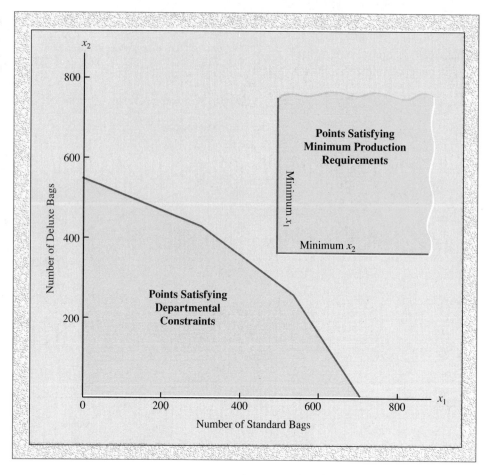

Table 2.2

Resources Needed to Manufacture 500
Standard Bags and 360 Deluxe Bags

Operation	Minimum Required Resources (hours)	Available Resources (hours)	Additional Resources Needed (hours)
Cutting and dyeing	$\frac{7}{10}(500) + 1(360) = 710$	630	80
Sewing	$\frac{1}{2}(500) + \frac{5}{6}(360) = 550$	600	None
Finishing	$1(500) + \frac{2}{3}(360) = 740$	708	32
Inspection and packaging	$\frac{1}{10}(500) + \frac{1}{4}(360) = 140$	135	5

having the sewing people help out periodically with the inspection and packaging. As you can see, there are many possibilities for corrective management action, once we discover that there is no feasible solution. The important thing to realize is that linear programming analysis can help determine whether management's plans are feasible. By analyzing the problem using linear programming, we are often able to point out infeasible conditions and initiate corrective action.

Unboundedness

A solution to a linear programming problem is *unbounded* if the value of the solution may be made infinitely large without violating any of the constraints. This condition might be termed "managerial utopia." If this condition were to occur in a profit maximization problem, it would be true that the manager could achieve an unlimited profit.

In linear programming models of real-world problems, the occurrence of an unbounded solution means that the problem has been improperly formulated. We know that it is not possible to increase profits indefinitely. Therefore, we must conclude that if a profit maximization problem results in an unbounded solution, the mathematical model is not a sufficiently accurate representation of the real-world problem. Usually, what has happened is that a constraint has been inadvertently omitted in the problem formulation.

As an illustration, consider the simple numerical example:

$$\text{Max} \quad 20x_1 + 10x_2$$

$$\text{s.t.}$$

$$1x_1 \qquad \geq 2$$

$$1x_2 \leq 5$$

$$x_1, x_2 \geq 0$$

You should now be able to recognize whether a linear program involves alternative optima, infeasibility, or is unbounded. Try Problems 40 and 41.

In Figure 2.19 we have graphed the feasible region associated with this problem. Note that we can only indicate part of the feasible region since the feasible region extends indefinitely in the direction of the x_1 axis. Looking at the objective function lines in Figure 2.19, we see that the solution to this problem may be made as large as we desire. That is, no matter what solution we pick, there will always be some feasible solution with a larger value. Thus, we say that the solution to this linear program is *unbounded*.

NOTES & COMMENTS

1. Infeasibility is independent of the objective function. It exists because the constraints are so restrictive that there is no feasible region for the linear programming model. Thus, when you encounter infeasibility, making changes in the coefficients of the objective function will not help; the problem will remain infeasible.

2. Unboundedness is often the result of a missing constraint. However, a change in the objective function may cause a previously unbounded problem to become bounded with an optimal solution. For example, the graph in Figure 2.19 shows an unbounded solution for the objective function max $20x_1 + 10x_2$. However, changing the objective function to max $-20x_1 - 10x_2$ will provide the optimal solution $x_1 = 2$ and $x_2 = 0$ even though no changes have been made in the constraints.

Figure 2.19
Example of an Unbounded
Problem

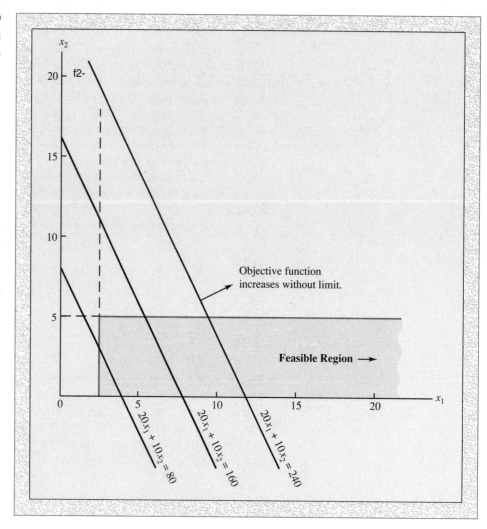

2.9 Introduction to Sensitivity Analysis

Sensitivity analysis is the study of how changes in the coefficients of a linear program affect the optimal solution. Using sensitivity analysis, we can answer questions such as the following:

1. How will a *change in a coefficient of the objective function* affect the optimal solution?
2. How will a *change in the right-hand-side value for a constraint* affect the optimal solution?

Since sensitivity analysis is concerned with how the above changes affect the optimal solution, the analysis does not begin until the optimal solution to the original linear programming problem has been obtained. For this reason, sensitivity analysis is often referred to as *postoptimality analysis*.

The primary reason that sensitivity analysis is important to decision makers is that real-world problems exist in a dynamic environment. Prices of raw materials change, demand fluctuates, companies purchase new machinery to replace old, global labor markets cause changes in production costs, employee turnover occurs, and so on. If a linear programming model has been used in such an environment, we can expect some of the coefficients to change over time. A manager will want to determine how such changes affect the optimal solution to the original linear programming problem. Sensitivity analysis provides the information needed to respond to such changes without requiring the complete solution of a revised linear program.

Recall the Par, Inc., problem introduced in Section 2.1.

$$\text{Max} \quad 10x_1 + 9x_2$$

s.t.

$$\frac{7}{10}x_1 + 1x_2 \leq 630 \quad \text{Cutting and dyeing}$$

$$\frac{1}{2}x_1 + \frac{5}{6}x_2 \leq 600 \quad \text{Sewing}$$

$$1x_1 + \frac{2}{3}x_2 \leq 708 \quad \text{Finishing}$$

$$\frac{1}{10}x_1 + \frac{1}{4}x_2 \leq 135 \quad \text{Inspection and packaging}$$

$$x_1, x_2 \geq 0$$

The optimal solution, $x_1 = 540$ standard bags and $x_2 = 252$ deluxe bags, is based on profit figures of \$10 per standard bag and \$9 per deluxe bag. However, suppose we later learn that because of a price reduction the profit contribution per standard bag has been reduced to \$7. Sensitivity analysis can be used to determine whether the production schedule calling for 540 standard bags and 252 deluxe bags is still the best solution. If it is, there will be no need to solve a modified linear program with $7x_1 + 9x_2$ as the objective function.

Sensitivity analysis can also be used to determine which coefficients in a linear programming model are most critical. For instance, suppose Par's management believes that the \$9 profit contribution per deluxe bag is only a rough estimate of the profit contribution that will actually be obtained. If sensitivity analysis shows that 540 standard bags and 252 deluxe bags will be the optimal solution as long as the profit contribution for the deluxe bag is between \$5 and \$13, management should feel comfortable with the rough estimate of \$9 per bag and the recommended production quantities. However, if sensitivity analysis shows that 540 standard bags and 252 deluxe bags will be the optimal solution only if the profit contribution for the deluxe bag is between \$8.90 and \$9.25, management may want to review the accuracy of the \$9-per-bag profit estimate.

Another aspect of sensitivity analysis is concerned with changes in the right-hand sides of the constraints. Recall that in the Par, Inc., problem the optimal solution used all the cutting and dyeing time and all the finishing time. How would the optimal solution and the total profit contribution change if Par's management could obtain additional time for either of these operations? Sensitivity analysis can help determine how much each additional hour is worth and how many hours can be added before diminishing returns set in.

2.10 Graphical Sensitivity Analysis

For linear programming problems with two decision variables, graphical solution methods can be used to perform sensitivity analysis on the objective function coefficients and the right-hand-side values for the constraints.

Objective Function Coefficients

Let us consider how changes in the objective function coefficients might affect the optimal solution to the Par, Inc., problem. The current contribution to profit is $10 per unit for the standard bag and $9 per unit for the deluxe bag. It seems obvious that an increase in the profit contribution for one of the bags might lead management to increase production of that bag and a decrease in the profit contribution for one of the bags might lead management to decrease production of that bag. But it is not as obvious how much the profit contribution would have to change before management would want to change the production quantities.

The current optimal solution to this problem calls for producing 540 standard golf bags and 252 deluxe golf bags. The *range of optimality* for each objective function coefficient provides the range of values over which the current solution will remain optimal. Managerial attention should be focused on those objective function coefficients that have a narrow range of optimality and coefficients near the endpoints of the range. These are the coefficients where a small change can necessitate modifying the optimal solution. Let us now compute the ranges of optimality for this problem.

Figure 2.20 shows the graphical solution. A careful inspection of this graph shows that as long as the slope of the objective function is between the slope of line A (which coincides with the cutting and dyeing constraint line) and the slope of line B (which coincides with the finishing constraint line), extreme point ③ with $x_1 = 540$ and $x_2 = 252$ will be optimal. Changing an objective function coefficient for x_1 or x_2 will cause the slope of the objective function to change. In Figure 2.20 we see that such changes cause the objective function line to rotate around extreme point ③. However, as long as the objective function line stays within the shaded region, extreme point ③ will remain optimal.

Students often have difficulty setting up the lower and upper bounds for the slope of the objective function line. The problem seems to be that the slope of the line is usually negative and hence a clockwise rotation of the objective function line makes the line steeper even though the slope is getting smaller (more negative).

Rotating the objective function line *counterclockwise* causes the slope to become less negative, and the slope increases. When the objective function line has been rotated counterclockwise (slope increased) enough to coincide with line A, we obtain alternative optimal solutions between extreme points ③ and ④. Any further counterclockwise rotation of the objective function line will cause extreme point ③ to be nonoptimal. Hence, the slope of line A provides an upper limit for the slope of the objective function line.

Rotating the objective function line *clockwise* causes the slope to become more negative, and the slope decreases. When the objective function line has been rotated clockwise (slope decreased) enough to coincide with line B, we obtain alternative optimal solutions between extreme points ③ and ②. Any further clockwise rotation of the objective function line will cause extreme point ③ to be nonoptimal. The slope of line B thus provides a lower limit for the slope of the objective function line.

From the above discussion, it should be clear that extreme point ③ will be the optimal solution as long as

Slope of line B ≤ slope of objective function line ≤ slope of line A

Figure 2.20
Graphical Solution of Par, Inc.,
Problem with Slope of Objective
Function Between Slopes of Lines
A and B; Extreme Point ③ Is
Optimal

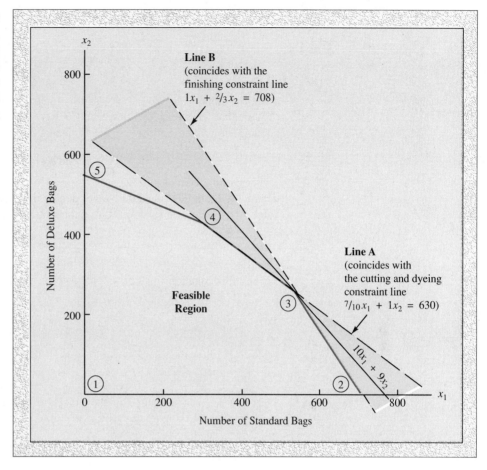

In Figure 2.20 we see that the equation for line A, the cutting and dyeing constraint line, is as follows:

$$\tfrac{7}{10} x_1 + 1x_2 = 630$$

By solving the above equation for x_2, we can write the equation for line A in its slope–intercept form. This yields

$$x_2 = -\tfrac{7}{10} x_1 + 630$$

↑ Slope of line A ↑ Intercept of line A on x_2 axis

Thus, the slope for line A is $-\tfrac{7}{10}$, and its intercept on the x_2 axis is 630.
 The equation for line B in Figure 2.20 is

$$1x_1 + \tfrac{2}{3} x_2 = 708$$

Solving for x_2 provides the slope–intercept form for line B. Doing so yields

$$\tfrac{2}{3}x_2 = -1x_1 + 708$$

$$x_2 = -\tfrac{3}{2}x_1 + 1062$$

Thus, the slope of line B is $-\tfrac{3}{2}$, and its intercept on the x_2 axis is 1062.

Now that the slopes of lines A and B have been computed, we see that for extreme point ③ to remain optimal we must have

$$-\tfrac{3}{2} \leq \text{slope of objective function} \leq -\tfrac{7}{10} \qquad (2.5)$$

Let us now consider the general form of the slope of the objective function. Let c_1 denote the profit of a standard bag, c_2 denote the profit of a deluxe bag, and z denote the value of the objective function. Using this notation, the objective function can be written as

$$z = c_1x_1 + c_2x_2$$

Writing this equation in slope–intercept form, we obtain

$$c_2x_2 = -c_1x_1 + z$$

and

$$x_2 = -\frac{c_1}{c_2}x_1 + \frac{z}{c_2}$$

Thus, we see that the slope of the objective function is given by $-c_1/c_2$. Substituting $-c_1/c_2$ into expression (2.12), we see that extreme point ③ will be optimal as long as the following expression is satisfied:

$$-\tfrac{3}{2} \leq -\frac{c_1}{c_2} \leq -\tfrac{7}{10} \qquad (2.6)$$

To compute the range of optimality for the standard-bag profit contribution, we hold the profit contribution for the deluxe bag fixed at its initial value $c_2 = 9$. Doing so in expression (2.13), we obtain

$$-\tfrac{3}{2} \leq -\frac{c_1}{9} \leq -\tfrac{7}{10}$$

Using the left-hand inequality, we have

$$-\tfrac{3}{2} \leq -\frac{c_1}{9} \qquad \text{or} \qquad \tfrac{3}{2} \geq \frac{c_1}{9}$$

Thus,

$$\tfrac{27}{2} \geq c_1 \qquad \text{or} \qquad c_1 \leq \tfrac{27}{2} = 13.5$$

Using the right-hand inequality, we have

$$-\frac{c_1}{9} \leq -\tfrac{7}{10} \qquad \text{or} \qquad \frac{c_1}{9} \geq \tfrac{7}{10}$$

Thus,

$$c_1 \geq \tfrac{63}{10} \qquad \text{or} \qquad c_1 \geq 6.3$$

You should now be able to compute the range of optimality using the graphical solution procedure. Try Problem 52.

Combining the above limits for c_1 provides the following range of optimality for the standard-bag profit contribution:

$$6.3 \leq c_1 \leq 13.5$$

In the original problem for Par, Inc., the standard bag had a profit contribution of $10. The resulting optimal solution was 540 standard bags and 252 deluxe bags. The range of optimality for c_1 tells Par's management that, with other coefficients unchanged, the profit contribution for the standard bag can be anywhere between $6.30 and $13.50 and the production quantities of 540 standard bags and 252 deluxe bags will remain optimal. Note, however, that while the production quantities will not change, the total profit contribution (value of objective function) will change due to the change in profit contribution per standard bag.

The above computations can be repeated, holding the profit contribution for standard bags constant at $c_1 = 10$. In this case, the range of optimality for the deluxe-bag profit contribution can be determined. Check to see that this range is $6.67 \leq c_2 \leq 14.29$.

In cases where the rotation of the objective function line about an optimal extreme point causes the objective function line to become *vertical*, there will be either no upper limit or no lower limit for the slope as it appears in the form of expression (2.13). To see how this special situation can happen in graphical sensitivity analysis, assume that the objective function for the Par, Inc. problem is $18x_1 + 9x_2$; in this case, extreme point ② in Figure 2.21 provides the optimal solution. Rotating the objective function line counterclockwise around extreme point ② provides an upper limit for the slope when the

Figure 2.21
Graphical Solution of Par, Inc.,
Problem with an Objective
Function of $18x_1 + 9x_2$; Optimal
Solution at Extreme Point ②

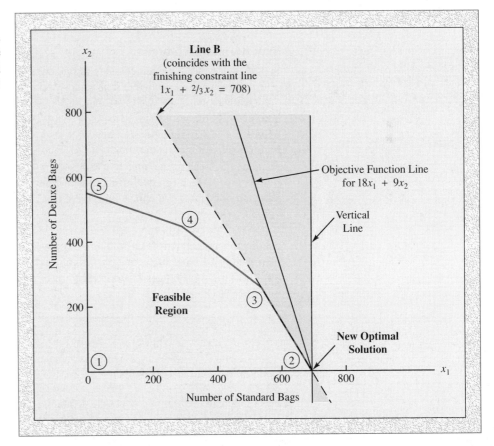

objective function line coincides with line B. Since we have previously seen that the slope of line B is $-\frac{3}{2}$, the upper limit for the slope of the objective function line must be $-\frac{3}{2}$. However, rotating the objective function line clockwise results in the slope becoming more and more negative, approaching a value of minus infinity as the objective function line becomes vertical; in this case, there is no lower limit for the slope of the objective function. Using the upper limit of $-\frac{3}{2}$, we can write

$$-\frac{c_1}{c_2} \leq -\frac{3}{2}$$

Slope of the
objective function line

Following our previous procedure of holding c_2 constant at its original value, $c_2 = 9$, we have

$$-\frac{c_1}{9} \leq -\frac{3}{2} \qquad \text{or} \qquad \frac{c_1}{9} \geq \frac{3}{2}$$

Solving for c_1 provides the following result:

$$c_1 \geq \frac{27}{2} = 13.5$$

In reviewing Figure 2.21 we note that extreme point ② remains optimal for all values of c_1 above 13.5. Thus, we obtain the following range of optimality for c_1 at extreme point ②:

$$13.5 \leq c_1 < \infty$$

Simultaneous Changes.   The range of optimality for objective function coefficients is only applicable for changes made to one coefficient at a time. All other coefficients are assumed to be fixed at their initial values. If two or more objective function coefficients are changed simultaneously, further analysis is necessary to determine whether the optimal solution will change. However, when solving two variable problems graphically, expression (2.13) suggests an easy way to determine whether simultaneous changes in both objective function coefficients will cause a change in the optimal solution. Simply compute the slope of the objective function $(-c_1/c_2)$ for the new coefficient values. If this ratio is greater than or equal to the lower limit on the slope of the objective function and less than or equal to the upper limit, then the changes made will not cause a change in the optimal solution.

Let us illustrate this approach by considering changes in both of the objective function coefficients for the Par, Inc., problem. Suppose the profit contribution per standard bag is increased to $13 and the profit contribution per deluxe bag is simultaneously reduced to $8. Recall that the ranges of optimality for c_1 and c_2 (both computed in a one-at-a-time manner) are

$$6.3 \leq c_1 \leq 13.5 \qquad\qquad\qquad (2.7)$$

$$6.67 \leq c_2 \leq 14.29 \qquad\qquad\qquad (2.8)$$

Given these ranges of optimality, we can conclude that changing either c_1 to $13 or c_2 to $8 (but not both) would not cause a change in the optimal solution of $x_1 = 540$ and $x_2 = 252$. But we cannot conclude from the ranges of optimality that changing both coefficients simultaneously would not result in a change in the optimal solution.

In expression (2.13) we showed that extreme point ③ remains optimal as long as

$$-\frac{3}{2} \le -\frac{c_1}{c_2} \le -\frac{7}{10}$$

If c_1 is changed to 13 and simultaneously c_2 is changed to 8, the new objective function slope will be given by

$$-\frac{c_1}{c_2} = -\frac{13}{8} = -1.625$$

Since this value is less than the lower limit of $-\frac{3}{2}$, the current solution of $x_1 = 540$ and $x_2 = 252$ will no longer be optimal. By resolving the problem with $c_1 = 13$ and $c_2 = 8$ we will find that extreme point ② is the new optimal solution.

Looking at the ranges of optimality, we concluded that changing either c_1 to \$13 or c_2 to \$8 (but not both) would not cause a change in the optimal solution. But in recomputing the slope of the objective function with simultaneous changes for both c_1 and c_2, we saw that the optimal solution did change. This emphasizes the fact that a range of optimality, by itself, can only be used to draw a conclusion about changes made to *one objective function coefficient at a time*.

Right-Hand Sides

Let us now consider how a change in the right-hand side for a constraint may affect the feasible region and perhaps cause a change in the optimal solution to the problem. To illustrate this aspect of sensitivity analysis, let us consider what happens if an additional 10 hours of production time becomes available in the cutting and dyeing department of Par, Inc. The right-hand side of the cutting and dyeing constraint is changed from 630 to 640, and the constraint is rewritten as

$$\tfrac{7}{10} x_1 + x_2 \le 640$$

By obtaining an additional 10 hours of cutting and dyeing time, we have expanded the feasible region for the problem, as shown in Figure 2.22. Since the feasible region has been enlarged, we now want to determine whether one of the new feasible solutions provides an improvement in the value of the objective function. Application of the graphical solution procedure to the problem with the enlarged feasible region shows that the extreme point with $x_1 = 527.5$ and $x_2 = 270.75$ now provides the optimal solution. The new value for the objective function is $10(527.5) + 9(270.75) = \$7711.75$; this provides an increase in profit of $\$7711.75 - \$7668.00 = \$43.75$. Thus, the increased profit occurs at a rate of $\$43.75/10$ hours $= \$4.375$ per hour added.

The *improvement* in the value of the optimal solution per unit increase in the right-hand side of the constraint is called the *dual price*. Here, the dual price for cutting and dyeing and production time is \$4.375 per hour; in other words, if we increase the right-hand side of the production and dyeing time constraint by 1 hour, the value of the objective function will improve by \$4.375. Conversely, if the right-hand side of the production and dyeing time constraint were to decrease by 1 hour, the objective function would get worse by \$4.375. The dual price can generally be used to determine what will happen to the value of the objective function when we make a one-unit change in the right-hand side of a constraint.

Can you compute and interpret the dual price for a constraint? Try Problem 53.

We caution here that the value of the dual price may be applicable only for small changes in the right-hand side. As more and more resources are obtained and the

Figure 2.22

Effect of a 10-Unit Change in the
Right-Hand Side of the Cutting
and Dyeing Constraint

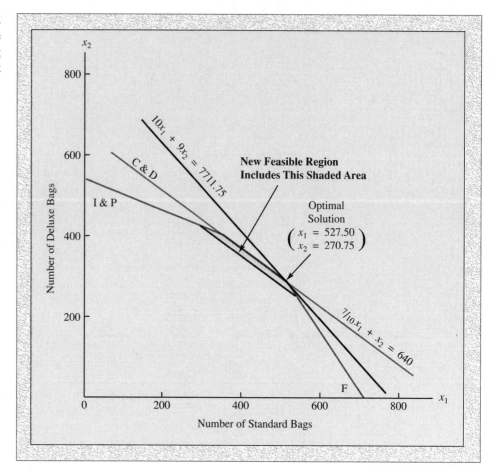

right-hand-side value continues to increase, other constraints will become binding and limit the change in the value of the objective function. For example, in the problem for Par, Inc., we would eventually reach a point where more cutting and dyeing time would be of no value; this would occur at the point where the cutting and dyeing constraint becomes nonbinding. At this point, the dual price would equal zero. In the next chapter we will show how to determine the range of values for a right-hand side over which the dual price will accurately predict the improvement in the objective function. Finally, we note that the dual price for any nonbinding constraint will be zero because an increase in the right-hand side of such a constraint will affect only the value of the slack or surplus variable for that constraint.

To illustrate the correct interpretation of dual prices for a minimization problem, suppose we had solved a problem involving the minimization of total cost and that the value of the optimal solution was $100. Furthermore, suppose that the dual price for a particular constraint was −$10. The *negative dual price* tells us that the objective function *will not improve* if the value of the right-hand side is increased by one unit. Thus, if the right-hand side of this constraint is increased by one unit, the value of the objective function will get worse by the amount of $10. Since becoming worse means an increase in the total cost, the value of the objective function will become $110 if the right-hand side is increased by one unit. Conversely, a decrease in the right-hand side of one unit will decrease the total cost by $10.

NOTES & COMMENTS

1. If two objective function coefficients change simultaneously, it is possible for both to move outside their respective ranges of optimality and not affect the optimal solution. For instance, in a two-variable linear program, the slope of the objective function will not change at all if both coefficients are changed by the same percentage.

2. Some texts associate the term *shadow price* with each constraint. The concept of a shadow price is closely related to the concept of a dual price. The shadow price associated with a constraint is the *change* in the value of the optimal solution per unit increase in the right-hand side of the constraint. In general, the dual price and the shadow price are the *same* for all *maximization* linear programs. In *minimization* linear programs, the shadow price is the *negative* of the corresponding dual price.

Summary

Mathematical programming is a name given to quantitative methods for solving problems involving constrained or unconstrained optimization. Linear, integer, and nonlinear programs are three mathematical programming problems.

Two problems, Par, Inc., and M&D Chemicals, were formulated as linear programs and solved by a graphical solution procedure. In studying the graphical solution procedure, we noted that if an optimal solution to a linear programming problem exists, it can be found at an extreme point.

In the process of formulating mathematical models of the problems presented in this chapter, the following general definition of a linear program was developed. A linear program is a mathematical model that has the following properties:

1. A linear objective function that is to be maximized or minimized
2. A set of linear constraints
3. Variables that are all restricted to nonnegative values

We have seen how slack variables can be used to write less-than-or-equal-to constraints in equality form and how surplus variables can be used to write greater-than-or-equal-to constraints in equality form. The value of a slack variable can usually be interpreted as the amount of unused resource, while the value of a surplus variable indicates the amount over and above some stated minimum requirement. When all constraints have been written as equalities, the linear program has been written in its standard form. In the special cases of infeasibility and unboundedness, we showed that there is no optimal solution to the problem. In the case of infeasibility, there are no feasible solutions; in the case of unboundedness, the objective function can be made infinitely large for a maximization problem and infinitely small for a minimization problem. A third special case, alternative optimal solutions, was also discussed. In this case, we have two optimal extreme points, and all the points on the line segment connecting them are also optimal.

The chapter concluded with a discussion of sensitivity analysis, the study of how changes in the coefficients of a linear program affect the optimal solution. We showed how a graphical solution method can be used to determine how a change in one of the objective function coefficients or a change in the right-hand-side value for a constraint will affect the optimal solution to the problem.

Glossary

Constraint An equation or inequality that rules out certain combinations of decision variables as feasible solutions.

Constraint function The left-hand side of a constraint (i.e., the portion of the constraint containing the variables).

Objective function All linear programs have a linear objective function that is to be either maximized or minimized. In many linear programming problems, the objective function will be used to measure the profit or cost of a particular solution.

Solution Any set of values for the variables.

Optimal solution A feasible solution that maximizes or minimizes the value of the objective function.

Nonnegativity constraints A set of constraints that requires all variables to be nonnegative.

Mathematical model A representation of a problem where the objective and all constraint conditions are described by mathematical expressions.

Linear program A mathematical model with a linear objective function, a set of linear constraints, and nonnegative variables.

Linear functions Mathematical expressions in which the variables appear in separate terms and are raised to the first power.

Feasible solution A solution that satisfies all the constraints.

Feasible region The set of all feasible solutions.

Slack variable A variable added to the left-hand side of a less-than-or-equal-to constraint to convert the constraint into an equality. The value of this variable can usually be interpreted as the amount of unused resource.

Standard form A linear program in which all the constraints are written as equalities. The optimal solution of the standard form of a linear program is the same as the optimal solution of the original formulation of the linear program.

Redundant constraint A constraint that does not affect the feasible region. If a constraint is redundant, it can be removed from the problem without affecting the feasible region.

Extreme point Graphically speaking, extreme points are the feasible solution points occurring at the vertices or "corners" of the feasible region. With two-variable problems, extreme points are determined by the intersection of the constraint lines.

Surplus variable A variable subtracted from the left-hand side of a greater-than-or-equal-to constraint to convert the constraint into an equality. The value of this variable can usually be interpreted as the amount over and above some required minimum level.

Alternative optimal solutions The case in which more than one solution provides the optimal value for the objective function.

Infeasibility The situation in which there is no solution to the linear programming problem that satisfies all the constraints.

Unboundedness A maximization linear programming problem is said to be unbounded if the value of the solution may be made infinitely large without violating any of the constraints. A minimization problem is unbounded if the value of the solution may be made infinitely small.

Sensitivity analysis The evaluation of how changes in the coefficients of a linear programming problem affect the optimal solution to the problem.

Postoptimality analysis Another name for sensitivity analysis, indicating that the analysis is performed after the optimal solution to the original linear programming problem has been obtained.

Range of optimality The range of values over which an objective function coefficient may vary without causing any change in the values of the decision variables in the optimal solution.

Dual price The improvement in the value of the optimal solution per unit increase in a constraint right-hand-side value.

 # Problems

SELF TEST

1. Determining acceptable mathematical relationships

1. Which of the following mathematical relationships could be found in a linear programming model, and which could not? For the relationships that are unacceptable for linear programs, state your reason for your answer.

   a. $-1x_1 + 2x_2 - 1x_3 \leq 70$

   b. $2x_1 - 2x_3 = 50$

   c. $1x_1 - 2x_2^2 + 4x_3 \leq 10$

d. $3\sqrt{x_1} + 2x_2 - 1x_3 \geq 15$

e. $1x_1 + 1x_2 + 1x_3 = 6$

f. $2x_1 + 5x_2 + 1x_1x_2 \leq 25$

2. Find the feasible solution points for the following constraints:

a. $4x_1 + 2x_2 \leq 16$

b. $4x_1 + 2x_2 \geq 16$

c. $4x_1 + 2x_2 = 16$

3. Graphing constraint lines is an essential step in the graphical method. Show a separate graph of the constraint lines and feasible solutions for each of the following constraints:

a. $3x_1 + 2x_2 \leq 18$

b. $12x_1 + 8x_2 \geq 480$

c. $5x_1 + 10x_2 = 200$

4. Show a separate graph of the constraint lines and feasible solutions for each of the following constraints:

a. $3x_1 - 4x_2 \geq 60$

b. $-6x_1 + 5x_2 \leq 60$

c. $5x_1 - 2x_2 \leq 0$

5. Show a separate graph of the constraint lines and feasible solutions for each of the following constraints:

a. $x_1 \geq 0.25 (x_1 + x_2)$

b. $x_2 \leq 0.10 (x_1 + x_2)$

c. $x_1 \leq 0.50 (x_1 + x_2)$

6. Given below are three objective functions for linear programming problems:

$$z = 7x_1 + 10x_2$$

$$z = 6x_1 + 4x_2$$

$$z = -4x_1 + 7x_2$$

Determine the slope of each objective function. Show the graph of each of the three objective functions for $z = 420$.

7. Identify the feasible region for the following set of constraints:

$$\tfrac{1}{2} x_1 + \tfrac{1}{4} x_2 \geq 30$$

$$1x_1 + 5x_2 \geq 250$$

$$\tfrac{1}{4} x_1 + \tfrac{1}{2} x_2 \leq 50$$

$$x_1, x_2 \geq 0$$

8. Identify the feasible region for the following set of constraints:

$$2x_1 - 1x_2 \leq 0$$

$$-1x_1 + 1.5x_2 \leq 200$$

$$x_1, x_2 \geq 0$$

9. Identify the feasible region for the following set of constraints:

$$3x_1 - 2x_2 \geq 0$$

$$2x_1 - 1x_2 \leq 200$$

$$1x_1 \leq 150$$

$$x_1, x_2 \geq 0$$

10. Graphical solution

10. Solve the following linear program:

$$\text{Max}\quad 5x_1 + 5x_2$$

s.t.

$$1x_1 \qquad\qquad \leq 100$$
$$\qquad\qquad 1x_2 \leq 80$$
$$2x_1 + 4x_2 \leq 400$$
$$x_1, x_2 \geq 0$$

SELF TEST ▷

11. Graphical solution

11. Consider the following linear programming problem:

$$\text{Max}\quad 2x_1 + 3x_2$$

s.t.

$$1x_1 + 2x_2 \leq 6$$
$$5x_1 + 3x_2 \leq 15$$
$$x_1, x_2 \geq 0$$

Find the optimal solution. What is the value of the objective function at the optimal solution?

12. Graphical solution; finding extreme points

12. Consider the following linear programming problem:

$$\text{Max}\quad 3x_1 + 3x_2$$

s.t.

$$2x_1 + 4x_2 \leq 12$$
$$6x_1 + 4x_2 \leq 24$$
$$x_1, x_2 \geq 0$$

a. Find the optimal solution.
b. If the objective function is changed to $2x_1 + 6x_2$, what will the optimal solution be?
c. How many extreme points are there? What are the values of x_1 and x_2 at each extreme point?

13. Graphical solution; redundant constraints

13. Consider the following linear programming problem:

$$\text{Max}\quad 3x_1 + 2x_2$$

s.t.

$$2x_1 + 2x_2 \leq 8$$
$$3x_1 + 2x_2 \leq 12$$
$$1x_1 + 0.5x_2 \leq 3$$
$$x_1, x_2 \geq 0$$

a. Find the optimal solution. What is the value of the objective function?
b. Does this problem have a redundant constraint? If so, what is it? Does the solution change if the redundant constraint is removed from the problem? Explain.

14. Consider the following linear program:

$$\text{Max} \quad 1x_1 + 2x_2$$

s.t.

$$
\begin{aligned}
1x_1 & & \leq 5 \\
& 1x_2 & \leq 4 \\
2x_1 + 2x_2 & & = 12 \\
x_1, x_2 & \geq 0 &
\end{aligned}
$$

  a. Show the feasible region.
  b. What are the extreme points of the feasible region?
  c. Find the optimal solution using the graphical procedure.

15. What constraint lines combine to form extreme point ④ of the Par, Inc., problem (see Figures 2.6 and 2.14)? Solve the simultaneous linear equations to show that the exact values of x_1 and x_2 at this extreme point are $x_1 = 300$ and $x_2 = 420$.

16. Suppose that Par's management encounters each of the following situations:
  a. The accounting department revises its estimate of the profit contribution for the deluxe bag to $18 per bag.
  b. A new low-cost material is available for the standard bag, and the profit contribution per standard bag can be increased to $20 per bag. (Assume the profit contribution of the deluxe bag is the original $9 value.)
  c. New sewing equipment is available that would increase the sewing operation capacity to 750 hours. (Assume $10x_1 + 9x_2$ is the appropriate objective function.)
  If each of the above conditions is encountered separately, what are the optimal solution and the total profit contribution for each situation?

17. Refer to the feasible region for the Par, Inc., problem in Figure 2.14.
  a. Develop an objective function that will make extreme point ⑤ the optimal extreme point.
  b. What is the optimal solution using the objective function you selected in part (a)?
  c. What are the values of the slack variables associated with this solution?

18. Write the following linear program in standard form:

$$\text{Max} \quad 5x_1 + 2x_2 + 8x_3$$

s.t.

$$
\begin{aligned}
1x_1 - 2x_2 + \tfrac{1}{2}x_3 & \leq 420 \\
2x_1 + 3x_2 - 1x_3 & \leq 610 \\
6x_1 - 1x_2 + 3x_3 & \leq 125 \\
x_1, x_2, x_3 & \geq 0
\end{aligned}
$$

19. For the linear program

$$\text{Max} \quad 4x_1 + 1x_2$$

s.t.

$$
\begin{aligned}
10x_1 + 2x_2 & \leq 30 \\
3x_1 + 2x_2 & \leq 12 \\
2x_1 + 2x_2 & \leq 10 \\
x_1, x_2 & \geq 0
\end{aligned}
$$

a. Write this problem in standard form.
b. Solve the problem.
c. What are the values of the three slack variables at the optimal solution?

20. Given the linear program

$$\text{Max} \quad 3x_1 + 4x_2$$

s.t.

$$-1x_1 + 2x_2 \leq 8$$

$$1x_1 + 2x_2 \leq 12$$

$$2x_1 + 1x_2 \leq 16$$

$$x_1, x_2 \geq 0$$

a. Write the problem in standard form.
b. Solve the problem.
c. What are the values of the three slack variables at the optimal solution?

21. RMC, Inc., is a small firm that produces a variety of chemical products. In a particular production process, three raw materials are blended (mixed together) to produce two products: a fuel additive and a solvent base. Each ton of fuel additive is a mixture of $\frac{2}{5}$ ton of material 1 and $\frac{3}{5}$ ton of material 3. A ton of solvent base is a mixture of $\frac{1}{2}$ ton of material 1, $\frac{1}{5}$ ton of material 2, and $\frac{3}{10}$ ton of material 3. After deducting relevant costs, the profit contribution is \$40 for every ton of fuel additive produced and \$30 for every ton of solvent base produced.

RMC's production is constrained by a limited availability of the three raw materials. For the current production period, RMC has available the following quantities of each raw material:

Raw Material	Amount Available for Production
Material 1	20 tons
Material 2	5 tons
Material 3	21 tons

Assuming that RMC is interested in maximizing the total profit contribution, answer the following:
a. What is the linear programming model for this problem?
b. Find the optimal solution. How many tons of each product should be produced, and what is the projected total profit contribution?
c. Is there any unused material? If so, how much?
d. Are there any redundant constraints? If so, which ones?

22. Kelson Sporting Equipment, Inc., makes two different types of baseball gloves: a regular model and a catcher's model. The firm has 900 hours of production time available in its cutting and sewing department, 300 hours available in its finishing department, and 100 hours available in its packaging and shipping department. The production time requirements and the profit contribution per glove are given in the table at the top of the next page.

| | Production Time (hours) | | | |
Model	Cutting and Sewing	Finishing	Packaging and Shipping	Profit/Glove
Regular model	1	½	⅛	$5
Catcher's model	3⁄2	⅓	¼	$8

Assuming that the company is interested in maximizing the total profit contribution, answer the following:

a. What is the linear programming model for this problem?

b. Find the optimal solution. How many gloves of each model should Kelson manufacture?

c. What is the total profit contribution Kelson can earn with the above production quantities?

d. How many hours of production time will be scheduled in each department?

e. What is the slack time in each department?

23. Formulation and graphical solution; maximization problem; 3 ≤ constraints

23. The Erlanger Manufacturing Company makes two products. The profit estimates are $25 for each unit of product 1 sold and $30 for each unit of product 2 sold. The labor-hour requirements for the products in each of three production departments are summarized below:

Department	Product 1	Product 2
A	1.50	3.00
B	2.00	1.00
C	.25	.25

The production supervisors in the departments have estimated that the following number of labor-hours will be available during the next month: 450 hours in department A, 350 hours in department B, and 50 hours in department C. Assuming that the company is interested in maximizing the total profit contribution, answer the following:

a. What is the linear programming model for this problem?

b. Find the optimal solution. How much of each product should be produced, and what is the projected total profit contribution?

c. What are the scheduled production time and slack time in each department?

24. Formulation and graphical solution; maximization problem; 3 ≤ constraints

24. Yard Care, Inc., manufactures a variety of lawn care products, including two well-known lawn fertilizers. Each fertilizer product is a blend of two raw materials known as K40 and K50. During the current production period, 900 pounds of K40 and 400 pounds of K50 are available. Each pound of the product known as "Green Lawn" uses ⅗ pound of K40 and ⅖ pound of K50. Each pound of the product known as "Lawn Care" uses ¾ pound of K40 and ¼ pound of K50. In addition, a current limit on the availability of packaging materials restricts the production of Lawn Care to a maximum of 500 pounds. Assume that the profit contribution for both products is $3 per pound.

a. What is the linear programming model for this problem?

b. Find the optimal solution. How many pounds of each product should be manufactured?

c. Should it be a concern to the company that the availability of packaging materials is restricting the production of Lawn Care? What would happen to the production quantities and the projected total profit contribution if the firm were able to remove the restriction on the amount of Lawn Care that could be produced?

25. Formulation and graphical solution; maximization problem; 3 ≤ constraints

25. Investment Advisors, Inc., is a brokerage firm that manages stock portfolios for a number of clients. A new client has requested that the firm handle an $80,000 investment portfolio. As an initial investment strategy, the client would like to restrict the portfolio to a mix of the following stocks:

Stock	Price/Share	Estimated Annual Return/Share	Risk Index/Share
U.S. Oil	$25	$3	0.50
Hub Properties	$50	$5	0.25

The risk index for the stock is a rating of the relative risk of the two investment alternatives. For the data given, U.S. Oil is judged to be the riskier investment. By constraining the total risk for the portfolio, the investment firm avoids placing excessive amounts of the portfolio in potentially high-return, but also high-risk, investments. For the current portfolio, an upper limit of 700 has been set for the total risk index of all investments. The firm has also set an upper limit of 1000 shares for the more risky U.S. Oil stock. How many shares of each stock should be purchased to maximize the total annual return?

26. Formulation and graphical solution; maximization problem; 3 ≤ constraints

26. Wilkinson Motors, Inc., sells standard automobiles and station wagons. The firm makes $400 profit for each automobile it sells and $500 profit for each station wagon it sells. The company is planning next quarter's order, which the manufacturer says cannot exceed 300 automobiles and 150 station wagons. Dealer preparation requires 2 hours for each automobile and 3 hours for each station wagon. Next quarter the company has 900 hours of shop time available for new car preparation. How many automobiles and station wagons should be ordered so that profit is maximized?
a. What is the linear programming model for this problem?
b. Write the linear program in standard form.
c. Find the optimal solution.
d. What are the values and interpretations of all slack and surplus variables?
e. Which constraints are binding?

27. Formulation and graphical solution; maximization problem; 3 ≤ constraints

27. Ryland Farms in northwestern Indiana grows soybeans and corn on its 500 acres of land. An acre of soybeans brings a $100 profit, and an acre of corn brings a $200 profit. Because of a government program, no more than 200 acres may be planted in soybeans. During the planting season, 1200 hours of planting time will be available. Each acre of soybeans requires 2 hours, while each acre of corn requires 6 hours. How many acres of soybeans and how many acres of corn should be planted to maximize profits?
a. What is the linear programming model for this problem?
b. Write the linear program in standard form.
c. Find the optimal solution.
d. What are the values and interpretations of all slack and surplus variables?
e. If the farm could get either more hours of labor for planting or additional land, which should it attempt to obtain? Why?

28. Formulation and graphical solution; maximization problem; 1 ≤ constraint, 2 ≥ constraints

28. Car Phones, Inc., sells two models of car telephones: model *x* and model *y*. Records show that 3 hours of sales time are used for each model *x* phone that is sold and 5 hours of sales

time for each model y phone. A total of 600 hours of sales time is available for the next 4-week period. In addition, management planning policies call for minimum sales goals of 25 units for both model x and model y.

   a. Show the feasible region for the Car Phones, Inc., problem.

   b. Assuming the company makes a \$40 profit contribution for each model x sold and a \$50 profit contribution for each model y sold, what is the optimal sales goal for the company for the next 4-week period?

   c. Develop a constraint and show the feasible region if management adds the restriction that Car Phones must sell at least as many model y phones as model x phones.

   d. What is the new optimal solution if the constraint in part (c) is added to the problem?

S E L F   T E S T

29. Graphical solution

29. Consider the following linear program:

$$\text{Min} \quad 3x_1 + 4x_2$$

s.t.

$$1x_1 + 3x_2 \geq 6$$

$$1x_1 + 1x_2 \geq 4$$

$$x_1, x_2 \geq 0$$

Identify the feasible region and find the optimal solution. What is the value of the objective function?

30. Identifying extreme points; graphical solution

30. Identify the three extreme-point solutions for the M&D Chemicals problem (see Section 2.7). Identify the value of the objective function and the values of the slack and surplus variables at each extreme point.

31. Graphical solution; determining slack and surplus

31. Consider the following linear programming problem:

$$\text{Min} \quad x_1 + 2x_2$$

s.t.

$$x_1 + 4x_2 \leq 21$$

$$2x_1 + x_2 \geq 7$$

$$3x_1 + 1.5x_2 \leq 21$$

$$-2x_1 + 6x_2 \geq 0$$

$$x_1, x_2 \geq 0$$

   a. Find the optimal solution and the value of the objective function.

   b. Determine the amount of slack or surplus for each constraint.

   c. Suppose the objective function is changed to max $5x_1 + 2x_2$. Find the optimal solution and the value of the objective function.

S E L F   T E S T

32. Graphical solution; finding extreme points

32. Consider the following linear program:

$$\text{Min} \quad 2x_1 + 2x_2$$

s.t.

$$1x_1 + 3x_2 \leq 12$$

$$3x_1 + 1x_2 \geq 13$$

$$1x_1 - 1x_2 = 3$$

$$x_1, x_2 \geq 0$$

a. Show the feasible region.
b. What are the extreme points of the feasible region?
c. Find the optimal solution using the graphical solution procedure.

SELF TEST

33. Standard form; graphical solution; determining slack and surplus

33. For the linear program

$$\text{Min} \quad 6x_1 + 4x_2$$

s.t.

$$2x_1 + 1x_2 \geq 12$$

$$1x_1 + 1x_2 \geq 10$$

$$1x_2 \leq 4$$

$$x_1, x_2 \geq 0$$

a. Write the problem in standard form.
b. Solve the problem using the graphical solution procedure.
c. What are the values of the slack and surplus variables?

34. Formulation and graphical solution; minimization problem; 2 ≥ constraints

34. Greentree Kennels, Inc., provides overnight lodging for a variety of pets. A particular feature at Greentree is the quality of care the pets receive, including excellent food. The kennel's dog food is made by mixing two brand-name dog food products to obtain what the kennel calls the "well-balanced dog diet." The data for the two dog foods are as follows:

Dog Food	Cost/ Ounce	Protein (%)	Fat (%)
Bark Bits	$.06	30	15
Canine Chow	$.05	20	30

If Greentree wants to be sure that the dogs receive at least 5 ounces of protein and at least 3 ounces of fat per day, what is the minimum cost mix of the two dog food products?

35. Formulation and graphical solution; minimization problem; 3 ≥ constraints

35. Jack Kammer has been trying to figure out the correct amount of fertilizer that should be applied to his lawn. After getting his soil analyzed at the local agricultural agency, he was advised to put at least 60 pounds of nitrogen, 24 pounds of phosphorous compounds, and 40 pounds of potassium compounds on the lawn this season. One-third of the mixture is to be applied in May, one-third in July, and one-third in late September. After checking the local discount stores, Jack finds that one store is currently having a sale on packaged fertilizer. One type on sale is the 20-5-20 mixture containing 20% nitrogen, 5% phosphorous compounds, and 20% potassium compounds, and it is selling at $4 for a 20-pound bag. The other type on sale is a 10-10-5 mixture; it is selling for $5 for a 40-pound bag. Jack would like to know how many bags of each type he should purchase so he can combine the ingredients to form a mixture that will meet the minimum agricultural agency requirements. Like all homeowners plagued by large lawns, Jack would like to spend as little as possible to keep his lawn healthy. What should Jack do?

36. Formulation and graphical solution; minimization problem; 2 ≥ constraints, 1 = constraint

36. Kats is a new pet food product. Each 16-ounce can of Kats consists of a blend, or mixture, of two pet food ingredients. Let

$x_1 = $ the number of ounces of ingredient A in a 16-ounce can
$x_2 = $ the number of ounces of ingredient B in a 16-ounce can

Each ounce of ingredient A contains ½ ounce of protein and ⅛ ounce of fat. Each ounce of ingredient B contains 1/10 ounce of protein and ⅓ ounce of fat. Restrictions are that a 16-ounce can of Kats must have at least 4 ounces of protein and 2.5 ounces of fat. If ingredient A costs $0.04 per ounce and ingredient B costs $0.03 per ounce, what is the minimum-cost blend of ingredients A and B in each 16-ounce can of Kats? Identify and interpret the values of the surplus variables for the problem.

37. Formulation and graphical solution; minimization problem; 2 ≥ constraints, 1 ≤ constraint

37. Innis Investments manages funds for a number of companies and wealthy clients. The investment strategy is tailored to each client's needs. For a new client, Innis has been authorized to invest up to $1.2 million in two investment funds: a stock fund and a money market fund. Each unit of the stock fund costs $50 and provides an annual rate of return of 10%; each unit of the money market fund costs $100 and provides an annual rate of return of 4%.

The client wants to minimize risk subject to the requirement that the annual income from the investment be at least $60,000. According to Innis's risk measurement system, each unit invested in the stock fund has a risk index of 8, and each unit invested in the money market fund has a risk index of 3; the higher risk index associated with the stock fund simply indicates that it is the riskier investment. Innis's client has also specified that at least $300,000 be invested in the money market fund.

a. Determine how many units of each fund Innis should purchase for the client to minimize the total risk index for the portfolio.
b. How much annual income will this investment strategy generate?
c. Suppose the client desires to maximize annual return. How should the funds be invested?

38. Formulation and graphical solution; minimization problem; 3 ≥ constraints

38. Photo Chemicals produces two types of photographic developing fluids. Both products cost Photo Chemicals $1 per gallon to produce. Based on an analysis of current inventory levels and outstanding orders for the next month, Photo Chemicals' management has specified that at least 30 gallons of product 1 and at least 20 gallons of product 2 must be produced during the next 2 weeks. Management has also stated that an existing inventory of highly perishable raw material required in the production of both fluids must be used within the next 2 weeks. The current inventory of the perishable raw material is 80 pounds. While more of this raw material can be ordered if necessary, any of the current inventory that is not used within the next 2 weeks will spoil—hence, the management requirement that at least 80 pounds be used in the next 2 weeks. Furthermore, it is known that product 1 requires 1 pound of this perishable raw material per gallon and product 2 requires 2 pounds of the raw material per gallon. Since Photo Chemicals' objective is to keep its production costs at the minimum possible level, the firm's management is looking for a minimum-cost production plan that uses all the 80 pounds of perishable raw material and provides at least 30 gallons of product 1 and at least 20 gallons of product 2. What is the minimum-cost solution?

39. Formulation, standard form, and graphical solution; maximization problem; 2 ≤ constraints, 2 ≥ constraints

39. Bryant's Pizza, Inc., is a producer of frozen pizza products. The company makes a profit of $1.00 for each regular pizza it produces and $1.50 for each deluxe pizza produced. Each pizza includes a combination of dough mix and topping mix. The firm currently has 150 pounds of dough mix and 50 pounds of topping mix. Each regular pizza uses 1 pound of dough mix and 4 ounces of topping mix. Each deluxe pizza uses 1 pound of dough mix and 8 ounces of topping mix. Based on past demand, Bryant can sell at least 50 regular pizzas and at least 25 deluxe pizzas. How many regular and deluxe pizzas should the company make to maximize profits?

a. What is the linear programming model for this problem?
b. Write the linear program in standard form.
c. Find the optimal solution.
d. What are the values and interpretations of all slack and surplus variables?
e. Which constraints are binding?

40. Does the following linear program involve infeasibility, unboundedness, and/or alternative optimal solutions? Explain.

$$\text{Max} \quad 4x_1 + 8x_2$$

s.t.

$$2x_1 + 2x_2 \leq 10$$

$$-1x_1 + 1x_2 \geq 8$$

$$x_1, x_2 \geq 0$$

41. Does the following linear program involve infeasibility, unboundedness, and/or alternative optimal solutions? Explain.

$$\text{Max} \quad 1x_1 + 1x_2$$

s.t.

$$8x_1 + 6x_2 \geq 24$$

$$4x_1 + 6x_2 \geq -12$$

$$2x_2 \geq 4$$

$$x_1, x_2 \geq 0$$

42. Consider the following linear program:

$$\text{Max} \quad 1x_1 + 1x_2$$

s.t.

$$5x_1 + 3x_2 \leq 15$$

$$3x_1 + 5x_2 \leq 15$$

$$x_1, x_2 \geq 0$$

a. What is the optimal solution for this problem?
b. Suppose that the objective function is changed to $1x_1 + 2x_2$. Find the new optimal solution.
c. By adjusting the coefficient of x_2 in the objective function, develop a new objective function that will make the solutions found in parts (a) and (b) alternative optimal solutions.

43. Consider the following linear program:

$$\text{Max} \quad 1x_1 - 2x_2$$

s.t.

$$-4x_1 + 3x_2 \leq 3$$

$$1x_1 - 1x_2 \leq 3$$

$$x_1, x_2 \geq 0$$

a. Graph the feasible region for the problem.
b. Is the feasible region unbounded? Explain.
c. Find the optimal solution.
d. Does an unbounded feasible region imply that the optimal solution to the linear program will be unbounded?

44. The manager of a small independent grocery store is trying to determine the best use of her shelf space for soft drinks. The store carries national and generic brands and currently has 200 square feet of shelf space available. The manager wants to allocate at least 60% of the space to the national brands and, regardless of the profitability, allocate at least 10% of the space to the generic brands. How many square feet of space should the manager allocate to the national brands and the generic brands if

a. The national brands are more profitable than the generic brands?

b. Both brands are equally profitable?

c. The generic brand is more profitable than the national brand?

45. Discuss what happens to the M&D Chemicals problem (see Section 2.7) if the cost per gallon for product 1 is increased to $3.00 per gallon. What would you recommend? Explain.

46. For the M&D Chemicals problem in Section 2.7, discuss the effect of management's requiring total production of 500 gallons for the two products. List two or three actions M&D should consider to correct the situation you encounter.

47. Reconsider the RMC situation in Problem 21.

a. Identify all the extreme points of the feasible region.

b. Suppose RMC discovers a way to increase the profit of solvent base to $60 per ton. Does this change the optimal solution? If so, how?

c. Suppose the profit for the solvent base is $50 per ton. What is the optimal solution now? Comment on any special characteristics that may exist with this profit for the solvent base.

48. Reconsider the RMC situation in Problem 21. Suppose that management adds the requirements that at least 30 tons of fuel additive and at least 15 tons of solvent base must be produced.

a. Graph the constraints for this revised RMC problem. What happens to the feasible region? Explain.

b. If there are no feasible solutions, explain what is needed to produce 30 tons of fuel additive and 15 tons of solvent base.

49. Reconsider the Kelson Sporting Equipment, Inc., production example (Problem 22). Discuss the concepts of infeasibility, unboundedness, and alternative optimal solutions as they occur in each of the following situations:

a. Management has requested that the production of baseball gloves (regular model plus catcher's model) be such that the total number of gloves produced is at least 750. That is, $1x_1 + 1x_2 \geq 750$.

b. The original problem has to be solved again because the profit contribution for the regular model is adjusted downward to $4 per glove.

c. What would have to happen for this problem to be unbounded?

50. Reconsider the RMC situation in Problem 21. Use the graphical sensitivity analysis approach to determine what ranges of values for the profit per ton of the fuel additive and solvent base can exist without causing RMC to change from the current optimal solution of 25 tons of fuel additive and 20 tons of solvent base.

51. For the RMC situation (Problem 21), use the graphical sensitivity analysis approach to determine what happens if an additional 3 tons of material 3 become available. What is the corresponding dual price?

52. Consider the linear program given below.

$$\text{Max} \quad 2x_1 + 3x_2$$

s.t.

$$x_1 + x_2 \leq 10$$

$$2x_1 + x_2 \geq 4$$

$$x_1 + 3x_2 \leq 24$$

$$2x_1 + x_2 \leq 16$$

$$x_1, x_2 \geq 0$$

a. Solve this problem using the graphical solution procedure.
b. Compute the range of optimality for c_1.
c. Compute the range of optimality for c_2.
d. Suppose c_1 is increased from 2 to 2.5. What is the new optimal solution?
e. Suppose c_2 is decreased from 3 to 1. What is the new optimal solution?

53. Refer to problem 52. Compute the dual prices for constraints 1 and 2 and interpret them.

54. Consider the linear program given below.

$$\text{Min} \quad x_1 + x_2$$

s.t.

$$x_1 + 2x_2 \geq 7$$

$$2x_1 + x_2 \geq 5$$

$$x_1 + 6x_2 \geq 11$$

$$x_1, x_2 \geq 0$$

a. Solve this problem using the graphical solution procedure.
b. Compute the range of optimality for c_1.
c. Compute the range of optimality for c_2.
d. Suppose c_1 is increased to 1.5. Find the new optimal solution.
e. Suppose c_2 is decreased to $\frac{1}{3}$. Find the new optimal solution.

55. Refer to problem 54. Compute and interpret the dual prices for the constraints.

56. Consider the linear program given below.

$$\text{Max} \quad 5x_1 + 7x_2$$

s.t.

$$2x_1 + x_2 \geq 3$$

$$-x_1 + 5x_2 \geq 4$$

$$2x_1 - 3x_2 \leq 6$$

$$3x_1 + 2x_2 \leq 35$$

$$\tfrac{3}{7}x_1 + x_2 \leq 10$$

$$x_1, x_2 \geq 0$$

a. Solve this problem using the graphical solution procedure.
b. Compute the range of optimality for c_1.
c. Compute the range of optimality for c_2.
d. Suppose c_1 is decreased to 2. What is the new optimal solution?
e. Suppose c_2 is increased to 10. What is the new optimal solution?

57. Refer to Problem 56. Suppose the objective function coefficient for c_2 is reduced to 3.
    a. Resolve using the graphical solution procedure.
    b. Compute the dual prices for constraints 2 and 3.

58. Refer again to Problem 52.
    a. Suppose c_1 is increased to 3 and c_2 is increased to 4. Find the new optimal solution.
    b. Suppose c_1 is increased to 3 and c_2 is decreased to 2. Find the new optimal solution.

59. Refer again to Problem 56.
   a. Suppose c_1 is decreased to 4 and c_2 is increased to 10. Find the new optimal solution.
   b. Suppose c_1 is decreased to 4 and c_2 is increased to 8. Find the new optimal solution.

60. Expedition Outfitters manufactures a variety of specialty clothing for hiking, skiing, and mountain climbing. They have decided to begin production on two new parkas designed for use in extremely cold weather; the names selected for the two models are the Mount Everest Parka and the Rocky Mountain Parka. Their manufacturing plant has 120 hours of cutting time and 120 hours of sewing time available for producing these two parkas. Each Mount Everest Parka requires 30 minutes of cutting time and 45 minutes of sewing time, and each Rocky Mountain Parka requires 20 minutes of cutting time and 15 minutes of sewing time. The labor and material cost is $150 for each Mount Everest Parka and $50 for each Rocky Mountain Parka, and the retail prices through the firm's mail order catalog are $250 for the Mount Everest Parka and $200 for the Rocky Mountain Parka. Because management believes that the Mount Everest Parka is a unique coat that will enhance the image of the firm, they have specified that at least 20% of the total production must consist of this model. Assuming that Expedition Outfitters can sell as many coats of each type as they can produce, how many units of each model should they manufacture to maximize the total profit contribution?

61. The NOW Computer Corporation would like to determine how many units of the NOW-100 and the NOW-200 personal computers to manufacture during the current production period. Both models use a Motorola 68040 microprocessor. The assembly times are 1.5 hours for each NOW-100 and 3 hours for each NOW-200. The firm has 3400 microprocessors and 6000 hours of assembly time available for the current production period. Management has specified that at least 25% of total production must be NOW-200 computers. If the profit contributions are $500 for each NOW-100 and $750 for each NOW-200, how many units of each model should they manufacture? Assume that NOW can sell as many units as they can produce.

62. Creative Sports Designs (CSD) manufactures a standard-size racket and an oversize racket. The firm's rackets are extremely light due to the use of a magnesium–graphite alloy that was invented by the firm's founder. Each standard-size racket uses 0.125 kilograms of the alloy and each oversize racket uses 0.4 kilograms; over the next 2-week production period only 80 kilograms of the alloy are available. Each standard-size racket uses 10 minutes of manufacturing time and each oversize racket uses 12 minutes. The profit contributions are $10 for each standard-size racket and $15 for each oversize racket, and 40 hours of manufacturing time are available each week. Management has specified that at least 20% of the total production must be the standard-size racket. How many rackets of each type should CSD manufacture over the next 2 weeks to maximize the total profit contribution? Assume that because of the unique nature of their products, CSD can sell as many rackets as they can produce.

63. Management of High Tech Services (HTS) would like to develop a model that will help allocate their technicians' time between service calls to regular contract customers and new customers. A maximum of 80 hours of technician time is available over the 2-week planning period. To satisfy cash flow requirements, at least $800 in revenue (per technician) must be generated during the 2-week period. Technician time for regular customers generates $25 per hour. However, technician time for new customers only generates an average of $8 per hour because in many cases a new customer contact does not provide billable services. To ensure that new customer contacts are being maintained, the technician time spent on new customer contacts must be at least 60% of the time spent on regular customer contacts. Given the above revenue and policy requirements, HTS would like to determine how to allocate technician time between regular customers and new customers so that the total number of customers contacted during the 2-week period will be maximized. Technicians require an average of 50 minutes for each regular customer contact and 1 hour for each new customer contact.
   a. Develop a linear programming model that will enable HTS to allocate technician time between regular customers and new customers.

b. Graph the feasible region.
c. Solve the appropriate simultaneous linear equations to determine the values of x_1 and x_2 at each extreme point of the feasible region.
d. Find the optimal solution.

Case Problem: Advertising Strategy

Midtown Motors, Inc., has hired a marketing services firm to develop an advertising strategy for promoting Midtown's used-car sales. The marketing firm has recommended that Midtown use spot announcements on both television and radio as the advertising media for the proposed promotional campaign. Advertising strategy guidelines are expressed as follows:

1. Use at least 30 announcements for combined television and radio coverage.
2. Do not use more than 25 radio announcements.
3. The number of radio announcements cannot be less than the number of television announcements.

The television station has quoted a cost of $1200 per spot announcement, and the radio station has quoted a cost of $300 per spot announcement. Midtown's advertising budget has been set at $25,500. The marketing services firm has rated the various advertising media in terms of audience coverage and recall power of the advertisement. For Midtown's media alternatives, the television announcement is rated at 600, and the radio announcement is rated at 200. Midtown's president would like to know how many television and how many radio spot announcements should be used to maximize the overall rating of the advertising campaign.

Midtown's president believes the television station will consider running the Midtown spot announcement on its highly rated evening news program (at the same cost) if Midtown will consider using additional television announcements.

Managerial Report

Perform an analysis of advertising strategy for Midtown Motors, and prepare a report to Midtown's president presenting your findings and recommendations. Include (but do not limit your discussion to) a consideration of the following:

1. The recommended number of television and radio spot announcements
2. The relative merits of each advertising medium
3. The news program rating that would be necessary before it would make sense to increase the number of television spots
4. The number of television spots that should be purchased if the news program is rated highly enough to make increasing the number of television spots advisable
5. The restrictions placed on the advertising strategy that Midtown might want to consider relaxing or altering
6. The best use of any possible increase in the advertising budget
7. Any other information that may help Midtown's president make the advertising strategy decision

Include a copy of your linear programming model and graphical solution in the appendix to your report.

Linear Programming: Formulation, Computer Solution, and Interpretation

In this chapter we provide an introduction to the use of computers for solving linear programming problems. We begin by showing how The Management Scientist, a microcomputer software package for solving a wide variety of management science problems, can be used to solve the Par, Inc. and M&D Chemicals problems presented in Chapter 2. Then we extend the discussion by formulating and solving two slightly larger problems with three decision variables. In discussing the computer solution for each of these problems, we focus on the interpretation of the computer output including both the optimal solution and sensitivity analysis information. The final section provides both general guidelines for problem formulation and further practice in the formulation, computer solution, and interpretation of output; the problem we consider involves four decision variables and various types of constraints. A chapter appendix describes how LINDO/PC, a popular microcomputer package developed by Linus Schrage at the University of Chicago, can be used to solve linear programs.

3.1 Computer Solution of Linear Programs

Computer programs designed to solve linear programming problems are now widely available. Most large companies, as well as most universities, have access to these computer programs. The developmental effort for large-scale "software packages" has come primarily from computer manufacturers and/or software service companies such as IBM, Control Data, and Ketron. After a short period of familiarization with the specific features of the package, users can usually solve linear programming problems with few difficulties. Problems involving thousands of variables and thousands of constraints are now routinely solved with computer packages. Most large linear programs can be solved with just a few minutes of computer time; small linear programs usually require only a few seconds.

In January 1952 the first successful computer solution of a linear programming problem was performed on the SEAC (Standards Eastern Automatic Computer). The SEAC, the first digital computer built by the National Bureau of Standards under U.S. Air Force sponsorship, had a 512-word memory and magnetic tape for external storage.

Using microcomputers that can be purchased for less than $5000, certain linear programming computer codes can now be used to solve problems with several thousand constraints and variables.

More recently there has been a virtual explosion of software for microcomputers. A large number of user-friendly computer programs that can solve linear programs on microcomputers are now available. These programs, developed by academicians and small software companies, are almost all easy to use. Most of these programs are designed to solve smaller linear programs (a few hundred variables). But, some can be used to solve problems involving thousands of variables and constraints.

The Management Scientist, a microcomputer software package developed by the authors of this text, contains a linear programming module. Let us demonstrate its usage by solving the Par, Inc., problem we introduced in Chapter 2. Since computer input must utilize decimal rather than fractional data values, we restate the problem with decimal coefficients:

$$\text{Max} \quad 10x_1 + 9x_2$$

s.t.

$$0.7x_1 + 1x_2 \leq 630 \quad \text{Cutting and dyeing}$$
$$0.5x_1 + 0.83333x_2 \leq 600 \quad \text{Sewing}$$
$$1.0x_1 + 0.66667x_2 \leq 708 \quad \text{Finishing}$$
$$0.1x_1 + 0.25x_2 \leq 135 \quad \text{Inspection and packaging}$$
$$x_1, x_2 \geq 0$$

Note that in the above form, the coefficient of x_2 in the sewing constraint is written as 0.83333, which is the closest five-place decimal value to the fraction $\frac{5}{6}$. A similar rounding occurs for the x_2 coefficient in the finishing constraint, where the decimal 0.66667 is used as the closest five-place decimal value to the fraction $\frac{2}{3}$. When this rounding of the input data is required, we may expect the computer solution to be slightly different than the hand-calculated solution based on the exact fractional values. However, as you will see, the two solutions are extremely close, and the slight rounding of the input data causes no serious problem.

After the user selects the linear programming module of The Management Scientist, the problem selection menu appears as shown in Figure 3.1. In the following figures, user responses are shown in color; the information printed by the computer is shown in black.

Figure 3.1
Problem Selection Menu from The Management Scientist (User Response Shown in Color)

```
                      PROBLEM SELECTION MENU

              Choices

                   1    Create a New Problem

                   2    Retrieve a Previously Saved Problem

                   3    Continue with the Current Problem

                   4    Delete a Previously Saved Problem

                   5    Return to the Top Level Menu

         PLEASE MAKE YOUR SELECTION AND PRESS RETURN 1
```

Note that the user has made choice 1, Create a New Problem. After making this choice, the user is requested to type in the objective function and constraints.

In using linear programming software, students often think that they need to enter the nonnegativity constraints. All software packages we are aware of automatically assume nonnegative values for the decision variables.

Figure 3.2 shows the computer prompts and how the user types in the problem. The computer prints OBJECTIVE FUNCTION: ; the user then types the objective function as shown. After the user presses the return or enter key, the computer prints CONSTRAINT 1: ; the user then types in the constraint and again presses the return key. Note that the symbol < is interpreted as ≤ by The Management Scientist. The computer will continue to ask for constraints until the user types END. Figure 3.2 shows that the user has typed in the four constraints and then typed END when asked for constraint 5.

Typing END tells The Management Scientist that the complete problem has been entered. The computer then prints the problem disposition menu as shown in Figure 3.3. At this point, the user can make choice 1 to solve the problem, choice 2 to save the problem for future use, choice 3 to display/edit the problem, or choice 4 to return to the problem selection menu. Choice 1 was selected, and the solution generated by The Management Scientist is shown in Figure 3.4.

Interpretation of Computer Output

Let us look more closely at The Management Scientist output in Figure 3.4 and interpret the computer solution provided for the Par, Inc., problem. First, note the number 7667.99463, which appears to the right of Objective Function Value. Rounding this value,

Figure 3.2
User Input for Par, Inc. Problem with The Management Scientist

```
OBJECTIVE FUNCTION:  MAX 10X1 + 9X2

CONSTRAINT  1:  .7X1 + 1X2 < 630

CONSTRAINT  2:  .5X1 + .83333X2 < 600

CONSTRAINT  3:  1X1 + .66667X2 < 708

CONSTRAINT  4:  1X1 + .25X2 < 135

CONSTRAINT  5:  END
```

Figure 3.3
User Makes Choice 1 Directing The Management Scientist to Solve the Par, Inc., Problem

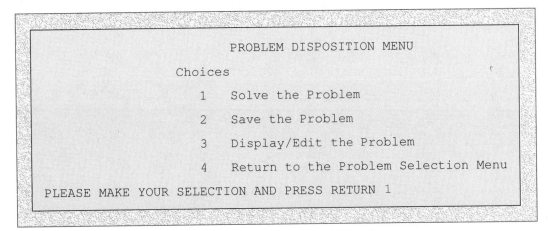

```
                    PROBLEM DISPOSITION MENU

        Choices

            1   Solve the Problem

            2   Save the Problem

            3   Display/Edit the Problem

            4   Return to the Problem Selection Menu

PLEASE MAKE YOUR SELECTION AND PRESS RETURN 1
```

we can conclude that the optimal solution to this problem will provide a profit of $7668. Directly below the objective function value, we find the values of the decision variables at the optimal solution. After rounding we have $x_1 = 540$ standard bags and $x_2 = 252$ deluxe bags as the optimal production quantities.

The information in the Reduced Costs column indicates how much the objective function coefficient of each decision variable would have to improve[1] before it would be possible for that variable to assume a positive value in the optimal solution. If a decision variable is already positive in the optimal solution, its reduced cost is zero. For the Par,

---

[1]For a maximization problem, improve means get bigger; for a minimization problem, improve means get smaller.

Figure 3.4 The Managment Scientist Solution for the Par, Inc. Problem

```
Objective Function Value =          7667.99463

     Variable              Value            Reduced Costs
   -------------        ------------       ----------------
        X1               539.99841             0.00000
        X2               252.00113             0.00000


    Constraint         Slack/Surplus          Dual Prices
   -------------       -------------         ---------------
        1                 0.00000               4.37496
        2               120.00070               0.00000
        3                 0.00000               6.93753
        4                17.99988               0.00000


OBJECTIVE COEFFICIENT RANGES

   Variable        Lower Limit       Current Value       Upper Limit
   ----------      ------------      --------------      ------------
      X1             6.30000            10.00000           13.49993
      X2             6.66670             9.00000           14.28572


RIGHT HAND SIDE RANGES

   Constraint      Lower Limit       Current Value       Upper Limit
   ----------      ------------      --------------      ------------
       1            495.59998          630.00000           682.36316
       2            479.99930          600.00000         No Upper Limit
       3            580.00146          708.00000           900.00000
       4            117.00012          135.00000         No Upper Limit
```

Inc., problem, the optimal solution is $x_1 = 540$ and $x_2 = 252$. Since both variables already have positive values, their corresponding reduced costs are zero. In Section 3.2 we will interpret the reduced cost for a decision variable that does not have a positive value in the optimal solution.

Immediately following the optimal x_1 and x_2 values and the reduced cost information, the computer output provides information about the status of the constraints. Recall that the Par, Inc., problem had four less-than-or-equal-to constraints corresponding to the hours available in each of four production departments. The information shown in the Slack/Surplus column provides the value of the slack variable for each of the departments. This information (after rounding) is summarized below:

Constraint Number	Constraint Name	Slack
1	Cutting and dyeing	0
2	Sewing	120
3	Finishing	0
4	Inspection and packaging	18

From the above information, we see that the binding constraints (the cutting and dyeing and the finishing constraints) have zero slack at the optimal solution. The sewing department has 120 hours of slack, or unused capacity, and the inspection and packaging department has 18 hours of slack or unused capacity.

The Dual Prices column contains information about the value of each of the four resources at the optimal solution. In Chapter 2 we defined the *dual price* as follows.

> The dual price associated with a constraint is the *improvement* in the value of the solution per-unit increase in the right-hand side of the constraint.

You should be able to use computer output to determine the optimal solution, and you should be able to interpret the values of the dual prices. Try Problem 1.

Thus, we see that the nonzero dual prices of 4.37496 for constraint 1 (cutting and dyeing constraint) and 6.93753 for constraint 3 (finishing constraint) tell us that an additional hour of cutting and dyeing time improves (increases) the value of the optimal solution by $4.37 and an additional hour of finishing time improves (increases) the value of the optimal solution by $6.94. Thus, if the cutting and dyeing time were increased from 630 to 631 hours, with all other coefficients in the problem remaining the same, Par's profit would be increased by $4.37 from $7668 to $7668 + $4.37 = $7672.37. A similar interpretation for the finishing constraint implies that an increase from 708 to 709 hours of available finishing time, with all other coefficients in the problem remaining the same, would increase Par's profit to $7668 + $6.94 = $7674.94. Since the sewing and the inspection and packaging constraints both have slack or unused capacity available, the dual prices of zero show that additional hours of these two resources will not improve the value of the objective function.

Referring again to the computer output in Figure 3.4, we see that after providing the constraint information on slack/surplus variables and dual prices, The Management

Scientist prints the ranges on the objective function coefficients and the right-hand sides of the constraints.

Considering the information provided under the computer output heading labeled OBJECTIVE COEFFICIENT RANGES, we see that variable x_1, which has a current profit coefficient of 10, has the following *range of optimality* for c_1:

$$6.30 \leq c_1 \leq 13.50$$

This tells us that as long as the profit contribution associated with the standard bag is between \$6.30 and \$13.50, the production of $x_1 = 540$ standard bags and $x_2 = 252$ deluxe bags will remain the optimal solution. Note that this is the range of optimality that we obtained by performing graphical sensitivity analysis for c_1 in Section 2.10.

Using the objective function coefficient range information for deluxe bags, we see that The Management Scientist has computed the following range of optimality:

$$6.67 \leq c_2 \leq 14.29$$

This tells us that as long as the profit contribution associated with the deluxe bag is between \$6.67 and \$14.29, the production of $x_1 = 540$ standard bags and $x_2 = 252$ deluxe bags will remain the optimal solution.

You should now be able to use computer output to determine the ranges of optimality and the ranges of feasibility. Try Problem 2.

The final section of the computer printout (RIGHT HAND SIDE RANGES) contains ranging information for the constraint right-hand sides. As long as the constraint right-hand side stays within this range, the associated dual price gives the improvement in the value of the optimal solution per-unit increase in the right-hand side. For example, let us consider the cutting and dyeing constraint with a current right-hand-side value of 630. Since the dual price for this constraint is \$4.37, we can conclude that additional hours will increase the objective function by \$4.37 per hour. It is also true that a reduction in the hours available will reduce the value of the objective function by \$4.37 per hour. From the range information given, we see that the dual price of \$4.37 is valid for increases up to 682.36316 and decreases down to 495.59998. A similar interpretation for the finishing constraint's right-hand side (constraint 3) shows that the dual price of \$6.94 is applicable for increases up to 900 hours and decreases down to 580.00146 hours.

As mentioned, the right-hand-side ranges provide limits within which the dual prices are applicable. For changes outside the range, the problem must be resolved to find the new optimal solution and the new dual price. We shall call the range over which the dual price is applicable the *range of feasibility*. The ranges of feasibility for the Par, Inc., problem are summarized below.

Constraint	Min RHS	Max RHS
Cutting and dyeing	495.6	682.4
Sewing	480.0	No upper limit
Finishing	580.0	900.0
Inspection and packaging	117.0	No upper limit

As long as the values of the right-hand sides are within these ranges, the dual prices shown on the computer output will not change. Right-hand-side values outside these limits will result in changes in the dual price information.

Simultaneous Changes

It is important to note that the sensitivity analysis information in computer output is based on the assumption that only one coefficient changes; it is assumed that all other coefficients will remain as stated in the original problem. Thus, the ranges for the objective function coefficients and the constraint right-hand sides are only applicable for changes in a single coefficient. In many cases, however, we may be interested in what would happen if two or more coefficients are changed simultaneously. As we will demonstrate, some analysis of simultaneous changes is possible with the help of the *100 percent rule*.[2] We begin by showing how the 100 percent rule applies to simultaneous changes in the objective function coefficients.

Suppose that in the Par, Inc., problem the accounting department concluded that the original profit contributions of $10 and $9 for the standard and deluxe bags, respectively, were incorrectly computed; the correct values should have been $11.50 and $8.25. To determine what effect, if any, these simultaneous changes have on the optimal solution, we need to first define the terms "allowable increase" and "allowable decrease." For an objective function coefficient, the *allowable increase* is the maximum amount the coefficient may be increased without exceeding the upper limit of the range of optimality; the *allowable decrease* is the maximum amount the coefficient may be decreased without dropping below the lower limit of the range of optimality.

From Figure 3.4 we see that the upper limit for the objective function coefficient of x_1 is 13.49993; thus, the allowable increase is $3.49993 = 13.49993 - 10$. In terms of percentage change, the increase of $1.50 in the objective function coefficient (from 10 to 11.50) for the standard bags is $(1.50/3.49993)(100) = 42.86\%$ of the allowable increase. Given the lower limit of 6.66670 for x_2, the allowable decrease for x_2 is $2.33330 = 9 - 6.66670$. In terms of percentage change, the decrease of $0.75 in the objective function coefficient (from 9 to 8.25) for the deluxe bags is $(0.75/2.33330)(100) = 32.14\%$ of the allowable decrease. The sum of the percentage change of the allowable increase (42.86%) and the percentage change of the allowable decrease (32.14%) is 75.00%.

Let us now state the 100 percent rule as it applies to simultaneous changes in the objective function coefficients.

---

1 0 0 PERCENT RULE FOR OBJECTIVE FUNCTION COEFFICIENTS

For all objective function coefficients that are changed, sum the percentages of the allowable increases and the allowable decreases represented by the changes. If the sum of the percentage changes does not exceed 100%, the optimal solution will not change.

Thus, since the sum of the two percentage changes in the objective function coefficients for the Par, Inc., problem is 75%, these simultaneous changes will not affect the optimal solution. Note, however, that although the optimal solution is still $x_1 = 539.99841$ and $x_2 = 252.00113$, the value of the optimal solution will change since the profit contribution for the standard bags has increased to $11.50 and the profit contribution of the deluxe bags has decreased to $8.25.

---

[2]See S. P. Bradley, A. C. Hax, and T. L. Magnanti, *Applied Mathematical Programming* (Reading, Mass.: Addison-Wesley, 1977).

The 100 percent rule does not, however, say that the optimal solution will change if the sum of the percentage changes exceeds 100%. It is possible that the optimal solution will not change even though the sum of the percentage changes exceeds 100%. When the 100 percent rule is not satisfied, we must resolve the problem to determine what affect such changes will have on the optimal solution.

A similar version of the 100 percent rule also applies to simultaneous changes in the constraint right-hand sides.

---

100 PERCENT RULE FOR CONSTRAINT RIGHT-HAND SIDES

For all right-hand sides that are changed, sum the percentages of allowable increases and allowable decreases. If the sum of percentages does not exceed 100%, then the dual prices will not change.

Let us illustrate the 100 percent rule for constraint right-hand sides by considering simultaneous changes in the right-hand sides for the Par, Inc., problem. Suppose, for instance, that in this problem we could obtain 20 additional hours of cutting and dyeing time and 100 additional hours of finishing time. The allowable increase for cutting and dyeing time is $682.36316 - 630.0 = 52.36316$, and the allowable increase for finishing time is $900.0 - 708.0 = 192.0$ (see Figure 3.4). The 20 additional hours of cutting and dyeing time are $(20/52.36316)(100) = 38.19\%$ of the allowable increase in the constraint's right-hand side. The 100 additional hours of finishing time are $(100/192)(100) = 52.08\%$ of the allowable increase in the finishing time constraint's right-hand side. The sum of the percentage changes is $38.19\% + 52.08\% = 90.27\%$. Since the sum of the percentage changes does not exceed 100%, we can conclude that the dual prices are applicable and that the objective function will improve by $(20)(4.37) + (100)(6.94) = 781.40$.

Interpretation of Computer Output—A Second Example

As another example of interpreting computer output, let us reconsider the M&D Chemicals minimization problem introduced in Section 2.7. The linear programming model for this problem is restated below, where $x_1 =$ number of gallons of product 1 and $x_2 =$ number of gallons of product 2 and it is desired to minimize production cost.

$$\text{Min} \quad 2x_1 + 3x_2$$

s.t.

$$1x_1 \qquad \geq 125 \quad \text{Demand for product 1}$$

$$1x_1 + 1x_2 \geq 350 \quad \text{Total production}$$

$$2x_1 + 1x_2 \leq 600 \quad \text{Processing time}$$

$$x_1, x_2 \geq 0$$

The solution obtained using The Management Scientist is presented in Figure 3.5. The computer output shows that the minimum-cost solution yields an objective function value of \$800. The values of the decision variables show that 250 gallons of product 1 ($x_1 = 250$) and 100 gallons of product 2 ($x_2 = 100$) provide the minimum-cost solution.

The Slack/Surplus column shows that the $\geq$ constraint corresponding to the demand for product 1 (see constraint 1) has a surplus of 125 units. This tells us that production of

Figure 3.5 The Management Scientist Solution for the M&D Chemicals Problem

```
Objective Function Value =              800.000

         Variable              Value              Reduced Costs
         --------              -----              -------------
            X1                250.000                 0.000
            X2                100.000                 0.000


        Constraint         Slack/Surplus            Dual Prices
        ----------         -------------            -----------
            1                125.000                  0.000
            2                  0.000                 -4.000
            3                  0.000                  1.000


OBJECTIVE COEFFICIENT RANGES

     Variable       Lower Limit       Current Value      Upper Limit
     --------       -----------       -------------      -----------
        X1       No Lower Limit           2.000             3.000
        X2              2.000             3.000         No Upper Limit


RIGHT HAND SIDE RANGES

    Constraint      Lower Limit       Current Value      Upper Limit
    ----------      -----------       -------------      -----------
        1        No Lower Limit          125.000           250.000
        2              300.000           350.000           475.000
        3              475.000           600.000           700.000
```

product 1 in the optimal solution exceeds demand by 125 gallons. The Slack/Surplus values are zero for the total production requirement (constraint 2) and the processing time limitation (constraint 3); this indicates that these constraints are binding at the optimal solution.

The Dual Prices column again shows us the *improvement* in the value of the optimal solution per-unit increase in the right-hand side of the constraint. Focusing first on the dual price of 1.00 for the processing time constraint (constraint 3), we see that if we can increase the processing time from 600 to 601 hours, the objective function value will *improve* by $1. Since the objective is to minimize costs, improvement in this case means a lowering of costs. Thus, if 601 hours of processing time are available, the value of the optimal solution will improve to $800 − $1 = $799. The RIGHT HAND SIDE RANGES section of the output shows that the upper limit for the processing time constraint (constraint 3) is 700 hours. Thus, the dual price of $1 per unit would be applicable for every additional hour of processing time up to a total of 700 hours.

Let us again return to the Dual Prices section of the output and consider the dual price for the total production constraint (constraint 2). The *negative dual price* tells us that the value of the optimal solution *will not improve* if the value of the right-hand side is increased by one unit. In fact, the dual price of −4.00 tells us that if the right-hand side of the total production constraint is increased from 350 to 351 units, the value of the optimal solution will worsen by the amount of $4. Since worsening means an increase in cost, the value of the optimal solution will become $800 + $4 = $804 if the one-unit increase in the total production requirement is made.

Since the dual price refers to improvement in the value of the optimal solution per-unit increase in the right-hand side, a constraint with a negative dual price should not have its right-hand side increased. In fact, if the dual price is negative, efforts should be made to reduce the right-hand side of the constraint. If the right-hand side of the total production constraint were decreased from 350 to 349 units, the dual price tells us the total cost could be lowered by $4 to $800 − $4 = $796.

The dual price is the improvement in the value of the optimal solution per-unit increase in the right-hand side of a constraint. However, as we have seen, the interpretation of an *improvement* in the value of an objective function depends on whether we are solving a maximization or a minimization problem. The dual price for a ≤ constraint will always be greater than or equal to zero because increasing the right-hand side cannot make the value of the objective function worse. Similarly, the dual price for a ≥ constraint will always be less than or equal to zero because increasing the right-hand side cannot improve the value of the optimal solution.

Finally, consider the right-hand-side ranges provided in Figure 3.5. The ranges of feasibility for the M&D Chemicals problem are summarized below.

Constraint	Min RHS	Max RHS
Product 1 demand	None	250
Total production	300	475
Processing time	475	700

You should now be able to interpret the computer output for a minimization problem. Try Problem 6.

As long as the right-hand sides are within the above ranges, the dual prices shown on the computer printout are applicable.

Cautionary Note on the Interpretation of Dual Prices

As stated previously, the dual price is the improvement in the value of the optimal solution per-unit increase in the right-hand side of a constraint. When the right-hand side of the constraint represents the amount of a resource available, the associated dual price is often interpreted as the maximum amount one should be willing to pay for one additional unit of the resource. However, such an interpretation is not always correct. To see why, we need to understand the difference between sunk and relevant costs. A *sunk cost* is one that is not affected by the decision made. It will be incurred no matter what values the decision variables assume. A *relevant cost* is one that depends on the decision made. The amount of a relevant cost will vary depending on the values of the decision variables.

Let us reconsider the Par, Inc., problem. The amount of cutting and dyeing time available is 630 hours. The cost of the time available is a sunk cost if it must be paid regardless of the number of standard and deluxe golf bags produced. It would be a relevant cost if Par only had to pay for the number of hours of cutting and dyeing time actually used to produce golf bags. All relevant costs should be reflected in the objective function of a linear program. Sunk costs should not be reflected in the objective function. For Par, Inc., we have been assuming that the company must pay its employees' wages whether or not their time on the job is completely utilized. Therefore, the cost of the labor-hours resource for Par, Inc., is a sunk cost and has not been reflected in the objective function.

Only relevant costs should be included in the objective function.

When the cost of a resource is *sunk,* the dual price can be interpreted as the maximum amount the company should be willing to pay for one additional unit of the resource. When the cost of a resource used is relevant, the dual price can be interpreted as the amount by which the value of the resource exceeds its cost. Thus, when the resource cost is relevant, the dual price can be interpreted as the maximum premium over the normal cost that the company should be willing to pay for one unit of the resource.

NOTES & COMMENTS

1. Computer software packages for solving linear programs are readily available. Most of these provide the optimal solution, dual or shadow price information, the range of optimality for the objective function coefficients, and the range of feasibility for the right-hand sides. The labels used for the ranges of optimality and feasibility may vary, but the meaning is the same as what we have described here.

2. Whenever one of the right-hand sides is at an end point of its range of feasibility, the dual and shadow prices only provide one-sided information. In this case, they only predict the change in the optimal value of the objective function for changes toward the interior of the range.

3. A condition called *degeneracy* can cause a subtle difference in how we interpret changes in the objective function coefficients beyond the end points of the range of optimality. Degeneracy occurs when the dual price equals zero for one of the binding constraints. Degeneracy does not affect the interpretation of changes toward the interior of the range of optimality. However, when degeneracy is present, changes beyond the end points of the range do not necessarily mean a different solution will be optimal. From a practical point of view, changes beyond the end points of the range of optimality necessitate resolving the problem.

4. The 100 percent rule permits an analysis of multiple changes in the right-hand sides or multiple changes in the objective function coefficients. But the 100 percent rule cannot be applied to changes in both objective function coefficients *and* right-hand sides at the same time. In order to consider simultaneous changes for *both* right-hand-side values and objective function coefficients, the problem must be resolved.

5. Managers are frequently called on to provide an economic justification for new technology. Often the new technology is developed, or purchased, in order to conserve resources. The dual price can be helpful in such cases because it can be used to determine the savings attributable to the new technology by showing the savings per unit of resource conserved.

3.2 More Than Two Decision Variables

The graphical solution procedure is useful only for linear programs involving two decision variables. Computer software packages are designed to handle linear programs involving large numbers of variables and constraints. In this section we discuss the formulation and computer solution for two linear programs with three decision variables. In doing so, we will show how to interpret the reduced-cost portion of the computer output and will also illustrate the interpretation of dual prices for constraints that involve percentages.

The Modified Par, Inc., Problem

In Section 3.1 we demonstrated how the linear programming module of The Management Scientist could be used to solve the Par, Inc., problem. The original problem is restated below with decimal coefficients:

$$\text{Max} \quad 10x_1 + 9x_2$$

s.t.

$$0.7x_1 + 1x_2 \leq 630 \quad \text{Cutting and dyeing}$$

$$0.5x_1 + 0.83333x_2 \leq 600 \quad \text{Sewing}$$

$$1x_1 + 0.66667x_2 \leq 708 \quad \text{Finishing}$$

$$0.1x_1 + 0.25x_2 \leq 135 \quad \text{Inspection and packaging}$$

$$x_1, x_2 \geq 0$$

Recall that x_1 is the number of standard golf bags produced and x_2 is the number of deluxe golf bags produced. Suppose that management is also considering producing a lightweight model designed specifically for golfers who prefer to carry their bags. It is estimated that each new lightweight model will require 0.8 hours for cutting and dyeing, 1 hour for sewing, 1 hour for finishing, and 0.25 hours for inspection and packaging. Because of the unique capabilities designed into the new model, Par's management feels that they will realize a profit contribution of $12.85 for each lightweight model produced during the current production period.

Let us consider the modifications in the original linear programming model that are needed to incorporate the effect of this additional decision variable. We will let x_3 denote the number of lightweight bags produced. After adding x_3 to the objective function and to each of the four constraints, we obtain the following linear program for the modified problem:

$$\text{Max} \quad 10x_1 + 9x_2 + 12.85x_3$$

s.t.

$$0.7x_1 + 1x_2 + 0.8x_3 \leq 630 \quad \text{Cutting and dyeing}$$

$$0.5x_1 + 0.83333x_2 + 1x_3 \leq 600 \quad \text{Sewing}$$

$$1x_1 + 0.66667x_2 + 1x_3 \leq 708 \quad \text{Finishing}$$

$$0.1x_1 + 0.25x_2 + 0.25x_3 \leq 135 \quad \text{Inspection and packaging}$$

$$x_1, x_2, x_3 \geq 0$$

Figure 3.6 shows the solution to the modified problem using The Management Scientist. We see that the optimal solution calls for the production of 280 standard bags, 0 deluxe bags, and 428 of the new lightweight bags; the value of the optimal solution after rounding is $8299.80.

Let us now look at the information contained in the Reduced Costs column. Recall that the reduced costs indicate how much each objective function coefficient would have to

Figure 3.6 The Management Scientist Solution for the Modified Par, Inc., Problem

```
Objective Function Value =          8299.80078

        Variable              Value            Reduced Costs
     --------------      --------------      ------------------
          X1                280.00000              0.00000
          X2                  0.00000              1.15003
          X3                428.00000              0.00000


        Constraint         Slack/Surplus          Dual Prices
     --------------      --------------      ------------------
          1                 91.60001              0.00000
          2                 32.00000              0.00000
          3                  0.00000              8.10000
          4                  0.00000             19.00000



OBJECTIVE COEFFICIENT RANGES

      Variable       Lower Limit       Current Value      Upper Limit
     -----------    --------------    --------------     --------------
         X1              5.14000           10.00000          12.07007
         X2         No Lower Limit          9.00000          10.15003
         X3             11.90907           12.85000          25.00000


RIGHT HAND SIDE RANGES

      Constraint      Lower Limit      Current Value      Upper Limit
     -----------    --------------    --------------     --------------
          1            538.40002          630.00000       No Upper Limit
          2            568.00000          600.00000       No Upper Limit
          3            540.00000          708.00000         852.63159
          4             70.80000          135.00000         144.60001
```

improve before the corresponding decision variable could assume a positive value in the optimal solution. As the computer output shows, the reduced costs for x_1 and x_3 are zero since the corresponding decision variables already have positive values in the optimal solution. The reduced cost of 1.15003 for decision variable x_2 tells us that the profit contribution for the deluxe bag would have to increase to at least $9 + $1.15003 = $10.15003 before x_2 *could* assume a positive value in the optimal solution.[3] In other words, unless the profit contribution for x_2 increases by at least $1.15 the value of x_2 will remain at zero in the optimal solution.

Suppose we increase the coefficient of x_2 by exactly $1.15003 and then resolve the problem using The Management Scientist. Figure 3.7 shows the new solution. Note that although x_2 assumes a positive value in the new solution, the value of the optimal solution has not changed. In other words, increasing the profit contribution of x_2 by *exactly* the amount of the reduced cost has resulted in alternative optimal solutions. Using a different computer software package, you may not see x_2 assume a positive value if you resolve the problem with an objective function coefficient of exactly 1.15003 for x_2; that is, the software package may show a different alternative optimal solution. However, if the profit contribution of x_2 is increased by *more than* $1.15003, then x_2 will not remain at zero in the optimal solution.

We also note from Figure 3.6 that the dual prices for constraints 3 and 4 are 8.1 and 19, respectively, indicating that these two constraints are binding in the optimal solution. Thus, each additional labor-hour in the finishing department would increase the value of the optimal solution by $8.10 and each additional labor-hour in the inspection and packaging department would increase the value of the optimal solution by $19.00. Since there is a slack of 91.6 hours in the cutting and dyeing department and 32 hours in the sewing department (see Figure 3.6), management might want to consider the possibility of utilizing these unused labor-hours in the finishing or inspection and packaging departments. For example, some of the employees in the cutting and dyeing department could be used to perform certain operations in either the finishing department or the inspection and packaging department. In the future, Par's management may want to explore the possibility of cross-training employees so that unused capacity in one department could be shifted to other departments. In the next chapter we will consider modeling situations like this.

Suppose that after reviewing the solution shown in Figure 3.6, management states that they will not consider any solution that does not include the production of some deluxe bags. Management then decides to add the requirement that the number of deluxe bags produced must be at least 30% of the number of standard bags produced. Writing this requirement using the decision variables x_1 and x_2, we obtain

$$x_2 \geq 0.3x_1$$

or

$$-0.3x_1 + x_2 \geq 0$$

Adding this new constraint to the modified Par, Inc., linear program and resolving the problem using The Management Scientist, we obtain the optimal solution shown in Figure 3.8.

---

[3]In the case of degeneracy, a variable may not assume a positive value in the optimal solution even when the improvement in the profit contribution exceeds the value of the reduced cost. Our definition of reduced costs, stated as "... *could* assume a positive value ....," provides for such special cases. More advanced texts on mathematical programming discuss these special types of situations.

Figure 3.7 The Management Scientist Solution for the Modified Par, Inc., Problem with the Coefficient of x_2 Increased by \$1.15003

```
Objective Function Value =        8299.80078

       Variable            Value           Reduced Costs
     --------------    --------------    ------------------

         X1              403.78317            0.00000
         X2              222.81198            0.00000
         X3              155.67476            0.00000


      Constraint       Slack/Surplus         Dual Prices
     --------------    --------------    ------------------

         1                0.00000             0.00000
         2               56.75776             0.00000
         3                0.00000             8.10000
         4                0.00000            19.00000


OBJECTIVE COEFFICIENT RANGES

    Variable      Lower Limit      Current Value      Upper Limit
   -----------   -------------    ---------------    -------------

       X1          10.00000          10.00000          12.51072
       X2          10.15003          10.15003          15.40790
       X3          10.65313          12.85000          12.85000


RIGHT HAND SIDE RANGES

   Constraint     Lower Limit      Current Value      Upper Limit
   -----------   -------------    ---------------    -------------

       1           538.40002         630.00000         682.36316
       2           543.24225         600.00000      No Upper Limit
       3           580.00140         708.00000         852.63159
       4           117.00012         135.00000         151.15410
```

Let us consider the interpretation of the dual price for constraint 5, the requirement that the number of deluxe bags produced must be at least 30% of the number of standard bags produced. The dual price of -1.38 indicates that a one-unit increase in the right-hand side of the constraint will lower profits by \$1.38. Thus, what the dual price of -1.38 is really telling us is what will happen to the value of the optimal solution if the constraint is changed to

$$x_2 \geq 0.3x_1 + 1$$

Figure 3.8 The Management Scientist Solution for the Modified Par, Inc., Problem with the 30% Deluxe-Bag Requirement

```
Objective Function Value =        8183.87793

       Variable              Value              Reduced Costs
    --------------       --------------       ------------------
         X1                335.99933               0.00000
         X2                100.79980               0.00000
         X3                304.80048               0.00000


     Constraint         Slack/Surplus             Dual Prices
    --------------       --------------       ------------------
          1                 50.16031               0.00000
          2                 43.20037               0.00000
          3                  0.00000               7.40998
          4                  0.00000              21.76006
          5                  0.00000              -1.38003


OBJECTIVE COEFFICIENT RANGES

     Variable         Lower Limit        Current Value        Upper Limit
    ------------     --------------     --------------      --------------
        X1               6.29500           10.00000            12.07007
        X2              -3.35000            9.00000            10.15003
        X3              11.90907           12.85000            18.14286


RIGHT HAND SIDE RANGES

    Constraint        Lower Limit        Current Value        Upper Limit
    ------------     --------------     --------------      --------------
         1             579.83972          630.00000        No Upper Limit
         2             556.79962          600.00000        No Upper Limit
         3             540.00000          708.00000           765.00049
         4             103.24991          135.00000           147.00008
         5             -84.00000            0.00000           101.67704
```

The correct interpretation of the dual price of -1.38 can now be stated as follows: If we are forced to produce one deluxe bag over and above the minimum 30% requirement, total profits will decrease by \$1.38. Conversely, if we relax the minimum 30% requirement by one bag ($x_2 \geq 0.3x_1 - 1$), total profits will increase by \$1.38.

The dual price for a percentage (or ratio) constraint such as this will not directly provide answers to questions concerning a percentage increase or decrease in the right-hand side of the constraint. For example, we might wonder what would happen to the value of the optimal solution if the number of deluxe bags has to be at least 31% of the number of standard bags. To answer such a question, we would resolve the problem using the constraint $-0.31x_1 + x_2 \geq 0$.

Because percentage (or ratio) constraints frequently occur in linear programming models, let us consider another example. For instance, suppose that Par's management states that the number of lightweight bags produced may not exceed 20% of the total golf bag production. Since the total production of golf bags is $x_1 + x_2 + x_3$, we can write this constraint as

$$x_3 \leq 0.2(x_1 + x_2 + x_3)$$

$$x_3 \leq 0.2x_1 + 0.2x_2 + 0.2x_3$$

$$-0.2x_1 - 0.2x_2 - 0.8x_3 \leq 0$$

The solution obtained using The Management Scientist for the model that incorporates both the effects of this new percentage requirement and the previous requirement ($-0.3x_1 + x_2 \geq 0$) is shown in Figure 3.9. After rounding, the dual price corresponding to the new constraint (constraint 6) is 0.89. Thus, every additional lightweight bag we are allowed to produce over the current 20% limit will increase the value of the objective function by $0.89; moreover, the right-hand-side range for this constraint shows that this interpretation is valid for increases of up to 156 units.

The Bluegrass Farms Problem

To provide additional practice in formulating and interpreting the computer solution for linear programs involving more than two decision variables, we consider a minimization problem involving three decision variables. Bluegrass Farms, located in Lexington, Kentucky, has been experimenting with a special diet for its racehorses. The feed components available for the diet are a standard horse feed product, a vitamin-enriched oat product, and a new vitamin and mineral feed additive. The nutritional values in units per pound and the costs for the three feed components are summarized in Table 3.1; for example, each pound of the standard feed component contains 0.8 unit of ingredient A, 1 unit of ingredient B, and 0.1 unit of ingredient C. The minimum daily diet requirements for each horse are three units of ingredient A, six units of ingredient B, and four units of ingredient C. In addition, to control the weight of the horses, the total daily feed for a horse should not exceed 6 pounds. Bluegrass Farms would like to determine the minimum-cost mix that will satisfy the daily diet requirements.

Formulation of the Bluegrass Farms Problem

To formulate a linear programming model for the Bluegrass Farms problem, we introduce the following three decision variables:

x_1 = number of pounds of the standard horse feed product
x_2 = number of pounds of the enriched oat product
x_3 = number of pounds of the vitamin and mineral feed additive

Using the data in Table 3.1, the objective function for minimizing the total cost associated with the daily feed can be written as follows:

$$\min 0.25x_1 + 0.50x_2 + 3x_3$$

Figure 3.9 The Management Scientist Solution for the Modified Par, Inc., Problem Incorporating the 20% Lightweight-Bag Requirement and the 30% Deluxe-Bag Requirement

```
Objective Function Value =          8044.25488

        Variable              Value            Reduced Costs
    --------------        --------------      ------------------

          X1               403.44730              0.00000
          X2               222.20738              0.00000
          X3               156.41367              0.00000


        Constraint        Slack/Surplus         Dual Prices
    --------------        --------------      ------------------

           1                 0.24859              0.00000
           2                56.69057              0.00000
           3                 0.00000              8.87330
           4                 0.00000             13.05157
           5               101.17319              0.00000
           6                 0.00000              0.89226


OBJECTIVE COEFFICIENT RANGES

       Variable        Lower Limit        Current Value        Upper Limit
    ------------      --------------      --------------      --------------

          X1              3.13800            10.00000            12.07007
          X2              6.47670             9.00000            10.15003
          X3             11.90907            12.85000         No Upper Limit


RIGHT HAND SIDE RANGES

      Constraint        Lower Limit        Current Value        Upper Limit
    ------------      --------------      --------------      --------------

           1             629.75140           630.00000        No Upper Limit
           2             543.30945           600.00000        No Upper Limit
           3             396.00146           708.00000           708.69653
           4             118.96714           135.00000           135.08900
           5          No Lower Limit            0.00000           101.17319
           6              -0.77936              0.00000           156.48053
```

Table 3.1

Nutritional Value and Cost Data for the Bluegrass Farms Problem

Feed Component	Standard	Enriched Oat	Additive
Ingredient A	0.8	0.2	0.0
Ingredient B	1.0	1.5	3.0
Ingredient C	0.1	0.6	2.0
Cost per pound	$0.25	$0.50	$3.00

Since the minimum daily requirement for ingredient A is three units, we obtain the constraint

$$0.8x_1 + 0.2x_2 \geq 3$$

The constraint for ingredient B is

$$1.0x_1 + 1.5x_2 + 3.0x_3 \geq 6$$

and the constraint for ingredient C is

$$0.1x_1 + 0.6x_2 + 2.0x_3 \geq 4$$

Finally, the constraint that restricts the mix to at most 6 pounds is

$$x_1 + x_2 + x_3 \leq 6$$

Combining all the constraints with the nonnegativity requirements enables us to write the complete linear programming model for the Bluegrass Farms problem as follows:

$$\text{Min} \quad 0.25x_1 + 0.50x_2 + 3x_3$$

s.t.

$$
\begin{aligned}
0.8x_1 + 0.2x_2 &\geq 3 \quad \text{Ingredient A} \\
1.0x_1 + 1.5x_2 + 3.0x_3 &\geq 6 \quad \text{Ingredient B} \\
0.1x_1 + 0.6x_2 + 2.0x_3 &\geq 4 \quad \text{Ingredient C} \\
x_1 + x_2 + x_3 &\leq 6 \quad \text{Weight} \\
x_1, x_2, x_3 &\geq 0
\end{aligned}
$$

Computer Solution and Interpretation for the Bluegrass Farms Problem

The output obtained using The Management Scientist to solve the Bluegrass Farms problem is shown in Figure 3.10. After rounding, we see that the optimal solution calls for a daily diet consisting of 3.51 pounds of the standard horse feed product, 0.95 pound of the enriched oat product, and 1.54 pounds of the vitamin and mineral feed additive. Thus, with feed component costs of $0.25, $0.50, and $3.00, the total cost of the optimal diet is

$$
\begin{aligned}
3.51 \text{ pounds @ } \$0.25 \text{ per pound} &= \$0.88 \\
0.95 \text{ pound @ } \$0.50 \text{ per pound} &= 0.47 \\
1.54 \text{ pounds @ } \$3.00 \text{ per pound} &= \underline{4.62} \\
\text{Total cost} &= \$5.97
\end{aligned}
$$

Figure 3.10 The Management Scientist Solution for the Bluegrass Farms Problem Solution

```
Objective Function Value =              5.973

        Variable              Value            Reduced Costs
      ---------------      ---------------    ---------------
          X1                  3.514               0.000
          X2                  0.946               0.000
          X3                  1.541               0.000


       Constraint          Slack/Surplus         Dual Prices
      ---------------      ---------------    ---------------
           1                  0.000               1.216
           2                  3.554               0.000
           3                  0.000              -1.959
           4                  0.000               0.919


OBJECTIVE COEFFICIENT RANGES

      Variable        Lower Limit        Current Value      Upper Limit
    ------------    ---------------    ---------------    ---------------
        X1                 -0.393            0.250        No Upper Limit
        X2          No Lower Limit           0.500                 0.925
        X3                  1.522            3.000        No Upper Limit


RIGHT HAND SIDE RANGES

     Constraint       Lower Limit        Current Value      Upper Limit
    ------------    ---------------    ---------------    ---------------
         1                  1.143            3.000                 3.368
         2          No Lower Limit           6.000                 9.554
         3                  2.100            4.000                 4.875
         4                  5.562            6.000                 8.478
```

Note that after rounding, this is the same as the objective function value in the computer output (Figure 3.10).

Looking at the Slack/Surplus section of the computer output, we find a value of 3.554 for constraint 2. Since constraint 2 is a greater-than-or-equal-to constraint, 3.554 is the surplus; the optimal solution exceeds the minimum daily diet requirement for ingredient B (six units) by 3.554 units. Since the surplus values for constraints 1 and 3 are both zero, we see that the optimal diet just meets the minimum requirements for ingredients A and C; moreover, a slack value of zero for constraint 4 shows that the optimal solution provides a total daily feed weight of 6 pounds.

After rounding, we see that the dual price for the ingredient A constraint (constraint 1) is -1.22. To interpret this value properly, we first look at the sign; since it is negative, we know that increasing the right-hand side of constraint 1 will cause the solution value to worsen. Since this is a minimization problem, "worsen" means that the total daily cost will increase. A one-unit increase in the right-hand side of constraint 1 will increase the total cost of the daily diet by $1.22. Conversely, it is also correct to conclude that a decrease of one unit in the right-hand side will decrease the total cost by $1.22. Looking at the RIGHT HAND SIDE RANGES section of the computer output, we see that these interpretations are correct as long as the right-hand side is between 1.143 and 3.368.

Suppose that the Bluegrass management is willing to reconsider their position regarding the maximum weight of the daily diet. The dual price of 0.92 (after rounding) for constraint 4 shows that a one-unit increase in the right-hand side of constraint 4 will reduce total cost by $0.92. The RIGHT HAND SIDE RANGES section of the output shows that this interpretation is correct for increases in the right-hand side up to a maximum of 8.478 pounds. Thus, the effect of increasing the right-hand side of constraint 4 from 6 to 8 pounds is a decrease in the total daily cost of $2 \times \$0.92$ or $1.84. Keep in mind that if this change were made, the feasible region would change, and we would obtain a new optimal solution.

The OBJECTIVE COEFFICIENT RANGES section of the computer output shows a lower limit of -0.393 for x_1. Clearly, in a real-world problem, the objective function coefficient of x_1 (the cost of the standard horse feed product) cannot take on a negative value. So, from a practical point of view, we can think of the lower limit for the objective function coefficient of x_1 as being zero. We can thus conclude that no matter how much the cost of the standard mix were to decrease, the optimal solution would not change. Even if Bluegrass Farms could obtain the standard horse feed product for free, the optimal solution would still specify a daily diet of 3.51 pounds of the standard horse feed product, 0.95 pound of the enriched oat product, and 1.54 pounds of the vitamin and mineral feed additive. However, any decrease in the per-unit cost of the standard feed would result in a decrease in the total cost for the optimal daily diet.

It is interesting to note that there is no upper limit on the objective function coefficient values for x_1 and x_3. Even if the cost of x_3 were to increase, for example, from $3.00 to $13.00 per pound, the optimal solution would not change; the total cost of the solution, however, would increase by $10 (the amount of the increase) times 1.541 or $15.41. You must always keep in mind that the interpretations that we have made using the sensitivity analysis information in the computer output are only appropriate if all other coefficients in the problem do not change. To consider simultaneous changes you must use the 100 percent rule or resolve the problem after making the changes.

3.3 Modeling

Modeling is the process of translating a verbal statement of a problem into a mathematical statement. In linear programming, the mathematical statement of the problem is a linear program. Up to this point, the problems that we have considered have been small and not particularly difficult to model. But, as problems become larger and more complex, some general guidelines for model formulation are useful.

As used in this text, problem formulation and modeling mean the same thing.

Guidelines for Model Formulation

The process of formulating linear programming models is an art that can only be mastered with practice and experience. Although every problem has *some* unique features, most problems also have common features. As a result, some general guidelines for model formulation can be helpful, especially for beginners.

1. **Understand the problem thoroughly.**
    Read the problem description quickly to get a feel for what is involved. Identify those items that you feel should be included in the model. If the problem is especially complex, take notes; these notes will help you focus on the key ideas and facts.
2. **Write a verbal statement of the objective function and each constraint.**
    Later you will translate these verbal statements into mathematical statements. At this step, you might write the objective function as, for instance, maximize profit or minimize monthly operating costs. You might write a constraint limiting funds borrowed as follows: funds borrowed ≤ line of credit. Even experienced management scientists find they sometimes make mistakes when skipping this step.
3. **Define the decision variables.**
    Ask yourself what decisions the manager must make. What does she or he control? The decision variables should be chosen to represent these decisions. The decision variables should also be defined in such a fashion that writing a mathematical statement of the objective function and the left-hand side of the constraints is facilitated.
4. **Write the objective function in terms of the decision variables.**
    Translate your verbal statement of the objective function developed in Step 2 into a mathematical statement; the mathematical statement must be a linear function of the decision variables.
5. **Write the constraints in terms of the decision variables.**
    Translate your verbal statement of each constraint developed in Step 2 into a mathematical statement; the left-hand side of the resulting equation or inequality must be a linear function of the decision variables.

After carrying out the above steps, we have a linear programming model that represents the problem, or application, under study. Solution of the model will provide the optimal solution, the values of decision variables, the values of the slack/surplus variables, and a variety of information concerning the sensitivity analysis aspects of the problem. Proper interpretation of the solution can provide valuable decision-making information for the manager.

In the next subsection we illustrate the modeling process for the Electronic Communications problem. After reading the written description of the problem, we encourage you to attempt a formulation following the guidelines given above. Then, solve the problem using a linear programming software package, and compare your solution with the one provided.

The Electronic Communications Problem

Electronic Communications manufactures portable radio systems that can be used for two-way communications. The company's new product, which has a range of up to 25 miles, is particularly suitable for use in a variety of business and personal applications. The distribution channels for the new radio are as follows:

1. Marine equipment distributors
2. Business equipment distributors
3. National chain of retail stores
4. Mail order

Because of differing distribution and promotional costs, the profitability of the product will vary with the distribution channel. In addition, the advertising cost and the personal sales effort required will vary with the distribution channels. Table 3.2 summarizes the contribution to profit, advertising cost, and personal sales effort data pertaining to the Electronic Communications problem. The firm has set the advertising budget at $5000 and there is a maximum of 1800 hours of sales force time available for allocation to the sales effort. Management has also decided to produce exactly 600 units for the current production period. Finally, an ongoing contract with the national chain of retail stores requires that at least 150 units be distributed through this distribution channel.

Electronic Communications is now faced with the problem of establishing a strategy that will provide for the distribution of the radios in such a way that overall profitability of the new radio production will be maximized. Decisions must be made as to how many units should be allocated to each of the four distribution channels, as well as how to allocate the advertising budget and sales force effort to each of the four distribution channels.

Formulation of the Electronic Communications Problem

A written statement of the problem has been presented. Let us now attempt to write a verbal statement of the objective function and each constraint. For the objective function, we can write

Objective function: Maximize profit

There appear to be four constraints necessary for this problem. They are necessary because of (1) a limited advertising budget, (2) limited sales force availability, (3) a production requirement, and (4) a retail stores distribution requirement.

Constraint 1: Advertising expenditures ≤ Budget

Constraint 2: Sales time used ≤ Time available

Constraint 3: Radios produced = Management requirement

Constraint 4: Retail distribution ≥ Contract requirement

This provides a verbal description of the objective function and the constraints. We are now ready to define the decision variables such that they represent the decisions that the manager must make.

For the Electronic Communications problem, we introduce the following four decision variables:

x_1 = the number of units produced for the marine equipment distribution channel
x_2 = the number of units produced for the business equipment distribution channel
x_3 = the number of units produced for the national retail chain distribution channel
x_4 = the number of units produced for the mail-order distribution channel

Table 3.2

Profit, Advertising Cost, and Personal Sales Time Data for the Electronic Communications Problem

Distribution Channel	Profit per Unit Sold	Advertising Cost per Unit Sold	Personal Sales Effort per Unit Sold
Marine distributors	$90	$10	2 hours
Business distributors	$84	$ 8	3 hours
National retail stores	$70	$ 9	3 hours
Mail order	$60	$15	None

Using the data in Table 3.2, the objective function for maximizing the total contribution to profit associated with the radios can be written as follows:

$$\max 90x_1 + 84x_2 + 70x_3 + 60x_4$$

Let us now develop a mathematical statement of the constraints for the problem. Since the advertising budget has been set at \$5000, the constraint that limits the amount of advertising expenditure can be written as follows:

$$10x_1 + 8x_2 + 9x_3 + 15x_4 \leq 5000$$

Similarly, since the sales time is limited to 1800 hours, we obtain the constraint

$$2x_1 + 3x_2 + 3x_3 \leq 1800$$

Management's decision to produce exactly 600 units during the current production period is expressed as

$$1x_1 + 1x_2 + 1x_3 + 1x_4 = 600$$

Finally, to account for the fact that the number of units distributed by the national chain of retail stores must be at least 150, we add the constraint

$$1x_3 \geq 150$$

Combining all of the constraints with the nonnegativity requirements enables us to write the complete linear programming model for the Electronic Communications problem as follows:

$$\text{Max} \quad 90x_1 + 84x_2 + 70x_3 + 60x_4$$

s.t.

$10x_1 +$	$8x_2 +$	$9x_3 +$	$15x_4 \leq$	5000	Advertising budget
$2x_1 +$	$3x_2 +$	$3x_3$	$\leq$	1800	Sales force availability
$1x_1 +$	$1x_2 +$	$1x_3 +$	$1x_4 =$	600	Production level
		$1x_3$	$\geq$	150	Retail stores requirement

$$x_1, x_2, x_3, x_4 \geq 0$$

Computer Solution and Interpretation for the Electronic Communications Problem

A portion of the output obtained using The Management Scientist to solve the Electronic Communications problem is shown in Figure 3.11. The Objective Function Value section shows that the optimal solution to the problem will provide a maximum profit of \$48,450. The optimal values of the decision variables are given by $x_1 = 25$, $x_2 = 425$, $x_3 = 150$, and $x_4 = 0$. Thus, the optimal strategy for Electronic Communications is to concentrate on the business equipment distribution channel with $x_2 = 425$ units. In addition, the firm should allocate 25 units to the marine distribution channel ($x_1 = 25$) and meet its 150-unit commitment to the national retail chain store distribution channel ($x_3 = 150$). With $x_4 = 0$, the optimal solution indicates that the firm should not use the mail-order distribution channel.

Figure 3.11 A Portion of the Management Scientist Computer Output for the Electronic Communications Problem

```
Objective Function Value =            48450.000

        Variable            Value            Reduced Costs
     --------------     --------------     ------------------

           X1              25.000               0.000
           X2             425.000               0.000
           X3             150.000               0.000
           X4               0.000              45.000


        Constraint      Slack/Surplus         Dual Prices
     --------------     --------------     ------------------

           1               0.000                3.000
           2              25.000                0.000
           3               0.000               60.000
           4               0.000              -17.000
```

It may be worthwhile to show the student that the reduced costs are also available from the objective coefficient ranges. For example, the reduced cost of $45 for x_4 is the difference between the upper limit of $105 and the current value of the objective function coefficient, $60 (see Figure 3.6).

Let us now look at the information contained in the Reduced Costs column. Recall that the reduced costs indicate how much each objective function coefficient would have to improve before the corresponding decision variable could assume a positive value in the optimal solution. As the computer output shows, the first three reduced costs are zero since the corresponding decision variables already have positive values in the optimal solution. However, the reduced cost of 45 for decision variable x_4 tells us that the profit for the new radios distributed via the mail-order channel would have to increase from its current value of $60 per unit to at least $60 + $45 = $105 per unit before it would be profitable to use the mail-order distribution channel.

The computer output information for the slack/surplus variables and the dual prices is restated below.

Constraint Number	Constraint Name	Type of Constraint	Slack or Surplus	Dual Price
1	Advertising budget	≤	0	3
2	Sales force availability	≤	25	0
3	Production level	=	0	60
4	Retail stores requirement	≥	0	−17

We see that the advertising budget constraint has a slack of zero, indicating that the entire budget of $5000 has been used. The corresponding dual price of 3 tells us that an additional dollar added to the advertising budget will improve the objective function (increase the profit) by $3. Thus, the possibility of increasing the advertising budget should be seriously considered by the firm. The slack of 25 hours for the sales force availability constraint shows that the allocated 1800 hours of sales time are adequate to distribute the radios produced and that 25 hours of sales time will remain unused. Since the production level constraint is an equality, the zero slack/surplus shown on the output is expected. However, the dual price of 60 associated with this constraint shows that if the firm were to consider increasing the production level for the radios, the value of the objective function, or profit, would improve at the rate of $60 per radio produced. Finally, the surplus of zero associated with the retail store distribution channel commitment is a result of this constraint being binding. The negative dual price indicates that increasing the commitment from 150 to 151 units will actually decrease the profit by $17. Thus, Electronic Communications may want to consider reducing its commitment to the retail store distribution channel. A *decrease* in the commitment will actually improve profit at the rate of $17 per unit.

Let us now consider the additional sensitivity analysis information provided by the computer output shown in Figure 3.12. The ranges of optimality for the objective function coefficients are

$$84 \leq c_1 < \text{No upper limit}$$

$$50 \leq c_2 \leq 90$$

$$\text{No lower limit} < c_3 \leq 87$$

$$\text{No lower limit} < c_4 \leq 105$$

Figure 3.12 Objective Coefficient and Right-Hand-Side Ranges Provided by the Management Scientist for the Electronic Communications Problem

```
OBJECTIVE COEFFICIENT RANGES

   Variable        Lower Limit        Current Value       Upper Limit
  -----------     --------------     --------------     --------------
      X1                84.000             90.000        No Upper Limit
      X2                50.000             84.000             90.000
      X3          No Lower Limit           70.000             87.000
      X4          No Lower Limit           60.000            105.000


RIGHT HAND SIDE RANGES

   Constraint      Lower Limit        Current Value       Upper Limit
  -----------     --------------     --------------     --------------
      1               4950.000           5000.000           5850.000
      2               1775.000           1800.000        No Upper Limit
      3                515.000            600.000            603.571
      4                  0.000            150.000            200.000
```

The current solution, or strategy, remains optimal, provided that the objective function coefficients remain in the above ranges of optimality. Note in particular the range of optimality associated with the mail-order distribution channel coefficient, c_4. This information is consistent with the earlier observation for the Reduced Costs portion of the output. In both instances, we see that the per-unit profit would have to increase to $105 before the mail-order distribution channel could be in the optimal solution with a positive value.

Finally, the sensitivity analysis information on RIGHT HAND SIDE RANGES, as shown in Figure 3.12, provides the ranges of feasibility for the right-hand-side values.

Constraint	Min RHS	Current Value	Max RHS
Advertising budget	4950	5000	5850
Sales force	1775	1800	No upper limit
Production level	515	600	603.57
Retail stores requirement	0	150	200

Do you feel comfortable interpreting the computer output for problems involving more than two decision variables? Try Problems 8 and 9.

Several interpretations of these ranges are possible. In particular, recall that the dual price for advertising budget enabled us to conclude that each $1 increase in the budget would improve the profit by $3. The range for the advertising budget shows that this statement about the value of increasing the budget is appropriate up to an advertising budget of $5850. Increases above this level would not necessarily be beneficial. Also note that the dual price of -17 for the retail stores requirement suggested the desirability of reducing this commitment. The range of feasibility for this constraint shows that the commitment could be reduced to zero and the value of the reduction would be at the rate of $17 per unit.

Let us again point out that the *sensitivity analysis* or *postoptimality analysis* provided by computer software packages for linear programming problems considers only *one change at a time,* with all other coefficients of the problem remaining as originally specified. As mentioned earlier, simultaneous changes can sometimes be analyzed without resolving the problem, provided that the cumulative changes are not large enough to violate the 100 percent rule.

Finally, recall that the complete solution to the Electronic Communications problem requested information not only on the number of units to be distributed over each channel, but also on the allocation of the advertising budget and the sales force effort to each distribution channel. Since the optimal solution is $x_1 = 25$, $x_2 = 425$, $x_3 = 150$, and $x_4 = 0$, we can simply evaluate each term in a given constraint to determine how much of the constraint resource is allocated to each distribution channel. For example, the advertising budget constraint of

$$10x_1 + 8x_2 + 9x_3 + 15x_4 \leq 5000$$

shows that $10x_1 = 10(25) = \$250$, $8x_2 = 8(425) = \$3400$, $9x_3 = 9(150) = \$1350$, and $15x_4 = 15(0) = \$0$. Thus, the advertising budget allocations are, respectively, $250, $3400, $1350, and $0 for each of the four distribution channels. Making similar calculations for the sales force constraint results in the managerial summary of the Electronic Communications optimal solution as shown in Table 3.3.

Table 3.3
Profit-Maximizing Strategy for the
Electronic Communications Problem

Distribution Channel	Volume	Advertising Allocation	Sales Force Allocation (hours)
Marine distributors	25	$ 250	50
Business distributors	425	3400	1275
National retail stores	150	1350	450
Mail order	0	0	0
Totals	600	$5000	1775

Projected total profit = $48,450

Summary

In this chapter we have shown how computer software packages can be used to solve linear programming problems. Since the graphical method and graphical sensitivity analysis are limited to linear programs with two decision variables, a computer solution procedure was presented as a practical method of solving linear programming problems with any number of decision variables. Although many software packages are available for computer solution, we used The Management Scientist to illustrate linear programming solutions on a microcomputer. We demonstrated the user-friendly aspect of the data input. Then we showed the computer output for several example problems to demonstrate the use and interpretation of the results. In addition to the value of the objective function and the optimal values of the decision variables, the computer output provides a variety of additional information concerning slack, surplus, and dual prices, as well as objective function coefficient and right-hand-side ranges. In the final section of the chapter, we provided some general guidelines for model formulation and then applied them to a sample problem. In the chapter appendix we show how LINDO/PC, a popular software package developed by Linus E. Schrage at the University of Chicago, is used.

Glossary

Reduced cost The amount by which an objective function coefficient would have to improve (increase for a maximization problem, decrease for a minimization problem), before it would be possible for the corresponding variable to assume a positive value in the optimal solution.

Dual price The improvement in the value of the objective function per-unit increase in a constraint right-hand side.

Range of optimality The range of values over which an objective function coefficient may vary without causing any change in the values of the decision variables in the optimal solution.

Range of feasibility The range of values over which a right-hand side may vary without changing the value and interpretation of the dual price.

100 percent rule A rule indicating when simultaneous changes in two or more objective function coefficients will not cause a change in the optimal values for the decision variables. It can also be applied to indicate when two or more right-hand-side changes will not cause a change in any of the dual prices.

Sunk cost A cost that is not affected by the decision made. It will be incurred no matter what values the decision variables assume.

Relevant cost A cost that depends upon the decision made. The amount of a relevant cost will vary depending on the values of the decision variables.

Modeling The process of translating a verbal statement of a problem into a mathematical statement.

Sensitivity analysis The evaluation of how changes in the coefficients of a linear programming problem affect the optimal solution to the problem.

Postoptimality analysis Another name for sensitivity analysis, indicating that the analysis is performed after the optimal solution to the original linear programming problem has been obtained.

Problems

S ELF T EST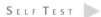

1. Interpreting computer output; maximization problem

1. Recall the Kelson Sporting Equipment problem (Chapter 2, Problem 22). Letting

$$x_1 = \text{number of regular gloves}$$
$$x_2 = \text{number of catcher's mitts}$$

leads to the following formulation:

$$\text{Max} \quad 5x_1 + 8x_2$$

s.t.

$$x_1 + \tfrac{3}{2}x_2 \leq 900 \quad \text{Cutting and sewing}$$

$$\tfrac{1}{2}x_1 + \tfrac{1}{3}x_2 \leq 300 \quad \text{Finishing}$$

$$\tfrac{1}{8}x_1 + \tfrac{1}{4}x_2 \leq 100 \quad \text{Packaging and shipping}$$

$$x_1, x_2 \geq 0$$

The computer solution obtained using The Management Scientist is shown in Figure 3.13.
a. What is the optimal solution, and what is the value of the total profit contribution?
b. Which constraints are binding?
c. What are the dual prices for the resources? Interpret each.
d. If overtime can be scheduled in one of the departments, where would you recommend doing so?

S ELF T EST

2. Interpreting computer output; maximization problem

2. Refer to the computer solution of the Kelson Sporting Equipment problem in Figure 3.13 (see Problem 1 above).
a. Compute the ranges of optimality for the objective function coefficients.
b. Interpret the ranges in part (a).
c. Interpret the range of feasibility for the right-hand sides.
d. How much will the value of the optimal solution improve if 20 extra hours of packaging and shipping time are made available?

3. Interpreting computer output; maximization problem

3. Recall the Investment Advisors problem (Chapter 2, Problem 25). Letting

$$x_1 = \text{shares of U.S. Oil}$$
$$x_2 = \text{shares of Hub Properties}$$

leads to the following formulation:

$$\text{Max} \quad 3x_1 + 5x_2 \qquad \text{Maximize total annual return}$$

s.t.

$$25x_1 + 50x_2 \leq 80{,}000 \quad \text{Funds available}$$

$$0.50x_1 + 0.25x_2 \leq 700 \quad \text{Risk maximum}$$

$$1x_1 \leq 1000 \quad \text{U.S. Oil maximum}$$

$$x_1, x_2 \geq 0$$

Figure 3.13   The Management Scientist Solution for the Kelson Sporting Equipment
Problem

```
Objective Function Value =        3700.00146

        Variable              Value            Reduced Costs
      --------------      --------------      ------------------
          X1               500.00153              0.00000
          X2               149.99924              0.00000


       Constraint         Slack/Surplus          Dual Prices
      --------------      --------------      ------------------
           1               174.99962              0.00000
           2                 0.00000              2.99999
           3                 0.00000             28.00006


OBJECTIVE COEFFICIENT RANGES

      Variable        Lower Limit        Current Value        Upper Limit
    ------------    --------------      --------------      --------------
        X1             4.00000             5.00000             12.00012
        X2             3.33330             8.00000             10.00000


RIGHT HAND SIDE RANGES

     Constraint      Lower Limit        Current Value        Upper Limit
    ------------    --------------      --------------      --------------
         1            725.00037           900.00000        No Upper Limit
         2            133.33199           300.00000           400.00000
         3             75.00000           100.00000           134.99982
```

The computer solution of this problem is shown in Figure 3.14.
  a. What is the optimal solution, and what is the value of the total estimated annual return?
  b. Which constraints are binding? What is your interpretation of this in terms of the problem?
  c. What are the dual prices for the constraints? Interpret each.
  d. Would it be beneficial to relax the constraint on the amount invested in U.S. Oil? Why or why not?

4. Interpreting computer output; maximization problem

4. Refer to Figure 3.14, which shows the computer solution of Problem 3.
  a. How much would the estimated per-share return for U.S. Oil have to increase before it would be beneficial to increase the investment in this stock?
  b. How much would the estimated per-share return for Hub Properties have to decrease before it would be beneficial to reduce the investment in this stock?
  c. How much would the total annual return be reduced if the U.S. Oil maximum were reduced to 900 shares?

Figure 3.14   The Management Scientist Solution for the Investment Advisors
Problem

```
Objective Function Value =          8400.000

        Variable            Value           Reduced Costs
    ---------------     ---------------     ---------------
          X1              800.000               0.000
          X2             1200.000               0.000


      Constraint       Slack/Surplus          Dual Prices
    ---------------     ---------------     ---------------
          1                0.000                0.093
          2                0.000                1.333
          3              200.000                0.000


OBJECTIVE COEFFICIENT RANGES

    Variable      Lower Limit     Current Value     Upper Limit
   -----------   ---------------  ---------------  ---------------
      X1              2.500           3.000           10.000
      X2              1.500           5.000            6.000


RIGHT HAND SIDE RANGES

   Constraint     Lower Limit     Current Value     Upper Limit
   -----------   ---------------  ---------------  ---------------
       1          65000.000        80000.000       140000.000
       2            400.000          700.000          775.000
       3            800.000         1000.000        No Upper Limit
```

5. Interpreting computer output;
maximization problem

5.   Recall the Wilkinson Motors problem (Chapter 2, Problem 26). Letting

$$x_1 = \text{number of automobiles}$$
$$x_2 = \text{number of station wagons}$$

leads to the following formulation:

Max $400x_1 + 500x_2$ Maximize total profit contribution

s.t.

$$2x_1 + 3x_2 \leq 900 \quad \text{Dealer preparation time}$$
$$1x_1 \quad\quad\quad \leq 300 \quad \text{Auto limit}$$
$$1x_2 \leq 150 \quad \text{Wagon limit}$$

$$x_1, x_2 \geq 0$$

The computer solution of this problem is shown in Figure 3.15.

a. How many regular automobiles and station wagons should Wilkinson order? What will the total profit contribution be if all the units ordered are sold?

b. How much would the total profit contribution of the regular automobiles have to decrease before Wilkinson would consider modifying its optimal solution?

c. Should Wilkinson consider raising the limit on the number of station wagons ordered beyond 150?

d. If the profit contribution for regular automobiles is reduced by $30 and the profit contribution for station wagons is increased by $50, should Wilkinson consider changing the order? Explain.

SELF TEST ▶   6. Recall the Innis Investments problem (Chapter 2, Problem 37). Letting

6. Interpreting computer output; minimization problem

x_1 = units purchased in the stock fund
x_2 = units purchased in the money market fund

Figure 3.15 The Management Scientist Solution for the Wilkinson Motors Problem

```
Objective Function Value =          170000.000

        Variable              Value              Reduced Costs
     --------------     ----------------      ------------------
           X1               300.000                  0.000
           X2               100.000                  0.000


        Constraint        Slack/Surplus            Dual Prices
     --------------     ----------------      ------------------
            1                  0.000                166.667
            2                  0.000                 66.667
            3                 50.000                  0.000


OBJECTIVE COEFFICIENT RANGES

     Variable        Lower Limit       Current Value       Upper Limit
   ------------    ---------------   ----------------    ---------------
        X1             333.333           400.000         No Upper Limit
        X2               0.000           500.000             600.000


RIGHT HAND SIDE RANGES

    Constraint       Lower Limit       Current Value       Upper Limit
   ------------    ---------------   ----------------    ---------------
        1              600.000           900.000            1050.000
        2              225.000           300.000             450.000
        3              100.000           150.000         No Upper Limit
```

leads to the following formulation:

$$\text{Min} \quad 8x_1 + 3x_2$$

s.t.

$$50x_1 + 100x_2 \leq 1{,}200{,}000 \quad \text{Funds available}$$

$$5x_1 + 4x_2 \geq 60{,}000 \quad \text{Annual income}$$

$$x_2 \geq 3{,}000 \quad \text{Units in money market}$$

$$x_1, x_2 \geq 0$$

The computer solution is shown in Figure 3.16.

a. What is the optimal solution, and what is the minimum total risk?

b. Specify the range of optimality for the objective function coefficients.

c. How much annual income will be earned by the portfolio?

Figure 3.16 The Management Scientist Solution for the Innis Investments Problem

```
Objective Function Value =          62000.000

        Variable              Value            Reduced Costs
        --------              -----            -------------

          X1               4000.000                 0.000
          X2              10000.000                 0.000


        Constraint        Slack/Surplus          Dual Prices
        ----------        -------------          -----------

           1                 0.000                  0.057
           2                 0.000                 -2.167
           3              7000.000                  0.000


OBJECTIVE COEFFICIENT RANGES

     Variable         Lower Limit      Current Value      Upper Limit
     --------         -----------      -------------      -----------

       X1                 3.750            8.000        No Upper Limit
       X2          No Lower Limit          3.000               6.400


RIGHT HAND SIDE RANGES

    Constraint        Lower Limit      Current Value      Upper Limit
    ----------        -----------      -------------      -----------

        1            780000.000        1200000.000        1500000.000
        2             48000.000          60000.000         102000.000
        3          No Lower Limit         3000.000          10000.000
```

d. What is the rate of return for the portfolio?

e. What is the dual price for the funds available constraint?

f. What is the marginal rate of return on extra funds added to the portfolio?

7. Refer to Problem 6 and the computer solution shown in Figure 3.16.

a. Suppose the risk index for the stock fund (the value of c_1) increases from its current value of 8 to 12. How does the optimal solution change, if at all?

b. Suppose the risk index for the money market fund (the value of c_2) increases from its current value of 3 to 3.5. How does the optimal solution change, if at all?

c. Suppose c_1 increases to 12 and c_2 increases to 3.3. How does the optimal solution change, if at all?

8. Suppose that in a product-mix problem x_1, x_2, x_3, and x_4 indicate the units of products 1, 2, 3, and 4, respectively, and the linear program is

$$\text{Max} \quad 4x_1 + 6x_2 + 3x_3 + 1x_4$$

s.t.

$$1.5x_1 + 2x_2 + 4x_3 + 3x_4 \leq 550 \quad \text{Machine A hours}$$

$$4x_1 + 1x_2 + 2x_3 + 1x_4 \leq 700 \quad \text{Machine B hours}$$

$$2x_1 + 3x_2 + 1x_3 + 2x_4 \leq 200 \quad \text{Machine C hours}$$

$$x_1, x_2, x_3, x_4 \geq 0$$

The computer solution developed using The Management Scientist is shown in Figure 3.17.

a. What is the optimal solution, and what is the value of the objective function?

b. Which constraints are binding?

c. Which machines have excess capacity available? How much?

d. If the objective function coefficient of x_1 is increased by 0.50, will the optimal solution change?

9. Refer to the computer solution of Problem 8 in Figure 3.17.

a. Identify the range of optimality for each objective function coefficient.

b. Suppose the objective function coefficient for x_1 is decreased by 3, the objective function coefficient of x_2 is increased by 1.5, and the objective function coefficient for x_4 is increased by 1. What will the new optimal solution be?

c. Identify the range of feasibility for the right-hand-side values.

d. If the number of hours available on machine A is increased by 300, will the dual price for that constraint change?

10. Consider the following linear program and computer solution shown in Figure 3.18.

$$\text{Min} \quad 15x_1 + 15x_2 + 16x_3$$

s.t.

$$1x_1 \qquad\quad + 1x_3 \leq 30$$

$$0.5x_1 - 1x_2 + 6x_3 \geq 15$$

$$3x_1 + 4x_2 - 1x_3 \geq 20$$

$$x_1, x_2, x_3 \geq 0$$

a. What is the optimal solution, and what is the optimal value for the objective function?

b. Which constraints are binding?

c. What are the dual prices? Interpret each.

d. If you could change the right-hand side of one constraint by one unit, which one would you choose? What would be the new value of the right-hand side?

Figure 3.17   The Management Scientist Solution for Problem 8

```
Objective Function Value =            525.000

        Variable            Value            Reduced Costs
      --------------    --------------      --------------
          X1                0.000                0.050
          X2               25.000                0.000
          X3              125.000                0.000
          X4                0.000                3.500


      Constraint       Slack/Surplus          Dual Prices
      --------------    --------------      --------------
           1                0.000                0.300
           2              425.000                0.000
           3                0.000                1.800


OBJECTIVE COEFFICIENT RANGES

    Variable       Lower Limit      Current Value      Upper Limit
   ------------    --------------   --------------    --------------
       X1         No Lower Limit        4.000             4.050
       X2              5.923            6.000             9.000
       X3              2.000            3.000            12.000
       X4         No Lower Limit        1.000             4.500


RIGHT HAND SIDE RANGES

    Constraint     Lower Limit      Current Value      Upper Limit
   ------------    --------------   --------------    --------------
       1             133.333           550.000           800.000
       2             275.000           700.000       No Upper Limit
       3             137.500           200.000           825.000
```

11. Interpreting computer output; minimization problem

11.   Refer to the computer solution of Problem 10 in Figure 3.18.
  a.   Interpret the ranges of optimality for the objective function coefficients.
  b.   Suppose c_1 is increased by 0.25. What is the new optimal solution?
  c.   Suppose c_1 is increased by 0.25 and c_2 is decreased by 0.25. What is the new optimal solution?

12. Interpreting computer output; maximization problem

12.   Supersport Footballs, Inc., has to determine the best number of All-Pro (x_1), College (x_2), and High School (x_3) models of footballs to produce in order to maximize profits. Constraints include production capacity limitations (time available in minutes) in each of three departments (cutting and dyeing, sewing, and inspection and packaging) as well as a

Figure 3.18 The Management Scientist Solution for Problem 10

```
Objective Function Value =            139.730

        Variable            Value            Reduced Costs
      --------------      --------------      ------------------
          X1                7.297                0.000
          X2                0.000                0.676
          X3                1.892                0.000


      Constraint         Slack/Surplus          Dual Prices
      --------------      --------------      ------------------
          1                20.811                0.000
          2                0.000                -3.405
          3                0.000                -4.432


OBJECTIVE COEFFICIENT RANGES

      Variable         Lower Limit       Current Value        Upper Limit
      ------------      --------------    ---------------    ---------------
          X1                1.333            15.000              15.543
          X2               14.324            15.000          No Upper Limit
          X3               13.500            16.000             180.000


RIGHT HAND SIDE RANGES

      Constraint       Lower Limit       Current Value        Upper Limit
      ------------      --------------    ---------------    ---------------
          1                9.189            30.000          No Upper Limit
          2                3.333            15.000             111.250
          3               -2.500            20.000              90.000
```

constraint that requires the production of at least 1000 All-Pro footballs. The linear programming model of Supersport's problem is shown below:

$$\text{Max} \quad 3x_1 + 5x_2 + 4x_3$$

s.t.

$$12x_1 + 10x_2 + 8x_3 \le 18{,}000 \quad \text{Cutting and dyeing}$$

$$15x_1 + 15x_2 + 12x_3 \le 18{,}000 \quad \text{Sewing}$$

$$3x_1 + 4x_2 + 2x_3 \le 9{,}000 \quad \text{Inspection and packaging}$$

$$1x_1 \qquad\qquad\qquad \ge 1{,}000 \quad \text{All-Pro model}$$

$$x_1, x_2, x_3 \ge 0$$

Figure 3.19 The Management Scientist Solution for the Supersport Footballs
Problem

```
Objective Function Value =          4000.000

        Variable              Value           Reduced Costs
        --------           ---------          -------------
           X1               1000.000              0.000
           X2                200.000              0.000
           X3                  0.000              0.000


        Constraint         Slack/Surplus         Dual Prices
        ----------         -------------         -----------
            1                4000.000              0.000
            2                   0.000              0.333
            3                5200.000              0.000
            4                   0.000             -2.000


OBJECTIVE COEFFICIENT RANGES

    Variable        Lower Limit        Current Value      Upper Limit
    --------        -----------        -------------      -----------
       X1         No Lower Limit           3.000             5.000
       X2               5.000              5.000         No Upper Limit
       X3         No Lower Limit           4.000             4.000


RIGHT HAND SIDE RANGES

   Constraint       Lower Limit        Current Value      Upper Limit
   ----------       -----------        -------------      -----------
       1            14000.000           18000.000       No Upper Limit
       2            15000.000           18000.000          24000.000
       3             3800.000            9000.000       No Upper Limit
       4                0.000            1000.000           1200.000
```

The computer solution to the Supersport problem is shown in Figure 3.19.
  a. How many footballs of each type should Supersport produce to maximize the total profit contribution?
  b. Which constraints are binding?
  c. Interpret the slack and/or surplus in each constraint.
  d. Interpret the ranges of optimality for the profit contributions of the three footballs.

13. Interpreting computer output; maximization problem

13. Refer to the computer solution of Problem 12 (see Figure 3.19).
  a. Overtime rates in the sewing department are $12 per hour. Would you recommend that the company consider using overtime in that department? Explain.
  b. What is the dual price for the fourth constraint? Interpret its value for management.

c. Note that the reduced cost for x_3 is zero, but x_3 is not in the solution at a positive value. What is your interpretation of this?

d. Suppose that the profit contribution of the College ball is increased by $1. How do you expect the solution to change?

Note: Problems 14–19 and the case problems require computer solution and interpretation of the results.

14. Better Products, Inc., manufactures three products on two machines. In a typical week, 40 hours are available on each machine. The profit contribution and production time in hours per unit are as follows:

Category	Product 1	Product 2	Product 3
Profit/unit	$30	$50	$20
Machine 1 time/unit	0.5	2.0	0.75
Machine 2 time/unit	1.0	1.0	0.5

Two operators are required for machine 1; thus, 2 hours of labor must be scheduled for each hour of machine 1 time. Only one operator is required for machine 2. A maximum of 100 labor hours is available for assignment to the machine during the coming week. Other production requirements are that product 1 cannot account for more than 50% of the units produced and that product 3 must account for at least 20% of the units produced.

a. How many units of each product should be produced to maximize the total profit contribution? What is the projected weekly profit associated with your solution?

b. How many hours of production time will be scheduled on each machine?

c. What is the value of an additional hour of labor?

d. Assume that labor capacity can be increased to 120 hours. Would you be interested in using the additional 20 hours available for this resource? Develop the optimal product mix assuming the extra hours are made available.

15. A manufacturer makes three components for sale to refrigeration companies. The components are processed on two machines: a shaper and a grinder. The times (in minutes) required on each machine are given below.

Component	Machine	
	Shaper	Grinder
1	6	4
2	4	5
3	4	2

The shaper is available for 120 hours, and the grinder is available for 110 hours. No more than 200 units of component 3 can be sold, but up to 1000 units of each of the other components can be sold. In fact, the company already has orders for 600 units of component 1 that must be satisfied. The profit contributions for components 1, 2, and 3 are $8, $6, and $9, respectively.

a. Formulate and solve for the recommended production quantities. Use any computer code available.

b. What are the ranges of optimality for the profit contributions of the three components? Interpret these ranges for company management.

c. What are the ranges of feasibility for the right-hand sides? Interpret these ranges for company management.

d. If more time could be made available on the grinder, how much would it be worth?

e. If more units of component 3 can be sold by reducing the sales price by $4, should the company reduce the price?

16. Formulation and computer solution; maximization problem; 3 decision variables; 2 ≤ constraints, 3 ≥ constraints

16. The Pfeiffer Company manages approximately $15 million for clients. For each client, Pfeiffer chooses a mix of three investment vehicles: a growth stock fund, an income fund, and a money market fund. Each client has different investment objectives and different tolerances for risk. To accommodate these differences, Pfeiffer places limits on the percentage of each portfolio that may be invested in the three funds and assigns a portfolio risk index to each client.

Here's how the system works for Dennis Hartmann, one of Pfeiffer's clients. Based on an evaluation of Hartmann's risk tolerance, Pfeiffer has assigned Hartmann's portfolio a risk index of 0.05. Furthermore, to maintain diversity, the fraction of Hartmann's portfolio invested in the growth and income funds must be at least 10% for each, and at least 20% must be in the money market fund.

The risk ratings for the growth, income, and money market funds are 0.10, 0.05, and 0.01, respectively. A portfolio risk index is computed as a weighted average of the risk ratings for the three funds where the weights are the fraction of the portfolio invested in each of the funds. Hartmann has given Pfeiffer $300,000 to manage. Pfeiffer is currently forecasting a yield of 20% on the growth fund, 10% on the income fund, and 6% on the money market fund.

a. Develop a linear programming model to select the best mix of investments for Hartmann's portfolio.

b. Use any linear programming computer code to solve the model you developed in part (a).

c. How much may the yields on the three funds vary before it will be necessary for Pfeiffer to modify Hartmann's portfolio?

d. If Hartmann were more risk tolerant, how much of a yield increase could he expect? For instance, what if his portfolio risk index is increased to 0.06?

e. If Pfeiffer revised his yield estimate for the growth fund downward to 0.10, how would you recommend modifying Hartmann's portfolio?

f. What information must Pfeiffer maintain on each client in order to use this system to manage client portfolios?

g. On a weekly basis Pfeiffer revises the yield estimates for the three funds. Suppose Pfeiffer has 50 clients. Describe how you would envision Pfeiffer making weekly modifications in each client's portfolio and allocating the total funds managed among the three investment funds.

17. Formulation and computer solution; maximization problem; 3 decision variables; 3 ≤ constraints, 2 ≥ constraints, 1 = constraint

17. La Jolla Beverage Products is considering producing a wine cooler that would be a blend of a white wine, a rosé wine, and fruit juice. To meet taste specifications, the wine cooler must consist of at least 50% white wine, at least 20% and no more than 30% rosé, and exactly 20% fruit juice. La Jolla purchases the wine from local wineries and the fruit juice from a processing plant in San Francisco. For the current production period, 10,000 gallons of white wine and 8000 gallons of rosé wine can be purchased; there is no limit on the amount of fruit juice that can be ordered. The costs for the wine are $1.00 per gallon for the white and $1.50 per gallon for the rosé; the fruit juice can be purchased for $0.50 per gallon. La Jolla Beverage Products can sell all of the wine cooler they can produce for $2.50 per gallon.

a. Is the cost of the wine and fruit juice a sunk cost or a relevant cost in this situation? Explain.

b. Formulate a linear program to determine the blend of the three ingredients that will maximize the total profit contribution. Solve the linear program to determine the number of gallons of each ingredient La Jolla should purchase and the total profit contribution they will realize from this blend.

c. If La Jolla could obtain additional amounts of the white wine, should they do so? If so, how much should they be willing to pay for each additional gallon, and how many additional gallons would they want to purchase?

d. If La Jolla Beverage Products could obtain additional amounts of the rosé wine, should they do so? If so, how much should they be willing to pay for each additional gallon, and how many additional gallons would they want to purchase?

e. Interpret the dual price for the constraint corresponding to the requirement that the wine cooler must contain at least 50% white wine. What is your advice to management given this dual price?

f. Interpret the dual price for the constraint corresponding to the requirement that the wine cooler must contain exactly 20% fruit juice. What is your advice to management given this dual price?

18. Formulation and computer solution; minimization problem; 4 decision variables; $2 \leq$ constraints, $3 \geq$ constraints, $1 =$ constraint

18. The program manager for Channel 10 would like to determine the best way to allocate the time for the 11:00–11:30 evening news broadcast. Specifically, she would like to determine the number of minutes of broadcast time to devote to local news, national news, weather, and sports. Over the 30-minute broadcast, 10 minutes are set aside for advertising. The station's broadcast policy states that at least 15% of the time available should be devoted to local news coverage; the time devoted to local news or national news must be at least 50% of the total broadcast time; the time devoted to the weather segment must be less than or equal to the time devoted to the sports segment; the time devoted to the sports segment should be no longer than the total time spent on the local and national news; and at least 20% of the time should be devoted to the weather segment. The production costs per minute are $300 for local news, $200 for national news, $100 for weather, and $100 for sports.

a. Formulate and solve a linear program that can determine how the 20 available minutes should be used to minimize the total cost of producing the program.

b. Interpret the dual price for the constraint corresponding to the available time. What advice would you give the station manager given this dual price?

c. Interpret the dual price for the constraint corresponding to the requirement that at least 15% of the available time should be devoted to local coverage. What advice would you give the station manager given this dual price?

d. Interpret the dual price for the constraint corresponding to the requirement that the time devoted to the local and the national news must be at least 50% of the total broadcast time. What advice would you give the station manager given this dual price?

e. Interpret the dual price for the constraint corresponding to the requirement that the time devoted to the weather segment must be less than or equal to the time devoted to the sports segment. What advice would you give the station manager given this dual price?

19. Formulation and computer solution; minimization problem; 3 decision variables; $3 \leq$ constraints, $2 \geq$ constraints, $1 =$ constraint

19. Gulf Coast Electronics is ready to award contracts for printing their annual report. For the past several years, the four-color annual report has been printed by Johnson Printing and Lakeside Litho. A new firm, Benson Printing, has inquired into the possibility of doing a portion of the printing. The quality and service level provided by Lakeside Litho has been extremely high; in fact, only 0.5% of their reports have had to be discarded because of quality problems. Johnson Printing has also had a high quality level historically, producing an average of only 1% unacceptable reports. Since Gulf Coast Electronics has had no experience with Benson Printing, they have estimated their defective rate to be 10%. Gulf Coast would like to determine how many reports should be printed by each firm to obtain 75,000 acceptable-quality reports. To ensure that Benson Printing will receive some of the contract, management has specified that the number of reports awarded to Benson Printing must be at least 10% of the volume given to Johnson Printing. In addition, the total volume assigned to Benson Printing, Johnson Printing, and Lakeside Litho should not exceed 30,000, 50,000, and 50,000 copies, respectively. Because of the long-term relationship that has developed with Lakeside Litho, management has also specified that at least 30,000 reports should be awarded to Lakeside Litho. The cost per copy is $2.45 for Benson Printing, $2.50 for Johnson Printing, and $2.75 for Lakeside Litho.

a. Formulate and solve a linear program for determining how many copies should be assigned to each printing firm to minimize the total cost of obtaining 75,000 acceptable-quality reports.

b. Suppose that the quality level for Benson Printing is much better than estimated. What effect, if any, would this have?

c. Suppose that management is willing to reconsider their requirement that Lakeside Litho be awarded at least 30,000 reports. What effect, if any, would this have?

Case Problem: Product Mix

TJ's, Inc., makes three nut mixes for sale to grocery chains located in the Southeast. The three mixes, referred to as the Regular Mix, the Deluxe Mix, and the Holiday Mix, are made by mixing different percentages of five types of nuts.

In preparation for the fall season, TJ's has just purchased the following shipments of nuts at the prices shown:

Type of Nut	Shipment Amount (pounds)	Cost per Shipment
Almond	6000	$7500
Brazil	7500	$7125
Filbert	7500	$6750
Pecan	6000	$7200
Walnut	7500	$7875

The Regular Mix consists of 15% almonds, 25% Brazil nuts, 25% filberts, 10% pecans, and 25% walnuts. The Deluxe Mix consists of 20% of each type of nut, and the Holiday Mix consists of 25% almonds, 15% Brazil nuts, 15% filberts, 25% pecans, and 20% walnuts.

TJ's accountant has analyzed the cost of packaging materials, sales price per pound, and so forth, and has determined that the profit contribution per pound is $1.65 for the Regular Mix, $2.00 for the Deluxe Mix, and $2.25 for the Holiday Mix. These figures do not include the cost of specific types of nuts in the different mixes because that cost can vary greatly in the commodity markets.

Customer orders already received are summarized below:

Type of Mix	Orders (pounds)
Regular	10,000
Deluxe	3,000
Holiday	5,000

Because demand is running high, it is expected that TJ's will receive many more orders than can be satisfied.

TJ's is committed to using the available nuts to maximize profit over the fall season; nuts not used will be given to the Free Store. But even if it is not profitable to do so, TJ's president has indicated that the orders already received must be satisfied.

Managerial Report

Perform an analysis of TJ's product-mix problem, and prepare a report for TJ's president that summarizes your findings. Be sure to include information and analysis on the following:

1. The cost per pound of the nuts included in the Regular, Deluxe, and Holiday mixes
2. The optimal product mix and the total profit contribution
3. Recommendations regarding how the total profit contribution can be increased if additional quantities of nuts can be purchased
4. A recommendation as to whether TJ's should purchase an additional 1000 pounds of almonds for $1000 from a supplier who overbought
5. Recommendations on how profit contribution could be increased (if at all) if TJ's does not satisfy all existing orders

Case Problem: Truck Leasing Strategy

Reep Construction has recently won a contract for the excavation and site preparation of a new rest area on the Pennsylvania turnpike. In preparing his bid for the job, Bob Reep, founder and president of Reep Construction, estimated that it would take 4 months to perform the work, and that the number of trucks needed in months 1 through 4 would be 10, 12, 14, and 8, respectively.

The firm currently has 20 trucks of the type that will be needed to perform the work on the new project. These trucks were obtained last year when Bob signed a long-term lease with PennState Leasing. While most of these trucks are currently being used on existing jobs, Bob estimates that one truck will be available for use on the new project in month 1, two trucks will be available in month 2, three trucks will be available in month 3, and one truck will be available in month 4. Thus, to complete the project, Bob will have to lease additional trucks.

The long-term leasing contract with PennState has a monthly cost of $600 per truck. Reep Construction pays their truck drivers $20 per hour, and daily fuel costs are approximately $100 per truck. All maintenance costs are paid by PennState Leasing. For planning purposes, Bob estimates that each truck used on the new project will be operating 8 hours per day, 5 days per week, and that there are approximately 4 weeks in each month.

Bob does not feel that current business conditions justify committing the firm to additional long-term leases. In discussing the short-term leasing possibilities with PennState Leasing, Bob has learned that he can obtain short-term leases of 1–4 months in length. Short-term leases differ from long-term leases in that the short-term leasing plans include the cost of both a truck and a driver. Maintenance costs for short-term leases are also paid by PennState Leasing. The following cost figures show the monthly leasing cost for each truck and driver:

Length of Lease (months)	Cost per Month
1	$4000
2	$3700
3	$3225
4	$3040

Bob Reep would like to acquire a lease that would minimize the cost of meeting the monthly trucking requirements for his new project, but he also takes great pride in the fact that his company has never laid off employees. Bob is committed to maintaining his no-layoff policy; that is, he will use his own drivers even if costs are higher.

Managerial Report

Perform an analysis of Reep Construction's leasing problem, and prepare a report for Bob Reep that summarizes your findings. Be sure to include information and analysis on the following:

1. The optimal leasing plan.
2. The costs associated with the optimal leasing plan.
3. Information as to what it will cost Reep Construction to maintain their current policy of no layoffs.

APPENDIX

Solving Linear Programs with LINDO/PC

LINDO/PC, developed by Linus E. Schrage at the University of Chicago, is a microcomputer version of the popular LINDO computer package that is widely available on mainframe computers. LINDO/PC allows the user to interact with the computer in a conversational mode. By this we mean that once the program has been loaded in the microcomputer, the user inputs the objective function and constraints as requested by the computer program. When satisfied that all data have been entered correctly, the user enters the command GO, and the LINDO/PC system solves the problem. The optimal solution and its related information are available at the user's computer monitor.

We will use the Par, Inc., problem to demonstrate LINDO/PC. The data input portion of a LINDO/PC computer session on an IBM Personal Computer is shown in Figure 3.20. The information keyed in by the user is shown in color, and the response from the computer package is shown in black. Note in particular the interactive nature of the system with the alternating user input and LINDO/PC response. Specific commands and symbols shown in Figure 3.20 are described as follows:

1. The "A>" is the user prompt for the IBM Personal Computer. The user command LINDO causes the LINDO/PC program to be loaded.
2. LINDO/PC begins by sending the symbol ":" to indicate that it is waiting for an instruction from the user.
3. The user keys in the objective function as it appears in the mathematical statement of the problem.
4. LINDO/PC then sends the symbol "?" to indicate that it is waiting for additional input concerning the linear program being solved.
5. The user input ST stands for *subject to*, notifying the program that information about the constraints is to follow.
6. After inputting each of the constraints with the symbol "<" (interpreted as ≤ by LINDO/PC) the user inputs END to signal that the data input is complete.
7. LINDO/PC again responds with ":" to indicate that it is waiting for an instruction.
8. The user inputs the optional instruction LOOK ALL; LINDO/PC then prints the linear programming problem that has been entered. LOOK ALL is not a required instruction, but using it provides an easy check on the accuracy of the input data. With LINDO/PC the objective function is identified as row 1. Thus, under the SUBJECT TO heading, we see the cutting and dyeing constraint identified as row 2, the sewing constraint as row 3, the finishing constraint as row 4, and the inspection and packaging constraint as row 5.

With the input data complete, the LINDO/PC package proceeds to develop the solution of the problem when given the command GO. The output from LINDO/PC is shown in Figure 3.21.

The first section of the output is self-explanatory. After printing the values of the slack variables and dual prices, LINDO/PC asks the user the following question: DO RANGE (SENSITIVITY) ANALYSIS? The user response of YES requests ranges on the objective function coefficients and the right-hand sides of the constraints.

Figure 3.20 Data Input Session with LINDO/PC (User Response Shown in Color)

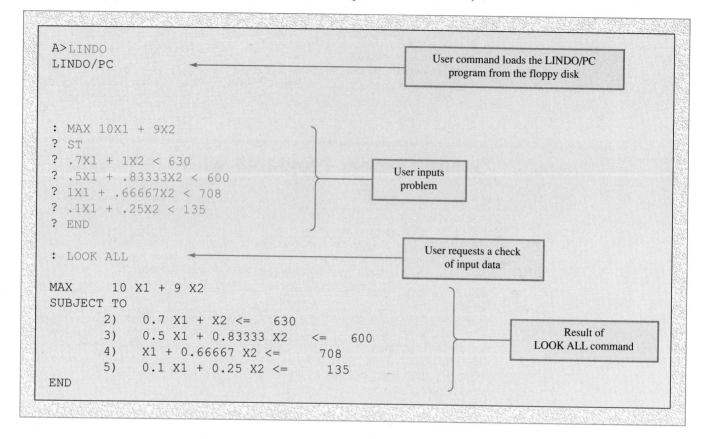

Considering the information provided under the computer output heading labeled OBJ COEFFICIENT RANGES, we see that variable x_1, with a current profit coefficient of 10, has an allowable increase of 3.5 and an allowable decrease of 3.7. Adding 3.5 to and subtracting 3.7 from the current coefficient of 10 provides the following range of optimality for c_1:

$$6.3 \leq c_1 \leq 13.5$$

Similarly, the range of optimality for c_2 is found to be

$$6.67 \leq c_2 \leq 14.29$$

The information under the heading labeled RIGHT HAND SIDE RANGES permits computing the range of feasibility for each right-hand side. Simply subtract the allowable decrease from the current value to get the lower limit, and add the allowable increase to the current value to get the upper limit. Doing so, we obtain

Constraint	Min RHS	Max RHS
Cutting and dyeing	495.6	682.4
Sewing	480.0	No upper limit
Finishing	580.0	900.0
Inspecting and packaging	117.0	No upper limit

Figure 3.21   Par, Inc., Solution Using LINDO/PC

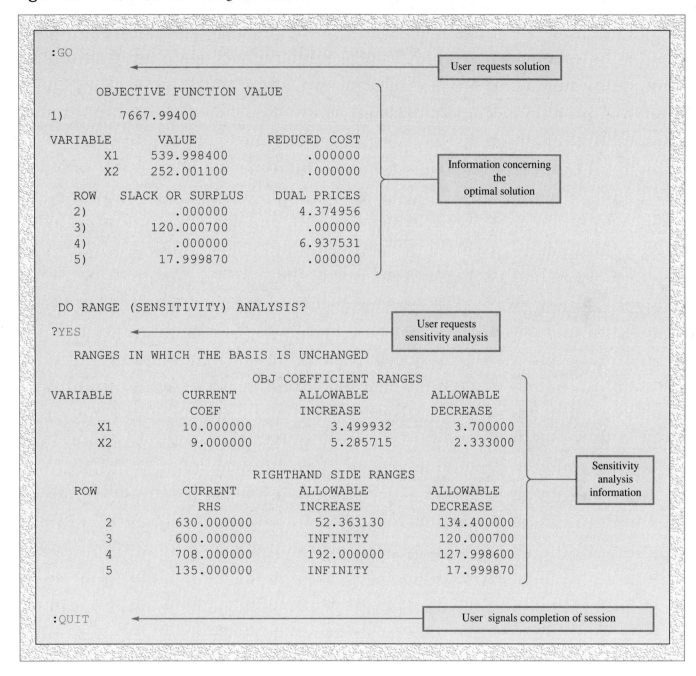

```
:GO                                                    ┌──────────────────────┐
                                         ◄─────────────│ User requests solution │
                                                       └──────────────────────┘
        OBJECTIVE FUNCTION VALUE

1)        7667.99400

VARIABLE        VALUE        REDUCED COST
      X1      539.998400          .000000          ┌──────────────────────┐
      X2      252.001100          .000000          │ Information concerning │
                                                   │          the           │
   ROW    SLACK OR SURPLUS     DUAL PRICES         │  optimal solution      │
    2)            .000000        4.374956          └──────────────────────┘
    3)         120.000700         .000000
    4)            .000000        6.937531
    5)          17.999870         .000000


DO RANGE (SENSITIVITY) ANALYSIS?
                                              ┌──────────────────────┐
?YES                            ◄─────────────│ User requests          │
                                              │ sensitivity analysis   │
   RANGES IN WHICH THE BASIS IS UNCHANGED     └──────────────────────┘

                     OBJ COEFFICIENT RANGES
VARIABLE           CURRENT        ALLOWABLE       ALLOWABLE
                    COEF          INCREASE        DECREASE
      X1         10.000000         3.499932        3.700000
      X2          9.000000         5.285715        2.333000
                                                          ┌────────────┐
                                                          │ Sensitivity │
                     RIGHTHAND SIDE RANGES                │ analysis    │
   ROW             CURRENT        ALLOWABLE       ALLOWABLE│ information │
                    RHS           INCREASE        DECREASE └────────────┘
     2           630.000000        52.363130      134.400000
     3           600.000000        INFINITY       120.000700
     4           708.000000       192.000000      127.998600
     5           135.000000        INFINITY        17.999870

                                              ┌─────────────────────────────┐
:QUIT                           ◄─────────────│ User signals completion of session │
                                              └─────────────────────────────┘
```

Note in Figure 3.21 that at the completion of the sensitivity analysis, LINDO/PC sends ":" and waits for another instruction. In this case, the user selected QUIT to signal the end of the LINDO/PC session. An optional instruction at this point would be ALT, which would have enabled the user to alter or modify one or more aspects of the problem and seek additional solution information.

MANAGEMENT SCIENCE IN PRACTICE

Eastman Kodak*
Rochester, New York

In 1880 entrepreneur/inventor George Eastman formed the Eastman Dry Plate Company with a vision that it would become a worldwide manufacturer and marketer of photographic goods. Today, Eastman Kodak is a 20-billion-dollar enterprise with manufacturing operations on four continents, and customers in over 150 countries. Headquartered in Rochester, New York, Kodak's imaging products include amateur roll film, photographic paper, medical and industrial X-ray film, motion picture film, and graphic arts materials. In addition, Kodak is a manufacturer of imaging equipment and chemicals.

Management Science at Kodak

Management science applications at Kodak can be traced back to pioneering efforts in the 1950s. Since then, management science has been employed to solve a variety of problems involving most of the operational areas of the company. Today, the majority of management science work is conducted by the Management Services Division, while a small group called Distribution Operations Research focuses on applying management science to worldwide logistics issues.

Assigning Products to Worldwide Facilities

The sensitizing operation is the heart of the manufacturing process for photographic paper and film. In this operation, a light-sensitive emulsion is coated on a base to produce a sensitized master roll. The sensitized master rolls are then sent to a finishing operation where they are cut into proper dimensions. The sensitizing operation, by virtue of its centrality to the overall process and the peculiarity of the manufacturing technologies required, receives a great deal of managerial attention, both at the operational and strategic levels.

One of Kodak's major planning issues involves the allocation of product to the various sensitizing facilities located throughout the world. The assignment of product to facilities is called the "world load." In determining the world load, Kodak is confronted with a number of interesting trade-offs. For instance, in terms of manufacturing costs, not all sensitizing facilities are equally efficient for all products. Some facilities tend to be more cost efficient over a broad range of products, but the margins by which they are better varies from product to product. However, there are many product–facility combinations that are essentially impossible because of unique product specifications and machine capabilities. Nonetheless, there is a choice of facilities for practically every product.

The product–facility manufacturing costs are only part of the picture. The cheapest place to sensitize a particular product might, for example, be Australia. But, if most of the customers

for that product are in Europe, then Australia becomes less favorable because of the high transportation costs involved. Transportation costs are therefore among the costs considered in determining the world load.

Another cost that must be considered involves the duties and duty drawbacks for the various countries throughout the world. Duty drawback is the "forgiving" of duty for a manufacturer who brings a semifinished product into a country, adds value to it, and then ships it out of that country. The effects of duty and duty drawback can significantly affect the allocation decision.

To assist in determining the world load, Kodak developed a linear programming model that accounts for the physical nature of the distribution problem and the various cost elements described above. More specifically, the program's objective is to minimize total cost (manufacturing, transportation, and duties) subject to "natural" constraints such as satisfying demand and capacity constraints for each facility.

Sensitivity Analysis and Interpretation

The linear programming model is a static representation of the problem situation, and the real world is always changing. Thus, Kodak cannot simply solve the linear program and implement the optimal solution; the static linear programming model must be used in a dynamic way. For instance, when demand expectations change, the model can be used to determine the effect the change will have on the world load. Or, suppose that country A and country B tear down duty barriers between them; what effect will this have on the world load? Suppose that the currency of country A rises compared to the currency of country B; how should the world load be modified? These are but a few of the situations of how the world load must be reevaluated based on the impact of external stimuli.

In addition to using the linear programming model in a "how-to-react" mode, the model is useful in a more active mode by considering questions such as the following: Is it worthwhile for facility F to spend D dollars to lower the unit manufacturing cost of product P from X to Y? If such an investment is made, the effect may go well beyond the simple first-order impact at facility F; in fact, it is likely that the change at facility F will result in a reshuffling of the world load. The linear programming model helps evaluate the overall effect of possible changes at any facility.

—Continued on next page

*The authors are indebted to Greg Sampson of Eastman Kodak for providing this application.

—Continued from previous page

Managerial Use

The world-load model gives excellent directional advice and integrates the complex interaction of many factors, but there are many aspects of the world-load problem that do not fall neatly into the cost categories discussed above. Although it might be possible to construct a model that would account for almost every aspect of the real-world situation, the time and cost needed to develop it would be prohibitive. Kodak has chosen to use a simpler world-load model; sensitivity analysis is then used to explore many of the questions that management may want to address. In the final analysis, managers recognize that they cannot use the model by simply turning it on, reading the results, and executing the solution. The model's recommendations combined with managerial judgment provide the final decisions and actions for world-load allocation.

Questions

1. What are some of the trade-offs associated with allocating the products to the various sensitizing facilities?
2. What costs are included in the objective function of the world-load model?
3. Briefly describe the role of sensitivity analysis in this application.
4. The world-load model does not account for all the various issues involved in assigning products to sensitizing facilities. What reason did Kodak have for not addressing *all* the issues, and what implications does this have for management?

Linear Programming Applications

Our study of linear programming thus far has been primarily directed at understanding the graphical solution method, sensitivity analysis, and the interpretation of computer solutions. This background is essential for knowing when linear programming is an appropriate problem-solving tool and for interpreting the results of a linear programming solution.

In practice, linear programming has proven to be one of the most successful quantitative approaches to managerial decision making. Numerous applications have been reported in the chemical, airline, steel, paper, petroleum, and other industries. The specific problems that have been studied are diverse and have included production scheduling, media selection, financial planning, capital budgeting, transportation, plant location, product mix, staffing, blending, and many others.

As the variety of applications mentioned above would suggest, linear programming is a flexible problem-solving tool with applications in many disciplines. In this chapter we present applications from the areas of marketing, finance, and production management. Computer solutions obtained using The Management Scientist software package are presented for many of the examples.

In Section 3.3 we provided some general guidelines for modeling more complex linear programming problems. Students should review Section 3.3 before proceeding with the linear programming applications in Chapter 4.

4.1 Marketing Applications

Applications of linear programming in marketing are numerous. In this section we discuss applications in media selection and marketing research.

Media Selection

Media selection applications of linear programming are designed to help marketing managers allocate a fixed advertising budget across various advertising media. Potential media include newspapers, magazines, radio, television, and direct mail. In most of these applications, the objective is to maximize audience exposure. Restrictions on the allowable allocation usually arise through considerations such as company policy, contract requirements, and availability of media. In the application that follows, we illustrate how a media selection problem might be formulated and solved using a linear programming model.

Relax-and-Enjoy Lake Development Corporation is developing a lakeside community at a privately owned lake. The primary market for the lakeside lots and homes they hope to sell includes all middle- and upper-income families within approximately 100 miles of the development. Relax-and-Enjoy has employed the advertising firm of Boone, Phillips and Jackson (BP&J) to design the promotional campaign for the project.

After considering possible advertising media and the market to be covered, BP&J has recommended that the first month's advertising be restricted to five sources. At the end of the month, BP&J will then reevaluate its strategy based on the month's results. BP&J has collected data on the number of potential purchase families reached, the cost per advertisement, the maximum number of times each is available, and the media exposure rating for each of the five media. The exposure rating is measured in terms of an exposure unit, a measure of the relative value of one advertisement in each of the media. These measures, based on BP&J's experience in the advertising business, take into account such factors as audience profile (age, income, and education of the audience reached), image presented, and quality of the advertisement. The information collected is presented in Table 4.1.

Relax-and-Enjoy has provided BP&J with an advertising budget of $30,000 for the first month's campaign. In addition, Relax-and-Enjoy has imposed the following restrictions on how BP&J may allocate these funds: at least 10 television commercials must be used, at least 50,000 potential purchasers must be reached during the month, and no more than $18,000 may be spent on television advertisements. What advertising media selection plan should the advertising firm recommend?

Table 4.1

Advertising Media Alternatives for the Relax-and-Enjoy Lake Development Corporation

Advertising Media	Number of Potential Purchase Families Reached	Cost Per Advertisement	Maximum Times Available Per Month*	Exposure Units
1. Daytime TV (1 min), station WKLA	1000	$1500	15	65
2. Evening TV (30 sec), station WKLA	2000	$3000	10	90
3. Daily newspaper (full page), *The Morning Journal*	1500	$ 400	25	40
4. Sunday newspaper magazine (½ page color), *The Sunday Press*	2500	$1000	4	60
5. Radio, 8:00 A.M. or 5:00 P.M. news (30 sec), station KNOP	300	$ 100	30	20

*The maximum number of times the medium is available is either the maximum number of times the advertising medium occurs (e.g., four Sundays for medium 4) or the maximum number of times BP&J recommends the medium be used.

We begin by defining the decision variables as follows:

x_1 = number of times daytime TV is used
x_2 = number of times evening TV is used
x_3 = number of times daily newspaper is used
x_4 = number of times Sunday newspaper is used
x_5 = number of times radio is used

Using the data on expected exposure in Table 4.1, we see that each daytime TV advertisement is rated at 65 exposure units. Thus, an advertising plan with x_1 daytime TV advertisements will provide a total of $65x_1$ exposure units. Continuing with the data in Table 4.1, we find evening TV (x_2) rated at 90 exposure units, daily newspaper (x_3) rated at 40 exposure units, Sunday newspaper (x_4) rated at 60 exposure units, and radio (x_5) rated at 20 exposure units. With the objective of maximizing the total exposure units for the overall media selection plan, the objective function becomes

$$\text{Max} \quad 65x_1 + 90x_2 + 40x_3 + 60x_4 + 20x_5$$

The constraints for the model can now be formulated from the information given:

$$
\left.
\begin{aligned}
x_1 & & & & & \leq 15 \\
& x_2 & & & & \leq 10 \\
& & x_3 & & & \leq 25 \\
& & & x_4 & & \leq 4 \\
& & & & x_5 & \leq 30
\end{aligned}
\right\} \begin{aligned} \text{Availability} \\ \text{of media} \end{aligned}
$$

$$1500x_1 + 3000x_2 + 400x_3 + 1000x_4 + 100x_5 \leq 30{,}000 \quad \text{Budget}$$

$$
\left.
\begin{aligned}
x_1 + x_2 & \geq 10 \\
1500x_1 + 3000x_2 & \leq 18{,}000
\end{aligned}
\right\} \begin{aligned} \text{Television} \\ \text{restrictions} \end{aligned}
$$

$$1000x_1 + 2000x_2 + 1500x_3 + 2500x_4 + 300x_5 \geq 50{,}000 \quad \text{Families reached}$$

$$x_1, x_2, x_3, x_4, x_5 \geq 0$$

The solution to this five-variable, nine-constraint linear programming model is presented in Table 4.2.

Care must be taken to ensure the linear programming formulation accurately reflects the problem being analyzed. Students should review their formulation thoroughly before any attempt is made to solve the problem.

Table 4.2
Advertising Plan for the Relax-and-Enjoy Lake Development Corporation

Media	Frequency	Budget
Daytime TV	10	$15,000
Daily newspaper	25	10,000
Sunday newspaper	2	2,000
Radio	30	3,000
		$30,000

Total audience contacted = 61,500

Exposure units = 2,370

More complex media selection models may include considerations such as the reduced exposure value for repeat media usage, cost discounts for repeat media usage, audience overlap by different media, and/or timing recommendations for the advertisements.

Problem 1 provides practice at formulating a similar media selection model.

A possible shortcoming of this model is that even if the expected exposure measure were not subject to error, there is no guarantee that maximization of total expected exposure will lead to a maximization of profit or of sales (a common surrogate for profit). However, this is not a shortcoming of linear programming; rather, it is a shortcoming of the use of exposure as a criterion. Were we able to directly measure the effect of an advertisement on profit, we would certainly use total profit as the objective to be maximized.

A more complex formulation—more variables and constraints—can often be used to overcome some of these limitations, but it will not always be possible to overcome all of them with a linear programming model. However, even in these cases, a linear programming model can often be used to arrive at an approximation of the best decision. Management evaluation combined with the linear programming solution should then make possible the selection of an effective advertising strategy.

NOTES & COMMENTS

1. In general, we use x_1, x_2, and so on to denote the decision variables in a linear programming model. At the beginning of the model formulation, we carefully present the notation used and the definition of each decision variable. While the notation x_1, x_2, and so on can be used in any linear programming model, some management scientists prefer to use a notation that is more descriptive of each decision variable. For example, the media selection model could have been formulated with DTV denoting the daytime TV, ETV denoting the evening TV, DN denoting the daily newspaper, and so on. In this case, the objective function would have been written as

$$\max 65DTV + 90ETV + 40DN + 60SN + 20R$$

The constraints would be restated in terms of the DTV, ETV, DN, SN, and R notation.

2. The media selection model required subjective evaluations of the exposure ratings for the media alternatives. While marketing managers may have substantial data concerning advertising exposure, the final coefficients used in the objective function include considerations based primarily on managerial judgment. Judgment input is an acceptable way of obtaining data for a linear programming model.

Marketing Research

Marketing research is conducted to learn about consumer characteristics, attitudes, and preferences toward products and/or services offered by an organization. The actual research is often performed by a marketing research firm that specializes in providing client organizations with the desired market information. Typical services offered by a marketing research firm include designing the study, conducting market surveys, analyzing the data collected, and providing summary reports and recommendations for the client. In the research design phase, targets or quotas may be established for the number and types of respondents to be reached by a survey. With quota guidelines established, the objective of the marketing research firm is to conduct the survey so as to meet the client's needs at a minimum cost.

Market Survey, Inc. (MSI), specializes in evaluating consumer reaction to new products, services, and advertising campaigns. A client firm has requested assistance from MSI in ascertaining consumer reaction to a recently marketed product for household use. During meetings with the client it was agreed that door-to-door personal interviews would be used to obtain information from both households with children and households without children. In addition, it was agreed that both day and evening interviews would be conducted to allow for a variety of household work schedules. Specifically, the client's contract called for MSI to conduct 1000 interviews with the following quota guidelines:

1. At least 400 households with children would be interviewed.
2. At least 400 households without children would be interviewed.
3. The total number of households interviewed during the evening would be at least as great as the number of households interviewed during the day.
4. At least 40% of the interviews for households with children would be conducted during the evening.
5. At least 60% of the interviews for households without children would be conducted during the evening.

Since the interviews for households with children take additional interviewer time, and since evening interviewers are paid more than daytime interviewers, the cost of an interview varies with the type of interview. Based on previous research studies, estimates of the interview costs are as follows:

	Interview Cost	
Household	Day	Evening
Children	$20	$25
No children	$18	$20

What is the household, time-of-day interview plan that will satisfy the contract requirements at a minimum total interviewing cost?

The formulation of a linear programming model for the MSI problem is a good opportunity to introduce the use of double-subscripted decision variables. Using x to represent the decision variables, the first subscript of x will indicate whether the interview involves children and the second subscript will indicate whether the interview is in the day or evening. Using 1 for children and 2 for no children, and 1 for day and 2 for evening, we obtain the following four decision variables:

x_{11} = the number of interviews for households with children that are conducted during the day

x_{12} = the number of interviews for households with children that are conducted during the evening

x_{21} = the number of interviews for households without children that are conducted during the day

x_{22} = the number of interviews for households without children that are conducted during the evening

We begin the linear programming model formulation by using the cost-per-interview data to develop the following objective function:

$$\text{Min } 20x_{11} + 25x_{12} + 18x_{21} + 20x_{22}$$

The constraint requiring a total of 1000 interviews is written as

$$x_{11} + x_{12} + x_{21} + x_{22} = 1000$$

The five specifications concerning the types of interviews are as follows.

- Households with children:

$$x_{11} + x_{12} \geq 400$$

- Households without children:

$$x_{21} + x_{22} \geq 400$$

- At least as many evening interviews as day interviews:

$$x_{12} + x_{22} \geq x_{11} + x_{21}$$

The usual format for linear programming model formulation and computer input places all decision variables on the left-hand side of the inequality and a constant (possibly zero) on the right-hand side. Thus, we will rewrite this constraint as

$$-x_{11} + x_{12} - x_{21} + x_{22} \geq 0$$

- At least 40% of interviews for households with children during the evening:

$$x_{12} \geq 0.4(x_{11} + x_{12})$$

or

$$-0.4x_{11} + 0.6x_{12} \geq 0$$

- At least 60% of interviews for households without children during the evening:

$$x_{22} \geq 0.6(x_{21} + x_{22})$$

or

$$-0.6x_{21} + 0.4x_{22} \geq 0$$

By adding the nonnegativity requirements, the four-variable, six-constraint linear programming model becomes

$$\text{Min} \quad 20x_{11} + 25x_{12} + 18x_{21} + 20x_{22}$$

s.t.

$$
\begin{aligned}
x_{11} + x_{12} + x_{21} + x_{22} &= 1000 \quad \text{Total interviews} \\
x_{11} + x_{12} &\geq 400 \quad \text{Households with children} \\
x_{21} + x_{22} &\geq 400 \quad \text{Households without children} \\
-x_{11} + x_{12} - x_{21} + x_{22} &\geq 0 \quad \text{Evening interviews} \\
-0.4x_{11} + 0.6x_{12} &\geq 0 \quad \text{Evening households with children} \\
-0.6x_{21} + 0.4x_{22} &\geq 0 \quad \text{Evening households without children}
\end{aligned}
$$

$$x_{11}, x_{12}, x_{21}, x_{22} \geq 0$$

The computer solution to the above linear program is shown in Figure 4.1. From this solution, we see that the minimum cost of $20,320 occurs with the following interview schedule:

	Number of Interviews		
Household	Day	Evening	**Totals**
Children	240	160	400
No children	240	360	600
Totals	480	520	1000

As can be seen, 480 interviews will be scheduled during the day and 520 during the evening. Households with children will be covered by 400 interviews, and households without children will be covered by 600 interviews.

Selected sensitivity analysis information from Figure 4.1 shows a dual price of -19.2 for constraint 1. This tells us that the objective function will get worse (the cost will increase) by $19.20 if the number of interviews is increased from 1000 to 1001. Thus, $19.20 is the incremental cost of obtaining additional interviews. It is also the savings that could be realized by reducing the number of interviews from 1000 to 999. The dual price for the requirement of 400 households with children (constraint 2) indicates that requesting additional interviews of households with children will not improve the

Figure 4.1 The Management Scientist Solution for the Market Survey Problem

```
Objective Function Value =          20320.000

      Variable              Value            Reduced Costs
   --------------        --------------     ------------------
        X11                 240.000              0.000
        X12                 160.000              0.000
        X21                 240.000              0.000
        X22                 360.000              0.000


      Constraint          Slack/Surplus         Dual Prices
   --------------        --------------     ------------------
          1                   0.000              -19.200
          2                   0.000               -2.800
          3                 200.000                0.000
          4                  40.000                0.000
          5                   0.000               -5.000
          6                   0.000               -2.000
```

objective function. In fact, additional interviews of households with children will add to the total cost at a rate of approximately $2.80 per interview.

The surplus variable, with a value of 200, for constraint 3 shows that 200 more households without children will be interviewed than required. Similarly, the surplus variable, with a value of 40, for constraint 4 shows that the number of evening interviews exceeds the number of daytime interviews by 40. The zero values for the surplus variables in constraints 5 and 6 indicate that the more expensive evening interviews are being held at a minimum.

4.2 Financial Applications

In finance, linear programming has been applied in problem situations involving capital budgeting, make-or-buy decisions, asset allocation, portfolio selection, and many more. In this section, we describe a portfolio selection problem and a problem involving choosing an appropriate balance between internally generated and borrowed funds.

Portfolio Selection

Portfolio selection problems involve situations in which a financial manager must select specific investments—for example, stocks, bonds—from a variety of investment alternatives. This type of problem is frequently encountered by managers of mutual funds, credit unions, insurance companies, and banks. The objective function for portfolio selection problems is usually maximization of expected return or minimization of risk. The constraints usually take the form of restrictions on the type of permissible investments, state laws, company policy, maximum permissible risk, and so on.

Problems of this type have been formulated and solved using a variety of mathematical programming techniques. In this section we show how a portfolio selection problem can be formulated and solved as a linear program.

Consider the case of Welte Mutual Funds, Inc., located in New York City. Welte has just obtained $100,000 by converting industrial bonds to cash and is now looking for other investment opportunities for these funds. Considering Welte's current investments, the firm's top financial analyst recommends that all new investments should be made in the oil or steel industry, or in government bonds. Specifically, the analyst has identified five investment opportunities and projected their annual rates of return. The investments and rates of return are shown in Table 4.3.

Management of Welte has imposed the following investment guidelines:

1. Neither industry (oil or steel) should receive more than $50,000 of the total investment.
2. Government bonds should be at least 25% of the steel industry investments.
3. The investment in Pacific Oil, the high-return but high-risk investment, cannot be more than 60% of the total oil industry investment.

What portfolio recommendations—investments and amounts—should be made for the available $100,000? Given the objective of maximizing projected return subject to the budgetary and managerially imposed constraints, we can answer this question by formulating a linear programming model of the problem. The solution to this linear programming model will then provide investment recommendations for the management of Welte Mutual Funds.

Table 4.3
Investment Opportunities for Welte Mutual Funds

Investment	Projected Rate of Return (%)
Atlantic Oil	7.3
Pacific Oil	10.3
Midwest Steel	6.4
Huber Steel	7.5
Government bonds	4.5

Let

$$x_1 = \text{dollars invested in Atlantic Oil}$$
$$x_2 = \text{dollars invested in Pacific Oil}$$
$$x_3 = \text{dollars invested in Midwest Steel}$$
$$x_4 = \text{dollars invested in Huber Steel}$$
$$x_5 = \text{dollars invested in government bonds}$$

Using the projected rates of return shown in Table 4.3, the objective function for maximizing the total return for the portfolio can be written as

$$\text{Max } 0.073x_1 + 0.103x_2 + 0.064x_3 + 0.075x_4 + 0.045x_5$$

The constraint specifying the available $100,000 is written as

$$x_1 + x_2 + x_3 + x_4 + x_5 = 100,000$$

The requirements that neither the oil nor the steel industry should receive more than $50,000 are as follows:

$$x_1 + x_2 \leq 50,000 \quad \text{Oil industry maximum}$$

$$x_3 + x_4 \leq 50,000 \quad \text{Steel industry maximum}$$

The requirement that government bonds be at least 25% of the steel industry investment is expressed as follows:

$$x_5 \geq 0.25\,(x_3 + x_4)$$

Converting the verbal description of a problem into constraint expressions may result in decision variables appearing on both sides of an equality or inequality. Students should be reminded that, while this is helpful and appropriate when formulating the problem, decision variables must be placed on the left-hand side and a constant (possibly zero) must be placed on the right-hand side before attempting a computer solution.

or

$$-0.25x_3 - 0.25x_4 + x_5 \geq 0$$

Finally, the constraint that Pacific Oil cannot be more than 60% of the total oil industry investment becomes

$$x_2 \leq 0.60(x_1 + x_2)$$

or

$$-0.60x_1 + 0.40x_2 \leq 0$$

By adding the nonnegativity restrictions, the complete linear programming model for the Welte Mutual Fund investment problem is as follows:

$$\text{Max} \quad 0.073x_1 + 0.103x_2 + 0.064x_3 + 0.075x_4 + 0.045x_5$$

s.t.

$x_1 +$	$x_2 +$	$x_3 +$	$x_4 +$	$x_5 = 100,000$	Available funds
$x_1 +$	x_2			$\leq\ 50,000$	Oil industry maximum
		$x_3 +$	x_4	$\leq\ 50,000$	Steel industry maximum

$$-0.25x_3 - 0.25x_4 + x_5 \geq 0 \quad \text{Government bonds minimum}$$

$$-0.6x_1 + 0.4x_2 \qquad\qquad\qquad \leq 0 \quad \text{Pacific Oil restriction}$$

$$x_1, x_2, x_3, x_4, x_5 \geq 0$$

This problem was solved using The Management Scientist; the output is shown in Figure 4.2. In Table 4.4 we show how the funds are divided among the securities. Note that the optimal solution indicates that the portfolio should be diversified among all the

Figure 4.2 The Management Scientist Solution for the Welte Mutual Funds Problem

```
Objective Function Value =          8000.000

        Variable            Value            Reduced Costs
    ---------------    ---------------    ------------------
         X1              20000.000               0.000
         X2              30000.000               0.000
         X3                  0.000               0.011
         X4              40000.000               0.000
         X5              10000.000               0.000


       Constraint       Slack/Surplus         Dual Prices
    ---------------    ---------------    ------------------
          1                  0.000               0.069
          2                  0.000               0.022
          3              10000.000               0.000
          4                  0.000              -0.024
          5                  0.000               0.030
```

Table 4.4

Optimal Portfolio Selection for Welte Mutual Funds

Investment	Amount	Expected Annual Return
Atlantic Oil	$ 20,000	$1,460
Pacific Oil	30,000	3,090
Huber Steel	40,000	3,000
Government bonds	10,000	450
	$100,000	$8,000

Expected annual return of $8,000

Overall rate of return = 8%

investment opportunities except Midwest Steel. The projected annual return for this portfolio is $8000, which is an overall return of 8%.

Using the computer printout for the Welte investment problem as shown in Figure 4.2, we see that the dual price for constraint 3 is zero. This is because the steel industry maximum is not a binding constraint; increases in the steel industry limit of $50,000 will not improve the value of the objective function. Indeed, the slack variable for this constraint shows that the current steel industry investment is $10,000 below its limit of $50,000. The dual prices for the other constraints are nonzero, indicating that these constraints are binding.

> The dual price for the available funds constraint provides information on the rate of return from additional investment funds.

The dual price of 0.069 for constraint 1 shows that the objective function can be increased by 0.069 if one more dollar can be made available for the portfolio investment. If more funds can be obtained at a cost of less than 6.9%, management should consider obtaining them. On the other hand, if a return in excess of 6.9% can be obtained by investing funds elsewhere (other than in these five securities), management should question the wisdom of investing the entire $100,000 in this portfolio.

Similar interpretations can be given to the other dual prices. Note, however, that the dual price for constraint 4 is negative; its value is −0.024. This indicates that increasing the value on the right-hand side of the constraint by one unit can be expected to cause a change in the objective function of −0.024. In terms of the optimal portfolio, this means that if Welte invests one more dollar in government bonds, the total return will decrease by 2.4 cents. To see why this is so, note again from the dual price for constraint 1 that the marginal return on the funds invested in the portfolio is 6.9% (the average return is 8%). The rate of return on government bonds is 4.5%. Thus, the cost of investing one more dollar in government bonds is the difference between the marginal return on the portfolio and the marginal return on government bonds: 6.9% − 4.5% = 2.4%.

> Practice formulating another portfolio selection problem by working Problem 9.

Note that the optimal solution shows that Midwest Steel should not be included in the portfolio ($x_3 = 0$). The associated reduced cost for x_3 of 0.011 tells us that the objective function coefficient for Midwest Steel would have to increase by 0.011 before it would be possible to consider the Midwest Steel investment alternative. With this increase the Midwest Steel return would be $0.064 + 0.011 = 0.075$, making this investment just as desirable as the currently used Huber Steel investment alternative.

Finally, a simple modification of the Welte linear programming model permits determining the fraction of available funds invested in each security. That is, we divide each of the right-hand-side values by 100,000. Then the optimal values for the variables

NOTES & COMMENTS

The optimal solution to the Welte Mutual Funds problem indicates that $20,000 is to be spent on the Atlantic Oil stock. If Atlantic Oil sells for $75 per share, we would have to purchase exactly 266⅔ shares in order to spend exactly $20,000. The difficulty of purchasing fractional shares is usually handled by purchasing the largest possible integer number of shares with the allotted funds (e.g., 266 shares of Atlantic Oil). This approach guarantees that the budget constraint will not be violated. This, of course, introduces the possibility that the solution will no longer be optimal, but the danger is slight if a large number of securities are involved. In cases where the analyst believes it is critical for the decision variables to have integer values, the problem must be formulated as an integer linear programming model. Integer linear programming is the topic of Chapter 8.

will give the fraction of funds that should be invested in each security for a portfolio of any size.

Financial-Mix Strategy

Financial-mix strategies involve the selection of means for financing company projects, inventories, production operations, and various other activities. In this section we illustrate how linear programming can be used to solve problems of this type by formulating and solving a problem involving the financing of production operations. In this particular application, a financial decision must be made with regard to how much production is to be supported by internally generated funds and how much is to be supported by external funds.

The Jefferson Adding Machine Company will begin production of two new models of electronic calculators during the next 3 months. Since these models require an expansion of the current production operation, the company will need operating funds to cover material, labor, and other expenses during the initial production period. Revenue from this initial production period will not be available until after the end of the period. Thus, the company must arrange financing for these operating expenses before production can begin.

Jefferson has set aside $3000 in internal funds to cover expenses of this operation. If additional funds are needed, they will have to be generated externally. A local bank has offered a line of short-term credit in an amount not to exceed $10,000. The interest rate over the life of the loan will be 12% per year on the average amount borrowed. One stipulation set by the bank requires that the remainder of the company cash set aside for this operation plus the accounts receivable for this product line be at least twice as great as the outstanding loan plus interest at the end of the initial production period.

In addition to the financial restrictions placed on this operation, labor capacity is also a factor. Only 2500 hours of assembly time and 150 hours of packaging and shipping time are available for the new product line during the initial 3-month production period. Relevant cost, price, and production time requirements for the two models, referred to as models Y and Z, are shown in Table 4.5.

Additional restrictions have been imposed by company management to guarantee that the market reaction to both products can be tested; that is, at least 50 units of model Y and at least 25 units of model Z must be produced in this first production period.

Since the cost of the units produced using borrowed funds will in effect experience an interest charge, the profit contributions for the units of models Y and Z produced on borrowed funds will be reduced. Hence, we adopt the following notation for the decision variables in this problem:

$$x_1 = \text{units of model Y produced with company funds}$$
$$x_2 = \text{units of model Y produced with borrowed funds}$$
$$x_3 = \text{units of model Z produced with company funds}$$
$$x_4 = \text{units of model Z produced with borrowed funds}$$

Table 4.5
Cost, Price, and Labor Data for the Jefferson Adding Machine Company

Model	Unit Cost (Materials and Other Variable Expenses)	Selling Price	Profit Margin	Labor Hours Required Assembly	Labor Hours Required Packaging and Shipping
Y	$ 50	$ 58	$ 8	12	1
Z	$100	$120	$20	25	2

How much will the profit contribution be reduced for units produced on borrowed funds? To answer this question, one must know how long the loan will be outstanding. We assume that all units of each model are sold, as they are produced, to independent distributors and that the average rate of turnover of accounts receivable is 3 months. Since company management has specified that the loan is to be repaid by funds generated by the units produced on borrowed funds, the funds borrowed to produce one unit of model Y or Z will be repaid approximately 3 months later. Hence, the profit contribution for each unit of model Y produced on borrowed funds is reduced from $8 to $8 − ($50 × 0.12 × ¼ yr) = $6.50, and the profit contribution for each unit of model Z produced on borrowed funds is reduced from $20 to $20 − ($100 × 0.12 × ¼ yr) = $17. With this information, we can now formulate the objective function for Jefferson's financial-mix problem:

$$\text{Max } 8x_1 + 6.5x_2 + 20x_3 + 17x_4$$

We can also specify the following constraints for the model:

$$
\begin{array}{llllll}
12x_1 & + 12x_2 & + 25x_3 & + 25x_4 & \le & 2{,}500 \quad \text{Assembly capacity} \\
x_1 & + x_2 & + 2x_3 & + 2x_4 & \le & 150 \quad \text{Packaging and shipping capacity} \\
50x_1 & & + 100x_3 & & \le & 3{,}000 \quad \text{Internal funds available} \\
& 50x_2 & & + 100x_4 & \le & 10{,}000 \quad \text{External funds available} \\
x_1 & + x_2 & & & \ge & 50 \quad \text{Model Y requirement} \\
& & x_3 & + x_4 & \ge & 25 \quad \text{Model Z requirement}
\end{array}
$$

In addition, the following constraint must be included to satisfy the bank loan requirement:

$$\text{Cash} + \text{accounts receivable} \ge 2(\text{loan} + \text{interest})$$

This restriction must be satisfied at the end of the period. Recalling that accounts receivable are outstanding for an average of 3 months, the following relationships can be used to derive a mathematical expression for the above inequality at the end of the period:

$$\text{Cash} = 3000 - 50x_1 - 100x_3$$

$$\text{Accounts receivable} = 58x_1 + 58x_2 + 120x_3 + 120x_4$$

$$\text{Loan} = 50x_2 + 100x_4$$

$$\text{Interest} = (0.12 \times \tfrac{1}{4} \text{ yr})(50x_2 + 100x_4) = 1.5x_2 + 3x_4$$

Therefore, the constraint resulting from the bank restriction can be written as

$$(3000 - 50x_1 - 100x_3) + (58x_1 + 58x_2 + 120x_3 + 120x_4) \ge 2(51.5x_2 + 103x_4)$$

or

$$3000 \ge -8x_1 + 45x_2 - 20x_3 + 86x_4$$

which is equivalent to

$$-8x_1 + 45x_2 - 20x_3 + 86x_4 \le 3000$$

Adding the nonnegativity constraints, the complete linear programming model for the Jefferson Adding Machine Company can now be stated:

$$\text{Max} \quad 8x_1 + 6.5x_2 + 20x_3 + 17x_4$$

s.t.

$$12x_1 + 12x_2 + 25x_3 + 25x_4 \leq 2{,}500$$

$$x_1 + x_2 + 2x_3 + 2x_4 \leq 150$$

$$50x_1 + 100x_3 \leq 3{,}000$$

$$50x_2 + 100x_4 \leq 10{,}000$$

$$x_1 + x_2 \geq 50$$

$$x_3 + x_4 \geq 25$$

$$-8x_1 + 45x_2 - 20x_3 + 86x_4 \leq 3{,}000$$

$$-0x_1, x_2, x_3, x_4 \geq 0$$

The computer solution to this four-variable, seven-constraint financial-mix problem is shown in Figure 4.3. The profit of $1191.86 is realized with the optimal solution of $x_1 = 0$, $x_2 = 50$, $x_3 = 30$, and $x_4 = 15.7$. Note that the reduced cost of zero for x_1 tells us that the objective function coefficient *does not have to increase* for management to consider bringing x_1 into the optimal solution. This is an indication that alternative optimal solutions exist for the problem. Figure 4.4 shows a computer solution yielding an alternative optimal solution. The profit of $1191.86 is now associated with the solution $x_1 = 50$, $x_2 = 0$, $x_3 = 5$, and $x_4 = 40.7$.

Figure 4.3 The Management Scientist Solution for the Jefferson Adding Machine Problem

```
Objective Function Value =          1191.860

        Variable            Value           Reduced Costs
     --------------     --------------     ------------------
          X1                0.000                0.000
          X2               50.000                0.000
          X3               30.000                0.000
          X4               15.698                0.000


       Constraint        Slack/Surplus        Dual Prices
     --------------     --------------     ------------------
           1               757.558               0.000
           2                 8.605               0.000
           3                 0.000               0.240
           4              5930.232               0.000
           5                 0.000              -2.395
           6                20.698               0.000
           7                 0.000               0.198
```

Figure 4.4 The Management Scientist Solution for an Alternative Optimal Solution of the Jefferson Adding Machine Problem

```
Objective Function Value =            1191.860

        Variable              Value              Reduced Costs
     --------------      --------------        ------------------
           X1                50.000                  0.000
           X2                 0.000                  0.000
           X3                 5.000                  0.000
           X4                40.698                  0.000


       Constraint         Slack/Surplus             Dual Prices
     --------------      --------------        ------------------
            1               757.558                  0.000
            2                 8.605                  0.000
            3                 0.000                  0.240
            4              5930.232                  0.000
            5                 0.000                 -2.395
            6                20.698                  0.000
            7                 0.000                  0.198
```

Obviously, management could implement either of the solutions shown in the figures and maximize profit. The solution in Figure 4.3 is summarized in Table 4.6 along with the expected profit and borrowed funds for each model of calculator. This solution requires the company to use all its internal funds ($3000), but only slightly more than $4000 of the available $10,000 line of credit.

NOTES & COMMENTS

The profit contributions for the two Jefferson Adding Machine products were based on the difference between the selling price per unit and the "cost" per unit. An important consideration in the determination of the cost per unit is the difference between sunk costs and relevant costs. *Sunk costs* are costs already incurred, such as for previously purchased materials, overhead, and indirect labor. Since they have already been incurred or will be incurred regardless of the decisions being made, these costs are not relevant or affected by the values of the decision variables. Sunk costs *should not be considered* when developing the objective function for a linear programming model. Note that Table 4.5 shows that the unit costs are based on the relevant variable costs of the materials as well as on other variable expenses. The environmental protection case at the end of the chapter will give you a chance to identify relevant costs in the development of a linear programming model.

Table 4.6
Optimal Financial Mix for the
Jefferson Adding Machine Problem

Model	Units	Expected Profit	Amount of Borrowed Funds
Model Y			
Borrowed funds	50.0	$ 325	$2500
Model Z			
Company funds	30.0	600	—
Borrowed funds	15.7	267	1570
Totals		$1192	$4070

Some additional interpretations from the computer output in Figure 4.3 show that assembly capacity (constraint 1, slack = 757.6 hours) and packaging and shipping capacity (constraint 2, slack = 8.6 hours) are adequate to meet the production requirements. Additional hours of these resources will not improve the value of the optimal solution. The dual price associated with the internal funds constraint (constraint 3) shows that a profit improvement of $0.24 can be made from an additional dollar of internal funds. With this high return on the internal funds investment, Jefferson may want to seriously consider allocating additional internal funds to this project. The negative dual price for constraint 5 tells us that increases in the model Y production requirement will reduce the profit margin. In fact, the negative dual price shows that reducing the current 50-unit requirement for model Y will actually increase profits at the rate of approximately $2.40 per unit reduction in the requirement.

4.3 Production Management Applications

There are a wealth of linear programming applications in production and operations management. Many of these are in the areas of scheduling, inventory control, and capacity planning. In this section we describe applications in production scheduling and labor allocation.

Production Scheduling

One of the most important areas of linear programming deals with multiperiod planning applications such as production scheduling. The solution to a production scheduling problem enables the manager to establish an efficient low-cost production schedule for one or more products over several time periods, such as weeks, months, and so on. Essentially, a production scheduling problem can be viewed as a product-mix problem for each of several periods in the future. The manager must determine the production levels that will allow the company to meet product demand requirements, given limitations on production capacity, labor capacity, and storage space. At the same time, it is desired to minimize the total cost of carrying out this task.

One advantage of using linear programming for production scheduling problems is that these problems are of a recurring nature. A production schedule must be established for the current month, then again for the next month, for the month after that, and so on. When the production manager looks at the problem each month, he or she will find that while demands for the products have changed, production times, production capacities, storage space limitations, and so on are roughly the same. Thus, the production manager is basically resolving the same problem handled in previous months, and a general linear programming model of the production scheduling procedure may be frequently applied. Once the model has been formulated, the manager can simply supply the data—demands, capacities, and so on—for the given production period and use the linear programming model repeatedly to develop the production schedule.

Let us consider the case of the Bollinger Electronics Company, which produces two different electronic components for a major airplane engine manufacturer. The airplane engine manufacturer notifies the Bollinger sales office each quarter as to what the monthly requirements for components will be during each of the next 3 months. The monthly requirements for the components may vary considerably depending on the type of engine the airplane engine manufacturer is producing. The order shown in Table 4.7 has just been received for the next 3-month period.

After the order is processed, a demand statement is sent to the production control department. The production control department must then develop a 3-month production plan for the components. Knowing the preference of the production department manager for constant demand levels that result in balanced workloads and constant machine and labor utilization, the production scheduler might consider the alternative of producing at a constant rate for all 3 months. This would set monthly production quotas at 3000 units per month for component 322A and 1500 units per month for component 802B.

While this schedule would be quite appealing to the production department, it may be undesirable from a total-cost point of view. In particular, this schedule ignores inventory costs. Consider the projected inventory levels that would result from this schedule calling for constant production (Figure 4.5). We see that this production schedule would lead to high inventory levels. When we consider the cost of tied-up capital and storage space, a schedule that provides lower inventory levels might be economically more desirable.

At the other extreme of the constant rate production schedule is the produce-to-meet-demand approach. While this schedule eliminates the inventory holding cost problem, the wide monthly fluctuations in production levels may cause some serious production problems and costs. For example, production capacity would have to be available to meet the total 8000-unit peak demand in June. Also, unless other components could be scheduled on the same production equipment in April and May, there would be significant unused capacity and thus low machine utilization in those months. These large production variations might also require substantial labor adjustments which in turn could lead to increased employee turnover and training problems. Thus, it appears that the best production schedule will be one that is a compromise between the two alternatives.

Table 4.7

Three-Month Demand Schedule for Bollinger Electronics Company

Component	April	May	June
322A	1000	3000	5000
802B	1000	500	3000

Figure 4.5

Projected Inventory Levels Under a Constant-Rate Production Schedule

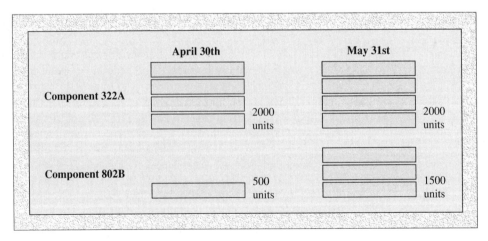

The production manager will want to identify and consider the following costs:

1. Production costs
2. Inventory holding cost
3. Change-in-production-level costs

In the remainder of this section we show how a linear programming model of the production and inventory process for Bollinger Electronics can be formulated to account for these costs in such a fashion that the total cost is minimized.

To develop the model, we will let x_{im} denote the production volume in units for product i in month m. Here $i = 1, 2$, and $m = 1, 2, 3$; $i = 1$ refers to component 322A, $i = 2$ refers to component 802B, $m = 1$ refers to April, $m = 2$ refers to May, and $m = 3$ refers to June. The purpose of the double subscript is to provide a more descriptive notation. We could simply use x_6 to represent the number of units of product 2 produced in month 3, but x_{23} is more descriptive in that we know directly the product and month represented by the variable.

If component 322A costs $20 per unit produced and component 802B costs $10 per unit produced, the total production cost part of the objective function is

$$\text{Total production cost} = 20x_{11} + 20x_{12} + 20x_{13} + 10x_{21} + 10x_{22} + 10x_{23}$$

However, since in this problem the production cost per unit is the same each month, we do not need to include production costs in the objective function; that is, no matter what production schedule is selected, the total production cost will remain the same. In other words, the production costs are not relevant costs for the production scheduling decision under consideration. In cases where the production cost per unit is expected to change each month, the variable production costs per unit per month must be included in the objective function. Since the solution for the Bollinger Electronics problem will be the same whether or not these costs are included, we have elected to include them so that the value of the linear programming objective function will include all the costs associated with the problem.

To incorporate the relevant inventory holding costs into the model, we let s_{im} denote the inventory level for product i at the end of month m. Bollinger has determined that on a monthly basis, inventory holding costs are 1.5% of the cost of the product; that is, $(0.015)(\$20) = \$0.30$ per unit for component 322A and $(0.015)(\$10) = \$0.15$ per unit for component 802B. A common assumption made in using the linear programming approach to production scheduling is that monthly ending inventories are an acceptable approximation to the average inventory levels throughout the month. Given this assumption, the total inventory holding cost portion of the objective function can be written as follows:

$$\text{Total inventory holding cost} = 0.30s_{11} + 0.30s_{12} + 0.30s_{13} + 0.15s_{21} + 0.15s_{22}$$

$$+ 0.15s_{23}$$

To incorporate the costs due to fluctuations in production levels from month to month, we need to define the following additional decision variables:

$$I_m = \text{increase in the total production level during}$$

$$= \text{month } m \text{ compared with month } m - 1$$

$$D_m = \text{decrease in the total production level during}$$

$$= \text{month } m \text{ compared with month } m - 1$$

After estimating the effects of employee layoffs, turnovers, reassignment training costs, and other costs associated with fluctuating production levels, Bollinger estimates that the cost associated with increasing the production level for any given month is \$0.50 per unit increase. A similar cost associated with decreasing the production level for any given month is \$0.20 per unit. Thus, the third portion of the objective function can be written as follows:

$$\text{Total change in production level cost} = 0.50I_1 + 0.50I_2 + 0.50I_3$$
$$+ 0.20D_1 + 0.20D_2$$
$$+ 0.20D_3$$

Note that Bollinger has elected to measure the cost associated with changes in production level as a function of the change in the total number of units produced in month m compared with the total number of units produced in month $m - 1$. In other production scheduling applications, fluctuations in production level might be measured in terms of machine hours or labor hours required rather than in terms of the total number of units produced.

Combining all three costs, the complete objective function becomes

$$\text{Min } 20x_{11} + 20x_{12} + 20x_{13} + 10x_{21} + 10x_{22} + 10x_{23} + 0.30s_{11}$$
$$+ 0.30s_{12} + 0.30s_{13} + 0.15s_{21} + 0.15s_{22} + 0.15s_{23} + 0.50I_1$$
$$+ 0.50I_2 + 0.50I_3 + 0.20D_1 + 0.20D_2 + 0.20D_3$$

Now let us consider the constraints. First, we must guarantee that the schedule meets customer demand. Since the units shipped can come from the current month's production or from inventory carried over from previous periods, the demand requirement takes the form

$$\begin{pmatrix} \text{Ending} \\ \text{inventory} \\ \text{from previous} \\ \text{month} \end{pmatrix} + \begin{pmatrix} \text{Current} \\ \text{production} \end{pmatrix} - \begin{pmatrix} \text{Ending} \\ \text{inventory} \\ \text{for this} \\ \text{month} \end{pmatrix} = \begin{pmatrix} \text{This month's} \\ \text{demand} \end{pmatrix}$$

Suppose that the inventories at the beginning of the 3-month scheduling period were 500 units for component 322A and 200 units for component 802B. Recalling that the demand for both products in the first month (April) was 1000 units, the constraints for meeting demand in the first month become

$$500 + x_{11} - s_{11} = 1000$$
$$200 + x_{21} - s_{21} = 1000$$

Moving the constants to the right-hand side, we have

$$x_{11} - s_{11} = 500$$
$$x_{21} - s_{21} = 800$$

Similarly, we need demand constraints for both products in the second and third months. These can be written as follows:

Month 2

$$s_{11} + x_{12} - s_{12} = 3000$$

$$s_{21} + x_{22} - s_{22} = 500$$

Month 3

$$s_{12} + x_{13} - s_{13} = 5000$$

$$s_{22} + x_{23} - s_{23} = 3000$$

If the company specifies a minimum inventory level at the end of the 3-month period of at least 400 units of component 322A and at least 200 units of component 802B, we can add the constraints:

$$s_{13} \geq 400$$

$$s_{23} \geq 200$$

Let us suppose that we have the additional information available on machine, labor, and storage capacity given in Table 4.8. Machine, labor, and storage space requirements are given in Table 4.9. To reflect these limitations, the following constraints are necessary:

Machine Capacity

$$0.10x_{11} + 0.08x_{21} \leq 400 \qquad \text{Month 1}$$

$$0.10x_{12} + 0.08x_{22} \leq 500 \qquad \text{Month 2}$$

$$0.10x_{13} + 0.08x_{23} \leq 600 \qquad \text{Month 3}$$

Labor Capacity

$$0.05x_{11} + 0.07x_{21} \leq 300 \qquad \text{Month 1}$$

$$0.05x_{12} + 0.07x_{22} \leq 300 \qquad \text{Month 2}$$

$$0.05x_{13} + 0.07x_{23} \leq 300 \qquad \text{Month 3}$$

Table 4.8

Machine, Labor, and Storage Capacities for Bollinger Electronics

Month	Machine Capacity (hours)	Labor Capacity (hours)	Storage Capacity (square feet)
April	400	300	10,000
May	500	300	10,000
June	600	300	10,000

Table 4.9

Machine, Labor, and Storage Requirements for Components 322A and 802B

Component	Machine (hours/unit)	Labor (hours/unit)	Storage (square feet/unit)
322A	0.10	0.05	2
802B	0.08	0.07	3

Storage Capacity

$$2s_{11} + 3s_{21} \leq 10,000 \qquad \text{Month 1}$$

$$2s_{12} + 3s_{22} \leq 10,000 \qquad \text{Month 2}$$

$$2s_{13} + 3s_{23} \leq 10,000 \qquad \text{Month 3}$$

One final set of constraints must be added. These are necessary to guarantee that I_m and D_m will reflect the increase or decrease in the total production level for month m. Suppose that the production levels for March, the month before the start of the current production scheduling problem, had been 1500 units of component 322A and 1000 units of component 802B for a total production level of $1500 + 1000 = 2500$ units. We can find the amount of the change in production for April from the relationship

$$\text{April production} - \text{March production} = \text{change}$$

Using the April production decision variables, x_{11} and x_{21}, and the March production of 2500 units, the above relationship can be rewritten as

$$(x_{11} + x_{21}) - 2500 = \text{change}$$

Note that the change can be positive or negative. A positive change reflects an increase in the total production level, and a negative change reflects a decrease in the total production level. Using the above relationship, the increase in production variable for April, I_1, and the decrease in production variable for April, D_1, can be used to specify the following constraint for the change in total production for the month of April:

$$(x_{11} + x_{21}) - 2500 = I_1 - D_1$$

Of course, we cannot have an increase in production and a decrease in production during the same 1-month period; thus, either I_1 or D_1 will be zero. If April requires 3000 units of production, we will have $I_1 = 500$ and $D_1 = 0$. If April requires 2200 units of production, we will have $I_1 = 0$ and $D_1 = 300$. This approach of denoting the change in production level as the difference between two nonnegative variables, I_1 and D_1, permits both positive and negative changes in the total production level. If a single variable, say c_m, had been used to represent the change in production level, then because of the nonnegativity requirement, only positive changes would be possible.

Using the same approach in May and June (always subtracting the previous month's total production from the current month's total production), we have the following constraints for the second and third months of the production scheduling period:

$$(x_{12} + x_{22}) - (x_{11} + x_{21}) = I_2 - D_2$$

$$(x_{13} + x_{23}) - (x_{12} + x_{22}) = I_3 - D_3$$

Placing the variables on the left-hand side and the constants on the right-hand side, the complete set of what are commonly referred to as production-smoothing constraints can be written as

$$x_{11} + x_{21} \qquad\qquad\qquad\qquad - I_1 + D_1 = 2500$$

$$-x_{11} - x_{21} + x_{12} + x_{22} \qquad\qquad - I_2 + D_2 = \quad 0$$

$$- x_{12} - x_{22} + x_{13} + x_{23} - I_3 + D_3 = \quad 0$$

The initially rather small, 2-product, 3-month scheduling problem has now developed into an 18-variable, 20-constraint linear programming problem. Note that in this problem

Figure 4.6   The Management Scientist Solution for the Bollinger Electronics Problem

```
Objective Function Value =         225294.969

        Variable              Value            Reduced Costs
     --------------      ----------------     ------------------
          X11                500.000                0.000
          X12               3200.000                0.000
          X13               5200.000                0.000
          X21               2500.000                0.000
          X22               2000.000                0.000
          X23                  0.000                0.128
          S11                  0.000                0.172
          S12                200.000                0.000
          S13                400.000                0.000
          S21               1700.000                0.000
          S22               3200.000                0.000
          S23                200.000                0.000
          I1                 500.000                0.000
          I2                2200.000                0.000
          I3                   0.000                0.072
          D1                   0.000                0.700
          D2                   0.000                0.700
          D3                   0.000                0.628


       Constraint         Slack/Surplus           Dual Prices
     --------------      ----------------     ------------------
           1                  0.000               -20.000
           2                  0.000               -10.000
           3                  0.000               -20.128
           4                  0.000               -10.150
           5                  0.000               -20.428
           6                  0.000               -10.300
           7                  0.000               -20.728
           8                  0.000               -10.450
           9                150.000                 0.000
          10                 20.000                 0.000
          11                 80.000                 0.000
          12                100.000                 0.000
          13                  0.000                 1.111
          14                 40.000                 0.000
          15               4899.999                 0.000
          16                  0.000                 0.000
          17               8599.999                 0.000
          18                  0.000                 0.500
          19                  0.000                 0.500
          20                  0.000                 0.428
```

we were concerned only with one type of machine process, one type of labor, and one type of storage area. Since actual production scheduling problems usually involve several machine types, several labor grades, and/or several storage areas, we can see why large-scale linear programs are required. For instance, a problem involving 100 products over a 12-month horizon could have over 1000 variables and constraints.

The computer solution to the Bollinger Electronics production scheduling problem is shown in Figure 4.6. A portion of the managerial report based on the computer solution is shown in Table 4.10.

Let us now consider the monthly variation in the production and inventory schedule shown in Table 4.10. Recall that the inventory cost for component 802B is one-half the inventory cost for component 322A. Therefore, as might be expected, component 802B is produced heavily in the first month (April) and then held in inventory for the demand that will occur in future months. Component 322A tends to be produced when needed, and only small amounts are carried in inventory.

The costs of increasing and decreasing the total production volume tend to smooth the monthly variations. In fact, the minimum-cost schedule calls for a 500-unit increase in total production in April and a 2200-unit increase in total production in May. The May production level of 5200 units is then maintained during June.

The machine usage section of the report shows ample machine capacity available in all 3 months. However, labor capacity is at full utilization (slack = 0 for constraint 13 in Figure 4.6) in the month of May. The dual price shows that an additional hour of labor capacity in May will improve the objective function (lower cost) by approximately $1.11.

We have seen in this illustration that a linear programming model of a 2-product, 3-month production system has provided some valuable information in terms of identifying a minimum-cost production schedule. In larger production systems, where the number of variables and constraints is too large to track manually, linear programming models can provide a significant advantage in developing cost-saving production schedules.

Problem 19 involves a production scheduling application with labor smoothing constraints.

Linear programming models for production scheduling are often very large. Thousands of decision variables and constraints are necessary when there are numerous products, machines, and time periods. Generating the data for large-scale models can be more time-consuming than either the formulation of the model or the development of the computer solution.

Table 4.10

Minimum-Cost Production Schedule Information for the Bollinger Electronics Problem

Activity	April	May	June
Production			
Component 322A	500	3,200	5,200
Component 802B	2,500	2,000	0
Totals	3,000	5,200	5,200
Ending inventory			
Component 322A	0	200	400
Component 802B	1,700	3,200	200
Machine usage			
Scheduled hours	250	480	520
Slack capacity hours	150	20	80
Labor usage			
Scheduled hours	200	300	260
Slack capacity hours	100	0	40
Storage usage			
Scheduled storage	5,100	10,000	1,400
Slack capacity	4,900	0	8,600
Total production, inventory, and production smoothing cost = $225,295			

> ### NOTES & COMMENTS
>
> In checking the appropriateness of a linear programming model, it is always a good idea to review the units of measurement for the objective function and the constraints. For example, the machine capacities for the Bollinger Electronics problem were stated in units of *hours*. With component 322A requiring 0.10 hour (6 minutes) per unit and component 802B requiring 0.08 hour (4.8 minutes) per unit, the constraint for the 400 hours available in month one was correctly stated as
>
> $$0.10x_{11} + 0.08x_{12} \leq 400$$
>
> The unit of measurement is consistent in that hours is used for both the left-hand side and the right-hand side. The constraint
>
> $$6x_{11} + 4.8x_{12} \leq 400$$
>
> would be incorrect because the use of minutes on the left-hand side would be inconsistent with the use of hours on the right-hand side. This inconsistency could be corrected by converting the right-hand side capacity to 400 hours × (60 minutes/hour) = 24,000 minutes. Thus, while there is flexibility in selecting the unit of measurement to use, consistency is required.

Work Force Assignment

Work force assignment problems frequently occur when production managers must make decisions involving staffing requirements for a given planning period. Work force assignments often have some flexibility, and at least some personnel can be assigned to more than one department or work center. This is the case when employees have been cross-trained on two or more jobs or, for instance, when sales personnel can be transferred between stores. In the following application we show how linear programming can be used to determine not only an optimal product mix, but also an optimal work force allocation.

McCormick Manufacturing Company produces two products with contributions to per-unit profit of $10 and $9, respectively. The labor requirements per unit produced and the total hours of labor available from personnel assigned to each of four departments are shown in Table 4.11. Assuming that the number of hours available in each department is

Table 4.11

Departmental Labor-Hours Per Unit and Total Hours Available for the McCormick Manufacturing Company

Department	Labor-Hours Per Unit		Total Hours Available
	Product 1	Product 2	
1	0.65	0.95	6500
2	0.45	0.85	6000
3	1.00	0.70	7000
4	0.15	0.30	1400

fixed, we can formulate McCormick's problem as a standard product-mix linear program with the following decision variables:

$$x_1 = \text{units of product 1}$$
$$x_2 = \text{units of product 2}$$

The linear program can be written as

$$\text{Max} \quad 10x_1 + 9x_2$$

s.t.

$$0.65x_1 + 0.95x_2 \leq 6500$$

$$0.45x_1 + 0.85x_2 \leq 6000$$

$$1.00x_1 + 0.70x_2 \leq 7000$$

$$0.15x_1 + 0.30x_2 \leq 1400$$

$$x_1, x_2 \geq 0$$

The optimal solution to the linear programming model provides 5744 units of product 1, 1795 units of product 2, and a total profit of $73,590. With this optimal solution, departments 3 and 4 are operating at capacity while departments 1 and 2 have a slack of approximately 1062 and 1890 hours, respectively. We would anticipate that the product mix would change and that the total profit would increase if the work force assignment could be revised so that the slack, or unused hours, in departments 1 and 2 could be transferred to the departments currently working at capacity. However, the production manager may be uncertain as to how the work force should be reallocated among the four departments. Let us expand the linear programming model to include decision variables that will help determine the optimal work force allocation in addition to the profit-maximizing product mix.

Suppose McCormick has a cross-training program that enables some employees to be transferred between departments. By taking advantage of the cross-training skills, a limited number of employees and labor-hours may be transferred from one department to another. For example, suppose that the cross-training permits transfers as shown in Table 4.12. Row 1 of this table shows that some employees assigned to department 1 have cross-training skills that permit them to be transferred to department 2 or 3. The column in the right-hand margin of Table 4.12 shows that for the current production planning period, a maximum of 400 hours can be transferred out of department 1. Similar cross-training transfer capabilities and capacities are shown for departments 2, 3, and 4.

Table 4.12

Cross-Training Ability and Capacity Information

From Department	Cross-Training Transfers Permitted to Department				Maximum Hours Transferable
	1	2	3	4	
1	—	yes	yes	—	400
2	—	—	yes	yes	800
3	—	—	—	yes	100
4	yes	yes	—	—	200

When work force assignments are flexible, we do not automatically know how many hours of labor should be assigned to or transferred from each department. Let us add the following decision variables to the linear programming model:

b_i = the labor-hours allocated to department i for i = 1, 2, 3, and 4
t_{ij} = the labor-hours transferred from department i to department j

With the addition of decision variables b_1, b_2, b_3, and b_4, the capacity restrictions for the four departments can be written as follows:

$$0.65x_1 + 0.95x_2 \leq b_1$$

$$0.45x_1 + 0.85x_2 \leq b_2$$

$$1.00x_1 + 0.70x_2 \leq b_3$$

$$0.15x_1 + 0.30x_2 \leq b_4$$

Since b_1, b_2, b_3, and b_4 are now decision variables, we follow the standard practice of placing these variables on the left-hand side of the inequalities, and the first four constraints of the linear programming model become

$$0.65x_1 + 0.95x_2 - b_1 \qquad\qquad\qquad \leq 0$$

$$0.45x_1 + 0.85x_2 \qquad - b_2 \qquad\qquad \leq 0$$

$$1.00x_1 + 0.70x_2 \qquad\qquad - b_3 \qquad \leq 0$$

$$0.15x_1 + 0.30x_2 \qquad\qquad\qquad - b_4 \leq 0$$

The labor-hours ultimately allocated to each department must be determined by a series of balance equations or constraints that include the number of hours initially assigned to each department plus the number of hours transferred into the department minus the number of hours transferred out of the department. Using department 1 as an example, the work force allocation is determined as follows:

$$b_1 = \begin{pmatrix} \text{Hours} \\ \text{initially in} \\ \text{department 1} \end{pmatrix} + \begin{pmatrix} \text{Hours} \\ \text{transferred into} \\ \text{department 1} \end{pmatrix} - \begin{pmatrix} \text{Hours} \\ \text{transferred out of} \\ \text{department 1} \end{pmatrix}$$

Table 4.11 shows 6500 hours initially assigned to department 1. We use the transfer decision variables t_{i1} to denote transfers into department 1 and t_{1j} to denote transfers out of department 1. Table 4.12 shows that the cross-training capabilities involving department 1 are restricted to transfers from department 4 (variable t_{41}) and transfers out to either department 2 or department 3 (variables t_{12} and t_{13}). Thus, we can express the total work force allocation for department 1 as follows:

$$b_1 = 6500 + t_{41} - t_{12} - t_{13}$$

Moving the decision variables for the work force transfers to the left-hand side, we have the balance equation or constraint

$$b_1 - t_{41} + t_{12} + t_{13} = 6500$$

A constraint of the above form will be needed for each of the four departments. Thus, the following balance constraints for departments 2, 3, and 4 would be added to the model.

$$b_2 - t_{12} - t_{42} + t_{23} + t_{24} = 6000$$

$$b_3 - t_{13} - t_{23} + t_{34} \qquad = 7000$$

$$b_4 - t_{24} - t_{34} + t_{41} + t_{42} = 1400$$

Finally, since Table 4.12 shows that the number of hours transferred out of each department is limited, a transfer capacity constraint must be added for each of the four departments. The four additional constraints necessary are:

$$t_{12} + t_{13} \leq 400$$

$$t_{23} + t_{24} \leq 800$$

$$t_{34} \qquad \leq 100$$

$$t_{41} + t_{42} \leq 200$$

The complete linear programming model has two product decision variables (x_1 and x_2), four department work force assignment variables (b_1, b_2, b_3, and b_4), and seven transfer variables ($t_{12}, t_{13}, t_{23}, t_{24}, t_{34}, t_{41}$, and t_{42}). There are a total of 12 constraints. The optimal solution to this linear program provided by The Management Scientist software package is shown in Figure 4.7.

McCormick's profit can be increased to \$84,011 by taking advantage of work force transfers. The optimal product mix of 6825 units of product 1 and 1751 units of product 2 can be achieved if $t_{13} = 400$ hours are transferred from department 1 to department 3; $t_{23} = 751$ hours are transferred from department 2 to department 3; $t_{24} = 49$ hours are transferred from department 2 to department 4; and $t_{34} = 100$ hours are transferred from department 3 to department 4. The resulting work force assignments for departments 1–4 would provide 6100, 5200, 8051, and 1549 hours, respectively.

If a manager has the flexibility to assign personnel to different departments, then a reduction in work force idle time, an improved work force utilization, and an improved profit should result. The linear programming model in this section automatically assigns employees and labor-hours to the departments in the most profitable manner.

Variations in the work force assignment model could be used in situations such as allocating raw material resources to products, allocating machine time to products, and allocating sales force time to stores or sales territories.

4.4 Blending Problems

Blending problems arise whenever a manager must decide how to blend two or more resources to produce one or more products. In these situations, the resources contain one or more essential ingredients that must be blended in such a manner that the final products will contain specific percentages of them. In most of these applications, then, management must decide how much of each resource to purchase in order to satisfy product specifications and product demands at minimum cost.

Blending problems occur frequently in the petroleum industry (such as blending crude oil to produce different-octane gasolines), chemical industry (such as blending chemicals to produce fertilizers and weed killers), and food industry (such as blending ingredients to produce soft drinks and soups). Because of the widespread occurrence of blending problems, this section illustrates how linear programming can be applied to a blending problem in the petroleum industry.

The Grand Strand Oil Company produces regular-grade and premium-grade gasoline products for independent service stations in the southeastern United States. The Grand Strand refinery manufactures the gasoline products by blending three petroleum components. The gasolines are sold at different prices, and the petroleum components have

Figure 4.7 The Management Scientist Solution for the McCormick Manufacturing
Work Force Assignment Problem

```
Objective Function Value =          84011.297

       Variable               Value           Reduced Costs
    --------------       ---------------    ------------------
          X1                6824.858              0.000
          X2                1751.413              0.000
          B1                6100.000              0.000
          B2                5200.000              0.000
          B3                8050.847              0.000
          B4                1549.153              0.000
          T41                  0.000              7.458
          T12                  0.000              8.249
          T13                400.000              0.000
          T42                  0.000              8.249
          T23                750.847              0.000
          T24                 49.153              0.000
          T34                100.000              0.000


      Constraint          Slack/Surplus          Dual Prices
    --------------       ---------------    ------------------
           1                   0.000              0.791
           2                 640.113              0.000
           3                   0.000              8.249
           4                   0.000              8.249
           5                   0.000              0.791
           6                   0.000              0.000
           7                   0.000              8.249
           8                   0.000              8.249
           9                   0.000              7.458
          10                   0.000              8.249
          11                   0.000              0.000
          12                 200.000              0.000
```

different costs. The firm would like to determine how to mix or blend the three components into the two gasoline products in such a way as to maximize profits.

Data available show that the regular-grade gasoline can be sold for $0.50 per gallon and the premium-grade gasoline for $0.54 per gallon. For the current production planning period, Grand Strand can obtain the three petroleum components at the cost per gallon and in the quantities shown in Table 4.13.

The product specifications for the regular and premium gasolines restrict the amounts of each component that can be used in each gasoline product. The product specifications are listed in Table 4.14. Current commitments to distributors require Grand Strand to produce at least 10,000 gallons of regular-grade gasoline.

Table 4.13

Petroleum Cost and Supply for the Grand Strand Blending Problem

Petroleum Component	Cost/Gallon	Maximum Available
1	$0.25	5,000 gallons
2	$0.30	10,000 gallons
3	$0.42	10,000 gallons

Table 4.14

Product Specifications for the Grand Strand Blending Problem

Product	Specifications
Regular gasoline	At most 30% component 1
	At least 40% component 2
	At most 20% component 3
Premium gasoline	At least 25% component 1
	At most 40% component 2
	At least 30% component 3

The Grand Strand blending problem is to determine how many gallons of each component should be used in the regular-grade gasoline blend and how many should be used in the premium-grade gasoline blend. The optimal blending solution should maximize the firm's profit, subject to the constraints on the available petroleum supplies shown in Table 4.13, the product specifications shown in Table 4.14, and the required 10,000 gallons of regular-grade gasoline.

We can use the following notation to define the decision variables:

$$x_{ij} = \text{gallons of component } i \text{ used in gasoline } j$$
$$\text{where } i = 1, 2, \text{ or } 3 \text{ for components } 1, 2, \text{ or } 3,$$
$$\text{and } j = r \text{ if regular or } j = p \text{ if premium}$$

The six decision variables become

$$x_{1r} = \text{gallons of component 1 in regular gasoline}$$
$$x_{2r} = \text{gallons of component 2 in regular gasoline}$$
$$x_{3r} = \text{gallons of component 3 in regular gasoline}$$
$$x_{1p} = \text{gallons of component 1 in premium gasoline}$$
$$x_{2p} = \text{gallons of component 2 in premium gasoline}$$
$$x_{3p} = \text{gallons of component 3 in premium gasoline}$$

Note that previously we have always used numbers as the subscripts for decision variables. Continuing this use, we could have let $j = 1$ for regular gasoline and $j = 2$ for premium gasoline. However, the use of the r and p subscripts is descriptive and will enable us to easily identify the gasoline product being referred to by the decision variable.

The total number of gallons of each type of gasoline produced is the sum of the number of gallons produced using each of the three petroleum components. That is,

Total Gallons Produced

$$\text{Regular gasoline} = x_{1r} + x_{2r} + x_{3r}$$

$$\text{Premium gasoline} = x_{1p} + x_{2p} + x_{3p}$$

Similarly, the total gallons of each petroleum component are provided by the following sums:

Total Petroleum Component Usage

$$\text{Component 1} = x_{1r} + x_{1p}$$

$$\text{Component 2} = x_{2r} + x_{2p}$$

$$\text{Component 3} = x_{3r} + x_{3p}$$

The objective function of maximizing the profit contribution can be developed by identifying the difference between the total revenue from both gasolines and the total cost of the three petroleum components. By multiplying the $0.50 per-gallon price by the total gallons of regular gasoline, the $0.54 per-gallon price by the total gallons of premium gasoline, and the component cost per-gallon figures in Table 4.13 by the total gallons of each component used, the objective function can be written as follows:

$$\text{Max} \quad 0.50(x_{1r} + x_{2r} + x_{3r}) + 0.54(x_{1p} + x_{2p} + x_{3p})$$
$$- 0.25(x_{1r} + x_{1p}) - 0.30(x_{2r} + x_{2p}) - 0.42(x_{3r} + x_{3p})$$

By combining terms, the objective function can be written as

$$\text{Max} \quad 0.25x_{1r} + 0.20x_{2r} + 0.08x_{3r} + 0.29x_{1p} + 0.24x_{2p} + 0.12x_{3p}$$

The limitations on the availability of the three petroleum components can be expressed by the following three constraints:

$$x_{1r} + x_{1p} \leq 5{,}000 \quad \text{Component 1}$$

$$x_{2r} + x_{2p} \leq 10{,}000 \quad \text{Component 2}$$

$$x_{3r} + x_{3p} \leq 10{,}000 \quad \text{Component 3}$$

Six constraints are now required to meet the product specifications stated in Table 4.14. The first specification states that component 1 can account for at most 30% of the total gallons of regular gasoline produced. That is,

$$\frac{x_{1r}}{x_{1r} + x_{2r} + x_{3r}} \leq 0.30$$

or

$$x_{1r} \leq 0.30(x_{1r} + x_{2r} + x_{3r})$$

Rewriting this constraint with the variables on the left-hand side and a constant on the right-hand side, the first product specification constraint becomes

$$0.70x_{1r} - 0.30x_{2r} - 0.30x_{3r} \leq 0$$

The second product specification listed in Table 4.14 can be written as

$$\frac{x_{2r}}{x_{1r} + x_{2r} + x_{3r}} \geq 0.40$$

or

$$x_{2r} \geq 0.40(x_{1r} + x_{2r} + x_{3r})$$

and thus

$$-0.40x_{1r} + 0.60x_{2r} - 0.40x_{3r} \geq 0$$

Similarly, the four additional blending specifications shown in Table 4.14 can be written as

$$-0.20x_{1r} - 0.20x_{2r} + 0.80x_{3r} \leq 0$$

$$-0.75x_{1p} - 0.25x_{2p} - 0.25x_{3p} \geq 0$$

$$-0.40x_{1p} + 0.60x_{2p} - 0.40x_{3p} \leq 0$$

$$-0.30x_{1p} - 0.30x_{2p} + 0.70x_{3p} \geq 0$$

The constraint for at least 10,000 gallons of the regular-grade gasoline is written

$$x_{1r} + x_{2r} + x_{3r} \geq 10,000$$

The complete linear programming model with 6 decision variables and 10 constraints can be written as follows:

Max $\quad 0.25x_{1r} + 0.20x_{2r} + 0.08x_{3r} + 0.29x_{1p} + 0.24x_{2p} + 0.12x_{3p}$

s.t.

$$
\begin{array}{rcl}
x_{1r} \hphantom{+ x_{2r}} + x_{1p} \hphantom{+ x_{2p} + x_{3p}} & \leq & 5,000 \\[4pt]
x_{2r} \hphantom{+} + x_{2p} \hphantom{+ x_{3p}} & \leq & 10,000 \\[4pt]
x_{3r} \hphantom{+} + x_{3p} & \leq & 10,000 \\[4pt]
0.70x_{1r} - 0.30x_{2r} - 0.30x_{3r} & \leq & 0 \\[4pt]
-0.40x_{1r} + 0.60x_{2r} - 0.40x_{3r} & \geq & 0 \\[4pt]
-0.20x_{1r} - 0.20x_{2r} + 0.80x_{3r} & \leq & 0 \\[4pt]
0.75x_{1p} - 0.25x_{2p} - 0.25x_{3p} & \geq & 0 \\[4pt]
-0.40x_{1p} + 0.60x_{2p} - 0.40x_{3p} & \leq & 0 \\[4pt]
-0.30x_{1p} - 0.30x_{2p} + 0.70x_{3p} & \geq & 0 \\[4pt]
x_{1r} + x_{2r} + x_{3r} & \geq & 10,000
\end{array}
$$

$$-0.00x_{1r}, x_{2r}, x_{3r}, x_{1p}, x_{2p}, x_{3p} \geq 0$$

The computer solution to the Grand Strand blending problem is shown in Figure 4.8. The optimal solution providing a profit of $4650 is summarized in Table 4.15. The optimal blending strategy shows that 10,000 gallons of regular gasoline should be produced. The regular gasoline will be manufactured as a blend of 1250 gallons of component 1, 6750 gallons of component 2, and 2000 gallons of component 3. The 15,000 gallons of premium gasoline will be manufactured as a blend of 3750 gallons of component 1, 3250 gallons of component 2, and 8000 gallons of component 3.

Try Problem 15 as another example of a blending model. The interpretation of the slack and surplus variables associated with the product specification constraints (constraints 4–9) in Figure 4.8 needs some clarification. If the constraint is a $\leq$ constraint, the value of the slack can be interpreted as the gallons of component usage below the maximum amount of the component usage specified by the

Figure 4.8   The Management Scientist Solution for the Grand Strand Blending Problem

```
Objective Function Value =            4650.000

      Variable              Value            Reduced Costs
   ---------------      ---------------    ------------------

        X1R              1250.000               0.000
        X2R              6750.000               0.000
        X3R              2000.000               0.000
        X1P              3750.000               0.000
        X2P              3250.000               0.000
        X3P              7999.999               0.000


     Constraint        Slack/Surplus          Dual Prices
   ---------------     ---------------      -------------------

         1                 0.000                0.290
         2                 0.000                0.240
         3                 0.000                0.120
         4              1750.000                0.000
         5              2750.000                0.000
         6                 0.000                0.000
         7                 0.000                0.000
         8              2750.000                0.000
         9              3499.999                0.000
        10                 0.000               -0.040
```

Table 4.15

Grand Strand Gasoline Blending Solution

| | Gallons of Component (percentage) | | | |
Gasoline	Component 1	Component 2	Component 3	Total
Regular	1250 (12.5%)	6750 (67.5%)	2000 (20%)	10,000
Premium	3750 (25%)	3250 (22%)	8000 (53%)	15,000

constraint. For example, the slack of 1750 for constraint 4 shows that component 1 usage is 1750 gallons below the maximum amount of component 1 that could have been used in the production of 10,000 gallons of regular gasoline. If the product specification constraint is a $\geq$ constraint, a surplus variable shows the gallons of component usage above the minimum amount of component usage specified by the blending constraint. For example, the surplus of 2750 for constraint 5 shows that component 2 usage is 2750 gallons above the minimum amount of component 2 that must be used in the production of 10,000 gallons of regular gasoline.

> # NOTES & COMMENTS
>
> A convenient way to define the decision variables in a blending problem is to use a matrix in which the rows correspond to the raw materials and the columns correspond to the final products. For example, in the Grand Strand blending problem, we could define the decision variables as follows:
>
> | | | **Final Products** | |
> | --- | --- | --- | --- |
> | | | *Regular Gasoline* | *Premium Gasoline* |
> | **Raw Materials** | Component 1 | x_{1r} | x_{1p} |
> | | Component 2 | x_{2r} | x_{2p} |
> | | Component 3 | x_{3r} | x_{3p} |
>
> There are two advantages to this approach: (1) It provides a systematic way to define the decision variables for any blending problem. (2) It provides a visual image of the decision variables in terms of how they are related to the raw materials, products, and each other.

4.5 Data Envelopment Analysis

Data envelopment analysis (DEA) is an application of linear programming that has been used to measure the relative efficiency of operating units with the same goals and objectives. For example, DEA has been used to measure the relative efficiency of individual fast-food outlets in the same chain. In this case, the goal of DEA was to identify the inefficient outlets that should be targeted for further study and, if necessary, corrective action. Other applications of DEA have measured the relative efficiencies of hospitals, banks, courts, schools, and so on. In these applications, the performance of each institution or organization was measured relative to the performance of all operating units in the same system.

The operating units of most organizations have multiple inputs, such as staff size, salaries, hours of operation, and advertising budget, as well as multiple outputs, such as profit, market share, and growth rate. In these situations, it is often difficult for a manager to determine which operating units are inefficient in converting their multiple inputs into multiple outputs. This is where data envelopment analysis has proven to be a helpful managerial tool.

The DEA approach uses a linear programming model to construct a hypothetical composite operating unit based on all units in the reference group. The output of the composite unit is determined by computing a weighted average of the outputs of all units in the reference group. The input for the composite unit is determined by using the same weights to compute a weighted average of the inputs for all units in the reference group. Constraints in the linear programming model require all outputs of the composite unit to be *greater than or equal to* the outputs of the unit being evaluated. If the inputs for the composite unit can be shown to be *less than* the inputs for the unit being evaluated, the composite unit will be shown to have the same, or more, output for *less input*. In this case, the model will show that the composite unit is more efficient than the unit being evaluated. In other words, the unit being evaluated is *less efficient* than the composite unit. Since the composite unit is based on all units in the reference group, the unit being evaluated can be judged *relatively inefficient* when compared to the other units in the group.

Evaluating the Performance of Hospitals

Let us illustrate the application of data envelopment analysis by evaluating the performance of a group of four hospitals. In this example, we will consider three measures of input and four measures of output. These measures are as follows:

Input Measures

1. The number of full-time equivalent (FTE) nonphysician personnel
2. The amount spent on supplies
3. The number of bed-days available

Output Measures

1. Patient-days of service under Medicare
2. Patient-days of service not under Medicare
3. Number of nurses trained
4. Number of interns trained

Summaries of the input and output measures for a 1-year period at each of the four hospitals are shown in Tables 4.16 and 4.17. Let us show how DEA can use these data to identify relatively inefficient hospitals.

In this application of DEA, a linear programming model will have to be developed for each hospital whose efficiency is to be evaluated. In the following discussion, we will develop a model that can be used to assess the relative efficiency of County Hospital. (Problem 25 at the end of the chapter will ask you to develop a model to assess the relative efficiency of General Hospital.) In developing the linear programming model for County Hospital, the weights used to construct the composite hospital are the variables. They are defined as follows:

wg = weight applied to inputs and outputs for General Hospital
wu = weight applied to inputs and outputs for University Hospital
wc = weight applied to inputs and outputs for County Hospital
ws = weight applied to inputs and outputs for State Hospital

Table 4.16
Annual Resources Consumed (Inputs) for the Four Hospitals

| | Hospital | | | |
Input Measure	General	University	County	State
Full-time equivalent nonphysicians	285.20	162.30	275.70	210.40
Supply expense ($1000's)	123.80	128.70	348.50	154.10
Bed-days available (1000's)	106.72	64.21	104.10	104.04

Table 4.17
Annual Services Provided (Outputs) for the Four Hospitals

| | Hospital | | | |
Output Measure	General	University	County	State
Medicare patient-days (1000's)	48.14	34.62	36.72	33.16
Non-Medicare patient-days (1000's)	43.10	27.11	45.98	56.46
Nurses trained	253	148	175	160
Interns trained	41	27	23	84

As noted, the weights will be used to determine the inputs and outputs for the hypothetical composite hospital. The input/output relationships that will be included in the model will have the following general form:

$$
\begin{pmatrix} \text{Input/output} \\ \text{of the} \\ \text{composite} \\ \text{hospital} \end{pmatrix} = \begin{pmatrix} \text{Input/output} \\ \text{at} \\ \text{General} \\ \text{Hospital} \end{pmatrix} wg + \begin{pmatrix} \text{Input/output} \\ \text{at} \\ \text{University} \\ \text{Hospital} \end{pmatrix} wu
$$

$$
+ \begin{pmatrix} \text{Input/output} \\ \text{at} \\ \text{County} \\ \text{Hospital} \end{pmatrix} wc + \begin{pmatrix} \text{Input/output} \\ \text{at} \\ \text{State} \\ \text{Hospital} \end{pmatrix} ws
$$

In formulating the DEA linear programming model, we will use the above expression to develop a constraint for each input measure and each output measure. To compute the weights for the four hospitals forming the composite hospital, the DEA linear programming model will require the sum of the weights to equal 1. Thus, for the four-hospital example, the first constraint will be as follows:

$$wg + wu + wc + ws = 1$$

> A set of output criteria or measures must be identified for the facilities in a DEA model. A $\geq$ constraint is required from each output measure.

Using the general input/output relationship for each of the four output measures, the four output constraints for the DEA model are written as follows:

$$48.14wg + 34.62wu + 36.72wc + 33.16ws \geq 36.72 \quad \text{Medicare}$$

$$43.10wg + 27.11wu + 45.98wc + 56.46ws \geq 45.98 \quad \text{Non-Medicare}$$

$$253wg + 148wu + 175wc + 160ws \geq 175 \quad \text{Nurses}$$

$$41wg + 27wu + 23wc + 84ws \geq 23 \quad \text{Interns}$$

Output for the composite hospital · Output for County Hospital

The above four constraints require the linear programming solution to provide weights such that all four outputs for the composite hospital will be greater than or equal to the four outputs of County Hospital. If a solution satisfying the output constraints can be found, then the composite hospital produces at least as much of each output as County Hospital.

Next, we need to consider the three input measures. The DEA linear programming model contains the variable E, which determines the fraction of County Hospital's input required by the composite hospital. The use of E, which is referred to as the efficiency index, follows.

	Input Resources	
Input Measure	Used by County Hospital	Available to Composite Hospital
FTE nonphysicians	275.70	275.70E
Supplies ($1000's)	348.50	348.50E
Bed-days (1000's)	104.10	104.10E

A set of input resources must be identified for the facilities in a DEA model. A $\leq$ constraint is required for each input resource.

The resources available to the composite hospital are simply a multiple of the resources used at County Hospital. If $E = 1$, the resources available to the composite hospital are the same as those used by County Hospital. If E is greater than 1, the composite hospital would have available proportionally more resources, while if E is less than 1, the composite hospital would have available proportionally less resources. The linear programming constraints for the three input measures are written as follows:

$$285.20wg + 162.30wu + 275.70wc + 210.40ws \leq 275.70E \quad \text{FTE nonphysicians}$$

$$123.80wg + 128.70wu + 348.50wc + 154.10ws \leq 348.50E \quad \text{Supplies}$$

$$106.72wg + 64.21wu + 104.10wc + 104.04ws \leq 104.10E \quad \text{Bed-days}$$

Input for the composite hospital

Input capacities for the composite hospital

If a solution with $E < 1$ can be found, the composite hospital does not need as many resources as County Hospital needs.

The logic of a DEA model is to determine whether a composite facility can achieve the *same or more output* as the test facility while *requiring less input*. If this can be done, the test facility is judged to be relatively inefficient.

The objective function in a DEA model is always Min E. The facility being analyzed (County Hospital in this example) can be judged relatively inefficient if the optimal solution provides an E less than 1, indicating that the composite facility requires less input resources.

The objective function for the DEA model is to minimize the value of E, which is equivalent to minimizing the input resources available to the composite hospital. Thus, the objective function is written as

$$\text{Min } E$$

The DEA efficiency conclusion is based on the optimal objective function value for E. The decision rule is as follows:

If $E = 1$, the composite hospital requires *as much input* as County Hospital does. There is no evidence that County Hospital is inefficient.

If $E < 1$, the composite hospital requires *less input* to obtain the output achieved by County Hospital. The composite hospital is more efficient; thus, County Hospital can be judged relatively inefficient.

The DEA linear programming model for the efficiency evaluation of County Hospital has five decision variables and eight constraints. The complete model is rewritten below:

$$\text{Min} \qquad E$$

s.t.

$$wg + wu + wc + ws = 1$$

$$48.14wg + 34.62wu + 36.72wc + 33.16ws \geq 36.72$$

$$43.10wg + 27.11wu + 45.98wc + 56.46ws \geq 45.98$$

$$253wg + 148wu + 175wc + 160ws \geq 175$$

$$41wg + 27wu + 23wc + 84ws \geq 23$$

$$-275.50E + 285.20wg + 162.30wu + 275.70wc + 210.40ws \leq 0$$

$$-348.50E + 123.80wg + 128.70wu + 348.50wc + 154.10ws \leq 0$$

$$-104.10E + 106.72wg + 64.21wu + 104.10wc + 104.04ws \leq 0$$

$$E, wg, wu, wc, ws \geq 0$$

Note that in this formulation of the model, we have moved the terms involving E to the left-hand side of the three input constraints because E is a decision variable. The above linear program was solved using The Management Scientist software package. The computer printout of the solution is shown in Figure 4.9.

We first note that the objective function shows that the efficiency score for County Hospital is 0.905. This tells us that the composite hospital can obtain at least the level of each output that County Hospital obtains by having available no more than 90.5% of the input resources required by County Hospital. Thus, the composite hospital is more efficient, and the DEA analysis has identified County Hospital as being relatively inefficient.

From the solution in Figure 4.9, we see that the composite hospital is formed from the weighted average of General Hospital ($wg = 0.212$), University Hospital ($wu = 0.260$), and State Hospital ($ws = 0.527$). Each input and output of the composite hospital is determined by the same weighted average of the inputs and outputs of these three hospitals.

The Slack/Surplus column provides some additional information about the efficiency of County Hospital compared to the composite hospital. Specifically, the composite hospital has at least as much of each output as County Hospital has (constraints 2–5) and provides 1.6 more nurses trained (surplus for constraint 4) and 37 more interns trained (surplus for constraint 5). The slack of zero from constraint 8 shows that the composite hospital uses approximately 90.5% of the bed-days used by County Hospital. The slack

Figure 4.9 The Managment Scientist Solution for the Data Envelopment Analysis County Hospital Problem

```
Objective Function Value =              0.905

        Variable              Value              Reduced Costs
      --------------      --------------      -------------------

             E                0.905                0.000
            WG                0.212                0.000
            WU                0.260                0.000
            WC                0.000                0.095
            WS                0.527                0.000


      Constraint          Slack/Surplus            Dual Prices
      --------------      --------------      -------------------

             1                0.000                0.239
             2                0.000               -0.014
             3                0.000               -0.014
             4                1.615                0.000
             5               37.027                0.000
             6               35.643                0.000
             7              174.422                0.000
             8                0.000                0.010
```

values for constraints 6 and 7 show that less than 90.5% of the FTE nonphysician and the supplies expense resources used at County Hospital are used by the composite hospital.

It is clear that the composite hospital is more efficient than County Hospital and that we are justified in concluding that County Hospital is relatively inefficient compared to the hospitals in the group. Given the results of the DEA analysis, hospital administrators should examine operations to determine how County Hospital resources can be more effectively utilized.

NOTES & COMMENTS

1. Remember that the goal of data envelopment analysis is to identify operating units that are relatively inefficient. The method *does not* necessarily identify the operating units that are *relatively efficient*. Just because the efficiency index is $E = 1$, we cannot conclude that the unit being analyzed is relatively efficient. Indeed, any unit that has the largest output on any one of the output measures cannot be judged relatively inefficient.

2. It is possible for DEA to show all but one unit to be relatively inefficient. Such would be the case if a unit producing the most of every output also consumes the least of every input. Such cases are extremely rare in practice.

3. In applying data envelopment analysis to problems involving a large group of operating units, practitioners have found that roughly 50% of the operating units can be identified as inefficient. Comparing each relatively inefficient unit to the units contributing to the composite unit may be helpful in understanding how the operation of each relatively inefficient unit can be improved.

Summary

In this chapter we presented a broad range of applications that illustrate how linear programming can be used to assist in the decision-making process. We formulated and solved problems from the areas of marketing, finance, and production management, and illustrated how linear programming can be applied to blending problems and the relatively new area of data envelopment analysis.

Many of the illustrations presented in this chapter are scaled-down versions of actual situations where linear programming has been applied. In real-world applications, the problem may not be so concisely stated, the data for the problem may not be as readily available, and the problem will most likely involve more decision variables and/or constraints. However, a thorough study of the applications in this chapter is a good place to begin for an individual who wants to apply linear programming to real-world problems.

Problems

Note to Student: The following problems have been designed to give you an understanding and appreciation of the broad range of problems that can be formulated as linear programs. You should be able to formulate a linear programming model for each of the problems. However, you will need access to a linear programming computer package to develop the solution and make the requested interpretations.

1. *Media selection.* The Westchester Chamber of Commerce periodically sponsors public service seminars and programs. Currently, promotional plans are under way for this year's program. Advertising alternatives include television, radio, and newspaper. Audience estimates, costs, and maximum media usage limitations are shown below.

Constraint	Television	Radio	Newspaper
Audience per advertisement	100,000	18,000	40,000
Cost per advertisement	$2,000	$300	$600
Maximum media usage	10	20	10

To ensure a balanced usage of advertising media, radio advertisements must not exceed 50% of the total number of advertisements authorized. In addition, it has been requested that television account for at least 10% of the total number of advertisements authorized.

a. If the promotional budget is limited to $18,200, how many commercial messages should be run on each medium to maximize total audience contact? What is the allocation of the budget among the three media, and what is the total audience reached?

b. What is the estimated audience contact that would result from an extra $100 allocated to the advertising budget?

2. *Overtime planning.* The Hartman Company is trying to determine how much of each of two products should be produced over the coming planning period. Shown below is information concerning labor availability, labor utilization, and product profitability.

Department	Product (hours/unit)		Labor-Hours Available
	1	2	
A	1.00	0.35	100
B	0.30	0.20	36
C	0.20	0.50	50
Profit contribution/unit	$30.00	$15.00	—

a. Develop a linear programming model of the Hartman Company problem. Solve the model to determine the optimal production quantities of products 1 and 2.

b. In computing the per-unit profit contribution, Hartman does not deduct labor costs because they are considered fixed for the upcoming planning period. However, suppose overtime can be scheduled in some of the departments. Which departments would you recommend scheduling for overtime? How much would you be willing to pay per hour of overtime in each department?

c. Suppose that 10, 6, and 8 hours of overtime may be scheduled in departments A, B, and C, respectively. The cost per hour of overtime is $18 in department A, $22.50 in department B, and $12 in department C. Formulate a linear programming model that can be used to determine the optimal production quantities if overtime is made available. What are the optimal production quantities, and what is the revised total contribution profit? How much overtime do you recommend using in each department? What is the increase in the total contribution to profit if overtime is used?

3. Investment planning

3. *Investment and loan planning.* The employee credit union at State University is planning the allocation of funds for the coming year. The credit union makes four types of loans to its members. In addition, the credit union invests in risk-free securities to stabilize income. The various revenue-producing investments together with annual rates of return are as follows:

Type of Loan/Investment	Annual Rate of Return (%)
Automobile loans	8
Furniture loans	10
Other secured loans	11
Signature loans	12
Risk-free securities	9

The firm will have $2,000,000 available for investment during the coming year. State laws and credit union policies impose the following restrictions on the composition of the credit union's loans and investments:

1. Risk-free securities may not exceed 30% of the total funds available for investment.
2. Signature loans may not exceed 10% of the funds invested in all loans (automobile, furniture, other secured and signature loans).
3. Furniture loans plus other secured loans may not exceed the automobile loans.
4. Other secured loans plus signature loans may not exceed the funds invested in risk-free securities.

How should the $2,000,000 be allocated to each of the loan/investment alternatives to maximize total annual return? What is the projected total annual return?

4. Blending

4. *Quality assurance.* Hilltop Coffee manufactures a coffee product by blending three types of coffee beans. The cost per pound and the available pounds of each bean are as follows:

Bean	Cost Per Pound	Available Pounds
1	$0.50	500
2	$0.70	600
3	$0.45	400

Consumer tests with coffee products were used to provide ratings on a 0-to-100 scale, with higher ratings indicating higher quality. Product quality standards for the blended coffee require a consumer rating for aroma to be at least 75 and a consumer rating for taste to be at least 80. The individual ratings of the aroma and taste for coffee made from 100% of each bean are as follows:

Bean	Aroma Rating	Taste Rating
1	75	86
2	85	88
3	60	75

It can be assumed that the aroma and taste attributes of the coffee blend will be a weighted average of the attributes of the beans used in the blend.

   a. What is the minimum-cost blend that will meet the quality standards and provide 1000 pounds of the blended coffee product?
   b. What is the cost per pound for the coffee blend?
   c. Determine the aroma and taste ratings for the coffee blend.
   d. If additional coffee were to be produced, what would be the expected cost per pound?

5. Blending

5. *Blending problem.* Ajax Fuels, Inc., is developing a new additive for airplane fuels. The additive is a mixture of three ingredients: A, B, and C. For proper performance, the total amount of additive (amount of A + amount of B + amount of C) must be at least 10 ounces per gallon of fuel. However, because of safety reasons, the amount of additive must not exceed 15 ounces per gallon of fuel. The mix or blend of the three ingredients is critical. At least 1 ounce of ingredient A must be used for every ounce of ingredient B. The amount of ingredient C must be greater than one-half the amount of ingredient A. If the cost per ounce for ingredients A, B, and C is $0.10, $0.03, and $0.09, respectively, find the minimum-cost mixture of A, B, and C for each gallon of airplane fuel.

6. Labor planning

6. *Labor planning.* G. Kunz and Sons, Inc., manufactures two products used in the heavy equipment industry. Both products require manufacturing operations in two departments. Production time in hours and profit contribution figures for the two products are as follows:

Product	Profit Per Unit	Labor-Hours	
		Dept. A	Dept. B
1	$25	6	12
2	$20	8	10

For the coming production period, Kunz has available a total of 900 hours of labor that can be allocated to either of the two departments. Find the production plan and labor allocation (hours assigned in each department) that will maximize the total contribution to profit.

7. Transportation

7. *Transportation.* The C&P Company has two manufacturing plants, one located in Kansas City and another in Louisville. Each month's production is shipped to regional warehouses, which store the products until orders are received from customers. The production capacities and the warehouse demands for the coming month are as follows:

Plant	Capacity	Warehouse	Demand
Kansas City	500	Region 1	200
Louisville	400	Region 2	250
		Region 3	300

Transportation costs in dollars per unit shipped are as follows:

	Warehouses		
Plant	Region 1	Region 2	Region 3
Kansas City	2.10	2.25	3.00
Louisville	2.00	2.40	2.80

a. Develop a transportation schedule that will determine the number of units shipped from each plant to each warehouse so that warehouse demands are satisfied at a minimum total transportation cost. (*Note:* The problem is referred to as a transportation problem; transportation problems will be treated further in Chapter 7.)

b. If the production costs are 2.00 per unit at the Kansas City plant and 2.25 per unit at the Louisville plant, how would you revise your transportation schedule to minimize the total production and transportation costs?

8. *Staff scheduling.* The Clark County Sheriff's Department schedules police officers for 8-hour shifts. The beginning times for the shifts are 8:00 A.M., noon, 4:00 P.M., 8:00 P.M., midnight, and 4:00 A.M. An officer beginning a shift at one of the above times works for the next 8 hours. During normal weekday operations, the number of officers needed varies depending on the time of day. The department staffing guidelines require the following minimum number of officers on duty:

Time of Day	Minimum Officers on Duty
8:00 A.M.–noon	5
Noon–4:00 P.M.	6
4:00 P.M.–8:00 P.M.	10
8:00 P.M.–midnight	7
Midnight–4:00 A.M.	4
4:00 A.M.–8:00 A.M.	6

Determine the number of police officers that should be scheduled to begin the 8-hour shifts at each of the six times (8:00 A.M., noon, 4:00 P.M., 8:00 P.M., midnight, and 4:00 A.M.) such that the total number of officers required is minimized. (*Hint:* Let x_1 = the number of officers beginning work at 8:00 A.M., x_2 = the number of officers beginning work at noon, and so on.)

9. *Portfolio selection.* National Insurance Associates carries an investment portfolio of a variety of stocks, bonds, and other investment alternatives. Currently $200,000 of funds are available and must be considered for new investment opportunities. The four stock options National is considering and the relevant financial data are as follows:

	Stock			
Financial Data	A	B	C	D
Price per share	$100	$50	$80	$40
Annual rate of return	0.12	0.08	0.06	0.10
Risk measure per dollar invested	0.10	0.07	0.05	0.08

The risk measure indicates the relative uncertainty associated with the stock in terms of its realizing the projected annual return; higher values indicate greater risk. The risk measures are provided by the firm's top financial advisor.

National's top management has stipulated the following investment guidelines:

1. The annual rate of return for the portfolio must be at least 9%.
2. No one stock can account for more than 50% of the total dollar investment.

a. Use linear programming to develop an investment portfolio that minimizes risk.
b. If the firm ignores risk and uses a maximum return-on-investment strategy, what is the investment portfolio?
c. What is the dollar difference between the portfolios recommended in parts (a) and (b)? Why might the company prefer the model developed in part (a)?

10. *Production routing.* Lurix Electronics manufactures two products that can be produced on two different production lines. Both products have their lowest production costs when produced on the more modern of the two production lines. However, the modern production line does not have the capacity to handle the total production. As a result, some production will have to be routed to the older production line. Shown below are the data for total production requirements, production line capacities, and production costs.

Product	Production Cost/Unit		Minimum Production Requirements
	Modern Line	Old Line	
1	$3.00	$5.00	500 units
2	$2.50	$4.00	700 units
Production line capacities	800	600	

Formulate a linear programming model that can be used to make the production routing decision. What is the recommended decision and the total cost?

11. *Purchasing.* Edwards Manufacturing Company purchases two component parts from three different suppliers. The suppliers have limited capacity, and no one supplier can meet all of the company's needs. In addition, the suppliers differ in the prices charged for the components. Component price data (in price/unit) are as follows:

Component	Supplier		
	1	2	3
1	$12	$13	$14
2	$10	$11	$10

Each supplier has a limited capacity in terms of the total number of components it can supply. However, as long as Edwards provides sufficient advance orders, each supplier can devote its capacity to component 1, component 2, or any combination of the two components, as long as the total number of units ordered is within its capacity. Supplier capacities are as follows:

Supplier	Capacity
1	600
2	1000
3	800

If the Edwards production plan for the next production period includes 1000 units of component 1 and 800 units of component 2, what purchases do you recommend? That is, how many units of each component should be ordered from each supplier? What is the total purchase cost for the components?

12. *Make or buy.* The Carson Stapler Manufacturing Company forecasts a 5000-unit demand for its Sure-Hold model during the next quarter. This stapler is assembled from three major components: base, staple cartridge, and handle. Until now Carson has manufactured all three components. However, the forecast of 5000 units is a new high in sales volume, and it is doubtful that the firm will have sufficient production capacity to make all the components. The company is considering contracting a local firm to produce at least some of the components. The production time requirements per unit are as follows:

Department	Production Time (hours)			Total Available (hours)
	Base	Cartridge	Handle	
A	0.03	0.02	0.05	400
B	0.04	0.02	0.04	400
C	0.02	0.03	0.01	400

After considering the firm's overhead, material, and labor costs, the accounting department has determined the unit manufacturing cost for each component. These data, along with the purchase price quotations by the contracting firm, are as follows:

Component	Manufacturing Cost	Purchase Cost
Base	$0.75	$0.95
Cartridge	$0.40	$0.55
Handle	$1.10	$1.40

a. Determine the make-or-buy decision for Carson that will meet the 5000-unit demand at a minimum total cost. How many units of each component should be made, and how many purchased?

b. Which departments are limiting the manufacturing volume? If overtime could be considered at the additional cost of $3 per hour, which department(s) should be allocated the overtime? Explain.

c. Suppose that up to 80 hours of overtime could be scheduled in department A. What would you recommend?

13. *Work force assignments.* McCarthy's Everyday Glass Company is planning to produce two styles of drinking glasses during the next month. The glasses are processed in four separate departments. The labor-hours per cases produced (one dozen glasses) in each of the four departments are as follows:

Department	Product 1	Product 2
1	0.070	0.100
2	0.050	0.084
3	0.100	0.067
4	0.010	0.025

The company makes a profit of $1.00 per case of product 1 and $0.90 per case of product 2. In making the work force allocations to each department, McCarthy's production manager reviews the cross-training and experience qualifications of the employees. The possible labor assignments and hours of labor available are as follows:

Possible Labor Assignments	Hours of Labor Available
Department 1 only	430
Department 2 only	400
Department 3 only	500
Department 4 only	135
Departments 1 or 2	570
Departments 3 or 4	300
Total	2335

Of the 2335 hours available for the month's production, 870 hours can be assigned with management discretion. Determine the product mix and the work force assignment per department that will maximize profits.

14. *Production scheduling.* The production manager for the Classic Boat Corporation must determine how many units of the Classic 21 model should be produced over the next four quarters. The company has a beginning inventory of 100 Classic 21 boats, and demand for the four quarters is 2000 units in quarter 1, 4000 units in quarter 2, 3000 units in quarter 3, and 1500 units in quarter 4. The firm has limited production capacity in each quarter. That is, up to 4000 units can be produced in quarter 1, 3000 units in quarter 2, 2000 units in quarter 3, and 4000 units in quarter 4. Each boat that is held in inventory in quarters 1 and 2 incurs an inventory holding cost of $250 per unit; the holding cost for quarters 3 and 4 is $300 per unit. The production costs for the first quarter are $10,000 per unit; these costs are estimated to increase by 10% each quarter because of increases in labor and material costs. Management has specified that the ending inventory for quarter 4 must be at least 500 boats.

a. Formulate a linear programming model that can be used to determine the production schedule that will minimize the total cost of meeting demand in each quarter subject to the production capacities in each quarter and also to the required ending inventory in quarter 4.

   b. Solve the linear program formulated in part (a); then develop a table that will show for each quarter the number of units to manufacture, the ending inventory, and the costs incurred.
   c. Interpret each of the dual prices corresponding to the constraints developed to meet demand in each quarter. What advice would you give the production manager given these dual prices?
   d. Interpret each of the dual prices corresponding to the production capacity in each quarter. What advice would you give the production manager given each of these dual prices?

SELF TEST ▷ **15.** *Blending.* Seastrand Oil Company produces two grades of gasoline: regular and high octane. Both gasolines are produced by blending two types of crude oil. Although both types of crude oil contain the two important ingredients required to produce both gasolines, the percentage of important ingredients in each type of crude oil differs, as does the cost per gallon. The percentage of ingredients A and B in each type of crude oil and the cost per gallon are shown below.

15. Blending

Crude Oil	Cost	Ingredient A	Ingredient B	
1	$0.10	20%	60%	Crude oil 1 is 60% ingredient B
2	$0.15	50%	30%	

Each gallon of regular gasoline must contain at least 40% of ingredient A, whereas each gallon of high octane can contain at most 50% of ingredient B. Daily demand for regular- and high-octane gasoline is 800,000 and 500,000 gallons, respectively. How many gallons of each type of crude oil should be used in the two gasolines to satisfy daily demand at a minimum cost?

16. Cutting stock

16. *Cutting stock.* The Ferguson Paper Company produces rolls of paper for use in adding machines, desk calculators, and cash registers. The rolls, which are 200 feet long, are produced in widths of $1\frac{1}{2}$, $2\frac{1}{2}$, and $3\frac{1}{2}$ inches. The production process provides 200-foot rolls in 10-inch widths only. The firm must therefore cut the rolls to the desired final product sizes. The seven cutting alternatives and the amount of waste generated by each are as follows:

Cutting Alternative	Number of Rolls			Waste (inches)
	$1\frac{1}{2}$ in.	$2\frac{1}{2}$ in.	$3\frac{1}{2}$ in.	
1	6	0	0	1
2	0	4	0	0
3	2	0	2	0
4	0	1	2	$\frac{1}{2}$
5	1	3	0	1
6	1	2	1	0
7	4	0	1	$\frac{1}{2}$

The minimum requirements for the three products are as follows:

Roll Width (inches)	Units
1½	1000
2½	2000
3½	4000

a. If the company wants to minimize the number of 10-inch rolls that must be manufactured, how many 10-inch rolls will be processed on each cutting alternative? How many rolls are required, and what is the total waste (inches)?

b. If the company wants to minimize the waste generated, how many 10-inch units will be processed on each cutting alternative? How many rolls are required, and what is the total waste (inches)?

c. What are the differences in approaches (a) and (b) to this problem? In this case, which objective do you prefer? Explain. What are the types of situations that would make the other objective more desirable?

17. *Inspection.* The Carole Pill Company inspects capsule medicine products by passing the capsules over a special lighting table where inspectors visually check for cracked or partially filled capsules. Currently, any of three inspectors can be assigned to the visual inspection task. The inspectors, however, differ in accuracy and speed abilities and are paid at slightly different wage rates. The differences are as follows:

Inspector	Speed (units/hour)	Accuracy (%)	Hourly Wage
Davis	300	98	$5.90
Wilson	200	99	$5.20
Lawson	350	96	$5.50

Operating on a full 8-hour shift, the company needs at least 2000 capsules inspected with no more than 2% of these capsules having inspection errors. In addition, because of the fatigue factor of this inspection process, no one inspector can be assigned this task for more than 4 hours per day. How many hours should each inspector be assigned to the capsule inspection process during an 8-hour day to minimize the cost of inspection? What volume will be inspected per day, and what is the daily capsule inspection cost?

18. *Equipment acquisition.* The Two-Rivers Oil Company near Pittsburgh transports gasoline to its distributors by trucks. The company has recently contracted to supply gasoline distributors in southern Ohio, and it has $600,000 available to spend on the necessary expansion of its fleet of gasoline tank trucks. Three models of gasoline tank trucks are available:

Truck Model	Capacity (gallons)	Purchase Cost	Monthly Operating Cost, Including Depreciation
Super Tanker	5000	$67,000	$550
Regular Line	2500	$55,000	$425
Econo-Tanker	1000	$46,000	$350

The company estimates that the monthly demand for the region will be 550,000 gallons of gasoline. Due to the size and speed differences of the trucks, the different truck models will vary in terms of the number of deliveries or round trips possible per month. Trip capacities are estimated at 15 trips per month for the Super Tanker, 20 trips per month for the Regular Line, and 25 trips per month for the Econo-Tanker. Based on maintenance and driver availability, the firm does not want to add more than 15 new vehicles to its fleet. In addition, the company has decided to purchase at least three of the new Econo-Tankers for use on the short-run low-demand routes. As a final constraint, the company does not want more than half of the new models to be Super Tankers.

a. If the company wishes to satisfy the gasoline demand with a minimum monthly operating expense, how many models of each truck should be purchased?

b. If the company did not require at least three Econo-Tankers and did not limit the number of Super Tankers to at most half of the new models, how many models of each truck should be purchased?

SELF TEST ▶ **19.** *Multiperiod planning.* The Silver Star Bicycle Company will be manufacturing both men's and women's models for their Easy-Pedal 10-speed bicycles during the next 2 months. The company would like to develop a production schedule indicating how many bicycles of each model should be produced in each month. Current demand forecasts call for 150 men's and 125 women's models to be shipped during the first month and 200 men's and 150 women's models to be shipped during the second month. Additional data are shown below.

19. Production scheduling

Model	Production Costs	Labor Requirements (hours)		Current Inventory
		Manufacturing	Assembly	
Men's	$120	2.0	1.5	20
Women's	$ 90	1.6	1.0	30

Last month the company used a total of 1000 hours of labor. The company's labor relations policy will not allow the combined total hours of labor (manufacturing plus assembly) to increase or decrease by more than 100 hours from month to month. In addition, the company charges monthly inventory at the rate of 2% of the production cost based on the inventory levels at the end of the month. The company would like to have at least 25 units of each model in inventory at the end of the 2 months.

a. Establish a production schedule that minimizes production and inventory costs and satisfies the labor-smoothing, demand, and inventory requirements. What inventories will be maintained, and what are the monthly labor requirements?

b. If the company changed the constraints so that monthly labor increases and decreases could not exceed 50 hours, what would happen to the production schedule? How much will the cost increase? What would you recommend?

20. *Labor balancing.* The Williams Calculator Company manufactures two kinds of calculators: the TW100 and the TW200. The assembly process requires three people. The assembly times are as follows:

	Calculator		Maximum Labor Available
Assembler	**TW100**	**TW200**	**(hrs/day)**
1	4 min	3 min	8
2	2 min	4 min	8
3	3½ min	3 min	8

The company policy is to balance workloads on all assembly jobs. In fact, management wants to schedule work so that no assembler will have more than 30 minutes more work per day than other assemblers. This means that in a regular 8-hour shift, all assemblers will be assigned at least 7½ hours of work. If the firm makes a $2.50 profit for each TW100 and a $3.50 profit for each TW200, how many units of each calculator should be produced per day? How much time will each assembler be assigned per day?

21. *Multiperiod production and inventory planning.* Multiperiod production and inventory planning models determine a production schedule and an ending inventory schedule for each of several periods that will achieve a goal of maximizing profit or minimizing cost. Considering selling price, regular production costs, overtime costs, inventory carrying costs, and lost sales costs, develop a three-period production and inventory planning model for Allen Manufacturing Company. Relevant information is as follows:

Period	Selling Price Per Unit	Production Cost Per Unit	Demand	Ending Inventory Cost Per Unit
1	$5.00	$2.80	500	$0.50
2	$5.00	$2.90	300	$0.50
3	$5.50	$3.00	400	$0.55

	Production Capacity (units)	
Period	**Regular**	**Overtime**
1	250	100
2	300	100
3	300	125

The overtime cost per unit in each period is 20% greater than the production cost per unit shown above. The lost sales cost, which is $4 per unit in any period, accounts for lost customer goodwill, but does not account for the cost associated with the lost revenue. The beginning inventory for period 1 is 100 units. In addition, the firm would like to have at least 50 units in ending inventory for period 3 to prepare for period 4.

To account for the multiperiod aspects of the problem, each period t will require balance equations or constraints based on the following relationships:

$$\text{Lost sales } (t) = \text{demand } (t) - \text{sales } (t)$$

$$\text{Ending inventory } (t) = \text{beginning inventory } (t) + \text{production } (t) - \text{sales } (t)$$

Develop a linear program that can be used to determine the optimal production and inventory schedule for Allen Manufacturing. Determine the sales, regular production, overtime production, ending inventory, and lost sales for each of the three periods. What is the net profit associated with your solution?

22. Multiperiod financial planning

22. *Multiperiod financial planning.* The Morton Financial Instituion must decide what percentage of available funds to commit to each of two investments, referred to as A and B, over the next four periods. The following table shows the amount of new funds available for each of the four periods, as well as the cash expenditure required for each investment (negative values) or the cash income from the investment (positive values). Data shown are in thousands of dollars, and reflect the amount of expenditure or income if 100% of the funds available in any period are invested in either A or B. For example, if Morton elects to invest 100% of the funds available in any period in investment A, they will incur cash expenditures of $1,000 in month 1, $800 in month 2, $200 in month 3, and income of $200 in month 4. Note, however, if Morton made the decision to invest 80% in investment A, the cash expenditures or income would be 80% of the values shown.

Period	New Investment Funds Available	Investment A	Investment B
1	1500	−1000	−800
2	400	−800	−500
3	500	−200	−300
4	100	200	300

The amount of funds available in any period is the sum of the new investment funds for the period, the new loan funds, the savings from the previous period, the cash income from investment A, and the cash income from investment B. The funds available in any period can be used to pay the loan and interest from the previous period, placed in savings, used to pay the cash expenditures for investment A, or used to pay the cash expenditures for investment B.

Assume an interest rate of 10% per period for savings and an interest rate of 18% per period on borrowed funds. Let

$S(t)$ = the savings for period t
$L(t)$ = the new loan funds for period t

Then, in any period t, the savings income from the previous period is $1.1S(t-1)$ and the loan and interest expenditure from the previous period is $1.18L(t-1)$.

At the end of period 4, investment A is expected to have a cash value of $3200 (assuming a 100% investment in A), while investment B is expected to have a cash value of $2500 (assuming a 100% investment in B). Additional income and expenses at the end of period 4 will be income from savings in period 4 less the repayment of the period 4 loan plus interest.

Suppose the decision variables are defined as follows:

x_1 = the proportion of investment A undertaken
x_2 = the proportion of investment B undertaken

For example, if $x_1 = 0.5$, we would invest $500 in investment A during the first period, and all remaining cash flows and ending investment A values would be multiplied by 0.5. The same holds for investment B. The model must include constraints $x_1 \leq 1$ and $x_2 \leq 1$ to make sure that at most 100% of the investments can be undertaken.

If at most $200 can be borrowed in any period, determine the proportions of investments A and B and the amount of savings and borrowing in each period that will maximize the cash value for the firm at the end of the four periods.

Time	Total Number of Employees
11:00 A.M.–noon	9
Noon–1:00 P.M.	9
1:00 P.M.–2:00 P.M.	9
2:00 P.M.–3:00 P.M.	3
3:00 P.M.–4:00 P.M.	3
4:00 P.M.–5:00 P.M.	3
5:00 P.M.–6:00 P.M.	6
6:00 P.M.–7:00 P.M.	12
7:00 P.M.–8:00 P.M.	12
8:00 P.M.–9:00 P.M.	7
9:00 P.M.–10:00 P.M.	7

23. *Staff scheduling.* Western Family Steakhouse offers a variety of low-cost meals and quick service. Other than management, the steakhouse operates with two full-time employees who work 8 hours per day. The rest of the employees are part-time employees who are scheduled for 4-hour shifts during peak meal times. On Saturdays the steakhouse is open from 11:00 A.M. to 10:00 P.M. Management would like to develop a schedule for part-time employees that will minimize labor costs and still provide excellent customer service. The average wage rate for the part-time employees is $4.60 per hour. The total number of full-time and part-time employees needed varies with the time of the day as shown in the margin table at the left.

One of the full-time employees comes on duty at 11:00 A.M., works 4 hours, takes an hour off, and returns for another 4 hours. The other full-time employee comes to work at 1:00 P.M. and works the same 4-hour-on, 1-hour-off, 4-hour-on pattern.

a. Develop a minimum-cost schedule for part-time employees.

b. What is the total payroll for the part-time employees? How many part-time shifts are needed? Use the surplus variables to comment on the desirability of scheduling at least some of the part-time employees for 3-hour shifts.

c. Assume part-time employees can be assigned either a 3-hour or 4-hour shift. Develop a minimum-cost schedule for the part-time employees. How many part-time shifts are needed, and what is the cost savings compared with the previous schedule?

24. *Interpretation of computer output.* Shown in Figure 4.10 is a portion of the computer output when The Management Scientist is used to solve the media selection problem for the Relax-and-Enjoy Lake Development Corporation (see Section 4.1).

a. How much would the exposure increase per dollar added to the budget? Given the current budget, what is the average exposure per advertising dollar? Does the marginal return from enlarging the budget seem to make enlarging the budget a good investment?

b. From an analysis of the dual prices, comment on whether or not the television commercials are a good idea.

25. *Hospital efficiency analysis.* In Section 4.5 data envelopment analysis was used to evaluate the relative efficiencies of four hospitals. Data for three input measures and four output measures were provided in Tables 4.16 and 4.17.

a. Use these data to develop a linear programming model that could be used to evaluate the performance of General Hospital.

b. The computer solution obtained using The Management Scientist is shown below. Does the solution indicate that General Hospital is relatively inefficient?

c. Which hospital or hospitals make up the composite unit used to evaluate General Hospital? State why this is true.

```
Objective Function Value =   1.000000
```

Variable	Value	Reduced Costs
E	1.000	0.000
WG	1.000	0.000
WU	0.000	0.000
WC	0.000	0.331
WS	0.000	0.215

Figure 4.10

```
Objective Function Value =          2370.000

       Variable              Value            Reduced Costs
    --------------       --------------      ------------------

         X1                 10.000                0.000
         X2                  0.000               65.000
         X3                 25.000                0.000
         X4                  2.000                0.000
         X5                 30.000                0.000


      Constraint         Slack/Surplus          Dual Prices
    --------------       --------------      ------------------

          1                  5.000                0.000
          2                 10.000                0.000
          3                  0.000               16.000
          4                  2.000                0.000
          5                  0.000               14.000
          6                  0.000                0.060
          7                  0.000              -25.000
          8               3000.000                0.000
          9              11500.003                0.000
```

Media
Availability

Budget

Television
Restrictions

Audience
Coverage

26. Hospital efficiency analysis

26. *Hospital efficiency analysis.* Data envelopment analysis has been used to measure the relative efficiency of a group of hospitals (H. David Sherman, "Hospital Efficiency Measurement and Evaluation," *Medical Care* (October 1984)). Sherman's study involved seven teaching hospitals; data on three input measures are contained in Table 4.18, and data on four output measures are contained in Table 4.19.

a. Formulate a linear programming model so that data envelopment analysis can be used to evaluate the performance of hospital D.

b. Solve the model using a computer software package.

Table 4.18
Annual Resources Consumed for
Seven Hospitals

Hospital	Full-Time Equivalent Nonphysicians	Supply Expense ($1000's)	Bed-Days Available (1000's)
A	310.0	134.60	116.00
B	278.5	114.30	106.80
C	165.6	131.30	65.52
D	250.0	316.00	94.40
E	206.4	151.20	102.10
F	384.0	217.00	153.70
G	530.1	770.80	215.00

Table 4.19
Annual Services Provided for Seven Hospitals

Hospital	Patient-Days (65 or older) (000's)	Patient-Days (under 65) (000's)	Nurses Trained	Interns Trained
A	55.31	49.52	291	47
B	37.64	55.63	156	3
C	32.91	25.77	141	26
D	33.53	41.99	160	21
E	32.48	55.30	157	82
F	48.78	81.92	285	92
G	58.41	119.70	111	89

    c. Is hospital D relatively inefficient? What is the interpretation of the value of the objective function?

    d. How many patient-days of each type are produced by the composite hospital?

    e. Which hospitals would you recommend hospital D consider emulating to improve the efficiency of its operation?

27. Hospital efficiency analysis

27. *Hospital efficiency analysis.* Refer again to the data presented in Problem 26.

    a. Formulate a linear programming model that can be used to perform data envelopment analysis for hospital E.

    b. Solve the model using a computer software package.

    c. Is hospital E relatively inefficient? What is the interpretation of the value of the objective function?

    d. Which hospitals are involved in making up the composite hospital? Can you make a general statement about which hospitals will make up the composite unit associated with a unit that is not inefficient?

28. Restaurant efficiency analysis

28. *Efficiency of fast-food restaurants.* The Ranch House, Inc., operates five fast-food restaurants. Input measures for the restaurants include weekly hours of operation, full-time equivalent staff, and weekly supply expenses. Output measures of performance include average weekly contribution to profit, market share, and annual growth rate. Data for the input and output measures are shown in Tables 4.20 and 4.21.

    a. Develop a linear programming model that can be used to evaluate the performance of the Clarksville Ranch House restaurant.

    b. Solve the model using a computer software package.

    c. Is the Clarksville Ranch House restaurant relatively inefficient? Discuss.

    d. Where does the composite restaurant have more output than the Clarksville restaurant? How much less of each input resource does the composite restaurant require when compared to the Clarksville restaurant?

    e. What other restaurants should be studied to find suggested ways for the Clarksville restaurant to improve its efficiency?

Table 4.20
Input Data for Five Fast-Food Restaurants

Restaurant	Hours of Operation	FTE Staff	Supplies ($)
Bardstown	96	16	850
Clarksville	110	22	1400
Jeffersonville	100	18	1200
New Albany	125	25	1500
St. Matthews	120	24	1600

Table 4.21
Output Data for Five Fast-Food Restaurants

Restaurant	Weekly Profit	Market Share (%)	Growth Rate (%)
Bardstown	$3800	25	8.0
Clarksville	$4600	32	8.5
Jeffersonville	$4400	35	8.0
New Albany	$6500	30	10.0
St. Matthews	$6000	28	9.0

Case Problem: Environmental Protection

Skillings Industrial Chemicals, Inc., operates a refinery in southwestern Ohio near the Ohio River. The company's primary product is manufactured from a chemical process that requires the use of two raw materials denoted as material A and material B. The production of 1 pound of the finished product requires the use of 1 pound of material A and 2 pounds of material B. The output of the chemical process is 1 pound of finished product, 1 pound of liquid waste material, and 1 pound of solid waste by-product. The solid waste by-product is given to a local fertilizer plant as payment for picking it up and disposing of it. Since the liquid waste material has no market value, the refinery has been dumping it directly into the Ohio River. The company's manufacturing process is shown schematically in Figure 4.11.

Governmental pollution guidelines established by the Environmental Protection Agency will not permit disposal of the liquid waste directly into the river. The refinery's research group has developed the following set of alternative uses for the liquid waste material:

1. Produce a secondary product K by adding 1 pound of raw material A to every pound of liquid waste.
2. Produce a secondary product M by adding 1 pound of raw material B to every pound of liquid waste.
3. Specially treat the liquid waste so that it meets pollution standards before dumping it into the river.

These three alternatives are depicted in Figure 4.12.

Figure 4.11
Manufacturing Process at Skillings Industrial Chemicals, Inc.

Figure 4.12
Alternatives for Handling the
Refinery Liquid Waste

The company's management knows that the secondary products will be low in quality and may not be very profitable. However, management is also aware of the fact that the special treatment alternative will be a relatively expensive operation. The company's problem is to determine how to satisfy the pollution regulations and still maintain the highest possible profit. How should the liquid waste material be handled? Should Skillings produce product K, produce product M, use the special treatment, or employ some combination of the three alternatives?

Last month 10,000 pounds of the company's primary product were produced. The accounting department has prepared a cost report showing the breakdown of fixed and variable expenses that were incurred during the month.

Cost Analysis for 10,000 Pounds of Primary Product

Fixed costs	
Administrative expenses	$12,000
Refinery overhead	4,000
Variable costs	
Raw material A	15,000
Raw material B	16,000
Direct labor	5,000
Total	$52,000

In the above cost analysis, the fixed-cost portion of the expenses is the same every month regardless of production level. Direct labor costs are expected to run $0.20 per pound for product K and $0.10 per pound for product M.

The company's primary product sells for $5.70 per pound. Secondary products K and M sell for $0.85 and $0.65 per pound, respectively. The special treatment of the liquid waste will cost $0.25 per pound.

One of the company's accountants feels that product K is too expensive to manufacture and cannot be sold at a price that recovers its material and labor cost. The accountant's recommendation is to eliminate product K as an alternative.

For the upcoming production period, 5000 pounds of raw material A and 7000 pounds of raw material B will be available. Develop a production and waste disposal plan for the production period.

Managerial Report

Develop an approach to the problem that will allow the company to determine how much primary product to produce, given the limitations on the amounts of the raw material available. Include recommendations as to how the company should dispose of the liquid waste to satisfy the environmental protection guidelines. How many pounds of product K should be produced? How many pounds of product M should be produced? How many pounds of liquid waste should be specially treated and dumped into the river? Include a discussion and analysis of the following in your report:

1. A cost analysis showing the profit contribution per pound for the primary product, product K, and product M.
2. The optimal production quantities and waste disposal plan, including the projected profit.
3. A discussion of the value of additional pounds of each raw material.
4. A discussion of the sensitivity analysis of the objective function coefficients.
5. Comments on the accountant's recommendation to eliminate product K as an alternative. Does the recommendation appear reasonable? What is your reaction to the recommendation? How would the optimal solution change if product K were eliminated?

Case Problem: Investment Strategy

J. D. Williams, Inc., is an investment advisory firm that manages over $120 million in funds for its numerous clients. The company employs an asset allocation model that recommends the portion of each client's portfolio that should be invested in a growth stock fund, an income fund, and a money market fund. To maintain diversity in each client's portfolio, the firm places limits on the percentage of each portfolio that may be invested in each of the three funds. General guidelines indicate that the amount invested in the growth fund must be between 20 and 40% of the total portfolio value. Similar percentages for the other two funds stipulate that between 20 and 50% of the total portfolio value must be in the income fund and at least 30% of the total portfolio value must be in the money market fund.

In addition, the company attempts to assess the risk tolerance of each client and adjust the portfolio to meet the needs of the individual investor. For example, Williams has just contracted with a new client who has $800,000 to invest. Based on their evaluation of the client's risk tolerance, Williams has assigned a maximum risk index of 0.05 for the client. The firm's risk indicators show the risk of the growth fund at 0.10, the income fund at 0.07, and the money market fund at 0.01. An overall portfolio risk index is computed as a weighted average of the risk rating for the three funds where the weights are the fraction of the client's portfolio invested in each of the funds.

Additionally, Williams is currently forecasting annual yields of 18% for the growth fund, 12.5% for the income fund, and 7.5% for the money market fund. Given the information provided, how should the new client be advised to allocate the $800,000 among the growth, income, and money market funds? Develop a linear programming model that will provide the maximum yield for the portfolio. Use your model to develop a managerial report as described below.

Managerial Report

1. Recommend how much of the $800,000 should be invested in each of the three funds. What is the annual yield you anticipate for the investment recommendation?
2. Assume the client's risk index could be increased to 0.055. How much would the yield increase and how would the investment recommendation change?
3. Refer again to the original situation where the client's risk index was assessed to be 0.05. How would your investment recommendation change if the annual yield for the growth fund were revised downward to 16% or even to 14%?

4. Assume that the client has expressed some concern about having too much money in the growth fund. How would the original recommendation change if the amount invested in the growth fund is not allowed to exceed the amount invested in the income fund?

5. The asset allocation model you have developed may be useful in modifying the portfolios for all of the firm's clients whenever the anticipated yields for the three funds are periodically revised. What is your recommendation as to whether or not this is possible?

Case Problem: Textile Mill Scheduling

The Scottsville Textile Mill[1] produces five different fabrics. Each fabric can be woven on one or more of the mill's 38 looms. The sales department has forecast demand for the next month. The demand data are shown in Table 4.22 along with data on the selling price per yard, variable cost per yard, and purchase price per yard. The mill operates 24 hours per day and is scheduled for 30 days during the coming month.

Table 4.22

Monthly Demand, Selling Price, Variable Cost, and Purchase Price Data for Scottsville Fabrics

Fabric	Demand (yards)	Selling Price ($/yard)	Variable Cost ($/yard)	Purchase Price ($/yard)
1	16,500	0.99	0.66	0.80
2	22,000	0.86	0.55	0.70
3	62,000	1.10	0.49	0.60
4	7,500	1.24	0.51	0.70
5	62,000	0.70	0.50	0.70

The mill has two types of looms: dobbie and regular. The dobbie looms are more versatile and can be used for all five fabrics. The regular looms can produce only three of the fabrics. There are a total of 38 looms—8 dobbie and 30 regular. The rate of production for each fabric on each type of loom is given in Table 4.23. The time required to change over from producing one fabric to another is negligible and does not have to be considered.

The Scottsville Textile Mill satisfies all demand with either its own fabric or with fabric purchased from another mill. That is, fabrics that cannot be woven at the Scottsville Mill because of limited loom capacity will be purchased from another mill. The purchase price of each fabric is also shown in Table 4.22.

Table 4.23

Loom Production Rates for the Scottsville Textile Mill

Fabric	Loom Rate (yards/hour)	
	Dobbie	Regular
1	4.63	*
2	4.63	*
3	5.23	5.23
4	5.23	5.23
5	4.17	4.17

*Fabrics 1 and 2 can be manufactured only on the dobbie loom.

Managerial Report

Develop a model that can be used to schedule production for the Scottsville Textile Mill, and at the same time, determine how many yards of each fabric must be purchased from another mill. Include a discussion and analysis of the following in your report:

1. The final production schedule and loom assignments for each fabric.
2. The projected total contribution to profit.
3. A discussion of the value of additional loom time. The mill is considering purchasing a ninth dobbie loom. What is your estimate of the monthly profit contribution of this additional loom?
4. A discussion of the ranges for the objective function coefficients.
5. A discussion of how the objective of minimizing total costs would provide a different model than the objective of maximizing total profit contribution. How would the interpretation of the ranges for the objective function coefficients differ for these two models?

---

[1]This case is based on the Calhoun Textile Mill Case by Jeffrey D. Camm, P. M. Dearing, and Suresh K. Tadisina, 1987.

MANAGEMENT SCIENCE IN PRACTICE

Marathon Oil Company*

Findlay, Ohio

Marathon Oil Company was founded in 1887 when 14 oilmen pooled their properties to organize an oil-producing company in the Trenton Rock oil fields of Ohio. In 1924 Marathon entered the refining and marketing phase of the petroleum industry. Today Marathon is a fully integrated oil company with significant international operations. In the United States the company markets petroleum products in 21 states, primarily in the Midwest and Southeast. Marathon is a unit of USX.

Management Science at Marathon Oil Company

Marathon Oil's Operations Research Department was formed in 1963 in order to aid problem solving and decision making in all areas of the company. Approximately 50% of the applications involve linear programming. Typical problems include refinery models, distribution models, gasoline and fuel oil blending models, and crude oil evaluation studies. Another 30% of the applications involve complex chemical engineering simulation models of process operations. The remainder of the management science applications involves solution techniques using nonlinear programming, network flow algorithms, and statistical techniques such as regression analysis.

A Marketing Planning Model

Marathon Oil Company has four refineries within the United States, operates 50 light products terminals, and has product demand at over 95 locations. The Supply and Transportation Division is faced with the problem of determining which refinery should supply which terminal and, at the same time, determining which products should be transported via which pipeline, barge, or tanker in order to achieve a minimum cost. Product demand must be satisfied, and the supply capability of each refinery must not be exceeded. To help solve this difficult problem, Marathon's Operations Research Department developed a marketing planning model for the Operations Planning Department.

The marketing planning model is a large-scale linear programming model that takes into account sales not only at Marathon product terminals but also at all exchange locations. An exchange contract is an agreement with other oil product marketers that involves exchanging or trading Marathon's products for theirs at different locations. Thus, some geographic imbalance between supply and demand can be reduced. Both sides of the exchanges are represented since this not only affects the net requirements at a demand location, but in addition has important financial implications. All pipelines, barges, and tankers within Marathon's marketing area are also represented in the linear programming model. The objective of the linear programming model is to minimize the cost of meeting a given demand structure, taking into account sales price, pipeline tariffs, exchange contract costs, product demand, terminal operating costs, refining costs, and product purchases.

The marketing planning model is used to solve a wide variety of planning problems. These vary from evaluating gasoline blending economics to analyzing the economics of a new terminal or pipeline. Although the types of problems that can be solved are almost unlimited, the model is most effective in handling the following:

1. Evaluating additional product demand locations, pipelines, and exchange contracts
2. Determining profitability of shifting sales from one product demand location to another
3. Determining the effects on supply and distribution when a pipeline increases its tariff
4. Optimizing production of the grades at the five refineries based on distribution

The linear programming model not only solves these problems, but also gives the financial impact of each solution.

Benefits

With daily sales of about 10 million gallons of refined light product, a saving of even one-thousandth of a cent per gallon can result in significant long-term savings. At the same time, what may appear to be a savings in one area, such as refining or transportation, may actually add to overall costs when the effects are fully realized throughout the system. The marketing planning model allows a simultaneous examination of this total effect.

Questions

1. What is the primary objective of Marathon's marketing planning model?
2. Describe the types of problems the marketing planning model is most effective in handling.
3. If daily savings using the model are one-tenth of a cent per gallon sold, what is the projected daily savings?

---

*The authors are indebted to Robert W. Wernert of Marathon Oil Company, Findlay, Ohio, for providing this application.

CHAPTER 5

Linear Programming: The Simplex Method

The simplex method was developed by George Dantzig while working for the U.S. Air Force. It was first published in 1949.

In Chapter 2 we showed how the graphical solution procedure can be used to solve linear programming problems involving two decision variables. However, most linear programming problems are too large to be solved graphically, and an algebraic solution procedure must be employed. The most widely used algebraic procedure for solving linear programming problems is called the *simplex method*.[1] Computer programs based on this method can routinely solve linear programming problems with thousands of variables and constraints.

5.1 An Algebraic Overview of the Simplex Method

Let us introduce the problem we will use to demonstrate the simplex method. HighTech Industries imports electronic components that are used to assemble two different models of personal computers. One model is called the HT Deskpro Computer, and the other model is called the HT Portable Computer. HighTech's management is currently interested in developing a weekly production schedule for both products.

The Deskpro generates a profit contribution of $50 per unit, and the Portable generates a profit contribution of $40 per unit. For next week's production, a maximum of 150 hours of assembly time can be made available. Each unit of the Deskpro requires 3 hours of assembly time, and each unit of the Portable requires 5 hours of assembly time. In addition, HighTech currently has only 20 Portable display components in inventory; thus, no more than 20 units of the Portable may be assembled. Finally, only 300 square feet of warehouse space can be made available for new production. Assembly of each Deskpro requires 8 square feet of warehouse space; similarly, each Portable requires 5 square feet.

---

[1] N. Karmarkar, at Bell Labs, has developed a linear programming solution procedure that may eventually supersede the simplex method. Some results indicate it is better for very large problems, but at this time, the simplex method is by far the most widely used.

To develop a linear programming model for the HighTech problem, we will use the following decision variables:

$$x_1 = \text{number of units of the Deskpro assembled}$$
$$x_2 = \text{number of units of the Portable assembled}$$

The complete mathematical model for this problem is presented below.

Max $50x_1 + 40x_2$

s.t.

$$3x_1 + 5x_2 \leq 150 \quad \text{Assembly time}$$
$$1x_2 \leq 20 \quad \text{Portable display}$$
$$8x_1 + 5x_2 \leq 300 \quad \text{Warehouse capacity}$$
$$x_1, x_2 \geq 0$$

Adding a slack variable to each of the constraints permits us to write the problem in standard form.

$$\text{Max} \quad 50x_1 + 40x_2 + 0s_1 + 0s_2 + 0s_3 \tag{5.1}$$

s.t.

$$3x_1 + 5x_2 + 1s_1 \qquad\qquad = 150 \tag{5.2}$$
$$1x_2 \qquad + 1s_2 \qquad = 20 \tag{5.3}$$
$$8x_1 + 5x_2 \qquad\qquad + 1s_3 = 300 \tag{5.4}$$
$$x_1, x_2, s_1, s_2, s_3 \geq 0 \tag{5.5}$$

Algebraic Properties of the Simplex Method

Constraint equations (5.2) to (5.4) form a system of three simultaneous linear equations with five variables. When a set of simultaneous linear equations has more variables than constraints, one can expect an infinite number of solutions. The simplex method can be viewed as an algebraic procedure for finding the best solution to such a system of equations. In the process, any solutions not satisfying the nonnegativity conditions given by equation (5.5) are eliminated.

Determining a Basic Solution

Since the HighTech Industries constraint equations have more variables (five) than equations (three), the simplex method finds solutions for these equations by assigning zero values to two of the variables and then solving for the values of the remaining three variables. For example, if we set $x_2 = 0$ and $s_1 = 0$, the system of constraint equations becomes

$$3x_1 \qquad\qquad = 150 \tag{5.6}$$
$$1s_2 \qquad = 20 \tag{5.7}$$
$$8x_1 \qquad + 1s_3 = 300 \tag{5.8}$$

By setting $x_2 = 0$ and $s_1 = 0$, we have reduced the system of three simultaneous linear equations with five variables to a system of three equations with three variables (x_1, s_2, and s_3).

Using equation (5.6) to solve for x_1, we have

$$3x_1 = 150$$

and hence $x_1 = 150/3 = 50$. Equation (5.7) provides $s_2 = 20$. Finally, substituting $x_1 = 50$ into equation (5.8) results in

$$8(50) + 1s_3 = 300$$

Solving for s_3, we obtain $s_3 = -100$.

Thus, we have obtained the following solution to the three-equation, five-variable set of linear equations determined by the HighTech constraints:

$$
\begin{aligned}
x_1 &= & 50 \\
x_2 &= & 0 \\
s_1 &= & 0 \\
s_2 &= & 20 \\
s_3 &= & -100
\end{aligned}
$$

The above solution is referred to as a *basic solution* for the HighTech linear programming problem. To provide a general procedure for determining a basic solution, we must consider a standard-form linear programming problem consisting of n variables (including decision variables, slack variables, and surplus variables) and m linear equations, where n is greater than m.

It is not always possible to find a unique solution to a set of m linear equations in m variables. However, the use of slack, surplus, and artificial variables guarantees that this will not occur when employing the simplex method.

> ### BASIC SOLUTION
>
> To determine a basic solution, set $n - m$ of the variables equal to zero, and solve the m linear constraint equations for the remaining m variables.[2]

In terms of the HighTech problem, a basic solution can be obtained by setting any two variables equal to zero and then solving the system of three linear equations for the remaining three variables. We shall refer to the $n - m$ variables set equal to zero as the *nonbasic variables* and the remaining m variables (allowed to be nonzero) as the *basic variables*. Thus, in the example above, x_2 and s_1 are the nonbasic variables, and x_1, s_2, and s_3 are the basic variables.

Basic Feasible Solutions

A basic solution can be either feasible or infeasible. A *basic feasible solution* is a basic solution that also satisfies the nonnegativity conditions. The basic solution found by setting x_2 and s_1 equal to zero and then solving for x_1, s_2, and s_3 is not a feasible solution because $s_3 = -100$. However, suppose that we had chosen to make x_1 and x_2 nonbasic variables by setting, $x_1 = 0$ and $x_2 = 0$. Solving for the corresponding basic solution is easy because with $x_1 = x_2 = 0$, the three constraint equations reduce to

---

[2]There are cases where a unique solution cannot be found for the resulting system of m equations in m variables. However, these cases will never be encountered when using the simplex method.

Figure 5.1
Feasible Region and Extreme
Points for the HighTech Industries
Problem

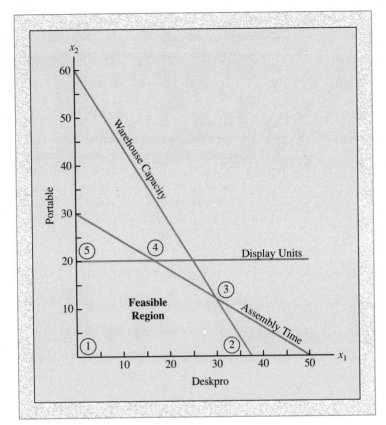

In the HighTech problem, the maximum possible number of basic solutions is given by the number of different sets of two variables that can be set to zero: $\binom{5}{2} = 10$. Actually, there are only nine basic solutions because no solution is obtained by setting x_2 and s_2 equal to zero. These solutions, five of which are also feasible, are shown in the graph below.

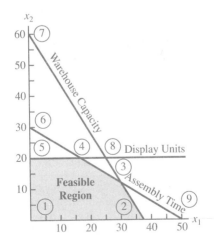

You should be able to find basic and basic feasible solutions to a system of equations at this point. Try Problem 3.

$$1s_1 \qquad\qquad = 150$$
$$1s_2 \qquad\quad = \;\; 20$$
$$1s_3 = 300$$

The complete solution (including the nonbasic variables) corresponding to $x_1 = 0$ and $x_2 = 0$ is

$$x_1 = \quad 0$$
$$x_2 = \quad 0$$
$$s_1 = 150$$
$$s_2 = \quad 20$$
$$s_3 = 300$$

This solution is a basic solution since it was obtained by setting two of the variables equal to zero and solving for the other three variables. Moreover, it is a basic *feasible* solution since all of the variables are greater than or equal to zero.

In Figure 5.1 we show a graph of the feasible region for the HighTech problem. We see that the basic feasible solution obtained by setting $x_1 = 0$ and $x_2 = 0$ corresponds to extreme point ① of the feasible region. This is not just a coincidence; all basic feasible solutions correspond to extreme points of the feasible region. Thus, for every extreme point of the feasible region of a linear programming problem, there is a corresponding basic feasible solution.

In Chapter 2 we showed that the optimal solution to a linear programming problem can be found at an extreme point. Since for every extreme point there is a corresponding basic feasible solution, we can now conclude that there is an optimal basic feasible solution.[3] The simplex method is an iterative procedure for moving from one basic feasible solution (extreme point) to another until the optimal solution is reached.

5.2 Tableau Form

A basic feasible solution to the system of m linear constraint equations and n variables is required as a starting point for the simplex method. From this starting point, the simplex method successively generates better basic feasible solutions to the system of linear equations. When the objective function can no longer be improved in this fashion, the optimal solution has been reached. The purpose of the tableau form is to provide the starting point: an initial basic feasible solution.

Recall that for the HighTech problem, the standard-form representation is

$$\text{Max} \quad 50x_1 + 40x_2 + 0s_1 + 0s_2 + 0s_3$$

s.t.

$$3x_1 + 5x_2 + 1s_1 \qquad\qquad = 150$$
$$1x_2 \qquad + 1s_2 \qquad = 20$$
$$8x_1 + 5x_2 \qquad\qquad + 1s_3 = 300$$

$$x_1, x_2, s_1, s_2, s_3 \geq 0$$

When a linear programming problem with all less-than-or-equal-to constraints is written in standard form, it is easy to find a basic feasible solution. We simply set the decision variables equal to zero and solve for the values of the slack variables. Note that doing this results in the values of the slack variables being set equal to the right-hand-side values of the constraint equations. For the HighTech problem, this yields $x_1 = 0$, $x_2 = 0$, $s_1 = 150$, $s_2 = 20$, and $s_3 = 300$ as the initial basic feasible solution. This solution corresponds to using the origin, extreme point ① in Figure 5.1, as the initial basic feasible solution.

If we study the standard-form representation of the HighTech constraint equations closely, we can identify two properties that make it possible to find an initial basic feasible solution. The first property, which enables us to find a basic solution, requires that the following conditions be satisfied:

a. For each constraint equation, the coefficient of one of the m basic variables in that equation must be 1, and the coefficients for all the remaining basic variables in that equation must be 0.

b. The coefficient for each basic variable may be 1 in only one constraint equation.

When these conditions are satisfied, there is exactly one basic variable with a coefficient of 1 associated with each constraint equation, and for each of the m constraint equations, it is a different basic variable. Thus, if the $n - m$ nonbasic variables are set equal to zero, the values of the basic variables can be read from the right-hand side of the constraint equations.

---

[3]We are only considering cases where there is an optimal solution. That is, in the cases of infeasibility and unboundedness, there is no optimal solution, so there cannot be an optimal basic feasible solution.

The second property enables us to find a feasible solution; it requires that the values on the right-hand sides of the constraint equations be nonnegative. This ensures that the basic solution obtained by setting the basic variables equal to the right-hand-side values is feasible.

If a linear programming problem satisfies the two properties above, it is said to be in *tableau form*. Thus, we see that the standard-form representation of the HighTech problem is already in tableau form. In fact, standard form and tableau form for linear programs that have all less-than-or-equal-to constraints and nonnegative right-hand-side values are the same. Later in this chapter we will show how to set up the tableau form for problems involving equality and greater-than-or-equal-to constraints; in these cases, the standard-form representation of the problem and the tableau-form representation are not the same.

To summarize, the following three steps are necessary to prepare a linear programming problem for solution using the simplex method:

Step 1 Formulate the problem.

Step 2 Set up the standard-form representation by adding slack and/or subtracting surplus variables.

Step 3 Set up the tableau-form representation.

5.3   Setting Up the Initial Simplex Tableau

After a linear programming problem has been converted to tableau form, we have an initial basic feasible solution that can be used to begin the simplex method. To provide a convenient means for performing the calculations required by the simplex solution procedure, we will first develop what is referred to as the initial *simplex tableau*.

For linear programs with less-than-or-equal-to constraints, the slack variables provide the initial basic feasible solution identified in tableau form.

Part of the initial simplex tableau is a table containing all the coefficients shown in the tableau-form representation of a linear program. If we adopt the general notation

$$c_j = \text{objective function coefficient for variable } j$$
$$b_i = \text{right-hand-side value for constraint } i$$
$$a_{ij} = \text{coefficient associated with variable } j \text{ in constraint } i$$

we can show this portion of the initial simplex tableau as follows:

c_1	c_2	$\ldots c_n$	
a_{11}	a_{12}	$\ldots a_{1n}$	b_1
a_{21}	a_{22}	$\ldots a_{2n}$	b_2
.	.	. . . .	.
.	.	. . . .	.
a_{m1}	a_{m2}	$\ldots a_{mn}$	b_m

Thus, for the HighTech problem, we obtain the following partial initial simplex tableau:

50	40	0	0	0	
3	5	1	0	0	**150**
0	1	0	1	0	**20**
8	5	0	0	1	**300**

Note that the row above the first horizontal line contains the coefficients of the objective function in tableau form. The elements appearing between the horizontal lines and to the left of the vertical line are the coefficients of the constraint equations, and the elements to the right of the vertical line are the corresponding right-hand-side values.

Later we may want to refer to the objective function coefficients, all the right-hand-side values, or all the coefficients in the constraints as a group. To do this, we will find the following general notation helpful:

c row = row of objective function coefficients

b column = column of right-hand-side values of the constraint equations

A matrix = m rows and n columns of coefficients of the variables in the constraint equations

Using this notation, we can show the above portion of the initial simplex tableau as follows:

c row	
A matrix	b column

To help us recall that each of the columns contains the coefficients of one variable, we will write the variable associated with each column directly above the column. Doing this, we obtain

> You should be able to set up the portion of the simplex tableau corresponding to the objective function and constraints at this point. Try Problem 6.

x_1	x_2	s_1	s_2	s_3	
50	40	0	0	0	
3	5	1	0	0	**150**
0	1	0	1	0	**20**
8	5	0	0	1	**300**

> The simplex tableau is nothing more than a table that helps keep track of the simplex method calculations and the equivalent system of constraint equations at each iteration. Students should be able to reconstruct the original problem from the initial simplex tableau.

The initial simplex tableau contains the tableau-form representation; thus, it is easy to identify the initial basic feasible solution. First, we note that for each basic variable, there is a corresponding column that has a 1 in the only nonzero position. Such columns are known as *unit columns* or *unit vectors*. Second, there is a row of the tableau associated with each basic variable. This row has a 1 in the unit column corresponding to the basic variable. The value of each basic variable is then given by the b_i value in the row associated with the basic variable. For example, in the HighTech problem, row 3 of the simplex tableau is associated with basic variable s_3 since this row has a 1 in the unit column corresponding to s_3; therefore, the value of this basic variable is given by $s_3 = b_3 = 300$. Table 5.1 shows the column corresponding to basic variable s_2, the row associated with s_2, and its value, $s_2 = 20$.

5.4 Improving the Solution

To improve the initial basic feasible solution, the simplex method must generate a new basic feasible solution (extreme point) that yields a better value for the objective function.

Table 5.1

Identifying Values of
Basic Variables from the Simplex
Tableau

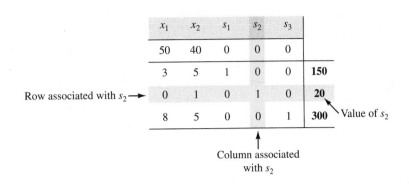

	x_1	x_2	s_1	s_2	s_3	
	50	40	0	0	0	
	3	5	1	0	0	**150**
Row associated with s_2 →	0	1	0	1	0	**20**
	8	5	0	0	1	**300**

Value of s_2

Column associated
with s_2

To do so requires changing the set of basic variables; this is accomplished by selecting
one of the current nonbasic variables to be made basic and one of the current basic
variables to be made nonbasic in such a fashion that the new basic feasible solution yields
an improved value for the objective function. The simplex method provides an easy way
to carry out this change of variables.

For computational convenience, we will add two new columns to the present form of
the simplex tableau. One column is labeled "*Basis*" and the other column is labeled
"c_B." In the *Basis* column, we list the current basic variables, and in the c_B column, we
list the corresponding objective function coefficient for each of these basic variables. For
the HighTech problem, this results in the following initial simplex tableau:

		x_1	x_2	s_1	s_2	s_3	
Basis	c_B	50	40	0	0	0	
s_1	0	3	5	1	0	0	**150**
s_2	0	0	1	0	1	0	**20**
s_3	0	8	5	0	0	1	**300**

Note that in the column labeled *Basis*, s_1 is listed as the first basic variable since its value
is given by the right-hand-side value for the first equation (i.e., $s_1 = b_1 = 150$); s_2 is listed
second since its value is given by $s_2 = b_2 = 20$; and $s_3 = b_3 = 300$ is listed last. In each
row, the basic variable and its current value are shown in boldface.

Can we improve the value of the objective function by moving to a new basic feasible
solution? To find out whether this is possible, we add two rows to the bottom of the
tableau. The first row, labeled z_j, represents the decrease in the value of the objective
function that will result if one unit of the variable corresponding to the jth column of the
A matrix is brought into the basis—that is, if this variable is made a basic variable with
a value of 1. The term *basis* is used here to refer to the set of basic variables. The second
row, labeled $c_j - z_j$, represents the net change in the value of the objective function if one
unit of the variable corresponding to the jth column of the A matrix is brought into the
solution. We refer to the $c_j - z_j$ row as the *net evaluation row*.

Let us first see how the entries in the z_j row are computed. Suppose that we consider
increasing the value of the nonbasic variable x_1 by one unit—that is, from $x_1 = 0$ to
$x_1 = 1$. In order to make this change and at the same time continue to satisfy the
constraint equations, the values of some of the other variables will have to be changed. As

we will show, the simplex method requires that the necessary changes be made to basic variables only. For example, in the first constraint we have

$$3x_1 + 5x_2 + 1s_1 = 150$$

The current basic variable in this constraint equation is s_1. Assuming that x_2 remains a nonbasic variable with a value of 0, if x_1 is increased in value by 1, then s_1 must be decreased by 3 for the constraint to be satisfied. Similarly, if we were to increase the value of x_1 by 1 (and keep $x_2 = 0$), we can see from the second and third equations that although s_2 would not decrease, s_3 would decrease by 8.

From analyzing all the constraint equations, we see that making x_1 a basic variable with a value of 1 will result in a decrease of three units in s_1, a decrease of zero units in s_2, and a decrease of eight units in s_3. Thus, we see that the coefficients in the x_1 column indicate the amount of decrease in the current basic variables when the nonbasic variable x_1 is increased from 0 to 1. In general, all the column coefficients can be interpreted this way. For instance, if we make x_2 a basic variable at a value of 1 (while keeping x_1 a nonbasic variable at a value of 0), s_1 will decrease by 5, s_2 will decrease by 1, and s_3 will decrease by 5.

Recall that the values in the c_B column of the simplex tableau are the objective function coefficients for the current basic variables. Hence, to compute the values in the z_j row (the decrease in value of the objective function when x_j is increased by one), we form the sum of the products obtained by multiplying the elements in the c_B column by the corresponding elements in the jth column of the A matrix. Doing this, we obtain

> The coefficients in the incoming column can be viewed as substitution rates. The element in each row is the rate of substitution of the incoming variable for the current basic variable in that row. Since the current basic variables are slack variables here, the coefficients in the x_1 column are the rate of substitution of x_1 for the right-hand resources.

$$z_1 = 0(3) + 0(0) + 0(8) = 0$$

$$z_2 = 0(5) + 0(1) + 0(5) = 0$$

$$z_3 = 0(1) + 0(0) + 0(0) = 0$$

$$z_4 = 0(0) + 0(1) + 0(0) = 0$$

$$z_5 = 0(0) + 0(0) + 0(1) = 0$$

Since the objective function coefficient of x_1 is 50, the value of $c_1 - z_1$ is $50 - 0 = 50$. This indicates that the net result of bringing one unit of x_1 into the current basis will be an increase in profit of \$50. Hence, in the net evaluation row corresponding to x_1, we enter 50. In the same manner, we can calculate the $c_j - z_j$ values for the remaining variables. The result is the following complete initial simplex tableau:

Basis	c_B	x_1 50	x_2 40	s_1 0	s_2 0	s_3 0	
s_1	0	3	5	1	0	0	**150**
s_2	0	0	1	0	1	0	**20**
s_3	0	8	5	0	0	1	**300**
z_j		0	0	0	0	0	**0**
$c_j - z_j$		50	40	0	0	0	↑
							Profit

In this tableau we also see a boldfaced 0 in the z_j row in the last column. This zero represents the profit associated with the current basic feasible solution. It was computed by multiplying the values of the basic variables, which are the boldfaced values given in the last column of the simplex tableau, by their corresponding contribution to profit as given in the c_B column. That is, profit $= 150(0) + 20(0) + 300(0) = 0$.

From the net evaluation row, we see that each unit of the Deskpro (x_1) increases the value of the objective function by 50 and each unit of the Portable (x_2) increases the value of the objective function by 40. Since x_1 causes the largest per-unit increase, we choose it as the variable to bring into the basis. We must next determine which of the current basic variables to make nonbasic. In doing so, we first note that since each unit of x_1 brought into the solution increases the objective function by $50, we would like to make x_1 as large as possible.

In discussing how to compute the z_j values, we noted that each of the coefficients in the x_1 column indicates the amount of decrease in the corresponding basic variable that would result from increasing x_1 by one unit. Hence, only the positive coefficients need to be considered in determining the current basic variable that will become nonbasic at a value of zero. Considering the first row, we see that every unit of the Deskpro produced will cause us to use 3 hours of assembly time (i.e., reduce s_1 by 3). In the current solution, $s_1 = 150$ and $x_1 = 0$. Thus—considering this row only—the maximum possible value of x_1 can be calculated by solving

$$3x_1 = 150$$

which provides

$$x_1 = 50$$

If x_1 is 50 (and x_2 remains a nonbasic variable with a value of 0), s_1 will have to be reduced to zero in order to satisfy the first constraint:

$$3x_1 + 5x_2 + 1s_1 = 150$$

Considering the second row, $0x_1 + 1x_2 + 1s_2 = 20$, we see that the coefficient of x_1 is 0. Thus, increasing x_1 will not have any effect on s_2; that is, increasing x_1 cannot drive the basic variable in the second row (s_2) to zero. Indeed, increases in x_1 will leave s_2 unchanged.

Finally, since the coefficient of x_1 is 8 in the third row, every unit that we increase x_1 will cause a decrease of eight units in s_3. Since the value of s_3 is currently 300, we can solve

$$8x_1 = 300$$

to find the maximum possible increase in x_1 before s_3 will become nonbasic at a value of zero; thus, we see that x_1 cannot be any larger than $300/8 = 37.5$.

Considering the three rows (constraints) simultaneously, we see that row 3 is the most restrictive. That is, producing 37.5 units of the Deskpro will use all of the warehouse space and force the corresponding slack variable to become nonbasic at a value of $s_3 = 0$.

In making the decision to produce as many Deskpro units as possible, we must change the set of variables in the basic feasible solution (i.e., obtain a new basis). The nonbasic variable x_1 will now become a basic variable while the previous basic variable s_3 will become a nonbasic variable with $s_3 = 0$. This interchange of roles between two variables is the essence of the simplex method. The way the simplex method moves from one basic feasible solution to another is by selecting a nonbasic variable to replace one of the current basic variables. This process of moving from one basic feasible solution to another is called an *iteration*. We now summarize the rules for selecting a nonbasic variable to be made basic and for selecting a current basic variable to be made nonbasic.

You should now be able to set up the complete initial simplex tableau for a problem with less-than-or-equal constraints. Try Problem 7(a).

CRITERION FOR ENTERING A NEW VARIABLE
INTO THE BASIS

Look at the net evaluation row $(c_j - z_j)$, and select the variable to enter the basis that will cause the largest per-unit improvement in the value of the objective function. In the case of a tie, we follow the convention of selecting the variable to enter the basis that corresponds to the leftmost of the columns.

CRITERION FOR REMOVING A VARIABLE FROM
THE CURRENT BASIS (MINIMUM RATIO TEST)

Suppose the incoming basic variable corresponds to column j in the A portion of the simplex tableau. For each row i, compute the ratio b_i/a_{ij} for each a_{ij} greater than zero. The basic variable that will be removed from the basis corresponds to the minimum of these ratios. In case of a tie, we follow the convention of selecting the variable that corresponds to the uppermost of the tied rows.

Let us illustrate the above procedure by applying it to the HighTech problem. To illustrate the computations involved, we add an extra column to the right of the tableau showing the b_i/a_{ij} ratios.

Basis	c_B	x_1 50	x_2 40	s_1 0	s_2 0	s_3 0		$\dfrac{b_i}{a_{i1}}$
s_1	0	3	5	1	0	0	**150**	$\dfrac{150}{3} = 50$
s_2	0	0	1	0	1	0	**20**	—
s_3	0	⑧	5	0	0	1	**300**	$\dfrac{300}{8} = 37.5$
z_j		0	0	0	0	0	**0**	
$c_j - z_j$		50	40	0	0	0		

We see that $c_1 - z_1 = 50$ is the largest positive value in the $c_j - z_j$ row. Hence, x_1 is selected to become the new basic variable. Checking the ratios b_i/a_{i1} for values of a_{i1} greater than zero, we see that $b_3/a_{31} = 300/8 = 37.5$ is the minimum of these ratios. Thus, the current basic variable associated with row 3 (s_3) is the variable selected to leave the basis. In the tableau we have circled $a_{31} = 8$ to indicate that the variable corresponding to the first column is to enter the basis and that the basic variable corresponding to the third row is to leave the basis. Adopting the usual linear programming terminology, we refer to this circled element as the *pivot element*. The column and the row containing the pivot element are called the *pivot column* and the *pivot row*, respectively.

> The circled value is the pivot element; the corresponding column and row are called the pivot column and pivot row.

To improve the current solution of $x_1 = 0$, $x_2 = 0$, $s_1 = 150$, $s_2 = 20$, and $s_3 = 300$, we should increase x_1 to 37.5. The production of 37.5 units of the Deskpro results in a profit of $50(37.5) = 1875$. In producing 37.5 units of the Deskpro, we will use all the available warehouse space, and s_3 will thus be reduced to zero. Hence, x_1 will become the new basic variable, replacing s_3 in the previous basis.

5.5 Calculating the Next Tableau

In the previous section we concluded that the initial basic feasible solution obtained by setting $x_1 = 0$ and $x_2 = 0$ could be improved by introducing x_1 into the basis to replace s_3. To determine the new basic feasible solution with x_1 as a basic variable, it will be necessary to update the simplex tableau.

Recall that the initial simplex tableau contains the coefficients of the tableau-form representation of the linear program. Because of the special properties of the tableau form, the initial simplex tableau contains a unit column corresponding to each basic variable.

We now want to update the simplex tableau in such a fashion that the column associated with the new basic variable is a unit column; in this way its value will be given by the right-hand-side value of the corresponding row. We would like the column in the new tableau corresponding to x_1 to look just like the column corresponding to s_3 in the original tableau, so our goal is to make the column in the A matrix corresponding to x_1 appear as

$$0$$
$$0$$
$$1$$

The way in which we transform the simplex tableau so that it still represents an equivalent system of constraint equations with the above properties is to use the following *elementary row operations.*

ELEMENTARY ROW OPERATIONS

1. Multiply any row (equation) by a nonzero number.
2. Replace any row (equation) by the result of adding or subtracting a multiple of another row (equation) to it.

The application of these elementary row operations to a system of simultaneous linear equations will not change the solution to the system of equations; however, the elementary row operations will change the coefficients of the variables and the values of the right-hand sides.

The objective in performing elementary row operations is to transform the system of constraint equations into a form that makes it easy to identify the new basic feasible solution. Consequently, we must perform the elementary row operations in such a manner that we transform the column for the variable entering the basis into a unit column. We emphasize that the feasible solutions to the original constraint equations are the same as the feasible solutions to the modified constraint equations obtained by performing elementary row operations. However, many of the numerical values in the simplex tableau will change as the result of performing these row operations. Thus, the present method of referring to elements in the simplex tableau may lead to confusion.

Up to now we have made no distinction between the A matrix and b column coefficients in the tableau form of the problem and the corresponding coefficients in the simplex tableau. Indeed, we showed that the initial simplex tableau is formed by properly placing the a_{ij}, c_j, and b_i elements as given in the tableau form of the problem into the simplex tableau. To avoid confusion in subsequent simplex tableaus, we will refer to the portion of the simplex tableau that initially contained the a_{ij} values with the symbol $\bar{A}$, and the portion of the tableau that initially contained the b_i values with the symbol $\bar{b}$. In terms of the simplex tableau, elements in $\bar{A}$ will be denoted by $\bar{a}_{ij}$, and elements in $\bar{b}$ will be denoted by $\bar{b}_i$. We recognize that $\bar{A} = A$ and $\bar{b} = b$ in the initial simplex tableau. However, in subsequent simplex tableaus, elementary row operations will change the tableau elements. The overbar notation should avoid any confusion when we wish to distinguish between (1) the original constraint coefficient values a_{ij} and right-hand-side values b_i of the tableau form, and (2) the simplex tableau elements $\bar{a}_{ij}$ and $\bar{b}_i$.

Now let us see how elementary row operations are used to create the next simplex tableau for the HighTech problem. Recall that the goal is to transform the column in the $\bar{A}$ portion of the simplex tableau corresponding to x_1 to a unit column; that is,

$$\bar{a}_{11} = 0$$
$$\bar{a}_{21} = 0$$
$$\bar{a}_{31} = 1$$

To set $\bar{a}_{31} = 1$, we perform the first elementary row operation by multiplying the pivot row (row 3) by $\frac{1}{8}$ to obtain the equivalent equation

$$\tfrac{1}{8}(8x_1 + 5x_2 + 0s_1 + 0s_2 + 1s_3) = \tfrac{1}{8}(300)$$

or

$$1x_1 + \tfrac{5}{8}x_2 + 0s_1 + 0s_2 + \tfrac{1}{8}s_3 = \tfrac{75}{2} \tag{5.9}$$

We refer to equation (5.9) in the updated simplex tableau as the **new pivot row**.

To set $\bar{a}_{11} = 0$, we perform the second elementary row operation by first multiplying the new pivot row by 3 to obtain the equivalent equation

$$3(1x_1 + \tfrac{5}{8}x_2 + 0s_1 + 0s_2 + \tfrac{1}{8}s_3) = 3(\tfrac{75}{2})$$

or

$$3x_1 + \tfrac{15}{8}x_2 + 0s_1 + 0s_2 + \tfrac{3}{8}s_3 = \tfrac{225}{2} \tag{5.10}$$

Subtracting equation (5.10) from the equation represented by row 1 of the simplex tableau completes the application of the second elementary row operation; thus, after dropping the terms with zero coefficients, we obtain

$$(3x_1 + 5x_2 + 1s_1) - (3x_1 + \tfrac{15}{8}x_2 + \tfrac{3}{8}s_3) = 150 - \tfrac{225}{2}$$

or

$$0x_1 + \tfrac{25}{8}x_2 + 1s_1 - \tfrac{3}{8}s_3 = \tfrac{75}{2} \tag{5.11}$$

Since $\bar{a}_{21} = 0$, no row operations need be performed on the second row of the simplex tableau. Replacing rows 1 and 3 with the coefficients in equations (5.11) and (5.9), respectively, we obtain the new simplex tableau

		x_1	x_2	s_1	s_2	s_3	
Basis	c_B	50	40	0	0	0	
s_1	0	0	$\frac{25}{8}$	1	0	$-\frac{3}{8}$	$\frac{75}{2}$
s_2	0	0	1	0	1	0	**20**
x_1	50	1	$\frac{5}{8}$	0	0	$\frac{1}{8}$	$\frac{75}{2}$
z_j							**1875**
$c_j - z_j$							

Dropping terms with zero coefficients, the corresponding system of equations is

$$\tfrac{25}{8}x_2 + 1s_1 \qquad - \tfrac{3}{8}s_3 = \tfrac{75}{2}$$

$$1x_2 \qquad + 1s_2 \qquad = 20$$

$$1x_1 + \tfrac{5}{8}x_2 \qquad + \tfrac{1}{8}s_3 = \tfrac{75}{2}$$

Assigning zero values to the nonbasic variables x_2 and s_3 permits us to identify the following new basic feasible solution:

$$s_1 = \tfrac{75}{2}$$
$$s_2 = 20$$
$$x_1 = \tfrac{75}{2}$$

This solution is also provided by the last column in the new simplex tableau. The profit associated with this solution is obtained by multiplying the solution values for the basic variables as given in the $\bar{b}$ column by their corresponding objective function coefficients as given in the c_B column; that is,

$$0(\tfrac{75}{2}) + 0(20) + 50(\tfrac{75}{2}) = 1875$$

Interpreting the Results of an Iteration

Starting with the initial simplex tableau, elementary row operations are used to change the elements in the simplex tableau in such a manner that we are able to identify a new basic feasible solution that improves the value of the objective function. Carrying out the process of determining a new simplex tableau is referred to as an iteration of the simplex method. In our example, the initial basic feasible solution was

$$x_1 = 0$$
$$x_2 = 0$$
$$s_1 = 150$$
$$s_2 = 20$$
$$s_3 = 300$$

with a corresponding profit of $0. One iteration of the simplex method moved us to another basic feasible solution with an objective function value of $1875. This new basic feasible solution is

$$x_1 = \tfrac{75}{2}$$
$$x_2 = 0$$
$$s_1 = \tfrac{75}{2}$$
$$s_2 = 20$$
$$s_3 = 0$$

Barring degeneracy, the simplex method moves from one extreme point to an adjacent extreme point at each iteration.

In Figure 5.2 we see that the initial basic feasible solution corresponds to extreme point ①. The first iteration moved us in the direction of the greatest increase per unit in profit—that is, along the x_1 axis. We moved away from extreme point ① in the x_1 direction until we could not move farther without violating one of the constraints. The tableau we calculated after one iteration is the basic feasible solution corresponding to extreme point ②.

We note from Figure 5.2 that at extreme point ② the warehouse capacity constraint is binding and also that there is slack in the other two constraints. From the simplex tableau,

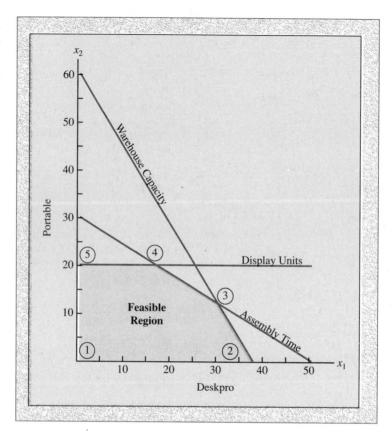

we see that the amount of slack for these two constraints is given by $s_1 = 75/2$
$s_2 = 20$.

Moving Toward a Better Solution

To see if a new better basic feasible solution can be found, we need to calculate the z_j
and $c_j - z_j$ rows for the new simplex tableau. Recall that the elements in the z_j row are
the sum of the products obtained by multiplying the elements in the c_B column of the
simplex tableau by the corresponding elements in the columns of the $\bar{A}$ matrix. Thus,
we obtain

$$z_1 = 0(0) \quad + 0(0) + 50(1) \; = 50$$

$$z_2 = 0(25/8) \quad + 0(1) + 50(5/8) = 250/8$$

$$z_3 = 0(1) \quad + 0(0) + 50(0) = 0$$

$$z_4 = 0(0) \quad + 0(1) + 50(0) = 0$$

$$z_5 = 0(-3/8) + 0(0) + 50(1/8) = 50/8$$

Subtracting z_j from c_j to compute the net evaluation row, we obtain the following simplex
tableau:

Basis	c_B	x_1 50	x_2 40	s_1 0	s_2 0	s_3 0	
s_1	0	0	$25/8$	1	0	$-3/8$	$75/2$
s_2	0	0	1	0	1	0	**20**
x_1	50	1	$5/8$	0	0	$1/8$	$75/2$
z_j		50	$250/8$	0	0	$50/8$	**1875**
$c_j - z_j$		0	$70/8$	0	0	$-50/8$	

Let us now analyze the $c_j - z_j$ row to see if we can introduce a new variable into the basis and continue to improve the value of the objective function. Using the rule for determining which variable should enter the basis next, we select x_2 since it has the highest positive coefficient in the $c_j - z_j$ row.

To determine which variable will be removed from the basis when x_2 enters, we must compute for each row i the ratio $\bar{b}_i/\bar{a}_{i2}$ (remember, though, that we should compute this ratio only if $\bar{a}_{i2}$ is greater than zero); then we select the variable to leave the basis that corresponds to the minimum ratio. As before, we will show these ratios in an extra column of the simplex tableau:

Basis	c_B	x_1 50	x_2 40	s_1 0	s_2 0	s_3 0		$\dfrac{\bar{b}_i}{\bar{a}_{i2}}$
s_1	0	0	$\boxed{25/8}$	1	0	$-3/8$	$75/2$	$\dfrac{75/2}{25/8} = 12$
s_2	0	0	1	0	1	0	**20**	$\dfrac{20}{1} = 20$
x_1	50	1	$5/8$	0	0	$1/8$	$75/2$	$\dfrac{75/2}{5/8} = 60$
z_j		50	$250/8$	0	0	$50/8$	**1875**	
$c_j - z_j$		0	$70/8$	0	0	$-50/8$		

Since 12 is the minimum ratio, s_1 will leave the basis. The pivot element is $\bar{a}_{12} = 25/8$, which is circled in the above tableau. The nonbasic variable x_2 must now be made a basic variable in row 1. This means that we must perform the elementary row operations that will convert the x_2 column into a unit column with a 1 in row 1; that is, we will have to transform the second column in the tableau to the form

$$1$$
$$0$$
$$0$$

We can do this by performing the following elementary row operations:

Step 1 Multiply every element in row 1 (the pivot row) by $8/25$ in order to make $\bar{a}_{12} = 1$.

Step 2 Subtract the new row 1 (i.e., the new pivot row) from row 2 to make $\bar{a}_{22} = 0$.

Step 3 Multiply the new pivot row by $5/8$, and subtract the result from row 3 to make $\bar{a}_{32} = 0$.

Although the above elementary row operations again change the appearance of the simplex tableau, they do not alter the solutions to the system of equations contained in the tableau. The only difference is that now we have x_2, s_2, and x_1 as the basic variables and s_1 and s_3 as the nonbasic variables. The new tableau resulting from these row operations is as follows:

Basis	c_B	x_1 50	x_2 40	s_1 0	s_2 0	s_3 0	
x_2	40	0	1	$8/25$	0	$-3/25$	**12**
s_2	0	0	0	$-8/25$	1	$3/25$	**8**
x_1	50	1	0	$-5/25$	0	$5/25$	**30**
z_j		50	40	$14/5$	0	$26/5$	**1980**
$c_j - z_j$		0	0	$-14/5$	0	$-26/5$	

Note that the values of the basic variables are $x_2 = 12$, $s_2 = 8$, and $x_1 = 30$, and the corresponding profit is $40(12) + 0(8) + 50(30) = 1980$.

We must now determine whether or not to bring any other variable into the basis and thereby move to another basic feasible solution. Looking at the net evaluation row, we see that every element is zero or negative. Since $c_j - z_j$ is less than or equal to zero for both of the nonbasic variables s_1 and s_3, any attempt to bring a nonbasic variable into the basis at this point will result in a lowering of the current value of the objective function. Hence, the above tableau represents the optimal solution. In general, the simplex method uses the following criterion to determine if the optimal solution has been obtained.

OPTIMALITY CRITERION

The optimal solution to a linear programming problem has been reached when all of the entries in the net evaluation row ($c_j - z_j$) are zero or negative. In such cases, the optimal solution is the current basic feasible solution.

Interpreting the Optimal Solution

The optimal solution to the HighTech problem, consisting of the basic variables x_1, x_2, and s_2 and nonbasic variables s_1 and s_3, is written as follows:

$$x_1 = 30$$
$$x_2 = 12$$
$$s_1 = 0$$
$$s_2 = 8$$
$$s_3 = 0$$

The value of the objective function is $1980. If management wants to maximize total profit contribution, HighTech should produce 30 units of the Deskpro and 12 units of the Portable. Since $s_2 = 8$, management should note that there will be eight unused Portable display units. Moreover, since $s_1 = 0$ and $s_3 = 0$, there is no slack associated with the assembly time constraint and the warehouse capacity constraint; in other words, these constraints are both binding. Consequently, if it is possible to obtain additional assembly time and/or additional warehouse space, management should consider doing so.

Referring to Figure 5.2, we can see graphically the process that the simplex method used to determine an optimal solution. The initial basic feasible solution corresponds to the origin ($x_1 = 0$, $x_2 = 0$, $s_1 = 150$, $s_2 = 20$, $s_3 = 300$). The first iteration caused x_1 to enter the basis and s_3 to leave. The second basic feasible solution corresponds to extreme point ② ($x_1 = 75/2$, $x_2 = 0$, $s_1 = 75/2$, $s_2 = 20$, $s_3 = 0$). At the next iteration, x_2 entered the basis and s_1 left. This brought us to extreme point ③, the optimal solution ($x_1 = 30$, $x_2 = 12$, $s_1 = 0$, $s_2 = 8$, $s_3 = 0$).

For the HighTech problem with only two decision variables, we had a choice of using the graphical or simplex method. For problems with more than two variables, we shall always use the simplex method.

Summary of the Simplex Method

Let us now summarize the steps followed to solve a linear program using the simplex method. We assume that the problem has all less-than-or-equal-to constraints and involves maximization.

Step 1 Formulate a linear programming model of the problem.

The only difference in the application of the simplex method for problems with equality and greater-than-or-equal-to constraints is in setting up tableau form. Section 5.7 explains how to set up tableau form for such cases.

Step 2 Add slack variables to each constraint to obtain standard form. This is also the tableau form necessary to identify an initial basic feasible solution for problems involving all less-than-or-equal-to constraints.

Step 3 Set up the initial simplex tableau.

Step 4 Choose the nonbasic variable with the largest entry in the net evaluation row to bring into the basis. This identifies the pivot column: the column associated with the incoming variable.

Step 5 Choose as the pivot row that row with the smallest ratio of $\bar{b}_i/\bar{a}_{ij}$ for $\bar{a}_{ij} > 0$ *where j is the pivot column.* This identifies the pivot row: the row of the variable leaving the basis when variable j enters.

Step 6 Perform the necessary elementary row operations to convert the column for the incoming variable to a unit column with a 1 in the pivot row.
   a. Divide each element of the pivot row by the pivot element (the element in the pivot row and pivot column).
   b. Obtain zeroes in all other positions of the pivot column by adding or subtracting an appropriate multiple of the new pivot row.

Once the row operations have been completed, the value of the new basic feasible solution can be read from the $\bar{b}$ column of the tableau.

Step 7 Test for optimality. If $c_j - z_j \leq 0$ for all columns, we have the optimal solution. If not, return to step 4.

The algorithm is basically the same for problems with equality and greater-than-or-equal-to constraints except that setting up tableau form requires a little more work. We discuss what is involved in Section 5.7. The simple modification necessary for minimization problems is covered in Section 5.8.

5.6 Solution of a Sample Problem

In this section we illustrate the use of the simplex method for a linear programming problem involving four decision variables. To check your understanding of the previous sections, you should attempt to solve the problem before studying the solution presented.

Solve the following linear program using the simplex method:

$$\text{Max} \quad 4x_1 + 6x_2 + 3x_3 + 1x_4$$

s.t.

$$\tfrac{3}{2}x_1 + 2x_2 + 4x_3 + 3x_4 \le 550$$

$$4x_1 + 1x_2 + 2x_3 + 1x_4 \le 700$$

$$2x_1 + 3x_2 + 1x_3 + 2x_4 \le 200$$

$$x_1, x_2, x_3, x_4 \ge 0$$

First, we add slack variables to convert the problem to standard form:

$$\text{Max} \quad 4x_1 + 6x_2 + 3x_3 + 1x_4 + 0s_1 + 0s_2 + 0s_3$$

s.t.

$$\tfrac{3}{2}x_1 + 2x_2 + 4x_3 + 3x_4 + 1s_1 \qquad\qquad = 550$$

$$4x_1 + 1x_2 + 2x_3 + 1x_4 \qquad + 1s_2 \qquad = 700$$

$$2x_1 + 3x_2 + 1x_3 + 2x_4 \qquad\qquad + 1s_3 = 200$$

$$x_1, x_2, x_3, x_4, s_1, s_2, s_3 \ge 0$$

The next step is to write the problem in tableau form. Since all the constraints are less-than-or-equal-to constraints, and since the right-hand-side values for the constraints are all nonnegative, the standard form and tableau form are the same. Thus, we can set up the initial simplex tableau and begin the simplex method.

		x_1	x_2	x_3	x_4	s_1	s_2	s_3		$\dfrac{\bar{b}_i}{\bar{a}_{i2}}$
Basis	c_B	4	6	3	1	0	0	0		
s_1	0	$\tfrac{3}{2}$	2	4	3	1	0	0	550	$550/2 = 275$
s_2	0	4	1	2	1	0	1	0	700	$700/1 = 700$
s_3	0	2	③	1	2	0	0	1	200	$200/3 = 66\tfrac{2}{3}$
z_j		0	0	0	0	0	0	0	0	
$c_j - z_j$		4	6	3	1	0	0	0		

Two iterations of the simplex method are required to reach the optimal solution.

Result of Iteration 1

		x_1	x_2	x_3	x_4	s_1	s_2	s_3		$\dfrac{\bar{b}_i}{\bar{a}_{i3}}$
Basis	c_B	4	6	3	1	0	0	0		
s_1	0	$\tfrac{1}{6}$	0	⑩⁄₃	$\tfrac{5}{3}$	1	0	$-\tfrac{2}{3}$	$416\tfrac{2}{3}$	125
s_2	0	$\tfrac{10}{3}$	0	$\tfrac{5}{3}$	$\tfrac{1}{3}$	0	1	$-\tfrac{1}{3}$	$633\tfrac{1}{3}$	380
x_2	6	$\tfrac{2}{3}$	1	$\tfrac{1}{3}$	$\tfrac{2}{3}$	0	0	$\tfrac{1}{3}$	$66\tfrac{2}{3}$	200
z_j		4	6	2	4	0	0	2	400	
$c_j - z_j$		0	0	1	-3	0	0	-2		

Result of Iteration 2

Basis	c_B	x_1 4	x_2 6	x_3 3	x_4 1	s_1 0	s_2 0	s_3 0	
x_3	3	$3/60$	0	1	$15/30$	$3/10$	0	$-6/30$	125
s_2	0	$195/60$	0	0	$-15/30$	$-5/10$	1	0	425
x_2	6	$39/60$	1	0	$15/30$	$-1/10$	0	$12/30$	25
z_j		$81/20$	6	3	$9/2$	$3/10$	0	$54/30$	525
$c_j - z_j$		$-1/20$	0	0	$-7/2$	$-3/10$	0	$-54/30$	

Since the $c_j - z_j$ elements are all less than or equal to zero, there is no nonbasic variable that we can introduce into solution and obtain an increase in the value of the objective function. Therefore, the current solution is optimal. The complete optimal solution is given by

$$x_1 = \ \ 0$$
$$x_2 = \ 25$$
$$x_3 = 125$$
$$x_4 = \ \ 0$$
$$s_1 = \ \ 0$$
$$s_2 = 425$$
$$s_3 = \ \ 0$$

You should now be able to solve a problem employing the simplex method. Try Problem 8.

The value of the objective function is 525.

NOTES & COMMENTS

The entries in the net evaluation row are closely related to the reduced costs that appear in the computer solution to a linear program. Recall that in Chapter 3 we defined the reduced cost as the amount by which an objective function coefficient would have to improve before it would be possible for the corresponding variable to assume a positive value in the optimal solution. The reduced costs are the absolute value of the entries in the net evaluation row.

5.7 Tableau Form: The General Case

This section explains how to get started with the simplex method for problems with greater-than-or-equal-to and equality constraints.

When a linear program contains all less-than-or-equal-to constraints with nonnegative right-hand-side values, it is easy to set up the tableau form. In this case, we simply add a slack variable to each constraint. However, obtaining tableau form is somewhat more complex if the linear program contains greater-than-or-equal-to constraints, equality constraints, and/or negative right-hand-side values. In this section we describe how to develop tableau form for each of these situations and also how to solve linear programs involving equality and greater-than-or-equal-to constraints using the simplex method.

Greater-Than-or-Equal-to Constraints

Suppose that in the HighTech Industries problem, management wanted to ensure that the combined total production for both models would be at least 25 units. This requirement means that the following constraint must be added to the current linear program:

$$1x_1 + 1x_2 \geq 25$$

Adding this constraint results in the following modified problem:

Max $50x_1 + 40x_2$

s.t.

$3x_1 +$	$5x_2 \leq$	150	Assembly time
	$1x_2 \leq$	20	Portable display
$8x_1 +$	$5x_2 \leq$	300	Warehouse space
$1x_1 +$	$1x_2 \geq$	25	Minimum total production
$x_1, x_2 \geq 0$			

A graph of the feasible region for this modified problem is shown in Figure 5.3. Extreme points ②, ③, and ④ have not changed, but the extreme points we have labeled ① and ⑤ are in different locations than they were in the original problem. The origin ($x_1 = 0$ and $x_2 = 0$) is no longer feasible. We note, however, that extreme point ③ remains feasible. Thus, even though part of the original feasible region has been cut off, we should expect to obtain the same optimal solution. To use the simplex method to solve this modified problem, we need to describe how to set up the tableau form for a linear programming problem that contains greater-than-or-equal-to constraints.

Figure 5.3
Feasible Region and Extreme Points for Modified HighTech Industries Problem

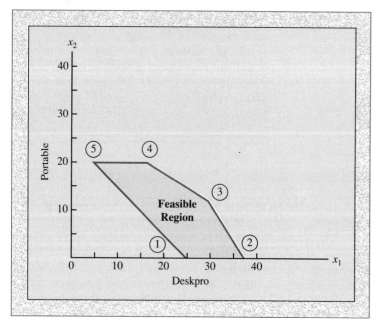

First, we use three slack variables and one surplus variable to write the problem in standard form. This provides the following:

$$\text{Max} \quad 50x_1 + 40x_2 + 0s_1 + 0s_2 + 0s_3 + 0s_4$$

s.t.

$$
\begin{array}{llllll}
3x_1 + & 5x_2 + & 1s_1 & & = 150 & \quad (5.12) \\
& 1x_2 & + 1s_2 & & = 20 & \quad (5.13) \\
8x_1 + & 5x_2 & & + 1s_3 & = 300 & \quad (5.14) \\
1x_1 + & 1x_2 & & - 1s_4 & = 25 & \quad (5.15)
\end{array}
$$

$$x_1, x_2, s_1, s_2, s_3, s_4 \geq 0$$

Now let us consider how we obtain an initial basic feasible solution to start the simplex method. Previously, we set $x_1 = 0$ and $x_2 = 0$ and selected the slack variables as the initial basic variables. The extension of this notion to the modified HighTech problem would suggest setting $x_1 = 0$ and $x_2 = 0$ and selecting the slack and surplus variables as the initial basic variables. However, in looking at the graph in Figure 5.3, we can see that the solution corresponding to $x_1 = 0$ and $x_2 = 0$, which is the origin, is no longer a feasible solution. The inclusion of the greater-than-or-equal-to constraint has eliminated the origin from the feasible region.

To see this another way, refer to equation (5.15) in the standard-form representation. When x_1 and x_2 are set equal to zero, equation (5.15) reduces to $-1s_4 = 25$, and hence, $s_4 = -25$. Thus, setting x_1 and x_2 to zero results in the basic solution

$$
\begin{array}{rr}
x_1 = & 0 \\
x_2 = & 0 \\
s_1 = & 150 \\
s_2 = & 20 \\
s_3 = & 300 \\
s_4 = & -25
\end{array}
$$

Here $s_4 = -25$ represents the amount by which this solution falls short of the newly specified minimum total production constraint. Clearly this is not a basic feasible solution since s_4 violates the nonnegativity requirement. The difficulty is that the standard-form representation and the tableau-form representation are not equivalent when the problem contains greater-than-or-equal-to constraints.

To set up the tableau form, we shall resort to a mathematical "trick" that will enable us to find an initial basic feasible solution in terms of the slack variables s_1, s_2, and s_3 and a new variable we shall denote a_4. The new variable constitutes the mathematical "trick." Variable a_4 really has nothing to do with the HighTech problem; it merely enables us to set up the tableau form and thus obtain an initial basic feasible solution. Since this new variable has been artificially created to start the simplex method, we will refer to it as an *artificial variable*.

Artificial variables are appropriately named; they have no physical meaning in the real problem.

The notation for artificial variables is similar to the notation used to refer to the elements of the A matrix. To avoid any confusion between the two, the elements of the A matrix (constraint coefficients) always have two subscripts, whereas artificial variables always have only one subscript.

With the addition of an artificial variable, we can convert the standard form of the problem into tableau form. We add artificial variable a_4 to constraint equation (5.15) to obtain the following representation of the system of equations in tableau form:

$$3x_1 + 5x_2 + 1s_1 \qquad\qquad\qquad = 150$$
$$1x_2 \qquad + 1s_2 \qquad\qquad = 20$$
$$8x_1 + 5x_2 \qquad\qquad + 1s_3 \qquad = 300$$
$$1x_1 + 1x_2 \qquad\qquad\qquad - 1s_4 + 1a_4 = 25$$

Note that the subscript on the artificial variable identifies the constraint with which it is associated. This is also the convention we have followed for slack and surplus variables; s_1 is associated with the first constraint, s_2 is associated with the second constraint, and so on. Thus, a_4 is the artificial variable associated with the fourth constraint.

Since the variables s_1, s_2, s_3, and a_4 each appear in a different constraint with a coefficient of 1, and since the right-hand-side values are nonnegative, both requirements of the tableau form have been satisfied. We can now obtain an initial basic feasible solution by setting $x_1 = x_2 = s_4 = 0$. The complete solution is

$$x_1 = \quad 0$$
$$x_2 = \quad 0$$
$$s_1 = 150$$
$$s_2 = \quad 20$$
$$s_3 = 300$$
$$s_4 = \quad 0$$
$$a_4 = \quad 25$$

A basic feasible solution containing one or more artificial variables at positive values is not feasible for the real-world problem.

Is this solution feasible in terms of our real-world problem? No, it is not. It does not satisfy the combined total production requirement of 25 units. We must make an important distinction between a basic feasible solution for the tableau form of our problem and a feasible solution for the real-world problem. A basic feasible solution for the tableau form of a linear programming problem is not always a feasible solution for the real-world problem.

The reason for creating the tableau form is to obtain the initial basic feasible solution that is required to start the simplex method. Thus, we see that whenever it is necessary to introduce artificial variables, the initial simplex solution will not in general be feasible for the real-world problem. This situation is not as difficult as it might seem, however, since the only time we must have a feasible solution for the real-world problem is at the last iteration of the simplex method. Thus, if we could devise a way to guarantee that any artificial variable would be eliminated from the basic feasible solution before the optimal solution is reached, there would be no difficulty.

The way in which we guarantee that artificial variables will be eliminated before the optimal solution is reached is to assign each artificial variable a very large cost in the objective function. For example, in the modified HighTech problem, we could assign a very large negative number as the profit coefficient for artificial variable a_4. Hence, if this variable is in the basis, it will substantially reduce profits. As a result, this variable will be eliminated from the basis as soon as possible, and this is precisely what we want to happen.

As an alternative to picking a large negative number like $-100,000$ for the profit coefficient, we will denote the profit coefficient of each artificial variable by $-M$. Here it is assumed that M represents a very large number—in other words, a number of very large magnitude and hence, the letter M. This notation will make it easier to keep track of the elements of the simplex tableau that depend on the profit coefficients of the artificial variables. Using $-M$ as the profit coefficient for artificial variable a_4 in the modified HighTech problem, we can write the objective function for the tableau form of the problem as follows:

$$\text{Max} \quad 50x_1 + 40x_2 + 0s_1 + 0s_2 + 0s_3 + 0s_4 - Ma_4$$

The initial simplex tableau for the problem is shown below.

Basis	c_B	x_1 50	x_2 40	s_1 0	s_2 0	s_3 0	s_4 0	a_4 $-M$	
s_1	0	3	5	1	0	0	0	0	**150**
s_2	0	0	1	0	1	0	0	0	**20**
s_3	0	8	5	0	0	1	0	0	**300**
a_4	$-M$	①	1	0	0	0	-1	1	**25**
z_j		$-M$	$-M$	0	0	0	M	$-M$	$-25M$
$c_j - z_j$		$50+M$	$40+M$	0	0	0	$-M$	0	

The above tableau corresponds to the solution $s_1 = 150$, $s_2 = 20$, $s_3 = 300$, $a_4 = 25$, and $x_1 = x_2 = s_4 = 0$. In terms of the simplex tableau, this is a basic feasible solution since all the variables are greater than or equal to zero and $n - m = 7 - 4 = 3$ of the variables are equal to zero. However, in terms of the modified HighTech problem, $x_1 = x_2 = 0$ is clearly not feasible. This situation is caused by the fact that the artificial variable is in the current basic solution at a positive value. Let us complete the simplex solution to this problem and see if the artificial variable is driven out of solution, as we hope it will be.

Since $c_1 - z_1 = 50 + M$ is the largest value in the net evaluation row, we see that x_1 will become a basic variable during the first iteration of the simplex method. Further calculations with the simplex method (the minimum ratio test) show that x_1 will replace a_4 in the basic solution. The simplex tableau after the first iteration is presented below.

Result of Iteration 1

Basis	c_B	x_1 50	x_2 40	s_1 0	s_2 0	s_3 0	s_4 0	a_4 $-M$	
s_1	0	0	2	1	0	0	3	-3	**75**
s_2	0	0	1	0	1	0	0	0	**20**
s_3	0	0	-3	0	0	1	8	-8	**100**
x_1	50	1	1	0	0	0	-1	1	**25**
z_j		50	50	0	0	0	-50	50	**1250**
$c_j - z_j$		0	-10	0	0	0	50	$-M-50$	

Graphically, we see in Figure 5.4 that this iteration has moved us from the origin (labeled A) to extreme point ①. The current solution is now feasible since there are no artificial variables in the solution. We now have the situation where the basic feasible

Figure 5.4
Sequence of Simplex Solutions for
the Modified HighTech Industries
Problem

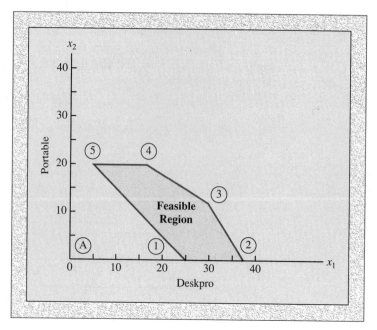

solution contained in the simplex tableau is also a feasible solution to the real-world problem.

Since a_4 is an artificial variable that was added simply to obtain an initial basic feasible solution, we can now drop its associated column from the simplex tableau. Indeed, whenever artificial variables are used, they can be dropped from the simplex tableau as soon as they have been eliminated from the basic feasible solution.

Artificial variables can be dropped from the tableau once they leave the basis. Leaving them in will not lead to the wrong solution, but it will cause more work.

When artificial variables are required to obtain an initial basic feasible solution, the iterations required to eliminate the artificial variables are referred to as *phase I* of the simplex method. When all the artificial variables have been eliminated from the basis, phase I is complete, and a basic feasible solution to the real-world problem has been obtained. Thus, by dropping the column associated with a_4 from the current tableau, we obtain the following simplex tableau at the end of phase I.

		x_1	x_2	s_1	s_2	s_3	s_4	
Basis	c_B	50	40	0	0	0	0	
s_1	0	0	2	1	0	0	3	75
s_2	0	0	1	0	1	0	0	20
s_3	0	0	−3	0	0	1	⑧	100
x_1	50	1	1	0	0	0	−1	25
z_j		50	50	0	0	0	−50	1250
$c_j - z_j$		0	−10	0	0	0	50	

We are now ready to begin phase II of the simplex method. This phase simply continues the simplex method computations after all artificial variables have been removed. At the next iteration, variable s_4 with $c_j - z_j = 50$ is entered into the solution, and variable s_3 is eliminated. The simplex tableau after this iteration is:

Basis	c_B	x_1 50	x_2 40	s_1 0	s_2 0	s_3 0	s_4 0	
s_1	0	0	㉕⁄₈	1	0	$-3/8$	0	$75/2$
s_2	0	0	1	0	1	0	0	**20**
s_4	0	0	$-3/8$	0	0	$1/8$	1	$25/2$
x_1	50	1	$5/8$	0	0	$1/8$	0	$75/2$
z_j		50	$250/8$	0	0	$50/8$	0	**1875**
$c_j - z_j$		0	$70/8$	0	0	$-50/8$	0	

In Figure 5.4 we see that this solution corresponds to extreme point ②. One more iteration is required. This time x_2 comes into the solution, and s_1 is eliminated. After performing this iteration, the following simplex tableau shows that the optimal solution has been reached.

Basis	c_B	x_1 50	x_2 40	s_1 0	s_2 0	s_3 0	s_4 0	
x_2	40	0	1	$8/25$	0	$-3/25$	0	**12**
s_2	0	0	0	$-8/25$	1	$3/25$	0	**8**
s_4	0	0	0	$3/25$	0	$2/25$	1	**17**
x_1	50	1	0	$-5/25$	0	$5/25$	0	**30**
z_j		50	40	$14/5$	0	$26/5$	0	**1980**
$c_j - z_j$		0	0	$-14/5$	0	$-26/5$	0	

From Figure 5.4 we see that this optimal solution corresponds to extreme point ③. Thus, the optimal solution to the modified HighTech problem is the same as the solution for the original problem. However, the simplex method required more iterations to reach this extreme point. This was so because it required an extra iteration to eliminate the artificial variable (a_4) in phase I to obtain a basic feasible solution for the real-world problem.

Fortunately, once we obtain an initial simplex tableau using artificial variables, we need not concern ourselves with whether or not the basic solution at a particular iteration is feasible for the real-world problem. We need only follow the rules for the simplex method. If we reach the optimality criterion (i.e., all $c_j - z_j \leq 0$) and all the artificial variables have been eliminated from the solution, then we have found the optimal solution. On the other hand, if we reach the stopping criterion and one or more of the artificial variables remain in solution at a positive value, then there is no feasible solution to the problem. This special case will be discussed further in Section 5.9.

Equality Constraints

When an equality constraint occurs in a linear programming problem, we need to add an artificial variable to obtain tableau form and an initial basic feasible solution. For example, if the equality constraint is

$$6x_1 + 4x_2 - 5x_3 = 30$$

we would simply add an artificial variable—say, a_1—to create a basic feasible solution in the initial simplex tableau. With the artificial variable, the above equation becomes

$$6x_1 + 4x_2 - 5x_3 + 1a_1 = 30$$

Now a_1 can be selected as the basic variable for this row, and its value is given by the right-hand side. Once we have created tableau form by adding an artificial variable to each equality constraint, the simplex method proceeds exactly as before.

Eliminating Negative Right-Hand-Side Values

One of the properties of the tableau form of a linear program is that the values on the right-hand sides of the constraints have to be nonnegative. In formulating a linear programming problem, we may find one or more of the constraints have negative right-hand-side values. To see how this might happen, suppose that the management of HighTech has specified that the number of units of the Portable model, x_2, has to be less than or equal to the number of units of the Deskpro model, x_1, after setting aside five units of the Deskpro for internal company use. We could formulate this constraint as

$$x_2 \leq x_1 - 5 \tag{5.16}$$

Subtracting x_1 from both sides of the inequality places both variables on the left-hand side of the inequality. Thus,

$$-x_1 + x_2 \leq -5 \tag{5.17}$$

Since this is a constraint with a negative right-hand-side value, we can develop an equivalent constraint with a nonnegative right-hand-side value by multiplying both sides of the constraint by -1. In doing so, we recognize that multiplying an inequality constraint by -1 changes the direction of the inequality.

Thus, to convert inequality (5.17) to an equivalent constraint with a nonnegative right-hand-side value, we multiply by -1 to obtain

$$x_1 - x_2 \geq 5 \tag{5.18}$$

We now have an acceptable nonnegative right-hand-side value. Tableau form for this constraint can now be obtained by subtracting a surplus variable and adding an artificial variable.

For a greater-than-or-equal-to constraint, multiplying by -1 creates an equivalent less-than-or-equal-to constraint. For example, suppose we had the following greater-than-or-equal-to constraint:

$$6x_1 + 3x_2 - 4x_3 \geq -20$$

Multiplying by -1 to obtain an equivalent constraint with a nonnegative right-hand-side value leads to the following less-than-or-equal-to constraint

$$-6x_1 - 3x_2 + 4x_3 \leq 20$$

Tableau form can be created for this constraint by adding a slack variable.

For an equality constraint with a negative right-hand-side value, we simply multiply by -1 to obtain an equivalent constraint with a nonnegative right-hand-side value. An artificial variable can then be added to create the tableau form.

Summary of the Steps to Create Tableau Form

Step 1 If the original formulation of the linear programming problem contains one or more constraints with negative right-hand-side values, multiply each of these constraints by -1. Doing this will change the direction of the inequalities. This step will provide an equivalent linear program with nonnegative right-hand-side values.

Step 2 For $\leq$ constraints, add a slack variable to obtain an equality constraint. The coefficient of the slack variable in the objective function is assigned a value of zero. This provides the tableau form for the constraint, and the slack variable becomes one of the basic variables in the initial basic feasible solution.

Step 3 For $\geq$ constraints, subtract a surplus variable to obtain an equality constraint, and then add an artificial variable to obtain the tableau form. The coefficient of the surplus variable in the objective function is assigned a value of zero. The coefficient of the artificial variable in the objective function is assigned a value of $-M$. The artificial variable becomes one of the basic variables in the initial basic feasible solution.

Step 4 For equality constraints, add an artificial variable to obtain the tableau form. The coefficient of the artificial variable in the objective function is assigned a value of $-M$. The artificial variable becomes one of the basic variables in the initial basic feasible solution.

To obtain some practice in applying the above steps, convert the following example problem into tableau form, and then set up the initial simplex tableau:

$$\text{Max} \quad 6x_1 + 3x_2 + 4x_3 + 1x_4$$

s.t.

$$-2x_1 - \tfrac{1}{2}x_2 + 1x_3 - 6x_4 = -60$$

$$1x_1 \qquad\quad + 1x_3 + \tfrac{2}{3}x_4 \leq 20$$

$$\qquad - 1x_2 - 5x_3 \qquad\quad \leq -50$$

$$x_1, x_2, x_3, x_4 \geq 0$$

To eliminate the negative right-hand-side values in constraints 1 and 3, we apply step 1. Multiplying both constraints by -1, we obtain the following equivalent linear program:

$$\text{Max} \quad 6x_1 + 3x_2 + 4x_3 + 1x_4$$

s.t.

$$2x_1 + \tfrac{1}{2}x_2 - 1x_3 + 6x_4 = 60$$

$$1x_1 \qquad\quad + 1x_3 + \tfrac{2}{3}x_4 \leq 20$$

$$\qquad 1x_2 + 5x_3 \qquad\quad \geq 50$$

$$x_1, x_2, x_3, x_4 \geq 0$$

Note that the direction of the $\leq$ inequality in constraint 3 has been reversed as a result of multiplying the constraint by -1. By applying step 4 for constraint 1, step 2 for constraint 2, and step 3 for constraint 3, we obtain the following tableau form:

$$\text{Max} \quad 6x_1 + 3x_2 + 4x_3 + 1x_4 + 0s_2 + 0s_3 - Ma_1 - Ma_3$$

s.t.

$$2x_1 + \tfrac{1}{2}x_2 - 1x_3 + 6x_4 \qquad\qquad + 1a_1 \qquad\quad = 60$$

$$1x_1 \qquad\quad + 1x_3 + \tfrac{2}{3}x_4 + 1s_2 \qquad\qquad\qquad = 20$$

$$1x_2 + 5x_3 \qquad\qquad - 1s_3 \qquad + 1a_3 = 50$$

$$x_1, x_2, x_3, x_4, s_2, s_3, a_1, a_3 \geq 0$$

The optimal solution to this problem is given by $x_2 = 160$ and $x_3 = 20$ with optimal value equal to 560.

The initial simplex tableau corresponding to this tableau form is

Basis	c_B	x_1	x_2	x_3	x_4	s_2	s_3	a_1	a_3	
		6	3	4	1	0	0	$-M$	$-M$	
a_1	$-M$	2	$\tfrac{1}{2}$	-1	⑥	0	0	1	0	60
s_2	0	1	0	1	$\tfrac{2}{3}$	1	0	0	0	20
a_3	$-M$	0	1	5	0	0	-1	0	1	50
z_j		$-2M$	$-\tfrac{3}{2}M$	$-4M$	$-6M$	0	M	$-M$	$-M$	$-110M$
$c_j - z_j$		$6 + 2M$	$3 + \tfrac{3}{2}M$	$4 + 4M$	$1 + 6M$	0	$-M$	0	0	

You should now be able to set up tableau form and develop the initial simplex tableau for problems with any constraint form. Try Problem 23.

Note that we have circled the pivot element above indicating that x_4 will enter and a_1 will leave the basis at the first iteration.

NOTES & COMMENTS

We have shown how to convert constraints with negative right-hand sides to equivalent constraints with positive right-hand sides. Actually, there is nothing wrong with formulating a linear program and including negative right-hand sides. But if you want to use the ordinary simplex method to solve the linear program, you must first eliminate the negative right-hand sides.

5.8 Solving a Minimization Problem

There are two ways in which we can use the simplex method to solve a minimization problem. The first approach requires that we change the rule used to introduce a variable into the basis. Recall that in the maximization case, we select the variable with the largest positive $c_j - z_j$ as the variable to introduce next into the basis. This is because the value of $c_j - z_j$ tells us the amount the objective function will increase if one unit of the variable in column j is brought into solution. To solve the minimization problem, we can simply

Minimization problems can be solved by simply bringing in the variable at each iteration with the most negative $c_j - z_j$ value and stopping when all $c_j - z_j \geq 0$. Alternatively, one can convert a minimization problem to a maximization problem by multiplying the objective function by (-1) and bringing in the variable with the largest positive value for $c_j - z_j$ at each iteration.

reverse this rule. That is, we can select the variable with the most negative $c_j - z_j$ as the one to introduce next. Of course, this approach means the stopping rule for the optimal solution will also have to be changed. Using this approach to solve a minimization problem, we would stop when every value in the net evaluation row is zero or positive.

The second approach to solving a minimization problem is the one we shall employ in this book. It is based on the fact that any minimization problem can be converted to an equivalent maximization problem by multiplying the objective function by -1. Solving the resulting maximization problem will provide the optimal solution to the minimization problem.

Let us illustrate this second approach by using the simplex method to solve the M&D Chemicals problem introduced in Chapter 2. Recall that in this problem, management wanted to minimize the cost of producing two products subject to a demand constraint for product 1, a minimum total production quantity requirement, and a constraint on available processing time. The mathematical statement of the M&D Chemicals problem is shown below.

$$\text{Min} \quad 2x_1 + 3x_2$$

s.t.

$$1x_1 \qquad\qquad \geq 125 \quad \text{Demand for product 1}$$
$$1x_1 + 1x_2 \geq 350 \quad \text{Total production}$$
$$2x_1 + 1x_2 \leq 600 \quad \text{Processing time}$$
$$x_1, x_2 \geq 0$$

To solve this problem using the simplex method, we first multiply the objective function by -1 to convert the minimization problem into the following equivalent maximization problem:

$$\text{Max} \quad -2x_1 - 3x_2$$

s.t.

$$1x_1 \qquad\qquad \geq 125 \quad \text{Demand for product 1}$$
$$1x_1 + 1x_2 \geq 350 \quad \text{Total production}$$
$$2x_1 + 1x_2 \leq 600 \quad \text{Processing time}$$
$$x_1, x_2 \geq 0$$

The tableau form for this problem is as follows:

$$\text{Max} \quad -2x_1 - 3x_2 + 0s_1 + 0s_2 + 0s_3 - Ma_1 - Ma_2$$

s.t.

$$1x_1 \qquad - 1s_1 \qquad\qquad + 1a_1 \qquad = 125$$
$$1x_1 + 1x_2 \qquad - 1s_2 \qquad\qquad + 1a_2 = 350$$
$$2x_1 + 1x_2 \qquad\qquad + 1s_3 \qquad\qquad = 600$$
$$x_1, x_2, s_1, s_2, s_3, a_1, a_2 \geq 0$$

The initial simplex tableau is shown below:

		x_1	x_2	s_1	s_2	s_3	a_1	a_2	
Basis	c_B	-2	-3	0	0	0	$-M$	$-M$	
a_1	$-M$	①	0	-1	0	0	1	0	125
a_2	$-M$	1	1	0	-1	0	0	1	350
s_3	0	2	1	0	0	1	0	0	600
z_j		$-2M$	$-M$	M	M	0	$-M$	$-M$	$-475M$
$c_j - z_j$		$-2+2M$	$-3+M$	$-M$	$-M$	0	0	0	

At the first iteration, x_1 is brought into the basis and a_1 is eliminated. After dropping the a_1 column from the tableau, the result of the first iteration is as follows:

		x_1	x_2	s_1	s_2	s_3	a_2	
Basis	c_B	-2	-3	0	0	0	$-M$	
x_1	-2	1	0	-1	0	0	0	125
a_2	$-M$	0	1	1	-1	0	1	225
s_3	0	0	1	②	0	1	0	350
z_j		-2	$-M$	$2-M$	M	0	$-M$	$-250-225M$
$c_j - z_j$		0	$-3+M$	$-2+M$	$-M$	0	0	

Continuing with two more iterations of the simplex method provides the final simplex tableau shown below.

		x_1	x_2	s_1	s_2	s_3	
Basis	c_B	-2	-3	0	0	0	
x_1	-2	1	0	0	1	1	250
x_2	-3	0	1	0	-2	-1	100
s_1	0	0	0	1	1	1	125
z_j		-2	-3	0	4	1	-800
$c_j - z_j$		0	0	0	-4	-1	

In Chapter 2 we used the graphical solution procedure to determine the optimal solution to this problem. The feasible region and solution are shown again in Figure 5.5. The simplex method has provided the same optimal solution with $x_1 = 250$, $x_2 = 100$, $s_1 = 125$, $s_2 = 0$, and $s_3 = 0$. Note, however, that the value of the objective function is -800 in the final simplex tableau. We must now multiply this value by -1 to obtain the value of the objective function to the original minimization problem (total cost $= 800$).

In the next section we shall concentrate on discussing some important special cases that may occur when trying to solve any linear programming problem. We will only consider the case for maximization problems, recognizing that all minimization problems may be placed into this form by multiplying the objective function by -1.

You should now be able to solve a minimization problem with the simplex method. Try Problem 25.

Figure 5.5
Graphical Solution for the M&D
Chemicals Problem

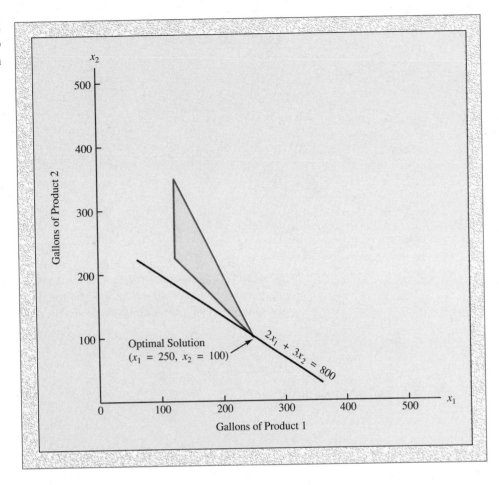

5.9 Special Cases

In Chapter 2 we discussed how infeasibility, unboundedness, and alternative optimal solutions could occur when solving linear programming problems using the graphical solution procedure. These special cases can also arise when using the simplex method. In addition, a special case referred to as *degeneracy* can theoretically cause difficulties for the simplex method. In this section we show how these special cases can be recognized and handled when the simplex method is used.

Infeasibility

Infeasibility occurs whenever there is no solution to the linear program that satisfies all the constraints, including the nonnegativity constraints. From the perspective of the graphical solution procedure, this means that there is no feasible region. Let us now see how infeasibility is recognized when the simplex method is used.

In Section 5.7, when discussing artificial variables, we mentioned that infeasibility can be recognized when the optimality criterion indicates that an optimal solution has been obtained and one or more of the artificial variables remain in the solution at a positive value. As an illustration of this situation, let us consider another modification of the

HighTech Industries problem. Suppose management had imposed a minimum combined total production requirement of 50 units. The revised problem formulation is shown below.

$$\text{Max} \quad 50x_1 + 40x_2$$

s.t.

$$3x_1 + 5x_2 \leq 150 \quad \text{Assembly time}$$
$$1x_2 \leq 20 \quad \text{Portable display}$$
$$8x_1 + 5x_2 \leq 300 \quad \text{Warehouse space}$$
$$1x_1 + 1x_2 \geq 50 \quad \text{Minimum total production}$$
$$x_1, x_2 \geq 0$$

A graph of the solution region for the problem is shown in Figure 5.6. We can see that there are no solutions that satisfy both the original HighTech problem constraints and the minimum combined total production constraint ($1x_1 + 1x_2 \geq 50$). Let us solve this modified problem using the simplex method. The simplex tableaus are shown on page 221.

Figure 5.6
Graph of Solution Region for Modified HighTech Problem

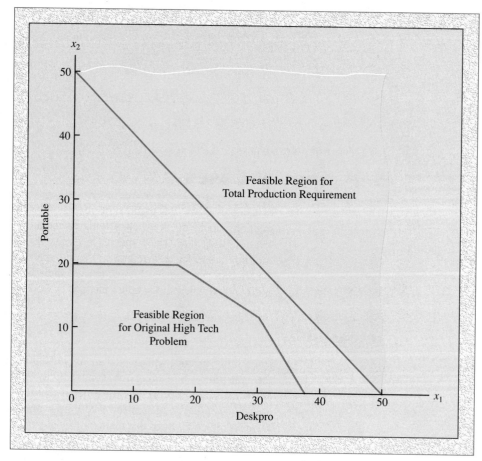

Initial Tableau

Basis	c_B	x_1 50	x_2 40	s_1 0	s_2 0	s_3 0	s_4 0	a_4 $-M$	
s_1	0	3	5	1	0	0	0	0	150
s_2	0	0	1	0	1	0	0	0	20
s_3	0	⑧	5	0	0	1	0	0	300
a_4	$-M$	1	1	0	0	0	-1	1	50
z_j		$-M$	$-M$	0	0	0	M	$-M$	$-50M$
$c_j - z_j$		$50 + M$	$40 + M$	0	0	0	$-M$	0	

Result of the First Iteration

Basis	c_B	x_1 50	x_2 40	s_1 0	s_2 0	s_3 0	s_4 0	a_4 $-M$	
s_1	0	0	㉕⁄₈	1	0	$-3/8$	0	0	$75/2$
s_2	0	0	1	0	1	0	0	0	20
x_1	50	1	$5/8$	0	0	$1/8$	0	0	$75/2$
a_4	$-M$	0	$3/8$	0	0	$-1/8$	-1	1	$25/2$
z_j		50	$\dfrac{250 - 3M}{8}$	0	0	$\dfrac{50 + M}{8}$	M	$-M$	$1875 - \dfrac{25M}{2}$
$c_j - z_j$		0	$\dfrac{70 + 3M}{8}$	0	0	$\dfrac{-50 - M}{8}$	$-M$	0	

Final Tableau

Basis	c_B	x_1 50	x_2 40	s_1 0	s_2 0	s_3 0	s_4 0	a_4 $-M$	
x_2	40	0	1	$8/25$	0	$-3/25$	0	0	12
s_2	0	0	0	$-8/25$	1	$3/25$	0	0	8
x_1	50	1	0	$-5/25$	0	$5/25$	0	0	30
a_4	$-M$	0	0	$-3/25$	0	$-2/25$	-1	1	8
z_j		50	40	$\dfrac{70 + 3M}{25}$	0	$\dfrac{130 + 2M}{25}$	M	$-M$	$1980 - 8M$
$c_j - z_j$		0	0	$\dfrac{-70 - 3M}{25}$	0	$\dfrac{-130 - 2M}{25}$	$-M$	0	

If an artificial variable is positive, the solution is not feasible for the real-world problem.

In the final tableau, just as you might have suspected, the artificial variable a_4 is in solution at a positive value; thus, phase I has not been completed. Note that $c_j - z_j \leq 0$ for all the variables; therefore, according to the optimality criterion, this should be the optimal solution. But this solution is not feasible for the modified HighTech problem since $x_1 = 30$ and $x_2 = 12$ results in a combined total production of 42 units instead of at least 50 units. The fact that the artificial variable is in solution at a value of $a_4 = 8$ tells us that the final solution violates the fourth constraint $(1x_1 + 1x_2 \geq 50)$ by eight units.

If management is interested in knowing which of the first three constraints is preventing us from satisfying the total production requirement, a partial answer can be obtained from the final simplex tableau. Note that $s_2 = 8$, but that s_1 and s_3 are nonbasic variables at values of zero. This tells us that the assembly time and warehouse capacity constraints are binding. Since there are not enough assembly time and warehouse space available, we cannot satisfy the minimum combined total production requirement.

The management implications here are that additional assembly time and/or warehouse space must be made available to satisfy the total production requirement. If more time and/or space cannot be made available, management will have to relax the total production requirement by at least eight units.

In summary, a linear program is infeasible if there is no solution that satisfies all the constraints simultaneously. Graphically, we recognize this situation as the case where there is no feasible region. *In terms of the simplex method, we recognize infeasibility as the case where one or more of the artificial variables remains in the final solution at a positive value.* In closing, we note that for linear programming problems with all $\leq$ constraints and nonnegative right-hand sides, there will always be a feasible solution. Since it is not necessary to introduce artificial variables to set up the initial simplex tableau for these types of problems, there could not possibly be an artificial variable in the final solution.

> You should now be able to recognize when there is no feasible solution to a problem using the simplex method. Try Problem 33.

Unboundedness

> Usually a constraint has been overlooked.

For maximization problems, we say that a linear program is unbounded if the value of the solution may be made infinitely large without violating any constraints. While discussing unboundedness for the graphical method in Section 2.8, we mentioned that unbounded profit maximization problems do not occur in practice. Thus, when unboundedness occurs, we can generally look for an error in the formulation of the problem.

The simplex method will automatically identify any unboundedness that exists before the final simplex tableau is reached. What will happen is that the rule for determining the variable to be removed from the basis will not identify one. Recall that in order to determine which variable should be removed from the current basis, we calculate the ratio $\bar{b}_i/\bar{a}_{ij}$ for each $\bar{a}_{ij}$ greater than zero. Then we pick the smallest ratio to tell us which variable to remove from the current basic feasible solution.

The coefficients in the column of the $\bar{A}$ matrix associated with the incoming variable indicate how much each of the current basic variables will decrease if one unit of the incoming variable is brought into solution. Suppose then, that for a particular linear programming problem, we reach a point where the rule for determining which variable should enter the basis results in the decision to enter variable x_2. Assume that for this variable, $c_2 - z_2 = 5$, and that all $\bar{a}_{i2}$ in column 2 are ≤ 0. Thus, each unit of x_2 brought into solution increases the objective function by five units. Furthermore, since $\bar{a}_{i2} \leq 0$ for all i, this means that none of the current basic variables will be driven to zero, no matter how many units of x_2 we introduce. Thus, we can introduce an infinite amount of x_2 into solution and still maintain feasibility. Since each unit of x_2 increases the objective function by 5, we will have an unbounded solution. Hence, *the way we recognize the unbounded situation is that all the $\bar{a}_{ij}$ are less than or equal to zero in the column associated with the incoming variable.*

To illustrate this concept, let us consider the example of an unbounded problem we introduced in Chapter 2:

$$\text{Max} \quad 20x_1 + 10x_2$$

$$\text{s.t.} \quad 1x_1 \qquad\qquad \geq 2$$

$$1x_2 \leq 5$$

$$x_1, x_2 \geq 0$$

We subtract a surplus variable s_1 from the first constraint equation and add a slack variable s_2 to the second constraint equation to obtain the standard-form representation. We then add an artificial variable a_1 to the first constraint equation to obtain the tableau form and to set up the initial simplex tableau in terms of the basic variables a_1 and s_2. After bringing in x_1 and deleting a_1 at the first iteration, the simplex tableau is as follows:

		x_1	x_2	s_1	s_2	
		20	10	0	0	
Basis	c_B					
x_1	20	1	0	-1	0	**2**
s_2	0	0	1	0	1	**5**
z_j		20	0	-20	0	**40**
$c_j - z_j$		0	10	20	0	

Since s_1 has the largest positive $c_j - z_j$, we know we can increase the value of the objective function most rapidly by bringing s_1 into the basis. But $\bar{a}_{13} = -1$ and $\bar{a}_{23} = 0$; hence, we cannot form the ratio $\bar{b}_i/\bar{a}_{i3}$ for any $\bar{a}_{i3} > 0$; there are no values of $\bar{a}_{i3}$ that are greater than zero. This is our indication that the solution to the linear program is unbounded. The reason the solution is unbounded is that each unit of s_1 that is brought into solution drives zero units of s_2 out of solution (since $\bar{a}_{23} = 0$) and provides one extra unit of x_1 (since $\bar{a}_{13} = -1$). The reason for this is that s_1 is a surplus variable and can be interpreted as the amount of product 1 we produce over the minimum amount required. Since the simplex tableau indicates that we can introduce as much of s_1 as we desire without violating any constraints, this tells us that we can make as much as we want above the minimum amount of x_1 required. Thus, there will be no upper bound on the value of the objective function since the objective function coefficient associated with x_1 is positive.

In summary, a maximization linear program is unbounded if it is possible to make the value of the optimal solution as large as desired without violating any of the constraints. We can recognize this condition graphically as the case where the feasible region extends to infinity in a direction in which the objective function increases. When employing the simplex solution procedure, an unbounded linear program is easy to recognize. *If, at some iteration, the simplex method tells us to introduce variable j into the solution and all the $\bar{a}_{ij}$ are less than or equal to zero in the jth column, the linear program has an unbounded solution.*

We emphasize that the case of an unbounded solution will never occur in real-world cost minimization or profit maximization problems because it is not possible to reduce costs to minus infinity or to increase profits to plus infinity. Thus, if we encounter an

Try Problem 35 for another example of an unbounded problem.

unbounded solution to a linear programming problem, we should carefully reexamine the formulation of the problem to determine if there has been a formulation error.

Alternative Optimal Solutions

A linear program with two or more optimal solutions is said to have alternative optimal solution. In Chapter 2 we saw that alternative optimal solution are recognized in the graphical solution procedure when the objective function line is parallel to one of the binding constraint lines. When using the simplex method, we cannot recognize that a linear program has alternative optimal solution until the final simplex tableau is reached. Then if the linear program has alternative optimal solution, $c_j - z_j$ will equal zero for one or more of the *nonbasic* variables.

To illustrate the case of alternative optimal solution when using the simplex method, consider changing the objective function for the HighTech problem from $50x_1 + 40x_2$ to $30x_1 + 50x_2$; in doing so, we obtain the revised linear program:

$$\text{Max} \quad 30x_1 + 50x_2$$

s.t.

$$3x_1 + 5x_2 \le 150$$
$$1x_2 \le 20$$
$$8x_1 + 5x_2 \le 300$$
$$x_1, x_2 \ge 0$$

The graphical solution to this problem is shown in Figure 5.7. Clearly, extreme points ③ and ④ are alternative optimal solutions. The final simplex tableau for this problem is shown below.

		x_1	x_2	s_1	s_2	s_3	
Basis	c_B	30	50	0	0	0	
x_2	50	0	1	0	1	0	**20**
s_3	0	0	0	$-8/3$	$25/3$	1	200/3
x_1	30	1	0	$1/3$	$-5/3$	0	50/3
z_j		30	50	10	0	0	**1500**
$c_j - z_j$		0	0	-10	0	0	

All values in the net evaluation row are less than or equal to zero, indicating that an optimal solution has been found. This solution is given by $x_1 = 50/3$, $x_2 = 20$, $s_1 = 0$, $s_2 = 0$, and $s_3 = 200/3$ and corresponds to extreme point ④ in Figure 5.7. The value of the objective function is 1500.

In looking at the net evaluation row in the optimal simplex tableau, we see that the $c_j - z_j$ value for nonbasic variable s_2 is equal to zero. This indicates that the linear program has alternative optimal solutions. In other words, since the net evaluation row entry for s_2 is zero, we can introduce s_2 into the basis without changing the value of the solution. The tableau obtained after introducing s_2 is at the top of page 225.

Basis	c_B	x_1 30	x_2 50	s_1 0	s_2 0	s_3 0	
x_2	50	0	1	$8/25$	0	$-3/25$	**12**
s_2	0	0	0	$-8/25$	1	$3/25$	**8**
x_1	30	1	0	$-5/25$	0	$5/25$	**30**
z_j		30	50	10	0	0	**1500**
$c_j - z_j$		0	0	-10	0	0	

After introducing s_2, we have a different basic feasible solution: $x_1 = 30$, $x_2 = 12$, $s_1 = 0$, $s_2 = 8$, and $s_3 = 0$. However, this new solution is also optimal since $c_j - z_j \leq 0$ for all j. Another way to confirm that this solution is still optimal is to note that the value of the solution has remained equal to 1500. This solution corresponds to extreme point ③ in Figure 5.7.

Try Problem 34 for another example of alternative optimal solutions.

In summary, we can recognize that a linear programming problem has alternative optimal solutions when using the graphical approach by observing that the objective function is parallel to one of the binding constraints. *When using the simplex method, we*

Figure 5.7

Graphical Solution to HighTech Problem with Alternative Optimal Solutions

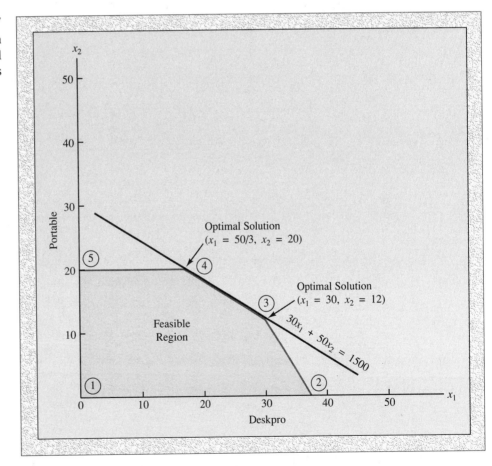

can recognize alternative optimal solutions if $c_j - z_j$ equals zero for one or more of the nonbasic variables in the final simplex tableau.

Degeneracy

A linear program is said to be *degenerate* if one or more of the basic variables have a value of zero. Degeneracy does not cause any particular difficulties for the graphical solution procedure; however, degeneracy can theoretically cause difficulties when the simplex method is used to solve a linear programming problem.

To see how a degenerate linear program could occur, consider a change in the right-hand-side value of the assembly time constraint for the HighTech problem. For example, what if the number of hours available had been 175 instead of 150? The modified linear program is shown below.

$$\text{Max} \quad 50x_1 + 40x_2$$

s.t.

$$3x_1 + 5x_2 \leq 175 \quad \text{Assembly time increased to 175 hours}$$

$$1x_2 \leq 20 \quad \text{Portable display}$$

$$8x_1 + 5x_2 \leq 300 \quad \text{Warehouse space}$$

$$x_1, x_2 \geq 0$$

The simplex tableau after one iteration is presented below.

		x_1	x_2	s_1	s_2	s_3	
Basis	c_B	50	40	0	0	0	
s_1	0	0	$25/8$	1	0	$-3/8$	$125/2$
s_2	0	0	1	0	1	0	**20**
x_1	50	1	$5/8$	0	0	$1/8$	$75/2$
z_j		50	$250/8$	0	0	$50/8$	**1875**
$c_j - z_j$		0	$70/8$	0	0	$-50/8$	

The entries in the net evaluation row indicate that x_2 should enter the basis. By calculating the appropriate ratios to determine the pivot row, we obtain

$$\frac{\bar{b}_1}{\bar{a}_{12}} = \frac{125/2}{25/8} = 20$$

$$\frac{\bar{b}_2}{\bar{a}_{22}} = \frac{20}{1} = 20$$

$$\frac{\bar{b}_3}{\bar{a}_{32}} = \frac{75/2}{5/8} = 60$$

We see that there is a tie between the first and second rows. This is an indication that we will have a degenerate basic feasible solution at the next iteration. Recall that when there is a tie, we follow the convention of selecting the uppermost row as the pivot row.

This means that s_1 will leave the basis. But from the tie for the minimum ratio we see that the basic variable in row 2, s_2, will also be driven to zero. Since it does not leave the basis, we will have a basic variable with a value of zero after performing this iteration. The simplex tableau after this iteration is as follows:

		x_1	x_2	s_1	s_2	s_3	
Basis	c_B	50	40	0	0	0	
x_2	40	0	1	$8/25$	0	$-3/25$	**20**
s_2	0	0	0	$-8/25$	1	$3/25$	**0**
x_1	50	1	0	$-5/25$	0	$5/25$	**25**
z_j		50	40	$70/25$	0	$130/25$	**2050**
$c_j - z_j$		0	0	$-70/25$	0	$-130/25$	

Transportation and assignment problems have degenerate solutions at every iteration.

As expected, we have a basic feasible solution with one of the basic variables, s_2, equal to zero. Whenever we have a tie in the minimum $\bar{b}_i/\bar{a}_{ij}$ ratio, there will always be a basic variable equal to zero in the next tableau. Since we are at the optimal solution in the above case, we do not care that s_2 is in solution at a zero value. However, if degeneracy occurs at some iteration prior to reaching the optimal solution, it is theoretically possible for the simplex method to cycle; that is, the procedure could possibly alternate between the same set of nonoptimal basic feasible solutions and never reach the optimal solution. Cycling has not proved to be a significant difficulty in practice. Therefore, we do not recommend introducing any special steps into the simplex method to eliminate the possibility that degeneracy will occur. If while performing the iterations of the simplex algorithm a tie occurs for the minimum $\bar{b}_i/\bar{a}_{ij}$ ratio, then we recommend simply selecting the upper row as the pivot row.

NOTES & COMMENTS

1. We have stated that infeasibility is recognized when the stopping rule is encountered but one or more artificial variables are in solution at a positive value. This does not necessarily mean that all artificial variables must be nonbasic to have a feasible solution. An artificial variable could be in solution at a zero value.

2. An unbounded feasible region must exist for a problem to be unbounded, but this does not guarantee that a problem will be unbounded. A minimization problem may be bounded whereas a maximization problem is unbounded with the same feasible region.

Summary

In Chapter 2 we showed how linear programming problems with two decision variables can be solved using the graphical method. In this chapter the simplex method was introduced as an algebraic procedure for solving linear programming problems. Although the simplex method can be used to solve small linear programs by hand calculations, this becomes too cumbersome as problems get larger. As a result, we must utilize a computer if we want to solve large linear programs in any reasonable length of time. The computational procedures of most computer software packages are based on the simplex method.

We described how developing the tableau form of a linear program is a necessary step in the simplex solution procedure, including learning how to convert greater-than-or-equal-to constraints, equality constraints, and constraints with negative right-hand-side values into tableau form.

For linear programs with greater-than-or-equal-to constraints and/or equality constraints, artificial variables are used to obtain tableau form. An objective function coefficient of $-M$, where M is a very large number, is assigned to each artificial variable. If there is a feasible solution to the real-world problem, all artificial variables will be driven out of solution (or to zero) before the simplex method reaches its optimality criterion. The iterations required to remove the artificial variables from solution constitute what is called phase I of the simplex method.

Two techniques were mentioned for solving minimization problems. The first approach involved changing the rule for introducing a variable into solution (choose the most negative $c_j - z_j$) and changing the optimality criterion (all $c_j - z_j \geq 0$). The second approach involved multiplying the objective function by -1 to obtain an equivalent maximization problem. With this change, any minimization problem can be solved using the steps required for a maximization problem, but the value of the optimal solution must be multiplied by (-1) to obtain the optimal value of the original minimization problem.

As a review of the material in this chapter we now present a detailed step-by-step procedure for solving linear programs using the simplex method.

Step 1   Formulate a linear programming model of the problem.

Step 2   Define an equivalent linear program by performing the following operations:
    a.   Multiply each constraint with a negative right-hand-side value by -1, and change the direction of the constraint inequality.
    b.   For a minimization problem, convert the problem to an equivalent maximization problem by multiplying the objective function by -1.

Step 3   Set up the standard-form representation of the linear program by adding appropriate slack and surplus variables.

Step 4   Set up the tableau-form representation of the linear program to obtain an initial basic feasible solution. All linear programs must be set up this way before the initial simplex tableau can be obtained.

Step 5   Set up the initial simplex tableau to keep track of the calculations required by the simplex method.

Step 6   Choose the nonbasic variable with the largest $c_j - z_j$ to bring into the basis. The column associated with that variable is the pivot column.

Step 7   Choose as the pivot row that row with the smallest ratio of $\bar{b}_i/\bar{a}_{ij}$ for $\bar{a}_{ij} > 0$. This ratio is used to determine which variable will leave the basis when variable j enters the basis. This ratio also indicates how many units of variable j can be introduced into solution before the basic variable in the ith row equals zero.

Step 8   Perform the necessary elementary row operations to convert the pivot column to a unit column.
    a.   Divide each element in the pivot row by the pivot element. The result is a new pivot row containing a 1 in the pivot column.
    b.   Obtain zeroes in all other positions of the pivot column by adding or subtracting an appropriate multiple of the new pivot row.

Step 9   Test for optimality. If $c_j - z_j \leq 0$ for all columns, we have the optimal solution. If not, return to step 6.

In Section 5.9 we discussed how the special cases of infeasibility, unboundedness, alternative optimal solutions, and degeneracy can occur when solving linear programming problems with the simplex method.

Glossary

Simplex method An algebraic procedure for solving linear programming problems. The simplex method uses elementary row operations to iterate from one basic feasible solution (extreme point) to another until the optimal solution is reached.

Basic solution Given a linear program in standard form, with n variables and m constraints, a basic solution is a solution obtained by setting $n - m$ of the variables equal to zero and solving the constraint equations for the values of the other m variables. If a unique solution exists, it is a basic solution.

Nonbasic variable One of $n - m$ variables set equal to zero in a basic solution.

Basic variable One of the m variables not required to equal zero in a basic solution.

Basic feasible solution A basic solution that is also feasible; that is, it satisfies the nonnegativity constraints. A basic feasible solution corresponds to an extreme point.

Tableau form The form in which a linear program must be written before setting up the initial simplex tableau. When a linear program is written in tableau form, its A matrix contains m unit columns corresponding to the basic variables, and the values of these basic variables are given by the values in the b column. A further requirement is that the entries in the b column be greater than or equal to zero.

Simplex tableau A table used to keep track of the calculations made when the simplex method is employed.

Unit vector or unit column A vector or column of a matrix that has a zero in every position except one. In the nonzero position there is a 1. There is a unit column in the simplex tableau for each basic variable.

Basis The set of variables that is not restricted to equal zero in the current basic solution. The variables that make up the basis are termed basic variables, and the remaining variables are called nonbasic variables.

Net evaluation row The row in the simplex tableau that contains the value of $c_j - z_j$ for every variable (column).

Elementary row operations Operations that may be performed on a system of simultaneous equations without changing the solution to the system of equations.

Iteration An iteration of the simplex method consists of the sequence of elementary row operations performed in moving from one basic feasible solution to another.

Pivot column The column in the simplex tableau corresponding to the nonbasic variable that is about to be introduced into solution.

Pivot row The row in the simplex tableau corresponding to the basic variable that will leave the solution.

Pivot element The element of the simplex tableau that is in both the pivot row and the pivot column.

Artificial variable A variable that has no physical meaning in terms of the original linear programming problem, but serves merely to enable a basic feasible solution to be created for starting the simplex method. Artificial variables are assigned an objective function coefficient of $-M$, where M is a very large number.

Phase I When artificial variables are present in the initial simplex tableau, phase I refers to the iterations of the simplex method that are used to drive the artificial variables out of solution. At the end of phase I, the basic feasible solution in the simplex tableau is also feasible for the real-world problem.

Degeneracy When one or more of the basic variables has a value of zero.

Problems

1. Solve the following system of linear equations; that is, find the values of x_1 and x_2 that satisfy both equations.

$$6x_1 + 3x_2 = 33$$

$$10x_1 - 2x_2 = 6$$

2. Solve the following system of linear equations; that is, find the values of x_1, x_2, and x_3 that satisfy all three equations.

$$1x_1 + 3x_2 - 1x_3 = 4$$

$$2x_1 + 4x_2 + 2x_3 = 22$$

$$5x_1 - 2x_2 + 1x_3 = 27$$

3. Consider the following system of linear equations:

$$3x_1 + x_2 \quad = 6$$

$$2x_1 + 4x_2 + x_3 = 12$$

   a. Find the basic solution with $x_1 = 0$.
   b. Find the basic solution with $x_2 = 0$.
   c. Find the basic solution with $x_3 = 0$.
   d. Which of the above would be basic feasible solutions for a linear program?

4. Consider the following linear program:

$$\text{Max} \quad x_1 + 2x_2$$

s.t.

$$x_1 + 5x_2 \le 10$$

$$2x_1 + 6x_2 \le 16$$

$$x_1, x_2 \ge 0$$

   a. Write the problem in standard form.
   b. How many variables will be set equal to zero in a basic solution for this problem?
   c. Find all the basic solutions, and indicate which are also feasible.
   d. Find the optimal solution by computing the value of each basic feasible solution.

5. Consider the following linear program:

$$\text{Max} \quad 5x_1 + 9x_2$$

s.t.

$$\tfrac{1}{2}x_1 + 1x_2 \le 8$$

$$1x_1 + 1x_2 \ge 10$$

$$\tfrac{1}{4}x_1 + \tfrac{3}{2}x_2 \ge 6$$

$$x_1, x_2 \ge 0$$

   a. Write the problem in standard form.
   b. How many variables will be set equal to zero in a basic solution for this problem? Explain.
   c. Find the basic solution that corresponds to s_1 and s_2 equal to zero.

d. Find the basic solution that corresponds to x_1 and s_3 equal to zero.

e. Are your solutions for part (c) and/or (d) basic feasible solutions? Extreme-point solutions? Explain.

f. Use the graphical approach to identify the solutions found in parts (c) and (d). Do the graphical results agree with your answer to part (e)? Explain.

S E L F   T E S T

6. Standard form and partial initial simplex tableau

6. Consider the following linear programming problem:

$$\text{Max} \quad 60x_1 + 90x_2$$

s.t.

$$15x_1 + 45x_2 \le 90$$

$$5x_1 + 5x_2 \le 20$$

$$x_1, x_2 \ge 0$$

a. Write the problem in standard form.

b. Develop the portion of the simplex tableau involving the objective function coefficients, the coefficients of the variables in the constraints, and the constants for the right-hand sides.

S E L F   T E S T

7. Complete initial tableau, choose entering variable, reconstruct original problem

7. A partially completed initial simplex tableau is given:

		x_1	x_2	s_1	s_2	
Basis	c_B	5	9	0	0	
s_1	0	10	9	1	0	90
s_2	0	−5	3	0	1	15
z_j						
$c_j - z_j$						

a. Complete the initial tableau.

b. Which variable would be brought into solution at the first iteration?

c. Write the original linear program.

S E L F   T E S T

8. Tableau form and simplex solution

8. The following partial initial simplex tableau is given:

		x_1	x_2	x_3	s_1	s_2	s_3	
Basis	c_B	5	20	25	0	0	0	
		2	1	0	1	0	0	40
		0	2	1	0	1	0	30
		3	0	−½	0	0	1	15
z_j								
$c_j - z_j$								

a. Complete the initial tableau.

b. Write the problem in tableau form.

c. What is the initial basis? Does this correspond to the origin? Explain.

d. What is the value of the objective function at this initial solution?

e. For the next iteration, what variable should enter the basis, and what variable should leave the basis?

f. How many units of the entering variable will be in the next solution? Before making this first iteration, what do you think will be the value of the objective function after the first iteration?

g. Find the optimal solution using the simplex method.

9. Graphical and simplex solution

9. Solve the following linear program using the graphical approach:

$$\text{Max} \quad 4x_1 + 5x_2$$

s.t.

$$2x_1 + 2x_2 \leq 20$$

$$3x_1 + 7x_2 \leq 42$$

$$x_1, x_2 \geq 0$$

Put the linear program in tableau form, and solve using the simplex method. Show the sequence of extreme points generated by the simplex method on your graph.

10. Standard form and tableau form

10. Explain in your own words why the tableau form and the standard form are the same for problems with less-than-or-equal-to constraints and nonnegative b_i's.

11. Simplex and graphical solution, maximization problem

11. Solve the Ryland Farm problem (Chapter 2, Problem 27) using the simplex method. Locate the solution found at each iteration on the graph of the feasible region. The formulation is shown below.

$$\text{Max} \quad 100x_1 + 200x_2$$

s.t.

$$
\begin{array}{llll}
x_1 + & x_2 \leq & 500 & \text{Land} \\
x_1 & \leq & 200 & \text{Soybean limit} \\
2x_1 + & 6x_2 \leq & 1200 & \text{Labor hours} \\
\end{array}
$$

$$x_1, x_2 \geq 0$$

where

$$x_1 = \text{acres of soybeans}$$
$$x_2 = \text{acres of corn}$$

12. Simplex solution and interpretation

12. Recall the problem for Par, Inc., introduced in Section 2.1. The complete mathematical model for this problem, originally presented in Section 2.4, is restated below:

$$\text{Max} \quad 10x_1 + 9x_2$$

s.t.

$$
\begin{array}{lll}
\tfrac{7}{10}x_1 + 1x_2 \leq 630 & \text{Cutting and dyeing} \\
\tfrac{1}{2}x_1 + \tfrac{5}{6}x_2 \leq 600 & \text{Sewing} \\
1x_1 + \tfrac{2}{3}x_2 \leq 708 & \text{Finishing} \\
\tfrac{1}{10}x_1 + \tfrac{1}{4}x_2 \leq 135 & \text{Inspection and packaging} \\
\end{array}
$$

$$x_1, x_2 \geq 0$$

where

$$x_1 = \text{number of standard bags produced}$$
$$x_2 = \text{number of deluxe bags produced}$$

a. Use the simplex method to determine how many bags of each model Par should manufacture.
b. What is the profit Par can earn with the above production quantities?
c. How many hours of production time will be scheduled for each operation?
d. What is the slack time in each operation?

13. Simplex solution compared to graphical solution

13. Solve the RMC problem (Chapter 2, Problem 21) using the simplex method. At each iteration, locate the basic feasible solution found by the simplex method on the graph of the feasible region. The problem formulation is shown below:

$$\text{Max} \quad 40x_1 + 30x_2$$

s.t.

$$\tfrac{2}{5}x_1 + \tfrac{1}{2}x_2 \leq 20 \quad \text{Material 1}$$

$$\tfrac{1}{5}x_2 \leq 5 \quad \text{Material 2}$$

$$\tfrac{3}{5}x_1 + \tfrac{3}{10}x_2 \leq 21 \quad \text{Material 3}$$

$$x_1, x_2 \geq 0$$

where

$$x_1 = \text{tons of fuel additive produced}$$
$$x_2 = \text{tons of solvent base produced}$$

14. Simplex solution

14. Solve the following linear program:

$$\text{Max} \quad 5x_1 + 5x_2 + 24x_3$$

s.t.

$$15x_1 + 4x_2 + 12x_3 \leq 2800$$

$$15x_1 + 8x_2 \leq 6000$$

$$x_1 + 8x_3 \leq 1200$$

$$x_1, x_2, x_3 \geq 0$$

15. Simplex and graphical solution

15. Solve the following linear program using both the graphical and the simplex methods:

$$\text{Max} \quad 2x_1 + 8x_2$$

s.t.

$$3x_1 + 9x_2 \leq 45$$

$$2x_1 + 1x_2 \geq 12$$

$$x_1, x_2 \geq 0$$

Show graphically how the simplex method moves from one basic feasible solution to another. Find the coordinates of all extreme points of the feasible region.

16. Basic solutions

16. How many basic solutions are possible for a linear program that has seven variables and four constraints when written in standard form?

17. Solve the following linear program:

$$\text{Max} \quad 120x_1 + 80x_2 + 14x_3$$

s.t.

$$4x_1 + 8x_2 + x_3 \leq 200$$
$$2x_2 + x_3 \leq 300$$
$$32x_1 + 4x_2 + 2x_3 = 400$$

$$x_1, x_2, x_3 \geq 0$$

18. Refer to Problem 12.
   a. Suppose that instead of introducing x_1 into the solution at the first iteration of the simplex method, you had mistakenly introduced x_2. Continue with the simplex method until an optimal solution has been reached.
   b. Do we always have to introduce the variable into the solution that has the largest $c_j - z_j$ value?
   c. Why does the criterion for introducing the variable into the solution use the largest $c_j - z_j$ value?

19. Suppose that we did not remove the basic variable with the smallest ratio of $\bar{b}_i/\bar{a}_{ij}$ at a particular iteration. What effect would this have on the simplex tableau for our next solution?

20. Suppose a company manufactures three products from two raw materials where the amount of raw material in each unit of each product is given.

Raw Material	Product A	Product B	Product C
I	7 lb	6 lb	3 lb
II	5 lb	4 lb	2 lb

If the company has available 100 pounds of material I and 200 pounds of material II, and if the profits for the three products are $20, $20, and $15 respectively, how much of each product should be produced to maximize profits?

21. Liva's Lumber, Inc., manufactures three types of plywood. The table below summarizes the production hours per unit in each of three production operations and other data for the problem.

Plywood	Operations (hours)			Profit/Unit
	I	II	III	
Grade A	2	2	4	$40
Grade B	5	5	2	$30
Grade X	10	3	2	$20
Maximum time available	900	400	600	

How many units of each grade of lumber should be produced?

22. Modeling, simplex solution and interpretation, maximization problem

22. Ye Olde Cording Winery in Peoria, Illinois, makes three kinds of authentic German wine: Heidelberg Sweet, Heidelberg Regular, and Deutschland Extra Dry. The raw materials, labor, and profit for a gallon of each of these wines are summarized below.

Wine	Grade A Grapes (bushels)	Grade B Grapes (bushels)	Sugar (pounds)	Labor (hours)	Profit/ Gallon
Heidelberg Sweet	1	1	2	2	$1.00
Heidelberg Regular	2	0	1	3	$1.20
Deutschland Extra Dry	0	2	0	1	$2.00

If the winery has 150 bushels of grade A grapes, 150 bushels of grade B grapes, 80 pounds of sugar, and 225 labor-hours available during the next week, what product mix of wines will maximize the company's profit?
a. Solve using the simplex method.
b. Interpret all slack variables.
c. An increase in what resources could improve the company's profit?

S E L F T E S T ▷

23. Set up the tableau form for the following linear program (do not attempt to solve):

23. General tableau form

$$\text{Max} \quad 4x_1 + 2x_2 - 3x_3 + 5x_4$$

s.t.

$$2x_1 - 1x_2 + 1x_3 + 2x_4 \geq 50$$

$$3x_1 \qquad\quad - 1x_3 + 2x_4 \leq 80$$

$$1x_1 + 1x_2 \qquad\quad + 1x_4 = 60$$

$$x_1, x_2, x_3, x_4 \geq 0$$

24. General tableau form

24. Set up the tableau form for the following linear program (do not attempt to solve):

$$\text{Min} \quad 4x_1 + 5x_2 + 3x_3$$

s.t.

$$4x_1 \qquad\quad + 2x_3 \geq 20$$

$$1x_2 - 1x_3 \leq -8$$

$$1x_1 - 2x_2 \qquad\quad = -5$$

$$2x_1 + 1x_2 + 1x_3 \leq 12$$

$$x_1, x_2, x_3 \geq 0$$

S E L F T E S T ▷

25. Simplex solution, artificial variables

25. Solve the following linear program:

$$\text{Min} \quad 3x_1 + 4x_2 + 8x_3$$

s.t.

$$4x_1 + 2x_2 \qquad\quad \geq 12$$

$$4x_2 + 8x_3 \geq 16$$

$$x_1, x_2, x_3 \geq 0$$

26. Solve the following linear program:

$$\text{Min} \quad 84x_1 + 4x_2 + 30x_3$$

s.t.

$$8x_1 + x_2 + 3x_3 \leq 240$$
$$16x_1 + x_2 + 7x_3 \geq 480$$
$$8x_1 - x_2 + 4x_3 \geq 160$$
$$x_1, x_2, x_3 \geq 0$$

27. Captain John's Yachts, Inc., located in Fort Lauderdale, Florida, rents three types of ocean-going boats: sailboats, cabin cruisers, and Captain John's favorite, the luxury yachts. Captain John advertises his boats with his famous "you rent—we pilot" slogan, which means that the company supplies the captain and crew for each rented boat. Each rented boat has one captain, of course, but the crew sizes (deck hands, galley hands, etc.) differ. The crew requirements, in addition to a captain, are one for sailboats, two for cabin cruisers, and three for yachts. Ten employees are captains, and an additional 18 employees fill the various crew positions. Currently, Captain John has rental requests for all of his boats: four sailboats, eight cabin cruisers, and three luxury yachts. If Captain John's daily profit contribution is $50 for sailboats, $70 for cruisers, and $100 for luxury yachts, how many boats of each type should he rent?

28. The Our-Bags-Don't-Break (OBDB) plastic bag company manufactures three plastic refuse bags for home use: a 20-gallon garbage bag, a 30-gallon garbage bag, and a 33-gallon leaf-and-grass bag. Using purchased plastic material, three operations are required to produce each end product: cutting, sealing, and packaging. The production time required to process each type of bag in every operation and the maximum production time available for each operation are shown below (note that the production time figures in this table are per box of each type of bag).

Type of Bag	Production Time (seconds/box)		
	Cutting	Sealing	Packaging
20 gallons	2	2	3
30 gallons	3	2	4
33 gallons	3	3	5
Time available	2 hours	3 hours	4 hours

If OBDB's profit contribution is $0.10 for each box of 20-gallon bags produced, $0.15 for each box of 30-gallon bags, and $0.20 for each box of 33-gallon bags, what is the optimal product mix?

29. Kirkman Brothers ice cream parlors sell three different flavors of Dairy Sweet ice milk: chocolate, vanilla, and banana. Due to extremely hot weather and a high demand for its products, Kirkman has run short of its supply of ingredients: milk, sugar, and cream. Hence, Kirkman will not be able to fill all the orders received from its retail outlets, the ice cream parlors. Due to these circumstances, Kirkman has decided to make the most profitable amounts of the three flavors, given the constraints on supply of the basic ingredients. The company will then ration the ice milk to the retail outlets.

Kirkman has collected the following data on profitability of the various flavors, availability of supplies, and amounts required for each flavor.

Flavor	Profit/ Gallon	Usage/Gallon		
		Milk (gallons)	Sugar (pounds)	Cream (gallons)
Chocolate	$1.00	0.45	0.50	0.10
Vanilla	$0.90	0.50	0.40	0.15
Banana	$0.95	0.40	0.40	0.20
Maximum available		200	150	60

Determine the optimal product mix for Kirkman Brothers. What additional resources could be used profitably?

30. Maximization problem, 6 variables, 3 ≤ constraints

30. Uforia Corporation sells two different brands of perfume: Incentive and Temptation No. 1. Uforia sells exclusively through department stores and employs a three-person sales staff to call on its customers. The amount of time necessary for each sales representative to sell one case of each product varies with experience and ability. Data on the average time for each of Uforia's three sales representatives is presented below.

Salesperson	Average Sales Time per Case (minutes)	
	Incentive	Temptation No. 1
John	10	15
Brenda	15	10
Red	12	6

Each sales representative spends approximately 80 hours per month in the actual selling of these two products. Cases of Incentive and Temptation No. 1 sell at profits of $30 and $25, respectively. How many cases of each perfume should each person sell during the next month to maximize the firm's profits? (Hint: Let x_1 = number of cases of Incentive sold by John, x_2 = number of cases of Temptation No. 1 sold by John, x_3 = number of cases of Incentive sold by Brenda, etc.)

31. Maximization problem, 2 variables, 3 ≤ constraints, 2 ≥ constraints

31. Recall the RMC problem (Chapter 2, Problem 21). The formulation is shown in Problem 13. Suppose management required that at least 10 tons of each product be produced. Modify the previous formulation, as appropriate, and solve using the simplex method.

32. Maximization problem, 3 variables, 4 ≤ constraints

32. Catalina Yachts, Inc., is a builder of cruising sailboats. It manufactures three models of sailboats: the C-32, the C-40, and the C-48. The company, because of its excellent reputation, is in the position of being able to sell all the boats it manufactures. Catalina is currently in the process of taking orders for the coming year. How many orders for each model should be accepted to maximize total profit contribution?

The manufacture of each model requires different amounts of time spent on each of three operations: molding, carpentry, and finishing. The number of days required to perform each of these activities on the three models is given below.

	Production Time (person-days)		
Model	Molding	Carpentry	Finishing
C-32	3	5	4
C-40	5	12	5
C-48	10	18	8

Based on past experience, management expects the profit contribution per boat to be $5000 on the C-32, $10,000 on the C-40, and $20,000 on the C-48.

Catalina currently has 40 people employed in manufacturing these sailboats: 10 in molding, 20 in carpentry, and 10 in finishing. On average, each employee works 240 days per year. The only other constraint is a management-imposed restriction on the number of C-48 models that may be sold. Because Catalina does not want the C-48 to become commonplace, it will not take orders for more than 20 of this model.

Note: In Problems 33–38, we provide examples of linear programs that result in one or more of the following situations:

1. Optimal solution
2. Infeasible solution
3. Unbounded solution
4. Alternative optimal solutions
5. Degenerate solution

For each linear program, determine the solution situation that exists, and indicate how you identified each situation using the simplex method. For the problems with alternative optimal solutions, calculate at least two optimal solutions.

SELF TEST ▷ **33.**

33. Infeasibility

$$\text{Max} \quad 4x_1 + 8x_2$$

s.t.

$$2x_1 + 2x_2 \le 10$$

$$-1x_1 + 1x_2 \ge 8$$

$$x_1, x_2 \ge 0$$

SELF TEST ▷ **34.**

34. Alternate optimal solution

$$\text{Min} \quad 3x_1 + 3x_2$$

s.t.

$$2x_1 + 0.5x_2 \ge 10$$

$$2x_1 \qquad \ge 4$$

$$4x_1 + 4x_2 \ge 32$$

$$x_1, x_2 \ge 0$$

SELF TEST ▷ **35.**

35. Unbounded

$$\text{Max} \quad 1x_1 + 1x_2$$

s.t.

$$8x_1 + 6x_2 \ge 24$$

$$4x_1 + 6x_2 \ge -12$$

$$2x_2 \ge 4$$

$$x_1, x_2 \ge 0$$

36. Alternate optimal solution

36.

$$\text{Max} \quad 2x_1 + 1x_2 + 1x_3$$

s.t.

$$4x_1 + 2x_2 + 2x_3 \geq 4$$
$$2x_1 + 4x_2 \qquad \leq 20$$
$$4x_1 + 8x_2 + 2x_3 \leq 16$$
$$x_1, x_2, x_3 \geq 0$$

37. Degeneracy

37.

$$\text{Max} \quad 2x_1 + 4x_2$$

s.t.

$$1x_1 + \tfrac{1}{2}x_2 \leq 10$$
$$1x_1 + 1x_2 = 12$$
$$1x_1 + \tfrac{3}{2}x_2 \leq 18$$
$$x_1, x_2 \geq 0$$

38. Infeasibility

38.

$$\text{Min} \quad -4x_1 + 5x_2 + 5x_3$$

s.t.

$$-1x_2 + 1x_3 \geq 2$$
$$-1x_1 + 1x_2 + 1x_3 \geq 1$$
$$-1x_3 \geq 1$$
$$x_1, x_2, x_3 \geq 0$$

39. a. Infeasibility
b. Alternate optimal solution

39. Supersport Footballs, Inc., manufactures three kinds of football: an All-Pro model, a College model, and a High School model. All three footballs require operations in the following departments: cutting and dyeing, sewing, and inspection and packaging. The production times and maximum production availabilities are shown below.

	Production Time (minutes)		
Model	Cutting and Dyeing	Sewing	Inspection and Packaging
All-Pro	12	15	3
College	10	15	4
High School	8	12	2
Time available	300 hours	200 hours	100 hours

Current orders indicate that at least 1000 All-Pro footballs must be manufactured.
a. If Supersport realizes a profit contribution of $3 for each All-Pro model, $5 for each College model, and $4 for each High School model, how many footballs of each type should be produced? What occurs in the solution of this problem? Why?
b. If Supersport can increase sewing time to 300 hours and inspection and packaging time to 150 hours by using overtime, what is your recommendation?

Simplex-Based Sensitivity Analysis and Duality

In Chapter 2 we defined sensitivity analysis as the study of how the optimal solution and the value of the optimal solution to a linear program change, given changes in the various coefficients of the problem. First, we showed how graphical sensitivity analysis can be performed for linear programs involving two decision variables; then in Chapter 3, as part of the discussion of the computer solution of linear programs, we showed how sensitivity analysis can be performed with the help of computer output. In this chapter we discuss how the sensitivity analysis information contained in the computer solution of linear programs is developed. As we will show, the final simplex tableau contains the information that is used to compute the dual prices, the ranges for the objective function coefficients, and the ranges for the right-hand-side values. The topic of duality is also introduced. We will see that associated with every linear programming problem is a dual problem that has an interesting economic interpretation.

6.1 Sensitivity Analysis with the Simplex Tableau

The usual sensitivity analysis for linear programs involves computing ranges for the objective function coefficients and the right-hand-side values, as well as the dual prices.

Objective Function Coefficients

At the end points of this range, the corresponding variable is a candidate for entering the basis if it is currently out or for leaving the basis if it is currently in.

Sensitivity analysis for an objective function coefficient involves placing a range on the coefficient's value. We call this range the *range of optimality*. As long as the actual value of the objective function coefficient is within the range of optimality, *the current basic feasible solution will remain optimal*. Thus, for a nonbasic variable, the range of optimality defines the coefficient values for which that variable will remain nonbasic. In contrast, the range of optimality for a basic variable defines the objective function

240

coefficient values for which that variable will remain part of the current optimal basic feasible solution.

In computing the range of optimality for an objective function coefficient, all other coefficients in the problem are assumed to remain at their original values; in other words, *only one coefficient is allowed to change at a time*. To illustrate the process of computing ranges for objective function coefficients, recall the HighTech Industries problem introduced in Chapter 5. The linear program that we developed for this problem is restated below.

$$\text{Max} \quad 50x_1 + 40x_2$$

s.t.

$$3x_1 + 5x_2 \leq 150 \quad \text{Assembly time}$$
$$1x_2 \leq 20 \quad \text{Portable display}$$
$$8x_1 + 5x_2 \leq 300 \quad \text{Warehouse capacity}$$
$$x_1, x_2 \geq 0$$

where

$$x_1 = \text{number of units of the Deskpro assembled}$$
$$x_2 = \text{number of units of the Portable assembled}$$

The final simplex tableau for the HighTech problem is reproduced below.

Basis	c_B	x_1 50	x_2 40	s_1 0	s_2 0	s_3 0	
x_2	40	0	1	$8/25$	0	$-3/25$	12
s_2	0	0	0	$-8/25$	1	$3/25$	8
x_1	50	1	0	$-5/25$	0	$5/25$	30
z_j		50	40	$14/5$	0	$26/5$	1980
$c_j - z_j$		0	0	$-14/5$	0	$-26/5$	

An objective function coefficient change causes changes in the z_j and $c_j - z_j$ rows, but not in the variable values.

Recall that when the simplex method is used to solve a linear program, an optimal solution is recognized when all entries in the net evaluation row $(c_j - z_j)$ are ≤ 0. Since the above simplex tableau satisfies this criterion, the solution shown is optimal. However, if a change in one of the objective function coefficients were to cause one or more of the $c_j - z_j$ values to become positive, then the current solution would no longer be optimal; in such a case, one or more additional simplex iterations would be necessary to find the new optimal solution. *The range of optimality for an objective function coefficient, then, is determined by those coefficient values that maintain*

$$c_j - z_j \leq 0 \tag{6.1}$$

for all values of j. Thus, to determine the range of optimality for an objective function coefficient, say c_k, we compute the value of the left-hand side of inequality (6.1) using c_k as the objective function coefficient for x_k.

By substituting c_1 for its numerical value, we quickly see how changing the value of c_1 affects the z_j and $c_j - z_j$ row.

Let us illustrate this approach by computing the range of optimality for c_1, the profit contribution per unit of the Deskpro. Using c_1 (instead of 50) as the objective function coefficient of x_1, the revised final simplex tableau is as follows:

		x_1	x_2	s_1	s_2	s_3	
Basis	c_B	c_1	40	0	0	0	
x_2	40	0	1	$8/25$	0	$-3/25$	12
s_2	0	0	0	$-8/25$	1	$3/25$	8
x_1	c_1	1	0	$-5/25$	0	$5/25$	30
z_j		c_1	40	$\dfrac{64 - c_1}{5}$	0	$\dfrac{c_1 - 24}{5}$	$480 + 30c_1$
$c_j - z_j$		0	0	$\dfrac{c_1 - 64}{5}$	0	$\dfrac{24 - c_1}{5}$	

Note that this tableau is the same as the previous optimal tableau except for c_1 replacing 50. Thus, we have a c_1 in the objective function coefficient row and the c_B column, and the z_j and $c_j - z_j$ rows have been recomputed using c_1 instead of 50. The $c_j - z_j$ entries for the basic variables are all still zero; thus the current solution will remain optimal as long as the value of c_1 results in $c_j - z_j \leq 0$ for the two nonbasic variables s_1 and s_3. Hence, we must have

$$\frac{c_1 - 64}{5} \leq 0$$

and

$$\frac{24 - c_1}{5} \leq 0$$

Using the first inequality, we obtain

$$c_1 - 64 \leq 0$$

or

$$c_1 \leq 64 \qquad (6.2)$$

Similarly, from the second inequality, we obtain

$$24 - c_1 \leq 0$$

or

$$24 \leq c_1 \qquad (6.3)$$

Since c_1 must satisfy both (6.2) and (6.3), the range of optimality for c_1 is given by

$$24 \leq c_1 \leq 64 \qquad (6.4)$$

To see how management of HighTech can make use of the above sensitivity analysis information, suppose an increase in material costs reduces the profit contribution per unit for the Deskpro to $30. The range of optimality indicates that the current solution

$(x_1 = 30, x_2 = 12, s_1 = 0, s_2 = 8, s_3 = 0)$ is still optimal. To verify this, let us recompute the final simplex tableau after reducing the value of c_1 to 30.

Basis	c_B	x_1 30	x_2 40	s_1 0	s_2 0	s_3 0	
x_2	40	0	1	$8/25$	0	$-3/25$	12
s_2	0	0	0	$-8/25$	1	$3/25$	8
x_1	30	1	0	$-5/25$	0	$5/25$	30
z_j		30	40	$34/5$	0	$6/5$	1380
$c_j - z_j$		0	0	$-34/5$	0	$-6/5$	

We have simply set $c_1 = 30$ everywhere it appears in the previous tableau.

Since $c_j - z_j \leq 0$ for all variables, the original solution is still optimal. That is, the optimal solution with $c_1 = 30$ is the same as the optimal solution with $c_1 = 50$. Note, however, that the decrease in profit contribution per unit of the Deskpro has caused a reduction in total profit from \$1980 to \$1380.

What if the profit contribution per unit were reduced even further—say, to \$20? Referring to the range of optimality for c_1 given by expression (6.4), we see that $c_1 = 20$ is outside the range; thus, we know that a change this large will cause a new basis to be optimal. To verify this, we have modified the final simplex tableau by replacing c_1 by 20 (instead of 30).

Basis	c_B	x_1 20	x_2 40	s_1 0	s_2 0	s_3 0	
x_2	40	0	1	$8/25$	0	$-3/25$	12
s_2	0	0	0	$-8/25$	1	$3/25$	8
x_1	20	1	0	$-5/25$	0	$5/25$	30
z_j		20	40	$44/5$	0	$-4/5$	1080
$c_j - z_j$		0	0	$-44/5$	0	$4/5$	

As expected, the current solution ($x_1 = 30$, $x_2 = 12$, $s_1 = 0$, $s_2 = 8$, and $s_3 = 0$) is no longer optimal since the entry in the s_3 column of the net evaluation row is greater than zero. This implies that at least one more simplex iteration must be performed to reach the optimal solution. You should continue to perform the simplex iterations (by introducing s_3) in the above tableau to verify that the new optimal solution will require the production of $16\frac{2}{3}$ units of the Deskpro and 20 units of the Portable.

The procedure we used to compute the range of optimality for c_1 can be used for any basic variable. Compute inequality (6.1) for each nonbasic variable; the smallest upper bound is the upper limit, and the largest lower bound is the lower limit of the range. The procedure for computing the range of optimality for nonbasic variables is even easier since a change in the objective function coefficient for a nonbasic variable causes only the corresponding $c_j - z_j$ entry to change in the final simplex tableau. To illustrate the approach, we show the following final simplex tableau for the original HighTech problem after replacing 0, the objective function coefficient for s_1, with the coefficient c_{s_1}:

Basis	c_B	x_1 50	x_2 40	s_1 c_{s_1}	s_2 0	s_3 0	
x_2	40	0	1	$8/25$	0	$-3/25$	**12**
s_2	0	0	0	$-8/25$	1	$3/25$	**8**
x_1	50	1	0	$-5/25$	0	$5/25$	**30**
z_j		50	40	$14/5$	0	$26/5$	**1980**
$c_j - z_j$		0	0	$c_{s_1} - 14/5$	0	$-26/5$	

Note that the only changes in the tableau are in the s_1 column. In applying inequality (6.1) to compute the range of optimality, we get

$$c_{s_1} - 14/5 \leq 0$$

and hence

$$c_{s_1} \leq 14/5$$

Therefore, as long as the objective function coefficient for s_1 is less than or equal to $14/5$, the current solution will be optimal. Since there is no lower bound on how much the coefficient may be decreased, we write the range of optimality for c_{s_1} as

$$c_{s_1} \leq 14/5$$

The same approach works for all nonbasic variables. In a maximization problem, there is no lower limit on the range of optimality, and the upper limit is given by z_j. Thus, the range of optimality for the objective function coefficient of any nonbasic variable is given by

$$c_j \leq z_j \tag{6.5}$$

Since s_1 is a slack variable in the HighTech problem, its objective function coefficient is not subject to variability. That is, the objective function coefficient for s_1 will always be zero, and hence, s_1 would never be brought into the solution. But, as we will see in the next section, the upper limit on the range for a nonbasic slack variable provides the daul price for the corresponding constraint.

Let us summarize the steps necessary to compute the range of optimality for objective function coefficients. In stating the following steps, we assume that computing the range of optimality for c_k, the coefficient of x_k, in a maximization problem is the desired goal. Keep in mind that x_k in this context may refer to one of the original decision variables, a slack variable, or a surplus variable.

Steps to Compute the Range of Optimality

Step 1 Replace the numerical value of the objective function coefficient for x_k with c_k everywhere it appears in the final simplex tableau.

Step 2 Recompute $c_j - z_j$ for each nonbasic variable (if x_k is a nonbasic variable, it is only necessary to recompute $c_k - z_k$).

Step 3 Requiring that $c_j - z_j \leq 0$, solve each inequality for any upper or lower bounds on c_k. If there are two or more upper bounds on c_k, the smaller of these is the upper bound on the range of optimality. If there are two or more lower bounds, the largest of these is the lower bound on the range of optimality.

Step 4 If the original problem is a minimization problem that was converted to a maximization problem in order to apply the simplex method, multiply the inequalities obtained in step 3 by -1, and change the direction of the inequalities to obtain the ranges of optimality for the original minimization problem.

You should now be able to compute the range of optimality for objective function coefficients by working with the final simplex tableau. Try Problem 1.

By using the range of optimality to determine whether a change in an objective function coefficient is large enough to cause a change in the optimal solution, we can often avoid the process of formulating and solving a modified linear programming problem.

Right-Hand-Side Values

In many linear programming problems, we can interpret the right-hand-side values (the b_i's) as the resources available. For instance, in the HighTech Industries problem, the right-hand side of constraint 1 represents the available assembly time, the right-hand side of constraint 2 represents the number of Portable display units available, and the right-hand side of constraint 3 represents the available warehouse space. Dual prices provide information on the value of additional resources in these cases; the ranges over which these dual prices are valid are given by the ranges for the right-hand-side values.

Dual Prices. In Chapter 2 we stated that the improvement in value of the optimal solution per-unit increase in a constraint's right-hand-side value is called a *dual price*.[1] When the simplex method is used to solve a linear programming problem, the values of the dual prices are easy to obtain. They are found in the z_j row of the final simplex tableau. To illustrate this point, the final simplex tableau for the HighTech problem is again reproduced.

		x_1	x_2	s_1	s_2	s_3	
Basis	c_B	50	40	0	0	0	
x_2	40	0	1	$8/25$	0	$-3/25$	**12**
s_2	0	0	0	$-8/25$	1	$3/25$	**8**
x_1	50	1	0	$-5/25$	0	$5/25$	**30**
z_j		50	40	$14/5$	0	$26/5$	**1980**
$c_j - z_j$		0	0	$-14/5$	0	$-26/5$	

The z_j values for the three slack variables are $14/5$, 0, and $26/5$, respectively. Thus, the dual prices for the assembly time constraint, portable display constraint, and warehouse

---

[1]The closely related term *shadow price* is used by some authors. The shadow price is the same as the dual price for maximization problems; for minimization problems, the dual and shadow prices are equal in absolute value but have opposite signs. LINDO/PC and The Management Scientist provide dual prices as part of the computer output. Some software packages provide shadow prices.

capacity constraint are respectively $14/5 = 2.80$, 0.00, and $26/5 = 5.20$. We see that obtaining more warehouse space will have the biggest positive impact on HighTech's profit.

To see why the z_j values for the slack variables in the final simplex tableau are the dual prices, let us first consider the case for slack variables that are part of the optimal basic feasible solution. Each of these slack variables will have a z_j value of zero, implying a dual price of zero for the corresponding constraint. For example, consider slack variable s_2, a basic variable in the HighTech problem. Since $s_2 = 8$ in the optimal solution, HighTech will have eight Portable display units unused. Consequently, how much would management of HighTech Industries be willing to pay to obtain additional Portable display units? Clearly the answer is nothing since at the optimal solution HighTech has an excess of this particular component. Additional amounts of this resource are of no value to the company, and, consequently, the dual price for this constraint is zero. In general, if a slack variable is a basic variable in the optimal solution, the value of z_j—and hence, the dual price of the corresponding resource—is zero.

Consider now the nonbasic slack variables—for example, s_1. In the previous subsection we determined that the current solution will remain optimal as long as the objective function coefficient for s_1 (denoted c_{s_1}) stays in the following range:

$$c_{s_1} \leq 14/5$$

This implies that the variable s_1 should not be increased from its current value of zero unless it is worth more than $\$14/5 = \$2.80$ to do so. In other words, HighTech should use all of its assembly time unless it is paid more than $2.80 per hour not to use it. We can conclude then that $2.80 is the marginal value to HighTech of 1 hour of assembly time used in the production of Deskpro and Portable computers. Thus, if additional time can be obtained, HighTech should be willing to pay up to $2.80 per hour for it. A similar interpretation can be given to the z_j value for each of the nonbasic slack variables. That is, z_j is the value of one additional unit of the resource in the row corresponding to that slack variable.

With a greater-than-or-equal-to constraint, the value of the dual price for a maximization problem will be less than or equal to zero because a one-unit increase in the value of the right-hand side cannot be helpful; a one-unit increase makes it more difficult to satisfy the constraint. For a maximization problem, then, the optimal value can be expected to decrease when the right-hand side of a greater-than-or-equal-to constraint is increased. The dual price gives the amount of the expected improvement—a negative number, since we expect a decrease. As a result, the dual price for a greater-than-or-equal-to constraint is given by the negative of the z_j entry for the corresponding surplus variable in the optimal simplex tableau.

Finally, it is possible to compute dual prices for equality constraints. They are given by the z_j values for the corresponding artificial variables. We will not develop this case in detail here since we have recommended dropping each artificial variable column from the simplex tableau as soon as the corresponding artificial variable leaves the basis.

To summarize, when the simplex method is used to solve a linear programming problem, the dual prices for the constraints are contained in the final simplex tableau. Table 6.1 summarizes the rules for determining the dual prices for the various constraint types in a maximization problem solved by the simplex method.

Try Problem 3, parts (a), (b), and (c) for practice at finding dual prices from the optimal simplex tableau.

Recall that we convert a minimization problem to a maximization problem by multiplying the objective function by -1 before using the simplex method. Nevertheless, the dual price is given by the same z_j values since improvement for a minimization problem is a decrease in the optimal value.

Table 6.1	Constraint Type	Dual Price Given by
Tableau Location of Dual Price by Constraint Type	$\leq$	z_j value for the slack variable associated with the constraint
	$\geq$	Negative of the z_j value for the surplus variable associated with the constraint
	$=$	z_j value for the artificial variable associated with the constraint

To illustrate the approach for computing dual prices for a minimization problem, recall the M&D Chemicals problem that we solved in Section 5.8 as an equivalent maximization problem by multiplying the objective function by -1. The linear programming model for this problem and the final simplex tableau are restated below, with x_1 and x_2 representing manufacturing quantities of products 1 and 2, respectively.

$$\text{Min} \quad 2x_1 + 3x_2$$

s.t.

$$1x_1 \qquad\qquad \geq 125 \quad \text{Demand for product 1}$$

$$1x_1 + 1x_2 \geq 350 \quad \text{Total production}$$

$$2x_1 + 1x_2 \leq 600 \quad \text{Processing time}$$

$$x_1, x_2 \geq 0$$

		x_1	x_2	s_1	s_2	s_3	
Basis	c_B	-2	-3	0	0	0	
x_1	-2	1	0	0	1	1	**250**
x_2	-3	0	1	0	-2	-1	**100**
s_1	0	0	0	1	1	1	**125**
	z_j	-2	-3	0	4	1	**-800**
	$c_j - z_j$	0	0	0	-4	-1	

Following the rules in Table 6.1 for identifying the dual price for each constraint type, the dual prices for the constraints in the M&D Chemicals problem are given in Table 6.2.

Table 6.2	Constraint	Constraint Type	Dual Price
Dual Prices for M&D Chemicals Problem	Demand for product 1	$\geq$	0
	Total production	$\geq$	-4
	Processing time	$\leq$	1

Since constraint 1 is not binding, its dual price is zero. The dual price for constraint 2 shows that the marginal cost of increasing the total production requirement is $4 per unit. Finally, the dual price of one for the third constraint shows that the per-unit value of additional processing time is $1.

Range of Feasibility. As we have just seen, the z_j row in the final simplex tableau can be used to determine the dual price and, as a result, predict the change in the value of the objective function corresponding to a unit change in a b_i. This interpretation is only valid, however, as long as the change in b_i is not large enough to make the current basic solution infeasible. Thus, we will be interested in calculating a range of values over which a particular b_i can vary without any of the current basic variables becoming infeasible (i.e., less than zero). This range of values will be referred to as the *range of feasibility*.

> A change in b_i does not affect optimality ($c_j - z_j$ is unchanged), but it does affect feasibility. One of the current basic variables may become negative.

To demonstrate the effect of changing a b_i, consider increasing the amount of assembly time available in the HighTech problem from 150 to 160 hours. Will the current basis still yield a feasible solution? If so, given the dual price of $2.80 for the assembly time constraint, we can expect an increase in the value of the solution of $10(2.80) = 28$. Shown below is the final simplex tableau corresponding to an increase in the assembly time of 10 hours.

Basis	c_B	x_1 50	x_2 40	s_1 0	s_2 0	s_3 0	
x_2	40	0	1	$8/25$	0	$-3/25$	**15.2**
s_2	0	0	0	$-8/25$	1	$3/25$	**4.8**
x_1	50	1	0	$-5/25$	0	$5/25$	**28.0**
z_j		50	40	$14/5$	0	$26/5$	**2008**
$c_j - z_j$		0	0	$-14/5$	0	$-26/5$	

The same basis, consisting of the basic variables x_2, s_2, and x_1, is feasible since all the basic variables are nonnegative. Note also that, just as we predicted using the dual price, the value of the optimal solution has increased by 28 (from 1980 to 2008).

You may wonder whether we had to resolve the problem completely to find this new solution. The answer is no! The only changes in the final simplex tableau (as compared with the final simplex tableau with $b_1 = 150$) are the differences in the values of the basic variables and the value of the objective function. That is, only the last column of the simplex tableau has changed. The entries in this new last column of the simplex tableau were obtained by merely adding 10 times the first four entries in the s_1 column to the last column in the previous tableau:

$$
\begin{array}{c}
\text{New} \\
\text{solution}
\end{array}
=
\begin{array}{c}
\text{Old} \\
\text{solution} \\
\downarrow \\
\begin{bmatrix} 12 \\ 8 \\ 30 \\ \hline 1980 \end{bmatrix}
\end{array}
+
\begin{array}{c}
\text{Change} \\
\text{in } b_1 \\
\downarrow \\
10
\end{array}
\begin{array}{c}
s_1 \text{ column} \\
\downarrow \\
\begin{bmatrix} 8/25 \\ -8/25 \\ -5/25 \\ \hline 14/5 \end{bmatrix}
\end{array}
=
\begin{array}{c}
\text{New} \\
\text{solution} \\
\downarrow \\
\begin{bmatrix} 15.2 \\ 4.8 \\ 28.0 \\ \hline 2008 \end{bmatrix}
\end{array}
$$

Let us now consider why this procedure can be used to find the new solution. First, recall that each of the coefficients in the s_1 column indicates the amount of decrease in a basic variable that would result from increasing s_1 by one unit. In other words, these coefficients tell us how many units of each of the current basic variables will be driven out of solution if one unit of variable s_1 is brought into solution. Bringing one unit of s_1 into solution, however, is the same as reducing the availability of assembly time (decreasing b_1) by one unit; increasing b_1, the available assembly time, by one unit has just the opposite effect. Therefore, the entries in the s_1 column can also be interpreted as the changes in the values of the current basic variables corresponding to a one-unit increase in b_1.

> You should now be able to find the new solution after a change in a right-hand side without resolving the problem when the same basis remains feasible. Try Problem 3, parts (d) and (e).

The change in the value of the objective function corresponding to a one-unit increase in b_1 is given by the value of z_j in that column (the dual price). In the foregoing case, the availability of assembly time increased by 10 units; thus, we multiplied the first four entries in the s_1 column by 10 to obtain the change in the value of the basic variables and the optimal value.

How do we know when a change in b_1 is so large that the current basis will become infeasible? We shall first answer this question specifically for the HighTech Industries problem and then state the general procedure for less-than-or-equal-to constraints. The approach taken with greater-than-or-equal-to and equality constraints will then be discussed.

We begin by showing how to compute upper and lower bounds for the maximum amount that b_1 can be changed before the current optimal basis becomes infeasible. We have seen how to find the new basic feasible solution values, given a 10-unit increase in b_1. In general, given a change in b_1 of Δb_1, the new values for the basic variables in the HighTech problem are given by

$$\begin{bmatrix} x_2 \\ s_2 \\ x_1 \end{bmatrix} = \begin{bmatrix} 12 \\ 8 \\ 30 \end{bmatrix} + \Delta b_1 \begin{bmatrix} 8/25 \\ -8/25 \\ -5/25 \end{bmatrix} = \begin{bmatrix} 12 + 8/25\,\Delta b_1 \\ 8 - 8/25\,\Delta b_1 \\ 30 - 5/25\,\Delta b_1 \end{bmatrix} \qquad (6.6)$$

> Changing a b_i has no effect on the $c_j - z_j$ row.

As long as the new value of each basic variable remains nonnegative, the current basis will remain feasible and therefore optimal. We can keep the basic variables nonnegative by limiting the change in b_1 (i.e., Δb_1) so that we satisfy each of the following conditions:

$$12 + 8/25\,\Delta b_1 \geq 0 \qquad (6.7)$$

$$8 - 8/25\,\Delta b_1 \geq 0 \qquad (6.8)$$

$$30 - 5/25\,\Delta b_1 \geq 0 \qquad (6.9)$$

The left-hand sides of the above inequalities represent the new values of the basic variables after b_1 has been changed by Δb_1.

Solving for Δb_1 in inequalities (6.7), (6.8), and (6.9), we obtain

$$\Delta b_1 \geq (25/8)(-12) = -37.5$$

$$\Delta b_1 \leq (-25/8)(-8) = 25$$

$$\Delta b_1 \leq (-25/5)(-30) = 150$$

Since all three inequalities must be satisfied, the most restrictive limits on b_1 must be satisfied for all the current basic variables to remain nonnegative. Therefore, Δb_1 must satisfy

$$-37.5 \leq \Delta b_1 \leq 25 \qquad (6.10)$$

The initial amount of assembly time available was 150 hours. Therefore, $b_1 = 150 + \Delta b_1$, where b_1 is the amount of assembly time available. We add 150 to each of the three terms in expression (6.10) to obtain

$$112.5 \leq 150 + \Delta b_1 \leq 175 \qquad (6.11)$$

Replacing $150 + \Delta b_1$ with b_1, we obtain the range of feasibility for b_1:

$$112.5 \leq b_1 \leq 175$$

This range of feasibility for b_1 indicates that as long as the available assembly time is between 112.5 and 175 hours, the current optimal basis will remain feasible. This is why we call this range the range of feasibility.

Since the dual price for b_1 (assembly time) is $14/5$, we know profit can be increased by $2.80 by obtaining an additional hour of assembly time. Suppose then that we increase b_1 by 25; that is, we increase b_1 to the upper limit of its range of feasibility, 175. The profit will increase to $1980 + ($2.80)25 = $2050, and the values of the optimal basic variables become

$$x_2 = 12 + 25(8/25) = 20$$

$$s_2 = 8 + 25(-8/25) = 0$$

$$x_1 = 30 + 25(-5/25) = 25$$

What has happened to the solution? The increased assembly time has caused a revision in the optimal production plan. HighTech should produce more of the Portable and less of the Deskpro. Overall, the profit will be increased by ($2.80)(25) = $70. Note that although the optimal solution has changed, the basic variables that were optimal before are still optimal.

The procedure for determining the range of feasibility has been illustrated with the assembly time constraint. The procedure for calculating the range of feasibility for the right-hand side of any less-than-or-equal-to constraint is the same. The first step (paralleling equation (6.6)) for a general constraint i is to calculate the range of values for b_i that satisfy the inequalities shown below.

$$\begin{bmatrix} \bar{b}_1 \\ \bar{b}_2 \\ \cdot \\ \cdot \\ \cdot \\ \bar{b}_m \end{bmatrix} + \Delta b_i \begin{bmatrix} \bar{a}_{1j} \\ \bar{a}_{2j} \\ \cdot \\ \cdot \\ \cdot \\ \bar{a}_{mj} \end{bmatrix} \geq \begin{bmatrix} 0 \\ 0 \\ \cdot \\ \cdot \\ \cdot \\ 0 \end{bmatrix} \qquad (6.12)$$

Current solution (last column of the final simplex tableau)

Column of the final simplex tableau corresponding to the slack variable associated with constraint i

The inequalities are used to identify lower and upper limits on Δb_i. The range of feasibility can then be established by the maximum of the lower limits and the minimum of the upper limits.

Similar arguments presented can be used to develop a procedure for determining the range of feasibility for the right-hand-side value of a greater-than-or-equal-to constraint. Essentially the procedure is the same, with the column corresponding to the surplus variable associated with the constraint playing the central role. For a general greater-than-or-equal-to constraint i, we first calculate the range of values for Δb_i that satisfy the inequalities shown in equation (6.13).

$$
\begin{bmatrix} \bar{b}_1 \\ \bar{b}_2 \\ \cdot \\ \cdot \\ \cdot \\ \bar{b}_m \end{bmatrix} - \Delta b_i \begin{bmatrix} \bar{a}_{1j} \\ \bar{a}_{2j} \\ \cdot \\ \cdot \\ \cdot \\ \bar{a}_{mj} \end{bmatrix} \geq \begin{bmatrix} 0 \\ 0 \\ \cdot \\ \cdot \\ \cdot \\ 0 \end{bmatrix} \qquad (6.13)
$$

Current solution (last column of the final simplex tableau)

Column of the final simplex tableau corresponding to the surplus variable associated with constraint i

Try Problem 4 to make sure you can compute the range of feasibility by working with the final simplex tableau.

Once again, these inequalities establish lower and upper limits on Δb_i. Given these limits, the range of feasibility is easily determined.

A range of feasibility for the right-hand side of an equality constraint can also be computed. To do so for equality constraint i, one could use the column of the final simplex tableau corresponding to the artificial variable associated with constraint i in equation (6.12). Since we have suggested dropping the artificial variable columns from the simplex tableau as soon as the artificial variable becomes nonbasic, these columns will not be available in the final tableau. Thus, more involved calculations are required to compute a range of feasibility for equality constraints. Details may be found in more advanced texts.

As long as the change in a right-hand-side value is such that b_i stays within its range of feasibility, the same basis will remain feasible and optimal. Changes that force b_i outside its range of feasibility will force us to resolve the problem to find the new optimal solution consisting of a different set of basic variables. (More advanced linear programming texts show how this can be done without completely resolving the problem.) In any case, the calculation of the range of feasibility for each b_i is valuable management information and should be included as part of the management report on any linear programming project. The range of feasibility is typically made available as part of the computer solution to the problem.

Such changes are normally accompanied by changes in the dual prices.

Simultaneous Changes

In reviewing the procedures for developing the range of optimality and the range of feasibility, we note that only one coefficient at a time was permitted to vary. That is why our statements concerning changes within these ranges were made with the understanding that no other coefficients are permitted to change. However, sometimes we can make the same statements when either two or more objective function coefficients or two or more right-hand sides are varied simultaneously. When the simultaneous changes satisfy the 100 percent rule, the same statements are applicable. The 100 percent rule was explained in Chapter 3, but we will briefly review it here.

Let us define allowable increase as the amount a coefficient can be increased before reaching the upper limit of its range, and allowable decrease as the amount a coefficient can be decreased before reaching the lower limit of its range. Now suppose simultaneous changes are made in two or more objective function coefficients. For each coefficient changed, we compute the percentage of the allowable increase, or allowable decrease, represented by the change. If the sum of the percentages for all changes does not exceed 100%, we say that the 100 percent rule is satisfied and that the simultaneous changes will not cause a change in the optimal solution. However, just as with a single objective function coefficient change, the value of the solution will change because of the change in the coefficients.

Similarly, if two or more changes in constraint right-hand-side values are made, we again compute the percentage of allowable increase or allowable decrease represented by each change. If the sum of the percentages for all changes does not exceed 100%, we say that the 100 percent rule is satisfied. The dual prices are then valid for determining the change in value of the objective function associated with the right-hand-side changes.

NOTES & COMMENTS

1. Sometimes, interpreting dual prices and choosing the appropriate sign can be confusing. It often helps to think of this process as follows. Relaxing a $\geq$ constraint means decreasing its right-hand side, and relaxing a $\leq$ constraint means increasing its right-hand side. Relaxing a constraint permits improvement in value; restricting a constraint (decreasing the right-hand side of a $\leq$ constraint or increasing the right-hand side of a $\geq$ constraint) has the opposite effect. In every case, the absolute value of the dual price gives the improvement in the optimal value associated with relaxing the constraint.

2. The Notes & Comments in Chapters 2 and 3 concerning sensitivity analysis are also applicable here. In particular, recall that the 100 percent rule cannot be applied to simultaneous changes in the objective function *and* the right-hand sides; it applies only to simultaneous changes in one or the other. Also note that this rule *does not* mean that simultaneous changes that do not satisfy the rule will necessarily cause a change in the solution. For instance, any proportional change in *all* the objective function coefficients will leave the optimal solution unchanged, and any proportional change in *all* the right-hand sides will leave the dual prices unchanged.

6.2 Duality

Every linear programming problem has an associated linear programming problem called the *dual*. Referring to the original formulation of the linear programming problem as the *primal,* we will see how the primal can be converted into its corresponding dual. Then we will solve the dual linear programming problem and interpret the results. A fundamental property of the primal–dual relationship is that the optimal solution to either the primal or the dual problem also provides the optimal solution to the other. In cases where the primal and the dual problems differ in terms of computational difficulty, we can choose the easier problem to solve.

Let us return to the HighTech Industries problem. The original formulation—the primal—is as follows:

$$\text{Max} \quad 50x_1 + 40x_2$$

s.t.

$$3x_1 + 5x_2 \leq 150 \quad \text{Assembly time}$$
$$1x_2 \leq 20 \quad \text{Portable display}$$
$$8x_1 + 5x_2 \leq 300 \quad \text{Warehouse space}$$
$$x_1, x_2 \geq 0$$

A maximization problem with all less-than-or-equal-to constraints and nonnegativity requirements for the variables is said to be in *canonical form*. For a maximization problem in canonical form, such as the HighTech Industries problem, the conversion to the associated dual linear program is relatively easy. Let us state the dual of the HighTech problem and then identify the steps taken to make the primal–dual conversion. The HighTech dual problem is as follows:

$$\text{Min} \quad 150u_1 + 20u_2 + 300u_3$$

s.t.

$$3u_1 \qquad + \quad 8u_3 \geq 50$$
$$5u_1 + 1u_2 + 5u_3 \geq 40$$
$$u_1, u_2, u_3 \geq 0$$

This is *canonical form for a minimization problem:* a minimization problem with all greater-than-or-equal-to constraints and nonnegativity requirements for the variables. Thus, the dual of a maximization problem in canonical form is a minimization problem in canonical form. The variables u_1, u_2, and u_3 are referred to as *dual variables.*

With the above example in mind, we make the following general statements about the *dual of a maximization problem in canonical form.*

> The canonical forms of the maximization and minimization problems are often called the symmetric primal and dual problems.

1. The dual is a minimization problem in canonical form.
2. When the primal has n decision variables ($n = 2$ in the HighTech problem), the dual will have n constraints. The first constraint of the dual is associated with variable x_1 in the primal, the second constraint in the dual is associated with variable x_2 in the primal, and so on.
3. When the primal has m constraints ($m = 3$ in the HighTech problem), the dual will have m decision variables. Dual variable u_1 is associated with the first primal constraint, dual variable u_2 is associated with the second primal constraint, and so on.
4. The right-hand sides of the primal constraints become the objective function coefficients in the dual.
5. The objective function coefficients of the primal become the right-hand sides of the dual constraints.
6. The constraint coefficients of the ith primal variable become the coefficients in the ith constraint of the dual.

Try part (a) of Problem 17 for practice in finding the dual of a maximization problem in canonical form.

The above six statements are the general requirements that must be satisfied when converting a maximization problem in canonical form to its associated dual: a minimization problem in canonical form. While these requirements may seem cumbersome at first, practice with a few simple problems will show that the primal–dual conversion process is relatively easy to implement.

Since we have formulated the HighTech dual linear programming problem, let us now proceed to solve it. With three variables in the dual, we will use the simplex method. After subtracting surplus variables s_1 and s_2 to obtain the standard form, adding artificial variables a_1 and a_2 to obtain the tableau form, and multiplying the objective function by -1 to convert the dual problem to an equivalent maximization problem, we arrive at the following initial simplex tableau.

Basis	c_B	u_1 -150	u_2 -20	u_3 -300	s_1 0	s_2 0	a_1 $-M$	a_2 $-M$	
a_1	$-M$	3	0	⑧	-1	0	1	0	50
a_2	$-M$	5	1	5	0	-1	0	1	40
	z_j	$-8M$	$-M$	$-13M$	M	M	$-M$	$-M$	$-90M$
	$c_j - z_j$	$-150 + 8M$	$-20 + M$	$-300 + 13M$	$-M$	$-M$	0	0	

At the first iteration, u_3 is brought into the basis, and a_1 is removed. The second tableau, with the a_1 column dropped, is shown below.

Basis	c_B	u_1 -150	u_2 -20	u_3 -300	s_1 0	s_2 0	a_2 $-M$	
u_3	-300	$3/8$	0	1	$-1/8$	0	0	$50/8$
a_2	$-M$	$\text{㉕}/8$	1	0	$5/8$	-1	1	$70/8$
	z_j	$\dfrac{-900 - 25M}{8}$	$-M$	-300	$\dfrac{300 - 5M}{8}$	M	$-M$	$\dfrac{-15{,}000 - 70M}{8}$
	$c_j - z_j$	$\dfrac{-300 + 25M}{8}$	$-20 + M$	0	$\dfrac{-300 + 5M}{8}$	$-M$	0	

At the second iteration, u_1 is brought into the basis, and a_2 is removed. The third tableau, with the a_2 column removed, is

Basis	c_B	u_1 -150	u_2 -20	u_3 -300	s_1 0	s_2 0	
u_3	-300	0	$-3/25$	1	$-5/25$	$3/25$	$26/5$
u_1	-150	1	$8/25$	0	$5/25$	$-8/25$	$14/5$
	z_j	-150	-12	-300	30	12	-1980
	$c_j - z_j$	0	-8	0	-30	-12	

Note that all of the artificial variables have now been driven out of the basis and that all the entries in the net evaluation row are less than or equal to zero. The optimal solution has been reached; it is $u_1 = 14/5$, $u_2 = 0$, $u_3 = 26/5$, $s_1 = 0$, and $s_2 = 0$. Since we have been maximizing the negative of the dual objective function, the value of the objective function for the optimal dual solution must be $-(-1980) = 1980$.

Shown below is the final simplex tableau for the original HighTech Industries problem.

		x_1	x_2	s_1	s_2	s_3	
Basis	c_B	50	40	0	0	0	
x_2	40	0	1	$8/25$	0	$-3/25$	**12**
s_2	0	0	0	$-8/25$	1	$3/25$	**8**
x_1	50	1	0	$-5/25$	0	$5/25$	**30**
z_j		50	40	$14/5$	0	$26/5$	**1980**
$c_j - z_j$		0	0	$-14/5$	0	$-26/5$	

The optimal solution to the primal problem is $x_1 = 30$, $x_2 = 12$, $s_1 = 0$, $s_2 = 8$, and $s_3 = 0$. The optimal value of the objective function is 1980.

What observation can we make about the relationship between the optimal value of the objective function in the primal and the optimal value in the dual for the HighTech problem? The optimal value of the objective function is the same (1980) for both. This relationship is true for all primal and dual linear programming problems and is stated as property 1.

PROPERTY 1

If the dual problem has an optimal solution, the primal problem has an optimal solution, and vice versa. Furthermore, the values of the optimal solutions to the dual and primal problems are equal.

If one of the problems is unbounded, its dual must be infeasible. However, both the primal and dual may be infeasible.

This property tells us that if we had solved only the dual problem, we would have known that HighTech could make a maximum of $1980.

Economic Interpretation of the Dual Variables

Before making further observations about the relationship between the primal and the dual solutions, let us consider the meaning or interpretation of the dual variables $u_1, u_2,$ and u_3. Remember that in setting up the dual problem, each dual variable is associated with one of the constraints in the primal. Specifically, u_1 is associated with the assembly time constraint, u_2 with the Portable display constraint, and u_3 with the warehouse space constraint.

To understand and interpret these dual variables, let us return to property 1 of the primal–dual relationship, which stated that the objective function values for the primal and dual problems must be equal. At the optimal solution, the primal objective function results in

$$50x_1 + 40x_2 = 1980 \qquad (6.14)$$

while the dual objective function is

$$150u_1 + 20u_2 + 300u_3 = 1980 \qquad (6.15)$$

Using equation (6.14), let us restrict our interest to the interpretation of the primal objective function. Since x_1 and x_2 are the number of units of the Deskpro and the Portable that are assembled respectively, we have

$$\begin{pmatrix} \text{Dollar value} \\ \text{per unit of} \\ \text{Deskpro} \end{pmatrix} \begin{pmatrix} \text{Number of} \\ \text{units of} \\ \text{Deskpro} \end{pmatrix} + \begin{pmatrix} \text{Dollar value} \\ \text{per unit of} \\ \text{Portable} \end{pmatrix} \begin{pmatrix} \text{Number of} \\ \text{units of} \\ \text{Portable} \end{pmatrix} = \begin{matrix} \text{Total dollar} \\ \text{value of} \\ \text{production} \end{matrix}$$

From equation (6.15), we see that the coefficients of the dual objective function (150, 20, and 300) can be interpreted as the number of units of resources available. Thus, since the primal and dual objective functions are equal at optimality, we have

$$\begin{pmatrix} \text{Units of} \\ \text{resource} \\ 1 \end{pmatrix} u_1 + \begin{pmatrix} \text{Units of} \\ \text{resource} \\ 2 \end{pmatrix} u_2 + \begin{pmatrix} \text{Units of} \\ \text{resource} \\ 3 \end{pmatrix} u_3 = \begin{matrix} \text{Total dollar value} \\ \text{of production} \end{matrix}$$

Thus, we see that the dual variables must carry the interpretation of being the value per unit of resource. For the HighTech problem,

$$u_1 = \text{dollar value per hour of assembly time}$$
$$u_2 = \text{dollar value per unit of the Portable display}$$
$$u_3 = \text{dollar value per square foot of warehouse space}$$

Have we attempted to identify the value of these resources previously? Recall that in Section 6.1, when we considered sensitivity analysis of the right-hand sides, we identified the value of an additional unit of each resource. These values were called dual prices and are helpful to the decision maker in determining whether additional units of the resources should be made available.

The analysis in Section 6.1 led to the following dual prices for the resources in the HighTech problem.

Resource	Value per Additional Unit (dual price)
Assembly time	$2.80
Portable display	$0.00
Warehouse space	$5.20

The dual variables are the shadow prices. But, since this is a maximization problem, they also equal the dual prices. For a minimization problem, the dual prices are the negative of the dual variables.

Let us now return to the optimal solution for the HighTech dual problem. The values of the dual variables at the optimal solution are $u_1 = {}^{14}\!/_5 = 2.80$, $u_2 = 0$, and $u_3 = {}^{26}\!/_5 = 5.20$. For this maximization problem, the values of the dual variables and the dual prices are the same. For a minimization problem, the dual prices and the dual variables are the same in absolute value but have opposite signs. Thus, the optimal values of the dual variables identify the dual prices of each additional resource or input unit at the optimal solution.

In light of the above discussion, the following interpretation of the primal and dual problems can be made when the primal is a product-mix problem.

Primal Problem. Given a per-unit value of each product, determine how much of each should be produced to maximize the value of the total production. Constraints require the amount of each resource used to be less than or equal to the amount available.

Dual Problem. Given the availability of each resource, determine the per-unit value such that the total value of the resources used is minimized. Constraints require the resource value per unit be greater than or equal to the value of each unit of output.

Using the Dual to Identify the Primal Solution

At the beginning of this section, we mentioned that an important feature of the primal–dual relationship is that when an optimal solution is reached, the value of the optimal solution for the primal problem is the same as the value of the optimal solution for the dual problem; see property 1. However, the question remains: If we solve only the dual problem, can we identify the optimal values for the primal variables?

Recall that in Section 6.1 we showed that when a primal problem is solved by the simplex method, the optimal values of the primal variables appear in the right-most column of the final tableau, and the dual prices (values of the dual variables) are found in the z_j row. Since the final simplex tableau of the dual problem provides the optimal values of the dual variables, the values of the primal variables should be found in the z_j row of the optimal dual tableau. This is, in fact, the case and is formally stated as property 2.

P R O P E R T Y **2**

Given the simplex tableau corresponding to the optimal dual solution, the optimal values of the primal decision variables are given by the z_j entries for the surplus variables; furthermore, the optimal values of the primal slack variables are given by the negative of the $c_j - z_j$ entries for the u_j variables.

This property enables us to use the final simplex tableau for the dual of the HighTech problem to determine the optimal primal solution of $x_1 = 30$ units of the Deskpro and $x_2 = 12$ units of the Portable. These optimal values of x_1 and x_2, as well as the values for all primal slack variables, are given in the z_j and $c_j - z_j$ rows of the final simplex tableau of the dual problem, which is shown again below.

You should now be able to find the primal solution from the optimal simplex tableau for the dual and also be able to interpret the dual variables. Try parts (b) and (c) of Problem 17.

Basis	c_B	u_1 -150	u_2 -20	u_3 -300	s_1 0	s_2 0	
u_3	-300	0	$-3/25$	1	$-5/25$	$3/25$	$26/5$
u_1	-150	1	$8/25$	0	$5/25$	$-8/25$	$14/5$
z_j		-150	-12	-300	30	12	-1980
$c_j - z_j$		0	-8	0	-30	-12	

Finding the Dual of Any Primal Problem

The HighTech Industries primal problem provided a good introduction to the concept of duality since it was formulated as a maximization problem in canonical form. For this form of primal problem, we have seen that conversion to the dual problem is rather easy. If the primal problem is a minimization problem in canonical form, then the dual is a maximization problem in canonical form. Therefore, finding the dual of a minimization problem in canonical form is also easy. Consider the following linear program in canonical form for a minimization problem:

$$\text{Min} \quad 6x_1 + 2x_2$$

s.t.

$$5x_1 - 1x_2 \geq 13$$

$$3x_1 + 7x_2 \geq 9$$

$$x_1, x_2 \geq 0$$

The dual is the following maximization problem in canonical form:

$$\text{Max} \quad 13u_1 + 9u_2$$

s.t.

$$5u_1 + 3u_2 \leq 6$$

$$-1u_1 + 7u_2 \leq 2$$

$$-0u_1, u_2 \geq 0$$

Try Problem 19 for practice in finding the dual of a minimization problem in canonical form.

While we could state a special set of rules for converting each type of primal problem into its associated dual, we believe it is easier to first convert any primal problem into an equivalent problem in canonical form. Then, we follow the procedures already established for finding the dual of a maximization or minimization problem in canonical form.

Let us illustrate the procedure for finding the dual of any linear programming problem by finding the dual of the following minimization problem:

$$\text{Min} \quad 2x_1 - 3x_2$$

s.t.

$$1x_1 + 2x_2 \leq 12$$

$$4x_1 - 2x_2 \geq 3$$

$$6x_1 - 1x_2 = 10$$

$$x_1, x_2 \geq 0$$

Since this is a minimization problem, we obtain the canonical form by converting all constraints to greater-than-or-equal-to form. For this problem, the necessary steps are as follows:

1. Convert the first constraint to greater-than-or-equal-to form by multiplying both sides of the inequality by (-1). Doing so yields

$$-x_1 - 2x_2 \geq -12$$

2. Constraint 3 is an equality constraint. For an equality constraint, we first create two inequalities: one with $\leq$ form, the other with $\geq$ form. Doing so yields

$$6x_1 - 1x_2 \geq 10$$

$$6x_1 - 1x_2 \leq 10$$

Then, we multiply the $\leq$ constraint by (-1) to get two $\geq$ constraints.

$$6x_1 - 1x_2 \geq 10$$

$$-6x_1 + 1x_2 \geq -10$$

Now the original primal problem has been restated in the following equivalent form:

$$\text{Min} \quad 2x_1 - 3x_2$$

s.t.

$$-1x_1 - 2x_2 \geq -12$$

$$4x_1 - 2x_2 \geq \quad 3$$

$$6x_1 - 1x_2 \geq \quad 10$$

$$-6x_1 + 1x_2 \geq -10$$

$$-0x_1, x_2 \geq 0$$

With the primal problem now in canonical form for a minimization problem, we can easily convert to the dual linear programming problem by the primal–dual procedure presented earlier in this section. The dual becomes[2]

$$\text{Max} \quad -12u_1 + 3u_2 + 10u_3' - 10u_3''$$

s.t.

$$-1u_1 + 4u_2 + 6u_3' - 6u_3'' \leq \quad 2$$

$$-2u_1 - 2u_2 - 1u_3' + 1u_3'' \leq -3$$

$$-00u_1, u_2, u_3', u_3'' \geq 0$$

Since the equality primal constraint required two $\geq$ constraints, we denote the dual variables associated with these constraints as u_3' and u_3''. This reminds us that u_3' and u_3'' both refer to the third constraint in the initial primal problem. Since there are two dual variables associated with an equality constraint, the interpretation of the dual variable must be modified slightly. The dual variable for the equality constraint $6x_1 - x_2 = 10$ is given by the value of $u_3' - u_3''$ in the optimal solution to the dual. Hence, the dual variable for an equality constraint can be negative.

You should now be able to write the dual of any linear programming problem. Try Problem 21.

Computational Considerations

We have shown that solving either the primal or the dual problem provides the solution to the other as well. Thus, whenever computation time and effort are important considerations in solving linear programs, practitioners have the option of solving either the primal or the dual, depending on which is easier to solve.

---

[2]Note that the right-hand side of the second constraint is negative. Thus, we must multiply both sides of the constraint by -1 to obtain a positive value for the right-hand side before attempting to solve the problem with the simplex method.

With modern computer codes and recent advances in computer speed, computational considerations are no longer a serious issue.

Recall that if the primal problem has m constraints and n variables, the dual problem will have n constraints and m variables. Also recall that the basic solution identified at each iteration of the simplex method contains as many basic variables as constraints in the problem. For most computer implementations of the simplex method, the number of computations performed at each iteration and the total number of iterations are proportional to the number of basic variables in the problem. Thus, in general, we expect linear programs with a larger number of constraints, and therefore a larger number of basic variables, to require greater computational time and effort. As a result, when there is a substantial difference in the number of constraints in the primal and dual problems, practitioners often recommend solving the form of the problem (primal or dual) with fewer constraints.

NOTES & COMMENTS

1. Care must be exercised in performing sensitivity analysis when a degenerate solution exists (i.e. one or more basic variables are equal to zero). When the solution to the primal problem is degenerate, the dual prices are not unique.

2. With today's high-speed computers and linear programming software packages, converting to the dual to gain a computational advantage is usually not necessary.

Summary

In this chapter we showed how sensitivity analysis can be performed using the information in the final simplex tableau. This included computing the range of optimality for objective function coefficients, dual prices, and the range of feasibility for the right-hand sides. This sensitivity information is routinely made available as part of the solution report provided by most linear programming computer packages.

We stress here that the sensitivity analysis is based on the assumption that only one coefficient is allowed to change at a time; all other coefficients are assumed to remain at their original values. It is possible to do some limited sensitivity analysis on the effect of changing more than one coefficient at a time; the 100 percent rule was mentioned as being useful in this context.

In studying duality, we saw how the original linear programming problem, called the primal, can be converted into its associated dual linear programming problem. Solving either the primal or the dual provides the solution to the other. In cases where the primal has relatively few variables but many constraints, the dual often possesses computational advantages. Finally, we learned that the value of the dual variable identifies the economic contribution or value of additional resources in the primal problem.

Glossary

Range of optimality The range of values over which an objective function coefficient may vary without causing any change in the optimal solution (i.e., the values of all the variables will remain the same, but the value of the objective function will change).

Dual price The improvement in value of the optimal solution per-unit increase in the value of the right-hand side associated with a linear programming constraint.

Range of feasibility The range of values over which a b_i may vary without causing the current basic solution to become infeasible. The values of the variables in solution will change, but the same variables will remain basic. The dual prices for constraints do not change within these ranges.

Dual problem A linear programming problem related to the primal problem. Solution of the dual also provides the solution to the primal.

Primal problem The original formulation of a linear programming problem.

Canonical form for a maximization problem A maximization problem with all less-than-or-equal-to constraints and nonnegativity requirements for the decision variables.

Canonical form for a minimization problem A minimization problem with all greater-than-or-equal-to constraints and nonnegativity requirements for the decision variables.

Dual variable The variable in a dual linear programming problem. Its optimal value provides the dual price for the associated primal resource.

Problems

SELF TEST ▶

1. Consider the linear programming problem given below.

1 . Compute range of optimality

$$\text{Max} \quad 5x_1 + 6x_2 + 4x_3$$

s.t.

$$3x_1 + 4x_2 + 2x_3 \leq 120$$
$$x_1 + 2x_2 + x_3 \leq 50$$
$$x_1 + 2x_2 + 3x_3 \geq 30$$
$$x_1, x_2, x_3 \geq 0$$

The optimal simplex tableau is as follows:

Basic	c_B	x_1	x_2	x_3	s_1	s_2	s_3	
		5	6	4	0	0	0	
s_3	0	0	4	0	−2	7	1	80
x_3	4	0	2	1	−1	3	0	30
x_1	5	1	0	0	1	−2	0	20
z_j		5	8	4	1	2	0	220
$c_j - z_j$		0	−2	0	−1	−2	0	

   a. Compute the range of optimality for c_1.
   b. Compute the range of optimality for c_2.
   c. Compute the range of optimality for c_{s_1}.

2. Compute range of optimality and interpret

2. For the HighTech problem, we found the range of optimality for c_1, the profit contribution per unit of the Deskpro. The final simplex tableau is given in Section 6.1. Find
   a. The range of optimality for c_2.
   b. The range of optimality for c_{s_2}.
   c. The range of optimality for c_{s_3}.
   d. Suppose the per-unit profit contribution of the Portable (c_2) dropped to $35. How would the optimal solution change? What is the new value for total profit?

3. Refer to the problem formulation and optimal simplex tableau given in Problem 1.
   a. Find the dual price for the first constraint.
   b. Find the dual price for the second constraint.
   c. Find the dual price for the third constraint.
   d. Suppose the right-hand side of the first constraint is increased from 120 to 125. Find the new optimal solution and its value.
   e. Suppose the right-hand side of the first constraint is decreased from 120 to 110. Find the new optimal solution and its value.

4. Refer again to the problem formulation and optimal simplex tableau given in Problem 1.
   a. Find the range of feasibility for b_1.
   b. Find the range of feasibility for b_2.
   c. Find the range of feasibility for b_3.

5. For the HighTech problem, we found the range of feasibility for b_1, the assembly time available (see Section 6.1).
   a. Find the range of feasibility for b_2.
   b. Find the range of feasibility for b_3.
   c. How much will HighTech's profit increase if there is a 20-square-foot increase in the amount of warehouse space available (b_3)?

6. Consider the linear program

$$\text{Max} \quad 7.5x_1 + 15x_2 + 10x_3$$

s.t.

$$2x_1 + \qquad\quad 2x_3 \leq 8$$
$$\tfrac{1}{2}x_1 + 2x_2 + 1x_3 \leq 3$$
$$1x_1 + 1x_2 + 2x_3 \leq 6$$
$$x_1, x_2, x_3 \geq 0$$

   a. Find the optimal solution.
   b. Calculate the range of optimality for c_1.
   c. What would be the effect of a 2.5-unit increase in c_1 (from 7.5 to 10) on the optimal solution and the value of that solution?
   d. Calculate the range of optimality for c_3.
   e. What would be the effect of a five-unit increase in c_3 (from 10 to 15) on the optimal solution and the value of that solution?

7. Consider the linear programming problem presented in Problem 6.
   a. Compute the ranges of feasibility for b_1, b_2, and b_3.
   b. How much will the value of the objective function change if b_1 is increased from 8 to 9?
   c. How much will the value of the objective function change if b_2 is increased from 3 to 4?
   d. How much will the value of the objective function change if b_3 is increased from 6 to 7?

8. Recall the Par, Inc., problem introduced in Chapter 2. The linear program for this problem is

$$\text{Max} \quad 10x_1 + 9x_2$$

s.t.

$$\tfrac{7}{10}x_1 + 1x_2 \leq 630 \quad \text{Cutting and dyeing time}$$
$$\tfrac{1}{2}x_1 + \tfrac{5}{6}x_2 \leq 600 \quad \text{Sewing time}$$

$$1x_1 + \tfrac{2}{3}x_2 \leq 708 \quad \text{Finishing time}$$

$$\tfrac{1}{10}x_1 + \tfrac{1}{4}x_2 \leq 135 \quad \text{Inspection and packaging time}$$

$$x_1, x_2 \geq 0$$

where

$$x_1 = \text{number of standard bags produced}$$
$$x_2 = \text{number of deluxe bags produced}$$

The final simplex tableau is

		x_1	x_2	s_1	s_2	s_3	s_4	
Basis	c_B	10	9	0	0	0	0	
x_2	9	0	1	$\tfrac{30}{16}$	0	$-\tfrac{21}{16}$	0	252
s_2	0	0	0	$-\tfrac{15}{16}$	1	$\tfrac{5}{32}$	0	120
x_1	10	1	0	$-\tfrac{20}{16}$	0	$\tfrac{30}{16}$	0	540
s_4	0	0	0	$-\tfrac{11}{32}$	0	$\tfrac{9}{64}$	1	18
z_j		10	9	$\tfrac{70}{16}$	0	$\tfrac{111}{16}$	0	7668
$c_j - z_j$		0	0	$-\tfrac{70}{16}$	0	$-\tfrac{111}{16}$	0	

a. Calculate the range of optimality for the profit contribution, c_1, of the standard bag.
b. Calculate the range of optimality for the profit contribution, c_2, of the deluxe bag.
c. If the profit contribution per deluxe bag drops to $7 per unit, how will the optimal solution be affected?
d. What unit profit contribution would be necessary for the deluxe bag before Par, Inc., would consider changing its current production plan?
e. If the profit contribution of the deluxe bags can be increased to $15 per unit, what is the optimal production plan? State what you think will happen before you compute the new optimal solution.

9. For the Par, Inc., problem (Problem 8):
   a. Calculate the range of feasibility for b_1 (cutting and dyeing capacity).
   b. Calculate the range of feasibility for b_2 (sewing capacity).
   c. Calculate the range of feasibility for b_3 (finishing capacity).
   d. Calculate the range of feasibility for b_4 (inspection and packaging capacity).
   e. Which of these four departments are you interested in scheduling for overtime? Explain.

10. a. Calculate the final simplex tableau for the Par, Inc., problem (Problem 8) after increasing b_1 from 630 to $682\tfrac{4}{11}$.
    b. Would the current basis be optimal if b_1 were increased further? If not, what would be the new optimal basis?

11. Also for the Par, Inc., problem (Problem 8):
    a. How much would profit increase if an additional 30 hours became available in the cutting and dyeing department (i.e., if b_1 were increased from 630 to 660)?
    b. How much would profit decrease if 40 hours were removed from the sewing department?
    c. How much would profit decrease if, because of an employee accident, there were only 570 hours instead of 630 available in the cutting and dyeing department?

12. Below are additional conditions encountered by Par, Inc. (Problem 8).
    a. Suppose because of some new machinery Par, Inc., was able to make a small reduction in the amount of time it took to do the cutting and dyeing (constraint 1) for a standard bag. What effect would this have on the objective function?

b. Management believes that by buying a new sewing machine, the sewing time for standard bags can be reduced from $\frac{1}{2}$ to $\frac{1}{3}$ hour. Do you think this machine would be a good investment? Why?

13. Compute range of optimality and dual price; interpret both

13. Recall the RMC problem (Chapter 2, Problem 21). Letting

$$x_1 = \text{tons of fuel additive produced}$$
$$x_2 = \text{tons of solvent base produced}$$

leads to the following formulation of the RMC problem:

$$\text{Max} \quad 40x_1 + 30x_2$$

s.t.

$$\frac{2}{5}x_1 + \frac{1}{2}x_2 \le 20 \quad \text{Material 1}$$

$$\frac{1}{5}x_2 \le 5 \quad \text{Material 2}$$

$$\frac{3}{5}x_1 + \frac{3}{10}x_2 \le 21 \quad \text{Material 3}$$

$$x_1, x_2 \ge 0$$

The final simplex tableau is shown below.

		x_1	x_2	s_1	s_2	s_3	
Basis	c_B	40	30	0	0	0	
x_2	30	0	1	$\frac{10}{3}$	0	$-\frac{20}{9}$	20
s_2	0	0	0	$-\frac{2}{3}$	1	$\frac{4}{9}$	1
x_1	40	1	0	$-\frac{5}{3}$	0	$\frac{25}{9}$	25
z_j		40	30	$\frac{100}{3}$	0	$\frac{400}{9}$	1600
$c_j - z_j$		0	0	$-\frac{100}{3}$	0	$-\frac{400}{9}$	

a. Compute the ranges of optimality for c_1 and c_2.
b. Suppose that because of an increase in production costs, the profit per ton on the fuel additive is reduced to $30 per ton. What effect will this have on the optimal solution?
c. What is the dual price for the material 1 constraint? What is the interpretation?
d. If RMC had an opportunity to purchase additional materials, which material would be the most valuable? How much should the company be willing to pay for this material?

14. Compute range of feasibility; relate to dual price

14. Refer to Problem 13.
a. Compute the range of feasibility for b_1 (material 1 availability).
b. Compute the range of feasibility for b_2 (material 2 availability).
c. Compute the range of feasibility for b_3 (material 3 availability).
d. What is the dual price for material 3? Over what range of values for b_3 is this dual price valid?

15. Simplex solution, compute and interpret range of optimality

15. Consider the following linear program:

$$\text{Max} \quad 3x_1 + 1x_2 + 5x_3 + 3x_4$$

s.t.

$$3x_1 + 1x_2 + 2x_3 \quad\quad = 30$$

$$2x_1 + 1x_2 + 3x_3 + 1x_4 \ge 15$$

$$2x_2 \quad\quad + 3x_4 \le 25$$

$$x_1, x_2, x_3, x_4 \ge 0$$

   a. Find the optimal solution.
   b. Calculate the range of optimality for c_3.
   c. What would be the effect of a four-unit decrease in c_3 (from 5 to 1) on the optimal solution and the value of that solution?
   d. Calculate the range of optimality for c_2.
   e. What would be the effect of a three-unit increase in c_2 (from 1 to 4) on the optimal solution and the value of that solution?

16. Compute range of feasibility

16. Consider the final simplex tableau shown below.

		x_1	x_2	x_3	x_4	s_1	s_2	s_3	
Basis	c_B	4	6	3	1	0	0	0	
x_3	3	$3/60$	0	1	$1/2$	$3/10$	0	$-6/30$	**125**
s_2	0	$195/60$	0	0	$-1/2$	$-5/10$	1	-1	**425**
x_2	6	$39/60$	1	0	$1/2$	$-1/10$	0	$12/30$	**25**
z_j		$81/20$	6	3	$9/2$	$3/10$	0	$54/30$	**525**
$c_j - z_j$		$-1/20$	0	0	$-7/2$	$-3/10$	0	$-54/30$	

The original right-hand-side values were $b_1 = 550$, $b_2 = 700$, and $b_3 = 200$.
   a. Calculate the range of feasibility for b_1.
   b. Calculate the range of feasibility for b_2.
   c. Calculate the range of feasibility for b_3.

S E L F T E S T

17. Find and solve dual; find primal solution from dual; interpret dual variables

17. Suppose that in a product-mix problem $x_1, x_2, x_3,$ and x_4 indicate the units of products 1, 2, 3, and 4, respectively, and we have

$$\text{Max} \quad 4x_1 + 6x_2 + 3x_3 + 1x_4$$

s.t.

$$1.5x_1 + 2x_2 + 4x_3 + 3x_4 \leq 550 \quad \text{Machine A hours}$$

$$4x_1 + 1x_2 + 2x_3 + 1x_4 \leq 700 \quad \text{Machine B hours}$$

$$2x_1 + 3x_2 + 1x_3 + 2x_4 \leq 200 \quad \text{Machine C hours}$$

$$x_1, x_2, x_3, x_4 \geq 0$$

   a. Formulate the dual to this problem.
   b. Solve the dual. Use the dual solution to show that the profit-maximizing product mix is $x_1 = 0, x_2 = 25, x_3 = 125,$ and $x_4 = 0$.
   c. Use the dual variables to identify the machine or machines that are producing at maximum capacity. If the manager can select one machine for additional production capacity, which machine should have priority? Why?

18. Find dual

18. Find the dual problem for the following linear program:

$$\text{Max} \quad 10x_1 + 9x_2 + 4x_3 + 6x_4$$

s.t.

$$3x_1 + 2x_2 + 4x_3 + 2x_4 \leq 70$$

$$5x_1 + 5x_2 + 1x_3 + 3x_4 \leq 60$$

$$5x_1 + 6x_2 + 3x_3 + 1x_4 \leq 25$$

$$x_1, x_2, x_3, x_4 \geq 0$$

S E L F   T E S T ▷

19. Find dual

19. Find the dual for the following linear program:

$$\text{Min} \quad 2800x_1 + 6000x_2 + 1200x_3$$

s.t.

$$
\begin{array}{rrrr}
15x_1 + & 15x_2 + & x_3 \geq & 5 \\
4x_1 + & 8x_2 & \geq & 5 \\
12x_1 & + & 8x_3 \geq & 24
\end{array}
$$

$$x_1, x_2, x_3 \geq 0$$

20. Comment on computational issues

20. Write the following primal linear program in canonical form for a maximization problem:

$$\text{Max} \quad 5x_1 + 1x_2 + 3x_3$$

s.t.

$$
\begin{array}{rrrr}
1x_1 + & 1x_2 & & \geq 40 \\
2x_1 + & 3x_2 + & 1x_3 & \leq 50 \\
3x_1 + & 2x_2 + & 2x_3 & \leq 25 \\
& 1x_2 + & 1x_3 & \geq 10
\end{array}
$$

$$x_1, x_2, x_3 \geq 0$$

From a computational point of view, would you rather solve the above linear programming problem or its dual?

S E L F   T E S T ▷

21. Find canonical form and write dual

21. Write the following primal problem in canonical form, and find its dual.

$$\text{Max} \quad 3x_1 + 1x_2 + 5x_3 + 3x_4$$

s.t.

$$
\begin{array}{rrrrr}
3x_1 + & 1x_2 + & 2x_3 & & = 30 \\
2x_1 + & 1x_2 + & 3x_3 + & 1x_4 & \geq 15 \\
& 2x_2 + & & 3x_4 & \leq 25
\end{array}
$$

$$x_1, x_2, x_3, x_4 \geq 0$$

22. Find dual; solve primal and dual graphically; compare results

22. Consider the following linear program:

$$\text{Max} \quad 2x_1 + 3x_2$$

s.t.

$$
\begin{array}{rr}
1x_1 + 2x_2 \leq & 8 \\
3x_1 + 2x_2 \leq & 12
\end{array}
$$

$$x_1, x_2 \geq 0$$

a. Write the dual of this problem.
b. Solve both the primal and the dual problems using the graphical procedure.
c. Solve both the primal and the dual problems using the simplex method.
d. Using your results from parts (b) and (c), identify where and how you can observe properties 1 and 2 of the primal–dual relationship.

23. Find and solve dual; find primal solution from dual; interpret dual variables

23. Photo Chemicals produces two types of photograph-developing fluids at a cost of $1.00 per gallon. Let

$$x_1 = \text{gallons of product 1}$$
$$x_2 = \text{gallons of product 2}$$

Photo Chemicals management has required that at least 30 gallons of product 1 and at least 20 gallons of product 2 be produced. They have also required that at least 80 pounds of a perishable raw material be used in production. A linear programming formulation of the problem is as follows:

$$\text{Min} \quad 1x_1 + 1x_2$$

s.t.

$$1x_1 \qquad \geq 30 \quad \text{Minimum product 1}$$
$$1x_2 \geq 20 \quad \text{Minimum product 2}$$
$$1x_1 + 2x_2 \geq 80 \quad \text{Minimum raw material}$$
$$x_1, x_2 \geq 0$$

a. Show the dual problem.
b. Solve the dual problem, and show from it that the optimal production plan is $x_1 = 30$ and $x_2 = 25$.
c. The third constraint involves a management request that the current 80 pounds of a perishable raw material be used. However, after learning that the optimal solution calls for an excess production of five units of product 2, management is reconsidering the raw material requirement. Specifically, you have been asked to identify the cost effect if this constraint is relaxed. Use the dual variable to indicate the change in the cost if only 79 pounds of raw material have to be used.

24. Find canonical form and write dual

24. Write the dual problem for the following linear program:

$$\text{Min} \quad 3x_1 + 1x_2 + 2x_3$$

s.t.

$$2x_1 + 1x_2 + 3x_3 = 5$$
$$4x_1 + 1x_2 + 1x_3 = 4$$
$$2x_1 \qquad + 1x_3 \leq 7$$
$$1x_1 + 2x_2 \qquad \geq 4$$
$$x_1, x_2, x_3 \geq 0$$

25. Find and solve dual; find primal solution from dual; show primal and dual optimal values are equal

25. Consider the following linear programming problem:

$$\text{Min} \quad 4x_1 + 3x_2 + 6x_3$$

s.t.

$$1x_1 + 0.5x_2 + 1x_3 \geq 15$$
$$2x_2 + 1x_3 \geq 30$$
$$1x_1 + 1x_2 + 2x_3 \geq 20$$
$$x_1, x_2, x_3 \geq 0$$

a. Write the dual problem.
b. Solve the dual.

c. Use the dual solution to identify the optimal solution to the original primal problem.

d. Verify that the optimal values for the primal and dual problems are equal.

26. Modeling; find and solve dual; find primal solution from dual; interpret dual variables

26. A sales representative who sells two products is trying to determine the number of sales calls that should be made during the next month to promote each product. Based on past experience, there is an average $10 commission for every call on product 1 and a $5 commission for every call on product 2. The company requires at least 20 calls per month for each product and not more than 100 calls per month on any one product. In addition, the sales representative spends about 3 hours on each call for product 1 and 1 hour on each call for product 2. If there are a total of 175 selling hours available next month, how many calls should be made for each of the two products to maximize the commission?

a. Formulate a linear program for this problem.

b. Formulate and solve the dual problem.

c. Use the final simplex tableau for the dual to determine the optimal number of calls for the products. What is the maximum commission?

d. Interpret the values of the dual variables.

27. Solve primal and dual; note that value of any primal feasible solution ≤ any dual feasible solution

27. Consider the linear program

$$\text{Max} \quad 3x_1 + 2x_2$$

s.t.

$$1x_1 + 2x_2 \leq 8$$

$$2x_1 + 1x_2 \leq 10$$

$$x_1, x_2 \geq 0$$

a. Solve this problem using the simplex method. Keep a record of the value of the objective function at each extreme point.

b. Formulate and solve the dual of this problem using the graphical procedure.

c. Compute the value of the dual objective function for each extreme-point solution of the dual problem.

d. Compare the values of the objective functions for each primal and dual extreme-point solution.

e. Can a dual feasible solution yield a value less than a primal feasible solution? Can you state a result concerning bounds on the value of the primal solution provided by any feasible solution to the dual problem?

28. Solve; find dual prices and note relation to binding constraints; find all ranges

28. Consider the following linear program:

$$\text{Max} \quad 15x_1 + 30x_2 + 20x_3$$

s.t.

$$1x_1 \qquad + \ 1x_3 \leq 4$$

$$0.5x_1 + \ 2x_2 + \ 1x_3 \leq 3$$

$$1x_1 + \ 1x_2 + \ 2x_3 \leq 6$$

$$x_1, x_2, x_3 \geq 0$$

Solve using the simplex method, and answer the following questions:

a. What is the optimal solution?

b. What is the value of the objective function?

c. Which constraints are the binding constraints?

d. How much slack is available in the nonbinding constraints?

e. What are the dual prices associated with the three constraints? Which right-hand-side value would have the greatest effect on the value of the objective function if it could be changed?

f. Develop the appropriate ranges for the coefficients of the objective function. What is your interpretation of these ranges?

g. Develop and interpret the ranges of feasibility for the right-hand-side values.

29. Suppose the optimal solution to a three-variable linear programming problem has $x_1 = 10$, $x_2 = 30$, and $x_3 = 15$. It is later discovered that the following two constraints were inadvertently omitted when formulating the problem.

$$6x_1 + 4x_2 - x_3 \leq 170$$

$$\tfrac{1}{4}x_1 + x_2 \geq 25$$

Find the new optimal solution if possible. If this is not possible, state that it is not possible and why.

30. Recall the Innis Investments problem (Chapter 2, Problem 37). Letting

x_1 = units purchased in the stock fund
x_2 = units purchased in the money market fund

leads to the following formulation:

$$\text{Min} \quad 8x_1 + 3x_2 \qquad \text{Total risk}$$

s.t.

$$50x_1 + 100x_2 \leq 1{,}200{,}000 \quad \text{Funds available}$$

$$5x_1 + 4x_2 \geq 60{,}000 \quad \text{Annual income}$$

$$x_2 \geq 3{,}000 \quad \text{Minimum units in money market}$$

$$x_1, x_2 \geq 0$$

a. Solve this problem using the simplex method.

b. The value of the optimal solution is a measure of the riskiness of the portfolio. What effect will increasing the annual income requirement have on the riskiness of the portfolio?

c. Find the range of feasibility for b_2.

d. How will the optimal solution and its value change if the annual income requirement is increased from $60,000 to $65,000?

e. How will the optimal solution and its value change if the risk measure for the stock fund is increased from 8 to 9?

MANAGEMENT SCIENCE IN PRACTICE

Performance Analysis Corporation*
Chapel Hill, North Carolina

Performance Analysis Corporation, founded in 1979, is a management consulting company that specializes in the use of management science to design more efficient and effective operations for a wide variety of chain stores. Performance Analysis Corporation has evaluated the operation of banks, savings and loans, and grocery chains. Recently, the company has been involved in evaluating the efficiency of fast-food outlets. In the following application, we describe how linear programming methodology has been used to provide an evaluation model for a chain of fast-food restaurants.

Fast-Food Business

The fast-food business for a chain such as McDonalds or Kentucky Fried Chicken is characterized by hundreds, or even thousands, of individual restaurants, some of which are company owned and some of which are franchised. A typical restaurant may gross close to a million dollars annually; thus, the impact of relatively minor improvements at a large proportion of the restaurants can have a substantial effect on a chain's profitability and market share.

Although each individual restaurant in a given chain usually offers the same type of menu (with some minor geographical variations), they must often deal with vastly different environments and competition. In addition, the age of the restaurant, facade used, ease of access and egress, hours of operation, scale of operation, and so on can vary substantially from restaurant to restaurant.

A major objective of company management in the fast-food industry involves the performance evaluations of managers of individual restaurants in the chain. These evaluations are the basis for awarding year-end bonuses and for personal advancement purposes. Unfortunately, there is not a single measure of performance such as profit that can be used as the basis for the evaluation since other measures such as market share and rate of growth are also important.

A Linear Programming Evaluation Model

One approach to the store evaluation problem utilizes the concept of Pareto optimality. According to this concept, a restaurant in a given chain is *relatively* inefficient if there are other restaurants in the same chain that have the following characteristics:

1. Have the same or worse environment.
2. Produce at least the same levels of *all* outputs.
3. Utilize no more of *any* resource and *less* of at least one of the resources.

The mechanism for discovering which of the restaurants are Pareto inefficient involves the development and solution of a linear programming model.** Constraints on the problem involve requirements concerning the minimum acceptable levels of output (e.g., profit and market share) and conditions imposed by uncontrollable elements in the environment. The objective function calls for the minimization of the resources necessary to produce the output. Solution of the model produces the following output for each restaurant:

1. A score that assesses the level of so-called relative technical efficiency achieved by the particular restaurant over the time period in question.
2. The reduction in controllable resources and/or the augmentation of outputs over the time period in question for an inefficient restaurant to have been rated as efficient.
3. A peer group of other restaurants with which each restaurant can be compared in the future.

Sensitivity analysis, especially that concerning the dual prices, provides important managerial information. For each constraint concerning a minimum acceptable output level, the dual price tells the manager how much one more unit of output would increase his/her efficiency measure. Analysis of the ranges for each of the constraint coefficients (the a_{ij} values) provides information concerning how much outputs could be reduced or inputs increased before the restaurant would become inefficient.

Types of Factors Utilized

The approach is capable of handling three types of factors: quantitative controllable factors such as salaries paid or local advertising expenditures; noncontrollable quantitative factors such as the median income in the geographic area served by the restaurant or the unemployment rate; and qualitative factors such as the degree of competition or appearance of restaurant. The outputs include total sales of various types (e.g., by time of day), profits, market share, rate of growth of sales, and so forth.

Benefits

The analysis typically identifies 40–50% of the restaurants as underperforming, given the previously stated conditions concerning the inputs available and outputs produced. Performance

—Continued on next page

---

*The authors are indebted to Richard C. Morey for providing this application.
**The model used is the data envelopment analysis model discussed in Section 4.5.

—Continued from previous page

Analysis Corporation has found that if all of the relative inefficiencies identified are eliminated simultaneously, the resulting increase in corporate profits is typically in the neighborhood of 5–10%. This is truly a substantial increase given the large scale of operations involved.

The district manager has an objective score card for each restaurant manager that indicates areas (e.g., overtime salary) where improvements may be in order. The efficient restaurants can be used to generate a set of best practices that can be models for other restaurants. Of primary benefit are the reactions of restaurant managers who appreciate that the evaluation process that they are subject to recognizes the environment they are forced to operate within; deals with noncommensurability of outputs involved; is theory based and nonpolitical; and is defensible, understandable, and equitable.

Questions

1. State in your own words what it means for one restaurant in a chain to be relatively inefficient relative to another restaurant in the same chain.

2. Suppose the evaluation model showed that for a particular restaurant the resource mix necessary to produce a given output mix was 90% of what another restaurant was using to produce that same mix of output. Would you conclude that the restaurant was relatively efficient or inefficient? Why?

CHAPTER 7

Transportation, Assignment, and Transshipment Problems

Sections 7.5 and 7.6, and Problems 32–43, deal with special-purpose algorithms; these sections and problems may be skipped without loss of continuity.

Transportation, assignment, and transshipment problems belong to a special class of linear programming problems called *network flow problems.* A separate chapter is devoted to these problems for two reasons. First, a wide variety of applications can be modeled as transportation, assignment, or transshipment problems. Second, these problems have a mathematical structure that has enabled management scientists to develop efficient specialized solution procedures for solving them; as a result, very large problems can be solved with just a few seconds of computer time.

We will approach the network flow problems by illustrating each type with a specific application. We first develop a graphical representation, called a *network,* of the problem, then show how a linear programming model of the problem can be formulated. The network representation makes it easy to see the close relationship among the three types of problems. After showing how the three types of problems can be formulated and solved as linear programs, we present special-purpose solution procedures for the transportation and assignment problems in the last two sections of the chapter.

An applications-oriented introduction to the transportation, assignment, and transshipment problems can be obtained by covering Sections 7.1 through 7.4. Sections 7.5 and 7.6, involving special-purpose algorithms, can be skipped without loss of continuity.

7.1 The Transportation Problem: The Network Model and a Linear Programming Formulation

The *transportation problem* arises frequently in planning for the distribution of goods and services from several supply locations to several demand locations. Typically, the quantity of goods available at each supply location (origin) is limited, and the goods are needed at each of several demand locations (destinations). The usual objective in a transportation problem is to minimize the cost of shipping goods from the origins to the destinations.

272

Let us illustrate by considering the transportation problem faced by Foster Generators. This problem involves the transportation of a product from three plants to four distribution centers. Foster Generators has production operations in Cleveland, Ohio; Bedford, Indiana; and York, Pennsylvania. Production capacities for these plants over the next 3-month planning period for one particular type of generator are as follows:

Origin	Plant	3-Month Production Capacity (units)
1	Cleveland	5,000
2	Bedford	6,000
3	York	2,500
	Total	13,500

The firm distributes its generators through four regional distribution centers located in Boston, Chicago, St. Louis, and Lexington; the 3-month forecast of demand for the distribution centers is as follows:

Destination	Distribution Center	3-Month Demand Forecast (units)
1	Boston	6,000
2	Chicago	4,000
3	St. Louis	2,000
4	Lexington	1,500
	Total	13,500

Management would like to determine how much of its production should be shipped from each plant to each distribution center. Figure 7.1 shows graphically the 12 distribution routes Foster can use. Such a graph is called a *network;* the circles are referred to as *nodes* and the lines connecting the nodes as *arcs.* Each origin and destination is represented by a node, and each possible shipping route is represented by an arc. The amount of the supply is written next to each origin node, and the amount of the demand is written next to each destination node. The goods shipped from the origins to the destinations represent the flow in the network. Note that the direction of flow (from origin to destination) is indicated by the arrows.

Try Problem 1 for practice in developing a network model of a transportation problem.

For Foster's transportation problem, the objective is to determine the routes to be used and the quantity to be shipped via each route that will provide the minimum total transportation cost. The cost for each unit shipped on each route is given in Table 7.1 and is shown on each arc in Figure 7.1.

A linear programming model can be used to solve this transportation problem. We shall use double-subscripted decision variables, with x_{11} denoting the number of units shipped from origin 1 (Cleveland) to destination 1 (Boston), x_{12} denoting the number of units shipped from origin 1 (Cleveland) to destination 2 (Chicago), and so on. In general,

The first subscript identifies the "from" node of the corresponding arc and the second subscript identifies the "to" node of the arc.

Figure 7.1
The Network Representation of
the Foster Generators
Transportation Problem

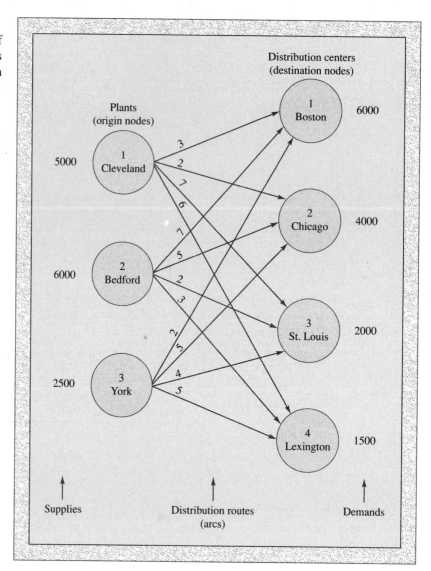

Table 7.1

Transportation Cost Per Unit for the
Foster Generators Transportation
Problem

	Destination			
Origin	Boston	Chicago	St. Louis	Lexington
Cleveland	3	2	7	6
Bedford	7	5	2	3
York	2	5	4	5

the decision variables for a transportation problem having m origins and n destinations are written as follows:

$$x_{ij} = \text{number of units shipped from origin } i \text{ to destination } j$$
$$\text{where } i = 1, 2, \ldots, m \text{ and } j = 1, 2, \ldots, n$$

Note that there is one decision variable for each arc in Figure 7.1. Using this notation, $x_{24} = 500$ would correspond to shipping 500 units from Bedford (origin 2) to Lexington (destination 4).

Since the objective of the transportation problem is to minimize the total transportation cost, we can use the cost data in Table 7.1 or on the arcs in Figure 7.1 to develop the following cost expressions:

Transportation costs for
units shipped from Cleveland $= 3x_{11} + 2x_{12} + 7x_{13} + 6x_{14}$

Transportation costs for
units shipped from Bedford $= 7x_{21} + 5x_{22} + 2x_{23} + 3x_{24}$

Transportation costs for
units shipped from York $= 2x_{31} + 5x_{32} + 4x_{33} + 5x_{34}$

The sum of the above expressions provides the objective function showing the total transportation cost for Foster Generators.

Transportation problems need constraints because each origin has a limited supply and each destination has a specific demand. We will consider the supply constraints first. The capacity at the Cleveland plant is 5000 units. With the total number of units shipped from the Cleveland plant expressed as $x_{11} + x_{12} + x_{13} + x_{14}$, the supply constraint for the Cleveland plant can be written as

$$x_{11} + x_{12} + x_{13} + x_{14} \leq 5000 \quad \text{Cleveland supply}$$

With three origins (plants), the Foster transportation problem has three supply constraints. Given the capacity of 6000 units at the Bedford plant and 2500 units at the York plant, the two additional supply constraints are as follows:

$$x_{21} + x_{22} + x_{23} + x_{24} \leq 6000 \quad \text{Bedford supply}$$

$$x_{31} + x_{32} + x_{33} + x_{34} \leq 2500 \quad \text{York supply}$$

To obtain a feasible solution, the total supply must be greater than or equal to the total demand.

With the four distribution centers as the destinations, the following four demand constraints are needed to ensure that destination demands will be satisfied:

$$x_{11} + x_{21} + x_{31} = 6000 \quad \text{Boston demand}$$

$$x_{12} + x_{22} + x_{32} = 4000 \quad \text{Chicago demand}$$

$$x_{13} + x_{23} + x_{33} = 2000 \quad \text{St. Louis demand}$$

$$x_{14} + x_{24} + x_{34} = 1500 \quad \text{Lexington demand}$$

Combining the objective function and constraints into one model provides the following 12-variable, 7-constraint linear programming formulation of the Foster Generators transportation problem:

$$\text{Min} \quad 3x_{11} + 2x_{12} + 7x_{13} + 6x_{14} + 7x_{21} + 5x_{22} + 2x_{23} + 3x_{24} + 2x_{31} + 5x_{32} + 4x_{33} + 5x_{34}$$

$$
\begin{aligned}
\text{s.t.} \quad & \\
x_{11} + x_{12} + x_{13} + x_{14} & \leq 5000 \\
x_{21} + x_{22} + x_{23} + x_{24} & \leq 6000 \\
x_{31} + x_{32} + x_{33} + x_{34} & \leq 2500 \\
x_{11} \quad\quad + x_{21} \quad\quad + x_{31} & = 6000 \\
x_{12} \quad\quad + x_{22} \quad\quad + x_{32} & = 4000 \\
x_{13} \quad\quad + x_{23} \quad\quad + x_{33} & = 2000 \\
x_{14} \quad\quad + x_{24} \quad\quad + x_{34} & = 1500 \\
x_{ij} \geq 0 \quad \text{for } i = 1, 2, 3 \text{ and } j = 1, 2, 3, 4
\end{aligned}
$$

You should now be able to use the computer to solve a linear programming model of a transportation problem. Try Problem 2.

Several observations can be made when we compare the linear programming formulation to the network in Figure 7.1. All the information needed for the linear programming formulation is on the network. There is one constraint for each node and one variable for each arc. The sum of the variables corresponding to arcs out of an origin node must be less than or equal to the origin's supply, and the sum of the variables corresponding to the arcs into a destination node must be equal to the destination's demand.

The Foster Generators problem was solved using the linear programming module of The Management Scientist. The computer solution (see Figure 7.2) shows that the minimum total transportation cost is $39,500. The values for the decision variables show

Figure 7.2 The Management Scientist Solution for the Foster Generators Transportation Problem

```
Objective Function Value =        39500.000

         Variable            Value            Reduced Costs
      --------------    ---------------    --------------------
           X11            3500.000                0.000
           X12            1500.000                0.000
           X13               0.000                8.000
           X14               0.000                6.000
           X21               0.000                1.000
           X22            2500.000                0.000
           X23            2000.000                0.000
           X24            1500.000                0.000
           X31            2500.000                0.000
           X32               0.000                4.000
           X33               0.000                6.000
           X34               0.000                6.000
```

the optimal amounts to ship over each route. For example, with $x_{11} = 3500$, we see that 3500 units should be shipped over the Cleveland–Boston route, and with $x_{12} = 1500$, 1500 units should be shipped from Cleveland to Chicago. Other values of the decision variables indicate the remaining shipping quantities and routes. The minimum-cost transportation schedule is shown in Table 7.2. Figure 7.3 summarizes the optimal solution on the network.

Problem Variations

The Foster Generators problem is an illustration of the basic transportation model. Variations of the basic transportation problem may involve one or more of the following situations:

1. Total supply not equal to total demand
2. Maximization objective function rather than minimization
3. Route capacities or route minimums
4. Unacceptable routes

With slight modifications in the linear programming model, these situations can be easily accommodated.

Supply Not Equal to Demand. Often *the total supply is not equal to the total demand.* If total supply exceeds total demand, no modification in the linear programming formulation is necessary. Excess supply will appear as slack in the linear programming solution. Slack for any particular origin can be interpreted as the unused supply or amount not shipped from the origin.

Whenever total supply is less than total demand, how the unsatisfied demand is handled (e.g., backorders) is not determined by the model; this aspect of the problem must be handled by the manager.

If total supply is less than total demand, the linear programming model of a transportation problem will not have a feasible solution. In this case, it is often desirable to provide a minimum-cost shipping schedule for the available supply and also to indicate which destinations will have unsatisfied demand. To obtain such a solution, we modify the network representation by adding a *dummy origin* with a supply equal to the difference between the total demand and the total supply. With the addition of the dummy origin, and an arc from the dummy origin to each destination, the linear programming model will have a feasible solution. A zero per-unit cost is assigned to each arc leaving the dummy origin so that the value of the optimal solution for the revised problem will represent the shipping cost for the units actually shipped (no shipments will actually be made from the dummy origin). When the optimal solution is implemented, the destina-

Table 7.2

Optimal Solution to the Foster Generators Transportation Problem

From	To	Units Shipped	Per-Unit Cost	Total Cost
Cleveland	Boston	3500	$3	$10,500
Cleveland	Chicago	1500	$2	3,000
Bedford	Chicago	2500	$5	12,500
Bedford	St. Louis	2000	$2	4,000
Bedford	Lexington	1500	$3	4,500
York	Boston	2500	$2	5,000
				$39,500

Figure 7.3

Optimal Solution to the Foster Generators Transportation Problem

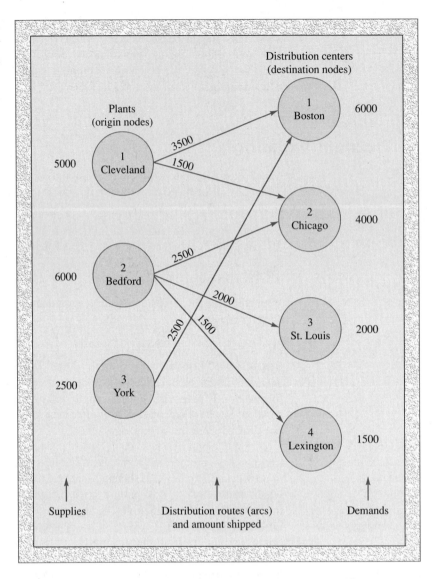

tions showing shipments being received from the dummy origin will be the destinations experiencing a shortfall or unsatisfied demand.

Maximization Objective. In some transportation problems, the objective is to find a solution that maximizes profit or revenue. Using the profit- or revenue-per-unit values as coefficients in the objective function, we simply solve a maximization rather than a minimization linear program. The constraints are not affected by this change.

Try Problem 8 to see if you can handle a case where demand is greater than supply with a maximization objective.

Arc Capacities. The linear programming formulation of the transportation problem can also accommodate capacities on one or more of the arcs. For example, suppose that in the Foster Generators problem the York–Boston route (origin 3 to destination 1) was found to have a capacity of 1000 units because of limited space availability on its normal mode of transportation. This route capacity can be accommodated by adding a constraint to the linear programming model that provides an upper limit on the corresponding decision variable. With x_{31} denoting the amount shipped from York to Boston, the route capacity constraint for the York–Boston route would appear as

$$x_{31} \leq 1000$$

Similarly, route minimums can be specified. For example,

$$x_{22} \geq 2000$$

would guarantee that a previously committed order for a Bedford–Chicago delivery of 2000 units would be maintained in the optimal solution.

Unacceptable Routes. As a final special situation, we note that in transportation problems it may not be possible to establish a route from every origin to every destination. That is, some routes may be unacceptable. To handle this situation, we simply drop the corresponding arc from the network and remove the corresponding variable from the linear programming formulation. For example, if the Cleveland–St. Louis route were determined to be unacceptable or unusable, the arc from Cleveland to St. Louis could be dropped in Figure 7.1, and x_{13} could be removed from the linear programming formulation. Solving the resulting 11-variable, 7-constraint model would provide the optimal solution while guaranteeing that the Cleveland–St. Louis route is not used.

A General Linear Programming Model of the Transportation Problem

To show the general linear programming model of the transportation problem, we use the following notation:

$$i = \text{index for origins, } i = 1, 2, \ldots, m$$
$$j = \text{index for destinations, } j = 1, 2, \ldots, n$$
$$x_{ij} = \text{number of units shipped from origin } i \text{ to destination } j$$
$$c_{ij} = \text{cost per unit of shipping from origin } i \text{ to destination } j$$
$$s_i = \text{supply or capacity in units at origin } i$$
$$d_j = \text{demand in units at destination } j$$

The general linear programming model of the m-origin, n-destination transportation problem is

$$\text{Min} \quad \sum_{i=1}^{m} \sum_{j=1}^{n} c_{ij} x_{ij}$$

s.t.

$$\sum_{j=1}^{n} x_{ij} \leq s_i \qquad i = 1, 2, \ldots, m \quad \text{Supply}$$

$$\sum_{i=1}^{m} x_{ij} = d_j \qquad j = 1, 2, \ldots, n \quad \text{Demand}$$

$$x_{ij} \geq 0 \qquad \text{for all } i \text{ and } j$$

As mentioned above, additional constraints of the form $x_{ij} \leq L_{ij}$ can be added if the route from origin i to destination j has capacity L_{ij}. A transportation problem that includes constraints of this type is called a *capacitated transportation problem.*

NOTES & COMMENTS

1. Transportation problems encountered in practice usually lead to very large linear programs. It is not unusual to encounter a transportation problem with 100 origins and 100 destinations. Such a problem would involve 10,000 = (100)(100) variables. For such a problem, special-purpose solution procedures (see Section 7.5) are much more efficient than general-purpose linear programming codes. But if speed is not an issue, a general-purpose linear programming code that has the capability to solve large problems will solve most transportation problems.

2. To handle a situation in which some routes may be unacceptable, we stated that you could drop the corresponding arc from the network and remove the corresponding variable from the linear programming formulation. Another approach that is often used assigns an extremely large objective function coefficient to any unacceptable arcs. If the problem has already been formulated, another option is to add a constraint to the formulation that sets the variable you want to remove equal to zero.

3. The optimal solution to a transportation model will consist of integer values for the decision variables as long as all supply and demand values are integers. This is because of the special mathematical structure of the linear programming model. Each variable appears in exactly one supply and one demand constraint, and all coefficients in the constraint equations are 1's and 0's.

7.2   The Assignment Problem: The Network Model and a Linear Programming Formulation

The *assignment problem* arises in a variety of decision-making situations; typical assignment problems involve assigning jobs to machines, agents to tasks, sales personnel to sales territories, contracts to bidders, and so on. A distinguishing feature of the assignment problem is that *one* agent is assigned to *one and only one* task. Specifically, we look for the set of assignments that will optimize a stated objective, such as minimize cost, minimize time, or maximize profits.

As an illustration of the assignment problem, let us consider the case of Fowle Marketing Research which has just received requests for market research studies from three new clients. The company is faced with the task of assigning project leaders (agents) to each of these three new research studies (tasks). Currently, three individuals are free from other commitments and available for the project leader assignments. Fowle's management realizes, however, that the time required to complete each study will depend on the experience and ability of the project leader assigned to the study. Since the three projects have been judged to have approximately the same priority, the company would like to assign project leaders such that the total number of days required to complete all three projects is minimized. If a project leader is to be assigned to one and only one client, what assignments should be made?

To answer the assignment question, Fowle's management must first consider all possible project leader–client assignments and then estimate the corresponding project completion times. With three project leaders and three clients, there are nine possible assignment alternatives. The alternatives and the estimated project completion times in days are summarized in Table 7.3. Using these data, we see that Terry would require 10 days to complete client 1's project, while Carle would require 9 days for the same project. Similar completion time statements can be made about the other possible assignments.

In Figure 7.4 we show the network representation of Fowle's assignment problem. The nodes correspond to the project leaders and clients, and the arcs represent the possible assignments of project leaders to clients. The supply at each origin node and the demand

Try part (a) of Problem 12 to see if you can develop a network model for an assignment problem.

Table 7.3

Estimated Project Completion Times (Days) for the Fowle Marketing Research Assignment Problem

| | Client | | |
Project Leader	1	2	3
1. Terry	10	15	9
2. Carle	9	18	5
3. McClymonds	6	14	3

Figure 7.4

A Network Model of the Fowle Marketing Research Assignment Problem

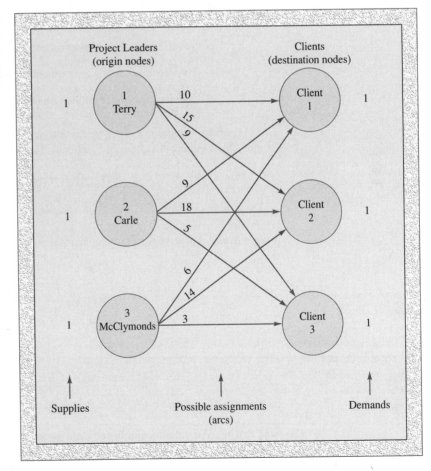

at each destination node are both 1; the cost of assigning a project leader to a client is the time it takes that project leader to complete the client's task. Note the similarity between the network models of the assignment problem (Figure 7.4) and of the transportation problem (Figure 7.1). The assignment problem is a special case of the transportation problem in which all supply and demand values equal 1 and the amount shipped over each arc is 0 or 1.

Since the assignment problem is a special case of the transportation problem, the linear programming formulation can be developed quickly from the graphical model provided by the network. Again, we need a constraint for each node and a variable for each arc. As in the transportation problem, we shall find it helpful to use double-subscripted decision variables, with x_{11} denoting the assignment of project leader 1 (Terry) to client 1, x_{12} denoting the assignment of project leader 1 (Terry) to client 2, and so on. Thus, the decision variables for Fowle's assignment problem are defined as follows:

$$x_{ij} = \begin{cases} 1 \text{ if project leader } i \text{ is assigned to client } j \\ 0 \text{ otherwise} \end{cases}$$

$$\text{where } i = 1, 2, 3, \text{ and } j = 1, 2, 3$$

Using this notation, $x_{21} = 1$ and $x_{31} = 0$ would tell us that project leader 2 (Carle) is assigned to client 1, and project leader 3 (McClymonds) is not assigned to client 1.

Following this notation and using the completion time data in Table 7.3, we can develop the following completion time expressions:

$$\text{Days required for Terry's assignment } = 10x_{11} + 15x_{12} + 9x_{13}$$

$$\text{Days required for Carle's assignment } = 9x_{21} + 18x_{22} + 5x_{23}$$

$$\text{Days required for McClymonds's assignment} = 6x_{31} + 14x_{32} + 3x_{33}.$$

The sum of the completion times for the three project leaders will provide the total days required to complete the three assignments. Thus, the objective function is

$$\text{Min} \quad 10x_{11} + 15x_{12} + 9x_{13} + 9x_{21} + 18x_{22} + 5x_{23} + 6x_{31} + 14x_{32} + 3x_{33}.$$

The constraints for the assignment problem reflect the conditions that each project leader can be assigned to at most one client and that each client must have one assigned project leader. These constraints are written as follows:

$$x_{11} + x_{12} + x_{13} \leq 1 \quad \text{Terry's assignment}$$

$$x_{21} + x_{22} + x_{23} \leq 1 \quad \text{Carle's assignment}$$

$$x_{31} + x_{32} + x_{33} \leq 1 \quad \text{McClymonds's assignment}$$

$$x_{11} + x_{21} + x_{31} = 1 \quad \text{Client 1}$$

$$x_{12} + x_{22} + x_{32} = 1 \quad \text{Client 2}$$

$$x_{13} + x_{23} + x_{33} = 1 \quad \text{Client 3}$$

Since the number of project leaders equals the number of clients, all the constraints could be written as equalities. But when the number of project leaders exceeds the number of clients, less-than-or-equal-to constraints must be used for the project leader constraints.

Note that there is one constraint for each node in Figure 7.4.

Combining the objective function and constraints into one model provides the following nine-variable, six-constraint linear programming model of the Fowle Marketing Research assignment problem:

$$\text{Min} \quad 10x_{11} + 15x_{12} + 9x_{13} + 9x_{21} + 18x_{22} + 5x_{23} + 6x_{31} + 14x_{32} + 3x_{33}$$

s.t.

$$
\begin{array}{lcccccccccc}
x_{11} + & x_{12} + & x_{13} & & & & & & & \leq 1 \\
& & & x_{21} + & x_{22} + & x_{23} & & & & \leq 1 \\
& & & & & & x_{31} + & x_{32} + & x_{33} & \leq 1 \\
x_{11} & & & + \; x_{21} & & & + \; x_{31} & & & = 1 \\
& x_{12} & & & + \; x_{22} & & & + \; x_{32} & & = 1 \\
& & x_{13} & & & + \; x_{23} & & & + \; x_{33} & = 1 \\
\end{array}
$$

$$x_{ij} \geq 0 \text{ for } i = 1, 2, 3, \text{ and } j = 1, 2, 3$$

At this point, you should be able to formulate and solve a linear programming model for an assignment problem on the computer. Try part (b) of Problem 12.

Figure 7.5 shows the computer solution for this model. Terry is assigned to client 2 ($x_{12} = 1$), Carle is assigned to client 3 ($x_{23} = 1$), and McClymonds is assigned to client 1 ($x_{31} = 1$). The total completion time required is 26 days. This solution is summarized in Table 7.4.

Problem Variations

Since the assignment problem can be viewed as a special case of the transportation problem, the problem variations that may arise in an assignment problem parallel those for the transportation problem. Specifically, we can handle the following:

1. The number of agents not equal to the number of tasks
2. A maximization objective function
3. Unacceptable assignments

The situation in which the number of agents is not equal to the number of tasks is analogous to total supply not equaling total demand in a transportation problem. If the

Figure 7.5 The Management Scientist Solution for the Fowle Marketing Research Assignment Problem

```
Objective Function Value =          26.000

        Variable            Value           Reduced Costs
     ---------------    ---------------    --------------------
          X11               0.000               0.000
          X12               1.000               0.000
          X13               0.000               3.000
          X21               0.000               0.000
          X22               0.000               4.000
          X23               1.000               0.000
          X31               1.000               0.000
          X32               0.000               3.000
          X33               0.000               1.000
```

Table 7.4

Optimal Project Leader Assignments for the Fowle Marketing Research Problem

Project Leader	Assigned Client	Days
Terry	2	15
Carle	3	5
McClymonds	1	6
	Total	26

In the linear programming formulation, we could get by with one dummy project leader by placing a 2 on the right-hand side of the constraint for the dummy project leader.

number of agents exceeds the number of tasks, there is no difficulty in the linear programming model; the extra agents simply remain unassigned. For instance, if there were four project leaders in the Fowle Marketing Research problem, one would remain unassigned in the optimal solution. If the number of tasks exceeds the number of agents, the linear programming model will have no feasible solution. In this situation, a simple modification is to add enough dummy agents to make the number of agents equal to the number of tasks. For instance, in the Fowle problem we might have had five clients (tasks) and only three project leaders (agents). By adding two dummy project leaders, we can create a new assignment problem with the number of project leaders equal to the number of clients. The objective function coefficients for the assignment of dummy project leaders would be set equal to zero so that the value of the optimal solution would represent the total number of days required by the assignments actually made (no assignments will actually be made to the clients receiving dummy project leaders). The optimal solution would then call for assigning project leaders to three of the five clients; the other two clients would not receive project leaders at this time.

If the assignment alternatives are evaluated in terms of revenue or profit rather than time or cost, the linear programming formulation can be solved as a maximization rather than a minimization problem. In addition, if one or more assignments are unacceptable, the corresponding decision variable can be removed from the linear programming formulation. This could happen, for example, if an agent did not have the experience necessary for one or more of the tasks.

A General Linear Programming Model of the Assignment Problem

The general assignment problem involves m agents and n tasks. If we let $x_{ij} = 1$ or 0 according to whether agent i is assigned to task j or not, and if c_{ij} denotes the cost of assigning agent i to task j, then we can write the general assignment model as follows:

$$\text{Min} \quad \sum_{i=1}^{m} \sum_{j=1}^{n} c_{ij} x_{ij}$$

s.t.

$$\sum_{j=1}^{n} x_{ij} \leq 1 \qquad i = 1, 2, \ldots, m \quad \text{Agents}$$

$$\sum_{i=1}^{m} x_{ij} = 1 \qquad j = 1, 2, \ldots, n \quad \text{Tasks}$$

$$x_{ij} \geq 0 \qquad \text{for all } i \text{ and } j$$

If the number of tasks n exceeds the number of agents m (i.e., if demand exceeds supply), $n - m$ dummy agents must be included for us to obtain a feasible solution.

Multiple Assignments

At the beginning of this section, we indicated that a distinguishing feature of the assignment problem is that *one* agent is assigned to *one and only one* task. In situations where one agent can be assigned to two or more tasks, the linear programming formulation of the problem can be easily modified to account for such cases. For example, let us assume that in the Fowle Marketing Research problem Terry was permitted to be assigned up to two clients; in this case, the constraint representing Terry's assignment would be rewritten as $x_{11} + x_{12} + x_{13} \leq 2$. In general, if a_i denotes the upper limit for the number of tasks to which agent i can be assigned, we can write the agent constraints as

If some tasks require more than one agent, the linear programming formulation can also accommodate the stiuation. Use the number of agents required as the right-hand side of the appropriate task constraint.

$$\sum_{j=1}^{n} x_{ij} \leq a_i \qquad i = 1, 2, \ldots, m$$

Thus, we see that one advantage of formulating and solving assignment problems as linear programs is that special cases such as the situation involving multiple assignments can be easily handled.

NOTES & COMMENTS

1. As noted, the assignment model is a special case of the transportation model. We stated in the notes and comments at the end of the previous section that the optimal solution to the transportation problem will consist of integer values for the decision variables as long as the supplies and demands are integer valued. For the assignment problem, all supplies and demands equal 1; thus, the optimal solution must be integer valued and the integer values must be 0 or 1.

2. Combining the method for handling multiple assignments with the notion of a dummy agent provides another means of dealing with situations when the number of tasks exceeds the number of agents. That is, we add one dummy agent, but provide the dummy agent with the capability to handle multiple tasks. The number of tasks the dummy agent can handle is equal to the difference between the number of tasks and the number of agents.

7.3 The Transshipment Problem: The Network Model and a Linear Programming Formulation

The *transshipment problem* is an extension of the transportation problem in which intermediate nodes, referred to as *transshipment nodes,* are added to account for locations such as warehouses. In this more general type of distribution problem, shipments are permitted to occur between any pair of the three general types of nodes: origin nodes, transshipment nodes, and destination nodes. For example, the transshipment problem permits shipments of goods from one supply location (origin) to another supply location, from one transshipment location to another, from one destination location to another, and directly from origins to destinations.

As was true for the transportation problem, the supply available at each origin is limited, and the demand at each destination is known. The objective in the transshipment problem is to determine how many units should be shipped over each arc in the network so that all destination demands are satisfied with the minimum possible transportation cost.

Let us consider the transshipment problem faced by Ryan Electronics. Ryan is an electronics company with production facilities located in Denver and Atlanta. Components produced at either facility may be shipped to either of the firm's regional warehouses, which are located in Kansas City and Louisville. From the regional warehouses, the firm supplies retail outlets in Detroit, Miami, Dallas, and New Orleans.

Try part (a) of Problem 23 for practice in developing a network representation of a transshipment problem.

Figure 7.6 Network Representation of the Ryan Electronics Transshipment Problem

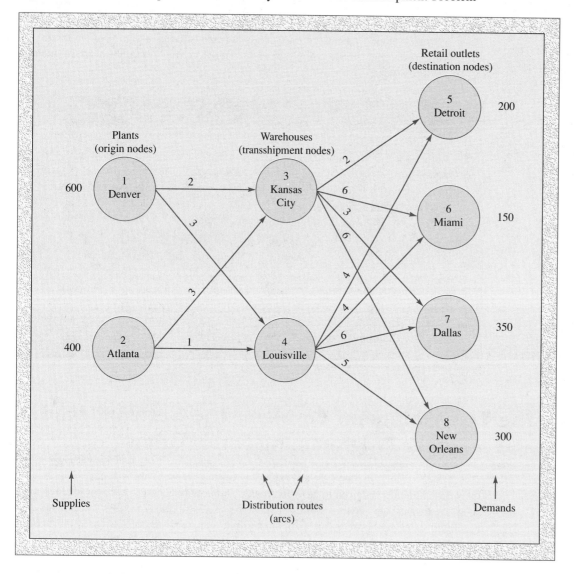

The key features of the problem are shown in the network model depicted in Figure 7.6. Note that the supply at each plant and the demand at each retail outlet are shown in the left and right margins, respectively. Nodes 1 and 2 are the origin nodes; nodes 3 and 4 are the transshipment nodes; and nodes 5, 6, 7, and 8 are the destination nodes. The transportation cost per unit for each distribution route is shown in Table 7.5 and on the arcs of the network model.

As with the transportation and assignment problems, it is easy to formulate a linear programming model of the transshipment problem given the network representation. Again, we need a constraint for each node and a variable for each arc. Let x_{ij} denote the number of units shipped from node i to node j. For example, x_{13} denotes the number of units shipped from the Denver plant to the Kansas City warehouse, x_{14} denotes the number of units shipped from the Denver plant to the Louisville warehouse, and so on. Since the supply at the Denver plant is 600 units, the amount shipped out of the Denver plant must be less than or equal to 600. Mathematically, this supply constraint is written

$$x_{13} + x_{14} \leq 600$$

Similarly, for the Atlanta plant we have

$$x_{23} + x_{24} \leq 400$$

Let us now consider how we must write the constraints corresponding to the two transshipment nodes. For node 3 (the Kansas City warehouse), we must guarantee that the number of units shipped out must equal the number of units shipped into the warehouse. Since

$$\text{Number of units shipped out of node 3} = x_{35} + x_{36} + x_{37} + x_{38}$$

and

$$\text{Number of units shipped into node 3} = x_{13} + x_{23}$$

we obtain

$$x_{35} + x_{36} + x_{37} + x_{38} = x_{13} + x_{23}$$

Table 7.5

Unit Transportation Costs for the Ryan Electronics Transshipment Problem

	Warehouse	
Plant	Kansas City	Louisville
Denver	2	3
Atlanta	3	1

	Retail Outlet			
Warehouse	Detroit	Miami	Dallas	New Orleans
Kansas City	2	6	3	6
Louisville	4	4	6	5

Placing all the variables on the left-hand side of the expression enables us to write the constraint corresponding to node 3 as

$$-x_{13} - x_{23} + x_{35} + x_{36} + x_{37} + x_{38} = 0$$

In a similar manner, the constraint corresponding to node 4 is

$$-x_{14} - x_{24} + x_{45} + x_{46} + x_{47} + x_{48} = 0$$

To develop the constraints associated with the destination nodes, we recognize that for each node the amount shipped to the destination must equal the demand. For example, to satisfy the demand for 200 units at node 5 (the Detroit retail outlet), we can write

$$x_{35} + x_{45} = 200$$

Similarly, for nodes 6, 7, and 8, we have the following constraints:

$$x_{36} + x_{46} = 150$$

$$x_{37} + x_{47} = 350$$

$$x_{38} + x_{48} = 300$$

As usual, the objective function reflects the total shipping cost over the 12 shipping routes. Combining the objective function and constraints leads to a 12-variable, 8-constraint linear programming model of the Ryan Electronics transshipment problem (see Figure 7.7).

The optimal solution was obtained using the linear programming module of The Management Scientist. Figure 7.8 shows the computer output, and Table 7.6 summarizes the optimal solution.

As mentioned at the beginning of this section, in the transshipment problem it is possible to have arcs between any pair of nodes. All such shipping patterns are possible in a transshipment problem. We still only require one constraint per node, but the constraint must include a variable for every arc entering or leaving the node. For origin nodes, we require that the sum of the shipments out minus the sum of the shipments in be less than or equal to the origin supply. For destination nodes, the sum of the shipments in

Try parts (b) and (c) of Problem 23 for practice in developing the linear programming model and in solving a transshipment problem on the computer.

Figure 7.7 Linear Programming Formulation of the Ryan Electronics Transshipment Problem

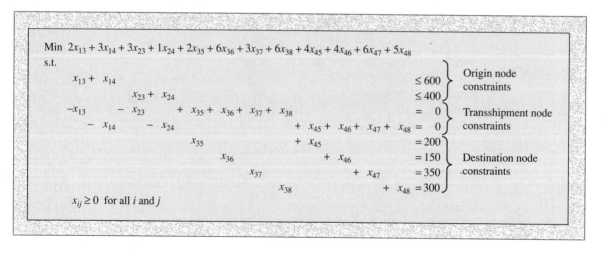

Figure 7.8 The Management Scientist Solution for the Ryan Electronics Transshipment Problem

```
Objective Function Value =            5200.000

       Variable             Value          Reduced Costs
   --------------      ---------------    ------------------
        X13               550.000              0.000
        X14                50.000              0.000
        X23                 0.000              3.000
        X24               400.000              0.000
        X35               200.000              0.000
        X36                 0.000              1.000
        X37               350.000              0.000
        X38                 0.000              0.000
        X45                 0.000              3.000
        X46               150.000              0.000
        X47                 0.000              4.000
        X48               300.000              0.000
```

Table 7.6

Optimal Solution to the Ryan Electronics Transshipment Problem

| Route | | | Cost | |
From	To	Units Shipped	Per-Unit	Total Cost
Denver	Kansas City	550	$2	$1100
Denver	Louisville	50	$3	150
Atlanta	Louisville	400	$1	400
Kansas City	Detroit	200	$2	400
Kansas City	Dallas	350	$3	1050
Louisville	Miami	150	$4	600
Louisville	New Orleans	300	$5	1500
				$5200

minus the sum of the shipments out must equal demand. For transshipment nodes, we require that the sum of the shipments out equal the sum of the shipments in, just as before.

For an illustration of this more general type of shipping pattern, let us modify the Ryan Electronics problem. Suppose it is possible to ship directly from Atlanta to New Orleans at $4 per unit and from Dallas to New Orleans at $1 per unit. The network model corresponding to this modified Ryan Electronics problem is shown in Figure 7.9, the linear programming formulation is shown in Figure 7.10, and the computer solution is shown in Figure 7.11.

In Figure 7.9 we see that two new arcs have been added to the network model. This means two new variables are necessary in the linear programming formulation. Figure 7.10 shows that the new variables appear in the objective function and in the constraints

Try Problem 24 for practice working with transshipment problems with this more general structure.

Figure 7.9 Network Representation of the Modified Ryan Electronics Transshipment Problem

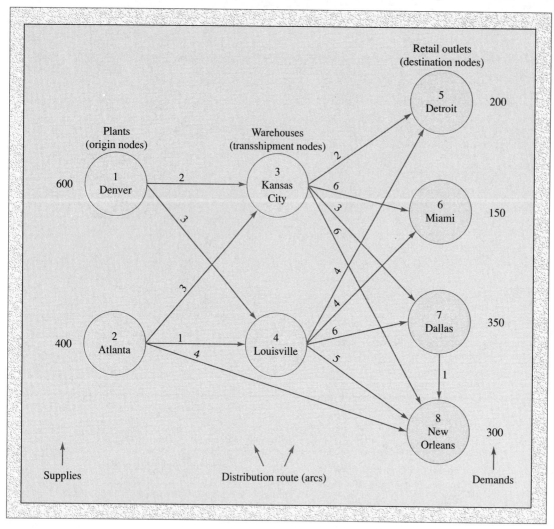

Figure 7.10 Linear Programming Formulation of the Modified Ryan Electronics Transshipment Problem

Min $2x_{13} + 3x_{14} + 3x_{23} + 1x_{24} + 2x_{35} + 6x_{36} + 3x_{37} + 6x_{38} + 4x_{45} + 4x_{46} + 6x_{47} + 5x_{48} + 4x_{28} + 1x_{78}$
s.t.

$$
\begin{array}{llll}
x_{13} + x_{14} & & & \leq 600 \\
\qquad\quad x_{23} + x_{24} & & + x_{28} & \leq 400 \\
-x_{13} \quad - x_{23} \quad + x_{35} + x_{36} + x_{37} + x_{38} & & = 0 \\
\quad - x_{14} \quad - x_{24} \quad\quad + x_{45} + x_{46} + x_{47} + x_{48} & & = 0 \\
\qquad\qquad\qquad x_{35} \qquad\qquad + x_{45} & & = 200 \\
\qquad\qquad\qquad\quad x_{36} \qquad\qquad + x_{46} & & = 150 \\
\qquad\qquad\qquad\qquad x_{37} \qquad\qquad + x_{47} & - x_{78} & = 350 \\
\qquad\qquad\qquad\qquad\quad x_{38} \qquad\qquad + x_{48} + x_{28} & + x_{78} & = 300 \\
\end{array}
$$

Origin node constraints
Transshipment node constraints
Destination node constraints

$x_{ij} \geq 0$ for all i and j

290

Figure 7.11   The Management Scientist Solution for the Modified Ryan Electronics
Transshipment Problem

```
Objective Function Value =            4600.000

        Variable              Value              Reduced Costs
      --------------      ---------------      ------------------
          X13              600.000                 0.000
          X14                0.000                 0.000
          X23                0.000                 3.000
          X24              150.000                 0.000
          X35              200.000                 0.000
          X36                0.000                 1.000
          X37              400.000                 0.000
          X38                0.000                 2.000
          X45                0.000                 3.000
          X46              150.000                 0.000
          X47                0.000                 4.000
          X48                0.000                 2.000
          X28              250.000                 0.000
          X78               50.000                 0.000
```

corresponding to the nodes the new arcs are connected to. Figure 7.11 shows that the value of the optimal solution has been reduced $600 by adding the two new shipping routes; 250 units are being shipped directly from Atlanta to New Orleans, and 50 units are being shipped from Dallas to New Orleans.

A General Linear Programming Model of the Transshipment Problem

The general linear programming model of the transshipment problem is

$$\text{Min} \quad \sum_{\text{all arcs}} c_{ij} x_{ij}$$

s.t.

$$\sum_{\text{arcs out}} x_{ij} - \sum_{\text{arcs in}} x_{ij} \leq s_i \qquad \text{Origin nodes } i$$

$$\sum_{\text{arcs out}} x_{ij} - \sum_{\text{arcs in}} x_{ij} = 0 \qquad \text{Transshipment nodes}$$

$$\sum_{\text{arcs in}} x_{ij} - \sum_{\text{arcs out}} x_{ij} = d_j \qquad \text{Destination nodes } j$$

$$x_{ij} \geq 0 \quad \text{for all } i \text{ and } j$$

where

$$c_{ij} = \text{per-unit cost of shipping from node } i \text{ to node } j$$
$$s_i = \text{supply at origin node } i$$
$$d_j = \text{demand at destination node } j$$

One final case deserves mention. Sometimes there are capacities on arcs. In this case, we simply add an upper bound constraint on the variable representing the amount shipped over the capacitated route. This is the same way route capacities are handled for the transportation problem. This more general type of transshipment problem is called the *capacitated transshipment problem.*

NOTES & COMMENTS

1. In more advanced treatments of linear programming and network flow problems, the capacitated transshipment problem is called the pure network problem. Very efficient special-purpose solution procedures are available for network problems and their special cases. In Sections 7.5 and 7.6 we present special-purpose solution procedures for the transportation and assignment problems.

2. In the general linear programming formulation of the transshipment problem, the constraints for the destination nodes are often written as

$$\sum_{\text{arcs out}} x_{ij} - \sum_{\text{arcs in}} x_{ij} = -d_j$$

The advantage of writing the constraints this way is that the left-hand side of each constraint then represents the flow out of the node minus the flow in. But such a constraint would then have to be multiplied by -1 to obtain a nonnegative right-hand side before solving the problem by many linear programming codes.

7.4 A Production and Inventory Application

Some applications of the transportation and transshipment models have nothing to do with the transportation of goods. For instance, in Section 7.2 we saw that the assignment problem can be viewed as a transportation problem involving the assignment of agents to tasks. Another type of problem that can be formulated and solved as a transportation or transshipment problem involves production and inventory scheduling. Let us illustrate this type of application by considering the problem faced by Contois Carpets.

When Contois Carpets installs new carpeting, one of the services offered is free removal of the existing carpet. Steve Contois, the owner, has observed that much of the carpeting removed is in good shape; he feels that if the carpet were cleaned and sanitized, it could be resold. As a result, Contois has invested in carpet cleaning and sanitizing equipment.

Contois would now like to develop a production and inventory schedule for the cleaning and sanitizing operation that will minimize the total production and inventory costs for the next four quarters. Table 7.7 shows the production capacity, demand, and

Table 7.7

Production, Demand, and Cost
Estimates for Contois Carpets

Quarter	Production Capacity (square yards)	Demand (square yards)	Production Cost ($/square yard)	Inventory Cost ($/square yard)
1	600	400	2	0.25
2	300	500	5	0.25
3	500	400	3	0.25
4	400	400	3	0.25

cost estimates for each quarter. Note that production capacity, demand, and production cost vary by quarter; however, the cost to carry inventory from one quarter to the next is a constant $0.25 per yard. Let us now see how Contois's production and inventory scheduling problem can be formulated and solved as a transshipment problem.

We begin by developing a network representation of the problem. First, we create four nodes corresponding to the production center in each quarter and four nodes corresponding to the demand center in each quarter. Each production center node is connected by an outgoing arc to the demand center node for the same period. The flow on the arc represents the number of square yards of carpet cleaned and sanitized in that period. For each demand center node, an outgoing arc is used to represent the amount of inventory (square yards of carpet) carried over to the demand center node for the next period. Figure 7.12 shows the network model. Note that nodes 1–4 represent the production facility for each quarter and nodes 5–8 represent the demand center for each quarter. The quarterly production capacities are shown in the left margin, and the quarterly demands are shown in the right margin.

The objective is to determine a production and inventory schedule that will minimize the total production and inventory cost over all periods. Constraints involve production capacity in each quarter and demand that must be satisfied in each quarter. As usual, a linear programming model can be developed from the network model by establishing a constraint for each node and a variable for each arc. Let us begin by showing how the constraint corresponding to node 1 is developed.

Let x_{15} denote the number of square yards of carpet cleaned and sanitized in quarter 1. Since the capacity of the facility is at most 600 square yards in quarter 1, the production capacity constraint for quarter 1 can be written as

$$x_{15} \leq 600$$

Using similar decision variables for the other three quarters allows us to write the production capacities for quarters 2–4 as shown below.

$$x_{26} \leq 300$$

$$x_{37} \leq 500$$

$$x_{48} \leq 400$$

Note that there is only one variable in each production capacity constraint; this is because there is only one arc out of the production node for each quarter.

Let us now consider the development of the constraints for each of the demand nodes. For node 5 we have one arc entering the node, which represents the number of square yards of carpet that were cleaned and sanitized in quarter 1, and one arc leaving the node, which represents the number of square yards of carpet that were not sold in quarter 1 and

Figure 7.12
Network Representation of
Contois Carpets Problem

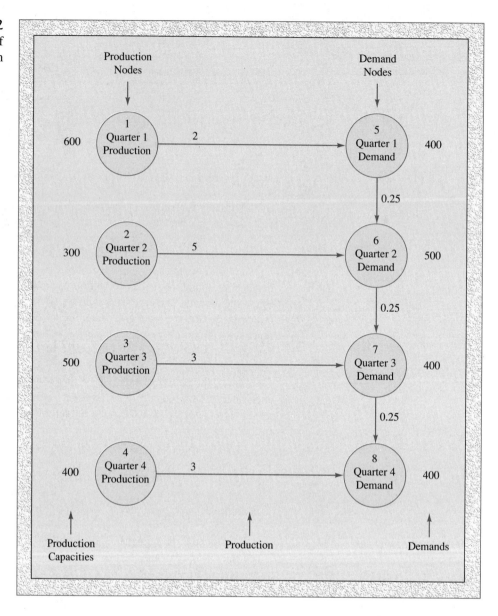

are carried over for possible sale in quarter 2. In general, for each quarter the beginning inventory plus the production minus the ending inventory must equal demand. However, for quarter 1 there is no beginning inventory; thus, the constraint for node 5 can be written as

$$x_{15} - x_{56} = 400$$

The constraints associated with the demand nodes in quarters 2, 3, and 4 are written as

$$x_{56} + x_{26} - x_{67} = 500$$

$$x_{67} + x_{37} - x_{78} = 400$$

$$x_{78} + x_{48} \qquad = 400$$

Note that the constraint for node 8 (4th-quarter demand) only involves two variables since there is no provision for ending inventory.

Since the objective is to minimize total production and inventory cost, the objective function can be written as

$$\text{Min} \quad 2x_{15} + 5x_{26} + 3x_{37} + 3x_{48} + 0.25x_{56} + 0.25x_{67} + 0.25x_{78}$$

The complete linear programming formulation of the Contois Carpets problem can now be written as shown below.

$$\text{Min} \quad 2x_{15} + 5x_{26} + 3x_{37} + 3x_{48} + 0.25x_{56} + 0.25x_{67} + 0.25x_{78}$$

s.t.

$$
\begin{aligned}
x_{15} & & & & & & & & & & \leq 600 \\
& x_{26} & & & & & & & & & \leq 300 \\
& & x_{37} & & & & & & & & \leq 500 \\
& & & x_{48} & & & & & & & \leq 400 \\
x_{15} & & & & - & x_{56} & & & & & = 400 \\
& x_{26} & & & + & x_{56} & - & x_{67} & & & = 500 \\
& & x_{37} & & & & + & x_{67} & - & x_{78} & = 400 \\
& & & x_{48} & & & & & + & x_{78} & = 400
\end{aligned}
$$

$$x_{ij} \geq 0 \quad \text{for all } i \text{ and } j$$

The Contois Carpets problem was solved using the linear programming module of The Management Scientist. The results are shown in Figure 7.13. We see that Contois Carpets should clean and sanitize 600 square yards of carpet in quarter 1, 300 square yards in quarter 2, 400 square yards in quarter 3, and 400 square yards in quarter 4. Note also that 200 square yards will be carried over from quarter 1 to quarter 2. The total production and inventory cost for this production and inventory schedule is $5150.

Figure 7.13 The Management Scientist Solution for the Contois Carpets Problem

```
Objective Function Value =          5150.000

      Variable            Value          Reduced Costs
   ---------------    ---------------    ------------------
        X15             600.000             0.000
        X26             300.000             0.000
        X37             400.000             0.000
        X48             400.000             0.000
        X56             200.000             0.000
        X67               0.000             2.250
        X78               0.000             0.000
```

7.5 The Transportation Simplex Method: A Special-Purpose Solution Procedure

Solving transportation problems using a general-purpose linear programming code is fine for small- to medium-sized problems. However, these problems often grow very large (a problem with 100 origins and 1000 destinations would have 100,000 variables), and more efficient solution procedures are needed. The special network structure of the transportation problem has enabled management scientists to develop special-purpose solution procedures that greatly simplify the computations.

Research has shown that special-purpose network algorithms provide substantial computational advantages over general-purpose linear programming codes.

In Section 7.1 we introduced the Foster Generators, Inc., transportation problem and showed how it could be formulated and solved as a linear program. The linear programming formulation involved 12 variables and 7 constraints. In this section we show a special-purpose solution procedure, called the *transportation simplex method,* that takes advantage of the network structure of the transportation problem and makes it possible to solve large transportation problems efficiently on a computer and small transportation problems by hand.

Let us see how the transportation simplex method works by applying it to the Foster Generators problem. The transportation simplex method, like the simplex method for linear programs, is a two-phase procedure; it involves first finding an initial feasible solution and then proceeding iteratively to make improvements in the solution until an optimal solution is reached. In order to summarize the data conveniently and to keep track of the calculations, a *transportation tableau* is usually employed. The transportation tableau for the Foster Generators problem is presented in Table 7.8.

Note that the 12 *cells* in the tableau correspond to the 12 arcs shown in Figure 7.1; that is, each cell corresponds to the route from one origin to one destination. Thus, each cell in the transportation tableau corresponds to a variable in the linear programming formulation. The entries in the right-hand margin of the tableau represent the supply

Table 7.8

Transportation Tableau for the Foster Generators Transportation Problem

Origin	Destination				Origin Supply
	Boston	Chicago	St. Louis	Lexington	
Cleveland	3	2	7	6	5,000
Bedford	7	5	2	3	6,000
York	2	5	4	5	2,500
Destination Demand	6000	4000	2000	1500	13,500

Cell corresponding
to shipments from
Bedford to Boston

Total supply
and total demand

available at each origin, and the entries in the bottom margin represent the demand at each destination. Each row corresponds to a supply node, and each column corresponds to a demand node in the network model of the problem. The number of rows plus the number of columns equals the number of constraints in the linear programming formulation of the problem. The entries in the upper right-hand corner of each cell represent the per-unit cost of shipping over the corresponding route. These are the objective function coefficients in the linear programming formulation. Note also that total supply equals total demand. The transportation simplex method can be applied only to a balanced (total supply = total demand) problem; if a problem is not balanced, a dummy origin or dummy destination must be added.

Phase I: Finding an Initial Feasible Solution

The first phase of the transportation simplex method involves finding an initial feasible solution. An initial feasible solution is a set of arc flows that satisfies each demand requirement without shipping more from any origin node than the supply available. The procedures most often used to find an initial feasible solution to a transportation problem are called heuristics. A *heuristic* is a common-sense procedure for quickly finding a solution to a problem.

The northwest corner rule is a heuristic that finds an initial feasible solution very quickly. However, the minimum-cost method is fairly quick and usually finds one closer to the optimal solution.

There are several heuristics that have been developed to find an initial feasible solution to a transportation problem. Although some heuristics can find an initial feasible solution very quickly, often the solution they find is not very good in terms of minimizing total cost. On the other hand, some heuristics may not find an initial solution as quickly, but the solution they find is often very good in terms of minimizing total cost. The heuristic we describe for finding an initial feasible solution to a transportation problem is called *the minimum-cost method.* This heuristic strikes a compromise between finding a feasible solution quickly and finding a feasible solution that is close to the optimal solution.

The minimum-cost method for identifying an initial feasible solution requires that we begin by allocating as much flow as possible to the minimum-cost arc. In Table 7.8 we see that the Cleveland–Chicago, Bedford–St. Louis, and York–Boston routes each qualify as the minimum-cost arc since they each have a per-unit transportation cost of 2. When ties such as this occur, we follow the convention of selecting the arc to which the most flow can be allocated. Since this corresponds to shipping 4000 units from Cleveland to Chicago, we write 4000 in the Cleveland–Chicago cell of the transportation tableau. This reduces the supply at Cleveland from 5000 to 1000; hence, we cross out the 5000-unit supply value and replace it with the reduced value of 1000. In addition, since allocating 4000 units to this arc satisfies the demand at Chicago, we reduce the Chicago demand to zero and eliminate the corresponding column from further consideration by drawing a line through it. The transportation tableau now appears as shown in Table 7.9.

Now we look at the reduced tableau consisting of all unlined cells to identify the next minimum-cost arc. There is a tie between the Bedford–St. Louis and York–Boston routes. More units of flow can be allocated to the York–Boston route, so we choose it for the next allocation. This results in an allocation of 2500 units over the York–Boston route. To update the tableau, the York supply is reduced to zero, and we eliminate this row from further consideration by lining through it. Continuing the process results in an allocation of 2000 units over the Bedford–St. Louis route and the elimination of the St. Louis column since its demand goes to zero. The transportation tableau obtained after carrying out the second and third iterations is shown in Table 7.10.

We now have two arcs that qualify for the minimum-cost arc with a value of 3: Cleveland–Boston and Bedford–Lexington. A flow of 1000 units can be allocated to the Cleveland–Boston route and a flow of 1500 to the Bedford–Lexington route, so we allocate 1500 units to the Bedford–Lexington route. Doing so results in a demand of zero at Lexington, and this column is eliminated. The next minimum-cost allocation is 1000 over the Cleveland–Boston route. After making these two allocations, the transportation tableau appears as shown in Table 7.11.

Table 7.9

Transportation Tableau After One Iteration of the Minimum-Cost Method

	Boston	Chicago	St. Louis	Lexington	**Supply**
Cleveland	3	2 ~~4000~~	7	6	1000 ~~5000~~
Bedford	7	5	2	3	6000
York	2	5	4	5	2500
Demand	6000	~~4000~~ 0	2000	1500	

Table 7.10

Transportation Tableau After Three Iterations of the Minimum-Cost Method

	Boston	Chicago	St. Louis	Lexington	Supply
Cleveland	3	2 4000	7	6	1000 ~~5000~~
Bedford	7	5	2 2000	3	4000 ~~6000~~
~~York~~	2 ~~2500~~	5	4	5	0 ~~2500~~
Demand	~~6000~~ 3500	~~4000~~ ~~0~~	~~2000~~ ~~0~~	1500	

Table 7.11

Transportation Tableau After Five Iterations of the Minimum-Cost Method

	Boston	Chicago	St. Louis	Lexington	Supply
~~Cleveland~~	3 ~~1000~~	2 4000	7	6	0 ~~1000~~ ~~5000~~
Bedford	7	5	2 2000	3 1500	2500 ~~4000~~ ~~6000~~
~~York~~	2 ~~2500~~	5	4	5	0 ~~2500~~
Demand	~~6000~~ ~~3500~~ 2500	~~4000~~ ~~0~~	~~2000~~ ~~0~~	~~1500~~ ~~0~~	

The only remaining unlined cell is now Bedford–Boston. Allocating 2500 units to the corresponding arc uses up the remaining supply at Bedford and satisfies all the demand at Boston. The resulting tableau is shown in Table 7.12.

This solution is feasible since all the demand is satisfied and all the supply is used. The total transportation cost resulting from this initial feasible solution is calculated in Table 7.13. Phase I of the transportation simplex method is now complete; we have an initial feasible solution.

Table 7.12

Final Tableau Showing the Initial Feasible Solution Obtained Using the Minimum-Cost Method

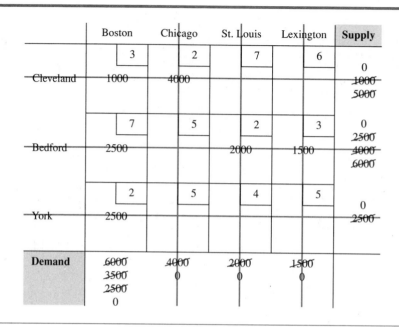

	Boston	Chicago	St. Louis	Lexington	**Supply**
~~Cleveland~~	3 ~~1000~~	2 ~~4000~~	7	6	0 ~~1000~~ ~~5000~~
~~Bedford~~	7 ~~2500~~	5	2 ~~2000~~	3 ~~1500~~	0 ~~2500~~ ~~4000~~ ~~6000~~
~~York~~	2 ~~2500~~	5	4	5	0 ~~2500~~
Demand	~~6000~~ ~~3500~~ ~~2500~~ 0	~~4000~~ 0	~~2000~~ 0	~~1500~~ 0	

Summary of the Minimum-Cost Method. Before applying phase II of the transportation simplex method, let us summarize the steps for obtaining an initial feasible solution to the transportation problem.

Step 1   Identify the cell in the transportation tableau with the lowest cost, and allocate as much flow as possible to this cell. In case of a tie, choose the cell corresponding to the arc over which the most units can be shipped. If ties still exist, choose any of the tied cells.

Step 2   Reduce the row supply and the column demand by the amount of flow allocated to the cell identified in step 1.

Step 3   If *all* row supplies and column demands have been exhausted, then stop; the allocations made will provide an initial feasible solution. Otherwise, continue with step 4.

Step 4   If the row supply is now zero, eliminate the row from further consideration by drawing a line through it. If the column demand is now zero, eliminate the column by drawing a line through it.

Step 5   Continue with step 1 for all unlined rows and columns.

You should be able to use the minimum-cost method to find an initial feasible solution. Try part (a) of Problem 32.

Phase II: Iterating to the Optimal Solution

Phase II of the transportation simplex method is a procedure for iterating from the initial feasible solution identified in phase I to the optimal solution. Recall that each cell in the transportation tableau corresponds to an arc (route) in the network model of the transportation problem. The first step at each iteration of phase II is to identify an incoming arc. The *incoming arc* is the currently unused route (unoccupied cell) where

Table 7.13

Total Cost of the Initial Feasible Solution Obtained Using the Minimum-Cost Method

| Route | | Units | Cost | |
From	To	Shipped	Per-Unit	Total Cost
Cleveland	Boston	1000	$3	$ 3,000
Cleveland	Chicago	4000	$2	8,000
Bedford	Boston	2500	$7	17,500
Bedford	St. Louis	2000	$2	4,000
Bedford	Lexington	1500	$3	4,500
York	Boston	2500	$2	5,000
				$42,000

making a flow allocation will cause the largest per-unit reduction in total cost. Flow is then assigned to the incoming arc, and the amounts being shipped over all other arcs to which flow had previously been assigned (occupied cells) are adjusted as necessary to maintain a feasible solution. In the process of adjusting the flow assigned to the occupied cells, an *outgoing arc* is identified and dropped from the solution. Thus, at each iteration in phase II, a currently unused arc (unoccupied cell) is brought into solution, and an arc to which flow had previously been assigned (occupied cell) is removed from solution.

To show how phase II of the transportation simplex method works, we must explain how the incoming arc (cell) is identified, how the adjustments are made to the other occupied cells when flow is allocated to the incoming arc, and how the outgoing arc (cell) is identified. Let us first turn to the issue of identifying the incoming arc.

As mentioned, the incoming arc is the one that will cause the largest per-unit reduction in the total cost of the current solution. To identify this arc, we must compute for each unused arc the amount by which total cost will be reduced by shipping one unit over that arc. The *MODI method* is a simple approach for making this computation.

The MODI method requires that we define an index u_i for each row of the tableau and an index v_j for each column of the tableau. These row and column indices are computed by requiring that the cost coefficient for each occupied cell equal $u_i + v_j$. If c_{ij} is the per-unit shipping cost from origin i to destination j, then we require that $u_i + v_j = c_{ij}$ for each occupied cell. Let us return to the initial feasible solution for the Foster Generators problem, which we found using the minimum-cost method (see Table 7.14), and use the MODI method to identify the incoming arc.

Requiring that $u_i + v_j = c_{ij}$ for all the occupied cells in the initial feasible solution leads to a system of six equations and seven indices or variables:

Occupied Cell	$u_i + v_j = c_{ij}$
Cleveland–Boston	$u_1 + v_1 = 3$
Cleveland–Chicago	$u_1 + v_2 = 2$
Bedford–Boston	$u_2 + v_1 = 7$
Bedford–St. Louis	$u_2 + v_3 = 2$
Bedford–Lexington	$u_2 + v_4 = 3$
York–Boston	$u_3 + v_1 = 2$

Since there is one more index than equation in the above system, we can freely pick a value for one of the indices and then solve for the others. We shall always choose

Table 7.14

Initial Feasible Solution to the Foster Generators Problem

	Boston	Chicago	St. Louis	Lexington	**Supply**
Cleveland	3 / 1000	2 / 4000	7 /	6 /	5000
Bedford	7 / 2500	5 /	2 / 2000	3 / 1500	6000
York	2 / 2500	5 /	4 /	5 /	2500
Demand	6000	4000	2000	1500	

$u_1 = 0$ and then solve for the values of the other indices. Setting $u_1 = 0$, we get the following system of equations:

$$0 + v_1 = 3$$

$$0 + v_2 = 2$$

$$u_2 + v_1 = 7$$

$$u_2 + v_3 = 2$$

$$u_2 + v_4 = 3$$

$$u_3 + v_1 = 2$$

Solving these equations leads to the following values for $u_1, u_2, u_3, v_1, v_2, v_3$, and v_4:

$$u_1 = 0 \qquad v_1 = 3$$

$$u_2 = 4 \qquad v_2 = 2$$

$$u_3 = -1 \qquad v_3 = -2$$

$$v_4 = -1$$

Management scientists have shown that for each *unoccupied* cell, $e_{ij} = c_{ij} - u_i - v_j$ provides the per-unit change in total cost that will be obtained by allocating one unit of flow to the corresponding arc. Thus, we will call e_{ij} the *net evaluation index*. Because of the way u_i and v_j are computed, the net evaluation index for each occupied cell equals zero.

The net evaluation indices serve the same purpose as the net evaluation row when using the simplex method.

Rewriting the tableau containing the initial feasible solution for the Foster Generators problem, and replacing the previous marginal information with the values of u_i and v_j, we obtain Table 7.15. In Table 7.15 the net evaluation index (e_{ij}) has been computed for each unoccupied cell; it is the circled number in the cell. Thus, we see that shipping one unit

Table 7.15

Per-Unit Cost Changes for the Initial Feasible Solution to the Foster Generators Problem Computed Using the MODI Method

u_i	v_j			
	3	2	−2	−1
0	3 1000	2 4000	7 ⑨	6 ⑦
4	7 2500	5 ⊝1	2 2000	3 1500
−1	2 2500	5 ④	4 ⑦	5 ⑦

over the route from origin 1 to destination 3 (Cleveland–St. Louis) will increase total cost by $9; shipping one unit from origin 1 to destination 4 (Cleveland–Lexington) will increase total cost by $7; shipping one from origin 2 to destination 2 (Bedford–Chicago) will decrease total cost by $1; and so on.

On the basis of the net evaluation indices, we see that the best arc in terms of cost reduction is associated with the Bedford–Chicago route (origin 2–destination 2); thus, the cell in row 2 and column 2 is chosen as the incoming cell. There will be a $1 decrease in total cost for every unit of flow assigned to this arc. The question now is this: How much flow should we assign to this arc? Since the total cost decreases by $1 per unit assigned, we would like to allocate the maximum possible flow. To find that maximum, we must recognize that to maintain feasibility, each unit of flow assigned to this arc will require adjustments in the flow over the other currently used arcs. The *stepping-stone method* can be used to determine what adjustments are necessary and to identify an outgoing arc.

The Stepping-Stone Method for Adjusting Flow and Identifying the Outgoing Arc.

Suppose we allocate one unit of flow to the incoming arc (the Bedford–Chicago route). To maintain feasibility—that is, not exceed the number of units to be shipped to Chicago—we would have to reduce the flow assigned to the Cleveland–Chicago arc to 3999. But then we would have to increase the flow on the Cleveland–Boston arc to 1001 so that the total Cleveland supply of 5000 units could be shipped. Finally, we would have to reduce the flow on the Bedford–Boston arc by 1 to satisfy the Boston demand exactly. Table 7.16 summarizes the cycle of adjustments just described.

We have seen that the cycle of adjustments necessary when an allocation is made to the Bedford–Chicago cell required changes in four cells: the incoming cell (Bedford–Chicago) and three currently occupied cells. We can view these four cells as forming a stepping-stone path in the tableau, where the corners of the path are currently occupied cells. The idea behind the stepping-stone path name is to view the tableau as a pond with the occupied cells as stones sticking up in the pond. To identify the stepping-stone path for an incoming cell, we start at the incoming cell and move in horizontal and vertical directions, using occupied cells as the stones at the corners of the path; the objective is to

Table 7.16

Cycle of Adjustments in Occupied Cells Necessary to Maintain Feasibility When Shipping One Unit from Bedford to Chicago

	Boston	Chicago	St. Louis	Lexington	**Supply**
Cleveland	3 1001 ~~1000~~	2 3999 ~~4000~~	7	6	5000
Bedford	7 2499 ~~2500~~	5 1	2 2000	3 1500	6000
York	2 2500	5	4	5	2500
Demand	6000	4000	2000	1500	

step from stone to stone and return to the incoming cell where we started. To focus attention on which occupied cells are part of the stepping-stone path, we draw each occupied cell in the stepping-stone path as a cylinder; this should reinforce the image of these cells as stones sticking up in the pond. Table 7.17 depicts the stepping-stone path associated with the incoming arc of the Bedford–Chicago route.

In Table 7.17 we have placed a plus sign ($+$) or a minus sign ($-$) in each occupied cell on the stepping-stone path. A plus sign indicates that the allocation to that cell will increase by the same amount we allocate to the incoming cell. A minus sign indicates that the allocation to that cell will decrease by the amount allocated to the incoming cell. Thus, to determine the maximum amount that may be allocated to the incoming cell, we simply look to the cells on the stepping-stone path identified with a minus sign. Since no arc can have a negative flow allocated to it, the minus-sign cell with the smallest amount allocated to it will determine the maximum amount that can be allocated to the incoming cell. After allocating this maximum amount to the incoming cell, we then make all the adjustments necessary on the stepping-stone path to maintain feasibility. The incoming cell becomes an occupied cell, and the outgoing cell is dropped from the current solution.

In the Foster Generators problem, the Bedford–Boston and Cleveland–Chicago cells are the ones where the allocation will decrease (the ones with a minus sign) as flow is allocated to the incoming arc (Bedford–Chicago). Since the 2500 units currently assigned to Bedford–Boston is less than the 4000 units assigned to Cleveland–Chicago, we identify Bedford–Boston as the outgoing arc. The new solution is then obtained by allocating 2500 units to the Bedford–Chicago arc, making the appropriate adjustments on the stepping-stone path, and dropping Bedford–Boston from the solution (its allocation has been driven to zero). Table 7.18 shows the tableau associated with the new solution. Note that the only changes from the previous tableau are located on the stepping-stone path originating in the Bedford–Chicago cell.

We are now ready to see if further improvement in the current solution can be made. Again, the first step is to apply the MODI method to find the best incoming arc, so we recompute the row and column indices by requiring that $u_i + v_j = c_{ij}$ for all occupied cells. The values of u_i and v_j can easily be computed directly on the tableau. Recall that we begin the MODI method by setting $u_1 = 0$. Thus, for the two occupied cells in row 1

Table 7.17

Stepping-Stone Path with the Bedford–Chicago Route as Incoming Arc

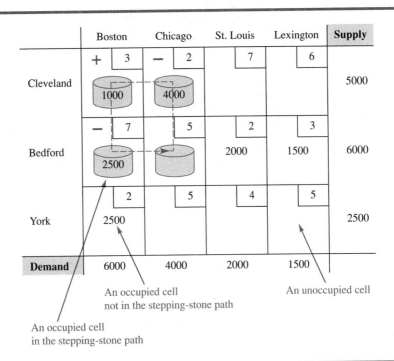

An occupied cell
in the stepping-stone path

An occupied cell
not in the stepping-stone path

An unoccupied cell

Table 7.18

New Solution After One Iteration in Phase II of the Transportation Simplex Method

	Boston	Chicago	St. Louis	Lexington	**Supply**
Cleveland	3 3500	2 1500	7	6	5000
Bedford	7	5 2500	2 2000	3 1500	6000
York	2 2500	5	4	5	2500
Demand	6000	4000	2000	1500	

of the table, $v_j = c_{1j}$; as a result, $v_1 = 3$ and $v_2 = 2$. Moving down the column associated with each newly computed column index, we can compute the row index associated with each occupied cell in that column by subtracting v_j from c_{ij}. Doing so for the newly found column indices, v_1 and v_2, we find that $u_3 = 2 - 3 = -1$ and $u_2 = 5 - 2 = 3$. Next, we use these newly found row indices to compute the column indices wherever there are occupied cells in the associated rows. Doing so allows us to compute $v_3 = 2 - 3 = -1$ and $v_4 = 3 - 3 = 0$. Table 7.19 shows these new row and column indices.

Also shown in Table 7.19 are the net changes (the circled numbers) in the value of the solution that will result from allocating one unit to each unoccupied cell. Recall that these are the net evaluation indices given by $e_{ij} = c_{ij} - u_i - v_j$. Reviewing Table 7.19, we see that the net evaluation index for every unoccupied cell is now greater than or equal to zero. Since there is no arc to which flow can be assigned to decrease the total cost, we have reached the optimal solution. The optimal solution, together with its total cost, is summarized in Table 7.20. As expected, this solution is exactly the same as the one obtained using the linear programming solution approach (Figure 7.2).

Maintaining $m + n - 1$ Occupied Cells. Recall that m represents the number of origins and n represents the number of destinations. A solution to a transportation problem that has less than a $m + n - 1$ cells with positive allocations is said to be *degenerate*. The solution to the Foster Generators problem is not degenerate; there are six occupied cells and $m + n - 1 = 3 + 4 - 1 = 6$. The problem with degeneracy is that there

Table 7.19

MODI Evaluation of Each Cell in Solution

Table 7.20

Optimal Solution to the Foster Generators Transportation Problem

Route				
From	To	Units Shipped	Per-Unit Cost	Total Cost
Cleveland	Boston	3500	$3	$10,500
Cleveland	Chicago	1500	$2	3,000
Bedford	Chicago	2500	$5	12,500
Bedford	St. Louis	2000	$2	4,000
Bedford	Lexington	1500	$3	4,500
York	Boston	2500	$2	5,000
				$39,500

This corresponds to having two or more basic variables equal to zero in the simplex solution. Thus, it is not the same as degeneracy with the LP simplex method; that is, where one or more basic variables equal zero.

must be $m + n - 1$ occupied cells in order to use the MODI method to compute all the row and column indices. When degeneracy occurs, we must artificially create an occupied cell in order to compute the row and column indices. Let us illustrate how degeneracy could occur and how to deal with it.

Table 7.21 shows the initial feasible solution obtained using the minimum-cost method for a transportation problem involving $m = 3$ origins and $n = 3$ destinations. To use the MODI method for this problem, we must have $m + n - 1 = 3 + 3 - 1 = 5$ occupied cells. Since the initial feasible solution has only four occupied cells, the solution is degenerate.

Suppose we try to use the MODI method to compute row and column indices to begin phase II for this problem. Setting $u_1 = 0$, and computing the column indices for each occupied cell in row 1, we obtain $v_1 = 3$ and $v_2 = 6$ (see Table 7.21). Continuing, we would then compute the row indices for all occupied cells in columns 1 and 2. Doing so yields $u_2 = 5 - 6 = -1$. At this point, we would be unable to compute any more row and column indices because there are no occupied cells in rows 1 or 2 of column 3.

The artificially occupied cell must be in either row 3 or column 3 of Table 7.21.

To compute all the row and column indices when there are less than $m + n - 1$ occupied cells, we must create one or more "artificially" occupied cells with a flow of zero. In Table 7.21 one artificially occupied cell must be created to make the number of occupied cells equal to 5. Any currently unoccupied cell can be made an artificially occupied cell if doing so makes it possible to compute the remaining row and column indices. For instance, treating the cell in row 2 and column 3 of Table 7.21 as an artificially occupied cell will enable us to compute u_3 and v_3, but placing it in row 2 and column 1 will not.

As we previously stated, whenever an artificially occupied cell is created, we assign a flow of zero to the corresponding arc. Table 7.22 shows the results of creating an artificially occupied cell in row 2 and column 3 of Table 7.21. Since the creation of the artificially occupied cell results in five occupied cells, we can now compute the remaining row and column indices. Using the row 2 index ($u_2 = -1$) and the artificially occupied cell in row 2, we compute the column index for column 3; thus, $v_3 = c_{23} - u_2 = 7 -$

Table 7.21

Transportation Tableau with a Degenerate Initial Feasible Solution

u_i	v_j			Supply
	3	6		**Supply**
0	3 / 35	6 / 25	7 /	60
−1	8 /	5 / 30	7 /	30
	4 /	9 /	11 / 30	30
Demand	35	55	30	

Table 7.22

Transportation Tableau with an Artificial Cell in Row 2 and Column 3

u_i	v_j 3	6	8	Supply
0	3 35	6 25	7 (−1)	60
−1	8 (6)	5 30	7 0	30
3	4 (−2)	9 (0)	11 30	30
Demand	35	55	30	

Artificial cell

$(-1) = 8$. Then, using the column 3 index ($v_3 = 8$) and the occupied cell in row 3 and column 3 of the tableau, we can compute the row 3 index; thus, $u_3 = c_{33} - v_3 = 11 - 8 = 3$. Table 7.22 shows the complete set of row and column indices as well as the net evaluation index for each unoccupied cell.

Reviewing the net evaluation indices in Table 7.22, we identify the cell in row 3 and column 1 (net evaluation index $= -2$) as the incoming cell. The stepping-stone path showing the adjustments necessary to maintain feasibility is shown in Table 7.23 where we see that the stepping-stone path can be more complex than the simple one obtained for the incoming cell in the Foster Generators problem. The path in Table 7.23 requires adjustments in all five occupied cells to maintain feasibility. Again, the plus- and minus-sign labels simply show where increases and decreases in the allocation will occur as units of flow are added to the incoming cell. The smallest flow in a decreasing cell is a tie between the cell in row 2 and column 2 and the cell in row 3 and column 3.

Since the smallest amount in a decreasing cell is 30, the allocation we make to the incoming cell is 30 units. However, when 30 units are allocated to the incoming cell and the appropriate adjustments are made to the occupied cells on the stepping-stone path, the allocations to two cells go to zero (row 2, column 2 and row 3, column 3). We may choose either one as the outgoing cell, but not both. One will be treated as unoccupied; the other will become an artificially occupied cell with a flow of zero allocated to it. The reason we cannot let both become unoccupied cells is that doing so would lead to a degenerate solution, and as before, we could not use the MODI method to compute the row and column indices for the next iteration. When ties occur in choosing the outgoing cell, any one of the tied cells can be chosen as the artificially occupied cell, and the MODI method can then be used to recompute the row and column indices. As long as no more than one cell is dropped at each iteration, the MODI method will work.

The solution obtained after allocating 30 units to the incoming cell in row 3 and column 1 and making the appropriate adjustments on the stepping-stone path leads to the tableau shown in Table 7.24. Note that we have chosen to treat the cell in row 2 and column 2 as the artificially occupied cell. The new row and column indices have been

Table 7.23
Stepping-Stone Path for the Incoming Cell in Row 3 and Column 1

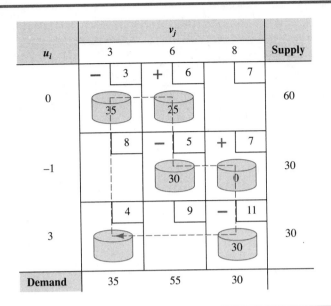

	v_j			
u_i	3	6	8	**Supply**
0	− [3] 35	+ [6] 25	[7]	60
−1	[8]	− [5] 30	+ [7] 0	30
3	[4] ◄	[9]	− [11] 30	30
Demand	35	55	30	

Table 7.24
New Row and Column Indices Obtained After Allocating 30 Units to the Incoming Cell

	v_j			
u_i	3	6	8	**Supply**
0	[3] 5	[6] 55	[7] (−1)	60
−1	[8] (6)	[5] 0	[7] 30	30
1	[4] 30	[9] (2)	[11] (2)	30
Demand	35	55	30	

computed, and we see that the cell in row 1 and column 3 will be the next incoming cell. Each unit allocated to this cell will further decrease the value of the solution by 1. The stepping-stone path associated with this incoming cell is shown in Table 7.25. The cell in row 2 and column 3 is the outgoing cell; the tableau after this iteration is shown in Table 7.26. Note that the optimal solution has been found and that, even though several earlier iterations were degenerate, the final solution is not degenerate.

Table 7.25
Stepping-Stone Path Associated with
the Incoming Cell in Row 1 and
Column 3

u_i	v_j 3	6	8	Supply
0	3 —	6	7	60
		55	(incoming)	
−1	8 +	5	7 —	30
		0	30	
1	4	9	11	30
Demand	35	55	30	

Table 7.26
Optimal Solution to a Problem with a
Degenerate Initial Feasible Solution

u_i	v_j 3	6	7	Supply
0	3 5	6 25	7 30	60
−1	8 ④	5 30	7 ①	30
1	4 30	9 ②	11 ③	30
Demand	35	55	30	

Summary of the Transportation Simplex Method

The transportation simplex method is a special-purpose solution procedure applicable to any network model having the special structure of the transportation problem. It is actually a clever implementation of the general simplex method for linear programming that takes advantage of the special mathematical structure of the transportation problem;

but because of the special structure, the transportation simplex method is hundreds of times faster than the general simplex method.

To apply the transportation simplex method, we must have a transportation problem with total supply equal to total demand; thus, for some problems we may need to add a dummy origin or dummy destination to put the problem in this form. The transportation simplex method takes the problem in this form and applies a two-phase solution procedure. In phase I, the minimum-cost method is applied to find an initial feasible solution. Phase II starts with the initial feasible solution and iterates until an optimal solution is reached. The steps of the transportation simplex method for a minimization problem are summarized below.

Try part (b) of Problem 32 for practice using the transportation simplex method.

PHASE I

Find an initial feasible solution using the minimum-cost method.

PHASE II

Step 1 If the initial feasible solution is degenerate, add an artificially occupied cell wherever necessary. Then use the MODI method to find u_i, v_j, and identify the incoming cell. The incoming cell is the one with the smallest net evaluation index: $c_{ij} - u_i - v_j$. If $c_{ij} - u_i - v_j \geq 0$ for all unoccupied cells, stop; in this case, the optimal solution has been found. Otherwise, go to step 2.

Step 2 Find the stepping-stone path associated with the incoming cell. Label each cell on the stepping-stone path whose flow will increase with a plus sign and each cell whose flow will decrease with a minus sign.

Step 3 Choose as the outgoing cell the minus-sign cell on the stepping-stone path with the smallest flow. If there is a tie, choose any one of the tied cells. The tied cells that are not chosen will be artificially occupied with a flow of zero at the next iteration.

Step 4 Allocate to the incoming cell the amount of flow currently given to the outgoing cell; make the appropriate adjustments to all cells on the stepping-stone path, and continue with step 1.

Problem Variations

Let us see how the following problem variations are handled with the transportation simplex method:

1. Total supply not equal to total demand
2. Maximization objective
3. Unacceptable transportation routes (arcs)

The case where the total supply is not equal to the total demand can be handled easily by the transportation simplex method if we first introduce a dummy origin or dummy destination. If total supply is greater than total demand, we introduce a *dummy destination* with demand exactly equal to the excess of supply over demand. Similarly, if total demand is greater than total supply, we introduce a *dummy origin* with supply exactly equal to the excess of demand over supply. In either the excess demand or the excess supply case, we assign cost coefficients of zero to every arc into a dummy destination and to every arc out of a dummy origin. This is because no shipments will actually be made from a dummy origin or to a dummy destination when the solution is implemented.

The transportation simplex method can also be used to solve maximization problems. The only modification necessary involves the selection of an incoming cell. Instead of picking the cell with the most negative e_{ij} value (smallest), we pick that cell for which e_{ij} is largest. That is, we pick the cell that will cause the largest per-unit increase in the objective function.

To handle unacceptable transportation routes in a minimization problem, we require that infeasible arcs carry an extremely high cost, denoted M, in order to keep them out of solution. Thus, if we have a transportation route (arc) from an origin to a destination that for some reason cannot be used, we simply assign this arc a per-unit cost of M, and it will not enter the solution. Unacceptable arcs would be assigned a per-unit cost of $-M$ in a maximization problem.

Let us now consider another example to show how the above difficulties can be resolved. In the process we will also show how production costs can be taken into account in a transportation problem. Suppose we have three plants (origins) with production capacities as follows:

Plants	Production Capacity
P_1	50
P_2	40
P_3	30
Total	120

We also have demand for the product at three retail outlets (destinations). The demand forecasts for the current planning period are presented below.

Retail Outlets	Forecasted Demand
R_1	45
R_2	15
R_3	30
Total	90

Table 7.27

Profit Per Unit Produced at Plant i and Sold at Retail Outlet j

Plants	Retail Outlets		
	R_1	R_2	R_3
P_1	10	6	7
P_2	6	11	6
P_3	12	7	11

The production cost at each plant is different, and the sales prices at the retail outlets vary. Taking prices, production costs, and shipping costs into consideration, the profits for producing one unit at plant i, shipping it to retail outlet j, and selling it at retail outlet j are presented in Table 7.27.

We note first that the total production capacity exceeds the total demand at the retail outlets. Thus, we must introduce a dummy retail outlet with demand exactly equal to the excess production capacity. We therefore add retail outlet R_4 with a demand of 30 units. The per-unit profit for shipping from each plant to retail outlet R_4 is set to zero since these units will not actually be shipped. To obtain an initial feasible solution, we use the minimum-cost method. However, since this is a maximization problem, the minimum-cost method must be changed to a corresponding maximum-profit method. That is, we select the shipping route that will maximize profit instead of minimizing cost. The initial feasible solution obtained using this approach is shown in Table 7.28.

Now let us compute the net evaluation indices: $e_{ij} = c_{ij} - u_i - v_j$. Table 7.29 shows the values of u_i, v_j, and e_{ij} obtained. Since this is a maximization problem, the cell with the largest positive value for e_{ij} is the incoming cell. This is the cell in row 3 and column 3

Table 7.28

Initial Feasible Solution to the Maximization Transportation Problem with a Dummy Destination

	R_1	R_2	R_3	R_4	
	10	6	7	0	
P_1	15		30	5	50
	6	11	6	0	
P_2		15		25	40
	12	7	11	0	
P_3	30				30
	45	15	30	30	

Table 7.29

MODI Method Identifies Cell in Row 3, Column 3 as Incoming Cell

u_i	v_j 10	11	7	0	Supply
0	+ ⌐10⌐ 15	6 (−5)	− 7 30	0 5	50
0	6 (−4)	11 15	6 (−1)	0 25	40
2	− 12 30	7 (−6)	11 2	0 (−2)	30
Demand	45	15	30	30	

Table 7.30

Optimal Solution to the Maximization Problem

u_i	v_j = 10	11	7	0	Supply
0	10 / 45	6 / (−5)	7 / 0	0 / 5	50
0	6 / (−4)	11 / 15	6 / (−1)	0 / 25	40
4	12 / (−2)	7 / (−8)	11 / 30	0 / (−4)	30
Demand	45	15	30	30	

(the route between P_3 and R_3). The stepping-stone path includes two minus-sign cells ($P_1 - R_3$ and $P_3 - R_1$), and there is a tie between them for the outgoing cell. Either may be chosen; we have decided to treat the cell in row 1 and column 3 as being artificially occupied. After allocating 30 units of flow to the incoming cell and making the appropriate adjustments on the stepping-stone path, we obtain the solution shown in Table 7.30.

The MODI method has been used in Table 7.30 to obtain new values for u_i, v_j, and e_{ij}. All values of e_{ij} are negative, indicating that making an allocation to any unoccupied cell will decrease the value of the solution. Since this is a maximization problem, we conclude that the current solution is optimal. When implementing this solution, we would ship 45 units from plant P_1 to retail outlet R_1, 15 units from P_2 to R_2, and 30 units from P_3 to R_3. The shipments to the dummy destination R_4 will not be made indicating that we are left with an excess supply of 5 units at P_1 and 25 units at P_2. Note that nothing will be shipped over the artificially occupied cell in row 1, column 3.

NOTES & COMMENTS

1. Much research in the 1970s and 1980s was devoted to developing efficient special-purpose solution procedures for network problems. The transportation simplex method is generally recognized as one of the best; it is used in The Management Scientist software package. A simple extension of this method can also be used to solve transshipment problems.

2. As we have previously noted, each cell in the transportation tableau corresponds to an arc (route) in the network model of the problem and a variable in the linear programming formulation. Phase II of the transportation simplex method is thus the same as phase II of the simplex method for linear programming. At each iteration, one variable is brought into solution and another variable is dropped from solution. The reason the method works so much better for transportation problems

—Continued on the next page

—Continued from previous page

is that the special mathematical structure of the constraint equations means that only addition and subtraction operations are necessary. We can implement the entire procedure in a transportation tableau that has one row for each origin and one column for each destination. A simplex tableau for such a problem would require a row for each origin, a row for each destination, and a column for each arc; thus, the simplex tableau would be much larger.

7.6 The Assignment Problem: A Special-Purpose Solution Procedure

Small assignment problems can be solved by enumeration; a 3 × 3 problem only has six possible solutions. But, the number of solutions grows rapidly. A 6 × 6 problem has 720 solutions, and an 8 × 8 problem has over 40,000 solutions. Efficient algorithms, such as the Hungarian method, are necessary for even moderate-sized problems.

As mentioned previously, the assignment problem is a special case of the transportation problem. Thus, the transportation simplex method can be used to solve the assignment problem. However, the assignment problem has an even more special structure; all supplies and demands equal 1. Because of this additional special structure, special-purpose solution procedures have been specifically designed to solve the assignment problem; one such procedure is called the *Hungarian method*. In this section we will show how the Hungarian method can be used to solve the Fowle Marketing Research problem.

Recall that the Fowle problem (see Section 7.2) involved assigning project leaders to research projects; there were three project leaders available and three research projects to be completed. Fowle's assignment alternatives and estimated project completion times in days are restated in Table 7.31.

The Hungarian method involves what is called *matrix reduction*. By subtracting and adding appropriate values in the matrix, the method determines an optimal solution to the assignment problem. There are three major steps associated with the procedure. Step 1 involves row and column reduction.

Step 1   Reduce the initial matrix by subtracting the smallest element in each row from every element in that row. Then, using the row-reduced matrix, subtract the smallest element in each column from every element in that column.

Thus, we first reduce the matrix in Table 7.31 by subtracting the minimum value in each row from each element in the row. With the minimum values of 9 for row 1, 5 for row 2, and 3 for row 3, the row-reduced matrix becomes

	1	2	3
Terry	1	6	0
Carle	4	13	0
McClymonds	3	11	0

The assignment problem represented by this reduced matrix is equivalent to our original assignment problem in the sense that the same solution will be optimal. To understand why, first note that the row 1 minimum element, 9, has been subtracted from every element in the first row. Since Terry must still be assigned to one of the clients, the only change is that in this revised problem, the time for any assignment will be 9 days

Table 7.31

Estimated Project Completion Times (Days) for the Fowle Assignment Problem

	Client		
Project Leader	1	2	3
Terry	10	15	9
Carle	9	18	5
McClymonds	6	14	3

less. Similarly, Carle and McClymonds are shown with completion times requiring 5 and 3 fewer days, respectively.

Continuing with step 1 in the matrix reduction process, we now subtract the minimum element in each column of the row-reduced matrix from every element in the column. This also leads to an equivalent assignment problem; that is, the same solution will still be optimal, but the times required to complete each project are reduced. With the minimum values of 1 for column 1, 6 for column 2, and 0 for column 3, the reduced matrix becomes

	1	2	3
Terry	0	0	0
Carle	3	7	0
McClymonds	2	5	0

The goal of the Hungarian method is to continue reducing the matrix until the value of one of the solutions is zero—that is, until an assignment of project leaders to clients can be made that, in terms of the reduced matrix, requires a total time expenditure of zero days. Then, as long as there are no negative elements in the matrix, the zero-valued solution will be optimal. The way in which we perform this further reduction and recognize when we have reached an optimal solution is described in the following two steps.

Step 2 Find the minimum number of straight lines that must be drawn through the rows and the columns of the current matrix so that all the zeros in the matrix will be covered. If the minimum number of straight lines is the same as the number of rows (or equivalently, columns) in the matrix, an optimal assignment with a value of zero can be made. If the minimum number of lines is less than the number of rows, go to step 3.

Applying step 2 as shown below, we see that the minimum number of lines required to cover all the zeros is 2. Thus, we must continue to step 3.

	1	2	3	
Terry	~~0~~	~~0~~	~~0~~	Two straight lines will cover
Carle	3	7	0	all the zeros (step 2)
McClymonds	②	5	0	

Step 3   Subtract the value of the smallest unlined element from every unlined element, and add this same value to every element at the intersection of two lines. All other elements remain unchanged. Return to step 2, and continue until the minimum number of lines necessary to cover all the zeros in the matrix is equal to the number of rows.

The minimum unlined element is 2. In the matrix above, we have circled this element. Subtracting 2 from all unlined elements and adding 2 to the intersection element for Terry and client 3 produces the new matrix shown below.

	1	**2**	**3**
Terry	0	0	2
Carle	1	5	0
McClymonds	0	3	0

Returning to step 2, we find that the minimum number of straight lines required to cover all the zeros in the current matrix is 3. The following matrix illustrates the step 2 calculations:

	1	**2**	**3**
Terry	0	0	2
Carle	1	5	0
McClymonds	0	3	0

Three lines must be drawn to cover all zeros; therefore, the optimal solution has been reached

According to step 2, then, it must be possible to find an assignment with a value of zero. Such an assignment can be found by first locating any row or column that contains only one zero. (If all have more than one zero, choose the assignment with the fewest assignments tied with it.) We draw a square around the zero, indicating an assignment, and eliminate that row and column from further consideration. Since row 2 has only one zero in the Fowle problem, we assign Carle to client 3 and eliminate row 2 and column 3 from further consideration. McClymonds must then be assigned to client 1 (the only remaining zero in row 3) and, finally, Terry to client 2. The solution to the Fowle problem is shown below; in terms of the reduced matrix, it requires a time expenditure of zero days.

	1	**2**	**3**
Terry	0	[0]	0
Carle	1	5	[0]
McClymonds	[0]	3	0

The value of the optimal assignment can be found by referring to the original assignment problem and summing the solution times associated with the optimal assignment—in this case, Terry to client 2, Carle to client 3, and McClymonds to client 1. Thus, we obtain the solution time of $15 + 5 + 6 = 26$ days.

Finding the Minimum Number of Lines

Sometimes it is not obvious how the lines should be drawn through rows and columns of the matrix in order to cover all the zeros with the smallest number of lines. In these cases, the following heuristic works well. Choose any row or column with a single zero. If it is a row, draw a line through the column the zero is in; if it is a column, draw a line through the row the zero is in. Continue in this fashion until all the zeros are covered.

You should be able to solve an assignment problem using the Hungarian method. Try Problem 38.

If you make the mistake of drawing too many lines to cover the zeros in the reduced matrix and thus conclude an optimal solution has been reached when it has not, you will find you cannot identify a zero-value assignment. Thus, if you think you have reached the optimal solution, but a set of zero-value assignments cannot be found, go back to the previous step, and check to see if you can cover all the zeros with fewer lines.

Problem Variations

We now discuss how to handle the following problem variations when using the Hungarian method:

1. Number of agents not the same as the number of tasks
2. Maximization objective
3. Unacceptable assignments

Number of Agents ≠ Number of Tasks. The Hungarian method requires that the number of rows (agents) equal the number of columns (tasks). Suppose that in the Fowle problem four project leaders (agents) had been available for assignment to the three new clients (tasks). Fowle still faces the same basic problem—namely, which project leaders should be assigned to which clients to minimize the total days required. The project completion time estimates with a fourth project leader are shown in Table 7.32.

We have seen how to apply the Hungarian method when the number of rows and the number of columns are equal. Therefore, we can apply the same procedure if we can add a new client. Since we do not have another client, we simply add a *dummy column,* or a dummy client. This dummy client is nonexistent, so the project leader assigned to the dummy client in the optimal assignment solution will in effect be the unassigned project leader.

What project completion time estimates should we show in this new dummy column? Actually, any arbitrary value is acceptable as long as all project leaders are given the same completion time. However, since the dummy client assignment will not actually take

Table 7.32

Estimated Project Completion Time (Days) for the Fowle Assignment Problem with Four Project Leaders

Project Leader	Client		
	1	2	3
Terry	10	15	9
Carle	9	18	5
McClymonds	6	14	3
Higley	8	16	6

place, a zero project completion time for all project leaders seems logical. The Fowle assignment problem with a dummy client, labeled D, is shown in Table 7.33. (Problem 40 at the end of the chapter asks you to use the Hungarian method to determine the optimal solution to this problem.)

Note that if we had considered the case of four new clients and only three project leaders, we would have had to add a *dummy row* (dummy project leader) in order to apply the Hungarian method. The client receiving the dummy leader would not actually be assigned an immediate project leader and would have to wait until one becomes available. To obtain a problem form compatible with the solution algorithm, it may be necessary to add several dummy rows or dummy columns, but never both.

Maximization Objective.   To illustrate how maximization assignment problems can be handled, let us consider the problem facing management of Salisbury Discounts, Inc. Suppose that Salisbury Discounts has just leased a new store and is attempting to determine where various departments should be located within the store. The store manager has four locations that have not yet been assigned a department and is considering five departments that might occupy the four locations. The departments under consideration are a shoe, a toy, an auto parts, a housewares, and a video department. The store manager would like to determine the optimal location assignment of the departments that will maximize profits. After a careful study of the layout of the remainder of the store, the store manager has made estimates, based on his experience with similar stores, of the expected annual profit for each department in each location. These are presented in Table 7.34.

We now have an assignment problem that requires a maximization objective. However, we also have a problem involving more rows than columns. Thus, we must first add a dummy column, corresponding to a dummy or fictitious location, in order to apply the Hungarian method. After adding a dummy column, we obtain the 5 × 5 Salisbury Discounts, Inc., assignment problem shown in Table 7.35.

Table 7.33

Estimated Project Completion Time (Days) for the Fowle Assignment Problem with a Dummy Client

	Client			Dummy client
Project Leader	1	2	3	D
Terry	10	15	9	0
Carle	9	18	5	0
McClymonds	6	14	3	0
Higley	8	16	6	0

Table 7.34

Estimated Annual Profit (Thousands of Dollars) for Each Department–Location Combination

	Location			
Department	1	2	3	4
Shoe	10	6	12	8
Toy	15	18	5	11
Auto parts	17	10	13	16
Housewares	14	12	13	10
Video	14	16	6	12

Table 7.35

Estimated Annual Profit (Thousands of Dollars) for Each Department–Location Combination, Including a Dummy Location

Department	Location 1	2	3	4	5 (Dummy location)
Shoe	10	6	12	8	0
Toy	15	18	5	11	0
Auto parts	17	10	13	16	0
Housewares	14	12	13	10	0
Video	14	16	6	12	0

Table 7.36

Opportunity Loss (Thousands of Dollars) for Each Department–Location Combination

Department	Location 1	2	3	4	5 (Dummy location)
Shoe	7	12	1	8	0
Toy	2	0	8	5	0
Auto parts	0	8	0	0	0
Housewares	3	6	0	6	0
Video	3	2	7	4	0

We can obtain an equivalent minimization assignment problem by converting all the elements in the matrix to *opportunity losses*. This conversion is accomplished by subtracting every element in each column from the largest element in the column.

It turns out that finding the assignment that minimizes opportunity loss leads to the same solution that maximizes the value of the assignment in the original problem. Thus, any maximization assignment problem can be converted to a minimization problem by converting the assignment matrix to one in which the elements represent opportunity losses. Hence, we begin our solution to this maximization assignment problem by developing an assignment matrix where each element represents the opportunity loss from not making the "best" assignment. The opportunity losses are presented in Table 7.36.

The opportunity loss from putting the shoe department in location 1 is $7000. That is, if we put the shoe department, instead of the best department (auto parts), in that location, we forgo the opportunity to make an additional $7000 in profit. The opportunity loss associated with putting the toy department in location 2 is zero since it yields the highest profit in that location. What about the opportunity losses associated with the dummy column? Well, the assignment of a department to this dummy location means that the department will not be assigned a store location in the optimal solution. Since all departments earn the same amount from this dummy location, zero, the opportunity loss for each department is zero.

Try Problem 41 for practice in using the Hungarian method for a maximization problem.

Following steps 1, 2, and 3 of the Hungarian method, we can proceed to determine the maximum profit assignment. (Problem 41 at the end of this chapter asks you to use the Hungarian method to determine the optimal solution to this problem.)

Unacceptable Assignments.   As an illustration of how we can handle unacceptable assignments, suppose that in the Salisbury Discounts, Inc., assignment problem the store manager believed that the toy department should not be considered for location 2

Table 7.37

Estimated Profit for the Salisbury
Department–Location Combinations

		Location			
Department	1	2	3	4	5
Shoe	10	6	12	8	0
Toy	15	$-M$	5	11	0
Auto parts	17	10	13	$-M$	0
Housewares	14	12	13	10	0
Video	14	16	6	12	0

and the auto parts department should not be considered for location 4. Essentially the store manager is saying that, based on other considerations, such as size of the area, adjacent departments, and so on, these two assignments are unacceptable alternatives.

Using the same approach for the assignment problem as we did for the transportation problem, we define a value of M for unacceptable minimization assignments and a value of $-M$ for unacceptable maximization assignments, where M is an arbitrarily large value. In fact, M is assumed to be so large that M plus or minus any value is still extremely large. Thus, an M-valued cell in an assignment matrix retains its M value throughout the matrix reduction calculations. An M-valued cell can never be zero, so it can never be an assignment in the final solution.

The Salisbury Discounts, Inc., assignment problem with the two unacceptable assignments is shown in Table 7.37. When this assignment matrix is converted to an opportunity loss matrix, the $-M$ profit value will be changed to M. (Problem 42 at the end of this chapter asks you to solve this assignment problem.)

Summary

In this chapter we introduced transportation, assignment, and transshipment problems. All three types of problems belong to the special category of linear programs called *network flow problems.* The network model of a transportation problem consists of nodes representing a set of origins and a set of destinations. In the basic model, an arc is used to represent the route from each origin to each destination. Each origin has a supply and each destination has a demand. The problem is to determine the optimal amount to ship from each origin to each destination.

The assignment model is a special case of the transportation model in which all supply and all demand values are equal to 1. We represent each agent as an origin node and each task as a destination node. The transshipment model is an extension of the transportation model to distribution problems involving transfer points referred to as transshipment nodes. In this more general model, we allow for arcs between any pair of nodes. A variation of the transshipment problem allows for placing capacities on the arcs. This variation, called the *capacitated transshipment problem,* is also known in the network flow literature as the pure network problem.

We showed how each of these network flow problems could be modeled as a linear program, and we solved each using a general-purpose linear programming computer package. However, many practical applications of network flow models lead to very large problems for which general-purpose linear programming codes are not very efficient. The transportation simplex method was presented as an efficient special-purpose solution procedure for solving transportation problems. The procedure, and its extension to the transshipment problem, has been shown to be hundreds of times faster than the general-purpose simplex method for large transportation and transshipment problems.

In network flow problems, the optimal solution will be integral as long as all supplies and demands are integral. Therefore, when solving any transportation, assignment, or transshipment problem in which the supplies and demands are integral, we can expect to obtain an integer-valued solution.

Glossary

Transportation problem A network flow problem that often involves minimizing the cost of shipping goods from a set of origins to a set of destinations; it can be formulated and solved as a linear program by including a variable for each arc and a constraint for each node.

Network A graphical representation of a problem consisting of numbered circles (nodes) interconnected by a series of lines (arcs); arrowheads on the arcs show the direction of flow. Transportation, assignment, and transshipment problems are network flow problems.

Nodes The intersection or junction points of a network (shown as circles).

Arcs The lines connecting the nodes in a network.

Capacitated transportation problem A variation of the basic transportation problem in which there are capacities on some or all of the arcs.

Assignment problem A network flow problem that often involves the assignment of agents to tasks; it can be formulated as a linear program and is a special case of the transportation problem.

Transshipment problem An extension of the transportation problem to distribution problems involving transfer points and possible shipments between any pair of nodes.

Capacitated transshipment problem A variation of the transshipment problem in which there are capacities on some or all of the arcs.

Transportation simplex method A special-purpose solution procedure for the transportation problem.

Heuristic A common-sense procedure for quickly finding a solution to a problem. Heuristics are used to find initial feasible solutions for the transportation simplex method as well as in other applications.

Minimum-cost method A heuristic used to find an initial feasible solution to a transportation problem; it is easy to use and usually provides a good (but not optimal) solution.

Incoming arc The unused arc (represented by an unoccupied cell in the transportation tableau) to which flow is assigned during an iteration of the transportation simplex method.

MODI method The MOdified DIstribution method is a procedure for determining the net evaluation index for unused arcs in the transportation simplex method.

Net evaluation index The per-unit cost change associated with assigning flow to an unused arc in the transportation simplex method.

Stepping-stone path The sequence of occupied cells that receive flow adjustments when flow is assigned to an unused arc in the transportation simplex method.

Outgoing arc The arc corresponding to an occupied cell that is dropped from solution during an iteration of the transportation simplex method.

Degenerate solution A solution to a transportation problem in which fewer than $m + n - 1$ arcs (cells) have positive flow; m is the number of origins and n is the number of destinations.

Dummy destination A destination added to a transportation problem to make the total supply equal to the total demand. The demand assigned to the dummy destination is the difference between the total supply and the total demand.

Dummy origin An origin added to a transportation problem in order to make the total supply equal to the total demand. The supply assigned to the dummy origin is the difference between the total demand and the total supply.

Hungarian method A special-purpose solution procedure for solving the assignment problem.

Opportunity loss For each cell in an assignment matrix, the opportunity loss is the difference between the largest value in the column and the value in the cell. The entries in the cells of an assignment matrix must be converted to opportunity losses to solve maximization problems using the Hungarian method.

Problems

NOTE: For Problems 1–31 a variety of solution methods can be used. In many cases, we ask you to formulate and solve the problem as a linear program. Where the solution method is not specified, you may also use the transportation or assignment modules of The Management Scientist or some other software package. Problems 32–43 are intended to be solved using the special-purpose algorithms of Sections 7.5 and 7.6. These special-purpose algorithms could also be used for many of the first 31 problems.

SELF TEST ▷

1. Transportation problem;
network model

1. A company imports goods at two ports: Philadelphia and New Orleans. Shipments of one of its products are made to customers in Atlanta, Dallas, Columbus, and Boston. For the next planning period, the supplies at each port, customer demands, and the per-case shipping costs from each port to each customer are given as follows:

Port	Customers				Port Supply
	Atlanta	Dallas	Columbus	Boston	
Philadelphia	2	6	6	2	5000
New Orleans	1	2	5	7	3000
Demand	1400	3200	2000	1400	

Develop a network model of the distribution system (transportation problem).

SELF TEST ▷

2. Transportation solution;
formulate and solve LP

2. Consider the following network representation of a transportation problem:

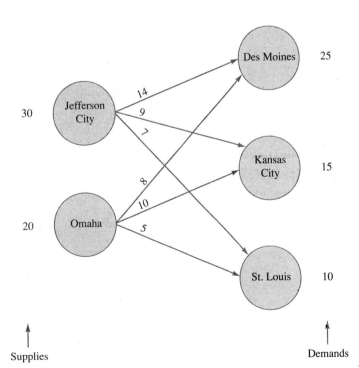

The supplies, demands, and per-unit transportation costs are shown on the network.

a. Develop a linear programming model for this problem; be sure to define the variables in your model.

b. Solve the linear program to determine the optimal solution.

3. Reconsider the distribution system described in Problem 1.

a. Develop a linear programming model that can be solved to minimize transportation cost.

b. Solve the linear program to determine the minimum-cost shipping pattern.

4. A product is produced at three plants and shipped to three warehouses (the transportation costs per unit are shown in the table below).

| | Warehouse | | | Plant |
Plant	W_1	W_2	W_3	Capacity
P_1	20	16	24	300
P_2	10	10	8	500
P_3	12	18	10	100
Warehouse demand	200	400	300	

a. Show a network representation of the problem.

b. Develop a linear programming model for minimizing transportation costs; solve this model to determine the minimum-cost solution.

c. Suppose the entries in the table above represent profit per unit produced at plant i and sold to warehouse j. How does the model formulation change from that in part (b)?

5. Consider the following information concerning a transportation problem:

| | Destination | | | |
Origin	Boston	Atlanta	Houston	Supply
Detroit	5	2	3	100
St. Louis	8	4	3	300
Denver	9	7	5	300
Demand	300	200	200	

Cost/unit

a. Develop a network representation of this problem.

b. Develop a linear programming model for this transportation problem.

c. Solve the linear program formulated in part (b). What is the minimum-cost solution? How many units are shipped over each transportation route?

d. Assume that 100 units must be shipped over the Detroit–Boston route. How would the linear programming model have to be modified to reflect this change?

e. Suppose that a labor dispute temporarily eliminates the Denver–Boston and the St. Louis–Atlanta routes. How would the linear programming model have to be revised to reflect these changes?

f. First, solve the transportation problem with the modification in part (d), and then resolve with the modification in part (e). What effect will each of these changes have on the total transportation cost and the specific transportation schedule?

6. Transportation solution; network model

6. Arnoff Enterprises manufactures the central processing unit (CPU) for a line of personal computers. The CPUs are manufactured in Seattle, Columbus, and New York and shipped to warehouses in Pittsburgh, Mobile, Denver, Los Angeles, and Washington, D.C., for further distribution. The transportation tableau below shows the number of CPUs available at each plant and the number of CPUs required by each warehouse. The shipping costs (dollars per unit) are also shown in each cell.

| Plant | Warehouse | | | | | CPUs Available |
	Pittsburgh	Mobile	Denver	Los Angeles	Washington	
Seattle	10	20	5	9	10	9000
Columbus	2	10	8	30	6	4000
New York	1	20	7	10	4	8000
CPUs Required	3000	5000	4000	6000	3000	21,000

a. Develop a network representation of this problem.
b. Determine the amount that should be shipped from each plant to each warehouse to minimize the total shipping cost.
c. The Pittsburgh warehouse has just increased its order by 1000 units, and Arnoff has authorized the Columbus plant to increase its production by 1000 units. Will this lead to an increase or decrease in total shipping costs? Solve for the new optimal solution.

7. Transportation solution; excess supply

7. Solve the following minimum-cost transportation problem. The numbers in the upper right-hand corner of each cell are the shipping costs.

| Origin | Destination | | | Supply |
	D_1	D_2	D_3	
O_1	1	3	4	200
O_2	2	6	8	500
O_3	2	5	7	300
Demand	200	100	400	

Since total supply (1000 units) exceeds total demand (700 units), which origins may consider alternative uses for their excess supply and still maintain a minimum-cost solution?

SELF TEST ▷

8. Transportation solution; network and LP model; excess demand

8. Klein Chemicals, Inc., produces a special oil-base material that is currently in short supply. Four of Klein's customers have already placed orders that together exceed the combined capacity of Klein's two plants. Klein's management faces the problem of deciding how many units it should supply to each customer. Since the four customers are in different industries, different prices can be charged to these customers because of the various industry pricing structures. However, slightly different production costs at the two plants and varying transportation costs between the plants and customers make a "sell to the highest bidder" strategy unacceptable. After considering price, production costs, and transportation costs, Klein has established the following profit per unit for each plant–customer alternative.

	Customer			
Plant	D_1	D_2	D_3	D_4
Clifton Springs	$32	$34	$32	$40
Danville	$34	$30	$28	$38

The plant capacities and customer orders are as follows:

Plant Capacity (units)	Distributor Orders (units)
Clifton Springs 5000	D_1 2000
	D_2 5000
Danville 3000	D_3 3000
	D_4 2000

How many units should each plant produce for each customer to maximize profits? Which customer demands will not be met? Show your network model and linear programming formulation.

9. Transportation solution; unacceptable route

9. Sound Electronics, Inc., produces a battery-operated tape recorder at plants located in Martinsville, North Carolina; Plymouth, New York; and Franklin, Missouri. The unit transportation cost for shipments from the three plants to distribution centers in Chicago, Dallas, and New York are as follows:

	To		
From	Chicago	Dallas	New York
Martinsville	1.45	1.60	1.40
Plymouth	1.10	2.25	0.60
Franklin	1.20	1.20	1.80

After considering transportation costs, management has decided that under no circumstances will it use the Plymouth–Dallas route. The plant capacities and distributor orders for the next month are as follows:

Plant	Capacity (units)		Distributor	Orders (units)
Martinsville	400		Chicago	400
Plymouth	600		Dallas	400
Franklin	300		New York	400

Because of different wage scales at the three plants, the unit production cost varies from plant to plant. Assuming the costs are $29.50 per unit at Martinsville, $31.20 per unit at Plymouth, and $30.35 per unit at Franklin, find the production and distribution plan that minimizes production and transportation costs.

10. Transportation solution; LP model

10.   The Ace Manufacturing Company has orders for three similar products:

Product	Orders (units)
A	2000
B	500
C	1200

Three machines are available for the manufacturing operations. All three machines can produce all the products at the same production rate. However, due to varying defect percentages of each product on each machine, the unit costs of the products vary depending on the machine used. Machine capacities for the next week, and the unit costs, are as follows:

Machine	Capacity (units)
1	1500
2	1500
3	1000

Machine	Product		
	A	B	C
1	$1.00	$1.20	$0.90
2	$1.30	$1.40	$1.20
3	$1.10	$1.00	$1.20

Use the transportation model to develop the minimum-cost production schedule for the products and machines. Show the linear programming formulation.

11. Forbelt Corporation has a 1-year contract to supply motors for all refrigerators produced by the Ice Age Corporation. Ice Age manufactures the refrigerators at four locations around the country: Boston, Dallas, Los Angeles, and St. Paul. Plans call for the following number (in thousands) of refrigerators to be produced at each location:

Boston	50
Dallas	70
Los Angeles	60
St. Paul	80

Forbelt has three plants that are capable of producing the motors. The plants and production capacities (in thousands) are as follows:

Denver	100
Atlanta	100
Chicago	150

Because of varying production and transportation costs, the profit Forbelt earns on each lot of 1000 units depends on which plant produced the lot and which destination it was shipped to. The following table gives the accounting department estimates of the profit per unit (shipments will be made in lots of 1000 units):

	Shipped To			
Produced At	Boston	Dallas	Los Angeles	St. Paul
Denver	7	11	8	13
Atlanta	20	17	12	10
Chicago	8	18	13	16

Given profit maximization as a criterion, Forbelt would like to determine how many motors should be produced at each plant and how many motors should be shipped from each plant to each destination.

a. Develop a network representation of this problem.
b. Find the optimal solution.

12. Scott and Associates, Inc., is an accounting firm that has three new clients. Three project leaders will be assigned to the three clients. Based on the different backgrounds and experiences of the leaders, the various leader–client assignments differ in terms of projected completion times. The possible assignments and the estimated completion times in days are shown below.

Project Leader	Client		
	1	2	3
Jackson	10	16	32
Ellis	14	22	40
Smith	22	24	34

a. Develop a network representation of this problem.

b. Formulate the problem as a linear program, and solve. What is the total time required?

13. Assignment solution

13. Assume that in Problem 12 an additional employee is available for possible assignment. The following table shows the assignment alternatives and the estimated completion times:

Project Leader	Client		
	1	2	3
Jackson	10	16	32
Ellis	14	22	40
Smith	22	24	34
Burton	14	18	36

a. What is the optimal assignment?

b. How did the assignment change compared to the best assignment possible in Problem 12? Was there any savings associated with considering Burton as one of the possible project leaders?

c. Which project leader remains unassigned?

14. Assignment solution; network and LP model

14. Wilson Distributors, Inc., is opening two new sales territories in the western states. Three individuals currently selling in the Midwest and the East are being considered for promotion to regional sales manager positions in the new sales territories. Management has estimated total annual sales (in thousands of dollars) for the assignment of each individual to each sales territory. The management sales projections are as follows:

Regional Managers	Sales Region	
	Northwest	Southwest
Bostock	$100	$95
McMahon	$ 85	$80
Miller	$ 90	$75

a. Develop a network representation of the problem.

b. Formulate and solve a linear programming model to obtain the optimal solution to this problem.

15. Assignment solution

15. Solve the Fowle Marketing Research assignment problem (Section 7.6) with four project leaders available for assignment to the three clients. The estimated project completion times in days are as follows:

Project Leader	Client		
	1	2	3
Terry	10	15	9
Carle	9	18	5
McClymonds	6	14	3
Higley	8	16	6

16. **a.** Develop a network representation of the Salisbury Discount, Inc., department–location assignment problem using the estimated annual profit data provided in Table 7.34.
b. Formulate a linear programming model, and solve for the department–location assignment that maximizes profit.

17. Consider the Salisbury Discount, Inc., assignment problem with two unacceptable assignments (see Table 7.37).
a. Develop a network representation of the problem.
b. Formulate and solve a linear programming model.

18. In a job shop operation, four jobs may be performed on any of four machines. The numbers of hours required for each job on each machine are summarized below. What is the minimum total time job–machine assignment?

	Machine			
Job	A	B	C	D
1	32	18	32	26
2	22	24	12	16
3	24	30	26	24
4	26	30	28	20

19. Mayfax Distributors, Inc., has four sales territories, each of which must be assigned a sales representative. From past experience the firm's sales manager has estimated the sales volume for each sales representative in each sales territory. Find the sales representative–territory assignments that will maximize sales (data given in thousands).

	Sales Territory			
Sales Representative	A	B	C	D
Washington	44	80	52	60
Benson	60	56	40	72
Fredricks	36	60	48	48
Hodson	52	76	36	40

20. Four trucks must be dispatched to each of four customer locations. The assignments and the distances traveled by each truck in making the trips are shown below. What truck–customer assignments minimize the total distance traveled by the four trucks? Note that two unacceptable assignments are indicated because the specific truck involved is not equipped to carry the type of shipment involved. The unacceptable assignments show M as the distance traveled.

	Customer			
Truck	A	B	C	D
1	130	125	120	135
2	120	110	100	120
3	125	120	M	140
4	150	150	140	M

21. Assignment solution; LP model; sensitivity analysis

21. A market research firm has three clients who have each requested that the firm conduct a sample survey. Four available statisticians can be assigned to these three projects; however, all four statisticians are busy, and therefore each can handle at most one of the clients. The following data show the number of hours it would take for each statistician to complete each job; the differences in time are due to differences in experience and ability among the statisticians.

| | Client | | |
Statistician	A	B	C
1	150	210	270
2	170	230	220
3	180	230	225
4	160	240	230

a. Formulate and solve a linear programming model for this problem.
b. Suppose that the time it takes statistician 4 to complete the job for client A is increased from 160 to 165 hours. What effect will this have on the solution?
c. Suppose that the time it takes statistician 4 to complete the job for client A is decreased to 140 hours. What effect will this have on the solution?
d. Suppose that the time it takes statistician 3 to complete the job for client B increases to 250 hours. What effect will this have on the solution?

22. Identify costs; assignment solution

22. Hatcher Enterprises uses a chemical called Rbase in production operations at five divisions. There are only six suppliers of Rbase that meet Hatcher's quality control standards. All six of the suppliers can produce Rbase in sufficient quantities to accommodate the needs of each division. The quantity of Rbase needed by each of Hatcher's divisions and the price per gallon charged by each supplier are given below.

Division	Demand (000's of gallons)	Supplier	Price Per Gallon
1	40	1	$12.60
2	45	2	$14.00
3	50	3	$10.20
4	35	4	$14.20
5	45	5	$12.00
		6	$13.00

The cost per gallon for shipping from each supplier to each division is provided in the following table:

| | Supplier | | | | | |
Division	1	2	3	4	5	6
1	2.75	2.50	3.15	2.80	2.75	2.75
2	.80	.20	5.40	1.20	3.40	1.00
3	4.70	2.60	5.30	2.80	6.00	5.60
4	2.60	1.80	4.40	2.40	5.00	2.80
5	3.40	.40	5.00	1.20	2.60	3.60

Hatcher believes it is important to spread business among suppliers so that the company will be less affected by supplier problems (e.g., labor strikes or resource availability). Company policy requires that each division should have a separate supplier.

a. For each supplier–division combination, compute the total cost of supplying the division's demand.

b. Determine the optimal assignment of suppliers to divisions.

S ELF T EST
23. Transshipment solution; network and LP model

23. The distribution system for the Herman Company consists of three plants, two warehouses, and four customer demand zones. Plant capacities and shipping costs (in $) from each plant to each warehouse are given below.

	Warehouses		
Plants	1	2	**Capacity**
1	4	7	450
2	8	5	600
3	5	6	380

Customer demand and per-unit shipping costs (in $) from each warehouse to each customer are as follows:

	Customers			
Warehouses	1	2	3	4
1	6	4	8	4
2	3	6	7	7
Demand	300	300	300	400

a. Develop a network model of this problem.
b. Formulate a linear programming model of the problem.
c. Use a computer code (e.g., The Management Scientist) to find the optimal shipping plan.

S ELF T EST
24. Complex transshipment network; LP model and solution

24. Refer to Problem 23. Suppose shipments between the two warehouses are permitted at $2 per unit and that direct shipments can be made from plant 3 to customer zone 4 at a cost of $7 per unit.

a. Develop a network model of this problem.
b. Formulate a linear programming model of this problem.
c. Use a computer code (e.g., The Management Scientist) to find the optimal shipping plan.

25. Transshipment solution; LP model; arc capacity

25. A company has two plants (P_1 and P_2), one regional warehouse (W), and two retail outlets (R_1 and R_2). The plant capacities, retail outlet demands, and per-unit shipping costs are shown in the following network:

a. Formulate a linear programming model to minimize shipping costs for this problem.
b. If you have access to a linear programming computer code, determine the optimal solution for the model formulated in part (a).
c. What change would have to be made in the linear programming model if the maximum amount of goods that can be shipped from W to R_1 is 500? How would this change the optimal solution?

26. Transshipment solution; LP model

26. Adirondack Paper Mills, Inc., has paper plants located in Augusta, Maine, and Tupper Lake, New York. Warehouse facilities are located in Albany, New York, and Portsmouth, New Hampshire. Distributors are located in Boston, New York, and Philadelphia. The plant capacities and distributor demands for the next month are as follows:

Plant	Capacity (units)	Distributor	Demand (units)
Augusta	300	Boston	150
Tupper Lake	100	New York	100
		Philadelphia	150

The unit transportation costs for shipments from the two plants to the two warehouses and from the two warehouses to the three distributors are shown below.

	Warehouse	
Plant	Albany	Portsmouth
Augusta	7	5
Tupper Lake	3	4

Warehouse	Distributor		
	Boston	New York	Philadelphia
Albany	8	5	7
Portsmouth	5	6	10

a. Draw the network representation of the Adirondack Paper Mills problem.
b. Formulate the Adirondack Paper Mills problem as a linear programming problem.
c. If you have access to a linear programming computer code, determine the minimum-cost shipping schedule for the problem.

27. Consider a transshipment problem consisting of three origin nodes, two transshipment nodes, and four destination nodes. The supplies at the origin nodes and the demands at the destination nodes are as follows:

Origin	Supply		Destination	Demand
1	400		1	200
2	450		2	500
3	350		3	300
			4	200

The per-unit shipping costs are provided in the following table:

		To					
		Transshipment		Destination			
From		1	2	1	2	3	4
Origin	1	6	8	—	—	—	—
	2	8	12	—	—	—	—
	3	10	5	—	—	—	—
Transshipment	1	—	—	9	7	6	10
	2	—	—	7	9	6	8

a. Draw the network representation of this problem.
b. Formulate this as a linear programming problem.
c. Solve for the optimal solution.

28. The Moore & Harman Company is in the business of buying and selling grain. An important aspect of the company's business is arranging for the purchased grain to be shipped to customers. If the company can keep freight costs low, profitability will be improved.

Currently, the company has purchased three rail cars of grain at Muncie, Indiana; six rail cars at Brazil, Indiana; and five rail cars at Xenia, Ohio. Twelve carloads of grain have been sold. The locations and the amount sold at each location are as follows:

Location	Number of Rail Car Loads
Macon, Ga.	2
Greenwood, S.C.	4
Concord, S.C.	3
Chatham, N.C.	3

All shipments must be routed through either Louisville or Cincinnati. Given below are the shipping costs per bushel (in cents) from the origins to Louisville and Cincinnati as well as the costs per bushel to ship from Louisville and Cincinnati to the destinations.

	To	
From	Louisville	Cincinnati
Muncie	8	6 ← Cost per bushel
Brazil	3	8 from Muncie to
Xenia	9	3 Cincinnati is 6¢

	To			
From	Macon	Greenwood	Concord	Chatham
Louisville	44	34	34	32
Cincinnati	57	35	28	24

Cost per bushel
from Cincinnati to
Greenwood is 35¢

Determine a shipping schedule that will minimize the freight costs necessary to satisfy demand. Which (if any) rail cars of grain must be held at the origin until buyers can be found?

29. Transshipment solution; complex network; LP model

29. A rental car company has an imbalance of cars at seven of its locations. The network below shows the locations of concern (the nodes) and the cost to move a car between locations. A positive number by a node indicates an excess supply at the node, and a negative number indicates an excess demand.

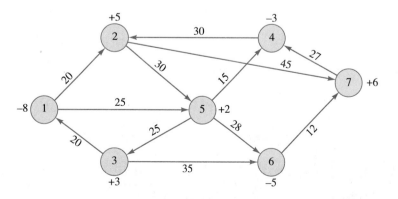

a. Develop a linear programming model of this problem.

b. Solve the model formulated in part (a) to determine how the cars should be redistributed among the locations.

30. Develop network model from LP

30. Shown below is the linear programming formulation of a transshipment problem.

$$\text{Min} \quad 11x_{13} + 12x_{14} + 10x_{21} + 8x_{34} + 10x_{35} + 11x_{42} + 9x_{45} + 12x_{52}$$

s.t.

$$
\begin{array}{llllllllr}
x_{13} + & x_{14} - & x_{21} & & & & & & \leq 5 \\
& & x_{21} & & & - x_{42} & & - x_{52} & \leq 3 \\
x_{13} & & & - x_{34} - & x_{35} & & & & = 6 \\
& - x_{14} & & - x_{34} & & + x_{42} + & x_{45} & & \leq 2 \\
& & & & x_{35} & & + x_{45} - & x_{52} & = 4
\end{array}
$$

$$x_{ij} \geq 0 \quad \text{for all } i, j$$

Show the network representation of this problem.

31. Transshipment solution; network and LP model

31. Refer to the Contois Carpets problem for which the network representation is shown in Figure 7.12. Suppose Contois has a beginning inventory of 50 yards of carpet and requires an inventory of 100 yards at the end of quarter 4.

a. Develop a network representation of this modified problem.

b. Develop a linear programming model, and solve for the optimal solution.

NOTE: The remaining problems involve the use of the special-purpose algorithms described in Sections 7.5 and 7.6 for solving transportation and assignment problems.

SELF TEST

32. Minimum-cost method, transportation simplex

32. Consider the following minimum-cost transportation problem:

Origin	Destination			Supply
	Los Angeles	San Francisco	San Diego	
San Jose	4	10	6	100
Las Vegas	8	16	6	300
Tucson	14	18	10	300
Demand	200	300	200	700

a. Use the minimum-cost method to find an initial feasible solution.

b. Use the transportation simplex method to find an optimal solution.

c. How would the optimal solution change if we must ship 100 units on the Tucson–San Diego route?

d. Because of road construction, the Las Vegas–San Diego route is now unacceptable. Resolve the initial problem.

33. Minimum-cost method

33. Refer to Problem 2.
a. Set up the transportation tableau for the problem.
b. Use the minimum-cost method to find an initial feasible solution.

34. Transportation simplex

34. Refer again to Problem 4. Use the transportation simplex method to find an optimal solution.

35. Minimum-cost method; transportation simplex

35. Consider the following minimum-cost transportation problem:

Origin	Destination			Supply
	D_1	D_2	D_3	
O_1	6	8	8	250
O_2	18	12	14	150
O_3	8	12	10	100
Demand	150	200	150	

a. Use the minimum-cost method to find an initial feasible solution.
b. Use the transportation simplex method to find an optimal solution.
c. Using your solution to part (b), identify an alternative optimal solution.

36. Compare MODI and stepping-stone methods

36. Use the per-unit cost changes for each unoccupied cell shown in Table 7.15 to answer the following problem statements:
a. Consider the arc connecting Bedford and Chicago as a candidate for the incoming arc. Allocate 1 unit of flow, and make the necessary adjustments on the stepping-stone path to maintain feasibility. Compute the value of the new solution, and show that the change in value is exactly what had been indicated by the per-unit cost change obtained using the MODI method.
b. Repeat part (a) for the arc connecting York and Lexington.

37. Transportation formulation of transshipment problem

37. Refer again to the Contois Carpets problem for which the network representation is shown in Figure 7.12. This problem can also be formulated and solved as a transportation problem.
a. Develop a network representation of this as a transportation problem. (*Hint:* Eliminate the inventory arcs, and add arcs showing that quarterly production can be used to satisfy demand in the current quarter and all future quarters.)
b. Solve the problem using the transportation simplex method.

SELF TEST ▶

38. Consider Problem 12 once again. Using the Hungarian method, obtain the optimal solution.

38. Hungarian method

39. Refer once again to Problem 14. Using the Hungarian method, obtain the optimal solution.

40. Refer once again to Problem 15. Using the Hungarian method, find an optimal solution.

41. Use the Hungarian method to solve the Salisbury Discount, Inc., problem using the profit data in Table 7.34.

42. Use the Hungarian method to solve the Salisbury Discount, Inc., problem as described in Problem 17.

43. Refer to Problem 19. Use the Hungarian method to find an optimal solution.

Case Problem: Assigning Umpire Crews*

The American Baseball League consists of 14 professional baseball teams organized into two divisions: the Western Division, with Seattle, Oakland, California, Texas, Kansas City, Minnesota, and Chicago, and the Eastern Division, with Milwaukee, Detroit, Cleveland, Toronto, Baltimore, New York, and Boston.

In addition to the schedules for each team, the American League must determine the best way to assign the umpire crews to the various games played throughout the league. Umpire crews are assigned to specific home-team cities for the two-, three-, or four-game series in that city, but are not assigned on an individual-game basis. Since there are 14 American League teams, there can be as many as seven games (double-headers count as one game in assigning crews); hence, seven umpire crews must be assigned.

Several considerations are important in making the umpire crew assignments. Because of the amount of travel required, airline costs can be substantial. Thus, from a cost point of view, umpire crew assignments with minimum travel distances are desirable. However, a second consideration in the assignment of the umpire crews is that there should be a balance such that each crew works approximately the same number of games with each team and in each city. The considerations of minimizing travel distances and, at the same time, balancing the crew assignments among the teams and cities are in conflict.

In addition to the above considerations, a number of requirements must be satisfied. The most important of these are

1. A crew cannot travel from city A to city B if the last game in city A is a night game and the first game in city B is an afternoon game on the next day.
2. A crew cannot travel from a West Coast location (Seattle, Oakland, or California) to Chicago or any Eastern Division city without a day off.
3. Because of flight scheduling difficulties, a crew traveling into or out of Toronto must have a day off unless coming from or going to New York, Boston, Detroit, or Cleveland.
4. Any crew traveling from a night game in Seattle, Oakland, or California cannot be assigned to Kansas City or Texas for a game on the next day.
5. No crew should be assigned to the same team for more than two series in a row.

The umpire crews have already been scheduled for the first four series of the five-series schedule shown in Table 7.38. Table 7.39 summarizes the crew assignments for the first four series in the schedule and shows the pairings for the fifth series. The number next to each team identification

*The authors are indebted to James R. Evans, consultant to the American League, New York, N.Y., for providing this case problem.

Table 7.38 Segment of the American League Schedule Showing Five Series

		Home Team													
Series	Date	SEA	OAK	CAL	TEX	KC	MIN	CHI	MKE	DET	CLE	TOR	BAL	NY	BOS
1	Mon.		CAL*		BOS*		SEA		TOR*	NY*			CHI*		
	Tues.		CAL*		BOS*		SEA		TOR*	NY*	KC*		CHI*		
	Wed.		CAL		BOS*		SEA		TOR*	NY	KC*		CHI*		
2	Thurs.	DET*		MKE*	KC*						CHI*		TOR*		MIN*
	Fri.	DET*	NY*	MKE*	KC*						CHI*		TOR*		MIN*
	Sat.	DET*	NY	MKE*	KC*						CHI		TOR*		MIN*
	Sun.	DET	NY(2)	MKE	KC*						CHI		TOR		MIN*
3	Mon.	MKE*		NY*		BOS*							MIN*		
	Tues.	MKE*	DET*	NY*	CHI*	BOS*						CLE*	MIN*		
	Wed.	MKE*	DET*	NY*	CHI*	BOS*						CLE*	MIN*		
	Thurs.	MKE*	DET	NY*	CHI*							CLE*			
4	Fri.	NY*	MKE*	DET*	BAL*		CLE*	KC*				BOS*			
	Sat.	NY*	MKE	DET*	BAL*		CLE*	KC*				BOS			
	Sun.	NY*	MKE	DET	BAL*		CLE	KC				BOS			
5	Mon.					TEX*		CLE*		SEA*		BOS*			
	Tues.					TEX*	BOS*	CLE*	CAL*	SEA*		BAL*		OAK*	
	Wed.					TEX*	BOS*	CLE*	CAL*	SEA*		BAL*		OAK*	
	Thurs.					TEX*	BOS		CAL	SEA*		BAL*		OAK*	

*Denotes night game or early-evening start.   (2)Denotes doubleheader (two games in one day).

Table 7.39 Umpire Crew Assignments for the First Four Series

		Home Team													
Series		SEA	OAK	CAL	TEX	KC	MIN	CHI	MKE	DET	CLE	TOR	BAL	NY	BOS
1			CAL[5]		BOS[3]		SEA[7]		TOR[4]	NY[1]	KC[6]		CHI[2]		
2		DET[3]	NY[2]	MKE[7]	KC[5]						CHI[6]		TOR[4]		MIN[1]
3		MKE[2]	DET[7]	NY[3]	CHI[6]	BOS[5]						CLE[1]	MIN[4]		
4		NY[7]	MKE[3]	DET[2]	BAL[6]		CLE[5]	KC[4]				BOS[1]			
5						TEX	BOS	CLE	CAL	SEA		BAL		OAK	

Example: For the fourth series, umpire crew 1 is assigned to the Boston at Toronto series

Table 7.40

Cost Matrix for Umpire Crew
Assignments (Series 5)

Crew From	To						
	KC	MIN	CHI	MKE	DET	TOR	NY
SEA(7)	1825	1399	2007	1694	1939	2124	2421
OAK(3)	1498	1589	2125	1845	2079	2286	2586
CAL(2)	1363	1536	2035	1756	1979	2175	2475
TEX(6)	506	853	798	843	982	1186	1383
MIN(5)	394	0	334	297	528	780	1028
CHI(4)	403	334	0	74	235	430	740
TOR(1)	968	897	497	583	206	0	366

Note: The numbers in parentheses reference umpire crews.

indicates the umpire crew assigned for that pairing. For example, for the fourth series, crew 1 is assigned to the Boston–Toronto games, crew 2 is assigned to the Detroit–California games, and so on.

Table 7.40 shows the distances from the cities where the fourth series is being played to the cities where the fifth series is being played. There are some other issues league management would like considered in assigning crews to the next series. Over the past nine series, crew 4 has umpired three series with Kansas City and three series with Milwaukee. Also, crew 5 has not been assigned to any games with New York, Toronto, or Detroit over the past month.

Managerial Report

Prepare a written recommendation to league management concerning the assignment of umpire crews to the fifth series that will minimize the distance traveled.

Case Problem: Distribution System Design

The Darby Company manufactures and distributes meters used to measure electric power consumption. The company started with a small production plant in El Paso and gradually built up a customer base throughout Texas. A distribution center was established in Ft. Worth, Texas, and later, as business expanded to the north, a second distribution center was established in Santa Fe, New Mexico.

The El Paso plant was expanded when the company began marketing its meters in Arizona, California, Nevada, and Utah. With the growth of the West Coast business, the Darby Company opened a third distribution center in Las Vegas and just two years ago opened a second production plant in San Bernardino, California.

Manufacturing costs differ between the company's production plants. The cost of each meter produced at the El Paso plant is $10.50. The San Bernardino plant utilizes newer and more efficient equipment; as a result, manufacturing costs are $0.50 per meter less than at the El Paso plant.

Due to the company's rapid growth, not much attention has been paid to the efficiency of the distribution system, and Darby's management has decided it is time to address this issue. As noted above, there are two plants and three distribution centers. The cost of shipping a meter from each plant to each distribution center is shown in Table 7.41.

The quarterly production capacity is 30,000 meters at the older El Paso plant and 20,000 meters at the San Bernardino plant. Note that no shipments are allowed from the San Bernardino plant to the Ft. Worth distribution center.

The company serves nine customer zones from the three distribution centers. The forecast of the number of meters needed in each customer zone for the next quarter is shown in Table 7.42.

The per-unit cost of shipping from each distribution center to each customer zone is given in Table 7.43; note that some of the distribution centers cannot serve certain customer zones.

Table 7.41

Shipping Cost Per Unit from
Production Plants to Distribution
Centers (in $)

| | Distribution Center | | |
Plant	Ft. Worth	Santa Fe	Las Vegas
El Paso	3.20	2.20	4.20
San Bernardino	—	3.90	1.20

Table 7.42

Quarterly Demand Forecast

Customer Zone	Demand (meters)
Dallas	6300
San Antonio	4880
Wichita	2130
Kansas City	1210
Denver	6120
Salt Lake City	4830
Phoenix	2750
Los Angeles	8580
San Diego	4460

Table 7.43

Shipping Cost from the Distribution
Centers to the Customer Zones

| | Customer Zone | | | | | | | | |
Distribution Center	Dallas	San Antonio	Wichita	Kansas City	Denver	Salt Lake City	Phoenix	Los Angeles	San Diego
Ft. Worth	0.3	2.1	3.1	4.4	6.0	—	—	—	—
Santa Fe	5.2	5.4	4.5	6.0	2.7	4.7	3.4	3.3	2.7
Las Vegas	—	—	—	—	5.4	3.3	2.4	2.1	2.5

In the current distribution system, demand at the Dallas, San Antonio, Wichita, and Kansas City customer zones is satisfied by shipments from the Ft. Worth distribution center. In a similar manner, the Denver, Salt Lake City, and Phoenix customer zones are served by the Santa Fe distribution center, and the Los Angeles and San Diego customer zones are served by the Las Vegas distribution center. To determine how many units to ship from each plant, the quarterly demand forecasts are aggregated at the distribution centers, and a transportation model is used to minimize the cost of shipping from the production plants to the distribution centers.

Managerial Report

You have been called in to make recommendations for improving the distribution system. Your report should address, but not be limited to, the following issues:

1. If the company does not change its current distribution strategy, what will its distribution costs be for the following quarter?
2. Suppose the company is willing to consider dropping the distribution center limitations; that is, customers could be served by any of the distribution centers. Can costs be reduced? By how much?

3. The company wants to explore the possibility of satisfying some of the customer demand directly from the production plants. In particular, the per-unit shipping cost is $0.30 from San Bernardino to Los Angeles and $0.70 from San Bernardino to San Diego. The per-unit cost for direct shipments from El Paso to San Antonio is $3.50. Can distribution costs be further reduced by considering these direct plant–customer shipments?

4. Over the next 5 years, Darby is anticipating moderate growth (around 5000 meters) to the North and West. Would you recommend that they consider plant expansion at this time?

MANAGEMENT SCIENCE IN PRACTICE

Optimal Decision Systems, Inc.*
Cincinnati, Ohio

Optimal Decision Systems, Inc. (ODS), is a management consulting firm that specializes in the development and implementation of decision support systems for manufacturing, transportation, and distribution applications. ODS was formed in 1978 and has a clientele that includes many Fortune 500 companies.

Systems developed by ODS use computerized models to provide managers with a menu of "good" alternatives from which the "best" alternative can be selected. Several examples of the types of problems for which ODS has developed decision support systems are listed below.

1. Locating manufacturing and distribution facilities
2. Designing sales territories, including how various distribution centers should supply the territories
3. Routing and scheduling truck fleets
4. Scheduling production systems to minimize inventory costs while maintaining desired service levels
5. Allocating capital to various investment opportunities

The majority of these applications (80%) have involved the development and implementation of large-scale mathematical programming models (linear programming, network, or mixed-integer linear programming models). Probability models and simulation have been the primary quantitative methodologies employed in the remaining applications. In addition, in almost every application, statistical analysis has played a heavy support role, particularly in the estimation of the parameters of the models.

Truck Fleet Management

The Fleet Management System (FMS) was developed by ODS for the management of private truck fleets. The heart of this system is a transshipment model that schedules and routes the company fleet over a user-specified time horizon (usually 1–7 days) in a way that optimizes one of the following measures of performance:

1. Savings over the use of common carrier truck fleets
2. Minimum total cost
3. Maximum total net revenue
4. Maximum load ratio (ratio of loaded miles to total miles driven by the fleet)
5. Some weighted combination of the above

In determining the optimal solution, all user-specified constraints on the operation of the truck fleet are simultaneously satisfied. Examples of such constraints are

1. Specified load movement, pickup, and delivery times
2. Minimum or maximum levels of utilization of the fleet
3. Operating hours at pickup points and delivery points
4. Restrictions on driver work hours

The Fleet Management System (FMS) accurately models the operation of a fleet, and thus, the results of the optimization are extremely useful input to strategic (long-term), tactical (intermediate-term), and operational (short-term) planning. Some of the strategic issues that can be addressed by FMS are fleet sizing, the location of driver domiciles, equipment selection and mix, alternative operating practices (one-shift versus two-shift operation, use of double teams and/or trailer pools), and location of maintenance and refueling facilities. Tactical issues might include the timing and level of seasonal capacity such as leased drivers and equipment, the determination of which freight should be handled by common carrier and by private fleet, the determination of appropriate internal pricing mechanisms, the timing of the increase or decrease of capacity by driver domicile, and/or the determination of scheduling rules and procedures that yield efficient driver tours. The primary issue of operational planning is the determination of an efficient work tour for each driver.

A Transshipment Model for Truck Fleet Management

The primary function of the Fleet Management System is to determine an optimal schedule and route for each driver over the appropriate time horizon. For illustrative purposes, assume that all drivers (each with tractor and trailer) are located at a single domicile and that the objective is to maximize the savings that can be obtained using the private fleet over common carriers for the same shipments. The system assumes the structure of a transshipment model. Capacity nodes represent the location of a driver at a particular point in time. Demand nodes represent the load origin, which requires a truck to be made available for a load pickup. A driver at a capacity node is assigned to an arc connecting to a demand node. For each unit of flow on this arc (each driver assigned), the incurred cost is the sum of the cost to travel to the location of the load origin plus any holding or delay

—Continued on next page

---

*The authors are indebted to Richard A. Murphy and Thomas E. Thompson, Optimal Decision Systems, Inc., for providing this application.

—Continued from previous page

costs that will be incurred if the driver experiences idle time. Arcs in the transshipment network are then used to assign the picked-up load to delivery locations. The net contribution on these delivery arcs is a savings the company realizes by using its own fleet of trucks rather than employing common carriers. This savings is the common carrier cost less the fuel, labor, idle time, and any other costs incurred by the company in making its own deliveries. Note that on completion of the delivery, the driver's location is defined as a capacity node, and the driver thus becomes available for reassignment at another point in time. Through the use of this transshipment model, the flow of the company's fleet of trucks can be scheduled over the time period of interest.

An Application and Results

The Fleet Management System was used to develop schedules for a Fortune 500 manufacturing company that operates a private fleet of over 100 drivers and tractors. The fleet is used primarily to move raw materials into and out of the company's manufacturing facilities located in over 40 locations throughout the United States and Canada. The fleet is also used to deliver finished goods to high-priority customer accounts where service levels are critical for continued business with the customer. Prior to implementation of the Fleet Management System, the fleet had been dispatched and managed on a purely manual basis, and the company was concerned about the high cost of the truck fleet operation.

The company's objective was to use the Fleet Management System to identify a set of short- and long-range changes in the operation that could yield significant improvements in cost and efficiency. In this case, an annual saving of $1.9 million was possible by improving freight selection and by scheduling the trucks more efficiently (with fewer empty miles). In addition, specific recommendations were made to alter the size, location, and equipment mix of the truck fleet.

Questions

1. Draw a network that shows the transshipment model for truck fleet management.
2. What are the units of supply and demand at the nodes in your network? What are the units of flow over the shipping routes?

CHAPTER 8

Integer Linear Programming

In this chapter we turn our attention to a class of problems that are modeled as linear programs with the additional requirement that some or all of the decision variables must be integer. Such problems are called *integer linear programming* problems. The use of integer variables provides additional modeling flexibility. As a result, the number of practical applications that can be addressed with linear programming methodology is enlarged. The cost of the added flexibility is that problems involving integer variables are usually much more difficult to solve. In fact, although linear programming problems involving several thousand continuous variables can be routinely solved with commercial linear programming codes, the solution of integer linear programming problems involving less than 100 variables can cause great difficulty. However, experienced management scientists can usually identify the types of integer linear programs that are easiest to solve; in such cases, problems with hundreds (and sometimes thousands) of integer variables can be solved with available computer codes such as IBM's MPSX-MIP and LINDO.

The plan of this chapter is to provide an applications-oriented introduction to integer linear programming. After a short section describing the different types of integer linear programming models, we show how a graphical procedure can be used to solve problems involving two decision variables. We then discuss, in some detail, two common integer linear programming applications: capital budgeting and distribution system design. The next section concerns the computer solution of integer linear programs. An application involving bank location is introduced, formulated, and solved using LINDO/PC. Finally, we have included a section detailing the branch-and-bound solution procedure for integer linear programs with more than two variables. This solution procedure is employed by almost all commercial integer linear programming computer codes and is regarded as the most efficient general-purpose solution procedure.

As noted in Chapter 7, the LP solution of network flow problems (transportation, assignment, and transshipment) will automatically be integer. No special procedures are necessary to obtain integer solutions.

8.1 Types of Integer Linear Programming Models

The only difference between the problems studied in this chapter and the ones studied in the earlier chapters on linear programming is that some of the variables are required to be integer. If all of the variables are required to be integer, we say we have an *all-integer linear program.* Stated below is a two-variable, all-integer linear programming model.

$$\text{Max} \quad 2x_1 + 3x_2$$

s.t.

$$3x_1 + 3x_2 \leq 12$$

$$\tfrac{2}{3}x_1 + 1x_2 \leq 4$$

$$1x_1 + 2x_2 \leq 6$$

$$x_1, x_2 \geq 0 \text{ and integer}$$

You will note that if the phrase "and integer" is dropped from the above model, we are left with the familiar two-variable linear program. The linear program that results from dropping the integer requirements for the decision variables is referred to as the *LP* (linear programming) *Relaxation* of the integer linear program.

If some, but not necessarily all, of the decision variables in a problem are required to be integer, we say we have a *mixed-integer linear program.* The following is a two-variable, mixed-integer linear program:

$$\text{Max} \quad 3x_1 + 4x_2$$

s.t.

$$-1x_1 + 2x_2 \leq 8$$

$$1x_1 + 2x_2 \leq 12$$

$$2x_1 + 1x_2 \leq 16$$

$$x_1, x_2 \geq 0 \text{ and } x_2 \text{ integer}$$

You should now be able to recognize the various types of integer programs and their LP Relaxations. Try Problem 1.

The LP Relaxation of the above mixed-integer linear program is obtained by dropping the requirement that x_2 be integer. Sometimes the variables required to assume integer values in a problem are called *discrete variables;* the others are said to be *continuous.*

In most practical applications of integer linear programming, the integer variables are only permitted to assume the values 0 or 1. In such cases, we say we have a *binary* or a *0–1 integer linear program.* Such *0–1* problems may be of either the all-integer or the mixed-integer type. The capital budgeting, distribution system design, and bank location problems discussed in later sections of this chapter all make use of *0–1* variables.

In practice, most integer problems involve only 0–1 variables. Such variables provide a way to handle situations involving either/or types of considerations—for example, invest/ do not invest, locate a plant/do not locate a plant, and so on.

8.2 Graphical Solution

Security Realty Investors currently has $1,365,000 available for new rental property investments. After an initial screening, Security has reduced the investment alternatives to a series of townhouses and a group of apartment buildings in a large apartment complex. The townhouses can be purchased in blocks of three for the price of $195,000 per block, but there are only four blocks of townhouses available for purchase at this time. Each building in the apartment complex contains 12 dwelling units and sells for $273,000. The individual apartment buildings can be purchased separately, and the complex developer has agreed to build as many 12-unit buildings as Security Realty would like to purchase.

Security's property manager is free to devote 140 hours per month to these investments. Each block of townhouses will require 4 hours of the property manager's time each month, while each apartment building will require 40 hours per month. The yearly cash flow after deducting mortgage payments and operating expenses, is estimated at $2000 per block of townhouses and $3000 per apartment building. Security would like to allocate its investment funds to apartment buildings and townhouses such that the yearly cash flow is maximized.

To develop an appropriate mathematical model for this problem, let us introduce the following definitions for the decision variables:

$$x_1 = \text{number of blocks of townhouses purchased}$$
$$x_2 = \text{number of apartment buildings purchased}$$

The objective function, measuring cash flow in thousands of dollars, can be written as

$$\text{Max} \quad 2x_1 + 3x_2$$

There are three constraints that must be satisfied:

$$195x_1 + 273x_2 \leq 1365 \quad \text{Funds available in thousands of dollars}$$

$$4x_1 + 40x_2 \leq 140 \quad \text{Manager's time in hours}$$

$$x_1 \quad\quad\quad \leq 4 \quad \text{Townhouse availability in blocks}$$

These variables must be restricted to nonnegative values. Also, since fractional values for the blocks of townhouses and/or number of apartment buildings are unacceptable, the decision variables x_1 and x_2 must be integer. Thus, we see that the proper model for the Security Realty problem is the following all-integer linear program:

$$\text{Max} \quad 2x_1 + 3x_2$$
$$\text{s.t.}$$
$$195x_1 + 273x_2 \leq 1365$$
$$4x_1 + 40x_2 \leq 140$$
$$x_1 \quad\quad\quad \leq 4$$
$$x_1, x_2 \geq 0 \text{ and integer}$$

If the problem has only less-than-or-equal-to constraints with positive coefficients on the decision variables, rounding down the solution to the LP Relaxation will always produce a feasible integer solution. Rounding down is discussed further in Section 8.5.

A first approach to solving such a problem might be to drop the integer requirements and solve the resulting LP Relaxation. You might then round the decision variables in an attempt to find the optimal solution to the integer linear program. However, as we shall see, such an approach may not yield the optimal solution. In fact, rounding values of the decision variables can sometimes result in an infeasible solution.

The linear program resulting from dropping the integer requirements for the decision variables (the LP Relaxation) is written as follows:

$$\text{Max} \quad 2x_1 + 3x_2$$

s.t.

$$195x_1 + 273x_2 \leq 1365$$

$$4x_1 + 40x_2 \leq 140$$

$$x_1 \leq 4$$

$$x_1, x_2 \geq 0$$

The optimal solution to the LP Relaxation (see Figure 8.1) is given by $x_1 = 2.44$ and $x_2 = 3.26$. The objective function value for this solution is 14.66, corresponding to a cash flow of \$14,660. However, this solution is not feasible for the integer linear programming problem since the decision variables assume fractional values.

Rounding the decision variables to the nearest integer value yields a solution of $x_1 = 2$ and $x_2 = 3$ for an objective function value of 13, or a \$13,000 annual cash flow. In Figure 8.2 we show the feasible solution points that provide integer values for x_1 and x_2. Is the rounded solution of $x_1 = 2$ and $x_2 = 3$ the optimal integer solution? The answer is no! As can be seen in Figure 8.2, the optimal integer solution is $x_1 = 4$ and $x_2 = 2$, with an objective function value of 14.00, or a \$14,000 annual cash flow. For Security Realty, the approach of rounding the linear programming solution to the nearest integer solution was not a good strategy. The rounded solution of $x_1 = 2$ and $x_2 = 3$ would have cost Security Realty \$1000 a year in cash flow.

In problems where the variables assume large values (e.g., cases of cereal produced), rounding the *linear programming* solution is usually acceptable. Very little deviation from feasibility or optimality will be caused.

Figure 8.1
Graphical Solution to the LP Relaxation of the Security Realty Problem

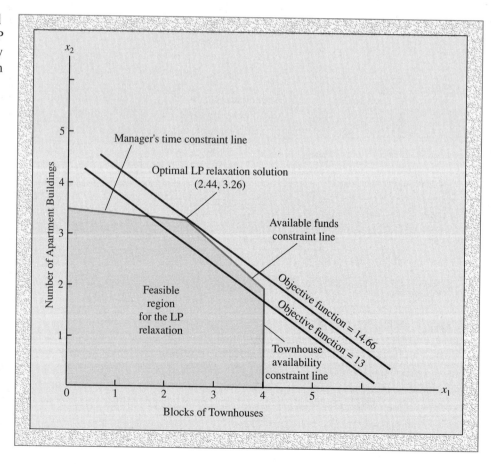

Figure 8.2
The Integer Solution to the
Security Realty Problem

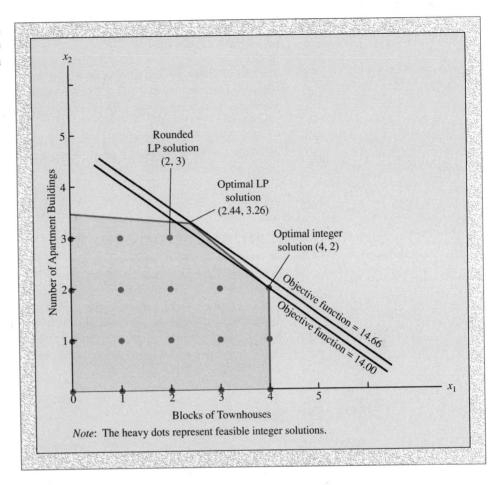

Note: The heavy dots represent feasible integer solutions.

Try Problem 2 for practice in solving
an integer programming problem
graphically.

As can be seen from the Security Realty problem, the graphical procedure for solving two-variable integer linear programs is quite similar to the graphical procedure for solving linear programs. First, a graph of the feasible region for the LP Relaxation is constructed. Then the feasible integer points are denoted by heavy dots. The integer solution point on the best objective function line can then be located; this point is the optimal solution to the integer linear programming program.

An important observation can be made from our analysis of the Security Realty Investors problem; it has to do with the relationship between the value of the optimal integer solution and the value of the optimal LP Relaxation solution. This observation is stated for maximization problems[1] as property 1.

Property 1 is the basis for
establishing bounds in the
branch-and-bound solution
procedure discussed in Section 8.5.

PROPERTY **1**

The value of the optimal solution to any integer or mixed-integer linear program involving maximization yields a value *less than* or *equal to* the value of the optimal solution to its LP Relaxation.

---

[1]For minimization problems, property 1 would be stated with "greater than or equal to" substituted for "less than or equal to."

This property means that an *upper bound* on the value of any maximization inte- ger or mixed-integer linear program can be found by solving its associated LP Relaxation. This property can be seen in Figure 8.2. The optimal LP Relaxation solution is on the highest objective function line and has a value of $14.66. The optimal integer solution is on a lower objective function line and has a smaller value, $14.00. As we shall see in Section 8.5, property 1 is used in the branch-and-bound solution procedure for solving integer linear programs.

We note in closing this section that mixed-integer linear programs with two-decision variables can be solved by a simple modification of the graphical procedure outlined above.

Try Problem 5 for practice in solving a mixed-integer linear programming problem graphically.

8.3 Applications of Integer Linear Programming

In the previous section we saw an illustration of an all-integer linear program: the Security Realty Investors problem. In this section we discuss two applications involving *0–1* or binary integer variables: the capital budgeting and distribution system design problems. We have chosen these applications because they represent two areas in which integer linear programming has been used widely in practice, and through them you should begin to gain an appreciation of the flexibility in model development provided by *0–1* variables.

Capital Budgeting

Capital budgeting is an area where management science has often led to considerable savings and/or increased profits. To provide an idea of what is involved in capital budgeting, let us consider the Ice-Cold Refrigerator problem and develop a linear programming formulation for it.

The Ice-Cold Refrigerator Company can invest capital funds in a variety of projects that have varying capital requirements over the next 4 years. Faced with limited capital resources, the company must select the most profitable projects and budgets for the capital expenditures. The estimated present values of the projects, the capital require- ments, and the available capital projections[2] are shown in Table 8.1.

_____
[2]The estimated present value is the net return for the project discounted back to the beginning of year 1.

Table 8.1

Project Present Values, Capital Requirements, and Available Capital Projections for the Ice-Cold Refrigerator Company

Project	Estimated Present Value ($)	Capital Requirements ($)			
		Year 1	Year 2	Year 3	Year 4
Plant expansion	90,000	15,000	20,000	20,000	15,000
Warehouse expansion	40,000	10,000	15,000	20,000	5,000
New machinery	10,000	10,000	0	0	4,000
New product research	37,000	15,000	10,000	10,000	10,000
Available capital funds		40,000	50,000	40,000	35,000

The following definitions are chosen for the decision variables:

$x_1 = 1$ if the plant expansion project is accepted; 0 if rejected
$x_2 = 1$ if the warehouse expansion project is accepted; 0 if rejected
$x_3 = 1$ if the new machinery project is accepted; 0 if rejected
$x_4 = 1$ if the new product research project is accepted; 0 if rejected

The linear programming relaxation of this capital budgeting problem has a separate constraint for each year's available funds and a separate constraint requiring each variable to be less than or equal to 1. The linear programming relaxation is given below (monetary units are expressed in thousands of dollars).

$$\text{Max} \quad 90x_1 + 40x_2 + 10x_3 + 37x_4$$

s.t.

$$15x_1 + 10x_2 + 10x_3 + 15x_4 \leq 40$$
$$20x_1 + 15x_2 \qquad\quad + 10x_4 \leq 50$$
$$20x_1 + 20x_2 \qquad\quad + 10x_4 \leq 40$$
$$15x_1 + 5x_2 + 4x_3 + 10x_4 \leq 35$$
$$x_1 \qquad\qquad\qquad\qquad \leq 1$$
$$x_2 \qquad\qquad\qquad \leq 1$$
$$x_3 \qquad\quad \leq 1$$
$$x_4 \leq 1$$
$$x_1, x_2, x_3, x_4 \geq 0$$

The optimal solution to this linear program is $x_1 = 1$, $x_2 = 0.5$, $x_3 = 0.5$, and $x_4 = 1$, with a total estimated present value of \$152,000. The difficulty with a linear programming approach to the capital budgeting problem is now readily apparent. Unless it is possible to implement the warehouse expansion and new machinery projects in 50% increments, the current solution is not feasible. Thus, some adjustment in the linear programming solution, such as rounding x_2 and x_3 (possibly leading to a nonoptimal solution), must be made prior to implementation.

The *0–1* integer linear programming formulation of the Ice-Cold Refrigerator Company problem is shown below:

$$\text{Max} \quad 90x_1 + 40x_2 + 10x_3 + 37x_4$$

s.t.

$$15x_1 + 10x_2 + 10x_3 + 15x_4 \leq 40$$
$$20x_1 + 15x_2 \qquad\quad + 10x_4 \leq 50$$
$$20x_1 + 20x_2 \qquad\quad + 10x_4 \leq 40$$
$$15x_1 + 5x_2 + 4x_3 + 10x_4 \leq 35$$
$$x_1, x_2, x_3, x_4 = 0, 1$$

The optimal integer solution[3] is given by $x_1 = 1$, $x_2 = 1$, $x_3 = 1$, and $x_4 = 0$, with a total estimated present value of $140,000. We note that this optimal solution could not have been discovered by simply rounding the linear programming solution. In fact, the best feasible solution that can be found by considering all possible roundings of the fractional variables in the linear programming solution is $x_1 = 1$, $x_2 = 0$, $x_3 = 0$, $x_4 = 1$, with a total estimated present value of $127,000. This is substantially less than the value of the optimal integer solution to the capital budgeting problem.

The ability to avoid fractional values is one of two main reasons that an integer programming formulation (as opposed to a linear programming formulation) is usually preferred for capital budgeting problems. The second reason most management scientists prefer a *0–1* integer programming model for the capital budgeting problem is the flexibility provided in developing certain nonbudgetary constraints. These constraints are often important in capital budgeting problems and can be formulated only through the use of *0–1* (sometimes called logical) variables.

Multiple-Choice and Mutually Exclusive Constraints

The modeling flexibility provided by *0–1* variables is illustrated in this subsection.

Suppose that instead of one warehouse expansion project, the Ice-Cold Refrigerator Company actually has three warehouse expansion projects under consideration. Assume one of the warehouses *must* be expanded because of increasing product demand, but there is not sufficient new demand to make expansion of more than one warehouse necessary. The following variable definitions and *multiple-choice constraint* could be incorporated into the previous *0–1* integer linear programming model to reflect this situation. Let

$x_2 = 1$ if the original warehouse expansion project is accepted; 0 if rejected
$x_5 = 1$ if the second warehouse expansion project is accepted; 0 if rejected
$x_6 = 1$ if the third warehouse expansion project is accepted; 0 if rejected

The multiple-choice constraint reflecting the requirement that one and only one of these projects may be selected is written as follows:

$$x_2 + x_5 + x_6 = 1$$

It is easy to see why this is called a multiple-choice constraint. Since x_2, x_5, and x_6 are allowed to assume only the values 0 or 1, one and only one of these projects must be selected from among the three choices. Note that if fractional values (as in linear programming) were allowed for the decision variables, we could not enforce the requirement of selecting one and only one project (e.g., $x_2 = \frac{1}{3}$, $x_5 = \frac{1}{3}$, $x_6 = \frac{1}{3}$ would satisfy the constraint).

If it had not been required that one warehouse be expanded, then our multiple-choice constraint could be modified as follows:

$$x_2 + x_5 + x_6 \leq 1$$

This modification allows for the case of no warehouse expansion ($x_2 = x_5 = x_6 = 0$), but does not permit more than one warehouse to be expanded. This type of constraint is often called a *mutually exclusive constraint*.

---

[3]This solution was found using the branch-and-bound solution procedure that will be presented in Section 8.5. (Problem 19 at the end of this chapter asks you to develop the branch-and-bound solution of this problem.)

k Out of *n* Alternatives Constraint

An extension of the notion of a multiple-choice constraint can be used to model situations in which *k out of a set of n* projects must be selected. Suppose x_2, x_5, x_6, x_7, and x_8 represent five potential warehouse expansion projects, and it is necessary to accept two of the five projects. The following constraint ensures satisfaction of this new requirement:

$$x_2 + x_5 + x_6 + x_7 + x_8 = 2$$

If it is required that no more than two of the projects be selected, we would use the following less-than-or-equal-to constraint:

$$x_2 + x_5 + x_6 + x_7 + x_8 \leq 2$$

Once again, each of the above variables must be restricted to *0–1* values.

Conditional and Corequisite Constraints

Sometimes the acceptance of one project is conditional on the acceptance of another. For example, suppose for the Ice-Cold Refrigerator Company that the warehouse expansion project was conditional on the plant expansion project. That is, the company will not consider expanding the warehouse unless the plant is expanded. With x_1 representing plant expansion and x_2 representing warehouse expansion, the following *conditional constraint* could be introduced to enforce this requirement:

$$x_2 \leq x_1$$

or

$$x_2 - x_1 \leq 0$$

Since both x_1 and x_2 are required to be 0 or 1, we see that whenever x_1 is 0, x_2 will be forced to 0. When x_1 is 1, x_2 is also allowed to be 1; thus, both the plant and the warehouse can be expanded. However, we note that the above constraint does not force the warehouse expansion project (x_2) to be accepted if the plant expansion project (x_1) is accepted.

If it were required that the warehouse expansion project be accepted whenever the plant expansion project was, and vice versa, then we would say that x_1 and x_2 represented *corequisite* projects. To model such a situation, we simply write the above constraint as an equality

$$x_2 = x_1$$

Try Problem 7 for practice with the modeling flexibility provided by *0–1* variables.

or

$$x_2 - x_1 = 0$$

This constraint forces x_1 and x_2 to take on the same value.

A Cautionary Note on Sensitivity Analysis

Sensitivity analysis is often more critical for integer linear programming problems than for linear programming problems. A very small change in one of the coefficients in the constraints can cause a relatively large change in the value of the optimal solution. To see why this is so, consider the following integer programming model of a simple capital budgeting problem involving four projects and a budgetary constraint for a single time period:

$$\text{Max} \quad 40x_1 + 60x_2 + 70x_3 + 160x_4$$

$$\text{s.t.}$$

$$16x_1 + 35x_2 + 45x_3 + 85x_4 \leq 100$$

$$x_1, x_2, x_3, x_4 = 0, 1$$

The optimal solution to this problem can be found by enumerating the alternatives. It is $x_1 = 1$, $x_2 = 1$, $x_3 = 1$, and $x_4 = 0$, with an objective function value of $170. However, note that if the budget available is increased by $1 (from 100 to 101), the optimal solution changes to $x_1 = 1$, $x_2 = 0$, $x_3 = 0$, and $x_4 = 1$, with an objective function value of $200. That is, one additional dollar in the budget would lead to a $30 increase in the return. Surely management, when faced with such a situation, would increase the budget by $1. Because of the extreme sensitivity of the value of the optimal solution to the constraint coefficients, practitioners usually recommend resolving the integer linear program several times with slight variations in the coefficients before attempting to choose an optimal solution for implementation.

> Dual prices cannot be used for sensitivity analysis like they are for linear programs. Multiple computer runs are usually necessary for sensitivity analysis of integer linear programs.

Distribution System Design

> A network description of the problem is a helpful way to introduce the distribution system design problem.

In Chapter 7 the following linear programming formulation for the transportation problem was developed:

$$\text{Min} \quad \sum_{i=1}^{m} \sum_{j=1}^{n} c_{ij} x_{ij}$$

$$\text{s.t.}$$

$$\sum_{j=1}^{n} x_{ij} \leq s_i \quad i = 1, 2, \ldots, m \quad \text{Supply}$$

$$\sum_{i=1}^{m} x_{ij} = d_j \quad j = 1, 2, \ldots, n \quad \text{Demand}$$

$$x_{ij} \geq 0 \quad \text{for all } i \text{ and } j$$

where

i = index for origins, $i = 1, 2, \ldots, m$
j = index for destinations, $j = 1, 2, \ldots, n$
x_{ij} = number of units shipped from origin i to destination j
c_{ij} = cost per unit of shipping from origin i to destination j
s_i = supply or capacity in units at origin i
d_j = demand in units at destination j

In the transportation problem, it is assumed that the origins and destinations are fixed. Consequently, the problem is to determine how much of the product to ship from each origin to each destination to minimize the total transportation cost. However, in more general distribution system design problems, it is necessary to select the best locations for the origins as well as the amounts to ship from each origin to each destination.

Suppose the origins represent m potential locations for plants with capacities s_i and the destinations represent n retail outlets with demand d_j. A more complex distribution system design problem must now be solved. If site i is selected for a plant location, there will be a fixed cost associated with plant operation and then a variable cost associated with the number of units shipped from plant i to the various retail outlets. On the other hand, if site i is not selected, then there is no fixed cost, and no units can be shipped from site i. The introduction of one integer $0-1$ variable for each potential plant location allows us to develop a mixed-integer linear programming model for this distribution system design problem. Let

$y_i = 1$ if a plant is constructed at site i; 0 if not
f_i = fixed cost of constructing a plant at site i with capacity s_i

To represent the constraint that nothing can be shipped from site i if a plant is not selected, the supply constraints in the transportation model are modified as follows:

$$\sum_{j=1}^{n} x_{ij} \leq s_i y_i \qquad i = 1, 2, \ldots, m$$

The use of $0-1$ variables allows us to formulate and solve more complete distribution system design problems than those solved in Chapter 7.

or

$$\sum_{j=1}^{n} x_{ij} - s_i y_i \leq 0 \quad i = 1, 2, \ldots, m$$

Also, another term must be added to the objective function to represent the fixed cost of plant operation at each site selected:

$$\text{Fixed cost of plant operation } = \sum_{i=1}^{m} f_i y_i$$

The complete model for our distribution system design problem can now be written as

$$\text{Min } \sum_{i=1}^{m} \sum_{j=1}^{n} c_{ij} x_{ij} + \sum_{i=1}^{m} f_i y_i$$

s.t.

$$\sum_{j=1}^{n} x_{ij} - s_i y_i \leq 0 \qquad i = 1, 2, \ldots, m \quad \text{Plant capacities}$$

$$\sum_{i=1}^{m} x_{ij} = d_j \qquad j = 1, 2, \ldots, n \quad \text{Demand at retail outlets}$$

$$x_{ij} \geq 0 \qquad \text{for all } i \text{ and } j$$

$$y_i = 0, 1 \qquad i = 1, 2, \ldots, m$$

Note that when $y_i = 1$ in this model, it represents a plant being opened at site i. Thus, the fixed cost f_i gets added to the objective function, and the ith plant capacity constraint permits an amount s_i to be shipped. When $y_i = 0$, no fixed cost for plant i is added to the objective function, and the ith plant capacity constraint does not allow anything to be shipped.

This basic model[4] can be expanded to accommodate distribution systems involving shipments from plants, to warehouses, to retail outlets, and multiple products. Using the special properties of $0-1$ variables, it can also be expanded to accommodate a variety of configuration constraints on the plant locations. For example, suppose site 1 were in Dallas and site 2 in Fort Worth. A company might not want to locate plants in both Dallas and Fort Worth because the cities are so close together. To prevent this, the following constraint can be added to the model:

$$y_1 + y_2 \leq 1$$

This constraint is an example of the mutually exclusive constraint discussed in the previous subsection. It allows either y_1 or y_2 to equal 1, but not both. If we had written the constraint as an equality, it would be the same as the multiple-choice constraint we encountered in the capital budgeting problem. Other constraints such as the conditional or corequisite constraint can be introduced to satisfy managerially specified requirements on the configuration of plant locations.

Try Problem 11 for practice in formulating a distribution system design problem involving 0–1 variables.

NOTES & COMMENTS

1. The general linear programming formulation of the assignment problem (see Chapter 7) is really a $0-1$ integer linear program. However, the special structure of the assignment problem allows the problem to be solved as a regular linear program and still obtain integer values for the decision variables.

2. The optimal solution to a transportation or transshipment problem with integer values for the supply and demand nodes will always be integer valued. Thus, these problems can be modeled as general linear programs or as integer programs.

8.4 Computer Solution

As mentioned in the chapter introduction, computer packages for solving integer linear programs are now widely available. Such codes are generally reliable for problems involving up to 100 or so integer variables and have often been used to solve specially structured problems with a few thousand variables.

Most of the general-purpose codes use a linear-programming-based branch-and-bound solution procedure similar to the one described in Section 8.5. While the branch-and-bound solution procedure can be used to solve small problems by hand, in practice a computer code is needed to solve integer linear programs. In this section we will show how another application of integer programming can be formulated and solved using LINDO/PC.

Most computer packages that solve all-integer programs solve mixed-integer and linear programs as well.

---

[4]For computational reasons, it is usually preferable to replace the m plant capacity constraints with mn shipping route capacity constraints of the form $x_{ij} \leq \text{Min} \{s_i \, d_j\} \, y_i$ for $i = 1, \ldots, m$ and $j = 1, \ldots, n$. The coefficient for y_i in each of these constraints is the smaller of the origin capacity or the destination demand. These additional constraints often cause the solution of the LP Relaxation to be integer.

A Bank Location Application

The long-range planning department for the Ohio Trust Company is considering expanding its operation into a 20-county region in northeastern Ohio (see Figure 8.3). Currently, Ohio Trust does not have a principal place of business in any of the 20 counties under consideration. According to the banking laws in Ohio, if a banking firm establishes a principal place of business (PPB) in any county, then branch banks can be established in that county and in any adjacent county. However, to establish a new principal place of business, Ohio Trust must either obtain approval for a new bank from the state's superintendent of banks or purchase an existing bank.

Table 8.2 lists the 20 counties in the region together with the adjacent counties, and from it we can see that Ashtabula County is adjacent to Lake, Geauga, and Trumbull counties; Lake County is adjacent to Ashtabula, Cuyahoga, and Geauga counties; and so on.

As an initial step in its planning, Ohio Trust would like to determine the minimum number of PPBs necessary to do business throughout the 20-county region. A *0–1* integer programming model can be used to solve this problem for Ohio Trust. Let us define the following variable:

$$x_i = 1 \text{ if a PPB is established in county } i; 0 \text{ otherwise}$$

Figure 8.3
The 20-County Area in Northeastern Ohio

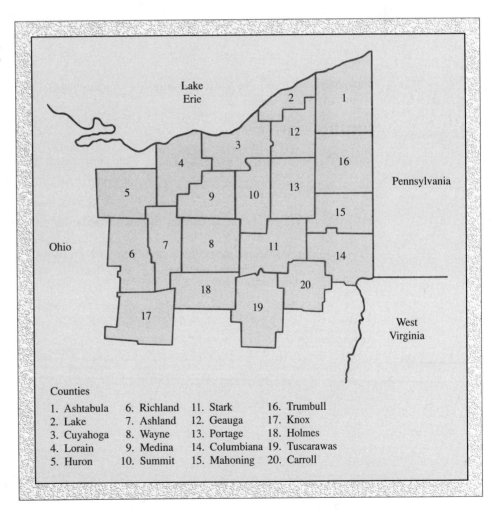

Counties

1. Ashtabula	6. Richland	11. Stark	16. Trumbull
2. Lake	7. Ashland	12. Geauga	17. Knox
3. Cuyahoga	8. Wayne	13. Portage	18. Holmes
4. Lorain	9. Medina	14. Columbiana	19. Tuscarawas
5. Huron	10. Summit	15. Mahoning	20. Carroll

Table 8.2
Counties in the Ohio Trust Expansion Region

Counties Under Consideration	Adjacent Counties (by Number)
1. Ashtabula	2, 12, 16
2. Lake	1, 3, 12
3. Cuyahoga	2, 4, 9, 10, 12, 13
4. Lorain	3, 5, 7, 9
5. Huron	4, 6, 7
6. Richland	5, 7, 17
7. Ashland	4, 5, 6, 8, 9, 17, 18
8. Wayne	7, 9, 10, 11, 18
9. Medina	3, 4, 7, 8, 10
10. Summit	3, 8, 9, 11, 12, 13
11. Stark	8, 10, 13, 14, 15, 18, 19, 20
12. Geauga	1, 2, 3, 10, 13, 16
13. Portage	3, 10, 11, 12, 15, 16
14. Columbiana	11, 15, 20
15. Mahoning	11, 13, 14, 16
16. Trumbull	1, 12, 13, 15
17. Knox	6, 7, 18
18. Holmes	7, 8, 11, 17, 19
19. Tuscarawas	11, 18, 20
20. Carroll	11, 14, 19

With the goal of minimizing the number of PPBs needed, the objective function can be written as

$$\text{Min} \quad x_1 + x_2 + \cdots + x_{20}$$

In order to place branch banks in a county, the county must either contain a PPB or be adjacent to another county with a PPB. Thus, there will be one constraint for each county. For example, the constraint for Ashtabula County would be written as follows:

$$x_1 + x_2 + x_{12} + x_{16} \geq 1 \quad \text{Ashtabula}$$

Note that satisfaction of this constraint ensures that a PPB will be placed in Ashtabula County *or* in one or more of the adjacent counties. This constraint thus guarantees that Ohio Trust will be able to place branch banks in Ashtabula County.

The complete statement of the bank location problem is shown below.

$$\text{Min} \quad x_1 + x_2 + \quad \cdots \quad + x_{20}$$

s.t.

$$x_1 + x_2 \quad + x_{12} + x_{16} \qquad \geq 1 \quad \text{Ashtabula}$$

$$x_1 + x_2 + x_3 + x_{12} \qquad \geq 1 \quad \text{Lake}$$

$$\vdots \qquad\qquad\qquad \vdots$$

$$x_{11} + x_{14} + x_{19} + x_{20} \geq 1 \quad \text{Carroll}$$

$$x_i = 0, 1 \quad i = 1, 2, \ldots, 20$$

Given this 20-variable, 20-constraint problem formulation, we can now solve it using LINDO/PC.[5] The input data are entered in the same manner as for a linear program. Then to make LINDO/PC treat each of the 20 decision variables as *0–1* integer variables, we enter the LINDO/PC command INTEGER 20. When the GO command is given, the LINDO/PC program will determine the optimal integer solution.

In Figure 8.4 we show a portion of the computer output. Note that the variable names correspond to the first four letters in the name of each county. Using the output, we see that the optimal solution calls for principal places of business in Ashland, Stark, and Geauga counties. With PPBs in these three counties, Ohio Trust can place branch banks in all 20 counties (see Figure 8.5). All other decision variables have an optimal value of zero, indicating that a PPB should not be placed in these counties. Clearly the integer programming model could be enlarged to allow for expansion into a larger area or throughout the entire state.[6]

Figure 8.4
LINDO/PC Solution for Bank
Location Problem

```
        OBJECTIVE FUNCTION VALUE

1)      3.00000000

VARIABLE            VALUE          REDUCED COST
    ASHT          .000000            .000000
    LAKE          .000000            .000000
    CUYA          .000000            .000000
    LORA          .000000            .000000
    HURO          .000000            .000000
    RICH          .000000           1.000000
    ASHL         1.000000            .000000
    WAYN          .000000            .000000
    MEDI          .000000            .000000
    SUMM          .000000            .000000
    STAR         1.000000            .000000
    GEAU         1.000000            .000000
    PORT          .000000            .000000
    COLU          .000000            .000000
    MAHO          .000000            .000000
    TRUM          .000000            .000000
    KNOX          .000000           1.000000
    HOLM          .000000            .000000
    TUSC          .000000            .000000
    CARR          .000000            .000000
```

[5]One could also solve this problem using the integer programming module of The Management Scientist.

[6]A model of this type allowing for expansion throughout the state and some other variations is presented in D. J. Sweeney, L. Mairose, and R. Martin, "Strategic Planning in Bank Location, *Decision Sciences Proceedings* (November 1979).

Figure 8.5
Principal Place of Business
Counties for Ohio Trust

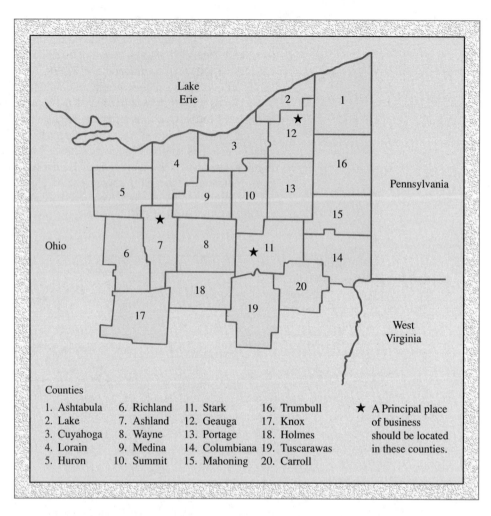

Lake
Erie

Pennsylvania

Ohio

West
Virginia

Counties

1. Ashtabula	6. Richland	11. Stark	16. Trumbull	★ A Principal place
2. Lake	7. Ashland	12. Geauga	17. Knox	of business
3. Cuyahoga	8. Wayne	13. Portage	18. Holmes	should be located
4. Lorain	9. Medina	14. Columbiana	19. Tuscarawas	in these counties.
5. Huron	10. Summit	15. Mahoning	20. Carroll	

NOTES & COMMENTS

1. Most practical applications of integer linear programming involve only *0–1* integer variables. Indeed, some mixed-integer computer codes are designed to handle only integer variables with binary values. However, if a clever mathematical trick is employed, these codes can still be used for problems involving general integer variables. The trick is called *binary expansion* and requires that an upper bound be established for each integer variable. More advanced texts on integer programming show how this can be done.

2. General-purpose mixed-integer linear programming codes can be used for linear programming problems, all-integer problems, and problems involving some continuous and some integer variables. General-purpose codes are seldom the fastest for solving problems with special structure (such as the transportation, assignment, and transshipment problems); however, unless the problems are very large, speed is usually not a critical issue. Thus, for most practitioners, it is probably

—Continued on the next page

—Continued from previous page

better to become familiar with one general-purpose computer package that can be used on a variety of problems than to maintain a variety of computer codes designed for special problems.

3. Several computer software packages can provide solutions to both general linear programming problems and integer linear programming problems. Note, however, that the sensitivity analysis information for integer linear programs shown in some of these software outputs does not have the same meaning as it does for linear programming problems and should ordinarily be disregarded.

8.5 Branch-and-Bound Solution

Branch and *bound* is currently the most efficient general-purpose solution procedure for integer linear programs. Almost all commercially available integer programming computer codes employ the branch-and-bound approach.

The branch-and-bound procedure divides the set of feasible solutions to an integer programming problem into smaller subsets (branching). Then various rules are used to (1) identify the subsets that are most likely to contain the optimal solution and (2) identify the subsets that need not be explored further because they could not possibly contain the optimal solution.

An upper bound on the value of the best solution in each subset is obtained by solving an LP Relaxation. Any time the solution to the LP Relaxation results in an integer solution, the best solution in the subset has been found, and a *lower bound* for the subset is also obtained. The best of the integer feasible solutions (considering all the subsets) is the optimal solution.

In this section we show how the branch-and-bound approach can be used to solve integer programming problems by applying it to the all-integer Security Realty Investors problem discussed in Section 8.2. We then comment on how it can be extended to mixed-integer linear programs and present a flowchart summarizing the steps in the procedure.

The branch-and-bound procedure begins by solving the LP Relaxation of the integer linear program. The LP Relaxation of the Security Realty Investors problem is restated below, where:

$$x_1 = \text{blocks of townhouses purchased}$$
$$x_2 = \text{apartment buildings purchased}$$

Max $\quad 2x_1 + 3x_2$

s.t.

$$195x_1 + 273x_2 \leq 1365 \qquad \text{Funds available}$$
$$4x_1 + 40x_2 \leq 140 \qquad \text{Manager's time}$$
$$x_1 \qquad \leq 4 \qquad \text{Townhouse availability}$$
$$x_1, x_2 \geq 0$$

The solution is $x_1 = 2.44$ and $x_2 = 3.26$, with an objective function value equal to 14.66. Had the optimal solution to the LP Relaxation satisfied the integer requirements, we would have had the optimal solution to the integer linear program. Since this did not occur, we will continue with the branch-and-bound procedure. As a first step, note that property 1 in Section 8.2 indicates that solving the LP Relaxation of an integer linear program provides an upper bound on the value of the solution to the integer linear programming problem. Thus, we know that the value of the integer optimal solution to the Security Realty problem cannot exceed 14.66.

Since the coefficients of all the variables in the constraints are nonnegative and since the constraints are all of the $\leq$ type, a feasible integer solution can be found by rounding down for each decision variable; that is, rounding down can only reduce the left-hand side of the inequality and hence must always provide a feasible solution. The feasible solution found by rounding down is $x_1 = 2$ and $x_2 = 3$, with an objective function value of 13. The value of this feasible solution provides a lower bound on the value of the optimal solution to the integer linear program since we know that the value of the optimal solution must yield a value greater than or equal to the value of any feasible solution. Thus, a lower bound of 13 can be established. The first node of the branch-and-bound solution tree appears as shown below, where UB refers to upper bound and LB to lower bound.

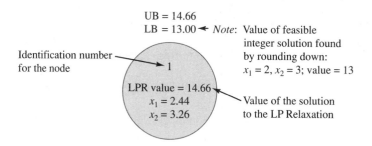

We now know that the value of the optimal solution must be between the upper bound of 14.66 and the lower bound of 13. Although we have already found a feasible solution with a value of 13, we must continue to see if a better solution can be found. This is where the branching part of the branch-and-bound solution procedure comes into play.

The set of feasible solutions to the LP Relaxation is partitioned into two subsets. These subsets are created by choosing the integer variable that is furthest from being integral to branch on; hence, x_1 with a value of 2.44 is selected. In the optimal integer solution, x_1 must be integer, so we see that either x_1 will be less than or equal to 2 or x_1 will be greater than or equal to 3. Thus, two branches and two *descendant nodes* are created for our branch-and-bound solution tree. One descendant node corresponds to the subset of solutions with $x_1 \leq 2$; the other corresponds to the subset of solutions with $x_1 \geq 3$. Since x_1 must be integral, the optimal solution must be contained in one of these two subsets.

The first branch is created by adding the constraint $x_1 \leq 2$ to the Security Realty problem. We will refer to the node created as node 2. Thus, at node 2 the following LP Relaxation is solved.

LP Relaxation at Node 2

$$\text{Max} \quad 2x_1 + 3x_2$$

s.t.

$$195x_1 + 273x_2 \leq 1365$$

$$4x_1 + 40x_2 \leq 140$$

$$x_1 \qquad \leq \quad 4$$

$$x_1 \qquad \leq \quad 2$$

$$x_1, x_2 \geq 0$$

We note that the added constraint ($x_1 \leq 2$) makes the constraint $x_1 \leq 4$ redundant. The solution to this linear program yields $x_1 = 2$ and $x_2 = 3.30$, with value equal to 13.90.

The second branch from node 1 is created by adding the constraint $x_1 \geq 3$ to the LP Relaxation of the Security Realty problem. Thus, at node 3 the following LP Relaxation is solved.

LP Relaxation at Node 3

$$\text{Max} \qquad 2x_1 + \quad 3x_2$$

s.t.

$$195x_1 + 273x_2 \leq 1365$$

$$4x_1 + \quad 40x_2 \leq \quad 140$$

$$x_1 \qquad\qquad \leq \quad 4$$

$$x_1 \qquad\qquad \geq \quad 3$$

$$x_1, x_2 \geq 0$$

The solution to this linear program yields $x_1 = 3$, and $x_2 = 2.86$, with value equal to 14.58.

From property 1 we know that the value of the LP Relaxation at node 2 is an upper bound on all solutions with $x_1 \leq 2$ and that the value of the LP Relaxation at node 3 is an upper bound on all solutions with $x_1 \geq 3$. Since these two subsets include all solutions to the Security Realty problem, we can compute a new upper bound. It is the maximum of the LP Relaxation value for node 2 (13.90) and for node 3 (14.58). (Hence, our new upper bound on the solution value to the Security Realty problem is 14.58.) In general, we will recompute the upper bound each time the two branches from a node have been completed.

At this time, the lower bound is also recomputed. The new value for the lower bound is the maximum value of all feasible integer solutions found so far. Since the LP Relaxation solutions at nodes 2 and 3 did not yield a feasible integer solution, the lower bound of 13 established at node 1 is not revised. At this point of the branch-and-bound solution procedure, we have UB = 14.58 and LB = 13.00. The current partial branch-and-bound solution tree is shown in Figure 8.6.

We have established (at node 2) that 13.90 is an upper bound on all solutions with $x_1 \leq 2$ and (at node 3) that 14.58 is an upper bound on all solutions with $x_1 \geq 3$. Property 2 below shows how these results can be used in continuing with the branch-and-bound solution procedure.

PROPERTY **2**

The LP Relaxation value at each node of a maximization problem is an upper bound on the LP Relaxation value at any descendant node.

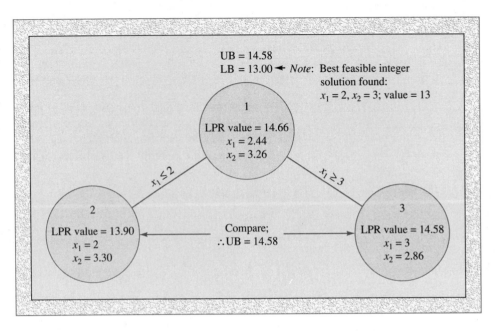

Using this property, we see that if we were to branch from node 2, we could not find any solution with a value greater than 13.90. If we were to branch from node 3, no solution with a value greater than 14.58 could be found. Since node 3 could potentially lead to a better solution, we choose to select it (rather than node 2) to branch from. In general for a maximization problem, we will always select the node with the largest LP Relaxation value to continue branching.

Since x_2 is the only variable with a fractional value at node 3, we choose to branch on it. Thus, two branches are created from node 3: one with $x_2 \leq 2$ and another with $x_2 \geq 3$. Two descendent nodes are then created by solving the following LP Relaxations at nodes 4 and 5.

LP Relaxation at Node 4

$$\text{Max} \quad 2x_1 + 3x_2$$

s.t.

$$195x_1 + 273x_2 \leq 1365$$
$$4x_1 + 40x_2 \leq 140$$
$$x_1 \leq 4$$
$$x_1 \geq 3$$
$$x_2 \leq 2$$
$$x_1, x_2 \geq 0$$

LP Relaxation at Node 5

$$\text{Max} \quad 2x_1 + 3x_2$$

s.t.

$$195x_1 + 273x_2 \leq 1365$$

$$4x_1 + 40x_2 \leq 140$$

$$x_1 \qquad \leq \quad 4$$

$$x_1 \qquad \geq \quad 3$$

$$x_2 \geq \quad 3$$

$$x_1, x_2 \geq \quad 0$$

Note that since we are branching from node 3, we require $x_1 \geq 3$ in both LP Relaxations.

After solving these linear programming problems, we can construct the branch-and-bound approach solution tree shown in Figure 8.7. Note that at node 4, which corresponds to adding the constraint $x_2 \leq 2$, we find a feasible integer solution. At node 5, however, we find that after adding the constraint $x_2 \geq 3$, there is no feasible solution.

At this point, we have found a feasible solution ($x_1 = 4$, $x_2 = 2$) with a value of 14.00 (see node 4). Thus, the lower bound is revised to LB = 14.00. From UB = 14.00 we know that the optimal solution cannot yield a value greater than 14.00. Therefore, the solution $x_1 = 4$, $x_2 = 2$ with a value 14 is optimal for the Security Realty problem. We can now state the stopping rule for the branch-and-bound solution procedure.

Figure 8.7
Complete Branch-and-Bound
Solution Tree for Security Realty
Problem

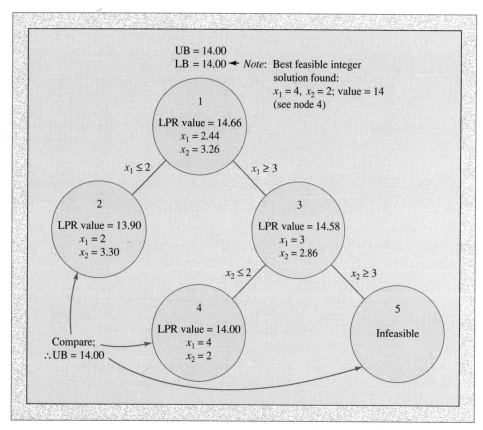

S T O P P I N G   R U L E

When UB = LB, the optimal solution has been found. It is the feasible solution with value equal to LB.

We have seen how the branch-and-bound solution procedure is applied to solve the all-integer Security Realty Investors problem. A summary of the general procedure for the all-integer linear program is presented in flowchart form in Figure 8.8 for maximization problems. For minimization problems, the solution of the LP Relaxation provides a lower bound. So lower bound must be replaced by upper bound in the algorithm, maximum by minimum, and greatest by smallest.

Try Problem 18 for practice in solving an all-integer problem using branch and bound.

Figure 8.8
Branch-and-Bound Solution
Procedure for the
All-Integer Linear Program
Maximization Objective

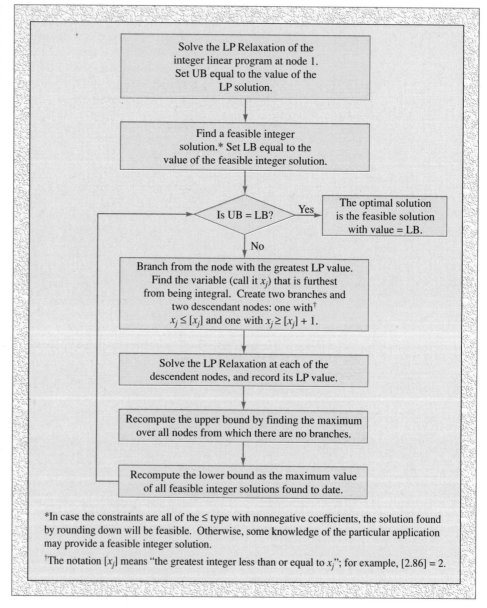

Solve the LP Relaxation of the integer linear program at node 1. Set UB equal to the value of the LP solution.

Find a feasible integer solution.* Set LB equal to the value of the feasible integer solution.

Is UB = LB? Yes → The optimal solution is the feasible solution with value = LB.

No

Branch from the node with the greatest LP value. Find the variable (call it x_j) that is furthest from being integral. Create two branches and two descendant nodes: one with† $x_j \leq [x_j]$ and one with $x_j \geq [x_j] + 1$.

Solve the LP Relaxation at each of the descendent nodes, and record its LP value.

Recompute the upper bound by finding the maximum over all nodes from which there are no branches.

Recompute the lower bound as the maximum value of all feasible integer solutions found to date.

*In case the constraints are all of the ≤ type with nonnegative coefficients, the solution found by rounding down will be feasible. Otherwise, some knowledge of the particular application may provide a feasible integer solution.

†The notation $[x_j]$ means "the greatest integer less than or equal to x_j"; for example, $[2.86] = 2$.

Extension to Mixed-Integer Linear Programs

A big advantage of the branch-and-bound solution procedure for integer programming is that it is applicable to both all-integer and mixed-integer linear programs. To see how the branch-and-bound solution approach can be applied to a mixed-integer linear program, let us return to the Security Realty problem and suppose that x_2 was not required to be integer. This would be the case if fractional shares could be purchased in the apartment buildings. In this situation, the LP Relaxation solved at node 1 would be exactly the same, yielding a value of 14.66 as an upper bound. But the lower bound would be found by rounding down on x_1 only. Thus, the value of the lower bound at node 1 would be 13.78, given by the feasible mixed-integer solution $x_1 = 2$, $x_2 = 3.26$. This is shown below.

UB = 14.66
LB = 13.78 ◄ *Note*: Best feasible mixed-integer solution found:
$x_1 = 2$, $x_2 = 3.26$; value = 13.78

1
LPR value = 14.66
$x_1 = 2.44$
$x_2 = 3.26$

Try Problem 20 for practice solving a mixed-integer problem using branch and bound.

In order to branch, we now restrict consideration to only those variables that are required to be integer. Selecting the integer variable with the largest fractional part leads us to again branch on x_1; we require $x_1 \leq 2$ on one branch and $x_1 \geq 3$ on the other. Thus, the LP Relaxations solved at nodes 2 and 3 would be the same as before (see Figure 8.9). However, note that a feasible mixed-integer solution exists whenever the linear programming solution at a node yields x_1 integer. Thus, the solutions at both nodes 2 and 3 are feasible for the mixed-integer linear program. A new lower bound of LB = 14.58 can be established by comparing the values of all the feasible mixed-integer solutions found. A

Figure 8.9

Branch-and-Bound Tree for Security Realty Mixed-Integer Linear Program (x_1 Integer, x_2 Not Integer)

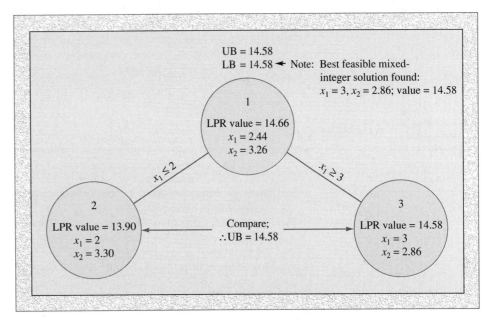

new upper bound of UB = 14.58 can be established by comparing the LP Relaxation values at nodes 2 and 3. Since the upper and lower bounds are equal, the optimal solution to the Security Realty problem with only x_1 required to be integer has been found. It is given by $x_1 = 3$ and $x_2 = 2.86$, with an objective function value of 14.58. The branch-and-bound tree for this mixed-integer linear program is shown in Figure 8.9.

Summary

We have introduced an important extension of the linear programming model: the integer linear program. The only difference between the integer linear programming problem and the linear programming problem studied in previous chapters is the added restriction on some of the variables. If all of the variables are required to be integer, we have an all-integer linear program; if some, but not necessarily all, of the variables are required to be integer, we have a mixed-integer linear program. Finally, in case the integer variables are only permitted to assume the values 0 or 1, we have a *0–1* (binary) integer linear program. Binary integer linear programs may be either all integer or mixed integer.

There are two primary reasons for studying integer linear programming. First, in many applications, fractional values of the decision variables are not permitted. Since we have seen that rounding the linear programming solution can provide poor results, methods for finding the optimal integer solution are needed. For any two-variable problem, a simple extension of the graphical procedure for linear programs can be used to find solutions. The branch-and-bound solution procedure was presented for solving larger integer linear programs. A major advantage of the branch-and-bound solution procedure is its flexibility; it can be used for both all-integer and mixed-integer linear programs. Almost all existing commercial computer codes employ the branch-and-bound approach.

A second reason for studying integer linear programming is that it increases modeling flexibility through the use of *0–1* variables. In our discussion of the capital budgeting and distribution system design problems, we saw how a number of important managerial considerations can be incorporated through the use of multiple-choice constraints, conditional constraints, and so on. In addition, the Ohio Trust problem presented in Section 8.4 provided another example of the modeling flexibility available using integer variables.

In recent years, with the availability of commercial integer linear programming computer codes, we have seen a rapid growth in the use of integer linear programming. As researchers develop solution procedures capable of solving integer linear programs with larger numbers of variables and as computer speeds increase, we can expect to see a continuation of this growth and the development of new applications.

Glossary

Integer linear program A linear program with the additional requirement that some or all of the decision variables must be integer.

All-integer linear program An integer linear program in which all the decision variables are required to be integer.

LP Relaxation The linear program that results from dropping the integer requirements for the decision variables. For a maximization problem, the value of the optimal solution to the LP Relaxation is an upper bound on the value of the optimal integer solution.

Mixed-integer linear program An integer linear program in which some, but not all, of the decision variables are required to be integer.

Discrete variable Another name for a variable that may only assume integer values.

Continuous variable A variable that may take on any real number as a value. The variables in a linear program are continuous.

0–1 integer linear program Also called *binary integer program.* An all-integer or mixed-integer linear program in which the integer variables are only permitted to assume the values 0 or 1.

Multiple-choice constraint A constraint requiring that the sum of two or more *0–1* variables equal 1. Thus, any feasible solution makes a choice of one of these variables to set equal to 1.

Mutually exclusive constraint A constraint requiring that the sum of two or more *0–1* variables be less than or equal to 1. Thus, if one of the variables equals 1, the others must equal 0. However, all variables could equal 0.

k Out of n alternatives constraint An extension of the multiple-choice constraint. This constraint requires that the sum of *n 0–1* variables equal *k*.

Conditional constraints Constraints involving *0–1* variables that do not allow certain variables to equal 1 unless certain other variables are equal to 1.

Corequisite constraint A constraint requiring that two *0–1* variables be equal. Thus, they are both in or out of solution together.

Branch and bound A solution procedure for integer linear programs that sequentially partitions the set of feasible solutions into smaller and smaller subsets until the optimal solution is found.

Upper bound A value that is known to be greater than or equal to the value of any feasible solution. The solution to the LP Relaxation of an integer linear program provides an upper bound for a maximization problem.

Lower bound A value that is less than or equal to the value of the optimal solution. For a maximization problem, the value of any feasible integer solution to an integer linear program is a lower bound.

Descendant node A node in a branch-and-bound solution tree created by adding a constraint to the LP Relaxation solved at the previous node.

Problems

SELF TEST ▶

1. Types of IP models

1. Indicate which of the following are all-integer linear programs, which are mixed-integer linear programs, and which are ordinary linear programs. For each of the all-integer and mixed-integer linear programs, write the LP Relaxation. (Do not attempt to solve.)

a. Max $\quad 30x_1 + 25x_2$

s.t.

$$3x_1 + 1.5x_2 \le 400$$

$$1.5x_1 + 2x_2 \le 250$$

$$1x_1 + 1x_2 \le 150$$

$$x_1, x_2 \ge 0 \text{ and } x_2 \text{ integer}$$

b. Min $\quad 3x_1 + 4x_2$

s.t.

$$2x_1 + 4x_2 \ge 8$$

$$2x_1 + 6x_2 \ge 12$$

$$x_1, x_2 \ge 0 \text{ and integer}$$

c. Min $30x_1 + 4x_2$

s.t.

$$3x_1 + 2x_2 \geq 50$$

$$0.1x_1 + 0.2x_2 \geq 2$$

$$x_1, x_2 \geq 0 \text{ and } x_1 \text{ integer}$$

d. Max $3x_1 + 4x_2$

s.t.

$$-1x_1 + 2x_2 \leq 8$$

$$1x_1 + 2x_2 \leq 12$$

$$2x_1 + 1x_2 \leq 16$$

$$x_1, x_2 \geq 0 \text{ and integer}$$

e. Max $20x_1 + 5x_2$

s.t.

$$5x_1 + 1x_2 \leq 15$$

$$6x_1 + 4x_2 \leq 24$$

$$1x_1 + 1x_2 \leq 5$$

$$x_1, x_2 \geq 0$$

SELF TEST

2. Graphical solution, LP Relaxation, rounding

2. Consider the all-integer linear program given below.

$$\text{Max} \quad 5x_1 + 8x_2$$

s.t.

$$6x_1 + 5x_2 \leq 30$$

$$9x_1 + 4x_2 \leq 36$$

$$1x_1 + 2x_2 \leq 10$$

$$x_1, x_2 \geq 0 \text{ and integer}$$

a. Graph the constraints for this problem. Use heavy dots to indicate all the feasible integer solutions.
b. Find the optimal solution to the LP Relaxation. Round down to find a feasible integer solution.
c. Find the optimal integer solution. Is it the same as the solution found in part (b) by rounding down?

3. Graphical solution, LP Relaxation

3. Consider the all-integer linear program given below.

$$\text{Max} \quad 1x_1 + 1x_2$$

s.t.

$$4x_1 + 6x_2 \leq 22$$

$$1x_1 + 5x_2 \leq 15$$

$$2x_1 + 1x_2 \leq 9$$

$$x_1, x_2 \geq 0 \text{ and integer}$$

a. Graph the constraints for this problem. Use heavy dots to indicate all the feasible integer solutions.
b. Solve the LP Relaxation of this problem.
c. Find the optimal integer solution.

4. Graphical solution, LP Relaxation, finding bounds

4. Consider the all-integer linear program given below.

$$\text{Max} \quad 10x_1 + 3x_2$$

s.t.

$$6x_1 + 7x_2 \le 40$$

$$3x_1 + 1x_2 \le 11$$

$$x_1, x_2 \ge 0 \text{ and integer}$$

a. Formulate and solve the LP Relaxation of the problem. Solve it graphically, and round down to find a feasible solution. Specify upper and lower bounds on the value of the optimal solution.
b. Solve the integer linear program graphically. Compare the value of this solution with the solution found in part (a).
c. Suppose the objective function changes to Max $3x_1 + 6x_2$. Repeat parts (a) and (b).

S ELF T EST ▶

5. Graphical solution, LP Relaxation, rounding

5. Consider the mixed-integer linear program given below.

$$\text{Max} \quad 2x_1 + 3x_2$$

s.t.

$$4x_1 + 9x_2 \le 36$$

$$7x_1 + 5x_2 \le 35$$

$$x_1, x_2 \ge 0 \text{ and } x_1 \text{ integer}$$

a. Graph the constraints for this problem. Indicate on your graph all feasible mixed-integer solutions.
b. Find the optimal solution to the LP Relaxation. Round the value of x_1 down to find a feasible mixed-integer solution. Is this solution optimal? Why or why not?
c. Find the optimal solution for the mixed-integer linear program.

6. Graphical solution, LP Relaxation, finding bounds

6. Consider the mixed-integer linear program given below.

$$\text{Max} \quad 1x_1 + 1x_2$$

s.t.

$$7x_1 + 9x_2 \le 63$$

$$9x_1 + 5x_2 \le 45$$

$$3x_1 + 1x_2 \le 12$$

$$x_1, x_2 \ge 0 \text{ and } x_2 \text{ integer}$$

a. Graph the constraints for this problem. Indicate on your graph all feasible mixed-integer solutions.
b. Find the optimal solution to the LP Relaxation. Round the value of x_2 down to find a feasible mixed-integer solution. Specify upper and lower bounds on the value of the optimal solution to the mixed-integer linear program.
c. Find the optimal solution to the mixed-integer linear program.

S ELF T EST ▶

7. Modeling with 0–1 variables

7. The following questions refer to a capital budgeting problem with six projects represented by $0-1$ variables $x_1, x_2, x_3, x_4, x_5,$ and x_6.

a. Write a constraint modeling a situation in which two and only two of the projects 1, 3, 5, and 6 must be undertaken.

b. Write a constraint modeling a situation in which projects 3 and 5 must be undertaken simultaneously.

c. Write a constraint modeling a situation in which project 1 or 4 must be undertaken, but not both.

d. Write constraints modeling a situation where project 4 cannot be undertaken unless projects 1 and 3 are also undertaken.

e. Revise the requirement in part (d) to accommodate the case in which, when projects 1 and 3 are undertaken, project 4 must also be undertaken.

8. Capital budgeting

8. Spencer Enterprises is attempting to choose among a series of new investment alternatives. The potential investment alternatives, the net present value of the future stream of returns, the capital requirements, and the available capital funds over the next 3 years are summarized below.

Alternative	Net Present Value ($)	Capital Requirements ($)		
		Year 1	Year 2	Year 3
Limited warehouse expansion	4,000	3,000	1,000	4,000
Extensive warehouse expansion	6,000	2,500	3,500	3,500
Test market new product	10,500	6,000	4,000	5,000
Advertising campaign	4,000	2,000	1,500	1,800
Basic research	8,000	5,000	1,000	4,000
Purchase new equipment	3,000	1,000	500	900
Capital funds available		10,500	7,000	8,750

a. Develop and solve an integer programming model for maximizing the net present value.

b. Assume that only one of the warehouse expansion projects can be implemented. Modify your model of part (a).

c. Suppose that if the test marketing of the new product is carried out, then the advertising campaign must also be conducted. Modify your formulation of part (b) to reflect this new situation.

9. Solving a 0–1 problem

9. The integer programming formulation of the Ice-Cold Refrigerator Company capital budgeting problem is presented below.

$$\text{Max} \quad 90x_1 + 40x_2 + 10x_3 + 37x_4$$

s.t.

$$15x_1 + 10x_2 + 10x_3 + 15x_4 \leq 40$$

$$20x_1 + 15x_2 \qquad + 10x_4 \leq 50$$

$$20x_1 + 20x_2 \qquad + 10x_4 \leq 40$$

$$15x_1 + 5x_2 + 4x_3 + 10x_4 \leq 35$$

$$x_1, x_2, x_3, x_4 = 0, 1$$

a. Solve by trial and error.

b. If you have a computer code for solving integer programs, use it to solve the problem.

10. Formulation, set covering problem

10. Grave City is considering the relocation of a number of police substations to obtain better enforcement in high-crime areas. The locations under consideration together with the areas that can be covered from these locations are given in the following table.

Potential Locations for Substations	Areas Covered
A	1, 5, 7
B	1, 2, 5, 7
C	1, 3, 5
D	2, 4, 5
E	3, 4, 6
F	4, 5, 6
G	1, 5, 6, 7

a. Formulate an integer programming model that could be used to find the minimum number of locations necessary to provide coverage to all areas.

b. Solve the problem in part (a) using any means at your disposal.

S ELF T EST ▶ **11.** The Martin-Beck Company is in the process of planning for new production facilities and developing a more efficient distribution system design. At present they have one plant at St. Louis with a capacity of 30,000 units. But because of increased demand, management is considering four potential new plant sites: Detroit, Denver, Toledo, and Kansas City. The transportation tableau below summarizes the projected plant capacities (in 1,000s), the cost per unit of shipping from each plant to each destination (upper right-hand corner of each cell), and the demand forecasts (in 1,000s) over a 1-year planning horizon.

11. Formulation, *0–1* variables, distribution system

Plant Sites	Destination			Capacities (in 1000's)
	Boston	Atlanta	Houston	
Detroit	5	2	3	10
Toledo	4	3	4	20
Denver	9	7	5	30
Kansas City	10	4	2	40
St. Louis	8	4	3	30
Demand (in 1000's)	30	20	20	

Suppose that the fixed costs of constructing the new plants, in thousands, are

Detroit	$175
Toledo	$300
Denver	$375
Kansas City	$500

The Martin-Beck Company would like to minimize the total cost of plant construction and distribution of goods.

a. Develop a $0-1$ mixed-integer linear programming model of this problem. If you have access to a computer code, use it to solve the problem.

b. Modify your formulation in part (a) to account for the policy restriction that one plant, but not two, must be located in Detroit or in Toledo.

c. Modify your formulation in part (a) to account for the policy restriction that at most two plants can be located in Denver, Kansas City, and St. Louis.

12. Formulation, $0-1$ variables

12. An automobile manufacturer has five outdated plants located in Michigan, New York (two plants), Ohio, and California. Management is considering modernizing these plants in order to manufacture engine blocks and transmissions for a new model car. The cost to modernize each plant and the manufacturing capacity after modernization are as follows:

Plant	Cost (millions)	Engine Blocks (1000's)	Transmissions (1000's)
Michigan	25	500	300
New York	35	800	400
New York	35	400	800
Ohio	40	900	600
California	20	200	300

The projected needs are for total capacities of 900,000 engine blocks and 900,000 transmissions. Management would like to determine which plants to modernize so as to be able to meet projected manufacturing needs and, at the same time, minimize the total cost of modernization.

a. Use total enumeration to develop a table that shows every possible option available to management. As part of your table, indicate the total engine block capacity and transmission capacity for each possible option, whether the option is feasible given the projected needs, and what the total modernization cost is for each option.

b. Based upon your analysis in part (a), what recommendation would you provide management?

c. Formulate a $0-1$ integer programming model that could be used to determine the optimal solution to the modernization question facing management.

d. Solve the model formulated in part (c) to provide a recommendation for management.

13. Formulation, $0-1$ variables, location problem

13. CHB, Inc., is a bank holding company that is evaluating the potential for expanding into a 13-county region in the southwestern part of the state. State law permits establishing branches in any county that is adjacent to a county in which a PPB (principal place of business) is located. Following is a map of the 13-county region with the population of each county indicated.

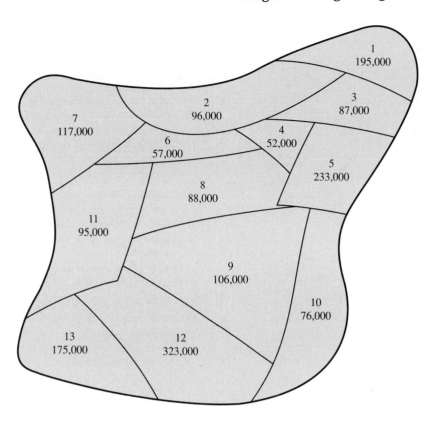

a. Assume that only one PPB can be established in the region. Where should it be located to maximize the population served? (*Hint:* Review the Ohio Trust formulation in Section 8.4. Consider minimizing the population not served, and introduce variable $y_i = 1$ if it is not possible to establish a branch in county i and $y_i = 0$ otherwise.)

b. Suppose that two PPBs can be established in the region. Where should they be located to maximize the population served?

c. Management has learned that a bank located in county 5 is considering selling. If CHB purchases this bank, the requisite PPB will be established in county 5, and a base for beginning expansion in the region will also be established. What advice would you give the management of CHB?

14. Formulation, general integer variables, teller scheduling

14. The Northshore Bank is working to develop an efficient work schedule for full-time and part-time tellers. The schedule must provide for efficient operation of the bank including adequate customer service, employee breaks, and so on. On Fridays the bank is open from 9:00 A.M. to 7:00 P.M. The number of tellers necessary to provide adequate customer service during each hour of operation is summarized below.

Time	9–10	10–11	11–12	12–1	1–2	2–3	3–4	4–5	5–6	6–7
Number of Tellers	6	4	8	10	9	6	4	7	6	6

Each full-time employee starts on the hour and works a 4-hour shift, followed by 1 hour for lunch and then a 3-hour shift. Part-time employees work one 4-hour shift beginning on the hour. Considering salary and fringe benefits, full-time employees cost the bank $15 per hour ($105 per day), and part-time employees cost the bank $8 per hour ($32 per day).

a. Formulate an integer programming model that can be used to develop a schedule that will satisfy customer service needs at a minimum employee cost. (*Hint:* Let x_i = number of full-time employees coming on duty at the beginning of hour i and y_i = number of part-time employees coming on duty at the beginning of hour i.)

b. Solve the LP Relaxation of your model in part (a).

c. Solve for the optimal schedule of tellers. Comment on the solution.

d. After reviewing the solution to part (c), the bank manager has realized that some additional requirements must be specified. Specifically, she wants to ensure that one full-time employee is on duty at all times and that there is a staff of at least five full-time employees. Revise your model to incorporate these additional requirements, and solve for the optimal solution.

15. Refer to the Ohio Trust bank location problem introduced in Section 8.4. Table 8.2 shows the counties under consideration and the adjacent counties.

a. Write the complete integer programming model where Ohio Trust is considering expanding into the following counties only: Lorain, Huron, Richland, Ashland, Wayne, Medina, and Knox.

b. Solve the problem in part (a) using trial and error.

c. If you have a computer code for integer programs, use it to solve the problem.

16. Refer to Problem 12. Suppose that management determined that their cost estimates to modernize their New York plants were too low. Specifically, suppose that the actual cost is $40 million to modernize each of these plants.

a. What changes in your previous $0–1$ integer linear programming model are needed to incorporate these changes in costs for the New York plants?

b. Given these cost changes, what recommendations would you now provide management regarding the modernization plan?

c. Reconsider the solution obtained using the revised cost figures. Suppose that management decides that closing two plants in the same state is not acceptable. How could this policy restriction be added to your $0–1$ integer programming model?

d. Given the cost revisions and the policy restrictions presented in part (c), what recommendations would you now provide management regarding the modernization plan?

17. The Bayside Art Gallery is considering installing a video camera security system to reduce their insurance premiums. A diagram of the eight display rooms that Bayside uses for exhibitions is shown in Figure 8.10; the openings between the rooms are numbered 1–13. A security firm has proposed that two-way cameras be installed at some of the room openings. Each camera has the ability to monitor the two rooms between which the camera is located. For example, if a camera were located at opening number 4, rooms 1 and 4 would be covered; if a camera were located at opening 11, rooms 7 and 8 would be covered; and so on. Bayside has decided not to locate a camera system at the entrance to the display rooms. Bayside's objective is to provide security coverage for all eight rooms using the minimum number of two-way cameras.

a. Formulate a $0–1$ integer linear programming model that will enable Bayside to determine the locations for the camera systems.

b. Solve the model formulated in part (a) to determine how many two-way systems Bayside will need to purchase and where they should be located.

c. Suppose that management wants to provide additional security coverage for room 7. Specifically, management wants room 7 to be covered by exactly two cameras. How would your model formulated in part (a) have to change to accommodate this policy restriction?

d. Given the policy restriction specified in part (c), determine how many two-way camera systems Bayside will need to purchase and where they will be located.

NOTE: Problems 18–20 request solution by the branch-and-bound method.

Figure 8.10
Diagram of Display Rooms for
Problem 17

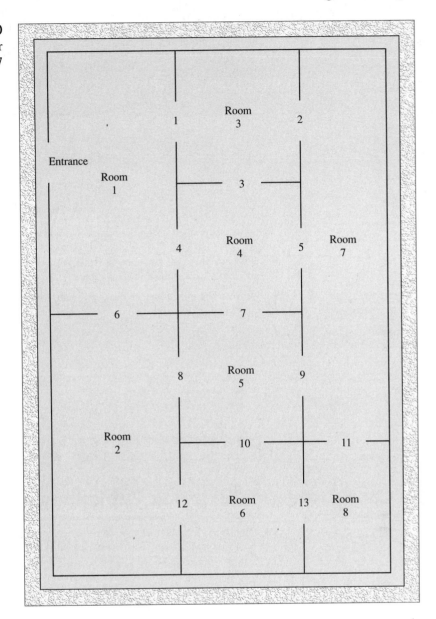

SELF TEST ▶

18. Consider again the all-integer linear program in Problem 4. It is restated below.

$$\text{Max} \quad 10x_1 + 3x_2$$

s.t.

$$6x_1 + 7x_2 \leq 40$$

$$3x_1 + 1x_2 \leq 11$$

$$x_1, x_2 \geq 0 \text{ and integer}$$

Solve this problem using the branch-and-bound procedure.

18. Branch-and-bound solution,
all-integer problem

19. Branch-and-bound solution, *0–1* variables

19. The integer programming formulation of the Ice-Cold Refrigerator Company capital budgeting problem is presented below.

$$\text{Max} \quad 90x_1 + 40x_2 + 10x_3 + 37x_4$$

s.t.

$$15x_1 + 10x_2 + 10x_3 + 15x_4 \leq 40$$
$$20x_1 + 15x_2 \qquad\quad + 10x_4 \leq 50$$
$$20x_1 + 20x_2 \qquad\quad + 10x_4 \leq 40$$
$$15x_1 + 5x_2 + 4x_3 + 10x_4 \leq 35$$
$$x_1, x_2, x_3, x_4 = 0, 1$$

Solve this problem using the branch-and-bound procedure. Note that in the case of variables restricted to 0 or 1, each branch corresponds to setting one of the variables equal to 0 or 1. Thus, the branching variable is treated as a constant in the linear programming problem solved at the descendant node.

SELF TEST ▶

20. Branch-and-bound solution, mixed-integer problem

20. Consider the mixed-integer linear program given below.

$$\text{Max} \quad 1x_1 + 2x_2 + 1x_3$$

s.t.

$$7x_1 + 4x_2 + 3x_3 \leq 28$$
$$4x_1 + 7x_2 + 2x_3 \leq 28$$
$$x_1, x_2, x_3 \geq 0 \text{ and } x_1, x_2 \text{ integer}$$

Solve this problem using the branch-and-bound procedure.

Case Problem: Textbook Publishing

ASW Publishing, Inc., a small publisher of college textbooks, must reach a decision regarding which books to publish next year. The books under consideration are listed in the following table, along with the projected 3-year sales expected from each book:

Book Subject	Type of Book	Projected Sales (1000s)
Business calculus	New	20
Finite mathematics	Revision	30
General statistics	New	15
Mathematical statistics	New	10
Business statistics	Revision	25
Finance	New	18
Financial accounting	New	25
Managerial accounting	Revision	50
English literature	New	20
German	New	30

The books that are listed as revisions are texts that ASW already has under contract; these texts are being considered for publication as new editions. The books that are listed as new have been reviewed by the company, but contracts as yet have not been signed.

The company has three individuals who can be assigned to these projects, all of whom have varying amounts of time available; John has 60 days available, and Susan and Monica both have 40 days available. The days required by each person to complete each project are shown below, and an "X" indicates that the person will not be used for the project because of a lack of expertise in the area, a personality conflict with the author(s), or some other reason. At least 2 staff members are capable of being assigned to each project except the finance book.

Book Subject	John	Susan	Monica
Business calculus	30	40	X
Finite mathematics	16	24	X
General statistics	24	X	30
Mathematical statistics	20	X	24
Business statistics	10	X	16
Finance	X	X	14
Financial accounting	X	24	26
Managerial accounting	X	28	30
English literature	40	34	30
German	X	50	36

ASW will not publish more than two statistics books or more than one accounting text in a single year. In addition, management has decided that one of the mathematics books (business calculus or finite math) must be published, but not both.

Managerial Report

Prepare a report for the general manager of ASW that describes your findings and recommendations regarding the best publication strategy for ASW to follow next year. In carrying out your analysis, assume that the fixed costs and the per-unit sales revenues are approximately equal for all books; management is interested primarily in maximizing the total sales volume.

The general manager has also asked that you include recommendations regarding the following possible changes:

1. If it would be advantageous to do so, Susan can be moved off another project to allow her to work 12 more days.
2. If it would be advantageous to do so, Monica can also be made available for another 10 days.
3. If one or more of the revisions could be postponed for another year, should they be? Clearly the company will risk losing market share by postponing a revision.

Include details of your analysis in an appendix to your report.

MANAGEMENT SCIENCE IN PRACTICE

KETRON*
Arlington, Virginia

Ketron Division of The Bionetics Corporation is an operations research organization with offices throughout the United States. An important part of Ketron's business involves work for local, state, and national governmental agencies.

The Ketron Management Science group is responsible for the development, enhancement, marketing, and support of MPSIII, a proprietary mathematical programming system that runs on a wide range of computers—from PC's to mainframes. Ketron Management Science provides consulting services for the design and implementation of mathematical programming applications. One such mixed-integer programming (MIP) application developed for a major sporting equipment company is outlined below.

A Customer Order Allocation Model

A major sporting equipment company satisfies demand for its products by making shipments from its factories and other locations around the country where inventories are maintained. The company markets approximately 300 products and has about 30 sources of supply (factory and warehouse locations). The problem of interest is to determine how best to allocate customer orders to the various sources of supply such that the total manufacturing cost is minimized. Although transportation cost is not directly considered, it can be accounted for indirectly by not including variables corresponding to shipments from distant locations. Figure 8.11 provides a graphical representation of this problem. Note in the figure that each customer can receive shipments from only a few of the various sources of supply. For example, we see that customer 1 may be supplied by source A or B, customer 2 may be supplied only by source A, and so on.

The customer order allocation problem is solved periodically. In a typical period, there are between 30 and 40 customers to be supplied. Since most customers require several products, there are usually between 600 and 800 orders that must be assigned to the sources of supply.

The sporting equipment company classifies each customer order as either a "guaranteed" or a "secondary" order. Guaranteed orders are single-source orders in that they must be filled by a single supplier to ensure that the complete order will be delivered to the customer at one time. It is this single-source requirement that necessitates the use of integer variables in the model. Approximately 80% of the company's orders are guaranteed orders.

Secondary orders can be split among the various sources of supply. These orders are made by customers restocking inventory, and there is no problem in receiving partial shipments from different sources at different times. The total of all secondary orders for a given product is treated as a goal or target in the model formulation. Deviations below the goal are permitted, but a penalty cost is associated with these deviations in the objective function. When deviations occur in the optimal solution, the secondary orders will not be completely satisfied; the shortfall is spread among customers in specified proportions.

Manufacturing considerations are such that raw material availability and the type of process used constrain the amount of production. In addition, groups of items that are similar may belong to a "model group" that must be jointly constrained at some factories. There are also several restrictions on international shipping. For various policy reasons, shipments between sources and customers in certain countries may not be made. This reduces the number of variables in the model, but necessi-

Figure 8.11
Graphical Representation of the Customer Order Allocation Problem

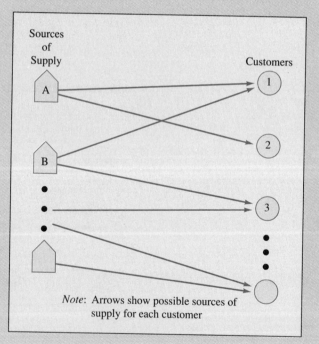

Note: Arrows show possible sources of supply for each customer

---

*The authors are indebted to J. A. Tomlin for providing this application.

—Continued on next page

—Continued from previous page

tates extensive data checking to ensure that all guaranteed orders have a permissible source. If they do not, some means must be found to make the problem feasible before beginning to solve the mixed-integer programming model.

The primary objective of the model is to minimize the total manufacturing costs, subject to the requirement that the guaranteed orders be met. As indicated previously, the deviations below the secondary demand goals are dealt with by defining shortfall-variables with an associated cost. This cost represents a penalty for not having the item in inventory when it is required.

A description of the constraints and the objective function for the model follows.

Constraints

- *Guaranteed orders:* Each customer's order for each product is assigned to a single supplier. (This is a multiple-choice constraint.)
- *Secondary orders:* For each product, the total amount of secondary demand assigned plus the shortfall must equal the total demand goal (target).
- *Raw material capacities:* The amount of each type of raw material used at a supply source cannot exceed the amount available.
- *Manufacturing capacities:* At each supply source, the capacity for each type of production process cannot be exceeded.
- *Individual product capacities:* The amount of product produced at a site cannot exceed that site's capacity for the product.
- *Group capacities:* The total production for a group of similar products at a site cannot exceed that site's capacity for the group of products.

Objective Function

The objective is to minimize the sum of (1) the manufacturing cost for guaranteed orders, (2) the manufacturing cost for secondary orders, and (3) the penalty cost for unsatisfied secondary demand.

Model Solution

It is unreasonable to expect to obtain an optimal solution for a problem of this complexity. Furthermore, the goal programming methodology for handling the secondary demand means that an "optimum" is of questionable interpretation. What is needed is a "good" feasible mixed-integer solution. This is one of the advantages of the branch-and-bound approach. If an integer solution is found whose value is within a few percent of the value of the lower bound, the room for improvement is obviously small.

The solution procedure used is as follows: A sequence of runs is made, each beginning where the previous one terminated. Each run allows at most 40 linear programming evaluations (boundings), though many more variables will usually be set to some integer value (branched on). In almost every case, the first such run, which includes finding the LP Relaxation solution, produces a solution satisfactory to the user.

A fairly typical problem has about 800 constraints, 2000 *0–1* assignment variables for the guaranteed orders, and 500 continuous variables associated with the secondary orders. This model is solved using Ketron's MPSIII system.

Implementation Notes

In large-scale applications such as this, considerable systems work is involved in generating the data for the model and the managerial reports. Special data processing languages are often available to ease the programming burden of these phases. The DATAFORM language facility of MPSIII is used to generate the data for this model and to prepare the reports.

In this application, it is necessary to make a completely separate preprocessing run to check for internal consistency and errors in the data. Only when the data appear logically error-free is the model generated and solved. Although tedious, this kind of preprocessing effort is critical for mixed-integer models since the cost of solving the wrong model can be significant. Furthermore, in some cases the data preprocessing step permits the size of the model to be reduced. Such a reduction is possible in this application when a demand for a product has only one legitimate source. The computational benefits of such reductions can be substantial.

Questions

1. Discuss the relationship between the method for handling secondary orders and feasibility.
2. It is mentioned that an "optimum" is of questionable interpretation. Discuss what is meant by this statement. Does it mean that any feasible solution is acceptable?

Network Models

Many managerial problems in areas such as transportation systems design, information systems design, and project scheduling have been successfully solved with the aid of network models and network analysis techniques. In Chapter 7 we showed how *networks* consisting of nodes and arcs can be used to provide graphical representations of transportation, assignment, and transshipment problems. In this chapter we present three additional network problems: the shortest-route problem, the minimal spanning tree problem, and the maximal flow problem. In each case, we will show how a network model can be developed and solved in order to provide an optimal solution to the problem.

9.1 The Shortest-Route Problem

Alternative criteria are minimizing cost or travel time between a pair of nodes.

In this section we consider a network application where the primary objective is to determine the *shortest route* or *path* between any pair of nodes in a network. Let us demonstrate the shortest-route problem by considering the situation facing the Gorman Construction Company. Gorman has several construction projects located throughout a three-county area. Construction sites are sometimes located as far as 50 miles from Gorman's main office. With multiple daily trips carrying personnel, equipment, and supplies to and from the construction locations, the costs associated with transportation activities are substantial. For any given construction site, the travel alternatives between the site and the office can be described by a network of roads, streets, and highways. The network shown in Figure 9.1 describes the travel alternatives to and from six of Gorman's newest construction sites. The circles or *nodes* of the network correspond to the site locations. The roads, streets, and highways appear as the *arcs* in the network. The distances between the sites are shown above the corresponding arcs. Gorman would like to determine the routes or paths that will minimize the total travel distance from the office to each site.

Figure 9.1
Road Network for the Gorman
Company Shortest-Route Problem

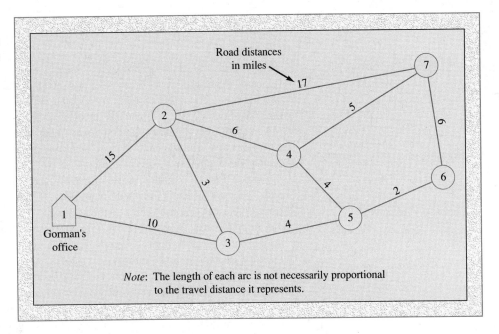

A Shortest-Route Algorithm

To solve Gorman's problem, we need to determine the shortest route from Gorman's office, node 1, to each of the other nodes in the network. The algorithm we present uses a labeling procedure to find the shortest distance from node 1 to each of the other nodes. As we perform the steps of the labeling procedure, we will identify a *label* consisting of two numbers enclosed in brackets for each node. The first number in the label for a particular node indicates the distance from node 1 to that node, while the second number indicates the preceding node on the route from node 1 to that node. We will show the label for each node directly above or below the node in the network. For example, a label for a particular node might appear as shown in Figure 9.2.

At any step of the labeling procedure, a node is said to be either labeled or unlabeled. A labeled node is any node for which we have identified a path from node 1 to that node, and an unlabeled node is any node for which a path has not yet been identified. A labeled node is also said to be either permanently or tentatively labeled. That is, whenever the algorithm has determined the *shortest* distance from node 1 to a particular node, the node is said to have a *permanent* label. If, however, the shortest distance from node 1 to a particular labeled node has not yet been determined, the node is said to have a *tentative*

Figure 9.2
An Example of a Node Label

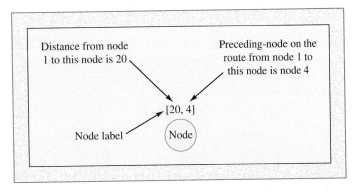

label. Now that we have an idea of what a label is, let us see how labels are computed and how the labeling process can be used to determine the shortest route to each of the nodes in the network.

We begin the labeling process by giving node 1 the permanent label [0,S]. The 0 indicates that the distance from node 1 to itself is zero and the S identifies node 1 as the starting node. To distinguish between tentatively and permanently labeled nodes, we use dark shading for all permanently labeled nodes in the network. In addition, an arrow indicates the permanently labeled node being investigated at each step of the labeling algorithm. The initial identification of Gorman's network is shown in Figure 9.3 when only node 1 is permanently labeled.

To perform the first step or iteration of the labeling procedure, we must consider every node that can be reached directly from node 1; hence, we look first at node 2 and then at node 3. We see that the direct distance from node 1 to node 2 is 15 miles. Thus, node 2 can be tentatively labeled [15,1], with the second number indicating that the preceding node on this route to node 2 is node 1. Next, we consider node 3 and find that the direct distance from node 1 to node 3 is 10 miles. Thus, the tentative label at node 3 is [10,1]. Figure 9.4 shows the results thus far with nodes 2 and 3 tentatively labeled.

Refer to Figure 9.4. We now consider all tentatively labeled nodes and identify the node with the smallest distance value in its label; thus, node 3 with a travel distance of 10 miles is selected. Could we get to node 3 following a shorter route? Since any other route to node 3 would require passing through other nodes, and since the distance from node 1 to all other nodes is greater than or equal to 10, a shorter route to node 3 cannot be found. Accordingly, node 3 is permanently labeled with a distance of 10 miles. Dark shading indicates that node 3 is a permanently labeled node and the arrow indicates that node 3 will be used to start the next step of the labeling process; these steps are shown in Figure 9.5.

We proceed by considering all nodes that are not permanently labeled and that can be reached directly from node 3; these are nodes 2 and 5. Note that the direct distance is 3 miles from node 3 to node 2 and it is 4 miles from node 3 to node 5. Since node 3's permanent label indicates that the shortest distance to node 3 is 10 miles, we see that we can reach node 2 in 10 + 3 = 13 miles and node 5 in 10 + 4 = 14 miles. Thus, the tentative label at node 2 is revised to [13,3] to indicate that we have now found a route

Figure 9.3
Initial Network Identification for Gorman's Shortest-Route Problem

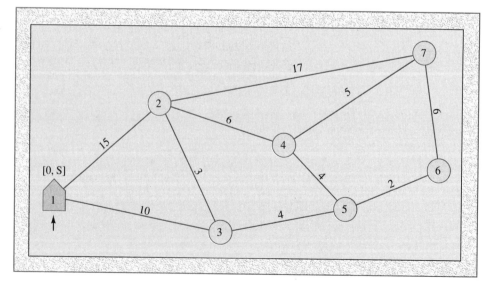

Figure 9.4
Gorman's Network with Tentative
Labels for Nodes 2 and 3

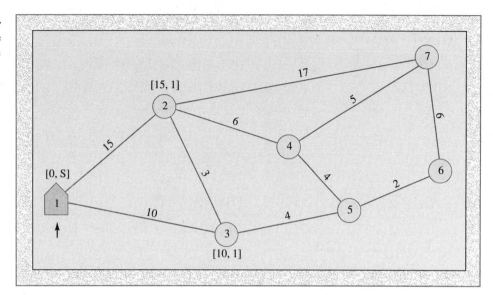

Figure 9.5
Gorman's Network with Node 3
Identified as a Permanently
Labeled Node

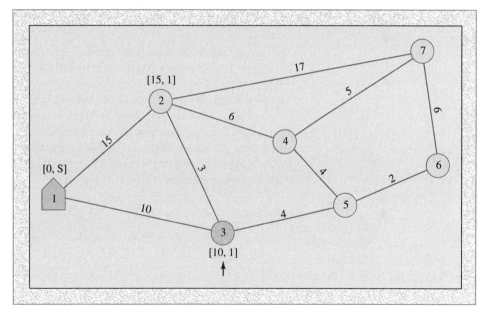

from node 1 to node 2 that has a distance of 13 miles and is routed through node 3. Similarly, the tentative label for node 5 is [14,3]. Figure 9.6 shows the network computations up to this point.

We next consider all tentatively labeled nodes in order to find the node with the smallest distance value in its label. From Figure 9.6 we see that this is node 2 with a distance of 13 miles. Node 2 is now permanently labeled because we now know that node 2 can be reached from node 1 in the shortest possible distance of 13 miles by going through node 3.

The next step or iteration begins at node 2, the most recently permanently labeled node. As before, we consider every nonpermanently labeled node that can be reached directly from node 2; that is, nodes 4 and 7. Starting with the distance value of 13 in the permanent label at node 2 and adding the direct distance from node 2 to both nodes 4 and

Figure 9.6
Gorman's Network with New
Tentative Labels for Nodes 2
and 5

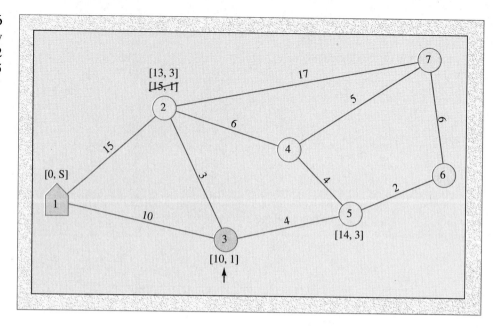

Figure 9.6
Gorman's Network with New
Tentative Labels for Nodes 2
and 5

7, we see that node 4 can be reached in $13 + 6 = 19$ miles, while node 7 can be reached in $13 + 17 = 30$ miles. Thus, the tentative labels at nodes 4 and 7 are as shown in Figure 9.7.

From among the tentatively labeled nodes (nodes 4, 5, and 7), we select the node with the smallest distance value and declare that node permanently labeled. Thus node 5, with a distance of 14, becomes the new permanently labeled node. From node 5, then, we consider all nonpermanently labeled nodes that can be reached directly from node 5. Thus, the tentative label on node 4 is revised, and node 6 is tentatively labeled. Figure 9.8 depicts these calculations.

Figure 9.7
Gorman's Network with a
Permanent Label at Node 2 and
New Tentative Labels for Nodes 4
and 7

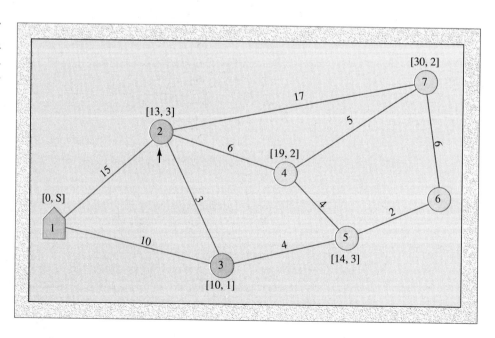

Figure 9.8
Gorman's Network with a
Permanent Label at Node 5 and
New Tentative Labels for Nodes 4
and 6

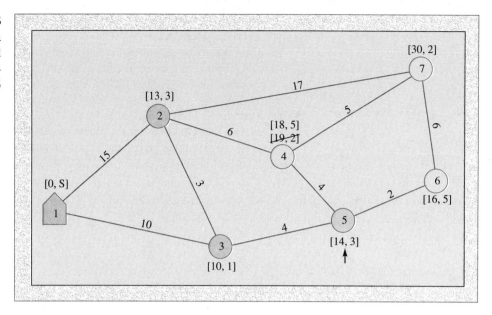

The smallest distance is again identified for the remaining tentatively labeled nodes, and this results in node 6 being permanently labeled. From node 6 we can determine a new tentative label with a distance value of 22 for node 7. After this step, the network appears as shown in Figure 9.9.

We now have only two remaining nonpermanently labeled nodes. Since the distance value at node 4 is smaller than that at node 7, node 4 becomes the new permanently labeled node. Since node 7 is the only nonpermanently labeled node that can be reached directly from node 4, we compare its distance value of 22 with the sum of the distance value at node 4 and the direct distance from node 4 to node 7, that is, $18 + 5 = 23$. Since

Figure 9.9
Gorman's Network with a
Permanent Label at Node 6 and a
New Tentative Label for Node 7

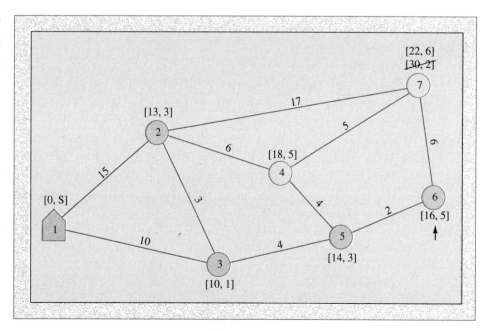

the [22,6] tentative label at node 7 is smaller, it remains unchanged. Figure 9.10 shows the network at this point.

Since node 7 is the only remaining node with a tentative label, it is now permanently labeled. Figure 9.11 shows the final network with all nodes permanently labeled.

We can now use the information in the permanent labels to find the shortest route from node 1 to each node in the network. For example, node 7's permanent label tells us the shortest distance from node 1 to node 7 is 22 miles. To find the particular route that enables us to reach node 7 in 22 miles, we *start* at node 7 and work back. Node 7's label gives us the next direct link—node 6—and node 6's label indicates that node 5 is the next shortest-route link. Continuing this process, we note that we reach node 5 from node 3

Figure 9.10
Gorman's Network with a
Permanent Label at Node 4

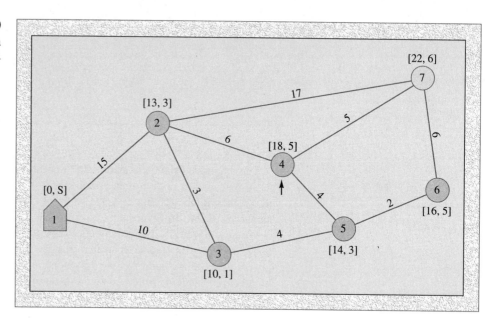

Figure 9.11
Gorman's Network with All Nodes
Permanently Labeled

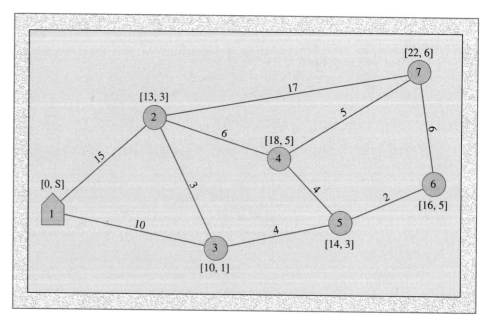

and, finally, that we reach node 3 from node 1. Therefore, the shortest route from node 1 to node 7 is $1-3-5-6-7$. Using this approach, the following shortest routes are identified for the Gorman transportation network:

Node	Shortest Route from Node 1	Distance in Miles
2	$1-3-2$	13
3	$1-3$	10
4	$1-3-5-4$	18
5	$1-3-5$	14
6	$1-3-5-6$	16
7	$1-3-5-6-7$	22

Perhaps for a problem as small as the Gorman problem you could have found the shortest routes just as fast, if not faster, by inspection. However, when we begin to investigate problems with 15 to 20 or more nodes, it becomes very time-consuming to find the shortest routes by inspection. In fact, because of the increased number of alternate routes in a larger network, it is very easy to miss one or more routes and come up with the wrong answer. Thus, for larger problems a systematic procedure such as the labeling procedure described above is required. Even with the labeling method, we find that as the networks grow in size, it becomes necessary to implement the algorithm on a computer.

As we summarize the shortest-route algorithm, think of a network consisting of N nodes. The following procedure can be used to find the shortest route from node 1 to each of the other nodes in the network:

Step 1 Assign node 1 the permanent label [0, S]; The 0 indicates that the distance from node 1 to itself is zero and the S indicates that node 1 is the starting node.

Step 2 Compute tentative labels for the nodes that can be reached directly from node 1. The first number in each label is the direct distance from node 1 to the node in question; we refer to this portion of the label as the distance value. The second number in each label, which we refer to as the preceding-node value, indicates the preceding node on the route from node 1 to the node in question; thus, in this step the preceding-node value is 1 since we are only considering nodes that can be directly reached from node 1.

Step 3 Identify the tentatively labeled node with the smallest distance value, and declare that node permanently labeled. If all nodes are permanently labeled, go to step 5.

Step 4 Consider the remaining nodes that are not permanently labeled and that can be reached directly from the new permanently labeled node identified in step 3. Compute new tentative labels for these nodes as follows:
   a. If the node in question has a tentative label, add the distance value at the new permanently labeled node to the direct distance from the new permanently labeled node to the node in question. If this sum is less than the distance value for the node in question, set the distance value for this node equal to this sum; in addition, set the preceding-node value equal to the new permanently labeled node that provided the smaller distance. Go to step 3.

b. If the node in question is not yet labeled, create a tentative label by adding the distance value at the new permanently labeled node to the direct distance from the new permanently labeled node to the node in question. The preceding-node value is set equal to the new permanently labeled node. Go to step 3.

Step 5 The permanent labels identify both the shortest distance from node 1 to each node and the preceding node on the shortest route. The shortest route to a given node can be found by starting at the given node and moving to its preceding node. Continuing this backward movement through the network will provide the shortest route from node 1 to the node in question.

The shortest-route problem can also be formulated and solved as a transshipment problem. Simply set the supply at the start node and the demand at the end node equal to 1. However, unlike the labeling algorithm, this approach does not find the shortest route from the start node to every other node.

The above algorithm will determine the shortest distance from node 1 to each of the other nodes in the network. Note that $N - 1$ iterations of the algorithm are required to find the shortest distance to all other nodes. If the shortest distance to every node is not needed, the algorithm can be stopped when those nodes of interest have been permanently labeled. The algorithm can also be easily modified to find the shortest distance from any

Figure 9.12
The Management Scientist
Solution of the Gorman
Shortest-Route
Problem

```
****    NETWORK DESCRIPTION    ****

        7 NODES AND 10 ARCS

  ARC     START NODE     END NODE     DISTANCE
  ---     ----------     --------     --------

   1          1             2            15
   2          1             3            10
   3          2             3             3
   4          2             4             6
   5          2             7            17
   6          3             5             4
   7          4             5             4
   8          4             7             5
   9          5             6             2
  10          6             7             6


THE SHORTEST ROUTE FROM NODE 1 TO NODE 7
*****************************************

  START NODE          END NODE          DISTANCE
  ----------          --------          --------
      1                  3                 10
      3                  5                  4
      5                  6                  2
      6                  7                  6

           TOTAL DISTANCE                  22
```

node, say node *k*, to all other nodes in the network. To make such a change, we would merely begin by labeling node *k* with the permanent label [0,S]. Then by applying the steps of the algorithm, we can find the shortest route from node *k* to each of the other nodes in the network.

The microcomputer package, The Management Scientist, can be used to solve small shortest-route problems. Input for the program includes the number of nodes, the number of arcs, and the length of each arc. The output shown in Figure 9.12 provides the shortest route from node 1 to node 7 for the Gorman problem.

You should now be able to use the labeling algorithm to solve a shortest-route problem. Try Problem 1.

NOTES & COMMENTS

1. Many applications of the shortest-route algorithm involve criteria such as time or cost instead of distance. In these cases, the shortest-route algorithm provides the minimum-time or minimum-cost solution. However, since the shortest-route algorithm always identifies a minimum-value solution, it would not make sense to apply the algorithm to problems that involve a profit criterion.

2. In some applications, the value associated with an arc may be negative. For example, in situations where cost is the criterion, a negative arc value would denote a negative cost; in other words, a profit would be realized by traversing the arc. The shortest-route algorithm presented in this section can only be applied to networks with nonnegative arc values. More advanced texts discuss algorithms that can solve problems with negative arc values.

9.2 The Minimal Spanning Tree Problem

In network terminology, the minimal spanning tree problem involves using the arcs of the network to reach *all* nodes of the network in such a fashion that the total length of all the arcs used is minimized. To better understand this problem, let us consider the communications system design problem encountered by a regional computer center.

The Southwestern Regional Computer Center must have special computer communications lines installed to connect five satellite users with a new central computer. The telephone company will install the new communications network. However, the installation is an expensive operation. To reduce costs, the center's management group wants the total length of the new communications lines to be as small as possible. While the central computer could be connected directly to each user, it appears to be more economical to install a direct line to some users and let other users tap into the system by linking them with users already connected to the system. The determination of this minimal length communications system design is an example of the *minimal spanning tree* problem. The network for this problem with possible connection alternatives and distances is shown in Figure 9.13. An algorithm that can be used to solve this network model is explained below.

A Minimal Spanning Tree Algorithm

For a network consisting of *N* nodes, any spanning tree will consist of *N* − 1 arcs.

A *spanning tree* for an *N*-node network is a set of *N* − 1 arcs that connects every node to every other node. A minimal spanning tree is the set of arcs that does this at minimal total

Figure 9.13
Communications Network for the
Regional Computer System

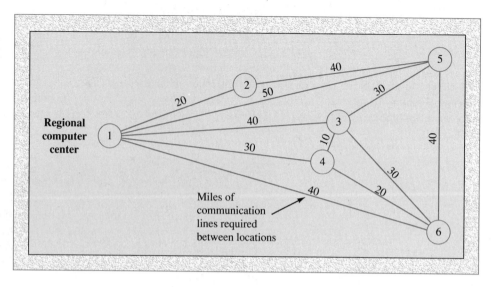

arc cost, distance, etc. The network algorithm that can be used to solve the minimal spanning tree problem is very simple. The steps of the algorithm are as follows:

Step 1 Arbitrarily begin at any node and connect it to the closest node in terms of the criterion being used (e.g. time, cost, or distance). The two nodes are referred to as *connected* nodes, and the remaining nodes are referred to as *unconnected* nodes.

Step 2 Identify the unconnected node that is closest to one of the connected nodes. Break ties arbitrarily if two or more nodes qualify as the closest node. Add this new node to the set of connected nodes. Repeat this step until all nodes have been connected.

This network algorithm is easily implemented by making the connection decisions directly on the network.

Referring to the communications network for the regional computer center and arbitrarily beginning at node 1, we find the closest node is node 2 with a distance of 20. Using a bold line to connect nodes 1 and 2, step 1 of the algorithm provides the following result:

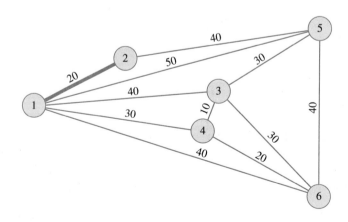

In step 2 of the algorithm, we find that the unconnected node closest to one of the connected nodes is node 4, with a distance of 30 miles from node 1. Adding node 4 to the set of connected nodes provides the following result:

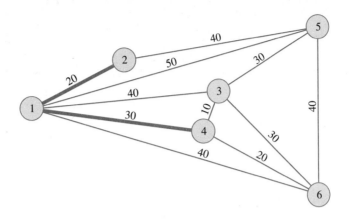

Repeating the step of always adding the closest unconnected node to the connected segment of the network provides the minimal spanning tree solution shown in Figure 9.14. Follow the steps of the algorithm, and see if you obtain this solution. The minimal length of the spanning tree is given by the sum of the distances on the arcs forming the spanning tree. In this case, the total distance is 110 miles for the computer center's communications network. Note that while the computer center's network arcs were measured in distance, other network models may measure the arcs in terms of other criteria such as cost, time, and so on. In such cases, the minimal spanning tree algorithm will identify the optimal solution (minimal cost, minimal time, etc.) for the criterion being considered.

The computer solution to the regional computer center's problem is shown in Figure 9.15. The Management Scientist was used to obtain the minimal spanning tree solution of 110 miles.

You should now be able to find a minimal spanning tree for a network. Try Problem 10.

Figure 9.14
Minimal Spanning Tree Communications Network for the Regional Computer Center

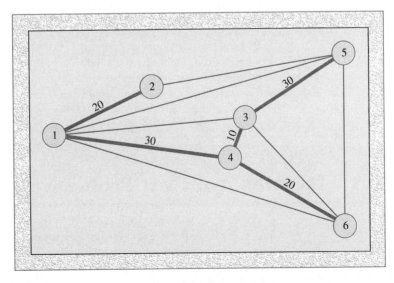

Figure 9.15
The Management Scientist
Solution for the Regional
Computer Center Minimal
Spanning Tree Problem

```
    ****   NETWORK DESCRIPTION   ****
           6 NODES AND 11 ARCS
   ARC      START NODE      END NODE       DISTANCE
   ---      ----------      --------       --------
    1          1               2              20
    2          1               3              40
    3          1               4              30
    4          1               5              50
    5          1               6              40
    6          2               5              40
    7          3               4              10
    8          3               5              30
    9          3               6              30
   10          4               6              20
   11          5               6              40

          MINIMAL SPANNING TREE
       *********************

   START NODE        END NODE          DISTANCE
   ----------        --------          --------
       1                2                 20
       1                4                 30
       4                3                 10
       4                6                 20
       3                5                 30

       TOTAL LENGTH                      110
```

NOTES & COMMENTS

The minimal spanning tree algorithm is considered a *greedy algorithm* since at each stage we can be "greedy" and take the best action available at that stage. Following this strategy at each successive stage will provide the overall optimal solution. Cases such as this, where a greedy algorithm provides the optimal solution, are rare. For many problems, however, greedy algorithms are excellent heuristics.

9.3 The Maximal Flow Problem

Consider a network with one input or *source* node and one output or *sink* node. The *maximal flow* problem asks: What is the maximum amount of flow (vehicles, messages, fluid, etc.) that can enter and exit the network system in a given period of time? In this problem, we attempt to transmit flow through all arcs of the network as efficiently as possible. The amount of flow is limited due to capacity restrictions on the various arcs of

Figure 9.16
Network of Highway System and Flow Capacities (1000's/Hour) for Cincinnati

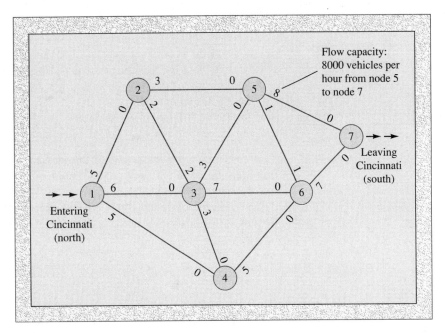

the network. For example, highway types limit vehicle flow in a transportation system, while pipe sizes limit oil flow in an oil distribution system. The maximum or upper limit on the flow in an arc is referred to as the *flow capacity* of the arc. While we do not specify capacities for the nodes, we do assume that the flow out of a node is equal to the flow into the node.

As an example of the maximal flow problem, consider the north–south interstate highway system passing through Cincinnati, Ohio. The north–south vehicle flow reaches a level of 15,000 vehicles per hour at peak times. Due to a summer highway maintenance program, which calls for the temporary closing of lanes and lower speed limits, a network of alternate routes through Cincinnati has been proposed by a transportation planning committee. The alternate routes include other highways as well as city streets. Because of differences in speed limits and traffic patterns, flow capacities vary, depending on the particular streets or roads used. The proposed network with arc flow capacities is shown in Figure 9.16.

The flow capacities are based on the direction of the flow. For example, highway section or arc 1–2 shows a capacity of 5000 vehicles per hour in the 1–2 direction; however, a zero capacity exists in the 2–1 direction. This means that the highway network planners do not want vehicles flowing from node 2 into node 1. Logically speaking, since node 1 is the input, or source, and a potential traffic jam location, it would be undesirable to permit traffic flow into the node 1 intersection from node 2. The directional capacities on arc 1–2 can also be interpreted as indicating a one-way street leading from the node 1 intersection. In any case, this example shows that the flow capacities of arcs can be dependent on the direction of the flow. Do you believe the highway system network shown in Figure 9.16 can accommodate the north–south maximum flow of 15,000 vehicles per hour? What is the maximal flow in vehicles per hour for the network? How much flow should go over each arc?

A Maximal Flow Algorithm

The maximal flow problem can also be formulated and solved as a linear program.

As we shall see, the maximal flow algorithm presented in this section uses the following common-sense approach:

1. Find any path from the input (source) node to the output (sink) node that has flow capacities in the direction of the flow greater than zero for all arcs on the path.
2. Increase the flow along the path by as much as possible.
3. Continue looking for source-to-sink paths that have remaining flow capacities in the direction of the flow greater than zero for all arcs, and increase the flow along these paths as much as possible.
4. Stop when it is no longer possible to find a source-to-sink path with flow capacities in the direction of the flow greater than zero for all arcs on the path.

Before presenting the details of the maximal flow algorithm, let us briefly discuss a procedure that will ensure that these intuitive steps result in an optimal solution to this maximal flow problem.

The procedure permits previously assigned flow to take an alternate route by permitting fictional flows in the reverse direction. For example, consider the 3–6 arc:

Here we see that the initial flow capacity in the 3–6 direction is 7000 vehicles per hour, while no flow is permitted in the 6–3 direction.

If we choose to let 6000 vehicles per hour flow in the 3–6 direction, we will revise the flow capacities as follows:

Note that we have decreased the flow capacity in the 3–6 direction by 6000 vehicles per hour and simultaneously increased the flow capacity in the 6–3 direction by the same amount. The revised flow capacity of 1000 vehicles per hour in the 3–6 direction is readily interpreted as the remaining flow capacity for the arc. However, note that the 6–3 direction that had an initial flow capacity of zero now shows a revised flow capacity of 6000 vehicles per hour. This revised capacity in the 6–3 direction is actually indicating that a fictitious flow of up to 6000 vehicles per hour is permitted in this direction. Fictitious flow would not actually send vehicles in the 6–3 direction but would rather decrease the amount of flow originally committed to the 3–6 arc direction. In effect, fictitious flow in the 6–3 direction would result in diverting flow originally committed to the 3–6 direction to other arcs in the network.

The above process of tracking flow capacities is an important part of the maximal flow algorithm. For example, in an earlier step of the algorithm, we might commit flow along a certain arc. Later, due to flows identified in other arcs, it may be desirable to decrease the flow along the original arc. This procedure will identify the extent to which our original decision to commit some flow needs to be revised in order to increase the total flow through the network.

Let us now look at the steps of the maximal flow algorithm.

Step 1 Find any path from the source (input) node to the sink (output) node that has flow capacities in the direction of the flow greater than zero for all arcs on the path. If no path is available, the optimal solution has been reached.

Step 2 Find the smallest arc capacity, P_f, on the path selected in step 1. Increase the flow through the network by sending an amount P_f over the path selected in step 1.

Step 3 For the path selected in step 1, reduce all arc flow capacities in the direction of flow by P_f, and increase all arc flow capacities in the reverse direction by P_f. Go to step 1.

While the procedure will vary depending on the analyst's choice of paths in step 1, the algorithm will eventually provide the maximal flow solution. Our calculations for the highway flow network are as follows:

ITERATION 1

The path selected is 1–3–6–7; P_f, determined by arc 1–3, is 6. The revised network is as follows:

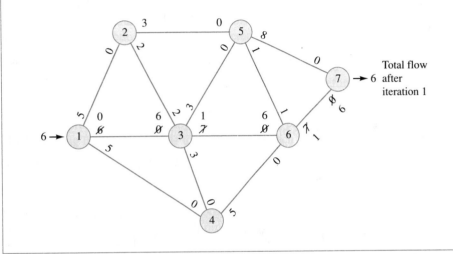

ITERATION 2

The path selected is 1–2–5–7; P_f, determined by arc 2–5, is 3. The revised network is as follows:

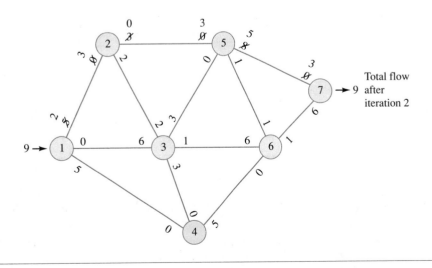

The total flow through the network at each iteration can be found by summing the P_f values from all iterations.

While we will not show the revised network after each iteration, you should attempt to update the network flow capacities as you follow the discussion. For example, what will this network look like after the following three iterations?

ITERATION 3

The path selected is 1–2–3–5–7; P_f, determined by arc 1–2 (or 2–3), is 2.

ITERATION 4

The path selected is 1–4–6–7; P_f, determined by arc 6–7, is 1.

ITERATION 5

The path selected is 1–4–6–5–7; P_f, determined by arc 6–5, is 1.

At this point, we have a total flow of 13,000 vehicles per hour, and the revised network capacities are as follows:

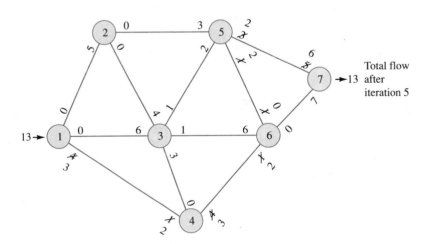

Total flow 13 after iteration 5

Are there any other paths from node 1 to node 7 that have flow capacities in the direction of the flow greater than zero? Try 1–4–6–3–5–7, with a flow of $P_f = 1$ determined by arc 3–5. This increases the flow to 14,000 vehicles per hour. However, as you can see from the following revised network, there are no more paths from node 1 to node 7 that have flow capacities greater than zero on all arcs of the path; thus, 14,000 vehicles per hour is the maximal flow for this network.

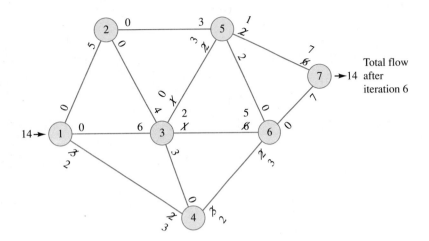

Note that in iteration 6 a flow of 1000 vehicles per hour was permitted in the 6–3 direction. From the initial network, however, we know that the flow capacity in the 6–3 direction is zero; thus, the 1000 units of flow in the 6–3 direction represent a fictitious flow. The real effect of this flow is to divert 1000 units of flow originally committed to the 3–6 arc in iteration 1 along the 3–5 arc to enable us to get 1000 units more of flow through the network. Let us now determine the amount and direction of flow in each arc so that the total flow of 14,000 vehicles per hour can be attained.

Arc flows for the maximal flow solution can be found by comparing the final arc flow capacities with the initial arc flow capacities. If the final flow capacity is *less* than the initial flow capacity, flow is occurring over the arc with an amount equal to the difference between the initial and final flow capacities. For example, consider the 3–6 arc with initial and final flow capacities shown below.

Initial Capacities

Final Capacities

Since the final flow capacity in the 3–6 direction is less than the initial flow capacity, the arc has a flow of $7 - 2 = 5$ in the 3–6 direction. This arc flow is summarized as follows:

$$3 \xrightarrow{\ 5 \ } 6$$

Comparing final and initial arc flow capacities for all arcs in the network enables us to determine the final flow pattern as shown in Figure 9.17.

The results of the maximal flow analysis indicate that the planned highway network system will not handle the peak flow of 15,000 vehicles per hour. The transportation planners will have to expand the highway network, increase current arc flow capacities, or be prepared for serious traffic jam problems. If the network is extended or modified, another maximal flow analysis will determine the extent of any improved flow.

Try Problem 15 for practice in solving a maximal flow problem.

Figure 9.17
Maximal Flow Pattern for the
Highway System Network

Summary

In this chapter we extended the discussion of the use of network models in managerial decision making. We introduced the shortest-route, minimal spanning tree, and maximal flow problems and presented specialized solution algorithms for each. The key to success in network approaches to problem solving is in seeing how the problem can be represented as a network model. While some network formulations are obvious, other problems may require substantial ingenuity to develop the appropriate network representation. In any case, once the network representation has been developed, specialized solution algorithms are available to solve the problem.

NOTES & COMMENTS

Network models can be used to describe a variety of management science problems. Unfortunately, there is no one network solution algorithm or computer code that can be used to solve every network problem. It is important to recognize the specific type of problem being modeled in order to select the correct specialized solution algorithm and computer code.

Glossary

Shortest route Shortest path between two nodes in a network.

Minimal spanning tree The spanning tree with the minimum length.

Spanning tree A set of $N - 1$ arcs that connect every node in the network with all other nodes where N is the number of nodes.

Arc capacity The maximum flow for an arc of the network. The arc capacity in one direction may not equal the arc capacity in the reverse direction.

Source A node that generates flow such that flow can only move away from it and never into it.
Sink A node that absorbs flow such that flow can only move into it and never away from it.
Maximal flow The maximum amount of flow that can enter and exit a network system during a
given period of time.

Problems

S ELF T EST

1. Shortest route

1. Find the shortest route from node 1 to each of the other nodes in the transportation
network shown.

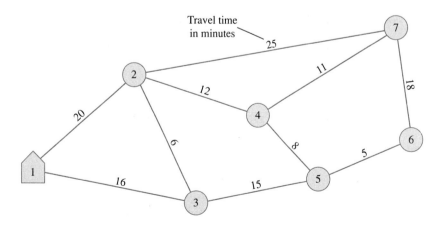

2. Variation of Gorman problem;
find shortest route from different
node

3. Variation of Gorman problem;
minimize travel time

2. For the Gorman Construction Company problem (see Figure 9.1), assume that node 7 is
the company's warehouse and supply center. Several daily trips are commonly made from
node 7 to the other nodes or construction sites. Using node 7 as the starting node, find the
shortest route from this node to each of the other nodes in the network.

3. In the original Gorman Construction Company problem, we found the shortest distance
from the office (node 1) to each of the other nodes or construction sites. Because some of
the roads are highways and others are city streets, the shortest-distance routes between the
office and the construction sites may not necessarily provide the quickest or shortest-time
routes. Shown below is the Gorman road network with travel time values rather than
distance values. Find the shortest route from Gorman's office to each of the construction
sites if the objective is to minimize travel time rather than distance.

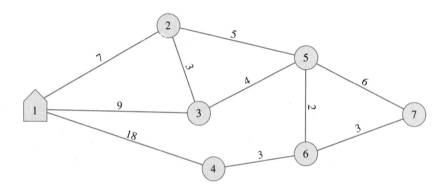

4. Find the shortest route between nodes 1 and 8 in the following network:

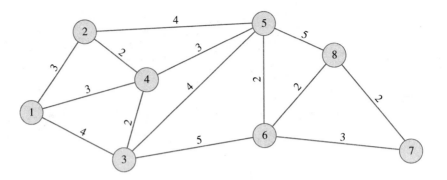

5. Shortest route

5. Find the shortest route between nodes 1 and 10 in the following network:

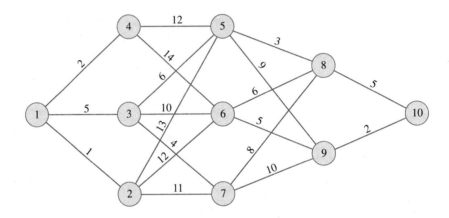

6. Shortest route to all cities

6. Morgan Trucking Company operates a special fast-service pickup and delivery service between Chicago and 10 other cities located in a four-state area. When Morgan receives a request for service, it dispatches a truck from Chicago to the city requesting service as soon as possible. Since both fast service and minimum travel costs are objectives for Morgan, it is important that the dispatched truck take the shortest route from Chicago to the specified city. Assume that the following network (not drawn to scale) with distances given in miles represents the highway network for this problem:

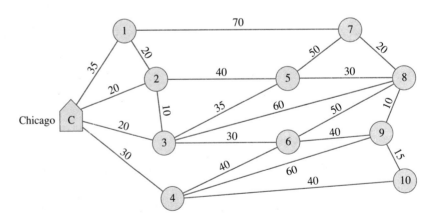

a. Find the shortest-route distances from Chicago to all 10 cities.
b. What is the shortest route to city 7? To city 9?

7. Shortest route

7. City Cab Company has identified 10 primary pickup and drop locations for cab riders in New York City. In an effort to minimize travel time and improve customer service and the utilization of the company's fleet of cabs, management would like the cab drivers to take the shortest route between locations whenever possible. Using the network of roads and streets shown below, what is the route a driver beginning at location 1 should take to reach location 10? The travel times in minutes are shown on the arcs of the network.

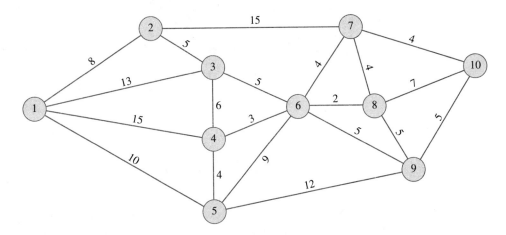

8. Shortest route

8. The Wisman Candy Company manufactures a variety of candy products. Company trucks are used to deliver local orders directly to retail outlets. When the business was small, the drivers of the trucks were free to take routes of their choice as they made the delivery rounds to the retail outlets. However, as the business has grown, transportation and delivery costs have become significant. In an effort to improve the efficiency of the delivery operation, Wisman's management would like to determine the shortest delivery routes between retail outlets. For example, the network below shows the roads that may be taken between a retail outlet at node 1 and a retail outlet at node 11. Determine the shortest route for a truck that must make deliveries to both outlets.

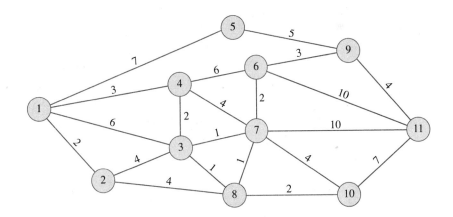

9. Use shortest-route model for equipment replacement

9. The five nodes in the network shown below represent points 1 year apart over a 4-year period. Each node indicates a time when a decision is made to keep or replace a firm's computer equipment. If a decision is made to replace the equipment, a decision must also be made as to how long the new equipment will be used. The arc from node 0 to node 1 represents the decision to keep the current equipment 1 year and replace it at the end of the year. The arc from node 0 to node 2 represents the decision to keep the current equipment 2 years and replace it at the end of year 2. The numbers above the arcs indicate the total cost associated with the equipment replacement decisions. These costs include discounted purchase price, trade-in value, operating costs, and maintenance costs. Determine the minimum-cost equipment replacement policy for the 4-year period.

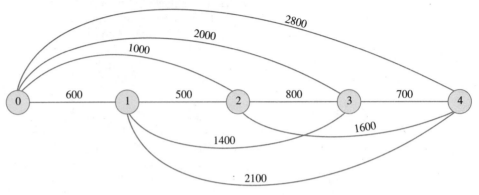

10. The State of Ohio recently purchased land for a new state park, and park planners have identified the ideal locations for the lodge, cabins, picnic groves, boat dock, and scenic points of interest. These locations are represented by the nodes of the network below. The arcs of the network represent possible road alternatives in the park. If the state park designers want to minimize the total road miles that must be constructed in the park and still permit access to all facilities (nodes), which road alternatives should be constructed?

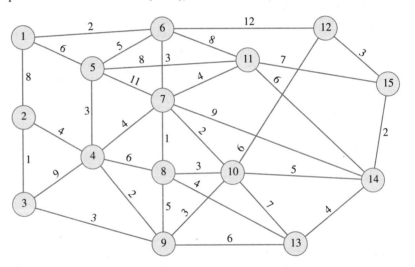

11. Develop the minimal spanning tree solution for the following emergency communications network.

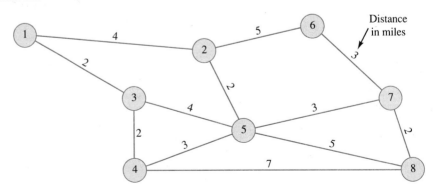

12. Minimal spanning tree

12. In a large soap products plant, quality control inspectors take samples of various products from the different production areas and deliver them to the lab for analysis. The inspection process is slow, and the inspectors spend substantial time transporting samples from the production areas to the lab. The company is considering installing a pneumatic tube conveyor system that could transport the samples between the production areas and the lab. The network below shows the locations of the lab and the production areas (nodes) where the samples must be collected. The arcs are the alternatives being considered for the conveyor system. What is the minimum total length and layout of the conveyor system that will enable all production areas to send samples to the lab?

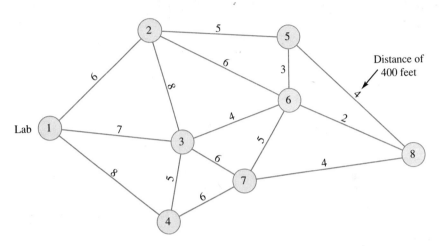

13. Minimal spanning tree

13. Midwest University is installing a computerized electronic mail system that will enable messages to be transmitted instantly among eight college offices. The network with possible electronic connections among the offices is shown below. Distances between offices are shown in thousands of feet. Develop a design for the office communication system that will enable all offices to have access to the electronic mail service. Provide the design that minimizes the total length of connections among the eight offices.

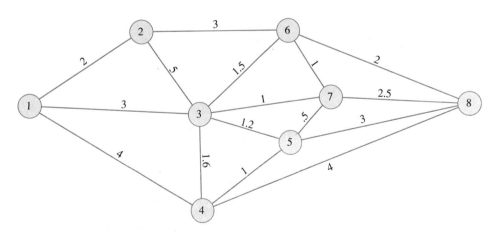

14. Minimal spanning tree

14. The Metrovision Cable Company has just received approval to begin providing cable television service to a suburb of Memphis, Tenn. The nodes of the network below show the distribution points that must be reached by the company's primary cable lines. The arcs of the network show the number of miles between the distribution points. Determine the solution that will enable the company to reach all distribution points with the minimum length of primary cable line.

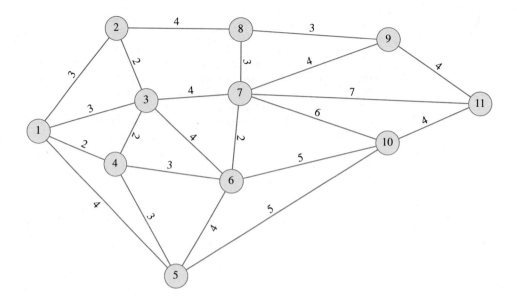

S ELF T EST ▶

15. Maximal flow

15. The north–south highway system passing through Albany, N.Y., can accommodate the capacities shown.

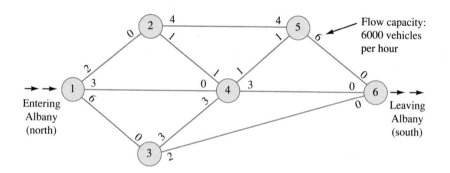

Do you believe the highway system can accommodate a north–south flow of 10,000 vehicles per hour?

16. Maximal flow

16. If the Albany highway system problem (see Problem 15) has revised flow capacities as shown in the following network, what is the maximal flow in vehicles per hour through the system?

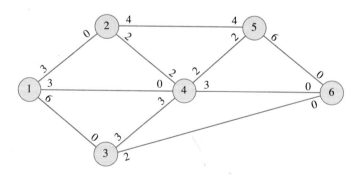

How many vehicles per hour must travel over each road (arc) to obtain this maximal flow?

17. Maximal flow

17. A long-distance telephone company uses an underground cable network of communication lines to provide high-quality audio communication between two major cities. Calls are carried through series cable lines and connecting nodes in the network as shown below. Also shown are the number of telephone calls (in thousands) that may occur simultaneously at any point in time. What is the maximum number of telephone calls that can be transmitted simultaneously between the two cities? What are the connecting nodes and cable flows when the system is operating at capacity?

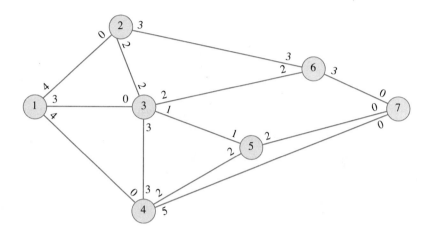

18. Maximal flow, variations

18. The High-Price Oil Company owns a pipeline network that is used to transmit oil from its source to several storage locations. A portion of the network is as follows:

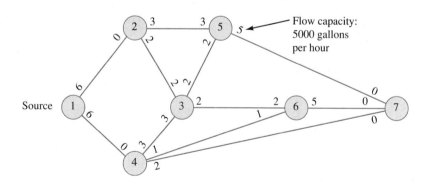

Due to the varying pipe sizes, the flow capacities also vary. By selectively opening and closing sections of the pipeline network, the firm can supply any of the storage locations.

a. If the firm wants to supply storage location 7 and fully utilize the system capacity, how long will it take to satisfy a location 7 demand of 100,000 gallons? What is the maximal flow for this pipeline system?

b. If a break occurs on line 2–3 and it is closed down, what is the maximal flow for the system? How long will it take to transmit 100,000 gallons to location 7?

19. Maximal flow, variations

19. For the highway network system shown below, determine the maximal flow in vehicles per hour.

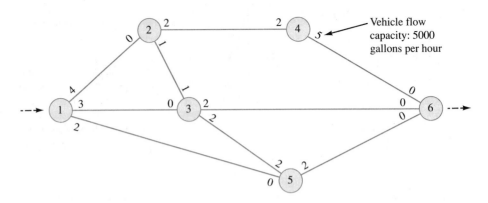

The highway commission is considering adding highway section 3–4 to permit a flow of 2000 vehicles per hour or, at an additional cost, a flow of 3000 vehicles per hour. What is your recommendation for the 3–4 arc of the network?

20. A chemical processing plant has a network of pipes that are used to transfer liquid chemical products from one part of the plant to another. The pipe network and pipe flow capacities in gallons per minute are shown below. What is the maximum flow capacity for the system if the company wishes to transfer as much liquid chemical as possible from location 1 to location 9? How much of the chemical will flow through the section of pipe from node 3 to node 5?

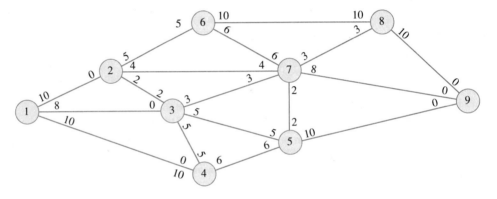

Case Problem: Ambulance Routing

The city of Binghamton is served by two major hospitals: Western Medical and Binghamton General. Western Medical is located in the southwest part of the city, and Binghamton General is in the northeast.

Bob Jones, the hospital administrator at Western Medical, has been discussing the problem of scheduling and routing ambulances with Margaret Johnson, the hospital administrator at Binghamton General. Both administrators feel that some type of system needs to be developed to better coordinate the use of the ambulance services at the two hospitals so that together they can provide the fastest possible emergency service for the city.

A proposal being considered is for all ambulance service calls to be handled through a central dispatcher, who could assign a call to the hospital capable of providing the fastest service. In studying this proposal, a project team consisting of employees from both hospitals met and decided that the best approach would be to divide the city into 20 service zones. In the proposed configuration, Western Medical would be located in zone 1 and Binghamton General in zone 20. A map showing the placement of the 20 zones and the travel time (in minutes) between adjacent zones is provided in Figure 9.18.

Figure 9.18
Network for Proposed Ambulance
Service

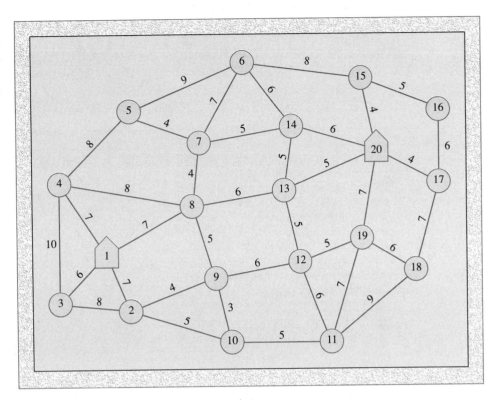

According to the proposed operating procedure, incoming emergency calls would be identified by zone number, and an ambulance from the hospital closest to that zone would be assigned the service call. However, if all ambulances from the closest hospital were occupied with other emergencies, the service call would be assigned to the other hospital. Regardless of which hospital responded to the service call, the individual or individuals requiring the emergency service would be taken to the closest hospital.

To make the coordinated service as efficient as possible, the ambulance drivers must know in advance the quickest route to take to each zone, which hospital the individual or individuals in that zone should be taken to, and the quickest route to that hospital.

Managerial Report

Prepare a report for the two hospital administrators describing your analysis of the problem. Include in your report recommendations regarding the following items:

1. A chart for the dispatcher that identifies the primary hospital ambulance service for every zone in the city.
2. A chart for the Western Medical ambulance drivers that provides the minimum-time routes from Western Medical to every zone in the city, including Binghamton General. Include a chart that tells Western Medical drivers which hospital the individuals should be taken to and the route that should be followed.
3. A chart for the Binghamton General ambulance drivers that provides the minimum-time routes from Binghamton General to every zone in the city, including Western Medical. Include a chart that tells Binghamton General drivers which hospital the individuals should be taken to and the route that should be followed.
4. Include recommendations regarding how the system could be modified to take into account varying traffic conditions that occur throughout the day and/or changes in driving conditions resulting from temporary road construction projects.

EDS

Plano, Texas[1]

EDS is a global leader in providing information technology services. For more than 30 years, the company has provided hardware, software, communications, and process solutions to companies and governments around the world. Headquartered in Plano, Texas, EDS helps customers become more competitive by focusing technology on business goals. Customers come from a variety of industries and include leaders in the automotive, government services, financial, insurance, communications, manufacturing, retail, energy, distribution, transportation, utilities, and health care industries. In 1984, EDS was acquired by the world's leading auto manufacturer, General Motors, and became an independently-operated subsidiary.

Minimal Spanning Tree Network Problem

EDS designs communication systems and information networks for many of its customers. In one application, a customer had 64 locations that needed to be linked together for information flow, information processing, and communications. Interactive data including voice, video, and digital data had to be accommodated in the information flow between the various sites. The customer's locations included approximately 50 offices and information

—Continued on next page

[1]The authors are indebted to Greg A. Dennis of EDS for providing this application.

Figure 9.19
A Portion of the Information Network Designed by EDS

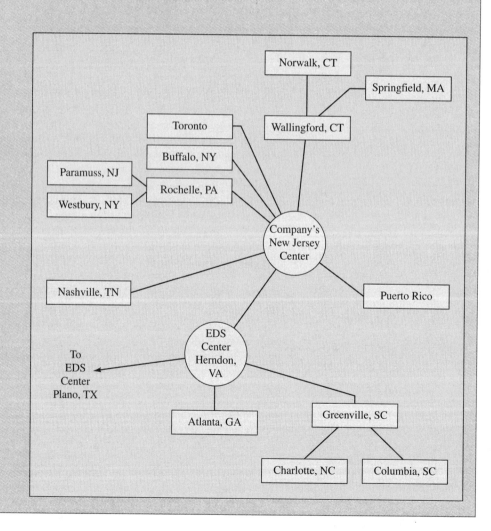

—Continued from previous page

centers in the continental United States; they ranged from Connecticut to Florida to Michigan to Texas to California. Additional locations existed in Canada, Mexico, Hawaii, and Puerto Rico. The total of 64 company locations formed the nodes of the information network.

EDS's task was to span the network by finding the most cost effective way to link 64 customer locations or nodes with the other customer locations as well as with existing EDS data centers. The arcs of the network were formed by connecting pairs of nodes in the network. In cases where land communication lines were available, the arcs consisted of fiber optic telephone lines. In other cases, the arcs were formed by satellite communication connections.

Using cost as the criterion, the information network design was a minimal spanning tree problem with the ultimate goal being the development of a minimum-cost network design such that all locations (nodes) could communicate with all other locations (nodes). Figure 9.19 shows a portion of the information network developed by EDS. With a communication arc

between the company's New Jersey center and the EDS center in Herndon, Virginia, the network enabled the company to communicate through Herndon with locations in Texas, Arizona, California, Hawaii, and Mexico by taking advantage of the existing EDS center in Plano, Texas. The use of the EDS centers in Herndon and Plano meant that the client could span its network without developing its own independent information network. An effective and economical communication system was developed for the customer.

Questions

1. What were the nodes and the arcs of the information network?
2. Where does the minimal spanning tree problem enter into design of the information network?
3. Why were the number of nodes expanded to include existing EDS centers in addition to the 64 company locations? What advantages did this provide in developing the minimum-cost network design?

CHAPTER 10

Project Scheduling: PERT/CPM

In many situations, managers assume the responsibility for planning, scheduling, and controlling projects that consist of numerous separate jobs or activities performed by a variety of departments and individuals. Often these projects are so large or complex that the manager cannot possibly keep all the information pertaining to the plan, schedule, and progress of the project in his or her head. In these situations, the techniques of PERT (*Program Evaluation and Review Technique*) and CPM (*Critical Path Method*) have proven to be extremely valuable in assisting managers in carrying out their project management responsibilities.

PERT and CPM have been used for a wide variety of projects, including

1. Research and development of new products and processes
2. Construction of plants, buildings, and highways
3. Maintenance of large and complex equipment
4. Design and installation of new systems

In projects such as these, project managers must schedule the various jobs or *activities* so that the entire project is completed on time. A complicating factor in carrying out this task is the interdependence of the activities; for example, some activities depend on the completion of other activities before they can be started. When we realize that projects can have as many as several thousand activities, we see why project managers look for procedures that will help them answer questions such as the following:

1. What is the total time to complete the project?
2. What are the scheduled start and finish dates for each specific activity?
3. Which activities are "critical" and must be completed *exactly* as scheduled to keep the project on schedule?
4. How long can "noncritical" activities be delayed before they cause a delay in the total project?

As you will see, PERT and CPM can be used to help answer the above questions.

A NASA project management team was responsible for landing Apollo 11 safely on the moon. Project scheduling techniques helped ensure that over 300,000 activities performed by over 400,000 people came together at the right time to make the mission successful.

Henry L. Gantt developed the Gantt Chart as a graphical aid to scheduling jobs on machines in 1918. This was the first application of what we know of as project scheduling techniques.

PERT (Navy) and CPM (Du Pont and Remington Rand) were developed for the same basic project scheduling purpose; they differ, however, because they were developed by different people working on different projects. Today, the best aspects of each have been combined to provide a valuable project scheduling technique.

While PERT and CPM have the same general purpose and utilize much of the same terminology, the techniques were actually developed independently. PERT was introduced in the late 1950s specifically for the Polaris missile project. Since many jobs or activities associated with the Polaris missile project had never been attempted previously, it was difficult to predict the completion times of the various jobs or activities. Consequently, PERT was developed to handle uncertainties in activity completion times.

On the other hand, CPM was developed primarily for industrial projects where activity times were considered known. CPM offers the option of reducing activity times by adding more workers and/or resources, usually at an increased cost. Thus, a distinguishing feature of CPM is that it enables trade-offs in time and cost for the various project activities.

Today's computerized versions of PERT/CPM often contain options for considering uncertainty in activity times as well as activity time–cost trade-offs. In this regard modern project scheduling procedures have essentially combined the features of PERT and CPM such that a distinction between the techniques is no longer necessary.

10.1　PERT/CPM Networks

The planning effort that goes into identifying the activities and their interrelationships is the critical first step of project scheduling. A team approach involving creativity and attention to detail is required. A significant amount of time may be needed to complete this step.

Immediate predecessor information determines whether activities can be completed in parallel (worked on simultaneously) or in series (one completed before another begins). Generally, with more series relationships present in a project, more time will be required to complete the project.

The first step in the PERT/CPM project scheduling process is the determination of the specific activities that will make up the project. As a simple illustration involving the process of buying a small business, consider the list of four activities shown in Table 10.1. The development of an accurate list of activities such as this is a key step in any project. Since we will base the entire project plan and completion date estimates on this list of activities, poor planning and omission of activities would be disastrous and would lead to inaccurate schedules. However, we will assume that the activities have been carefully planned. Table 10.1 lists all activities for the small business project.

Note that Table 10.1 contains additional information in the column labeled Immediate Predecessor. The *immediate predecessors* for a particular activity are the activities that, when completed, enable the start of the activity in question. For example, the information in Table 10.1 tells us we can start work on activities A and B anytime since neither of these activities depends on the completion of any prior activities. However, activity C cannot be started until activity B has been completed, and activity D cannot be started until both activities A and C have been completed. As you will see, immediate predecessor information must be known for each activity in order to describe the interdependencies among the activities.

In Figure 10.1 we have drawn a network that depicts the activities listed in Table 10.1 and shows the predecessor relationships among the activities. This graphical representation is referred to as the PERT/CPM network for the project. The activities are shown on

Table 10.1
Activity List for Small Business Project

Activity	Activity Description	Immediate Predecessor
A	Develop a list of sources for financing	—
B	Analyze the financial records of the business	—
C	Develop a business plan (sales projections, cash flow projections, etc.)	B
D	Submit a proposal to a lending institution	A, C

Figure 10.1
PERT/CPM Network for Small
Business Project

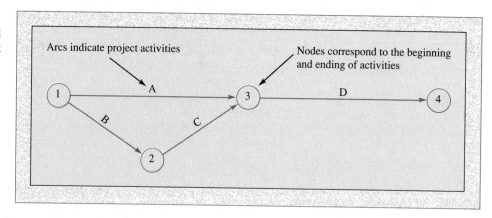

the arcs of the network. The circles, or nodes, correspond to the beginning and ending of the activities. The completion of all the activities that lead into a node is referred to as an *event*. For example, node 2 corresponds to the event that activity B has been completed, and node 3 corresponds to the event that both activities A and C have been completed.

Let us now attempt to develop the network for another project having the following activities and immediate predecessors:

Activity	Immediate Predecessor
A	—
B	—
C	B
D	A, C
E	C
F	C
G	D, E, F

A portion of the PERT/CPM network that could be used for the first four activities is as follows:

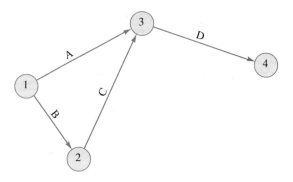

This portion of the network causes no particular problem for activity D since it shows activities A and C as the correct immediate predecessors. However, when we attempt to add activity E, we encounter a problem. At first we might attempt to show activity E beginning at node 3. However, this indicates that both activities A and C are the immediate predecessors for activity E, which is incorrect. Referring to the original activity schedule for the project, we see that activity E only has activity C as its immediate predecessor.

We can avoid the above problem by inserting a *dummy activity,* which, as the name implies, is not an actual activity, but rather a fictitious activity used to ensure that the proper precedence relationships among the activities are depicted in the network. For example, we can add node 5 and insert a dummy activity, indicated by a dashed line from node 5 to node 3, forming the network shown below.

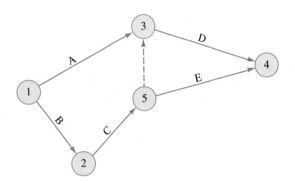

With this change in the network, activity E only has activity C as its immediate predecessor. The dummy activity does not have a time requirement but is merely used to maintain the proper precedence relationships in the network. Note that the insertion of the dummy activity also correctly shows activities A and C as the immediate predecessors for activity D.

Completion of the seven-activity network could be shown as follows:

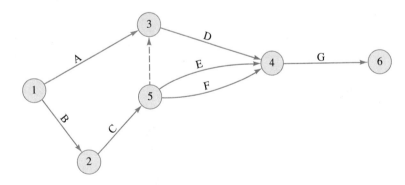

A project network is extremely helpful in visualizing the interrelationships of activities. In large and complex projects, several dummy activities may be needed to maintain the immediate predecessor relationships. The ability to take an activity list and draw a project network, including the identification of dummy activities, is not trivial and will improve as students gain practice and experience.

Note how the network correctly identifies activities D, E, and F as the immediate predecessors for activity G. However, note that activities E and F both start at node 5 and end at node 4. This situation causes problems for certain computer programs that use starting and ending nodes to identify the activities in a PERT/CPM network. In these programs, the computer procedure would recognize activities E and F as the same activity since they have the same starting and ending nodes. When this condition occurs, dummy activities can be added to make sure that two or more activities do not have the same starting and ending nodes. The use of node 7 and a dummy activity as shown below eliminates this problem for activities E and F.

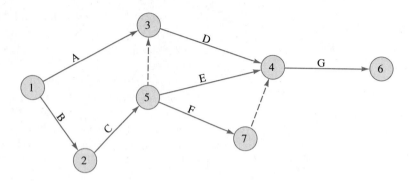

Try Problem 3. This problem provides the immediate predecessor information for a project with seven activities and asks you to develop the project network.

Dummy activities can be used to identify precedence relationships correctly as well as to eliminate the possible confusion of two or more activities having the same starting and ending nodes. Although dummy activities may not be required for all PERT/CPM networks, larger or more complex projects may require many dummy activities to depict the network properly.

10.2 Project Scheduling with PERT/CPM

The owner of the Western Hills Shopping Center is considering modernizing and expanding the current 32-business shopping complex. Financing for the expansion has been arranged through a private investor. If the expansion project is undertaken, the owner hopes to add 8 to 10 new businesses or tenants to the shopping complex.

The specific activities that make up the expansion project are listed in Table 10.2. Note that the list includes the immediate predecessor for each activity as well as the number of weeks required to complete the activity. The PERT/CPM network for the project is shown in Figure 10.2. Check to see that the network does in fact maintain the immediate predecessor relationships shown in Table 10.2.

Table 10.2

Activity List for the Western Hills Shopping Center Project

Activity	Activity Description	Immediate Predecessor	Completion Time (weeks)
A	Prepare architectural drawings	—	5
B	Identify potential new tenants	—	6
C	Develop prospectus for tenants	A	4
D	Select contractor	A	3
E	Prepare building permits	A	1
F	Obtain approval for building permits	E	4
G	Perform construction	D, F	14
H	Finalize contracts with tenants	B, C	12
I	Tenants move in	G, H	2
		Total	51

Figure 10.2 PERT/CPM Network for the Western Hills Shopping Center Project

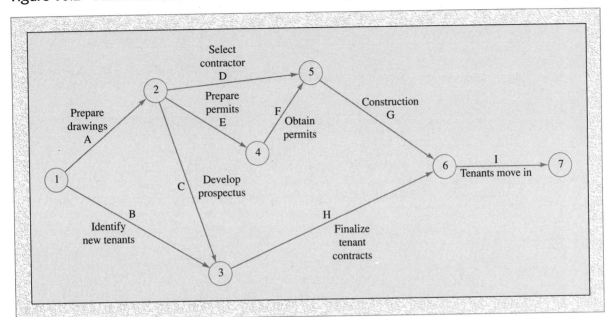

Information in Table 10.2 indicates that the total time required to complete all activities in the shopping center expansion project is 51 weeks. However, we can see from the network (Figure 10.2) that several of the activities can be conducted simultaneously (e.g., A and B). Being able to work on two or more activities at the same time will shorten the total project completion time to less than 51 weeks. However, the total time required to complete the project is not directly available from the data in Table 10.2.

To facilitate the PERT/CPM computations that we will be making, the project network has been redrawn as shown in Figure 10.3. Note that each activity letter and activity time are written, respectively, above and below the corresponding arc.

The Critical Path

We use the convention of referencing activities with letters and events (nodes) with numbers; this is done for convenience. Generally, we assign the letters and the numbers in order as we move from left to right through the project network.

Once we have the PERT/CPM network and the activity times, we are ready to determine the total time required to complete the project. We will use the results of our calculations to develop a detailed schedule for each activity.

To determine the project completion time, we must identify what is called the critical path. A *path* is a sequence of connected activities that leads from the starting node (1) to the completion node (7). The connected activities defined by nodes 1–2–3–6–7 form a path consisting of activities A, C, H, and I. Since *all* paths must be traversed in order to complete the project, we need to determine the amount of time the various paths require. The longest path through the network determines the total time required to complete the project. If activities on the longest path are delayed, the entire project will be delayed. Thus, the longest-path activities are the *critical path activities* of the project, and the longest path is called the *critical path*. If managers wish to reduce the project completion time, they will have to reduce the length of the critical path by shortening the duration of the critical path activities. The following discussion presents a step-by-step procedure for finding the critical path of a project network.

Figure 10.3 Western Hills Shopping Center Project Network with Activity Times

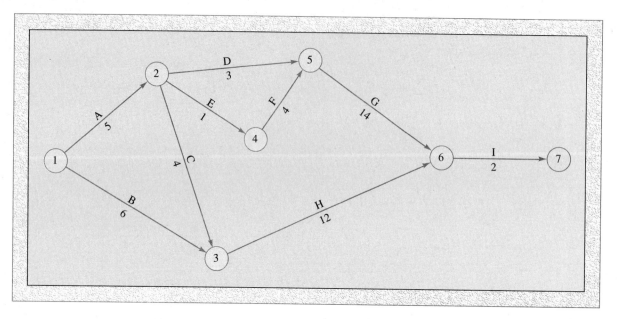

Starting at the network's origin (node 1) and using a starting time of 0, we will compute an *earliest start* and *earliest finish time* for each activity in the network. Let

ES = earliest start time for a particular activity
EF = earliest finish time for a particular activity
t = expected activity time for the activity

The following expression can be used to find the earliest finish time for a given activity:

$$EF = ES + t \qquad (10.1)$$

For example, for activity A, $ES = 0$ and $t = 5$; thus, the earliest finish time for activity A is $EF = 0 + 5 = 5$.

We will write the earliest start and finish times directly on the network in brackets next to the letter of the activity. Using activity A as an example, we have

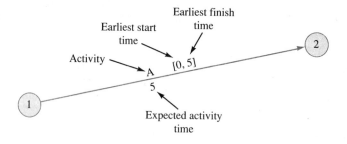

Since activities leaving a node cannot be started until *all* immediately preceding activities have been completed, the following rule determines the earliest start times for activities.

> ### Earliest Start Time Rule
>
> The earliest start time for an activity leaving a particular node is equal to the *largest* of the earliest finish times for all activities entering the node.

In applying this rule to a portion of the network involving activities A, B, C, and H, we obtain the following:

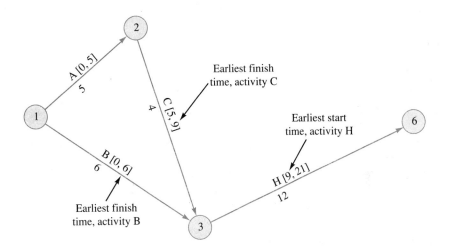

Note that in applying the earliest start time rule to activity C, which leaves node 2, we first recognize that activity A is the only activity entering node 2. Since the earliest finish time for activity A is 5, the earliest start time for activity C is 5. Thus, the earliest finish time for activity C must be EF = ES + t = 5 + 4 = 9.

The above diagram also shows that the earliest finish time for activity B is 6. Applying the earliest start time rule for activity H, we see that the earliest start time for this activity must be equal to the largest of the earliest finish times for the two activities that enter node 3, activities B and C. Thus, the earliest start time for activity H is 9, and the earliest finish time is EF = ES + t = 9 + 12 = 21.

Proceeding in a *forward pass* through the network, we can establish the earliest start time and then the earliest finish time for each activity. The Western Hills Shopping Center PERT/CPM network, with the ES and EF values for each activity, is shown in Figure 10.4. Note that the earliest finish time for activity I, the last activity, is 26 weeks; therefore, the total time required to complete the project is 26 weeks.

We now continue the algorithm for finding the critical path by making a *backward pass* calculation. Starting at the completion point (node 7) and using a latest finish time of 26 for activity I, we trace back through the network, computing a *latest start* and *latest finish time* for each activity. Let

LS = latest start time for a particular activity
LF = latest finish time for a particular activity

The following expression can be used to find the latest start time for a given activity:

$$LS = LF - t \qquad (10.2)$$

Figure 10.4 Western Hills Shopping Center Project with Earliest Start and Earliest Finish Times Shown Above the Activity Arcs

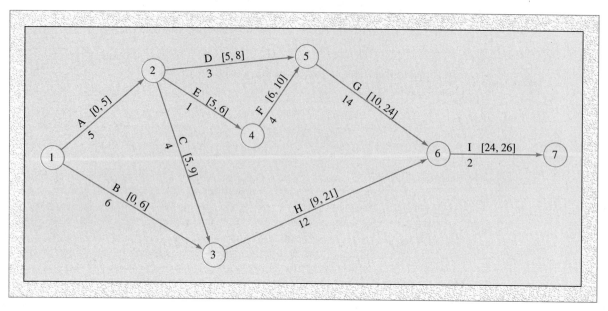

Given LF = 26 and t = 2 for activity I, the latest start time for this activity can be computed as LS = 26 − 2 = 24.

The following rule determines the latest finish time for any activity in the network:

LATEST FINISH TIME RULE

The latest finish time for an activity entering a particular node is equal to the *smallest* of the latest start times for all activities leaving the node.

Logically, the above rule states that the latest time an activity can be finished is equal to the earliest (smallest) value for the latest start time of following activities. The complete network with the LS and LF backward pass calculations is shown in Figure 10.5. The latest start and latest finish times are written in brackets directly under the earliest start and earliest finish times.

Note the application of the latest finish time rule to activity A, which enters node 2. The latest finish time for activity A (LF = 5) is the smallest of the latest start times for the activities that leave node 2; that is, the smallest LS value for activities C (LS = 8), E (LS = 5), and D (LS = 7) is 5.

Using Figure 10.5, we can now find the amount of slack or free time associated with each of the activities. *Slack* is defined as the length of time an activity can be delayed without affecting the total time required to complete the project. The amount of slack for each activity is computed as follows:

$$\text{Slack} = \text{LS} - \text{ES} = \text{LF} - \text{EF} \qquad (10.3)$$

For example, we see that the slack associated with activity C is LS − ES = 8 − 5 = 3 weeks. This means that activity C can be delayed up to 3 weeks (start anywhere between

---

The slack for each activity indicates the length of time the activity can be delayed without increasing the time to complete the project.

One of the primary advantages of PERT/CPM is the identification of the *critical* path activities. The project manager will want to monitor critical path activities closely, because a delay in any one of them will delay the entire project.

Figure 10.5 Western Hills Shopping Center Project with Latest Start and Latest Finish Times Shown Below the Activity Arcs

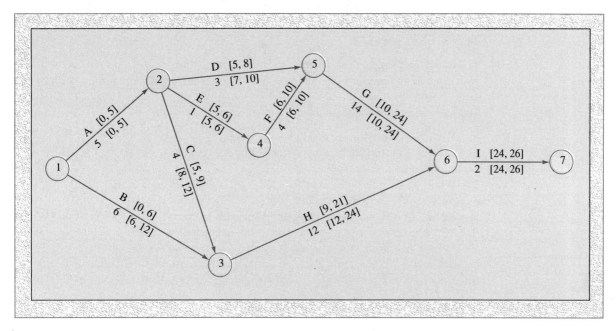

weeks 5 and 8) and the entire project can still be completed in 26 weeks. Thus, activity C is not a critical path activity. Using equation (10.3), we see that the slack associated with activity E is LS − ES = 5 − 5 = 0. Thus, activity E has no slack time and cannot be delayed without affecting the entire project. In general, the *critical path activities* are the activities with zero slack.

The start and finish times shown in Figure 10.5 provide a detailed schedule for all activities. That is, from this network we know the earliest and latest start and finish times for the activities. Putting this information in tabular form gives us the activity schedule shown in Table 10.3. Note that by computing the slack associated with each activity, we see that activities A, E, F, G, and I each have zero slack; hence, these activities form the *critical path* in the shopping center expansion network. Note that Table 10.3 also shows

> The critical path algorithm is essentially a *longest-path* algorithm. In traveling from the first to the last node, we will find that the critical path identifies the sequence of nodes and arcs that has the longest or most time.

Table 10.3
Activity Schedule for the Western Hills Shopping Center Project

Activity	Earliest Start (ES)	Latest Start (LS)	Earliest Finish (EF)	Latest Finish (LF)	Slack (LS − ES)	Critical Path?
A	0	0	5	5	0	Yes
B	0	6	6	12	6	
C	5	8	9	12	3	
D	5	7	8	10	2	
E	5	5	6	6	0	Yes
F	6	6	10	10	0	Yes
G	10	10	24	24	0	Yes
H	9	12	21	24	3	
I	24	24	26	26	0	Yes

the slack or delay that can be tolerated for the noncritical activities before these activities will cause a project delay.

Contributions of PERT/CPM

If the total time required to complete the project is too long, good judgment about where and how to shorten the time of critical path activities must be exercised. If any activity times are altered, the critical path calculations should be repeated to determine the impact on the activity schedule as well as the impact on the total project completion time. In Section 10.4 we show how linear programming can be used to find the least-cost way to shorten the project completion time.

Software packages such as The Management Scientist perform the critical path calculations quickly and efficiently. The project manager can modify any aspect of the project and quickly determine how the modification affects the activity schedule and the total time required to complete the project.

Previously, we stated that project managers look for procedures that will help answer many important questions regarding the planning, scheduling, and controlling of projects. Let us reconsider these questions in light of the information that the PERT/CPM network and the critical path calculations have given us.

1. What is the total time to complete the project?
   Answer: The project can be completed in 26 weeks if the individual activities are completed on schedule.
2. What are the scheduled start and completion times for each activity?
   Answer: The activity schedule (see Table 10.3) shows the earliest start, latest start, earliest finish, and latest finish times for each activity.
3. Which activities are critical and must be completed *exactly* as scheduled in order to keep the project on schedule?
   Answer: A, E, F, G, and I are the critical path activities.
4. How long can noncritical activities be delayed before they cause a delay in the completion time for the project?
   Answer: The activity schedule (see Table 10.3) shows the slack time associated with each activity.

The above information is important and valuable in managing any project. While larger projects may substantially increase the time required to make the necessary calculations, the procedure and contributions of PERT/CPM to larger projects are identical to those observed in the shopping center expansion project. Furthermore, computer packages exist that carry out the steps of the PERT/CPM procedure. Figure 10.6 shows the activity schedule for the shopping center expansion project developed by The Management Scientist computer software package. Input to the program included the activities, their immediate predecessors, and the expected activity times. Only a few minutes were required to input the information and generate the critical path and activity schedule information.

Summary of the PERT/CPM Critical Path Procedure

Test your ability to do the critical path calculations by working Problem 6. This problem asks you to develop the activity schedule, identify the activity slack time, and determine the total project completion time.

Before leaving this section, let us summarize the PERT/CPM critical path procedure that can be used to plan, schedule, and control projects.

Step 1 Develop a list of activities that make up the project.

Step 2 Determine the immediate predecessor activities for each activity in the project.

Step 3 Estimate the completion time for each activity.

Step 4 Draw a network depicting the activities and immediate predecessors listed in steps 1 and 2.

Step 5 Using the network and the activity time estimates, determine the earliest start and the earliest finish time for each activity by making a forward pass through the network. The earliest finish time for the last activity in the project identifies the total time required to complete the project.

Figure 10.6   The Management Scientist Activity Schedule for the Western Hills
Shopping Center Project

```
          ***    ACTIVITY SCHEDULE   ***

            EARLIEST  LATEST   EARLIEST  LATEST            CRITICAL
  ACTIVITY  START     START    FINISH    FINISH   SLACK    ACTIVITY
  ----------------------------------------------------------------
     A        0         0         5         5       0       YES
     B        0         6         6        12       6
     C        5         8         9        12       3
     D        5         7         8        10       2
     E        5         5         6         6       0       YES
     F        6         6        10        10       0       YES
     G       10        10        24        24       0       YES
     H        9        12        21        24       3
     I       24        24        26        26       0       YES
  ----------------------------------------------------------------

     CRITICAL PATH:  A-E-F-G-I

     PROJECT COMPLETION TIME = 26
```

Step 6   Using the project completion time identified in step 5 as the latest finish time for the last activity, make a backward pass through the network to identify the latest start and latest finish time for each activity.

Step 7   Use the difference between the latest start time and the earliest start time for each activity to identify the slack time available for the activity.

Step 8   Find the activities with zero slack; these are the critical path activities.

Step 9   Use the information from steps 5 and 6 to develop the activity schedule for the project.

NOTES & COMMENTS

If after analyzing a PERT/CPM network and finding that the project completion time is unacceptable (i.e., the project is going to take too long), a manager must take one or both of the following steps. First, review the original PERT/CPM network to see if the immediate predecessor relationships can be modified so that at least some of the critical path activities can be done simultaneously. Second, consider adding resources to critical path activities in an attempt to shorten the critical path; this alternative, referred to as *crashing,* is discussed in Section 10.4.

10.3 Project Scheduling with Uncertain Activity Times

In this section we consider the details of project scheduling for a problem involving the research and development of a new product. Because many of the activities in this project have never been previously attempted, the project manager wants to account for the uncertainties in the activity times. Let us show how project scheduling can be conducted with uncertain activity times.

The Daugherty Porta-Vac Project

The H. S. Daugherty Company has manufactured industrial vacuum cleaning systems for a number of years. Recently, a member of the company's new-product research team submitted a report suggesting that the company consider manufacturing a cordless vacuum cleaner. The new product, referred to as a Porta-Vac, could contribute to Daugherty's expansion into the household market. Management hopes that it can be manufactured at a reasonable cost and that its portability and no-cord convenience will make it extremely attractive.

Daugherty's management would like to study the feasibility of manufacturing the Porta-Vac product. The feasibility study will recommend the action to be taken. To complete this study, information must be obtained from the firm's research and development (R&D), product testing, manufacturing, cost estimating, and market research groups. How long will this feasibility study will take? When should we tell the product testing group to schedule its work? Obviously, we do not have enough information to answer these questions at this time. In the following discussion, we will learn how to answer these questions and provide an activity schedule for the project.

Again, the first step in the project scheduling process is to identify all the activities that make up the project and then determine the immediate predecessors for each activity. For the Porta-Vac project, these data are shown in Table 10.4

The PERT/CPM network for the Porta-Vac project is shown in Figure 10.7. Check for yourself to see that the network does in fact maintain the immediate predecessor relationships shown in Table 10.4.

Table 10.4
Activity List for the Porta-Vac Project

Activity	Description	Immediate Predecessor
A	Develop product design	—
B	Plan market research	—
C	Prepare routing (manufacturing engineering)	A
D	Build prototype model	A
E	Prepare marketing brochure	A
F	Prepare cost estimates (industrial engineering)	C
G	Do preliminary product testing	D
H	Complete market survey	B, E
I	Prepare pricing and forecast report	H
J	Prepare final report	F, G, I

Figure 10.7
Network for the Porta-Vac Project

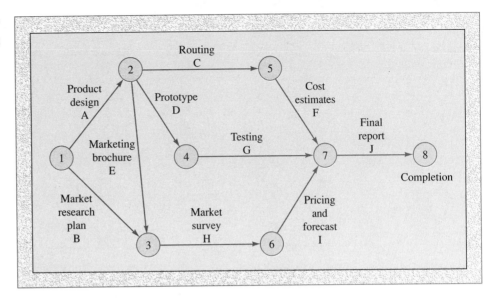

Uncertain Activity Times

Accurate activity time estimates are important in the development of an activity schedule. When activity times are uncertain, the three time estimates—optimistic, most probable, and pessimistic—allow the project manager to take uncertainty into consideration in determining the critical path and the activity schedule. This approach was developed by the designers of PERT.

Once we have developed a PERT/CPM network for the project, we will need information on the time required to complete each activity. This information will be used in the calculation of the total time required to complete the project and in the scheduling of specific activities. For repeat projects, such as construction and maintenance projects, managers may have the experience and historical data necessary to provide accurate activity time estimates. However, for new or unique projects, activity time estimation may be significantly more difficult. In fact, in many cases, activity times are uncertain and are best described by a range of possible values rather than by one specific time estimate. In these instances, the uncertain activity times are treated as random variables with associated probability distributions. As a result, probability statements will be provided about the ability to meet a specific project completion date.

To incorporate uncertain activity times into the network analysis, we will need to obtain three time estimates for each activity. The three estimates are

Optimistic time a = the activity time if everything progresses in an ideal manner
Most probable time m = the most probable activity time under normal conditions
Pessimistic time b = the activity time if significant delays are encountered

The three time estimates require the manager to provide the *most probable time* and express the uncertainty by providing time estimates ranging from the best possible (*optimistic*) time to the worst possible (*pessimistic*) time.

As an illustration of the PERT/CPM procedure with uncertain activity times, let us consider the optimistic, most probable, and pessimistic time estimates for the Porta-Vac activities as presented in Table 10.5. Using activity A as an example, we see that the manager estimates the most probable time to be 5 weeks with a range from 4 weeks (optimistic) to 12 weeks (pessimistic). If the activity could be repeated a large number of times, what would be the average time for the activity? This average or *expected time* (*t*) can be determined from the following formula:

$$t = \frac{a + 4m + b}{6} \qquad (10.4)$$

Table 10.5

Optimistic, Most Probable, and Pessimistic Activity Time Estimates (in Weeks) for the Porta-Vac Project

Activity	Optimistic (a)	Most Probable (m)	Pessimistic (b)
A	4	5	12
B	1	1.5	5
C	2	3	4
D	3	4	11
E	2	3	4
F	1.5	2	2.5
G	1.5	3	4.5
H	2.5	3.5	7.5
I	1.5	2	2.5
J	1	2	3

For activity A we have an estimated average or expected completion time of

$$t_A = \frac{4 + 4(5) + 12}{6} = \frac{36}{6} = 6 \text{ weeks}$$

With uncertain activity times, we can use the common statistical measure of the *variance* to describe the dispersion or variation in the activity time values. The variance of the activity time is given by the following formula:[1]

$$\sigma^2 = \left(\frac{b - a}{6}\right)^2 \tag{10.5}$$

As you can see, the difference between the pessimistic (b) and optimistic (a) time estimates greatly affects the value of the variance. Large differences in these two values reflect a high degree of uncertainty in the activity time. Accordingly, the variance given by equation (10.5) will be large. Using equation (10.5), we see that the measure of uncertainty—that is, the variance—of activity A, denoted σ_A^2, is

$$\sigma_A^2 = \left(\frac{12 - 4}{6}\right)^2 = \left(\frac{8}{6}\right)^2 = 1.78$$

Problem 10 involves a project with uncertain activity times and asks you to compute the expected completion time and the variance for the project.

Equations (10.4) and (10.5) are based on the assumption that the activity distribution can be described by a *beta probability distribution.*[2] With this assumption, the probability distribution for the time to complete activity A is as shown in Figure 10.8. Using equations (10.4) and (10.5) and the data in Table 10.5, the expected times and variances for all of the Porta-Vac activities are as summarized in Table 10.6.

A network depicting the Porta-Vac project and expected activity times is shown in Figure 10.9. Note that above each arc we write the letter of the corresponding activity, and directly under the arc we write the expected time of the activity.

[1] The variance equation is based on the notion that a standard deviation is approximately ⅙ of the difference between the extreme values of the distribution: $(b - a)/6$. The variance is simply the square of the standard deviation.

[2] For the equations for t and σ^2 to be exact, additional assumptions are required about the parameters of the beta probability distribution. However, even when these additional assumptions are not made, the equations still tend to provide very good and useful approximations of t and σ^2.

Figure 10.8
Activity Time Distribution for Product Design Activity A of the Porta-Vac Project

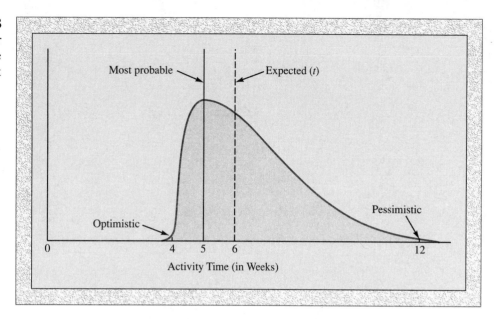

Table 10.6
Expected Times and Variances for the Porta-Vac Project Activities

Activity	Expected Time (weeks)	Variance
A	6	1.78
B	2	0.44
C	3	0.11
D	5	1.78
E	3	0.11
F	2	0.03
G	3	0.25
H	4	0.69
I	2	0.03
J	2	0.11
Total	32	

The Critical Path

When uncertain activity times are used, the critical path calculations will only determine the expected or average time to complete the project. The actual time required to complete the project may differ. However, for planning purposes, the expected time should be valuable information for the project manager.

Once we have the network and the expected activity times, we are ready to proceed with the critical path calculations necessary to determine the expected time required to complete the project and the activity schedule. In these calculations, we will treat the expected activity times (Table 10.6) as the *fixed length* or *known duration* of each activity. As a result, we can use the critical path calculation procedure introduced in Section 10.2 to find the critical path for the Porta-Vac project. After the critical activities and the expected time to complete the project have been determined, we will analyze the effect of the activity time variability.

Proceeding with a forward pass through the network shown in Figure 10.9, we can establish the earliest start (ES) and earliest finish (EF) times for each activity. The PERT/CPM network with the ES and EF values is shown in Figure 10.10. Note that the

Figure 10.9
Porta-Vac Project Network with
Expected Activity Times

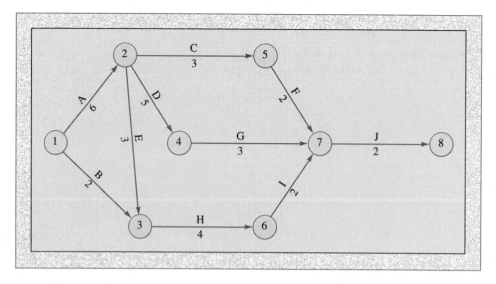

Figure 10.10
Porta-Vac Network with Earliest
Start and Earliest Finish Times
Shown Above Activities

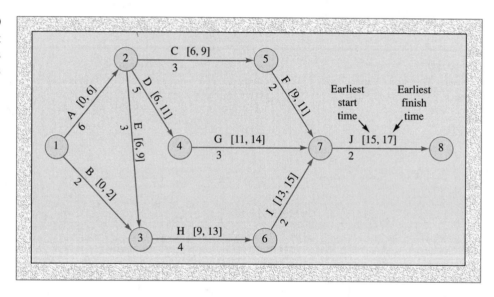

Activities that have larger variances show a greater degree of uncertainty. The project manager should monitor the progress of any activity with a large variance even if the expected times do not identify the activity as a critical activity.

earliest finish time for activity J, the last activity, is 17 weeks. Thus, the expected completion time for the entire project is also 17 weeks. Next, we make a backward pass through the network. The backward pass provides the latest start (LS) and latest finish (LF) times shown in Figure 10.11.

Figure 10.11 provides a detailed schedule for all activities. Putting this information in tabular form provides the activity schedule shown in Table 10.7. Note that the slack time (LS − ES) is also shown for each activity. The activities with zero slack (A, E, H, I, and J) form the critical path for the Porta-Vac project network.

Variability in the Project Completion Time

Recall that for the Porta-Vac project the critical path of A–E–H–I–J resulted in an expected total project completion time of 17 weeks. Variation in critical path activities can cause variation in the project completion time. Variation in noncritical path activities

Figure 10.11
Porta-Vac Network with Latest
Start and Latest Finish Times
Shown Below Activities

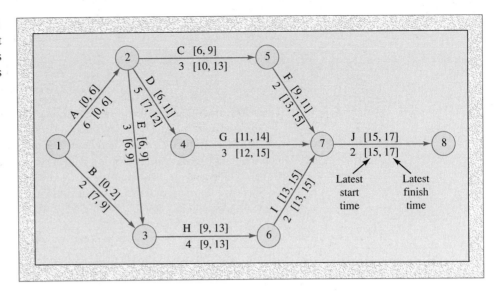

Table 10.7
Activity Schedule for the Porta-Vac
Project

Activity	Earliest Start (ES)	Latest Start (LS)	Earliest Finish (EF)	Latest Finish (LF)	Slack (LS − ES)	Critical Path?
A	0	0	6	6	0	Yes
B	0	7	2	9	7	
C	6	10	9	13	4	
D	6	7	11	12	1	
E	6	6	9	9	0	Yes
F	9	13	11	15	4	
G	11	12	14	15	1	
H	9	9	13	13	0	Yes
I	13	13	15	15	0	Yes
J	15	15	17	17	0	Yes

ordinarily has no effect on the project completion time because of the slack time associated with these activities. However, if a noncritical path activity is delayed long enough to expend its slack time, then it becomes part of a new critical path and may affect the project completion time. Variability leading to a longer-than-expected total time for the critical path activities will always extend the project completion time, and conversely, variability that results in a shorter critical path will produce a shorter-than-expected project completion time, unless other activities become critical. Let us now use the variance in the critical path activities to determine the variance in the project completion time.

Let T denote the total time required to complete the project. The expected value of T, which is determined by the critical activities A–E–H–I–J in the Porta-Vac problem, is

$$E(T) = t_A + t_E + t_H + t_I + t_J$$

$$= 6 + 3 + 4 + 2 + 2 = 17 \text{ weeks}$$

where t_A, t_E, t_H, t_I, and t_J are the expected completion times for the critical path activities.

The variance in the project completion time is the sum of the variances of the critical path activities. Thus, the variance for the Porta-Vac project completion time is given by

$$\sigma^2 = \sigma_A^2 + \sigma_E^2 + \sigma_H^2 + \sigma_I^2 + \sigma_J^2$$

$$= 1.78 + 0.11 + 0.69 + 0.03 + 0.11 = 2.72$$

where σ_A^2, σ_E^2, σ_H^2, σ_I^2, and σ_J^2 are the variances of the critical path activities.

The above formula for σ^2 is based on the assumption that the activity times are independent. If two or more activities are dependent, the formula only provides an approximation to the variance of the project completion time. The closer the activities are to being independent, the better the approximation.

Since we know that the standard deviation is the square root of the variance, we can compute the standard deviation σ for the Porta-Vac project completion time as follows:

$$\sigma = \sqrt{\sigma^2} = \sqrt{2.72} = 1.65$$

The normal distribution tends to be a better approximation of the distribution of total time for larger projects where the critical path has many activities.

A final assumption that the distribution of the project completion time T follows a normal or bell-shaped distribution[3] allows us to draw the distribution shown in Figure 10.12. With this distribution, we can compute the probability of meeting a specified project completion date. For example, suppose that management has allotted 20 weeks for the Porta-Vac project. What is the probability that we will meet the 20-week deadline? Using the normal distribution shown in Figure 10.13, we are asking for the probability that $T \leq 20$. This is shown graphically as the shaded area in Figure 10.13. The z value for the normal distribution at $T = 20$ is given by

$$z = \frac{20 - 17}{1.65} = 1.82$$

Figure 10.12
PERT Normal Distribution of the Project Completion Time for the Porta-Vac Project

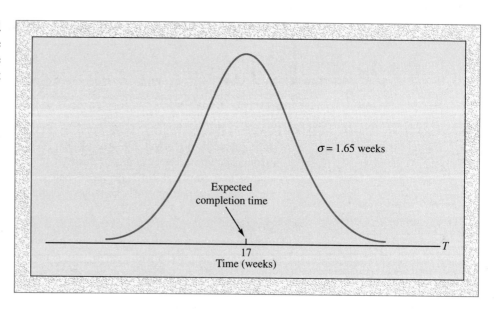

$\sigma = 1.65$ weeks

Expected completion time

17
Time (weeks)

T

---

[3]The use of the normal distribution as an approximation is based on the central limit theorem, which indicates that the sum of independent activity times follows a normal distribution as the number of activities becomes large.

Figure 10.13
Probability of a Porta-Vac Project
Completion Date Prior to the
20-Week Deadline

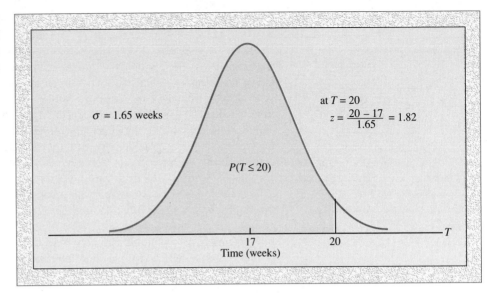

$\sigma = 1.65$ weeks

at $T = 20$
$z = \dfrac{20 - 17}{1.65} = 1.82$

$P(T \leq 20)$

17   20
Time (weeks)

T

Using $z = 1.82$ and the table for the normal distribution (see Appendix A), we see that the probability of the project meeting the 20-week deadline is $0.4656 + 0.5000 = 0.9656$. Thus, while activity time variability may cause the completion time to exceed 17 weeks, there is an excellent chance that the project will be completed before the 20-week deadline. Similar probability calculations can be made for other project deadline alternatives.

Thus, we see that the PERT/CPM procedure can be used to schedule projects with uncertain activity times. A procedure using three time estimates for each activity (optimistic time, most probable time, and pessimistic time) enables the computation of an expected time and a variance for each activity. Using the expected time as the fixed time, the critical activities and the critical path can be found using the procedure presented in Section 10.2. The sum of the expected times of the critical path activities provides the expected project completion time. The sum of the variances of the critical path activities provides the project completion time variance. Using the normal probability distribution assumption for the project completion time, standard procedures from probability can be used to compute the probability of the project being completed in a specified amount of time.

NOTES & COMMENTS

For projects involving uncertain activity times, the probability that the project can be completed within a specified amount of time is helpful managerial information. However, remember that this probability estimate is based *only* on the critical path activities. When uncertain activity times exist, longer-than-expected completion times for one or more noncritical path activities may cause an original noncritical path to become critical and hence increase the time required to complete the project. By frequently monitoring the progress of the project to make sure all activities are on schedule, the project manager will be better prepared to take corrective action if a noncritical activity begins to lengthen the duration of the project.

10.4 Considering Time–Cost Trade-Offs

The original developers of CPM provided the project manager with the capability of adding resources to selected activities in an attempt to reduce project completion time. Since added resources (such as more workers, overtime, and so on) generally increase project costs, the decision to reduce activity times must take into consideration the additional cost involved. In effect, the project manager has to make a decision that involves trading decreased activity time for increased project cost.

Using more resources to reduce activity times was proposed by the developers of CPM. The shortening of activity times is referred to as crashing.

In the Porta-Vac project, the 17-week scheduled completion time could be reduced if management were willing to add resources to shorten any of the critical path activities: A, E, H, I, and J. Since the Porta-Vac project has a high probability of meeting the 20-week project deadline, it is doubtful that management would be willing to add costs to reduce activity times for this particular project. Thus, let us consider another project where time–cost trade-offs would most likely need to be considered.

Table 10.8 defines a two-machine maintenance project consisting of five activities. Since management has had substantial experience with similar projects, the times for maintenance activities are considered known; hence, a single time estimate is given for each activity. The network for this project is shown in Figure 10.14.

Critical path calculations for the maintenance project network are computed following the procedure we used to find the critical path in the networks for both the Western Hills Shopping Center expansion project and the Porta-Vac project. Making the forward pass and backward pass calculations for the network in Figure 10.14, we can obtain the

Table 10.8
Activity List for the Two-Machine Maintenance Project

Activity	Description	Immediate Predecessor	Expected Time (days)
A	Overhaul machine I	—	7
B	Adjust machine I	A	3
C	Overhaul machine II	—	6
D	Adjust machine II	C	3
E	Test system	B, D	2

Figure 10.14
Network of the Two-Machine Maintenance Project

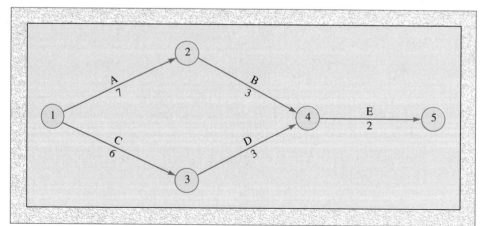

activity schedule shown in Table 10.9. As you can see, the zero slack times, and thus the critical path, are associated with activities A–B–E or nodes 1–2–4–5. The length of the critical path, and thus the total time required to complete the project, is 12 days.

Crashing Activity Times

Now suppose that the current production levels make it imperative for the maintenance project to be completed within 2 weeks, or 10 working days. By looking at the length of the critical path of the network (12 days), we realize that it is impossible to meet the desired project completion time unless we can shorten selected activity times. This shortening of activity times, which usually can be achieved by adding resources such as labor or overtime, is referred to as *crashing*. However, since the added resources associated with crashing activity times usually result in added project costs, we will want to identify the activities that cost least to crash and then crash those activities only the amount necessary to meet the desired project completion time.

To determine just where and how much to crash activity times, we will need information on how much each activity can be crashed and how much the crashing process costs. To accomplish this, we must ask management for the following information on each activity:

1. Estimated activity cost under the normal or expected activity time
2. Estimated time to complete the activity under maximum crashing (i.e., the shortest possible activity time)
3. Estimated activity cost under maximum crashing

Let

$$\tau_j = \text{normal time for activity } j$$
$$\tau_j' = \text{time for activity } j \text{ under maximum crashing}$$
$$M_j = \text{maximum possible reduction in time for activity } j \text{ due}$$
$$\text{to maximum crashing}$$

Given τ_j and τ_j', we can compute M_j as follows:

$$M_j = \tau_j - \tau_j' \tag{10.6}$$

Next, let C_j denote the estimated cost for activity j under the normal or expected activity time and C_j' denote the estimated cost for activity j under maximum crashing. Thus, on a per-unit time basis (e.g., per day), the crashing cost K_j for each activity is given by

$$K_j = \frac{C_j' - C_j}{M_j} \tag{10.7}$$

Table 10.9		Earliest Start (ES)	Latest Start (LS)	Earliest Finish (EF)	Latest Finish (LF)	Slack (LS − ES)	Critical Path?
Activity Schedule for the Two-Machine Maintenance Project	**Activity**						
	A	0	0	7	7	0	Yes
	B	7	7	10	10	0	Yes
	C	0	1	6	7	1	
	D	6	7	9	10	1	
	E	10	10	12	12	0	Yes

For example, if the normal or expected time for activity A is 7 days at a cost of $C_A = \$500$ and the time under maximum crashing is 4 days at a cost of $C'_A = \$800$, equations (10.6) and (10.7) show that the maximum possible reduction in time for activity A is

$$M_A = 7 - 4 = 3 \text{ days}$$

with a crashing cost of

$$K_A = \frac{C'_A - C_A}{M_A} = \frac{800 - 500}{3} = \frac{300}{3} = \$100 \text{ per day}$$

We will make the assumption that any portion or fraction of the activity crash time can be achieved for a corresponding portion of the activity crashing cost. For example, if we decided to crash activity A by only 1½ days, we would assume that this could be accomplished with an added cost of 1½($100) = $150, which results in a total activity cost of $500 + $150 = $650. Figure 10.15 shows the graph of the time–cost relationship for activity A. The complete normal and crash activity data for the two-machine maintenance project are given in Table 10.10.

Now the question is, which activities should be crashed—and by how much—in order to meet the 10-day project completion deadline at minimum cost? Your first reaction to this question may be to consider crashing the critical path activities—A, B, or E. Activity A has the lowest crashing costs of the three, and crashing this activity by 2 days will reduce the A–B–E path to the desired 10 days. While this is correct, keep in mind that as you crash the current critical path activities, other paths may become critical. Thus, you will need to check the critical path in the revised network and perhaps either identify additional activities to crash or modify your initial crashing decision. For a small network, this trial-and-error approach can be used to make crashing decisions; in larger networks, however, a mathematical procedure is required to determine the optimal crashing decisions. The following discussion shows how linear programming can be used to solve the network crashing problem.

Figure 10.15
Time–Cost Relationship for
Activity A

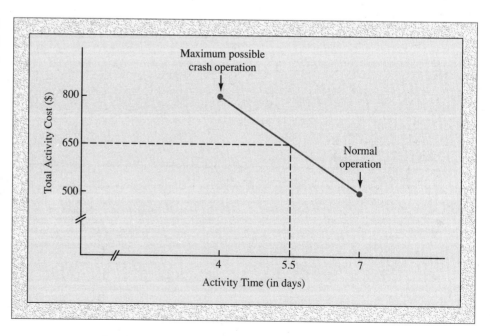

Table 10.10

Normal and Crash Activity Data for the Two-Machine Maintenance Project

Activity	Time (days) Normal	Time (days) Crash	Total Cost Normal (C_j)	Total Cost Crash (C_j')	Maximum Reduction in Time (M_j)	Crash Cost Per Day $\left(K_j = \dfrac{C_j' - C_j}{M_j}\right)$
A	7	4	$ 500	$ 800	3	$100
B	3	2	200	350	1	150
C	6	4	500	900	2	200
D	3	1	200	500	2	150
E	2	1	300	550	1	250
			$1700	$3100		

A Linear Programming Model for Crashing Decisions

First, recall that an event refers to the completion of all the activities that lead into a node. Since we have five nodes or events in the two-machine maintenance project, we need five decision variables to identify the time of occurrence for each event. In addition, we will need five decision variables to represent the amount of crash time used for each of the five activities. Thus, we define the following decision variables:

x_i = time of occurrence of event i $i = 1, 2, 3, 4, 5$
y_j = amount of crash time used for activity j $j = $ A, B, C, D, E

A linear programming model is used to determine optimal crashing decisions. Because of the complexity of the model computer-based solutions must be used for most practical applications.

Since the total project cost for a normal completion time is fixed at $1700 (see Table 10.10), we can minimize the total project cost (normal cost plus crash cost) by minimizing the total crashing costs. Thus, the linear programming objective function becomes

$$\text{Min} \sum_j K_j y_j \tag{10.8}$$

or

$$\text{Min } 100y_A + 150y_B + 200y_C + 150y_D + 250y_E \tag{10.9}$$

where K_j is the crash cost for activity j and $j = $ A, B, C, D, E, on a per-unit time basis.[4]

The constraints for the model involve describing the network, limiting the activity crash times, and meeting the project completion date. Of these, the constraints used to describe the network are perhaps the most difficult. These constraints are based on the following conditions:

1. The time of occurrence of event i (x_i) must be greater than or equal to the activity completion time for all activities leading into the node or event.
2. An activity start time is equal to the occurrence time of its preceding node or event.
3. The time to complete an activity time is equal to its normal time less the length of time it is crashed.

---

[4]Note that the x_i variables indicating event occurrences do not result in costs; thus, they have zero coefficients in the objective function.

Starting with a time of occurrence of zero at node 1 ($x_1 = 0$), we can create the following set of network description constraints:

Event 2

$$x_2 \geq \tau_A - y_A + 0$$

Occurrence time for event 2

Actual time for activity A

Start time for activity A ($x_1 = 0$)

or with $\tau_A = 7$

$$x_2 + y_A \geq 7 \tag{10.10}$$

Event 3

$$x_3 \geq \tau_C - y_C + 0$$

or with $\tau_C = 6$

$$x_3 + y_C \geq 6 \tag{10.11}$$

Since two activities enter event or node 4, we have the following two constraints:

Event 4

$$x_4 \geq \tau_B - y_B + x_2$$
$$x_4 \geq \tau_D - y_D + x_3 \tag{10.12}$$

or with $\tau_B = 3$ and $\tau_D = 3$

$$-x_2 + x_4 + y_B \geq 3$$
$$-x_3 + x_4 + y_D \geq 3 \tag{10.13}$$

Event 5

$$x_5 \geq \tau_E - y_E + x_4$$

or with $\tau_E = 2$

$$-x_4 + x_5 + y_E \geq 2 \tag{10.14}$$

Constraints (10.10) through (10.14) are all necessary to describe the network.

The maximum allowable crash time constraints are

$$y_A \leq 3 \tag{10.15}$$

$$y_B \leq 1 \tag{10.16}$$

$$y_C \leq 2 \tag{10.17}$$

$$y_D \leq 2 \tag{10.18}$$

$$y_E \leq 1 \tag{10.19}$$

and the desired project completion time provides another constraint for event 5:

$$x_5 \leq 10 \tag{10.20}$$

Table 10.11

New Activity Schedule for the
Two-Machine Maintenance Project
After Crashing Activities A and D

Activity	Time After Crashing	ES	LS	EF	LF	Slack
A	5	0	0	5	5	0
B	3	5	5	8	8	0
C	6	0	0	6	6	0
D	2	6	6	8	8	0
E	2	8	8	10	10	0

In general, a linear programming model for crashing a network with m activities and n nodes will have $m + n - 1$ variables and $2m + 1$ constraints.

Test your ability to formulate a linear programming model for crashing decisions by working Problem 22. A computer solution of your linear programming model will determine the activities that should be crashed.

Adding the nonnegativity restrictions and solving the above linear programming model provides the following solution:

$$x_2 = 5 \qquad y_A = 2$$

$$x_3 = 6 \qquad y_B = 0$$

$$x_4 = 8 \qquad y_C = 0$$

$$x_5 = 10 \qquad y_D = 1$$

$$y_E = 0$$

Objective function = $350

The solution values of $y_A = 2$ and $y_D = 1$ tell us activity A must be crashed 2 days ($200) and activity D must be crashed 1 day ($150) in order to meet the 10-day project completion deadline. Because of this crashing, the time for activity A will be reduced to $7 - 2 = 5$ days, while the time for activity D will be reduced to $3 - 1 = 2$ days. The total project cost (normal cost plus crashing cost) will be $1700 + $200 + $150 = $2050. To generate the new activity schedule under crashing, we use the crashed activity times and repeat the critical path calculations for the network. Doing this provides the activity schedule shown in Table 10.11. Note that in the final solution all activities are critical. Resolving the linear programming model with alternative desired project completion times—constraint (10.20)—will show the project manager the costs associated with crashing the project to meet alternative deadlines.

Due to the substantial formulation and computational effort associated with activity crashing, most applications of this technique use specialized computer programs developed to handle crashing and the related network analyses.

10.5 PERT/Cost

As you have seen, PERT/CPM concentrates on the *time* aspect of a project and provides information that can be used to schedule activities so that the entire project is completed on time. Although project time is a primary consideration for almost every project, there are many situations in which the *cost* associated with the project is just as important as time. In this section we show how the technique referred to as PERT/Cost can be used to help plan, schedule, and control project costs. The ultimate objective of a PERT/Cost system is to provide information that can be used to maintain project costs within a specified budget.

Planning and Scheduling Project Costs

The budgeting process for a project usually involves identifying all costs associated with the project and then developing a schedule or forecast of when the costs are expected to occur. Then at various stages of project completion, the actual project costs incurred can be compared to the scheduled or budgeted costs; if actual costs exceed budgeted costs, corrective action may be taken to keep the total project cost within the budget.

The first step in a PERT/Cost control system is to divide the entire project into components that are convenient in terms of measuring and controlling costs. While a PERT/CPM network may already show detailed activities for the project, we may find that these activities are too detailed for conveniently controlling project costs. In such cases, related activities that are under the control of one department, subcontractor, or other entity, are often grouped together to form what are referred to as *work packages*. By identifying costs of each work package, a project manager can use a PERT/Cost system to help plan, schedule, and control project costs.

Since the projects we discuss in this chapter have a relatively small number of activities, we will find it convenient to define work packages as having only one activity. Thus, in our discussion of the PERT/Cost technique we will treat each activity as a separate work package. Realize, however, that in large and complex projects we would almost always group related activities such that a cost control system could be developed for a more reasonable number of work packages.

To illustrate the PERT/Cost technique, let us consider the research and development project network shown in Figure 10.16. We are assuming that each activity is a work package and that a detailed cost analysis has been made on an activity basis. The activity cost estimates, along with the expected activity times, are shown in Table 10.12. In using the PERT/Cost technique, we assume that activities (work packages) are defined such that their costs occur at a constant rate over the duration of the activity. For example, activity B, with an estimated cost of $30,000 and an expected 3-month duration, is assumed to have a cost rate of $30,000/3 = $10,000 per month. The cost rates for all activities are also provided in Table 10.12. Note that the total estimated or budgeted cost for the project is $87,000.

Using the expected activity times, we can compute the critical path for the project. A summary of the critical path calculations and the resulting activity schedule is shown in Table 10.13. Activities B, D, and F determine the critical path and provide an expected project completion time of 8 months.

Figure 10.16
R&D Project Network

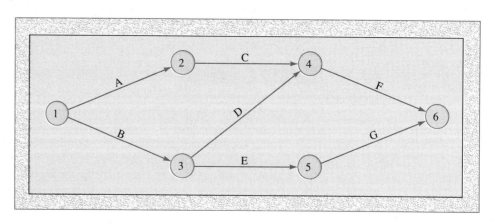

Table 10.12

Activity Times and Cost Estimates for R&D Project

Activity	Expected Time (Months)	Budgeted or Estimated Cost	Budgeted Cost Per Month
A	2	$10,000	$ 5,000
B	3	30,000	10,000
C	1	3,000	3,000
D	3	6,000	2,000
E	2	20,000	10,000
F	2	10,000	5,000
G	1	8,000	8,000
	Total budget	$87,000	

Table 10.13

Activity Schedule for R&D Project

Activity	Earliest Start (ES)	Latest Start (LS)	Earliest Finish (EF)	Latest Finish (LF)	Slack	Critical Path?
A	0	3	2	5	3	
B	0	0	3	3	0	Yes
C	2	5	3	6	3	
D	3	3	6	6	0	Yes
E	3	5	5	7	2	
F	6	6	8	8	0	Yes
G	5	7	6	8	2	

Table 10.14

Budgeted Costs for an Earliest Starting Time Schedule ($000's) for R&D Project

Activity	Month							
	1	2	3	4	5	6	7	8
A	5	5						
B	10	10	10					
C			3					
D				2	2	2		
E				10	10			
F							5	5
G						8		
Monthly cost	15	15	13	12	12	10	5	5
Total cost	15	30	43	55	67	77	82	87

We are now ready to develop a budget for the project that will show when costs should occur during the 8 months. First, let us assume that all activities begin at their earliest possible start time. Using the monthly activity cost rates shown in Table 10.12 and the earliest start times, we can prepare the month-by-month cost forecast as shown in Table 10.14. For example, using the earliest start date for activity A as 0, we expect activity A, which has a 2-month duration, to show a cost of $5000 in each of the first 2 months of the project. By similarly using the earliest start time and monthly cost rate for each activity, we are able to complete Table 10.14 as shown. Note that by summing the costs in each column, we obtain the total cost anticipated for each month of the project. Finally, by accumulating the monthly costs, we can show the budgeted total cost schedule, provided all activities are started at the *earliest* starting times. Table 10.15 shows the budgeted total cost schedule when all activities are started at the *latest* starting times.

Provided the project progresses on its PERT/CPM time schedule, each activity will be started somewhere between its earliest and latest starting times. This implies that the total project costs should occur at levels between the earliest start and latest start costs schedules. For example, using the data in Tables 10.14 and 10.15, we see that at the end of month 3, total project costs should be between $30,000 (latest starting time schedule) and $43,000 (earliest starting time schedule).

In Figure 10.17 we show the forecasted total project costs for both the earliest and the latest starting time schedules. The shaded region between the two cost curves shows the possible feasible budgets for the project. If the project manager is willing to commit activities to specific starting times, a specific project forecast or budget can be prepared. However, based on the above analysis, we know that such a budget will have to be in the region of the feasible budgets shown in Figure 10.17.

Controlling Project Costs

The information that we have developed thus far is helpful in terms of scheduling total project costs. However, if we are going to have an effective cost control system, we will need to identify costs on a more detailed basis. For example, information that the project's actual total cost is exceeding the budgeted total cost will be of little value unless we can identify the activity or group of activities that are causing the cost overruns.

The PERT/Cost system provides the desired cost control by budgeting and then recording actual costs on an activity (i.e., work package) basis. Periodically throughout the project's duration, actual costs for all completed and in-process activities are compared with the appropriate budgeted costs. The project manager is then provided with up-to-date information on the cost status of each activity. If at any point in time actual costs exceed budgeted costs, a cost overrun has occurred. On the other hand, if actual

Table 10.15

Budgeted Costs for a Latest Starting Time Schedule ($000's) for R&D Project

Activity	Month 1	2	3	4	5	6	7	8
A				5	5			
B	10	10	10					
C						3		
D				2	2	2		
E						10	10	
F							5	5
G								8
Monthly cost	10	10	10	7	7	15	15	13
Total cost	10	20	30	37	44	59	74	87

Figure 10.17
Feasible Budgets for Total R&D
Project Costs

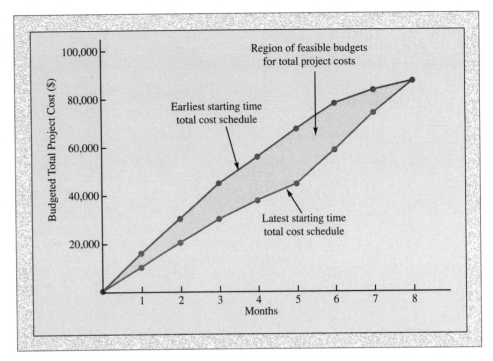

Table 10.16
Activity Cost Estimates for R&D
Project

Activity	Budgeted Cost	Activity	Budgeted Cost
A	$10,000	E	$20,000
B	30,000	F	10,000
C	3,000	G	8,000
D	6,000		

costs are less than the budgeted costs, we have a condition referred to as a cost underrun. By identifying the sources of cost overruns and cost underruns, the manager can take corrective action where necessary. Note that the budgeted or estimated activity costs for the R&D project network of Figure 10.16 are shown in Table 10.16.

Now at any point during the project's duration, the manager can use a PERT/Cost procedure to obtain an activity cost status report by collecting the following information for *each activity:*

1. Actual cost to date
2. Percent completion to date

A PERT/Cost system will require periodic—perhaps biweekly or monthly—collection of the above information. Let us suppose we are at the end of the fourth month of the project and have the actual cost and percent completion data for each activity, as shown in Table 10.17. This current status information shows that activities A and B have been completed; activities C, D, and E are in process; and activities F and G have not yet been started.

Table 10.17

Activity Cost and Percent Completion Data at the End of Month 4 for R&D Project

Activity	Actual Cost	Percent Completion
A	$12,000	100
B	30,000	100
C	1,000	50
D	2,000	33
E	10,000	25
F	0	0
G	0	0
Total	$55,000	

To prepare a cost status report, we will need to compute the value for all work completed to date. Let

$$V_i = \text{value of work completed for activity } i$$
$$p_i = \text{percent completion for activity } i$$
$$B_i = \text{budgeted cost for activity } i$$

The following relationship is used to find the value of work completed for each activity:

$$V_i = (p_i/100)B_i \tag{10.21}$$

For example, the values of work completed for activities A and C are as follows:[5]

$$V_A = (^{100}/_{100})(\$10,000) = \$10,000$$

$$V_C = (^{50}/_{100})(\$3000) = \$1500$$

Cost overruns and underruns can now be found by comparing the actual cost of each activity with its appropriate budget value. Let

$$AC_i = \text{actual cost to date for activity } i$$
$$D_i = \text{difference between actual cost and value of work completed}$$
$$\text{for activity } i$$

We have

$$D_i = AC_i - V_i \tag{10.22}$$

A positive D_i indicates the activity has a cost *overrun,* while a negative D_i indicates a cost *underrun,* and $D_i = 0$ indicates that actual costs are in agreement with the budgeted costs. For example,

$$D_A = AC_A - V_A = \$12,000 - \$10,000 = \$2000$$

shows that activity A, which has already been completed, has a $2000 cost overrun. However, activity C, with $D_C = \$1000 - \$1500 = -\$500$, is currently showing a cost underrun, or savings, of $500. A complete cost status report such as the one shown in Table 10.18 can now be prepared for the project manager.

---

[5]Equation (10.21) and the succeeding calculations are based on the PERT/Cost assumption that activity costs occur at a constant rate over the duration of the activity.

Table 10.18

Project Cost Status Report at Month 4 for R&D Project

Activity	Actual Cost (AC)	Value of Work Completed (V)	Differences (D)
A	$12,000	$10,000	$2,000
B	30,000	30,000	0
C	1,000	1,500	−500
D	2,000	2,000	0
E	10,000	5,000	5,000
F	0	0	0
G	0	0	0
Totals	$55,000	$48,500	$6,500

↑
Total project cost
overrun to date

Work PERT/Cost Problem 26 and develop the feasible budgets for the Daugherty Porta-Vac project.

This cost report shows the project manager that the costs to date are $6500 over the estimated or budgeted costs. On a percentage basis, we would say the project is experiencing a $6500/$48,500 100 = 13.4% cost overrun, which for most projects is a serious situation. By checking each activity, we see that activities A and E are causing the cost overrun. Since activity A has been completed, its cost overrun cannot be corrected; however, activity E is in process and is only 25% complete. Thus, activity E should be reviewed immediately. Corrective action for activity E can help to bring actual costs closer to the budgeted costs. The manager may also want to consider cost reduction possibilities for activities C, D, F, and G to keep the total project cost within the budget.

While the PERT/Cost procedure described above can be an effective cost control system, it is not without potential drawbacks and implementation problems. First, the activity-by-activity cost recording system can require significant clerical effort, especially for firms with large and/or numerous projects. Thus, the personnel and other costs associated with maintaining a PERT/Cost system may offset some of the advantages. Second, questions can arise as to how costs should be allocated to activities or work packages. Overhead, indirect, and even material costs can cause cost allocation and measurement problems. Third, and perhaps most critical, is the fact that PERT/Cost requires a system of cost recording and control that is significantly different from most cost accounting systems. Firms using departments or other organizational units as cost centers will need a substantially revised accounting system to handle the PERT/Cost activity-oriented system. Problems of modifying accounting procedures and carrying dual accounting systems are not trivial matters.

There are potential problems in the implementation of PERT/Cost due to the clerical effort required to monitor costs of work packages. In addition, existing cost accounting procedures may differ from the procedures best suited for PERT/Cost.

Summary

In this chapter we introduced PERT/CPM and PERT/Cost as procedures designed to assist managers schedule and control projects. The key to these techniques is the development of a PERT/CPM network that depicts the activities and their precedence relationships. Given this network and the activity time estimates, the critical path for the network and the associated critical path activities can be identified. In the process, an activity schedule showing the earliest start and finish times, the latest start and finish times, and the slack for each activity can be identified.

We showed how we can include capabilities for handling variable or uncertain activity times and how this information can be used to provide a probability statement about the chances the project can be completed in a specified period of time. Crashing was introduced as a procedure for reducing activity times to meet project completion deadlines. A linear programming model can be used to determine the crashing decisions that will minimize the cost of reducing the project completion time.

In the final section of this chapter we described how the PERT/Cost technique can be used to monitor project costs. Because of the numerous computations associated with planning, updating, and revising PERT/CPM and PERT/Cost networks, computer programs are frequently used to implement these project management techniques. For modest-sized projects, computerized procedures are available on microcomputers.

Glossary

Program evaluation and review technique (PERT) A network-based project scheduling procedure.

Critical path method (CPM) A network-based project scheduling procedure.

Activities Specific jobs or tasks that are components of a project. These are represented by arcs in a PERT/CPM network.

Immediate predecessors The activities that must immediately precede a given activity.

Event An event occurs when *all* the activities leading into a node have been completed.

Dummy activity A fictitious activity with zero activity time used to maintain predecessor relationships in a PERT/CPM network.

Critical path The longest path in a PERT/CPM network. The time it takes to traverse this path is the total time required to complete the project.

Path A sequence of arcs (activities) connecting the first node and the last node of a network.

Critical path activities The activities on the critical path.

Earliest start time The earliest time at which an activity may begin.

Earliest finish time The earliest time at which an activity may be completed.

Forward pass That part of the PERT/CPM calculation procedure that involves moving forward through the network in order to determine the earliest start and earliest finish times for each activity.

Latest start time The latest time at which an activity may begin without delaying the entire project.

Latest finish time The latest time at which an activity may be completed without delaying the entire project.

Backward pass That part of the PERT/CPM calculation procedure that involves moving backward through the network in order to determine the latest start and latest finish times for each activity.

Optimistic time An activity time estimate based on the assumption that the activity will progress in an ideal manner.

Most probable time An activity time estimate for the most likely activity time.

Pessimistic time An activity time estimate based on the assumption that the most unfavorable conditions occur.

Expected time The average activity time.

Beta distribution A probability distribution used to describe activity times.

Slack The length of time an activity can be delayed without affecting the project completion time.

Crashing The process of reducing an activity time by adding resources and hence usually increasing cost.

PERT/Cost A technique designed to assist in the monitoring of project costs.

Work package A natural grouping of interrelated activities for purposes of cost control. A work package is a unit of cost control in a PERT/Cost system.

Problems

1. PERT/CPM networks

1. The Mohawk Discount Store is designing a management training program for individuals at its corporate headquarters. The company would like to design the program so that the trainees can complete it as quickly as possible. There are important precedence relationships that must be maintained between assignments or activities in the program. For example, a trainee cannot serve as an assistant to the store manager until the trainee has obtained experience in the credit department and at least one sales department. The activities shown below are the assignments that must be completed by each trainee in the program.

Activity	Immediate Predecessor
A	—
B	—
C	A
D	A, B
E	A, B
F	C
G	D, F
H	E, G

Construct a PERT/CPM network for this problem. Do not attempt to perform any further analysis.

2. PERT/CPM networks

2. Consider the PERT/CPM network shown below.

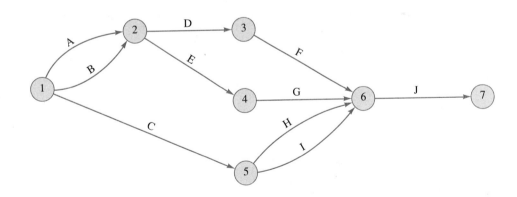

a. Add the dummy activities that will eliminate the problem that activities have the same starting and ending nodes.

b. Add dummy activities that will satisfy the following immediate predecessor requirements:

Activity	Immediate Predecessor
H	B, C
I	B, C
G	D, E

S ELF T EST

3. PERT/CPM networks

3. Construct a PERT/CPM network for a project having the following activities:

Activity	Immediate Predecessor
A	—
B	—
C	A
D	A
E	C, B
F	C, B
G	D, E

The project is completed when activities F and G are both complete.

4. Critical path

4. Assume that the project in Problem 3 has the following activity times:

Activity	Time (months)
A	4
B	6
C	2
D	6
E	3
F	3
G	5

  a. Find the critical path.
  b. The project must be completed in 1½ years. Do you anticipate difficulty in meeting the deadline? Explain.

5. PERT/CPM networks

5. Management Decision Systems (MDS) is a consulting company specializing in the development of decision support systems. MDS has just obtained the contract to develop a computer system to assist the management of a large company in formulating its capital expenditure plan. The project leader has developed the following list of activities and immediate predecessors:

Activity	Immediate Predecessor
A	—
B	—
C	—
D	B
E	A
F	B
G	C, D
H	B, E
I	F, G
J	H

Construct a PERT/CPM network for this problem.

SELF TEST ▷   **6.** Consider the following project network (the times shown are in weeks):

6. Critical path

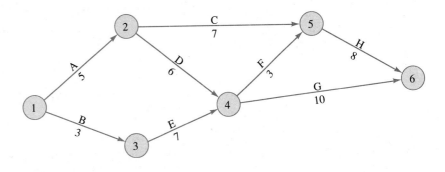

   a. Identify the critical path.
   b. How long will it take to complete this project?
   c. Can activity D be delayed without delaying the entire project? If so, how many weeks?
   d. Can activity C be delayed without delaying the entire project? If so, how many weeks?
   e. What is the schedule for activity E?

7. Network and critical path   **7.** A project involving the installation of a computer system consists of eight activities. The immediate predecessors and activity times are shown below.

Activity	Immediate Predecessor	Time (weeks)
A	—	3
B	—	6
C	A	2
D	B, C	5
E	D	4
F	E	3
G	B, C	9
H	F, G	3

a. Draw the PERT/CPM network for this project.
b. What are the critical path activities?
c. What is the expected project completion time?

8. Colonial State College is considering building a new multipurpose athletic complex on campus. The complex would provide a new gymnasium for intercollegiate basketball games, expanded office space, classrooms, and intramural facilities. The activities that would have to be undertaken before beginning construction are shown below.

Activity	Description	Immediate Predecessor	Time (weeks)
A	Survey building site	—	6
B	Develop initial design	—	8
C	Obtain board approval	A, B	12
D	Select architect	C	4
E	Establish budget	C	6
F	Finalize design	D, E	15
G	Obtain financing	E	12
H	Hire contractor	F, G	8

a. Develop a PERT/CPM network for this project.
b. Identify the critical path.
c. Develop the activity schedule for the project.
d. Does it appear reasonable that construction of the athletic complex could begin 1 year after the decision to begin the project with the site survey and initial design plans? What is the expected completion time for the project?

9. Hamilton County Parks is planning to develop a new park and recreational area on a recently purchased 100-acre tract. Project development activities include clearing playground and picnic areas, constructing roads, constructing a shelter house, purchasing picnic equipment, and so on. The PERT/CPM network shown below is being used in the planning, scheduling, and controlling of this project.

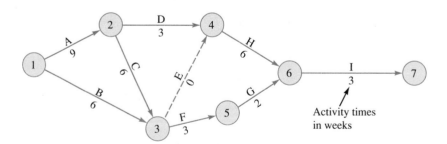

a. What is the critical path for this network?
b. Show the activity schedule for this project.
c. The park commissioner would like to open the park to the public within 6 months from the time the work on the project is started. Does this opening date appear feasible? Explain.

10. The following estimates of activity times (days) are available for a small project:

Activity	Optimistic	Most Probable	Pessimistic
A	4	5.0	6
B	8	9.0	10
C	7	7.5	11
D	7	9.0	10
E	6	7.0	9
F	5	6.0	7

a. Compute the expected activity completion times and the variance for each activity.

b. An analyst has found that the critical path consists of activities B–D–F. Compute the expected project completion time and the variance.

11. The project of building a backyard swimming pool consists of nine major activities. The activities and their immediate predecessors are shown below. Develop the PERT/CPM network for this project.

Activity	Immediate Predecessor
A	—
B	—
C	A, B
D	A, B
E	B
F	C
G	D
H	D, F
I	E, G, H

12. Assume that the activity time estimates in days for the swimming pool construction project from Problem 11 are as follows:

Activity	Optimistic	Most Probable	Pessimistic
A	3	5	6
B	2	4	6
C	5	6	7
D	7	9	10
E	2	4	6
F	1	2	3
G	5	8	10
H	6	8	10
I	3	4	5

a. What are the critical path activities?
b. What is the expected time to complete the project?
c. What is the probability that the project can be completed in 25 working days or less?

SELF TEST

13. Critical path, uncertain activity times

13. Suppose that the following estimates of activity times (weeks) were provided for the network shown in Problem 6:

Activity	Optimistic	Most Probable	Pessimistic
A	4.0	5.0	6.0
B	2.5	3.0	3.5
C	6.0	7.0	8.0
D	5.0	5.5	9.0
E	5.0	7.0	9.0
F	2.0	3.0	4.0
G	8.0	10.0	12.0
H	6.0	7.0	14.0

What is the probability that the project will be completed
a. Within 21 weeks?
b. Within 22 weeks?
c. Within 25 weeks?

14. Critical path, uncertain activity times

14. Consider the project network given below.

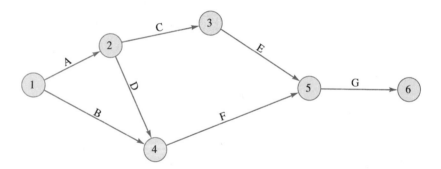

Estimates of the optimistic, most probable, and pessimistic times (in days) for the activities are as follows:

Activity	Optimistic	Most Probable	Pessimistic
A	5	6	7
B	5	12	13
C	6	8	10
D	4	10	10
E	5	6	13
F	7	7	10
G	4	7	10

a. Find the critical path.
b. How much slack time, if any, is there in activity C?
c. Determine the expected project completion time and the variance.
d. Find the probability that the project will be completed in 30 days or less.

15. Doug Casey is in charge of planning and coordinating next spring's sales management training program for his company. Doug has listed the following activity information for this project:

			Times (weeks)		
Activity	**Description**	**Immediate Predecessor**	Optimistic	Most Probable	Pessimistic
A	Plan topic	—	1.5	2.0	2.5
B	Obtain speakers	A	2.0	2.5	6.0
C	List meeting locations	—	1.0	2.0	3.0
D	Select location	C	1.5	2.0	2.5
E	Finalize speaker travel plans	B, D	0.5	1.0	1.5
F	Make final check with speakers	E	1.0	2.0	3.0
G	Prepare and mail brochure	B, D	3.0	3.5	7.0
H	Take reservations	G	3.0	4.0	5.0
I	Handle last-minute details	F, H	1.5	2.0	2.5

a. Show the PERT/CPM network for this project.
b. Prepare the activity schedule for this project.
c. What are the critical path activities and the expected project completion time?
d. If Doug wants a 0.99 probability of completing the project on time, how far ahead of the scheduled meeting date should he begin working on the project?

16. The Daugherty Porta-Vac project discussed in Section 10.3 had an expected project completion time of 17 weeks. The probability that the project could be completed in 20 weeks or less was found to be 0.9656. Shown below are the noncritical paths in the Porta-Vac project network.

A–D–G–J
A–C–F–J
B–H–I–J

a. Using the information in Table 10.6, compute the expected time and variance for each of the above paths.
b. Compute the probability that each path will be completed in the desired 20-week period.
c. Why is the computation of the probability of completing a project on time based on the analysis of the critical path? In what case, if any, would it be desirable to make the probability computation for a noncritical path?

17. Refer to the Porta-Vac project network shown in Figure 10.7. Suppose Daugherty's management revises the activity time estimates (in weeks) as follows:

Activity	Optimistic	Most Probable	Pessimistic
A	3.0	7.0	11.0
B	2.0	2.5	6.0
C	2.0	3.0	4.0
D	6.0	7.0	14.0
E	2.0	3.0	4.0
F	2.5	3.0	3.5
G	2.5	4.0	5.5
H	4.5	5.5	9.5
I	1.0	2.0	3.0
J	1.0	2.0	3.0

a. Compute the expected time and variance for each activity.
b. Show the new activity schedule.
c. What are the critical path activities?
d. What is the expected project completion time?
e. What is the new probability that the project will be completed within the 20-week deadline?

18. The manager of the Oak Hills Swimming Club is planning the club's swimming team program. The first team practice is scheduled for May 1. The activities, their immediate predecessors, and the activity time estimates are as follows:

Activity	Description	Immediate Predecessor	Time (weeks)		
			Optimistic	Most Probable	Pessimistic
A	Meet with board	—	1	1	2
B	Hire coaches	A	4	6	8
C	Reserve pool	A	2	4	6
D	Announce program	B, C	1	2	3
E	Meet with coaches	B	2	3	4
F	Order team suits	A	1	2	3
G	Register swimmers	D	1	2	3
H	Collect fees	G	1	2	3
I	Plan first practice	E, H, F	1	1	1

a. Show the PERT/CPM network for this project.
b. Develop an activity schedule for the project.
c. What are the critical path activities, and what is the expected project completion time?
d. If the club manager plans to start the project on February 1, what is the probability the swimming program will be ready by the scheduled May 1 date (13 weeks)? Should the manager begin planning the swimming program prior to February 1?

19. The product development group at Landon Corporation has been working on a new computer software product that has the potential to capture a large market share. Through outside sources, Landon's management has learned that a competitor is working to bring a similar product to the market. As a result, Landon's top management has increased its pressure on the product development group. The group's leader has turned to PERT/CPM as an aid to scheduling the activities remaining before the new product can be brought to the market. The PERT/CPM network is as follows.

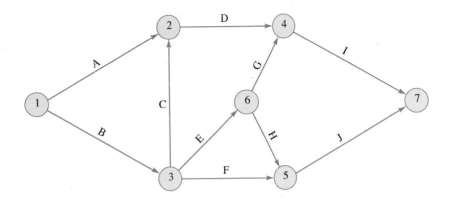

The activity time estimates in weeks are given below.

Activity	Optimistic	Most Probable	Pessimistic
A	3.0	4.0	5.0
B	3.0	3.5	7.0
C	4.0	5.0	6.0
D	2.0	3.0	4.0
E	6.0	10.0	14.0
F	7.5	8.5	12.5
G	4.5	6.0	7.5
H	5.0	6.0	13.0
I	2.0	2.5	6.0
J	4.0	5.0	6.0

a. Develop an activity schedule for this project, and identify the critical path activities.
b. What is the probability that the project will be completed so that Landon Corporation may introduce the new product within 25 weeks? Within 30 weeks?

20. LP for crashing decisions

20. Using the computer installation project referred to in Problem 7, assume that the project has to be completed in 16 weeks. Crashing of the project is necessary. Relevant information is shown.

	Time (weeks)		Cost ($)	
Activity	Normal	Crash	Normal	Crash
A	3	1	900	1700
B	6	3	2000	4000
C	2	1	500	1000
D	5	3	1800	2400
E	4	3	1500	1850
F	3	1	3000	3900
G	9	4	8000	9800
H	3	2	1000	2000

a. Formulate a linear programming model that can be used to make the crashing decisions for the above project.
b. Solve the linear programming model and make the minimum-cost crashing decisions. What is the added cost of meeting the 16-week completion time?
c. Develop a complete activity schedule using the crashed activity times.

SELF TEST ▶

21. Crashing the critical path

21. Consider the following network with activity times shown in days:

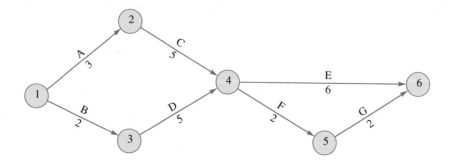

The crash data for this project are as follows:

	Time (days)		Total Cost ($)	
Activity	Normal	Crash	Normal	Crash
A	3	2	800	1400
B	2	1	1200	1900
C	5	3	2000	2800
D	5	3	1500	2300
E	6	4	1800	2800
F	2	1	600	1000
G	2	1	500	1000

a. Find the critical path and the expected project completion time.
b. What is the total project cost using the normal times?

SELF TEST ▶

22. LP for crashing decisions

22. Refer to Problem 21. Assume that management desires a 12-day project completion time.
a. Formulate a linear programming model that can be used to assist with the crashing decisions.
b. What activities should be crashed?
c. What is the total project cost for the 12-day completion time?

23. LP for crashing decisions

23. Assume that the following crash data are available for the project described in Problem 4:

	Time (months)		Total Cost ($000's)	
Activity	Normal	Crash	Normal	Crash
A	4	2	50	70
B	6	3	40	55
C	2	1	20	24
D	6	4	100	130

—Table continues on next page

—Table continued from previous page

	Time (months)		Total Cost ($000's)	
Activity	Normal	Crash	Normal	Crash
E	3	2	50	60
F	3	3	25	25
G	5	3	60	75

    a. Develop a linear programming model that could be used to make the crashing decisions if the project has to be completed in *T* months.

    b. If $T = 12$ months, what activities should be crashed, what is the crashing cost, and what are the critical path activities?

24. Crashing the critical path

24. Office Automation, Inc., has developed a proposal for introducing a new computerized office system that will improve word processing and interoffice communications for a particular company. Contained in the proposal is a list of activities that must be accomplished to complete the new office system project. Information about the activities is shown below.

		Immediate Predecessor	Time (weeks)		Cost ($000's)	
Activity	**Description**	**Predecessor**	Normal	Crash	Normal	Crash
A	Plan needs	—	10	8	30	70
B	Order equipment	A	8	6	120	150
C	Install equipment	B	10	7	100	160
D	Set up training lab	A	7	6	40	50
E	Conduct training course	D	10	8	50	75
F	Test system	C, E	3	3	60	—

    a. Show the network for the project.

    b. Develop an activity schedule for the project.

    c. What are the critical path activities, and what is the expected project completion time?

    d. Assume that the company wishes to complete the project in 6 months or 26 weeks. What crashing decisions would be recommended to meet the desired completion time at the least possible cost? Work through the network, and attempt to make the crashing decisions by inspection.

    e. Develop an activity schedule for the crashed project.

    f. What is the added project cost to meet the 6-month completion time?

25. LP for crashing decisions

25. Because Landon Corporation (see Problem 19) is being pressured to complete the product development project at the earliest possible date, the project leader has requested that the possibility of crashing the project be evaluated.

    a. Develop a linear programming model that could be used in making the crashing decisions.

    b. What information would have to be provided before the linear programming model could be implemented?

S E L F   T E S T ▶

26. PERT/Cost

26. For the Daugherty Porta-Vac project shown in Figure 10.7, suppose that the expected activity costs are as follows:

Activity	Expected Cost ($000's)
A	90
B	16
C	3
D	100
E	6
F	2
G	60
H	20
I	4
J	2

Develop a total cost budget based on both an earliest start and a latest start schedule. Show the graph of feasible budgets for the total project cost.

27. PERT/Cost

27. Using the Daugherty Porta-Vac project cost data given in Problem 26, prepare a PERT/Cost analysis for each of the following points in time. For each case, show the percent overrun or underrun for the project to date, and indicate any corrective action that should be undertaken. (Note: If an activity is not listed below, assume that it has not been started.)
   a. At the end of the 5th week:

Activity	Actual Cost ($000's)	Percent Completion
A	62	80
B	6	50

   b. At the end of the 10th week:

Activity	Actual Cost ($000's)	Percent Completion
A	85	100
B	16	100
C	1	33
D	100	80
E	4	100
H	10	25

c. At the end of the 15th week:

Activity	Actual Cost ($000's)	Percent Completion
A	85	
B	16	
C	3	
D	105	
E	4	100
F	3	
G	55	
H	25	
I	4	

28. PERT/Cost

28. The network for the two-machine maintenance project discussed in Section 10.4 is shown below:

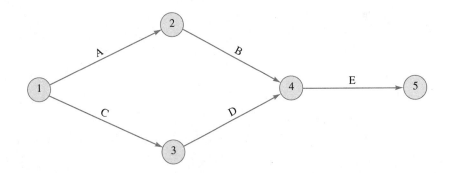

The recommended crashed activity schedule is shown in Table 10.11. Final times and costs for the project are as follows:

Activity	Expected Time (days)	Cost ($)
A	5	700
B	3	200
C	6	500
D	2	350
E	2	300
	Total	2050

a. Show the graph of feasible budgets for the project's total cost. Does this represent an unusual feasible budget region? Explain.

b. Suppose that at the start of day 8 we find the following activity status report:

Activity	Actual Cost ($)	Percent Completion
A	800	100
B	100	67
C	450	100
D	250	50
E	0	0

In terms of both time and cost, is the project on schedule? What action should be recommended?

29. PERT/Cost

29. A firm is modifying its warehouse operation with the installation of an automated stock handling system. Specific activities include redesigning the warehouse layout, installing the new equipment, and testing the new equipment. The project network is shown below.

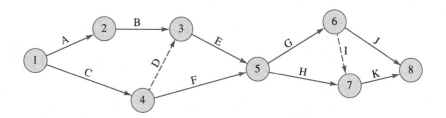

Pertinent time and cost data are as follows:

Activity	Expected Time (weeks)	Variance	Budgeted Cost ($)
A	3	0.3	6,000
B	2	0.5	4,000
C	8	2.0	16,000
D	0	0.0	0
E	6	1.0	18,000
F	4	0.2	20,000
G	5	0.4	15,000
H	1	0.1	2,000
I	0	0.0	0
J	5	1.0	5,000
K	6	0.6	12,000

a. Develop an activity schedule for the project.
   (1) What is the critical path?
   (2) What is the expected completion time?
   (3) What is the probability of meeting a desired 6-month (26-week) completion time?

b. Develop a PERT/Cost budget for total project costs over the project's duration. What should the range be for expenditures after 12 weeks of the project?

30. PERT/Cost

30. Refer to the network in Problem 29. Suppose that after 12 weeks of operation the following data are available on all completed and in-process activities:

Activity	Actual Cost ($)	Percent Completion
A	5,000	100
B	4,000	100
C	18,000	100
E	9,000	50
F	18,000	75

Is the project in control based on both time and cost considerations? What corrective action, if any, is desirable?

Case Problem: Warehouse Expansion

R. C. Coleman distributes a variety of food products that are sold through grocery store and supermarket outlets. The company receives orders directly from the individual outlets, with a typical order requesting the delivery of several cases of anywhere from 20 to 50 different products. Under the company's current warehouse operation, warehouse clerks dispatch order-picking personnel to fill each order and have the goods moved to the warehouse shipping area. Because of the high labor costs and relatively low productivity of hand order-picking, the company has decided to automate the warehouse operation by installing a computer-controlled order-picking system, along with a conveyor system for moving goods from storage to the warehouse shipping area.

R. C. Coleman's director of material management has been named the project manager in charge of the automated warehouse system. After consulting with members of the engineering staff and warehouse management personnel, the director has compiled a list of activities associated with the project. The optimistic, most probable, and pessimistic times in weeks have also been provided for each activity. This information is as follows:

Activity	Description	Immediate Predecessor
A	Determine equipment needs	—
B	Obtain vendor proposals	—
C	Select vendor	A, B
D	Order system	C
E	Design new warehouse layout	C
F	Design warehouse	E
G	Design computer interface	C
H	Interface computer	D, F, G
I	Install system	D, F
J	Train system operators	H
K	Test system	I, J

	Time (weeks)		
Activity	Optimistic	Most Probable	Pessimistic
A	4	6	8
B	6	8	16
C	2	4	6
D	8	10	24
E	7	10	13
F	4	6	8
G	4	6	20
H	4	6	8
I	4	6	14
J	3	4	5
K	2	4	6

Managerial Report

Develop a report that presents the activity schedule and expected project completion time for the warehouse expansion project. Include a PERT/CPM network of the project in the report. In addition, take into consideration the following issues.

1. R. C. Coleman's top management has established a required 40-week completion time for the project. Can this completion time be achieved? Include probability information in your discussion. What recommendations do you have if the 40-week completion time is required?
2. Suppose that management requests that activity times be shortened to provide an 80% chance of meeting the 40-week completion time. Assuming the variance in the project completion time is the same as you found in part (a), how much should the expected project completion time be shortened to achieve the goal of an 80% chance of completion within 40 weeks?
3. Using the expected activity times as the normal times and the following crashing information, determine the activity crashing decisions and revised activity schedule for the warehouse expansion project.

	Crashed Activity Time	Cost ($)	
Activity	(weeks)	Normal	Crashed
A	4	1,000	1,900
B	7	1,000	1,800
C	2	1,500	2,700
D	8	2,000	3,200
E	7	5,000	8,000
F	4	3,000	4,100
G	5	8,000	10,250
H	4	5,000	6,400
I	4	10,000	12,400
J	3	4,000	4,400
K	3	5,000	5,500

Seasongood & Mayer

Cincinnati, Ohio

Seasongood & Mayer, established in 1887, is an investment securities firm that engages in the following areas of municipal finance:

1. Underwriting new issues of municipal bonds
2. Trading—for example, acting as a market maker for the buying and selling of previously issued bonds
3. Investment banking—that is, the process of obtaining money from the capital markets at the lowest possible cost

The major applications of management science at Seasongood & Mayer are in the investment banking area. One particular application involved the use of PERT/CPM in the introduction of a $31 million hospital revenue bond issue.

Scheduling the Introduction of a Bond Issue

In any major building project there are certain common steps:

1. Defining the project
2. Determining the cost of the project
3. Financing the project

The investment banker's role in building projects is to develop the method of financing that will result in the owner's receiving the necessary funds in a timely manner. In a hospital building project, such as the one we will be discussing, the typical method of financing is tax-free hospital revenue bonds.

The construction cost for the building project is an important factor in determining the best approach to financing. Normally, the construction cost is based on a bid submitted by a contractor or a construction manager. However, this cost is usually guaran-

teed only for a specified period of time, such as 60–90 days. The major function of the hospital's investment banker is to arrange the timing of the financing in such a way that the proceeds of the bond issue can be made available within the time limit of the guaranteed-price construction bid. Since most hospitals must have the proceeds of their permanent long-term financing in hand prior to committing to major construction contracts, the investment banker's role is a significant one.

To arrange for the financing, the investment banker must coordinate the activities of hospital attorneys, the bond counsel, and so on. The cooperation of all parties and the coordination of project activities are best achieved if everyone recognizes the interdependency of the activities and the necessity of completing individual tasks in a timely manner. Seasongood & Mayer has found PERT/CPM to be useful in scheduling and coordinating such a project.

As managing underwriter for a $31,050,000 issue of Hospital Facilities Revenue Bonds for Providence Hospital in Hamilton County, Ohio, Seasongood & Mayer used a critical path procedure to coordinate and schedule the project financing activities. Descriptions of the activities, times required, and immediate predecessors are given in Table 10.19. The complete network is shown in Figure 10.18. The critical path activities K–L–M–N–P–Q–R–S–U–W resulted in a scheduled project completion time of 29.14 weeks. Specific schedules showing start and finish times for all activities were used to keep the entire project on track. The use of PERT/CPM was instrumental in helping Seasongood & Mayer obtain financing for this project within the time specified in the construction bid.

Figure 10.18
Seasongood & Mayer
PERT/CPM Network for
Providence Hospital Project

Critical path:
Activities K–L–M–N–P–Q–R–S–U–W

—Continued on next page

—Continued from previous page

Table 10.19

Activities for the Providence Hospital Project

Activity	Time Required (weeks)	Description of Activity	Immediate Predecessor
A	4	Drafting and distribution of legal documents	—
B	3	Preparation and distribution of unaudited financial statements of hospital	—
C	2	Drafting and distribution of hospital history, description of services, and existing facilities for Preliminary Official Statement (POS)	—
D	8	Drafting and distribution of demand portion of feasibility study	—
E	4	Review (additions/deletions) and approval as to form of legal documents	A
F	1	Review (additions/deletions) and approval of history, etc., for POS	C
G	4	Review (additions/deletions) and approval of demand portion of feasibility study	D
H	2	Drafting and distribution of financial portion (as to form) of feasibility study	E, G
I	2	Drafting and distribution of plan of financing and all pertinent facts relevant to the bond transaction for POS	E
J	0.5	Review and approval of unaudited financial statements	B
K	20	Receipt of firm price for project	—
L	1	Review (additions/deletions), approval, and completion of financial portion of feasibility study	H, K
M	1	Drafting of POS completed	F, I, J, L
N	0.14	Distribution of all material to bond rating services	M
O	0.28	Printing and distribution of POS to all interested parties	M
P	1	Presentation to bond rating services (Standard & Poor's, Moody's)	N
Q	1	Receipt of bond rating	P
R	2	Marketing of bonds	O, Q
S	0*	Execution of purchase Contract	R
T	0.14	Authorization and completion of Final Official Statement, completion of legal documents	S
U	3	Fulfillment of all terms and conditions of Purchase Contract	S
V	0	Bond proceeds available to hospital	T, U
W	0*	Hospital able to sign construction contract	T, U

*Occurs instantaneously.

Questions

1. What is the role of the investment banker in building projects?
2. For the hospital project described, what is the primary objective of the investment banker?
3. Perform the critical path calculations for the network shown in Figure 10.18. Is there more than one critical path? Discuss.

CHAPTER 11

Inventory Models

The cost associated with developing and maintaining inventory is larger than many people think. Quantitative models such as the ones presented in this chapter can be used to develop cost-effective inventory management decisions.

Inventory refers to idle goods or materials that are held by an organization for use sometime in the future. Items carried in inventory include raw materials, purchased parts, components, subassemblies, work-in-process, finished goods, and supplies. One reason organizations maintain inventory is that it is rarely possible to predict sales levels, production times, demand, and usage needs exactly. Thus, inventory serves as a buffer against uncertain and fluctuating usage and keeps a supply of items available in case the items are needed by the organization or its customers. While inventory serves an important and essential role, the expense associated with financing and maintaining inventories is a substantial part of the cost of doing business. In large organizations, the cost associated with inventory can run into the millions of dollars.

Two important questions that managers must answer in order to effectively manage inventories are as follows:

1. *How much* should be ordered when the inventory for the item is replenished?
2. *When* should the inventory for a given item be replenished?

The purpose of this chapter is to show how quantitative models can assist in making the above decisions.

We will first consider *deterministic* inventory models where it is reasonable to assume that the rate of demand for the item is constant or nearly constant. Later we will consider *probabilistic* inventory models where the demand for the item fluctuates and can be described only in probabilistic terms. In addition, we will describe an inventory management procedure referred to as *material requirements planning* (MRP); this approach is suited for managing inventories of raw materials, subassemblies, and components whose demand is directly dependent on the demand for the final products in the inventory system. Finally, in the last section of the chapter, we discuss a philosophy of material management and control known as *just-in-time* (JIT); the primary objective of JIT is to eliminate all sources of waste, including unnecessary inventory.

11.1 Economic Order Quantity (EOQ) Model

The best known and most fundamental inventory model is the *economic order quantity (EOQ) model*. This model is applicable when the demand for an item has a constant, or nearly constant, rate and when the entire quantity ordered arrives in inventory at one point in time. The *constant demand rate* assumption means that the same number of units is taken from inventory each period of time, such as 5 units every day, 25 units every week, 100 units every 4-week period, and so on.

To illustrate the EOQ model, let us consider the situation faced by the R & B Beverage Company. R & B Beverage is a distributor of beer, wine, and soft drink products. From a main warehouse located in Columbus, Ohio, R & B supplies nearly 1000 retail stores with beverage products. The beer inventory, which constitutes about 40% of the company's total inventory, averages approximately 50,000 cases. With an average cost per case of approximately $8, R & B estimates the value of its beer inventory to be $400,000.

The warehouse manager has decided to do a detailed study of the inventory costs associated with Bub Beer, the number-one-selling R & B beer. The purpose of the study is to establish the *how-much*-to-order and the *when*-to-order decisions for Bub Beer that will result in the lowest possible total cost. As the first step in the study, the warehouse manager has obtained the following historical demand data for the past 10 weeks:

> One of the most criticized assumptions of the EOQ model is the constant demand rate. Obviously, the model would be inappropriate for items with widely fluctuating and variable demand rates. However, as this example attempts to show, the EOQ model can provide a realistic approximation of the optimal order quantity when demand is relatively stable and occurs at a nearly constant rate.

Week	Demand (cases)
1	2,000
2	2,025
3	1,950
4	2,000
5	2,100
6	2,050
7	2,000
8	1,975
9	1,900
10	2,000
Total cases	20,000
Average cases per week	2,000

Strictly speaking, the above weekly demand figures do not show a constant demand rate. However, given the relatively low variability exhibited by the weekly demand, inventory planning with a constant demand rate of 2000 cases per week appears acceptable. In practice, you will find that the actual inventory situation seldom, if ever, satisfies the assumptions of the model exactly. Thus, in any particular application, it is the job of the manager to determine whether the model assumptions are close enough to reality for the model to be useful. In this situation, since demand varies from a low of 1900 cases to a high of 2100 cases, it appears that the assumption of constant demand of 2000 cases per week is a reasonable approximation.

The how-much-to-order decision involves selecting an order quantity that draws a compromise between (1) keeping small inventories and ordering frequently and (2) keeping large inventories and ordering infrequently. The first alternative can result in undesirably high ordering costs, while the second alternative can result in undesirably high inventory holding costs. To find an optimal compromise between these conflicting alternatives, let us consider a mathematical model that will show the total cost[1] as the sum of the holding cost and the ordering cost.

Holding costs are the costs associated with maintaining or carrying a given level of inventory; these costs depend on the size of the inventory. First, there is the cost of financing the inventory investment. If money is borrowed, an interest charge is incurred; if the firm's own money is used, there is an opportunity cost associated with not being able to use the money for other investments. In either case, an interest cost exists for the capital tied up in inventory. This *cost of capital* is usually expressed as a percentage of the amount invested. R & B estimates its cost of capital at an annual rate of 18%.

There are a number of other holding costs, such as insurance, taxes, breakage, pilferage, and warehouse overhead, that also depend for the most part on the value of the inventory. R & B estimates these other costs at an annual rate of approximately 7% of the value of its inventory. Thus, the total holding cost for the R & B beer inventory is 25% of the value of the inventory.

Assume that the cost of one case of Bub Beer is $8. Since R & B estimates its annual holding cost to be 25% of the value of its inventory, the cost of holding one case of Bub Beer in inventory for 1 year is 0.25($8) = $2.00. Note that defining the holding cost as a percentage of the value of the product is convenient because it is easily transferable to other products. For example, a case of Carle's Red Ribbon Beer, which costs $7.00 per case, would have an annual holding cost of 0.25($7.00) = $1.75 per case.

The next step in the inventory analysis is to determine the *ordering cost*. This cost, which is considered fixed regardless of the order quantity, covers the preparation of the voucher, the processing of the order including payment, postage, telephone, transportation, invoice verification, receiving, and so on. For R & B Beverage, the largest portion of the ordering cost involves the salaries of the purchasers. An analysis of the purchasing process showed that a purchaser spends approximately 45 minutes preparing and processing an order for Bub Beer. With a wage rate and fringe benefit cost for purchasers of $20 per hour, the labor portion of the ordering cost is $15. Making allowances for paper, postage, telephone, transportation, and receiving costs at $17 per order, the manager estimates that the ordering cost is $20 per order. That is, R & B is paying $32 per order regardless of the quantity requested in the order.

The holding cost, ordering cost, and demand information are the three data items that must be known prior to the use of the EOQ model. Since these data have now been developed for the R & B problem, let us see how they are used to develop a total-cost model. We begin by defining Q to be the order quantity. Thus, the how-much-to-order decision involves finding the value of Q that will minimize the sum of holding and ordering costs.

The inventory level for Bub will have a maximum value of Q units when an order of size Q is received from the supplier. R & B will then satisfy customer demand from inventory until the inventory is depleted, at which time another shipment of Q units will be received. Suppose that R & B is open 5 days each week. Thus, assuming a constant demand rate of 2000 cases per week or 400 cases per day, the graph of the inventory level for Bub Beer is as shown in Figure 11.1. Note that the graph indicates that the average

As with other quantitative models, accurate estimates of cost parameters are critical inputs. In the EOQ model, estimates of both the inventory holding cost and the ordering cost are needed. Point out to the students that in many firms these costs are not necessarily automatically available. Also point out footnote[1], which refers to *variable* or *relevant* costs.

---

[1]While management scientists typically refer to "total-cost" models for inventory systems, often these models describe only the total *variable* or total *relevant* costs for the decision being considered. Costs that are not affected by the how-much-to-order decision are considered fixed or constant and are not included in the model.

Figure 11.1
Inventory Level for Bub Beer

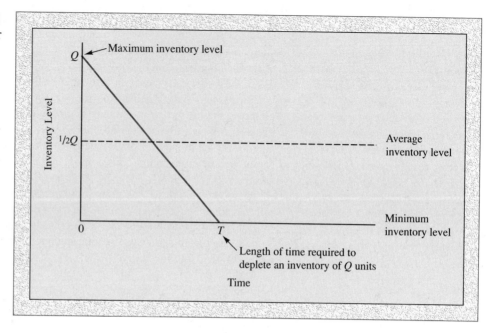

inventory level for the period in question is $\frac{1}{2}Q$. This should appear reasonable since the maximum inventory level is Q, the minimum is zero, and the inventory level declines at a constant rate over the period.

Figure 11.1 shows the inventory pattern during one order cycle of length T. As time goes on, this pattern will repeat. The complete inventory pattern is shown in Figure 11.2. If the average inventory during each cycle is $\frac{1}{2}Q$, the average inventory level over any number of cycles is also $\frac{1}{2}Q$.

The holding cost can be calculated using the average inventory level. That is, we can calculate the holding cost by multiplying the average inventory level by the cost of carrying one unit in inventory for the stated period. The period selected for the model is up to you; it could be 1 week, 1 month, 1 year, or more. However, since the holding cost for many industries and businesses is expressed as an *annual* percentage, most inventory models are developed on an *annual cost* basis.

Reemphasize that most inventory cost models will use an *annual cost*. Thus, demand should be expressed in units per year and inventory holding cost should be based on an annual rate. The ordering cost should be expressed as a cost per order with the model providing the calculation of the total annual ordering cost.

Figure 11.2
Inventory Pattern for the EOQ
Inventory Model

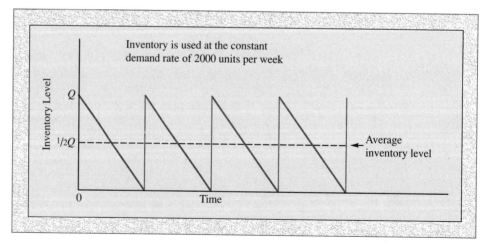

Let

$$I = \text{annual holding cost rate}$$
$$C = \text{unit cost of the inventory item}$$
$$C_h = \text{annual cost of holding one unit in inventory}$$

The annual cost of holding one unit in inventory is

$$C_h = IC \tag{11.1}$$

The cost of one case of Bub Beer is $C = \$8$. With the annual holding cost rate of 25%, ($I = 0.25$), the annual holding cost for one case of Bub Beer would be $C_h = IC = (0.25)(\$8) = \$2$. The general equation for the annual holding cost for the average inventory of $\frac{1}{2}Q$ units is as follows:

$$\text{Annual holding cost} = \left(\begin{array}{c}\text{Average} \\ \text{inventory} \\ \text{level}\end{array}\right)\left(\begin{array}{c}\text{Annual holding} \\ \text{cost} \\ \text{per unit}\end{array}\right)$$

$$= \frac{1}{2}QC_h \tag{11.2}$$

C_h is the cost of holding one unit in inventory for one year. Since smaller order quantities Q will result in lower inventory levels, total annual holding cost can be reduced by using smaller order quantities.

To complete the total-cost model, we must now include the annual ordering cost. The goal is to express the annual ordering cost in terms of the order quantity Q. The first question is, How many orders will be placed during the year? Let D denote the annual demand for the product (for R & B Beverage, D = (52 weeks)(2000 cases per week) = 104,000 cases per year). We know that by ordering Q units every time we order, we will have to place D/Q orders per year. If C_o is the cost of placing one order, the general equation for the annual ordering cost is as follows:

$$\text{Annual ordering cost} = \left(\begin{array}{c}\text{Number of} \\ \text{orders} \\ \text{per year}\end{array}\right)\left(\begin{array}{c}\text{Cost} \\ \text{per} \\ \text{order}\end{array}\right)$$

$$= \left(\frac{D}{Q}\right)C_o \tag{11.3}$$

C_o is the fixed cost per order regardless of the amount ordered. For a given annual demand of D units, the total annual ordering cost can be reduced by using larger order quantities.

Thus, the total annual cost, denoted TC, can be expressed as follows:

$$\begin{array}{c}\text{Total} \\ \text{annual} \\ \text{cost}\end{array} = \begin{array}{c}\text{Annual} \\ \text{holding} \\ \text{cost}\end{array} + \begin{array}{c}\text{Annual} \\ \text{ordering} \\ \text{cost}\end{array}$$

$$TC = \frac{1}{2}QC_h + \frac{D}{Q}C_o \tag{11.4}$$

The cost of goods (DC) is not included in the total annual cost equation (11.4) because it is *not a relevant cost* for the EOQ model. The choice of order quantity has no effect on the cost per unit.

Using the Bub Beer data ($C_h = \$2$, $C_o = \$32$, and $D = 104,000$), the total annual cost model is

$$TC = \frac{1}{2}Q(\$2) + \frac{104,000}{Q}(\$32) = Q + \frac{3,328,000}{Q}$$

The development of the above total-cost model has gone a long way toward solving the inventory problem. We now are able to express the total annual cost as a function of *how much* should be ordered. The development of a realistic total-cost model is perhaps the most important part of the application of quantitative techniques to inventory decision making. Equation (11.4) is the general total-cost equation for inventory situations in which the assumptions of the economic order quantity model are valid.

The How-Much-to-Order Decision

The next step is to find the order quantity Q that will minimize the total annual cost for Bub Beer. Using a trial-and-error approach, we can compute the total annual cost for several possible order quantities. As a starting point, let us consider $Q = 8000$. The total annual cost for Bub Beer is

$$TC = Q + \frac{3,328,000}{Q}$$

$$= 8000 + \frac{3,328,000}{8000} = \$8416$$

A trial order quantity of 5000 gives

$$TC = 5000 + \frac{3,328,000}{5000} = \$5666$$

The results of several other trial order quantities are shown in Table 11.1. As can be seen, the lowest cost solution is around 2000 cases. Graphs of the annual holding and ordering costs, and total annual costs are shown in Figure 11.3.

The advantage of the trial-and-error approach is that it is rather easy to do and provides the total annual cost for a number of possible order quantity decisions. Also, we can see that approximately 2000 cases appears to be the minimum-cost order quantity. The disadvantage of this approach, however, is that it does not provide the exact minimum-cost order quantity.

Refer to Figure 11.3. The minimum total-cost order quantity is denoted by an order size of Q^*. By using differential calculus, it can be shown (see Appendix 11.1) that the value of Q^* that minimizes the total annual cost is given by the formula

> The EOQ formula determines the optimal order quantity by balancing the annual holding cost and the annual ordering cost. Problem 2 at the end of the chapter will ask the student to show that an order quantity of Q^* causes the annual holding cost to equal the annual ordering cost.

$$Q^* = \sqrt{\frac{2DC_o}{C_h}} \tag{11.5}$$

This formula is referred to as the *economic order quantity (EOQ) formula*.

Using (11.5), the minimum total-annual-cost order quantity for Bub Beer is

> In 1915 F. W. Harris derived the mathematical formula for the economic order quantity. This was the first application of quantitative methods to the area of inventory management.

$$Q^* = \sqrt{\frac{2(104,000)32}{2}} = 1824 \text{ cases}$$

The use of an order quantity of 1824 in equation (11.4) shows that the minimum-cost inventory policy for Bub Beer has a total annual cost of $3649. Note that $Q^* = 1824$ has balanced the holding and ordering costs. Check for yourself to see that these costs are

---

Table 11.1

Annual Holding, Ordering, and Total Costs for Various Order Quantities of Bub Beer

Order Quantity	Annual Cost		
	Holding	Ordering	Total
5000	$5000	$ 666	$5666
4000	4000	832	4832
3000	3000	1109	4109
2000	2000	1664	3664
1000	1000	3328	4328

Figure 11.3
Annual Holding, Ordering, and
Total Costs for Bub Beer

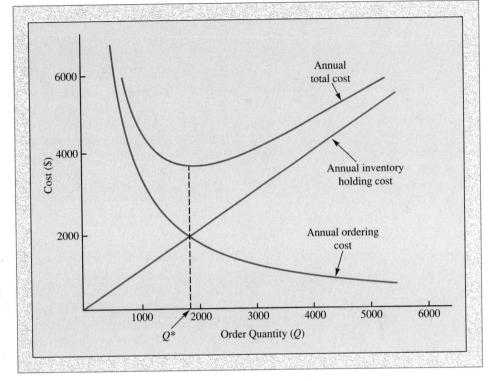

The reorder point is expressed in terms of *inventory position*, the amount of inventory on hand plus the amount on order. Students often think that the reorder point is expressed in terms of inventory on hand. With short lead times, inventory position is usually the same as the inventory on hand. However, with long lead times, inventory position may be larger than inventory on hand.

equal.[2] (Problem 2 at the end of the chapter will ask you to show that equal holding and ordering costs is a property of the EOQ model.)

The When-to-Order Decision

Now that we know how much to order, we want to address the question of *when* to order. To answer this question, we need to introduce the concept of inventory position. The *inventory position* for an item is defined as the amount of inventory on hand plus the amount of inventory on order. The when-to-order decision is expressed in terms of a *reorder point*—the inventory position at which a new order should be placed.

Given the assumptions of a constant demand rate and a fixed lead time, the reorder point can be computed such that the new order will arrive exactly when the inventory level reaches zero. Since this condition is rarely encountered in practice, most managers will increase the reorder point to guard against a slightly higher-than-anticipated demand and/or a slightly longer-than-expected lead time

The manufacturer of Bub Beer guarantees a 2-day delivery on any order placed by R & B Beverage. Hence, assuming a constant demand rate of 2000 cases per week or 400 cases per day, we expect (2 days)(400 cases/day) = 800 cases of Bub to be sold during the 2 days it takes a new order to reach the R & B warehouse. In inventory terminology, the 2-day delivery period is referred to as the *lead time* for a new order, and the 800 cases of demand anticipated during this period is referred to as the *lead-time demand*. Thus, R & B should order a new shipment of Bub Beer from the manufacturer when the inventory level reaches 800 cases. For inventory systems using the constant demand rate assumption and a fixed lead time, the reorder point is the same as the lead-time demand. For these systems, the general expression for the reorder point is as follows:

$$r = dm \tag{11.6}$$

---

[2]Actually, Q^* from equation (11.5) is 1824.28, but since we cannot order fractional cases of beer, a Q^* of 1824 is shown. This value of Q^* may cause a few cents deviation between the two costs. If Q^* is used at its exact value, the holding and ordering costs will be exactly the same.

where

$$r = \text{reorder point}$$
$$d = \text{demand per day}$$
$$m = \text{lead time for a new order in days}$$

The cycle time can be expressed in units of years with $T = Q^*/D$. Since inventory managers may wish to think of cycle time in other units, T can be adjusted to months by multiplying by 12, to weeks by multiplying by 52, or as we show, to days by multiplying by the number of working days per year, which may vary from firm to firm.

The question of how frequently the order will be placed can now be answered. This period between orders is referred to as the *cycle time*. Previously (see equation (11.2)), we defined D/Q as the number of orders that will be placed in a year. Thus, $D/Q^* = 104{,}000/1824 = 57$ is the number of orders R & B Beverage will place for Bub Beer each year. If R & B purchasers place 57 orders over 250 working days, they will order approximately every $250/57 = 4.4$ working days. Thus, the cycle time is 4.4 working days. The general expression[3] for a cycle time of T days is given by

$$T = \frac{250}{D/Q^*} = \frac{250Q^*}{D} \tag{11.7}$$

Sensitivity Analysis in the EOQ Model

Even though substantial time may have been spent in arriving at the cost per order ($32) and the holding cost rate (25%), we should realize that these figures are at best good estimates. Thus, we may want to consider how much the recommended order quantity would change if the estimated ordering and holding costs had been different. To determine this, we can calculate the recommended order quantity under several different cost conditions; Table 11.2 shows the minimum total-cost order quantity for several cost possibilities. As you can see from the table, the value of Q^* appears relatively stable, even with some variations in the cost estimates. Based on these results, it appears that the best order quantity for Bub Beer is somewhere around 1700–2000 cases. If operated properly, the total cost for the Bub Beer inventory system should be close to $3400–$3800 per year. We also note that there is very little risk associated with implementing the calculated order quantity of 1824. In the worst case (holding cost rate 24%, $C_o = \$34$, and the true optimal order quantity $Q^* = 1919$), there is only a $5 increase in the total annual cost; that is, $3690 - \$3685 = \$5$, with $Q = 1824$.

Table 11.2

Optimal Order Quantities for Several Cost Possibilities

Possible Inventory Holding Cost (%)	Possible Cost Per Order	Optimal Order Quantity (Q^*)	Projected Total Annual Cost	
			Using Q^*	Using $Q = 1824$
24	$30	1803	$3461	$3462
24	34	1919	3685	3690
26	30	1732	3603	3607
26	34	1844	3835	3836

---

[3]This general expression for cycle time is based on 250 working days per year. If the firm operated 300 working days per year and wanted to express cycle time in terms of working days, the cycle time would be given by $T = 300Q^*/D$.

From the above analysis, we would say that this EOQ model is insensitive to small variations or errors in the cost estimates. This is a property of EOQ models in general, which indicates that if we have at least reasonable estimates of ordering costs and holding costs, we can expect to obtain a good approximation of the true minimum-cost order quantity.

The Manager's Use of the EOQ Model

The EOQ model results in a recommended order quantity of 1824 units. Is this the final decision, or should the manager's judgment enter into the establishment of the final inventory policy? Although the model has provided a good order-quantity recommendation, it may not have taken into account all aspects of the inventory situation. As a result, the decision maker may want to modify the final order-quantity recommendation to meet the unique circumstances of his or her inventory situation. In this case, the warehouse manager felt that it would be desirable to increase the order quantity from 1824 cases to 2000 cases in order to have an order quantity equal to 5 working days' demand. By doing so, R & Beverage can maintain a weekly order cycle.

The total-cost curve in Figure 11.3 is relatively flat near the value of Q^*. This means that the inventory manager may choose to adjust the EOQ slightly to a more convenient level without seriously affecting the total cost.

The warehouse manager also realized that the EOQ model was based on the constant demand rate assumption of 2000 cases per week. While this is a good approximation, we must also recognize that sometimes the demand exceeds 2000 cases per week. If a reorder point of 800 cases is used, we would be expecting an 800-case demand during the lead time and the new order to arrive exactly when the inventory level reached zero. Such close timing would have little room for error, and the scheduling of arrivals would be very critical if stockouts were to be avoided. To protect against shortages due to higher-than-expected demands or slightly delayed incoming orders, the warehouse manager recommended a 1200-case reorder point. Thus, under normal conditions, R & B Beverage will order 2000 cases of Bub whenever the current inventory reaches 1200 cases. During the expected 2-day lead time, 800 cases should be demanded, and 400 cases should be in inventory when an order arrives. The extra 400 cases serve as a safety precaution against a higher-than-expected demand or a delayed incoming order. In general, the amount by which the reorder point exceeds the expected lead-time demand is referred to as *safety stock*.

The decisions to adjust the order quantity and reorder point were purely judgment decisions and were not necessarily made with a minimum-cost objective in mind. However, they are examples of how managerial judgment might interface with the inventory decision model to arrive at a sound inventory policy. The final decision of $Q = 2000$ with a 400-case safety stock resulted in a total annual cost of \$4464.[4]

How Has the EOQ Decision Model Helped?

The EOQ model has objectively included holding and ordering costs and, with the aid of some management judgment, has led to a low-cost inventory policy. In addition, the general optimal order-quantity model, equation (11.5), is potentially applicable to other R & B products. For example, Red Ribbon Beer (\$7/case), which has an ordering cost of

[4]A Q of 2000 units resulted in a total cost of \$3664 (see Table 11.1). The additional safety stock inventory of 400 units increases the average inventory by 400 units since it is on hand all year long. Thus, the inventory carrying charge is increased by 2(400) = \$800, the total cost of the revised policy is \$3664 + \$800 = \$4464.

Table 11.3

Summary of the EOQ Model
Assumptions

1. Demand D is deterministic and occurs at a constant rate.
2. The order quantity Q is the same for each order. The inventory level increases by Q units each time an order is received.
3. The cost per order, C_o, is constant and does not depend on the quantity ordered.
4. The purchase cost per unit, C, is constant and does not depend on the quantity ordered.
5. The inventory holding cost per unit per time period, C_h, is constant. The total inventory holding cost depends on both C_h and the size of the inventory.
6. Shortages such as stockouts or backorders are not permitted.
7. The lead time for an order is constant.
8. The inventory position is reviewed continuously. As a result, an order is placed as soon as the inventory position reaches the reorder point.

$32, a constant demand rate of 1200 cases per week (62,400 cases/year), and a 2-day lead-time period, has a recommended order quantity of

Problem 1 provides practice in
applying the EOQ model to another
R & B product.

$$Q^* = \sqrt{\frac{2(62,400)(32)}{(0.25)(7)}} = 1511 \text{ cases}$$

a cycle time of $T = [250(1511)]/62,400 = 6.05$ days, and a reorder point of $r = (240)\,(2) = 480$ cases.

A Summary of the EOQ Model Assumptions

To use the optimal order-quantity and reorder-point model described here, an analyst must make assumptions about how the inventory system operates. The EOQ model with its economic order quantity formula is based on some very specific assumptions about the R & B inventory system. A summary of the assumptions for this model is provided in Table 11.3. Before using the EOQ formula, you should carefully review these assumptions to ensure that they are applicable to the inventory system being analyzed. If the assumptions are not reasonable, a different inventory model should be sought.

One should carefully review the
assumptions of the inventory model
before applying it in an actual
situation. Several of the inventory
models discussed in this chapter
alter one or more of the
assumptions for the EOQ model.

There are various types of inventory systems in practice, and the inventory models presented in the following sections alter one or more of the EOQ model assumptions shown in Table 11.3 to meet the needs of the different systems. When the assumptions change, a different inventory model with different optimal operating policies becomes necessary.

NOTES & COMMENTS

With relatively long lead times, the lead-time demand and the resulting reorder point r, determined by equation (11.6), may exceed Q^*. If this condition occurs, there will be at least one order outstanding when a new order is placed. For example, assume that Bub Beer has a lead time of $m = 6$ days. With a daily demand of $d = 400$ cases, equation (11.6) shows that the reorder point would be $r = dm = 6 \times 400 = 2400$ cases. Thus, a new order for Bub Beer should be placed whenever the inventory position (the amount of inventory on hand plus the amount of inventory on order) reaches 2400. With an economic order quantity of $Q^* = 1824$ cases, the inventory position of 2400 cases occurs when one order of 1824 cases is outstanding and $2400 - 1824 = 576$ cases are on hand.

11.2 Economic Production Lot Size Model

The inventory model in this section alters assumption 2 of the EOQ model (see Table 11.3). The assumption concerning the arrival of Q units each time an order is received is changed to a constant production supply rate.

The inventory model presented in this section is similar to the EOQ model in that we are attempting to determine *how much* we should order and *when* the order should be placed. We will again assume a constant demand rate. However, instead of assuming that the goods arrive in a shipment of size Q^*, as in the EOQ model, we will assume that units are supplied to inventory at a constant rate over several days or several weeks. The *constant supply rate* assumption implies that the same number of units is supplied to inventory each period of time (e.g., 10 units every day or 50 units every week). This model is designed for production situations in which, once an order is placed, production begins and a constant number of units is added to inventory each day until the production run has been completed.

If we have a production system that produces 50 units per day and we decide to schedule 10 days of production, we have a $50(10) = 500$-unit production lot size. In general, if we let Q indicate the production lot size, the approach to the inventory decisions will be similar to the EOQ model; that is, we will attempt to build a holding and ordering cost model that expresses the total cost as a function of the production lot size. Then we will attempt to find the production lot size that minimizes the total cost.

One other condition that should be mentioned at this time is that the model will only apply to situations where the production rate is greater than the demand rate; the production system must be able to satisfy demand. For instance, if the constant demand rate is 2000 units per week, the production rate must be at least 2000 units per week to satisfy demand.

During the production run, demand will be reducing the inventory while production will be adding to inventory. Since we have assumed that the production rate exceeds the demand rate, each day during a production run we will be producing more units than are demanded. Thus, the excess production will cause a gradual inventory buildup during the production period. When the production run is completed, the continuing demand will cause the inventory to gradually decline until a new production run is started. The inventory pattern for this system is shown in Figure 11.4.

Figure 11.4
Inventory Pattern for the
Production Lot Size Inventory
Model

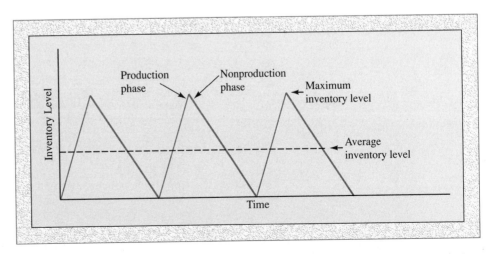

This model differs from the EOQ model in that a setup cost replaces the ordering cost and the saw-tooth inventory pattern shown in Figure 11.4 differs from the inventory pattern shown in Figure 11.2.

As in the EOQ model, we are now dealing with two costs, the holding cost and the ordering cost. While the holding cost is identical to the definition in the EOQ model, the interpretation of the ordering cost is slightly different. In fact, in a production situation the ordering cost is more correctly referred to as the production *setup cost*. This cost, which includes labor, material, and lost production costs incurred while preparing the production system for operation, is a fixed cost that occurs for every production run regardless of the production lot size.

The Total Cost Model

Let us begin building the production lot size model by writing the holding cost in terms of the production lot size Q. Again, the approach will be to develop an expression for average inventory and then establish the holding costs associated with the average inventory level. We will use a 1-year time period and an annual cost for the model.

We saw in the EOQ model that the average inventory is one-half the maximum inventory or $\frac{1}{2}Q$. Since Figure 11.4 shows a constant inventory buildup rate during the production run and a constant inventory depletion rate during the nonproduction period, the average inventory for the production lot size model will be one-half of the maximum inventory level. However, in this inventory system the production lot size Q does not go into inventory at one point in time, and thus the inventory level never reaches a level of Q units.

Let us show how we can compute the maximum inventory level. Let

$$d = \text{daily demand rate for the product}$$
$$p = \text{daily production rate for the product}$$
$$t = \text{number of days for a production run}$$

At this point, the logic of the production lot size model is easier to follow using a daily demand rate d and a daily production rate p. However, when the total annual cost model is eventually developed (see equation (11.15)), we recommend that inputs to the model be expressed in terms of the annual demand rate D and the annual production rate P.

Since we are assuming p will be larger than d, the daily inventory buildup rate during the production phase is $p - d$. If we run production for t days and place $p - d$ units in inventory each day, the inventory level at the end of the production run will be $(p - d)t$. From Figure 11.4 we can see that the inventory level at the end of the production run is also the maximum inventory level. Thus

$$\text{Maximum inventory level} = (p - d)t \tag{11.8}$$

If we know we are producing a production lot size of Q units at a daily production rate of p units, then $Q = pt$, and the length of the production run t must be

$$t = \frac{Q}{p} \text{ days} \tag{11.9}$$

Thus

$$\text{Maximum inventory level} = (p - d)t = (p - d)\left(\frac{Q}{p}\right) \tag{11.10}$$

$$= \left(1 - \frac{d}{p}\right)Q$$

The average inventory level, which is one-half of the maximum inventory level, is given by

$$\text{Average inventory level} = \frac{1}{2}\left(1 - \frac{d}{p}\right)Q \tag{11.11}$$

With an annual per unit holding cost of C_h, the general equation for annual holding cost is as follows:

$$\text{Annual holding cost} = \begin{pmatrix} \text{Average} \\ \text{inventory} \\ \text{level} \end{pmatrix} \begin{pmatrix} \text{Annual holding} \\ \text{cost} \\ \text{per unit} \end{pmatrix} \tag{11.12}$$

$$= \frac{1}{2}\left(1 - \frac{d}{p}\right)QC_h$$

If D is the annual demand for the product and C_o is the setup cost for a production run, then the annual setup cost, which takes the place of the annual ordering cost in the EOQ model, is as follows:

$$\text{Annual setup cost} = \begin{pmatrix} \text{Number of production} \\ \text{runs per year} \end{pmatrix} \begin{pmatrix} \text{Setup cost} \\ \text{per run} \end{pmatrix} \tag{11.13}$$

$$= \frac{D}{Q}C_o$$

Thus, the total annual cost (TC) model is

$$TC = \frac{1}{2}\left(1 - \frac{d}{p}\right)QC_h + \frac{D}{Q}C_o \tag{11.14}$$

Suppose that a production facility operates 250 days per year; 115 days are idle due to weekends and holidays. Then we can write daily demand d in terms of annual demand D as follows:

$$d = \frac{D}{250}$$

Now let P denote the annual production for the product if the product were produced every day. Then

$$P = 250p \quad \text{and} \quad p = \frac{P}{250}$$

Thus[5]

$$\frac{d}{p} = \frac{D/250}{P/250} = \frac{D}{P}$$

Therefore, we can write the total annual cost model as follows:

$$TC = \frac{1}{2}\left(1 - \frac{D}{P}\right)QC_h + \frac{D}{Q}C_o \tag{11.15}$$

Equations (11.14) and (11.15) are equivalent. However, equation (11.15) may be used more frequently since an *annual* cost model tends to make the analyst think in terms of collecting *annual* demand data (D) and *annual* production data (P) rather than daily data.

Finding the Economic Production Lot Size

Given estimates of the holding cost (C_h), setup cost, (C_o), annual demand rate (D), and annual production rate (P), we could use a trial-and-error approach to compute the total

---

[5]The ratio $d/p = D/P$ regardless of the number of days of operation; 250 days is used here merely as an illustration.

As the production rate P approaches infinity, D/P approaches zero. In this case, equation (11.16) is equivalent to the EOQ model in equation (11.5).

annual cost for various production lot sizes (Q). However, this is not necessary; we can use the minimum-cost formula for Q^* that has been developed using differential calculus (see Appendix 11.2). The equation is as follows:

$$Q^* = \sqrt{\frac{2DC_o}{(1 - D/P)C_h}} \tag{11.16}$$

An Example Beauty Bar Soap is produced on a production line that has an annual capacity of 60,000 cases. The annual demand is estimated at 26,000 cases, with the demand rate essentially constant throughout the year. The cleaning, preparation, and setup of the production line cost approximately $135.00. The manufacturing cost per case is $4.50, and the annual holding cost is figured at a 24% rate. Thus, $C_h = IC = 0.24(\$4.50) = \$1.08$. What is the recommended production lot size?

Using equation (11.16), we have

$$Q^* = \sqrt{\frac{2(26,000)(135)}{(1 - 26,000/60,000)(1.08)}} = 3387$$

The total annual cost using equation (11.15) and $Q^* = 3387$ is estimated to be $2073.

Other relevant data include a 1-week lead time to schedule and set up a production run. Thus, the lead-time demand of $26,000/52 = 500$ cases is the reorder point. The cycle time between production runs, using equation (11.7), is estimated to be $T = 250Q^*/D = [(250)(3387)]/26,000$, or about 33 working days. Thus, we should plan a production run of 3387 units about every 33 working days.

Certainly the manager will want to review the model recommendations. Adjusting the recommended $Q^* = 3387$ to a slightly different figure and/or adding safety stock may be desirable.

Work Problem 13 as an example of an economic production lot size model.

11.3 An Inventory Model with Planned Shortages

A shortage or stockout is a demand that cannot be supplied. In many situations, shortages are undesirable and should be avoided if at all possible. However, there are other cases in which it may be desirable—from an economic point of view—to plan for and allow shortages. In practice, these types of situations are most commonly found where the value per unit of the inventory is very high and hence the holding cost is high. An example of this type of situation is a new-car dealer's inventory. It is uncommon for a specific car you want to be in stock. However, if you are willing to wait a few weeks, the dealer is usually able to order it for you.

The assumptions of the EOQ model in Table 11.3 apply to this inventory model with the exception that shortages, referred to as backorders, are now permitted.

The model developed in this section takes into account a type of shortage known as a *backorder*. In a backorder situation, we assume that when a customer places an order and discovers that the supplier is out of stock, the customer waits until the new shipment arrives, and then the order is filled. Frequently, the waiting period in backordering situations is relatively short; thus, by promising the customer top priority and immediate delivery when the goods become available, companies may be able to convince the customer to wait until the order arrives. In these cases, the backorder assumption is valid.

The backorder model that we will develop is an extension of the EOQ model presented in Section 11.1. We will use the EOQ model assumptions in which the goods arrive in inventory all at one time and there is a constant demand rate (see Table 11.3). If we let S indicate the number of backorders that are accumulated when a new shipment of size Q is received, then the inventory system for the backorder case has the following characteristics:

- If S backorders exist when a new shipment of size Q arrives, the S backorders are shipped to the appropriate customers, and the remaining $Q - S$ units are placed in inventory. Therefore, $Q - S$ is the maximum inventory level.
- The inventory cycle of T days is divided into two distinct phases; t_1 days when inventory is on hand and orders are filled as they occur, and t_2 days when there are stockouts and all new orders are placed on backorder.

The inventory pattern for the inventory model with backorders, where negative inventory represents the number of backorders, is shown in Figure 11.5.

With the inventory pattern now defined, we can proceed with the basic step of all inventory models—namely, the development of a total-cost model. For the inventory model with backorders, we will encounter the usual holding costs and ordering costs. We will also incur a backorder cost in terms of the labor and special delivery costs directly associated with the handling of the backorders. Another portion of the backorder cost accounts for the loss of goodwill due to the fact that some customers will have to wait for their orders. Since the *goodwill cost* depends on how long the customer has to wait, it is customary to adopt the convention of expressing all backorder costs in terms of how much it costs to have a unit on backorder for a stated period of time. This method of costing backorders on a time basis is similar to the method used to compute the inventory holding cost, and we can use it to compute a total annual cost of backorders once the average backorder level and the backorder cost per unit per period are known.

Let us begin the development of a total-cost model by calculating the inventory holding costs for a small hypothetical problem. If we have an average inventory of two units for 3 days and no inventory on the fourth day, what is the average inventory level over the 4-day period? It is

$$\frac{2 \text{ units } (3 \text{ days}) + 0 \text{ units } (1 \text{ day})}{4 \text{ days}} = \frac{6}{4} = 1.5 \text{ units}$$

Figure 11.5
Inventory Pattern for an Inventory Model with Backorders

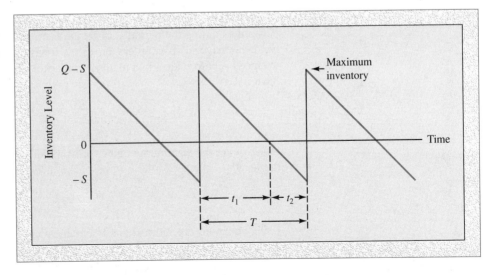

Refer to Figure 11.5. You can see that the above situation is what happens in the backorder model. With a maximum inventory of $Q - S$ units, the t_1 days we have inventory on hand will have an average inventory of $(Q - S)/2$. No inventory is carried for the t_2 days in which we experience backorders. Thus, over the total cycle time of $T = t_1 + t_2$ days, we can compute the average inventory level as follows:

$$\text{Average inventory level} = \frac{\frac{1}{2}(Q - S)t_1 + 0t_2}{t_1 + t_2} = \frac{\frac{1}{2}(Q - S)t_1}{T} \tag{11.17}$$

Can we find other ways of expressing t_1 and T? Since we know that the maximum inventory is $Q - S$ and that d represents the constant daily demand, we have

$$t_1 = \frac{Q - S}{d} \text{ days} \tag{11.18}$$

That is, the maximum inventory level of $Q - S$ units will be used up in $(Q - S)/d$ days. Since Q units are ordered each cycle, we know the length of a cycle must be

$$T = \frac{Q}{d} \text{ days} \tag{11.19}$$

Combining equations (11.18) and (11.19) with equation (11.17), we can write the following:

$$\text{Average inventory level} = \frac{\frac{1}{2}(Q - S)[(Q - S)/d]}{Q/d} = \frac{(Q - S)^2}{2Q} \tag{11.20}$$

Thus, the average inventory level is expressed in terms of two inventory decisions: how much we order (Q) and the maximum number of backorders we will allow (S).

The formula for the annual number of orders placed under this model is identical to that for the EOQ model. With D representing the annual demand, we have

$$\text{Annual number of orders} = \frac{D}{Q} \tag{11.21}$$

The next step is to develop an expression for the average backorder level. Since there is a maximum of S backorders, we can use the same logic we used to establish average inventory in finding the average number of backorders. We have an average number of backorders during the period t_2 of $\frac{1}{2}$ the maximum number of backorders or $\frac{1}{2} S$. Since we do not have any backorders during the t_1 days we have inventory, we can calculate the average backorder level in a manner similar to equation (11.17). Using this approach, we have

$$\text{Average backorder level} = \frac{0t_1 + (S/2)t_2}{T} = \frac{(S/2)t_2}{T} \tag{11.22}$$

Since we let the maximum number of backorders reach an amount S at a daily rate of d, the length of the backorder portion of the inventory cycle is

$$t_2 = \frac{S}{d} \tag{11.23}$$

Using equations (11.23) and (11.19) in equation (11.22), we have

$$\text{Average backorder level} = \frac{(S/2)(S/d)}{Q/d} = \frac{S^2}{2Q} \tag{11.24}$$

Let

$$C_h = \text{cost to maintain one unit in inventory for 1 year}$$
$$C_o = \text{cost per order}$$
$$C_b = \text{cost to maintain one unit on backorder for 1 year}$$

The backorder cost C_b is one of the most difficult costs to estimate in inventory models. The reason is that it attempts to measure the cost associated with the loss of goodwill when a customer must wait for an order. Expressing this cost on an annual basis adds to the difficulty.

The total annual cost model (TC) for the inventory model with backorders becomes

$$TC = \frac{(Q - S)^2}{2Q}C_h + \frac{D}{Q}C_o + \frac{S^2}{2Q}C_b \tag{11.25}$$

Given the cost estimates C_h, C_o, and C_b and the annual demand D, the minimum-cost values for the order quantity Q^* and the planned backorders S^* are as follows (see Appendix 11.3):

$$Q^* = \sqrt{\frac{2DC_o}{C_h}\left(\frac{C_h + C_b}{C_b}\right)} \tag{11.26}$$

$$S^* = Q^*\left(\frac{C_h}{C_h + C_b}\right) \tag{11.27}$$

An Example Suppose the Higley Radio Components Company has a product for which the assumptions of the inventory model with backorders are valid. Information obtained by the company is as follows:

$$D = 2000 \text{ units per year}$$

$$I = 0.20$$

$$C = \$50 \text{ per unit}$$

$$C_h = IC = (0.20)(\$50) = \$10 \text{ per unit per year}$$

$$C_o = \$25 \text{ per order}$$

The company is considering the possibility of allowing some backorders to occur for the product. The annual backorder cost has been estimated to be $30 per unit per year. Using equations (11.26) and (11.27), we have

$$Q^* = \sqrt{\frac{2(2000)(25)}{10}\left(\frac{10 + 30}{30}\right)} = 115$$

and

$$S^* = 115\left(\frac{10}{10 + 30}\right) = 29$$

An inventory situation that incorporates backorder costs is considered in Problem 15.

If this solution is implemented, the system will operate with the following properties:

$$\text{Maximum inventory} = Q - S = 115 - 29 = 86$$

$$\text{Cycle time} = T = \frac{Q}{D}(250) = \frac{115}{2000}(250) = 14.4 \text{ working days}$$

The total annual cost is

$$\text{Holding cost} = \frac{(86)^2}{2(115)}(10) = \$322$$

$$\text{Ordering cost} = \frac{2000}{115}(25) = \$435$$

$$\text{Backorder cost} = \frac{(29)^2}{2(115)}(30) = \underline{\$110}$$

$$\text{Total cost} = \$867$$

If backorders can be tolerated, the total cost including the backordering cost will be less than the total cost of the EOQ model. Students tend to think the model with backordering will have a greater cost because it includes a backordering cost in addition to the usual inventory holding and ordering costs. You can point out the fallacy in this thinking by noting that the backorder model leads to lower inventory levels and hence lower inventory holding costs.

If the company had chosen to prohibit backorders and had adopted the regular EOQ model, the recommended inventory decision would have been

$$Q^* = \sqrt{\frac{2(2000)(25)}{10}} = \sqrt{10{,}000} = 100$$

This order quantity would have resulted in a holding cost and an ordering cost of $500 each or a total annual cost of $1000. Thus, in this problem, allowing backorders is projecting a $1000 − $867 = $133 or 13.3% savings in cost from the no-stockout EOQ model. The above comparison and conclusion are based on the assumption that the backorder model with an annual cost per backordered unit of $30 is a valid model for the actual inventory situation. If the company is concerned that stockouts might lead to lost sales, then the above savings might not be enough to warrant switching to an inventory policy that allowed for planned shortages.

NOTES & COMMENTS

Equation (11.27) shows that the optimal number of planned backorders S^* is proportional to the ratio $C_h/(C_h + C_b)$, where C_h is the annual holding cost per unit and C_b is the annual backorder cost per unit. Whenever C_h increases, the above ratio becomes larger, and the number of planned backorders increases. This explains why items that have a high per-unit cost and a correspondingly high annual holding cost are more economically handled on a backorder basis. On the other hand, whenever the backorder cost C_b increases, the above ratio becomes smaller, and the number of planned backorders decreases. Thus, the model provides the intuitive result that items with high backordering costs will be handled with very few backorders. In fact, with high backorder costs, the backorder model and the EOQ model with no backordering allowed provide very similar inventory policies.

11.4 Quantity Discounts for the EOQ Model

Quantity discounts occur in numerous situations where suppliers provide an incentive for large order quantities by offering a lower purchase cost when items are ordered in larger lots or quantities. In this section we show how the EOQ model can be used when quantity discounts are available.

In the quantity discount model, assumption 4 of the EOQ model in Table 11.3 is altered. The cost per unit varies depending on the quantity ordered.

Assume that we have a product where the basic EOQ model (see Table 11.3) is applicable, but instead of a fixed unit cost, the supplier quotes the following discount schedule:

Discount Category	Order Size	Discount (%)	Unit Cost
1	0 to 999	0	$5.00
2	1000 to 2499	3	4.85
3	2500 and over	5	4.75

The 5% discount for the 2500-unit minimum order quantity looks tempting; however, realizing that higher order quantities result in higher inventory holding costs, we should prepare a thorough cost analysis before making a final ordering and inventory policy recommendation.

Suppose the data and cost analyses show an annual holding cost of 20%, an ordering cost of $49 per order, and an annual demand of 5000 units; what order quantity should we select? The following three-step procedure shows the calculations necessary to make this decision. In the preliminary calculations, we will use Q_1 to indicate the order quantity for discount category 1, Q_2 for discount category 2, and Q_3 for discount category 3.

Step 1 For each discount category, compute a Q^* using the EOQ formula based on the unit cost associated with the discount category.

Recall that the EOQ model provides $Q^* = \sqrt{2DC_o/C_h}$, where $C_h = IC = (0.20)C$. With three discount categories providing three different unit costs C, we obtain

$$Q_1^* = \sqrt{\frac{2(5000)49}{(0.20)(5.00)}} = 700$$

$$Q_2^* = \sqrt{\frac{2(5000)49}{(0.20)(4.85)}} = 711$$

$$Q_3^* = \sqrt{\frac{2(5000)49}{(0.20)(4.75)}} = 718$$

Since the only differences in the EOQ formulas are slight differences in the holding cost, the economic order quantities resulting from this step will be approximately the same. However, these order quantities will usually not all be of the size necessary to qualify for the discount price assumed. In the above case, both Q_2^* and Q_3^* are insufficient order quantities to obtain their assumed discounted costs of $4.85 and $4.75, respectively. For those order quantities for which the assumed price cannot be obtained, the following procedure must be used.

Step 2 For the Q^* that is too small to qualify for the assumed discount price, adjust the order quantity upward to the nearest order quantity that will allow the product to be purchased at the assumed price.

In our example, this causes us to set

$$Q_2^* = 1000$$

and

$$Q_3^* = 2500$$

Table 11.4

Total Annual Cost Calculations for the EOQ Model with Quantity Discounts

Discount Category	Unit Cost	Order Quantity	Annual Cost			
			Holding	Ordering	Purchase	Total
1	$5.00	700	$ 350	$350	$25,000	$25,700
2	4.85	1000	485	245	24,250	24,980
3	4.75	2500	1188	98	23,750	25,036

In the EOQ model with quantity discounts, the annual purchase cost must be included because purchase cost depends on the order quantity, and it is thus a relevant cost in the decision process.

If a calculated Q^* for a given discount price is large enough to qualify for a bigger discount, that value of Q^* cannot lead to an optimal solution. While the reason may not be obvious, it does turn out to be a property of the EOQ quantity discount model. (Problem 23 at the end of the chapter will ask you to show that this property is true.)

In the previous inventory models considered, the annual purchase cost of the item was not included because it was constant and never affected by the inventory-order policy decision. However, in the quantity discount model, the annual purchase cost depends on the order-quantity decision and the associated unit cost. Thus, annual purchase cost (annual demand D × unit cost C) is included in the total cost model as shown below.

$$TC = \frac{Q}{2}C_h + \frac{D}{Q}C_o + DC \qquad (11.28)$$

Using this total-cost formula, we can determine the optimal order quantity for the EOQ discount model in step 3 below.

Step 3   For each of the order quantities resulting from steps 1 and 2, compute the total annual cost using the unit price from the appropriate discount category and equation (11.28). The order quantity yielding the minimum total annual cost is the optimal order quantity.

Working Problem 21 will give you practice in applying the EOQ model to situations with quantity discounts.

The step 3 calculations for the example problem are summarized in Table 11.4. As you can see, a decision to order 1000 units at the 3% discount rate yields the minimum-cost solution. While the 2500-unit order quantity would result in a 5% discount, its excessive holding cost makes it the second best solution. Figure 11.6 shows the total-cost curves for the three discount categories. Note that $Q^* = 1000$ provides the minimum-cost order quantity.

11.5   A Single-Period Inventory Model with Probabilistic Demand

This is the first inventory model in the chapter that explicitly treats probabilistic demand. Unlike the EOQ model, it is for a single period with unused inventory not carried over to future periods.

The inventory models that we have discussed thus far have been based on the assumption that the demand rate is constant and *deterministic* throughout the year. We developed minimum-cost order quantity and reorder-point policies based on this assumption. In situations where the demand rate is not deterministic, models have been developed that treat demand as *probabilistic* and best described by a probability distribution. In this section we consider a *single-period* inventory model with probabilistic demand.

The single-period inventory model refers to inventory situations in which *one* order is placed for the product; at the end of the period, the product has either sold out, or there

Figure 11.6
Total-Cost Curves for the Three
Discount Categories

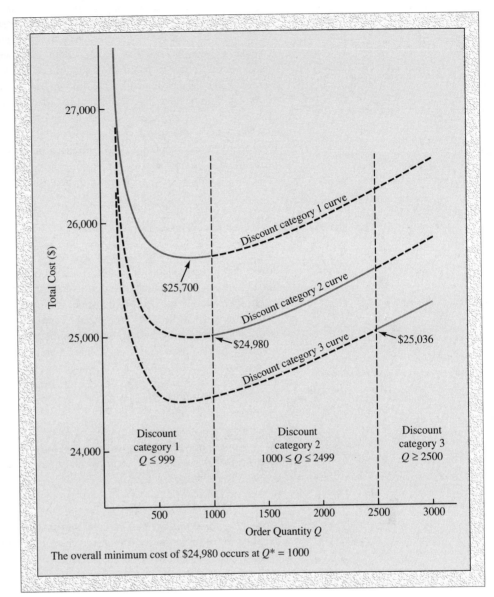

The overall minimum cost of $24,980 occurs at $Q^* = 1000$

is a surplus of unsold items that will be sold for a salvage value. The single-period inventory model is applicable in situations involving seasonal or perishable items that cannot be carried in inventory and sold in future periods. Seasonal clothing (such as bathing suits and winter coats) are typically handled in a single-period manner. In these situations, a buyer places one preseason order for each item and then experiences a stockout or holds a clearance sale on the surplus stock at the end of the season. No items are carried in inventory and sold the following year. Newspapers are another example of a product that is ordered one time and is either sold or not sold during the single period. While newspapers are ordered daily, they cannot be carried in inventory and sold in later periods. Thus, newspaper orders may be treated as a sequence of single-period models; that is, each day or period is separate, and a single-period inventory decision must be made each period (day). Since we order only once for the period, the only inventory decision we must make is *how much* of the product to order at the start of the period. Because newspaper sales is an excellent example of a single-period situation, the single-period inventory problem is sometimes referred to as the *newsboy problem.*

Obviously, if the demand were known for a single-period inventory situation, the solution would be easy; we would simply order the amount we knew would be demanded. However, in most single-period models, the exact demand is not known. In fact, forecasts may show that demand can have a wide variety of values. If we are going to analyze this type of inventory problem in a quantitative manner, we will need information about the probabilities associated with the various demand values. Thus, the single-period model presented in this section is based on probabilistic demand.

The Johnson Shoe Company Problem

Let us consider a single-period inventory model that could be used to make a how-much-to-order decision for the Johnson Shoe Company. The buyer for the Johnson Shoe Company has decided to order a shoe for men that has just been shown at a buyers' meeting in New York City. The shoe will be part of the company's spring-summer promotion and will be sold through nine retail stores in the Chicago area. Since the shoe is designed for spring and summer months, it cannot be expected to sell in the fall. Johnson plans to hold a special August clearance sale in an attempt to sell all shoes that have not been sold by July 31. The shoes cost $40 per pair and retail for $60 per pair. At the sale price of $30 per pair, it is expected that all surplus shoes can be sold during the August sale. If you were the buyer for the Johnson Shoe Company, how many pairs of the shoes would you order?

An obvious question at this time is, What are the possible values of demand for the shoe? We will need this information to answer the question of how much to order. Let us suppose that the uniform probability distribution shown in Figure 11.7 can be used to describe the demand for the size 10D shoes. In particular, note that the range of demand is from 350 to 650 pairs of shoes, with an average, or expected, demand of 500 pairs of shoes.

Incremental analysis is a method that can be used to determine the optimal order quantity for a single-period inventory model. Incremental analysis addresses the how-much-to-order question by comparing the cost or loss of *ordering one additional unit*

Figure 11.7

Uniform Probability Distribution of Demand for the Johnson Shoe Company Problem

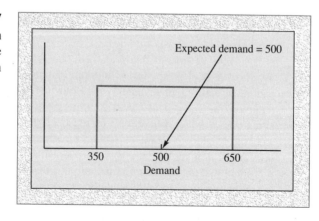

Expected demand = 500

350   500   650
Demand

with the cost or loss of *not ordering one additional unit.* The costs involved are defined as follows:

$$c_o = \text{cost per unit of } overestimating \text{ demand}$$

This cost represents the loss of ordering one additional unit and finding that it cannot be sold.

$$c_u = \text{cost per unit of } underestimating \text{ demand}$$

This cost represents the opportunity loss of not ordering one additional unit and finding that it could have been sold.

The cost of underestimating demand is usually harder to determine than the cost of overestimating demand. The reason is that the cost of underestimating demand includes a lost profit and may include a customer goodwill cost because the customer is unable to purchase the item when desired.

In the Johnson Shoe Company problem, the company will incur the cost of overestimating demand whenever it orders too much and has to sell the extra shoes during the August sale. Thus, the cost per unit of overestimating demand is equal to the purchase cost per unit minus the August sales price per unit; that is, $c_o = \$40 - \$30 = \$10$. Therefore, Johnson will lose \$10 for each pair of shoes that it orders over the quantity demanded. The cost of underestimating demand is the lost profit due to the fact that a pair of shoes that could have been sold was not available in inventory. Thus, the per-unit cost of underestimating demand is the difference between the regular selling price per unit and the purchase cost per unit; that is, $c_u = \$60 - \$40 = \$20$.

Since the exact level of demand for the size 10D shoes is unknown, we will have to consider the probability of demand and thus the probability of obtaining the above costs or losses. For example, let us assume that the Johnson Shoe Company wishes to consider an order quantity equal to the average or expected demand for 500 pairs of shoes. In incremental analysis, we will consider the possible losses associated with an order quantity of 501 (ordering one additional unit) and an order quantity of 500 (not ordering one additional unit). The order-quantity alternatives and the possible losses are summarized below.

Order-Quantity Alternatives	Loss Occurs If	Possible Loss	Probability Loss Occurs
$Q = 501$	Demand overestimated; the additional unit *cannot* be sold.	$c_o = \$10$	$P(\text{demand} \leq 500)$
$Q = 500$	Demand underestimated; an additional unit *could have* been sold.	$c_u = \$20$	$P(\text{demand} > 500)$

By looking at the demand probability distribution in Figure 11.7, we see that $P(\text{demand} \leq 500) = 0.50$ and that $P(\text{demand} > 500) = 0.50$. By multiplying the possible losses, $c_o = \$10$ and $c_u = \$20$, by the probability of obtaining the loss, we can compute the expected value of the loss, or simply the *expected loss* (EL), associated with the order-quantity alternatives. Thus

$$\text{EL}(Q = 501) = c_o P(\text{demand} \leq 500) = \$10(0.50) = \$\ 5$$

$$\text{EL}(Q = 500) = c_u P(\text{demand} > 500) = \$20(0.50) = \$10$$

Based on the above expected losses, do you prefer an order quantity of 501 or 500 pairs of shoes? Since the expected loss is greater for $Q = 500$, and since we want to avoid this higher cost or loss, we should make $Q = 501$ the preferred decision. We could now consider incrementing the order quantity one additional unit to $Q = 502$ and repeating the above expected loss calculations.

While we could continue this unit-by-unit analysis, it would be very time-consuming and cumbersome. We would have to evaluate $Q = 502$, $Q = 503$, $Q = 504$, and so on, until we found the value of Q where the expected loss of ordering one incremental unit is equal to the expected loss of not ordering one incremental unit; that is, the optimal order quantity $Q*$ occurs when the incremental analysis shows that

$$EL(Q* + 1) = EL(Q*) \tag{11.29}$$

When the above relationship holds, there is no economic advantage to increasing the order quantity by one additional unit. Using the logic with which we computed the expected losses for the order quantities of 501 and 500, the general expressions for $EL(Q* + 1)$ and $EL(Q*)$ can be written

$$EL(Q* + 1) = c_o P(\text{demand} \leq Q*) \tag{11.30}$$

$$EL(Q*) = c_u P(\text{demand} > Q*) \tag{11.31}$$

Since we know from basic probability that

$$P(\text{demand} \leq Q*) + P(\text{demand} > Q*) = 1 \tag{11.32}$$

we can write

$$P(\text{demand} > Q*) = 1 - P(\text{demand} \leq Q*) \tag{11.33}$$

Using this expression, equation (11.31) can be rewritten as

$$EL(Q*) = c_u[1 - P(\text{demand} \leq Q*)] \tag{11.34}$$

Equations (11.30) and (11.34) can be used to show that $EL(Q* + 1) = EL(Q*)$ whenever

$$c_o P(\text{demand} \leq Q*) = c_u[1 - P(\text{demand} \leq Q*)] \tag{11.35}$$

Solving for $P(\text{demand} \leq Q*)$, we have

$$P(\text{demand} \leq Q*) = \frac{c_u}{c_u + c_o} \tag{11.36}$$

The above expression provides the general condition for the optimal order quantity $Q*$ in the single-period inventory model.

In the Johnson Shoe Company problem, $c_o = \$10$ and $c_u = \$20$. Thus, equation (11.36) shows that the optimal order size for Johnson shoes must satisfy the following condition:

$$P(\text{demand} \leq Q*) = \frac{c_u}{c_u + c_o} = \frac{20}{20 + 10} = \frac{20}{30} = \frac{2}{3}$$

We can find the optimal order quantity $Q*$ by referring to the assumed probability distribution shown in Figure 11.7 and finding the value of Q that will provide $P(\text{demand} \leq Q*) = 2/3$. To do this, we note that in the uniform distribution the probability is evenly distributed over the entire range of 350–650 pairs of shoes. Thus, we can satisfy the expression for $Q*$ by moving two-thirds of the way from 350 to 650. Since this is a range of $650 - 350 = 300$, we move 200 units from 350 toward 650. Doing so provides the optimal order quantity of 550 pairs of size 10D shoes.

In summary, the key to establishing an optimal order quantity for single-period inventory models is to identify the probability distribution that describes the demand for the item and the costs of overestimation and underestimation. Then, using the information for the costs of overestimation and underestimation, equation (11.36) can be used to find the location of Q^* in the probability distribution.

The Kremer Chemical Company Problem

As another example of a single-period inventory model with probabilistic demand, consider the situation faced by the Kremer Chemical Company. Kremer has a contract with one of its customers to supply a unique liquid chemical product. Historically, the customer places orders approximately every 6 months. Since a 2-month aging condition exists for the product, Kremer will have to make its production quantity decision before the customer places an order. Kremer's inventory problem is to determine the number of pounds of the chemical to produce in anticipation of the customer's order.

Kremer's manufacturing costs for the chemical are $15 per pound, and the product sells at the fixed contract price of $20 per pound. If Kremer underproduces, it will be unable to satisfy the customer's demand. When this condition occurs, Kremer has agreed to absorb the added cost of filling the order by purchasing a higher-quality substitute product from another chemical firm. The substitute product, including additional transportation expenses, will cost Kremer $19 per pound. If Kremer overproduces, it will have more product in inventory than the customer requires. Because of the spoilage potential for the product, Kremer cannot store excess production until the customer's next order. As a result, Kremer reprocesses the excess production and sells the surplus for $5 per pound.

Based on previous experience with the customer's orders, Kremer believes that the normal probability distribution shown in Figure 11.8 best describes the possible demand. Note that the normal distribution shows an average or expected demand of $\mu = 1000$ pounds with a standard deviation of $\sigma = 100$ pounds. Using Kremer's price and cost data as well as the probability distribution of demand shown in Figure 11.8, how much production should Kremer plan for in anticipation of the customer's order for the liquid chemical?

Let us begin by computing the cost of underestimation, c_u, and the cost of overestimation, c_o, as required for equation (11.36). First, if Kremer underproduces, it will have to purchase a substitute product at a higher cost per unit to satisfy the customer's demand for the product. Since the substitute product costs $19 per pound and Kremer could have manufactured the product for $15 per pound, a cost of $c_u = \$19 -$

Figure 11.8

Normal Probability Distribution of Demand for the Kremer Chemical Company Problem

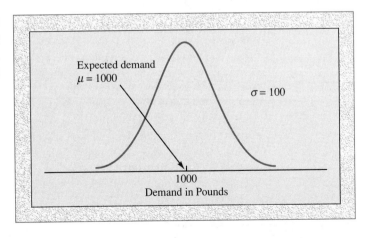

$15 = $4 exists for every pound of underestimated demand. If Kremer overestimates demand, the company incurs a cost of $15 per pound to manufacture the product and then sells the reprocessed excess product for $5 per pound. Thus, Kremer has a per-unit cost of $c_o = \$15 - \$5 = \$10$ for overestimating demand.

Applying equation (11.36) indicates that the optimal order quantity must satisfy the following condition:

$$P(\text{demand} \leq Q^*) = \frac{c_u}{c_u + c_o} = \frac{4}{4 + 10} = 0.29$$

We can use the normal probability distribution for demand as shown in Figure 11.9 to find the order quantity that satisfies the condition that $P(\text{demand} \leq Q^*) = 0.29$. From Appendix C we see that 0.29 of the area in the left tail of the curve of the normal probability distribution occurs at $z = 0.55$ standard deviations *below* the mean. Since the mean or expected demand is given by $\mu = 1000$ and the standard deviation is $\sigma = 100$, we have

$$Q^* = \mu - 0.55\sigma$$

$$= 1000 - 0.55(100) = 945$$

An example of a single-period inventory model with probabilistic demand described by a normal probability distribution is considered in Problem 25.

Thus, with the assumed normal probability distribution of demand, the Kremer Chemical Company should produce 945 pounds of the chemical in anticipation of the customer's order. Note that in this case the cost of underestimation is less than the cost of overestimation. Thus, Kremer is willing to risk a higher probability of underestimation and hence a higher probability of a stockout. In fact, Kremer's optimal order quantity has a 0.29 probability of having a surplus and a $1 - 0.29 = 0.71$ probability of a stockout.

NOTES & COMMENTS

1. In any probabilistic inventory model, the assumption about the probability distribution for demand is critical and can affect the recommended inventory decision. In the problems presented in this section, we used the uniform and the normal probability distributions to describe demand. In some situations, other probability distributions may be more appropriate. In using probabilistic inventorymodels, we must exercise care in selecting the probability distribution that most realistically describes demand.

2. In the single-period inventory model, the value of $c_u/(c_u + c_o)$ plays a critical role in selecting the order quantity (see equation (11.36)). Whenever $c_u = c_o$, $c_u/(c_u + c_o)$ equals 0.50; in this case, we should select an order quantity corresponding to the median demand. With this choice, it is just as likely to have a stockout as it is to have a surplus; this makes sense because the two costs are equal. However, whenever $c_u < c_o$, a smaller order quantity will be recommended. In this case, there will be a higher probability of a stockout; however, the more expensive cost of overestimating demand and having a surplus will tend to be avoided. Finally, whenever $c_u > c_o$, a larger order quantity will be recommended. In this case, the larger order quantity provides a lower probability of a stockout in an attempt to avoid the more expensive cost of underestimating demand and experiencing a stockout.

Figure 11.9
Probability Distribution of
Demand for the Kremer Chemical
Company Problem Showing the
Location of the Optimal Order
Quantity Q^*

11.6 An Order-Quantity, Reorder-Point Model with Probabilistic Demand

The inventory model in this section
is based on the assumptions of the
EOQ model shown in Table 11.3
with the exception that demand is
probabilistic rather than
deterministic. With probabilistic
demand, occasional shortages
cannot be prevented.

In the previous section we considered a single-period inventory model with probabilistic demand. In this section we extend our discussion to a multiperiod order-quantity, reorder-point inventory model with probabilistic demand. In the multiperiod model, the inventory system operates continuously with many repeating periods or cycles; inventory can be carried from one period to the next. Whenever the inventory position reaches the reorder point, an order for Q units is placed. Since demand is probabilistic, the time the reorder point will be reached, the time between orders, and the time the order of Q units will arrive in inventory cannot be determined in advance.

The inventory pattern for the order-quantity, reorder-point model with probabilistic demand will have the general appearance shown in Figure 11.10. Note that the increases or jumps in the inventory level occur whenever an order of Q units arrives. The inventory level decreases at a nonconstant rate based on the probabilistic demand. A new order is

Figure 11.10
Inventory Pattern for an
Order-Quantity, Reorder-Point
Model with Probabilistic Demand

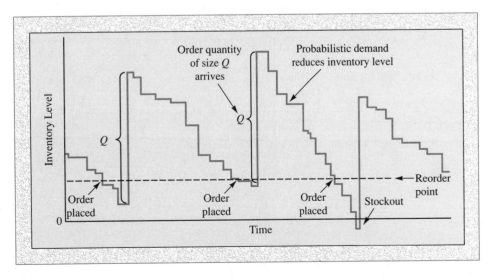

placed whenever the reorder point is reached. At times, the order quantity of Q units will arrive before inventory reaches zero. However, at other times, higher demand will cause a stockout before a new order is received. As with other order-quantity, reorder-point models, the manager must determine the order quantity Q and the reorder point r for the inventory system.

The exact mathematical formulation of an order-quantity, reorder-point inventory model with probabilistic demand is beyond the scope of this text. However, we will present a procedure that can be used to obtain good, workable order-quantity and reorder-point inventory policies. While the solution procedure can be expected to provide only an approximation of the optimal solution, it has been found to yield very good solutions in many practical situations.

Let us consider the inventory problem of Dabco Industrial Lighting Distributors. Dabco purchases a special high-intensity light bulb for industrial lighting systems from a well-known light bulb manufacturer. Dabco would like a recommendation on how much to order and when to order so that a low-cost inventory policy can be maintained. Pertinent facts are that the ordering cost is $12 per order, one bulb costs $6, and Dabco uses a 20% annual holding cost for its inventory ($C_h = IC = 0.20 \times \$6 = \$1.20$). Dabco, which has over 1000 different customers, experiences a probabilistic demand; in fact, the number of units demanded varies considerably from day to day and from week to week. The lead time for a new order of light bulbs is 1 week. Historical sales data indicate that demand during a 1-week lead time can be described by a normal probability distribution with a mean of 154 light bulbs and a standard deviation of 25 light bulbs. The normal distribution of demand during the lead time is shown in Figure 11.11. Since the mean demand during 1-week is 154 units, Dabco can anticipate a mean or expected annual demand of 154 units/week $\times$ 52 weeks/year = 8008 units/year.

The How-Much-to-Order Decision

Although we are in a probabilistic demand situation, we have an estimate of the expected annual demand of 8008 units. We can apply the EOQ model from Section 11.1 as an approximation of the best order quantity, with the expected annual demand used for D. In Dabco's case

$$Q^* = \sqrt{\frac{2DC_o}{C_h}} = \sqrt{\frac{2(8008)(12)}{(1.20)}} = 400 \text{ units}$$

Figure 11.11
Lead-Time Demand Probability Distribution for Dabco Light Bulbs

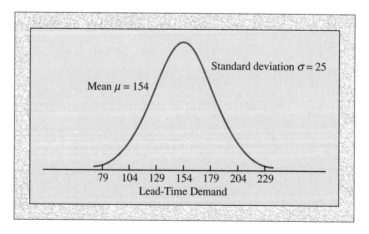

When we studied the sensitivity of the EOQ model, we learned that the total cost of operating an inventory system was relatively insensitive to order quantities that were in the neighborhood of Q^*. Using this knowledge, we expect 400 units per order to be a good approximation of the optimal order quantity. Even if annual demand were as low as 7000 units or as high as 9000 units, an order quantity of 400 units should be a relatively good low-cost order size. Thus, given our best estimate of annual demand at 8008 units, we will use $Q^* = 400$.

We have established the 400-unit order quantity by ignoring the fact that demand is probabilistic. Using $Q^* = 400$, Dabco can anticipate placing approximately $D/Q^* = 8008/400 = 20$ orders per year with an average of approximately $250/20 = 12.5$ working days between orders.

The When-to-Order Decision

We now want to establish a when-to-order decision rule or reorder point that will trigger the ordering process. With a mean lead-time demand of 154 units, you might first suggest a 154-unit reorder point. However, it now becomes extremely important to consider the probability of demand. If 154 is the mean lead-time demand, and if demand is symmetrically distributed about 154, then the lead-time demand will be more than 154 units roughly 50% of the time. When the demand during the 1-week lead time exceeds 154 units, Dabco will experience a shortage or stockout. Thus, using a reorder point of 154 units, approximately 50% of the time (10 of the 20 orders a year) Dabco will be short of bulbs before the new supply arrives. This shortage rate would most likely be viewed as unacceptable.

Refer to the *lead-time demand distribution* shown in Figure 11.11. Given this distribution, we can now determine how the reorder point r affects the probability of a stockout. Since stockouts occur whenever the demand during the lead time exceeds the reorder point, we can find the probability of a stockout by using the lead-time demand distribution to compute the probability that demand will exceed r.

We could now approach the when-to-order problem by defining a cost per stockout and then attempting to include this cost in a total-cost equation. Alternatively, we can ask management to specify the average number of stockouts that can be tolerated per year; this number is referred to as the service level. If demand for a product is probabilistic, a manager who will never tolerate a stockout is being somewhat unrealistic because attempting to avoid stockouts completely will require high reorder points, high inventory levels, and an associated high holding cost.

The probability of a stockout during any one inventory cycle is easiest to estimate by first determining the number of orders that are expected during the year. The inventory manager can usually state a willingness to allow perhaps one, two, or three stockouts during the year. The allowable stockouts per year divided by the number of orders per year will provide the desired probability of a stockout.

Suppose in this case that Dabco management is willing to tolerate an average of one stockout per year. Since Dabco places 20 orders per year, this implies management is willing to allow demand during lead time to exceed the reorder point one time in 20, or 5% of the time. This suggests that the reorder point r can be found by using the lead-time demand distribution to find the value of r for which there is only a 5% chance of having a lead-time demand that will exceed it. This situation is shown graphically in Figure 11.12.

From the standard normal probability distribution table in Appendix A, we see that the r value is 1.645 standard deviations above the mean. Therefore, for the assumed normal distribution for lead-time demand with $\mu = 154$ and $\sigma = 25$, the reorder point r is

$$r = 154 + 1.645(25) = 195$$

Figure 11.12
Reorder Point *r* That Allows a 5%
Chance of a Stockout for Dabco
Light Bulbs

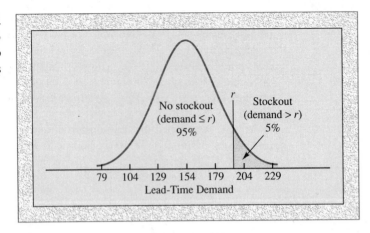

If a normal distribution is used for lead-time demand, the general equation for *r* is

$$r = \mu + z\sigma \qquad (11.37)$$

where *z* is the number of standard deviations necessary to obtain the acceptable stockout probability.

Thus, the recommended inventory decision is to order 400 units whenever the inventory level reaches the reorder point of 195. Since the mean or expected demand during the lead time is 154 units, the 195 − 154 = 41 units serve as a safety stock, which absorbs higher-than-usual demand during the lead time. Roughly 95% of the time, the 195 units will be able to satisfy demand during the lead time. The anticipated annual cost for this system is as follows:

Ordering cost	$(D/Q)C_o = (8000/400)12$	$= \$240.00$
Holding cost, normal inventory	$(Q/2)C_h = (400/2)(1.20)$	$= \$240.00$
Holding cost, safety stock	$(41)C_h = 41(1.20)$	$= \$\ 49.20$
	Total	$\overline{\$529.20}$

Try Problem 29 as an example of an order-quantity, reorder-point model with probabilistic demand.

If Dabco could have assumed that a known, constant demand rate of 8008 units per year existed for the light bulbs, then $Q^* = 400$, $r = 154$, and a total annual cost of $240 + $240 = $480 would have been optimal. When demand is uncertain and can only be expressed in probabilistic terms, a larger total cost can be expected. The larger cost occurs in the form of larger holding costs due to the fact that more inventory must be maintained to limit the number of stockouts. For Dabco, this additional inventory or safety stock was 41 units, with an additional annual holding cost of $49.20.

11.7   A Periodic-Review Model with Probabilistic Demand

The order-quantity, reorder-point inventory models previously discussed require a *continuous-review* inventory system. In a continuous-review inventory system, the inventory position is monitored continuously so that an order can be placed whenever the reorder point is reached. Computerized inventory systems can easily provide the continuous review required by the order-quantity, reorder-point models.

Up to this point, we have assumed that the inventory position is reviewed continuously so that an order can be placed as soon as the inventory position reaches the reorder point. The inventory model in this section assumes probabilistic demand and a periodic review of the inventory position.

The biggest advantage of a periodic-review model is that many items and products can be placed on the same periodic review. Thus, orders for multiple items can be coordinated such that ordering, shipping, and receiving of the items occur simultaneously.

An alternative to the continuous-review system is the *periodic-review* system. With a periodic-review system, the inventory level is checked and reordering is done only at specified points in time. For example, inventory levels may be checked and orders placed on a weekly, biweekly, monthly, or some other periodic basis. When a firm or business handles multiple products, the periodic-review system has the advantage of requiring that the orders for several items be placed at the same preset periodic-review time. With this type of inventory system, the shipping and receiving of orders for multiple products are easily coordinated. Under the previously discussed order-quantity, reorder-point systems, the reorder points for various products can be encountered at substantially different points in time, making the coordination of orders for multiple products more difficult.

To illustrate this system, let us consider Dollar Discounts, a firm with several retail stores that carry a wide variety of products for household use. The company operates its inventory system with a two-week periodic review. Under this system, a retail store manager may order any number of units of any product from the Dollar Discounts central warehouse every 2 weeks. The orders for all products going to a particular store are combined into one shipment. When making the order-quantity decision for each product at a given review period, the store manager knows that a reorder for the product cannot be made until the next review period.

Assuming that the lead time is less than the length of the review period, an order placed at a review period will be received prior to the next review period. In this case, the how-much-to-order decision at any review period is determined using the following:

$$Q = M - H \qquad (11.38)$$

where

$$Q = \text{the order quantity}$$
$$M = \text{the replenishment level}$$
$$H = \text{the inventory on hand at the review period}$$

Since the demand is probabilistic, the inventory on hand at the review period, *H*, will vary. Thus, the order quantity that must be sufficient to bring the inventory position back to its maximum or replenishment level *M* can be expected to vary each period. For example, if the replenishment level for a particular product is 50 units, and the inventory on hand at the review period is $H = 12$ units, an order of $Q = M - H = 50 - 12 = 38$ units should be made. Thus, under the periodic-review model, enough units are ordered each review period to bring the inventory position back up to the replenishment level.

A typical inventory pattern for a periodic-review system with probabilistic demand is shown in Figure 11.13. Note that the time between periodic reviews is predetermined and fixed. The order quantity *Q* at each review period can vary and is shown to be the difference between the replenishment level and the inventory on hand. Finally, as with other probabilistic models, an unusually high demand can result in an occasional stockout.

The decision variable in the periodic-review model is the replenishment level *M*. To determine *M,* we could begin by developing a total-cost model, including holding, ordering, and stockout costs. Instead, we will describe an approach that is often used in practice. In this approach, the objective is to determine a replenishment level that will meet a desired performance level, such as a reasonably low probability of stockout or a reasonably low number of stockouts per year.

In the Dollar Discounts problem, we will assume that management's objective is to determine the replenishment level for which there is only a 1% chance of a stockout. In the periodic-review model, the order quantity at each review period must be sufficient to cover demand for the *review period plus the demand for the following lead time.* That is,

Figure 11.13
Inventory Pattern for
Periodic-Review Model with
Probabilistic Demand

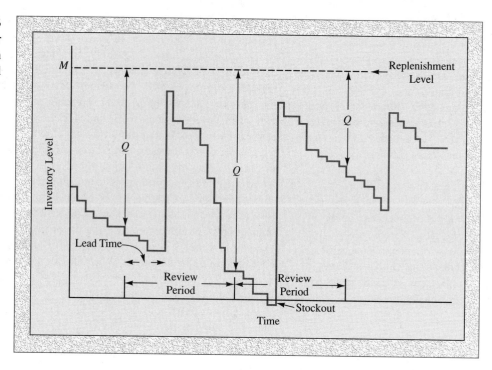

the order quantity that brings the inventory position up to the replenishment level M must last until the order made at the next review period is received in inventory. The length of this time is equal to the review period plus the lead time. Figure 11.14 shows the normal probability distribution of demand during the review period plus the lead-time period for one of the Dollar Discounts products. The mean demand is 250 units, and the standard deviation of demand is 45 units. Given this situation, the logic used to establish M is similar to the logic used to establish the reorder point in Section 11.7. Figure 11.15 shows the replenishment level M, for which there is a 1% chance that demand will exceed that replenishment level. In other words, Figure 11.15 shows the replenishment level that allows a 1% chance of a stockout associated with the replenishment decision. Using the normal probability distribution table in Appendix A, we see that a value of M that is 2.33 standard deviations above the mean will allow stockouts with a 1% probability.

Figure 11.14
Probability Distribution of
Demand During the Review
Period and Lead Time for the
Dollar Discounts Problem

Figure 11.15
Replenishment Level *M* That
Allows a 1% Chance of a
Stockout for the Dollar Discounts
Problem

Therefore, for the assumed normal probability distribution with $\mu = 250$ and $\sigma = 45$, the replenishment level is determined by

$$M = 250 + 2.33(45) = 355$$

Problem 33 will give you practice in computing the replenishment level for a periodic-review model with probabilistic demand.

While other probability distributions can be used to express the demand during the review period plus the lead-time period, if the normal probability distribution is used, the general expression for *M* is

$$M = \mu + z\sigma \qquad (11.39)$$

where z is the number of standard deviations necessary to obtain the acceptable stockout probability.

Periodic-review systems provide advantages of coordinated orders for multiple items. However, periodic-review systems require larger safety stock levels than corresponding continuous-review systems.

If demand had been deterministic rather than probabilistic, the replenishment level would have been the demand during the review period plus the demand during the lead-time period. In this case, the replenishment level would have been 250 units, and no stockout would have occurred. However, with the probabilistic demand, we have seen that higher inventory levels are necessary to allow for uncertain demand and to control the probability of a stockout. In the Dollar Discounts problem, $355 - 250 = 105$ is the safety stock that is necessary to absorb any higher-than-usual demand during the review period plus the demand during the lead-time period. It is this safety stock that limits the probability of a stockout to 1%.

More Complex Periodic-Review Models

The periodic-review model that we have just discussed is one approach to determining a replenishment level for the periodic-review inventory system with probabilistic demand. More complex versions of the periodic-review model incorporate a reorder point as another decision variable. That is, instead of ordering at every periodic review, a reorder point is established. If the inventory on hand at the periodic review is at or below the reorder point, a decision is made to order up to the replenishment level. However, if the inventory on hand at the periodic review is greater than the reorder level, such an order is not placed, and the system continues until the next periodic review. In this case, the cost of ordering is a relevant cost and can be included in a cost model along with holding and stockout costs. Optimal policies can be reached based on minimizing the expected total cost. Situations with lead times longer than the review period add to the complexity of the model. The mathematical level required to treat these more extensive periodic-review models is beyond the scope of this text.

NOTES & COMMENTS

1. The periodic-review model presented in this section is based on the assumption that the lead time for an order is less than the periodic-review period. Most periodic-review systems operate under this condition. However, the case in which the lead time is longer than the review period can be handled by defining H in equation (11.38) as the inventory position, where H includes the inventory on hand plus the inventory on order. In this case, the order quantity at any review period is the amount needed for the inventory on hand plus *all* outstanding orders needed to reach the replenishment level.

2. In the order-quantity, reorder-point model discussed in Section 11.6, a continuous review was used to initiate an order whenever the reorder point was reached. The safety stock for this model was based on the probabilistic demand during the lead time. The periodic-review model presented in this section also determined a recommended safety stock. However, since the inventory review was only periodic, the safety stock was based on the probabilistic demand during the *review period plus the lead-time period.* This longer period for the safety stock computation means that periodic-review systems tend to require larger safety stocks than do continuous-review systems.

11.8 Material Requirements Planning

Independent demand is the demand generated by customers external to the firm. Dependent demand is the demand for an item generated by another product in which the item is a component (part).

The inventory models we have discussed thus far have been found to be most appropriate for managing the inventories of finished goods. Finished goods are characterized as having *independent demands* that may be forecast. In this section we focus on the planning and controlling of manufacturing inventories such as raw materials, components, and subassemblies. The demand for these types of items is *dependent* on the amounts of finished goods that are scheduled to be produced and can be *calculated* from the forecasts and scheduled production of finished goods. A technique that can be used to manage dependent-demand inventories is called *material requirements planning* (MRP).

Dependent Demand and the MRP Concept

The first book on material requirements planning, written by Joseph Orlicky, was published in 1975. In 1973, while preparing a study guide on material requirements planning for the American Production and Inventory Control Society (APICS), Orlicky found that the entire MRP literature consisted of only 26 items.

Let us consider a finished product with one component part to illustrate dependent demand and the MRP concept. The demand for the finished product consists of many independent demands from many customers. Since these demands occur somewhat randomly, the demand rate is often fairly constant, and the assumptions of the production lot size model are reasonable. The inventory level for the finished product is shown at the top of Figure 11.16. Assume that the single component is purchased from an outside supplier. When production of the finished product is initiated (point A on the time axis), the component parts are withdrawn from inventory in order to meet the manufacturing needs. The inventory level of the component part is shown at the bottom of Figure 11.16. When the component inventory level falls below its reorder point, an order for the component is placed with the supplier. The shipment is received at point B, and the

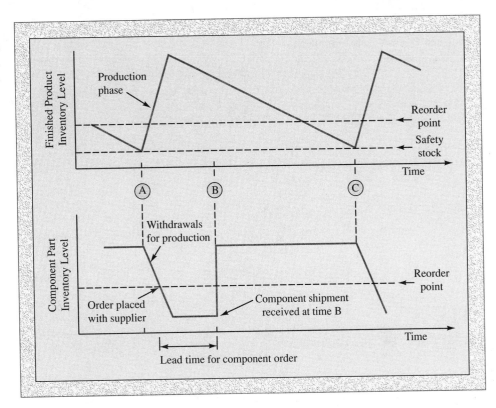

Figure 11.16
Finished Product and Component Part Inventory Levels Without an MRP System

component inventory is replenished. However, note that the component is not needed again until the next production run for the finished product, which is scheduled to occur at point C. Clearly, the investment in the component inventory from points B to C is unnecessary. We can eliminate this unnecessary component inventory by "backing up" from point C according to the purchase lead time so that the components will arrive just at time C. This situation is illustrated in Figure 11.17. Note that the component inventory level and corresponding inventory investment are less in Figure 11.17 than in Figure 11.16.

The philosophy of basing component inventory orders on the demand and production needs of other items is the approach followed by MRP. When operating properly, the MRP system will reduce inventory investment, improve work flow, reduce the shortage of materials and components, and help achieve more reliable delivery schedules.

Information System for MRP

What makes the MRP process difficult to implement is that many finished products consist of dozens or hundreds of parts, many of which are in turn dependent on other parts. Therefore, there must be accurate data and a reliable computer information system to perform the many calculations required for MRP.

Material requirements planning calculations begin with the *master production schedule,* which states the number of units of each finished product to be produced during each time period. With the information in the master production schedule, we can begin to determine when the various components that make up the final products must be available. Thus, the next step will be to identify the list of components that are required by the products. This information is available from the *bill of materials* (BOM).

The master production schedule should be a statement of what will be produced; it should not represent a management wish list of what management would like to produce.

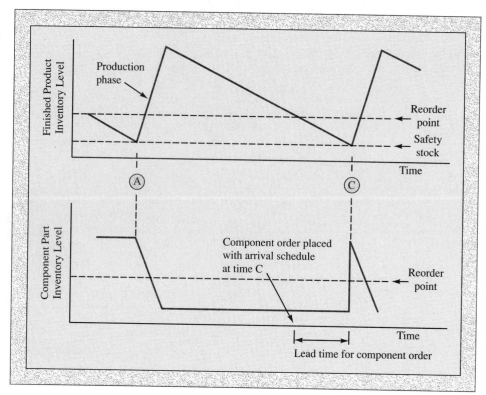

The BOM is a structured parts list; however, it differs from an ordinary parts list in that it shows the hierarchical relationship between the finished product and its various components. An example of a BOM for the Spiecker Company is shown in Figure 11.18. This figure shows the bill of materials for a 14-inch snowblower. The finished product is

Figure 11.18
Bill of Materials for the Spiecker
14-inch Snowblower

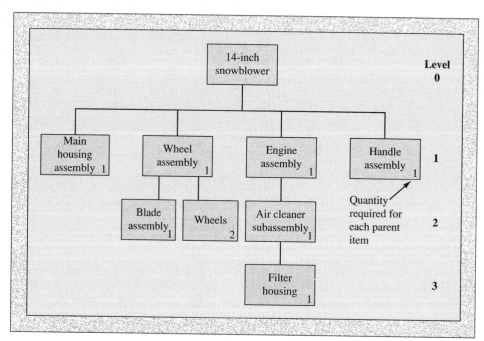

shown at the top of the hierarchy (called level 0). It consists of one main housing assembly, one wheel assembly, one engine assembly, and one handle assembly. If we consider the BOM as a "family tree," then the 14-inch snowblower is the "parent" item for each of these assemblies. These assemblies, in turn, are parent items for all the components included in them. Thus, the wheel assembly is the parent item of one blade assembly and two wheels. In general, items at level k are parent items for components at level $k + 1$. From the BOM, we can determine exactly how many components are needed to produce the quantity of finished products stated in the master production schedule.

A schematic diagram of an MRP information system is given in Figure 11.19. Forecasts and orders are used to develop the master production schedule. The master production schedule, BOM, and current inventory files are the inputs needed to begin the MRP computations. The outputs from the MRP system are the requirements for each item in the BOM along with the dates each item is needed. This information is used to plan order releases for production and purchasing. To illustrate how these calculations are performed, let us consider an MRP system for the Spiecker snowblower problem.

MRP Calculations

In MRP terminology, the time periods, which are called *buckets,* are often 1 week in length. Buckets, such as 1 week, are good for scheduling production over a short time horizon but may be too precise for long-range planning; larger buckets are used as the planning horizon gets longer. However, for the Spiecker Manufacturing problem, we assume that all buckets are 1 week in length.

The master production schedule calls for the final assembly of 1250 units of the 14-inch snowblower during week 21 of the current planning period. The assembly lead

Figure 11.19
An MRP System

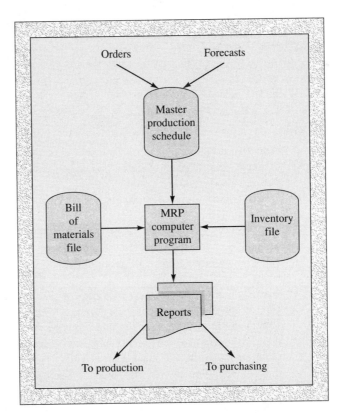

Table 11.5

Inventory on Hand and Lead Time for the Spiecker Manufacturing Problem

Component	Units in Inventory	Lead Time (weeks)
Engine assembly	450	4
Air cleaner subassembly	250	1
Filter housing	500	2

time is 1 week; thus, to meet this schedule, the four main assemblies in the bill of materials must be completed no later than the end of week 20. We now examine the production and inventory control aspects for the engine assembly in detail, concentrating on how the MRP approach can be applied. Relevant data regarding the number of units in inventory and lead time are given in Table 11.5.

Before the advent of MRP, the net requirement for each component was often found using the following formula:

$$\text{Net component requirement} = \left(\begin{array}{c}\text{Number of components} \\ \text{required to meet} \\ \text{demand for} \\ \text{finished good}\end{array}\right) - \left(\begin{array}{c}\text{Number of} \\ \text{components} \\ \text{in inventory}\end{array}\right)$$

Thus, the net requirements based on 1250 snowblowers are calculated as follows:

A primary function of material requirements planning is to convert gross requirements into net requirements. Once the net requirements are established, shop orders and purchase orders can be issued to cover the net requirements.

Components	Number of Components Required to Meet Demand for 1250 Snowblowers	−	Number in Inventory	=	Net Requirement
Engines	1250	−	450	=	800
Air cleaners	1250	−	250	=	1000
Filter housings	1250	−	500	=	750

However, note that this approach does not recognize the nature of dependent demand; for example, the number of filter housings required is dependent on the number of air cleaners produced, and so on.

The approach to determining net requirements whenever a dependent demand situation exists is

$$\text{Net component requirement} = \left(\begin{array}{c}\text{Gross component} \\ \text{requirement}\end{array}\right) - \left(\begin{array}{c}\text{Scheduled} \\ \text{receipts}\end{array}\right) - \left(\begin{array}{c}\text{Number of} \\ \text{components} \\ \text{in inventory}\end{array}\right)$$

where the gross component requirement is the quantity of the component needed to support production at the next higher level of assembly. For example, the gross component requirement for the filter housing is the number of filter housings required to meet the net requirement for the air cleaner subassembly; the gross component requirement for the air cleaner subassembly is the number of air cleaners needed to meet the net requirement for the engine assembly; and so on. Let us see how these requirements can be computed for Spiecker Manufacturing. (We assume, for simplicity, that scheduled receipts are zero.)

The computation of MRP net requirements is the subject of Problem 37.

	Units
Quantity of snowblowers to be produced:	1250
Gross requirements, engines:	1250
Less engines in inventory:	450
Net requirements, engines:	800 ← Engines
Gross requirements, air cleaners:	800
Less air cleaners in inventory:	250
Net requirements, air cleaners:	550 ← Air cleaners
Gross requirements, filter housings:	550
Less filter housings in inventory:	500
Net requirements, filter housings:	50 ← Filter housings

The time-phasing aspect of MRP focuses on the timing of orders and production.

While the net requirement for engines under the MRP approach is still 800 units, note how MRP has used the dependent-demand information to show that fewer air cleaners and filter housings will be needed. In addition to considering dependent demand in the determination of net requirements for components, an MRP system also determines when the net requirements are needed. MRP handles this aspect of production and inventory control using the *time-phasing* concept. By starting with the time that the finished product must be completed, we can work backward to determine when an order for each component must be placed. For example, the time-phasing calculations for the Spiecker snowblower problem might appear as follows:

	Week
Complete order for engines:	20
Minus lead time for engines:	4
Place an order for engines:	16 ← Order engines
Complete order for air cleaners:	16
Minus lead time for air cleaners:	1
Place an order for air cleaners:	15 ← Order air cleaners
Complete order for filter housings:	15
Minus lead time for filter housings:	2
Place an order for filter housings:	13 ← Order filter housings

The components are scheduled so that they are made available only when required for the next higher level of assembly. Similar calculations can be made for all the other components of the snowblower, and if the bill of materials is exploded into detailed part requirements, a complete schedule for shop orders and purchase requisitions is available.

Until the development of large-scale computers, the sheer volume of calculations prohibited the implementation of an MRP system. For example, even in our small illustration, you can begin to appreciate the complexity involved in keeping track of the production and inventory status for every component.

11.9 The Just-in-Time Approach to Inventory Management

The Japanese have captured a sizable share of world markets for many products because of the progress they have made in manufacturing. Among the reasons for this success are the Japanese style of management, the development of new technologies, and the use of new methods of material management and control. One new method that has received much attention in recent years is known as *just-in-time* (JIT). JIT represents a philosophy whose objective is the elimination of all sources of waste including unnecessary inventory.

The fundamental principle of JIT is to produce the right units in the right quantity at the right time. With JIT, units are produced only when they are required. Ideally, the number of parts produced or purchased at any one time should be just enough to produce one unit of the finished product. Inventories are not needed, or are at least minimized. For JIT to function effectively, fundamental changes in traditional production systems must take place. These changes require modifications in the production layout design and material flow process; in addition, setup times must be reduced.

Poor equipment layout is one of the major causes of inefficiencies in manufacturing. In a typical U.S. manufacturing environment, material is transported from the supplier to the warehouse and then to the plant. Within the plant, material may be transported from department to department. When production is completed, the finished goods may be returned to the warehouse, where they are stored until later distribution to the customer. Even with optimal inventory models, inventory and material handling costs can be substantial. The JIT approach helps reduce inventory and material handling costs by providing a flow of raw materials and finished goods in which material introduced at one end of the manufacturing process moves without delays into the finished products.

The driving force behind JIT production is the coordination of successive production activities. A key component of this coordination is an information system called a *Kanban*—the Japanese word for *card*. The type and number of units required by the production process are written on Kanbans, which are used to initiate the withdrawal and the production of units through the production process. By beginning at the final assembly, the Kanban "pulls" parts and components from preceding work stations. Thus, the entire manufacturing operation is synchronized to the final assembly stage. In this fashion, JIT prohibits earlier sources of supply and production from "pushing" units forward and building unnecessary and excessive inventories.

It is important to realize that the total quality concept is critical in the implementation of the JIT philosophy. Since lot sizes are small and inventory levels are minimal, there is no safety stock to replace nonconforming or defective units. Any quality problems disrupt the flow of materials throughout the plant and can be disastrous to the JIT system.

Finally, the coordination of the materials flow from suppliers to the manufacturer is another critical component of JIT. The JIT philosophy does not permit the shipment of large lots from suppliers that would build unnecessarily high inventory levels and costs. To maintain the smooth flow required by JIT, suppliers must make just-in-time deliveries. Instead of the large shipments that must be counted, inspected, and stored, suppliers make smaller deliveries on a daily basis or even more frequently as necessary to accommodate the manufacturer's daily production schedule. JIT requires a close partnership between the suppliers and the manufacturer to enable materials to be obtained on time and with zero defects.

The benefits of JIT are improved profits, resulting from reduced inventory costs, and improved quality. In the area of inventory management, the more obvious benefits of JIT are the reduced inventory levels, the increased inventory turnover, and the overall lower holding costs. While these benefits are significant, the behavioral and cultural differences between the Japanese and American people at both the management and the labor force levels make it unclear whether the Japanese success with JIT can be duplicated in American production systems. A few American companies have implemented the JIT philosophy, but most are still employing their traditional systems of inventory management.

Summary

In this chapter we presented some of the approaches management scientists use to assist managers in establishing low-cost inventory policies. We first considered cases where the demand rate for the product is constant. In analyzing these inventory systems, total-cost models were developed, which included ordering costs, holding costs, and, in some cases, backordering costs. Then minimum-cost formulas for the order quantity Q were presented. A reorder point r can be established by considering the lead-time demand for the item.

In addition, we discussed inventory models where a deterministic and constant rate could not be assumed, and thus, demand was described by a probability distribution. A critical issue with these probabilistic inventory models is obtaining a probability distribution that most realistically approximates the demand distribution for the item. We first described a single-period model where only one order is placed for the product and, at the end of the period, either the product has sold out or there is a surplus of unsold products that will be sold for a salvage value. Solution procedures were then presented for multiperiod models based on either an order-quantity, reorder-point, continuous-review system or a replenishment-level, periodic-review system.

We pointed out that the models presented in the earlier sections of the chapter are for independent-demand situations and are most applicable for managing finished goods inventory. For manufacturing inventories of subassemblies and component parts, where dependent demand exists, methods such as material requirements planning (MRP) offer significant advantages. Finally, we discussed the just-in-time philosophy that has evolved from the Japanese approach to material management and control. In inventory management, JIT is directed at reducing inventory levels and increasing inventory turnover.

In closing this chapter, we reemphasize that inventory and inventory systems can be an expensive phase of a firm's operation. It is of utmost economic importance for managers to be aware of the cost of inventory systems and to make the best possible operating policy decisions for the inventory system. Inventory models, as presented in this chapter, can help managers to develop good inventory policies.

Glossary

Economic order quantity (EOQ) The order quantity that minimizes the annual holding cost plus the annual ordering cost.

Constant demand rate An assumption of many inventory models that states that the same number of units are taken from inventory each period of time.

Holding cost The cost associated with maintaining an inventory investment; holding cost includes the cost of the capital investment in the inventory, insurance, taxes, warehouse overhead, and so on. This cost may be stated as a percentage of the inventory investment or as a cost per unit.

Cost of capital The cost a firm incurs in order to obtain capital for investment. The cost of capital, which may be stated as an annual percentage rate, is part of the holding cost associated with maintaining inventory levels.

Ordering cost The fixed cost (salaries, paper, transportation, etc.) associated with placing an order for an item.

Setup cost The fixed cost (labor, materials, lost production) associated with preparing a production system for a new production run.

Inventory position The inventory on hand plus the inventory on order.

Reorder point The inventory position at which a new order should be placed.

Lead time The time between the placing of an order and its receipt in the inventory system.

Lead-time demand The number of units demanded during the lead-time period.

Cycle time The length of time between the placing of two consecutive orders.

Safety stock Inventory maintained in order to reduce the number of stockouts resulting from higher-than-expected demand.

Constant supply rate The situation in which the inventory is built up at a constant rate over a period of time.

Backorder The receipt of an order for a product when there are no units in inventory. These backorders become shortages, which are eventually satisfied when a new supply of the product becomes available.

Goodwill cost A cost associated with a backorder, a lost sale, or any form of stockout or unsatisfied demand. This cost may be used to reflect the loss of future profits due to the fact a customer experienced an unsatisfied demand.

Quantity discounts Discounts or lower unit costs offered by the manufacturer when a customer purchases larger quantities of the product.

Deterministic demand rate A demand for an inventory item that is considered known and not subject to uncertainty.

Probabilistic demand rate When the demand for the inventory item is not known exactly, probabilities must be associated with the possible values for demand.

Single-period inventory models Inventory models in which only one order is placed for the product, and at the end of the period either the item has sold out, or there is a surplus of unsold items that will be sold for a salvage value.

Incremental analysis A method used to determine an optimal order quantity by comparing the cost of ordering an additional unit with the cost of not ordering an additional unit.

Lead-time demand distribution The distribution of demand that occurs during the lead-time period.

Service level The average number of stockouts tolerated per year.

Continuous review When the inventory position is monitored or reviewed on a continuous basis so that a new order can be placed as soon as the reorder point is reached.

Periodic review When the inventory position is checked or reviewed at predetermined periodic points in time. Reorders are placed only at periodic-review points.

Independent demand Demand for an item that is independent of the demand for other products or items. Usually independent demand is generated by customers placing orders for finished goods.

Dependent demand Demand for a product, component, subassembly, or item that is dependent on the demand for another product or item.

Material requirements planning (MRP) A computerized inventory management system whose functions are to schedule production and to control the level of inventory for components with dependent demand.

Master production schedule A statement of how many finished items are to be produced, and when.

Bill of materials (BOM) A structured parts list that shows the manner in which the product is put together.

Time phasing Adding the dimension of time to inventory status data in an MRP environment.

Just-in-time A philosophy that encourages the elimination of waste in time and resources. In inventory management, JIT works to reduce inventory levels and increase inventory turnover.

Kanban The Japanese word for *card,* which refers to the information system used for implementing JIT.

Problems

SELF TEST

1. EOQ

1. Suppose that the R & B Beverage Company has a soft-drink product that has a constant annual demand rate of 3600 cases. A case of the soft drink costs R & B $3. Ordering costs are $20 per order and holding costs are charged at 25% of the cost per unit. There are 250 working days per year and the lead time is 5 days. Identify the following aspects of the inventory policy.
   a. Economic order quantity
   b. Reorder point
   c. Cycle time
   d. Total annual cost

2. EOQ

2. A general property of the EOQ inventory model is that total inventory holding and total ordering costs are equal at the optimal solution. Use the data in Problem 1 to show that this result is true. Use equations (11.1), (11.2), and (11.3) to show that, in general, total holding costs and total ordering costs are equal whenever Q^* is used.

3. Reorder point

3. The reorder point (see equation (11.6)) is defined as the lead-time demand for the item. In cases of long lead times, the lead-time demand and thus the reorder point may exceed the economic order quantity Q^*. In such cases, the inventory position will not equal the inventory on hand when an order is placed and the reorder point may be expressed in terms of either the inventory position or the inventory on hand. Consider the economic order quantity model with $D = 5000$, $C_o = \$32$, $C_h = \$2$, and 250 working days per year. Identify the reorder point in terms of the inventory position and in terms of the inventory on hand for each of the following lead times.

  a. 5 days   **c.** 25 days
  b. 15 days   **d.** 45 days

4. EOQ

4. The XYZ Company purchases a component used in the manufacture of automobile generators directly from the supplier. XYZ's generator production operation, which is operated at a constant rate, will require 1000 components per month throughout the year (12,000 units annually). Assume that the ordering costs are $25 per order, the unit cost is $2.50 per component, and that annual holding costs are charged at 20%. There are 250 working days per year and the lead time is 5 days. Answer the following inventory policy questions for XYZ.

  a. What is the EOQ for this component?
  b. What is the reorder point?
  c. What is the cycle time?
  d. What are the total annual holding and ordering costs associated with your recommended EOQ?

5. EOQ

5. Suppose that XYZ's management in Problem 4 likes the operational efficiency of ordering once each month and in quantities of 1000 units. How much more expensive would this policy be than your EOQ recommendation? Would you recommend in favor of the 1000-unit order quantity? Explain. What would the reorder point be if the 1000-unit quantity were acceptable?

6. EOQ

6. Tele-Reco is a new specialty store that sells television sets, videotape recorders, video games, and other television-related products. A new Japanese-manufactured videotape recorder costs Tele-Reco $600 per unit. Tele-Reco's holding cost is figured at an annual rate of 22%. Ordering costs are estimated to be $70 per order.

  a. If demand for the new videotape recorder is expected to be constant with a rate of 20 units per month, what is the recommended order quantity for the videotape recorder?
  b. What are the estimated annual inventory holding and ordering costs associated with this product?
  c. How many orders will be placed per year?
  d. With 250 working days per year, what is the cycle time for this product?

7. EOQ

7. A large distributor of oil-well drilling equipment has operated over the past 2 years with EOQ policies based on an annual holding cost rate of 22%. Under the EOQ policy, a particular product has been ordered with a $Q^* = 80$. A recent evaluation of holding costs shows that because of an increase in the interest rate associated with bank loans, the annual holding cost rate should be 27%.

  a. What is the new economic order quantity for the product?
  b. Develop a general expression showing how the economic order quantity changes when the annual holding cost rate is changed from I to I'.

8. EOQ

8. Nation-Wide Bus Lines is proud of its 6-week bus driver training program that it conducts for all new Nation-Wide drivers. As long as the class size remains less than or equal to 35, a 6-week training program costs Nation-Wide $22,000 for instructors, equipment, and so on. The Nation-Wide training program must provide the company with approximately five new drivers per month. After completing the training program, new drivers are paid $1600 per month but do not work until a full-time driver position is open. Nation-Wide views the $1600 per month paid to each idle new driver as a holding cost necessary to maintain a supply of newly trained drivers available for immediate service. Viewing new drivers as inventory-type units, how large should the training classes be to minimize Nation-Wide's total annual training and new driver idle-time costs? How many training classes should the company hold each year? What is the total annual cost associated with your recommendation?

9. EOQ

9. Cress Electronic Products manufactures components used in the automotive industry. Cress purchases parts for use in its manufacturing operation from a variety of different suppliers. One particular supplier provides a part where the assumptions of the EOQ model are realistic. The annual demand is 500 units, ordering costs are $80 per order, and holding costs are figured at an annual rate of 25%.

   a. If the cost of the part is $20 per unit, what is the economic order quantity?

   b. Assume 250 days of operation per year. If the lead time for an order is 12 days, what is the reorder point?

   c. If the lead time for the part is 7 weeks (35 days), what is the reorder point?

   d. What is the reorder point for part (c) if the reorder point is expressed in terms of the inventory on hand rather than the inventory position?

10. Economic production lot size

10. All-Star Bat Manufacturing, Inc., supplies baseball bats to major and minor league baseball teams. After an initial order in January, demand over the 6-month baseball season is approximately constant at 1000 bats per month. Assuming that the bat production process can handle up to 4000 bats per month, the bat production setup costs are $150 per setup, the production cost is $10 per bat, and that holding costs are figured at a monthly rate of 2%, what production lot size would you recommend to meet the demand during the baseball season? If All-Star operates 20 days per month, how often will the production process operate, and what is the length of a production run?

11. Economic production lot size

11. Assume that a production line operates such that the production lot size model of Section 11.2 is applicable. Given $D = 6400$ units per year, $C_o = \$100$, and $C_h = \$2$ per unit per year, compute the minimum-cost production lot size for each of the following production rates:

   a. 8000 units per year   **c.** 32,000 units per year

   b. 10,000 units per year   **d.** 100,000 units per year

Compute the EOQ recommended lot size using equation (11.5). What two observations can you make about the relationship between the EOQ model and the production lot size model?

12. Economic production lot size

12. Assume that you are reviewing the production lot size decision associated with a production operation where $P = 8000$ units per year, $D = 2000$ units per year, $C_o = \$300$, and $C_h = \$1.60$ per unit per year. Also assume that current practice calls for production runs of 500 units every 3 months. Would you recommend changing the current production lot size? Why or why not? How much could be saved by converting to your production lot size recommendation?

SELF TEST

13. Economic production lot size

13. Wilson Publishing Company produces books for the retail market. Demand for a current book is expected to occur at a constant annual rate of 7200 copies. The cost of one copy of the book is $14.50. The holding cost is based on an 18% annual rate, and production setup costs are $150 per setup. The equipment on which the book is produced has an annual production volume of 25,000 copies. There are 250 working days per year and the lead time for a production run is 15 days. Use the production lot size model to compute the following values:

   a. Minimum-cost production lot size   **e.** Maximum inventory level

   b. Number of production runs per year   **f.** Total annual cost

   c. Cycle time   **g.** Reorder point

   d. Length of a production run

14. Economic production lot size

14. A well-known manufacturer of several brands of toothpaste uses the production lot size model to determine production quantities for its various products. The product known as Extra White is currently being produced in production lot sizes of 5000 units. The length of the production run for this quantity is 10 days. Because of a recent shortage of a particular raw material, the supplier of the material has announced a cost increase that will be passed along to the manufacturer of Extra White. Current estimates are that the new raw material cost will increase the manufacturing cost of the toothpaste products by 23% per unit. What will be the effect of this price increase on the production lot sizes for Extra White?

S E L F   T E S T

15. Planned shortages

15. Suppose that the XYZ Company of Problem 4, with $D = 12,000$ units per year, $C_h = (2.50)(0.20) = \$0.50$, and $C_o = \$25$, decided to operate with a backorder inventory policy. Backorder costs are estimated to be $5 per unit per year. Identify the following:
a. Minimum-cost order quantity
b. Maximum number of backorders
c. Maximum inventory level
d. Cycle time
e. Total annual cost

16. Planned shortages

16. Assuming 250 days of operation per year and a lead time of 5 days, what is the reorder point for the XYZ Company in Problem 15? Show the general formula for the reorder point for the EOQ model with backorders. In general, is the reorder point when backorders are allowed greater than or less than the reorder point when backorders are not allowed? Explain.

17. Planned shortages

17. A manager of an inventory system believes that inventory models are important decision-making aids. While often using an EOQ policy, the manager has never considered a backorder model because of the assumption that backorders were "bad" and should be avoided. However, with upper management's continued pressure for cost reduction, you have been asked to analyze the economics of a backordering policy for some products that can possibly be backordered. For a specific product with $D = 800$ units per year, $C_o = \$150$, $C_h = \$3$, and $C_b = \$20$, what is the difference in total annual cost between the EOQ model and the planned shortage or backorder model? If the manager adds constraints that no more than 25% of the units can be backordered and that no customer will have to wait more than 15 days for an order, should the backorder inventory policy be adopted? Assume 250 working days per year.

18. Reorder point with EOQ and planned shortages

18. If the lead time for new orders is 20 days for the inventory system discussed in Problem 17, find the reorder point for both the EOQ and the backorder models.

19. Planned shortages

19. The A&M Hobby Shop carries a line of radio-controlled model racing cars. Demand for the cars is assumed to be constant at a rate of 40 cars per month. The cars cost $60 each, and ordering costs are approximately $15 per order, regardless of the order size. The annual holding cost rate is 20%.
a. Determine the economic order quantity and total annual cost under the assumption that no backorders are permitted.
b. Using a $45 per unit per year backorder cost, determine the minimum-cost inventory policy and total annual cost for the model racing cars.
c. What is the maximum number of days a customer would have to wait for a backorder under the policy in part (b)? Assume that the Hobby Shop is open for business 300 days per year.
d. Would you recommend a no-backorder or a backorder inventory policy for this product? Explain.
e. If the lead time is 6 days, what is the reorder point for both the no-backorder and backorder inventory policies?

20. Assume that the following quantity discount schedule is appropriate:

Order Size	Discount (%)	Unit Cost
0 to 49	0	$30.00
50 to 99	5	28.50
100 or more	10	27.00

If annual demand is 120 units, ordering costs are $20 per order, and the annual holding cost rate is 25%, what order quantity would you recommend?

21. Apply the EOQ model to the following quantity discount situation where $D = 500$ units per year, $C_o = \$40$, and an annual holding cost rate of 20% are given:

Discount Category	Order Size	Discount (%)	Unit Cost
1	0 to 99	0	$10.00
2	100 or more	3	9.70

What order quantity do you recommend?

22. Keith Shoe Stores carries a basic black dress shoe for men that sells at an approximate constant rate of 500 pairs of shoes every 3 months. Keith's current buying policy is to order 500 pairs each time an order is placed. It costs Keith $30 to place an order. The annual holding cost rate is 20%. With the order quantity of 500, Keith obtains the shoes at the lowest possible unit cost of $28 per pair. Other quantity discounts offered by the manufacturer are as follows:

Order Quantity	Price Per Pair
0–99	$36
100–199	32
200–299	30
300 or more	28

What is the minimum-cost order quantity for the shoes? What are the annual savings of your inventory policy over the policy currently being used by Keith?

23. In the EOQ model with quantity discounts, we stated that if the Q^* for a price category is larger than necessary to qualify for the category price, the category cannot be optimal. Use the two discount categories in Problem 21 to show that this is true. That is, plot the total-cost curves for the two categories and show that if the category 2 minimum cost Q is an acceptable solution, we do not have to consider category 1.

24. Single period, probabilistic demand

24. The J&B Card Shop sells calendars with different Colonial pictures shown for each month. The once-a-year order for each year's calendar arrives in September. From past experience, the September-to-July demand for the calendars can be approximated by a normal distribution with $\mu = 500$ and $\sigma = 120$. The calendars cost $1.50 each, and J&B sells them for $3 each.
   a. If J&B throws out all unsold calendars at the end of July (i.e., salvage value is zero), how many calendars should be ordered?
   b. If J&B reduces the calendar price to $1 at the end of July and can sell all surplus calendars at this price, how many calendars should be ordered?

S ELF T EST

25. Single period, probabilistic demand

25. The Gilbert Air-Conditioning Company is considering the purchase of a special shipment of portable air conditioners manufactured in Japan. Each unit will cost Gilbert $80 and it will be sold for $125. Gilbert does not want to carry surplus air conditioners over until the following year. Thus, all surplus air conditioners will be sold to a wholesaler for $50 per unit. Assume that the air conditioner demand follows a normal probability distribution with $\mu = 20$ and $\sigma = 8$.
   a. What is the recommended order quantity?
   b. What is the probability that Gilbert will sell all units it orders?

26. Single period, probabilistic demand

26. A popular newsstand in a large metropolitan area is attempting to determine how many copies of the Sunday paper it should purchase each week. Demand for the newspaper on Sundays can be approximated by a normal probability distribution with $\mu = 450$ and $\sigma = 100$. The newspaper costs the newsstand 35¢ a copy and sells for 50¢ a copy. The newsstand does not receive any value from surplus papers and thus absorbs a 100% loss on all unsold papers.
   a. How many copies of the Sunday paper should be purchased each week?
   b. What is the probability that the newsstand will have a stockout?
   c. The manager of the newsstand is concerned about the newsstand's image if the probability of stockout is high. The customers often purchase other items after coming to the newsstand for the Sunday paper. Frequent stockouts would cause customers to go to another newsstand. The manager agrees that a 50¢ goodwill cost should be assigned to any stockout. What is the new recommended order quantity and the new probability of a stockout?

27. Single period, probabilistic demand

27. A perishable dairy product is ordered daily at a particular supermarket. The product, which costs $1.19 per unit, sells for $1.65 per unit. If units are unsold at the end of the day, the supplier takes them back at a rebate of $1 per unit. Assume that daily demand is approximately normally distributed with $\mu = 150$ and $\sigma = 30$.
   a. What is your recommended daily order quantity for the supermarket?
   b. What is the probability that the supermarket will see all the units it orders?
   c. In problems such as these, why would the supplier offer a rebate as high as $1? For example, why not offer a nominal rebate of, say, 25¢ per unit? What happens to the supermarket order quantity as the rebate is reduced?

28. Single period, probabilistic demand

28. A retail outlet sells a seasonal product for $10 per unit. The cost of the product is $8 per unit. All units not sold during the regular season are sold for half the retail price in an end-of-season clearance sale. Assume that demand for the product is uniformly distributed between 200 and 800.
   a. What is the recommended order quantity?
   b. What is the probability that at least some customers will ask to purchase the product after the outlet is sold out? That is, what is the probability of a stockout using your order quantity in part (a)?
   c. To keep customers happy and returning to the store later, the owner feels that stockouts should be avoided if at all possible. What is your recommended order quantity if the owner is willing to tolerate a 0.15 probability of a stockout?
   d. Using your answer to part (c), what is the goodwill cost you are assigning to a stockout?

29. Floyd Distributors, Inc., provides a variety of auto parts to small local garages. Floyd purchases parts from manufacturers according to the EOQ model and then ships the parts from a regional warehouse direct to its customers. For a particular type of muffler, Floyd's EOQ analysis recommends orders with $Q^* = 25$ to satisfy an annual demand of 200 mufflers. There are 250 working days per year and the lead time averages 15 days.

a. What is the reorder point if Floyd assumes a constant demand rate?

b. Suppose that an analysis of Floyd's muffler demand shows that the lead-time demand follows a normal probability distribution with $\mu = 12$ and $\sigma = 2.5$. If Floyd's management can tolerate one stockout per year, what is the revised reorder point?

c. What is the safety stock for part (b)? If $C_h = \$5$/unit/year, what is the extra cost due to the uncertainty of demand?

30. For Floyd Distributors in Problem 29, we were given $Q^* = 25$, $D = 200$, $C_h = \$5$, and a normal lead-time demand distribution with $\mu = 12$ and $\sigma = 2.5$.

a. What is Floyd's reorder point if the firm is willing to tolerate two stockouts during the year?

b. What is Floyd's reorder point if the firm wants to restrict the probability of a stockout on any one cycle to at most 1%?

c. What are the safety stock levels and the annual safety stock costs for the reorder points found in parts (a) and (b)?

31. A product with an annual demand of 1000 units has $C_o = \$25.50$ and $C_h = \$8$. The demand exhibits some variability such that the lead-time demand follows a normal probability distribution with $\mu = 25$ and $\sigma = 5$.

a. What is the recommended order quantity?

b. What are the reorder point and safety stock if the firm desires at most a 2% probability of stockout on any given order cycle?

c. If a manager sets the reorder point at 30, what is the probability of a stockout on any given order cycle? How many times would you expect to stockout during the year if this reorder point were used?

32. The B&S Novelty and Craft Shop in Bennington, Vermont, sells a variety of quality handmade items to tourists. B&S will sell 300 hand-carved miniature replicas of a Colonial soldier each year, but the demand pattern during the year is uncertain. The replicas sell for $20 each, and B&S uses a 15% annual inventory holding cost rate. Ordering costs are $5 per order, and demand during the lead time follows a normal probability distribution with $\mu = 15$ and $\sigma = 6$.

a. What is the recommended order quantity?

b. If B&S is willing to accept a stockout roughly twice a year, what reorder point would you recommend? What is the probability that B&S will have a stockout in any one order cycle?

c. What are the safety stock and annual safety stock costs for this product?

33. A firm uses a 1-week periodic review inventory system. There is a 2-day lead time for any order, and the firm is willing to tolerate an average of one stockout per year.

a. Using the firm's service guideline, what is the probability of a stockout associated with each replenishment decision?

b. What is the replenishment level if demand during the review period plus lead-time period is normally distributed with a mean of 60 units and a standard deviation of 12 units?

c. What is the replenishment level if demand during the review period plus lead-time period is uniformly distributed between 35 and 85 units?

34. Foster Drugs, Inc., handles a variety of health and beauty aid products. A particular hair conditioner product costs Foster Drugs $2.95 per unit. The annual holding cost rate is 20%. An order-quantity, reorder-point inventory model recommends an order quantity of 300 units per order.

a. Lead time is one week and the lead-time demand is normally distributed with a mean of 150 units and a standard deviation of 40 units. What is the reorder point if the firm is willing to tolerate a 1% chance of stockout on any one cycle?

b. What safety stock and annual safety stock cost is associated with your recommendation in part (a)?

c. The order-quantity, reorder-point model requires a continuous-review system. Foster is considering making a transition to a periodic-review system in an attempt to coordinate ordering for many of its products. The demand during the proposed two-week review period and the one-week lead-time period is normally distributed with a mean of 450 units and a standard deviation of 70 units. What is the recommended replenishment level for this periodic-review system if the firm is willing to tolerate the same 1% chance of stockout associated with any replenishment decision?

d. What safety stock and annual safety stock cost is associated with your recommendation in part (c)?

e. Compare your answers to parts (b) and (d). The company is seriously considering the periodic-review system. Would you support this decision? Explain.

f. Would you tend to favor the continuous-review system for more expensive items? For example, assume that the product in the above example sold for $295 per unit. Explain.

35. Periodic review

35. Statewide Auto Parts uses a 4-week periodic-review system to reorder parts for its inventory stock. A 1-week lead time is required to fill the order. Demand for one particular part during the 5-week replenishment period is normally distributed with a mean of 18 units and a standard deviation of 6 units.

a. At a particular periodic review, 8 units are in inventory. The parts manager places an order for 16 units. What is the probability that this part will have a stockout before an order that is placed at the next 4-week review period arrives?

b. Assume that the company is willing to tolerate a 2.5% chance of a stockout associated with a replenishment decision. How many parts should the manager have ordered in part (a)? What is the replenishment level for the 4-week periodic-review system?

36. Periodic review

36. Rose Office Supplies, Inc., which is open 6 days a week, uses a 2-week periodic review for its store inventory. On alternating Monday mornings, the store manager fills out an order sheet requiring a shipment of various items from the company's warehouse. A particular three-ring notebook sells at an average rate of 16 notebooks per week. The standard deviation in sales is 5 notebooks per week. The lead time for a new shipment is 3 days. The mean lead time demand is 8 notebooks with a standard deviation of 3.5.

a. What is the mean or expected demand during the review period plus the lead-time period?

b. Under the assumption of independent demand from week to week, the variances in demands are additive. Thus, the variance of the demand during the review period plus the lead-time period is equal to the variance of demand during the first week plus the variance of demand during the second week plus the variance of demand during the lead-time period. What is the variance of demand during the review period plus the lead-time period? What is the standard deviation of demand during the review period plus the lead-time period?

c. Assuming that demand has a normal probability distribution, what is the replenishment level that will provide an expected stockout rate of one per year?

d. On Monday, March 22, 18 notebooks remain in inventory at the store. How many notebooks should the store manager order?

SELF TEST ▶
37. Net requirements for MRP

37. Consider the Spiecker Manufacturing problem of Section 11.8. Determine the net requirements for the engine assembly, the air cleaner subassembly, and the filter housing if the number of units in inventory were 2000, 1500, and 1000, respectively. Assume that 5000 units of the 14-inch snowblower are required in week 21.

38. Time phasing for MRP

38. For the Spiecker Manufacturing problem of Section 11.8, determine the effect on time phasing if lead times were 10 for the engine assembly, 3 for the air cleaner subassembly, and 5 for the filter housing.

39. Net requirements for MRP

39. C & D Lawn Products manufactures a rotary spreader for applying fertilizer. A portion of the bill of materials is shown below:

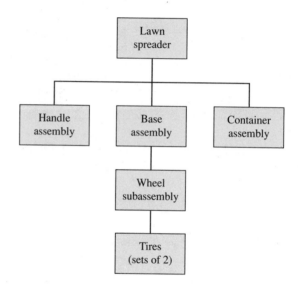

If 3000 lawn spreaders are needed to satisfy a customer's order, determine the net requirements for the base assembly, wheel subassembly, and tires (sets of two). Assume that 1000 base assemblies, 1500 wheel subassemblies, and 800 tires (sets of two) are currently in inventory.

40. Time phasing for MRP

40. In Problem 39, assume that the lead time for the base assembly, wheel subassembly, and tires are 2 weeks, 4 weeks, and 5 weeks, respectively. If all components must be completed no later than week 15 of the current production period, determine when orders must be placed to meet the production schedule.

Case Problem: A Make-or-Buy Analysis

Wagner Fabricating Company is reviewing the economic feasibility of manufacturing a part that it currently purchases from a supplier. Forecasted annual demand for the part is 3200 units. Wagner operates 250 days per year.

Wagner's financial analysts have established a cost of capital of 14% for the use of funds for investments within the company. In addition, over the past year $600,000 has been the average investment in the company's inventory. Accounting information shows that a total of $24,000 was spent on taxes and insurance related to the company's inventory. In addition, it has been estimated that $9000 was lost due to inventory shrinkage, which included damaged goods as well as pilferage. A remaining $15,000 was spent on warehouse overhead, including utility expenses for heating and lighting.

An analysis of the purchasing operation shows that approximately 2 hours are required to process and coordinate an order for the part regardless of the quantity ordered. Purchasing salaries average $28 per hour, including employee benefits. In addition, a detailed analysis of 125 orders showed that $2375 was spent on telephone, paper, and postage directly related to the ordering process.

A 1-week lead time is required to obtain the part from the supplier. An analysis of demand during the lead time shows that lead-time demand is approximately normally distributed with a mean of 64 units and a standard deviation of 10 units. Service level guidelines indicate that one stockout per year is acceptable.

Currently, the company has a contract to purchase the part from a supplier at a cost of $18 per unit. However, over the past few months, the company's production capacity has been expanded. As a result, excess capacity is now available in certain production departments and the company is considering the alternative of producing the parts itself.

Forecasted utilization of equipment shows that production capacity will be available for the part being considered. The production capacity is available at the rate of 1000 units per month, with up to 5 months of production time available. It is felt that with a 2-week lead time, schedules can be arranged so that the part can be produced whenever needed. The demand during the 2-week lead time is approximately normally distributed, with a mean of 128 units and a standard deviation of 20 units. Production costs are expected to be $17 per part.

A concern of management is that setup costs will be significant. The total cost of labor and lost production time is estimated to be $50 per hour, and it will take a full 8-hour shift to set up the equipment for producing the part.

Managerial Report

Develop a report for management of Wagner Fabricating that will address the question of whether the company should continue to purchase the part from the supplier or should begin to produce the part itself. Include the following factors in your report:

1. An analysis of the holding costs, including the appropriate annual holding cost rate.
2. An analysis of ordering costs, including the appropriate cost per order from the supplier.
3. An analysis of setup costs for the production operation.
4. A development of the inventory policy for the following two alternatives:
   a. Ordering a fixed quantity Q from the supplier
   b. Ordering a fixed quantity Q from in-plant production
5. Include the following in the policies of parts 4(a) and 4(b) above.
   a. Optimal quantity $Q*$
   b. Number of order or production runs per year
   c. Cycle time
   d. Reorder point
   e. Amount of safety stock
   f. Expected maximum inventory level
   g. Average inventory level
   h. Annual holding cost
   i. Annual ordering cost
   j. Annual cost of the units purchased or manufactured
   k. Total annual cost of the purchase policy and the total annual cost of the production policy
6. Make a recommendation as to whether the company should purchase or manufacture the part. What is the saving associated with your recommendation as compared with the other alternative?

Development of the Optimal Order-Quantity (Q*) Formula for the EOQ Model

Given equation (11.4) as the total annual cost for the EOQ model,

$$TC = \frac{1}{2}QC_h + \frac{D}{Q}C_o \tag{11.4}$$

we can find the order quantity Q that minimizes the total cost by setting the derivative, dTC/dQ, equal to zero and solving for Q^*.

$$\frac{dTC}{dQ} = \frac{1}{2}C_h - \frac{D}{Q^2}C_o = 0$$

$$\frac{1}{2}C_h = \frac{D}{Q^2}C_o$$

$$C_h Q^2 = 2DC_o$$

$$Q^2 = \frac{2DC_o}{C_h}$$

Hence,

$$Q^* = \sqrt{\frac{2DC_o}{C_h}} \tag{11.5}$$

The second derivative is

$$\frac{d^2TC}{dQ^2} = \frac{2D}{Q^3}C_o$$

Since the value of the second derivative is greater than zero for D, C_o, and Q greater than zero, Q^* from equation (11.5) is the minimum-cost solution.

Development of the Optimal Lot Size (Q*) Formula for the Production Lot Size Model

Given equation (11.15) as the total annual cost for the production lot size model,

$$TC = \frac{1}{2}\left(1 - \frac{D}{P}\right)QC_h + \frac{D}{Q}C_o \tag{11.15}$$

we can find the order quantity Q that minimizes the total cost by setting the derivative, dTC/dQ, equal to zero and solving for Q^*.

$$\frac{dTC}{dQ} = \frac{1}{2}\left(1 - \frac{D}{P}\right)C_h - \frac{D}{Q^2}C_o = 0$$

Solving for Q^*, we have

$$\frac{1}{2}\left(1 - \frac{D}{P}\right)C_h = \frac{D}{Q^2}C_o$$

$$\left(1 - \frac{D}{P}\right)C_h Q^2 = 2DC_o$$

$$Q^2 = \frac{2DC_o}{(1 - D/P)C_h}$$

Hence,

$$Q^* = \sqrt{\frac{2DC_o}{(1 - D/P)C_h}} \qquad (11.16)$$

The second derivative is

$$\frac{d^2 TC}{dQ^2} = \frac{2DC_o}{Q^3}$$

Since the value of the second derivative is greater than zero for D, C_o, and Q greater than zero, Q^* from equation (11.16) is a minimum-cost solution.

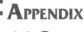

APPENDIX 11.3

Development of the Optimal Order-Quantity (Q^*) and Optimal Backorder (S^*) Formulas for the Planned Shortage Model

Given equation (11.25) as the total annual cost for the planned shortage case,

$$TC = \frac{(Q - S)^2}{2Q}C_h + \frac{D}{Q}C_o + \frac{S^2}{2Q}C_b \qquad (11.25)$$

we have two inventory decision variables, Q and S. To find the Q and S values that minimize equation (11.25), we must set the two partial derivatives, $\partial TC/\partial Q$ and $\partial TC/\partial S$, equal to zero.

First, let us rewrite equation (11.25) as follows:

$$TC = \left(\frac{Q^2 - 2QS + S^2}{2Q}\right)C_h + \frac{D}{Q}C_o + \frac{S^2}{2Q}C_b$$

$$= \frac{Q}{2}C_h - SC_h + \frac{C_h}{2Q}S^2 + \frac{DC_o}{Q} + \frac{C_b}{2Q}S^2$$

$$= \left(\frac{C_h + C_b}{2Q}\right)S^2 - SC_h + \frac{QC_h}{2} + \frac{DC_o}{Q}$$

Then, setting $\partial TC/\partial S = 0$, we obtain

$$\frac{\partial TC}{\partial S} = \left(\frac{C_h + C_b}{Q}\right)S - C_h = 0$$

Solving for $S*$, we have

$$\left(\frac{C_h + C_b}{Q}\right)S = C_h$$

Thus

$$S* = Q\left(\frac{C_h}{C_h + C_b}\right) \tag{11.27}$$

Setting $\partial TC/\partial Q = 0$, we obtain

$$\frac{\partial TC}{\partial Q} = \frac{-(C_h + C_b)S^2}{2Q^2} + \frac{C_h}{2} - \frac{DC_o}{Q^2} = 0$$

Substituting $S*$ of equation (11.27), we have

$$\frac{\partial TC}{\partial Q} = \frac{-(C_h + C_b)Q^2(C_h)^2/(C_h + C_b)^2}{2Q^2} + \frac{C_h}{2} - \frac{DC_o}{Q^2} = 0$$

We can solve for $Q*$ as follows:

$$\frac{-C_h^2}{2(C_h + C_b)} + \frac{C_h}{2} = \frac{DC_o}{Q^2}$$

$$\frac{-C_h^2 + C_h(C_h + C_b)}{2(C_h + C_b)} = \frac{DC_o}{Q^2}$$

$$Q^2 = \frac{2(C_h + C_b)DC_o}{C_hC_b}$$

$$Q^2 = \frac{2C_hDC_o}{C_hC_b} + \frac{2C_bDC_o}{C_hC_b}$$

$$Q^2 = \frac{2DC_o}{C_h}\left(\frac{C_h}{C_b} + \frac{C_b}{C_b}\right)$$

Hence

$$Q* = \sqrt{\frac{2DC_o}{C_h}\left(\frac{C_h + C_b}{C_b}\right)} \tag{11.26}$$

The second-order conditions will show that equations (11.26) and (11.27) are the minimum-cost solutions.

SupeRx, Inc.*
Cincinnati, Ohio

SupeRx, Inc., is a chain of conventional-size drugstores with locations in 15 states. The company operates a total of 345 stores that are part of Hook-SupeRx, Inc., which operates over 1100 stores, primarily in the Midwest and Northeast. As in any retail business, the company's primary functions and concerns revolve around sales growth, profit margins, expense control, and inventory management.

Inventory management is undergoing a rapid transformation from an art to a science. No longer can any retail business expect to operate profitably without a sound inventory management program, and SupeRx has recognized this. A key consideration for the company is product movement information that in turn determines reorder quantities at both the store and warehouse levels. Seasonal fluctuations and advertising can affect product movement, and their effects must be measured using historical data rather than seat-of-the-pants guesswork.

General inventory management for SupeRx involves several product categories: basic products carried on an everyday basis, seasonal products carried only during certain times of the year (such as fruitcakes during Christmas), and special items bought on an in-and-out basis throughout the year.

By far the most critical inventory issue is the replenishment of basic products. At SupeRx, as at most retail drug chains, this type of product is ordered under a periodic-review inventory system, with the review period being 1 week. The weekly review uses electronic ordering equipment that scans an order label affixed to the shelf. Such a label is located on the shelf directly below each item. Among other information on this label is the "order-to quantity." (*Note:* This is the replenishment level referred to in the periodic-review inventory model of Section 11.7.) The store employee placing the order determines the quantity to order by subtracting the number of units of product on the shelf from the order-to quantity (OTQ). For example, if the OTQ is 6 and there are two units of product on the shelf, the quantity ordered would be 4. The OTQ is the key factor in inventory control for basic products.

Several factors are considered in determining individual item OTQs. The most obvious is average weekly demand or movement. SupeRx uses movement figures from the warehouse to the stores. Suppose, for example, an item averages two units per week per store in warehouse deliveries. Setting the OTQ equal to 2 would not allow for sales fluctuations that exceeded the average of 2. To compensate for this and to avoid stockouts, SupeRx sets the OTQ equal to a 3-week demand or movement. Thus, in our example, the OTQ would become 6.

Another factor to consider is whether an item can be ordered in units or cases. In some instances, it is not feasible for the warehouse to deliver in anything less than case quantities. An example would be candy bars. Stores must order a minimum of one case (36 units), no matter what the movement indicates. Thus, the OTQ is 36 or a multiple of 36 to accommodate the case order restriction. Merchandising esthetics must also be considered when determining an OTQ. If an item has four facings or open positions on the shelf, but the optimum OTQ determined by movement is 3, there would be one space without product. This would create an out-of-stock impression to the customer, and, thus, the OTQ would be increased to at least 4. Seasonal fluctuations in movement must be considered when OTQs are determined. For example, the OTQ for a cough and cold item would be significantly higher in January than it would be in July. Adhesive bandages would be just the opposite, with higher usage in the summer than in the winter.

SupeRx is in the process of taking advantage of new technological breakthroughs in inventory management. Today, its OTQs are based on average company warehouse movement into the stores. Soon SupeRx will have a program in place to produce OTQs by item by individual store, based on that store's movement, rather than on the company movement. Once that is in place, SupeRx will be able to accommodate seasonal fluctuations by individual store as well.

The chain drug industry is well behind other retail industries (most notably the grocery industry) in the ability to capture point-of-sale information with the use of scanning registers. SupeRx is in the process of installing them, and once they are in place, the company will be able to use actual point-of-sale product information instead of warehouse movement. These scanning registers also have the ability to place an order to the warehouse automatically, based on what is actually sold that week, so the inventory movement management can only continue to improve.

Good inventory management does not occur in a vacuum, but must be interrelated with sales, gross margin, and expense control objectives. SupeRx is fortunate in that it has had planning software in place for some time. This system allows SupeRx merchandisers to act out "what if" scenarios relating to OTQs, product costs, retail sales prices, inventory carrying costs, sales, and other factors. As an example, optimum order-to quantities normally result in some percentage of missed sales due to individual item movement fluctuations. On the other hand, increasing the OTQs to maximize sales also increases

---

*The authors are indebted to Bob Carver of SupeRx, Inc., for providing this application.

—Continued on next page

—Continued from previous page

inventory, decreases inventory turnover, and thus ties up capital that could otherwise be used for building new stores, remodeling existing locations, and so on. By using the new inventory management techniques, SupeRx can maximize both sales and inventory turnover. Rapidly becoming a necessity rather than a luxury, the use of this modern technology ensures the maximization of sales, profits, and inventory turnovers that ultimately determine the success or failure of a drug chain.

Questions

1. Does SupeRx use a continuous-review or a periodic-review inventory system? Why would this system be preferred for a retail business such as SupeRx?
2. What is the decision rule that SupeRx uses to provide a safety stock and minimize stockouts?
3. What is SupeRx doing to obtain information that will help continue to improve inventory management?

CHAPTER 12

Waiting Line Models

Recall the last time that you had to wait at a supermarket checkout counter, for a teller at your local bank, or to be served at a fast-food restaurant. In these and many other waiting line situations, the time spent waiting is undesirable. Since adding more checkout clerks, bank tellers, or servers is not always the most economical strategy for improving service, businesses need to determine ways to keep waiting times within tolerable limits.

Models have been developed to help managers understand and make better decisions concerning the operation of waiting lines. In management science terminology, a waiting line is also known as a *queue*, and the body of knowledge dealing with waiting lines is known as *queuing theory*. In the early 1900s A. K. Erlang, a Danish telephone engineer, began a study of the congestion and waiting times occurring in the completion of telephone calls. Since then, queuing theory has grown far more sophisticated and has been applied to a wide variety of waiting line situations.

Waiting line models consist of mathematical formulas and relationships that can be used to determine the *operating characteristics* (performance measures) for a waiting line. Some of the operating characteristics that are of interest are the following:

1. The probability that there are no units in the system
2. The average number of units in the waiting line
3. The average number of units in the system (the number of units in the waiting line plus the number of units being served)
4. The average time a unit spends in the waiting line
5. The average time a unit spends in the system (the waiting time plus the service time)
6. The probability that an arriving unit has to wait for service
7. The probability of n units in the system

Managers who have the above information are better able to make decisions that balance desirable service levels against the cost of providing the service.

12.1 The Structure of a Waiting Line System

To illustrate the basic features of a waiting line model, we consider the waiting line at the Burger Dome fast-food restaurant. Burger Dome sells hamburgers, cheeseburgers, french fries, soft drinks, and milk shakes, as well as a limited number of specialty items and dessert selections. Although Burger Dome would like to serve each customer immediately, at times more customers arrive than can be handled by the Burger Dome food-service staff. Thus, customers wait in line to place and receive their orders.

Burger Dome is concerned that the methods they are currently using to serve customers are resulting in excessive waiting times. Management has asked that a waiting line study be performed to help determine the best approach to reducing waiting times and improving service.

The Single-Channel Waiting Line

In the current Burger Dome operation with one cash register, a server takes the customer's order, determines the total cost of the order, takes the money from the customer, and then fills the order. Once the first customer's order is filled, the server takes the order of the next customer waiting for service. This operation is an example of a *single-channel* waiting line. By this, we mean that each customer entering the Burger Dome restaurant must pass through the *one* channel—one order-taking and order-filling station—to place an order, pay the bill, and receive the food. When more customers arrive than can be immediately served, the customers form a waiting line and wait for the order-taking and order-filling station to become available. A diagram of the Burger Dome single-channel waiting line is shown in Figure 12.1.

The Process of Arrivals

Defining the arrival process for a waiting line involves determining the probability distribution for the number of arrivals in a given period of time. For many waiting line situations, the arrivals occur in a *random fashion;* that is, each arrival is independent of other arrivals, and we cannot predict when an arrival will occur. In such cases, management scientists have found that the *Poisson probability distribution* provides a good description of the arrival pattern.

Figure 12.1
The Burger Dome Single-Channel
Waiting Line

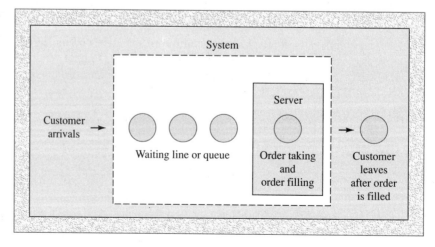

Using the Poisson probability function,[1] the probability of x arrivals in a specific time period is defined as follows:

$$P(x) = \frac{\lambda^x e^{-\lambda}}{x!} \quad \text{for } x = 0, 1, 2 \ldots \tag{12.1}$$

where

> x = the number of arrivals in the period
> λ = the average or mean number of arrivals per period
> e = 2.71828

Values of $e^{-\lambda}$ are provided in Table 12.1.

Suppose that Burger Dome has analyzed data on customer arrivals and has concluded that the mean arrival rate is 45 customers per hour. For a 1-minute period, the mean number of arrivals would be $\lambda = 45/60 = 0.75$ arrivals per minute. Thus, we can use the following Poisson probability function to compute the probability of x arrivals during a 1-minute period:

$$P(x) = \frac{\lambda^x e^{-\lambda}}{x!} = \frac{0.75^x e^{-0.75}}{x!} \tag{12.2}$$

Table 12.1 shows that $e^{-0.75} = 0.4724$. Thus, the probabilities of 0, 1, and 2 arrivals during a 1-minute period are as follows:

$$P(0) = \frac{(0.75)^0 e^{-0.75}}{0!} = e^{-0.75} = 0.4724$$

$$P(1) = \frac{(0.75)^1 e^{-0.75}}{1!} = 0.75 e^{-0.75} = 0.75(0.4724) = 0.3543$$

$$P(2) = \frac{(0.75)^2 e^{-0.75}}{2!} = \frac{0.75^2 e^{-0.75}}{2!} = \frac{(0.5625)(0.4724)}{2} = 0.1329$$

We see that the probability of no arrivals in a 1-minute period is 0.4724, the probability of exactly one arrival in a 1-minute period is 0.3543, and the probability of exactly two arrivals in a 1-minute period is 0.1329. The Poisson probability distribution of arrivals during a 1-minute period is shown in Table 12.2.

The waiting line models presented in Sections 12.2 and 12.3, use the Poisson distribution to describe the customer arrivals at Burger Dome. In practice, you will want to record the actual number of arrivals per time period for several days or weeks and compare the frequency distribution of the observed number of arrivals to the Poisson distribution in order to determine if the Poisson distribution provides a reasonable approximation of the arrival distribution.

The Distribution of Service Times

The service time is the time the customer spends at the service facility once the service has started. At Burger Dome, the service time starts when the customer begins to place

---

[1] The term $x!$, *x factorial*, is defined as $x! = x(x-1)(x-2) \ldots (2)(1)$. For example, $4! = (4)(3)(2)(1) = 24$. For the special case of $x = 0$, $0! = 1$ by definition.

Table 12.1
Values of $e^{-\lambda}$

λ	$e^{-\lambda}$	λ	$e^{-\lambda}$	λ	$e^{-\lambda}$
0.05	0.9512	2.05	0.1287	4.05	0.0174
0.10	0.9048	2.10	0.1225	4.10	0.0166
0.15	0.8607	2.15	0.1165	4.15	0.0158
0.20	0.8187	2.20	0.1108	4.20	0.0150
0.25	0.7788	2.25	0.1054	4.25	0.0143
0.30	0.7408	2.30	0.1003	4.30	0.0136
0.35	0.7047	2.35	0.0954	4.35	0.0129
0.40	0.6703	2.40	0.0907	4.40	0.0123
0.45	0.6376	2.45	0.0863	4.45	0.0117
0.50	0.6065	2.50	0.0821	4.50	0.0111
0.55	0.5769	2.55	0.0781	4.55	0.0106
0.60	0.5488	2.60	0.0743	4.60	0.0101
0.65	0.5220	2.65	0.0707	4.65	0.0096
0.70	0.4966	2.70	0.0672	4.70	0.0091
0.75	0.4724	2.75	0.0639	4.75	0.0087
0.80	0.4493	2.80	0.0608	4.80	0.0082
0.85	0.4274	2.85	0.0578	4.85	0.0078
0.90	0.4066	2.90	0.0550	4.90	0.0074
0.95	0.3867	2.95	0.0523	4.95	0.0071
1.00	0.3679	3.00	0.0498	5.00	0.0067
1.05	0.3499	3.05	0.0474	5.05	0.0064
1.10	0.3329	3.10	0.0450	5.10	0.0061
1.15	0.3166	3.15	0.0429	5.15	0.0058
1.20	0.3012	3.20	0.0408	5.20	0.0055
1.25	0.2865	3.25	0.0388	5.25	0.0052
1.30	0.2725	3.30	0.0369	5.30	0.0050
1.35	0.2592	3.35	0.0351	5.35	0.0047
1.40	0.2466	3.40	0.0334	5.40	0.0045
1.45	0.2346	3.45	0.0317	5.45	0.0043
1.50	0.2231	3.50	0.0302	5.50	0.0041
1.55	0.2122	3.55	0.0287	5.55	0.0039
1.60	0.2019	3.60	0.0273	5.60	0.0037
1.65	0.1920	3.65	0.0260	5.65	0.0035
1.70	0.1827	3.70	0.0247	5.70	0.0033
1.75	0.1738	3.75	0.0235	5.75	0.0032
1.80	0.1653	3.80	0.0224	5.80	0.0030
1.85	0.1572	3.85	0.0213	5.85	0.0029
1.90	0.1496	3.90	0.0202	5.90	0.0027
1.95	0.1423	3.95	0.0193	5.95	0.0026
2.00	0.1353	4.00	0.0183	6.00	0.0025
				7.00	0.0009
				8.00	0.000335
				9.00	0.000123
				10.00	0.000045

Table 12.2

Poisson Probabilities for the Number of Arrivals at a Burger Dome Restaurant During a 1-Minute Period ($\lambda = 0.75$)

Number of Arrivals	Probability
0	0.4724
1	0.3543
2	0.1329
3	0.0332
4	0.0062
5 or more	0.0010

the order with the food server and continues until the customer has received the order. Service times are rarely constant. At Burger Dome, the number of items ordered and the mix of items ordered vary considerably from one customer to the next. Small orders can be handled in a matter of seconds, while larger orders may require more than 2 minutes to process.

Management scientists have determined that the *exponential probability distribution* often provides a good approximation of service times in waiting line situations. If the probability distribution for the service times follows an exponential probability distribution, the probability that the service time will be less than or equal to a time of length t is given by

$$P(\text{service time} \leq t) = 1 - e^{-\mu t} \tag{12.3}$$

where

$$\mu = \text{the average or mean number of units that can be served per time period}$$

Suppose that Burger Dome has studied the order-taking and order-filling process and has found that the single food server can process an average of 60 customer orders per hour. On a 1-minute basis, the average or mean service rate would be $\mu = 60/60 = 1$ customer per minute. For example, using $\mu = 1$, equation (12.3) can be used to compute probabilities such as the probability an order can be processed in ½ minute or less, 1 minute or less, and 2 minutes or less. These computations are as follows:

$$P(\text{service time} \leq 0.5 \text{ min.}) = 1 - e^{-1(0.5)} = 1 - 0.6065 = 0.3935$$

$$P(\text{service time} \leq 1.0 \text{ min.}) = 1 - e^{-1(1.0)} = 1 - 0.3679 = 0.6321$$

$$P(\text{service time} \leq 2.0 \text{ min.}) = 1 - e^{-1(2.0)} = 1 - 0.1353 = 0.8647$$

A property of the exponential probability distribution is that there is a 0.6321 probability that the random variable takes on a value less than the mean. In waiting line applications, the exponential probability distribution indicates that approximately 63% of the services require less time than the mean service time and approximately 37% of the services require more time.

Thus, we would conclude that there is a 0.3935 probability that an order can be processed in ½ minute (30 seconds) or less, a 0.6321 probability that it can be processed in 1 minute or less, and a 0.8647 probability that it can be processed in 2 minutes or less.

In several of the waiting line models presented in this chapter, we will assume that the probability distribution for the service times follows an exponential probability distribution. In practice, you will want to collect data on actual service times to see if the exponential probability distribution is a reasonable approximation of the service times for your application.

Queue Discipline

In describing a waiting line system, we must define the manner in which the waiting units are arranged for service. For the Burger Dome waiting line, and in general for most customer-oriented waiting lines, the units waiting for service are arranged on a *first-come, first-served* basis; serving in this manner is referred to as an *FCFS* queue discipline. However, some situations call for different queue disciplines. For example, when people wait for an elevator, the last one on the elevator is usually the first one to complete service (i.e., the first to leave the elevator). Other types of queue disciplines assign priorities to the waiting units and then service the unit with the highest priority first. In this chapter we restrict our attention to waiting lines that use a first-come, first-served queue discipline.

Steady-State Operation

When the Burger Dome restaurant opens in the morning, no customers are in the restaurant. Gradually, the business activity builds up to a normal or steady state. The beginning or start-up period is referred to as the *transient period*. The transient period ends when the system reaches the normal or *steady-state* operation. Waiting line models describe the steady-state operating characteristics of the waiting line.

12.2 The Single-Channel Waiting Line Model with Poisson Arrivals and Exponential Service Times

In this section we will present formulas that can be used to determine the steady-state operating characteristics for a single-channel waiting line. The formulas can be used only if the following assumptions regarding the waiting line are applicable:

Waiting line models are often based on assumptions such as Poisson arrivals and exponential service times. When applying any waiting line model, students should collect data on the actual system to ensure that the assumptions of the model are reasonable.

1. The waiting line has a single channel.
2. The pattern of arrivals follows a Poisson probability distribution.
3. The service times follow an exponential probability distribution.
4. The queue discipline is first-come, first-served (FCFS).

Since these assumptions apply to the Burger Dome waiting line problem introduced in Section 12.1, we will show how the formulas can be used to determine Burger Dome's operating characteristics and thus provide management with helpful decision-making information.

The mathematical methodology used to derive the formulas for the operating characteristics of waiting lines is rather complex. However, our purpose in this chapter is not to provide the theoretical development of waiting line models, but rather to show how the formulas that have been developed can provide information about operating characteristics of the waiting line. Readers interested in the mathematical development of the formulas can consult any of the specialized texts listed in the References and Bibliography section at the end of the text.

The Operating Characteristics

The formulas that can be used to develop the steady-state operating characteristics for a single-channel waiting line with Poisson arrivals and exponential service times use the following notation:

$$\lambda = \text{the mean or average number of arrivals per time period}$$
$$\text{(the mean arrival rate)}$$

$$\mu = \text{the mean or average number of services per time period}$$
$$\text{(the mean service rate)}$$

Equations (12.4) through (12.10) show that waiting line models do not provide formulas for optimal conditions. Rather, these equations provide information about the operating characteristics of the system.

1. The probability that there are no units in the system

$$P_0 = 1 - \frac{\lambda}{\mu} \tag{12.4}$$

2. The average number of units in the waiting line

$$L_q = \frac{\lambda^2}{\mu(\mu - \lambda)} \tag{12.5}$$

3. The average number of units in the system

$$L = L_q + \frac{\lambda}{\mu} \qquad (12.6)$$

4. The average time a unit spends in the waiting line

$$W_q = \frac{L_q}{\lambda} \qquad (12.7)$$

5. The average time a unit spends in the system

$$W = W_q + \frac{1}{\mu} \qquad (12.8)$$

6. The probability that an arriving unit has to wait for service

$$P_w = \frac{\lambda}{\mu} \qquad (12.9)$$

7. The probability of n units in the system

$$P_n = \left(\frac{\lambda}{\mu}\right)^n P_0 \qquad (12.10)$$

The values of the *mean arrival rate* λ and the *mean service rate* μ are clearly important components in determining the operating characteristics. From equation (12.9) we see that the ratio of the mean arrival rate to the mean service rate, λ/μ, provides the probability that an arriving unit has to wait because the service facility is busy. Since λ/μ provides the probability the service facility is busy, it is often referred to as the *utilization factor* for the service facility.

The operating characteristics presented in equations (12.4) through (12.10) are applicable only when the mean service rate μ is *greater than* the mean arrival rate λ—in other words, when $\lambda/\mu < 1$. If this condition does not exist, the waiting line will continue to grow without limit since the service facility does not have sufficient capacity to handle the arriving units. Thus, in using equations (12.4) through (12.10), we must have $\mu > \lambda$.

Characteristics for the Burger Dome Problem

Recall that for the Burger Dome problem we had a mean arrival rate of $\lambda = 0.75$ customers per minute and a mean service rate of $\mu = 1$ customer per minute. Thus, since $\mu > \lambda$, equations (12.4) through (12.10) can be used to provide the following operating characteristics for the Burger Dome single-channel waiting line:

$$P_0 = 1 - \frac{\lambda}{\mu} = 1 - \frac{0.75}{1} = 0.25$$

$$L_q = \frac{\lambda^2}{\mu(\mu - \lambda)} = \frac{0.75^2}{1(1 - 0.75)} = 2.25 \text{ customers}$$

$$L = L_q + \frac{\lambda}{\mu} = 2.25 + \frac{0.75}{1} = 3 \text{ customers}$$

$$W_q = \frac{L_q}{\lambda} = \frac{2.25}{0.75} = 3 \text{ minutes}$$

$$W = W_q + \frac{1}{\mu} = 3 + \frac{1}{1} = 4 \text{ minutes}$$

$$P_w = \frac{\lambda}{\mu} = \frac{0.75}{1} = 0.75$$

Problem 5 asks you to compute the operating characteristics for a single-channel waiting line application.

Equation (12.10) can be used to determine the probability of any number of customers in the system, and applying it provides the probability information summarized in Table 12.3.

The Manager's Use of Waiting Line Models

Looking at the results of the single-channel waiting line for Burger Dome, we can learn several important things about the operation of the waiting line. In particular, customers wait an average of 3 minutes before beginning to place an order, and this appears somewhat long for a business based on fast service. In addition, the facts that the average number of customers waiting in line is 2.25 and that 75% of the arriving customers have to wait for service are indicators that something should be done to improve the efficiency of the waiting line operation. Table 12.3 shows that there is a 0.1335 probability that seven or more customers are in the Burger Dome system at one time. This indicates a fairly high probability that Burger Dome will periodically experience some very long waiting lines if it continues to use the single-channel operation.

Waiting line models often indicate where improvements in operating characteristics are desirable. However, the decision of how to modify the waiting line configuration to improve the operating characteristics must be based on the insights and creativity of the analyst.

If the operating characteristics are unsatisfactory in terms of meeting company standards for service, Burger Dome's management should consider alternative designs or plans for improving the waiting line operation.

Improving the Waiting Line Operation

After reviewing the operating characteristics provided by the waiting line model, Burger Dome's management concluded that improvements designed to reduce waiting times are desirable. Improvements in the waiting line operation most often focus on ways to improve the service rate. Generally, service improvements are made along the following lines:

1. Increase the mean service rate μ by making a creative design change or by employing new technology.
2. Add parallel service channels so that more units can be serviced at a time.

Table 12.3

The Probability of n Customers in the System for the Burger Dome Waiting Line Problem

Number of Customers	Probability
0	0.2500
1	0.1875
2	0.1406
3	0.1055
4	0.0791
5	0.0593
6	0.0445
7 or more	0.1335

Assume that in considering alternative 1, Burger Dome's management decides to employ an order filler who will assist the order taker at the cash register. The customer begins the service process by placing the order with the order taker. As the order is placed, the order taker announces the order over an intercom system, and the order filler begins filling the order. When the order is completed, the order taker handles the money, while the order filler continues to fill the order. With this design, Burger Dome's management estimates the mean service rate can be increased from the current service rate of 60 customers per hour to 75 customers per hour. On a per-minute basis, the mean service rate for the revised system is $\mu = 75/60 = 1.25$ customers per minute. Using $\lambda = 0.75$ and $\mu = 1.25$, equations (12.4) through (12.10) provide the operating characteristics summarized in Table 12.4.

As can be seen in Table 12.4, the operating characteristics or performance measures have all improved due to the increased service rate provided by the order filler. In particular, average time in the system has been reduced from 4 to 2 minutes. Are other alternatives possible for increasing the service rate? If other alternatives can be identified,

Table 12.4		
	Probability of no units in the system	0.400
Operating Characteristics for the	Average number of units in the waiting line	0.900
Burger Dome System with the Mean	Average number of units in the system	1.500
Service Rate Increased to $\mu = 1.25$	Average time in the waiting line	1.200 minutes
Customers per Minute	Average time in the system	2.000 minutes
	Probability an arriving unit has to wait	0.600
	Probability 7 or more are in system	0.028

Increasing the mean service rate is one way to improve the operation of a waiting line. Problem 11 asks you to determine whether a change in the mean service rate will meet the company's service guideline for its customers.

and if the mean service rate μ can be identified for these alternatives, equations (12.4) through (12.10) will provide the information needed to assess the amount of improvement from the proposed alternatives. The added cost of any proposed change can be compared with the corresponding service improvements to help the manager determine whether the proposed service improvements are worthwhile.

As mentioned previously, another option that is usually available is to provide one or more additional service channels so that more than one customer may be served at the same time. The extension of the single-channel waiting line model to the multiple-channel waiting line model is the topic of the next section.

NOTES & COMMENTS

1. The assumption that arrivals follow a Poisson probability distribution is equivalent to the assumption that the time between arrivals has an exponential probability distribution. For example, if the arrivals for a waiting line follow a Poisson probability distribution with a mean of 20 arrivals per hour, the time between arrivals will follow an exponential probability distribution, with a mean time between arrivals of $\frac{1}{20}$ or 0.05 hour.

2. Many individuals believe that whenever the mean service rate μ is greater than the mean arrival rate λ, the system should be able to handle or service all arrivals. However, as the Burger Dome example shows, the variability of arrival times and service times may result in long waiting times even when the mean service rate exceeds the mean arrival rate. A contribution of waiting line models is that they can point out undesirable waiting line operating characteristics even when the $\mu > \lambda$ condition appears satisfactory.

12.3 The Multiple-Channel Waiting Line Model with Poisson Arrivals and Exponential Service Times

A *multiple-channel* waiting line consists of two or more channels or service locations that are assumed to be identical in terms of service capability. In the multiple-channel system, arriving units wait in a single waiting line and then move to the first available channel to be served.

The single-channel Burger Dome operation could be expanded to a two-channel system by opening a second cash register and operating a second service channel. A diagram of the Burger Dome two-channel waiting line is shown in Figure 12.2.

Figure 12.2
The Burger Dome Two-Channel
Waiting Line

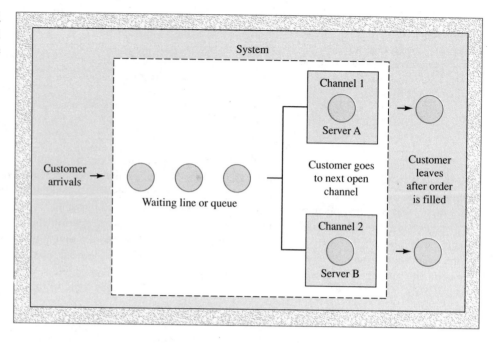

In this section we present formulas that can be used to determine the steady-state operating characteristics for a multiple-channel waiting line. These formulas are applicable if the following assumptions for the waiting line are reasonable:

1. The waiting line has two or more channels.
2. The pattern of arrivals follows a Poisson probability distribution.
3. The service time for each channel follows an exponential probability distribution.
4. The mean service rate μ is the same for each channel.
5. The arrivals wait in a single waiting line and then move to the first open channel for service.
6. The queue discipline is first-come, first-served (FCFS).

Students may be familiar with multiple-channel systems that also have multiple waiting lines. The waiting line model in this section has multiple channels, but only a single waiting line. Operating characteristics for a multiple-channel system are better when a single waiting line, rather than multiple waiting lines, is used.

The Operating Characteristics

The formulas used to compute the steady-state operating characteristics for multiple-channel waiting lines use the following notation:

$$\lambda = \text{the mean arrival rate for the system}$$
$$\mu = \text{the mean service rate for } each \text{ channel}$$
$$k = \text{the number of channels}$$

The ratio λ/μ is a measure of traffic density called an erlang. This measure was named after A. K. Erlang, the Danish pioneer in the study of waiting lines. In general, the number of erlangs indicates the minimum number of servers required to handle arrivals with no loss of customers.

Since μ is the mean service rate for each channel, $k\mu$ is the mean service rate for the multiple-channel system. As was true for the single-channel waiting line model, the formulas for the operating characteristics of multiple-channel waiting lines can be applied only in situations where the mean service rate for the system is greater than the mean arrival rate for the system; in other words, the formulas are applicable only if $k\mu$ is greater than λ.

1. The probability that there are no units in the system

$$P_0 = \frac{1}{\sum_{n=0}^{k-1} \dfrac{(\lambda/\mu)^n}{n!} + \dfrac{(\lambda/\mu)^k}{k!}\left(\dfrac{k\mu}{k\mu-\lambda}\right)} \qquad (12.11)$$

2. The average number of units in the waiting line

$$L_q = \frac{(\lambda/\mu)^k \lambda\mu}{(k-1)!(k\mu-\lambda)^2} P_0 \qquad (12.12)$$

3. The average number of units in the system

$$L = L_q + \frac{\lambda}{\mu} \qquad (12.13)$$

4. The average time a unit spends in the waiting line

$$W_q = \frac{L_q}{\lambda} \qquad (12.14)$$

5. The average time a unit spends in the system

$$W = W_q + \frac{1}{\mu} \qquad (12.15)$$

6. The probability that an arriving unit has to wait

$$P_w = \frac{1}{k!}\left(\frac{\lambda}{\mu}\right)^k \left(\frac{k\mu}{k\mu-\lambda}\right) P_0 \qquad (12.16)$$

7. The probability of n units in the system

$$P_n = \frac{(\lambda/\mu)^n}{n!} P_0 \quad \text{for } n \le k \qquad (12.17)$$

$$P_n = \frac{(\lambda/\mu)^n}{k! k^{(n-k)}} P_0 \quad \text{for } n > k \qquad (12.18)$$

While some of the above expressions for the operating characteristics of multiple-channel waiting lines are more complex than their single-channel counterparts, the expressions provide the same information. This information is used by managers in the same way as that for the single-channel model. To help simplify the use of the multiple-channel equations, we have provided Table 12.5, which contains values of P_0 for selected values of λ/μ and k. The values provided in the table correspond to cases where $k\mu > \lambda$, and hence the service rate is sufficient to process all arrivals.

Operating Characteristics for the Burger Dome Problem

As an illustration of the multiple-channel waiting line model, let us return to the Burger Dome fast-food restaurant waiting line problem. Suppose management wishes to evaluate the desirability of opening a second cash register and order-processing station so that two customers can be served simultaneously. Assume there will be a single waiting line with the next customer in line moving to the first available server. If this were done, Burger

Table 12.5

Values of P_0 for Multiple-Channel Waiting Lines with Poisson Arrivals and Exponential Service Times

Ratio λ/μ	Number of Channels (k)			
	2	3	4	5
0.15	0.8605	0.8607	0.8607	0.8607
0.20	0.8182	0.8187	0.8187	0.8187
0.25	0.7778	0.7788	0.7788	0.7788
0.30	0.7391	0.7407	0.7408	0.7408
0.35	0.7021	0.7046	0.7047	0.7047
0.40	0.6667	0.6701	0.6703	0.6703
0.45	0.6327	0.6373	0.6376	0.6376
0.50	0.6000	0.6061	0.6065	0.6065
0.55	0.5686	0.5763	0.5769	0.5769
0.60	0.5385	0.5479	0.5487	0.5488
0.65	0.5094	0.5209	0.5219	0.5220
0.70	0.4815	0.4952	0.4965	0.4966
0.75	0.4545	0.4706	0.4722	0.4724
0.80	0.4286	0.4472	0.4491	0.4493
0.85	0.4035	0.4248	0.4271	0.4274
0.90	0.3793	0.4035	0.4062	0.4065
0.95	0.3559	0.3831	0.3863	0.3867
1.00	0.3333	0.3636	0.3673	0.3678
1.20	0.2500	0.2941	0.3002	0.3011
1.40	0.1765	0.2360	0.2449	0.2463
1.60	0.1111	0.1872	0.1993	0.2014
1.80	0.0526	0.1460	0.1616	0.1646
2.00		0.1111	0.1304	0.1343
2.20		0.0815	0.1046	0.1094
2.40		0.0562	0.0831	0.0889
2.60		0.0345	0.0651	0.0721
2.80		0.0160	0.0521	0.0581
3.00			0.0377	0.0466
3.20			0.0273	0.0372
3.40			0.0186	0.0293
3.60			0.0113	0.0228
3.80			0.0051	0.0174
4.00				0.0130
4.20				0.0093
4.40				0.0063
4.60				0.0038
4.80				0.0017

Dome would have a two-channel waiting line. Let us evaluate the operating characteristics for this two-channel system.

We will use equations (12.11) through (12.18) for the $k = 2$ channel system. Given a mean arrival rate of $\lambda = 0.75$ customers per minute and mean service rate of $\mu = 1$ customer per minute for each channel, we have the following operating characteristics:

$$P_0 = 0.4545 \text{ (from Table 12.5 with } \lambda/\mu = 0.75)$$

$$L_q = \frac{(0.75/1)^2(0.75)(1)}{(2-1)![2(1) - 0.75]^2}(0.4545) = 0.1227 \text{ customer}$$

$$L = L_q + \frac{\lambda}{\mu} = 0.1227 + \frac{0.75}{1} = 0.8727 \text{ customer}$$

$$W_q = \frac{L_q}{\lambda} = \frac{0.1227}{0.75} = 0.16 \text{ minute}$$

$$W = W_q + \frac{1}{\mu} = 0.16 + \frac{1}{1} = 1.16 \text{ minutes}$$

$$P_w = \frac{1}{2!}\left(\frac{0.75}{1}\right)^2\left[\frac{2(1)}{2(1) - 0.75}\right](0.4545) = 0.2045$$

Try Problem 19, which will give you practice in determining the operating characteristics for a two-channel waiting line.

By using equations (12.17) and (12.18), the probabilities of n customers in the system can be computed. The results from these computations are summarized in Table 12.6.

We can now compare the steady-state operating characteristics of the two-channel service operation to the operating characteristics of the original single-channel system discussed in Section 12.2.

1. The average time required between when a customer enters the waiting line and when the customer receives the order (waiting time plus service time) is reduced from $W = 4$ minutes to $W = 1.16$ minutes.
2. The average length of the waiting line is reduced from $L_q = 2.25$ customers to $L_q = 0.1227$ customers.
3. The average time a customer waits for service to begin is reduced from $W_q = 3$ minutes to $W_q = 0.16$ minute.
4. The percentage of customers having to wait for service is reduced from $P_w = 0.75$ or 75% to $P_w = 0.2045$ or 20.45%.

It is clear that the two-channel system will greatly improve the operating characteristics of the waiting line. However, as we saw in the single-channel system, adding a separate order filler at each service station would increase the mean service rate and also improve the operating characteristics. The final decision regarding the staffing policy at Burger Dome rests with the Burger Dome management. The waiting line study has simply provided the operating characteristics that can be anticipated under three configurations: a single-channel system with one employee, a single-channel system with two employees, and a two-channel system with an employee for each channel. After considering these results, what action would you recommend? In this case, Burger Dome adopted the following policy statement: For periods when customer arrivals are expected to average 45 customers per hour, Burger Dome will open two cash-register, order-processing stations, with one employee assigned to each station.

Table 12.6

The Probability of n Customers in the System for the Burger Dome Two-Channel Waiting Line

Number of Customers	Probability
0	0.4545
1	0.3409
2	0.1278
3	0.0479
4	0.0180
5 or more	0.0109

N O T E S & C O M M E N T S

The multiple-channel waiting line model assumes a single waiting line. You may have also encountered situations where each of the k channels has its own waiting line. Management scientists have shown that the operating characteristics of multiple-channel systems are better if a single waiting line is used. People like them better also; no one who comes in after you can be served ahead of you. Thus, in practice, banks, airline reservation counters, food-service establishments, and other businesses typically use a single waiting line for a multiple-channel system.

By changing the mean arrival rate λ to reflect arrival rates at different times of the day, and then computing the operating characteristics, Burger Dome's management can establish guidelines and policies that tell the store managers when they should schedule service operations with a single channel, two channels, or perhaps even three or more channels.

12.4 Some General Relationships for Waiting Line Models

In Sections 12.2 and 12.3 we presented formulas for computing the operating characteristics for single-channel and multiple-channel waiting lines with Poisson arrivals and exponential service times. The operating characteristics of interest included

L_q = the average number of units in the waiting line
L = the average number of units in the system
W_q = the average time a unit spends in the waiting line
W = the average time a unit spends in the system

John D. C. Little showed that general relationships existing among these four characteristics apply to a variety of different waiting line systems. Two of the relationships, referred to as *Little's flow equations,* are as follows:

$$L = \lambda W \tag{12.19}$$

$$L_q = \lambda W_q \tag{12.20}$$

Equation (12.19) shows that the average number of units in the system, L, can be found by multiplying the mean arrival rate λ by the average time a unit spends in the system, W. Equation (12.20) shows that the same relationship holds between the average number of units in the waiting line, L_q, and the average time a unit spends in the waiting line, W_q.

Using equation (12.20) and solving for W_q, we obtain

$$W_q = \frac{L_q}{\lambda} \tag{12.21}$$

This equation, which follows directly from Little's second flow equation, was used for the single-channel waiting line model in Section 12.2 and the multiple-channel waiting line model in Section 12.3 (see equations (12.7) and (12.14)). Once L_q is computed for either of these models, equation (12.21) can then be used to compute W_q.

Another general expression that applies to waiting line models is that the average time in the system, W, is equal to the average time in the waiting line, W_q, plus the average service time. For a system with a mean service rate μ, the average or mean service time is $1/\mu$. Thus, we have the following general relationship:

$$W = W_q + \frac{1}{\mu} \tag{12.22}$$

Recall that this equation was used to provide the average time in the system for both the single- and multiple-channel waiting line models (see equations (12.8) and (12.15)).

The importance of Little's flow equations is that they apply to *any waiting line model* regardless of whether arrivals follow the Poisson probability distribution and regardless of whether service times follow the exponential probability distribution. For example, in a study of the grocery checkout counters at Murphy's Foodliner, an analyst concluded that

The advantage of Little's flow equations is that they show how operating characteristics L, L_q, W, and W_q are related in any waiting line system. Arrivals and service times do not have to follow specific probability distributions for the flow equations to be applicable.

arrivals follow the Poisson probability distribution with the mean arrival rate of 24 customers per hour or $\lambda = 24/60 = 0.40$ customers per minute. However, the analyst found that service times follow a normal probability distribution rather than an exponential probability distribution. The mean service rate was found to be 30 customers per hour or $\mu = 30/60 = 0.50$ customers per minute. A time study of actual customer waiting times showed that, on average, a customer spends 4.5 minutes in the system (waiting time plus checkout time); that is, $W = 4.5$. Using the waiting line relationships discussed in this section, we can now compute other operating characteristics for this waiting line.

First, using equation (12.22) and solving for W_q, we have

$$W_q = W - \frac{1}{\mu} = 4.5 - \frac{1}{0.50} = 2.5 \text{ minutes}$$

With both W and W_q known, we can use Little's flow equations, (12.19) and (12.20), to compute

$$L = \lambda W = 0.40(4.5) = 1.8 \text{ customers}$$

$$L_q = \lambda W_q = 0.40(2.5) = 1 \text{ customer}$$

The application of Little's flow equations are demonstrated in Problem 25.

The manager of Murphy's Foodliner can now review these operating characteristics to see if action should be taken to improve the service and to reduce the waiting time and the length of the waiting line.

NOTES & COMMENTS

1. The advantage of the general relationships presented in this section is that W, L, W_q, and L_q can be determined for any waiting line regardless of the arrival distribution, service time distribution, and number of channels. In fact, as soon as *any one* of the four operating characteristics—W, L, W_q, and L_q—has been determined, the other three can be computed. Thus, management scientists first compute the operating characteristic that is easiest to estimate. Given the value of this operating characteristic and the basic relationships presented in this section, the other operating characteristics can be easily determined.

2. In waiting line systems where the length of the waiting line is limited (e.g., a small waiting area), some of the arriving units will be blocked from joining the waiting line and will be lost. In this case, the blocked or lost arrivals will make the arrival rate in terms of units entering the system something less than the overall mean arrival rate. By defining λ as the mean arrival rate for units *joining the system*, rather than the overall mean arrival rate, the relationships used in this section can be used to determine W, L, W_q, and L_q.

12.5 Economic Analysis of Waiting Lines

Frequently, the decisions involving the design of waiting lines, such as determining the number of channels, will be based on a subjective evaluation of the waiting line characteristics. For example, a manager may decide that an average waiting time of

1 minute or less and an average of two customers or less in the system are reasonable goals. The waiting line models presented in the preceding sections can be used to determine the number of channels that will meet the manager's waiting line performance goals.

In other instances, it may be desirable to identify the cost of operating the waiting line system and then base the decisions regarding system design on a minimum hourly or daily operating cost. In order to conduct an economic analysis of a waiting line, a total-cost model, which includes the cost of waiting and the cost of service, must be developed.

To develop a total-cost model for a waiting line, we begin by defining the following notation:

Generally, c_s is easier to estimate than c_w. This is due to the fact the cost of customer waiting, c_w, is more subjective in that it often includes the cost of lost goodwill due to customer waiting time. This is analogous to the difficulty in estimating backordering costs for an inventory model with planned shortages.

c_w = the waiting cost per time period for each unit
L = the average number of units in the system
c_s = the service cost per time period for each channel
k = the number of channels
TC = the total cost per time period

The total cost is the sum of the waiting cost and the service cost; that is,

$$TC = c_w L + c_s k \qquad (12.23)$$

A critical issue in conducting an economic analysis of a waiting line is to obtain reasonable estimates of the waiting cost and service cost per period. Of these two costs, the waiting cost per period is usually the more difficult to evaluate. In the Burger Dome restaurant problem, the waiting cost per period would be the cost per minute for a customer waiting for service. This cost is not a direct cost to Burger Dome. However, if Burger Dome ignores this cost and allows long waiting lines, customers will ultimately take their business elsewhere. Thus, Burger Dome will experience lost sales and, in effect, incur a cost.

The service cost per period is generally easier to determine. This cost is the relevant cost associated with operating each service channel. In the Burger Dome problem, this cost would include the server's wages, benefits, and any other direct costs associated with operating the service channel. At Burger Dome, this cost is estimated to be $7 per hour.

Adding more channels always improves the operating characteristics of the waiting line and reduces the waiting cost. However, more channels increase the service cost. An economic analysis of waiting lines attempts to find the number of channels that will minimize total cost by balancing the waiting cost and the service cost.

In order to demonstrate equation (12.23), let us assume that Burger Dome is willing to assign a cost of $10 per hour for customer waiting time. Using the average number of units in the system, L, as computed in Sections 12.2 and 12.3, the total hourly cost for the single-channel and two-channel systems would be as follows:

Single-channel system ($L = 3$ customers):

$$TC = c_w L + c_s k$$

$$TC = \$10(3) + \$7(1) = \$37.00 \text{ per hour}$$

Two-channel system ($L = 0.8727$ customers):

$$TC = c_w L + c_s k$$

$$= \$10(0.8727) + \$7(2) = \$22.73 \text{ per hour}$$

Working Problem 21 will give you the chance to test your ability to conduct an economic analysis of proposed single-channel and two-channel waiting line systems.

Thus, given the cost data provided by Burger Dome, the two-channel system provides the most economical operation.

The general shapes of the cost curves in the economic analysis of waiting lines are shown in Figure 12.3. The service cost increases as the number of channels is increased.

Figure 12.3
The General Shape of Waiting
Cost, Service Cost, and Total-Cost
Curves in Waiting Line Models

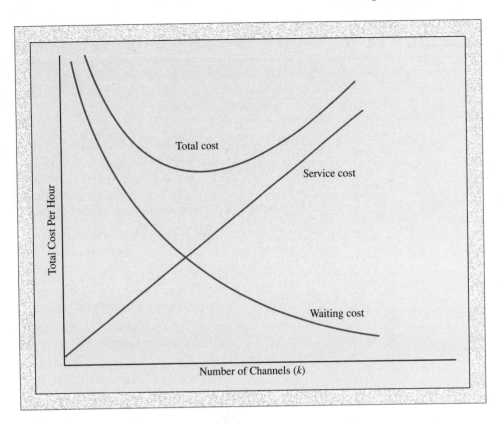

However, with more channels, the service is better. As a result, the waiting time, as well as the waiting cost, decreases as the number of channels is increased. The number of channels that will provide a good approximation of the minimum total-cost design can be found by evaluating the total cost for several design alternatives.

NOTES & COMMENTS

1. In dealing with many government agencies and utility companies, customers cannot take their business elsewhere. In these situations, no lost business occurs when long waiting times are encountered. This is one of the reasons why service in such organizations may be poor and why customers in such situations experience long waiting times.

2. In some instances, the organization providing the service also employs the units waiting for the service. For example, consider the case of a company that owns and operates the trucks used to deliver goods to and from its manufacturing plant. In addition to the costs associated with the trucks waiting to be loaded or unloaded, the firm also pays the wages of the truck loaders and unloaders who operate the service channel. In this case, the cost of having the trucks wait and the cost of operating the service channel are direct expenses to the firm. An economic analysis of the waiting line system is highly recommended for these types of situations.

12.6 Other Waiting Line Models

D. G. Kendall suggested a notation that is helpful in classifying the wide variety of different waiting line models that have been developed. The three-symbol Kendall notation is as follows:

$$A/B/s$$

where

    A denotes the probability distribution for the number of arrivals
    B denotes the probability distribution for the service time
    s denotes the number of channels

Depending on the value of the letter appearing in the *A* or *B* position, a wide variety of waiting line systems can be simply described. The values for *A* and *B* that are commonly used are as follows:

    M designates a Poisson probability distribution for the number of arrivals or an exponential probability distribution for service time

    D designates that the number of arrivals or service time is deterministic or constant

    G designates a general distribution with a known mean and variance for the number of arrivals or service time

Using the Kendall notation, the single-channel waiting line model with Poisson arrivals and exponential service times is classified as an *M/M/*1 model. The 2-channel waiting line model with Poisson arrivals and exponential service times, which we presented in Section 12.3, would be classified as an *M/M/*2 model.

NOTES & COMMENTS

In some cases, the Kendall notation is extended to five symbols. The fourth symbol indicates the largest number of units that can be in the system, and the fifth symbol indicates the size of the input or calling population. The fourth symbol is used in situations where the waiting line can hold a finite or maximum number of units, and the fifth symbol is necessary when the population of arriving units or customers is finite. When the fourth and fifth symbols of the Kendall notation are omitted, the waiting line system is assumed to have infinite capacity, and the calling population is assumed to be infinite.

12.7 The Single-Channel Waiting Line Model with Poisson Arrivals and Arbitrary Service Times

Let us return to the single-channel waiting line model where arrivals are described by a Poisson probability distribution. However, let us now assume that the probability distribution for the service times is not necessarily an exponential probability distribution. Thus, using the Kendall notation, the waiting line model that is appropriate is an *M/G/*1 model, where G denotes a general or unspecified probability distribution. Let us show how operating characteristics can be developed for the $M/G/1$ waiting line model.

Operating Characteristics for the M/G/1 Model

When providing input to the $M/G/1$ model, students should be consistent in terms of the time period. For example, if λ and μ are expressed in terms of the number of units per *hour*, the standard deviation of the service time should be expressed in *hours*. The example that follows uses minutes as the time period for the arrival and service data.

The following notation is used to describe the operating characteristics for the $M/G/1$ model:

$$\lambda = \text{the average or mean arrival rate}$$
$$\mu = \text{the average or mean service rate}$$
$$\frac{1}{\mu} = \text{the average or mean service time}$$
$$\sigma = \text{the standard deviation of the service time}$$

Using this notation, some of the steady-state operating characteristics of the $M/G/1$ waiting line model are as follows:

1. The probability that there are no units in the system

$$P_0 = 1 - \frac{\lambda}{\mu} \tag{12.24}$$

2. The average number of units in the waiting line

$$L_q = \frac{\lambda^2 \sigma^2 + (\lambda/\mu)^2}{2(1 - \lambda/\mu)} \tag{12.25}$$

3. The average number of units in the system

$$L = L_q + \frac{\lambda}{\mu} \tag{12.26}$$

4. The average time a unit spends in the waiting line

$$W_q = \frac{L_q}{\lambda} \tag{12.27}$$

5. The average time a unit spends in the system

$$W = W_q + \frac{1}{\mu} \tag{12.28}$$

6. The probability that an arriving unit has to wait

$$P_w = \frac{\lambda}{\mu} \tag{12.29}$$

Note that the relationships for L, W_q, and W are the same as the relationships used for the waiting line models in Sections 12.2 and 12.3. They are also based on Little's flow equations.

An Example. Retail sales at Hartlage's Seafood Supply are handled by one clerk. Customer arrivals are random, and the average arrival rate is 21 customers per hour or $\lambda = 21/60 = 0.35$ customers per minute. A study of the service process shows that the average or mean service time is 2 minutes per customer, with a standard deviation of $\sigma = 1.2$ minutes. The mean time of 2 minutes per customer shows that the clerk has a mean service rate of $\mu = \frac{1}{2} = 0.50$ customers per minute. The following calculations provide the operating characteristics of this M/G/1 waiting line system:

$$P_0 = 1 - \frac{\lambda}{\mu} = 1 - \frac{0.35}{0.50} = 0.30$$

$$L_q = \frac{(0.35)^2(1.2)^2 + (0.35/0.50)^2}{2(1 - 0.35/0.50)} = 1.11 \text{ customers}$$

$$L = L_q + \frac{\lambda}{\mu} = 1.11 + \frac{0.35}{0.50} = 1.81 \text{ customers}$$

$$W_q = \frac{L_q}{\lambda} = \frac{1.1107}{0.35} = 3.17 \text{ minutes}$$

$$W = W_q + \frac{1}{\mu} = 3.17 + \frac{1}{0.50} = 5.17 \text{ minutes}$$

$$P_w = \frac{\lambda}{\mu} = \frac{0.35}{0.50} = 0.70$$

Problem 27 provides another application of a single-channel waiting line with Poisson arrivals and arbitrary service times.

Hartlage's manager can review these operating characteristics to determine if scheduling a second clerk appears worthwhile.

Constant Service Times

Let us comment briefly on the single-channel waiting line model that assumes arrivals are random, but service times are constant. Such a waiting line can occur in production and manufacturing environments where machine-controlled service times are constant. This waiting line is described by the $M/D/1$ model, with the D referring to the deterministic service times. With the $M/D/1$ model, the average number of units in the waiting line, L_q, can be found by using equation (12.25) with the condition that the standard deviation of the constant service time is $\sigma = 0$. Thus, the expression for the average number of units in the waiting line for the $M/D/1$ waiting line becomes

$$L_q = \frac{(\lambda/\mu)^2}{2(1 - \lambda/\mu)} \tag{12.30}$$

The other expressions presented earlier in this section can be used to determine additional operating characteristics of the $M/D/1$ system.

NOTES & COMMENTS

Whenever the operating characteristics of a waiting line are unacceptable, managers often try to improve service by increasing the mean service rate μ. While this is a good idea, equation (12.25) shows that the variation in the service times also affects the operating characteristics of the waiting line. Since the standard deviation of service times, σ, appears in the numerator of equation (12.25), we see that a larger variation in service times results in a larger average number of units in the waiting line. This fact suggests that another alternative for improving the service capabilities of a waiting line is to reduce the variation in the service times. Thus, even when the mean service rate of the service facility cannot be increased, a reduction in σ will reduce the average number of units in the waiting line and, in general, improve the other operating characteristics of the system.

12.8 A Multiple-Channel Model with Poisson Arrivals, Arbitrary Service Times, and No Waiting Line

An interesting variation of the waiting line models discussed thus far involves a system in which no waiting is allowed. Arriving units or customers seek service from one of several service channels. If all the channels are busy, any units that arrive are denied access to the system. In waiting line terminology, the arrivals occurring when the system is full are *blocked* and cleared from the system. Such customers may be lost or may attempt a return to the system at a later point in time.

The specific model considered in this section is based on the following assumptions:

1. The system has k channels.
2. The pattern of arrivals follows a Poisson probability distribution, with mean arrival rate λ.
3. The service times for each channel may have any probability distribution.
4. The mean service rate μ is the same for each channel.
5. The arrivals enter the system only if at least one of the k channels is available. Arrivals occurring when all channels are busy are blocked—that is, denied service and not allowed to enter the system.

With G denoting a general or unspecified probability distribution for service times, the appropriate model for this situation is referred to as an *M/G/k* model with "blocked customers cleared." The question addressed in this type of situation is, How many channels or servers should be employed?

One of the primary applications of this model involves the design of telephone and other communication systems where the arrivals are the calls and the channels are the number of telephone or communication lines available. In this system, the calls are made to one telephone number, with each call automatically switched to an open channel if possible. When all channels are busy, additional calls receive a busy signal and are denied access to the system.

The Operating Characteristics for the M/G/k Model with Blocked Customers Cleared

The problem of selecting the best number of channels is approached by computing the steady-state probabilities that exactly j of the k channels will be busy. These probabilities are computed as follows:

$$P_j = \frac{(\lambda/\mu)^j/j!}{\sum_{i=0}^{k} (\lambda/\mu)^i/i!} \tag{12.31}$$

where

$$\begin{aligned}
\lambda &= \text{the mean arrival rate} \\
\mu &= \text{the mean service rate of each channel} \\
k &= \text{the number of channels in the system} \\
P_j &= \text{the probability that exactly } j \text{ of the } k \text{ channels are busy} \\
&\quad \text{for } j = 0, 1, 2, \ldots, k
\end{aligned}$$

With no waiting allowed, operating characteristics L_q and W_q considered in previous waiting line models are automatically zero regardless of the number of service channels. In this situation, the more important design consideration becomes how the percentage of blocked or lost customers is affected by the number of service channels.

The most important probability value is P_k, which is the probability that all k channels are busy. On a percentage basis, P_k indicates the percentage of arrivals that are blocked and denied access to the system.

Another operating characteristic of interest is the average number of units in the system; note that this is equivalent to the average number of channels in use. Letting L denote the average number of units in the system, we have

$$L = \frac{\lambda}{\mu}(1 - P_k) \qquad (12.32)$$

An Example. Microdata Software, Inc., uses a telephone ordering system for its computer software products. Callers place orders with Microdata by using the company's 800 telephone number. Assume that calls to this telephone number arrive at an average rate of 12 per hour. The time required to process a telephone order varies considerably from order to order. However, each Microdata sales representative can be expected to handle an average of six calls per hour. Currently, the Microdata 800 telephone number has three internal lines or channels, each operated by a separate sales representative. Calls received on the 800 number are automatically transferred to one of the open lines or channels if available.

Whenever all three lines are busy, callers receive a busy signal. In the past, Microdata has assumed that callers receiving a busy signal will call back later. However, recent research on telephone ordering has shown that a substantial portion of callers who are denied access do not call back later. Since these lost calls represent lost revenues for the firm, Microdata's management has requested an analysis of the telephone ordering system. Specifically, management would like to know the percentage of callers who are experiencing busy signals and are being blocked from the system. If management's goal is to provide sufficient capacity to handle 90% of the callers, how many telephone lines and sales representatives should Microdata use?

Let us demonstrate the use of equation (12.31) by computing P_3, the probability that all three of the currently available telephone lines will be in use and additional callers will be blocked.

$$P_3 = \frac{(^{12}\!/_6)^3/6}{(^{12}\!/_6)^0/1 + (^{12}\!/_6)^1/1 + (^{12}\!/_6)^2/2 + (^{12}\!/_6)^3/6} = \frac{1.3333}{6.3333} = 0.2105$$

With $P_3 = 0.2105$, we see that approximately 21% of the calls, or slightly more than one in five calls, are being blocked. Only 79% of the calls are being handled immediately by the three-telephone-line system.

Let us assume Microdata expands to a four-channel system. The following calculation shows the probability that all four channels will be in use and that callers will be blocked.

$$P_4 = \frac{(^{12}\!/_6)^4/24}{(^{12}\!/_6)^0/1 + (^{12}\!/_6)^1/1 + (^{12}\!/_6)^2/2 + (^{12}\!/_6)^3/6 + (^{12}\!/_6)^4/24} = \frac{0.6667}{7} = 0.0952$$

With only 9.52% of the callers blocked, 90.48% of the callers will reach the Microdata sales representatives. Thus, Microdata should expand its order-processing operation to four lines to meet management's goal of providing sufficient capacity to handle at least 90% of the callers. The following calculation shows the average number of calls in the four-channel system and thus the average number of lines and sales representatives that will be busy:

$$L = \lambda/\mu(1 - P_4) = {}^{12}\!/_6(1 - 0.0952) = 1.81$$

Table 12.7

Probabilities of Busy Lines for the Microdata 4-Line System

Number of Busy Lines	Probability
0	0.1429
1	0.2857
2	0.2857
3	0.1905
4	0.0952

Try Problem 30 to obtain practice in multiple-channel systems with no waiting line.

Although an average of less than 2 lines will be busy, the 4-line system is necessary to provide the capacity to handle at least 90% of the callers. By using equation (12.31), the probability that exactly j of the four channels will be busy can be computed. These probabilities are summarized in Table 12.7.

As we discussed in Section 12.5, an economic analysis of waiting lines can be used to guide the system design decisions. In the Microdata system, the cost of the additional line and additional sales representative should be relatively easy to establish. This cost can be balanced against the cost of the blocked calls. With 9.52% of the calls blocked and $\lambda = 12$ calls per hour, an 8-hour day will have an average of $8(12)(0.0952) = 9.1$ blocked calls. If Microdata can estimate the cost of possible lost sales, the cost of these blocked calls can be established. The economic analysis based on the service cost and the blocked-call cost can assist in determining the best number of lines for the system.

NOTES & COMMENTS

Many of the operating characteristics we have considered in previous sections are not applicable for the $M/G/k$ model with blocked customers cleared. In particular, the average time in the waiting line, W_q, and the average number of units in the waiting line, L_q, are no longer considered because waiting is not permitted in this type of system.

12.9 Waiting Line Models with Finite Calling Populations

In previous waiting line models, the arrival rate λ was constant and independent of the number of units in the system. With a finite calling population, the arrival rate decreases as the number of units in the system increases because, with more units in the system, there are fewer units in the population that can arrive for service.

For the waiting line models we have introduced thus far, the population of units or customers arriving for service has been considered to be unlimited. In technical terms, when there is no limit placed on how many units may seek service, the model is said to have an *infinite calling population*. Under this assumption, the mean arrival rate λ remains constant regardless of how many units are in the waiting line system. This assumption of an infinite calling population is made in most waiting line models.

In other cases, the maximum number of units or customers that may seek service is fixed at a finite value. In this situation, the mean arrival rate for the system changes depending on the number of units in the waiting line. Whenever a finite population is assumed, the waiting line model is said to have a *finite calling population*. The formulas for the operating characteristics of the previous waiting line models must be modified to account for the effect of the finite calling population.

The finite calling population model discussed in this section is based on the following assumptions:

1. The waiting line has a single channel.
2. The population of units that may seek service is finite.
3. The pattern of arrivals for *each unit* follows a Poisson probability distribution, with mean arrival rate λ.
4. The service times follow an exponential probability distribution, with mean service rate μ.
5. The queue discipline is first-come, first-served (FCFS).

The waiting line model that is appropriate in such cases is referred to as an *M/M/*1 model with a finite calling population.

Note that the mean arrival rate for the *M/M/*1 model with a finite calling population is defined in terms of how often *each unit* arrives or seeks service. This differs from previous waiting line models, which used λ to denote the mean arrival rate for the system. The difference in the definition of λ is due to the fact that with a finite calling population, the mean arrival rate for the system varies depending on how many units are in the system. Instead of trying to adjust for the changing system arrival rate, the finite calling population model uses λ to indicate the mean arrival on an individual unit basis. Each unit will be assumed to have the same arrival rate.

> The mean arrival rate λ is defined differently for the finite calling population model. Specifically, λ is defined in terms of the mean arrival rate for *each unit*.

The Operating Characteristics for the M/M/1 Model with a Finite Calling Population

The formulas used to determine the steady-state operating characteristics for an *M/M/*1 model with a finite calling population use the following notation:

$$\lambda = \text{the mean arrival rate for each unit}$$
$$\mu = \text{the mean service rate}$$
$$N = \text{the size of the population}$$

1. The probability that there are no units in the system

$$P_0 = \frac{1}{\displaystyle\sum_{n=0}^{N} \frac{N!}{(N-n)!} \left(\frac{\lambda}{\mu}\right)^n} \tag{12.33}$$

2. The average number of units in the waiting line

$$L_q = N - \frac{\lambda + \mu}{\lambda}(1 - P_0) \tag{12.34}$$

3. The average number of units in the system

$$L = L_q + (1 - P_0) \tag{12.35}$$

4. The average waiting time in the waiting line

$$W_q = \frac{L_q}{(N - L)\lambda} \tag{12.36}$$

5. The average waiting time in the system

$$W = W_q + \frac{1}{\mu} \tag{12.37}$$

6. The probability of *n* units in the system

$$P_n = \frac{N!}{(N - n)!}\left(\frac{\lambda}{\mu}\right)^n P_0 \quad \text{for } n = 0, 1, \ldots, N \tag{12.38}$$

One of the primary applications of the *M/M/*1 model with a finite calling population is referred to as the machine repair problem. In this problem, a group of machines is considered the finite population of "customers" that may request repair service.

Whenever a machine breaks down, an arrival occurs in the sense that a new repair request is initiated. If another machine breaks down before the repair work has been completed on the first machine, the second machine begins to form a "waiting line" as it waits for the repair service. Additional breakdowns by other machines will add to the length of the waiting line. The assumption of first-come, first-served indicates that machines are repaired in the order they break down. The M/M/1 model shows that one person or one channel is available to perform the repair service. To return the machine to operation, each machine with a breakdown must be handled by the single-channel repair operation.

An Example. The Kolkmeyer Manufacturing Company has a group of six identical machines; each machine operates an average of 20 hours between breakdowns. Thus, the mean arrival rate or request for repair service for each individual machine is $\lambda = 1/20 = 0.05$ machine per hour. With randomly occurring breakdowns, the Poisson probability distribution is used to describe the machine breakdown arrival process. One person from the maintenance department provides the single-channel repair service for the six machines. The exponentially distributed service times have a mean of 2 hours per machine or a mean service rate of $\mu = 1/2 = 0.50$ machines per hour.

With $\lambda = 0.05$ and $\mu = 0.50$, let us use equations (12.33) through (12.37) to compute the operating characteristics for this system. In using equation (12.33), note that the computations involved are somewhat cumbersome. Check for yourself to confirm that equation (12.30) provides the value $P_0 = 0.4845$. The computations for the other operating characteristics are shown below.

$$L_q = 6 - \left(\frac{0.05 + 0.50}{0.05}\right)(1 - 0.4845)$$

$$= 0.3295 \text{ machines}$$

$$L = 0.3295 + (1 - 0.4845)$$

$$= 0.845 \text{ machines}$$

$$W_q = \frac{0.3295}{(6 - 0.845)0.05}$$

$$= 1.28 \text{ hours}$$

$$W = 1.28 + \frac{1}{0.50}$$

$$= 3.28 \text{ hours}$$

Operating characteristics of an M/M/1 waiting line with a finite calling population are considered in Problem 34.

Formulas for the operating characteristics of the single-channel waiting line with a finite calling population of size N are relatively easy to use. However, the complexity of the multiple-channel model makes a computer solution essential.

Finally, equation (12.38) can be used to compute the probabilities of any number of machines being in the repair system.

As with other waiting line models, the operating characteristics provide the manager with information about the waiting line operation. Whether or not these operating characteristics suggest that better repair service is needed depends on the cost of the idle machine waiting time compared to the cost of assigning an additional person to make the repair operation either a two-channel system or a faster one-channel system.

Computations for the multiple-channel finite calling population model are more complex than those for the single-channel model. A computer solution is virtually mandatory in this case. The Management Scientist software package that accompanies this text has the capability of analyzing the finite calling population model. The computer output for the Kolkmeyer machine repair problem with a two-person, two-channel, repair system is shown in Figure 12.4.

Figure 12.4
The
Management
Scientist
Printout for the
Kolkmeyer
Two-Channel
Machine Repair
Problem

```
WAITING LINE MODELS
* * * * * * * * * * * * * * * * * * *
     NUMBER OF CHANNELS = 2
     POISSON ARRIVALS WITH MEAN RATE = .05
     EXPONENTIAL SERVICE TIMES WITH MEAN RATE = .5 PER CHANNEL
     FINITE CALLING POPULATION OF SIZE = 6

OPERATING CHARACTERISTICS
---------------------------
THE PROBABILITY OF NO UNITS IN THE SYSTEM              0.5602
THE AVERAGE NUMBER OF UNITS IN THE WAITING LINE        0.0227
THE AVERAGE NUMBER OF UNITS IN THE SYSTEM              0.5661
THE AVERAGE TIME A UNIT SPENDS IN THE WAITING LINE     0.0834
THE AVERAGE TIME A UNIT SPENDS IN THE SYSTEM           2.0834
THE PROBABILITY THAT AN ARRIVING UNIT HAS TO WAIT      0.1036


Number of Units in the System          Probability
------------------------------         -----------
              0                           0.5602
              1                           0.3361
              2                           0.0840
              3                           0.0168
              4                           0.0025
              5                           0.0003
              6                           0.0000
```

Summary

In this chapter we have presented a variety of waiting line models that have been developed to help managers understand and make better decisions concerning the operation of waiting lines. For each model, formulas were presented that could be used to develop operating characteristics for the system being studied. Some of the operating characteristics that were presented included:

1. The probability that there are no units in the system
2. The average number of units in the waiting line
3. The average number of units in the system
4. The average time a unit spends in the waiting line
5. The average time a unit spends in the system
6. The probability that arriving units will have to wait for service
7. The probability that the service facility is in use

We also showed how an economic analysis of the waiting line situation could be conducted by developing a total-cost model that includes the cost associated with units waiting for service and the cost required to operate the service facility.

The complexity and diversity of waiting line systems found in practice often prevents an analyst from finding an existing waiting line model that fits the specific application being studied. Computer simulation, the topic discussed in the next chapter, provides another approach to determining the operating characteristics of waiting line systems.

As many of the examples in this chapter show, the most obvious applications of waiting line models are situations in which customers arrive for service, such as at a grocery checkout counter, bank, or restaurant. However, with a little creativity, waiting line models can be applied to many different situations such as, telephone calls waiting for connections, mail orders waiting for processing, machines waiting for repairs, manufacturing jobs waiting to be processed, and money waiting to be spent or invested.

Glossary

Queue A waiting line.

Queuing theory The body of knowledge dealing with waiting lines.

Single-channel A waiting line with only one service facility.

Poisson probability distribution The probability distribution used to describe the arrival pattern for some waiting line models.

Exponential probability distribution The probability distribution used to describe the pattern of service times for some waiting line models.

FCFS The queue discipline that orders service of the waiting units on a first-come, first-served basis.

Transient period The start-up period for a waiting line, occurring before the waiting line reaches a normal or steady-state operation.

Steady-state The normal operation of the waiting line after it has gone through a start-up or transient period. General operating characteristics of waiting lines are computed for steady-state conditions.

Mean arrival rate The average number of customers or units arriving in a given period.

Mean service rate The average number of customers or units that can be serviced by one service facility in a given period.

Multiple-channel A waiting line with two or more parallel service facilities.

Blocking The condition that exists when arriving units cannot enter the waiting line because the system is full. Blocking can occur when waiting lines are not allowed or when waiting lines have a finite capacity.

Infinite calling population The population of customers or units who may seek service does not have a specified upper limit.

Finite calling population The population of customers or units who may seek service has a fixed and finite value.

Problems

1. Poisson distribution

1. Willow Brook National Bank operates a drive-in teller window, which allows customers to complete bank transactions without getting out of their cars. On weekday mornings, arrivals to the drive-in teller window occur at random, with a mean arrival rate of 24 customers per hour or 0.4 customer per minute.
   a. What is the mean or expected number of customers that will arrive in a 5-minute period?
   b. Since the arrival of customers is random, the Poisson probability distribution can be used to describe the arrival process. Using the mean in part (a), compute the probabilities that exactly 0, 1, 2, and 3 customers will arrive during a 5-minute period.
   c. Delay problems are expected if more than 3 customers arrive during any 5-minute period. What is the probability that delay problems will occur?

2. Exponential distribution

2. In the Willow Brook National Bank waiting line system (see Problem 1), assume that the service times for the drive-in teller follow an exponential probability distribution with a mean service rate of 36 customers per hour or 0.6 customer per minute. Use the exponential probability distribution to answer the following questions:
   a. What is the probability that the service time is 1 minute or less?
   b. What is the probability that the service time is 2 minutes or less?
   c. What is the probability that the service time is more than 2 minutes?

3. Using the single-channel drive-in bank teller operation referred to in Problems 1 and 2, determine the following operating characteristics for the system:
   a. The probability that there are no customers in the system
   b. The average number of customers waiting
   c. The average number of customers in the system
   d. The average time a customer spends waiting
   e. The average time a customer spends in the system
   f. The probability that arriving customers will have to wait for service

4. Using the single-channel drive-in bank teller operation referred to in Problems 1–3, find the probabilities of 0, 1, 2, and 3 customers in the system. What is the probability that more than 3 customers will be in the drive-in teller system?

5. The reference desk of a university library receives requests for assistance. Assume that a Poisson probability distribution with a mean rate of 10 requests per hour can be used to describe the arrival pattern and that service times follow the exponential probability distribution with a mean service rate of 12 requests per hour.
   a. What is the probability that there are no requests for assistance in the system?
   b. What is the average number of requests that will be waiting for service?
   c. What is the average waiting time in minutes before service begins?
   d. What is the average time at the reference desk in minutes (waiting time plus service time)?
   e. What is the probability that a new arrival has to wait for service?

6. Trucks using a single-channel loading dock arrive according to the Poisson probability distribution. The time required to load/unload follows the exponential probability distribution. The mean arrival rate is 12 trucks per day, and the mean service rate is 18 trucks per day.
   a. What is the probability that there are no trucks in the system?
   b. What is the average number of trucks waiting for service?
   c. What is the average time a truck waits for the loading/unloading service to begin?
   d. What is the probability that a new arrival will have to wait?

7. A mail-order nursery specializes in European beech trees. New orders, which are processed by a single shipping clerk, have a mean arrival rate of 6 per day and a mean service rate of 8 per day. Assume that arrivals follow a Poisson probability distribution and that service times follow an exponential probability distribution.
   a. What is the average number of orders in the system?
   b. What is the average time that an order spends waiting before the clerk is available to begin service?
   c. What is the average time an order spends in the system?

8. For the Burger Dome single-channel waiting line in Section 12.2, assume that the arrival rate is increased to 1 customer per minute and the mean service rate is increased to 1.25 customers per minute. Compute the following operating characteristics for the new system: P_0, L_q, L, W_q, W, and P_w. Does this system provide better or poorer service as compared to the original system? Discuss any differences and the reason for these differences.

9. Marty's Barber Shop has one barber. Customers arrive at the rate of 2.2 customers per hour, and haircuts are given at the average rate of 5 per hour. Use the Poisson arrivals and exponential service times model to answer the following questions:
   a. What is the probability that there are no units in the system?
   b. What is the probability that 1 customer is receiving a haircut and no one is waiting?
   c. What is the probability that 1 customer is receiving a haircut and 1 customer is waiting?
   d. What is the probability that 1 customer is receiving a haircut and 2 customers are waiting?

e. What is the probability that more than 2 customers are waiting?

f. What is the average time a customer waits for service?

10. Trosper Tire Company has decided to hire a new mechanic to handle all tire changes for customers ordering a new set of tires. Two mechanics have applied for the job. One mechanic has limited experience and can be hired for $14 per hour. It is expected that this mechanic can service an average of 3 customers per hour. The other mechanic has several years of experience. This mechanic can service an average of 4 customers per hour, but must be paid $20 per hour. Assume that customers arrive at the Trosper garage at the rate of 2 customers per hour.

a. Compute the waiting line characteristics for each mechanic, assuming Poisson arrivals and exponential service times.

b. If the company assigns a customer waiting cost of $30 per hour, which mechanic provides the lower operating cost?

11. Agan Interior Design provides home and office decorating assistance to its customers. In normal operation, an average of 2.5 customers arrive each hour. One design consultant is available to answer customer questions and make product recommendations. The consultant averages 10 minutes with each customer.

a. Compute the operating characteristics of the customer waiting line, assuming Poisson arrivals and exponential service times.

b. Service goals dictate that an arriving customer should not wait for service more than an average of 5 minutes. Is this goal being met? What action do you recommend?

c. If the consultant can reduce the average time spent per customer to 8 minutes, what is the mean service rate? Will the service goal be met?

12. Pete's Market is a small local grocery store with only one checkout counter. Assume that shoppers arrive at the checkout lane according to the Poisson probability distribution, with a mean arrival rate of 15 customers per hour. The checkout service times follow an exponential probability distribution, with a mean service rate of 20 customers per hour.

a. Compute the operating characteristics for this waiting line.

b. If the manager's service goal is to limit the waiting time prior to beginning the checkout process to at most 5 minutes, what recommendations would you provide regarding the current checkout system?

13. After reviewing the waiting line analysis of Problem 12, the manager of Pete's Market feels it would be desirable to improve service by considering one of the following alternatives:

a. Hire a second person to bag the groceries while the cash register operator is entering the cost data and collecting money from the customer. With this improved single-channel operation, the mean service rate could be increased to 30 customers per hour.

b. Hire a second person to operate a second checkout counter. The two-channel operation would have a mean service rate of 20 customers per hour for each channel.

What alternative would you recommend? Justify your recommendation.

14. Keuka Park Savings and Loan currently has one drive-in teller window. The arrivals follow a Poisson probability distribution, with a mean arrival rate of 10 cars per hour. The service times follow an exponential probability distribution, with a mean service rate of 12 cars per hour.

a. What is the probability there are no customers in the system?

b. If you were to drive up to the facility, how many cars would you expect to see waiting and being serviced?

c. What is the probability that at least one car will be waiting to be serviced?

d. What is the average time in the queue waiting for service?

e. As a potential customer of the system, would you be satisfied with the above waiting line characteristics?

15. To improve the service to the customer, Keuka Park Savings and Loan (see Problem 14) wants to investigate the effect of a second drive-in teller window. Assume a mean arrival rate of 10 cars per hour. In addition, assume a mean service rate of 12 cars per hour for each drive-in window. What effect would the addition of a new teller window have on the system? Does this system appear acceptable?

16. Fore and Aft Marina is a newly planned marina that will be located on the Ohio River near Madison, Indiana. Assume that Fore and Aft has decided to build a docking facility where one boat at a time can stop for gas and servicing. Assume that arrivals follow a Poisson probability distribution, with a mean of 5 boats per hour, and that service times follow an exponential probability distribution, with a mean of 10 boats per hour. Consider the following questions:
   a. What is the probability that there are no boats in the system?
   b. What is the average number of boats that will be waiting for service?
   c. What is the average time a boat will spend waiting for service?
   d. What is the average time a boat will spend at the dock?
   e. If you were the management of Fore and Aft Marina, would you be satisfied with the service level your system will be providing?

17. The management of the Fore and Aft Marina in Problem 16 wants to investigate the possibility of enlarging the docking facility so that two boats can stop for gas and servicing simultaneously. Assume that the mean arrival rate is 5 boats per hour and that the mean service rate for each of the channels is 10 boats per hour.
   a. What is the probability that the boat dock will be idle?
   b. What is the average number of boats that will be waiting for service?
   c. What is the average time a boat will spend waiting for service?
   d. What is the average time a boat will spend at the dock?
   e. If you were the manager of Fore and Aft Marina, would you be satisfied with the service level your system will be providing?

18. The City Beverage Drive-Thru is considering a two-channel service system. Cars arrive according to the Poisson probability distribution, with a mean arrival rate of 6 cars per hour. The service times have an exponential probability distribution, with a mean service rate of 10 cars per hour for each channel.
   a. What is the probability there are no cars in the system?
   b. What is the average number of cars waiting for service?
   c. What is the average time waiting for service?
   d. What is the average time in the system?
   e. What is the probability that an arrival will have to wait for service?

19. Consider a two-channel waiting line with Poisson arrivals and exponential service times. The mean arrival rate is 14 units per hour, and the mean service rate is 10 units per hour for each channel.
   a. What is the probability that there are no units in the system?
   b. What is the average number of units in the system?
   c. What is the average time a unit waits for service?
   d. What is the average time a unit is in the system?
   e. What is the probability of having to wait for service?

20. Refer to Problem 19. Assume that the system is expanded to a three-channel operation.
   a. Compute the operating characteristics for this waiting line system.
   b. If the service goal is to provide sufficient capacity so that at most 25% of the customers have to wait for service, is the two- or three-channel system preferred?

21. Refer to the Agan Interior Design situation in Problem 11. Agan would like to evaluate two alternatives:

   ■ Use one consultant with an average service time of 8 minutes per customer.
   ■ Expand to two consultants, each of whom has an average service time of 10 minutes per customer.

If the consultants are paid $16 per hour and the customer waiting time is valued at $25 per hour for waiting time prior to service, should Agan expand to the two-consultant system? Explain.

22. A fast-food franchise is considering operating a drive-up window food-service operation. Assume that customer arrivals follow a Poisson probability distribution, with a mean arrival rate of 24 cars per hour, and that service times follow an exponential probability distribution. Arriving customers place orders at an intercom station at the back of the parking lot and then drive up to the service window to pay for and receive their order. The following three service alternatives are being considered:

- A single-channel operation where one employee fills the order and takes the money from the customer. The average service time for this alternative is 2 minutes.
- A single-channel operation where one employee fills the order while a second employee takes the money from the customer. The average service time for this alternative is 1.25 minutes.
- A two-channel operation with two service windows and two employees. The employee stationed at each window fills the order and takes the money for customers arriving at the window. The average service time for this alternative is 2 minutes for each channel.

Compute the following operating characteristics for each alternative, and recommend an alternative design for the fast-food franchise:
a. What is the probability that there are no customers in the system?
b. What is the average number of cars waiting for service?
c. What is the average time a car waits for service?
d. What is the average time in the system?
e. What is the average number of cars in the system?
f. What is the probability an arriving car will have to wait for service?

23. The following cost information is available for the fast-food franchise in Problem 22.

- Customer waiting time is valued at $25.00 per hour to reflect the fact that waiting time is costly to the fast-food business.
- The cost of each employee is $6.50 per hour.
- To account for equipment and space, an additional cost of $20.00 per hour is attributable to each channel.

What is the lowest-cost design for the fast-food business?

24. Patients arrive at a dentist's office at a mean rate of 2.8 patients per hour. The dentist can service patients at the mean rate of 3 patients per hour. A study of patient waiting times shows that, on average, a patient waits 30 minutes before seeing the dentist.
a. What are the mean arrival rate and the mean service rate in terms of patients per minute?
b. What is the average number of patients in the waiting room?
c. If a patient arrives at 10:10 A.M., what is the expected time the patient will leave the office?

25. A study of the multichannel food-service operation at the Red Birds' baseball park shows that the average time between the arrival of a customer at the food-service counter and his or her departure with a filled order is 10 minutes. During the game, customers arrive at the average rate of 4 per minute. The food-service operation requires an average of 2 minutes per customer order.
a. What is the mean service rate per channel in terms of customers per minute?
b. What is average waiting time in the line prior to placing an order?
c. On average, how many customers are in the food-service system?

26. Manning Autos operates an automotive service counter. While completing the repair work, Manning mechanics arrive at the company's parts department counter at the mean rate of 4 per hour. The parts coordinator spends an average of 6 minutes with each mechanic, discussing what parts the mechanic needs and retrieving the parts from inventory.

a. Currently, there is one parts coordinator. On average, each mechanic waits 4 minutes before the parts coordinator is available to answer questions and/or retrieve parts from inventory. Find L_q, W, and L for this single-channel parts operation.

b. A trial period with a second parts coordinator showed that, on average, each mechanic waited only 1 minute before a parts coordinator was available. Find L_q, W, and L for this two-channel parts operation.

c. If the cost of each mechanic is $20 per hour and the cost of each parts coordinator is $12 per hour, is the one-channel or the two-channel system the more economical?

27. Gubser Welding, Inc., operates a welding service for construction and automotive repair jobs. Assume that the arrival of jobs at the company's office can be described by a Poisson probability distribution with a mean arrival rate of 2 jobs per 8-hour day. The time required to complete the jobs follows a normal probability distribution with a mean time of 3.2 hours and a standard deviation of 2 hours. Answer the following questions assuming Gubser uses one welder to complete all jobs.

a. What is the mean arrival rate in jobs per hour?
b. What is the mean service rate in jobs per hour?
c. What is the average number of jobs waiting for service?
d. What is the average time a job waits before the welder can begin working on it?
e. What is the average number of hours between when a job is received and when it is completed?
f. What percentage of the time is the Gubser welder busy?

28. Jobs arrive randomly at a particular assembly plant; assume that the mean arrival rate is 5 jobs per hour. Service times do not follow the exponential probability distribution. Two proposed designs for the plant's assembly operation are shown below.

Design	Service Times (in minutes per job)	
	Mean	Standard Deviation
A	6.0	3.0
B	6.25	0.6

a. What is the mean service rate in jobs per hour for each of the designs?
b. Using the mean service rates in part (a), what design appears to provide the best or fastest service rate?
c. What are the standard deviations of the service times expressed in hours?
d. Use the M/G/1 model in Section 12.7 to compute the operating characteristics for each of the designs.
e. Which design provides the best operating characteristics? Why?

29. The Burger Dome single-channel waiting line model discussed in Section 12.2 has a mean arrival rate of 0.75 customers per minute and a mean service rate of 1 customer per minute. The model was based on the assumption of Poisson arrivals and exponential service times. The mean service rate of 1 customer per minute implies that the standard deviation of service times is 1 minute. Burger Dome is considering a new computerized cash register, order-taking system that will maintain the current mean service rate of 1 customer per minute. However, the standard deviation of service times for the new system will be reduced to 0.50 minute. Use the M/G/1 waiting line model to determine if the proposed system is worthwhile. In what ways, if any, will the proposed system improve the operating characteristics of the waiting line?

30. A large insurance company has a central computing system that contains a variety of information about customer accounts. Insurance agents, located throughout a six-state area use telephone lines to access the customer information data base. Currently, the company's central computer system allows 3 users to simultaneously access the central computer. Agents who attempt to use the system when it is full are denied access; no waiting is allowed. The company realizes that with its expanding business, more requests will be made to the central information system. Being denied access to the system is inefficient as well as annoying for the agents. Access requests follow a Poisson probability distribution, with a mean of 42 calls per hour. The mean service rate per line is 20 calls per hour.

   a. What is the probability that 0, 1, 2, and 3 access lines will be in use?

   b. What is the probability that an agent will be denied access to the system?

   c. What is the average number of access lines in use?

   d. In planning for the future, the company would like to be able to handle $\lambda = 50$ calls per hour; in addition, the probability that an agent will be denied access to the system should be no greater than your answer to part (b). How many access lines should this system have?

31. Mid-West Publishing Company publishes college textbooks. The company operates an 800 telephone number where potential adopters can ask questions about forthcoming texts, request examination copies of texts, and place orders. Currently, two extension lines are used, with two representatives handling the telephone inquiries. Calls occurring when both extension lines are being used receive a busy signal; no waiting is allowed. Each representative can accommodate an average of 12 calls per hour.

   a. If the mean arrival rate is 20 calls per hour, what percentage of the calls receive a busy signal?

   b. How many extensions should be used if the company would like to handle 90% of the calls immediately?

   c. What is the average number of extensions that will be busy if your recommendation in part (b) is used?

32. City Cab, Inc., uses two dispatchers to handle requests for service and dispatch the cabs. The telephone calls that are made to City Cab use a common telephone number. When both dispatchers are busy, the caller hears a busy signal; no waiting is allowed. Callers who receive a busy signal can call back later or call another cab service. Assume that the arrival of calls follows a Poisson probability distribution, with a mean of 40 calls per hour, and that each dispatcher can handle a mean of 30 calls per hour.

   a. What percentage of the time are both dispatchers idle?

   b. What percentage of the time are both dispatchers busy?

   c. What is the probability callers will receive a busy signal if 2, 3, or 4 dispatchers are used?

   d. If the company wants at most 12% of the callers to receive a busy signal, how many dispatchers should be used?

33. Kolkmeyer Manufacturing Company (see Section 12.9) is considering adding 2 machines to its manufacturing operations; this will bring the number of machines to 8. Mr. Andrew, the president of Kolkmeyer, has asked for a study of the need to add a second employee to the repair process. The mean arrival rate is 0.05 machine per hour for each machine, and the mean service rate for each individual assigned to the repair operation is 0.50 machine per hour.

   a. Compute the following operating characteristics if the company retains the single-employee repair service:

   - The probability that all machines are in operation and the repair person is idle
   - The average number of machines waiting for repair
   - The average number of machines down (those waiting plus those being serviced)
   - The average waiting time before repair can begin
   - The average down time (waiting time plus servicing time)

b. Use The Management Scientist software package to compute the above characteristics if a second employee is added to the machine repair operation.

c. Each employee assigned to the service operation is paid $20 per hour. Machine down time is valued at $80 per hour. From an economic point of view, should one or two employees handle the machine repair operation?

34. Five secretaries use an office copier. The average time between arrivals for each secretary is 40 minutes, which is equivalent to a mean arrival rate of $1/40 = 0.025$ arrival per minute. The mean time each secretary spends at the copier is 5 minutes, which is equivalent to a mean service rate of $\frac{1}{5} = 0.20$ user per minute. Use the $M/M/1$ model with a finite calling population to determine the following:

a. The probability that the copier is idle

b. The average number of secretaries in the waiting line

c. The average number of secretaries at the copier

d. The average time a secretary spends waiting for the copier

e. The average time a secretary spends at the copier

f. During an 8-hour day, how many minutes does a secretary spend at the copier? How much of this time is waiting time?

g. Should the company consider purchasing a second copier? Explain.

35. Schips Department Store operates a fleet of 10 trucks. The trucks arrive at random times throughout the day at the store's truck dock to be loaded with new deliveries or to have incoming shipments from the regional warehouse unloaded. Each truck returns to the truck dock for service 2 times per 8-hour day. Thus, the mean arrival rate per truck is 0.25 truck per hour. The mean service rate is 4 trucks per hour. Using the Poisson arrivals and exponential service times model with a finite calling population of 10 trucks, determine the following operating characteristics:

a. The probability no trucks are at the truck dock

b. The average number of trucks waiting for loading/unloading

c. The average number of trucks in the truck dock area

d. The average waiting time before loading/unloading begins

e. The average waiting time in the system

f. What is the hourly cost of operation if the cost is $50 per hour for each truck and $30 per hour for the truck dock?

g. In considering a two-channel truck dock operation where the second channel could be operated for an additional $30 per hour, what would be the average number of trucks waiting for loading/unloading have to be reduced to with the two-channel operation to make the two-channel truck dock economically feasible?

h. Should the company consider expanding to the two-channel truck dock? Explain.

Case Problem: Airline Reservations

Regional Airlines is establishing a new telephone system for handling flight reservations. During the 10:00 A.M. to 11:00 A.M. time period, calls to the reservation agent occur randomly at an average of one call every 3.75 minutes. Historical service time data show that a reservation agent spends an average of 3 minutes with each customer. The waiting line model assumptions of Poisson arrivals and exponential service times appear reasonable for the telephone reservation system.

Regional Airlines' management feels that offering an efficient telephone reservation system is an important part of establishing an image as a service-oriented airline. If the system is properly implemented, Regional Airlines will establish good customer relations, which in the long run will increase business. However, if the telephone reservation system is frequently overloaded and customers have difficulty contacting an agent, a negative customer reaction may lead to an eventual loss of business. The cost of a ticket reservation agent is $20 per hour. Thus, management wants to provide good service, but does not want to incur the cost of overstaffing the telephone reservation operation by using more agents than necessary.

At a planning meeting, Regional's management team agreed that an acceptable customer service goal is to answer at least 85% of the incoming calls immediately. During the planning meeting, Regional's vice president of administration pointed out that the data show that the average service rate for an agent is faster than the average arrival rate of the telephone calls. His conclusion was that the personnel costs could be minimized by using one agent and that the single agent should be able to handle the telephone reservations and still have some idle time. The vice president of marketing restated the importance of customer service and expressed support for at least two reservation agents.

The current telephone reservation system design does not allow callers to wait. Callers who attempt to reach a reservation agent when all agents are occupied receive a busy signal and are blocked from the system. A representative from the telephone company suggested that Regional Airlines consider an expanded system that accommodates waiting. In the expanded system, when a customer calls and all agents are busy, a recorded message tells the customer that the call is being held in the order received and that an agent will be available shortly. The customer can stay on the line and listen to background music while waiting for an agent. Regional's management will need more information before switching to the expanded system.

Managerial Report

Prepare a managerial report for Regional Airlines analyzing the telephone reservation system. Evaluate both the system that does not allow waiting and the expanded system that allows waiting. Include the following information in your report:

1. A detailed analysis of the operating characteristics of the reservation system with one agent as proposed by the vice president of administration. What is your recommendation concerning a single-agent system?
2. A detailed analysis of the operating characteristics of the reservation system based on your recommendation regarding the number of agents Regional should use and whether the system should allow customers to wait.
3. What appear to be the advantages or disadvantages of the expanded system? Discuss the number of waiting callers the expanded system would need to accommodate.
4. The telephone arrival data presented above are for the 10:00 A.M. to 11:00 A.M. time period; however, the arrival rate of incoming calls is expected to change from hour to hour. Describe how your waiting line analysis could be used to develop a ticket agent staffing plan that would enable the company to provide different levels of staffing for the ticket reservation system at different times during the day. Indicate the information that you would need to develop this staffing plan.

MANAGEMENT SCIENCE IN PRACTICE

Goodyear Tire & Rubber Company*
Akron, Ohio

The Goodyear Tire & Rubber Company* had its beginning in an old converted strawboard factory in 1898. Its first product was bicycle tires. In 1916 it became the world's largest tire company, and in 1926, the world's largest rubber company.

Although tires are Goodyear's biggest single product line, the company has become a highly diversified corporate enterprise. The company's product line has changed from the original bicycle tires, carriage tires, and horseshoe pads to tires of all types, chemicals, automotive components, automotive belts and hose, industrial hose and conveyor belts, polyurethane and composite plastic panels, shoe soles and heels. Over the years the line has included polyester for tire cords and bottles, foam cushioning, metal wheels and rims, packaging films, aircraft brakes and wheels, aerospace products, computers, and enriched uranium for atomic energy. In recent years, a subsidiary, Celeron Corp., built the first oil pipeline to carry petroleum 1,200 miles from the West Coast to refineries in Texas and other points east.

Goodyear has more than 80 production facilities—about half in the United States and half overseas—and approximately 97,000 associates. Its sales and distribution operations involve virtually every nation in the world. Corporate headquarters are in Akron, Ohio.

Familiar to millions of people are the company airships named the "Eagle," based in Los Angeles, Ca., the "Stars & Stripes," based in Pompano Beach, Fla., and the newest state-of-the-art airship, the "Spirit of Akron," based in Akron, Ohio.

The global consolidation of the tire industry resulted in the purchase of two major U.S. tiremakers by foreign firms. One of those mergers put Goodyear in the number two position in worldwide tire sales, although it still leads in North and South America. Today, nearing its centennial, Goodyear stands alone as the only major publicly held tire and rubber company in the United States.

Management Science at Goodyear

Goodyear has many departments that make use of management science applications. Most analyses are performed by one of the computer programming departments under the guidance of a user (client) department. These computer programming departments work on applications ranging from routine data collection and systems maintenance to queuing analysis. For example, one department is responsible for maintaining a system that gathers records of orders and sales, another department is responsible for forecasting and assisting production schedulers, and a third department is responsible for quality control. The waiting line application discussed in the remainder of this presentation is the responsibility of yet another department. Many of the applica-

tions are interrelated, and one department will often use data generated by another department.

A Waiting Line Application

The following application involves a system for dispatching maintenance personnel to fix machines. Under the old manual system, whenever a machine needed repair, a production supervisor used a phone intercom system to call an individual referred to as a dispatcher. The dispatcher manually recorded the information provided by the production supervisor on cards. Then, whenever maintenance personnel called the dispatcher to request a new assignment, the information on these cards was used to tell the maintenance personnel which machine should be repaired.

Due primarily to a need to develop a computerized data base that could be analyzed to improve the maintenance function, Goodyear decided to replace the manual system with a computer-controlled system. In the computer-controlled system, the dispatcher function is performed by a person called a coordinator. The coordinator enters service information when received into the computer, using a remote computer terminal. As the amount of information needed to be entered has grown, the coordinator's task has become more time-consuming than that of the dispatcher in the old system. However, the computer-controlled system offers advantages in other areas.

The problem of expanding capacity in the computer-controlled system obviously had to be addressed. Determining how many coordinators (and, consequently, remote computer terminals) should be used was the main issue. With too few coordinators, production supervisors and maintenance personnel would have difficulty reaching a coordinator. For the computer system to be a success, people trying to reach the coordinator should not have long waits. However, with too many coordinators, excessive coordinator and computer terminal expenses would be incurred. Some of the questions that had to be answered were the following:

1. What percentage of the time will the coordinator be busy?
2. What is the maximum number of people waiting to reach the coordinator?
3. What is the average time spent waiting to reach the coordinator?

—Continued on next page

*The authors are indebted to Dr. Walter J. Fenske of The Goodyear Tire & Rubber Company for providing this application.

—Continued from previous page

4. How many calls does the coordinator receive?
5. How many callers have to wait longer than 4 minutes to reach the coordinator?
6. How many callers do not have to wait to reach the coordinator?

These questions suggested that the design of a new system could be aided through the use of a waiting line model. In this situation, the coordinators are the servers, and the people waiting to talk to the coordinators constitute the units in the waiting line. Thus, if one coordinator is used, the model is a single-channel waiting line model. Otherwise, it is a multiple-channel waiting line model.

The complexity of the proposed computer system can best be understood by considering the four types of arrivals that must be handled. The first type of arrival is a call received from a production supervisor stating that a machine needs repair. At this time, a *work order is initiated.* The second type of arrival is a call from a maintenance person stating that the repair work is being started; this is referred to as *placing the work order in process.* The third type of arrival, referred to as *completing the work order,* is a call from a maintenance person stating that the repair work has been completed. The fourth type of arrival is any other type of call. Note that each work order generates three calls to the coordinator.

For this problem, the arrivals were known to differ from the Poisson probability distribution. In addition, there were a number of complicating factors that precluded the use of the waiting line models introduced in this chapter. However, the simulation model of the system was implemented built using many of the basic waiting line principles discussed in this chapter. The General Purpose Simulation System (GPSS) was the programming language used for the simulation model.

Computer simulation runs were performed for a system with one coordinator and for a system with two coordinators. In the single-coordinator system, the simulation runs showed that the coordinator would be busy about 69% of the time and that the average time spent waiting to reach the coordinator would be 4.9 minutes. The average waiting time for the single-coordinator system was considered to be much too high.

For the two-coordinator system, the simulation results indicated that each coordinator would be busy approximately 35% of the time. However, the average time spent waiting to reach a coordinator dropped to 42 seconds. In fact, it was found that a call would get through immediately about 90% of the time. Since management believed that these times were reasonable, the new system included two coordinators and two remote computer terminals.

Questions

1. What is the primary reason that Goodyear decided to replace the manual system with a computer-controlled system?
2. What factors in this application led to the use of a simulation model rather than an analytical model of the waiting line?

Computer Simulation

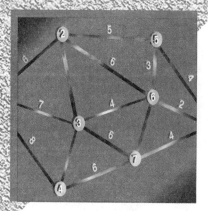

Computer simulation is a method that can be used to study the performance of a real-world system. First, a computer simulation model that "behaves like" or simulates the real system is developed; at this stage, great care is taken to ensure that the simulation model is descriptive of the real system. Then through a series of computer runs, or experiments, we learn about the behavior of the simulation model. The characteristics observed in the model are then used to make inferences about the real system.

Computer simulation is one of the most frequently used techniques of management science. Computer simulation has been applied in the following situations:

1. Simulating traffic flow through a busy intersection. The objective is to determine whether installing a left turn signal will improve traffic flow.
2. Simulating the behavior of an inventory system. The objective is to determine the lowest cost order quantity and reorder point.
3. Simulating the operation of a paper mill. The objective is to determine the benefits of expanding the production operation.

In many applications of computer simulation, an analyst adjusts the parameters of the model to improve the performance of the model. When good parameter values have been found for the model, these values can be used to improve the performance of the real system.

Computer simulation can be used to model the performance of a waiting line system. In Chapter 12 we showed how analytic procedures based on the use of mathematical formulas could be used to evaluate waiting line systems. The mathematics involved for simple waiting lines are difficult enough; for more complex systems, analytic procedures are more difficult and may not be available. Thus, computer simulation models are often used to evaluate and improve the operation of more complex waiting line systems.

In the material that follows, we introduce the concepts and procedures of computer simulation by studying how computer simulation can be applied to waiting line systems and inventory systems. Analytical techniques for these systems have been presented in

Chapters 11 and 12. These analytical techniques should be used whenever the assumptions underlying the techniques are adequate approximations of the real-world system. If this is not the case, computer simulation is a viable alternative to modeling the real-world system.

13.1   County Beverage Drive-Thru

County Beverage Drive-Thru, Inc., is building a chain of beverage supply stores throughout an area in northern Illinois. The stores will enable customers to pick up beverages, snacks, and party supplies without getting out of their cars. A typical store design is shown in Figure 13.1. A service lane runs through the store, and soft drinks, beer, and other supplies are available at various locations along both sides of the service lane. When a customer drives into the store, the store clerk takes the order, fills it, and collects the money. The customer remains in the car while receiving service. When additional customers arrive at the store, they wait in a line outside the store until the preceding customer's order is complete. Then the next customer in line drives into the store for service.

The County Beverage Drive-Thru operation is a *waiting line* or *queuing system*. This particular waiting line configuration has one service lane and is therefore a *single-channel waiting line* with a first-come, first-served (FCFS) queue discipline. If we are willing to assume that the number of cars arriving at the store has a Poisson probability distribution and that the length of time that the customer is actually in the store (service time) has an exponential probability distribution, the mathematical models presented in the previous chapter can be used to study this system. However, for the County Beverage Drive-Thru we are not willing to make these assumptions; thus, we will be using a computer simulation model to study the operation of the system.

One of the advantages of computer simulation is the ability to use observed probability distributions that are unique to the system being studied. The waiting line models in the previous chapter required assumptions such as Poisson arrivals and exponential service times.

The specific situation we will simulate is a new store that will be located near a major shopping center. Construction of the store will not begin for approximately 3 months. County Beverage's president has requested planning information on the projected operation of the store, including estimates of the number of customers served, the profitability of the store, and the number of lost sales due to long waiting lines.

In modeling the system, we will study the store's operation in terms of what happens during 3-minute periods. That is, we will count the number of customer arrivals and the number of customers lost and determine whether a customer is being serviced during each

Figure 13.1
County Beverage Drive-Thru
Store Design

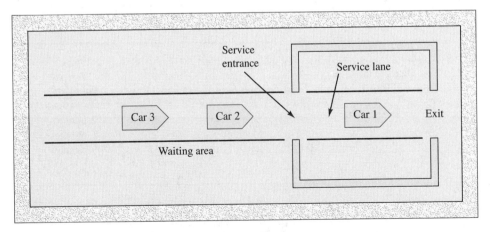

Table 13.1

Probability Distribution for the Number of Customers Arriving at the County Beverage Drive-Thru During a 3-Minute Period

Number of Customers Arriving	Probability
0	0.19
1	0.39
2	0.19
3	0.15
4	0.08
	1.00

3-minute interval. A simulation model such as this, that increments time in fixed intervals, is referred to as a *fixed-time simulation model*. Simulation models that increment time based on the occurrence of the next event (time of next arrival, time of next service, and so on) are referred to as *next-event simulation models*.

Based on a study of traffic flow, the company has estimated that the probability distribution of customer arrivals is as shown in Table 13.1. This probability distribution is believed to be representative of the number of arrivals during the peak business period occurring in the late afternoon and early evening. As the data show, there is a 0.19 probability of no customers arriving during a given 3-minute period, a 0.39 probability of 1 customer arriving during the same 3-minute period, and so on.

Sales records from the company's other stores show customer variability in terms of the size of the order placed. The probability for three classes of order size (small, medium, and large), the average time to fill the orders, and the average profit per order are shown in Table 13.2.

As an additional operating condition, experience with other company stores indicates that customers will wait for service only if there are fewer than four cars in the waiting line. If a customer arrives and there are already four cars in the waiting area, the customer will drive off. This failure to enter the waiting line is referred to as a *balking* and results in a lost customer and thus an opportunity loss corresponding to the lost profit.

Simulation of Customer Arrivals and Order Sizes

Before developing the computer simulation model, let us concentrate on simulating the number of customers that arrive at the store during any 3-minute period. In simulating this arrival rate for County Beverage, we will also be demonstrating how the probabilistic component of a real-world system is modeled.

The technique used to simulate customer arrivals is based on the use of random numbers. Tables of random numbers are available from a variety of handbooks[1] that contain page after page of random numbers. We have included one such page of random numbers in Appendix B. A portion of this page is shown in Table 13.3, and 20 random numbers from the first line of this table are as follows:

63271   59986   71744   51102

The digit appearing in a given position is a random selection of the digits 0, 1, 2, . . . , 9, with each digit having an equal chance of appearing. Grouping the numbers in sets of five simply makes the table easier to read.

Table 13.2

Order Size Data for the County Beverage Drive-Thru

Order Size	Probability	Average Time to Fill Order	Average Profit
Small	0.39	3 minutes	$1.50
Medium	0.50	6 minutes	3.00
Large	0.11	9 minutes	6.00
Total	1.00		

[1]See, for example, *A Million Random Digits with 100,000 Normal Deviates,* New York: The Free Press, 1983.

Table 13.3

Random Numbers

63271	59986	71744	51102	15141	80714	58683	93108	13554	79945
88547	09896	95436	79115	08303	01041	20030	63754	08459	28364
55957	57243	83865	09911	19761	66535	40102	26646	60147	15702
46276	87453	44790	67122	45573	84358	21625	16999	13385	22782
55363	07449	34835	15290	76616	67191	12777	21861	68689	03263
69393	92785	49902	58447	42048	30378	87618	26933	40640	16281
13186	29431	88190	04588	38733	81290	89541	70290	40113	08243
17726	28652	56836	78351	47327	18518	92222	55201	27340	10493
36520	64465	05550	30157	82242	29520	69753	72602	23756	54935
81628	36100	39254	56835	37636	02421	98063	89641	64953	99337
84649	48968	75215	75498	49539	74240	03466	49292	36401	45525
63291	11618	12613	75055	43915	26488	41116	64531	56827	30825
70502	53225	03655	05915	37140	57051	48393	91322	25653	06543
06426	24771	59935	49801	11082	66762	94477	02494	88215	27191
20711	55609	29430	70165	45406	78484	31639	52009	18873	96927
41990	70538	77191	25860	55204	73417	83920	69468	74972	38712
72452	36618	76298	26678	89334	33938	95567	29380	75906	91807
37042	40318	57099	10528	09925	89773	41335	96244	29002	46453
53766	52875	15987	46962	67342	77592	57651	95508	80033	69828
90585	58955	53122	16025	84299	53310	67380	84249	25348	04332
32001	96293	37203	64516	51530	37069	40261	61374	05815	06714
62606	64324	46354	72157	67248	20135	49804	09226	64419	29457
10078	28073	85389	50324	14500	15562	64165	06125	71353	77669
91561	46145	24177	15294	10061	98124	75732	00815	83452	97355
13091	98112	53959	79607	52244	63303	10413	63839	74762	50289

Suppose we select random numbers from the table in sets of 2 digits. There are 100 2-digit random numbers from 00 to 99, with each 2-digit random number having a $1/100 = 0.01$ chance of occurring. While we could select 2-digit random numbers from any part of the random number table, suppose we use the first row of random numbers from Table 13.3. The first 10 2-digit random numbers are

$$63 \quad 27 \quad 15 \quad 99 \quad 86 \quad 71 \quad 74 \quad 45 \quad 11 \quad 02$$

Now let us see how we can simulate the customer arrival rate in a 3-minute period by associating a given number of arrivals with each of the 100 2-digit random numbers. For example, let us consider the possibility of no customers arriving during a 3-minute interval. The probability distribution in Table 13.1 shows that this event has a 0.19 probability. Since each 2-digit random number has a 0.01 probability of occurrence, we can let 19 of the 100 possible 2-digit random numbers correspond to no customers arriving. Any 19 numbers from 00 to 99 will do, but for convenience we associate the arrival of 0 customers with the first 19 2-digit numbers: 00, 01, 02, 03, . . . , 18. Thus, any time one of these 2-digit numbers is observed in a random selection, we will say that no customers arrived. Since the numbers 00–18 include 19% of the possible 2-digit random numbers, we expect the arrival of no customers for any given 3-minute interval to have a probability of 0.19.

Now consider the possibility of one customer arriving during a 3-minute period, an event that has a 0.39 probability of occurring (see Table 13.1). Letting 39 of the 100

Problem 1 will give you the opportunity to establish intervals of random numbers and simulate demand for a product. Use the format of Table 13.5 to present the results of the 10 days of simulated demand.

The term *Monte Carlo* comes from the use of probabilistic inputs that are analogous to the outcomes of roulette and other gambling games played in the gambling casinos of Monte Carlo.

2-digit numbers (such as 19, 20, 21, 22, . . . , 57) correspond to a simulated arrival of one customer will provide a 0.39 probability for one customer arrival. Continuing to assign the number of customers arriving to sets of 2-digit numbers according to the probability distribution shown in Table 13.1 results in the sets of random numbers and customer arrival assignments shown in Table 13.4.

Using Table 13.4 and the 2-digit random numbers in the first row of Table 13.3 (63, 27, 15, 99, 86, . . .), we can simulate the number of customers arriving during the 3-minute periods. The results for 10 such 3-minute periods, or ½ hour of store operation, are shown in Table 13.5. The first 2-digit random number, 63, is in the interval 58–76; thus, according to Table 13.4 this corresponds to two customers arriving during the first 3-minute period. The second random number, 27, is in the interval 19–57; thus, the number of simulated customer arrivals during the second period is one, and so on.

By selecting a 2-digit random number for each 3-minute period, we can simulate the number of customer arrivals for as many 3-minute periods as desired. In doing so, the simulated probability distribution for customer arrivals will agree with the probability distribution shown in Table 13.1. A computer simulation model that involves generating probabilistic inputs such as the number of customer arrivals is referred to as a *Monte Carlo simulation*.

It is relatively easy to apply the above procedure to simulate values of a random variable for any computer simulation model. First, develop a table similar to Table 13.4

Table 13.4

Random Number Assignments for the Number of Customers Arriving at the County Beverage Drive-Thru During a 3-Minute Period

Number of Customers	Associated 2-Digit Random Numbers	Interval Description	Probability
0	00, 01, . . . , 18	00 but less than 19	0.19
1	19, 20, . . . , 57	19 but less than 58	0.39
2	58, 59, . . . , 76	58 but less than 77	0.19
3	77, 78, . . . , 91	77 but less than 92	0.15
4	92, 93, . . . , 99	92 but less than 100	0.08

Table 13.5

Simulated Customer Arrivals for 10 3-Minute Periods at the County Beverage Drive-Thru

Period	Random Number	Simulated Customer Arrivals
1	63	2
2	27	1
3	15	0
4	99	4
5	86	3
6	71	2
7	74	2
8	45	1
9	11	0
10	02	0
	Total	15

Since random digits are equally likely, the analyst can easily assign groups of random numbers to each outcome so that the probability of the outcome in the computer simulation model is identical to the probability of the outcome in the actual situation.

by associating an interval of random numbers with each possible value of the random variable. In doing so, make the probability of selecting a random number from each interval the same as the actual probability associated with the value of the random variable. Then each time a value of the random variable is needed, we simply select a new random number and use the corresponding interval of random numbers to find the value of the random variable.

Associating random number intervals with order sizes, we see that the random number intervals given in Table 13.6 can be used to simulate order sizes for customers stopping at the County Beverage Drive-Thru. Thus, the simulation model for the County Beverage Drive-Thru has two probabilistic components: customer arrivals and order size.

Logic of the Simulation Model for County Beverage Drive-Thru

Now that we know how to simulate the customer arrivals and the size of the customer's order, let us proceed with the development of the logic for the sequence of operations in the County Beverage simulation model. We will develop the model in a step-by-step manner. In doing so, we will carry out the necessary calculations to demonstrate how the simulation process works.

In the simulation calculations that follow, we will use the random numbers from row 10 of Table 13.3. Tables 13.4 and 13.6 will be used to determine the corresponding number of customer arrivals and the order sizes. For convenience, the first five 2-digit random numbers from row 10 are reproduced here:

$$81 \quad 62 \quad 83 \quad 61 \quad 00$$

In developing the logic for the model, we try to imitate the actual operation of the system as closely as possible. Suppose we begin with an idle or empty store and simulate what happens for each of the first three periods. Try to follow the logic of the model and see if you agree with the statements under the column labeled "Things That Happen." Each time we need to know what happens in the model, we will use the next random number in the sequence 81, 62, 83, 61, 00, and so on.

Period 1 (see Figure 13.2)

Random Number	Things That Happen
81	Three cars arrive for service; thus, the first car, identified as car 1, gets immediate service.
62	Car 1 places a medium order and hence will not finish service until the end of period 2 (6 minutes).
	Cars 2 and 3 join the waiting line.

Table 13.6
Random Number Assignments for Order Sizes at the County Beverage Drive-Thru

Order Size	Associated 2-Digit Random Numbers	Interval Description	Probability
Small	00, 01, . . . , 38	00 but less than 39	0.39
Medium	39, 40, . . . , 88	39 but less than 89	0.50
Large	89, 90, . . . , 99	89 but less than 100	0.11

Period 2 (see Figure 13.3)

Random Number	Things That Happen
83	Three more cars, identified as cars 4, 5, and 6, arrive for service. The drive-thru is still busy serving the customer from period 1; hence, no order size is generated. Five cars (two old customers plus three new customers) are wanting service this period, but only four cars will wait; hence, one customer (car 6) will be lost. Car 1 completes service at the end of this period; a profit of $3 is recorded.

Period 3 (see Figure 13.4)

Random Number	Things That Happen
61	Two more cars, identified as cars 7 and 8, arrive for service. The service area is free at the beginning of the period since the customer from period 1 (car 1) has completed service and left the drive-thru. One car from the waiting line (car 2) begins service, leaving five cars still wanting service; hence, one customer (car 8) will be lost and four cars will remain in the waiting line.
00	The customer in car 2 places a small order; thus, car 2 will finish service at the end of this period. Total profit as of the end of this period will be $3 (car 1) + $1.50 (car 2) = $4.50.

The flowchart containing the logic we have been using is shown in Figure 13.5 (page 564). Continue to use the random numbers from row 10 of Table 13.3 and see if you can conduct the simulation calculations for the first 10 periods of operation. Your simulation results should agree with those shown in Table 13.7.

At this point, we have succeeded in simulating 10 periods, or a total of 30 minutes of operation. Although the results in Table 13.7 show evidence of long waiting lines and

Figure 13.2
Status for the First 3-Minute
Simulation Period

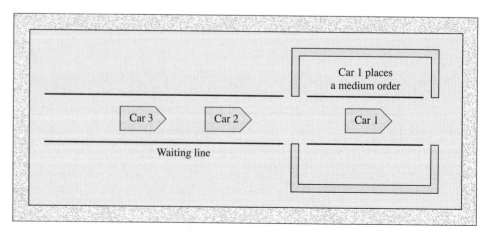

Figure 13.3
Status for the Second 3-Minute
Simulation Period

Figure 13.4
Status for the Third 3-Minute
Simulation Period

Table 13.7 Simulation Results for 10 3-Minute Periods at the County Beverage Drive-Thru

Period	Random Number	Number of New Customers	Is Service Area Available?	Random Number	Order Size	Service Periods	Number of Lost Customers	Number Waiting	Was Service Completed This Period?	Profit
1	81	3	Yes	62	Medium	2	0	2	No	—
2	83	3	No	—	—	—	1	4	Yes	$3.00
3	61	2	Yes	00	Small	1	1	4	Yes	1.50
4	39	1	Yes	25	Small	1	0	4	Yes	1.50
5	45	1	Yes	68	Medium	2	0	4	No	—
6	35	1	No	—	—	—	1	4	Yes	3.00
7	37	1	Yes	63	Medium	2	0	4	No	—
8	60	2	No	—	—	—	2	4	Yes	3.00
9	24	1	Yes	21	Small	1	0	4	Yes	1.50
10	98	4	Yes	06	Small	1	3	4	Yes	1.50

Total customers served 7   Total profit $15.00   Total lost customers 8

Figure 13.5
The County Beverage Drive-Thru
Simulation Model Logic

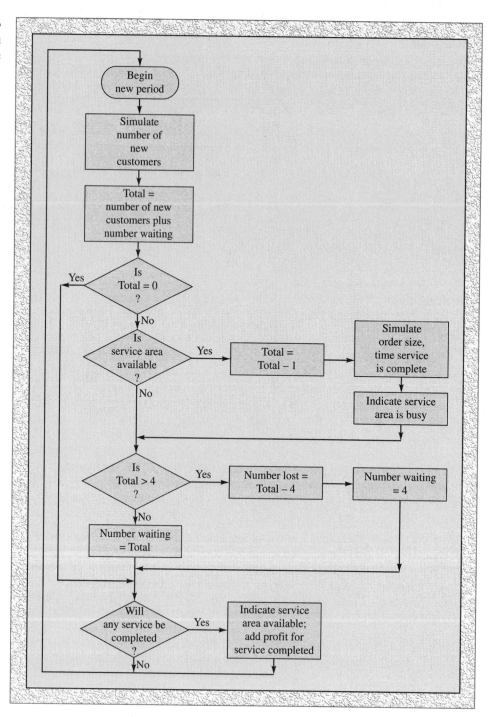

high lost customer rates (eight in the first ½ hour), a 30-minute simulation period is too short a time frame from which to draw general conclusions about the operation of the store. To take full advantage of the simulation model, we must continue to simulate the store's operation for many more periods. But even for this relatively small simulation problem, continuing the hand simulation computations as we have been doing is unrealistic. Thus, we will look to the computer to provide the computational assistance necessary.

Generating Pseudorandom Numbers

Cumulative probabilities are provided in Tables 13.8 and 13.9 in order to show how intervals are established for the pseudorandom numbers. The widths of the intervals provide the probabilities for the customer arrivals and order sizes.

If a computer procedure is going to be used to perform the simulation calculations, we will need a way for the computer to generate random numbers and values for the probabilistic components of the model. While the computer could be programmed to store random number tables and then follow the procedure outlined previously, the computer storage space required would result in an inefficient use of computer resources. For this reason, computer simulation models make use of mathematical formulas that generate numbers which, for all practical purposes, have the same properties as the numbers selected from random number tables. These numbers are called *pseudorandom numbers*. In computer simulation, pseudorandom numbers are used in the same way random numbers are used in hand simulation computations. We associate an interval of pseudorandom numbers with each value of the random variable. Most mathematical formulas designed to generate pseudorandom numbers will produce numbers from 0 up to, but not including, 1.

To generate customer arrivals for the County Beverage simulation model with the computer, we must associate an interval of pseudorandom numbers with each number of arrivals such that the probability of generating a pseudorandom number in the interval will be equal to the probability of the corresponding number of arrivals. Table 13.8 shows how this would be done for the number of arrivals at the County Beverage Drive-Thru. Using the probability and cumulative probability for the number of customer arrivals, we see that a pseudorandom number in the interval 0.00 but less than 0.19 corresponds to no arrivals; a pseudorandom number greater than or equal to 0.19 but less than 0.58

Table 13.8	Number of Customer Arrivals	Probability	Cumulative Probability	Interval of Pseudorandom Numbers
Pseudorandom Numbers for the Number of Customers Arriving at the County Beverage Drive-Thru	0	0.19	0.19	0.00 but less than 0.19
	1	0.39	0.58	0.19 but less than 0.58
	2	0.19	0.77	0.58 but less than 0.77
	3	0.15	0.92	0.77 but less than 0.92
	4	0.08	1.00	0.92 but less than 1.00
	Total	1.00		

Table 13.9

Pseudorandom Numbers for the Order Sizes of County Beverage Customers

Order Size	Probability	Cumulative Probability	Interval of Pseudorandom Numbers
Small	0.39	0.39	0.00 but less than 0.39
Medium	0.50	0.89	0.39 but less than 0.89
Large	0.11	1.00	0.89 but less than 1.00
Total	1.00		

corresponds to one arrival; and so on. Table 13.9 provides similar pseudorandom number intervals that can be used to generate the simulated order sizes.

Computer Program and Results

To simulate the operation of the County Beverage Drive-Thru, we need to develop a computer program containing the logic shown in Figure 13.5. Such a program would perform the calculations and keep track of the simulation results in a form similar to that shown in Table 13.7. Figure 13.6 shows a computer program written in the BASIC language that will simulate the County Beverage operation. This particular program was developed for and run on a personal computer.

Results from the computer simulation are shown in Table 13.10. The store's operation was simulated for a total of 30 hours. Based on the simulation results, we are able to make the following observations about the behavior of the system:

1. During the 30 hours of simulated operation, 365 customers were serviced. However, 575 customers (61.2%) were lost because of long waiting lines.
2. The average profit was $32.56 per hour or $2.68 per car serviced ($976.50/365 = $2.68).
3. The biggest problem with the store's operation appears to be the number of lost customers (an average of 19.17 per hour). An estimate of the average dollar loss per hour due to lost customers is 19.17($2.68 per car) = $51.38.

Try Problem 3. This is another example in setting up and simulating demand. Operational information such as average daily demand and number of lost customers is considered.

Recall for a moment that a primary objective of computer simulation is to describe the behavior of a real system. In the County Beverage Drive-Thru simulation, this is exactly what we have done. We have not determined an optimal solution or decision for the store; we have simply simulated what could happen in 30 hours of actual operation of the drive-thru. If the actual operation behaves as the computer simulation model indicates, County Beverage will have a significant waiting line problem with a sizable lost profit. In the next section we shall see how the computer simulation model can be modified to investigate ways to improve the operation of the County Beverage Drive-Thru.

Table 13.10

Computer Simulation Results for 30 Hours of Operation

Item of Interest	Total	Percent	Hourly Average
Number served	365	38.8	12.17
Number lost	575	61.2	19.17
Profit	$976.50	—	$32.56

Figure 13.6
BASIC Program for the Computer
Simulation of the County
Beverage Drive-Thru (See also
page 568.)

```
300   IF TOTAL.CARS.IN.LINE > 4 THEN GOTO 350
      CARS.WAITING = TOTAL.CARS.IN.LINE
      GOTO 400

350   CARS.LOST = TOTAL.CARS.IN.LINE - 4
      CARS.WAITING = 4
      TOTAL.CARS.LOST = TOTAL.CARS.LOST + CARS.LOST

REM
REM   RELEASE A CAR COMPLETING SERVICE AND RECORD THE PROFIT
REM

400   IF TIME.CAR.FINISHES.SERVICE > THREE.MINUTE.PERIOD THEN GOTO 200
      IF PERIODS.OF.SERVICE = 1 THEN PROFIT = 1.5
      IF PERIODS.OF.SERVICE = 2 THEN PROFIT = 3
      IF PERIODS.OF.SERVICE = 3 THEN PROFIT = 6
      TOTAL.PROFIT = TOTAL.PROFIT + PROFIT
      TOTAL.CARS.SERVED = TOTAL.CARS.SERVED + 1
      CAR.BEING.SERVICED$ = "NO"

REM
REM   SIMULATION RUNS FOR 30 HOURS
REM

      IF THREE.MINUTE.PERIOD < 20 THEN GOTO 200
      TIME.CAR.FINISHES.SERVICE = TIME.CAR.FINISHES.SERVICE - 20
      IF HOUR.OF.SIMULATION < 30 THEN GOTO 100

REM
REM   COMPUTE SUMMARY STATISTICS AND PRINT SUMMARY REPORT
REM

      AVERAGE.CARS.SERVED.PER.HOUR = TOTAL.CARS.SERVED / 30
      TOTAL.CARS.ARRIVING = TOTAL.CARS.SERVED + TOTAL.CARS.LOST
      PERCENT.SERVED = TOTAL.CARS.SERVED / TOTAL.CARS.ARRIVING * 100
      AVERAGE.CARS.LOST.PER.HOUR = TOTAL.CARS.LOST / 30
      PERCENT.LOST = 100 - PERCENT.SERVED
      AVERAGE.PROFIT.PER.HOUR = TOTAL.PROFIT / 30

      TCS = TOTAL.CARS.SERVED
      PS = PERCENT.SERVED
      ACS = AVERAGE.CARS.SERVED.PER.HOUR
      TCL = TOTAL.CARS.LOST
      PL = PERCENT.LOST
      ACL = AVERAGE.CARS.LOST.PER.HOUR
      TP = TOTAL.PROFIT
      AP = AVERAGE.PROFIT.PER.HOUR

      CLS
      PRINT : PRINT
      PRINT TAB(8); "ITEM OF INTEREST"; TAB(29); "TOTAL";
      PRINT TAB(41); "PERCENT"; TAB(55); "AVERAGE"
      PRINT : PRINT
      PRINT TAB(8); "NUMBER SERVED";
      PRINT USING "    #######        ###.#      #####.##"; TCS; PS; ACS
      PRINT
      PRINT TAB(8); "NUMBER LOST  ";
      PRINT USING "    #######        ###.#      #####.##"; TCL; PL; ACL
      PRINT
      PRINT TAB(8); "PROFIT       ";
      PRINT USING "    #######.##                #####.##"; TP; AP
      END
```

The BASIC program demonstrates
the step-by-step logic of a
computer simulation model and
shows the details of the simulation
process. However, special computer
simulation languages such as SLAM,
GPSSH, and SIMSCRIPT are typically
used in practice.

—Figure continues on next page

Figure 13.6
—Continued

```
      REM
      REM   THIS COMPUTER PROGRAM SIMULATES THE OPERATION OF THE
      REM   COUNTY BEVERAGE DRIVE-THRU
      REM
      REM   THE STATEMENT RANDOMIZE INITIALIZES THE PSEUDO RANDOM
      REM   NUMBER GENERATOR
      REM


            CLS
            RANDOMIZE


      REM
      REM   INITIALIZING THE SIMULATION MODEL
      REM

            HOUR.OF.SIMULATION = 0
            CAR.BEING.SERVICED$ = "NO"
            CARS.WAITING = 0
            TIME.CAR.FINISHES.SERVICE = 0
            TOTAL.CARS.SERVED = 0
            TOTAL.PROFIT = 0
            TOTAL.CARS.LOST = 0


      REM
      REM   THE CLOCK IS UPDATED AS THE SIMULATION PROGRESSES
      REM

      100   HOUR.OF.SIMULATION = HOUR.OF.SIMULATION + 1
            THREE.MINUTE.PERIOD = 0

      REM
      REM   SIMULATE THE NUMBER OF CARS ARRIVING IN A THREE MINUTE PERIOD
      REM

      200   THREE.MINUTE.PERIOD = THREE.MINUTE.PERIOD + 1
            X = RND(1!)
                IF X < .19 THEN NEW.CARS = 0
                IF X >= .19 AND X < .58 THEN NEW.CARS = 1
                IF X >= .58 AND X < .77 THEN NEW.CARS = 2
                IF X >= .77 AND X < .92 THEN NEW.CARS = 3
                IF X >= .92 THEN NEW.CARS = 4
            TOTAL.CARS.IN.LINE = CARS.WAITING + NEW.CARS
            IF TOTAL.CARS.IN.LINE = 0 THEN GOTO 400
            IF CAR.BEING.SERVICED$ = "YES" THEN GOTO 300
            TOTAL.CARS.IN.LINE = TOTAL.CARS.IN.LINE - 1

      REM
      REM   SIMULATE THE ORDER SIZE FOR THE NEXT CAR TO BE SERVICED
      REM

            Y = RND(1!)
                IF Y < .39 THEN PERIODS.OF.SERVICE = 1
                IF Y >= .39 AND Y < .89 THEN PERIODS.OF.SERVICE = 2
                IF Y >= .89 THEN PERIODS.OF.SERVICE = 3
            TIME.CAR.FINISHES.SERVICE = THREE.MINUTE.PERIOD + PERIODS.OF.SERVICE - 1
            CAR.BEING.SERVICED$ = "YES"

      REM
      REM   CALCULATE THE NUMBER OF LOST CUSTOMERS AND THE NUMBER OF CARS WAITING
      REM
```

A slightly more complicated simulation is discussed in Problem 11. The simulation application involves Markov processes, which will be considered in Chapter 17.

NOTES & COMMENTS

1. Most applications of computer simulation involve probabilistic components. However, computer simulation can also be used when there are no probabilistic components in the model. For instance, computer simulation can be used as a heuristic procedure to find a good solution to a complex optimization problem (such as a nonlinear integer program). In this case, computer simulation is a trial-and-error procedure; a variety of values are generated for the decision variables, and the best of the feasible solutions is chosen.

2. There are essentially two approaches to the logic and record keeping of a computer simulation model: fixed-time period and next-event. We have employed the fixed-time period approach for the County Beverage Drive-Thru problem. Each period is of equal length, and the state of the system is updated at either the beginning or the end of each period. The next-event approach would randomly generate the time between arrivals and the time to complete service for a customer. The state of the system would be updated each time there was either a customer arriving or a customer completing service. Thus, the time between system updates is variable. Either approach is acceptable; we have chosen to demonstrate the fixed-time period approach because, for an introductory treatment, we believe that it is easier to understand.

3. We have shown how to generate values of a random variable from a discrete probability distribution. With continuous random variables, the random number generation is the same, but there is only one (not an interval) random number corresponding to each value of the random variable. The value of the pseudorandom number (between 0 and 1) is taken to be the value of the cumulative distribution function, from which the corresponding value of the random variable is generated.

13.2 County Beverage Drive-Thru: Improving the System Design

The primary conclusion from the County Beverage computer simulation results presented in Section 13.1 is that the current store design cannot handle the amount of business that is anticipated. Undoubtedly, County Beverage management would like to explore alternative operating policies and designs that might improve service and enhance company profits. Certainly, the addition of a second store clerk should help the performance of the system. In addition, since construction of the building has not begun, management could consider a possible redesign of the store.

We are now ready to see how computer simulation can be used to improve system design. Once a model that is descriptive of the real system has been developed, we can think in terms of modifying the system design and using the computer simulation to see if the modifications improve system performance. The modifications explored are often called "*what if*" questions. The capability to ask "what if" questions is one of the biggest advantages of computer simulation. The simulation model serves as an experimental laboratory for answering such questions as "What if a second clerk is added?" and "What if the store is redesigned?" The two "what if" questions we want to address for County Beverage Drive-Thru deal with the performance of two modified designs, which we refer to as systems A and B.

Figure 13.7
The System A Design for the
County Beverage Drive-Thru

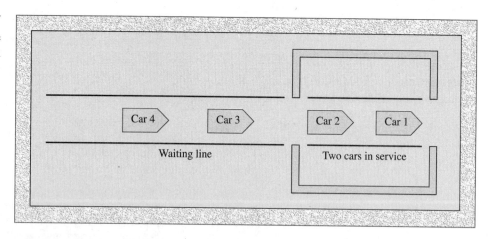

Figure 13.7
The System A Design for the
County Beverage Drive-Thru

System A (see Figure 13.7)

Computer simulation allows the user to consider design modifications and/or changes to input parameters and then observe the impact of the modifications and changes on operating characteristics such as profit, cost, waiting time, lost customers, and so on.

Two clerks will operate the store during the peak business period. Two cars will be permitted into the store area for servicing at the same time. Bottlenecks may still occur because both cars must use the same lane. If the second car completes service before the first car, it will have to wait for the first car to complete service before it can leave the store. Also, if the first car finishes service first, it can leave the store, but a new customer cannot enter the store until the car in the second position has its order filled.

System B (see Figure 13.8)

Two clerks will operate the store during the peak period. The service lane of the store will be widened to permit two cars to be serviced simultaneously, with each car being permitted to leave the store as soon as it is finished. Waiting cars move into the store as soon as either lane opens up.

To help the company determine which system should be adopted, computer simulation models were developed for both systems. Tables 13.11 and 13.12 show the results of 30

Figure 13.8
The System B Design for the
County Beverage Drive-Thru

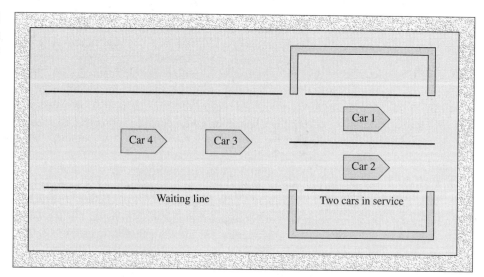

Table 13.11

System A Simulation Results for 30 Hours of Operation at the County Beverage Drive-Thru

Item of Interest	Total	Percent	Hourly Average
Number served	618	67.2	20.60
Number lost	302	32.8	10.07
Profit	$1672.50	—	$55.75

Table 13.12

System B Simulation Results for 30 Hours of Operation at the County Beverage Drive-Thru

Item of Interest	Total	Percent	Hourly Average
Number served	785	84.1	26.17
Number lost	148	15.9	4.93
Profit	$2068.50	—	$68.96

hours of simulation for each system. These results provide answers to "what if" questions and other useful information to the individual responsible for the final design decision.

System A shows an average profit of $55.75 per hour, an increase of $23.20 per hour over the original one-lane, one-server system. However, 302 customers (32.8%) were lost because of long waiting lines. Although system B shows a higher average profit ($68.96 per hour) and a lower lost customer rate (15.9%), the advantage of system B may be offset by the added construction cost required to widen the service lane. The final decision may still take more study, but the computer simulation results provide important information for the decision maker.

NOTES & COMMENTS

With the County Beverage Drive-Thru problem, we have seen how "what if" questions can play an important role in improving system design. If the original model is representative of the real system, the behavior of the model in response to the "what if" questions will be representative of how the real system will respond to the proposed modifications. Thus, the computer simulation model will help by predicting what can be expected in practice.

13.3 Modeling, Validation, and Statistical Considerations

The value of a computer simulation model depends on the accuracy of its description of the real system and on the proper use of statistical experimental design procedures in evaluating the simulation results. In this section we discuss some of the issues to consider in developing, validating, and using the results of simulations.

Selecting a Simulation Language

The computational and record-keeping aspects of computer simulation models are aided by special computer simulation languages. These languages ease the programming task associated with developing the computer simulation.

In developing a computer simulation model, a computer language must be chosen, and general-purpose programming languages such as BASIC, FORTRAN, PASCAL, and PL/1 can certainly be used. However, as computer simulation applications have increased, users as well as computer software manufacturers have recognized that most computer simulations have many common features: values of random variables must be generated from probability distributions, tables that track simulation results, and so on. Thus, special computer programming languages have been developed to enable analysts and programmers to describe simulation models more easily.

Some of the more common computer simulation languages in use today are SLAM, GPSSH, and SIMSCRIPT. These special simulation languages have automatic or built-in time indicators, simplified procedures for generating probabilistic components, and automatic collection and printout of simulation results. One programming statement of a computer simulation language often performs the computation and record keeping that would require several BASIC, FORTRAN, PASCAL, or PL/1 statements to duplicate. Complete textbooks are devoted to a discussion of the use of computer languages in simulation, and the interested reader can refer to one of the references listed at the end of this text.

Validation

An important step in any simulation study involves confirming that the simulation model accurately represents the real-world system it is designed to simulate. Models that do not adequately reflect the behavior of the real system cannot be expected to provide worthwhile information. Thus, before implementing any computer simulation results, the analyst must be sure that the model has been thoroughly validated.

If the computer simulation model has been developed for a system currently in operation, the simulation results can be compared with the current and past behavior of the real system to determine the validity of the model. In the procedure usually followed, the computer simulation program is run using an actual set of past observations. In this way, the output of the computer simulation can be compared directly with the behavior of the actual system. Any major difference in the results is indicative of problems with the accuracy of the model.

In another approach to model validation, the overall logic of the model is reviewed by experts who are most familiar with the operation of the real system. This review is subjective in nature, with the appropriate individuals evaluating the reasonableness of the computer simulation model and the simulation results.

In addition, careful attention should also be paid to the programming effort. Even if the model is formulated correctly, improper programming of the model can lead to inaccurate results. Standard quality control steps and good computer programming practice can be the best safeguards against this type of error.

A further check in the validation procedure is the comparison of the simulated distributions for the probabilistic components with the corresponding probability distributions in the real system. For example, in the County Beverage study, the probability distribution for the number of cars arriving in a 3-minute period was considered known and was an important input for the computer simulation model. Recall that the simulation results shown in Table 13.10 were based on 30 hours of simulated operation. Since each hour has 20 3-minute periods, the total simulation contained $30(20) = 600$ 3-minute periods. Thus, if the model is correctly simulating the number of customers arriving at the

Table 13.13

Model Validation Step: Comparing the Simulated Relative Frequencies and the Actual Probabilities for the Number of Customer Arrivals at the County Beverage Drive-Thru

Number of Customer Arrivals	Number of Simulated Periods Having This Number of Arrivals	Simulated Relative Frequencies	Actual Probabilities (See Table 13.1)
0	124	0.207	0.19
1	229	0.382	0.39
2	104	0.173	0.19
3	86	0.143	0.15
4	57	0.095	0.08
Totals	600	1.000	1.00

store, the relative frequencies of customer arrivals should approximate the probability distribution for the real system as shown in Table 13.1.

Table 13.13 shows the relative frequencies for the number of customers arriving during the simulated 600 3-minute periods. A comparison of the simulated distribution and the actual probability distribution from Table 13.1 shows no major differences. Thus, we conclude that the number of customer arrivals is being simulated correctly.[2] A similar comparison of the actual and simulated distributions for the size of the customer orders resulted in the conclusion that the model was valid in terms of its simulation of this probabilistic component.

Start-Up Problems

Most computer simulation studies are concerned with the operation of a system during its normal, or *steady-state,* condition. Steady state for a system refers to the system behavior after it has been operating long enough for the effect of any start-up conditions to have dissipated. In the County Beverage problem, the firm is interested in what happens during a typical steady-state hour of operation. Recall, however, that when we started the computer simulation calculations, we assumed that no cars were waiting and that no cars were being served. Therefore, data collected during the first part of the simulation can be expected to differ from data collected during time intervals later in the simulation. To avoid start-up difficulties, the computer simulation program is usually run for a specified period without collecting any data. The length of this start-up period must be sufficient for the system to have stabilized. Data are then collected on the system after it has reached a stable, or steady-state, condition. For the County Beverage simulation, the first hour of operation was considered a start-up period. The data for the 30 hours of simulation reported in Table 13.10 are the simulation results for hours 2–31.

Statistical Considerations

The results of any computer simulation actually represent a sample. For example, the simulation results in Table 13.10 can be viewed as a sample of 30 hours of operation.

---

[2]Standard statistical procedures, such as the chi-square goodness-of-fit test, can be performed to test whether the results observed are representative of those expected. The use of such tests is described in most standard statistics texts. For example, see D. R. Anderson, D. J. Sweeney, and T. A. Williams, *Statistics for Business and Economics,* 5th ed. (St. Paul, Minn.: West Publishing Company, 1993).

Thus, $32.56 is an estimate of the average hourly profit for the County Beverage operation. The important thing to keep in mind is that different values for average hourly profit would be observed if the computer simulation used a different sequence of random numbers. To illustrate this, we ran two additional computer simulations each for 30 hours of operation. The results are as follows:

	Simulation Results		
Item of Interest	Sample 1	Sample 2	Sample 3
Number served	365	361	356
Number lost	575	558	622
Average hourly profit	$32.56	$32.26	$32.20

Relatively long simulated periods are recommended as a way of obtaining useful simulation results.

Although slightly different results are obtained in each case, by using the computer simulation model for a long period of time, most analysts are willing to use the values obtained from a single computer simulation program run to estimate the true mean value of interest.

Determining the best statistical approach to estimating the statistical significance of differences due to design modifications is not a simple problem. A complete study of this issue would require a background in the area of statistics referred to as experimental design. Consequently, the interested reader is referred to one of the more advanced texts in simulation listed at the end of the text.

13.4 An Inventory Simulation Model

In this section we present another illustration of computer simulation by modeling an auto supply company's inventory system. While we are interested in accurately describing how the inventory system operates, we are also interested in making decisions concerning the reorder point and order quantity for a particular inventory item. By designing a set of experiments, we will simulate the operation of the inventory system for a variety of "what if" questions concerning reorder-point and order-quantity alternatives. Upon completion of the computer simulation experiments, we should be able to select a good reorder point and order quantity for the item.

Art's Auto Supplies, Inc., is a specialty auto supply store that carries over 1000 items in inventory. Although the store's manager has used inventory models to determine how much to order and when to order for most of the products, the manager has become concerned about the inventory problem for a deluxe tool cabinet. Demand for the cabinets has been relatively low, but subject to some variability. On approximately one-half of the days the store is open for business, no one orders a cabinet, but on about 1 day per month, three or four orders occur. If variable demand were the only source of uncertainty, the store manager believes that the order-quantity and reorder-point decisions could be based on an inventory model, perhaps similar to the inventory model discussed in Section 12.1. However, the tool cabinet inventory problem is further complicated by the fact that the lead time—the time between order placement and order arrival—also varies. Historically, the lead time has been between 1 and 5 days. The variable lead times have caused the store to run out of inventory on several occasions and orders received during the out-of-stock period have caused lost sales. Given this situation, the store manager would like to establish order-quantity and reorder-point decisions that minimize total relevant inventory costs—that is, ordering, holding, and stockout or shortage costs.

After an analysis of delivery charges and other costs associated with each order, the store manager was able to estimate the order cost at $20 per order. An analysis of interest, insurance, and other inventory carrying costs led to an estimate of $0.10 per unit per day for the holding cost. Finally, the shortage cost was estimated to be $50 per unit. The total relevant cost of the inventory system is given by the sum of the ordering cost, the holding cost, and the shortage cost. The objective is to find the order-quantity and reorder-point combination that will result in the lowest possible total cost.

A first step in the computer simulation approach to this problem is the development of a model that can simulate the total relevant costs corresponding to a specific order size and reorder point. Then, using this model, "what if" questions can be posed by systematically varying the two decision variables to determine what appears to be the lowest-cost combination. Let us begin by developing such a model to carry out a 1-day simulation of the inventory process.

Assume that a specific reorder point and order quantity have already been selected. We begin each day of the simulation by checking whether any inventory previously ordered has arrived. If so, the current inventory on hand is increased by the quantity of goods received. This assumes that orders are received and inventory on hand is updated at the start of each day. If such an assumption is not appropriate, a different model, perhaps calling for goods to be received at the end of the day, would have to be developed.

Next, the computer simulation must randomly generate a value for the daily demand from the appropriate probability distribution. If there is sufficient inventory on hand to meet the daily demand, the inventory on hand will be decreased by the amount of the daily demand. If, however, inventory on hand is not sufficient to satisfy all the demand, as much demand as possible will be satisfied. The inventory will be reduced to zero, and a shortage cost will be computed for all unsatisfied demand. Updating the process in this fashion, we are assuming that if a customer orders more cabinets than the store has in inventory, the customer will take what is available and shop elsewhere for the remainder of the order. With another auto supply store only two blocks away, the store manager is sure that unsatisfied demand will result in lost sales, and a $50 per unit shortage cost is appropriate.

After the daily demand has been processed, the next step is to determine whether the ending inventory has reached the reorder point and a new order should be placed. However, prior to placing a new order, we must check to see if the most recent order is outstanding. If so, we do not place another order.[3] Otherwise, an order is placed, and the company incurs an ordering cost. When an order is placed, a lead time must be randomly generated to reflect the time between the placement of the order and the receipt of the goods.

Finally, holding cost, which is $0.10 for each unit in the daily ending inventory, is computed. The sum of the shortage costs, ordering costs, and holding costs becomes the total daily cost for the simulation. Performing the above sequence of operations would complete 1 day of simulation. Figure 13.9 depicts this daily simulation process for the deluxe tool cabinet inventory operation.

The daily simulation process should be repeated for as many days as are necessary to reach steady state and obtain meaningful results. The output from the computer

---

[3]We are assuming that it will never be necessary to have two orders outstanding simultaneously. However, in other computer simulation models, having several orders outstanding may be an entirely appropriate assumption.

Figure 13.9
The Art's Auto Supplies Inventory
Simulation Model

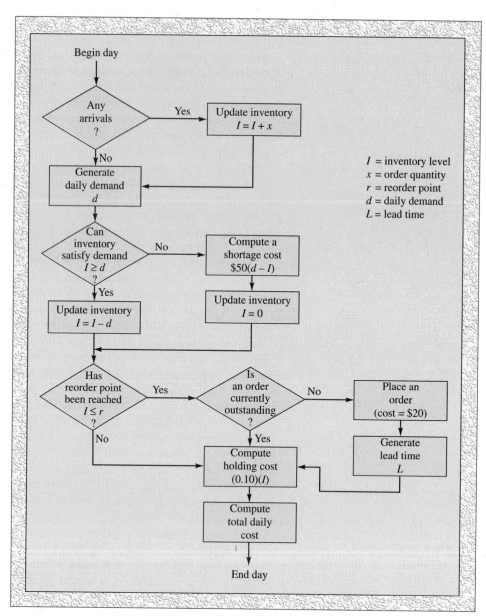

I = inventory level
x = order quantity
r = reorder point
d = daily demand
L = lead time

Table 13.14

Frequency and Relative Frequency
Distributions of Demand for Art's
Auto Supplies Problem

Demand (units)	Frequency (days)	Relative Frequency
0	150	0.50
1	75	0.25
2	45	0.15
3	15	0.05
4	15	0.05
Totals	300	1.00

simulation will show the total cost involved in using one particular order-quantity and reorder-point combination. By simulating the inventory operation with different order-quantity/reorder-point combinations, we can compare total operating costs and select the apparent "best" order-quantity and reorder-point decisions for the deluxe tool cabinets.

Suppose that the store has a complete set of records showing the demand for the deluxe tool cabinets for the past year (300 days). Furthermore, suppose that the records also show the number of days between placement and receipt of each order over the same period. Table 13.14 shows the frequency and relative frequency distributions for demand, and Table 13.15 shows the frequency and relative frequency distributions for lead time.

To carry out the computer simulation steps depicted in Figure 13.9, we must develop the procedure for generating values from the demand and lead-time distributions. As before, we will associate an interval of pseudorandom numbers with each value of the

Table 13.15

Frequency and Relative Frequency Distributions of Lead Time for Art's Auto Supplies Problem

Lead Time (days)	Frequency (days)	Relative Frequency
1	6	0.20
2	3	0.10
3	12	0.40
4	6	0.20
5	3	0.10
Totals	30	1.00

random variable such that the probability of generating a pseudorandom number in that interval is the same as the relative frequency of the associated demand and lead time. The intervals of pseudorandom numbers are shown in Tables 13.16 and 13.17.

To appreciate how the simulation method works for this problem, we will first perform a 10-day simulation of the process. Let us assume that the store manager wants to determine the effect of using an order quantity of 5 units with a reorder point of 3 units. For purposes of starting the simulation, let us assume that we have a beginning inventory of 5 units at the start of day 1 of the 10-day simulation.

Refer to the flowchart in Figure 13.9. The first step is to check to see whether any shipments have arrived. Since this is the first day of the simulation, we assume no arrivals and generate the daily demand for day 1. Let us assume that we use a computer program to generate pseudorandom numbers between 0 and 0.999 . . . and that the first number generated is 0.09. From Table 13.16 we see that this pseudorandom number corresponds to a demand of 0 units. There are no shortage costs to compute since the inventory on hand (5 units) is greater than the daily demand (0 units); moreover, since the inventory on hand is greater than the order point (3 units), we do not place an order. The holding cost for day 1 is computed to be ($0.10)5, or $0.50. With no shortages and no ordering, the total cost for day 1 is just the holding cost of $0.50. Continuing the simulation in this manner, we obtained the computer-generated results shown in Table 13.18.

At the start of day 4, the beginning inventory was 4 units. The random number selected to generate daily demand was 0.53; thus, a daily demand of 1 unit was generated. As a result, the ending inventory dropped to 3 units, and an order for 5 units was placed. Generating another random number—in this case, 0.62—indicates (see Table 13.18) a lead time of 3 days, which means that the new order will be available at the start of day 7. The day 4 costs thus far are ($0.10)3 = $0.30 for the holding cost and $20.00 for the

Table 13.16

Pseudorandom Numbers and Daily Demands for Art's Auto Supplies Problem

Daily Demand	Relative Frequency or Probability	Cumulative Probability	Interval of Pseudorandom Numbers
0	0.50	0.50	0.00 but less than 0.50
1	0.25	0.75	0.50 but less than 0.75
2	0.15	0.90	0.75 but less than 0.90
3	0.05	0.95	0.90 but less than 0.95
4	0.05	1.00	0.95 but less than 1.00
Total	1.00		

Table 13.17

Pseudorandom Numbers and Lead Times for Art's Auto Supplies Problem

Lead Time (days)	Relative Frequency or Probability	Cumulative Probability	Interval of Pseudorandom Numbers
1	0.20	0.20	0.00 but less than 0.20
2	0.10	0.30	0.20 but less than 0.30
3	0.40	0.70	0.30 but less than 0.70
4	0.20	0.90	0.70 but less than 0.90
5	0.10	1.00	0.90 but less than 1.00
	1.00		

Table 13.18 Simulation Results for 10 Days of Operation of Art's Auto Supplies (Order Quantity of 5, Reorder Point of 3)

Day	Beg Inv	Units Rec'd	Rndm Num	Units Dem'd	End Inv	Rndm Num	Lead Time	Holding	Order	Shortage	Total
								Cost ($)			
1	5	0	0.09	0	5			0.50	0.00	0.00	0.50
2	5	0	0.68	1	4			0.40	0.00	0.00	0.40
3	4	0	0.29	0	4			0.40	0.00	0.00	0.40
4	4	0	0.53	1	3	0.62	3	0.30	20.00	0.00	20.30
5	3	0	0.87	2	1			0.10	0.00	0.00	0.10
6	1	0	0.98	4	0			0.00	0.00	150.00	150.00
7	0	5	0.62	1	4			0.40	0.00	0.00	0.40
8	4	0	0.82	2	2	0.94	5	0.20	20.00	0.00	20.20
9	2	0	0.37	0	2			0.20	0.00	0.00	0.20
10	2	0	0.35	0	2			0.20	0.00	0.00	0.20
					Average cost for 10 simulated days			0.27	4.00	15.00	19.27

ordering cost. Since there is no shortage cost, the total cost for the day is $20.30. The figures at the bottom of Table 13.18 provide the average costs for holding, ordering, and shortages, and the average total cost for the 10-day simulation. Before we draw any firm conclusions based on these limited results, we should run the computer simulation for many more days. We will also want to test many other order-quantity/reorder-point combinations.

A computer programmer could develop a computer simulation program that would enable the store to explore a variety of order quantities and reorder points for a large number of simulated days. In Table 13.19 we present output from a computer program that was developed to solve inventory problems such as the Art's Auto Supplies problem. In this program, the decision maker has the option of selecting a variety of order quantities and reorder points. For purposes of illustration, the computer program output is shown for simulations with order quantities of from 5 to 50 units in increments of 5 and for reorder points of from 1 to 10 units in increments of 1. A total of 1000 days is represented in the simulation of each order-quantity/reorder-point combination.

We see that the results of this computer simulation indicate that the lowest-cost solution occurs at an order quantity of 25 units and a reorder point of 6 units; in this case,

Table 13.19

Simulated Average Daily Cost for 1000 Days of Art's Auto Supplies Problem (Order-Quantity Increments of 5)

Reorder Point	5	10	15	20	25	30	35	40	45	50
	Order Quantity									
1	14.35	8.30	6.58	5.20	5.35	4.16	3.30	4.42	3.98	5.22
2	11.51	5.93	5.46	3.92	3.91	3.44	2.96	3.69	3.62	3.71
3	9.34	5.64	3.37	3.01	3.03	2.84	3.96	3.29	2.90	3.07
4	6.90	4.12	3.47	2.78	3.14	2.79	3.29	3.25	3.37	3.42
5	5.41	3.31	2.85	2.42	2.61	3.24	3.25	2.93	3.18	3.22
6	4.72	2.75	2.69	2.60	2.39	2.74	2.93	3.06	3.13	3.34
7	4.72	2.85	2.52	2.60	2.76	2.71	3.06	2.99	3.02	3.28
8	5.50	2.89	2.66	2.50	2.62	2.75	2.99	3.05	3.33	3.56
9	4.36	3.11	2.62	2.62	2.66	2.77	3.05	3.18	3.34	3.49
10	4.68	3.05	2.75	2.72	2.80	2.85	3.18	3.28	3.31	3.72

Table 13.20

Simulated Average Daily Cost for 1000 Days of Art's Auto Supplies Problem (Order-Quantity Increments of 1)

Reorder Point	Order Quantity									
	21	22	23	24	25	26	27	28	29	30
4	2.94	3.02	3.13	2.74	2.89	2.56	2.74	3.07	2.67	3.24
5	2.59	2.58	2.84	2.70	2.66	2.59	2.88	2.57	2.48	2.75
6	2.55	2.33	2.87	2.35	2.75	2.45	2.81	2.79	2.61	2.60
7	2.52	2.45	2.47	2.51	2.57	2.62	2.61	2.63	2.62	2.67
8	2.50	2.69	2.48	2.49	2.63	2.57	2.63	2.69	2.69	2.71

You should now be able to work Problem 15. The inventory simulation results should be presented in the format of Table 13.8.

the resulting average total cost is $2.39 per day. After studying these results, the store manager might wish to explore other order quantities near the apparent "best" order quantity of 25. In Table 13.20 the results of varying the order quantity from 21 to 30 (in increments of 1) and the reorder point from 4 to 8 are shown. The smallest simulated average total cost of $2.33 now occurs when the order quantity is 22 units and the reorder point is 6 units. Note, however, that in this second set of simulation experiments the previously best order quantity of 25 units and reorder point of 6 units has a total cost of $2.75 per day. Since different random numbers were used in the two simulations, different total costs are to be expected. The selection of the "best" order quantity and reorder point is now up to the analyst. What decisions would you make? While you might want to run more or longer simulations, the simulation data of Tables 13.19 and 13.20 indicate that good solutions apparently exist with order quantities around 20–25 units and reorder points around 6 or 7 units. Thus, while computer simulation has not guaranteed an optimal solution, it has enabled us to identify apparent low-cost or "near-optimal" decisions for the inventory problem. The final decision for an order quantity and reorder point will be based on the store manager's preference from among the good or "near-optimal" solutions.

13.5 Advantages and Disadvantages of Computer Simulation

Through computer simulation experiments, we can ask "what if" questions and project how the real-world system will behave. While the experiments cannot guarantee optimality, they usually result in very good, near-optimal solutions. In addition, simulation models often warn against poor decisions and strategies where simulation results project disastrous outcomes such as system failures, large financial losses, and so on.

A primary advantage of computer simulation is that it is applicable in complex cases where analytical procedures cannot be employed. For example, the County Beverage waiting line system and the Art's Auto Supplies inventory system are sufficiently complex that the analytical approaches discussed in other chapters of this text do not apply. That is, the forms of the probability distributions involved do not satisfy the assumptions of the analytical models. In general, the larger the number of probabilistic components in the system, the more likely it is that computer simulation will be the best approach.

Another advantage of computer simulation is that the simulation model and its computer program provide a convenient experimental laboratory. Once the computer program has been developed, it is usually relatively easy to experiment with the model by asking "what if" questions. For example, if we want to know the effect of an increase in shortage cost on the recommended solution to the inventory problem, we could simply change the shortage cost input value and rerun the computer program. The effect of experimental changes in other inputs, such as the probability distributions of customer arrivals, lead time, and so on, could also be investigated.

Computer simulation is not without its disadvantages. One obvious disadvantage is that someone must develop the computer simulation program. For large simulation projects, this is usually a substantial undertaking. Hence, one should certainly not attempt to develop a simulation model unless the potential gains promise to outweigh the costs of model development. This disadvantage has been reduced with the development of computer simulation languages such as GPSSH, SIMSCRIPT, and SLAM. The use of these languages often leads to considerable savings in time and money as the computer simulation program is developed.

Another disadvantage of computer simulation is that it does not guarantee an optimal solution to a problem. One usually selects those values of the decision variables to test in the model that have a good chance of being near the optimal solution. However, since it is usually too costly to try all values of the decision variables, and since different simulations may provide different results, there is no guarantee that the best simulation solution found is the overall optimal solution. Nonetheless, the danger of obtaining bad solutions is slight if good judgment is exercised in developing the computer simulation model and the computer program. The decision maker usually has a good idea of reasonable values to try for the decision variables, and it is usually possible to run the computer simulation long enough to reach steady state and identify the apparent best decisions.

Summary

Computer simulation is used extensively today. Some of the reasons why it is so widely applied include the following:

1. It can be used for a large number of practical problems.
2. It can be used to obtain good solutions to problems that are too complex to be solved with analytic procedures such as waiting line models or inventory models.
3. The computer simulation approach is straightforward and hence relatively easy to explain and understand. As a result, management confidence is increased and acceptance of the model is more easily obtained.
4. Computer software firms have developed specialized computer simulation programming languages, thus facilitating the use of simulation in practice.

In this chapter we illustrated the use of computer simulation for a waiting line system and an inventory system. In both cases, we saw how a series of experiments with key design parameters of the model could be conducted to identify good values for these parameters of the real system. In the County Beverage problem, simulation experiments helped to identify the two-lane design as the one yielding the highest average hourly profit. In the computer simulation of Art's Auto Supplies, the simulation experiments helped identify an order quantity of around 20–25 units and a reorder level of 6 or 7 units as a good low-cost inventory policy.

A primary objective of computer simulation is the development of a model that is descriptive of the real system; the purpose of validation is to make sure that it is. Once validation has shown that the simulation model is acceptable, the model can be used to address "what if" questions and conduct experiments concerning system performance. We have stressed that proper experimental designs must be developed and appropriate statistical methodology must be employed in analyzing the experimental results.

Glossary

Simulation A technique used to describe the behavior of a real-world system. A computer program is used to perform the simulation computations.

Monte Carlo simulations Simulations that use a random number procedure to generate values for the probabilistic components.

Pseudorandom numbers Computer-generated numbers developed from mathematical expressions that have the properties of random numbers.

"What if" questions Modifications made to model parameters to explore the effect on simulation output.

Problems

Note to student: Most of the problems in this section are designed to enable you to perform simulations with hand calculations. To keep the calculations reasonable, we will ask you to consider only a few decision alternatives and relatively short periods of time. While this should give you a good understanding of the simulation process, the simulation results will not be sufficient for you to make final conclusions or decisions about the problem situation. If you have access to a computer, we suggest that you develop a computer program for some of the problems. Then, by using the program to test several decision alternatives over a much longer simulated period, you will be able to obtain the desired decision-making information.

S ELF T EST

1. Random number ranges and simulation, one event

1. A retail store has experienced the following historical daily demand for a particular product:

Sales (units)	Frequency (days)
0	4
1	6
2	14
3	12
4	7
5	5
6	2
Total	50

   a. Develop a relative frequency distribution for the above data.
   b. Use the random numbers from row 4 of Table 13.3 to simulate daily sales for a 10-day period. This row begins with the random numbers 46276 87453.
   c. What is the total sales for the 10 days?

2. Random number ranges and simulation, one event

2. A study was conducted to investigate the number of cars arriving at the drive-in window of Community Savings Bank. The following data were collected for 100 randomly selected 5-minute intervals:

Number of Arrivals	Number of Occurrences
0	12
1	24
2	37
3	19
4	8
Total	100

a.   Develop a relative frequency distribution for the above data.

b.   Use random numbers 08, 61, and 22 to simulate the number of customers that arrive between 9:00 A.M. and 9:15 A.M. on a given day.

SELF TEST

3. Random number ranges and simulation, one event

3.   A car rental agency has collected data on the demand for luxury-class automobiles over the past 25 days. The data are shown below.

Daily Demand	Number of Days
7	2
8	5
9	8
10	7
11	3
Total	25

Because customers drop cars at another location, the agency only has 9 cars available currently.

a.   Use the following five random numbers to generate 5 days of demand for the rental agency: 15   48   71   56   90.

b.   What is the average number of cars rented for the 5 days?

c.   How many rentals will be lost over the 5 days?

d.   What is the average daily demand for the 5 days?

4. Random number ranges and simulation, one event

4.   Refer to the data in Problem 2 concerning arrivals at the Community Savings Bank.

a.   Use the following random numbers to generate arrivals for the next six 5-minute intervals: 01   09   26   05   33   14.

b.   Compute the average number of arrivals for the 6 periods in part (a).

c.   Would you feel comfortable estimating the average number of arrivals using the arrivals generated in part (a)? Why or why not?

d.   Compute the expected number of arrivals in a 5-minute period using the relative frequencies in Problem 2 as the appropriate probabilities. Compare this with the average computed in part (b).

5. Random number ranges and simulation, one event

5.   Decca Industries has experienced the following weekly absenteeism over the past 20 weeks:

Number of Employees Absent	Frequency
1	2
2	4
3	7
4	3
5	2
6	2
Total	20

a.   Develop a relative frequency distribution for the above data.

b.   Use random numbers to simulate weekly absenteeism for a 15-week period.

6. Random number ranges and simulation, one event

6. Given below are 50 weeks of historical sales data for cars sold by Domoy Motors, Inc., a new-car dealer in Newton, Ohio.

Weekly Sales	Number of Weeks
0	2
1	5
2	8
3	22
4	10
5	3
	Total 50

  a. Develop the relative frequency distribution for these data.
  b. Use a random number procedure to simulate weekly automobile sales for a 12-week period.

7. Random number ranges and simulation, one event

7. Charlestown Electric Company is building a new generator for its Mount Washington plant. Even with good maintenance procedures, the generator will have periodic failures or breakdowns. Historical figures for similar generators indicate that the relative frequency of failures during a year is as follows:

Number of Failures	0	1	2	3
Relative Frequency	0.80	0.15	0.04	0.01

  Assume that the useful lifetime of the generator is 25 years. Use simulation to estimate the number of breakdowns that will occur in the 25 years of operation. Is it common to have 5 or more consecutive years of operation without a failure?

8. Random number ranges and simulation, one event

8. Use row 15 of Table 13.3 beginning with 20711 and 55609 to simulate 15 minutes of operation for the County Beverage Drive-Thru application presented in Section 13.1. Show your simulation results in the format of Table 13.7.

9. Random number ranges and simulation, two events

9. A service technician for a major photocopier company is trained to service two models of copier: the X100 and the Y200. Approximately 60% of the technician's service calls are for the X100, and 40% are for the Y200. The service time distributions for the two models are as follows:

X100 Copier		Y200 Copier	
Time (minutes)	Relative Frequency	Time (minutes)	Relative Frequency
25	0.50	20	0.40
30	0.25	25	0.40
35	0.15	30	0.10
40	0.10	35	0.10

  a. Show the random number intervals that can be used to simulate the type of machine to be serviced and the length of the service time for each model.
  b. Simulate 20 service calls. What is the total service time spent on the 20 calls?

10. Bushnell's Sand and Gravel (BSG) is a small firm that supplies sand, gravel, and topsoil to contractors and landscaping firms. BSG maintains an inventory of high-quality screened topsoil that is used to supply the weekly orders for two companies: Bath Landscaping Service and Pittsford Lawn Care, Inc. BSG must determine how many cubic yards of screened topsoil to have in inventory at the beginning of each week to satisfy the needs of both its customers. BSG would like to select the lowest possible inventory level that would have a 0.95 probability of satisfying the combined weekly orders from both customers. The demand distributions for the two customers are as follows:

Customer	Weekly Demand (cubic yards)	Relative Frequency
Bath Landscaping	10	0.20
	15	0.35
	20	0.30
	25	0.10
	30	0.05
Pittsford Lawn Care	30	0.20
	40	0.40
	50	0.30
	60	0.10

Simulate 20 weeks of operation for beginning inventories of 70 and 80 cubic yards. Based on your limited simulation results, how many cubic yards should BSG maintain in inventory? Discuss what you would want to do in a full-scale simulation of this problem.

11. Three discount pharmacies (Super Z, Devco, and Floorgreen) compete for business in a suburban area. Customers often make a purchase at one of the stores and then make their next purchase at another store. The matrix below shows the probability that a customer will switch stores from one purchase to the next.

Current Purchase	Next Purchase		
	Super Z	Devco	Floorgreen
Super Z	0.70	0.10	0.20
Devco	0.30	0.55	0.15
Floorgreen	0.10	0.10	0.80

a. Show the probability distribution and the intervals of random numbers that could be used to generate the next purchase for a customer who last made a purchase at Super Z.
b. Repeat part (a) for a customer who last made a purchase at Devco.
c. Repeat part (a) for a customer who last made a purchase at Floorgreen.
d. Gary Hatcher made his last purchase at Super Z. Use the following four random numbers to simulate the store at which he makes his next four purchases: 42, 81, 16, 57.

e. Suppose Gary Hatcher's last purchase in part (d) had been made at Devco. Use the same four random numbers to generate his next four purchases.

f. If the simulation were conducted for a large number of purchases (say, 1000), the fraction of Hatcher's purchases from each store would be about the same regardless of which store he made his last purchase from. This is what it means to reach steady state. Use your results from parts (d) and (e) to comment on whether simulating four purchases is enough to reach steady state.

12. Simulation, multiple events

12. A door-to-door magazine salesperson has the historical sales record shown below. If the salesperson talks to the woman of the house, there is a 15% chance of making a sale. Furthermore, if the salesperson convinces the woman of the house to purchase some magazines, the relative frequency distribution for the number of the subscriptions ordered is as follows:

Number of Subscriptions	1	2	3
Relative Frequency	0.60	0.30	0.10

On the other hand, if the man of the house answers the door, the salesperson's chances of making a sale are 25%. In addition, the relative frequency distribution for the number of subscriptions ordered is as follows:

Number of Subscriptions	1	2	3	4
Relative Frequency	0.10	0.40	0.30	0.20

The salesperson has found that no one answers the door at about 30% of the houses contacted. However, of the people who do answer the door, 80% are women and 20% are men. The salesperson's profit is $2 for each subscription sold.

a. Using simulation, show the house-by-house results for 25 calls.

b. What is the total profit projected for the 25 calls?

c. Based on your results from part (b), how many subscriptions should the salesperson expect to sell by calling on 100 houses per day? What is the salesperson's expected daily profit?

13. Simulation modeling: project times

13. A project has four activities (A, B, C, and D) that must be performed sequentially to complete the project. The probability distribution for the time required to complete each of the activities is as follows:

Activity	Activity Time (weeks)	Probability
A	5	0.25
	6	0.30
	7	0.30
	8	0.15
B	3	0.20
	5	0.55
	7	0.25

Activity	Activity Time (weeks)	Probability
C	10	0.10
	12	0.25
	14	0.40
	16	0.20
	18	0.05
D	8	0.60
	10	0.40

a. Use a random number procedure to simulate the completion time for each activity. Sum the activity times to establish a completion time for the entire project.

b. Use the simulation procedure developed in part (a) to simulate 20 completions of this project. Show the distribution of completion times, and estimate the probability that the project can be completed in 35 weeks or less.

14. Simulation modeling: inventory

14. The New York City corner newsstand orders 250 copies of *The New York Times* daily. Primarily due to weather conditions, the demand for newspapers varies from day to day. The probability distribution of the demand for newspapers is as follows:

Number of Newspapers	150	175	200	225	250
Probability	0.10	0.30	0.30	0.20	0.10

The newsstand makes a 15-cent profit on every paper sold, but it loses 10 cents on every paper unsold by the end of the day. Use 10 days of simulated results to determine whether the newsstand should order 200, 225, or 250 papers per day. What is the average daily profit the newsstand can anticipate based on your recommendation?

S E L F   T E S T

15. Simulation modeling: inventory

15. For the Art's Auto Supplies problem in Section 13.4, develop a 10-day simulation where the following demand distribution is assumed:

Demand	0	1	2	3	4
Relative Frequency	0.25	0.50	0.15	0.05	0.05

Using an order quantity of 5 and a reorder point of 3, show your results in the format of Table 13.18.

16. Simulation modeling: inventory

16. Bristol Bikes, Inc., would like to develop an order-quantity and reorder-point policy that would minimize the total costs associated with the company's inventory of exercise bikes. The relative frequency distribution for retail demand on a weekly basis is as follows:

Demand	0	1	2	3	4	5
Probability	0.20	0.50	0.10	0.10	0.05	0.05

The relative frequency distribution for lead time is as follows:

Lead Time (weeks)	1	2	3	4
Relative Frequency	0.10	0.25	0.60	0.05

The holding cost is $1 per unit per week, the ordering cost is $20 per order, the shortage cost is $25 per unit, and the beginning inventory is 7 units. Using an order quantity of 12 and a reorder point of 5, simulate 10 weeks of operation of this inventory system.

17. Stollar's Bakery Shop would like to determine how many 10-inch white cakes should be produced each day to maximize profits. The production cost is $2.50 per cake, and the selling price is $4.50. Any cakes that are not sold at the end of the day are sold for $1.50 to a local store that specializes in day-old goods. Assume that the following data showing the daily demand during the past month (20 days of operation) is available:

Daily Demand	Frequency (number of days observed)
0	1
1	2
2	1
3	2
4	3
5	6
6	3
7	1
8	1
Total	20

Develop a 10-day simulation for production sizes ranging from 1 to 8 cakes per day. Use the following random numbers to generate daily demand:

48   12   77   24   32   43   96   03   62   77

What appears to be the best production size?

18. Domoy Motors, Inc., purchases a certain model automobile for $5778. To finance the purchase of cars of this model, Domoy must pay an 18% annual interest rate on borrowed capital. This interest rate amounts to approximately $20 per car per week. Orders for additional cars can be placed each week, but a minimum order size of 5 cars is required on any given order. It currently takes 3 weeks to receive a new shipment of cars after the order is placed. The cost of placing an order is $50. If Domoy runs out of cars in inventory, a shortage cost of $300 per car is incurred. Currently, Domoy has 20 cars of this model in inventory. Historical data showing the weekly demand were given in Problem 6.

a. Assuming an order quantity of 15 cars and a reorder point of 10 cars, perform a 12-week simulation of Domoy's operation. Use the first 12 two-digit random numbers from row 2 of Table 13.3 beginning with the number 88547. Show your simulation results in the format of Table 13.18.

b. Write a computer program to simulate weekly sales at Domoy Motors. Use the program to determine the order policy that appears to minimize Domoy's overall costs.

19. A firm with a national chain of hotels and motels is interested in learning where individuals prefer to stay when on business trips. Three competing hotel and motel chains are included in the study. They are the Marimont Inn, the Harrison Inn, and the Hinton Hotel. The study found that where an individual stays on one trip is a good predictor of where the individual will stay the next trip. However, the study showed that sometimes individuals switch from one chain to another. The probabilities of staying at each chain are shown below. For example, if an individual stayed at the Marimont Inn on one trip, there is a 0.70 probability of staying at the Marimont Inn the next trip, a 0.10 probability of staying at the Harrison Inn the next trip, and a 0.20 probability of staying at the Hinton Hotel the next trip. Similar probability values are shown for individuals staying at the Harrison Inn and the Hinton Hotel on a particular trip.

Currently Staying at	Probability of Staying the Next Trip at		
	Marimont	Harrison	Hinton
Marimont	0.70	0.10	0.20
Harrison	0.20	0.60	0.20
Hinton	0.15	0.05	0.80

a. Show the random number assignments that can be used to simulate the next visit for an individual currently staying at the Marimont, Harrison, and Hinton chains.

b. Develop a flowchart that describes the process for simulating where an individual will stay during a series of business trips.

c. Assume that an individual most recently stayed at the Marimont Inn. Simulate where the individual would stay on the next 50 business trips. What percentage of time will the person select each chain? Which appears to be the most popular chain?

d. Repeat the simulation in part (c) starting with an individual most recently staying at the Harrison Inn. Repeat part (c) again with the individual most recently staying at the Hinton Hotel. Which is the most popular chain based on these simulation results?

20. Shown below is the probability distribution for the number of pins a bowler obtains on a first ball.

Number of Pins	6	7	8	9	10
Probability	0.02	0.08	0.20	0.30	0.40

The probability table showing the number of pins obtained on a second ball is as follows:

If Number of Pins on First Ball Is	Number of Pins on Second Ball Is				
	0	1	2	3	4
6	0.01	0.03	0.20	0.26	0.50
7	0.04	0.10	0.36	0.50	
8	0.05	0.25	0.70		
9	0.15	0.85			

a. Using the above information, simulate a game of bowling. What is the bowler's score?

b. Develop a computer program for this problem, and simulate several games of bowling. What is an estimate of the bowler's average score?

21. Mount Washington Garage sells regular and unleaded gasoline. Pump 1, a self-service facility, is used by customers who want to pump their own gas. Pump 2, a full-service facility, is used by customers who are willing to pay a higher cost per gallon to have an attendant pump the gas, check the oil, and so on. Both pumps can service 1 car at a time. Based on past data, the owner of the garage estimates that 70% of the customers select the self-service pump and 30% want full service. The arrival rate of cars for each minute of operation is given by the following probability distribution:

Number of Arrivals in 1 Minute of Operation	Probability
0	0.10
1	0.20
2	0.35
3	0.30
4	0.05
Total	1.00

The time it takes to service a car, which depends on whether the self-service or the full-service facility is used, is given by the following probability distribution:

Self-Service Pump		Full-Service Pump	
Service Time (minutes)	Probability	Service Time (minutes)	Probability
2	0.10	3	0.20
3	0.20	4	0.30
4	0.60	5	0.35
5	0.10	6	0.10
Total	1.00	7	0.05
		Total	1.00

Study the operation of the system for 10 minutes using simulation. As part of your analysis, consider the following types of questions: What is the average number of cars waiting for service per minute at both facilities? What is the average amount of time a car must wait for service? Prepare a brief report for Mount Washington Garage that describes your analysis and any conclusions.

22. Simulation design

22. A medical consulting firm has been asked to determine the facilities required in the X-ray laboratory of a new hospital. In particular, the firm should provide recommendations on the number of X-ray units for the laboratory. How could computer simulation assist in reaching a good decision? What factors would you consider in a simulation model of this problem?

23. Simulation design

23. Consider a medium-sized community that currently has only one fire station. You have been hired by the city manager to assist in the determination of the best location for a second fire station. What would be your objective for this problem? Explain how computer simulation might be used to evaluate alternative locations and help identify the best location.

24. Simulation design

24. A bus company is considering adding a new 10-stop route to its operation. The bus will be scheduled to complete the route once each hour. If the company has determined the approximate demand distribution for each location, discuss how computer simulation might be used to project the hourly profit associated with the new route. If the company can assign a regular bus or a more economical minibus to this route, discuss how computer simulation might help make this decision. Note that with the minibus the company's management is concerned about being unable to pick up customers if the bus is already carrying its maximum number of riders.

Case Problem: Machine Repair

Jerry Masters, president of Pacific Plastics, Inc. (PPI), has become concerned with reports that downtime for PPI's plastic injection-molding machines has been increasing. A machine's downtime includes the time the machine must wait for a repair service technician to arrive after a breakdown plus the actual repair time. Currently, PPI has three plastic injection-molding machines, which are repaired by one service technician. However, because of an increase in business, PPI is considering the purchase of three additional machines. Jerry is concerned that, with the additional machines, downtime will increase.

An analysis of historical data shows that the probability of each machine breaking down during 1 hour of operation is 0.10. In addition, the distribution of the repair time for a machine that breaks down is as follows:

Repair Time (hours)	1	2	3	4	5
Probability	0.20	0.35	0.25	0.15	0.05

The loss in revenue associated with a machine being down for 1 hour is $100. PPI pays its service technician $22 per hour, and it is believed that additional service technicians can be hired at the same wage rate.

In reviewing the breakdown problem, Jerry decided that the best way to learn about the machine repair operation would be to simulate the performance of the system. In considering the potential use of computer simulation, Jerry indicated that PPI must deal with the two conflicting sources of cost: the cost of the service technician(s) and the cost of machine downtime. He indicated that PPI could minimize salaries by employing only one service technician. On the other hand, PPI could minimize the cost of machine downtime by hiring so many service technicians that a machine could be serviced immediately after a breakdown.

Jerry would like you to develop a computer simulation model of the machine repair operation and use it to determine how many service technicians PPI should employ to minimize its total cost. When developing the model, you can assume that if a machine has a breakdown, the breakdown can be treated as occurring at the beginning of the hour of operation—that is, if a machine breaks down in hour 4, count the entire hour as downtime. If 1 hour is spent waiting for a service technician and the length of time required to service the machine is 2 hours, the machine will be down during hours 4, 5, and 6 and then ready for operation at the beginning of hour 7. You can also assume that the probability of any machine breakdown is independent of the breakdown of any other machine and that each service time is also independent of other service times.

Managerial Report

Prepare a report that discusses the general development of the computer simulation model, the conclusions that you plan to draw by using the model, and any recommendations that you have regarding the best decision for PPI. Include the following:

1. List the information the computer simulation model should generate so that a decision can be made about the desired number of service technicians.
2. Set up a flowchart of the machine repair operation for one machine and one service technician.
3. Use a random number table and hand computations to demonstrate the simulation of the machine repair operation with three machines and one service technician. Use a table similar to Table 13.7 to summarize 10 hours of simulation results.
4. Develop a computer program for the machine repair operation when PPI expands to six machines. Use your simulation results to make a recommendation about the number of service technicians that PPI should employ.

MANAGEMENT SCIENCE IN PRACTICE

The Upjohn Company*
Kalamazoo, Michigan

The Upjohn Company is a worldwide supplier of high-quality, innovative pharmaceutical products. While its largest business is in prescription pharmaceutical products, Upjohn also operates related businesses in animal health care products, agronomic and vegetable seeds, and specialty chemical products. Founded in 1886, Upjohn had sales of $3.6 billion in 1992. The company has approximately 19,000 employees worldwide, with major manufacturing facilities in Kalamazoo, Puerto Rico, and Belgium and research laboratories in Kalamazoo, England, and Japan. Committed to total quality improvement—in service to its customers, its products, and its performance in the work place—Upjohn is also dedicated to conducting businesses in an environmentally and socially responsible manner.

Management Science at Upjohn

The management science function at Upjohn is part of the Management Information and Office Services organization and offers a high-quality, professional problem-solving service to any part of the corporation. The mission of the group is to provide decision making support for the company's customers, strategies, and priorities by using management science techniques to solve business problems and exploit business opportunities in a cost-effective manner. The primary areas of application are problem definition and analysis, modeling and simulation, capacity planning, resource allocation, scheduling, and project management.

A Computer Simulation Application

Demand for one of Upjohn's long-standing products had remained stable for several years at a level easily satisfied by the company's manufacturing facility. However, changes in market conditions caused an increase in demand to a level beyond the capacity of the current facility. In the discussion that follows, we describe a simulation study successfully undertaken to determine the most cost-effective means of increasing production to meet the new level of demand.

The production process is shown in Figure 13.10. It consists of three independent subprocesses: raw material processing, bulk processing, and spent material reprocessing. Raw material processing takes purchased material as input and transforms it into material that can be used in bulk processing. Bulk processing (shown within the dashed line in Figure 13.10), which involves initial processing, assay, and final processing, converts the raw materials into a finished product. The key step occurs when an assay of the initial bulk processing output or intermediate is performed to determine whether the lot is ready for final processing. If the assay is acceptable, the lot proceeds to final

—Continued on next page

*The authors are indebted to Dr. David B. Magerlein, Dr. James M. Magerlein, and Mr. Michael J. Goodrich of The Upjohn Company for providing this application.

Figure 13.10
A Production Process at Upjohn

—Continued from previous page

processing and completion. If the assay is not acceptable, the intermediate is returned to initial bulk processing and several steps are repeated. The new intermediate material, which is input during the repeat processing, is obtained by reprocessing one of the spent materials generated during a prior initial bulk processing.

Each time the initial bulk process is run, a quantity of spent material is generated for possible reprocessing. Although the primary use of the reprocessed material is as input for repeat bulk processing, it also can be used as a replacement for the original raw material at the start of the bulk processing. Since the cost of the reprocessed material is significantly less than the cost of new raw material, it is beneficial to use as much reprocessed material as possible.

A simulation model of the production process was developed, and these questions were addressed:

1. What is the maximum throughput of the existing facility?
2. How can the production process be modified to increase the throughput of the existing facility?
3. How much equipment (tanks and centrifuges) must be added to the current facility to increase the capacity to meet the forecasted demand?
4. How should the reprocessed spent material be used to minimize the total production cost?
5. If a new facility is required, what is the optimal size and configuration?

The scope of the simulation model included the raw material, bulk- and spent-material processes defined above. The model was built in a modular flexible manner that allowed for the evaluation of resource levels within the facility, staffing levels and hours, changes in process times or equipment usage, changes in lot size, and/or yield changes. The logic of the process flow served as the core of the .nodel and was developed in collaboration with the lead operators and supervisors of the production area. Since a good logical model is the key to good simulation results, a significant amount of time was spent defining the logic of the process flow. The model development process provided a secondary benefit in that production personnel got to review and evaluate the process as they explained it.

The computer simulation model has been used on several occasions over the past 2 years. Simulation results have assisted management in addressing capacity, resource allocation, and operating policy issues. Each time a request to evaluate an issue is made, a detailed experimental design is developed that defines the alternatives to be evaluated. The appropriate simulation runs are made, the results evaluated and presented to production management and personnel, and follow-up actions defined.

The computer simulation model was developed using the SLAMSYSTEM Version 3.0 simulation language from the Pritsker Corporation. All simulation runs were made on a personal computer.

Benefits of the Simulation Model

The ongoing investigation of the production process using computer simulation has resulted in numerous benefits to the company, including the following:

1. Optimizing the use of reprocessed spent material to replace fresh raw material. Total material costs were reduced by approximately $3 million per year.
2. Demonstrating that the current facility, with some operating policy improvements, was large enough to satisfy the increased demand for the next several years. Expansion to a new facility was not necessary.
3. Determining the impact on facility throughput from alternative process changes. Numerous potential changes were investigated. The simulation model predicted how each change would affect total facility throughput. One change was identified that would increase throughput beyond what was needed for the 5-year forecasted demand.
4. Determining appropriate staffing levels within the facility. The model determined the number of operators that will be required as the production level increases in the future. This ensures that the proper number of operators will be trained by the time they are needed.
5. Determining the required size and configuration for a new facility. Although the current facility was found adequate to meet demand, the model still allowed management to determine the cost required to build a new facility.

The final actions taken based on the simulation results included alterations in policies for using reprocessed spent material, priority implementation of the process change that most impacted increasing facility throughput, establishment of appropriate staffing levels, and cost minimization because the expense of building a new or expanded facility was avoided.

Questions

1. Briefly describe the Upjohn production operation.
2. What is the primary reason Upjohn conducted a study of this operation?
3. Describe some of the factors that had to be included in the simulation model.
4. What were the advantages of computer simulation to Upjohn?

CHAPTER 14

Decision Analysis

Decision analysis can be used to determine optimal strategies when a decision maker is faced with several decision alternatives and an uncertain or risk-filled pattern of future events. For example, a manufacturer of a new line of seasonal clothing would like to manufacture large quantities if consumer acceptance and consequently demand for the product are going to be high. However, the manufacturer would like to produce much smaller quantities if consumer acceptance and demand for the product are going to be low. Unfortunately, seasonal clothing items require the manufacturer to make a production–volume decision before the demand is known. Actual consumer acceptance of the product will not be determined until the items have been placed in the stores and buyers have had the opportunity to purchase them. Selection of the best production–volume decision from among several alternatives when the decision maker is faced with the uncertainty of future demand is a problem suited for decision analysis.

We begin the study of decision analysis by considering problems in which there are reasonably few decision alternatives and reasonably few possible future events. The concepts of a payoff table and a decision tree are introduced to provide a structure for this type of decision situation and to illustrate the fundamentals of decision analysis. The discussion is then extended to show how additional information obtained through experimentation can be combined with the decision maker's preliminary information to develop an optimal decision strategy.

The last section of the chapter introduces the concepts of utility and the expected utility criterion. Utility takes into account the decision maker's attitude toward the profit, loss, and risk associated with an outcome. In situations where the decision maker feels that monetary values do not adequately reflect the preferences for the payoffs, a utility analysis of the problem should be considered.

593

14.1 Structuring the Decision Problem

To illustrate the decision analysis approach, let us consider the case of Political Systems, Inc. (PSI), a newly formed computer service firm specializing in information services such as surveys and data analysis for individuals running for political office. The firm is in the final stages of selecting a computer system for its Midwest branch, located in Chicago. While PSI has decided on a computer manufacturer, it is currently attempting to determine the size of the computer system that would be most economical. We will use decision analysis to help PSI make its computer decision.

The first step in the decision analysis approach is to identify the alternatives considered by the decision maker. For PSI, the final decision will be to select one of three computer systems, which differ in size and capacity. The three *decision alternatives,* denoted by d_1, d_2, and d_3, are as follows:

$$d_1 = \text{large computer system}$$
$$d_2 = \text{medium computer system}$$
$$d_3 = \text{small computer system}$$

Obviously, the selection of the *best* decision alternative will depend on what PSI management foresees as the possible market acceptance of the service and consequently the possible demand or load on the PSI computer system. Often, the future events associated with a decision situation are uncertain. That is, while a decision maker may have an idea of the variety of possible future events, that same person will be unsure as to which particular event will occur. Thus, the second step is to identify the future events that might occur. These events, which are not under the control of the decision maker, are referred to as the *states of nature*. It is assumed that the list of possible states of nature includes everything that can happen and that the individual states of nature do not overlap; that is, the states of nature are defined so that one and only one of the listed states of nature will occur.

When asked about the states of nature for the PSI decision problem, management viewed the possible acceptance of the PSI service as an either–or situation. That is, management believed that the firm's overall level of acceptance in the marketplace would be one of two possibilities: high acceptance or low acceptance. Thus, the PSI states of nature, denoted s_1 and s_2, are as follows:

$$s_1 = \text{high customer acceptance of PSI services}$$
$$s_2 = \text{low customer acceptance of PSI services}$$

Given the three decision alternatives and the two states of nature, which computer system should PSI select? To answer this question, we will need information on the profit associated with each combination of a decision alternative and a state of nature. For example, what profit would PSI experience if the firm selected the large computer system (d_1) and market acceptance was high (s_1)? What profit would PSI experience if the firm selected the large computer system (d_1) and market acceptance was low (s_2)?

Payoff Tables

In decision analysis terminology, we refer to the outcome resulting from a certain decision and the occurrence of a particular state of nature as the *payoff*. Using the best information available, management has estimated the payoffs or profits for the PSI problem. These estimates are presented in Table 14.1. A table of this form is referred to as

Table 14.1

Payoff Table (Profit in $) for the PSI Problem

		States of Nature	
Decision Alternatives		High Acceptance s_1	Low Acceptance s_2
Large system	d_1	200,000	−20,000
Medium system	d_2	150,000	20,000
Small system	d_3	100,000	60,000

a *payoff table*. In general, entries in a payoff table can be stated in terms of profits, costs, or any other measure of output that may be appropriate for the particular situation being analyzed. The notation we will use for the entries in the payoff table is $V(d_i, s_j)$, which denotes the payoff associated with decision alternative d_i and state of nature s_j. Using this notation, we see that $V(d_3, s_1) = \$100,000$.

Decision Trees

A *decision tree* provides a graphical representation of the decision-making process. Figure 14.1 shows a decision tree for the PSI problem. Note that the tree shows the natural or logical progression that will occur over time. First, the firm must make its decision ($d_1, d_2,$ or d_3); then, once the decision is implemented, the state of nature (s_1 or s_2) will occur. The number at each end point of the tree represents the payoff associated with a particular chain of events. For example, the topmost payoff of $200,000 arises whenever management selects a large system (d_1) and customer acceptance turns out to be high (s_1). The next-lower terminal point of −$20,000 is reached when management selects the large system (d_1) and the state of nature turns out to be a low

Figure 14.1

Decision Tree for the PSI Problem (Payoffs in $)

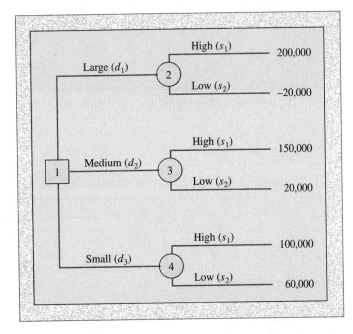

Given a payoff table, you should be able to develop a decision tree. Try Problem 1(a).

acceptance (s_2). Thus, we see that each possible sequence of events for the PSI leasing problem is represented in the decision tree.

Using the general terminology associated with decision trees, we will refer to the intersection or junction points of the tree as *nodes* and the arcs or connectors between the nodes as *branches*. Figure 14.1 shows the PSI decision tree with the nodes numbered 1 to 4. When the branches *leaving* a given node are decision branches, we refer to the node as a *decision node*. Decision nodes are denoted by squares. Similarly, when the branches leaving a given node are state-of-nature branches, we refer to the node as a *state-of-nature node*. State-of-nature nodes are denoted by circles. Using this node-labeling procedure, node 1 is a decision node, whereas nodes 2, 3, and 4 are state-of-nature nodes.

The identification of the decision alternatives, the states of nature, and the determination of the payoff associated with each decision alternative and state-of-nature combination are the first three steps in the decision analysis process. The question we now turn to is the following: How can the decision maker best utilize the information presented in the payoff table or the decision tree to arrive at a decision? As we will see, there are several approaches that may be used.

NOTES & COMMENTS

1. Experts in problem-solving agree that the first step in solving a complex problem is to decompose it into a series of smaller subproblems. Decision trees provide a useful means of showing how the problem can be decomposed, as well as showing the sequential nature of the decision process.

2. People often view the same problem from different perspectives. Thus, there is no one correct way to develop a decision tree for a problem. Often, the discussion regarding the most appropriate decision tree provides additional insight regarding the problem.

14.2 Decision Making Without Probabilities

Many students think of a good decision as one in which the outcome is favorable. It should be stressed that in some instances, a good, well-thought-out decision may still lead to a bad or undesirable outcome.

In this section we consider approaches to decision making that do not require knowledge of the probabilities of the states of nature. These approaches are appropriate in situations where the decision maker has very little confidence in his or her ability to assess the probabilities of the various states of nature, or where it is desirable to consider best- and worst-case analyses that are independent of state-of-nature probabilities. Because different approaches sometimes lead to different decision recommendations, it is important for the decision maker to understand the approaches available and then select the specific approach that, according to the decision maker's judgment, is the most appropriate.

Optimistic Approach

The *optimistic approach* evaluates each decision alternative in terms of the *best* payoff that can occur. The decision alternative that is recommended is the one that provides the best possible payoff. For a problem in which maximum profit is desired, as it is in the PSI

For a maximization problem, the optimistic approach is often referred to as the *maximax approach*; for a minimization problem, the corresponding terminology is *minimin*.

problem, the optimistic approach would lead the decision maker to choose the alternative corresponding to the largest profit. For problems involving minimization, this approach leads to choosing the alternative with the smallest payoff.

To illustrate the use of the optimistic approach, we will show how it can be used to develop a recommendation for the PSI problem. First, we determine the maximum payoff possible for each of the decision alternatives; then we select the decision alternative that provides the overall maximum profit. This is just a systematic way of identifying the decision alternative that provides the largest possible profit. Table 14.2 illustrates this process.

Since $200,000, corresponding to d_1, is the largest profit or payoff, the decision to lease a large system is the recommended decision alternative using the optimistic approach. It is easy to see why this is called an optimistic approach. It simply recommends the decision alternative that provides the best of all payoffs, $200,000.

Conservative Approach

For a maximization problem, the conservative approach is often referred to as the *maximin approach*; for a minimization problem, the corresponding terminology is *minimax*.

The *conservative approach* evaluates each decision alternative in terms of the *worst* payoff that can occur. The decision alternative recommended is the one that provides the best of the worst possible payoffs. For a problem in which the output measure is profit, as it is in the PSI problem, the conservative approach would lead the decision maker to choose the alternative that maximizes the minimum possible profit that could be obtained. For problems involving minimization, this approach identifies the alternative that will minimize the maximum payoff.

To illustrate the conservative approach, we will use it to develop a recommendation for the PSI problem. First, the decision maker would identify the minimum payoff for each of the decision alternatives; then, the decision maker would select the alternative that maximizes the minimum payoff. Table 14.3 illustrates this approach for the PSI problem.

Since $60,000, corresponding to d_3, yields the maximum of the minimum payoffs, the decision alternative of a small system is recommended. This decision approach is considered conservative because it concentrates on the worst possible payoffs and then recommends the decision alternative that avoids the possibility of extremely "bad" payoffs. In the conservative approach, PSI is guaranteed a profit of at least $60,000. While PSI may still make more, it *cannot* make less than $60,000.

Table 14.2
PSI Maximum Payoff for Each Decision Alternative

Decision Alternatives		Maximum Payoff	
Large system	d_1	200,000	◄——— Maximum of the maximum payoff values
Medium system	d_2	150,000	
Small system	d_3	100,000	

Table 14.3
PSI Minimum Payoff for Each Decision Alternative

Decision Alternatives		Minimum Payoff	
Large system	d_1	−20,000	
Medium system	d_2	20,000	
Small system	d_3	60,000	◄——— Maximum of the minimum payoff values

Minimax Regret Approach

Minimax regret is another approach to decision making without probabilities. This approach is neither purely optimistic nor purely conservative. Let us illustrate the minimax regret approach by showing how it can be used to select a decision alternative for the PSI problem.

Suppose that we make the decision to select the small system (d_3) and afterwards learn that customer acceptance of the PSI service is high (s_1). Table 14.1 shows the resulting profit to be $100,000. However, now that we know that state of nature s_1 has occurred, we see that the large-system decision (d_1), yielding a profit of $200,000, would have been the best decision. The difference between the best payoff ($200,000) and the payoff experienced ($100,000) is referred to as the *opportunity loss* or *regret* associated with the d_3 decision when state of nature s_1 occurs; thus, in this case the regret or opportunity loss is $200,000 − $100,000 = $100,000. If we had made decision d_2 and state of nature s_1 had occurred, the opportunity loss or regret would have been $200,000 − $150,000 = $50,000.

In maximization problems, the general expression for opportunity loss or regret is given by the following formula.

OPPORTUNITY LOSS OR REGRET

$$R(d_i, s_j) = V^*(s_j) - V(d_i, s_j) \qquad (14.1)$$

where

$R(d_i, s_j)$ = regret associated with decision alternative d_i and state of nature s_j
$V^*(s_j)$ = best payoff value[1] under state of nature s_j
$V(d_i, s_j)$ = payoff associated with decision alternative d_i and state of nature s_j

---

Using equation (14.1) and the payoffs in Table 14.1, we can compute the regret associated with all combinations of decision alternatives d_i and states of nature s_j. We simply replace each entry in the payoff table with the value found by subtracting the entry from the largest entry in its column. Table 14.4 shows the regret, or opportunity loss, table for the PSI problem.

The next step in applying the minimax regret approach requires the decision maker to identify the maximum regret for each decision alternative. These data are shown in Table 14.5. The choice of a best decision is made by selecting the alternative correspond-

Table 14.4
Regret or Opportunity Loss for the PSI Problem

		States of Nature	
Decision Alternatives		High Acceptance s_1	Low Acceptance s_2
Large system	d_1	0	80,000
Medium system	d_2	50,000	40,000
Small system	d_3	100,000	0

---

[1] In cost minimization problems, $V^*(s_j)$ will be the smallest entry in column j, and equation (14.1) must be changed to $R(d_i, s_j) = V(d_i, s_j) - V^*(s_j)$.

Table 14.5

PSI Maximum Regret or Opportunity Loss for Each Decision Alternative

Decision Alternatives		Maximum Regret or Opportunity Loss	
Large system	d_1	80,000	
Medium system	d_2	50,000	◄—— Minimum of the maximum regret
Small system	d_3	100,000	

ing to the *mini*mum of the *maxi*mum *regret* values—hence, the name *minimax regret*. For the PSI problem, the decision to select a medium-computer system, with a corresponding regret of $50,000, is the recommended minimax regret decision.

You should be able to develop a decision recommendation using the optimistic, conservative, and minimax regret approaches. Try Problem 1(b).

Note that the three approaches discussed in this section have provided different recommendations. This is not in itself bad. It simply reflects the difference in decision-making philosophies that underlie the various approaches. Ultimately, the decision maker will have to choose the most appropriate approach and then make the final decision accordingly. The major criticism of the approaches discussed in this section is that they do not consider any information about the probabilities of the various states of nature. In the next section we discuss an approach that utilizes probability information in selecting a decision alternative.

14.3 Decision Making with Probabilities

Even when probabilities are available, the approaches presented for decision making without probabilities still have value. They can provide a best case–worst case scenario for the problem being considered.

In many decision-making situations, it is possible to obtain probability estimates for each of the states of nature. When such probabilities are available, the *expected value approach* can be used to identify the best decision alternative. The expected value approach evaluates each decision alternative in terms of its expected value. The recommended decision alternative is the one that provides the best expected value. Let us first define the expected value of a decision alternative and then show how it can be used for the PSI problem.

Let

$$N = \text{the number of states of nature}$$
$$P(s_j) = \text{the probability of state of nature } s_j$$

Since one and only one of the N states of nature can occur, the associated probabilities must satisfy the following two conditions:

$$P(s_j) \geq 0 \qquad \text{for all states of nature} \tag{14.2}$$

$$\sum_{j=1}^{N} P(s_j) = P(s_1) + P(s_2) + \cdots + P(s_N) = 1 \tag{14.3}$$

The *expected value* (*EV*) of decision alternative d_i is defined as follows.

> ### EXPECTED VALUE OF DECISION ALTERNATIVE d_i
>
> $$\mathrm{EV}(d_i) = \sum_{j=1}^{N} P(s_j)V(d_i, s_j) \tag{14.4}$$

In words, the expected value of a decision alternative is the sum of weighted payoffs for the decision alternative. The weight for a payoff is the probability of the associated state of nature and therefore the probability that the payoff occurs. Let us return to the PSI problem to see how the expected value approach can be applied.

Suppose that PSI management believes that s_1, the high-acceptance state of nature, has a 0.3 probability of occurrence and that s_2, the low-acceptance state of nature, has a 0.7 probability. Thus, $P(s_1) = 0.3$ and $P(s_2) = 0.7$. Using the payoff values $V(d_i, s_j)$ shown in Table 14.1 and equation (14.4), expected values for the three decision alternatives can be calculated:

$$EV(d_1) = 0.3(200,000) + 0.7(-20,000) = \$46,000$$

$$EV(d_2) = 0.3(150,000) + 0.7(20,000) = \$59,000$$

$$EV(d_3) = 0.3(100,000) + 0.7(60,000) = \$72,000$$

You should now be able to use the expected value approach to develop a decision recommendation. Try Problem 5.

Thus, according to the expected value approach, d_3 is the recommended decision since d_3 has the highest expected value ($\$72,000$).

The calculations required to identify the decision alternative with the best expected value can be conveniently carried out on a decision tree. Figure 14.2 shows the decision tree for the PSI problem with state-of-nature branch probabilities. Working backward through the decision tree, we first compute the expected value at each state-of-nature node. That is, at each state-of-nature node, we weight each possible payoff by its chance of occurrence. By doing this, we obtain the expected values for nodes 2, 3, and 4 as shown in Figure 14.3.

Since the decision maker controls the branch leaving decision node 1 and since we are trying to maximize the expected profit, the best decision branch at node 1 is d_3. Thus, the decision tree analysis leads us to recommend d_3 with an expected value of $\$72,000$. Note that this is the same recommendation that was obtained using the expected value approach in conjunction with the payoff table.

Figure 14.2
PSI Decision Tree with
State-of-Nature Branch
Probabilities

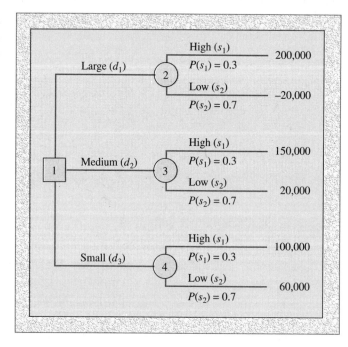

Figure 14.3

Applying the Expected Value
Approach Using Decision Trees

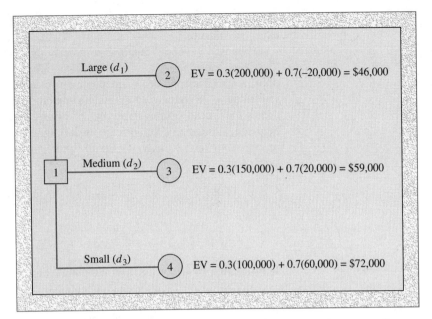

We have shown how decision trees can be used to analyze decisions with state-of-nature probabilities. While other decision problems may be substantially more complex than the PSI problem, if there are a reasonable number of decision alternatives and states of nature, the decision tree approach outlined in this section can be used. First, the analyst must draw a decision tree consisting of decision and state-of-nature nodes and branches that describe the sequential nature of the problem. Assuming that the expected value approach is to be used, the next step is to determine the probabilities for each of the state-of-nature branches and compute the expected value at each state-of-nature node. The decision branch leading to the state-of-nature node with the best expected value is then selected. The decision alternative associated with this branch is the recommended decision.

14.4 Sensitivity Analysis

For the PSI problem, management provided a 0.3 probability for s_1, the high-acceptance state of nature, and a 0.7 probability for s_2, the low-acceptance state of nature. Using these probabilities, we found that decision alternative d_3 had the highest expected value and was the recommended decision. In this section we consider how changes in the probability estimates for the states of nature affect or alter the recommended decision. The study of the effect of such changes is referred to as *sensitivity analysis*.

One approach to sensitivity analysis is to consider different probabilities for the states of nature and then recompute the expected value for each decision alternative. Repeating this several times, we can begin to learn how changes in the probabilities for the states of nature affect the recommended decision. For example, suppose that we consider a change in the probabilities for the states of nature such that $P(s_1) = 0.6$ and $P(s_2) = 0.4$. Using these probabilities and repeating the expected value computations, we find the following:

$$EV(d_1) = 0.6(200,000) + 0.4(-20,000) = \$112,000$$

$$EV(d_2) = 0.6(150,000) + 0.4(20,000) = \$\ 98,000$$

$$EV(d_3) = 0.6(100,000) + 0.4(60,000) = \$\ 84,000$$

Thus, with these probabilities, the recommended decision alternative is d_1, with an expected value of \$112,000.

Obviously, we could continue to modify the probabilities of the states of nature and thus learn more about how such changes affect the recommended decision. The only drawback to this approach is the numerous calculations required to evaluate the effect of several possible changes in the state-of-nature probabilities.

For the special case of two states of nature, the sensitivity analysis computations can be eased substantially through the use of a graphical procedure. Let us demonstrate this procedure by further analyzing the PSI problem. We begin by denoting the probability of state of nature s_1 by p. That is,

$$P(s_1) = p$$

and thus

$$P(s_2) = 1 - P(s_1) = 1 - p$$

The expected value for decision alternative d_1 can then be written as a function of p.

$$
\begin{aligned}
\text{EV}(d_1) &= P(s_1)(200{,}000) + P(s_2)(-20{,}000) \\
&= p(200{,}000) + (1 - p)(-20{,}000) \\
&= 220{,}000p - 20{,}000
\end{aligned}
\tag{14.5}
$$

Repeating the expected value computation for decision alternatives d_2 and d_3, we obtain the following expressions for expected value as a function of p:

$$\text{EV}(d_2) = 130{,}000p + 20{,}000 \tag{14.6}$$

$$\text{EV}(d_3) = 40{,}000p + 60{,}000 \tag{14.7}$$

Thus, we have developed three linear equations that express the expected value of the three decision alternatives as a function of the probability of state of nature s_1.

Let us continue by developing a graph with values of p on the horizontal axis and the associated expected values on the vertical axis. Since equations (14.5), (14.6), and (14.7) are all linear equations, we can graph each equation, or line, by finding any two points and drawing a line through the points. If we use $\text{EV}(d_1)$ in equation (14.5) as an example, we first let $p = 0$ and find that $\text{EV}(d_1) = -20{,}000$. Then, letting $p = 1$, we find that $\text{EV}(d_1) = 200{,}000$. Connecting these two points, $(0, -20{,}000)$ and $(1, 200{,}000)$, provides the line labeled $\text{EV}(d_1)$ in Figure 14.4. This figure also shows a line labeled $\text{EV}(d_2)$ and a line labeled $\text{EV}(d_3)$; these are the graphs of equations (14.6) and (14.7), respectively.

Figure 14.4 can now be used for sensitivity analysis. Recall that PSI is seeking to maximize profit. Note that for small values of p, decision alternative d_3 provides the largest expected value and is thus the recommended decision. Similarly, for large values of p, we see that decision alternative d_1 provides the largest expected value and is thus the recommended decision. Further, note that there is no section of the graph for which decision alternative d_2 provides the largest expected value. Thus, with the exception of the point where the three expected value lines intersect and all three expected values are equal, decision alternative d_2 can never be the decision alternative recommended by the expected value approach.

Referring to Figure 14.4 again, we see that the three lines intersect at a value of p between 0.4 and 0.5. In other words, at some point between 0.4 and 0.5, all three decision alternatives provide the same expected value.

Figure 14.4
Expected Value as a Function of *p*

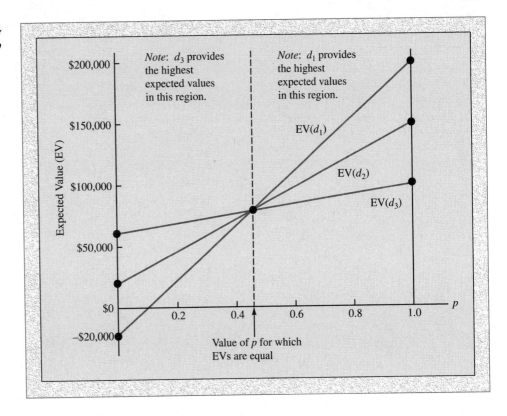

Whenever two or more lines intersect on a sensitivity analysis graph, we can set the equations for two of the intersecting lines equal to each other and solve for the value of *p*. Using the equations for decision alternative d_1 and decision alternative d_3, we obtain

$$220,000p - 20,000 = 40,000p + 60,000$$

Thus,

$$180,000p = 80,000$$

$$p = \frac{80,000}{180,000} = 0.44$$

Hence, whenever $p = 0.44$, each decision alternative will provide the same expected value. Using this value of *p* in Figure 14.4, we can now conclude that for $p < 0.44$, decision alternative d_3 provides the largest expected value and that for $p > 0.44$, decision alternative d_1 provides the largest expected value. Since *p* is simply the probability of state of nature s_1 and $(1 - p)$ is the probability of state of nature s_2, we now have the sensitivity analysis information that tells us how changes in the state-of-nature probabilities affect the recommended decision alternative.

The benefit of performing sensitivity analysis is that it can provide a better perspective on management's original judgment regarding the state-of-nature probabilities. Management originally estimated the probability of high customer acceptance as $P(s_1) = 0.3$. As a result, decision alternative d_3 was recommended. After carrying out the sensitivity analysis, we can now tell management that the original estimate of $P(s_1)$ is not extremely critical for d_3 to be the recommended decision. In fact, as long as $P(s_1) < 0.44$, the d_3 decision alternative remains optimal.

Sensitivity analysis can assist management in deciding when it is worth investing more time and money to obtain better probability estimates.

You should now be able to use graphical sensitivity analysis to determine how changes in the probability estimates affect the recommended decision. Try Problem 12.

Note that in the PSI problem, the three lines for the three decision alternatives graphed in Figure 14.4 intersect at the same point ($p = 0.44$). Similar sensitivity analysis computations for other decision analysis problems with two states of nature and three decision alternatives should not be expected to result in the same type of graph. With a different sensitivity analysis graph, d_1 could be the best decision alternative for certain values of p, d_2 the best decision alternative of other values of p, and d_3 the best decision alternative for the remaining values of p. This situation is demonstrated in the sensitivity analysis computation for Problem 13.

The graphical sensitivity analysis procedure we have described for the PSI problem applies only to decision analysis problems with two states of nature. However, sensitivity analysis is important in problems with more than two states of nature. In these cases, a computer software package can be used to assist with the computations. Basically, we return to the approach of testing a variety of likely changes for the state-of-nature probabilities. The software package is helpful in making the necessary expected value computations and providing the decision alternative recommendations with a minimum of time and effort on the part of the analyst.

14.5   Expected Value of Perfect Information

Suppose that PSI had the opportunity to conduct a market research study that would evaluate consumer need for the PSI service. Such a study could help by improving the probability assessments for the states of nature. However, if the cost of obtaining the market research information exceeds its value, PSI should not conduct the market research study.

The expected value of perfect information provides an upper limit on how much the decision maker should be willing to pay for sample information.

To determine the maximum possible value that PSI should pay for additional information, let us suppose that PSI could obtain perfect information regarding the states of nature; that is, we will assume that PSI could determine with certainty which state of nature will occur. To make use of perfect information, we need to develop a decision strategy for PSI to follow. As we will show, a decision strategy is simply a rule that is to be followed by the decision maker. In computing the *expected value of perfect information* (EVPI), the decision strategy is a rule that specifies which decision alternative should be selected given each state of nature.

To help determine the optimal decision strategy for PSI if perfect information were available, we have reproduced PSI's payoff table as Table 14.6. We see that if state of nature s_1 occurs, then the best decision alternative is d_1 with a profit of $200,000. Similarly, if state of nature s_2 occurs, then the best decision alternative is d_3 with a profit of $60,000. Thus, PSI's optimal decision strategy if perfect information were available can be stated as follows:

If s_1 occurs, then select d_1.

If s_2 occurs, then select d_3.

What is the expected value for this decision strategy? Since $P(s_1) = 0.3$ and $P(s_2) = 0.7$, we see that there is a 0.3 probability that PSI will make $200,000 and a 0.7 probability PSI will make $60,000. Thus, the expected value of the decision strategy that uses perfect information is

$$0.3(\$200,000) + 0.7(\$60,000) = \$102,000$$

We refer to $102,000 as the *expected value with perfect information* (EVwPI).

Table 14.6

Payoff Table for the PSI Problem

		States of Nature	
		High Acceptance s_1	Low Acceptance s_2
Decision Alternatives			
Large system	d_1	200,000	−20,000
Medium system	d_2	150,000	20,000
Small system	d_3	100,000	60,000

Recall that when perfect information was not available, the expected value approach resulted in recommending decision alternative d_3, with an expected value of $72,000. We refer to $72,000 as the *expected value without perfect information* (EVwoPI). Since $72,000 is the expected value without perfect information (EVwoPI) and $102,000 is the expected value with perfect information (EVwPI), $102,000 − $72,000 = $30,000 represents the expected value of perfect information (EVPI); that is,

$$\text{EVPI} = \text{EVwPI} - \text{EVwoPI}$$

$$= \$102,000 - \$72,000$$

$$= \$30,000$$

In other words, $30,000 represents the additional expected value that can be obtained if perfect information were available about the states of nature. Figure 14.5 provides a summary of the computation of the EVPI for the PSI problem.

Generally speaking, a market research study will not provide "perfect" information; however, the information provided might be worth a good portion of the $30,000. In any case, PSI's management knows it should never pay more than $30,000 for any information, no matter how good. Provided the market survey cost is reasonably small—say, $5000 to $10,000—it appears economically desirable for PSI to consider the market research study.

You should be able to determine the expected value of perfect information. Try Problem 17.

Figure 14.5

The Expected Value of Perfect Information

14.6 Decision Analysis with Sample Information

In applying the expected value approach, we have seen how probability information about the states of nature affects the expected value calculations and thus the decision recommendation. Frequently, decision makers have preliminary or prior probability estimates for the states of nature that are the best probability values available. However, to make the best possible decision, the decision maker may want to seek additional information about the states of nature. This new information can be used to revise or update the prior probabilities so that the final decision is based on better probability estimates for the states of nature.

The seeking of additional information is most often accomplished through experiments designed to provide sample information about the states of nature. Raw material sampling, product testing, and market research studies are examples of experiments that may enable a revision or updating of the state-of-nature probabilities. In the following discussion, we will reconsider the PSI problem and show how sample information can be used to revise the state-of-nature probabilities. We will then show how the revised probabilities can be used to develop an optimal decision strategy for PSI.

Recall that management had assigned a probability of $P(s_1) = 0.3$ to state of nature s_1 and a probability of $P(s_2) = 0.7$ to state of nature s_2. At this point, we will refer to these initial probability estimates, $P(s_1)$ and $P(s_2)$, as the *prior probabilities* for the states of nature. Using these prior probabilities, we found that d_3, the decision to select the small system was optimal, yielding an expected value of $72,000. Recall also that we showed that the expected value of new information about the states of nature could potentially be worth as much as EVPI = $30,000.

Suppose that PSI decides to consider hiring a market research firm to study the acceptance of the PSI service. The market research study will provide new information that can be combined with the prior probabilities through a Bayesian procedure to obtain updated or revised probability estimates for the states of nature. These *revised* probabilities are called *posterior probabilities*. The process of revising probabilities is depicted in Figure 14.6.

We will refer to the new information obtained through research or experimentation as an *indicator*. Since in many cases the experiment conducted to obtain the additional information will consist of taking a statistical sample, the new information is also often referred to as *sample information*.

Using the indicator terminology, we can denote the outcomes of the PSI marketing research study as follows:

I_1 = favorable market research report (i.e., the individuals contacted generally express interest in PSI's services)

I_2 = unfavorable market research report (i.e., the individuals contacted generally express little interest in PSI's services)

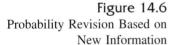

Figure 14.6
Probability Revision Based on
New Information

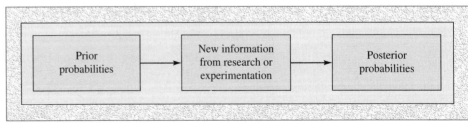

Given one of these possible indicators, the objective is to provide improved estimates of the probabilities of the two states of nature. The end result of the *Bayesian revision* process depicted in Figure 14.6 is a set of posterior probabilities of the form $P(s_j \mid I_k)$, where $P(s_j \mid I_k)$ represents the conditional probability that state of nature s_j will occur given that the outcome of the market research study was indicator I_k.

To make effective use of this indicator information, we must know something about the probability relationships between the indicators and the states of nature. For example, in the PSI problem, given that the state of nature ultimately turns out to be high customer acceptance, what is the probability that the market research study will result in a favorable report? In this case, we are asking about the conditional probability of indicator I_1 given state of nature s_1, written $P(I_1 \mid s_1)$. To carry out the analysis, we will need conditional probabilities for all indicators given all states of nature, that is, $P(I_1 \mid s_1)$, $P(I_1 \mid s_2)$, $P(I_2 \mid s_1)$, and $P(I_2 \mid s_2)$.

In the PSI problem, assume that the following estimates are available for the conditional probabilities:

	Market Research Report	
States of Nature	Favorable I_1	Unfavorable I_2
High acceptance s_1	$P(I_1 \mid s_1) = 0.8$	$P(I_2 \mid s_1) = 0.2$
Low acceptance s_2	$P(I_1 \mid s_2) = 0.1$	$P(I_2 \mid s_2) = 0.9$

Note that these probability estimates indicate that a good degree of confidence can be placed in the market research report. When the true state of nature is s_1, the market research report will be favorable 80% of the time and unfavorable only 20%. When the true state is s_2, the report will make the correct indication 90% of the time. Now let us see how this additional information can be incorporated into the decision-making process.

14.7 Developing a Decision Strategy

The student should understand that the analysis performed to develop an optimal decision strategy is done prior to actually collecting the indicator information. Its value is to help decide whether to seek the sample information, and what to do if the information is obtained.

A decision strategy is a rule that is to be followed by the decision maker. In the PSI problem, with the market research study, a decision strategy is a rule that recommends a particular decision based on whether the market research report is favorable or unfavorable. We will employ a decision tree analysis to find the optimal decision strategy for PSI.

Figure 14.7 shows the decision tree for the PSI problem provided that a market research study is conducted. Note that from left to right, the tree shows the natural or logical order that will occur in the decision-making process. First, the firm will obtain the market research report indicator (I_1 or I_2); then a decision (d_1, d_2, or d_3) will be made; finally, the state of nature (s_1 or s_2) will occur. The decision and the state of nature combine to provide the final profit or payoff.

Using decision tree terminology, we have now introduced an *indicator node,* node 1, and *indicator branches,* I_1 and I_2. Since the branches emanating from indicator nodes are not under the control of the decision maker, but are determined by chance, these nodes are depicted by a circle just like the state-of-nature nodes. We see that nodes 2 and 3 are decision nodes, while nodes 4, 5, 6, 7, 8, and 9 are state-of-nature nodes. For decision nodes, the decision maker must select the specific branch d_1, d_2, or d_3 that will be taken. Selecting the best decision branch is equivalent to making the best decision. However,

Figure 14.7
PSI Decision Tree Incorporating
the Results of the Market
Research Study (Payoffs in $)

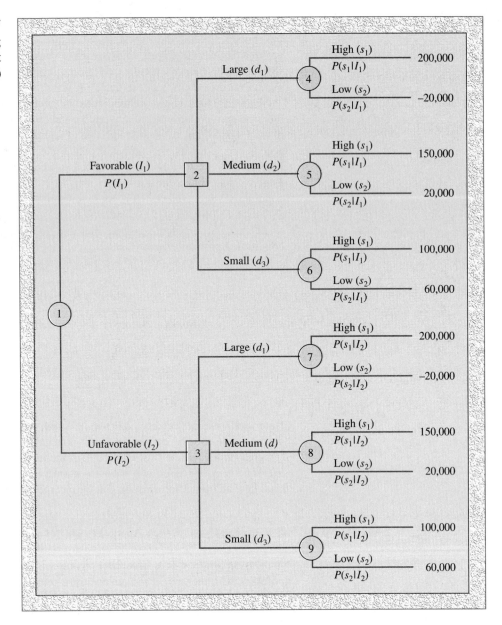

since the indicator and state-of-nature branches are not controlled by the decision maker, the specific branch leaving an indicator or a state-of-nature node will depend on the probability associated with the branch. Thus, before we can carry out an analysis of the decision tree and develop a decision strategy, we must compute the probability of each indicator branch and the probability of each state-of-nature branch. Note from the decision tree that the state-of-nature branches occur *after* the indicator branches. Thus, when we attempt to compute state-of-nature branch probabilities, we will need to consider which indicator was previously observed. That is, we will express the state-of-nature probabilities in terms of the probability of state of nature s_j *given* that indicator I_k was observed. Thus, all state-of-nature probabilities will be expressed in a $P(s_j \mid I_k)$ form.

Computing Branch Probabilities

The prior probabilities for the states of nature in the PSI problem were given as $P(s_1) = 0.3$ and $P(s_2) = 0.7$. In Section 14.6 we identified the relationships between the market research indicators and states of nature with the conditional probabilities

$$P(I_1 \mid s_1) = 0.8 \qquad P(I_2 \mid s_1) = 0.2$$

$$P(I_1 \mid s_2) = 0.1 \qquad P(I_2 \mid s_2) = 0.9$$

To develop a decision strategy utilizing the decision tree in Figure 14.7, we need indicator branch probabilities $P(I_k)$ and state-of-nature branch probabilities $P(s_j \mid I_k)$. The problem now facing us is to determine how to use the prior probability estimates $P(s_j)$ and conditional probability estimates $P(I_k \mid s_j)$ to calculate the branch probabilities $P(I_k)$ and $P(s_j \mid I_k)$. In this section we will show how the Bayesian revision process can be used to calculate the branch probabilities $P(I_k)$ and $P(s_j \mid I_k)$.

To see how this Bayesian procedure is applied and at the same time understand how the procedure works, let us look closely at the calculation of the indicator branch probability $P(I_1)$ for the PSI market research study. First, note that there are only two ways in which the outcome I_1 can occur:

1. The market research report is favorable (I_1) *and* the state of nature turns out to be high acceptance (s_1), written ($I_1 \cap s_1$).
2. The market research report is favorable (I_1) *and* the state of nature turns out to be low acceptance (s_2), written ($I_1 \cap s_2$).

The probabilities of these two outcomes are written $P(I_1 \cap s_1)$ and $P(I_1 \cap s_2)$, respectively. We can add these two probabilities to obtain the following branch probability:

$$P(I_1) = P(I_1 \cap s_1) + P(I_1 \cap s_2) \tag{14.8}$$

The multiplication law of probability provides the following formulas for $P(I_1 \cap s_1)$ and $P(I_1 \cap s_2)$:

$$P(I_1 \cap s_1) = P(I_1 \mid s_1)P(s_1) \tag{14.9}$$

$$P(I_1 \cap s_2) = P(I_1 \mid s_2)P(s_2) \tag{14.10}$$

Finally, substituting the above expressions for $P(I_1 \cap s_1)$ and $P(I_1 \cap s_2)$ in equation (14.8), we obtain

$$P(I_1) = P(I_1 \mid s_1)P(s_1) + P(I_1 \mid s_2)P(s_2) \tag{14.11}$$

Generalizing the above expression for any indicator branch probability, $P(I_k)$, and N states of nature, $s_1, s_2, \ldots, s_N$, we have

$$P(I_k) = P(I_k \mid s_1)P(s_1) + P(I_k \mid s_2)P(s_2) + \cdots + P(I_k \mid s_N)P(s_N) \tag{14.12}$$

or

$$P(I_k) = \sum_{j=1}^{N} P(I_k \mid s_j)P(s_j) \tag{14.13}$$

Returning to the PSI problem with the two prior probabilities $P(s_1) = 0.3$ and $P(s_2) = 0.7$ and the conditional probabilities $P(I_1 \mid s_1) = 0.8$, $P(I_1 \mid s_2) = 0.1$, $P(I_2 \mid s_1) = 0.2$, and $P(I_2 \mid s_2) = 0.9$, we can use equation (14.13) to compute the two indicator branch probabilities. These calculations are as follows:

$$P(I_1) = P(I_1 \mid s_1)P(s_1) + P(I_1 \mid s_2)P(s_2)$$

$$= (0.8)(0.3) + (0.1)(0.7) = 0.31$$

and

$$P(I_2) = P(I_2 \mid s_1)P(s_1) + P(I_2 \mid s_2)P(s_2)$$

$$= (0.2)(0.3) + (0.9)(0.7) = 0.69$$

The above probabilities indicate that the probability of I_1, a favorable market research report, is 0.31 and the probability of I_2, an unfavorable market research report, is 0.69.

Now that we know the indicator branch probabilities, let us show how the Bayesian process enables us to compute the revised, or posterior, state-of-nature branch probabilities $P(s_j \mid I_k)$. We will illustrate this procedure by considering the state-of-nature branch probability $P(s_1 \mid I_1)$, the probability the market acceptance is high (s_1) given that the market research report is favorable (I_1). The fundamental conditional probability relationship as presented in texts dealing with probability and statistics can be written

$$P(s_1 \mid I_1) = \frac{P(I_1 \cap s_1)}{P(I_1)} \tag{14.14}$$

Using equation (14.9) for $P(I_1 \cap s_1)$, we have

$$P(s_1 \mid I_1) = \frac{P(I_1 \mid s_1)P(s_1)}{P(I_1)} \tag{14.15}$$

With known probabilities $P(I_1 \mid s_1) = 0.8$, $P(s_1) = 0.3$, and $P(I_1) = 0.31$, the revised state-of-nature probability, $P(s_1 \mid I_1)$, becomes

$$P(s_1 \mid I_1) = \frac{(0.8)(0.3)}{0.31} = \frac{0.24}{0.31} = 0.7742$$

Recall that the prior probability of a high market acceptance was $P(s_1) = 0.3$. The preceding probability information now tells us that if the market research indicator is favorable, the probability of a high market acceptance should be revised to $P(s_1 \mid I_1) = 0.7742$.

Generalizing equation (14.15) for any state of nature s_j and any indicator I_k provides

$$P(s_j \mid I_k) = \frac{P(I_k \mid s_j)P(s_j)}{P(I_k)} \tag{14.16}$$

Thus, we can use equation (14.16) to compute the revised or posterior state-of-nature branch probabilities. For example, the revised probability of low market acceptance s_2 given the market research indicator is favorable I_1 becomes

$$P(s_2 \mid I_1) = \frac{P(I_1 \mid s_2)P(s_2)}{P(I_1)} = \frac{(0.1)(0.7)}{0.31} = \frac{0.07}{0.31} = 0.2258$$

Similar calculations for an unfavorable market research indicator I_2 will provide the revised state-of-nature branch probabilities $P(s_1 \mid I_2) = 0.0870$ and $P(s_2 \mid I_2) = 0.9130$. Figure 14.8 shows the PSI decision tree after all indicator and all revised state-of-nature branch probabilities have been computed.

You should now be able to compute revised or posterior probabilities. Try Problem 23.

Although the above procedure can be used to compute branch probabilities, the calculations can become quite cumbersome as the problem size grows larger. Thus, to

Figure 14.8
PSI Decision Tree with Branch
Probabilities

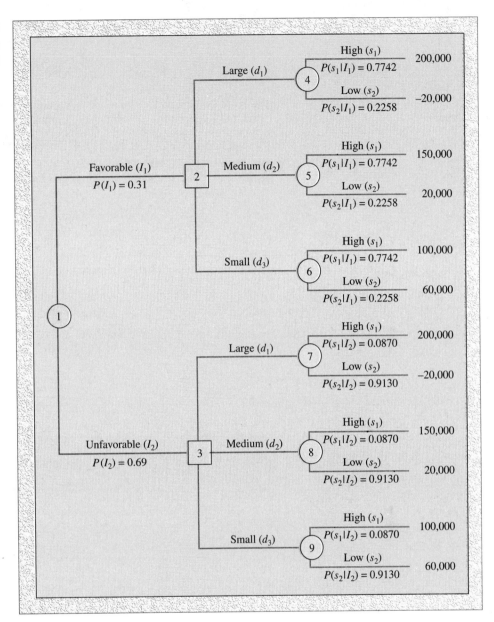

ease computations, especially for large decision analysis problems, we present the
following tabular procedure.

Computing Branch Probabilities: A Tabular Procedure

The procedure for computing the probabilities of the indicator and state-of-nature
branches can be accomplished using a tabular approach. First, for each indicator I_k we
form a table consisting of the following five columns:

- Column 1   States of nature s_j
- Column 2   Prior probabilities $P(s_j)$
- Column 3   Conditional probabilities $P(I_k \mid s_j)$

- Column 4   Joint probabilities $P(I_k \cap s_j)$
- Column 5   Posterior probabilities $P(s_j \mid I_k)$

Then, given any indicator I_k, the following procedure can be used to calculate $P(I_k)$ and the $P(s_j \mid I_k)$ values:

Step 1 In column 1, list the states of nature appropriate to the problem being analyzed.

Step 2 In column 2, enter the prior probability corresponding to each state of nature listed in column 1.

Step 3 In column 3, enter the appropriate value of $P(I_k \mid s_j)$ for each state of nature specified in column 1.

Step 4 To compute each entry in column 4, multiply each entry in column 2 by the corresponding entry in column 3.

Step 5 Add the entries in column 4. The sum is the value of $P(I_k)$. For convenience, write the sum below column 4.

Step 6 To compute each entry in column 5, divide the corresponding entry in column 4 by $P(I_k)$.

We will now use this procedure to compute $P(I_1)$ and the revised state-of-nature probabilities $P(s_j \mid I_1)$ for the PSI problem.

Steps 1, 2, and 3

s_j	$P(s_j)$	$P(I_1 \mid s_j)$	$P(I_1 \cap s_j)$	$P(s_j \mid I_1)$
s_1	0.3	0.8		
s_2	0.7	0.1		

Steps 4 and 5

s_j	$P(s_j)$	$P(I_1 \mid s_j)$	$P(I_1 \cap s_j)$	$P(s_j \mid I_1)$
s_1	0.3	0.8	0.24	
s_2	0.7	0.1	0.07	
			$P(I_1) = 0.31$	

Step 6

s_j	$P(s_j)$	$P(I_1 \mid s_j)$	$P(I_1 \cap s_j)$	$P(s_j \mid I_1)$
s_1	0.3	0.8	0.24	0.24/0.31 = 0.7742
s_2	0.7	0.1	0.07	0.07/0.31 = 0.2258
			$P(I_1) = 0.31$	

Note that $P(I_1)$, $P(s_1 \mid I_1)$, and $P(s_2 \mid I_1)$ are exactly the same as we calculated by applying equations (14.13) and (14.16) directly. The preceding tabular computations could be repeated to compute $P(I_2)$ and the revised state-of-nature probabilities $P(s_j \mid I_2)$.

An Optimal Decision Strategy

Once we have computed the branch probabilities, we can use the expected value approach to determine the decision strategy. Working *backward* through the decision tree in Figure 14.8, we first compute the expected value at each state-of-nature node. That is, at each state-of-nature node, the possible payoffs are weighted by their chance of occurrence. Thus, the expected values for nodes 4–9 are computed as follows:

$$EV(\text{node } 4) = 0.7742(200,000) + 0.2258(-20,000) = 150,324$$

$$EV(\text{node } 5) = 0.7742(150,000) + 0.2258(20,000) = 120,646$$

$$EV(\text{node } 6) = 0.7742(100,000) + 0.2258(60,000) = 90,968$$

$$EV(\text{node } 7) = 0.0870(200,000) + 0.9130(-20,000) = -860$$

$$EV(\text{node } 8) = 0.0870(150,000) + 0.9130(20,000) = 31,310$$

$$EV(\text{node } 9) = 0.0870(100,000) + 0.9130(60,000) = 63,480$$

Figure 14.9 shows the above calculations directly on the decision tree. Since the decision maker controls the branch leaving a decision node and since we are trying to maximize expected profits, the optimal decision at node 2 is d_1. Thus, since d_1 leads to an expected value of \$150,324, EV(node 2) = \$150,324.

A similar analysis of decision node 3 shows that the optimal decision branch at this node is d_3. Thus, EV(node 3) becomes \$63,480 when the optimal decision of d_3 is made.

As a final step, we continue working backward to the indicator node and establish its expected value. We see that since node 1 has probability branches, we cannot select the best branch. Rather, we must compute the expected value. Thus, we have

$$EV(\text{node } 1) = (0.31)EV(\text{node } 2) + (0.69)EV(\text{node } 3)$$

$$= 0.31(150,324) + 0.69(63,480) = \$90,402$$

The value of \$90,402 is viewed as the expected value of the optimal decision strategy when the market research study is used. In other words, it is the expected value using the sample information provided by the market research report.

Note that the final decision has not yet been determined. We will need to know the results of the market research study before deciding to select a large system (d_1) or a small system (d_3). The results of the decision analysis at this point, however, have provided the following optimal *decision strategy*

If	Then
Report favorable (I_1)	Select large system (d_1)
Report unfavorable (I_2)	Select small system (d_3)

Figure 14.9 Developing a Decision Strategy for the PSI Problem

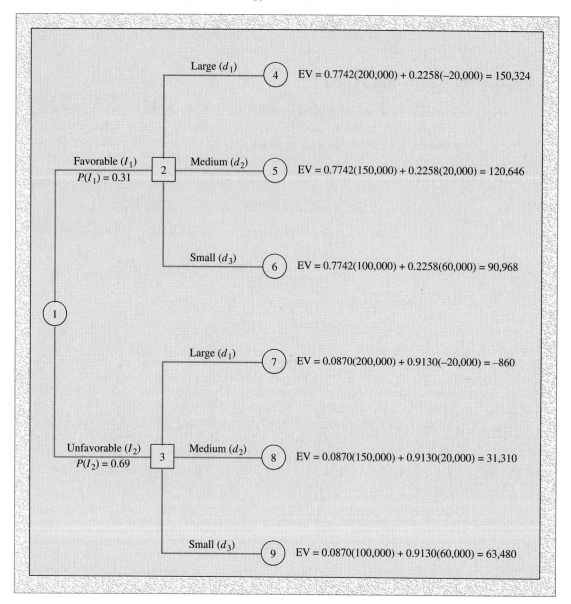

A decision tree provides a good visual description for small and relatively simple problems because it shows the overall structure of the problem. However, the tree size expands multiplicatively as additional stages are added to the tree; thus, for large problems, it becomes impossible to represent the complete tree in one figure or on one computer screen.

Thus, we have seen how to develop an optimal decision strategy when sample information is available. While other decision analysis problems may not be as simple as the PSI problem, the approach we have outlined is still applicable. First, draw a decision tree consisting of indicator, decision, and state-of-nature nodes and branches such that the tree describes the specific sequence of decisions and chance outcomes. Posterior probability calculations must be made to establish indicator and state-of-nature branch probabilities. Then, by working backward through the tree, computing expected values at state-of-nature and indicator nodes, and selecting the best decision branch at decision nodes, the analyst can determine an optimal decision strategy and its associated expected value.

14.8 Expected Value of Sample Information

In the PSI problem, management now has a decision strategy of selecting the large computer system if the market research report is favorable and selecting the small computer system if the market research report is unfavorable. Since the additional information provided by the market research firm will result in an added cost for PSI in terms of the fee paid to the research firm, PSI management may question the value of this market research information.

The value of sample information is often measured by calculating what is referred to as the *expected value of sample information* (EVSI). For maximization problems,[2] EVSI is computed as follows.

EXPECTED VALUE OF SAMPLE INFORMATION

$$EVSI = \begin{pmatrix} \text{Expected value of the} \\ \text{optimal decision } \textit{with} \\ \text{sample information} \end{pmatrix} - \begin{pmatrix} \text{Expected value of the} \\ \text{optimal decision } \textit{without} \\ \text{sample information} \end{pmatrix} \qquad (14.17)$$

> You should now be able to compute the expected value of sample information. Try Problem 26(a).

For PSI, the market research information is considered the sample information. The decision tree calculations indicated that the expected value of the optimal decision with the market research information was $90,402; thus, $90,402 is the *expected value with sample information* (EVwSI). When sample information is not available, the expected value approach resulted in recommending decision alternative d_3 with an expected value of $72,000; thus, $72,000 is the *expected value without sample information* (EVwoSI). Using equation (14.17), the expected value of the market research report is

$$EVSI = \$90,402 - \$72,000 = \$18,402$$

Thus, PSI should be willing to pay up to $18,402 for the market research information.

Efficiency of Sample Information

In Section 14.5 we saw that the expected value of perfect information (EVPI) for the PSI problem was $30,000. While we never expected the market research report to obtain perfect information, we can use an *efficiency* measure to express the value of the market research information. With perfect information having an efficiency rating of 100%, the efficiency rating E for sample information is computed as follows.

EFFICIENCY OF SAMPLE INFORMATION

$$E = \frac{EVSI}{EVPI} \times 100 \qquad (14.18)$$

---

[2]In minimization problems, the expected value of the optimal decision with sample information will be less than or equal to the expected value of the optimal decision without sample information. Thus, in minimization problems,

$$EVSI = \begin{pmatrix} \text{expected value of the} \\ \text{optimal decision } \textit{without} \\ \text{sample information} \end{pmatrix} - \begin{pmatrix} \text{expected value of the} \\ \text{optimal decision } \textit{with} \\ \text{sample information} \end{pmatrix}$$

For the PSI problem,

$$E = \frac{18,402}{30,000} \times 100 = 61.3\%$$

You should be able to determine the efficiency of sample information. Try Problem 26(b).

In other words, the information from the market research firm is 61.3% as efficient as perfect information.

Low efficiency ratings for sample information might lead the decision maker to look for other types of information. On the other hand, high efficiency ratings indicate that the sample information is almost as good as perfect information, and additional sources of information should not be worthwhile.

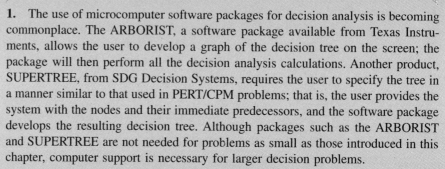

NOTES & COMMENTS

1. The use of microcomputer software packages for decision analysis is becoming commonplace. The ARBORIST, a software package available from Texas Instruments, allows the user to develop a graph of the decision tree on the screen; the package will then perform all the decision analysis calculations. Another product, SUPERTREE, from SDG Decision Systems, requires the user to specify the tree in a manner similar to that used in PERT/CPM problems; that is, the user provides the system with the nodes and their immediate predecessors, and the software package develops the resulting decision tree. Although packages such as the ARBORIST and SUPERTREE are not needed for problems as small as those introduced in this chapter, computer support is necessary for larger decision problems.

2. The expected value without perfect information (EVwoPI) defined in Section 14.5 and the expected value without sample information (EVwoSI) are always equal. This value simply represents the expected value of the best decision using the prior probabilities.

14.9   Utility and Decision Making

In the previous sections of this chapter we expressed the payoffs in terms of monetary values. When probability information was available about the states of nature, we recommended selecting the decision alternative with the best expected monetary value. However, there are situations in which the decision alternative with the best expected monetary value may not be the most desirable decision.

By the most desirable decision we mean the one that is preferred by the decision maker after taking into account not only monetary value, but also other factors such as the risk associated with the outcomes. Examples of situations in which selecting the decision alternative with the best expected monetary value may not lead to the selection of the most preferred decision are numerous. One such example is the decision to buy house insurance. Clearly, buying insurance for a house does not provide a higher expected monetary value than not buying such insurance. Otherwise, insurance companies could not pay expenses and make a profit. Similarly, many people buy tickets for state lotteries even though the expected monetary value of such a decision is negative.

Should we conclude that persons or businesses that buy insurance or participate in lotteries do so because they are unable to determine which decision alternative leads to the best expected monetary value? On the contrary, we take the view that in these cases monetary value is not the sole measure of the true worth of the outcome to the decision maker.

We will see that in cases where expected monetary value does not lead to the most preferred decision alternative, expressing the value (or worth) of an outcome in terms of its *utility* will permit the use of *expected utility* to identify the most desirable decision.

The Meaning of Utility

Until 1944, when Von Neumann and Morgenstern published the book *Theory of Games and Economic Behavior*, the literature on decisions involving risk consisted primarily of applications involving the use of probability in gambling.

Utility is a measure of the total worth of a particular outcome; it reflects the decision maker's attitude toward a collection of factors such as profit, loss, and risk. As an example of a case where utility can help in selecting the best decision alternative, let us consider the problem faced by Swofford, Inc., a relatively small real estate investment firm located in Atlanta, Georgia. Swofford currently has two investment opportunities, which require approximately the same cash outlay. The cash requirements necessary prohibit Swofford from making more than one investment at this time. Consequently, there are three possible decision alternatives that may be considered.

The three decision alternatives, denoted by d_1, d_2, and d_3, are as follows:

$$d_1 = \text{make investment A}$$
$$d_2 = \text{make investment B}$$
$$d_3 = \text{do not invest}$$

The monetary payoffs associated with the investment opportunities depend largely on what happens to the real estate market during the next 6 months. Real estate prices will go up, remain stable, or go down. Thus, the states of nature, denoted by s_1, s_2, and s_3, are as follows:

$$s_1 = \text{real estate prices go up}$$
$$s_2 = \text{real estate prices remain stable}$$
$$s_3 = \text{real estate prices go down}$$

Using the best information available, Swofford has estimated the profits or payoffs associated with each decision alternative and state-of-nature combination. The resulting payoff table is shown in Table 14.7.

The best estimate of the probability that prices will go up is 0.3, the best estimate of the probability that prices will remain stable is 0.5, and the best estimate of the probability that real estate prices will go down is 0.2. Thus, the expected values for the three decision alternatives are

$$\text{EV}(d_1) = 0.3(\$30,000) + 0.5(\$20,000) \quad + 0.2(-\$50,000) = \quad \$9,000$$

$$\text{EV}(d_2) = 0.3(\$50,000) + 0.5(-\$20,000) + 0.2(-\$30,000) = -\$1,000$$

$$\text{EV}(d_3) = 0.3(\$0) \quad\quad + 0.5(\$0) \quad\quad + 0.2(\$0) \quad\quad = \quad \$0$$

Table 14.7
Payoff Table (Profit in $) for Swofford, Inc.

| | | States of Nature | | |
| | | Prices Up | Prices Stable | Prices Down |
Decision Alternatives		s_1	s_2	s_3
Investment A	d_1	30,000	20,000	−50,000
Investment B	d_2	50,000	−20,000	−30,000
Do not invest	d_3	0	0	0

Using the expected value approach, the optimal decision is to select investment A, with an expected monetary value of $9000. Is this really the best decision alternative? Let us consider some other relevant factors that relate to Swofford's capability for absorbing the $50,000 loss if investment A is made and real estate prices go down.

It turns out that Swofford's financial position is very weak. This was partly reflected in Swofford's ability to undertake, at most, one investment at the current time. More important, however, the firm's president, Shari Kaplan, feels that if the next investment results in substantial losses, Swofford's future will be in jeopardy. Although the expected value approach leads to a recommendation for d_1, do you think this is the decision she would prefer? We suspect that d_2 or d_3 would be selected to avoid the possibility of incurring a $50,000 loss. In fact, it is reasonable to believe that if a loss as great as even $30,000 could drive Swofford out of business, the president would select d_3, feeling that both investment A and investment B are too risky for Swofford's current financial position.

The way we resolve Swofford's dilemma is first to determine Swofford's utility for the various monetary outcomes. Recall that the utility of any outcome is the total worth of that outcome, taking into account the risks and payoffs involved. If the utilities for the various outcomes are assessed correctly, then the decision alternative with the highest expected utility is the most preferred or best alternative.

Developing Utilities for Payoffs

The procedure we will use to establish utility values for the payoffs requires that we first assign a utility value to the best and worst possible payoffs in the decision situation. Any values will work as long as the utility assigned to the best payoff is greater than the utility assigned to the worst payoff. In Swofford's case, Table 14.7 shows that $50,000 is the best payoff and −$50,000 is the worst payoff. Suppose, then, that we arbitrarily make the following assignments to these two payoffs:

$$\text{Utility of } -\$50,000 = U(-\$50,000) = 0$$

$$\text{Utility of } \quad \$50,000 = U(\$50,000) \quad = 10$$

Utility values of 0 and 1 could have been selected here; we selected 0 and 10 to avoid any possible confusion between the utility value and the probability p.

Now let us see how we can determine the utility associated with every other payoff.

Consider the process of establishing the utility of a payoff of $30,000. First, we ask Swofford's president to state her preference between a guaranteed $30,000 payoff and the opportunity to engage in the following *lottery,* or bet:

Lottery: Swofford obtains a payoff of $50,000 with probability p
and a payoff of −$50,000 with probability $(1 − p)$.

p is often referred to as the indifference probability.

If p is very close to 1, Swofford's president would prefer the lottery to the certain payoff of $30,000 since the firm would virtually guarantee itself a payoff of $50,000. On the other hand, if p is very close to 0, she would clearly prefer the guarantee of $30,000. In any event, as p changes continuously from 0 to 1, the preference for the guaranteed payoff of $30,000 will change at some point into a preference for the lottery. At this value of p, she would have no greater preference for the guaranteed payoff of $30,000 than for the lottery. For example, let us assume that when $p = 0.95$, she is indifferent between the certain payoff of $30,000 and the lottery. Given this value of p, we can compute the utility of a $30,000 payoff as follows:

$$U(\$30,000) = pU(\$50,000) + (1 − p)U(-\$50,000)$$

$$= 0.95(10) + (0.05)(0)$$

$$= 9.5$$

Obviously, if we had started with a different assignment of utilities for payoffs of $50,000 and −$50,000, we would have ended up with a different utility for $30,000. Hence, we must conclude that the utility assigned to each payoff is not unique, but merely depends on the initial choice of utilities for the best and worst payoffs. We will discuss this further at the end of this section. For now, however, we will continue to use a value of 10 for the utility of $50,000 and a value of 0 for the utility of −$50,000.

Before computing the utility for the other payoffs, let us consider the significance of assigning a utility of 9.5 to a payoff of $30,000. Clearly, when $p = 0.95$, the expected value of the lottery is

$$\text{EV(lottery)} = 0.95(\$50,000) + 0.05(-\$50,000)$$
$$= \$47,500 - \$2,500$$
$$= \$45,000$$

The difference between the expected value of the lottery and the guaranteed payoff can be viewed as the risk premium the decision maker is willing to pay.

We see that although the expected value of the lottery when $p = 0.95$ is $45,000, Swofford's president would just as soon take a guaranteed payoff of $30,000 and thus take a conservative, or risk-avoiding, viewpoint. That is, she would rather have $30,000 for certain than risk anything greater than a 5% chance of incurring a loss of $50,000. One can view the difference between the EV of $45,000 and the $30,000 amount for certain as the risk premium that the president would be willing to pay to avoid the 5% chance of losing $50,000.

To compute the utility associated with a payoff of −$20,000, we must ask Swofford's president to state a preference between a guaranteed −$20,000 payoff and the opportunity to engage in the following lottery.

Lottery: Swofford obtains a payoff of $50,000 with probability p
and a payoff of −$50,000 with probability $(1 - p)$.

Note that this is exactly the same lottery we used to establish the utility of a payoff of $30,000. In fact, this will be the lottery used to establish the utility for any monetary value in the Swofford payoff table. Using this lottery, then, we must ask the president to state the value of p that would make her indifferent between a guaranteed payoff of −$20,000 and the lottery. For example, we might begin by asking her to choose between a certain loss of $20,000 and the lottery with a payoff of $50,000 with probability $p = 0.90$ and a payoff of −$50,000 with probability $(1 - p) = 0.10$. What answer do you think we would get? Surely, with this high probability of obtaining a payoff of $50,000, the president would elect the lottery. Next, we might ask if $p = 0.85$ would result in indifference between the loss of $20,000 for certain and the lottery. Again, she might tell us that the lottery would be preferred. Suppose that we continue in this fashion until we get to $p = 0.55$, where we find that with this value of p, the president is indifferent between the payoff of −$20,000 and the lottery. That is, for any value of p less than 0.55, the president would rather take a loss of $20,000 for certain than risk the potential loss of $50,000 with the lottery; for any value of p above 0.55, the president would elect the lottery. Thus, the utility assigned to a payoff of −$20,000 is

$$U(-\$20,000) = pU(\$50,000) + (1 - p)U(-\$50,000)$$
$$= 0.55(10) + 0.45(0)$$
$$= 5.5$$

Again, let us examine the significance of this assignment as compared with the expected value approach. When $p = 0.55$, the expected value of the lottery is

$$EV(\text{lottery}) = 0.55(\$50,000) + 0.45(-\$50,000)$$

$$= \$27,500 - \$22,500$$

$$= \$5,000$$

Thus, the president would just as soon absorb a loss of $20,000 for certain as take the lottery, even though the expected value of the lottery is $5000. Once again we see the conservative, or risk-avoiding, point of view of Swofford's president.

In the above two examples where we computed the utility for a specific monetary payoff, M, we first found the probability p where the decision maker was indifferent between a guaranteed payoff of M and a lottery with a payoff of $50,000 with probability p and $-\$50,000$ with probability $(1 - p)$. The utility of M was then computed as

$$U(M) = pU(\$50,000) + (1 - p)U(-\$50,000)$$

$$= p(10) + (1 - p)0$$

$$= 10p$$

Using the above procedure, utility values for the rest of the payoffs in Swofford's problem were developed. The results are presented in Table 14.8.

Now that we have determined the utility value of each of the possible monetary values, we can write the original payoff table in terms of utility values. Table 14.9 shows the utility for the various outcomes in the Swofford problem. The notation we will use for the entries in the utility table is $U(d_i, s_j)$, which denotes the utility associated with decision alternative d_i and state of nature s_j. Using this notation, we see that $U(d_2, s_3) = 4.0$.

Table 14.8

Utility of Monetary Payoffs for the Swofford, Inc., Problem

Monetary Value	Indifference Value of p	Utility Value
$ 50,000	Does not apply	10.0
30,000	0.95	9.5
20,000	0.90	9.0
0	0.75	7.5
−20,000	0.55	5.5
−30,000	0.40	4.0
−50,000	Does not apply	0

Table 14.9

Utility Table for Swofford, Inc., Problem

		States of Nature		
Decision Alternatives		Prices Up s_1	Prices Stable s_2	Prices Down s_3
Investment A	d_1	9.5	9.0	0
Investment B	d_2	10.0	5.5	4.0
Do not invest	d_3	7.5	7.5	7.5

The Expected Utility Approach

We can now apply the expected value computations introduced in Section 14.3 to the payoffs in Table 14.9 in order to select an optimal decision alternative for Swofford, Inc. However, since utility values represent such a special case of expected value, we will refer to the expected value when applied to utility values as the *expected utility* (EU). In this way, we will avoid any possible confusion between the expected value for the original payoff table and the expected value for the payoff table consisting of *utility values*. Thus, the expected utility approach requires the analyst to compute the expected utility for each decision alternative and then select the alternative yielding the best expected utility. If there are N possible states of nature, the expected utility of a decision alternative d_i is given by

$$\text{EU}(d_i) = \sum_{j=1}^{N} P(s_j)U(d_i, s_j) \tag{14.19}$$

The expected utility for each of the decision alternatives in the Swofford problem is computed as follows:

$$\text{EU}(d_1) = 0.3(9.5) + 0.5(9.0) + \quad 0.2(0) = 7.35$$

$$\text{EU}(d_2) = 0.3(10) \;+ 0.5(5.5) + 0.2(4.0) = 6.55$$

$$\text{EU}(d_3) = 0.3(7.5) + 0.5(7.5) + 0.2(7.5) = 7.50$$

You should now be able to use the expected utility approach to determine the optimal decision. Try Problem 28.

We see that the optimal decision using the expected utility approach is d_3, do not invest. The ranking of alternatives according to the president's utility assignments and the associated monetary values is as follows:

Ranking of Decision Alternatives	Expected Utility	Expected Monetary Value
Do not invest	7.50	$ 0
Investment A	7.35	9000
Investment B	6.55	− 1000

Note that whereas investment A had the highest expected monetary value of $9000, the analysis indicates that Swofford should decline this investment. The rationale behind not selecting investment A is that the 0.2 probability of a $50,000 loss was considered by Swofford's president to involve a very serious risk. The seriousness of this risk and its associated impact on the company were not adequately reflected by the expected monetary value of investment A. It was necessary to assess the utility for each payoff to adequately take this risk into account.

One difficulty in applying the expected utility approach is that some managers are uncomfortable with using a lottery to develop the indifference probabilities; in such cases, it becomes very difficult for the analyst to establish accurate utility values.

Unfortunately, the determination of the appropriate utilities is not a trivial task. As we have seen, measuring utility requires a degree of subjectivity on the part of the decision maker, and different decision makers will have different utility functions. This aspect of utility often causes decision makers to feel uncomfortable about using the expected utility approach in decision making. However, if we encounter a decision situation in which we are convinced monetary value is not the only relevant measure of performance, utility analysis should be considered.

NOTES & COMMENTS

1. In the Swofford problem, we used a utility of 10 for the largest possible payoff and 0 for the smallest. Had we chosen 1 for the utility of the largest payoff and 0 for the utility of the smallest, the utility for any monetary value M would have been the value of p at which the decision maker was indifferent between a payoff of M for certain and a lottery in which the best payoff is obtained with probability p and the worst payoff is obtained with probability $(1 - p)$. Thus, the utility for any monetary value would have been equal to the probability of earning the highest payoff. Often, this choice is made because of the ease in computation. We chose not to do so to emphasize the distinction between the utility values and the indifference probabilities for the lottery.

2. It is generally agreed that when the payoffs for a particular decision-making problem fall into a reasonable range—the best is not too good and the worst is not too bad—decision makers tend to express preferences in agreement with the expected value approach. Thus, as a general guideline we suggest asking the decision maker to consider the best and worst possible payoffs for a problem and assess their reasonableness. If the decision maker believes they are in the reasonable range, the expected monetary value criterion can be used. However, if the payoffs appear unreasonably large or unreasonably small (e.g., a huge loss), and if the decision maker feels monetary values do not adequately reflect her or his true preferences for the payoffs, a utility analysis of the problem should be considered.

Summary

In this chapter we have emphasized how decision analysis can be used to solve problems with a limited number of decision alternatives and a limited number of possible states of nature. The goal of decision analysis is to identify the best decision alternative given an uncertain or risk-filled pattern of future events (i.e., states of nature).

We presented three approaches to decision making without probabilities and discussed the use of the expected value approach for decision making with probabilities. Then we showed how additional information about the states of nature can be used to revise or update the probability estimates and develop an optimal decision strategy. The concepts of expected value of sample information, expected value of perfect information, and efficiency of information were used to evaluate the contribution of the sample information.

We suggested that the expected utility approach should be used in situations in which monetary value is not the only relevant measure of performance. Unlike monetary value, utility is a measure of the total worth of an outcome resulting from the choice of a decision alternative and the occurrence of a state of nature. As such, utility takes into account the decision maker's attitude toward the profit, loss, and risk associated with an outcome. In our examples, we have seen how the use of utility analysis can lead to decision recommendations that differ from those that would be selected using the expected monetary value approach.

Glossary

States of nature The uncontrollable future events that affect the payoff associated with a decision alternative.

Payoff The outcome measure, such as profit, cost, and time. Each combination of a decision alternative and a state of nature has an associated payoff.

Payoff table A tabular representation of the payoffs for a decision problem.

Decision tree A graphical representation of the decision problem that shows the sequential nature of the decision-making situation.

Nodes The intersection or junction points of the decision tree.

Branches Lines or arcs connecting nodes of the decision tree.

Optimistic approach An approach to choosing a decision alternative without using probabilities. For a maximization problem, it leads to choosing the decision alternative corresponding to the largest payoff; for a minimization problem, it leads to choosing the decision alternative corresponding to the smallest payoff.

Conservative approach An approach to choosing a decision alternative without using probabilities. For a maximization problem, it leads to choosing the decision alternative that maximizes the minimum payoff; for a minimization problem, it leads to choosing the decision alternative that minimizes the maximum payoff.

Minimax regret An approach to choosing a decision alternative without using probabilities. For each alternative, the maximum regret is computed. This approach leads to choosing the decision alternative that minimizes the maximum regret.

Expected value approach An approach to choosing a decision alternative that is based upon the expected value of each decision alternative. The recommended decision alternative is the one that provides the best expected value.

Sensitivity analysis The study of how changes in the probability estimates for the states of nature affect the recommended decision alternative.

Opportunity loss or regret The amount of loss (lower profit or higher cost) due to not making the best decision for each state of nature.

Expected value (EV) For a decision alternative, it is the weighted average of the payoffs. The weights are the state-of-nature probabilities.

Expected value of perfect information (EVPI) The expected value of information that would tell the decision maker exactly which state of nature is going to occur (i.e., perfect information).

Prior probabilities The probabilities of the states of nature prior to obtaining sample information.

Posterior (revised) probabilities The probabilities of the states of nature after revising the prior probabilities based on given indicator information.

Indicators Information about the states of nature. An indicator may be the result of a sample.

Bayesian revision The process of revising prior probabilities to create the posterior probabilities based on sample information.

Expected value of sample information (EVSI) The difference between the expected value of an optimal strategy based on sample information and the "best" expected value without any sample information.

Efficiency The ratio of EVSI to EVPI; perfect information is 100% efficient.

Utility A measure of the total worth of an outcome reflecting a decision maker's attitude toward considerations such as profit and loss, and intangibles such as risk.

Lottery A hypothetical investment alternative with a probability p of obtaining the best possible payoff and a probability of $(1 - p)$ of obtaining the worst possible payoff.

Expected utility (EU) approach An approach that considers the expected utility for each decision alternative and then selects the decision alternative yielding the highest expected utility.

Problems

SELF TEST ▶

1. Decision tree, decision making without probabilities

1. The payoff table showing profit for a decision analysis problem with two decisions and three states of nature is shown below.

Decision Alternatives	States of Nature		
	s_1	s_2	s_3
d_1	250	100	25
d_2	100	100	75

    a. Construct a decision tree for this problem.

    b. If the decision maker knows nothing about the chances or probability of occurrence of the three states of nature, what is the recommended decision using the optimistic, conservative, and minimax regret approaches?

2. Decision making without probabilities

2. Suppose that a decision maker faced with four decision alternatives and four states of nature develops the following profit payoff table:

Decision Alternatives	States of Nature			
	s_1	s_2	s_3	s_4
d_1	14	9	10	5
d_2	11	10	8	7
d_3	9	10	10	11
d_4	8	10	11	13

    a. If the decision maker knows nothing about the chances or probability of occurrence of the four states of nature, what is the recommended decision using the optimistic, conservative, and minimax regret approaches?

    b. Which approach do you prefer? Explain. Is it important for the decision maker to establish the most appropriate approach before analyzing the problem? Explain.

    c. Assume that the payoff table provides *cost* rather than profit payoffs. What is the recommended decision using the optimistic, conservative, and minimax regret approaches?

3. Decision tree, decision making without probabilities

3. Southland Corporation's decision to produce a new line of recreational products has resulted in the need to construct either a small plant or a large plant. The selection of plant size depends on how the marketplace reacts to the new product line. To conduct an analysis, marketing management has decided to view the possible long-run demand as either low, medium, or high. The following payoff table shows the projected profit in millions of dollars:

Decision	Long-Run Demand		
Alternatives	Low	Medium	High
Small plant	150	200	200
Large plant	50	200	500

a. Construct a decision tree for this problem.

b. Recommend a decision using the optimistic, conservative, and minimax regret approaches.

4. McHuffter Condominiums, Inc., of Pensacola, Florida, recently purchased land near the Gulf of Mexico and is attempting to determine the size of the condominium development it should build. Three sizes of developments are being considered: small, d_1; medium, d_2; and large, d_3. At the same time, an uncertain economy makes it difficult to ascertain the demand for the new condominiums. McHuffter's management realizes that a large development followed by a low demand could be very costly to the company. However, if McHuffter makes a conservative small-development decision and then finds a high demand, the firm's profits will be lower than they might have been. With the three levels of demand—low, medium, and high—McHuffter's management has prepared the following profit ($1000s) payoff table:

Decision	Demand		
Alternatives	Low	Medium	High
Small	400	400	400
Medium	100	600	600
Large	−300	300	900

a. Construct a decision tree for this problem.

b. If nothing is known about the demand probabilities, what are the recommended decisions using the optimistic, conservative, and minimax regret approaches?

5. The payoff table presented in Problem 1 is repeated here:

Decision	States of Nature		
Alternatives	s_1	s_2	s_3
d_1	250	100	25
d_2	100	100	75

Suppose that the decision maker has obtained the following probability estimates: $P(s_1) = 0.65$, $P(s_2) = 0.15$, $P(s_3) = 0.20$. Use the expected value approach to determine the optimal decision.

6. Expected value approach

6. The profit payoff table presented in Problem 2 is repeated here:

Decision Alternatives	States of Nature			
	s_1	s_2	s_3	s_4
d_1	14	9	10	5
d_2	11	10	8	7
d_3	9	10	10	11
d_4	8	10	11	13

Suppose that the decision maker obtains information that enables the following probability estimates to be made: $P(s_1) = 0.5, P(s_2) = 0.2, P(s_3) = 0.2, P(s_4) = 0.1$.
a. Use the expected value approach to determine the optimal decision.
b. Now assume that the entries in the payoff table are costs; use the expected value approach to determine the optimal decision.

7. Expected value approach

7. Hale's TV Productions is considering producing a pilot for a comedy series for a major television network. While the network may reject the pilot and the series, it may also purchase the program for 1 or 2 years. Hale may decide to produce the pilot or transfer the rights for the series to a competitor for $100,000. Hale's profits are summarized in the following profit ($1000s) payoff table:

	States of Nature		
	Reject	1 Year	2 Years
d_1 (Produce pilot)	−100	50	150
d_2 (Sell to competitor)	100	100	100

Assuming the probability estimates for the states of nature are $P(\text{reject}) = 0.2$, $P(1 \text{ year}) = 0.3$, and $P(2 \text{ years}) = 0.5$, what should the company do?

8. Expected value approach

8. Consider the McHuffter Condominiums problem presented in Problem 4. If $P(\text{low}) = 0.20$, $P(\text{medium}) = 0.35$, *and* $P(\text{high}) = 0.45$, *what is the recommended decision using the expected value approach?*

9. Decision tree, expected value approach

9. Martin's Service Station is considering investing in a heavy-duty snowplow this fall. Martin has analyzed the situation carefully and feels that this would be a very profitable investment if the snowfall is heavy. A small profit could still be made if the snowfall is moderate, but Martin would lose money if the snowfall is light. Specifically, Martin forecasts a profit of $7000 if the snowfall is heavy and $2000 if it is moderate, and a $9000 loss if the snowfall is light. Based on the weather bureau's long-range forecast, Martin estimates that $P(\text{heavy snowfall}) = 0.4$, $P(\text{moderate snowfall}) = 0.3$, and $P(\text{light snowfall}) = 0.3$.
a. Prepare a decision tree for Martin's problem.
b. What is the expected value at each state-of-nature node?
c. Using the expected value approach, would you recommend that Martin invest in the snowplow?

10. Decision tree, expected value approach

10. Joseph Software, Inc. (JSI), has been investigating the possibility of developing a grammar-and-style checker for use on microcomputers. Based on their experience with other software projects, JSI estimates that the total cost to develop a prototype of the software is $200,000. If the performance of the prototype is somewhat better than existing software, referred to as a *moderate success,* JSI believes they could sell the rights to the software to a larger software developer for $160,000. If the performance of the prototype is significantly better than existing software, referred to as a *major success,* they believe that the software can be sold for $1.2 million. However, if the performance of the prototype does not exceed the performance of existing software, referred to as a *failure,* JSI will not be able to sell the software and hence will lose all of their development costs.

   a. Prepare a decision tree for JSI.
   b. If the best estimates of the states of nature are $P(\text{failure}) = 0.70$, $P(\text{moderate success}) = 0.20$, and $P(\text{major success}) = 0.10$, what should JSI do if they use the expected value approach?

11. Expected value approach

11. Six months ago, Doug Reynolds paid $25,000 for an option to purchase a tract of land that he is considering developing. Another investor has offered to purchase Doug's option for $275,000. If Doug does not accept the investor's offer, he will purchase the property, clear the land, and prepare the site for building. He believes that once the site is prepared he can sell the land to a home builder. However, the success of the investment depends upon the real estate market at the time he sells the property. If the real estate market is down, Doug feels that he will lose $1.5 million. If market conditions stay at their current level, he estimates that his profit will be $1 million; if market conditions are up at the time he sells, he estimates a profit of $4 million. Because of other commitments Doug does not consider it feasible to hold the land once he has developed it; thus, the only two alternatives are to sell the option or to develop the land. Suppose that the probabilities of the real estate market being down, at the current level, or up are 0.6, 0.3, and 0.1, respectively. What decision should Doug make using the expected value approach?

S E L F   T E S T ▶

12. Graphical sensitivity analysis

12. The payoff table showing profit for a decision problem with two states of nature and two decision alternatives is shown below:

Decision Alternatives	States of Nature	
	s_1	s_2
d_1	10	1
d_2	4	3

Use graphical sensitivity analysis to determine the probability of state of nature s_1 for which each of the decision alternatives has the largest expected value.

13. Graphical sensitivity analysis

13. The payoff table showing profit for a decision problem with two states of nature and three decision alternatives is presented below:

Decision Alternatives	States of Nature	
	s_1	s_2
d_1	80	50
d_2	65	85
d_3	30	100

Use graphical sensitivity analysis to determine the values of the probability of state of nature s_1 for which each of the decision alternatives has the largest expected value.

14. Milford Trucking, located in Chicago, has requests to haul two shipments, one to St. Louis and one to Detroit. Because of a scheduling problem, Milford will be able to accept only one of these assignments. The St. Louis customer has guaranteed a return shipment, but the Detroit customer has not. Thus, if Milford accepts the Detroit shipment and cannot find a Detroit-to-Chicago return shipment, the truck will return to Chicago empty. The payoff table showing profit is as follows:

Shipment		Return Shipment from Detroit s_1	No Return Shipment from Detroit s_2
St. Louis	d_1	2000	2000
Detroit	d_2	2500	1000

a. If the probability of a Detroit return shipment is 0.4, what should Milford do?
b. Use graphical sensitivity analysis to determine the values of the probability of state of nature s_1 for which d_1 has the largest expected value.

15. Refer to Problem 11. Suppose that the probabilities of the real estate market being down, at the current level, or up are 0.5, 0.3, and 0.2, respectively. What decision should Doug make following the expected value approach? What if the probabilities are 0.4, 0.4, and 0.2? What do the above results suggest regarding the proposed investment?

16. Suppose that after further consideration, Doug Reynolds (Problems 11 and 15) concludes that 0.1 is a good estimate of the probability of the real estate market being up. However, Doug is unable to reach any definite conclusions regarding the probabilities for the other two states of nature. What would the value of the probability of the market being down have to be for the expected value approach to recommend that he should sell his option for $275,000? Do you think that this information would help Doug make a decision regarding whether to sell the option or develop the site? Explain.

17. The payoff table presented in Problems 1 and 5 is repeated here:

Decision Alternatives	States of Nature s_1	s_2	s_3
d_1	250	100	25
d_2	100	100	75

The probabilities for the states of nature are: $P(s_1) = 0.65$, $P(s_2) = 0.15$, $P(s_3) = 0.20$.
a. What is the optimal decision strategy if perfect information were available?
b. What is the expected value for the decision strategy developed in part (a)?
c. Using the expected value approach, what is the recommended decision? What is its expected value?
d. What is the expected value of perfect information?

18. The profit payoff table presented in Problems 2 and 6 is repeated here:

Decision Alternatives	States of Nature			
	s_1	s_2	s_3	s_4
d_1	14	9	10	5
d_2	11	10	8	7
d_3	9	10	10	11
d_4	8	10	11	13

The probabilities of the states of nature are: $P(s_1) = 0.5$, $P(s_2) = 0.2$, $P(s_3) = 0.2$, and $P(s_4) = 0.1$.
a. What is the optimal decision strategy if perfect information were available?
b. What is the expected value for the decision strategy developed in part (a)?
c. Using the expected value approach, what is the recommended decision? What is its expected value?
d. What is the expected value of perfect information?

19. Consider the Hale's TV Productions problem (Problem 7). What is the maximum that Hale should be willing to pay for inside information on what the network will do?

20. Consider the McHuffter Condominiums problem (Problems 4 and 8). What is the expected value of perfect information?

21. Refer again to the investment problem faced by Martin's Service Station (Problem 9). Martin can purchase a blade to attach to his service truck that can also be used to plow driveways and parking lots. Since this truck must also be available to start cars, Martin will not be able to generate as much revenue plowing snow if he elects this alternative. But he will keep his loss smaller if there is light snowfall. Under this alternative, Martin forecasts a profit of $3500 if the snowfall is heavy and $1000 if it is moderate and a $1500 loss if the snowfall is light.
a. Prepare a new decision tree showing all three alternatives.
b. Using the expected value approach, what is the optimal decision?
c. What is the expected value of perfect information?

22. Consider the Milford Trucking problem (Problem 14). What is the expected value of perfect information that would tell Milford Trucking whether Detroit has a return shipment?

23. Suppose that you are given a decision situation with three possible states of nature: s_1, s_2, and s_3. The prior probabilities are $P(s_1) = 0.2$, $P(s_2) = 0.5$, and $P(s_3) = 0.3$. Indicator information I is obtained, and it is known that $P(I \mid s_1) = 0.1$, $P(I \mid s_2) = 0.05$, and $P(I \mid s_3) = 0.2$. Compute the revised or posterior probabilities: $P(s_1 \mid I)$, $P(s_2 \mid I)$, and $P(s_3 \mid I)$.

24. The payoff table showing profit for a decision problem with two states of nature and three decision alternatives is presented in Table 14.10. The prior probabilities for s_1 and s_2 are $P(s_1) = 0.8$ and $P(s_2) = 0.2$.
a. Using only the prior probabilities and the expected value approach, find the optimal decision.
b. Use graphical sensitivity analysis to determine the values of the probability of state of nature s_1 for which each of the decision alternatives has the largest expected value.
c. Find the EVPI.
d. Suppose that some indicator information I is obtained with $P(I \mid s_1) = 0.2$ and $P(I \mid s_2) = 0.75$. Find the posterior probabilities $P(s_1 \mid I)$ and $P(s_2 \mid I)$. Recommend a decision alternative based on these probabilities.

Table 14.10

	s_1	s_2
d_1	15	10
d_2	10	12
d_3	8	20

25. Consider the following decision tree representation of a decision analysis problem with two indicators, two decision alternatives, and two states of nature:

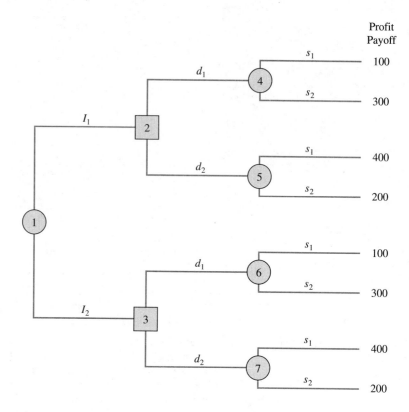

Assume that the following probability information is given:

$$P(s_1) = 0.4 \qquad P(I_1 \mid s_1) = 0.8 \qquad P(I_2 \mid s_1) = 0.2$$

$$P(s_2) = 0.6 \qquad P(I_1 \mid s_2) = 0.4 \qquad P(I_2 \mid s_2) = 0.6$$

a. What are the values for $P(I_1)$ and $P(I_2)$?
b. What are the values of $P(s_1 \mid I_1)$, $P(s_2 \mid I_1)$, $P(s_1 \mid I_2)$, and $P(s_2 \mid I_2)$?
c. Using the decision tree approach, determine the optimal decision strategy and its expected value.

26. For a particular decision problem, suppose that the expected value of the optimal decision with sample information is $45,000 and that the expected value of the optimal decision without sample information is $37,000. The expected value with perfect information is $60,000.
a. Compute EVSI.
b. What is the efficiency of the sample information?
c. If the study required to obtain the sample information had a cost of $10,000, what would you recommend?

27. Refer to Problem 25.
a. What is your decision without the indicator information?
b. What is the expected value of the indicator or sample information EVSI?
c. What is the expected value of perfect information EVPI?
d. What is the efficiency of the indicator information?

SELF TEST ▶

28. Decision tree, developing a decision strategy, EVSI

28. The payoff table (profit in $1000s) for Hale's TV Productions (Problems 7 and 19) is as follows:

Decision Alternatives		States of Nature		
		s_1	s_2	s_3
Produce pilot	d_1	-100	50	150
Sell to competitor	d_2	100	100	100
Probability of states of nature		0.2	0.3	0.5

For a consulting fee of $2500, an agency will review the plans for the comedy series and indicate the overall chances of a favorable network reaction to the series. If the special agency review results in a favorable (I_1) or an unfavorable (I_2) evaluation, what should Hale's decision strategy be? Assume that Hale believes that the following conditional probabilities are realistic appraisals of the agency's evaluation accuracy:

$$P(I_1 \mid s_1) = 0.3 \qquad P(I_2 \mid s_1) = 0.7$$

$$P(I_1 \mid s_2) = 0.6 \qquad P(I_2 \mid s_2) = 0.4$$

$$P(I_1 \mid s_3) = 0.9 \qquad P(I_2 \mid s_3) = 0.1$$

a. Show the decision tree for this problem.
b. What is the recommended decision strategy and the expected value, assuming that the agency information is obtained?
c. What is the EVSI? Is the agency information worth the $2500 consulting fee? What is the maximum that Hale should be willing to pay for the consulting information?

29. Developing a decision strategy, EVSI, EVPI

29. McHuffter Condominiums (Problems 4, 8, and 20) is conducting a survey that will help evaluate the demand for the new condominium development. McHuffter's payoff table (profit in $1000s) is as follows:

Decision Alternatives		States of Nature		
		Low s_1	Medium s_2	High s_3
Small	d_1	400	400	400
Medium	d_2	100	600	600
Large	d_3	-300	300	900
Probability of states of nature		0.20	0.35	0.45

Table 14.11

	$P(I_k \mid s_k)$		
	I_1	I_2	I_3
s_1	0.6	0.3	0.1
s_2	0.4	0.4	0.2
s_3	0.1	0.4	0.5

The survey will result in three indicators of demand: weak (I_1), average (I_2), or strong (I_3). The conditional probabilities are shown in Table 14.11.

a. What is McHuffter's optimal strategy?
b. What is the value of the survey information?
c. What are the EVPI and the efficiency of the survey information?

30. The payoff table ($) for Martin's Service Station (Problems 9 and 21) is as follows:

Decision Alternatives		Snowfall		
		Heavy s_1	Moderate s_2	Light s_3
Purchase snowplow	d_1	7000	2000	−9000
Do not invest	d_2	0	0	0
Purchase snowplow with blade	d_3	3500	1000	−1500
Probability of states of nature		0.4	0.3	0.3

Suppose that Martin decides to wait to check the September temperature pattern before making a final decision. Estimates of the probabilities associated with an unseasonably cold September (I_1) are as follows: $P(I_1 \mid s_1) = 0.30$, $P(I_1 \mid s_2) = 0.20$, $P(I_1 \mid s_3) = 0.05$. If Martin observes an unseasonably cold September, what is the recommended decision? If Martin does not observe an unseasonably cold September (I_2), what is the recommended decision?

31. Suppose that Joseph Software, Inc., in Problem 10, can hire an independent consultant to review their ideas for the new software. For a fee of $5000, the consultant will make a recommendation as to whether or not JSI should develop a prototype. Based on previous experience with this consultant, JSI has assigned the following conditional probabilities:

$$P(I_1 \mid s_1) = 0.2$$

$$P(I_1 \mid s_2) = 0.6$$

$$P(I_1 \mid s_3) = 0.9$$

where

I_1 = recommendation to develop a prototype
s_1 = failure
s_2 = moderate success
s_3 = major success

Should JSI hire the consultant? Explain.

32. Milford Trucking (Problems 14 and 22) has the following payoff table:

Shipment		Return Shipment from Detroit s_1	No Return Shipment from Detroit s_2
St. Louis	d_1	2000	2000
Detroit	d_2	2500	1000
Probabilities		0.40	0.60

a. Milford can phone a Detroit truck dispatch center and determine if the general Detroit shipping activity is busy (I_1) or slow (I_2). If the report is busy, the chances of obtaining a return shipment will increase. Suppose the following conditional probabilities are given:

$$P(I_1 \mid s_1) = 0.6 \qquad P(I_2 \mid s_1) = 0.4$$

$$P(I_1 \mid s_2) = 0.3 \qquad P(I_2 \mid s_2) = 0.7$$

What should Milford do?

b. If the Detroit report is busy (I_1), what is the probability that Milford will obtain a return shipment if it makes the trip to Detroit?

c. What is the efficiency of the phone information?

33. To save on gasoline expenses, Rona and Jerry agreed to form a carpool for traveling to and from work. After limiting the travel routes to two alternatives, Rona and Jerry could not agree on the best way to travel to work. Jerry preferred the expressway, since it was usually the fastest; however, Rona pointed out that traffic jams on the expressway sometimes led to long delays. Rona preferred the somewhat longer but more consistent Queen City Avenue. While Jerry still preferred the expressway, he agreed with Rona that they should take Queen City Avenue if the expressway had a traffic jam. Unfortunately, they do not know the state of the expressway ahead of time. The following payoff table provides the one-way time estimates in minutes for traveling to or from work:

| | | States of Nature | |
| | | Expressway Open s_1 | Expressway Jammed s_2 |
Route			
Expressway	d_1	25	45
Queen City Avenue	d_2	30	30

a. After driving to work on the expressway for 1 month (20 days), they found the expressway jammed three times. Assuming that these days are representative of future days, should they continue to use the expressway for traveling to work? Explain.

b. Use graphical sensitivity analysis to determine the values of the probability of state of nature s_1 for which d_1 has the best expected value.

c. Would it make sense to not use the expected value approach for this particular problem? Explain.

After a period of time, Rona and Jerry noted that the weather seemed to affect the traffic conditions on the expressway. They identified three weather conditions (indicators) with the following conditional probabilities:

$$I_1 = \text{clear} \qquad I_2 = \text{overcast} \qquad I_3 = \text{rain}$$

$$P(I_1 \mid s_1) = 0.8 \qquad P(I_2 \mid s_1) = 0.2 \qquad P(I_3 \mid s_1) = 0$$

$$P(I_1 \mid s_2) = 0.1 \qquad P(I_2 \mid s_2) = 0.3 \qquad P(I_3 \mid s_2) = 0.6$$

d. Show the decision tree for the problem of traveling to work.

e. What is the optimal decision strategy and the expected travel time?

f. What is the efficiency of the weather information?

34. The Gorman Manufacturing Company must decide whether it should purchase a component from a supplier or manufacture the component at its Milan, Michigan, plant. If demand is high, it would be to Gorman's advantage to manufacture the component. However, if demand is low, Gorman's unit manufacturing cost will be high due to underutilization of equipment. The projected profit in thousands of dollars for Gorman's make-or-buy decision is shown below:

Decision Alternatives	Demand		
	Low	Medium	High
Manufacture component	−20	40	100
Purchase component	10	45	70

The states of nature have the following probabilities: $P(\text{low demand}) = 0.35$, $P(\text{medium demand}) = 0.35$, and $P(\text{high demand}) = 0.30$.

a. Use a decision tree to recommend a decision.

b. Use EVPI to determine whether Gorman should attempt to obtain a better estimate of demand.

A test market study of the potential demand for the product is expected to report either a favorable (I_1) or unfavorable (I_2) condition. The relevant conditional probabilities are as follows:

$$P(I_1 \mid s_1) = 0.10 \qquad P(I_2 \mid s_1) = 0.90$$

$$P(I_1 \mid s_2) = 0.40 \qquad P(I_2 \mid s_2) = 0.60$$

$$P(I_1 \mid s_3) = 0.60 \qquad P(I_2 \mid s_3) = 0.40$$

c. What is the probability that the market research report will be favorable?

d. What is Gorman's optimal decision strategy?

e. What is the expected value of the market research information?

f. What is the efficiency of the information?

35. EVPI

35. A firm produces a perishable food product at a cost of $10 per case. The product sells for $15 per case. For planning purposes, the company is considering possible demands of 100, 200, or 300 cases. If the demand is less than production, the excess production is lost. If demand is more than production, the firm, in an attempt to maintain a good service image, will satisfy the excess demand with a special production run at a cost of $18 per case. The product, however, always sells at $15 per case.

a. Set up the payoff table for this problem.

b. If $P(100) = 0.2$, $P(200) = 0.2$, and $P(300) = 0.6$, should the company produce 100, 200, or 300 cases?

c. What is the EVPI?

36. Expected value approach, developing a decision strategy, EVSI, efficiency of sample information

36. Sealcoat, Inc., has a contract with one of its customers to supply a unique liquid chemical product that will be used by the customer in the manufacture of a lubricant for airplane engines. Because of the chemical process used by Sealcoat, batch sizes for the liquid chemical product must be 1000 pounds. The customer has agreed to adjust manufacturing to the full batch quantities and will order either one, two, or three batches every 3 months. Since an aging process of 1 month exists for the product, Sealcoat will have to make its production (how much to make) decision before the customer places an order. Thus, Sealcoat can list the product demand alternatives of 1000, 2000, or 3000 pounds, but the exact demand is unknown.

Sealcoat's manufacturing costs are $150 per pound, and the product sells at the fixed contract price of $200 per pound. If the customer orders more than Sealcoat has produced, Sealcoat has agreed to absorb the added cost of filling the order by purchasing a higher quality substitute product from another chemical firm. The substitute product, including transportation expenses, will cost Sealcoat $240 per pound. Since the product cannot be stored more than 2 months without spoilage, Sealcoat cannot inventory excess production until the customer's next 3-month order. Therefore, if the customer's current order is less than Sealcoat has produced, the excess production will be reprocessed and is valued at $50 per pound.

The inventory decision in this problem is how much should Sealcoat produce given the above costs and the possible demands of 1000, 2000, or 3000 pounds? Based on historical data and an analysis of the customer's future demands, Sealcoat has assessed the probability distribution for demand shown in Table 14.12.

a. Develop a payoff table for the Sealcoat problem.
b. How many batches should Sealcoat produce every 3 months?
c. How much of a discount should Sealcoat be willing to allow the customer for specifying in advance exactly how many batches will be purchased?

Sealcoat has identified a pattern in the demand for the product based on the customer's previous order quantity. Let

$$I_1 = \text{customer's last order was 1000 pounds}$$
$$I_2 = \text{customer's last order was 2000 pounds}$$
$$I_3 = \text{customer's last order was 3000 pounds}$$

The conditional probabilities are as follows:

$$P(I_1 \mid s_1) = 0.10 \qquad P(I_2 \mid s_1) = 0.40 \qquad P(I_3 \mid s_1) = 0.50$$

$$P(I_1 \mid s_2) = 0.22 \qquad P(I_2 \mid s_2) = 0.68 \qquad P(I_3 \mid s_2) = 0.10$$

$$P(I_1 \mid s_3) = 0.80 \qquad P(I_2 \mid s_3) = 0.20 \qquad P(I_3 \mid s_3) = 0.00$$

d. Develop an optimal decision strategy for Sealcoat.
e. What is the EVSI?
f. What is the efficiency of the information for the most recent order?

Table 14.12

Demand	Probability
1000	0.3
2000	0.5
3000	0.2

37. Expected value approach, decision tree, developing a decision strategy (binomial distribution)

37. A quality control procedure involves 100% inspection of parts received from a supplier. Historical records indicate that the defective rates shown in Table 14.13 have been observed. The cost to inspect 100% of the parts received is $250 for each shipment of 500 parts. If the shipment is not 100% inspected, defective parts will cause rework problems later in the production process. The rework cost is $25 for each defective part.

a. Complete the following payoff table, where the entries represent the total cost of inspection and reworking:

Table 14.13

Percent Defective	Probability
0	0.15
1	0.25
2	0.40
3	0.20

	Percent Defective			
Inspection	0	1	2	3
100% inspection	$250	$250	$250	$250
No inspection				

b. The plant manager is considering eliminating the inspection process to save the $250 inspection cost per shipment. Do you support this action? Use expected value to justify your answer.
c. Show the decision tree for this problem.
d. Suppose that a sample of five parts is selected from the shipment and one defect is found. Let $I = 1$ defect in a sample of 5. Use the binomial probability distribution to compute $P(I \mid s_1)$, $P(I \mid s_2)$, $P(I \mid s_3)$, and $P(I \mid s_4)$. The binomial probability function is as follows:

$$f(x) = \frac{n!}{x!(n-x)!} p^x (1-p)^{n-x}$$

where

$$n = \text{the sample size}$$
$$x = \text{the number of defects}$$
$$p = \text{the proportion defective}$$

In this problem, $n = 5$, $x = 1$, and $p = 0$, 0.01, 0.02, and 0.03.

e. If I occurs, what are the revised probabilities for the states of nature?
f. Should the entire shipment be 100% inspected whenever one defect is found in a sample of size 5?
g. What is the cost savings associated with the sample information?

38. A food processor considers daily production runs of 100, 200, and 300 cases. Possible demands for the product are 100, 200, and 300 cases. The payoff table is as follows:

		Demand		
		100	200	300
Production		s_1	s_2	s_3
100	d_1	500	200	-100
200	d_2	-400	800	700
300	d_3	-1000	-200	1600

a. If $P(s_1) = 0.2$, $P(s_2) = 0.2$, and $P(s_3) = 0.6$, what is your recommended production quantity?
b. On some days the firm receives phone calls for advance orders, and on some days it does not. Suppose that $I_1 = $ advance orders are received and $I_2 = $ no advance orders are received. If $P(I_2 \mid s_1) = 0.8$, $P(I_2 \mid s_2) = 0.4$, and $P(I_2 \mid s_3) = 0.1$, what is your recommended production quantity for days the company does not receive any advance orders?

39. The research and development manager for Beck Company is trying to decide whether the company should fund the development of a new lubricant. It is assumed that the project will be either a major technical success, a minor success, or a failure. The company has estimated that the value of a major success is $150,000, since the lubricant can be used in a number of products the company is making. If the project is a minor success, its value is $10,000, since Beck feels that the knowledge gained will benefit some other ongoing projects. If the project is a failure, it will cost the company $100,000.

Based on the opinion of the scientists involved and the manager's own subjective assessment, the assigned prior probabilities are as follows:

$$P(\text{major success}) = 0.15$$

$$P(\text{minor success}) = 0.45$$

$$P(\text{failure}) = 0.40$$

a. Using the expected value approach, should the project be funded?
b. Suppose that a group of expert scientists from a research institute could be hired as consultants to study the project and make a recommendation. If this study will cost $30,000, should the Beck Company consider hiring the consultants?

Suppose that an experiment can be conducted to shed some light on the technical feasibility of the project. There are three possible outcomes for the experiment:

I_1 = prototype lubricant works well at all temperatures
I_2 = prototype lubricant works well only at temperatures above 10°F
I_3 = prototype lubricant does not work well at any temperature

For this situation, Beck believes that the following conditional probabilities are appropriate:

$P(I_1 \mid$ major success$) = 0.70$ $P(I_2 \mid$ major success$) = 0.25$ $P(I_3 \mid$ major success$) = 0.05$

$P(I_1 \mid$ minor success$) = 0.10$ $P(I_2 \mid$ minor success$) = 0.70$ $P(I_3 \mid$ minor success$) = 0.20$

$P(I_1 \mid$ failure$) = 0.10$ $P(I_2 \mid$ failure$) = 0.30$ $P(I_3 \mid$ failure$) = 0.60$

c. Assuming that the experiment is conducted and the prototype lubricant works well at all temperatures, should the development project be funded?
d. Assuming that the experiment is conducted and the prototype lubricant works well only at temperatures above 10°F, should the project be funded?
e. Develop a decision strategy that Beck's R&D manager can use to recommend a funding decision based on the outcome of the experiment.
f. Find the EVSI for the experiment. How efficient is the information in the experiment?

40. Expected value approach, expected utility approach

40. A firm has three investment alternatives. The payoff table (in $1000s) and associated probabilities are as follows:

	Economic Conditions		
Investments	Up	Stable	Down
d_1	100	25	0
d_2	75	50	25
d_3	50	50	50
Probabilities	0.40	0.30	0.30

a. Using the expected value approach, which decision is preferred?
b. For the lottery having a payoff of $100,000 with probability p and $0 with probability $(1 - p)$, two decision makers expressed the following indifference probabilities:

	Indifference Probability (p)	
Profit	Decision Maker A	Decision Maker B
$75,000	0.80	0.60
50,000	0.60	0.30
25,000	0.30	0.15

Find the most preferred decision for each decision maker using the expected utility approach.
c. Why don't decision makers A and B select the same decision alternative?

41. Expected value approach, expected utility approach

41. Alexander Industries is considering purchasing an insurance policy for its new office building in St. Louis. The policy has an annual cost of $10,000. If Alexander Industries does not purchase the insurance and minor fire damage occurs to the office building, a cost of $100,000 is anticipated; the cost if major or total destruction occurs is $200,000. The payoff table in ($), including the state-of-nature probabilities, is as follows:

Decision Alternatives		Damage		
		None s_1	Minor s_2	Major s_3
Purchase insurance	d_1	10,000	10,000	10,000
Do not purchase insurance	d_2	0	100,000	200,000
Probabilities		0.96	0.03	0.01

a. Using the expected value approach, what decision do you recommend?
b. What lottery would you use to assess utilities? (Note that since the data are costs, the best payoff is $0.)
c. Assume we found the following indifference probabilities for the lottery defined in part (b):

Cost	Indifference Probability (p)
$ 10,000	0.99
100,000	0.60

What decision would you recommend?
d. Do you favor using expected value or expected utility for this decision problem? Why?

42. In a certain state lottery, a lottery ticket costs $2. In terms of the decision to purchase or not to purchase a lottery ticket, suppose the following payoff table (in $) applies:

Decision Alternatives		States of Nature	
		Win s_1	Lose s_2
Purchase lottery ticket	d_1	300,000	−2
Do not purchase lottery ticket	d_2	0	0

a. If a realistic estimate of the chances of winning are 1 in 250,000, use the expected value approach to recommend a decision.
b. If a particular decision maker assigns an indifference probability of 0.000001 to the $0 payoff, would this individual purchase a lottery ticket? Use expected utility to justify your answer.

43. There are two different routes for traveling between two cities. Route A normally takes 60 minutes, while route B normally takes 45 minutes. If traffic problems are encountered on route A, the travel time increases to 70 minutes; traffic problems on route B increase travel time to 90 minutes. The probability of the delay is 0.2 for route A and 0.3 for route B.

a. Using the expected value approach, what is the recommended route?

b. If utilities are to be assigned to the travel times, what is the appropriate lottery? Note that the smaller times should reflect higher utilities.

c. Using the lottery of part (b), assume the decision maker expresses indifference probabilities of

$$p = 0.8 \qquad \text{for 60 minutes}$$

$$p = 0.6 \qquad \text{for 70 minutes}$$

What route should this decision maker select?

44. Expected value approach, expected utility approach

44. Suppose that the point spread for a particular sporting event is 10 points and that with this spread you are convinced you would have a 0.6 probability of winning a bet on your team. However, the local bookie will accept only a $1000 bet. Assuming that such bets are legal, would you bet on your team? (Disregard any commission charged by the bookie.) Remember that *you* must pay losses out of your own pocket. Your payoff table (in $) is as follows:

		States of Nature	
Decision Alternatives		You Win s_1	You Lose s_2
Bet	d_1	1000	−1000
Don't bet	d_2	0	0

a. What decision does the expected value approach recommend?

b. What is *your* indifference probability for the $0 payoff? (While this is not easy, be as realistic as possible. Remember, this is required if we are to do an analysis that reflects your attitude toward risk.)

c. What decision would you make based on the expected utility approach?

d. Would other individuals assess the same utility values you do? Explain.

e. If your decision in part (c) was to place the bet, repeat the analysis, assuming a minimum bet of $10,000.

45. Expected value approach, expected utility approach

45. A Las Vegas roulette wheel has 38 different numerical values. If an individual bets on one number and wins, the payoff is 35 to 1.

a. Show a payoff table for a $10 bet on one number using decision alternatives of bet and do not bet.

b. What is the recommended decision using the expected value approach?

c. What range of utility values would a decision maker have to assign to the $0 payoff to have expected utility justify his or her decision to place the $10 bet?

46. Expected value approach, expected utility approach

46. A new product has the following profit projections and associated probabilities:

Profit	Probability
150,000	0.10
100,000	0.25
50,000	0.20
0	0.15
−50,000	0.20
−100,000	0.10

a. Use the expected value approach to make the decision of whether to market the new product.
b. Because of the high dollar values involved, especially the possibility of a $100,000 loss, the marketing vice president has expressed some concern about the use of the expected value approach. As a consequence, if a utility analysis is performed, what is the appropriate lottery? Assume the following indifference probabilities are assigned:

Profit	Indifference Probability (p)
$ 100,000	0.95
50,000	0.70
0	0.50
−50,000	0.25

c. Use expected utility to make a recommended decision.
d. Should the decision maker feel comfortable with the final decision recommended by the analysis?

47. Expected value approach, expected utility approach

47. A television network has been receiving low ratings for its programs. Currently, management is considering two alternatives for the Monday night 8:00 P.M.–9:00 P.M. time slot: a Western program with a well-known star and a musical variety program with a relatively unknown husband-and-wife team. The percentages of viewing audience estimates depend on the degree of program acceptance. The relevant data are as follows:

Program Acceptance	Percentage of Viewing Audience	
	Western	Musical Variety
High	30	40
Moderate	25	20
Poor	20	15

The probabilities associated with the program acceptance levels are as follows:

Program Acceptance	Probability	
	Western	Musical Variety
High	0.30	0.30
Moderate	0.60	0.40
Poor	0.10	0.30

a. Using the expected value approach, which program should the network choose?
b. Assuming a utility analysis is desired, what is the appropriate lottery?
c. Using the appropriate lottery in part (b), assume that the network's program manager has assigned the following indifference probabilities:

Percentage of Audience	Indifference Probability (p)
30	0.40
25	0.30
20	0.10

Using expected utility, which program would you recommend?

Case Problem: Property Purchase Strategy

Glenn Foreman, president of Oceanview Development Corporation, is considering submitting a bid to purchase property that will be sold by sealed bid at a county tax foreclosure. Glenn's initial judgment is to submit a bid of $5 million. From past experience, Glenn estimates that a bid of $5 million will have a 0.2 probability of being the highest bid and securing the property for Oceanview. The current date is June 1. Sealed bids for the property must be submitted by August 15. The winning bid will be announced on September 1.

If Oceanview submits the highest bid and obtains the property, the firm plans to build and sell a complex of luxury condominiums. However, a complicating factor is that the property is currently zoned for single-family residences only. Glenn feels that a referendum could be placed on the voting ballot in time for the November election. Passage of the referendum would change the zoning of the property and permit construction of the condominiums.

The sealed-bid procedure requires the bid to be submitted with a certified check for 10% of the amount bid. If the bid is rejected, the deposit is refunded. If the bid is accepted, the deposit is the down payment for the property. However, if the bid is accepted and the bidder does not follow through with the purchase and meet the remainder of the financial obligation within 6 months, the deposit will be forfeited. In this case, the county will offer the property to the next highest bidder.

To determine whether Oceanview should submit the $5 million bid, Glenn has done some preliminary analysis. This preliminary work provided an estimate of 0.3 for the probability that the referendum for a zoning change will be approved and resulted in estimates of the costs and revenues that will be incurred if the condominiums are built. The data obtained are shown below.

Cost and Revenue Estimates	
Revenue from condominium sales	$15,000,000
Cost	
Property	$ 5,000,000
Construction expenses	$ 8,000,000

If Oceanview obtains the property and the zoning change is not approved in November, Glenn feels that the best option would be for the firm not to complete the purchase of the property. In this case, Oceanview would forfeit the 10% deposit that accompanied the bid.

Because the likelihood that the zoning referendum will be approved is such an important factor in the decision process, Glenn has suggested that the firm hire a market research service to conduct a survey of voters. The survey would provide a better estimate of the likelihood that the referendum for a zoning change would be approved. The market research firm that Oceanview Development has worked with in the past has agreed to do the study for $15,000. The results of the study will be available August 1, so that Oceanview will have this information before the August 15 bid deadline. The results of the survey will be either a prediction that the zoning change will be approved or a prediction that the zoning change will not be approved. After considering the record of the market research service in previous studies conducted for Oceanview, Glenn has developed the following probability estimates concerning the accuracy of the market research information:

$$P(I_1 \mid s_1) = 0.9 \qquad P(I_2 \mid s_1) = 0.1$$

$$P(I_1 \mid s_2) = 0.2 \qquad P(I_2 \mid s_2) = 0.8$$

where

I_1 = prediction that the zoning change will be approved
I_2 = prediction that the zoning change will not be approved
s_1 = the zoning change is approved by the voters
s_2 = the zoning change is not approved by the voters

Managerial Report

Perform an analysis of the problem facing the Oceanview Development Corporation, and prepare a report that summarizes your findings and recommendations. Include the following information in your report:

1. A decision tree that shows the logical sequence of the decision problem.
2. A recommendation regarding what Oceanview should do if the market research information is not available.
3. A decision strategy that Oceanview should follow if the market research is conducted.
4. A recommendation as to whether Oceanview should employ the market research firm. What is the value of the information provided by the market research firm?

Include a copy of the details of your analysis in the appendix to your report.

MANAGEMENT SCIENCE IN PRACTICE

Ohio Edison Company*

Akron, Ohio

Ohio Edison Company is an investor-owned electric utility headquartered in northeastern Ohio. Ohio Edison and a Pennsylvania subsidiary provide electrical service to over 2 million people. Most of this electricity is generated by coal-fired power plants. To meet evolving air-quality standards, Ohio Edison replaced existing particulate control equipment at most of its generating plants with more efficient equipment. The combination of this program to upgrade air-quality control equipment with the continuing need to construct new generating plants to meet future power requirements resulted in a large capital investment program.

Management science activities at Ohio Edison are distributed throughout the company rather than centralized in a specific department, and are more or less evenly divided among the following areas: fossil and nuclear fuel planning, environmental studies, capacity planning, large equipment evaluation, and corporate planning. Applications include decision analysis, optimal ordering strategies, computer modeling, and simulation.

A Decision Analysis Application

The flue gas emitted by coal-fired power plants contains small ash particles and sulfur dioxide (SO_2). Federal and state regulatory agencies have established emission limits for both particulates and sulfur dioxide. In the late 1970s, Ohio Edison developed a plan to comply with new air-quality standards at one of its largest power plants. This plant, which consists of seven coal-fired units (most of which were constructed in the 1960s), constitutes about one-third of the generating capacity of Ohio Edison and its subsidiary company. Although all the units were initially constructed with particulate emission control equipment, that equipment was no longer capable of meeting new particulate emission requirements.

A decision had already been made to burn low-sulfur coal in four of the smaller units (units 1–4) at the plant in order to meet SO_2 emission standards. Fabric filters were to be installed on these units to control particulate emissions. Fabric filters, also known as baghouses, use thousands of fabric bags to filter out the particulates; they function in much the same way as a household vacuum cleaner.

It was considered likely, although not certain, that the three larger units (units 5–7) at this plant would burn medium- to high-sulfur coal. A method of controlling particulate emissions at these units had not yet been selected. Preliminary studies narrowed the particulate control equipment choice to a decision between fabric filters and electrostatic precipitators (which remove particulates suspended in the flue gas by passing the flue gas through a strong electric field). This decision was affected by a number of uncertainties, including the following:

- Uncertainty in the way some air-quality laws and regulations might be interpreted.
- Potential requirements that either low-sulfur coal or high-sulfur Ohio coal (or neither) be burned in units 5–7.
- Potential future changes to air quality laws and regulations.
- An overall plant reliability improvement program already under way at this plant.
- The outcome of this program itself, which would affect the operating costs of whichever pollution control technology was installed in these units.
- Uncertain construction costs of the equipment, particularly since limited space at the plant site made it necessary to install the equipment on a massive bridge deck over a four-lane highway immediately adjacent to the power plant.
- Uncertain costs associated with replacing the electrical power required to operate the particulate control equipment.
- Various other factors, including potential accidents and chronic operating problems that could increase the costs of operating the generating units (the degree to which each of these factors could affect operating costs varied with the choice of technology and with the sulfur content of the coal).

Decision Analysis

The air-quality program involved a choice between two types of particulate control equipment (fabric filters and electrostatic precipitators) for units 5–7. Because of the complexity of the problem, the high degree of uncertainty associated with factors affecting the decision, and the importance (because of potential reliability and cost impact on Ohio Edison) of the choice, decision analysis was used in the selection process.

The decision measure used to evaluate the outcomes of the particulate technology decision analysis was the annual revenue requirements for the three large units over their remaining lifetime. Revenue requirements are the monies that would have to be collected from the utility customers to recover costs resulting from the decision. They include not only direct costs, but also the cost of capital and return on investment.

—Continued on next page

---

*The authors are indebted to Thomas J. Madden and M. S. Hyrnick of Ohio Edison Company, Akron, Ohio, for providing this application.

—Continued from previous page

Figure 14.10
Simplified Particulate Control
Equipment Decision Tree

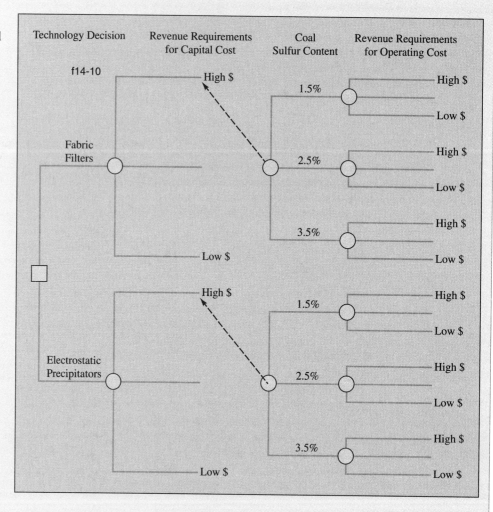

A decision tree was constructed to represent the particulate control decision and its uncertainties and costs. A simplified version of this decision tree is shown in Figure 14.10. The decision and state-of-nature nodes are indicated. Note that to conserve space, a type of shorthand notation is used. The coal sulfur content state-of-nature node should actually be located at the end of each branch of the capital cost state-of-nature node, as the dashed lines indicate. Each of the state-of-nature nodes actually represents several probabilistic cost models or submodels. The total revenue requirements are the sum of the revenue requirements for capital and operating costs. Costs associated with these models were obtained from engineering calculations or estimates. Probabilities were obtained from existing data or the subjective assessments of knowledgeable persons.

Results

A decision tree similar to that shown in Figure 14.10 was used to generate cumulative probability distributions for the annual revenue requirements outcomes calculated for each of the two particulate control alternatives. Careful study of these results led to the following conclusions:

- The expected value of annual revenue requirements for the electrostatic precipitator technology was approximately $1 million lower than that for the fabric filters.
- The fabric filter alternative had a higher upside risk—that is, a higher probability of high revenue requirements—than did the precipitator alternative.

—Continued on next page

—Continued from previous page

- The precipitator technology had nearly an 80% probability of lower annual revenue requirements than the fabric filters.
- Although the capital cost of the fabric filter equipment (the cost of installing the equipment) was lower than for the precipitator, this was more than offset by the higher operating costs associated with the fabric filter.

These results led Ohio Edison to select the electrostatic precipitator technology for the generating units in question. Had the decision analysis not been performed, the particulate control decision might have been based chiefly on capital cost, a decision measure that would have favored the fabric filter

equipment. Decision analysis offers a means for effectively analyzing the uncertainties involved in a decision. Because of this, it is felt that the use of decision analysis methodology in this application resulted in a decision that yielded both lower expected revenue requirements and lower risk.

Questions

1. Why was decision analysis used in the selection of particulate control equipment for units 5, 6, and 7?
2. List the decision alternatives for the decision analysis problem developed by Ohio Edison.
3. What were the benefits of using decision analysis in this application?

CHAPTER 15

Multicriteria Decision Problems

In previous chapters we have seen how a variety of management science techniques can help managers make better decisions. In each case, whenever we desired an optimal solution, we employed a single criterion (e.g., maximize profit, minimize cost, minimize expected cost). In this chapter we discuss techniques that are appropriate for situations in which the decision maker needs to consider multiple criteria in arriving at the overall best decision. For example, consider a company involved in selecting a location for a new manufacturing plant. Since the cost of land and construction may vary from location to location, one criterion in selecting the best site could be the cost involved in building the plant; if this were the sole criterion of interest, management would simply select the location where the land cost plus the construction cost is minimized. Before making any decision, however, management might also want to consider additional criteria such as the availability of transportation from the plant to the firm's distribution centers, the attractiveness of the proposed location in terms of hiring and retaining employees, energy costs at the proposed site, and state and local taxes. In situations such as this, the complexity of the problem increases since one location can be more desirable from the perspective of one criterion and less desirable from the perspective of one or more of the other criteria.

To introduce the topic of multicriteria decision making, we will first consider a technique referred to as *goal programming*. This technique was developed to handle multicriteria situations within the general framework of linear programming. The other approach we will consider, referred to as the *analytic hierarchy process* (AHP), permits the inclusion of subjective factors in arriving at a recommended decision. In this approach, the decision maker must make judgments about the relative importance of each of the decision criteria and then specify a preference for each decision alternative relative to each criterion; the output is a prioritized ranking indicating the overall preference for each of the decision alternatives.

646

15.1 Goal Programming: Formulation and Graphical Solution

To illustrate the goal programming approach to multicriteria decision problems, let us consider a problem facing Nicolo Investment Advisors. A particular client has $80,000 to invest and, as an initial strategy, would like the investment portfolio restricted to the following two stocks:

Stock	Price/Share	Estimated Annual Return/Share	Risk Index/Share
U.S. Oil	$25	$3	0.50
Hub Properties	50	5	0.25

U.S. Oil, which has a return of $3 on a $25 share price, provides an annual rate of return of 12%, while Hub Properties provides an annual rate of return of 10%. The risk index per share, 0.50 for U.S. Oil and 0.25 for Hub Properties, is a rating Nicolo has assigned to measure the relative risk of the two investment alternatives. Higher values imply greater risk; hence, we see that Nicolo has judged U.S. Oil to be the riskier investment. By specifying a maximum portfolio risk, Nicolo is able to avoid placing too much of the portfolio in high-risk investments.

To illustrate how the risk index per share can be used to measure the total portfolio risk, suppose Nicolo chooses a portfolio that invests all $80,000 in U.S. Oil, the highest-risk, but highest-return, investment. We could purchase $80,000/$25 = 3200 shares of U.S. Oil, and the portfolio would have a risk index of 3200(0.50) = 1600. On the other hand, if no shares of either stock are purchased, there will be no risk, but no return. Thus, the portfolio risk index will vary from 0 (least risk) to 1600 (most risk).

Nicolo's client would like to avoid a high-risk portfolio; thus, investing all funds in U.S. Oil would not be desirable. However, the client agreed that an acceptable level of risk would correspond to portfolios with a maximum total risk index of 700. Thus, considering only risk, the objective or *goal* is to find a portfolio with a risk index of 700 or less.

Another goal of the client is to obtain an annual return of at least $9000. This goal can be achieved with a portfolio consisting of 2000 shares of U.S. Oil (at a cost of 2000($25) = $50,000) and 600 shares of Hub Properties (at a cost of 600($50) = $30,000); the annual return in this case would be 2000($3) + 600($5) = $9000. Note, however, that the portfolio risk for this investment strategy would be 2000(0.50) + 600(0.25) = 1150; thus, this portfolio achieves the annual return goal but does not satisfy the portfolio risk goal.

It is now clear that the portfolio selection problem is a multicriteria decision problem involving two conflicting goals: one dealing with risk and one dealing with annual return. This is the kind of problem for which the goal programming approach was developed. Goal programming can be used to identify a portfolio that comes closest to achieving both goals. Before applying the methodology, the client must determine which, if either, goal is more important.

Suppose the top-priority goal is restricting the risk; that is, keeping the portfolio risk index at 700 or less is so important the client is not willing to trade the achievement of this goal for any amount of an increase in annual return. On the other hand, as long as the portfolio risk does not exceed 700, the client seeks the best possible return. Given this statement of priorities, the goals for the problem can be written as follows:

Primary Goal (Priority Level 1)

Goal 1: Find a portfolio that has a risk index of 700 or less.

Secondary Goal (Priority Level 2)

Goal 2: Find a portfolio that will provide an annual return of at least $9000.

In goal programming with preemptive priorities, we never permit trade-offs between higher- and lower-level goals.

We have noted, in parentheses above, that the primary goal is called a priority level 1 goal and the secondary goal is called a priority level 2 goal. In goal programming terminology, these are called *preemptive priorities* because the decision maker is not willing to sacrifice any amount of achievement of the priority level 1 goal for the lower priority goal. The portfolio risk index of 700 is the *target value* for the priority level 1 (primary) goal, and the annual return of $9000 is the target value for the priority level 2 (secondary) goal. The difficulty in finding a solution that will achieve these goals is that there is only $80,000 available for investment.

Developing the Constraints and the Goal Equations

To see how a goal programming model can be developed for the portfolio selection problem, we begin by defining the following decision variables:

$$x_1 = \text{number of shares of U.S. Oil purchased}$$
$$x_2 = \text{number of shares of Hub Properties purchased}$$

Constraints for goal programming problems are handled in the same way as in an ordinary linear programming problem. Using the decision variables, we write a constraint corresponding to the funds available. Since each share of U.S. Oil costs $25 and each share of Hub Properties costs $50, the constraint representing the funds available is

$$25x_1 + 50x_2 \leq 80,000$$

This is the only constraint for the problem.

To complete the formulation of the model, we must develop a *goal equation* for each goal. Let us begin by writing the goal equation for the primary goal. Since each share of U.S. Oil has a risk index of 0.50 and each share of Hub Properties has a risk index of 0.25, the portfolio risk index is $0.50x_1 + 0.25x_2$. Depending on the values of x_1 and x_2, the portfolio risk index may be less than, equal to, or greater than the target value of 700. To represent these possibilities mathematically, we create the following goal equation:

$$0.50x_1 + 0.25x_2 = 700 + d_1^+ - d_1^-$$

where

$$d_1^+ = \text{the amount by which the portfolio risk index exceeds the target value of 700}$$
$$d_1^- = \text{the amount by which the portfolio risk index is less than the target value of 700}$$

To achieve a goal exactly, the two deviation variables must both equal zero.

In goal programming, d_1^+ and d_1^- are called *deviation variables*. The purpose of deviation variables is to allow for the possibility of not meeting the target value exactly. Consider, for example, a portfolio that consists of $x_1 = 2000$ shares of U.S. Oil and $x_2 = 0$ shares of Hub Properties. The portfolio risk index is $0.50(2000) + 0.25(0) = 1000$. In this case, $d_1^+ = 300$ reflects the fact that the portfolio risk index exceeds the target value by 300 units; note also that since d_1^+ is greater than zero, the value of d_1^- must be zero. For a portfolio consisting of $x_1 = 0$ shares of U.S. Oil and $x_2 = 2000$ shares of Hub Properties, the portfolio risk index would be $0.50(0) + 0.25(1000) = 250$. In this case, $d_1^- = 450$ (and $d_1^+ = 0$), indicating that the solution provides a portfolio risk index of 450 less than the target value of 700.

In general, the letter d is used for deviation variables in a goal programming model. A superscript of plus ($+$) or minus ($-$) is used to indicate whether the variable corresponds to a positive or negative deviation from the target value. If we bring the deviation variables to the left-hand side, we can rewrite the goal equation for the primary goal as

$$0.50x_1 + 0.25x_2 - d_1^+ + d_1^- = 700$$

In the margin:

> Both d_1^+ and d_1^- cannot be simultaneously greater than zero in the simplex solution to a goal program because the corresponding columns are linearly dependent.

In general, the value on the right-hand side of the goal equation is the target value for the goal. The left-hand side of the goal equation consists of two parts:

1. A function that defines the amount of goal achievement in terms of the decision variables (e.g., $0.50x_1 + 0.25x_2$)
2. The difference between the target value for the goal and the amount of achievement, represented by the two deviation variables

To develop a goal equation for the secondary goal, we begin by writing a function representing the annual return for the investment.

$$\text{Annual return} = 3x_1 + 5x_2$$

Then we define two deviation variables that represent the amount of over- or under-achievement of the goal. Doing so, we obtain

$d_2^+ = $ the amount by which the annual return for the portfolio is greater than the target value of \$9000

$d_2^- = $ the amount by which the annual return for the portfolio is less than the target value of \$9000

Using these two deviation variables, we can write the goal equation for goal 2 as

$$3x_1 + 5x_2 = 9000 + d_2^+ - d_2^-$$

or

$$3x_1 + 5x_2 - d_2^+ + d_2^- = 9000$$

This completes the development of the goal equations and the constraints for the Nicolo portfolio problem. We are now ready to develop an appropriate objective function for the problem.

Developing an Objective Function with Preemptive Priorities

The objective function in a goal programming model calls for minimizing a function of the deviation variables. In the portfolio selection problem, the most important goal is to find a portfolio with a risk index of 700 or less. Since this is the most important goal, it is assigned the highest-priority level, which we will denote as P_1. There are only two goals in the problem, and the client is unwilling to incur a risk index greater than 700 to achieve the secondary goal. Therefore, the secondary goal, annual return, is assigned the priority level P_2. These priorities are referred to as preemptive priorities in goal programming terminology because the satisfaction of a higher-level goal cannot be traded for the satisfaction of a lower-level goal.

Goal programming problems with preemptive priorities are solved by treating priority level 1 goals (P_1) first in an objective function. The idea is to start with a solution that comes closest to satisfying the priority level 1 goals. The solution found is then modified by solving a problem with an objective function involving only priority level 2 goals (P_2); however, revisions in the solution minimizing deviations from the P_1 goals are permitted only if they do not cause a reduction in the achievement of the P_1 goals. In general, when we solve a goal programming problem with preemptive priorities, a sequence of linear programs with different objective functions is solved; P_1 goals are considered first, P_2 goals second, P_3 goals third, and so on. At each stage of the solution procedure, a revision in the solution is permitted only if it causes no reduction in the achievement of a higher-priority goal.

We must solve one linear program for each priority level.

The number of linear programs we must solve in sequence to develop the solution to a goal programming problem is determined by the number of priority levels. One linear program must be solved for each priority level. We will call the first linear program solved the priority level 1 problem, the second linear program solved the priority level 2 problem, and so on. Each of the linear programs is obtained from the one at the next higher level by changing the objective function and adding a constraint. Let us formulate the priority level 1 problem.

We first formulate the objective function. The client has stated that the portfolio risk index should not exceed 700. Is underachieving the target value of 700 a concern? Clearly, the answer is no since values less than 700 correspond to less risk. Is overachieving the target value of 700 a concern? The answer is yes since portfolios with a risk index greater than 700 correspond to levels of risk higher than the client is willing to accept. Thus, the objective function corresponding to the priority level 1 linear program should minimize the value of d_1^+.

The goal equations and the funds available constraint have already been developed. Thus, the priority level 1 linear program can now be stated.

P_1 Problem

$$\text{Min} \quad d_1^+$$

s.t.

$$
\begin{array}{llll}
25x_1 + 50x_2 & & \leq 80{,}000 & \text{Funds available} \\
0.50x_1 + 0.25x_2 - d_1^+ + d_1^- & = & 700 & P_1 \text{ goal} \\
3x_1 + 5x_2 & -d_2^+ + d_2^- = & 9000 & P_2 \text{ goal} \\
\end{array}
$$

$$x_1, x_2, d_1^+, d_1^-, d_2^+, d_2^- \geq 0$$

The Graphical Solution Procedure

One approach that can often be used to solve a difficult problem is to break the problem into two or more smaller or easier problems. The linear programming procedure we use to solve the goal programming problem uses this approach.

The graphical solution procedure for goal programming is similar to the graphical solution procedure for linear programming presented in Chapter 2. The only difference is that the procedure for goal programming involves a separate solution for each priority level. Recall that the linear programming graphical solution procedure used a graph to display the values for the decision variables. Since the decision variables are nonnegative, we only consider that portion of the graph where $x_1 \geq 0$ and $x_2 \geq 0$. Recall also that every point on the graph is called a *solution point*.

We will begin the graphical solution procedure for the Nicolo Investment problem by identifying all solution points that satisfy the available funds constraint:

$$25x_1 + 50x_2 \leq 80,000$$

The region in color in Figure 15.1, feasible portfolios, consists of all points that satisfy the above constraint—that is, values of x_1 and x_2 for which $25x_1 + 50x_2 \leq 80,000$.

The objective for the priority level 1 linear program is to minimize d_1^+, the amount by which the portfolio index exceeds the target value of 700. To show how this is done, recall that the P_1 goal equation is

$$0.50x_1 + 0.25x_2 - d_1^+ + d_1^- = 700$$

When the P_1 goal is met exactly, $d_1^+ = 0$ and $d_1^- = 0$; the goal equation then reduces to $0.50x_1 + 0.25x_2 = 700$. Figure 15.2 shows the graph of this equation; the region shown in color identifies all solution points that satisfy the available funds constraint and also result in the value of $d_1^+ = 0$. Since any solution point for which $d_1^+ = 0$ will achieve the priority level 1 goal, the region in color contains all the solution points that correspond to portfolios with a risk index of 700 or less.

At this point, we have solved the priority level 1 problem. Note that there are alternative optimal solutions; in fact, all solution points in the region shown in color in Figure 15.2 maintain a portfolio risk index of 700 or less, and hence $d_1^+ = 0$. We are now ready to consider the priority level 2 problem.

The priority level 2 goal for the Nicolo Investment problem is to find a portfolio that will provide an annual return of at least $9000. Is overachieving the target value of $9000 a concern? Clearly, the answer is no since values more than $9000 correspond to higher returns. Is underachieving the target value of $9000 a concern? The answer is yes since

Figure 15.1

The Goal Programming Graphical Solution Procedure: Portfolios That Satisfy the Available Funds Constraint

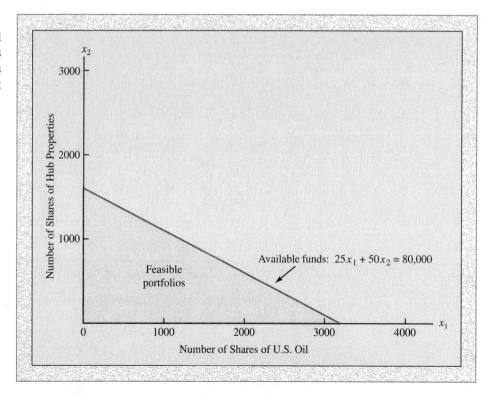

Figure 15.2

The Goal Programming Graphical
Solution Procedure: Portfolios
That Satisfy the P_1 Goal

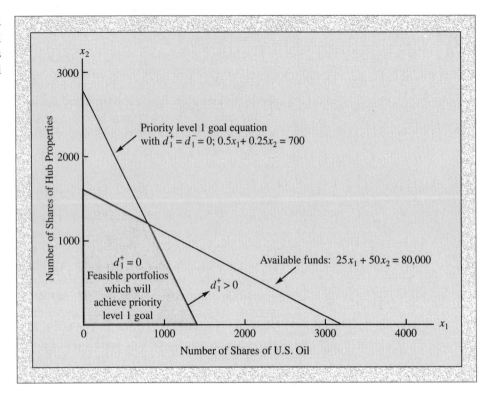

portfolios with an annual return of less than \$9000 are not acceptable to the client. Thus, the objective function corresponding to the priority level 2 linear program should minimize the value of d_2^-. However, since goal 2 is a secondary goal, the solution to the priority level 2 linear program must not degrade the optimal solution to the priority level 1 problem. Thus, the priority level 2 linear program is as follows:

P_2 Problem

Min d_2^-

s.t.

$$
\begin{array}{llll}
25x_1 + 50x_2 & & \le 80{,}000 & \text{Funds available} \\
0.50x_1 + 0.25x_2 - d_1^+ + d_1^- & = 700 & & P_1 \text{ goal} \\
3x_1 + 5x_2 & - d_2^+ + d_2^- = 9{,}000 & & P_2 \text{ goal} \\
d_1^+ & = 0 & & \text{Maintain achievement} \\
& & & \text{of } P_1 \text{ goal}
\end{array}
$$

$$x_1, x_2, d_1^+, d_1^-, d_2^+, d_2^- \ge 0$$

We note that the priority level 2 linear program differs from the priority level 1 linear program in two ways. The objective function involves minimizing the negative deviations from the level 2 goal, and another constraint has been added to ensure that no amount of achievement of the priority level 1 goal is sacrificed.

Let us now continue the graphical solution procedure. The goal equation for the priority level 2 goal is

$$3x_1 + 5x_2 - d_2^+ + d_2^- = 9000$$

When both d_2^+ and d_2^- equal zero, this equation reduces to $3x_1 + 5x_2 = 9000$; we show the graph with this equation in Figure 15.3.

At this stage, we cannot consider any solution point that will degrade the achievement of the priority level 1 goal. Figure 15.3 shows that there are no solution points that will achieve the priority level 2 goal and maintain the values we were able to achieve for the priority level 1 goal. In fact, the best solution that can be obtained when considering the priority level 2 goal is given by the point ($x_1 = 800$, $x_2 = 1200$); in other words, this point comes the closest to satisfying the priority level 2 goal from among those solutions satisfying the priority level 1 goal. Since the annual return corresponding to this solution point is $3(800) + $5(1200) = 8400, we see that it is impossible to identify a portfolio that will satisfy both the priority level 1 and the priority level 2 goals; in fact, the best solution point underachieves goal 2 by $d_2^- = $9000 - $8400 = 600.

Thus, the goal programming solution for the Nicolo Investment problem recommends that the $80,000 available for investment be used to purchase 800 shares of U.S. Oil and 1200 shares of Hub Properties. Note that the priority level 1 goal of a portfolio risk index of 700 or less has been achieved. However, the priority level 2 goal of at least a $9000 annual return is not achievable. The recommended portfolio projects a $8400 annual return.

In summary, the graphical solution procedure for goal programming is as follows:

1. Identify the feasible solution points; these are the ones that satisfy the problem constraints.
2. Identify all feasible solutions that achieve the highest-priority goal; if there are no feasible solutions that will achieve the highest-priority goal, identify the solution(s) that comes closest to achieving the highest-priority goal.

Figure 15.3

The Goal Programming Graphical Solution Procedure: Best Solution with Respect to Both Goals (Solution to P_2 Problem)

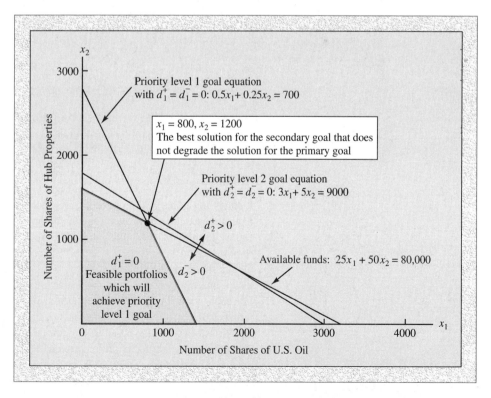

3. Move down one priority level, and determine the "best" solution possible without sacrificing any achievement of higher-priority goals.
4. Repeat step 3 until all priority levels have been considered.

You should be able to formulate a goal programming model and use the graphical solution procedure to obtain a solution. Try Problem 2.

Although the graphical solution procedure is a convenient method for solving goal programming problems involving two decision variables, the solution to larger problems requires a computer-based approach. In Section 15.2 we will illustrate how to use a computer software package to solve more complex goal programming problems.

The Goal Programming Model

As we have stated, goal programming problems are solved as a sequence of linear programs; there is one linear program for each priority level. However, it is helpful to have a notation that permits writing a goal programming problem in one concise statement. We show how this is done for the portfolio selection problem.

In writing the overall objective for the problem, we must write the objective function in a way that reminds us of the preemptive priorities inherent in the problem. We can do this by writing the objective function as follows:

$$\text{Min} \quad P_1(d_1^+) + P_2(d_2^-)$$

The priority levels P_1 and P_2 are not numerical weights on the deviation variables, but simply labels that remind us of the priority levels for the goals.

We now write the complete goal programming model as follows:

$$\text{Min} \quad P_1(d_1^+) + P_2(d_2^-)$$

s.t.

$$
\begin{array}{llll}
25x_1 + 50x_2 & & \leq 80{,}000 & \text{Funds available} \\
0.50x_1 + 0.25x_2 - d_1^+ + d_1^- & & = \quad 700 & P_1 \text{ goal} \\
3x_1 + 5x_2 & - d_2^+ + d_2^- = & 9000 & P_2 \text{ goal} \\
\end{array}
$$

$$x_1, x_2, d_1^+, d_1^-, d_2^+, d_2^- \geq 0$$

With the exception of the P_1 and P_2 priority levels in the objective function, this model is a linear programming model. It is understood that the solution to this linear program involves solving a sequence of linear programs involving goals at decreasing priority levels.

We now summarize the procedure used to develop a goal programming model.

1. Identify the goals and any constraints that reflect resource capacities or other restrictions that may prevent achievement of the goals.
2. Determine the priority level of each goal; goals with priority level P_1 are most important, those with priority level P_2 are next most important, and so on.
3. Define the decision variables.
4. Formulate the constraints in the usual linear programming fashion.
5. For each goal, develop a goal equation, with the right-hand side specifying the target value for the goal. Deviation variables d_i^+ and d_i^- are included in each goal equation to reflect the possible deviations above or below the target value.
6. Write the objective function in terms of minimizing a prioritized function of the deviation variables.

Notes & Comments

1. The constraints in the general goal programming model are of two types: goal equations and ordinary linear programming constraints. Some management scientists call the goal equations *goal constraints* and the ordinary linear programming constraints *system constraints*.

2. One can think of the general goal programming model as having "hard" and "soft" constraints. The hard constraints are the ordinary linear programming constraints that cannot be violated. The soft constraints are the ones resulting from the goal equations. Soft constraints can be violated, but there is a penalty for doing so. The penalty is reflected by the coefficient of the deviation variable in the objective function.

3. Note that the constraint added when moving from the linear programming problem at one priority level to the linear programming problem at the next-lower priority level becomes a hard constraint. No amount of achievement of a higher-priority goal may be sacrificed to achieve a lower-priority goal.

15.2 Goal Programming: Solving More Complex Problems

In Section 15.1 we formulated and solved a goal programming model that involved one priority level 1 goal and one priority level 2 goal. In this section we show how to formulate and solve goal programming models that involve multiple goals within the same priority level. Although computer programs have been specially developed to solve goal programming models, these programs are not as readily available as general purpose linear programming software packages. Thus, the computer solution procedure outlined in this section develops a solution to a goal programming model by solving a sequence of linear programming models with a general purpose linear programming package.

The Suncoast Office Supplies Problem

Management of Suncoast Office Supplies establishes monthly goals, or quotas, for the types of customers contacted. For the next 4 weeks, Suncoast's customer contact strategy calls for the sales force, which consists of four salespeople, to make 200 contacts with customers who have previously purchased supplies from the firm. In addition, the strategy calls for 120 contacts of new customers. The purpose of this latter goal is to ensure that the sales force is continuing to investigate new sources of sales.

Making allowances for travel and waiting time, as well as for demonstration and direct sales time, Suncoast has allocated 2 hours of sales force effort to each contact of a previous customer. New customer contacts tend to take longer and require 3 hours per contact. Normally, each salesperson works 40 hours per week, or 160 hours over the 4-week planning horizon; under a normal work schedule, the four salespeople will have 4(160) = 640 hours of sales force time available for customer contacts.

Management is willing to use some overtime, if needed, but is also willing to accept a solution that uses less than the scheduled 640 hours available. However, management wants both overtime and underutilization of the work force limited to at most 40 hours over the 4-week period. Thus, from an overtime perspective, management's goal is to use no more than $640 + 40 = 680$ hours of sales force time, and from a labor utilization perspective, management's goal is to use at least $640 - 40 = 600$ hours of sales force time.

In addition to the customer contact goals, Suncoast has established a goal regarding sales volume. Based on past experience, Suncoast estimates that each previous customer contacted will generate \$250 of sales and each new customer contacted will generate \$125 of sales. Management would like to generate sales of at least \$70,000 for the next month.

Given Suncoast's small sales force and the short time frame involved, management has decided that the overtime goal and the labor utilization goal are both priority level 1 goals. Management also concluded that the \$70,000 sales goal should be a priority level 2 goal and that the two customer contact goals should be priority level 3 goals. Given these priorities, we can now summarize the goals as follows:

Priority Level 1 Goals

Goal 1: Do not use any more than 680 hours of sales force time.

Goal 2: Do not use any less than 600 hours of sales force time.

Priority Level 2 Goal

Goal 3: Generate sales revenues of at least \$70,000.

Priority Level 3 Goals

Goal 4: Call on at least 200 previous customers.

Goal 5: Call on at least 120 new customers.

Formulating the Goal Equations

Next, we must define the decision variables whose values will be used to determine whether we are able to achieve the goals. Let

$$x_1 = \text{the number of previous customers contacted}$$
$$x_2 = \text{the number of new customers contacted}$$

Using these decision variables and appropriate deviation variables, a goal equation can be developed for each goal. The procedure used parallels the approach introduced in the previous section. A summary of the results obtained is shown for each goal.

Goal 1

$$2x_1 + 3x_2 - d_1^+ + d_1^- = 680$$

where

$$d_1^+ = \text{the amount by which the number of hours used by the sales force is greater than the target value of 680 hours}$$

$$d_1^- = \text{the amount by which the number of hours used by the sales force is less than the target value of 680 hours}$$

Goal 2

$$2x_1 + 3x_2 - d_2^+ + d_2^- = 600$$

where

d_2^+ = the amount by which the number of hours used by the sales force is greater than the target value of 600 hours

d_2^- = the amount by which the number of hours used by the sales force is less than the target value of 600 hours

Goal 3

$$250x_1 + 125x_2 - d_3^+ + d_3^- = 70,000$$

where

d_3^+ = the amount by which the sales revenue is greater than the target value of \$70,000

d_3^- = the amount by which the sales revenue is less than the target value of \$70,000

Goal 4

$$x_1 - d_4^+ + d_4^- = 200$$

where

d_4^+ = the amount by which the number of previous customer contacts exceeds the target value of 200 previous customer contacts

d_4^- = the amount by which the number of previous customer contacts falls short of the target value of 200 previous customer contacts

Goal 5

$$x_2 - d_5^+ + d_5^- = 120$$

where

d_5^+ = the amount by which the number of new customer contacts exceeds the target value of 120 new customer contacts

d_5^- = the amount by which the number of new customer contacts falls short of the target value of 120 new customer contacts

Formulating the Objective Function

To develop the objective function for the Suncoast Office Supplies problem, we begin by considering the priority level 1 goals. When considering goal 1, note that if $d_1^+ = 0$, we will have found a solution that uses no more than 680 hours of sales force time. Since solutions for which d_1^+ is greater than zero represent overtime beyond the desired level, the objective function should minimize the value of d_1^+. When considering goal 2, if $d_2^- = 0$, we will have found a solution that uses *at least* 600 hours of sales force time. If d_2^- is greater than zero, however, labor utilization will not have reached the acceptable level. Thus, the objective function for the priority level 1 goals should also minimize the value of d_2^-. Assuming that both of these priority level 1 goals are equally important, the objective function for the priority level 1 problem would be written as

$$\text{Min} \quad d_1^+ + d_2^-$$

In considering the priority level 2 goal, we note that management's objective is to achieve sales revenues of at least $70,000. Note that if $d_3^- = 0$, Suncoast will achieve revenues of *at least* $70,000, and if $d_3^- > 0$, revenues of less than $70,000 will be obtained. Thus, the objective function for the priority level 2 problem would be

$$\text{Min} \quad d_3^-$$

Next, let us consider what the objective function must be for the priority level 3 problem. When considering goal 4, note that if $d_4^- = 0$, we will have found a solution with *at least* 200 previous customer contacts; however, if $d_4^- > 0$, we will have underachieved the goal of contacting at least 200 previous customers. Thus, for goal 4 the objective is to minimize d_4^-. When considering goal 5, if $d_5^- = 0$, we will have found a solution with *at least* 120 new customer contacts; however, if $d_5^- > 0$, we will have underachieved the goal of contacting at least 120 new customers. Thus, for goal 5 the objective is to minimize d_5^-. If both goals 4 and 5 are equal in importance, the objective function for the priority level 3 problem would be

$$\text{Min} \quad d_4^- + d_5^-$$

However, suppose management believes that generating new customers is so vital to the long-run success of the firm that goal 5 should be weighted more than goal 4. Assuming management believes that goal 5 is two times as important as goal 4, we would write the objective function for the priority level 3 problem as

$$\text{Min} \quad d_4^- + 2d_5^-$$

Combining the objective functions for all three priority levels, we obtain the following objective function for the Suncoast Office Supplies problem:

$$\text{Min} \quad P_1(d_1^+) + P_1(d_2^-) + P_2(d_3^-) + P_3(d_4^-) + P_3(2d_5^-)$$

As we indicated previously, P_1, P_2, and P_3 are simply labels that remind us that goals 1 and 2 are the priority level 1 goals, goal 3 is the priority level 2 goal, and goals 4 and 5 are the priority level 3 goals. Since this completes the formulation of the goal programming model, we can now write the complete goal programming model for the Suncoast Office Supplies problem as follows:

$$\text{Min} \quad P_1(d_1^+) + P_1(d_2^-) + P_2(d_3^-) + P_3(d_4^-) + P_3(2d_5^-)$$

s.t.

$$
\begin{array}{lllllllll}
2x_1 & + & 3x_2 & - & d_1^+ & + & d_1^- & & & = & 680 & \text{Goal 1} \\
2x_1 & + & 3x_2 & & & - & d_2^+ & + & d_2^- & = & 600 & \text{Goal 2} \\
250x_1 & + & 125x_2 & & & & & - & d_3^+ + d_3^- & = & 70{,}000 & \text{Goal 3} \\
x_1 & & & & & & & - & d_4^+ + d_4^- & = & 200 & \text{Goal 4} \\
& & x_2 & & & & & - & d_5^+ + d_5^- & = & 120 & \text{Goal 5}
\end{array}
$$

$$x_1, x_2, d_1^+, d_1^-, d_2^+, d_2^-, d_3^+, d_3^-, d_4^+, d_4^-, d_5^+, d_5^- \geq 0$$

Computer Solution

The computer procedure develops a solution to a goal programming model by solving a sequence of linear programming problems. The first problem consists of all the constraints and all the goal equations for the complete goal programming model; however, the objective function for this problem involves only the P_1 priority level goals. We refer to this problem as the P_1 problem.

Whatever the solution is to the P_1 problem, a P_2 problem is formed by adding a constraint to the P_1 model that ensures that subsequent problems will not degrade the solution obtained for the P_1 problem. The objective function for this second-stage problem takes into consideration only the P_2 priority level goals. The process continues until all priority levels have been considered. We will illustrate the procedure for the Suncoast Office Supplies problem using the LINDO/PC microcomputer package.

To solve the Suncoast Office Supplies problem, we begin by solving the following P_1 problem:

$$\text{Min} \quad d_1^+ + d_2^-$$

s.t.

$$
\begin{array}{llllll}
2x_1 + & 3x_2 - d_1^+ + d_1^- & & = & 680 & \text{Goal 1} \\
2x_1 + & 3x_2 & - d_2^+ + d_2^- & = & 600 & \text{Goal 2} \\
250x_1 + & 125x_2 & - d_3^+ + d_3^- & = & 70{,}000 & \text{Goal 3} \\
x_1 & & - d_4^+ + d_4^- & = & 200 & \text{Goal 4} \\
& x_2 & - d_5^+ + d_5^- & = & 120 & \text{Goal 5}
\end{array}
$$

$$x_1, x_2, d_1^+, d_1^-, d_2^+, d_2^-, d_3^+, d_3^-, d_4^+, d_4^-, d_5^+, d_5^- \geq 0$$

In Figure 15.4 we show the LINDO/PC solution for this linear program. Note that

Figure 15.4

The LINDO/PC Solution of the P_1 Problem

```
                  OBJECTIVE FUNCTION VALUE

       1)                 .00000000

       VARIABLE           VALUE          REDUCED COST
        D1PLUS            .000000         1.000000
        D2MINUS           .000000         1.000000
            X1         200.000000          .000000
            X2          66.666660          .000000
        D1MINUS         80.000000          .000000
        D2PLUS            .000000          .000000
        D3PLUS            .000000          .000000
        D3MINUS       11666.670000         .000000
        D4PLUS            .000000          .000000
        D4MINUS           .000000          .000000
        D5PLUS            .000000          .000000
        D5MINUS          53.333330         .000000
```

D1MINUS refers to d_1^-, D1PLUS refers to d_1^+, D2MINUS refers to d_2^-, and so on. We see that the solution consisting of $x_1 = 200$ previous customer contacts and $x_2 = 66.67$ new customer contacts does achieve both goals 1 and 2 since D1PLUS and D2MINUS are equal to zero; alternatively, the objective function value of D1PLUS + D2MINUS = 0 also confirms that both priority level 1 goals have been achieved. Note that this solution underachieves the sales revenue goal by D3MINUS = $11,666.67, achieves goal 4, and underachieves goal 5 by D5MINUS = 53.33 new customers. Most important, however, we now know that a solution exists that achieves the priority level 1 goals.

The model for the P_2 problem is formed by adding a constraint to the P_1 problem that ensures that subsequent solutions will not degrade the solution already obtained for the priority level 1 goals. We can do this by requiring that all future solutions satisfy the constraint $d_1^+ + d_2^- = 0$. Adding this constraint to the model and writing the objective function in terms of the priority level 2 goal, we obtain the linear program and LINDO/PC solution shown in Figure 15.5.

The optimal solution to the P_2 problem is to contact $x_1 = 270$ previous customers and $x_2 = 20$ new customers. Since D3MINUS = 0, we now know that it is possible to achieve both the P_1 and the P_2 level goals. In other words, we now know that a solution can be

Figure 15.5

The LINDO/PC Solution of the P_2 Problem

```
MIN     D3MINUS
SUBJECT TO
      2)  - D1PLUS + 2 X1 + 3 X2 + D1MINUS =      680
      3)    D2MINUS + 2 X1 + 3 X2 - D2PLUS =      600
      4)    250 X1 + 125 X2 - D3PLUS + D3MINUS =      70000
      5)    X1 - D4PLUS + D4MINUS =      200
      6)    X2 - D5PLUS + D5MINUS =      120
      7)    D1PLUS + D2MINUS =      0
END


          OBJECTIVE FUNCTION VALUE

    1)          .00000000


    VARIABLE          VALUE          REDUCED COST
     D1PLUS           .000000           .000000
     D2MINUS          .000000           .000000
         X1        270.000000           .000000
         X2         20.000000           .000000
     D1MINUS        80.000000           .000000
     D2PLUS           .000000           .000000
     D3PLUS           .000000           .000000
     D3MINUS          .000000          1.000000
     D4PLUS         70.000000           .000000
     D4MINUS          .000000           .000000
     D5PLUS           .000000           .000000
     D5MINUS       100.000000           .000000
```

found that will achieve the labor utilization goals and also generate sales revenues of at least \$70,000. Note, however, that this solution overachieves the previous customer contact goal by D4PLUS = 70 previous customers and falls short of the new customer contact goal by D5MINUS = 100 new customers.

The third linear programming problem requires adding a constraint to the P_2 problem that will ensure that the P_2 sales revenue goal will continue to be achieved. Note that this can be done by adding the constraint $d_3^- = 0$. With the addition of this constraint and the objective function corresponding to the P_3 priority level goals, we obtain the priority level 3 linear program and LINDO/PC solution shown in Figure 15.6. We see that the optimal solution consisting of $x_1 = 250$ previous customer contacts and $x_2 = 60$ customer contacts overachieves goal 4 by D4PLUS = 50 previous customers; however, this solution underachieves goal 5 by D5MINUS = 60 new customers.

Since all the priority levels have been considered, the solution procedure is finished. The optimal solution for Suncoast is to contact 250 previous customers and 60 new customers. Although this solution will not achieve management's goal of contacting at least 120 new customers, it does achieve each of the other goals specified. If management

Figure 15.6
The LINDO/PC
Solution of the P_3 Problem

```
MIN      D4MINUS + 2 D5MINUS
SUBJECT TO
     2)  - D1PLUS + 2 X1 + 3 X2 + D1MINUS =     680
     3)    D2MINUS + 2 X1 + 3 X2 - D2PLUS =     600
     4)    250 X1 + 125 X2 - D3PLUS + D3MINUS =     70000
     5)    X1 - D4PLUS + D4MINUS =     200
     6)    X2 - D5PLUS + D5MINUS =     120
     7)    D1PLUS + D2MINUS =     0
     8)    D3MINUS =     0
END


            OBJECTIVE FUNCTION VALUE

     1)          120.000000


     VARIABLE          VALUE          REDUCED COST
       D1PLUS          .000000           .000000
      D2MINUS          .000000          1.000000
           X1       250.000000           .000000
           X2        60.000000           .000000
      D1MINUS          .000000          1.000000
       D2PLUS        80.000000           .000000
       D3PLUS          .000000           .000000
      D3MINUS          .000000           .000000
       D4PLUS        50.000000           .000000
      D4MINUS          .000000          1.000000
       D5PLUS          .000000          2.000000
      D5MINUS        60.000000           .000000
```

is still not happy with this solution, a different set of priorities could be considered. Management must keep in mind, however, that in any problem situation involving multiple goals at different priority levels, rarely will all the goals be achieved given the existing resources.

NOTES & COMMENTS

1. Not all goal programming problems involve multiple priority levels. For problems with one priority level, only one linear program needs to be solved to obtain the goal programming solution. One simply minimizes the weighted deviations from the goals. Trade-offs are permitted among the goals since they are all at the same priority level.

2. The goal programming approach can be employed when one is confronted with an infeasible solution to an ordinary linear program. By reformulating some of the constraints as goal equations with deviation variables, a solution can be found that minimizes the weighted sum of the deviation variables. Often, this approach will suggest a reasonable solution.

3. The approach we have utilized to solve goal programming problems with multiple priority levels is to solve a sequence of linear programs. These linear programs are closely related so that complete reformulation and solution are not necessary. By changing the objective function and adding a constraint, we can go from one linear program to the next.

15.3 The Analytic Hierarchy Process

Most people prefer a problem-solving approach that is conceptually simple so that it can be understood. A strength of the analytic hierarchy process is that it is easy to understand and still robust enough to handle the complexities of real-world decisions.

The analytic hierarchy process (AHP), developed by Thomas L. Saaty,[1] is designed to solve complex problems involving multiple criteria. The process requires the decision maker to provide judgments about the relative importance of each criterion and then specify a preference on each criterion for each decision alternative. The output of AHP is a prioritized ranking indicating the overall preference for each of the decision alternatives.

To introduce AHP, we consider the problem faced by Dave Payne, who is planning to purchase a new car. After a preliminary analysis of the makes and models available, Dave has narrowed the list of decision alternatives to three cars, which we will refer to as car A, car B, and car C. Table 15.1 provides a summary of the information he has collected regarding these cars.

Based on the information in Table 15.1—as well as his own personal feelings resulting from driving each car—Dave decided that there were several criteria that he needed to consider in making the purchase decision. After some thought, he selected purchase price, miles per gallon (MPG), comfort, and style as the four criteria he would like to consider. Quantitative data regarding the purchase price and MPG criteria are provided directly in Table 15.1. However, measures of comfort and style cannot be specified so easily. Dave will need to consider factors such as car interior, type of radio, ease of entry and exit, and

---

[1]Thomas L. Saaty, *The Analytic Hierarchy Process* (New York: McGraw-Hill, 1980).

Table 15.1

Information for the Car-Selection Problem

Category	Car A	Car B	Car C
Price	$13,100	$11,200	$9,500
MPG	18	23	29
Interior	Deluxe	Above average	Standard
Body	4-door midsize	2-door sport	2-door compact
Radio	AM/FM, tape	AM/FM	AM
Engine	6-cylinder	4-cylinder turbo	4-cylinder

seat-adjustment features to determine the comfort level of each car. The style criterion will need to be measured in terms of Dave's subjective evaluation of each car.

Even when we deal with a criterion as easily measured as purchase price, however, subjectivity becomes an issue whenever a particular decision maker indicates his or her personal preferences. For instance, car A costs $3600 more than car C; this difference might represent a great deal of money to one person, but not very much money to another person. Thus, whether car A is considered extremely more expensive than car C or only moderately more expensive is a subjective judgment that will depend primarily on the financial status of the person making the comparison. An advantage of AHP is that it is designed to handle situations such as this, in which the subjective judgments of individuals constitute an important part of the decision process.

Developing the Hierarchy

The first step in AHP is to develop a graphical representation of the problem in terms of the *overall goal, criteria,* and *decision alternatives.* Such a graph depicts the *hierarchy* for the problem. Figure 15.7 shows the hierarchy for the car-selection problem. Note that the first level of the hierarchy shows that the overall goal is to select the best car. At the second level, we see that the four criteria (purchase price, MPG, comfort, and style) will contribute to the achievement of the overall goal. Finally, at the third level, we see that each decision alternative (car A, car B, and car C) contributes to each criterion in a unique way.

Figure 15.7

Hierarchy for the Car-Selection Problem

AHP has the decision maker specify his or her judgments about the relative importance of each criterion in terms of its contribution to the achievement of the overall goal. At the next level, AHP asks the decision maker to indicate a preference or priority for each decision alternative in terms of how it contributes to each criterion. For example, in the car-selection problem, Dave will need to specify his judgment about the relative importance of each of the four criteria. He will also need to indicate his preference for each of the three cars relative to each criterion. Given the information on relative importance and preferences, a mathematical process is used to synthesize the information and provide a priority ranking of the three cars in terms of their overall preference.

15.4 Establishing Priorities Using AHP

In this section we will show how AHP utilizes pairwise comparisons to establish priority measures for both the criteria and the decision alternatives. What needs to be determined in the car-selection problem are the priorities of

1. The four criteria in terms of the overall goal
2. The three cars in terms of the purchase price criterion
3. The three cars in terms of the MPG criterion
4. The three cars in terms of the comfort criterion
5. The three cars in terms of the style criterion

In the following discussion, we will demonstrate how to establish priorities for the three cars in terms of the *comfort* criterion. The other sets of priorities can be determined in a similar fashion.

Pairwise Comparisons

Pairwise comparisons are fundamental building blocks of AHP. In establishing the priorities for the three cars in terms of comfort, we will ask Dave to state a preference for the comfort of the cars when the cars are considered two at a time (pairwise). That is, Dave must compare the comfort of car A to car B, car A to car C, and car B to car C in three separate comparisons.

AHP employs an underlying scale with values from 1 to 9 to rate the relative preferences for two items. Table 15.2 provides the numerical ratings recommended for the verbal preferences expressed by the decision maker. Research and experience have confirmed the nine-unit scale as a reasonable basis for discriminating between the preferences for two items.

In the car-selection problem, suppose that Dave has compared the comforts of car A with those of car B and is convinced that car A is more comfortable. Dave is then asked to state his preference for the comfort of car A compared to that of car B using one of the verbal descriptions shown in Table 15.2. If he believes that car A is *moderately* preferred to car B, a value of 3 is utilized in AHP; if he believes that car A is *strongly* preferred, a value of 5 is utilized; if he believes that car A is *very strongly* preferred, a value of 7 is utilized; if he believes that car A is *extremely* preferred, a value of 9 is utilized. Values of 2, 4, 6, and 8 are the intermediate values for the scale. A value of 1 is reserved for the case where the two items are judged to be *equally* preferred.

Suppose that when asked his preference between cars A and B with respect to the comfort criterion, Dave states that car A is equally to moderately more preferred than car

Table 15.2

Pairwise Comparison Scale for AHP Preferences

Verbal Judgment of Preference	Numerical Rating
Extremely preferred	9
Very strongly to extremely	8
Very strongly preferred	7
Strongly to very strongly	6
Strongly preferred	5
Moderately to strongly	4
Moderately preferred	3
Equally to moderately	2
Equally preferred	1

B; the numerical measure that reflects this judgment is 2. He is then asked to give his preference between car A and car C. Suppose in this case he states that car A is very strongly to extremely more preferred than car C; this corresponds to a numerical rating of 8. Finally, Dave is asked to state his preference for car B compared to car C. Suppose in this case he indicates that car B is strongly to very strongly preferred to car C; AHP would assign a numerical rating of 6.

The Pairwise Comparison Matrix

To develop the priorities for the three cars in terms of the comfort criterion, we need to construct a matrix of the pairwise comparison ratings. Since three cars are being considered, the pairwise comparison matrix will consist of three rows and three columns. Shown below is a portion of the *pairwise comparison matrix* based on the preferences Dave has specified.

	Comfort		
	Car A	Car B	Car C
Car A		2	8
Car B			6
Car C			

Note: In the pairwise comparison matrix, the value in row i and column j is the measure of preference of the car in row i when compared to the car in column j.

We see that the value in the matrix that corresponds to comparing car A with car B is 2, the value for comparing car A with car C is 8, and for comparing car B with car C, it is 6.

To determine the remaining entries in the pairwise comparison matrix, first note that when we compare any car against itself, the judgment must be "equally preferred." Thus, using the scale shown in Table 15.2, the rating of car A compared to car A, car B to car B, and car C to car C must be 1. Hence, AHP assigns a 1 to all elements on the diagonal of the pairwise comparison matrix.

Given these entries, all that remains is to determine the rating for car B compared to car A, car C compared to car A, and car C compared to car B. Obviously, we could follow the same procedure and ask Dave to provide his preferences for these pairwise comparisons. However, since we already know that Dave has rated his preference for car A compared to car B as 2, there is no need for him to make another pairwise comparison with these two cars. In fact, we will conclude that the preference rating for car B when compared to car A is simply the reciprocal of the preference rating for car A when compared to car B: ½. Using this procedure, AHP obtains the preference rating of car B compared to car A by computing the reciprocal of the rating of car A to car B. Using this inverse, or reciprocal, relationship, we find that the rating of car C compared to car A is ⅛ and the rating of car C to car B is ⅙. Using these numerical values of preference, the complete pairwise comparison matrix for the comfort criterion is shown in Table 15.3.

Table 15.3

Pairwise Comparison Matrix Showing Preferences for the Three Cars in Terms of Comfort

	Comfort		
	Car A	Car B	Car C
Car A	1	2	8
Car B	½	1	6
Car C	⅛	⅙	1

Synthesis

Once the matrix of pairwise comparisons has been developed, we can calculate what is called the *priority* of each of the elements being compared. For example, we would now like to use the pairwise comparison information in Table 15.3 to estimate the relative priority for each of the cars in terms of the comfort criterion. This part of AHP is referred to as *synthesization*.

The exact mathematical procedure required to perform this synthesization involves the computation of eigenvalues and eigenvectors and is beyond the scope of this text. However, the following three-step procedure provides a good approximation of the synthesized priorities.

Procedure for Synthesizing Judgments

Step 1   Sum the values in each column of the pairwise comparison matrix.

Step 2   Divide each element in the pairwise comparison matrix by its column total; the resulting matrix is referred to as the *normalized pairwise comparison matrix.*

Step 3   Compute the average of the elements in each row of the normalized matrix; these averages provide an estimate of the relative priorities of the elements being compared.

To see how the synthesization process works, we carry out the procedure using the pairwise comparison matrix shown in Table 15.3. The three steps are as follows:

Step 1   Sum the values in each column.

	Comfort		
	Car A	Car B	Car C
Car A	1	2	8
Car B	½	1	6
Car C	⅛	⅙	1
Column totals	1⅜	1⁹⁄₆	15

Step 2   Divide each element of the matrix by its column total.

	Comfort		
	Car A	Car B	Car C
Car A	$8/13$	$12/19$	$8/15$
Car B	$4/13$	$6/19$	$6/15$
Car C	$1/13$	$1/19$	$1/15$

Note: All columns in the normalized pairwise comparison matrix now have a sum of 1.

Step 3 Average the elements in each row. (The values in the normalized pairwise comparison matrix have been converted to decimal form.)

	Comfort			
	Car A	Car B	Car C	**Row Average**
Car A	0.615	0.631	0.533	0.593
Car B	0.308	0.316	0.400	0.341
Car C	0.077	0.053	0.067	0.066
			Total	1.000

This synthesis provides the relative priorities for the three cars with respect to the comfort criterion. Thus, we see that, considering comfort, the most preferred car is car A (with a priority of 0.593). Car B (with a priority of 0.341) is second, followed by car C (with a priority of 0.066). The priority vector showing the relative priorities of car A, car B, and car C with respect to the comfort criterion is written as follows:

$$\begin{bmatrix} 0.593 \\ 0.341 \\ 0.066 \end{bmatrix}$$

You should be able to set up the pairwise comparison matrix and determine priorities. Try Problem 12.

Consistency

A key step in AHP is the establishment of priorities through the use of the pairwise comparison procedure just described. An important consideration in terms of the quality of the ultimate decision relates to the *consistency* of judgments that the decision maker demonstrated during the series of pairwise comparisons.

Realize that perfect consistency is very difficult to achieve and that some lack of consistency is expected to exist in almost any set of pairwise comparisons. To handle the consistency question, AHP provides a method for measuring the degree of consistency among the pairwise judgments provided by the decision maker. If the degree of consistency is acceptable, the decision process can continue. However, if the degree of consistency is unacceptable, the decision maker should reconsider and possibly revise the pairwise comparison judgments before proceeding with the analysis.

AHP provides a measure of the consistency of pairwise comparison judgments by computing a *consistency ratio*. This ratio is designed in such a way that values of the ratio exceeding 0.10 are indicative of inconsistent judgments; in such cases, the decision maker would probably want to revise the original values in the pairwise comparison matrix. Values of the consistency ratio of 0.10 or less are considered to be a reasonable level of consistency in the pairwise comparisons.

Although the exact mathematical computation of the consistency ratio is beyond the scope of this text, an approximation of the ratio can be obtained. We will illustrate this computational procedure for the car-selection problem by considering Dave's pairwise comparisons for the comfort criterion. The steps of the computational procedure are demonstrated next.

Estimating the Consistency Ratio

Step 1   Multiply each value in the first column of the pairwise comparison matrix by the relative priority of the first item considered; multiply each value in the second column of the matrix by the relative priority of the second item considered; multiply each value in the third column of the matrix by the relative priority of the third item considered. Sum the values across the rows to obtain a vector of values labeled "weighted sum." This computation for the car-selection problem is

$$0.593 \begin{bmatrix} 1 \\ \frac{1}{2} \\ \frac{1}{8} \end{bmatrix} + 0.341 \begin{bmatrix} 2 \\ 1 \\ \frac{1}{6} \end{bmatrix} + 0.066 \begin{bmatrix} 8 \\ 6 \\ 1 \end{bmatrix}$$

Weighted Sum Vector

$$= \begin{bmatrix} 0.593 \\ 0.297 \\ 0.074 \end{bmatrix} + \begin{bmatrix} 0.682 \\ 0.341 \\ 0.057 \end{bmatrix} + \begin{bmatrix} 0.528 \\ 0.396 \\ 0.066 \end{bmatrix} = \begin{bmatrix} 1.803 \\ 1.034 \\ 0.197 \end{bmatrix}$$

Step 2   Divide the elements of the vector of weighted sums obtained in step 1 by the corresponding priority value. For the car-selection problem, we obtain

$$\frac{1.803}{0.593} = 3.040$$

$$\frac{1.034}{0.341} = 3.032$$

$$\frac{0.197}{0.066} = 2.985$$

Step 3   Compute the average of the values found in step 2; this average is denoted by λ_{max}. For the car-selection problem, we obtain

$$\lambda_{max} = \frac{3.040 + 3.032 + 2.985}{3} = 3.019$$

Step 4   Compute the consistency index (CI), which is defined as follows:

$$CI = \frac{\lambda_{max} - n}{n - 1}$$

where

n = the number of items being compared

For the car-selection problem with $n = 3$, we obtain

$$CI = \frac{3.019 - 3}{2} = 0.010$$

Step 5 Compute the consistency ratio (CR), which is defined as follows:

$$CR = \frac{CI}{RI}$$

where RI, the random index, is the consistency index of a randomly generated pairwise comparison matrix. It can be shown that RI depends on the number of elements being compared and takes on the following values:

n	3	4	5	6	7	8
RI	0.58	0.90	1.12	1.24	1.32	1.41

Thus, for our car-selection problem with $n = 3$ and $RI = 0.58$, we obtain the following consistency ratio:

$$CR = \frac{0.01}{0.58} = 0.017$$

You should now be able to determine whether the judgments are consistent. Try Problem 16.

As mentioned previously, a consistency ratio of 0.10 or less is considered acceptable. Since our example shows a consistency ratio of 0.017, the degree of consistency exhibited in the pairwise comparison matrix for comfort is acceptable.

Other Pairwise Comparisons for the Car-Selection Problem

Continuing with the AHP analysis of the car-selection problem, we need to use the pairwise comparison procedure to determine the priorities of the three cars in terms of the purchase price, MPG, and style criteria. This requires that Dave express pairwise comparison preferences for the cars, considering each of these criteria one at a time. Assume that this has been done and that his preferences are summarized in the pairwise comparison matrices shown in Table 15.4.

Following the same synthesis procedure that we used for the comfort criterion, the priority vectors for these criteria can be computed. The result of this synthesis is shown in Table 15.5. In interpreting these priorities, we see that car C is the most preferable in terms of purchase price (0.557) and miles per gallon (0.639). Car B is the most preferable

Table 15.4 Pairwise Comparison Matrices for Price, MPG, and Style in the Car-Selection Problem

	Price				**MPG**				**Style**		
	Car A	Car B	Car C		Car A	Car B	Car C		Car A	Car B	Car C
Car A	1	1/3	1/4	Car A	1	1/4	1/6	Car A	1	1/3	4
Car B	3	1	1/2	Car B	4	1	1/3	Car B	3	1	7
Car C	4	2	1	Car C	6	3	1	Car C	1/4	1/7	1

Table 15.5

Priority Vectors for Price, MPG, and Style in the Car-Selection Problem

Price	MPG	Style
$\begin{bmatrix} 0.123 \\ 0.320 \\ 0.557 \end{bmatrix}$	$\begin{bmatrix} 0.087 \\ 0.274 \\ 0.639 \end{bmatrix}$	$\begin{bmatrix} 0.265 \\ 0.655 \\ 0.080 \end{bmatrix}$

in terms of style (0.655). No car is the most preferred with respect to all criteria. Thus, before a final decision can be made, we must assess the relative importance of the criteria.

In addition to the pairwise comparisons for the decision alternatives, we must use the same pairwise comparison procedure to set priorities for all four criteria in terms of the importance of each in contributing toward the overall goal of selecting the best car. To develop this final pairwise comparison matrix, Dave would have to specify how important he thinks each criterion is compared to each of the other criteria. To do this, six pairwise judgments have to be made:

> Purchase price compared to MPG
> Purchase price compared to comfort
> Purchase price compared to style
>
> MPG compared to comfort
> MPG compared to style
>
> Comfort compared to style

For example, in the pairwise comparison of the purchase price and MPG, Dave indicates that purchase price is *moderately* more important than MPG. Using the AHP nine-point numerical rating scale (see Table 15.2), a value of 3 is recorded to show the higher importance of the purchase-price criterion. The summary of the pairwise comparison matrix preferences for the four criteria is shown in Table 15.6.

The synthesization process described earlier in this section can now be used to convert the pairwise comparison information into the priorities for the four criteria. The results obtained are as follows:

Priorities for the Four Criteria	
Price	0.398
MPG	0.085
Comfort	0.218
Style	0.299

Table 15.6

Pairwise Comparison Matrix for the Four Criteria in the Car-Selection Problem

	Criterion			
	Price	MPG	Comfort	Style
Price	1	3	2	2
MPG	1/3	1	1/4	1/4
Comfort	1/2	4	1	1/2
Style	1/2	4	2	1

We see that the purchase price (0.398) has been identified as the highest-priority, or most important, criterion in the car-selection decision. Style (0.299) and comfort (0.218) rank next in importance. Miles per gallon (0.085) is a relatively unimportant criterion in terms of the overall goal of selecting the best car. In the next section we show how AHP uses the priority information generated here to develop an overall priority ranking for the three cars.

15.5 Using AHP to Develop an Overall Priority Ranking

In the previous section we showed how a pairwise comparison matrix can be used to develop a prioritized ranking of the items being compared. Now we will show how the criterion priorities and the priorities of each decision alternative relative to each criterion can be combined to develop an overall priority ranking of the decision alternatives. Table 15.7 summarizes the priorities for each car in terms of each criterion as computed in Section 15.4. We will refer to this matrix as the *priority matrix*.

The procedure used to compute the overall priorities for each decision alternative can best be understood if we think of the priority for each criterion as a weight that reflects its importance. The overall priority for each decision alternative is obtained by summing the products of the criterion priority times the priority of its decision alternative. Recall that the criterion priorities were found to be 0.398 for purchase price, 0.085 for MPG, 0.218 for comfort, and 0.299 for style. Thus, the computation of the overall priority for car A is as follows:

$$\text{Overall car A priority} = 0.398(0.123) + 0.085(0.087) + 0.218(0.593) + 0.299(0.265)$$
$$= 0.265$$

Repeating this calculation for cars B and C provides their overall priorities as follows:

$$\text{Overall car B priority} = 0.398(0.320) + 0.085(0.274) + 0.218(0.341) + 0.299(0.655)$$
$$= 0.421$$

$$\text{Overall car C priority} = 0.398(0.557) + 0.085(0.639) + 0.218(0.066) + 0.299(0.080)$$
$$= 0.314$$

You should now be able to use AHP to determine overall priority ranking. Try Problem 20.

Ranking these priority values, we have the following AHP ranking of the decision alternatives:

Alternative	Priority
Car A	0.265
Car B	0.421
Car C	0.314
Total	1.000

Table 15.7		Price	MPG	Comfort	Style
The Priority Matrix for the Car-Selection Problem	Car A	0.123	0.087	0.593	0.265
	Car B	0.320	0.274	0.341	0.655
	Car C	0.557	0.639	0.066	0.080

These results provide a basis for Dave to make a decision regarding the purchase of a car. Based on the AHP priorities, Dave should select car B. Whether or not Dave actually decides to purchase car B based on the AHP analysis is still his decision to make. If Dave believes that the judgments that he has made regarding the importance of the criteria and his preferences for the cars in terms of the criteria are valid, then the AHP priorities show that car B is the preferred car. Whether Dave actually decides to purchase car B may not be as important as the additional understanding that he has gained through the AHP analysis. That is, the process may be as helpful to Dave as the actual decision recommendation itself.

15.6 Using Expert Choice to Implement AHP

Expert Choice (EC), a software package marketed by Decision Support Software, provides a user-friendly procedure for implementing AHP on a microcomputer. In this section we provide an introduction to this software package by using it to compute the priorities for the car-selection problem.

Expert Choice enables the user to construct a graphical representation of the hierarchy easily. For example, to create the hierarchy for the car-selection problem, the user selects the option to develop a new application; what appears on the computer's monitor is a request to define the overall goal. After the user defines the overall goal, select the best car, a rectangular box, or node, appears on the screen with this goal description written directly above it. The user selects the EDIT command and then the INSERT option; another rectangular box or node appears below the goal node, and the user now types the name of a criterion, such as price, which will be entered inside the box. This process continues until all four criterion nodes, including MPG, comfort, and style, have been specified. Figure 15.8 shows the partial hierarchy appearing on the computer screen after the four criteria have been entered.

In Figure 15.8 we see that in addition to the names of each criterion, the criterion nodes also contain the decimal value of 0.250. This value represents the initial weight, or priority, given to each criterion at the start of the EC session. The user can now continue to use the EDIT command with the INSERT option to define the decision alternative nodes associated with each of the criterion nodes. Figure 15.9 shows the result of defining

Figure 15.8
Partial Hierarchy Showing Criteria with Initial Priorities Equal to 0.250

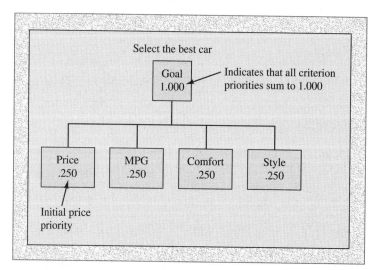

Figure 15.9
Partial Hierarchy Showing the
Price Criterion with Initial
Priorities for Cars A, B, and C

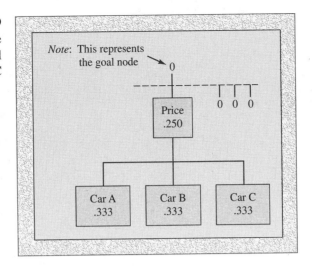

the decision alternative nodes of car A, car B, and car C for the price criterion; note that since there are three alternatives, the initial priorities are set at 0.333. A similar set of decision alternatives is then identified for each of the other three criteria.

Now that the hierarchy has been input to EC, we are ready to begin developing the pairwise comparisons needed to establish priorities for the decision alternatives. To illustrate the type of approach used, we moved back to the goal node and then selected the COMPARE command by typing C. After selecting the option to make comparisons based on the importance of the decision criteria, the EC system begins to go through the pairwise comparison analysis.

One portion of this analysis, which shows the approach used by EC to establish the comparative importance between the purchase price and MPG criteria, is shown in Figure 15.10. Note that this figure indicates to the EC system that price is moderately more important than MPG. This process continues until all the entries in the pairwise comparison matrix for criteria have been developed. The synthesization process is then performed to compute the priorities for the criteria; Figure 15.11 shows the priorities that were obtained after synthesization.[2]

The process of entering pairwise preferences for the cars relative to each of the criteria was performed in a similar manner. The overall decision was then arrived at by entering the command S, which is an abbreviation for synthesizing; this command is used only when all data for the pairwise comparison matrices have been entered and we want to obtain an overall prioritization of the decision alternatives. Figure 15.12 shows the results. Note that they indicate that the final priority for car B, the most preferable, is 0.422.

The EC system is much more powerful and comprehensive than our brief introduction can begin to show. It is very helpful in performing the multicriteria decision analysis of AHP. In addition to providing the overall priorities for the decision alternatives, EC has the capability of doing "what if" types of analyses, where the decision maker can begin to learn how the overall priorities for the decision alternative are affected by changes in the preference input data.

Practitioners in Japan originally viewed AHP as too complicated. However, in a 1985 symposium, Thomas L. Saaty, the founder of AHP, showed the Japanese that the method is simple, is easy to use, and has a great potential to solve a variety of decision problems. Since then, a Japanese version of Expert Choice has been developed, and research activities have been revitalized.

---

[2]The priorities computed by EC differ slightly from those we obtained previously. This is simply due to the fact that the method we used was an approximation to the EC synthesization procedure which involves the computation of eigenvalues and eigenvectors.

Figure 15.10 Determining the Rating for the Price and MPG Pairwise Comparison

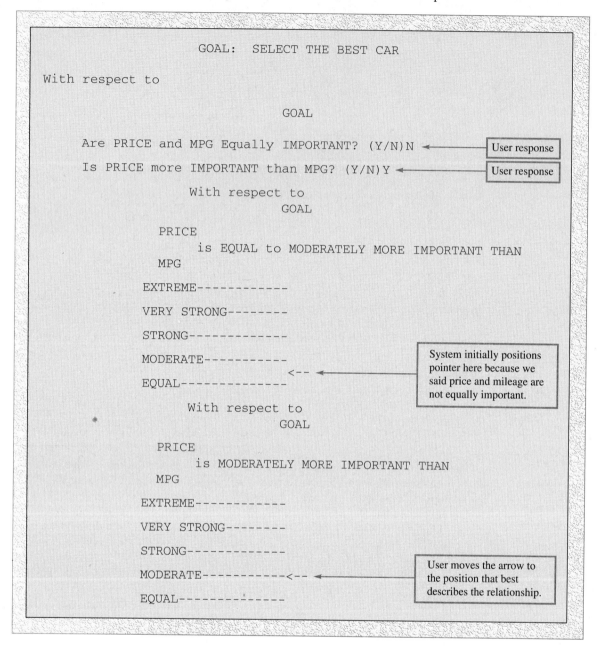

Figure 15.11
The Hierarchy Showing Priorities
After Synthesization for the
Criteria

Figure 15.12
AHP Final
Results
for the
Car-Selection
Problem

Summary

In this chapter we have used goal programming to solve problems with multiple objectives or goals within the linear programming framework. We have shown that the goal programming model contains one or more goal equations and an objective function that is designed to minimize the deviations from the goals. In situations where resource capacities or other restrictions affect the achievement of the goals, the model will contain constraints that are formulated and treated in the same manner as constraints in an ordinary linear programming model.

In goal programming problems with preemptive priorities, priority level 1 goals are treated first in an objective function to identify a solution that will best satisfy these goals. This solution is then revised by considering an objective function involving only the priority level 2 goals; solution modifications are considered only if they do not degrade the solution obtained for the priority level 1 goals. This process continues until all priority levels have been considered.

We showed how a variation of the linear programming graphical solution procedure can be used to solve goal programming problems with two decision variables. Specialized goal programming computer packages are available for solving the general goal programming problem, but such computer codes are not as readily available as are general purpose linear programming computer packages. As a result, we have shown how a general linear programming package such as LINDO/PC can be used in an iterative manner to provide a solution for a goal programming problem.

We presented an approach to multicriteria decision making known as the analytic hierarchy process (AHP). We showed that a key part of AHP is the development of judgments concerning the relative importance of, or preference for, the elements being compared. A consistency ratio is computed to determine the degree of consistency exhibited by the decision maker in making the pairwise comparisons. Values of the consistency ratio less than or equal to 0.10 are considered acceptable.

Once the set of all pairwise comparisons has been developed, a process referred to as synthesization is used to determine the priorities for the elements being compared. The final step of the analytic hierarchy process is an overall synthesization, in which the priority levels established for the decision alternatives relative to each criterion are multiplied by the priority levels reflecting the importance of the criteria themselves; the sum of these products over all the criteria is the overall priority level for the decision alternative. The chapter concluded with a brief introduction to Expert Choice, a software package designed to perform the computational steps of AHP.

Glossary

Goal programming A linear programming approach to problems involving multicriteria where the objective function is designed to minimize the deviations from goals.

Preemptive priorities Priorities assigned to goals which ensure that the satisfaction of a higher-level goal cannot be traded for the satisfaction of a lower-level goal.

Target value The value specified in the statement of the goal. Based on the context of the problem, management will want the solution to the goal programming problem to result in a value for the goal that is less than, equal to, or greater than the target value.

Goal equation An equation whose right-hand side is the target value for the goal; the left-hand side of the goal equation consists of (1) a function representing the level of achievement and (2) deviation variables representing the difference between the target value for the goal and the level achieved.

Deviation variables Variables that are added to the goal equation to allow the solution to deviate from the goal's target value.

Analytic hierarchy process (AHP) An approach to multicriteria decision making based in part on pairwise comparisons for elements in a hierarchy.

Hierarchy A figure that shows the levels of a problem in terms of the overall goal, the criteria, and the decision alternatives.

Pairwise comparison matrix A matrix that consists of the preference, or relative importance, ratings provided during a series of pairwise comparisons.

Synthesization A mathematical process that uses the preference values in the pairwise comparison matrix to develop priorities.

Normalized pairwise comparison matrix The matrix obtained by dividing each element of the pairwise comparison matrix by its column total. This matrix is computed as an intermediate step in the synthesization of priorities.

Consistency A concept developed to assess the quality of preference judgments made during a series of pairwise comparisons. It is a measure of the internal consistency of these comparisons.

Consistency ratio A numerical measure of the degree of consistency in a series of pairwise comparisons. Values less than or equal to 0.10 are considered acceptable.

Expert Choice (EC) A computer software package that performs the computations required by the analytic hierarchy process.

Problems

1. GP modeling and graphical solution procedure

1. The RMC Corporation blends three raw materials to produce two products: a fuel additive and a solvent base. Each ton of fuel additive is a mixture of $\frac{2}{5}$ ton of material 1 and $\frac{3}{5}$ ton of material 3. A ton of solvent base is a mixture of $\frac{1}{2}$ ton of material 1, $\frac{1}{5}$ ton of material 2, and $\frac{3}{10}$ ton of material 3. RMC's production is constrained by a limited availability of the three raw materials. For the current production period, RMC has the following quantities of each raw material: material 1, 20 tons; material 2, 5 tons; material 3, 21 tons. Management would like to achieve the following P_1 priority level goals:

   Goal 1: Produce at least 30 tons of fuel additive.

   Goal 2: Produce at least 15 tons of solvent base.

   Assume there are no other goals in the problem.
   a. Is it possible for management to achieve both P_1 level goals given the constraints on the amounts of each material available? Explain.
   b. Treating the amounts of each material available as constraints, formulate a goal programming model to determine the optimal product mix. Assume both of the P_1 priority level goals are equally important to management.
   c. Use the graphical goal programming procedure to solve the model formulated in part (b).
   d. If goal 1 is twice as important as goal 2, what is the optimal product mix?

SELF TEST ▷

2. GP modeling and graphical solution procedure

2. DJS Investment Services must develop an investment portfolio for a new client. As an initial investment strategy, the new client would like to restrict the portfolio to a mix of the following two stocks:

Stock	Price/Share	Estimated Annual Return (%)
AGA Products	$ 50	6
Key Oil	100	10

The client has $50,000 available to invest and has established the following two investment goals:

Priority Level 1 Goal

Goal 1: Obtain an annual return of at least 9%.

Priority Level 2 Goal

Goal 2: Limit the investment in Key Oil, the riskier investment, to at most 60% of the total investment.

a. Formulate a goal programming model for the DJS Investment problem.

b. Use the graphical goal programming procedure to obtain a solution.

3. The L. Young & Sons Manufacturing Company produces two products, which have the following profit and resource requirement characteristics:

Characteristic	Product 1	Product 2
Profit/unit	$4	$2
Dept. A hours/unit	1	1
Dept. B hours/unit	2	5

Last month's production schedule used 350 hours of labor in department A and 1000 hours of labor in department B.

Young's management has been experiencing work force morale and labor union problems during the past 6 months because of monthly departmental work load fluctuations. New hiring, layoffs, and interdepartmental transfers have been common because the firm has not attempted to stabilize work load requirements.

Management would like to develop a production schedule for the coming month that will achieve the following goals:

Goal 1: Use 350 hours of labor in department A.

Goal 2: Use 1000 hours of labor in department B.

Goal 3: Earn a profit of at least $1300.

a. Formulate a goal programming model for this problem assuming goals 1 and 2 are P_1 level goals and goal 3 is a P_2 level goal; assume goals 1 and 2 are equally important.

b. Solve the model formulated in part (a) using the graphical goal programming procedure.

c. Suppose the firm ignores the work load fluctuations and considers the 350 hours in department A and the 1000 hours in department B as the maximum available. Formulate and solve a linear programming problem to maximize profit subject to these constraints.

d. Compare the solutions obtained in parts (b) and (c). Discuss which approach you favor, and tell why.

e. Reconsider part (a) assuming the priority level 1 goal is goal 3 and the priority level 2 goals are goals 1 and 2; as before, assume goals 1 and 2 are equally important. Solve this revised problem using the graphical goal programming procedure, and compare your solution to the one obtained for the original problem.

4. Industrial Chemicals produces two adhesives that are used in the manufacturing process for airplanes. The two adhesives, which have different bonding strengths, require different amounts of production time: the IC–100 adhesive requires 20 minutes of production time per gallon of finished product, and the IC–200 adhesive uses 30 minutes of production time per gallon. Both products use 1 pound of a highly perishable resin for each gallon of finished product. There are 300 pounds of the resin in inventory, and more can be obtained if necessary. However, because of the shelf life of the material, any amount not used in the next 2 weeks will be discarded.

The firm has existing orders for 100 gallons of IC–100 and 120 gallons of IC–200. Under normal conditions, the production process operates 8 hours per day, 5 days per week. Management would like to schedule production for the next 2 weeks to achieve the following goals:

Priority Level 1 Goals

Goal 1:   Avoid underutilization of the production process.

Goal 2:   Avoid overtime in excess of 20 hours for the 2 weeks.

Priority Level 2 Goals

Goal 3:   Satisfy existing orders for the IC–100 adhesive; that is, produce at least 100 gallons of IC–100.

Goal 4:   Satisfy existing orders for the IC–200 adhesive; that is, produce at least 120 gallons of IC–200.

Priority Level 3 Goal

Goal 5:   Use up all the available resin.

a. Formulate a goal programming model for the Industrial Chemicals problem. Assume that both priority level 1 goals and both priority level 2 goals are equally important.

b. Use the graphical goal programming procedure to develop a solution for the model formulated in part (a).

5. Reconsider the RMC data presented in Problem 1. Assume that the two P_1 priority level goals remain the same and that both goals are equally important to management. Suppose management has learned that additional amounts of material 3 can be obtained from another RMC plant. Although management would like to obtain a solution that satisfies their production goals using the 21 tons of material 3 currently available, they are willing to consider using additional amounts of material 3 from the other plant. Introducing this new objective or goal as a P_2 priority level goal, the problem goals can now be restated as follows:

Priority Level 1 Goals

Goal 1:   Produce at least 30 tons of fuel additive.

Goal 2:   Produce at least 15 tons of solvent base.

Priority Level 2 Goal

Goal 3:   Use at most 21 tons of material 3.

a. Treating the amounts of materials 1 and 2 available as problem constraints, formulate a goal programming model for this problem.

b. Use the goal programming computer procedure illustrated in Section 15.2 to solve the model formulated in part (a).

c. How many tons of material 3 need to be obtained from RMC's other plant?

6. Michigan Motors Corporation (MMC) has just introduced a new luxury touring sedan. As part of its promotional campaign, the marketing department has decided to send personalized invitations to test drive the new sedan to two target groups: (1) current owners of an MMC luxury automobile and (2) owners of luxury cars manufactured by one of MMC's competitors. The cost of sending a personalized invitation to each customer is estimated to be $1 per letter. Based on previous experience with this type of advertising, MMC estimates that 25% of the customers contacted from group 1 and 10% of the customers contacted from group 2 will test drive the new sedan. As part of this campaign, MMC has set the following goals:

Goal 1:   Get at least 10,000 customers from group 1 to test drive the new sedan.

Goal 2:   Get at least 5000 customers from group 2 to test drive the new sedan.

Goal 3:   Limit the expenses for sending out the invitations to at most $70,000.

Assume that goals 1 and 2 are P_1 priority level goals and that goal 3 is a P_2 priority level goal.

a. Suppose goals 1 and 2 are equally important; formulate a goal programming model of the MMC problem.

b. Use the goal programming computer procedure illustrated in Section 15.2 to solve the model formulated in part (a).

c. If management believes that contacting customers from group 2 is twice as important as contacting customers from group 1, what should MMC do?

7. A committee in charge of promoting a Ladies Professional Golf Association tournament is trying to determine how best to advertise the event over the 2 weeks prior to the tournament. The following table shows the information obtained by the committee for the three advertising media they are considering using:

Category	Audience Reached per Advertisement	Cost per Advertisement	Maximum Number of Advertisements
TV	200,000	$2500	10
Radio	50,000	400	15
Newspaper	100,000	500	20

The last column in this table shows the maximum number of advertisements that can be run over the next 2 weeks; these values should be treated as constraints in the problem. The committee has established the following goals for the campaign:

Priority Level 1 Goal

Goal 1:   Reach at least 4 million people.

Priority Level 2 Goal

Goal 2:   The number of television advertisements should be at least 30% of the total number of advertisements.

Priority Level 3 Goal

Goal 3:   The number of radio advertisements should not exceed 20% of the total number of advertisements.

Priority Level 4 Goal

Goal 4:   Limit the total amount spent for advertising to at most $20,000.

a. Formulate a goal programming model for this problem.

b. Use the goal programming computer procedure illustrated in Section 15.2 to solve the model formulated in part (a).

8. Morley Company is attempting to determine the best location for a new machine in an existing layout of three machines. The existing machines are located at the following x_1, x_2 coordinates on the shop floor:

$$\text{Machine 1:} \ x_1 = 1, x_2 = 7$$

$$\text{Machine 2:} \ x_1 = 5, x_2 = 9$$

$$\text{Machine 3:} \ x_1 = 6, x_2 = 2$$

a. Develop a goal programming model that can be solved to minimize the total distance of the new machine from the three existing machines. The distance is to be measured rectangularly. For example, if the location of the new machine is $(x_1 = 3, x_2 = 5)$, it is considered to be a distance of $|3 - 1| + |5 - 7| = 2 + 2 = 4$ from machine 1. *Hint:* In the goal programming formulation, let

$$x_1 = \text{first coordinate of the new machine location}$$

$$x_2 = \text{second coordinate of the new machine location}$$

$$d_i^+ = \text{amount by which the } x_1 \text{ coordinate of the new machine}$$
$$\text{exceeds the } x_1 \text{ coordinate of machine } i \ (i = 1, 2, 3)$$

$$d_i^- = \text{amount by which the } x_1 \text{ coordinate of machine } i$$
$$\text{exceeds the } x_1 \text{ coordinate of the new machine } (i = 1, 2, 3)$$

$$e_i^+ = \text{amount by which the } x_2 \text{ coordinate of the new machine}$$
$$\text{exceeds the } x_2 \text{ coordinate of machine } i \ (i = 1, 2, 3)$$

$$e_1^- = \text{amount by which the } x_2 \text{ coordinate of machine } i$$
$$\text{exceeds the } x_2 \text{ coordinate of the new machine } (i = 1, 2, 3)$$

b. What is the optimal location for the new machine?

9. GP modeling and solution

9. A fast-food chain is attempting to determine the best location of a new outlet. Management would like to determine the best location for drawing customers from three population centers. Letting (x_1, x_2) represent the map coordinates of the three population centers, we can show their locations as follows:

Population center 1:	$x_1 = 2, x_2 = 8$
Population center 2:	$x_1 = 6, x_2 = 6$
Population center 3:	$x_1 = 1, x_2 = 1$

If the new outlet is located at coordinates $(x_1 = 3, x_2 = 2)$, then it is a distance of $(3 - 1) + (2 - 1) = 3$ miles from population center 3 (distance is measured as the sum of the east–west and north–south differences in coordinates).

a. Formulate and solve a goal programming model to determine what location for the new outlet will minimize the total distance from the three population centers. (*Hint:* Let x_1, x_2 represent the coordinates of the new location.)

b. Population center 1 is four times as large as center 3, and center 2 is twice as large as center 3. The firm feels that the importance of locating near a population center is proportional to its population. Develop and solve a new goal programming model where the weights on the deviations reflect this importance.

10. AHP priorities and consistency ratio

10. Using the pairwise comparison matrix for the price criterion as shown in Table 15.4, verify that the priorities after synthesization are 0.123, 0.320, and 0.557. Compute the consistency ratio, and comment on its acceptability.

11. AHP priorities and consistency ratio

11. Using the pairwise comparison matrix for the MPG criterion as shown in Table 15.4, verify that the priorities after synthesization are 0.087, 0.274, and 0.639. Compute the consistency ratio and comment on its acceptability.

S ELF T EST ▶

12. AHP priorities and consistency ratio

12. Using the pairwise comparison matrix for the style criterion as shown in Table 15.4, verify that the priorities after synthesization are 0.265, 0.655, and 0.080. Compute the consistency ratio and comment on its acceptability.

13. AHP priorities

13. Dan Joseph was considering entering one of two graduate schools of business to pursue studies for an MBA degree. When asked how he compared the two schools with respectto reputation, he responded that school A was strongly to very strongly preferred over school B.

a. Set up the pairwise comparison matrix for this problem.

b. Determine the priorities for the two schools relative to this criterion.

14. An organization was investigating relocating its corporate headquarters to one of three possible cities. The following pairwise comparison matrix shows the president's judgments regarding the desirability for the three cities:

	City 1	City 2	City 3
City 1	1	5	7
City 2	⅕	1	3
City 3	⅐	⅓	1

   a. Determine the priorities for the three cities.
   b. Is the president consistent in terms of the judgments provided? Explain.

15. The following pairwise comparison matrix contains the judgments of an individual regarding the fairness of two proposed tax programs, A and B:

	A	B
A	1	3
B	⅓	1

   a. Determine the priorities for the two programs.
   b. Are the individual's judgments consistent? Explain.

SELF TEST ▷

16. An individual was asked to compare three soft drinks with respect to flavor. The following judgments were obtained:

       A is moderately more preferable than B.
       A is equally to moderately more preferable than C.
       B is strongly more preferable than C.

   a. Set up the pairwise comparison matrix for this problem.
   b. Determine the priorities for the soft drinks with respect to the flavor criterion.
   c. Compute the consistency ratio. Are the individual's judgments consistent? Explain.

17. Refer to Problem 16. Suppose that the individual had provided the following judgments instead of those given in Problem 16:

       A is strongly more preferable than C.
       B is equally to moderately more preferable than A.
       B is strongly more preferable than C.

Answer parts (a), (b), and (c) as stated in Problem 16.

18. The national sales director for Jones Office Supplies needs to determine the best location for the next national sales meeting. Three locations have been proposed: Dallas, San Francisco, and New York. One criterion considered important in the decision is the desirability of the location in terms of restaurants, entertainment, and so on. The national sales manager provided the following judgments with regard to this criterion:

       New York is very strongly more preferred than Dallas.
       New York is moderately more preferred than San Francisco.
       San Francisco is moderately to strongly more preferred than Dallas.

a. Set up the pairwise comparison matrix for this problem.
b. Determine the priorities for the desirability criterion.
c. Compute the consistency ratio. Are the sales manager's judgments consistent? Explain.

19. A study comparing four personal computers resulted in the following pairwise comparison matrix for the performance criterion:

	Computer			
Computer	1	2	3	4
1	1	3	7	$1/3$
2	$1/3$	1	4	$1/4$
3	$1/7$	$1/4$	1	$1/6$
4	3	4	6	1

a. Determine the priorities for the four computers relative to the performance criterion.
b. Compute the consistency ratio. Are the judgments regarding performance consistent? Explain.

20. An individual was interested in determining which of two stocks to invest in, Central Computing Company (CCC) or Software Research, Inc. (SRI). The criteria thought to be most relevant in making the decision are the potential yield of the stock and the risk associated with the investment. The pairwise comparison matrices for this problem are as follows:

	Criterion			Yield			Risk	
	Yield	Risk		CCI	SRI		CCI	SRI
Yield	1	2	CCI	1	3	CCI	1	$1/2$
Risk	$1/2$	1	SRI	$1/3$	1	SRI	2	1

a. Draw the hierarchy for this problem.
b. Compute the priorities for each of the pairwise comparison matrices.
c. Determine the overall priority for the two investments.

21. The vice president of Harling Equipment needs to select a new director of marketing. The two possible candidates are Bill Jacobs and Sue Martin, and the criteria thought to be most relevant in the selection are leadership ability (L), personal skills (P), and administrative skills (A). The following pairwise comparison matrices were obtained:

	Criterion				Leadership	
	L	P	A		Jacobs	Martin
L	1	$1/3$	$1/4$	Jacobs	1	4
P	3	1	2	Martin	$1/4$	1
A	4	$1/2$	1			

	Personal			Administrative	
	Jacobs	Martin		Jacobs	Martin
Jacobs	1	⅓	Jacobs	1	2
Martin	3	1	Martin	½	1

a. Draw the hierarchy for this decision problem.
b. Compute the priorities for each of the pairwise comparison matrices.
c. Determine an overall priority for each of the candidates.

22. AHP: overall priority ranking

22. A woman considering the purchase of a custom sound stereo system for her car looked at three different systems that varied in terms of price (P), sound quality (Q), and FM reception (FM). The following pairwise consistency matrices were developed:

Criterion				Price			
	P	Q	FM		A	B	C
P	1	3	4	A	1	4	2
Q	⅓	1	3	B	¼	1	⅓
FM	¼	⅓	1	C	½	3	1

Quality				FM Reception			
	A	B	C		A	B	C
A	1	½	¼	A	1	4	2
B	2	1	⅓	B	¼	1	1
C	4	3	1	C	½	1	1

a. Draw the hierarchy for this decision problem.
b. Compute the priorities for each of the pairwise comparison matrices.
c. Determine an overall priority for each of the systems.

Case Problem: Production Scheduling

EZ Trailers, Inc., manufactures a variety of general purpose trailers, including a complete line of boat trailers. Two of their best-selling boat trailers are the EZ–190 and the EZ–250; the EZ–190 is designed for boats up to 19 feet in length, and the EZ–250 can be used for boats up to 25 feet in length.

EZ Trailers would like to schedule production for the next 2 months for these two models. Each unit of the EZ–190 requires 4 hours of production time, and each unit of the EZ–250 uses 6 hours of production time. The following orders have been received for March and April:

Model	March	April
EZ–190	800	600
EZ–250	1100	1200

The ending inventory from February was 200 units of the EZ–190 and 300 units of the EZ–250. The total number of hours of production time used in February was 6300 hours.

The management of EZ Trailers is very much concerned about being able to satisfy existing orders for the EZ–250 for both March and April. In fact, they feel that this is the most important goal they would like to achieve in developing a production schedule. Next in importance is satisfying existing orders for the EZ–190. In addition, management does not want to implement any production schedule that would involve significant labor fluctuations from month to month. In this regard, their goal is to find a production schedule that would limit fluctuations in labor-hours used to a maximum of 1000 hours from one month to the next.

Managerial Report

Perform an analysis of EZ Trailers' production scheduling problem, and prepare a report for EZ's president that summarizes your findings. Include a discussion and analysis of the following in your report:

1. The production schedule that best achieves the goals as specified by management.
2. Suppose EZ Trailers' storage facilities would only accommodate up to 300 trailers in any one month. What effect would this have on the production schedule?
3. Suppose EZ Trailers can only store up to 300 trailers in any one month. In addition, suppose management would like to have an ending inventory in April of at least 100 units of each model. What effect would both of these changes have on the production schedule?
4. What changes would occur in the production schedule if the labor fluctuation goal was the highest-priority goal?

CHAPTER 16

Forecasting

Most companies can forecast total demand for all products with errors of less than 5%. However, forecasting demand for individual products can result in significantly higher errors.

A forecast is simply a *prediction* of what will happen in the future. Managers must learn to accept the fact that regardless of the technique used, they will not be able to develop perfect forecasts.

A critical aspect of managing any organization is planning for the future. Indeed, the long-run success of an organization is closely related to how well management is able to foresee the future and develop appropriate strategies. Good judgment, intuition, and an awareness of the state of the economy may give a manager a rough idea or "feeling" of what is likely to happen in the future. However, it is often difficult to convert this feeling into a number that can be used as next quarter's sales volume or next year's raw material cost per unit. The purpose of this chapter is to introduce several methods that can help predict many future aspects of a business operation.

Suppose we have been asked to provide quarterly forecasts of the sales volume for a particular product during the coming 1-year period. Production schedules, raw material purchasing plans, inventory policies, and sales quotas will all be affected by the quarterly forecasts that we provide. Consequently, poor forecasts may result in increased costs for the firm. How should we go about providing the quarterly sales volume forecasts?

We will certainly want to review the actual sales data for the product in past periods. Suppose we have actual sales data for each quarter over the past 3 years. Using these historical data, we can identify the general level of sales and determine whether there is any trend, such as an increase or decrease in sales volume over time. A further review of the data might reveal a seasonal pattern, such as peak sales occurring in the third quarter of each year and sales volume bottoming out during the first quarter. By reviewing historical data over time, we can often develop a better understanding of the pattern of past sales; often this can lead to better predictions of future sales for the product.

The historical sales data form what is called a *time series*. A time series is a set of observations measured at successive points in time or over successive periods of time. In this chapter we will introduce several procedures that can be used to analyze time series data. The objective of this analysis will be to provide good *forecasts* or predictions of future values of the time series.

Forecasting methods can be classified as quantitative or qualitative. Quantitative forecasting methods are based on an analysis of historical data concerning a time series and possibly other related time series. If the historical data used are restricted to past

686

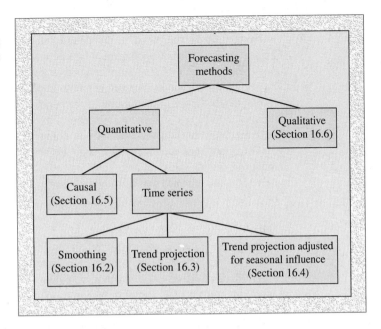

Figure 16.1
An Overview of Forecasting
Methods

values of the series that we are trying to forecast, the forecasting procedure is called a time series method. In this chapter we discuss three time series methods: smoothing (moving averages and exponential smoothing), trend projection, and trend projection adjusted for seasonal influence. If the historical data used in a quantitative forecasting method involve other time series that are believed to be related to the time series that we are trying to forecast, we say that we are using a causal method. In this chapter we also discuss the use of regression analysis as a causal forecasting method.

Qualitative forecasting methods generally utilize the judgment of experts to make forecasts. An advantage of these procedures is that they can be applied in situations where no historical data are available. We discuss some of these approaches in Section 16.6. Figure 16.1 provides an overview of the different types of forecasting methods.

16.1 The Components of a Time Series

To explain the pattern or behavior of the data in a time series, it is often helpful to think of the time series as consisting of several components. The usual assumption is that four separate components—trend, cyclical, seasonal, and irregular—combine to provide specific values for the time series. Let us look more closely at each of these components.

Trend Component

In time series analysis, the measurements may be taken every hour, day, week, month, or year, or at any other regular interval.[1] Although time series data generally exhibit random fluctuations, the time series may still show gradual shifts or movements to relatively

---

[1]We restrict our attention here to time series where the values of the series are recorded at equal intervals. Treatment of cases where the observations are not made at equal intervals is beyond the scope of this text.

higher or lower values over a longer period of time. The gradual shifting of the time series is referred to as the *trend* in the time series; this shifting or trend is usually due to long-term factors such as changes in the population, in demographic characteristics of the population, in technology, and in consumer preferences.

For example, a manufacturer of photographic equipment may see substantial month-to-month variability in the number of cameras sold. However, in reviewing the sales over the past 10–15 years, this manufacturer may find a gradual increase in the annual sales volume. Suppose the sales volume was approximately 1800 cameras per month in 1983, 2200 cameras per month in 1988, and 2600 cameras per month in 1993. While actual month-to-month sales volumes may vary substantially, this gradual growth in sales over time shows an upward trend for the time series. Figure 16.2 shows a straight line that may be a good approximation of the trend in camera sales. While the trend for camera sales appears to be linear and increasing over time, sometimes the trend in a time series is better described by other patterns.

Figure 16.3 shows some other possible time series trend patterns. In part (a) we see a nonlinear trend; in this case, the time series shows very little growth initially, followed by a period of rapid growth, and then a leveling off. This trend pattern might be a good approximation of sales for a product from introduction through a growth period and into a period of market saturation. The linear decreasing trend in part (b) is useful for time series displaying a steady decrease over time. The horizontal line in part (c), which shows a time series that does not have any consistent increase or decrease over time, is the case of no trend.

Cyclical Component

Although a time series may exhibit a trend over long periods of time, we cannot expect all future values of the time series to be exactly on the trend line. In fact, time series often show alternating sequences of points below and above the trend line. Any recurring

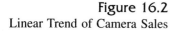

Figure 16.2
Linear Trend of Camera Sales

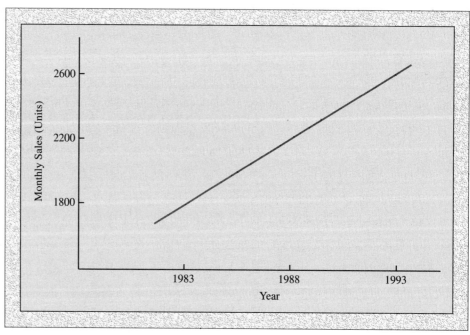

Figure 16.3
Examples of Some Possible Time Series Trend Patterns

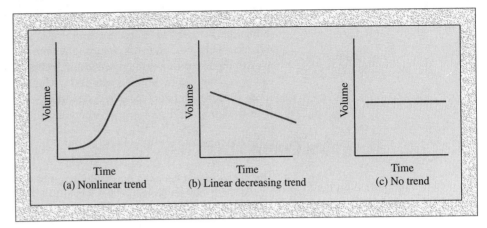

sequence of points above and below the trend line lasting more than 1 year can be attributed to the *cyclical component* of the time series. Figure 16.4 shows the graph of a time series with an obvious cyclical component. The observations are taken at intervals 1 year apart.

Many time series exhibit cyclical behavior with regular runs of observations below and above the trend line. The general belief is that this component of the time series represents multiyear cyclical movements in the economy. For example, periods of modest inflation followed by periods of rapid inflation can lead to many time series that alternate below and above a generally increasing trend line (e.g., a time series for housing costs). Many time series in the late 1970s and early 1980s displayed this type of behavior.

Seasonal Component

While the trend and cyclical components of a time series are identified by analyzing multiyear movements in historical data, many time series show a regular pattern of variability within 1-year periods. For example, a manufacturer of swimming pools expects low sales activity in the fall and winter months, with peak sales occurring in the spring and summer months. Manufacturers of snow removal equipment and heavy clothing, however, expect just the opposite yearly pattern. It should not be surprising that

Figure 16.4
Trend and Cyclical Components of a Time Series (Data Points Are 1 Year Apart)

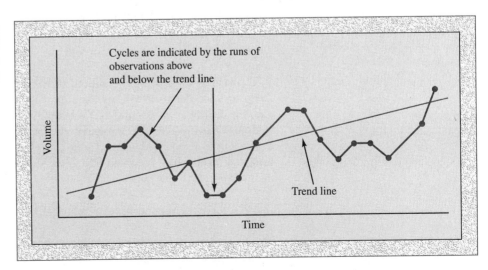

the component of the time series that represents the variability in the data due to seasonal influences is called the *seasonal component*. Although we generally think of seasonal movement in a time series as occurring within 1 year, the seasonal component can also be used to represent any regularly repeating pattern that is less than 1 year in duration. For example, daily traffic volume data show within-the-day "seasonal" behavior, with peak levels during rush hours, moderate flow during the rest of the day and early evening, and light flow from midnight to early morning.

Irregular Component

The *irregular component* of the time series is the residual or "catchall" factor that accounts for the deviations of the actual time series values from what we would expect given the effects of the trend, cyclical, and seasonal components. It accounts for the random variability in the time series. The irregular component is caused by the short-term, unanticipated, and nonrecurring factors that affect the time series. Since this component accounts for the random variability in the time series, it is unpredictable. We cannot attempt to predict its impact on the time series in advance.

16.2 Forecasting Using Smoothing Methods

In this section we discuss forecasting techniques that are appropriate for a fairly stable time series—that is, one that exhibits no significant trend, cyclical, or seasonal effects. In such situations the objective of the forecasting method is to "smooth out" the irregular component of the time series through an averaging process. We begin with the method known as moving averages.

Moving Averages

Many manufacturing environments require forecasts for thousands of items on a weekly or monthly basis. Thus, in choosing a forecasting technique, simplicity and ease of use are important criteria. The data requirements for the techniques in this section are minimal and the techniques are easy to use and understand.

The *moving averages* method uses the average of the *most recent n* data values in the time series as the forecast for the next period. Mathematically, the moving average calculation is made as follows:

$$\text{Moving average} = \frac{\Sigma(\text{most recent } n \text{ data values})}{n} \tag{16.1}$$

The term *moving* is based on the fact that as a new observation becomes available for the time series, it replaces the oldest observation in equation (16.1), and a new average is computed. As a result, the average will change, or move, as new observations become available.

To illustrate the moving averages method, consider the 12 weeks of data presented in Table 16.1 and Figure 16.5. These data show the number of gallons of gasoline sold by a gasoline distributor in Bennington, Vermont, over the past 12 weeks.

To use moving averages to forecast gasoline sales, we must first select the number of data values to be included in the moving average. As an example, let us compute forecasts using a 3-week moving average. The moving average calculation for the first 3 weeks of the gasoline sales time series is as follows:

$$\text{Moving average (weeks 1–3)} = \frac{17 + 21 + 19}{3} = 19$$

This moving average value is then used as the forecast for week 4. Since the actual value observed in week 4 is 23, we see that the forecast error in week 4 is $23 - 19 = 4$. In

Figure 16.5
Gasoline Sales Time Series

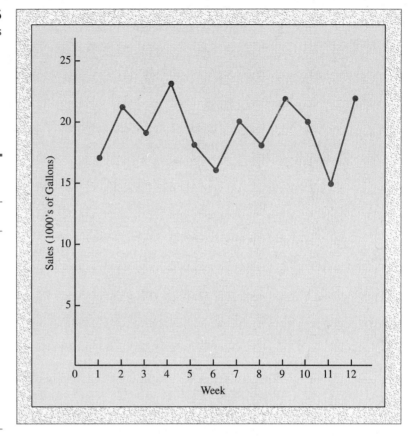

Table 16.1
Gasoline Sales Time Series Data

Week	Sales (1000s of gallons)
1	17
2	21
3	19
4	23
5	18
6	16
7	20
8	18
9	22
10	20
11	15
12	22

general, the error associated with any forecast is the difference between the observed value of the time series and the forecast.

The calculation for the second 3-week moving average is shown below.

$$\text{Moving average (weeks 2–4)} = \frac{21 + 19 + 23}{3} = 21$$

You should now be able to use moving averages to compute a forecast. Try Problem 1.

Hence, the forecast for week 5 is 21. The error associated with this forecast is $18 - 21 = -3$. Thus, we see that the forecast error can be positive or negative depending on whether the forecast is too low or too high. A complete summary of the 3-week moving average calculations for the gasoline sales time series is shown in Table 16.2 and Figure 16.6.

Forecast accuracy is not the only consideration. Sometimes the most accurate method utilizes data on related time series that are difficult or costly to obtain. Trade-offs are often made between cost and forecast accuracy.

An important consideration in using any forecasting method is the accuracy of the forecast. Clearly, we would like the forecast errors to be small. The last two columns of Table 16.2, which contain the forecast errors and the forecast errors squared, can be used to develop measures of forecast accuracy.

One measure of forecast accuracy that you might think of using would be to sum the forecast errors over time. The problem with this measure is that if the errors are random (as they should be if the forecasting method selected is appropriate), some errors will be positive and some errors will be negative, resulting in a sum near zero regardless of the size of the individual errors. Indeed, we see from Table 16.2 that the sum of forecast errors for the gasoline sales time series is zero. This difficulty can be avoided by squaring each of the individual forecast errors.

Table 16.2
Summary of 3-Week Moving Average
Calculations

Week	Time Series Value	Moving Average Forecast	Forecast Error	Squared Forecast Error
1	17			
2	21			
3	19			
4	23	19	4	16
5	18	21	−3	9
6	16	20	−4	16
7	20	19	1	1
8	18	18	0	0
9	22	18	4	16
10	20	20	0	0
11	15	20	−5	25
12	22	19	3	9
		Totals	0	92

For the gasoline sales time series, we can use the last column of Table 16.2 to compute the average of the sum of the squared errors. Doing so, we obtain

$$\text{Average of the sum of squared errors} = \frac{92}{9} = 10.22$$

This average of the sum of squared errors is commonly referred to as the *mean squared error* (MSE). The MSE is an often-used measure of the accuracy of a forecasting method and is the one we use in this chapter.

As we indicated previously, to use the moving averages method, we must first select the number of data values to be included in the moving average. It should not be too surprising that for a particular time series, different-length moving averages will differ in their ability to accurately forecast the time series. One possible approach to choosing the number of values to be included is to use trial and error to identify the length that minimizes the MSE. Then, if we are willing to assume that the length that is best for the past will also be best for the future, we would forecast the next value in the time series using the number of data values that minimized the MSE for the historical time series.

You should now be able to use MSE as a measure of forecast accuracy. Try Problem 2.

Weighted Moving Averages

In the moving averages method, each observation in the calculation receives the same weight. One possible variation, known as *weighted moving averages,* involves selecting different weights for each data value and then computing a weighted mean as the forecast. In most cases, the most recent observation receives the most weight, and the weight decreases for older data values. For example, using the gasoline sales time series, let us illustrate the computation of a weighted 3-week moving average, where the most recent observation receives a weight three times as great as that given the oldest observation, and the next oldest observation receives a weight twice as great as the oldest. The weighted moving averages forecast for week 4 would be computed as follows:

Weighted moving averages forecast for week 4 $= \frac{3}{6}(19) + \frac{2}{6}(21) + \frac{1}{6}(17) = 19.33$

Note that for the weighted moving average the sum of the weights is equal to 1. This was also true for the simple moving average, where each weight was $\frac{1}{3}$. However, recall that the simple or unweighted moving average provided a forecast of 19.

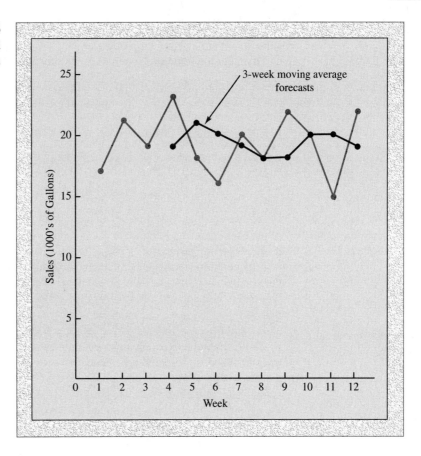

Figure 16.6
Gasoline Sales Time Series and
3-Week Moving Average Forecasts

Exponential Smoothing

Exponential smoothing is simple
and has few data requirements.
Thus, it is an inexpensive, useful
approach for firms that make many
forecasts each period.

Exponential smoothing uses a weighted average of past time series values as the forecast. The basic exponential smoothing model is as follows:

$$F_{t+1} = \alpha Y_t + (1 - \alpha)F_t \qquad (16.2)$$

where

$$F_{t+1} = \text{forecast of the time series for period } t + 1$$
$$Y_t = \text{actual value of the time series in period } t$$
$$F_t = \text{forecast of the time series for period } t$$
$$\alpha = \text{smoothing constant } (0 \leq \alpha \leq 1)$$

To see that the forecast for any period is a weighted average of *all the previous actual values* for the time series, suppose we have a time series consisting of three periods of data, Y_1, Y_2, and Y_3. To get the exponential smoothing calculations started, we let F_1 equal the actual value of the time series in period 1; that is, $F_1 = Y_1$. Hence, the forecast for period 2 is written as follows:

$$F_2 = \alpha Y_1 + (1 - \alpha)F_1$$
$$= \alpha Y_1 + (1 - \alpha)Y_1$$
$$= Y_1$$

In general, then, the exponential smoothing forecast for period 2 is equal to the actual value of the time series in period 1.

To obtain the forecast for period 3, we substitute $F_2 = Y_1$ in the expression for F_3; the result is

$$F_3 = \alpha Y_2 + (1 - \alpha)Y_1$$

Finally, substituting this expression for F_3 in the expression for F_4, we obtain

$$F_4 = \alpha Y_3 + (1 - \alpha)[\alpha Y_2 + (1 - \alpha)Y_1]$$

$$= \alpha Y_3 + \alpha(1 - \alpha)Y_2 + (1 - \alpha)^2 Y_1$$

The name exponential smoothing comes from the exponential nature of the weighting scheme for the historical values.

Hence, we see that F_4 is a weighted average of the first three time series values. The sum of the coefficients or weights for Y_1, Y_2, and Y_3 equals 1. A similar argument can be made to show that any forecast F_{t+1} is a weighted average of all the previous time series values.

Exponential smoothing is a simple procedure that requires very little historical data. Once the *smoothing constant* α has been selected, only two pieces of information are required to compute the forecast for the next period. Referring to equation (16.2), we see that with a given α we can compute the forecast for period $t + 1$ simply by knowing the actual and forecast time series values for period t—that is, Y_t and F_t.

To illustrate the exponential smoothing approach to forecasting, consider the gasoline sales time series presented previously in Table 16.1 and Figure 16.5. As we indicated in the discussion above, the exponential smoothing forecast for period 2 is equal to the actual value of the time series in period 1. Thus, with $Y_1 = 17$, we will set $F_2 = 17$ to get the exponential smoothing computations started. Referring to the time series data in Table 16.1, we find an actual time series value in period 2 of $Y_2 = 21$. Thus, period 2 has a forecast error of $21 - 17 = 4$.

Continuing with the exponential smoothing computations provides the following forecast for period 3:

$$F_3 = 0.2Y_2 + 0.8F_2 = 0.2(21) + 0.8(17) = 17.8$$

Once the actual time series value in period 3, $Y_3 = 19$, is known, we can generate a forecast for period 4 as follows:

$$F_4 = 0.2Y_3 + 0.8F_3 = 0.2(19) + 0.8(17.8) = 18.04$$

By continuing the exponential smoothing calculations, we are able to determine the weekly forecast values and the corresponding weekly forecast errors, as shown in Table 16.3. Note that we have not shown an exponential smoothing forecast or the forecast error for period 1 because F_1 was set equal to Y_1 in order to begin the smoothing computations. For week 12, we have $Y_{12} = 22$ and $F_{12} = 18.48$. Can you use this information to generate a forecast for week 13 before the actual value of week 13 becomes known? Using the exponential smoothing model, we have

$$F_{13} = 0.2Y_{12} + 0.8F_{12} = 0.2(22) + 0.8(18.48) = 19.18$$

You should now be able to develop forecasts using exponential smoothing. Try Problem 4.

Thus, the exponential smoothing forecast of the amount sold in week 13 is 19.18, or 19,180 gallons of gasoline. With this forecast, the firm can make plans and decisions accordingly. The accuracy of the forecast will not be known until the firm conducts its business through week 13.

Figure 16.7 shows the plot of the actual and the forecast time series values. Note in particular how the forecasts "smooth out" the irregular fluctuations in the time series.

Table 16.3

Summary of the Exponential
Smoothing Forecasts and Forecast
Errors for Gasoline Sales with
Smoothing Constant $\alpha = 0.2$

Week (t)	Time Series Value (Y_t)	Exponential Smoothing Forecast (F_t)	Forecast Error ($Y_t - F_t$)
1	17		
2	21	17.00	4.00
3	19	17.80	1.20
4	23	18.04	4.96
5	18	19.03	−1.03
6	16	18.83	−2.83
7	20	18.26	1.74
8	18	18.61	−0.61
9	22	18.49	3.51
10	20	19.19	0.81
11	15	19.35	−4.35
12	22	18.48	3.52

In the preceding exponential smoothing calculations, we used a smoothing constant of $\alpha = 0.2$. Although any value of α between 0 and 1 is acceptable, some values will yield better forecasts than others. Insight into choosing a good value for α can be obtained by rewriting the basic exponential smoothing model as follows:

$$F_{t+1} = \alpha Y_t + (1 - \alpha)F_t$$

$$F_{t+1} = \alpha Y_t + F_t - \alpha F_t \qquad (16.3)$$

$$F_{t+1} = F_t + \alpha(Y_t - F_t)$$

Forecast in period t

Forecast error in period t

Thus, we see that the new forecast F_{t+1} is equal to the previous forecast F_t plus an adjustment, which is α times the most recent forecast error, $Y_t - F_t$. That is, the forecast in period $t + 1$ is obtained by adjusting the forecast in period t by a fraction of the forecast error. If the time series contains substantial random variability, a small value of the smoothing constant is preferred. The reason for this choice is that since much of the forecast error is due to random variability, we do not want to overreact and adjust the forecasts too quickly. For a time series with relatively little random variability, larger values of the smoothing constant have the advantage of quickly adjusting the forecasts when forecasting errors occur and therefore allowing the forecast to react faster to changing conditions.

The criterion we will use to determine a desirable value for the smoothing constant α is the same as the criterion we proposed earlier for determining the number of periods of data to include in the moving averages calculation. That is, we choose the value of α that minimizes the mean squared error. A summary of the MSE calculations for the exponential smoothing forecast of gasoline sales with $\alpha = 0.2$ is shown in Table 16.4. Note that there is one less squared error term than the number of periods because we had no past values with which to make a forecast for period 1. Would a different value of α have provided better results in terms of a lower MSE value? Perhaps the most straightforward way to answer this question is simply to try another value for α. We will then compare its mean squared error with the MSE value of 8.98, obtained using a smoothing constant of 0.2.

The exponential smoothing results with $\alpha = 0.3$ are shown in Table 16.5. With MSE = 9.35, we see that for the current data set a smoothing constant of $\alpha = 0.3$ results

For a given set of data, you should now be able to determine whether moving averages or exponential smoothing provides the best forecasts. Try Problem 5.

Figure 16.7
Actual and Forecast Gasoline
Sales Time Series with
Smoothing Constant $\alpha = 0.2$

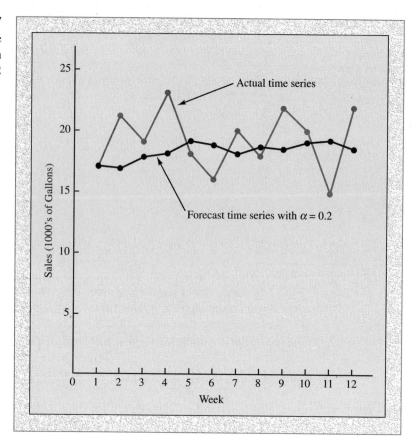

Table 16.4
Mean Squared Error Computations for
Forecasting Gasoline Sales with
$\alpha = 0.2$

Week (t)	Time Series Value (Y_t)	Forecast (F_t)	Forecast Error ($Y_t - F_t$)	Squared Forecast Error ($Y_t - F_t)^2$
1	17			
2	21	17.00	4.00	16.00
3	19	17.80	1.20	1.44
4	23	18.04	4.96	24.60
5	18	19.03	−1.03	1.06
6	16	18.83	−2.83	8.01
7	20	18.26	1.74	3.03
8	18	18.61	−0.61	0.37
9	22	18.49	3.51	12.32
10	20	19.19	0.81	0.66
11	15	19.35	−4.35	18.92
12	22	18.48	3.52	12.39
			Total	98.80

$$\text{MSE} = \frac{98.80}{11} = 8.98$$

Table 16.5
Mean Squared Error Computations for Forecasting Gasoline Sales with $\alpha = 0.3$

Week (t)	Time Series Value (Y_t)	Forecast (F_t)	Forecast Error ($Y_t - F_t$)	Squared Forecast Error ($Y_t - F_t)^2$
1	17			
2	21	17.00	4.00	16.00
3	19	18.20	0.80	0.64
4	23	18.44	4.56	20.79
5	18	19.81	−1.81	3.28
6	16	19.27	−3.27	10.69
7	20	18.29	1.71	2.92
8	18	18.80	−0.80	0.64
9	22	18.56	3.44	11.83
10	20	19.59	0.41	0.17
11	15	19.71	−4.71	22.18
12	22	18.30	3.70	13.69
			Total	102.83

$$\text{MSE} = \frac{102.83}{11} = 9.35$$

in less forecast accuracy than a smoothing constant of $\alpha = 0.2$. Thus, we would be inclined to use the original smoothing constant of 0.2. Using a trial-and-error calculation with other values of α, a "good" value for the smoothing constant can be found. This value can be used in the exponential smoothing model to provide forecasts for the future. At a later date, after a number of new time series observations have been obtained, it is good practice to analyze the newly collected time series data to see if the smoothing constant should be revised to provide better forecasting results.

NOTES & COMMENTS

Another commonly used measure of forecast accuracy is the *mean absolute deviation* (MAD). This measure is simply the average of the sum of the absolute values of all the forecast errors. Using the errors given in Table 16.2, we obtain

$$\text{MAD} = \frac{4 + 3 + 4 + 1 + 0 + 4 + 0 + 5 + 3}{9} = 2.67$$

One major difference between the MSE and the MAD is that the MSE measure is much more influenced by large forecast errors than by small errors (since for the MSE measure the errors are squared). The selection of the best measure of forecasting accuracy is not a simple matter. Indeed, forecasting experts often disagree as to which measure should be used. We will use the MSE measure in this chapter.

16.3 Forecasting Using Trend Projection

In this section we will see how to forecast the values of a time series that exhibits a long-term linear trend. Specifically, let us consider the time series data for bicycle sales of

Table 16.6
Bicycle Sales Data

Year (t)	Sales (1000s) (Y_t)
1	21.6
2	22.9
3	25.5
4	21.9
5	23.9
6	27.5
7	31.5
8	29.7
9	28.6
10	31.4

a particular manufacturer over the past 10 years, as shown in Table 16.6 and Figure 16.8. Note that 21,600 bicycles were sold in year 1, 22,900 were sold in year 2, and so on; in year 10, the most recent year, 31,400 bicycles were sold. Although Figure 16.8 shows some up-and-down movement over the past 10 years, the time series seems to have an overall increasing or upward trend in the number of bicycles sold.

We do not want the trend component of a time series to follow each and every "up" and "down" movement. Rather, the trend component should reflect the gradual shifting—in our case, growth—of the time series values. After we view the time series data in Table 16.6 and the graph in Figure 16.8, we might agree that a linear trend as shown in Figure 16.9 has the potential of providing a reasonable description of the long-run movement in the series.

Using the bicycle sales data to illustrate the calculations involved, we will now describe how regression analysis can be used to identify a linear trend. For a linear trend, the estimated sales volume expressed as a function of time can be written as follows:

$$T_t = b_0 + b_1 t \tag{16.4}$$

where

T_t = trend value for bicycle sales in period t
b_0 = intercept of the trend line
b_1 = slope of the trend line

Note that for the time series on bicycle sales, $t = 1$ corresponds to the oldest time series value and $t = 10$ corresponds to the most recent time series value. Formulas for computing b_1 and b_0 are shown below:

$$b_1 = \frac{\Sigma t Y_t - (\Sigma t \Sigma Y_t)/n}{\Sigma t^2 - (\Sigma t)^2/n} \tag{16.5}$$

Figure 16.8
Bicycle Sales Time Series

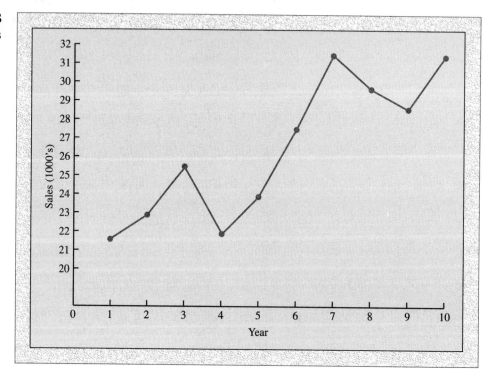

Figure 16.9
Trend Represented by a Linear
Function for Bicycle Sales

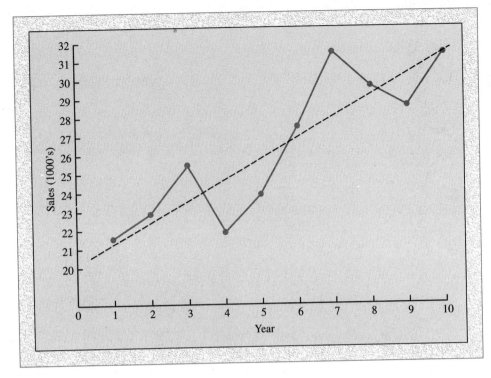

$$b_0 = \bar{Y} - b_1\bar{t} \tag{16.6}$$

where

Y_t = actual value of the time series in period t
n = number of periods
$\bar{Y}$ = average value of the time series; that is, $\bar{Y} = \Sigma Y_t/n$
$\bar{t}$ = average value of t; that is, $\bar{t} = \Sigma t/n$

Using these relationships for b_0 and b_1 and the bicycle sales data of Table 16.6, we have
the following calculations:

	t	Y_t	tY_t	t^2
	1	21.6	21.6	1
	2	22.9	45.8	4
	3	25.5	76.5	9
	4	21.9	87.6	16
	5	23.9	119.5	25
	6	27.5	165.0	36
	7	31.5	220.5	49
	8	29.7	237.6	64
	9	28.6	257.4	81
	10	31.4	314.0	100
Totals	55	264.5	1545.5	385

Figure 16.10
Some Possible Functional Forms
for Nonlinear Trend Patterns

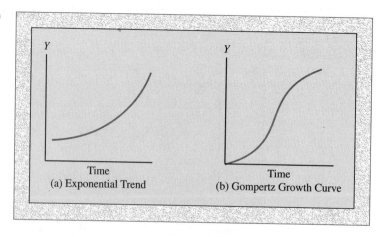

$$\bar{t} = \frac{55}{10} = 5.5$$

$$\bar{Y} = \frac{264.5}{10} = 26.45$$

$$b_1 = \frac{1545.5 - (55)(264.5)/10}{385 - (55)^2/10} = 1.10$$

$$b_0 = 26.45 - 1.10(5.5) = 20.4$$

Therefore,

$$T_t = 20.4 + 1.1t \qquad (16.7)$$

You should now be able to develop the equation for the linear trend component for a time series. Try Problem 14.

Before using the trend equation to develop a forecast, a statistical test of significance should be conducted for the slope estimate. Such a test on the slope of 1.1 would provide statistical evidence to support the conclusion that the slope is significantly different from zero. In practice, such a test would be a routine part of fitting the trend line.

is the expression for the linear trend component for the bicycle sales time series.

The slope of 1.1 in the trend equation indicates that over the past 10 years the firm has experienced an average growth in sales of around 1100 units per year. If we assume that the past 10-year trend in sales is a good indicator of the future, then equation (16.7) can be used to project the trend component of the time series. For example, substituting $t = 11$ into equation (16.7) yields next year's trend projection, T_{11}:

$$T_{11} = 20.4 + 1.1(11) = 32.5$$

Thus, using the trend component only, we would forecast sales of 32,500 bicycles next year.

The use of a linear function to model the trend is common. However, as we discussed earlier, sometimes time series exhibit a curvilinear, or nonlinear, trend similar to those shown in Figure 16.10. More advanced texts discuss in detail how to develop models for these more complex relationships.

16.4 Forecasting with Trend and Seasonal Components

We previously showed how to forecast the values of a time series that had a trend component. In this section we expand the discussion by showing how to forecast the values of a time series that has both trend and seasonal components. The approach we

Table 16.7
Quarterly Data for Television Set Sales

Year	Quarter	Sales (1000s)
1	1	4.8
	2	4.1
	3	6.0
	4	6.5
2	1	5.8
	2	5.2
	3	6.8
	4	7.4
3	1	6.0
	2	5.6
	3	7.5
	4	7.8
4	1	6.3
	2	5.9
	3	8.0
	4	8.4

will take is first to remove the seasonal effect or seasonal component from the time series. This step is referred to as *deseasonalizing* the time series. After deseasonalizing, the time series will have only a trend component. As a result, we can use the method described in the previous section to identify the trend component of the time series. Then, using a trend projection calculation, we will develop a forecast based upon the trend component of the time series. The final step in developing the forecast will be to reincorporate the seasonal component by using a seasonal index to adjust the trend projection. In this manner, we will be able to identify the trend and seasonal components and consider both in forecasting the time series.

In addition to a trend component T and a seasonal component S, we will assume that the time series also has an irregular component I. The irregular component accounts for any random effects in the time series that cannot be explained by the trend and seasonal components. Using T_t, S_t, and I_t to identify the trend, seasonal, and irregular components at time t, we will assume that the actual time series value, denoted by Y_t, can be described by the following *multiplicative time series model*:

$$Y_t = T_t \times S_t \times I_t \tag{16.8}$$

In this model, T_t is the trend measured in units of the item being forecast. However, the S_t and I_t components are measured in relative terms, with values above 1.00 indicating effects above the trend, and values below 1.00 indicating effects below the trend.

We illustrate the use of the multiplicative model with trend, seasonal, and irregular components by working with the quarterly data presented in Table 16.7 and Figure 16.11. These data show the television set sales (in thousands of units) for a particular manufacturer over the past 4 years. We begin by showing how to identify the seasonal component of the time series.

Figure 16.11
Quarterly Television Set Sales Time Series

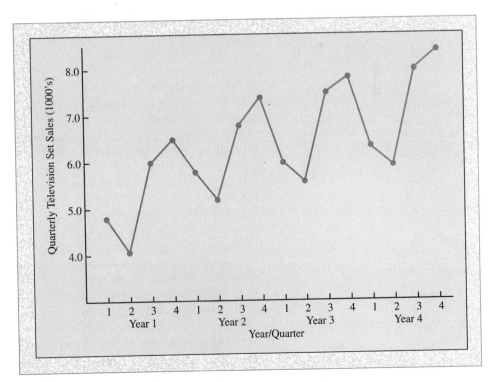

Calculating the Seasonal Indexes

Looking at Figure 16.11, we observe that sales are lowest in the second quarter of each year, followed by higher sales levels in quarters 3 and 4. Thus, we conclude that a seasonal pattern exists for the television set sales. The computational procedure used to identify each quarter's seasonal influence begins by computing a moving average to isolate the combined seasonal and irregular components, S_t and I_t.

To do this, we use 1 year of data in each calculation. Since we are working with a quarterly series, we will use four data values in each moving average. The moving average calculation for the first 4 quarters of the television set sales data is as follows:

$$\text{First moving average} = \frac{4.8 + 4.1 + 6.0 + 6.5}{4} = \frac{21.4}{4} = 5.35$$

Note that the moving average calculation for the first 4 quarters yields the average quarterly sales over the first year of the time series. Continuing the moving average calculation, we next add the 5.8 value for the first quarter of year 2 and drop the 4.8 for the first quarter of year 1. Thus, the second moving average is

$$\text{Second moving average} = \frac{4.1 + 6.0 + 6.5 + 5.8}{4} = \frac{22.4}{4} = 5.6$$

Similarly, the third moving average calculation is $(6.0 + 6.5 + 5.8 + 5.2)/4 = 5.875$.

Before we proceed with the moving average calculations for the entire time series, let us return to the first moving average calculation, which resulted in a value of 5.35. The 5.35 value represents an average quarterly sales volume (across all seasons) for year 1. As we look back at the calculation of the 5.35 value, perhaps it makes sense to associate 5.35 with the "middle" quarter of the moving average group. Note, however, that some difficulty in identifying the middle quarter is encountered; with 4 quarters in the moving average, there is no middle quarter. The 5.35 value corresponds to the last half of quarter 2 and the first half of quarter 3. Similarly, if we go to the next moving average value of 5.60, the middle corresponds to the last half of quarter 3 and the first half of quarter 4.

Recall that the reason we are computing moving averages is to isolate the combined seasonal and irregular components. However, the moving average values we have computed do not correspond directly to the original quarters of the time series. We can resolve this difficulty by using the midpoints between successive moving average values. For example, since 5.35 corresponds to the first half of quarter 3 and 5.60 corresponds to the last half of quarter 3, we will use $(5.35 + 5.60)/2 = 5.475$ as the moving average value for quarter 3. In a similar manner, we associate a moving average value of $(5.60 + 5.875)/2 = 5.738$ with quarter 4. What results is called a *centered moving average*. A complete summary of the moving average and centered moving average calculations for the television set sales data is shown in Table 16.8.

If the number of data points in a moving average calculation is an odd number, the middle point will correspond to one of the periods in the time series. In such cases, we would not have to center the moving average values to correspond to a particular time period, as we did in the calculations in Table 16.8.

Let us pause for a moment to consider what the centered moving averages in Table 16.8 tell us about this time series. Plots of the actual time series values and the corresponding centered moving average are shown in Figure 16.12. Note particularly how the centered moving average values tend to "smooth out" both the seasonal and irregular fluctuations in the time series. Since the moving average values were computed for 4 quarters of data, they do not include the fluctuations due to seasonal influences. Each

Table 16.8

Moving Average Calculations for the Television Set Sales Time Series

Year	Quarter	Sales (1000s)	4-Quarter Moving Average	Centered Moving Average
1	1	4.8		
	2	4.1		
			5.350	
	3	6.0		5.475
			5.600	
	4	6.5		5.738
			5.875	
2	1	5.8		5.975
			6.075	
	2	5.2		6.188
			6.300	
	3	6.8		6.325
			6.350	
	4	7.4		6.400
			6.450	
3	1	6.0		6.538
			6.625	
	2	5.6		6.675
			6.725	
	3	7.5		6.763
			6.800	
	4	7.8		6.838
			6.875	
4	1	6.3		6.938
			7.000	
	2	5.9		7.075
			7.150	
	3	8.0		
	4	8.4		

point in the centered moving average represents what the value of the time series would be if there were no seasonal or irregular influence.

By dividing each time series observation by the corresponding centered moving average value, we can identify the seasonal–irregular effect in the time series. For example, the third quarter of year 1 shows 6.0/5.475 = 1.096 as the combined seasonal–irregular component. The resulting seasonal–irregular values for the entire time series are summarized in Table 16.9.

Consider the third quarter. The results from years 1, 2, and 3 show third-quarter values of 1.096, 1.075, and 1.109, respectively. Thus, in all cases the seasonal–irregular component appears to have an above average influence in the third quarter. Since the year-to-year fluctuations in the seasonal–irregular component can be attributed primarily to the irregular component, we can average the computed values to eliminate the irregular influence and obtain an estimate of the third-quarter seasonal influence:

$$\text{Seasonal effect of third quarter} = \frac{1.096 + 1.075 + 1.109}{3} = 1.09$$

Figure 16.12
Quarterly Television Set Sales
Time Series and
Centered Moving Average

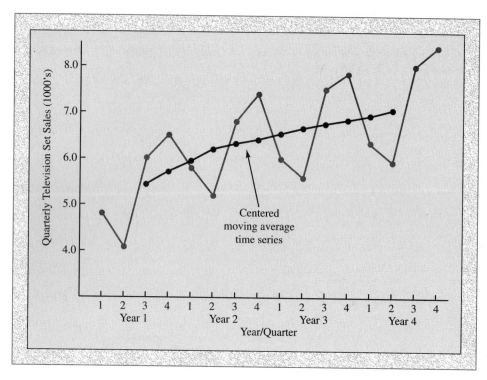

Table 16.9
Seasonal–Irregular Factors for the
Television Set Sales Time Series

Year	Quarter	Sales (1000s)	Centered Moving Average	Seasonal–Irregular Component
1	1	4.8		
	2	4.1		
	3	6.0	5.475	1.096
	4	6.5	5.738	1.133
2	1	5.8	5.975	0.971
	2	5.2	6.188	0.840
	3	6.8	6.325	1.075
	4	7.4	6.400	1.156
3	1	6.0	6.538	0.918
	2	5.6	6.675	0.839
	3	7.5	6.763	1.109
	4	7.8	6.838	1.141
4	1	6.3	6.938	0.908
	2	5.9	7.075	0.834
	3	8.0		
	4	8.4		

Table 16.10

Seasonal Index Calculations for the
Television Set Sales Time Series

Quarter	Seasonal–Irregular Component Values $(S_t I_t)$	Seasonal Index (S_t)
1	0.971, 0.918, 0.908	0.93
2	0.840, 0.839, 0.834	0.84
3	1.096, 1.075, 1.109	1.09
4	1.133, 1.156, 1.141	1.14

We refer to 1.09 as the *seasonal index* for the third quarter. In Table 16.10 we summarize the calculations involved in computing the seasonal indexes for the television set sales time series. Thus, we see that the seasonal indexes for all 4 quarters are as follows: quarter 1, 0.93; quarter 2, 0.84; quarter 3, 1.09; and quarter 4, 1.14.

Interpretation of the values in Table 16.10 provides some observations about the "seasonal" component in television set sales. The best sales quarter is the fourth quarter, with sales averaging 14% above the average quarterly value. The worst, or slowest, sales quarter is the second quarter, with its seasonal index at 0.84, showing the sales average 16% below the average quarterly sales. The seasonal component corresponds nicely to the intuitive expectation that television viewing interest and thus television purchase patterns tend to peak in the fourth quarter, with its coming winter season and fewer outdoor activities. The low second-quarter sales reflect the reduced television interest resulting from the spring and presummer activities of the potential customers.

One final adjustment is sometimes necessary in obtaining the seasonal indexes. The multiplicative model requires that the average seasonal index equal 1.00; that is, the sum of the four seasonal indexes in Table 16.10 must equal 4.00. This is necessary if the seasonal effects are to even out over the year, as they must. The average of the seasonal indexes in our example is equal to 1.00, and hence, this type of adjustment is not necessary. In other cases, a slight adjustment may be necessary. The adjustment can be made by multiplying each seasonal index by the number of seasons divided by the sum of the unadjusted seasonal indexes. For quarterly data, we would multiply each seasonal index by 4/(sum of the unadjusted seasonal indexes). Some of the problems at the end of the chapter will require this adjustment to obtain the appropriate seasonal indexes.

You should now be able to compute and interpret seasonal indexes for a time series. Try Problem 27.

Deseasonalizing the Time Series

With deseasonalized data, comparing sales in successive periods makes sense. With data that have not been deseasonalized, relevant comparisons can often be made between sales in the current period and sales in the same period 1 year ago.

The purpose of finding seasonal indexes is to remove the seasonal effects from a time series. This process is referred to as *deseasonalizing* the time series. Economic time series adjusted for seasonal variations (deseasonalized time series) are often reported in publications such as the *Survey of Current Business* and *The Wall Street Journal*. Using the notation of the multiplicative model, we have

$$Y_t = T_t \times S_t \times I_t$$

By dividing each time series observation by the corresponding seasonal index, we have removed the effect of season from the time series. The deseasonalized time series for television set sales is summarized in Table 16.11. A graph of the deseasonalized television set sales time series is shown in Figure 16.13.

Table 16.11

Deseasonalized Values for the
Television Set Sales Time Series

Year	Quarter	Sales (1000s) (Y_t)	Seasonal Index (S_t)	Deseasonalized Sales $(Y_t/S_t = T_t I_t)$
1	1	4.8	0.93	5.16
	2	4.1	0.84	4.88
	3	6.0	1.09	5.50
	4	6.5	1.14	5.70
2	1	5.8	0.93	6.24
	2	5.2	0.84	6.19
	3	6.8	1.09	6.24
	4	7.4	1.14	6.49
3	1	6.0	0.93	6.45
	2	5.6	0.84	6.67
	3	7.5	1.09	6.88
	4	7.8	1.14	6.84
4	1	6.3	0.93	6.77
	2	5.9	0.84	7.02
	3	8.0	1.09	7.34
	4	8.4	1.14	7.37

Using the Deseasonalized Time Series to Identify Trend

Looking at Figure 16.13, we see that while the graph shows some up-and-down movement over the past 16 quarters, the time series seems to have an upward linear trend. To identify this trend, we will use the same procedure we introduced for identifying trend when forecasting with annual data; in this case, since we have deseasonalized the data, quarterly sales values can be used. Thus, for a linear trend, the estimated sales volume expressed as a function of time can be written

$$T_t = b_0 + b_1 t$$

where

T_t = trend value for television set sales in period t
b_0 = intercept of the trend line
b_1 = slope of the trend line

As we did before, $t = 1$ corresponds to the time of the first observation for the time series, $t = 2$ corresponds to the time of the second observation, and so on. Thus, for the deseasonalized television set sales time series, $t = 1$ corresponds to the first deseasonalized quarterly sales value, and $t = 16$ corresponds to the most recent deseasonalized quarterly sales value. The formulas for computing the values of b_0 and b_1 are shown again

$$b_1 = \frac{\Sigma t Y_t - (\Sigma t \Sigma Y_t)/n}{\Sigma t^2 - (\Sigma t)^2/n}$$

$$b_0 = \bar{Y} - b_1 \bar{t}$$

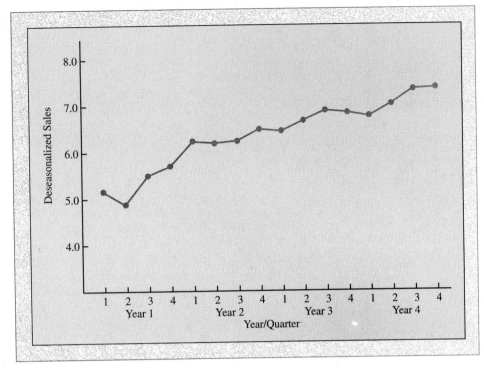

Figure 16.13
Deseasonalized Television Set
Sales Time Series

Note, however, that Y_t now refers to the deseasonalized time series value at time t and not to the actual value of the time series. Using the given relationships for b_0 and b_1 and the deseasonalized sales data of Table 16.11, we have the following calculations:

t	Y_t (deseasonalized)	tY_t	t^2
1	5.16	5.16	1
2	4.88	9.76	4
3	5.50	16.50	9
4	5.70	22.80	16
5	6.24	31.20	25
6	6.19	37.14	36
7	6.24	43.68	49
8	6.49	51.92	64
9	6.45	58.05	81
10	6.67	66.70	100
11	6.88	75.68	121
12	6.84	82.08	144
13	6.77	88.01	169
14	7.02	98.28	196
15	7.34	110.10	225
16	7.37	117.92	256
Totals 136	101.74	914.98	1496

$$\bar{t} = \frac{136}{16} = 8.5$$

$$\bar{Y} = \frac{101.74}{16} = 6.359$$

$$b_1 = \frac{914.98 - (136)(101.74)/16}{1496 - (136)^2/16} = 0.148$$

$$b_0 = 6.359 - 0.148(8.5) = 5.101$$

Therefore,

$$T_t = 5.101 + 0.148t$$

is the expression for the linear trend component of the time series.

The slope of 0.148 indicates that over the past 16 quarters the firm has experienced an average deseasonalized growth in sales of around 148 sets per quarter. If we assume that the past 16-quarter trend in sales data is a reasonably good indicator of the future, then this equation can be used to project the trend component of the time series for future quarters. For example, substituting $t = 17$ into the equation yields next quarter's trend projection, T_{17}:

$$T_{17} = 5.101 + 0.148(17) = 7.617$$

Using the trend component only, we would forecast sales of 7617 television sets for the next quarter. In a similar fashion, if we use the trend component only, we would forecast sales of 7765, 7913, and 8061 television sets in quarters 18, 19, and 20, respectively.

Seasonal Adjustments

Now that we have a forecast of sales for each of the next 4 quarters based on trend, we must adjust these forecasts to account for the effect of season. For example, since the seasonal index for the first quarter of year 5($t = 17$) is 0.93, the quarterly forecast can be obtained by multiplying the forecast based on trend ($T_{17} = 7617$) times the seasonal index (0.93). Thus, the forecast for the next quarter is 7617(0.93) = 7084. Table 16.12 shows the quarterly forecast for quarters 17–20. The forecasts show the high-volume fourth quarter with a 9190-unit forecast and the low-volume second quarter with a 6523-unit forecast.

Models Based on Monthly Data

The television set sales example provided in this section uses quarterly data to illustrate the computation of seasonal indexes, which requires relatively few computations. Many

Table 16.12

Quarterly Forecasts for the Television Set Sales Time Series

Year	Quarter	Trend Forecast	Seasonal Index (see Table 16.10)	Quarterly Forecast
5	1	7617	0.93	(7617)(0.93) = 7084
	2	7765	0.84	(7765)(0.84) = 6523
	3	7913	1.09	(7913)(1.09) = 8625
	4	8061	1.14	(8061)(1.14) = 9190

businesses use monthly rather than quarterly forecasts. In such cases, the procedures introduced in this section can be applied with minor modifications. First, a 12-month moving average replaces the 4-quarter moving average; second, 12 monthly seasonal indexes, rather than the 4 quarterly indexes, need to be computed. Other than these changes, the computational and forecasting procedures are identical.

Cyclical Component

Mathematically, the multiplicative model of equation (16.8) can be expanded to include a cyclical component as follows:

$$Y_t = T_t \times C_t \times S_t \times I_t \tag{16.9}$$

Just as with the seasonal component, the cyclical component is expressed as a percentage of trend. As mentioned in Section 16.1, this component is attributable to multiyear cycles in the time series. It is analogous to the seasonal component, but over a longer period of time. However, because of the length of time involved, it is often difficult to obtain enough relevant data to estimate the cyclical component. Another difficulty is that the length of cycles usually varies. We leave further discussion of the cyclical component to texts on forecasting methods.

16.5 Forecasting Using Regression Models

Regression analysis is a statistical technique that can be used to develop a mathematical equation showing how variables are related. In regression terminology, the variable that is being predicted is called the *dependent* or *response* variable. The variable or variables that predict the value of the dependent variable are called the *independent* or *predictor* variables. Regression analysis involving one independent variable and one dependent variable for which the relationship between the variables is approximated by a straight line is called *simple linear regression*. Regression analysis involving two or more independent variables is called *multiple regression analysis.*

The approach that we used in Section 16.3 to fit a linear trend to the bicycle sales time series is an example of how simple linear regression can be used to forecast future values of a time series. In that example, bicycle sales (dependent variable) and time (independent variable) were shown to be linearly related.[2] Regression analysis, however, can also be used to develop forecasts in situations where time series data are not available. To illustrate how regression analysis is used in this context, let us consider the sales forecasting problem faced by Armand, Inc.

Using Regression Analysis When Time Series Data Are Not Available

Armand, Inc., is a chain of Italian restaurants located in a five-state area. The most successful locations have been near college campuses. Prior to opening a new restaurant, management requires a forecast of the yearly sales revenues. Such an estimate is used in

---

[2]In a purely technical sense, the number of bicycles sold is not thought of as being causally related to time; instead, time is used as a surrogate for variables that the number of bicycles sold is actually related to but that are unknown or too difficult or too costly to measure.

planning the appropriate restaurant capacity, making initial staffing decisions, and deciding whether the potential revenue justifies the cost of operation. Since no historical data are available on sales at a new store, Armand cannot use time series data to develop the forecast.

Management believes that annual sales revenue is related to the size of the student population on the nearby campus. On an intuitive basis, management believes that restaurants located near large campuses generate more revenue than those located near

Table 16.13

Data on Annual Sales and Student Population for 10 Restaurants

Restaurant	y = **Annual Sales** ($1000s)	x = **Student Population** (1000s)
1	58	2
2	105	6
3	88	8
4	118	8
5	117	12
6	137	16
7	157	20
8	169	20
9	149	22
10	202	26

Figure 16.14

Scatter Diagram of Annual Sales Versus Student Population

small campuses. If a relationship can be established between sales revenue and the size of the campus population, Armand can use the size of the campus population to predict revenues for the new restaurant. To evaluate the relationship between annual sales y and student population x, Armand collected data from a sample of 10 of its restaurants located near college campuses. These data are summarized in Table 16.13. For example, we see that restaurant 1, with $y = 58$ and $x = 2$, had \$58,000 in sales revenue and is located near a campus with 2000 students.

Figure 16.14 shows graphically the data presented in Table 16.13. The size of the student population is shown on the horizontal axis, with annual sales on the vertical axis. A graph such as this is known as a *scatter diagram*. Usually the independent variable is plotted on the horizontal axis, and the dependent variable is plotted on the vertical axis. The advantage of a scatter diagram is that it provides an overview of the data and enables us to draw preliminary conclusions about a possible relationship between the variables.

What preliminary conclusions can we draw from Figure 16.14? It appears that low sales volumes are associated with small student populations and higher sales volumes are associated with larger student populations. It also appears that the relationship between the two variables can be approximated by a straight line. In Figure 16.15 we have drawn a straight line through the data that appears to provide a good linear approximation of the relationship between the variables. Observe that the relationship is not perfect. Indeed, few, if any, of the data items fall exactly on the line. However, if we can develop the mathematical expression for this line, we may be able to use it to predict or forecast the value of y corresponding to each possible value of x. We will refer to the resulting equation of the line as the *estimated regression equation*.

Figure 16.15
Straight-Line Approximation for Data on Annual Sales and Student Population

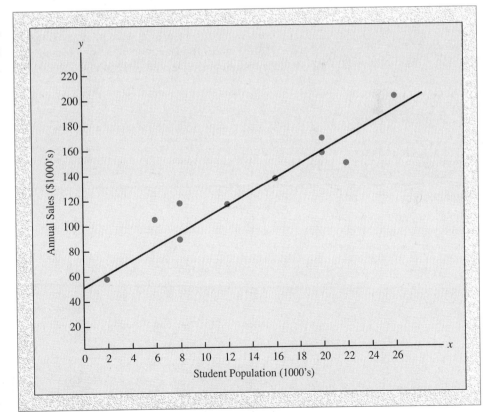

Using the least-squares method of estimation, we can develop the following estimated regression equation:

$$\hat{y} = b_0 + b_1 x \qquad (16.10)$$

where

$\hat{y}$ = estimated value of the dependent variable (sales revenue)
b_0 = intercept of the estimated regression equation
b_1 = slope of the estimated regression equation
x = value of the independent variable (student population)

Using the sample data, the intercept b_0 and slope b_1 can be computed using the following expressions:

$$b_1 = \frac{\Sigma x_i y_i - (\Sigma x_i \, \Sigma y_i)/n}{\Sigma x_i^2 - (\Sigma x_i)^2/n} \qquad (16.11)$$

$$b_0 = \bar{y} - b_1 \bar{x} \qquad (16.12)$$

where

x_i = value of the independent variable for the ith observation
y_i = value of the dependent variable for the ith observation
$\bar{x}$ = mean value for the independent variable
$\bar{y}$ = mean value for the dependent variable
n = total number of observations

Some of the calculations necessary to develop the least-squares estimated regression equation for the data on student population and annual sales are shown in Table 16.14. In our example there are 10 restaurants or observations; hence $n = 10$. Using equations (16.11) and (16.12), we can now compute the slope and intercept of the estimated regression equation. The calculation of the slope b_1 proceeds as follows:

$$b_1 = \frac{\Sigma x_i y_i - (\Sigma x_i \, \Sigma y_i)/n}{\Sigma x_i^2 - (\Sigma x_i)^2/n}$$

$$= \frac{21{,}040 - (140)(1300)/10}{2528 - (140)^2/10}$$

Table 16.14

Calculations Necessary to Develop the Least-Squares Estimated Regression Equation for the Armand Data

Restaurant (i)	y_i	x_i	$x_i y_i$	x_i^2
1	58	2	116	4
2	105	6	630	36
3	88	8	704	64
4	118	8	944	64
5	117	12	1,404	144
6	137	16	2,192	256
7	157	20	3,140	400
8	169	20	3,380	400
9	149	22	3,278	484
10	202	26	5,252	676
Totals	1300	140	21,040	2528

$$= \frac{2840}{568}$$

$$= 5$$

The calculation of the intercept b_0 is as follows:

$$\bar{x} = \frac{\Sigma x_i}{n} = \frac{140}{10} = 14$$

$$\bar{y} = \frac{\Sigma y_i}{n} = \frac{1300}{10} = 130$$

$$b_0 = \bar{y} - b_1\bar{x}$$

$$= 130 - 5(14)$$

$$= 60$$

Thus, the estimated regression equation found by using the method of least squares is

$$\hat{y} = 60 + 5x$$

We show the graph of this equation in Figure 16.16.

The slope of the estimated regression equation ($b_1 = 5$) is positive, implying that as student population increases, annual sales increase. In fact, we can conclude (since sales are measured in thousands of dollars and student population in thousands) that an increase

Figure 16.16
The Estimated Regression
Equation for the Armand Data

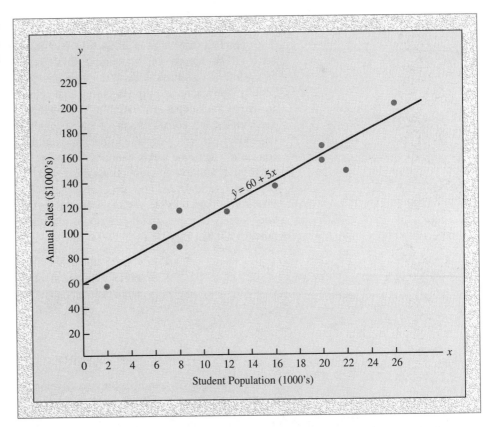

in the student population of 1000 is associated with an increase of $5000 in expected annual sales; that is, sales are expected to increase by $5 per student.

If we believe that the least-squares estimated regression equation adequately describes the relationship between x and y, then it would seem reasonable to use the estimated regression equation to forecast the value of y for a given value of x. For example, if we wanted to forecast annual sales for a new restaurant location near a campus with 16,000 students, we would compute

$$\hat{y} = 60 + 5(16)$$

$$= 140$$

Hence we would forecast sales of $140,000 per year.

The sales forecasting problem faced by Armand, Inc., illustrates how simple linear regression analysis can be used to develop forecasts when time series data are not available. Multiple regression analysis can also be applied in these situations provided additional data for other independent variables are available. For example, suppose that management of Armand, Inc., also believes that the number of competitors near the college campus is related to the annual sales. On an intuitive basis, management believes that restaurants located near campuses where there are fewer competitors generate more sales revenue than those located near campuses where there are more competitors. Given these additional data, multiple regression analysis could be used to develop an equation relating annual sales to the size of the student population and the number of competitors.

> You should now be able to use regression analysis to develop a forecast when time series data are not available. Try Problem 34.

Using Regression Analysis When Time Series Data Are Available

The approach that we used in Section 16.3 to fit a linear trend to the bicycle sales time series is an example of how simple linear regression analysis can be used to forecast future values of a time series when time series data are not available. Recall that for this problem the annual sales in year t was treated as the dependent variable and the year t was treated as the independent variable. The inherent complexity of most real-world problems necessitates the consideration of more than one independent variable to predict the dependent variable. Let us consider how multiple regression analysis is used to develop forecasts when time series data are available.

To use multiple regression analysis, we need a sample of observations for the dependent variable and all independent variables. In time series analysis, the n periods of time series data provide a sample of n observations for each variable. To describe the wide variety of regression-based models that can be developed, we will use the following notation:

$$Y_t = \text{actual value of the time series in period } t$$
$$x_{1t} = \text{value of independent variable 1 in period } t$$
$$x_{2t} = \text{value of independent variable 2 in period } t$$
$$\cdot$$
$$\cdot$$
$$\cdot$$
$$x_{kt} = \text{value of independent variable } k \text{ in period } t$$

The n periods of data necessary to develop the estimated regression equation would appear as follows:

Period	Time Series Value (Y_t)	Value of Independent Variables						
		x_{1t}	x_{2t}	x_{3t}	.	.	.	x_{kt}
1	Y_1	x_{11}	x_{21}	x_{31}	.	.	.	x_{k1}
2	Y_2	x_{12}	x_{22}	x_{32}	.	.	.	x_{k2}
.	.	.	.	.	.	.	.	.
.	.	.	.	.	.	.	.	.
.	.	.	.	.	.	.	.	.
n	Y_n	x_{1n}	x_{2n}	x_{3n}	.	.	.	x_{kn}

As you might imagine, there are a number of choices for the independent variables in a forecasting model. One possible choice is simply time. This is the choice we made in Section 16.3 when we estimated the trend of the time series using a linear function of the independent variable time. Letting

$$x_{1t} = t$$

we obtain an estimated regression equation of the form

$$\hat{Y}_t = b_0 + b_1 t$$

where $\hat{Y}_t$ is the estimate of the time series value Y_t and where b_0 and b_1 are the estimated regression coefficients. In a more complex model, additional terms could be added corresponding to time raised to other powers. For example, if

$$x_{2t} = t^2$$

and

$$x_{3t} = t^3$$

the estimated regression equation would then become

$$\hat{Y}_t = b_0 + b_1 x_{1t} + b_2 x_{2t} + b_3 x_{3t}$$
$$= b_0 + b_1 t + b_2 t^2 + b_3 t^3$$

Note that this model provides a forecast of a time series with curvilinear characteristics over time.

Other regression-based forecasting models employ a mixture of economic and demographic independent variables. For example, in forecasting the sale of refrigerators, we might select independent variables such as the following:

x_{1t} = price in period t
x_{2t} = total industry sales in period $t - 1$
x_{3t} = number of building permits for new houses in period $t - 1$
x_{4t} = population forecast for period t
x_{5t} = advertising budget for period t

According to the usual multiple regression procedure, an estimated regression equation with five independent variables would be used to develop forecasts.

Spyros Makridakis, a noted forecasting expert, has conducted research that shows simple techniques usually outperform more complex procedures for short-term forecasting. Using a more sophisticated and expensive procedure will not guarantee better forecasts.

Whether or not a regression approach provides a good forecast depends largely on how well we are able to identify and obtain data for independent variables that are closely related to the time series. Generally, during the development of an estimated regression equation, we will want to consider many possible sets of independent variables. Thus, part of the regression analysis procedure should focus on the selection of the set of independent variables that provides the best forecasting model.

In the chapter introduction we stated that *causal forecasting models* utilized time series related to the one being forecast in an effort to better explain the cause of a time series' behavior. Regression analysis is the tool most often used in developing these causal models. The related time series become the independent variables, and the time series being forecast is the dependent variable.

Another type of regression-based forecasting model occurs whenever the independent variables are all previous values of the *same* time series. For example, if the time series values are denoted by $Y_1, Y_2, \ldots, Y_n$, we might try to find an estimated regression equation relating Y_t to the most recent time series values, Y_{t-1}, Y_{t-2}, and so on. For instance, using the actual values of the time series for the three most recent periods as independent variables, the estimated regression equation would be

$$\hat{Y}_t = b_0 + b_1 Y_{t-1} + b_2 Y_{t-2} + b_3 Y_{t-3}$$

Regression models such as this, where the independent variables are previous values of the time series, are referred to as *autoregressive models*.

Finally, another regression-based forecasting approach is one that incorporates a mixture of the independent variables previously discussed. For example, we might select a combination of time variables, some economic/demographic variables, and some previous values of the time series variable itself.

16.6 Qualitative Approaches to Forecasting

If historical data are not available, managers must use a qualitative technique to develop forecasts. But, the cost of using qualitative techniques can be very high because of the time commitment required from the people involved.

Empirical evidence and theoretical arguments suggest that between 5 and 20 experts should be used in judgmental forecasting. However, in situations involving exponential growth, judgmental forecasts may be inappropriate.

In the previous sections we discussed several types of quantitative forecasting methods. Since each of these techniques requires historical data on the variable of interest, these techniques cannot be applied in situations where no historical data are available. Furthermore, even when such data are available, a significant change in environmental conditions affecting the time series may make the use of past data questionable in predicting future values of the time series. For example, a government-imposed gasoline rationing program would cause one to question the validity of a gasoline sales forecast based on historical data. Qualitative forecasting techniques offer an alternative in these and other cases.

One of the most commonly used qualitative forecasting methods is the *Delphi approach*. This technique, originally developed by a research group at the Rand Corporation, attempts to develop forecasts through "group consensus." In the usual application of this technique, the members of a panel of experts—all of whom are physically separated from and unknown to each other—are asked to respond to a series of questionnaires. The responses from the first questionnaire are tabulated and used to prepare a second questionnaire that contains information and opinions of the whole group. Each respondent is then asked to reconsider and possibly revise his or her previous response in light of the group information provided. This process continues until the coordinator feels that some degree of consensus has been reached. Note that the goal of the Delphi approach is not to produce a single answer as output, but to produce instead a relatively narrow spread of opinions within which the majority of experts concur.

The qualitative procedure referred to as *scenario writing* consists of developing a conceptual scenario of the future based on a well-defined set of assumptions. Thus, by starting with different sets of assumptions, many different future scenarios can be presented. The job of the decision maker is to decide which scenario is most likely to occur in the future and then to make decisions accordingly.

Subjective or *intuitive qualitative approaches* are based on the ability of the human mind to process a variety of information that is, in most cases, difficult to quantify. These techniques are often used in group work, wherein a committee or panel seeks to develop new ideas or solve complex problems through a series of "brainstorming sessions." In such sessions, individuals are freed from the usual group restrictions of peer pressure and criticism since any idea or opinion can be presented without regard to its relevancy and, even more importantly, without fear of criticism.

Summary

In this chapter we introduced the basic methods of time series analysis and forecasting. First, we showed that to explain the behavior of a time series, it is often helpful to think of the time series as consisting of four separate components: trend, seasonal, irregular, and cyclical. By isolating these components and measuring their apparent effect, it is possible to forecast future values of the time series.

We discussed how smoothing methods can be used to forecast a time series that exhibits no significant trend, seasonal, or cyclical effect. The moving averages approach consists of computing an average of past data values and then using this average as the forecast for the next period. The exponential smoothing method is the preferred technique; it uses a weighted average of past time series values to compute a forecast.

When the time series only exhibits a long-term trend, we showed how regression analysis could be used to make trend projections. When both trend and seasonal influences are significant, we showed how to isolate the effects of the two factors and prepare better forecasts. Finally, regression analysis was described as a procedure for developing so-called causal forecasting models. A causal forecasting model is one that relates the time series value (dependent variable) to other independent variables that are believed to explain (cause) the time series behavior.

Qualitative forecasting methods were discussed as approaches that could be used when little or no historical data are available. These methods are also considered most appropriate when the historical pattern of the time series is not expected to continue into the future.

It is important to realize that time series analysis and forecasting is a major field in its own right. In this chapter we have just scratched the surface of the field of time series and forecasting methodology.

Glossary

Time series A set of observations measured at successive points in time or over successive periods of time.

Forecast A projection or prediction of future values of a time series.

Trend The long-run shift or movement in the time series observable over several periods of data.

Cyclical component The component of the time series model that results in periodic above-trend and below-trend behavior of the time series lasting more than 1 year.

Seasonal component The component of the time series model that shows a periodic pattern over 1 year or less.

Irregular component The component of the time series model that reflects the random variation of the actual time series values beyond what can be explained by the trend, cyclical, and seasonal components.

Moving averages A method of forecasting or smoothing a time series by averaging each successive group of data points. The moving averages method can be used to isolate the seasonal component of the time series.

Mean squared error (MSE) One approach to measuring the accuracy of a forecasting model. This measure is the average of the sum of the squared differences between the forecasted values and the actual time series values.

Weighted moving averages A method of forecasting or smoothing a time series by computing a weighted average of past time series values. The sum of the weights must equal 1.

Exponential smoothing A forecasting technique that uses a weighted average of past time series values to arrive at smoothed time series values that can be used as forecasts.

Smoothing constant A parameter of the exponential smoothing model that provides the weight given to the most recent time series value in the calculation of the forecast.

Multiplicative time series model A model that assumes that the separate components of the time series can be multiplied together to identify the actual time series value. When the four components of trend, cyclical, seasonal, and irregular are assumed present, we obtain $Y_t = T_t \times C_t \times S_t \times I_t$. When cyclical effects are not modeled, we obtain $Y_t = T_t \times S_t \times I_t$.

Deseasonalized time series A time series that has had the effect of season removed by dividing each original time series observation by the corresponding seasonal index.

Regression analysis A statistical technique that can be used to develop a mathematical equation showing how variables are related.

Causal forecasting methods Forecasting methods that relate a time series to other variables that are believed to explain or cause its behavior.

Autoregressive model A time series model that uses a regression relationship based on historical time series values to predict the future time series values.

Delphi approach A qualitative forecasting method that obtains forecasts through group consensus.

Scenario writing A qualitative forecasting method that consists of developing a conceptual scenario of the future based on a well-defined set of assumptions.

Problems

S E L F T E S T

1. Moving averages

1. Corporate Triple A Bond interest rates for 12 consecutive months are shown below.

9.5 9.3 9.4 9.6 9.8 9.7 9.8 10.5 9.9 9.7 9.6 9.6

   a. Develop 3- and 4-month moving averages for this time series. Which moving average provides the better forecasts? Explain.
   b. What is the moving average forecast for the next month?

S E L F T E S T

2. Moving averages

2. Refer to the gasoline sales time series data in Table 16.1.
   a. Compute 4- and 5-week moving averages for the time series.
   b. Compute the MSE for the 4- and 5-week moving average forecasts.
   c. What appears to be the best number of weeks of past data to use in the moving average computation? Remember that the MSE for the 3-week moving average is 10.22.

3. Weighted moving averages

3. Refer again to the gasoline sales time series data in Table 16.1.
   a. Using a weight of ½ for the most recent observation, ⅓ for the second most recent, and ⅙ for third most recent, compute a 3-week weighted moving average for the time series.
   b. Compute the MSE for the weighted moving average in part (a). Do you prefer this weighted moving average to the unweighted moving average? Remember that the MSE for the unweighted moving average is 10.22.

c. Suppose you are allowed to choose any weights as long as they sum to 1. Could you always find a set of weights that would make the MSE smaller for a weighted moving average than for an unweighted moving average? Why or why not?

4. Use the gasoline time series data from Table 16.1 to show the exponential smoothing forecasts using $\alpha = 0.1$. Using the mean squared error criterion, would you prefer a smoothing constant of $\alpha = 0.1$ or $\alpha = 0.2$?

5. Data below show the monthly percentages of all shipments that were received on time over the past 12 months.

$$80 \quad 82 \quad 84 \quad 83 \quad 83 \quad 84 \quad 85 \quad 84 \quad 82 \quad 83 \quad 84 \quad 83$$

a. Compare a 3-month moving average forecast with an exponential smoothing forecast using $\alpha = 0.2$. Which provides the better forecasts?
b. What is the forecast for next month?

6. Using a smoothing constant of $\alpha = 0.2$, equation (16.2) shows that the forecast for the 13th week of the gasoline sales data from Table 16.1 is given by $F_{13} = 0.2Y_{12} + 0.8F_{12}$. However, the forecast for week 12 is given by $F_{12} = 0.2Y_{11} + 0.8F_{11}$. Thus, we could combine these two results to show that the forecast for the 13th week can be written

$$F_{13} = 0.2Y_{12} + 0.8(0.2Y_{11} + 0.8F_{11}) = 0.2Y_{12} + 0.16Y_{11} + 0.64F_{11}$$

a. Making use of the fact that $F_{11} = 0.2Y_{10} + 0.8F_{10}$ (and similarly for F_{10} and F_9), continue to expand the expression for F_{13} until it is written in terms of the past data values $Y_{12}, Y_{11}, Y_{10}, Y_9,$ and Y_8, and the forecast for period 8.
b. Refer to the coefficients or weights for the past data values $Y_{12}, Y_{11}, Y_{10}, Y_9,$ and Y_8; what observation do you make about how exponential smoothing weights past data values in arriving at new forecasts? Compare this weighting pattern with the weighting pattern of the moving averages method.

7. Alabama building contracts for a 12-month period are shown below. Data are in millions of dollars.

$$240 \quad 350 \quad 230 \quad 260 \quad 280 \quad 320 \quad 220 \quad 310 \quad 240 \quad 310 \quad 240 \quad 230$$

a. Compare a 3-month moving average forecast with an exponential smoothing forecast using $\alpha = 0.2$. Which provides the better forecasts?
b. What is the forecast for the next month?

8. The following time series shows the sales of a particular product over the past 12 months:

Month	Sales	Month	Sales
1	105	7	145
2	135	8	140
3	120	9	100
4	105	10	80
5	90	11	100
6	120	12	110

a. Use $\alpha = 0.3$ to compute the exponential smoothing values for the time series.
b. Use a smoothing constant of 0.5 to compute the exponential smoothing values. Does a smoothing constant of 0.3 or 0.5 appear to provide the better forecasts?

9. The Dow Jones Industrial Average is based on common stock prices of 30 industrial stocks. This average is used to describe what is happening in the stock market. The weekly closing levels of the Dow Jones average for 12 weeks are shown below.

Week	Dow Jones	Week	Dow Jones
1	2480	7	2520
2	2470	8	2470
3	2475	9	2440
4	2510	10	2480
5	2500	11	2530
6	2480	12	2550

    a. Compute the exponential smoothing forecasts using $\alpha = 0.2$.
    b. Compute the exponential smoothing forecasts using $\alpha = 0.3$.
    c. Which exponential smoothing model provides the better forecasts? What is the forecast of the Dow Jones Industrial Average for week 13?

10. Exponential smoothing

10. The number of component parts used in a production process during the last 10 weeks are shown below.

Week	Parts	Week	Parts
1	200	6	210
2	350	7	280
3	250	8	350
4	360	9	290
5	250	10	320

Using a smoothing constant of 0.25, develop the exponential smoothing values for this time series. Indicate your forecast for week 11.

11. Exponential smoothing

11. A chain of grocery stores experienced the following weekly demand (cases) for a particular brand of automatic-dishwasher detergent:

Week	Demand	Week	Demand
1	22	6	24
2	18	7	20
3	23	8	19
4	21	9	18
5	17	10	21

Use exponential smoothing with $\alpha = 0.2$ to develop a forecast for week 11.

12. Exponential smoothing

12. United Dairies, Inc., supplies milk to several independent grocers throughout Dade County, Fla. The management of United Dairies would like to develop a forecast of the number of half-gallons of milk sold per week. Sales data for the past 12 weeks are as follows:

Week	Sales (Units)	Week	Sales (Units)
1	2750	7	3300
2	3100	8	3100
3	3250	9	2950
4	2800	10	3000
5	2900	11	3200
6	3050	12	3150

Using exponential smoothing with $\alpha = 0.4$, develop a forecast of demand for week 13.

13. Exponential smoothing

13. Ten weeks of data on the Commodity Futures Index are shown below.

> 7.35   7.40   7.55   7.56   7.60   7.52   7.52   7.70   7.62   7.55

a. Compute the exponential smoothing forecasts using $\alpha = 0.2$.
b. Compute the exponential smoothing forecasts using $\alpha = 0.3$.
c. Which exponential smoothing model provides the better forecasts? What is the forecast for week 11?

SELF TEST ▶   **14.** The enrollment data (1000s) for a state college for the past 6 years are shown below.

14. Trend projection

Year	1	2	3	4	5	6
Enrollment	20.5	20.2	19.5	19.0	19.1	18.8

Develop the equation for the linear trend component for this time series. Comment on what is happening to enrollment at this institution.

15. Trend projection

15. The time series for the retail price index of consumer goods and services over a 9-year period is shown below.

Year	Price Index	Year	Price Index
1	66.9	6	94.6
2	74.8	7	97.8
3	81.2	8	101.9
4	85.0	9	106.9
5	89.2		

Use trend projection to forecast the retail price index for years 10 and 11.

16. Trend projection

16. Average attendance figures at home football games for a major university show the following pattern for the past 7 years:

Year	1	2	3	4	5	6	7
Attendance	28,000	30,000	31,500	30,400	30,500	32,200	30,800

Develop the equation for the linear trend component (equation (16.4)) for this time series.

17. Trend projection

17. Automobile sales at B. J. Scott Motors, Inc., provided the following 10-year time series:

Year	Sales	Year	Sales
1	400	6	260
2	390	7	300
3	320	8	320
4	340	9	340
5	270	10	370

Plot the time series, and comment on the appropriateness of a linear trend. What type of functional form do you believe would be most appropriate for the trend pattern of this time series?

18. Trend projection

18. The president of a small manufacturing firm has been concerned about the continual growth in manufacturing costs over the past several years. Shown below is a time series of the cost per unit for the firm's leading product over the past 8 years.

Year	Cost Per Unit ($)	Year	Cost Per Unit ($)
1	20.00	5	26.60
2	24.50	6	30.00
3	28.20	7	31.00
4	27.50	8	36.00

a. Show a graph of this time series. Does a linear trend appear to exist?
b. Develop the equation for the linear trend component for the above time series. What is the average cost increase that the firm has been realizing per year?

19. Trend projection

19. Earnings per share for the Walgreen Company for a 10-year period are as follows:

0.84   0.73   0.94   1.14   1.33   1.53   1.67   1.68   2.10   2.50

a. Use a linear trend projection to forecast this time series for the coming year.
b. What does this time series analysis tell you about the Walgreen Company? Do the historical data indicate the Walgreen Company is a good investment?

20. Trend projection

20. The gross revenue data for Delta Airlines for a 10-year period are shown below. Data are in millions of dollars.

Year	Revenue	Year	Revenue
1	2428	6	4264
2	2951	7	4738
3	3533	8	4460
4	3618	9	5318
5	3616	10	6915

a. Develop a linear trend expression for this time series. Comment on what the expression tells about the gross revenue for Delta Airlines for the 10-year period.

b. Provide the forecasts of gross revenue for years 11 and 12.

21. Trend projection

21. The vacancy rate for office rentals is reported in terms of the percentage of available offices that are not rented. Office vacancy rates for downtown Philadelphia over an 8-year period are shown below.

Year	Vacancy Rate	Year	Vacancy Rate
1	5.9	5	9.2
2	4.6	6	9.5
3	6.4	7	10.8
4	9.5	8	11.0

a. Develop a linear trend for this time series.

b. Provide forecasts of the vacancy rate for years 9, 10, and 11.

c. Should city planners be concerned with the forecasts of office vacancy? What conclusion should be reached, and what possible actions should the city planners consider?

22. Trend projection

22. Canton Supplies, Inc., is a service firm that employs approximately 100 individuals. Because of the necessity of meeting monthly cash obligations, the management of Canton Supplies would like to develop a forecast of monthly cash requirements. Because of a recent change in operating policy, only the past 7 months of data were considered to be relevant. Use the historical data shown below to develop a forecast of cash requirements for each of the next 2 months using trend projection.

Month	1	2	3	4	5	6	7
Cash Required ($1000s)	205	212	218	224	230	240	246

23. Trend projection

23. Data below show the time series of the most recent quarterly capital expenditures in billions of dollars for the 1000 largest manufacturing firms.

24 25 23 24 22 26 28 31 29 32 37 42

a. Develop a linear trend expression for the above time series.

b. Show a graph of the time series and the linear trend expression.

c. Using the time series, what appears to be happening to the capital expenditures? What is the forecast 1 year or 4 quarters into the future?

24. Trend projection

24. The Costello Music Company has been in business for 5 years. During this time, the sale of electric organs has grown from 12 units in the first year to 76 units in the most recent year. Fred Costello, the firm's owner, would like to develop a forecast of organ sales for the coming year. The historical data are shown below.

Year	1	2	3	4	5
Sales	12	28	34	50	76

a. Show a graph of this time series. Does a linear trend appear to exist?

b. Develop the equation for the linear trend component for the above time series. What is the average increase in sales that the firm has been realizing per year?

25. Hudson Marine has been an authorized dealer for C&D marine radios for the past 7 years. The number of radios sold each year is shown below.

Year	1	2	3	4	5	6	7
Number Sold	35	50	75	90	105	110	130

a. Show a graph of this time series. Does a linear trend appear to exist?
b. Develop the equation for the linear trend component for the above time series.
c. Use the linear trend developed in part (b) to prepare a forecast for annual sales in year 8.

26. Aggregate personal income data by month are as follows:

January	3.92	July	4.05
February	3.96	August	4.08
March	4.00	September	4.10
April	4.01	October	4.12
May	4.02	November	4.18
June	4.04	December	4.22

a. Develop a linear trend expression for the above time series. What was happening to aggregate personal income during the year?
b. Provide estimates of aggregate personal income for the first 6 months of the coming year.
c. Assume that in June of the coming year, the actual level of aggregate personal income turned out to be 4.41. Comment on the forecasting error based on your trend projection.

S ELF T EST ▶

27. The quarterly sales data (number of copies sold) for a college textbook over the past 3 years are as follows:

Quarter	Year 1	Year 2	Year 3
1	1690	1800	1850
2	940	900	1100
3	2625	2900	2930
4	2500	2360	2615

a. Show the 4-quarter moving average values for this time series. Plot both the original time series and the moving averages on the same graph.
b. Compute seasonal indexes for the 4 quarters.
c. When does the textbook publisher experience the largest seasonal index? Does this appear reasonable? Explain.

28. Identify the monthly seasonal indexes for the following 3 years of expenses for a 6-unit apartment house in southern Florida. Use a 12-month moving average calculation.

Month	Year 1	Year 2	Year 3
January	170	180	195
February	180	205	210
March	205	215	230
April	230	245	280
May	240	265	290
June	315	330	390
July	360	400	420
August	290	335	330
September	240	260	290
October	240	270	295
November	230	255	280
December	195	220	250

29. Seasonal indexes, trend, seasonal adjustments

29. Air pollution control specialists in southern California monitor the amount of ozone, carbon dioxide, and nitrogen dioxide in the air on an hourly basis. The hourly time series data exhibit seasonality, with the levels of pollutants showing similar patterns over the hours in the day. On July 15, 16, and 17, the observed levels of nitrogen dioxide in a city's downtown area for the 12 hours from 6:00 A.M. to 6:00 P.M. were as follows:

July 15	25	28	35	50	60	60	40	35	30	25	25	20
July 16	28	30	35	48	60	65	50	40	35	25	20	20
July 17	35	42	45	70	72	75	60	45	40	25	25	25

a. Identify the hourly seasonal indexes for the 12-hour daily readings.
b. Using the seasonal indexes from part (a), the trend equation developed for the deseasonalized data is $T_t = 32.983 + 0.3922t$. Using the trend component only, develop forecasts for the 12 hours for July 18.
c. Use the seasonal indexes from part (a) to adjust the trend forecasts developed in part (b).

30. Seasonal indexes

30. Refer to Problem 25. Suppose the quarterly sales values for the 7 years of historical data are as follows:

Year	Quarter 1	Quarter 2	Quarter 3	Quarter 4	Total Sales
1	6	15	10	4	35
2	10	18	15	7	50
3	14	26	23	12	75
4	19	28	25	18	90
5	22	34	28	21	105
6	24	36	30	20	110
7	28	40	35	27	130

a. Show the 4-quarter moving average values for this time series. Plot both the original time series and the moving averages on the same graph.

b. Compute the seasonal indexes for the 4 quarters.
c. When does Hudson Marine experience the largest seasonal effect? Does this seem reasonable? Explain.

31. Consider the Costello Music Company scenario presented in Problem 24. The quarterly sales data are shown below.

Year	Quarter 1	Quarter 2	Quarter 3	Quarter 4	Total Yearly Sales
1	4	2	1	5	12
2	6	4	4	14	28
3	10	3	5	16	34
4	12	9	7	22	50
5	18	10	13	35	76

a. Compute the seasonal indexes for the 4 quarters.
b. When does Costello Music experience the largest seasonal effect? Does this appear reasonable? Explain.

32. Refer to the Hudson Marine data presented in Problem 30.
a. Deseasonalize the data, and use the deseasonalized time series to identify the trend.
b. Use the results of part (a) above to develop a quarterly forecast for next year based on trend.
c. Use the seasonal indexes developed in Problem 30 to adjust the forecasts developed in part (b) above to account for the effect of season.

33. Consider the Costello Music Company time series presented in Problem 31.
a. Deseasonalize the data, and use the deseasonalized time series to identify the trend.
b. Use the results of part (a) above to develop a quarterly forecast for next year based on trend.
c. Use the seasonal indexes to adjust the forecasts developed in part (b) above to account for the effect of season.

S E L F   T E S T ▶

34. Eddie's Restaurants collected the following data on the relationship between advertising and sales at a sample of five restaurants:

Advertising Expenditures ($1000s)	1.0	4.0	6.0	10.0	14.0
Sales ($1000s)	19.0	44.0	40.0	52.0	53.0

a. Let x equal advertising expenditures and y equal sales. Use the method of least squares to develop a straight-line approximation to the relationship between the two variables.
b. Use the equation developed in part (a) to forecast sales for an advertising expenditure of $8000.

35. The management of a chain of fast-food restaurants would like to investigate the relationship between the daily sales volume of a company restaurant and the number of competitor restaurants within a 1-mile radius of the firm's restaurant. The following data have been collected:

Number of Competitors Within 1 Mile	Sales ($)
1	3600
1	3300
2	3100
3	2900
3	2700
4	2500
5	2300
5	2000

a. Develop the least-squares estimated regression equation that relates daily sales volume to the number of competitor restaurants within a 1-mile radius.

b. Use the estimated regression equation developed in part (a) to forecast the daily sales volume for a particular company restaurant that has four competitors within a 1-mile radius.

36. Forecast using regression analysis

36. In a manufacturing process, the assembly-line speed (feet/minute) was thought to affect the number of defective parts found during the inspection process. To test this theory, management devised a situation where the same batch of parts was inspected visually at a variety of line speeds. The following data were collected:

Line Speed	Number of Defective Parts Found
20	21
20	19
40	15
30	16
60	14
40	17

a. Develop the estimated regression equation that relates line speed to the number of defective parts found.

b. Use the equation developed in part (a) to forecast the number of defective parts found for a line speed of 50 feet per minute.

Case Problem: Forecasting Sales

The Vintage Restaurant is located on Captiva Island, a resort community located near Fort Meyers, Florida. The restaurant, which is owned and operated by Karen Payne, has just completed its third year of operation. During this time, Karen has sought to establish a reputation for the restaurant as a high-quality dining establishment that specializes in fresh seafood. The efforts made by Karen and her staff have proved successful, and her restaurant has become one of the best and fastest-growing restaurants on the island.

Karen has concluded that in order to plan better for the growth of the restaurant in the future, it is necessary to develop a system that will enable her to forecast food and beverage sales by month for up to 1 year in advance. Karen has available data on the total food and beverage sales that were realized during the previous 3 years of operation. These data are provided below.

Food and Beverage Sales for the Vintage Restaurant ($1000s)

Month	First Year	Second Year	Third Year
January	242	263	282
February	235	238	255
March	232	247	265
April	178	193	205
May	184	193	210
June	140	149	160
July	145	157	166
August	152	161	174
September	110	122	126
October	130	130	148
November	152	167	173
December	206	230	235

Managerial Report

Perform an analysis of the sales data for the Vintage Restaurant. Prepare a report for Karen that summarizes your findings, forecasts, and recommendations. Include information on the following:

1. A graph of the time series.
2. An analysis of the seasonality of the data. Include the seasonal indexes for each month, and comment on the high seasonal and low seasonal sales months. Do the seasonal indexes make intuitive sense? Discuss.
3. Forecast sales for January through December of the fourth year.
4. Assume that January sales for the fourth year turned out to be $295,000. What was your forecast error? If this is a large error, Karen may be puzzled as to why there is such a difference between your forecast and the actual sales value. What can you do to resolve her uncertainty in the forecasting procedure?
5. Develop recommendations as to when the system that you have developed should be updated to account for new sales data that will occur.
6. Include any detailed calculations of your analysis in the appendix of your report.

MANAGEMENT SCIENCE IN PRACTICE

The Cincinnati Gas & Electric Company*
Cincinnati, Ohio

The Cincinnati Gas Light and Coke Company was chartered by the state of Ohio on April 3, 1837. Under this charter, the company manufactured gas by distillation of coal and sold it for lighting purposes. During the last quarter of the 19th century, the company successfully marketed gas for lighting, heating, and cooking and as fuel for gas engines.

In 1901 the Cincinnati Gas Light and Coke Company and the Cincinnati Electric Light Company merged to form The Cincinnati Gas & Electric Company (CG&E). This new company was able to shift from manufactured gas to natural gas and adopt the rapidly emerging technologies in generating and distributing electricity. CG&E operated as a subsidiary of the Columbia Gas Electric Company from 1909 until 1944.

Today CG&E is a privately owned public utility serving approximately 420,000 gas customers and 700,000 electric customers. The company's service area covers approximately 3000 square miles in and around the Greater Cincinnati area.

Forecasting at CG&E

As in any modern company, forecasting at CG&E is an integral part of operating and managing the business. Depending on the decision to be made, the forecasting techniques used range from judgment and graphical trend projections to sophisticated multiple regression models.

Forecasting in the utility industry offers some unique perspectives. Since there are no finished-goods or in-process inventories of electricity, this product must be generated to meet the instantaneous requirements of the customers. Electrical shortages are not just lost sales, but "brownouts" or "blackouts." This situation places an unusual burden on the utility forecaster. On the positive side, the demand for energy and the sale of energy are more predictable than for many other products. Also, unlike the situation in a multiproduct firm, a great amount of forecasting effort and expertise can be concentrated on the two products: gas and electricity.

Forecasting Electric Energy and Peak Loads

The two types of forecasts discussed in this section are the long-range forecasts of electric peak load and electric energy. The largest observed electric demand for any given period, such as an hour, a day, a month, or a year, is defined as the peak load. The cumulative amount of energy generated and used over the period of an hour is referred to as electric energy.

Until the mid-1970s the seasonal patterns of both electric energy and electric peak load were very regular; the time series for both of these exhibited a fairly steady exponential growth.

Business cycles had little noticeable effect on either. Perhaps the most serious shift in the behavior of these time series came from the increasing installation of air conditioning units in the Greater Cincinnati area, which caused an accelerated growth in the trend component and also in the relative magnitude of the summer peaks. Nevertheless, the two time series were very regular and generally quite predictable.

Trend projection was the most popular method used to forecast electric energy and electric peak load. The forecast accuracy was quite acceptable and even enviable when compared to forecast errors experienced in other industries.

A New Era in Forecasting

In the mid-1970s a variety of actions by the government, the off-and-on energy shortages, and price signals to the consumer began to affect the consumption of electric energy. The behavior of the peak load and electric energy time series became less predictable, and a simple trend projection forecasting model was no longer adequate. As a result, a special forecasting model—referred to as an econometric model—was developed by CG&E to better account for the behavior of these time series.

The purpose of the econometric model is to forecast the annual energy consumption by residential, commercial, and industrial classes of service. These forecasts are then used to develop forecasts of summer and winter peak loads. First, energy consumption in the industrial and commercial classes is forecast. For an assumed level of economic activity, the projection of electric energy is made along with a forecast of employment in the area. The employment forecast is converted to a forecast of adult population through the use of unemployment rates and labor force participation rates. Household forecasts are then developed through the use of demographic statistics on the average number of persons per household. The resulting forecast of households is used as an indicator of residential customers.

At this point, a comparison is made with the demographic projections for the area population. The differences between the residential customers forecast and the population forecast are reconciled to produce the final forecast of residential customers. This forecast becomes the principal independent variable in forecasting residential electric energy.

—Continued on next page

*The authors are indebted to Dr. Richard Evans, The Cincinnati Gas & Electric Company, Cincinnati, Ohio, for providing this application.

—Continued from previous page

Summer and winter peak loads are then forecast by applying class peak contribution factors to the energy forecasts. The contributions that each class makes toward the peak are summed to establish the peak forecast.

A number of economic and demographic time series are used in the construction of the above econometric model. Simply speaking, the entire forecasting system is a compilation of several statistically verified multiple regression equations.

Impact and Value of the Forecasts

The forecast of the annual electric peak load guides the timing decisions for constructing future generating units, and the financial impact of these decisions is great. For example, a large generating unit built by the company cost nearly $600 million, and the interest rate on a recent first mortgage bond was 16%. At this rate, annual interest costs would be nearly $100 million. Obviously, a timing decision that leads to having the unit available no sooner than necessary is crucial.

The energy forecasts are important in other ways also. For example, purchases of coal as fuel for the generating units are based on the forecast levels of energy needed. The revenue from the electric operations of the company is determined from forecasted sales, which in turn enters into the planning of rate changes and external financing. These planning and decision-making processes are among the most important management activities in the company. It is imperative that the decision makers have the best forecast information available to assist them in arriving at these decisions.

Questions

1. Describe some of the unique perspectives associated with forecasting in the utility industry as compared with other industries.
2. What type of forecasting procedure was used by CG&E into the mid-1970s? What necessitated a change?
3. Briefly describe CG&E's current approach to forecasting.
4. What are the benefits of accurate forecasts for CG&E?

Markov Processes

Markov process models are useful in studying the evolution of certain systems over repeated trials. The repeated trials are often successive time periods where the state or outcome of the system in any particular period cannot be determined with certainty. Rather, transition probabilities are used to describe the manner in which the system makes transitions from one period to the next. Hence, we are interested in the probability of the system being in a particular state at a given time period.

Markov processes have been used to describe the probability that a machine that is functioning in one period will continue to function or will break down in the next period. They have also been used to describe the probability that a consumer purchasing brand A in one period will purchase brand B in the next period. In this chapter we present a marketing application that involves an analysis of the store-switching behavior of supermarket customers. As a second illustration, we will consider an accounting application that is concerned with the transitioning of accounts receivable dollars to different account-aging categories.

Since an in-depth treatment of Markov processes is beyond the scope of this text, the analysis in both illustrations will be restricted to situations in which there are a finite number of states, the transition probabilities remain constant over time, and the probability of being in a particular state at any one time period depends only on the state of the process in the immediately preceding time period. Such Markov processes are referred to as Markov chains with stationary transition probabilities.

17.1 Market Share Analysis

Suppose that we are interested in analyzing the market share and customer loyalty for Murphy's Foodliner and Ashley's Supermarket, the only two grocery stores in a small town. We focus on the sequence of shopping trips of one customer, and assume that the

Many applications of Markov processes use time periods as the trials of the process. Markov processes also can be applied to situations where there are trials representing successive steps of a process.

customer makes one shopping trip each week to either Murphy's Foodliner or Ashley's Supermarket, but not both.

Using the terminology of Markov processes, we refer to the weekly periods or shopping trips as the *trials of the process.* Thus, at each trial, the customer will shop at either Murphy's Foodliner or Ashley's Supermarket. The particular store selected in a given week is referred to as the *state of the system* in that period. Since the customer has two shopping alternatives at each trial, we say the system has two states, and since the number of states is finite, we can identify each state as follows:

State 1 The customer shops at Murphy's Foodliner

State 2 The customer shops at Ashley's Supermarket

If we say the system is in state 1 at trial 3, we are simply saying that the customer shops at Murphy's during the third weekly shopping period.

As we continue the shopping trip process into the future, we cannot say for certain where the customer will shop during a given week or trial. In fact, we realize that during any given week, the customer may be either a Murphy's customer or an Ashley's customer. However, using a Markov process model, we will be able to compute the probability that the customer shops at each store during any period. For example, we may find there is a 0.6 probability that the customer will shop at Murphy's during a particular week and a 0.4 probability that the customer will shop at Ashley's.

To determine the probabilities of the various states occurring at successive trials of the Markov process, we need information on the probability that a customer remains with the same store or switches to the competing store as the process continues from trial to trial or week to week.

Suppose as part of a market research study we collect data from 100 shoppers over a 10-week period. Suppose further that these data show each customer's weekly shopping trip pattern in terms of the sequence of visits to Murphy's and Ashley's. To develop a Markov process model for the sequence of weekly shopping trips, we need to express the probability of selecting each store (state) in a given period solely in terms of the store (state) that was selected during the previous period. In reviewing the data, suppose we find that of all customers who shopped at Murphy's in a given week, 90% shopped at Murphy's the following week while 10% switched to Ashley's. Suppose that similar data for the customers who shopped at Ashley's in a given week show that 80% shopped at Ashley's the following week while 20% switched to Murphy's. Probabilities based on these data are shown in Table 17.1. Since these are the probabilities that a customer moves, or makes a transition, from a state in a given period to each state in the following period, these probabilities are called *transition probabilities.*

Students should recall conditional probability from their probability and statistics courses. Transition probabilities are simply conditional probabilities. The probability the system will be in state A next period given that it is currently in state B can be written as the conditional probability $P(A \mid B)$.

An important property of the table of transition probabilities is that the sum of the entries in each row is 1; this indicates that each row of the table provides a probability distribution. For example, a customer who shops at Murphy's one week must shop at either Murphy's or Ashley's the next week. The entries in row 1 give the probabilities

Table 17.1

Transition Probabilities for Murphy's and Ashley's Grocery Stores

Current Weekly Shopping Period	Next Weekly Shopping Period	
	Murphy's Foodliner	Ashley's Supermarket
Murphy's Foodliner	0.9	0.1
Ashley's Supermarket	0.2	0.8

associated with each of these events. The 0.9 and 0.8 probabilities in Table 17.1 can be interpreted as measures of store loyalty in that they indicate the probability of a repeat visit to the same store. Similarly, the 0.1 and 0.2 probabilities are measures of the store-switching characteristics of the customers. .

It is important to realize that in developing a Markov process model for this problem, we are assuming that the transition probabilities will be the same for any customer and that the transition probabilities will not change over time.

Note that Table 17.1 has one row and one column for each state of the system. We will use the symbol p_{ij} to represent the transition probabilities and the symbol P to represent the matrix of transition probabilities; that is,

$$p_{ij} = \text{probability of making a transition from state } i \text{ in a given period to state } j \text{ in the next period}$$

A quick check for a valid matrix of transition probabilities is to make sure the sum of the probabilities in each row equals 1.

For the supermarket problem, we have

$$P = \begin{bmatrix} p_{11} & p_{12} \\ p_{21} & p_{22} \end{bmatrix} = \begin{bmatrix} 0.9 & 0.1 \\ 0.2 & 0.8 \end{bmatrix}$$

Using the matrix of transition probabilities, we can now determine the probability that a customer will be a Murphy's or an Ashley's customer at some period in the future. Let us begin by assuming that we have a customer whose last weekly shopping trip was to Murphy's. What is the probability that this customer will shop at Murphy's on the next weekly shopping trip, period 1? In other words, what is the probability that the system will be in state 1 after the first transition? The matrix of transition probabilities indicates that this probability is $p_{11} = 0.9$.

Now let us consider the state of the system in period 2. A useful way of depicting what can happen on the second weekly shopping trip is to draw a tree diagram of the possible outcomes (see Figure 17.1). Using this tree diagram, we see that the probability that the customer shops at Murphy's during both the first and the second weeks is $(0.9)(0.9) = 0.81$. Also, note that the probability of the customer switching to Ashley's on the first trip and then switching back to Murphy's on the second trip is $(0.1)(0.2) = 0.02$. Since these are the only two ways that the customer can be in state 1 (shopping at Murphy's) during the second period, the probability of the system being in state 1 during the second period is $0.81 + 0.02 = 0.83$. Similarly, the probability of the system being in state 2 during the second period is $0.09 + 0.08 = 0.17$.

As desirable as the tree diagram approach may be from an intuitive point of view, this approach becomes very cumbersome when we want to extend the analysis to three or more periods into the future. Fortunately, there is an easier way to calculate the probabilities of the system being in state 1 or state 2 for any subsequent period. First, we introduce notation that will allow us to represent these probabilities for any given period. Let

$$\pi_i(n) = \text{probability that the system is in state } i \text{ in period } n$$

Index denotes the state   Denotes the time period or number of transitions

For example, $\pi_1(1)$ would represent the probability of the system being in state 1 in period 1, while $\pi_2(1)$ denotes the probability of the system being in state 2 in period 1. Since $\pi_i(n)$ is the probability that the system is in state i in period n, this probability is referred to as a *state probability*.

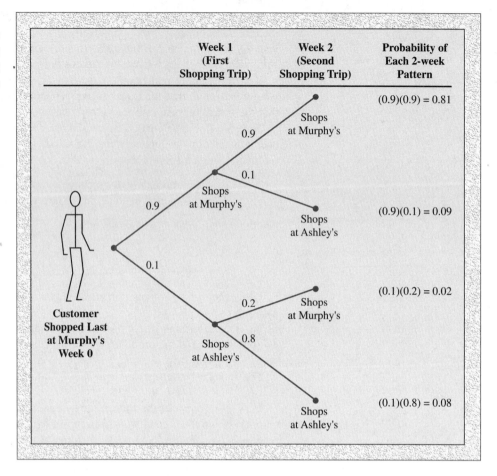

The terms $\pi_1(0)$ and $\pi_2(0)$ will denote the probability of the system being in state 1 or state 2 at some initial or starting period. Week 0 represents the most recent period, when we are beginning the analysis of a Markov process. If we set $\pi_1(0) = 1$ and $\pi_2(0) = 0$, we are saying that as an initial condition the customer shopped last week at Murphy's; alternatively, if we set $\pi_1(0) = 0$ and $\pi_2(0) = 1$, we would be starting the system with a customer who shopped last week at Ashley's. In the tree diagram of Figure 17.1, we consider the situation where the customer shopped last at Murphy's. Thus,

$$[\pi_1(0) \quad \pi_2(0)] = [1 \quad 0]$$

is a vector that represents the initial state probabilities of the system. In general, we use the notation

$$\Pi(n) = [\pi_1(n) \quad \pi_2(n)]$$

to denote the vector of state probabilities for the system in period n. In our example, $\Pi(1)$ is a vector representing the state probabilities for the first week, $\Pi(2)$ is a vector representing the state probabilities for the second week, and so on.

Using this notation, we can find the state probabilities for period $n + 1$ by simply multiplying the known state probabilities for period n by the transition probability matrix.

Using the vector of state probabilities and the matrix of transition probabilities, the multiplication[1] can be expressed as follows:

$$\Pi(\text{next period}) = \Pi(\text{current period})P$$

or

$$\Pi(n + 1) = \Pi(n)P \qquad (17.1)$$

Beginning with the system in state 1 at period 0, we have $\Pi(0) = [1 \ 0]$. We can compute the state probabilities for period 1 as follows:

$$\Pi(1) = \Pi(0)P$$

or

$$[\pi_1(1) \quad \pi_2(1)] = [\pi_1(0) \quad \pi_2(0)] \begin{bmatrix} p_{11} & p_{12} \\ p_{21} & p_{22} \end{bmatrix}$$

$$= [1 \quad 0] \begin{bmatrix} 0.9 & 0.1 \\ 0.2 & 0.8 \end{bmatrix}$$

$$= [0.9 \quad 0.1]$$

The state probabilities $\pi_1(1) = 0.9$ and $\pi_2(1) = 0.1$ are the probabilities that a customer who shopped at Murphy's during week 0 will shop at Murphy's or at Ashley's during week 1.

Using equation (17.1), we can compute the state probabilities for the second week as follows:

$$\Pi(2) = \Pi(1)P$$

or

$$[\pi_1(2) \quad \pi_2(2)] = [\pi_1(1) \quad \pi_2(1)] \begin{bmatrix} p_{11} & p_{12} \\ p_{21} & p_{22} \end{bmatrix}$$

$$= [0.9 \quad 0.1] \begin{bmatrix} 0.9 & 0.1 \\ 0.2 & 0.8 \end{bmatrix}$$

$$= [0.83 \quad 0.17]$$

We see that the probability of shopping at Murphy's during the second week is 0.83, while the probability of shopping at Ashley's during the second week is 0.17. These same results were previously obtained using the tree diagram of Figure 17.1. By continuing to apply equation (17.1), we can compute the state probabilities for any future period; that is,

$$\Pi(3) = \Pi(2)P$$

$$\Pi(4) = \Pi(3)P$$

$$\vdots \qquad \vdots$$

$$\Pi(n + 1) = \Pi(n)P$$

---

[1]Appendix E provides the step-by-step procedure for vector and matrix multiplication.

Table 17.2 shows the result of carrying out these calculations for ten periods.

The vectors $\Pi(1)$, $\Pi(2)$, $\Pi(3)$, . . . contain the probabilities that a customer who started out as a Murphy customer will be in state 1 or state 2 in the first period, the second period, the third period, and so on. In Table 17.2 we see that after a large number of periods these probabilities do not change much from one period to the next.

If we had started with 1000 Murphy customers—that is, 1000 consumers who last shopped at Murphy's—our analysis indicates that during the fifth weekly shopping period, 723 would be customers of Murphy's and 277 would be customers of Ashley's. Moreover, during the tenth weekly shopping period, 676 would be customers of Murphy's and 324 customers of Ashley's.

Now let us repeat the analysis, but this time we will begin the process with a customer who shopped last at Ashley's. Thus,

$$\Pi(0) = [\pi_1(0) \quad \pi_2(0)] = [0 \quad 1]$$

Using equation (17.1), the probability of the system being in state 1 or state 2 in period 1 is given by

$$\Pi(1) = \Pi(0)P$$

or

$$[\pi_1(1) \quad \pi_2(1)] = [\pi_1(0) \quad \pi_2(0)] \begin{bmatrix} p_{11} & p_{12} \\ p_{12} & p_{22} \end{bmatrix}$$

$$= [0 \quad 1] \begin{bmatrix} 0.9 & 0.1 \\ 0.2 & 0.8 \end{bmatrix}$$

$$= [0.2 \quad 0.8]$$

Proceeding as before, we can calculate subsequent state probabilities. Doing so, we obtain the results shown in Table 17.3.

In the fifth shopping period, the probability that the customer will be shopping at Murphy's is 0.555, and the probability that the customer will be shopping at Ashley's is 0.445. In the tenth period, the probability that a customer will be shopping at Murphy's is 0.648, and the probability that a customer will be shopping at Ashley's is 0.352.

Table 17.2

State Probabilities for Future Periods Beginning Initially with a Murphy's Customer

State Probability	Period (n)										
	0	1	2	3	4	5	6	7	8	9	10
$\pi_1(n)$	1	0.9	0.83	0.781	0.747	0.723	0.706	0.694	0.686	0.680	0.676
$\pi_2(n)$	0	0.1	0.17	0.219	0.253	0.277	0.294	0.306	0.314	0.320	0.324

Table 17.3

State Probabilities for Future Periods Beginning Initially with an Ashley's Customer

State Probability	Period (n)										
	0	1	2	3	4	5	6	7	8	9	10
$\pi_1(n)$	0	0.2	0.34	0.438	0.507	0.555	0.589	0.612	0.628	0.640	0.648
$\pi_2(n)$	1	0.8	0.66	0.562	0.493	0.445	0.411	0.388	0.372	0.360	0.352

As we continue the Markov process, we will find that the probability of the system being in a particular state after a large number of periods is independent of the beginning state of the system. The probabilities that we approach after a large number of transitions are referred to as the *steady-state probabilities*. We shall denote the steady-state probability for state 1 with the symbol π_1 and the steady-state probability for state 2 with the symbol π_2. In other words, in the steady-state case, we simply omit the period designation from $\pi_i(n)$ since it is no longer necessary.

The analysis of Tables 17.2 and 17.3 indicates that as n gets larger, the difference between the state probabilities for the nth shopping period and the $(n + 1)$th period becomes increasingly smaller. This leads us to the conclusion that as n gets extremely large, the state probabilities at the $(n + 1)$th period are very close to those at the nth period. This observation provides the basis for a simple method for computing the steady-state probabilities without having to actually carry out a large number of calculations.

In general, we know from equation (17.1) that

$$
\begin{bmatrix} \pi_1(n + 1) & \pi_2(n + 1) \end{bmatrix} = \begin{bmatrix} \pi_1(n) & \pi_2(n) \end{bmatrix} \begin{bmatrix} p_{11} & p_{12} \\ p_{21} & p_{22} \end{bmatrix}
$$

Since for sufficiently large n the difference between $\Pi(n + 1)$ and $\Pi(n)$ is negligible, we see that in the steady state $\pi_1(n + 1) = \pi_1(n) = \pi_1$ and $\pi_2(n + 1) = \pi_2(n) = \pi_2$. Thus, we have

$$
\begin{bmatrix} \pi_1 & \pi_2 \end{bmatrix} = \begin{bmatrix} \pi_1 & \pi_2 \end{bmatrix} \begin{bmatrix} p_{11} & p_{12} \\ p_{21} & p_{22} \end{bmatrix}
$$

$$
= \begin{bmatrix} \pi_1 & \pi_2 \end{bmatrix} \begin{bmatrix} 0.9 & 0.1 \\ 0.2 & 0.8 \end{bmatrix}
$$

After carrying out the above multiplications, we obtain

$$
\pi_1 = 0.9\pi_1 + 0.2\pi_2 \tag{17.2}
$$

and

$$
\pi_2 = 0.1\pi_1 + 0.8\pi_2 \tag{17.3}
$$

However, we also know the steady-state probabilities must sum to 1 with

$$
\pi_1 + \pi_2 = 1 \tag{17.4}
$$

Using equation (17.4) to solve for π_2 and substituting the result in equation (17.2), we obtain

$$
\pi_1 = 0.9\pi_1 + 0.2(1 - \pi_1)
$$

$$
\pi_1 = 0.9\pi_1 + 0.2 - 0.2\pi_1
$$

$$
\pi_1 - 0.7\pi_1 = 0.2
$$

$$
0.3\pi_1 = 0.2
$$

$$
\pi_1 = \tfrac{2}{3}
$$

Then, using equation (17.4), we can conclude that $\pi_2 = 1 - \pi_1 = \tfrac{1}{3}$. Thus, using equations (17.2) and (17.4), we can solve for the steady-state probabilities directly. You can check

The Markov process analysis provides the steady-state probabilities. The starting state of the system does not affect the eventual steady-state probabilities.

A linear programming computer code using an arbitrary objective function can be used to solve for the steady-state probabilities. For instance, using equations (17.2) and (17.4) as constraints, the linear programming model

$$
\begin{aligned}
\text{Max} \quad & \pi_1 + \pi_2 \\
\text{s.t.} \quad & 0.1\pi_1 - 0.2\pi_2 = 0 \\
& \pi_1 + \pi_2 = 1 \\
& \pi_1, \pi_2 \geq 0
\end{aligned}
$$

provides $\pi_1 = 0.667$ and $\pi_2 = 0.333$. The objective function is only included because it is a requirement of the linear programming computer code.

You should now be able to compute the steady-state probabilities for Markov processes with two states. Problem 3 provides an application.

With three states, the steady-state probabilities are found by solving three equations for the three unknown steady-state probabilities. Try Problem 7 as a slightly more difficult problem involving three states.

for yourself that we could have obtained the same result using equations (17.3) and (17.4).[2]

Thus, if we have 1000 customers in the system, the Markov process model tells us that in the long run, with steady-state probabilities $\pi_1 = \frac{2}{3}$ and $\pi_2 = \frac{1}{3}$, $\frac{2}{3}(1000) = 667$ customers would be Murphy's and $\frac{1}{3}(1000) = 333$ customers would be Ashley's. The steady-state probabilities can be interpreted as the market shares for the two stores.

Market share information is often quite valuable in decision making. For example, suppose Ashley's Supermarket is contemplating an advertising campaign to attract more of Murphy's customers to its store. Let us suppose further that Ashley's believes this promotional strategy will increase the probability of a Murphy's customer switching to Ashley's from 0.10 to 0.15. The new transition probabilities that would result are given in Table 17.4.

Given the new transition probabilities, we can modify equations (17.2) and (17.4) to solve for the new steady-state probabilities or market shares. Thus, we obtain

$$\pi_1 = 0.85\pi_1 + 0.20\pi_2$$

Substituting $\pi_2 = 1 - \pi_1$ from equation (17.4), we have

$$\pi_1 = 0.85\pi_1 + 0.20(1 - \pi_1)$$

$$\pi_1 = 0.85\pi_1 + 0.20 - 0.20\pi_1$$

$$\pi_1 - 0.65\pi_1 = 0.20$$

$$0.35\pi_1 = 0.20$$

$$\pi_1 = 0.57$$

and

$$\pi_2 = 1 - 0.57 = 0.43$$

We see that the proposed promotional strategy will increase Ashley's market share from $\pi_2 = 0.33$ to $\pi_2 = 0.43$. Suppose that the total market consists of 6000 customers per week. The new promotional strategy will increase the number of customers doing their weekly shopping at Ashley's from 2000 to 2580. If the average weekly profit per customer is $10, the proposed promotional strategy can be expected to increase Ashley's profits by $5800 per week. If the cost of the promotional campaign is less than $5800 per week, Ashley should consider implementing the strategy.

This is one illustration of how a Markov analysis of a firm's market share can be useful in decision making. Suppose that instead of trying to attract customers from Murphy's Foodliner, Ashley's directed a promotional effort at increasing the loyalty of its own

---

[2]Even though equations (17.2) and (17.3) provide two equations and two unknowns, we must include equation (17.4) when solving for π_1 and π_2 to ensure that the sum of steady-state probabilities will equal 1.

Table 17.4

New Transition Probabilities for Murphy's and Ashley's Grocery Stores

Current Weekly Shopping Period	Next Weekly Shopping Period	
	Murphy's Foodliner	Ashley's Supermarket
Murphy's Foodliner	0.85	0.15
Ashley's Supermarket	0.20	0.80

customers. In this case, p_{22} would increase, and p_{21} would decrease. Once we knew the amount of the change, we could calculate new steady-state probabilities and compute the impact on profits.

NOTES & COMMENTS

1. The Markov processes presented in this section have what is called the *memoryless* property: the current state of the system together with the transition probabilities contains all the information necessary to predict the future behavior of the system. The prior states of the system do not have to be considered. Such Markov processes are considered first-order Markov processes. Higher-order Markov processes are ones in which future states of the system depend on two or more previous states.

2. Analysis of a Markov process model is not intended to optimize any particular aspect of a system. Rather, the analysis predicts or describes the future and steady-state behavior of the system. For instance, in the grocery store example, the analysis of the steady-state behavior provided a forecast or prediction of the market shares for the two competitors. In other applications, management scientists have extended the study of Markov processes to what are called *Markov decision processes*. In these models, decisions can be made at each period that affect the transition probabilities and hence influence the future behavior of the system. Markov decision processes have been used in analyzing machine breakdown and maintenance operations, planning the movement of patients in hospitals, developing inspection strategies, determining newspaper subscription duration, and analyzing equipment replacement.

17.2 Accounts Receivable Analysis

An accounting application where Markov processes have produced useful results involves the estimation of the allowance for doubtful accounts receivable. This allowance is an estimate of the amount of accounts receivable that will ultimately prove to be uncollectible (i.e., bad debts).

Let us consider the accounts receivable situation for Heidman's Department Store. Heidman's has two aging categories for its accounts receivable: (1) accounts that are classified as 0–30 days old and (2) accounts that are classified as 31–90 days old. If any portion of an account balance exceeds 90 days, that portion is written off as a bad debt. Heidman's follows the procedure of aging the total balance in any customer's account according to the oldest unpaid bill. For example, suppose one customer's account balance on September 30 is as follows:

Date of Purchase	Amount Charged
August 15	$25
September 18	10
September 28	50
Total	$85

An aging of accounts receivable on September 30 would assign the total balance of $85 to the 31–90-day category because the oldest unpaid bill of August 15 is 46 days old. Let us assume that one week later, October 7, the customer pays the August 15 bill of $25. The remaining total balance of $60 would now be placed in the 0–30-day category since the oldest unpaid amount, corresponding to the September 18 purchase, is less than 31 days old. This method of aging accounts receivable is called the *total balance method* since the total account balance is placed in the age category corresponding to the oldest unpaid amount.

Note that under the total balance method of aging accounts receivable, dollars appearing in a 31–90-day category at one point in time may appear in a 0–30-day category at a later point in time. In the above example, this was true for $60 of September billings, which shifted from a 31–90-day to a 0–30-day category after the August bill had been paid.

Let us assume that on December 31 Heidman's shows a total of $3000 in its accounts receivable and that the firm's management would like an estimate of how much of the $3000 will eventually be collected and how much will eventually result in bad debts. The estimated amount of bad debts will appear as an allowance for doubtful accounts in the year-ending financial statements.

Let us see how we can view the accounts receivable operation as a Markov process. First, concentrate on what happens to *one* dollar currently in accounts receivable. As the firm continues to operate into the future, we can consider each week as a trial of a Markov process with a dollar existing in one of the following states of the system:

State 1 Paid category

State 2 Bad debt category

State 3 0–30-day category

State 4 31–90-day category

Thus, we can track the week-by-week status of one dollar by using a Markov analysis to identify the state of the system at a particular week or period.

Using a Markov process model with the above states, we define the transition probabilities as follows:

p_{ij} = probability of a dollar in state i in one week moving to state j in the next week

Based on historical transitions of accounts receivable dollars, the following matrix of transition probabilities, P, has been developed for Heidman's Department Store:

$$P = \begin{bmatrix} p_{11} & p_{12} & p_{13} & p_{14} \\ p_{21} & p_{22} & p_{23} & p_{24} \\ p_{31} & p_{32} & p_{33} & p_{34} \\ p_{41} & p_{42} & p_{43} & p_{44} \end{bmatrix} = \begin{bmatrix} 1.0 & 0.0 & 0.0 & 0.0 \\ 0.0 & 1.0 & 0.0 & 0.0 \\ 0.4 & 0.0 & 0.3 & 0.3 \\ 0.4 & 0.2 & 0.3 & 0.1 \end{bmatrix}$$

Note that the probability of a dollar in the 0–30-day category (state 3) moving to the paid category (state 1) in the next period is 0.4. Also, there is a 0.3 probability that this dollar will remain in the 0–30-day category (state 3) one week later, while there is a 0.3 probability that it will be in the 31–90-day category (state 4) one week later. Note also that a dollar in a 0–30-day account cannot make the transition to a bad debt (state 2) in one week.

An important property of the Markov process model for Heidman's accounts receivable situation is the presence of *absorbing states*. For example, once a dollar makes

The Markov processes in Section 17.2 have one or more states from which the system cannot transition. Such states are called *absorbing states*.

When absorbing states are present, each row of the transition matrix corresponding to an absorbing state will have a single 1 and all other probabilities will be 0.

a transition to state 1, the paid state, the probability of making a transition to any other state is zero. Similarly, once a dollar is in state 2, the bad debt state, the probability of a transition to any other state is zero. Thus, once a dollar reaches state 1 or state 2, the system will remain in this state indefinitely. This leads us to conclude that all accounts receivable dollars will eventually be absorbed into either the paid or the bad debt state, and hence the name *absorbing state*.

The Fundamental Matrix and Associated Calculations

Whenever a Markov process has absorbing states, we do not compute steady-state probabilities because each unit ultimately ends up in one of the absorbing states. With absorbing states present, we are interested in knowing the probability that a unit will end up in each of the absorbing states. For the Heidman's Department Store problem, we want to know the probability that a dollar currently in the 0–30-day age category will end up paid (absorbing state 1) as well as the probability that a dollar in this age category will end up a bad debt (absorbing state 2). We also want to know these absorbing-state probabilities for dollars currently in the 31–90-day age category.

The computation of the absorbing-state probabilities requires the determination and use of what is called a *fundamental matrix*. The mathematical logic underlying the fundamental matrix is beyond the scope of this text. However, as we will see, the fundamental matrix is derived from the matrix of transition probabilities and is relatively easy to compute for Markov processes with a small number of states. In the following example, we show the computation of the fundamental matrix and the determination of the absorbing-state probabilities for Heidman's Department Store.

We begin the computations by partitioning the matrix of transition probabilities into the following four parts:

$$P = \begin{bmatrix} 1.0 & 0.0 & | & 0.0 & 0.0 \\ 0.0 & 1.0 & | & 0.0 & 0.0 \\ - & - & - & - & - \\ 0.4 & 0.0 & | & 0.3 & 0.3 \\ 0.4 & 0.2 & | & 0.3 & 0.1 \end{bmatrix} = \begin{bmatrix} 1.0 & 0.0 & | & 0.0 & 0.0 \\ 0.0 & 1.0 & | & 0.0 & 0.0 \\ - & - & - & - & - \\ & R & | & & Q \end{bmatrix}$$

where

$$R = \begin{bmatrix} 0.4 & 0.0 \\ 0.4 & 0.2 \end{bmatrix} \quad Q = \begin{bmatrix} 0.3 & 0.3 \\ 0.3 & 0.1 \end{bmatrix}$$

A matrix *N*, called a *fundamental matrix*, can be calculated using the following formula:

$$N = (I - Q)^{-1} \tag{17.5}$$

where *I* is an identity matrix with 1's on the main diagonal and 0's elsewhere. The superscript -1 is used to indicate the inverse of the matrix $(I - Q)$. In Appendix E we present formulas for finding the inverse of a matrix with two rows and two columns.

Before proceeding, we note that to use equation (17.5), the identity matrix *I* must be chosen such that it has the *same size or dimensionality* as the matrix *Q*. In our example problem, *Q* has two rows and two columns, so we must choose

$$I = \begin{bmatrix} 1.0 & 0.0 \\ 0.0 & 1.0 \end{bmatrix}$$

Let us now continue with the example problem by computing the fundamental matrix.

$$I - Q = \begin{bmatrix} 1.0 & 0.0 \\ 0.0 & 1.0 \end{bmatrix} - \begin{bmatrix} 0.3 & 0.3 \\ 0.3 & 0.1 \end{bmatrix}$$

$$= \begin{bmatrix} 0.7 & -0.3 \\ -0.3 & 0.9 \end{bmatrix}$$

and (see Appendix E)

$$N = (I - Q)^{-1} = \begin{bmatrix} 1.67 & 0.56 \\ 0.56 & 1.30 \end{bmatrix}$$

If we multiply the fundamental matrix N times the R portion of the P matrix, we obtain the probabilities that accounts receivable dollars initially in states 3 or 4 will eventually reach each of the absorbing states. The multiplication of N times R for the Heidman's Department Store problem is shown below (again, see Appendix E for the steps of this matrix multiplication):

$$NR = \begin{bmatrix} 1.67 & 0.56 \\ 0.56 & 1.30 \end{bmatrix} \begin{bmatrix} 0.4 & 0.0 \\ 0.4 & 0.2 \end{bmatrix} = \begin{bmatrix} 0.89 & 0.11 \\ 0.74 & 0.26 \end{bmatrix}$$

The first row of the product NR is the probability that a dollar in the $0-30$-day age category will end up in each of the absorbing states. Thus, we see that there is a 0.89 probability that a dollar in the $0-30$-day category will eventually be paid and a 0.11 probability that it will become a bad debt. Similarly, the second row shows the probabilities associated with a dollar in the $31-90$-day category; that is, a dollar in the $31-90$-day category has a 0.74 probability of eventually being paid and a 0.26 probability of proving to be uncollectible. Using this information, we can predict the amount of money that will be paid and the amount that will be lost as bad debts.

Problem 14 at the end of the chapter is an interesting example for the students to consider. Since six states are involved, a computer solution is recommended.

Establishing the Allowance for Doubtful Accounts

Let B represent a two-element vector that contains the current accounts receivable balances in the $0-30$-day and the $31-90$-day age categories; that is,

$$B = [b_1 \quad b_2]$$

Total dollars in the $0-30$-day category   Total dollars in the $31-90$-day category

Suppose that the December 31 balance of accounts receivable for Heidman's shows $1000 in the $0-30$-day category (state 3) and $2000 in the $31-90$-day category (state 4).

$$B = [1000 \quad 2000]$$

We can multiply B times NR to determine how much of the $3000 will be collected and how much will be lost. For example

$$BNR = [1000 \quad 2000] \begin{bmatrix} 0.89 & 0.11 \\ 0.74 & 0.26 \end{bmatrix}$$

$$= [2370 \quad 630]$$

Thus, we see that $2370 of the accounts receivable balances will be collected and $630 will have to be written off as a bad debt expense. Based on this analysis, the accounting department would set up an allowance for doubtful accounts of $630.

The matrix multiplication of *BNR* is simply a convenient way of computing the eventual collections and bad debts of the accounts receivable. Recall that the *NR* matrix showed a 0.89 probability of collecting dollars in the 0–30-day category and a 0.74 probability of collecting dollars in the 31–90-day category. Thus, as was shown by the *BNR* calculation, we expect to collect a total of $(1000)0.89 + (2000)0.74 = 890 + 1480 = \$2370$.

Suppose that on the basis of the previous analysis Heidman's would like to investigate the possibility of reducing the amount of bad debts. Recall that our analysis indicated that a 0.11 probability or 11% of the dollars in the 0–30-day age category and 26% of the amount in the 31–90-day age category will prove to be uncollectible. Let us assume that Heidman's is considering instituting a new credit policy involving a discount for prompt payment.

Management believes that the policy under consideration will increase the probability of a transition from the 0–30-day age category to the paid category and decrease the probability of a transition from the 0–30-day to the 31–90-day age category. Let us assume that a careful study of the effects of this new policy leads management to conclude that the following transition matrix would be applicable:

$$P = \begin{bmatrix} 1.0 & 0.0 & | & 0.0 & 0.0 \\ 0.0 & 1.0 & | & 0.0 & 0.0 \\ - & - & - & - & - \\ 0.6 & 0.0 & | & 0.3 & 0.1 \\ 0.4 & 0.2 & | & 0.3 & 0.1 \end{bmatrix}$$

We see that the probability of a dollar in the 0–30-day age category making a transition to the paid category in the next period has increased to 0.6 and that the probability of a dollar in the 0–30-day age category making a transition to the 31–90-day category has decreased to 0.1. To determine the effect of these changes on bad debt expense, we must calculate *N*, *NR*, and *BNR*. We begin by using equation (17.5) to calculate the fundamental matrix *N*:

$$N = (I - Q)^{-1} = \left\{ \begin{bmatrix} 1.0 & 0.0 \\ 0.0 & 1.0 \end{bmatrix} - \begin{bmatrix} 0.3 & 0.1 \\ 0.3 & 0.1 \end{bmatrix} \right\}^{-1}$$

$$= \begin{bmatrix} 0.7 & -0.1 \\ -0.3 & 0.9 \end{bmatrix}^{-1}$$

$$= \begin{bmatrix} 1.5 & 0.17 \\ 0.5 & 1.17 \end{bmatrix}$$

By multiplying *N* times *R*, we obtain the new probabilities that the dollars in each age category will end up in the two absorbing states:

$$NR = \begin{bmatrix} 1.5 & 0.17 \\ 0.5 & 1.17 \end{bmatrix} \begin{bmatrix} 0.6 & 0.0 \\ 0.4 & 0.2 \end{bmatrix}$$

$$= \begin{bmatrix} 0.97 & 0.03 \\ 0.77 & 0.23 \end{bmatrix}$$

We see that with the new credit policy we would expect only 3% of the funds in the 0–30-day age category and 23% of the funds in the 31–90-day age category to prove to be uncollectible. If, as before, we assume that there is a current balance of $1000 in the 0–30-day age category and $2000 in the 31–90-day age category, we can calculate the total amount of accounts receivable that will end up in the two absorbing states by multiplying *B* times *NR*. We obtain

$$BNR = \begin{bmatrix} 1000 & 2000 \end{bmatrix} \begin{bmatrix} 0.97 & 0.03 \\ 0.77 & 0.23 \end{bmatrix}$$

$$= \begin{bmatrix} 2510 & 490 \end{bmatrix}$$

Problem 11, which provides a variation of Heidman's Department Store problem, will give you practice in analyzing Markov processes with absorbing states.

Under the previous credit policy, we found the bad debt expense to be $630. Thus, a savings of $630 − $490 = $140 could be expected as a result of the new credit policy. Given our total accounts receivable balance of $3000, this is a 4.7% reduction in bad debt expense. After considering the costs involved, management can evaluate the economics of adopting the new credit policy. If the cost, including discounts, is less than 4.7% of the accounts receivable balance, we would expect the new policy to lead to increased profits for Heidman's Department Store.

Summary

In this chapter we have presented Markov process models as well as examples of their application. We saw that a Markov analysis could provide helpful decision-making information about a situation that involves a sequence of repeated trials with a finite number of possible outcomes or states on each trial. A primary objective is obtaining information about the probability of each state having a large number of transitions or time periods in the future.

A market share application showed the computational procedure for determining the steady-state probabilities that could be interpreted as market shares for two competing supermarkets. In an accounts receivable application, we introduced the notion of absorbing states; the two absorbing states were the bad debt and paid categories, and we showed how to determine the percentage of an accounts receivable balance that would be absorbed in each of these states.

Glossary

Trials of the process The events that trigger transitions of the system from one state to another. In many applications, successive time periods represent the trials of the process.

State of the system The condition of the system at any particular trial or time period.

Transition probability Given the system is in state i during one period, the transition probability p_{ij} is the probability that the system will be in state j during the next period.

State probability The probability that the system will be in any particular state. (That is, $\pi_i(n)$ is the probability of the system being in state i in period n.)

Steady-state probability The probability that the system will be in any particular state after a large number of transitions. Once steady state has been reached, the state probabilities do not change from period to period.

Absorbing state A state is said to be absorbing if the probability of making a transition out of that state is zero. Thus, once the system has made a transition into an absorbing state, it will remain there.

Fundamental matrix A matrix necessary for the computation of probabilities associated with absorbing states of a Markov process.

Problems

1. Computing the state probabilities during each of several periods

1. In the market share analysis of Section 17.1, suppose that we are considering the Markov process associated with the shopping trips of one customer, but we do not know where the customer shopped during the last week. Thus, we might make the assumption that there is a 0.5 probability that the customer shopped at Murphy's and a 0.5 probability that the customer shopped at Ashley's at period 0; that is, $\pi_1(0) = 0.5$ and $\pi_2(0) = 0.5$. Given these initial state probabilities, develop a table similar to Table 17.2 showing the probability of each state in future periods. What do you observe about the long-run probabilities of each state?

2. Management of the New Fangled Softdrink Company believes that the probability of a customer purchasing Red Pop or the company's major competition, Super Cola, is based on the customer's most recent purchase. Suppose the following transition probabilities are appropriate:

	To	
From	Red Pop	Super Cola
Red Pop	0.9	0.1
Super Cola	0.1	0.9

a. Show the two-period tree diagram for a customer who last purchased Red Pop. What is the probability that this customer purchases Red Pop on the second purchase?

b. What is the long-run market share for each of these two products?

c. A Red Pop advertising campaign is being planned to increase the probability of attracting Super Cola customers. Management believes that the new campaign will increase the probability of a customer switching from Super Cola to Red Pop to 0.15. What is the projected effect of the advertising campaign on the market shares?

3. The computer center at Rockbottom University has been experiencing computer downtime. Let us assume that the trials of an associated Markov process are defined as 1-hour periods and that the probability of the system being in a running state or a down state is based on the state of the system in the previous period. Historical data show the following transition probabilities:

	To	
From	Running	Down
Running	0.90	0.10
Down	0.30	0.70

a. If the system is initially running, what is the probability of the system being down in the next hour of operation?

b. What are the steady-state probabilities of the system being in the running state and in the down state?

4. One cause of the downtime in Problem 3 was traced to a specific piece of computer hardware. Management believes that switching to a different hardware component will result in the following transition probability matrix:

	To	
From	Running	Down
Running	0.95	0.05
Down	0.60	0.40

a. What are the steady-state probabilities of the system being in the running and down states?

b. If the cost of the system being down for any period is estimated to be $500 (including lost profits for time down and maintenance), what is the breakeven cost for the new hardware component on a time-period basis?

5. A major traffic problem in the Greater Cincinnati area involves traffic attempting to cross the Ohio River from Cincinnati to Kentucky using Interstate I-75. Let us assume that the probability of no traffic delay in one period, given no traffic delay in the preceding period, is 0.85 and that the probability of finding a traffic delay in one period, given a delay in the preceding period, is 0.75. Traffic is classified as having either a delay or a no-delay state, and the period considered is 30 minutes.

   a. Assuming you are a motorist entering the traffic system and receive a radio report of a traffic delay, what is the probability that for the next 60 minutes (two time periods) the system will be in the delay state? Note that this is the probability of being in the delay state for two consecutive periods.

   b. What is the probability that in the long run the traffic will not be in the delay state?

   c. An important assumption of the Markov process models presented in this chapter has been the constant or stationary transition probabilities as the system operates in the future. Do you believe this assumption should be questioned in the above traffic problem? Explain.

6. Data collected from selected major metropolitan areas in the eastern United States show that 2% of individuals living within the city limits move to the suburbs during a 1-year period while 1% of individuals living in the suburbs move to the city during a 1-year period. Answer the following questions assuming this process is modeled by a Markov process with two states: city and suburbs.

   a. Show the matrix of transition probabilities.

   b. Compute the steady-state probabilities.

   c. In a particular metropolitan area, 40% of the population live in the city and 60% of the population live in the suburbs. What population changes do your steady-state probabilities project for this metropolitan area?

7. Assume a third grocery store, Quick Stop Groceries, enters the market share and customer loyalty situation described in Section 17.1. Quick Stop Groceries is smaller than either Murphy's Foodliner or Ashley's Supermarket. However, Quick Stop's convenience with faster service and gasoline for automobiles can be expected to attract some customers who currently make weekly shopping visits to either Murphy's or Ashley's. Assume the transition probabilities are as shown below:

	To		
From	Murphy's	Ashley's	Quick Stop
Murphy's Foodliner	0.85	0.10	0.05
Ashley's Supermarket	0.20	0.75	0.05
Quick Stop	0.15	0.10	0.75

a. Compute the steady-state probabilities for this three-state Markov process.

b. What market share will Quick Stop obtain?

c. With 1000 customers, the original two-state Markov process in Section 17.1 projected 667 weekly customer trips to Murphy's Foodliner and 333 weekly customer trips to Ashley's Supermarket. What impact will Quick Stop apparently have on the customer visits at Murphy's and Ashley's? Explain.

8. The purchase patterns of two brands of toothpaste can be expressed as a Markov process with the following transition probabilities:

	To	
From	Special B	MDA
Special B	0.90	0.10
MDA	0.05	0.95

a. Which brand appears to have the most loyal customers? Explain.
b. What are the projected market shares for the two brands?

9. Suppose that in Problem 8 a new toothpaste brand enters the market such that the following transition probabilities exist:

	To		
From	Special B	MDA	T-White
Special B	0.80	0.10	0.10
MDA	0.05	0.75	0.20
T-White	0.40	0.30	0.30

What are the new long-run market shares? Which brand will suffer most from the introduction of the new brand of toothpaste?

10. Given the following transition matrix with states 1 and 2 as absorbing states, what is the probability that units in states 3 and 4 end up in each of the absorbing states?

$$P = \begin{bmatrix} 1.0 & 0.0 & 0.0 & 0.0 \\ 0.0 & 1.0 & 0.0 & 0.0 \\ 0.2 & 0.1 & 0.4 & 0.3 \\ 0.2 & 0.2 & 0.1 & 0.5 \end{bmatrix}$$

11. In the Heidman's Department Store problem of Section 17.2, suppose the following transition matrix is appropriate:

$$P = \begin{bmatrix} 1.0 & 0.0 & 0.0 & 0.0 \\ 0.0 & 1.0 & 0.0 & 0.0 \\ 0.5 & 0.0 & 0.25 & 0.25 \\ 0.5 & 0.2 & 0.05 & 0.25 \end{bmatrix}$$

If Heidman's has $4000 in the 0–30-day age category and $5000 in the 31–90-day age category, what is your estimate of the amount of bad debts the company will experience?

12. The KLM Christmas Tree Farm owns a plot of land with 5000 evergreen trees. Each year KLM allows retailers of Christmas trees to select and cut trees for sale to individual customers. KLM protects small trees (usually less than 4 feet tall) so that they will be available for sale in future years. Currently 1500 trees are classified as protected trees, while the remaining 3500 are available for cutting. However, even though a tree is available for cutting in a given year, it may not be selected for cutting until future years.

While most trees not cut in a given year live until the next year, some diseased trees are lost every year.

In viewing the KLM Christmas tree operation as a Markov process with yearly periods, we define the following four states:

State 1 Cut and sold

State 2 Lost to disease

State 3 Too small for cutting

State 4 Available for cutting but not cut and sold

The following transition matrix is appropriate:

$$P = \begin{bmatrix} 1.0 & 0.0 & 0.0 & 0.0 \\ 0.0 & 1.0 & 0.0 & 0.0 \\ 0.1 & 0.2 & 0.5 & 0.2 \\ 0.4 & 0.1 & 0.0 & 0.5 \end{bmatrix}$$

How many of the farm's 5000 trees will be sold eventually, and how many will be lost?

13. Managerial promotions with two absorbing states

13. A large corporation has collected data on the reasons both middle managers and senior managers eventually leave the company. Some managers eventually retire, but others leave the company prior to retirement for personal reasons including more attractive positions with other firms. Assume that the following matrix of 1-year transition probabilities applies with the four states of the Markov process being retirement, leaves prior to retirement for personal reasons, stays as a middle manager, stays as a senior manager.

	Retirement	**Leaves— Personal**	**Middle Manager**	**Senior Manager**
Retirement	1.00	0.00	0.00	0.00
Leaves—Personal	0.00	1.00	0.00	0.00
Middle Manager	0.03	0.07	0.80	0.10
Senior Manager	0.08	0.01	0.03	0.88

a. What states are considered absorbing states? Why?
b. Interpret the transition probabilities for the middle managers.
c. Interpret the transition probabilities for the senior managers.
d. What percentage of the current middle managers will eventually retire from the company? What percentage will leave the company for personal reasons?
e. The company currently has 920 managers: 640 middle managers and 280 senior managers. How many of these managers will eventually retire from the company? How many will leave the company for personal reasons?

14. College dropout model with two absorbing states; computer solution suggested because the process has six states

14. Data for the progression of college students at a particular college are summarized in the following matrix of transition probabilities.

	Graduate	**Dropout**	**Freshmen**	**Sophomore**	**Junior**	**Senior**
Graduate	1.00	0.00	0.00	0.00	0.00	0.00
Dropout	0.00	1.00	0.00	0.00	0.00	0.00
Freshmen	0.00	0.20	0.15	0.65	0.00	0.00
Sophomore	0.00	0.15	0.00	0.10	0.75	0.00
Junior	0.00	0.10	0.00	0.00	0.05	0.85
Senior	0.90	0.05	0.00	0.00	0.00	0.05

a. What states are absorbing states?

b. Interpret the transition probabilities for a sophomore.

c. Use the Management Scientist software package to compute the probabilities that a sophomore will graduate and that a sophomore will drop out.

d. In an address to the incoming class of 600 freshmen, the dean asks the students to look around the auditorium and realize that about ½ of the freshmen present today will not make it to graduation day. Does your Markov process analysis support the dean's statement? Explain.

e. Currently, the college has 600 freshmen, 520 sophomores, 460 juniors, and 420 seniors. What percentage of the 2000 students attending the college will eventually graduate?

MANAGEMENT SCIENCE IN PRACTICE

U.S. General Accounting Office*
Washington, D.C.

The U.S. General Accounting Office (GAO) is an independent, nonpolitical audit organization in the legislative branch of the federal government. The GAO was created by the Budget and Accounting Act of 1921 and has three basic purposes:

1. To assist Congress, its committees, and its members in carrying out their legislative and oversight responsibilities, consistent with its role as an independent, nonpolitical agency.
2. To audit and evaluate the programs, activities, and financial operations of federal departments and agencies and to make recommendations toward more efficient and effective operations.
3. To carry out financial control and other functions with respect to federal government programs and operations including accounting, legal, and claims settlement work.

GAO evaluators, the main occupation in the GAO, determine the effectiveness of existing or proposed federal programs and the efficiency, economy, legality, and effectiveness with which federal agencies carry out their responsibilities. These evaluations culminate in reports to the Congress and to the heads of federal departments and agencies. Such reports typically include recommendations to Congress concerning the need for enabling or remedial legislation and suggestions to agencies concerning the need for changes in programs or operations to improve their economy, efficiency, and effectiveness.

GAO evaluators analyze policies and practices and the use of resources within and among federal programs, identify problem areas and deficiencies in meeting program goals, develop and analyze alternative solutions to problems of program execution, and develop and recommend changes to enable the programs to better conform to congressional goals and legislative intent. To effectively carry out their duties, evaluators must be proficient in interviewing, data processing, records review, legislative research, management science, and statistical analysis techniques.

Impact of Services on the Well-being of Older People

GAO evaluators obtained data from a random sample of noninstitutionalized persons aged 65 and older living in Cleveland, Ohio. The health conditions of the sampled individuals in the 65- to 69-year-old groups were defined by the following three states:

- **Best.** Individual able to perform 13 identified activities of daily living without help.

- **Next best.** Individual able to perform the same 13 activities, but required help for at least one activity.
- **Worst.** Individual unable to perform the same 13 activities even with help.

Using a 2-year period, GAO evaluators developed estimates of the year-to-year transition probabilities for individuals in the 65- to 69-year-old group. These estimates were then used to develop a transition probability matrix such as that shown in Table 17.5. Note that a death state has been added as an absorbing state.

Using the transition probabilities, a Markov process analysis can be used to determine the state probabilities for any number of periods (years) into the future. To verify the appropriateness of the Markov process model, GAO evaluators used the transition probabilities to determine the state probabilities for the 65- to 69-year-old age group 5 years into the future. The resulting state probabilities were compared with the health states of individuals in a known 70- to 74-year-old age group. There was no statistically significant difference between the probabilities provided by the model and the actual state probabilities of the 70- to 74-year-old group.

Table 17.5
Transition Probability Matrix for the Health Condition of Individuals 65–69 Years Old

Current Year Condition	Following Year Condition			
	Best	Next Best	Worst	Death
Best	p_{11}	p_{12}	p_{13}	p_{14}
Next Best	p_{21}	p_{22}	p_{23}	p_{24}
Worst	p_{31}	p_{32}	p_{33}	p_{34}
Death	0	0	0	1

—Continued on next page

---

*The authors are indebted to Bill Ammann, U.S. General Accounting Office, Washington, D.C., for providing this application.

—Continued from previous page

Estimating the Likely Effects of Health Care Programs

The individuals in the original study were subdivided into two groups: those receiving appropriate health care and those not receiving appropriate health care. For the purpose of the study, a person was classified as receiving appropriate health care if the person was taking medication and/or treatment for each illness present and if the person was receiving help to perform each of the 13 activities of daily living as specifically needed. As a result, GAO evaluators developed two matrices of transition probabilities: one for individuals receiving appropriate health care and one for individuals not receiving appropriate health care.

For any individuals not receiving appropriate help, the kind of additional help needed was determined, and the cost of that help was estimated. Then those persons were artificially aged using the transition probabilities to establish the likely benefits in terms of improved health states for the individuals. Over a 20-year period, there was a net savings for the health care program provided all other factors remained equal. That is, the increased cost to provide sufficient appropriate help to all persons was eventually offset by individuals either improving their health state or by not spending as much time in a worse state. Although benefits of health care are often proclaimed theoretically, the Markov process model provided evidence that indicated benefits would be achieved with the health care program.

This type of Markov analysis was also conducted for economic, social, and life view status as well as for the health status. In some instances, the Markov model showed that additional help and/or programs did not result in net savings over time.

Questions

1. Suppose the transition probabilities in Table 17.5 were as follows:

$$\begin{bmatrix} 0.80 & 0.10 & 0.06 & 0.04 \\ 0.05 & 0.75 & 0.15 & 0.05 \\ 0.00 & 0.05 & 0.75 & 0.20 \\ 0.00 & 0.00 & 0.00 & 1.00 \end{bmatrix}$$

   Assume a particular city has 1000 individuals in the best state, 2000 in the next best state, and 500 in the worst state. Estimate how many of each of these individuals will be in each state 2 years from now.

2. How might health care programs affect the matrix of transition probabilities in question (1)? What effect would you expect to see in the distribution of individuals across the four states 2 years from now?

Dynamic Programming

D*ynamic programming* is an approach to problem solving that permits decomposing one large mathematical model that may be very difficult to solve into a number of smaller problems that are usually much easier to solve. Moreover, the dynamic programming approach allows us to break up a large problem in such a fashion that once all the smaller problems have been solved, we are left with an optimal solution to the large problem. We shall see that each of the smaller problems is identified with a *stage* of the dynamic programming solution procedure. As a consequence, the technique has been applied to many decision problems that are multistage in nature. Often, multiple stages are created because a sequence of decisions must be made over time. For example, a problem of determining an optimal decision over a 1-year horizon might be broken into 12 smaller stages, where each stage requires an optimal decision over a 1-month horizon. In most cases, each of these smaller problems cannot be considered to be completely independent of the others, and this is where dynamic programming is helpful. Let us begin by discovering how to solve a shortest-route problem using dynamic programming.

18.1 A Shortest-Route Problem

In Chapter 9 we studied a labeling algorithm for solving the shortest-route problem. Let us now illustrate the dynamic programming approach by using it to solve a shortest-route problem. Consider the network presented in Figure 18.1. Assuming that the numbers above each arc denote the direct distance in miles between two nodes, find the shortest route from node 1 to node 10.

Before attempting to solve this problem, let us note an important characteristic of shortest-route problems. This characteristic is actually a restatement of Richard Bellman's famous *principle of optimality* as it applies to the shortest-route problem.[1]

---

[1]See S. Dreyfus, *Dynamic Programming and the Calculus of Variations* (New York: Academic Press, 1965).

Figure 18.1
Network for the Shortest-Route
Problem

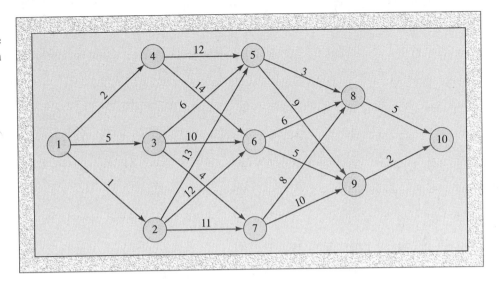

Figure 18.1
Network for the Shortest-Route
Problem

THE PRINCIPLE OF OPTIMALITY

If a particular node is on the optimal route, then the shortest path from that node to the end is also on the optimal route.

The dynamic programming approach to the shortest route problem essentially involves treating each node as if it were on the optimal route and making calculations accordingly. In doing so, work backward by starting at the terminal node, node 10, and calculating the shortest route from each node to node 10 until we reach the origin, node 1. Then we will have solved the original problem of finding the shortest route from node 1 to node 10.

As we stated in the introduction to this chapter, dynamic programming decomposes the original problem into a number of smaller problems that are much easier to solve. In the shortest-route problem for the network in Figure 18.1, the smaller problems that we will create define a four-stage dynamic programming problem. The first stage begins with nodes that are exactly one arc away from the destination and ends at the destination node. Note from Figure 18.1 that only nodes 8 and 9 are exactly one arc away from node 10. The second stage begins with all nodes that are exactly two arcs away from the destination and ends with all nodes that are exactly one arc away. Hence, in dynamic programming terminology, nodes 5, 6, and 7 would be considered the input nodes for stage 2, and nodes 8 and 9 would be considered the output nodes for stage 2. The output nodes for stage 2 are the input nodes for stage 1. The input nodes for the third-stage problem are those that are exactly three arcs away from the destination—that is, nodes 2, 3, and 4. The output nodes, all of which are one arc closer to the destination, are nodes 5, 6, and 7. Finally, the input to stage 4 is node 1, and the output nodes are 2, 3, and 4. The decision problem we shall want to solve at each stage is, Which arc is best to travel over in moving from each particular input node to an output node? Let us consider the stage 1 problem.

We arbitrarily begin the stage 1 calculations with node 9. Since there is only one way to travel from node 9 to node 10, this is obviously the shortest route and requires us to travel a distance of 2 miles. Similarly, there is only one path from node 8 to node 10. The

The dynamic programming procedure moves backwards through the sequence of decisions; the stage 1 problem involves finding the best choice for the last decision to actually be made. Here this means that we first find the best way to move from nodes 8 or 9 to the end (node 10).

shortest route from node 8 to the end is thus the length of that route, or 5 miles. The stage 1 decision problem is solved. For each input node, we have identified an optimal decision—that is, the best arc to travel over to reach the output node. The stage 1 results are summarized below.

	Stage 1	
Input Node	**Arc (decision)**	**Shortest Distance to Node 10**
8	8–10	5
9	9–10	2

To begin the solution to the stage 2 problem, we move to node 7. (We could have selected node 5 or 6; the order of the nodes selected at any stage is arbitrary.) There are two arcs that leave node 7 and are connected to input nodes for stage 1. These are arc 7–8, which has a length of 8, and arc 7–9, which has a length of 10. If we select arc 7–8, we will have a distance from node 7 to node 10 of 8 (i.e., the length of arc 7–8) plus the shortest distance to node 10 from node 8. Thus, the decision to select arc 7–8 has a total associated distance of $8 + 5 = 13$. With a distance of 10 for arc 7–9 and stage 1 results showing a distance of 2 from node 9 to node 10, the decision to select arc 7–9 has an associated distance of $10 + 2 = 12$. Thus, given we are at node 7, we should select arc 7–9 since it is on the path that will reach node 10 in the shortest distance (12 miles). By performing similar calculations for nodes 5 and 6, we can generate the following stage 2 results:

	Stage 2		
Input Node	**Arc (decision)**	**Output Node**	**Shortest Distance to Node 10**
5	5–8	8	8
6	6–9	9	7
7	7–9	9	12

In Figure 18.2 the number in the square by each node considered so far indicates the length of the shortest route from that node to the end. We have completed the solution to the first two subproblems (stages 1 and 2). We now know the shortest route from nodes 5, 6, and 7 to node 10.

To begin the third stage, let us start with node 2. To find the shortest route from node 2 to node 10, we must make three calculations because we have three arcs that connect node 2 to stage 2 input nodes. If we select arc 2–7 and then follow the shortest route to the end, we will travel $11 + 12 = 23$ miles. Similarly, selecting arc 2–6 requires $12 + 7 = 19$ miles, and selecting arc 2–5 requires $13 + 8 = 21$ miles. Thus, the shortest route from node 2 to node 10 is 19 miles, which indicates that arc 2–6 is the best decision, given that we are at node 2. Similarly, we find that the shortest route from node 3 to node 10 is given by Min $\{4 + 12, 10 + 7, 6 + 8\} = 14$; the shortest route from node 4 to node

Figure 18.2
Intermediate Solution to the
Shortest-Route Problem Using
Dynamic Programming

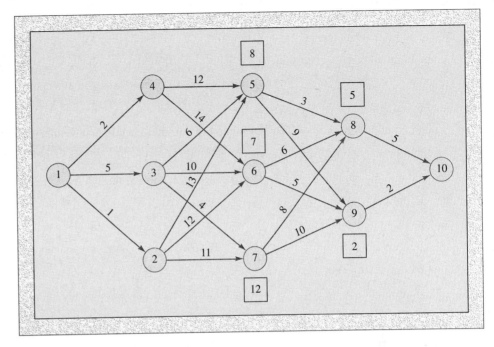

10 is given by Min {14 + 7, 12 + 8} = 20. This completes the stage 3 calculations. The results are summarized below.

		Stage 3	
Input Node	**Arc (decision)**	**Output Node**	**Shortest Distance to Node 10**
2	2–6	6	19
3	3–5	5	14
4	4–5	5	20

In solving the stage 4 subproblem, we find that the shortest route from node 1 to node 10 is given by Min {1 + 19, 5 + 14, 2 + 20} = 19. Thus, the optimal decision at stage 4 is the selection of arc 1–3. By moving through the network from stage 4 to stage 3 to stage 2 to stage 1, we can identify the best decision at each stage and therefore the shortest route from node 1 to node 10. This is as follows:

Stage	**Arc (decision)**
4	1– 3
3	3– 5
2	5– 8
1	8–10

Thus, the shortest route is through nodes 1–3–5–8–10 with a distance of 5 + 6 + 3 + 5 = 19 miles.

Note how the calculations at each successive stage make use of the calculations at prior stages. This characteristic is an important part of the dynamic programming procedure. Figure 18.3 illustrates the final network calculations. Note that in working back through the stages we have now determined the shortest route from every node to node 10.

Dynamic programming, while enumerating or evaluating several paths at each stage, does not require us to enumerate all possible paths from node 1 to node 10. Returning to the stage 4 calculations, we consider three alternatives for leaving node 1. The complete route associated with each of these alternatives is presented below.

Arc Alternatives at Node 1	Complete Path to Node 10	Distance	
1–2	1–2–6–9–10	20	
1–3	1–3–5–8–10	19	← Selected as best
1–4	1–4–5–8–10	22	

Try Problem 2, part (a), for practice solving a shortest-route problem using dynamic programming.

When you realize that there are a total of 16 alternate routes from node 1 to node 10, you can see that dynamic programming has provided substantial computational savings over a total enumeration of all possible solutions.

The fact that we did not have to evaluate all the paths at each stage as we moved backward from node 10 to node 1 is illustrative of the power of dynamic programming. Using dynamic programming, we need only make a small fraction of the number of

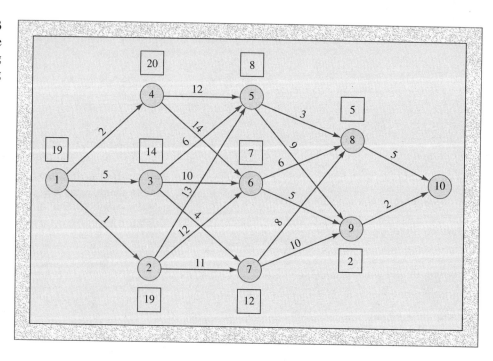

Figure 18.3
Final Solution to the Shortest-Route Problem Using Dynamic Programming

calculations that would be required using total enumeration. If our example network had been larger, the computational savings provided by dynamic programming would have been even greater.

18.2 Dynamic Programming Notation

Perhaps one of the most difficult aspects of learning to apply dynamic programming involves understanding the notation. The notation we will use is the same as that used by Nemhauser[2] and is fairly standard.

The *stages* of a dynamic programming solution procedure are formed by decomposing the original problem into a number of subproblems. Associated with each subproblem is a stage in the dynamic programming solution procedure. For example, the shortest-route problem introduced in the preceding section was solved using a four-stage dynamic programming solution procedure. We had four stages because we decomposed the original problem into the following four subproblems:

1. **Stage 1 Problem:** Where should we go from nodes 8 and 9 so that we will reach node 10 along the shortest route?
2. **Stage 2 Problem:** Using the results of stage 1, where should we go from nodes 5, 6, and 7 so that we will reach node 10 along the shortest route?
3. **Stage 3 Problem:** Using the results of stage 2, where should we go from nodes 2, 3, and 4 so that we will reach node 10 along the shortest route?
4. **Stage 4 Problem:** Using the results of stage 3, where should we go from node 1 so that we will reach node 10 along the shortest route?

Let us look closely at what occurs at the stage 2 problem. Consider the following representation of this stage:

Using dynamic programming notation, we define

x_2 = input to stage 2; represents the location in the network at the beginning of stage 2 (node 5, 6, or 7).

d_2 = decision variable at stage 2 (This represents the arc selected to move to stage 1.)

x_1 = output for stage 2 (This will be the node we reach (node 8 or 9) after considering the input x_2 and the decision d_2. This will also be the input to stage 1.)

---

[2]See G. L. Nemhauser, *Introduction to Dynamic Programming* (New York: Wiley, 1966).

Using this notation, the stage 2 problem can be represented as follows:

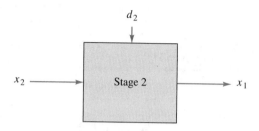

Recall that using dynamic programming to solve the shortest-route problem, we worked backward through the stages, beginning at node 10. When we reached stage 2, we did not know x_2 because the stage 3 problem had not yet been solved. The approach used was to consider *all* alternatives for the input x_2. Then we determined the best decision d_2 for each of the inputs x_2. Later, when we moved forward through the system to recover the optimal sequence of decisions, we saw that the stage 3 decision provided a specific x_2, node 5, and from our previous analysis we knew the best decision (d_2) to make as we continued on to stage 1.

Let us consider a general dynamic programming problem with N stages and adopt the following general notation:

$$x_n = \text{input to stage } n \text{ (output from stage } n + 1\text{)}$$
$$d_n = \textit{decision variable at stage } n$$

The general N-stage problem is decomposed as follows:

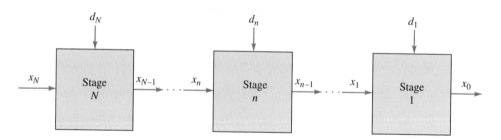

The four-stage shortest-route problem can be represented as follows:

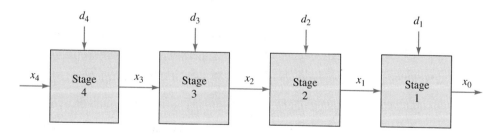

The values of the input and output variables x_4, x_3, x_2, x_1, and x_0 are important because they couple the four subproblems together. At any stage, we will ultimately need to know the input x_n to make the best decision d_n. These x_n variables can be thought of as defining the *state* or condition of the system as we move from stage to stage. Accordingly, these variables are referred to as the *state variables* of the problem. In the shortest-route problem, the state variables represented the location in the network at each stage (i.e., a particular node).

At stage 2 of the shortest-route problem, we considered the input x_2 and made the decision d_2 that would provide the shortest distance to the destination. The output x_1 was based on a combination of the input and the decision; that is, x_1 was a function of x_2 and d_2. In dynamic programming notation, we could write

$$x_1 = t_2(x_2, d_2)$$

where $t_2(x_2, d_2)$ is the function at stage 2 that determines the stage 2 output. Since $t_2(x_2, d_2)$ is the function that "transforms" the input to the stage into the output, this function is referred to as the *stage transformation function*.

The general expression for the stage transformation function is

$$x_{n-1} = t_n(x_n, d_n) \tag{18.1}$$

The mathematical form of the stage transformation function is dependent on the particular dynamic programming problem. In the shortest-route problem, the transformation function was based on a tabular type of calculation. For example, Table 18.1 shows the stage transformation function $t_2(x_2, d_2)$ for stage 2. The possible values of d_2 are the arcs selected in the body of the table.

Each stage also has a return associated with it. In the shortest-route problem, the return was the arc distance traveled in moving from an input node to an output node. For example, if node 7 were the input state for stage 2 and we selected arc 7–9 as d_2, the return for that stage would be the arc length, 10 miles. The return at a stage, which may be thought of as the payoff or value for a stage, is represented by the general notation $r_n(x_n, d_n)$.

Using the stage transformation function and the *return function*, our shortest-route problem can be shown as follows.

Table 18.1

Stage Transformation $x_1 = t_2(x_2, d_2)$ for Stage 2. A Table Showing the Value of x_1 Corresponding to Each Value of x_2.

x_2 Input State	x_1 Output State 8	9
5	5–8	5–9
6	6–8	6–9
7	7–8	7–9

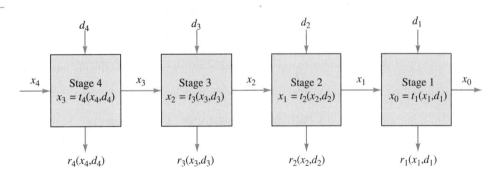

If we view a system or a process as consisting of N stages, we can represent a dynamic programming formulation schematically as follows:

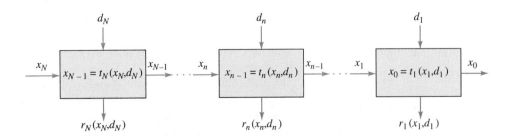

Each of the squares in the diagram represents a stage in the process. As indicated, there are two inputs to each stage: the state variable and the decision variable. There are also two outputs: a new value for the state variable and a return for the stage. The new value for the state variable is determined as a function of the inputs using $t_n(x_n, d_n)$. The value of the return for a stage is also determined as a function of the inputs using $r_n(x_n, d_n)$.

> The optimal total return depends only on the state variable.

In addition, we will use the notation $f_n(x_n)$ to represent the optimal total return from stage n and all remaining stages, given an input of x_n to stage n. For example, in the shortest-route problem, $f_2(x_2)$ represents the optimal total return (i.e., the minimum distance) from stage 2 and all remaining stages, given an input of x_2 to stage 2. Thus, we see from Figure 18.3 that $f_2(x_2 = \text{node } 5) = 8, f_2(x_2 = \text{node } 6) = 7,$ and $f_2(x_2 = \text{node } 7) = 12$. These are just the values in the squares at nodes 5, 6, and 7.

NOTES & COMMENTS

1. The primary advantage of dynamic programming is its "divide and conquer" solution strategy. Using dynamic programming, a large, complex problem can be divided into a sequence of smaller interrelated problems. By solving the smaller problems sequentially, the optimal solution to the larger problem is found. Dynamic programming is a general approach to problem solving; it is not a specific technique such as linear programming, which can be applied in the same fashion to a variety of problems. Although there are some common characteristics of all dynamic programming problems, each application requires some degree of creativity, insight, and expertise to recognize how the larger problems can be broken into a sequence of interrelated smaller problems.

2. Dynamic programming has been applied to a wide variety of problems including inventory control, production scheduling, capital budgeting, resource allocation, equipment replacement, and maintenance. In many of these applications, periods such as days, weeks, and months, provide the sequence of interrelated stages for the larger multiperiod problem.

18.3 The Knapsack Problem

The *knapsack problem* is another problem that can be solved using dynamic programming. The basic idea of the knapsack problem is that there are N different types of items that can be put into a knapsack. Each item has a certain weight associated with it as well as a value. The problem is to determine how many units of each item to place in the knapsack to maximize the total value. A constraint is placed on the maximum weight permissible.

Consider a manager of a manufacturing operation who must make a biweekly selection of jobs from each of 4 categories to process during the following 2-week period. A list showing the number of jobs waiting to be processed at the beginning of the current week is presented in Table 18.2. The estimated time required for completion and the value rating associated with each job category are also shown.

The value rating assigned to each job category is a subjective score assigned by the supervisor. A scale from 1 to 20 is used to measure the value of each job, where 1 represents jobs of the least value, and 20 represents jobs of most value. The value of a job

Table 18.2
Job Data for the Manufacturing
Operation

Category	Number of Jobs to Be Processed	Estimated Completion Time Per Job (days)	Value Rating
1	4	1	2
2	3	3	8
3	2	4	11
4	2	7	20

depends on such things as expected profit, length of time the job has been waiting to be processed, priority, and so on. In this situation, we would like to select certain jobs during the next 2 weeks such that all the jobs selected can be processed within 10 days and the total value of the jobs selected is maximized. In knapsack problem terminology, we are in essence selecting the best jobs for our 2-week (10 working days) knapsack, where the knapsack has a capacity equal to the 10-day production capacity. Let us formulate and solve this problem using dynamic programming.

This problem can be formulated as a dynamic programming problem involving four stages. At stage 1, we must decide how many jobs from category 1 to process; at stage 2, we must decide how many jobs from category 2 to process; and so on. Thus, we let

d_n = number of jobs in category n selected (decision variable at stage n)
x_n = number of days processing time remaining at beginning of stage n
(state variable for stage n)

Thus, with a 2-week production period, $x_4 = 10$ represents the total number of days available for processing jobs. The stage transformation functions are then defined so that

> The knapsack problem can also be solved as an integer programming problem. The following formulation is applicable here
>
> Max $2x_1 + 8x_2 + 11x_3 + 20x_4$
>
> s.t.
>
> $x_1 + 3x_2 + 4x_3 + 7x_4 \leq 10$
>
> $x_1 \leq 4, x_2 \leq 3, \ x_3 \leq 2, \ x_4 \leq 2$
>
> $x_i \geq 0$ for all i and integer

$$\text{Stage 4:} \quad x_3 = t_4(x_4, d_4) = x_4 - 7d_4$$

$$\text{Stage 3:} \quad x_2 = t_3(x_3, d_3) = x_3 - 4d_3$$

$$\text{Stage 2:} \quad x_1 = t_2(x_2, d_2) = x_2 - 3d_2$$

$$\text{Stage 1:} \quad x_0 = t_1(x_1, d_1) = x_1 - 1d_1$$

The return at each stage is based on the value rating of the associated job category and the number of jobs selected from that category. The return functions are as follows:

$$\text{Stage 4:} \quad r_4(x_4, d_4) = 20d_4$$

$$\text{Stage 3:} \quad r_3(x_3, d_3) = 11d_3$$

$$\text{Stage 2:} \quad r_2(x_2, d_2) = 8d_2$$

$$\text{Stage 1:} \quad r_1(x_1, d_1) = 2d_1$$

Figure 18.4 shows a schematic of the problem.

As with the shortest-route problem in Section 18.1, we will apply a backward solution procedure; that is, we will begin by assuming that decisions have already been made for stages 4, 3, and 2 and that the final decision remains (how many jobs from category 1 to select at stage 1). A restatement of the principle of optimality can be made in terms of this problem. That is, regardless of whatever decisions have been made at previous stages, if the decision at stage n is to be part of an optimal overall strategy, the decision made at stage n must necessarily be optimal for all remaining stages.

Figure 18.4
Dynamic Programming
Formulation of the Job Selection
Problem

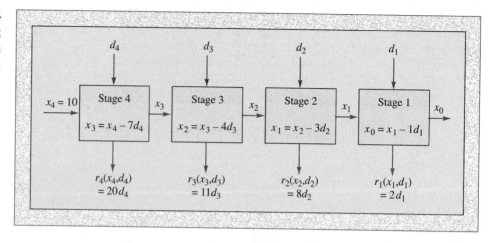

Let us set up a table that will help us calculate the optimal decisions for stage 1.

Stage 1 Note that stage 1's input (x_1), the number of days of processing time available at stage 1, is unknown because we have not yet identified the decisions at the previous stages. Therefore, in our analysis at stage 1, we will have to consider all possible values of x_1 and identify the best decision d_1 for each case; $f_1(x_1)$ will be the total return after decision d_1 is made. The possible values of x_1 and the associated d_1 and $f_1(x_1)$ values are as follows:

x_1	d_1^*	$f_1(x_1)$
0	0	0
1	1	2
2	2	4
3	3	6
4	4	8
5	4	8
6	4	8
7	4	8
8	4	8
9	4	8
10	4	8

The d_1^* column gives the optimal values of d_1 corresponding to a particular value of x_1, where x_1 can range from 0 to 10. The specific value of x_1 will depend on how much processing time has been used by the jobs in the other categories selected in stages 2, 3, and 4. Since each stage 1 job requires 1 day of processing time and has a positive return of 2 per job, we always select as many jobs at this stage as possible. The number of category 1 jobs selected will depend on the processing time available, but cannot exceed four.

Recall that $f_1(x_1)$ represents the value of the optimal total return from stage 1 and all remaining stages, given an input of x_1 to stage 1. Therefore, $f_1(x_1) = 2x_1$ for values of $x_1 \leq 4$. The optimization of stage 1 is accomplished. Let us now move on to stage 2 and carry out the optimization at that stage.

Stage 2 Again, we will use a table to help identify the optimal decision. Since stage 2's input (x_2), is unknown, we have to consider all possible values from 0 to 10. Also, we have to consider all possible values of d_2 (i.e., 0, 1, 2, or 3). The entries under the heading $r_2(x_2, d_2) + f_1(x_1)$ represent the total return that will be forthcoming from the final two stages, given the input of x_2 and the decision of d_2. For example, if stage 2 were entered with $x_2 = 7$ days of processing time remaining, and if a decision were made to select two jobs from category 2 (i.e., $d_2 = 2$), the total return for stages 1 and 2 would be 18.

d_2	$r_2(x_2, d_2) + f_1(x_1)$						$x_1 = t_2(x_2, d_2^*)$
x_2	0	1	2	3	d_2^*	$f_2(x_2)$	$= x_2 - 3d_2^*$
0	⓪	—	—	—	0	0	0
1	②	—	—	—	0	2	1
2	④	—	—	—	0	4	2
3	6	⑧	—	—	1	8	0
4	8	⑩	—	—	1	10	1
5	8	⑫	—	—	1	12	2
6	8	14	⑯	—	2	16	0
7	8	16	⑱	—	2	18	1
8	8	16	⑳	—	2	20	2
9	8	16	22	㉔	3	24	0
10	8	16	24	㉖	3	26	1

The return for stage 2 would be $r_2(x_2, d_2) = 8d_2 = 8(2) = 16$, and with $x_2 = 7$ and $d_2 = 2$, we would have $x_1 = x_2 - 3d_2 = 7 - 6 = 1$. From the previous table, we see that the optimal return from stage 1 with $x_1 = 1$ is $f_1(1) = 2$. Thus, the total return corresponding to $x_2 = 7$ and $d_2 = 2$ is given by $r_2(7,2) + f_1(1) = 16 + 2 = 18$. Similarly, with $x_2 = 5$, and $d_2 = 1$, we get $r_2(5,1) + f_1(2) = 8 + 4 = 12$. Note that some combinations of x_2 and d_2 are not feasible. For example, with $x_2 = 2$ days, $d_2 = 1$ is infeasible because category 2 jobs each require 3 days to process. The infeasible solutions are indicated by a dash.

After all the total returns in the rectangle have been calculated, we can determine an optimal decision at this stage for each possible value of the input or state variable x_2. For example, if $x_2 = 9$, there are four possible values we can select for d_2: 0, 1, 2, or 3. Clearly $d_3 = 3$ with a value of 24 yields the maximum total return for the last two stages. Therefore, we record this value in the d_2^* column. For additional emphasis, we circle the element inside the rectangle corresponding to the optimal return. The optimal total return, given that we are in state $x_2 = 9$ and must pass through two more stages, is thus 24, and we record this value in the $f_2(x_2)$ column. Given that we enter stage 2 with $x_2 = 9$ and make the optimal decision there of $d_2^* = 3$, we will enter stage 1 with $x_1 = t_2(9, 3) = x_2 - 3d_2 = 9 - 3(3) = 0$. This value is recorded in the last column in the table. We can now go on to stage 3.

Stage 3   The table we construct here is much the same as for stage 2. The entries under the heading $r_2(x_3, d_3) + f_2(x_2)$ represent the total return over stages 3, 2, and 1 for all possible inputs x_3 and all possible decisions d_3.

x_3 \\ d_3	$r_3(x_3, d_3) + f_2(x_2)$			d_3^*	$f_3(x_3)$	$x_2 = t_3(x_3, d_3^*)$ $= x_3 - 4d_3^*$
	0	1	2			
0	⓪	—	—	0	0	0
1	②	—	—	0	2	1
2	④	—	—	0	4	2
3	⑧	—	—	0	8	3
4	10	⑪	—	1	11	0
5	12	⑬	—	1	13	1
6	⑯	15	—	0	16	6
7	18	⑲	—	1	19	3
8	20	21	㉒	2	22	0
9	㉔	23	㉔	0,2	24	9,1
10	26	㉗	26	1	27	6

There are some features of interest in this table that were not present at stage 2. We note that if the state variable $x_3 = 9$, then there are two decisions that will lead to an optimal total return from stages 1, 2, and 3; that is, we may elect to process no jobs from category 3, in which case, we will obtain no return from stage 3, but will enter stage 2 with $x_2 = 9$. Since $f_2(9) = 24$, the selection of $d_3 = 0$ would result in a total return of 24. However, a selection of $d_3 = 2$ also leads to a total return of 24. We obtain a return of $11(d_3) = 11(2) = 22$ for stage 3 and a return of 2 for the remaining two stages since $x_2 = 1$. To show that there are alternative optimal solutions at this stage, we have placed two entries in the d_3^* and $x_2 = t_3(x_3, d_3^*)$ columns. The other entries in this table are calculated in the same manner as at stage 2. Let us now move on to the last stage.

Stage 4   Since we know that there are 10 days available in the planning period, the input to stage 4 is $x_4 = 10$. Thus, we have to consider only one row in the table, corresponding to stage 4.

x_4 \\ d_4	$r_4(x_4, d_4) + f_3(x_3)$		d_4^*	$f_4(x_4)$	$x_3 = t_4(x_4, d_4^*)$ $= 10 - 7d_4^*$
	0	1			
10	27	㉘	1	28	3

The optimal decision, given $x_4 = 10$, is $d_4^* = 1$.

We have completed the dynamic programming solution of this problem. To identify the overall optimal solution, we must now trace back through the tables, beginning at stage 4, the last stage considered. The optimal decision at stage 4 is $d_4^* = 1$. Thus, $x_3 = 10 - 7d_4^* = 3$, and we enter stage 3 with 3 days available for processing. With $x_3 = 3$, we see that the best decision at stage 3 is $d_3^* = 0$. Thus, we enter stage 2 with $x_2 = 3$. The optimal decision at stage 2 with $x_2 = 3$ is $d_2^* = 1$, resulting in $x_1 = 0$. Finally, the decision at stage 1 must be $d_1^* = 0$. The optimal strategy for our manufacturing operation is then as follows:

Decision	Return
$d_1^* = 0$	0
$d_2^* = 1$	8
$d_3^* = 0$	0
$d_4^* = 1$	20
Total	28

We should schedule one job from category 2 and one job from category 4 for processing over the next 10-day planning period.

Another advantage of the dynamic programming approach can now be illustrated. Suppose we wanted to schedule the jobs to be processed over an 8-day period only. We can solve this new problem simply by making a recalculation at stage 4. The new stage 4 table would appear as follows:

x_4 \ d_4	$r_4(x_4,d_4) + f_3(x_3)$ 0	1	d_4^*	$f_4(x_4)$	$x_3 = t_4(x_4, d_4^*)$ $= 8 - 7d_4^*$
8	㉒	㉒	0,1	22	8,1

> This ability to provide sensitivity analysis with respect to the number of days available is an advantage of dynamic programming over integer programming.

Actually, we are testing the sensitivity of our optimal solution to a small change in the total number of days available for processing. We have here the case of alternative optimal solutions. One solution can be found by setting $d_4^* = 0$ and tracing through the tables. Doing so, we obtain the following:

Decision	Return
$d_1^* = 0$	0
$d_2^* = 0$	0
$d_3^* = 2$	22
$d_4^* = 0$	0
Total	22

A second optimal solution can be found by setting $d_4^* = 1$ and tracing back through the tables. Doing so, we obtain another solution (which has exactly the same total return):

Decision	Return
$d_1^* = 1$	2
$d_2^* = 0$	0
$d_3^* = 0$	0
$d_4^* = 1$	20
Total	22

You should now be able to solve a knapsack problem using dynamic programming. Try Problem 3.

From the shortest-route and the knapsack examples you should start to become familiar with the basic stage-by-stage solution procedure of dynamic programming. In the next section we see how dynamic programming can be used to solve a production and inventory control problem.

18.4   A Production and Inventory Control Problem

Suppose we have developed forecasts of the demand for a particular product over a certain number of periods and we would like to decide on a production quantity for each of the periods so that demand can be satisfied at a minimum cost. There are two costs to be considered: production costs and holding costs. We will assume that one production setup will be made each period; thus, setup costs will be constant. As a result, setup costs are not considered in the analysis.

We will allow the production and holding costs to vary across periods. This makes the model more flexible since it also allows for the possibility of using different facilities for production and storage in different periods. Production and storage capacity constraints, which may vary across periods, will be included in the model. Let us adopt the following notation:

N = number of periods (stages in the dynamic programming formulation)
D_n = demand during stage n; $n = 1, 2, \ldots, N$
x_n = a state variable representing the amount of inventory on hand at the beginning of stage n; $n = 1, 2, \ldots, N$
d_n = decision variable for stage n; the production quantity for the corresponding period; $n = 1, 2, \ldots, N$
P_n = production capacity in stage n; $n = 1, 2, \ldots, N$
W_n = storage capacity at the end of stage n; $n = 1, 2, \ldots, N$
C_n = production cost per unit in stage n; $n = 1, 2, \ldots, N$
H_n = holding cost per unit of ending inventory for stage n; $n = 1, 2, \ldots, N$

We will develop the dynamic programming solution for a problem covering 3 months of operation. The data for our problem are presented in Table 18.3. We can think of each month as a stage in a dynamic programming formulation. Figure 18.5 shows a schematic of such a formulation. Note that the beginning inventory in January is one unit.

In Figure 18.5 we have numbered the periods backward; that is, stage 1 corresponds to March, stage 2 corresponds to February, and stage 3 corresponds to January. The stage

Table 18.3
Production and Inventory Control Problem Data

Month	Demand	Capacity		Cost Per Unit	
		Production	Storage	Production	Holding
January	2	3	2	$175	$30
February	3	2	3	150	30
March	3	3	2	200	40

The beginning inventory for January is one unit.

Figure 18.5
Production and Inventory Control
Problem as a Three-Stage
Dynamic Programming Problem

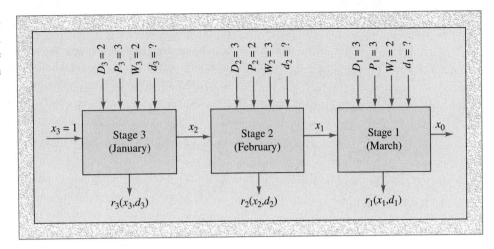

transformation functions take the form of ending inventory = beginning inventory + production − demand. Thus, we have

$$x_3 = 1$$

$$x_2 = x_3 + d_3 - D_3 = x_3 + d_3 - 2$$

$$x_1 = x_2 + d_2 - D_2 = x_2 + d_2 - 3$$

$$x_0 = x_1 + d_1 - D_1 = x_1 + d_1 - 3$$

The return functions for each stage represent the sum of production and holding costs for the month. For example, in stage 1 (March), $r_1(x_1, d_1) = 200d_1 + 40(x_1 + d_1 - 3)$ represents the total production and holding costs for the period. The production costs are $200 per unit, and the holding costs are $40 per unit of ending inventory. The other return functions are

$$r_2(x_2, d_2) = 150d_2 + 30(x_2 + d_2 - 3) \qquad \text{Stage 2, February}$$

$$r_3(x_3, d_3) = 175d_3 + 30(x_3 + d_3 - 2) \qquad \text{Stage 3, January}$$

This problem is particularly interesting because there are three constraints that must be satisfied at each stage as we perform the optimization procedure. Two are fairly straightforward, while the third is a little tricky. The first constraint is that the ending inventory must be less than or equal to the warehouse capacity. Mathematically, we have

$$x_n + d_n - D_n \le W_n$$

or

$$x_n + d_n \le W_n + D_n \tag{18.2}$$

The second constraint is that the production level in each period may not exceed the production capacity. Mathematically, we have

$$d_n \le P_n \tag{18.3}$$

The most difficult constraint to handle is the requirement that beginning inventory plus production must exceed demand for each period. The difficulty with this constraint becomes clear if we study stage 2. The demand for this period is 3, but the production capacity is 2. Therefore, we must require that the beginning inventory x_2 be greater than or equal to 1. In general, this means that for each stage we must have a constraint that requires beginning inventory plus production to be greater than or equal to demand. Mathematically, this constraint can be written as

$$x_n + d_n \geq D_n \qquad (18.4)$$

Let us now begin the stagewise solution procedure. At each stage, we want to minimize $r_n(x_n, d_n) + f_{n-1}(x_{n-1})$ subject to the constraints given by equations (18.2), (18.3), and (18.4).

Stage 1   The stage 1 problem is as follows:

$$\text{Min} \quad r_1(x_1, d_1) = 200d_1 + 40(x_1 + d_1 - 3)$$

s.t.

$$x_1 + d_1 \leq 5 \quad \text{Warehouse constraint}$$

$$d_1 \leq 3 \quad \text{Production constraint}$$

$$x_1 + d_1 \geq 3 \quad \text{Satisfy demand constraint}$$

Combining terms in the objective function, we can rewrite the problem:

$$\text{Min} \quad r_1(x_1, d_1) = 240d_1 + 40x_1 - 120$$

s.t.

$$x_1 + d_1 \leq 5$$

$$d_1 \leq 3$$

$$x_1 + d_1 \geq 3$$

Following the tabular approach we adopted in Section 18.3, we will consider all possible inputs to stage 1 (x_1) and make the corresponding minimum-cost decision. Since we are attempting to minimize cost, we will want the decision variable d_1 to be as small as possible and still satisfy the demand constraint. Thus, the table for stage 1 is as follows:

x_1	d_1^*		$\begin{array}{c} f_1(x_1) = r_1(x_1, d_1^*) \\ 240d_1 + 40x_1 - 120 \end{array}$
0	3		600
1	2		400
2	1	Production capacity of 3 for stage 1 limits d_1	200
3	0		0

Warehouse capacity of 3 from stage 2 limits value of x_1

Demand constraint: $x_1 + d_1 \geq 3$

Now let us proceed to stage 2.

Stage 2

$$\text{Min} \quad r_2(x_2, d_2) + f_1(x_1) = 150d_2 + 30(x_2 + d_2 - 3) + f_1(x_1)$$

$$= 180d_2 + 30x_2 - 90 + f_1(x_1)$$

s.t.

$$x_2 + d_2 \le 6$$

$$d_2 \le 2$$

$$x_2 + d_2 \ge 3$$

The stage 2 calculations are summarized in the table below:

d_2	$r_2(x_2, d_2) + f_1(x_1)$			Production capacity of 2 for stage 2		
x_2	0	1	2	d_2^*	$f_2(x_2)$	$x_1 = x_2 + d_2^* - 3$
0	—	—	—	—	M	—
1	—	—	⃝900	2	900	0
2	—	750	⃝730	2	730	1

Warehouse capacity of 2 from stage 3

Check demand constraint $x_2 + d_2 \ge 3$ for each x_2, d_2 combination (– indicates an infeasible solution)

The detailed calculations for $r_2(x_2, d_2) + f_1(x_1)$ when $x_2 = 1$ and $d_2 = 2$ are as follows:

$$r_2(1,2) + f_1(0) = 180(2) + 30(1) - 90 + 600 = 900$$

For $r_2(x_2, d_2) + f_1(x_1)$ when $x_2 = 2$ and $d_2 = 1$, we have

$$r_2(2,1) + f_1(0) = 180(1) + 30(2) - 90 + 600 = 750$$

For $x_2 = 2$ and $d_2 = 2$, we have

$$r_2(2,2) + f_1(1) = 180(2) + 30(2) - 90 + 400 = 730$$

Note that an arbitrarily high cost M is assigned to the $f_2(x_2)$ column for $x_2 = 0$. Since an input of 0 to stage 2 does not provide a feasible solution, the M cost associated with the $x_2 = 0$ input will prevent $x_2 = 0$ from occurring in the optimal solution.

Stage 3

$$\text{Min} \quad r_3(x_3, d_3) + f_2(x_2) = 175d_3 + 30(x_3 + d_3 - 2) + f_2(x_2)$$

$$= 205d_3 + 30x_3 - 60 + f_2(x_2)$$

s.t.

$$x_3 + d_3 \le 4$$

$$d_3 \le 3$$

$$x_3 + d_3 \ge 2$$

With $x_3 = 1$ already defined by the beginning inventory level, the table for stage 3 becomes

d_3	$r_3(x_3, d_3) + f_2(x_2)$						
x_3	0	1	2	3	d_3^*	$f_3(x_3)$	$x_2 = x_3 + d_3^* - 2$
1	—	M	⟨1280⟩	1315	2	1280	1

Production capacity of 3 at stage 3

Try Problem 10 for practice using dynamic programming to solve a production and inventory control problem.

Thus, we find that the total cost associated with the optimal production and inventory policy is $1280. To find the optimal decisions and inventory levels for each period, we may trace back through each stage and identify x_n and d_n^* as we go. Table 18.4 summarizes the optimal production and inventory policy.

Table 18.4
Optimal Production and Inventory Control Policy

Month	Beginning Inventory	Production	Production Cost	Ending Inventory	Holding Cost	Total Monthly Cost
January	1	2	$ 350	1	$30	$ 380
February	1	2	300	0	0	300
March	0	3	600	0	0	600
		Totals	$1250		$30	$1280

Summary

Dynamic programming is an attractive approach to problem solving when it is possible to break a large problem up into interrelated smaller problems. The solution procedure then proceeds recursively, solving one of the smaller problems at each stage. Dynamic programming is not a specific algorithm, but rather an approach to problem solving. Thus, the recursive optimization may be carried out differently for different problems. In any case, it is almost always easier to solve a series of smaller problems than one large one. This is how dynamic programming obtains its power.

NOTES & COMMENTS

1. With dynamic programming, as with other management science techniques, the computer can be a valuable computational aid. However, since dynamic programming is a general approach with stage decision problems differing substantially from application to application, no one algorithm or computer software package is available for solving dynamic programs. Some software packages exist for specific types; however, most new applications of dynamic programming will require specially designed software if a computer solution is to be obtained.

2. The introductory illustrations of dynamic programming presented in this chapter are deterministic and involve a finite number of decision alternatives and a finite number of stages. For problems such as these, computations can be organized and carried out in a tabular form. With this structure, the optimization problem at each stage can usually be solved by total enumeration of all possible outcomes.

—Continued on the next page

—Continued from previous page

More complex dynamic programming models may include probabilistic components, continuous decision variables, and/or an infinite number of stages. In cases where the optimization problem at each stage involves continuous decision variables, linear programming or the calculus-based procedures presented in the next chapter may be needed to obtain an optimal solution.

Glossary

Dynamic programming An approach to problem solving that permits decomposing a large problem that may be very difficult to solve into a number of interrelated smaller problems that are usually easier to solve.

Principle of optimality Regardless of the decisions that have been made at the previous stages, if the decision made at stage n is to be part of an overall optimal solution, the decision made at stage n must be optimal for all remaining stages.

Stages When a large problem is decomposed into a number of subproblems, the dynamic programming solution approach creates a stage to correspond to each of the subproblems.

State variables x_n and x_{n-1} An input state variable x_n and an output state variable x_{n-1} together define the condition of the process at the beginning and end of stage n.

Decision variable d_n A variable representing the possible decisions that can be made at stage n.

Stage transformation function $t_n(x_n, d_n)$ The rule or equation that relates the output state variable x_{n-1} for stage n to the input state variable x_n and the decision variable d_n.

Return function $r_n(x_n, d_n)$ A value (such as profit or loss) associated with making decision d_n at stage n for a specific value of the input state variable x_n.

Knapsack problem Finding the number of N items, each of which has a different weight and value, that can be placed in a knapsack with limited weight capacity so as to maximize the total value of the items placed in the knapsack.

Problems

1. Compare total enumeration with dynamic programming

1. In Section 18.1 we solved a shortest-route problem using dynamic programming. Find the optimal solution to this problem by total enumeration; that is, list all 16 possible routes from the origin, node 1, to the destination, node 10, and pick the one with the smallest value. Explain why dynamic programming results in fewer computations for this problem.

S ELF T EST

2. Shortest-route problem, compare total enumeration with dynamic programming

2. Consider the following network. The numbers above each arc represent the distance between the connected nodes.

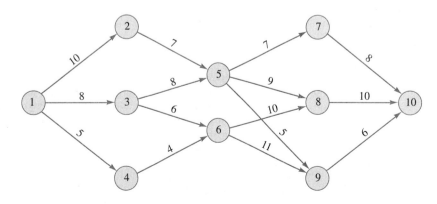

a. Find the shortest route from node 1 to node 10 using dynamic programming.

b. What is the shortest route from node 4 to node 10?

c. Enumerate all possible routes from node 1 to node 10. Explain how dynamic programming has reduced the number of computations to fewer than the number required by total enumeration.

3. A charter pilot has additional capacity for 2000 pounds of cargo on a flight from Dallas to Seattle. A transport company has four types of cargo in Dallas to be delivered to Seattle. The number of units of each cargo type, the weight per unit, and the delivery fee per unit are shown.

Cargo Type	Units Available	Weight Per Unit (100 pounds)	Delivery Fee ($100)
1	2	8	22
2	2	5	12
3	4	3	7
4	3	2	3

a. Use dynamic programming to find how many units of each cargo type the pilot should contract to deliver.

b. Suppose the pilot agrees to take another passenger and the additional cargo capacity is reduced to 1800 pounds. How does your recommendation change?

4. A firm has just hired eight new employees and would like to determine how to allocate their time to four activities. The firm has prepared the table below, which gives the estimated profit for each activity as a function of the number of new employees allocated to it:

Activities	\multicolumn{9}{c}{Number of New Employees}

Activities	0	1	2	3	4	5	6	7	8
1	22	30	37	44	49	54	58	60	61
2	30	40	48	55	59	62	64	66	67
3	46	52	56	59	62	65	67	68	69
4	5	22	36	48	52	55	58	60	61

a. Use dynamic programming to determine the optimal allocation of new employees to the activities.

b. Suppose only six new employees were hired. Which activities would you assign to these employees?

5. A sawmill receives logs in 20-foot lengths, cuts them to smaller lengths, and then sells these smaller lengths to a number of manufacturing companies. The company has orders for the following lengths:

$$l_1 = 3 \text{ ft}$$

$$l_2 = 7 \text{ ft}$$

$$l_3 = 11 \text{ ft}$$

$$l_4 = 16 \text{ ft}$$

The sawmill currently has an inventory of 2000 logs in 20-foot lengths and would like to select a cutting pattern that will maximize the profit made on this inventory. Assuming the sawmill has sufficient orders available, its problem becomes one of determining the cutting pattern that will maximize profits. The per-unit profit for each of the smaller lengths is as follows:

Length (feet)	3	7	11	16
Profit ($)	1	3	5	8

Any cutting pattern is permissible as long as

$$3d_1 + 7d_2 + 11d_3 + 16d_4 \le 20$$

where d_i is the number of pieces of length l_i cut, $i = 1, 2, 3, 4$.

a. Set up a dynamic programming model of this problem, and solve it. What are your decision variables? What is your state variable?

b. Explain briefly how this model can be extended to find the best cutting pattern in cases where the overall length l can be cut into N lengths, $l_1, l_2, \ldots, l_N$.

6. Shortest-route formulation

6. A large manufacturing company has a very well developed management training program. Each trainee is expected to complete a four-phase program, but there are a number of different assignments that each trainee can be given at each phase of the training program. The assignments available and the estimated completion times in months at each phase of the program are shown below:

Phase I	Phase II	Phase III	Phase IV
A–13	E–3	H–12	L–10
B–10	F–6	I–6	M–5
C–20	G–5	J–7	N–13
D–17		K–10	

Assignments made at subsequent phases depend on the previous assignment. For example, a trainee who completes assignment A at phase I may only go on to assignment F or G at phase II. That is, there is a precedence relationship for each assignment as shown below.

Assignment	Feasible Succeeding Assignments	Assignment	Feasible Succeeding Assignments
A	F, G	H	L, M
B	F	I	L, M
C	G	J	M, N
D	E, G	K	N
E	H, I, J, K	L	Finish
F	H, K	M	Finish
G	J, K	N	Finish

a. The company would like to determine the sequence of assignments that will minimize the time in the training program. Formulate and solve this as a dynamic programming problem. (*Hint*: Develop a network representation of the problem where each node represents completion of an activity.)

b. If a trainee has just completed assignment F and would like to complete the remainder of the training program in the shortest possible time, which assignment should be chosen next?

7. Crazy Robin, the owner of a small chain of Robin Hood Sporting Goods stores in Des Moines and Cedar Rapids, Iowa, has just purchased a new supply of 500 dozen top-line golf balls. Because she was willing to purchase the entire amount of a production overrun, Robin was able to buy the golf balls at one-half the usual price.

Three of Robin's stores do a good business in the sale of golf equipment and supplies, and, as a result, Robin has decided to retail the balls at these three stores. Thus, Robin is faced with the problem of determining how many dozen balls to allocate to each store. The following estimates show the expected profit from allocating 100, 200, 300, 400, or 500 dozen to each store:

	Number of Dozens of Golf Balls				
Store	100	200	300	400	500
1	$600	$1100	$1550	$1700	$1800
2	500	1200	1700	2000	2100
3	550	1100	1500	1850	1950

Assuming the lots cannot be broken into any sizes smaller than 100 dozen each, how many dozen golf balls should Crazy Robin send to each store?

8. The Max X. Posure Advertising Agency is conducting a 10-day advertising campaign for a local department store. The agency has determined that the most effective campaign would possibly include placing ads in four media: daily newspaper, Sunday newspaper, radio, and television. A total of $8000 has been made available for this campaign, and the agency would like to distribute this in $1000 increments across the media in such a fashion that an advertising exposure index is maximized. Research that has been conducted by the agency permits the following estimates to be made of the exposure per each $1000 expenditure in each of the media.

	Thousands of Dollars Spent							
Media	1	2	3	4	5	6	7	8
Daily newspaper	24	37	46	59	72	80	82	82
Sunday newspaper	15	55	70	75	90	95	95	95
Radio	20	30	45	55	60	62	63	63
Television	20	40	55	65	70	70	70	70

a. How much should the agency spend on each medium to maximize the department store's exposure?

b. How would your answer change if only $6000 were budgeted?

c. How would your answers in parts (a) and (b) change if television were not considered as one of the media?

9. Suppose we have a three-stage process where the yield for each stage is a function of the decision made. In mathematical notation, we may state our problem as follows:

$$\text{Max} \quad r_1(d_1) + r_2(d_2) + r_3(d_3)$$

s.t.

$$d_1 + d_2 + d_3 \leq 1000$$

The possible values the decision variables may take on at each stage and the corresponding returns are presented in tabular form below.

Stage 1		Stage 2		Stage 3	
d_1	$r_1(d_1)$	d_2	$r_2(d_2)$	d_3	$r_3(d_3)$
0	0	100	120	100	175
100	110	300	400	500	700
200	300	500	650		
300	400	600	700		
400	425	800	975		

a. Use total enumeration to list all feasible sequences of decisions for this problem. Which one is optimal (i.e., maximizes $r_1(d_1) + r_2(d_2) + r_3(d_3)$)?

b. Use dynamic programming to solve this problem.

10. Recall the production and inventory control problem of Section 18.4. Mills Manufacturing Company has just such a production and inventory control problem for an armature the company manufactures as a component for a generator. The available data for the next 3-month planning period are presented below.

Month	Demand	Capacity		Cost Per Unit	
		Production	Warehouse	Production	Holding
1	20	30	40	$2.00	$0.30
2	30	20	30	1.50	0.30
3	30	30	20	2.00	0.20

Use dynamic programming to find the optimal production quantities and inventory levels in each period for the Mills Manufacturing Company. Assume there is an inventory of 10 units on hand at the beginning of month 1 and production runs are completed in multiples of 10 units (i.e., 10, 20, or 30 units).

11. A chemical processing plant is considering introducing a new product. However, before making a final decision, management has requested that you provide estimates of profits associated with different process designs. The general flow process is represented:

Raw material is fed into a heater at the rate of 4500 pounds per week. The heated material is then routed to a reactor where a portion of the raw material is converted to pure product. A separator then withdraws the finished product for sale. The unconverted material is discarded as waste.

Profit considerations are to be based on a 2-year payback period on investments; that is, all capital expenditures must be recovered in 2 years (100 weeks). All calculations will be based on weekly operations. Raw material costs are expected to stay fixed at $1 per pound, and it has been forecast that the finished product will sell for $6 per pound.

It is your responsibility to determine the process design that will yield maximum profit per week. You and your co-workers have collected the following preliminary data.

One heater with an initial cost of $12,000 is being considered at stage 3. Two temperatures, 700°F and 800°F, are feasible. The operating costs for the heater depend directly on the temperature to be attained. These costs are as follows:

	Operating Costs at Stage 3	
	Decisions at Stage 3	
Input x_3	700°F	800°F
4500 lb	$280/week	$380/week

Stage 3's output x_2, which is also the input to stage 2, may be expressed as 4500 pounds of raw material heated to either 700°F or 800°F. One of the decisions you must make is to what temperature the raw material should be heated.

A reactor, which can operate with either of two catalysts, C1 or C2, is to be used for stage 2. The initial cost of this reactor is $50,000. The operating costs of this reactor are independent of the input x_2 and depend only on the catalyst selected. The costs of the catalysts are included in the operating costs. The output will be expressed in pounds of converted (or pure) material. The percentage of material converted depends on the incoming temperature and the catalyst used. The tables below summarize the pertinent information. Thus, a second decision you must make is to specify which catalyst should be used.

	Percent Conversion	
	Decisions at Stage 2	
x_2	C1	C2
(4500 lb, 700°F)	20	40
(4500 lb, 800°F)	40	60

Operating Costs Decision at Stage 2	
C1	C2
$450/week	$650/week

One of two separators, S1 or S2, will be purchased for stage 1. The S1 separator has an initial cost of $20,000 and a weekly operating cost of $0.10 per pound of pure product to be separated. Comparatively, S2 has an initial cost of $5000 and a weekly operating cost of $0.20. Included in these operating costs is the expense of discarding the unconverted raw material as waste.

Develop a dynamic programming model for this problem. What is your recommendation for the best temperature for the heater? The best catalyst to use with the reactor? The best separator to purchase? What is the maximum weekly profit?

MANAGEMENT SCIENCE IN PRACTICE

The U.S. Environmental Protection Agency*
Washington, D.C.

The U.S. Environmental Protection Agency (EPA) is an independent agency of the executive branch of the federal government. Fifteen components of five executive departments and independent agencies were consolidated to form the EPA on December 2, 1970, under Reorganization Plan No. 3 by President Nixon. Today, the EPA administers comprehensive environmental protection laws related to

- Water pollution control, water quality, and drinking water
- Air pollution and radiation
- Pesticides and toxic substances
- Solid and hazardous waste including emergency spill response and Superfund site remediation

Program offices for each of these media support the EPA administrator through policy development, standards and criteria development, and support and evaluation of regional activities. The 10 regional offices implement and enforce standards, conduct monitoring and surveillance programs, and provide technical and financial assistance to state and local governments.

Functional activities at EPA headquarters, which transcend all media, include planning and management, enforcement, and research and development. Management Science techniques are used extensively in the experimental design of research studies, providing quality assurance of monitoring surveys and enforcement actions, as well as environmental modeling and simulation studies to evaluate the cost effectiveness of alternative environmental policies, regulations, and control technologies.

The EPA's Office of Research and Development serves as the primary source of scientific and technical support to the agency's operating programs and regional offices by conducting in-house and extramural research at 14 locations throughout the country. Research activities focus on analytical methods, development and quality assurance, environmental processes and effects research, health effects research, and environmental engineering. Environmental modeling is conducted for all media at many of these research locations. The Office of Research and Development maintains a Center for Water Quality Modeling at its laboratory in Athens, Georgia. The following dynamic programming application was developed by the Municipal Environmental Research Laboratory in Cincinnati, Ohio, as part of an effort to evaluate the usefulness of seasonal discharge permits in reducing the cost of wastewater treatment while maintaining water quality.

Water-Quality Management Program

The EPA administers programs designed to maintain acceptable water-quality conditions for rivers and streams throughout the United States. To guard against polluted rivers and streams, the government requires companies to obtain a discharge permit from federal or state authorities before any form of pollutants can be discharged into a body of water. These permits specifically notify each discharger as to the amount of legally dischargeable waste that can be placed in the river or stream. The discharge limits are determined by ensuring that water-quality criteria are met even in unusually dry seasons when the river or stream has a critically low flow condition. Most often, this condition is based on the lowest flow recorded over the past 10 years. By ensuring that water quality is maintained under the low-flow conditions, there is a high degree of reliability that the water-quality criteria can be maintained throughout the year.

At different seasons of the year, water will flow at different rates in the various rivers and streams. With these seasonal variations, seasonal discharge permits can be issued that allow different discharge limits at the different times of the year. As a result, companies can take advantage of higher stream flow rates to reduce treatment requirements and to lower the discharge treatment costs. A goal of the EPA is to establish seasonal discharge limits that enable lower treatment costs while maintaining water-quality standards at a prescribed level of reliability.

A Dynamic Programming Model for Seasonal Discharge Limits

A dynamic programming model has been formulated for establishing the allowable waste discharge load during the various seasons of the year. The periods or stages of the model correspond to different seasons considered during the year; there is a separate stage for each season. The return function at each stage is the cost of the treatment for waste discharged during that stage. The decision variable at each stage is the design streamflow for the body of water receiving the waste. Once the design streamflow has been established, an allowable waste discharge and its associated treatment cost can be determined. The design streamflow decisions at each stage interact to determine the overall reliability that the annual water-quality conditions will be maintained. In this regard, the decision variable choice at any one stage, or period, is affected by the decision variable choices at the other stages.

—Continued on next page

*The authors are indebted to John Convery, Environmental Protection Agency, for providing this application.

—Continued from previous page

The probability that there will be no water-quality violations over the entire year is the product of the seasonal probabilities of no violations. To maintain reliability standards, the probability of no violation during the year must exceed a certain value. Suppose we let $P_j(q_j)$ represent the probability of no violation during season j when the design streamflow is q_j. Then the probability of no water-quality violation over the entire year is given by

$$\prod_{j=1}^{N} P_j(q_j) = \text{probability of no violation}$$

where N is the number of seasons during the year.

The reliability requirement is satisfied when this probability is sufficiently high. Suppose α is the minimal acceptable probability. The water-quality constraint is then

$$\prod_{j=1}^{N} P_j(q_j) \geq \alpha$$

By taking the logarithm of both sides, this constraint can be written as

$$\sum_{j=1}^{N} \log P_j(q_j) \geq \log \alpha$$

The state variable at stage j is then defined to be

$$s_j = \sum_{k=1}^{j} P_k(q_k)$$

The design streamflows (the decision variables) are chosen to minimize treatment cost subject to requirements that the allowable waste discharge be within given limits and that the state variable ensure sufficient reliability of no water-quality violations.

The solution to the model provides the design streamflows for each seasonal period. These streamflows combine with the water-quality criterion to establish the seasonal waste discharge load. With the return function measuring treatment cost, the model obtains the minimum-cost solution that will maintain the EPA water-quality standards.

Questions

1. Suppose there are four seasons and the probabilities of a water-quality violation in each season are 0.01, 0.05, 0.02, and 0.01, respectively. What is the probability that there will be no water-quality violation over the entire year?

2. Let P_j = the probability of no water-quality violation in season j. Suppose there are three seasons. Write a constraint specifying that the minimal acceptable probability of no violation over the three seasons is 0.90.

CHAPTER 19

Calculus-Based Solution Procedures

In this chapter we consider mathematical models where the functions or mathematical relationships involved are not all linear. For example, in formulating a profit or cost function for a specific problem, we may find that a linear function is inappropriate and that a curve or a nonlinear function is necessary. Recall that in the analysis of inventory models (see Section 11.1) we developed the following nonlinear function to show how total relevant cost could be expressed in terms of the order quantity Q:

$$TC = \frac{Q}{2} C_h + \frac{D}{Q} C_o$$

Differential calculus can be used as a tool for solving problems that involve the maximization or minimization of a function.

John von Neumann (1903–1957), one of the great mathematicians of the 20th century, stated that "The calculus was the first achievement of modern mathematics, and it is difficult to overstate its importance."

The graph of the total-cost curve for an economic order quantity inventory model is shown in Figure 19.1.

In determining the optimal values of the decision variables in nonlinear models, we will find calculus-based solution procedures quite valuable. In this chapter we show how differential calculus can be used to find maximum and minimum values for such models. We begin by using differential calculus to analyze nonlinear objective functions with only one decision variable. Then we discuss the procedures for handling nonlinear functions with two or more decision variables. Finally, we show how calculus-based solution procedures can be used to solve nonlinear models that have constraints.

This is the only chapter in this book where a working knowledge of calculus, specifically differential calculus, is a prerequisite. However, the reader with no calculus background may still find this chapter useful in terms of learning about nonlinear models and the role that calculus-based solution procedures play in analyzing these models.

19.1 Models with One Decision Variable

The Macon Psychiatric Institute, a nonprofit organization, is interested in redesigning its mental health care delivery system to maximize the number of people who can benefit from its services. Based on some recent studies, the institute has learned that the average

Figure 19.1
Total-Cost Curve for the
Economic Order Quantity
Inventory Model

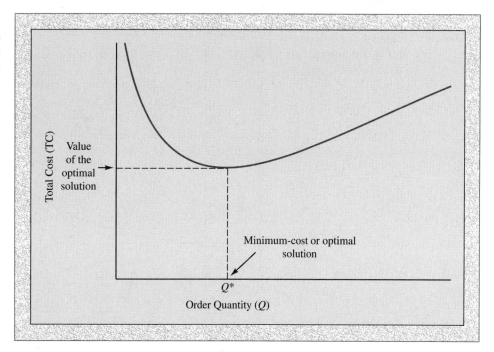

treatment time per patient is a function of the number of patients the clinic is simultaneously treating. With more patients receiving treatment, the patients remain in residence longer; that is, with more patients in the system, the clinic's staff becomes overloaded, and the patient's time in residence at the clinic increases. If the institute reduces the number of patients being treated, the patients can receive more personal attention, and the treatment time can be shortened. The institute's problem can be stated in terms of how many active or in-residence patients should be maintained by the clinic so that the total number of patients treated per year is maximized.

Based on patient records and recovery time estimates by the clinic's staff members, the following mathematical relationship can be used to describe how the number of in-residence patients affects the patient treatment or recovery time:

$$T = \frac{45}{180 - P} \qquad (19.1)$$

where

T = average patient treatment time in years
P = number of in-residence patients

This relationship is believed to be valid as long as the number of in-residence patients, P, remains between 45 and 135.

Using equation (19.1), we see that if the clinic operates with $P = 135$ patients, then $T = 45/(180 - 135) = 1$ year (i.e., on the average a patient receives 1 year of treatment before being released). However, if the clinic reduces its number of in-residence patients to 60, then the average recovery period can be shortened to $T = 45/(180 - 60) = 0.375$ year, or 4.5 months. The relationship between the number of in-residence patients and the average treatment time is shown in Figure 19.2.

The institute wants to maximize the total number of people treated per year. Since T is the average treatment time per patient and since the clinic treats P patients *simultaneously,* the total number of patients treated per year is given by

Figure 19.2
Average Treatment Time, *T*, as a
Function of the Number of
In-Residence Patients, *P*

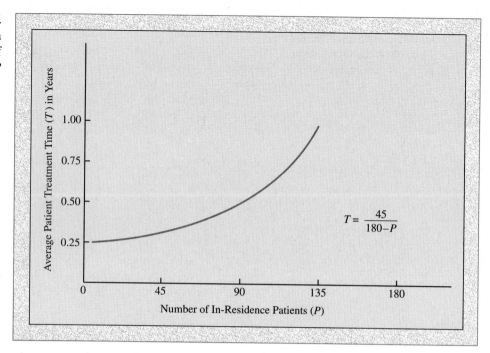

For *P* = 135, we saw earlier that *T* = 1 year; thus, *N* = *P*/*T* = 135/1 = 135 patients per year. However, for *P* = 60, *T* = 0.375 and *N* = 60/0.375 = 160 patients per year. Therefore, reducing the number of active patients to 60 does improve the effectiveness of the clinic; more patients can be treated over a specified period. However, the question of what the optimal number of in-residence patients is still needs to be answered.

Since *T* is a function of *P* (equation (19.1)), we can substitute into equation (19.2) and write the mathematical model for the problem as a function of the one variable *P*:

$$N = \frac{P}{T} = \frac{P}{45/(180 - P)} = \frac{(180 - P)P}{45} = 4P - \frac{1}{45}P^2 \qquad (19.3)$$

We are interested in maximizing the number of patients treated per year *N*. Thus, the above model provides a nonlinear objective function for a maximization problem with one decision variable *P*, and our problem becomes

$$\text{Max} \quad N = 4P - \frac{1}{45}P^2 \qquad (19.4)$$

With only one decision variable, we can observe how the number of patients treated per year *N* varies for different *P* values by graphing the relationship. This graph, shown in Figure 19.3, indicates that the maximum value of the objective function is 180, corresponding to an in-residence patient volume of 90. Since sketching the graph of a function may be time-consuming, and since the determination of the optimal solution is dependent on the accuracy of the graph, we will usually want to use a differential calculus procedure for solving such a problem.

Figure 19.3
Number of Patients Treated Per Year as a Function of the Number of Patients in Residence

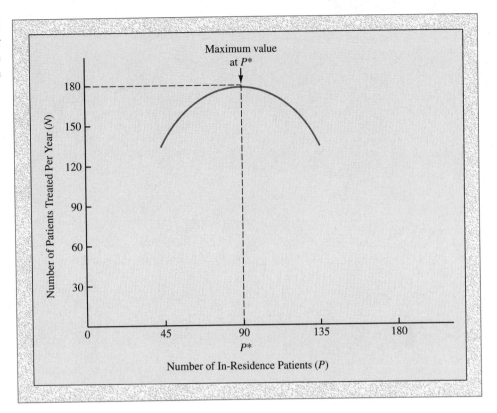

Recall from calculus that the first derivative of an unconstrained function must be equal to zero at a *local maximum* or *local minimum*. The reason for this is that the first derivative is the slope of the line tangent to the curve, and the slope of the tangent line is zero at any local maximum or local minimum value of the function. In the Macon Psychiatric Institute problem, we see that the function relating the number of patients treated per year to the number of in-residence patients has one local maximum (Figure 19.3). Many functions, however, possess a number of local maxima and/or minima. For example, consider the graph of the function depicted in Figure 19.4, which has two local maxima and one local minimum. At each of the local maxima and at the local minimum, the first derivatives, and hence the slope of the tangent lines, are equal to zero. Rule 1 below summarizes the above discussion in the form of a *necessary condition* for determining all the local maxima or minima of an unconstrained function of one variable:

It is possible for the derivative of a function to equal zero at points that are neither maximum nor minimum points of the curve.

Sir Isaac Newton (1642–1727) and Gottfried Wilhelm Leibniz (1647–1716) share credit for the development of a large part of the subject of calculus. The notation developed by Leibniz is still used today.

R U L E 1 (N E C E S S A R Y C O N D I T I O N)

The first derivative of an unconstrained function of one variable must equal zero at its local maximum or local minimum points.

Let us now calculate the first derivative for the institute's problem:[1]

$$\text{First derivative} = \frac{dN}{dP} = 4 - \frac{2}{45}P$$

---

[1] A short table of derivative formulas is provided in Appendix D.

Figure 19.4
Function $f(x)$ with Two Local
Maxima and One Local Minimum

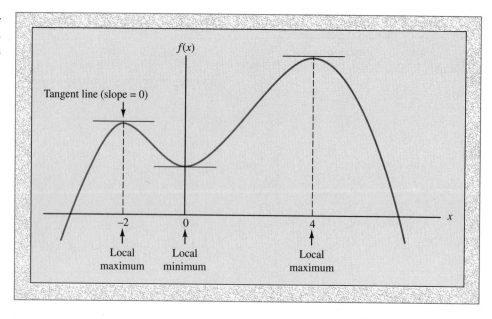

Setting the first derivative equal to zero and solving, we obtain

$$\frac{dN}{dP} = 4 - \tfrac{2}{45}P = 0$$

$$\tfrac{2}{45}P = 4$$

$$P^* = \frac{(4)(45)}{2} = 90$$

Thus, we see that $P^* = 90$ is the value of P that sets the first derivative equal to zero. Figure 19.5 shows that the slope of the line tangent to the curve at this local maximum point is in fact zero.

Unfortunately, while it is a necessary condition that the first derivative equal zero at a local maximum point, this is not sufficient to guarantee that we have in fact located a local maximum. Actually, a point where the first derivative equals zero could be a local maximum, a local minimum, or an inflection point. Thus, a second derivative test is needed to determine whether we have a local maximum.[2] Rule 2 provides such a test and establishes a *sufficient condition* that guarantees that we have reached a local maximum (or a local minimum) solution.

If the second derivative is zero, the point may be a local minimum, a local maximum, or an inflection point.

RULE 2 (SUFFICIENT CONDITION)

If rule 1 is satisfied at a point, and
a. If the second derivative is *greater than* zero, then the point is a local *minimum*.
b. If the second derivative is *less than* zero, then the point is a local *maximum*.

---

[2]The second derivative is found simply by applying the differentiation rule to the first derivative function.

Figure 19.5
Maximum Is at Value of P Where Derivative = 0

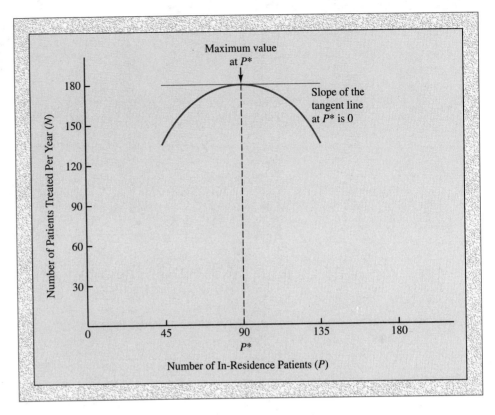

Let us apply this second derivative test to the Macon Psychiatric Institute problem. The second derivative is given by

$$\text{Second derivative} = \frac{d^2N}{dP^2} = -2/45 < 0$$

Since the second derivative is less than zero, rule 2 tells us that $P^* = 90$ does indeed yield a local maximum of the objective function for our problem.

We call a point a *global maximum* if it yields the highest value for the function. Similarly, we call a point a *global minimum* if it yields the lowest value. In this case, it is easy to verify that the local maximum, $P^* = 90$, is also a global maximum. Since the function has only one point at which rule 1 is satisfied, and since rule 2 says that this point is a local maximum, this local maximum must be the global maximum.

Assuming that the relationships we used in developing the mathematical model are accurate reflections of reality, the institute should admit 90 patients and maintain this many patients in residence all the time. This will maximize the number of patients the institute can treat per year at 180.

The problem we have just described illustrates how calculus can assist in finding the optimum for an unconstrained function of one variable. However, in some situations, we will find that it is of interest to consider finding the optimal value for a function over a restricted interval. This situation may come about because of constraints placed on the decision maker or because the function of interest is defined only over a specified interval, and, as a result, we choose to limit ourselves to finding the best value for the

At this point, you should be able to find the maximum or minimum of an unconstrained function. Try Problems 1(a) and 2(b).

Figure 19.6
Function
$f(x) = x^3 - 3x^2$

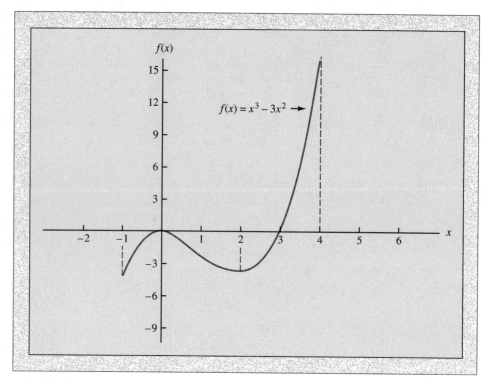

function over that interval. In problems of this type, the optimal solution could occur at the end points of the interval as well as at points where rules 1 and 2 hold.

As an illustration of this type of situation, suppose we are trying to find the maximum of the function $f(x) = x^3 - 3x^2$ over the interval $-1 \leq x \leq 4$. A graph of the function over this interval is shown in Figure 19.6.

Clearly, the global maximum of the function over this interval occurs at $x = 4$. However, rule 1 is not satisfied at this point because the first derivative (the slope of the tangent line) is not equal to zero. When we are constrained to a specific interval in the search for the optimum of a function of one variable, we must extend the solution procedure beyond checking points that satisfy rules 1 and 2. The general procedure for finding the global maximum or minimum of a function of one variable is as follows:

Step 1 Find all the points that satisfy rules 1 and 2. These are candidates for yielding the optimal solution to the problem.

Step 2 If the solution is restricted to a specified interval, evaluate the function at the end points of the interval.

Step 3 Compare the values of the function at all the points found in steps 1 and 2. The largest of these is the global maximum solution; the smallest is the global minimum solution.

Let us apply this procedure to the function in Figure 19.6. Following step 1, we first find all the points at which the first derivative equals zero:

$$\frac{df(x)}{dx} = 3x^2 - 6x = 0$$

Therefore,

$$x(3x - 6) = 0$$

and we see that both $x = 0$ and $x = 2$ satisfy rule 1. Checking rule 2, we find

$$\frac{d^2f(x)}{dx^2} = 6x - 6$$

At $x = 0$,

$$\frac{d^2f(0)}{dx^2} = -6 < 0$$

and we have a local maximum of the function at $x = 0$. The value of the function at $x = 0$ is $f(0) = 0^3 - 3(0)^2 = 0$. Looking back to Figure 19.6, we see that this is indeed a local maximum and the slope of the tangent line is equal to zero at this point. At $x = 2$,

$$\frac{d^2f(2)}{dx^2} = 6(2) - 6 = 6 > 0$$

Therefore, by rule 2 we have a local minimum at $x = 2$. The value of the function at $x = 2$ is $f(2) = (2)^3 - 3(2)^2 = -4$.

Proceeding to step 2, we evaluate the function at both of its end points:

$$f(-1) = (-1)^3 - 3(-1)^2 = -4$$

$$f(4) = (4)^3 - 3(4)^2 = 16$$

At step 3 we compare the values at the points found in steps 1 and 2. The largest value occurs at $x = 4$ and yields a global maximum value of 16 over the restricted interval. The smallest value occurs at both $x = -1$ and $x = 2$; that is, there is a tie for the global minimum, and we say that both $x = -1$ and $x = 2$ are global minima. The minimum value is -4. Note that one of these candidates was found in step 1 and the other in step 2 of the solution procedure. Figure 19.6 illustrates graphically the conclusions we have reached.

Let us return for a moment to the Macon Psychiatric Institute problem. The objective function for this problem was believed to be applicable only over the interval $45 \leq P \leq 135$. It may be reasonable to assume that this means the institute will not consider letting the number of in-residence patients fall below 45 or exceed 135. If this were the case then, why did we not need to check the end points of this interval in our search for a maximum? The reason is that there was only one point ($P^* = 90$) that satisfied rule 1, and it was a local maximum. Since P^* is a local maximum, the value of the function decreases as we move away from it, and since no other points satisfy rule 1, we know that the function does not turn up again anywhere. Therefore, no other point could yield a higher value than $P^* = 90$. Nevertheless, the three-step procedure we have specified for maximizing or minimizing a function of one variable would have led to the same conclusion. The value of the function is smaller at $P = 45$ and $P = 135$ than at the maximum, $P^* = 90$.

Before concluding this section, let us consider another numerical example to make sure that we know how to apply steps 1, 2, and 3.

Example   Suppose we want to minimize the function

$$f(x) = x^3 - 6x^2 + 50 \tag{19.5}$$

over the interval $0 \leq x \leq 5$.

Step 1 Setting the first derivative equal to zero, we find

$$\frac{df(x)}{dx} = 3x^2 - 12x = 0$$

or

$$x(3x - 12) = 0$$

This provides two possible values for x: either $x = 0$ or $3x - 12 = 0$ and $x = 4$. That is, $x = 0$ and $x = 4$ both set the first derivative equal to zero, satisfying rule 1. To see if either of these yields a local minimum, we must calculate the second derivative:

$$\frac{d^2f(x)}{dx^2} = 6x - 12$$

At $x = 0$, we have

$$\frac{d^2f(0)}{dx^2} = 6(0) - 12 = -12 < 0$$

Therefore, by rule 2, $x = 0$ yields a local maximum for $f(x)$. At $x = 4$ we have

$$\frac{d^2f(4)}{dx^2} = 6(4) - 12 = 12 > 0$$

Therefore, by rule 2, $x = 4$ yields a local minimum for $f(x)$. The graph of $f(x)$ (equation (19.5)) is shown in Figure 19.7. Again note that the slopes of the lines tangent to the curve at these local minimum and maximum points are both zero.

Step 2 Evaluating the function at the end points, we obtain

$$f(0) = 50$$

$$f(5) = 25$$

Figure 19.7
Function $f(x) = x^3 - 6x^2 + 50$

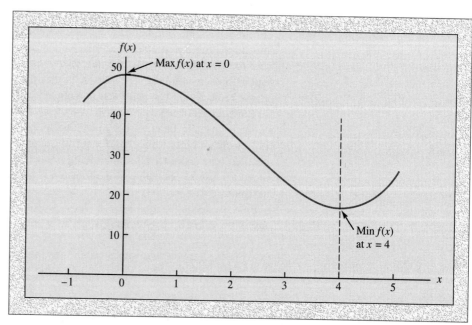

You should now be able to find the maximum or minimum of a function over a specified interval. Try Problems 1(b), 1(c), and 2(b).

Step 3 Since we are searching for a minimum and $f(4) = 18 < f(5) = 25$, we conclude that $x^* = 4$ is the global minimum solution. We note also in this example that the local maximum found in step 1 corresponded to one of the end points. This is purely a coincidence where the first derivative of the function happens to be zero at an end point of the interval.

NOTES & COMMENTS

1. The material in this chapter illustrates the development of models based on nonlinear relationships. When one realizes that many real-world relationships are nonlinear, the appeal of developing nonlinear models becomes apparent. However, nonlinear models are much more difficult to solve than linear models. For this reason, we recommend that a linear model be considered first. If a linear model is judged to be a reasonable approximation, solution procedures such as linear programming computer software are readily available. If a linear model does not provide an acceptable approximation, a nonlinear model should be used. Even if only an approximate solution can be found to the correct nonlinear model, this is usually better than having an optimal solution to an inappropriate linear model.

2. The difference between a local and a global optimal solution is a critical issue in solving calculus-based optimization models. The calculus-based necessary and sufficient conditions only permit us to identify local optimal solutions. Once all the local optimal solutions have been found, we can choose the best as the global optimal solution. Computer codes are available for helping identify local optimal solutions. Searching for the global optimal solution usually requires some trial-and-error experimentation with different starting solutions. The expertise of a management scientist is often critical in arriving at the global optimal solution to a nonlinear model.

19.2 Unconstrained Models with More Than One Decision Variable

Situations involving several independent variables are more common than situations involving only one independent variable.

As we have seen in the previous section and elsewhere in the text, there are a number of problem situations for which we can develop mathematical models involving only one decision variable. However, there are even more decision-making situations in which the decision maker must select the best values for two or more decision variables. In this section we discuss a problem that leads to the formulation of a nonlinear mathematical model involving two decision variables. Then we show how first and second derivative tests similar to rules 1 and 2 can be developed for finding the local maximum and local minimum values of unconstrained functions of two variables. We do not attempt to extend the analysis to the case where each of the variables is restricted to an interval. This case is inherently more difficult than the situation for one variable, and its analysis would take us too far afield for an introductory text of this nature.[3] For completeness, we will discuss the extension to unconstrained models involving several decision variables.

---

[3]The analysis of this case essentially involves treating each end point as a separate constraint. For a discussion, see B. S. Gottfried and J. Weisman, *Introduction to Optimization Theory* (Englewood Cliffs, N.J.: Prentice-Hall, 1973).

To see how a mathematical model involving two decision variables might arise, let us suppose that Lawn King, Inc., manufactures two styles of lawn mower. One is a riding mower, and the other is a standard walking power mower. Lawn King is interested in establishing a pricing policy for the two mowers that will maximize the total profit for the product line. Sales for these two products are not independent. Over time, Lawn King has observed that an increase in the price of the riding mower is usually accompanied by a decrease in the number of riding mowers sold and an increase in the number of walking mowers sold. Similarly, increases in the price of the walking mower have been accompanied by a decrease in sales of the walking mower and an increase in sales of the riding mower. Economists would say that the two types of lawn mowers are *substitutable products*. Because these two products are substitutable, we should expect that an appropriate mathematical model for maximizing total profit would involve the simultaneous consideration of the prices for both products.

Suppose that after a study of the relationships between sales prices and quantities sold, Lawn King has established the following expressions:

$$q_1 = 95 - 2p_1 + 0.7p_2 \tag{19.6}$$

$$q_2 = 188 + 0.3p_1 - 0.5p_2 \tag{19.7}$$

where

q_1 = number of walking mowers sold in thousands
q_2 = number of riding mowers sold in thousands
p_1 = price of walking mower in dollars
p_2 = price of riding mower in dollars

Further information, prepared by the accounting department, is available on the total cost of producing each type of mower:

$$c_1 = 100 + 90q_1 \tag{19.8}$$

$$c_2 = 50 + 250q_2 \tag{19.9}$$

where

c_1 = total cost of producing q_1 walking mowers in thousands of dollars
c_2 = total cost of producing q_2 riding mowers in thousands of dollars

Note that the production costs are in thousands of dollars and the number of lawn mowers are being measured in thousands of units. The fixed cost of producing walking mowers (the part that is independent of the number of units produced) is thus $100,000, and the variable cost is $90,000 per 1000 walking mowers, or $90 per mower. Similarly, the fixed production cost for riding mowers is $50,000, and the variable cost is $250,000 per 1000 mowers, or $250 per mower.

We would like to develop a mathematical model of the relationship between the controllable inputs, p_1 and p_2, and the output we would like to maximize, gross profit (GP). The appropriate relationship is established as follows:

$$GP = \text{total revenue} - \text{total cost}$$
$$= (p_1q_1 + p_2q_2) - (c_1 + c_2) \tag{19.10}$$

We can use equations (19.6) through (19.9) to eliminate q_1 and q_2 from the model, permitting us to write a mathematical model that is a function of only the two decision variables p_1 and p_2. Using equations (19.6) and (19.7) to substitute into equations (19.8) and (19.9), we obtain (in thousands of dollars)

$$c_1 = 100 + 90(95 - 2p_1 + 0.7p_2)$$

$$= 8650 - 180p_1 + 63p_2$$

and

$$c_2 = 50 + 250(188 + 0.3p_1 - 0.5p_2)$$

$$= 47{,}050 + 75p_1 - 125p_2$$

Substituting these two expressions along with equations (19.6) and (19.7) into the gross profit expression (equation (19.10)) allows us to write the gross profit model as a function of p_1 and p_2 only:

$$GP = p_1(95 - 2p_1 + 0.7p_2) + p_2(188 + 0.3p_1 - 0.5p_2)$$

$$- (8650 - 180p_1 + 63p_2) - (47{,}050 + 75p_1 - 125p_2)$$

After multiplying and collecting terms, we obtain

$$GP = -2p_1^2 - 0.5p_2^2 + p_1 p_2 + 200p_1 + 250p_2 - 55{,}700 \qquad (19.11)$$

This is the function we would like to maximize. The gross profit in this model is represented by an unconstrained nonlinear function of two variables. The rules for finding the local maximum and/or local minimum of the functions of two variables are similar to the ones we developed in the previous section for the functions of one variable. There is a first derivative test that serves as a necessary condition that must be satisfied by any local maximum or minimum point. In addition, there is a second derivative test that can be applied to determine whether a point satisfying the necessary condition is a local maximum, a local minimum, or neither. This second derivative test is referred to as a sufficient condition. The first derivative test is stated as rule 3:

RULE 3 (NECESSARY CONDITION)

Both partial derivatives of an unconstrained function of two variables must equal zero at any local maximum or local minimum point.

Let us apply the first derivative test to the gross profit function (equation (19.11)) in the Lawn King problem. Recall from calculus that when taking the partial derivative of a function of more than one variable, we treat all the variables as if they were constants, except for the one on which we are taking the partial derivative. Taking the two partial derivatives of the gross profit function yields

$$\frac{\partial GP}{\partial p_1} = -4p_1 + p_2 + 200 \qquad (19.12)$$

and

$$\frac{\partial GP}{\partial p_2} = -p_2 + p_1 + 250 \qquad (19.13)$$

Following rule 3 and setting both partial derivatives equal to zero, we obtain a system of two simultaneous equations in the two variables p_1 and p_2:

$$-4p_1 + p_2 + 200 = 0 \qquad (19.14)$$

$$p_1 - p_2 + 250 = 0 \qquad (19.15)$$

Adding equations (19.14) and (19.15) yields

$$-3p_1 + 450 = 0$$

Thus, we have

$$3p_1 = 450$$

or

$$p_1 = 150$$

Substituting $p_1 = 150$ into equation (19.15) yields

$$p_2 = 400$$

Hence, the point $p_1 = 150$ and $p_2 = 400$ satisfies the necessary condition given by rule 3. Since $p_1 = 150$ and $p_2 = 400$ are the only values of p_1 and p_2 satisfying the necessary condition, we know that if this point is a local maximum, it must also be the global maximum. Just as in the single-variable case, when there is only one point satisfying the necessary condition, the function cannot have more than one local maximum or minimum. To ensure that we have found a local maximum, and not perhaps a local minimum, a second derivative test is necessary.

The second derivative test requires that we know the values of all the second partial derivatives of the function. There are four second partial derivatives for a function of two variables; each of the two first partial derivatives has two partial derivatives itself. Let us calculate the second partial derivatives for our Lawn King problem.

To calculate the partial derivative of GP, first with respect to p_1 and then again with respect to p_1, we simply take the partial derivative of equation (19.12) with respect to p_1. Thus,

$$\frac{\partial^2 GP}{\partial p_1^2} = -4$$

The notation $\partial^2 GP/\partial p_1^2$ is used to indicate that the partial derivative of GP was taken first with respect to p_1 and then again with respect to p_1.

To calculate the second partial derivative denoted by $\partial^2 GP/\partial p_2 \partial p_1$ we first take the partial derivative of GP with respect to p_1 and then again with respect to p_2. Thus, we can compute this partial derivative by taking the partial derivative of equation (19.12) with respect to p_2. Doing so, we obtain

$$\frac{\partial^2 GP}{\partial p_2 \partial p_1} = 1$$

Similarly, the notation $\partial^2 GP/\partial p_1 \partial p_2$ is used to indicate that the partial derivative of GP was taken first with respect to p_2 and then with respect to p_1. Taking the partial derivative of equation (19.13) with respect to p_1, we obtain this second partial derivative:

$$\frac{\partial^2 GP}{\partial p_1 \partial p_2} = 1$$

Finally, the notation $\partial^2 GP/\partial p_2^2$ is used to indicate that the partial derivative of GP was taken first with respect to p_2 and then again with respect to p_2. Hence, we obtain this second partial derivative by taking the partial derivative of equation (19.13) with respect to p_2:

$$\frac{\partial^2 GP}{\partial p_2^2} = -1$$

We can make one observation as a result of calculating these second partial derivatives. In our Lawn King problem, the *mixed partials* (i.e., with respect to one variable, then the other) are equal. This is true except for certain rare cases. We shall not be interested in such cases and thus will assume that the second mixed partials are always equal. Rule 4 can now be stated as supplying sufficient conditions for a point (x_1, x_2) to give a local maximum, a local minimum, or a saddle point of an unconstrained function $f(x_1, x_2)$ of two variables:

RULE 4 (SUFFICIENT CONDITION)

If rule 3 is satisfied at the point (x_1, x_2) and

a. If

$$\frac{\partial^2 f}{\partial x_1^2} > 0$$

and

$$\left(\frac{\partial^2 f}{\partial x_1^2}\right)\left(\frac{\partial^2 f}{\partial x_2^2}\right) - \left(\frac{\partial^2 f}{\partial x_1 \partial x_2}\right)^2 > 0$$

then the point is a local *minimum.*

b. If

$$\frac{\partial^2 f}{\partial x_1^2} < 0$$

and

$$\left(\frac{\partial^2 f}{\partial x_1^2}\right)\left(\frac{\partial^2 f}{\partial x_2^2}\right) - \left(\frac{\partial^2 f}{\partial x_1 \partial x_2}\right)^2 > 0$$

then the point is a local *maximum.*

c. If

$$\left(\frac{\partial^2 f}{\partial x_1^2}\right)\left(\frac{\partial^2 f}{\partial x_2^2}\right) - \left(\frac{\partial^2 f}{\partial x_1 \partial x_2}\right)^2 < 0$$

then the point is a *saddle point,* which is neither a local maximum nor a local minimum.

Condition (c) of rule 4 referring to a saddle point means that the point we have found attains a maximum with respect to one of the variables, but a minimum with respect to the other. Hence, the function indeed looks like a saddle at that point, and the solution is neither a local maximum nor a local minimum value of the function.

Cases in which

$$\left(\frac{\partial^2 f}{\partial x_1^2}\right)\left(\frac{\partial^2 f}{\partial x_2^2}\right) - \left(\frac{\partial^2 f}{\partial x_1 \partial x_2}\right)^2 = 0$$

have not been mentioned. In this situation, the point could actually be a local minimum or a local maximum, but further analysis would be necessary to establish that fact. However, that further analysis is beyond the scope of this text.

Let us now apply rule 4 to the Lawn King problem to see if we have found a local maximum. We have

$$\frac{\partial^2 GP}{\partial p_1^2} = -4 < 0$$

and

$$\left(\frac{\partial^2 GP}{\partial p_1^2}\right)\left(\frac{\partial^2 GP}{\partial p_2^2}\right) - \left(\frac{\partial^2 GP}{\partial p_1 \partial p_2}\right)^2 = (-4)(-1) - (1)^2 = 3 > 0$$

Therefore, case (b) of rule 4 applies, and we have indeed found a local maximum, which from our previous discussion we know to be a global maximum.

Our analysis of the Lawn King problem is now complete. We have determined that a pricing policy of $150 for the walking mower and $400 for the riding mower will maximize the company's gross profit. Using equation (19.11), the gross profit the company can anticipate if it employs this pricing policy is

$$GP = -2(150)^2 - 0.5(400)^2 + (150)(400) + 200(150)$$
$$+ 250(400) - 55,700 = 9300$$

Since the model measures gross profit in thousands of dollars, Lawn King can anticipate a gross profit of $9,300,000 with this pricing policy. Of course, there are a number of other expenses that must yet be subtracted before we can determine the company's net profit.

At a price of $150 for the walking mower and $400 for the riding mower, we can now determine the number of mowers that will be sold by using equations (19.6) and (19.7). The number of walking mowers sold in thousands, q_1, is

$$q_1 = 95 - 2p_1 + 0.7p_2$$
$$= 95 - 2(150) + 0.7(400)$$
$$= 75$$

The number of riding mowers sold in thousands, q_2, is

$$q_2 = 188 + 0.3p_1 - 0.5p_2$$
$$= 188 + 0.3(150) - 0.5(400)$$
$$= 33$$

Thus, if Lawn King produces 75,000 walking mowers at a price of $150 each and 33,000 riding mowers at a price of $400 each, the company will maximize gross profit at an anticipated level of $9,300,000. Note that the confidence management has in the relationships established between the sales prices and quantities sold and costs and quantities sold is critical to the applicability of these results. That is, if management believes equations (19.6) through (19.9) are accurate representations of the true relationships between these factors, then the information developed using the calculus-based solution procedures can be valuable input to the decision-making process.

In our discussion of the Lawn King problem, we concluded that the local maximum point $p_1 = 150$ and $p_2 = 400$ was also the global maximum since $p_1 = 150$ and $p_2 = 400$ were the only values satisfying the necessary condition given by rule 3. Let us now discuss how we can in general determine the global optimal solution for any unconstrained function of two variables. We will state the procedure for a maximization problem to simplify the exposition. The modifications necessary to solve minimization problems should be apparent.

Step 1 Find all local maxima by applying rules 3 and 4.

Step 2 Select the largest of the local maxima as the global maximum (maxima).[4]

Note that a function can have more than one global maximum. Such situations are analogous to the case of alternative optimal soultions in a linear program.

To make sure that we understand the concepts involved in optimizing unconstrained mathematical models with two decision variables, let us consider the following numerical example.

Example Suppose we want to find all the minimum and maximum points of the function below.

$$f(x_1, x_2) = 5x_1^2 + 10x_2^2 + 10x_1x_2 - 22x_1 - 26x_2 + 25 \qquad (19.16)$$

Applying rule 3, we must set the partial derivatives with respect to x_1 and x_2 equal to zero and then solve the resulting equations for x_1 and x_2:

$$\frac{\partial f}{\partial x_1} = 10x_1 + 10x_2 - 22 = 0$$

$$\frac{\partial f}{\partial x_2} = 20x_2 + 10x_1 - 26 = 0$$

Solving these equations, we obtain the solution $x_1 = \frac{9}{5}$, $x_2 = \frac{2}{5}$. To see if this is a local maximum or a local minimum, we must calculate the second partial derivatives and apply rule 4. Calculating the second partial derivatives, we get

$$\frac{\partial^2 f}{\partial x_1^2} = 10 \qquad \frac{\partial^2 f}{\partial x_2^2} = 20 \qquad \frac{\partial^2 f}{\partial x_1 \partial x_2} = 10$$

Since

$$\frac{\partial^2 f}{\partial x_1^2} = 10 > 0$$

---

[4]For those unconstrained functions that go to infinity, a global maximum does not exist. Hence, in such cases, steps 1 and 2 will not yield a global maximum. However, such functions could never be realistic models of real-world optimization problems, and consequently we avoid a digression into such considerations in this text.

and

$$\left(\frac{\partial^2 f}{\partial x_1^2}\right)\left(\frac{\partial^2 f}{\partial x_2^2}\right) - \left(\frac{\partial^2 f}{\partial x_1 \partial x_2}\right)^2 = (10)(20) - (10)^2 = 100 > 0$$

case (a) of rule 4 applies, and the point $x_1 = \frac{9}{5}$, $x_2 = \frac{2}{5}$ yields a local minimum value for the function. Since this is the only point at which rule 3 applies, we can further conclude that this local minimum is the global minimum.

At this point, you should be able to determine the global optimal solution for an unconstrained function of two decision variables. Try Problem 7.

Let us pause for a moment to reflect on what we have learned in this section. Just as for unconstrained functions of a single variable, there is a first and second derivative test that must be applied to determine whether a point is a local maximum or a local minimum. The first derivative test, which must be satisfied by both local maximum and local minimum points, is called a necessary condition and is stated in rule 3. The second derivative test, just as with functions of a single variable, allows us to distinguish among a local maximum point, a local minimum point, and a point that may be neither a local maximum nor a local minimum. This is called a sufficient condition and is stated in rule 4.

We would like to comment, before closing this section, that for unconstrained functions of more than two variables, the first and second derivative tests are given by extensions of rules 3 and 4. For an unconstrained function of n variables, $f(x_1, x_2, \ldots, x_n)$, the first derivative test for a local maximum or a local minimum requires that all n of the partial derivatives equal zero. Since it is a simple extension of rule 3, we state it here as rule 5:

Rule 5 (Necessary Condition)

All n partial derivatives of an unconstrained function of n variables, $f(x_1, x_2, \ldots, x_n)$, must equal zero at any local maximum or local minimum point.

For an unconstrained function of n variables, the second derivative test requires that all the second partial derivatives be calculated. Although this test is similar to rule 4, a simple statement of the test requires that we construct a matrix of second partial derivatives and perform some tests on the matrix. The tests require a knowledge of determinants of matrices, which is not a prerequisite for the text. Thus, we omit an extension of rule 4 to a second derivative test for functions of n variables. This extension is discussed in a number of more advanced texts on mathematical programming.[5]

19.3   Models with Equality Constraints: Lagrange Multipliers

In this section we discuss a problem that leads to the formulation of a nonlinear mathematical model involving two decision variables and one constraint. After we have

---

[5]A good discussion of these tests is contained in D. G. Luenberger, *Introduction to Linear and Nonlinear Programming* (Reading, Mass.: Addison-Wesley, 1973).

seen how such a problem might arise, we present a solution procedure that once again involves a calculus-based first and second derivative test.

Green Lawns, Inc., provides a lawn fertilizer and weed control service. The company provides four treatments of fertilizer and weed control chemicals to its subscribers each year. In order to attract new customers, Green Lawns has decided to offer a special aeration treatment as a low-cost extra service. Management is planning to promote this new service in two media: radio and direct-mail advertising. A budget of $2000 is to be used on this promotional campaign over the next quarter. Based on past experience in promoting its other services, Green Lawns has been able to obtain an estimate of the relationship between sales and the amount spent on promotion in these two media:

$$s = -2x_1^2 - 10x_2^2 - 8x_1x_2 + 18x_1 + 34x_2 \tag{19.17}$$

where

s = sales in thousands of dollars
x_1 = thousands of dollars spent on radio advertising
x_2 = thousands of dollars spent on direct-mail promotion

Green Lawns would like to develop a promotional strategy that will lead to maximum sales subject to the restriction provided by the promotional budget. Recognizing that the promotional budget is $2000, we may state Green Lawn's problem as the following constrained optimization problem:

$$\text{Max} \quad -2x_1^2 - 10x_2^2 - 8x_1x_2 + 18x_1 + 34x_2$$

$$\text{s.t.} \tag{19.18}$$

$$x_1 + x_2 = 2$$

We note that the constraint is written as $x_1 + x_2 = 2$ because x_1 and x_2 are being measured in thousands of dollars. Also, the objective function calls for the maximization of sales in thousands of dollars.

In general, all problems involving the minimization or maximization of a function of two variables subject to an equality constraint can be written as follows:

$$\text{Min or Max} \quad f(x_1, x_2)$$

$$\text{s.t.} \tag{19.19}$$

$$g(x_1, x_2) = b$$

We shall solve the above class of problems by introducing a new variable, called a *Lagrange multiplier,* and using it to combine the constraint and objective function into a single function. The new single function is called a *Lagrangian function* and is written below, where λ denotes the Lagrange multiplier.

$$\text{Lagrangian function} = L(x_1, x_2, \lambda) \tag{19.20}$$

$$= f(x_1, x_2) + \lambda[g(x_1, x_2) - b]$$

The first derivative test that every local minimum or maximum point of a constrained problem must satisfy[6] is stated in rule 6:

Rule 6 (Necessary Condition)

For a function of two variables, x_1 and x_2, subject to one constraint to have a local minimum or a local maximum at a point, the partial derivatives of the Lagrangian function with respect to x_1, x_2, and λ must all equal zero at that point.

Thus, once we have set up the Lagrangian function, the first derivative test for a constrained problem turns out to be very similar to the first derivative test for unconstrained functions. Let us now apply this test to the problem faced by Green Lawns, Inc.

Introducing a Lagrange multiplier as indicated by equations (19.19) and (19.20), we obtain the following Lagrangian function:

$$L(x_1, x_2, \lambda) = -2x_1^2 - 10x_2^2 - 8x_1x_2 + 18x_1 + 34x_2$$
$$+ \lambda(x_1 + x_2 - 2) \qquad (19.21)$$

Following rule 6, we first determine the partial derivatives with respect to x_1, x_2, and λ, and then set them equal to zero:

$$\frac{\partial L}{\partial x_1} = -4x_1 - 8x_2 + 18 + \lambda = 0 \qquad (19.22)$$

$$\frac{\partial L}{\partial x_2} = -20x_2 - 8x_1 + 34 + \lambda = 0 \qquad (19.23)$$

$$\frac{\partial L}{\partial \lambda} = x_1 + x_2 - 2 = 0 \qquad (19.24)$$

We are left with three equations in three unknowns: x_1, x_2, and λ. Solving these will give us a point that satisfies rule 6 and is thus a candidate for a maximum solution of the Green Lawns problem. Subtracting equation (19.22) from equation (19.23) allows us to form a new equation not including λ:

$$-4x_1 - 12x_2 + 16 = 0 \qquad (19.25)$$

Multiplying equation (19.24) by 4 and adding the result to equation (19.25) yields

$$-8x_2 + 8 = 0$$

Hence,

$$x_2 = 1$$

Substituting $x_2 = 1$ into equation (19.24), we find that $x_1 = 1$. As a consequence, from equations (19.22) and (19.23) we find that $\lambda = -6$. Thus, the necessary condition of rule 1 is satisfied with

$$x_1^* = 1$$
$$x_2^* = 1$$
$$\lambda^* = -6$$

---

[6]There are certain examples that can be constructed for which the maximum or minimum does not satisfy rule 6, but since these exceptions rarely occur in practice, we shall not be concerned with them.

Since there is only one solution satisfying rule 6, we know that if it is a local maximum, it is also a global maximum. It remains to be seen if this point truly yields a local maximum solution for the Green Lawns problem. We must develop a second derivative rule to make that determination. Rule 7 provides such a test and thus gives sufficient conditions for a local maximum or minimum point.

RULE 7 (SUFFICIENT CONDITION)

If rule 6 is satisfied at a point $(x_1^*, x_2^*, \lambda^*)$, apply conditions (a) and (b) of rule 4 to the Lagrangian function with λ fixed at a value of λ^* to determine if the point (x_1^*, x_2^*) is a local maximum or a local minimum.

Rule 7 says first to fix λ at the value necessary to satisfy rule 6. Then the Lagrangian function is expressed as a function of the two variables x_1 and x_2, with λ fixed at the value λ^*. Conditions (a) and (b) of rule 4 may be applied to this new function to determine if we have a local maximum or a local minimum.[7]

Let us apply rule 7 to the Green Lawns problem to see if the solution we have found is a local maximum. The Lagrangian function (equation (19.21)) with λ fixed at $\lambda^* = -6$ is

$$L(x_1, x_2, \lambda = -6) = -2x_1^2 - 10x_2^2 - 8x_1x_2 + 18x_1 + 34x_2$$
$$- 6(x_1 + x_2 - 2)$$

We need to find the second partial derivatives of this function with respect to x_1 and x_2 to determine if the $x_1^* = 1$ and $x_2^* = 1$ solution yields a maximum. Taking the first partial derivatives with respect to x_1 and x_2, we obtain the same result we could have obtained by substituting $\lambda = -6$ into equations (19.22) and (19.23):

$$\frac{\partial L}{\partial x_1} = -4x_1 - 8x_2 + 18 - 6 = -4x_1 - 8x_2 + 12$$

$$\frac{\partial L}{\partial x_2} = -20x_2 - 8x_1 + 34 - 6 = -20x_2 - 8x_1 + 28$$

The second partial derivatives of this function with respect to x_1 and x_2 are

$$\frac{\partial^2 L}{\partial x_1^2} = -4 \qquad \frac{\partial^2 L}{\partial x_2^2} = -20 \qquad \frac{\partial^2 L}{\partial x_1 \partial x_2} = -8$$

To see whether the Lagrangian function with λ fixed at $\lambda^* = -6$ has an unconstrained minimum at $x_1^* = 1$ and $x_2^* = 1$, we apply the second derivative test developed in rule 4 for unconstrained functions of two variables:

$$\frac{\partial^2 L}{\partial x_1^2} = -4 < 0$$

$$\left(\frac{\partial^2 L}{\partial x_1^2}\right)\left(\frac{\partial^2 L}{\partial x_2^2}\right) - \left(\frac{\partial^2 L}{\partial x_1 \partial x_2}\right)^2 = (-4)(-20) - (-8)^2 = 16 > 0$$

---

[7]Condition (c) of rule 4 is not used for equality-constrained problems since a saddle point of the Lagrangian function need not correspond to a saddle point of the equality-constrained problem we want to solve.

Case (b) of rule 4 applies, and the point $x_1^* = 1$, $x_2^* = 1$ is an unconstrained maximum of the Lagrangian function with $\lambda = -6$. Thus, we see that $x_1^* = 1$ and $x_2^* = 1$ is the optimal solution to the Green Lawns problem. The company should invest \$1000 in radio advertising and \$1000 in direct-mail promotion. To determine the expected sales volume from this strategy, we must evaluate the objective function (equation (19.17)) with $x_1 = 1$ and $x_2 = 1$. Doing so, we obtain

$$\text{Sales} = -2(1)^2 - 10(1)^2 - 8(1)(1) + 18(1) + 34(1) = 32$$

Thus, the expected sales volume resulting from this promotional strategy is \$32,000.

The following numerical example provides another illustration of the use of the Lagrange multiplier method for solving equality-constrained optimization problems.

Example Suppose we have the following constrained optimization problem:

$$\text{Min} \quad x_1^2 + 2x_2^2 - 8x_1 - 12x_2 + 34$$

s.t.

$$x_1 + 2x_2 = 4$$

Setting up the Lagrangian function for this problem, we obtain

$$L(x_1, x_2, \lambda) = x_1^2 + 2x_2^2 - 8x_1 - 12x_2 + 34 + \lambda(x_1 + 2x_2 - 4) \qquad (19.26)$$

Applying rule 6, we set the partial derivatives of this Lagrangian function with respect to x_1, x_2, and λ equal to zero:

$$\frac{\partial L}{\partial x_1} = 2x_1 - 8 + \lambda = 0$$

$$\frac{\partial L}{\partial x_2} = 4x_2 - 12 + 2\lambda = 0$$

$$\frac{\partial L}{\partial \lambda} = x_1 + 2x_2 - 4 = 0$$

Solving the resulting three equations for the three unknowns, we obtain

$$x_1^* = 2 \qquad x_2^* = 1 \qquad \lambda^* = 4$$

Once again, there is only one solution satisfying rule 6. Thus, if it is a local maximum or minimum, it must also be a global maximum or minimum.

We must now apply rule 7 to see whether this is a local maximum or a local minimum point. Setting $\lambda^* = 4$ in equation (19.26), the second partial derivatives of the Lagrangian function with respect to x_1 and x_2 are

$$\frac{\partial^2 L}{\partial x_1^2} = 2 \qquad \frac{\partial^2 L}{\partial x_2^2} = 4 \qquad \frac{\partial^2 L}{\partial x_1 \partial x_2} = 0$$

Checking conditions (a) and (b) of the test procedures for rule 4, we have

$$\frac{\partial^2 L}{\partial x_1^2} = 2 > 0$$

and

$$\left(\frac{\partial^2 L}{\partial x_1^2}\right)\left(\frac{\partial^2 L}{\partial x_2^2}\right) - \left(\frac{\partial^2 L}{\partial x_1 \partial x_2}\right)^2 = (2)(4) - (0)^2 = 8 > 0$$

You should now be able to use Lagrange multipliers to solve equality-constrained optimization problems. Try Problem 11a.

Thus, we have a local minimum of the Lagrangian function with λ fixed at 4, and in light of the previous discussion, we have found a global minimum at $x_1 = 2$ and $x_2 = 1$.

The Green Lawns, Inc., problem and the above problem are examples of models having a nonlinear objective function and a linear equality constraint. In applying rules 6 and 7, we were able to develop the necessary and sufficient condition test relatively easily. However, for problems where the equality constraint is also nonlinear, you will find that the solution computations become somewhat more difficult. (Problems 12 and 14 at the end of this chapter ask you to use rules 6 and 7 to solve a problem with a nonlinear objective function and a nonlinear equality constraint.)

To complete our discussion, we mention briefly how rule 6 can be extended to supply a necessary condition for minimizing or maximizing a function of n variables subject to m equality constraints. This extended problem may be stated in the following general form:

$$\text{Min or Max} \quad f(x_1, x_2, \dots, x_n)$$

s.t.

$$g_1(x_1, x_2, \dots, x_n) = b_1$$
$$g_2(x_1, x_2, \dots, x_n) = b_2$$
$$\vdots \qquad \qquad \vdots \qquad \qquad (19.27)$$
$$g_m(x_1, x_2, \dots, x_n) = b_m$$

A Lagrangian function, combining the objective function and all the constraints into one function, can be formulated by introducing a separate Lagrange multiplier for each constraint:

$$L(x_1, x_2, \dots, x_n, \lambda_1, \lambda_2, \dots, \lambda_m)$$
$$= f(x_1, x_2, \dots, x_n) + \lambda_1[g_1(x_1, x_2, \dots, x_n) - b_1]$$
$$+ \lambda_2[g_2(x_1, x_2, \dots, x_n) - b_2] + \cdots \qquad (19.28)$$
$$+ \lambda_m[g_m(x_1, x_2, \dots, x_n) - b_m]$$

The extension of rule 6 to this problem can now be stated in terms of this new Lagrangian function:

RULE 8 (NECESSARY CONDITION)

For a function of n variables, $f(x_1, x_2, \dots, x_n)$, subject to m constraints to have a local minimum or a local maximum at a point, the partial derivatives of the Lagrangian function with respect to $x_1, x_2, \dots, x_n$ and $\lambda_1, \lambda_2, \dots, \lambda_m$ must all equal zero at that point.

The second derivative test for this problem is a natural extension to rule 7; that is, we would check for a local maximum or a local minimum of the Lagrangian function with $\lambda_1, \lambda_2, \ldots, \lambda_m$ fixed at the values found when applying rule 8. This would require that we have a second derivative test for an unconstrained function of n variables. A matrix of second partial derivatives provides the basis for this test; however, as we stated earlier, the methodology is beyond the scope of this text.

Before concluding this section, note the similarity of this problem to those in the previous two sections. Once again we have a first derivative test that any local maximum or local minimum point has to satisfy. Then we have a second derivative test that can be used to determine whether a point satisfying the first derivative test is indeed a local maximum or a local minimum. The only conceptual difference in solving these constrained problems is in the formulation of the Lagrangian function and the first and second derivative tests on that function. Only conditions (a) and (b) of the second derivative test are applicable for constrained problems.

19.4 Interpretation of the Lagrange Multiplier

In the previous section we saw that it is necessary to introduce an additional variable called a Lagrange multiplier in order to solve constrained problems. This variable was used in setting up the Lagrangian function. In meeting the necessary condition (rule 6), we actually found a value for the Lagrange multiplier. The value of this Lagrange multiplier can often be used to provide valuable managerial information about the sensitivity of an optimal solution to changes in resource levels.

To be more specific, let us reconsider the Green Lawns problem, which is restated below:

$$\text{Max} \quad -2x_1^2 - 10x_2^2 - 8x_1x_2 + 18x_1 + 34x_2$$

s.t.

$$x_1 + x_2 = 2$$

Here, x_1 represents the amount spent on radio advertising and x_2 the amount spent on direct-mail promotion. The constraint indicates that $2000 is to be used for the promotional campaign and that it is to be divided between the two media, x_1 and x_2. In the previous section we saw that the optimal allocation divided the budget equally between the two media: $x_1 = 1$ and $x_2 = 1$. Management might wonder what the effect on sales would be if a different amount—say, $1000 or $3000—were budgeted for the promotional campaign. The value of the Lagrange multiplier provides an estimate of that effect. Let us see how.

Recall that the general model with two decision variables and one equality constraint was written as

$$\text{Min or Max} \quad f(x_1, x_2)$$

s.t.

$$g(x_1, x_2) = b$$

The interpretation of the Lagrange multiplier for this problem is stated as property 1.

PROPERTY 1 (INTERPRETATION OF THE LAGRANGE MULTIPLIER)

The value of the Lagrange multiplier associated with the general model above is the negative of the rate of change of the objective function with respect to a change in b. More formally, it is the negative of the partial derivative of $f(x_1, x_2)$ with respect to b; that is, $\lambda = -\partial f/\partial b$ or

$$\frac{\partial f}{\partial b} = -\lambda \qquad (19.29)$$

The optimal solution to the Green Lawns problem has

$$x_1^* = 1 \qquad x_2^* = 1 \qquad \lambda^* = -6$$

Since $\lambda^* = -6$, property 1 indicates that with $\partial f/\partial b = -\lambda = -(-6) = 6$, the objective function should increase by approximately 6 if b is increased by 1. For example, if the budget is increased from \$2000 to \$3000 in the Green Lawns problem, the objective function should increase by approximately \$6000. Let us change the budget to \$3000 and see what happens.

After increasing the budget to \$3000, the Green Lawns problem can be written as follows:

$$\text{Max} \quad -2x_1^2 - 10x_2^2 - 8x_1x_2 + 18x_1 + 34x_2 \qquad (19.30)$$

s.t.

$$x_1 + x_2 = 3$$

Formulating the Lagrangian function and setting the partial derivatives equal to zero yield

$$L(x_1, x_2, \lambda) = -2x_1^2 - 10x_2^2 - 8x_1x_2 + 18x_1 + 34x_2 \qquad (19.31)$$
$$+ \lambda(x_1 + x_2 - 3)$$

and

$$\frac{\partial L}{\partial x_1} = -4x_1 - 8x_2 + 18 + \lambda = 0$$

$$\frac{\partial L}{\partial x_2} = -20x_2 - 8x_1 + 34 + \lambda = 0$$

$$\frac{\partial L}{\partial \lambda} = x_1 + x_2 - 3 = 0$$

Solving these three equations simultaneously for x_1, x_2, and λ yields

$$x_1^* = 2.5 \qquad x_2^* = 0.5 \qquad \lambda^* = -4$$

To check to see whether we have a maximum, we must determine the second partial derivatives of the Lagrangian with λ fixed at $\lambda^* = -4$. Using equation (19.31) with $\lambda = -4$, these second partial derivatives are

$$\frac{\partial^2 L}{\partial x_1^2} = -4 \qquad \frac{\partial^2 L}{\partial x_2^2} = -20 \qquad \frac{\partial^2 L}{\partial x_1 \partial x_2} = -8$$

Applying rule 4, we see that $x_1^* = 2.5$ and $x_2^* = 0.5$ does indeed yield an unconstrained maximum of the Lagrangian with λ fixed at $\lambda^* = -4$. According to rule 7, we have found the maximum for this new problem.

Now we would like to see how close the $6000 increase in the objective function predicted by $\lambda^* = -6$ comes to the true increase. The value of the objective function for $x_1^* = 2.5$ and $x_2^* = 0.5$ is

$$f(x_1, x_2) = \text{sales} = -2(2.5)^2 - 10(0.5)^2 - 8(2.5)(0.5)$$

$$+ 18(2.5) + 34(0.5) = 37$$

The maximum value of sales, given a budget of $3000, is thus $37,000. Since the maximum value for a budget of $2000 was previously found to be $32,000, the increase in sales is $5000 and not the $6000 the value of the Lagrange multiplier predicted. We should not be too surprised at this. What we are observing is the law of diminishing returns. As the amount of resources available increases (advertising budget in this case), the per-unit increase in the objective function decreases. Note that the value we obtained for the Lagrange multiplier when the budget was increased to $3000 was $\lambda^* = -4$. This would lead us to predict that sales would increase by another $4000 if the budget were further increased to $4000. The rate of return per unit increase in the budget has decreased from 6 to 4 as the budget has increased from 2 to 3.

Also, we should note that the Lagrange multiplier value associated with a budget of $3000, $\lambda^* = -4$, would lead us to predict that sales would decrease by $4000 if the budget were decreased to $2000. The actual change, as we now know, is $5000. Thus, if we used the Lagrange multiplier associated with $b = 2000$, $\lambda^* = -6$, to predict the change in sales associated with a $1000 change in the budget, we would overestimate the change. On the other hand, if we used the Lagrange multiplier associated with $b = 3000$, $\lambda^* = -4$, to predict the change in sales associated with changing the budget from $3000 to $2000, we would underestimate the change. The actual change, $5000, is halfway between.

In Table 19.1 we show the maximum sales levels for budget amounts varying between $1000 and $3000 in increments of $200 together with the maximum sales levels we would have predicted by using the property of the Lagrange multiplier.

Table 19.1 verifies that the estimates based on the Lagrange multiplier are good as long as the change in b is not large. For a $200 change in the budget, the estimate based on the Lagrange multiplier is pretty good. There is only a $40 error in the sales estimate. Of course, as we get farther away from a budget of $2000, the predictions continue to get worse. We can also see the effect of diminishing returns with respect to the advertising budget from studying the table. When the budget is set at $1000, a $200 increase causes an increase in sales of $1560. When the budget is set at $2800, a $200 increase causes an increase in sales of only $840.

From a managerial point of view, we see that the value of the Lagrange multiplier can provide important information. It is an indication of the sensitivity of the optimal solution to changes in resource levels. In most real-world problems, these resource levels are not some number that cannot be changed. For example, in the Green Lawns situation, management has initially budgeted $2000 for an advertising campaign. If the quantitative analyst can show the manager that an increase in the advertising budget of $1 can be expected to increase sales by $6, then the manager may want to consider expanding the budget. Of course, whether or not the manager chooses to expand it will depend on a number of other considerations as well. Can funds be freed from other uses for the

Table 19.1

Maximum Sales Levels for Varying Budgets Compared with Estimates Based on the Lagrange Multiplier of $\lambda = -6$ for the Green Lawns Problem

Budget	Actual Maximum Sales $f(x_1^*, x_2^*)$	Estimated Maximum Sales $\lambda^* = -6$	Difference
$1000	$25,000	$26,000	−1000
1200	26,560	27,200	− 640
1400	28,040	28,400	− 360
1600	29,440	29,600	− 160
1800	30,760	30,800	− 40
2000	32,000	32,000	0
2200	33,160	33,200	− 40
2400	34,240	34,400	− 160
2600	35,240	35,600	− 360
2800	36,160	36,800	− 640
3000	37,000	38,000	−1000

campaign? How much confidence do we have that our model is representative of the real relationship between advertising in the two media and sales? Also, since the $6 increase in sales will cost us $1 of advertising, is the remaining $5 enough to offset all the other costs associated with the increased sales? Regardless of how this sensitivity information is eventually used by the manager, it is important to know what it means and that it can be made available as a by-product of the model solution.

The Lagrange multiplier analysis can be extended to problems with more variables and more constraints. However, because of the additional complexity involved, we leave a discussion of this extension to more advanced texts on mathematical programming.

NOTES & COMMENTS

The managerial interpretation of the Lagrange multiplier in a constrained optimization model parallels the interpretation of dual prices in a linear programming model. The value of a Lagrange multiplier provides the marginal value of making a change in the right-hand side of a constraint. In applications where the right-hand side of a constraint represents the amount of a scarce resource, the multiplier identifies the marginal value of obtaining additional quantities of the resource. However, since nonlinear relationships are involved, the value of the multiplier can change as soon as any change is made in the value of the right-hand side. There is no "range of feasibility" over which the value of the Lagrange multiplier does not change. A manager should keep this in mind and recognize that using the Lagrange multiplier can only be interpreted as an approximation of the value of additional resources in a nonlinear model.

19.5 Models Involving Inequality Constraints

In this section we study problems that lead to nonlinear mathematical models involving two decision variables and one inequality constraint. We will find that this type of problem can be solved using the approaches we have already learned in the previous sections of this chapter.

Suppose that instead of stating that a budget of $2000 had to be spent on an advertising campaign for the aeration service, the management of Green Lawns, Inc., had stated that the amount spent had to be less than or equal to the $2000 budget. This is actually a more realistic interpretation of the budget constraint. Certainly if more sales could be realized by spending less on advertising, the company would be willing to do so. Given this less-than-or-equal-to interpretation of the constraint, the Green Lawns model would involve two decision variables and one inequality constraint as shown below.

$$\text{Max} \quad -2x_1^2 - 10x_2^2 - 8x_1x_2 + 18x_1 + 34x_2$$

$$\text{s.t.}$$

$$x_1 + x_2 \leq 2$$

In solving this problem, we recognize that there are actually two possibilities with respect to the constraint. The first is that the constraint $x_1 + x_2 \leq 2$ will be binding at the optimal solution. In this case, we could assume that the constraint has the form $x_1 + x_2 = 2$ and then solve the problem just as we did in Section 19.3 for problems with equality constraints. The second possibility is that at the optimal solution the constraint is not binding; that is, $x_1^* + x_2^* < 2$. In this case, we could simply ignore the constraint and solve the problem as we did in Section 19.2 for unconstrained problems. The recognition that these are the only two possibilities is what motivates the solution procedure we are about to present.

We state the solution procedure for a maximization problem in order to simplify the exposition. The modifications necessary to solve minimization problems should be apparent.

Step 1   Assume the constraint is not binding, and apply the procedures of Section 19.2 to find the global maximum of the function, if it exists. (Functions that go to infinity do not have a global maximum.) If this global maximum satisfies the constraint, stop. This is the global maximum for the inequality-constrained problem. If not, the constraint may be binding at the optimum. Record the value of any local maximum that satisfies the inequality constraint, and go on to step 2.

Step 2   Assume the constraint is binding, and apply the procedures of Section 19.3 to find all the local maxima of the resulting equality-constrained problem. Compare these values with any feasible local maxima found in step 1. The largest of these is the global maximum.

Let us apply this solution procedure to our new version of the Green Lawns problem. Applying step 1 and ignoring the constraint $x_1 + x_2 \leq 2$ would lead us to solve the unconstrained problem

$$\text{Max} \quad -2x_1^2 - 10x_2^2 - 8x_1x_2 + 18x_1 + 34x_2$$

Applying rule 3, we set the partial derivatives of the objective function equal to zero:

$$\frac{\partial f}{\partial x_1} = -4x_1 - 8x_2 + 18 = 0$$

$$\frac{\partial f}{\partial x_2} = -20x_2 - 8x_1 + 34 = 0$$

Solving these two equations simultaneously, we obtain $x_1^* = 5\frac{1}{2}$ and $x_2^* = -\frac{1}{2}$. Before checking the second derivatives for a local maximum or minimum, however, let us see if these values for x_1 and x_2 satisfy the constraint. Clearly, $x_1^* + x_2^* = 5\frac{1}{2} - \frac{1}{2} = 5$ is not less than or equal to 2, and, therefore, even if this solution did yield the global maximum to the unconstrained problem (which it does, by the way), it could not be optimal since it does not satisfy the inequality constraint. There are no other local maxima to record; therefore, we go on to step 2 and solve the following equality-constrained optimization problem:

$$\text{Max} \quad -2x_1^2 - 10x_2^2 - 8x_1x_2 + 18x_1 + 34x_2$$

s.t.

$$x_1 + x_2 = 2$$

The global maximum for this problem was found in Section 19.3 and is given by $x_1 = 1$ and $x_2 = 1$. Since there are no feasible local maxima from step 1, the optimal solution to the constrained optimization problem is also $x_1 = 1$, $x_2 = 1$, with an expected sales volume of \$32,000.

Let us now look at another example involving a minimization problem.

Example. Suppose we want to solve the following problem:

$$\text{Min} \quad f(x_1, x_2) = x_1^2 - 10x_1 + x_2^2 - 10x_2$$

s.t.

$$x_1 + 2x_2 \leq 20$$

Step 1 of the solution procedure says to ignore the constraint and solve the resulting unconstrained optimization problem. Applying rule 3, we set the partial derivatives of the objective function equal to zero:

$$\frac{\partial f}{\partial x_1} = 2x_1 - 10 = 0$$

$$\frac{\partial f}{\partial x_2} = 2x_2 - 10 = 0$$

Solving these two equations, we obtain $x_1^* = 5$ and $x_2^* = 5$. Since this point satisfies the constraint, we must check to see if it is a local minimum. Applying the second derivative test of rule 4, we obtain

$$\frac{\partial^2 f}{\partial x_1^2} = 2 > 0$$

and

$$\left(\frac{\partial^2 f}{\partial x_1^2}\right)\left(\frac{\partial^2 f}{\partial x_2^2}\right) - \left(\frac{\partial^2 f}{\partial x_1 \partial x_2}\right)^2 = (2)(2) - 0^2 = 4 > 0$$

Therefore, the point $x_1 = 5$, $x_2 = 5$ yields a local minimum for this function. Further, since no other values of x_1, x_2 satisfy rule 3, we can conclude that $x_1 = 5$, $x_2 = 5$ yields a global minimum for this unconstrained function. Thus, it is unnecessary to go on to step 2 since no point on the constraint boundary could possibly be better than the global minimum. We can therefore conclude that $x_1 = 5$, $x_2 = 5$ is the global minimum for the inequality-constrained problem.

We have seen how the solution procedure of this section can be applied both when the constraint is satisfied as an equality at the optimum and when it is satisfied as a strict inequality. Unfortunately, the solution procedure we have outlined here cannot be extended to problems with more than one inequality constraint or to problems with both equality and inequality constraints. We will comment briefly on what to do in such cases.

In some applications, the appropriate mathematical model may have a mixture of equality and inequality constraints. In these kinds of mathematical models, the solution approach invariably requires a computerized mathematical programming algorithm. There are many research papers and a number of mathematical programming textbooks devoted to these computerized algorithms. The approach taken by all these algorithms is iterative in nature. Initially a starting point, which is a guess at the optimal solution, is picked, and then an improved solution is determined by the computer algorithm. Another improvement is made, and so on, until eventually the optimal solution is reached. The details of these solution algorithms are beyond the scope of this text.

NOTES & COMMENTS

With linear programming models, we have shown how the computer plays an important role in determining the optimal solution to a particular problem. A number of computer codes are readily available for solving linear programming models. Computer codes are also helpful in solving nonlinear models. However, such codes are not as readily available nor as easy to use. This situation is complicated by the fact that many codes are especially designed to solve a particular type of nonlinear model. Thus, more mathematical expertise is required to understand the special characteristics of the given nonlinear model and then select a computer code that will solve the problem.

Summary

The kinds of problems discussed in this chapter have been examples of decision-making situations in which the appropriate mathematical model of the problem involved nonlinear relationships. When these decision-making situations arise, the linear programming procedures of Chapters 2 through 6 are not applicable, and calculus-based procedures must be employed.

For both unconstrained and constrained problems we saw that first and second derivative tests were required. In the unconstrained single-variable case, these tests were made on the first and second derivatives of the objective function. In the unconstrained two-variable case, these tests were made on the first and second partial derivatives of the objective function. Equality-constrained problems with two decision variables and one constraint were solved by first introducing a new variable called a Lagrange multiplier. A Lagrangian function was then formed by combining the objective function and constraint into one function. Tests on the first and second partial derivatives of the Lagrangian function were then developed to find the optimal solution. The Lagrange multiplier was found to provide valuable managerial information about the sensitivity of the optimal solution to changes in the value of the right-hand side of the constraint (the resource level).

Glossary

Local maximum (minimum) A point that gives at least as high (low) a value of the objective function as any nearby point.

Necessary conditions Conditions, usually requiring first derivatives to be equal to zero, that must be satisfied at an optimal solution. They do not guarantee an optimal solution.

Sufficient conditions Conditions, usually involving the sign of second derivatives, that determine whether a solution meeting the necessary conditions is a maximum solution, a minimum solution, or no solution.

Global maximum (minimum) The point, or points, at which a function takes on its greatest (lowest) value.

Saddle point A condition that occurs in models with two decision variables when one variable reaches its maximum value and another reaches its minimum value at the same point.

Lagrange multiplier A new variable added to a constrained nonlinear model to obtain a solution. In sensitivity analysis, this variable tells us what effect a change in the level of resources will have on the objective function.

Lagrangian function The function formed by using the Lagrange multiplier to combine the objective function and the constraint(s) into one function. For example, the constrained problem

$$\text{Min} \quad f(x_1, x_2)$$

s.t.

$$g(x_1, x_2) = b$$

has the following Lagrangian function:

$$L(x_1, x_2, \lambda) = f(x_1, x_2) + \lambda[g(x_1, x_2) - b]$$

where λ is the Lagrange multiplier.

Problems

S E L F   T E S T

1. Maximization, one variable

1. a. Maximize the function

$$f(x) = 12x - 6x^2 - 30$$

   b. Maximize the above function over the interval

$$0 \le x \le 10$$

   c. Maximize the above function over the interval

$$2 \le x \le 10$$

S E L F   T E S T

2. Minimization, one variable

2. a. Find the minimum of the function

$$f(x) = 3x^3 - 20x^2 + 60$$

   b. Find the minimum of the above function over the interval

$$0 \le x \le 4$$

3. Maximization, one variable

3. A large grocery chain is interested in determining the best size for a new store being built at a particular site. The chain has made an extensive study of the sector in which the new store will be located. Based on such factors as sector population, weekly per-capita food expenditures, and the competition, the grocery chain has developed the following model that relates sales (in thousands of dollars) to the size of the store x (in units of 10,000 square feet):

$$\text{Sales} = 100x - 10x^2 - 150$$

Determine the size of the store that will maximize sales. What are the maximum sales corresponding to the store size?

4. Maximization, one variable

4.   The manufacturer of King's Chunk Style Peanut Butter has determined that sales in any particular store are related to the amount of shelf space devoted to the peanut butter and the amount of traffic through the store. A detailed analysis led to the following equation relating the square feet on shelves and the number of store customers per week to the total weekly sales in dollars:

$$\text{Sales} = -20x^2 - 50C^2 - 60Cx + 220x - 340C + 610$$

where

$$x = \text{square feet of shelf space}$$
$$C = \text{thousands of customers}$$

King uses the above formula to determine the optimal amount of shelf space for its product in any particular store. Suppose a particular store averages a thousand customers per week. How many square feet of shelf space would be required to maximize sales?

5. Modeling, minimization, one variable

5.   Suppose the total cost (TC) of producing x pounds of a certain cleaning fluid is given by

$$TC = \tfrac{4}{3}x^4 - 3x^3 + 2x^2 + 5x$$

Write the mathematical expression for the cost per pound. If x must be at least 0.3, what batch size will lead to the minimum cost per pound?

6. Modeling, maximization, one variable

6.   A certain product sells for \$5 per unit. The total cost C of producing and selling this product is given by

$$TC(x) = x^2 - 15x + 20$$

a.   What is the fixed cost of production? That is, what portion of the cost is independent of the number of units produced?

b.   Develop a mathematical model that shows total profit as a function of the number of units produced.

c.   What level of production will maximize profit?

S E L F   T E S T ▶

7. Minimization, two variables

7.   The cost per batch of a certain production process is related to the setting of two control instruments. Suppose the total cost per batch is given by

$$f(x_1, x_2) = 4x_1^2 + 2x_2^2 + 4x_1x_2 - 8x_1 - 6x_2 + 35$$

Determine the settings for the two instruments that will minimize this cost.

8. Checking for local maximum, local minimum, or a saddle point

8.   Consider the function $f(x_1, x_2) = 2x_1^4 - 12x_1^2 + 2x_1^2x_2 + x_2^2 - 4x_2 + 20$. Determine whether the points below yield local minima, local maxima, saddle points, or none of these.

$$\begin{pmatrix} x_1 = 0 \\ x_2 = 2 \end{pmatrix} \qquad \begin{pmatrix} x_1 = +2 \\ x_2 = -2 \end{pmatrix} \qquad \begin{pmatrix} x_1 = -2 \\ x_2 = -2 \end{pmatrix}$$

9. Modeling, maximization, two variables

9.   The prices for two products, denoted by p_1 and p_2, are related to the quantities sold of the two products, x_1 and x_2, by the expressions

$$x_1 = 32 - 2p_1$$
$$x_2 = 22 - p_2$$

Further, the total cost (TC) of producing and selling the products is related to the quantities sold by the function

$$TC(x_1, x_2) = \tfrac{1}{2}x_1^2 + 2x_1x_2 + x_2^2 + 73$$

a. Develop a mathematical model that shows profit as a function of the quantities produced.
b. Determine the prices and quantities that maximize profit.

10. A shoe store has determined that its earnings $E(x_1, x_2)$, in thousands of dollars, can be approximated by a function of x_1, its investment in inventory in thousands of dollars, and x_2, its expenditure on advertising in thousands of dollars:

$$E(x_1, x_2) = -3x_1^2 + 2x_1x_2 - 6x_2^2 + 30x_1 + 24x_2 - 86$$

Find the maximum earnings, along with the amount of advertising expenditure and inventory investment, that yields this maximum.

11. Consider the problem

$$\text{Min} \quad x_1^2 - 14x_1 + x_2^2 - 16x_2 + 113$$

s.t.

$$2x_1 + 3x_2 = 12$$

a. Find the minimum solution to this problem.
b. How much would you expect the value of the solution to change if the right-hand side of the constraint were increased from 12 to 13?

12. Consider the problem

$$\text{Max} \quad -x_1^2 - 4x_1x_2 + 20x_1 - 5x_2^2 + 82x_2 - 397$$

s.t.

$$2x_1^2 - 16x_1 + 9x_2^2 - 18x_2 + 5 = 0$$

Determine whether or not the point $x_1 = 4$, $x_2 = 3$ provides an optimal solution.

13. Heller Manufacturing has two production facilities that manufacture baseball gloves. Production costs at the two facilities differ because of varying labor rates, local property taxes, type of equipment, capacity, and so on. The Dayton plant has weekly production costs that can be expressed as a function of the number of gloves produced:

$$TC_1(x_1) = x_1^2 - x_1 + 5$$

where x_1 is the weekly production volume in thousands of units and $TC_1(x_1)$ is the cost in thousands of dollars. The Hamilton plant's weekly production costs are given by

$$TC_2(x_2) = x_2^2 + 2x_2 + 3$$

where x_2 is the weekly production volume in thousands of units and $TC_2(x_2)$ is the cost, in thousands of dollars. Heller Manufacturing would like to produce 8000 gloves per week at the lowest possible cost.
a. Formulate a mathematical model that can be used to determine the number of gloves to produce each week at each facility.
b. Solve your mathematical model to determine the optimal number of gloves to produce at each facility.

14. Solve the problem

$$\text{Min} \quad x_1^2 + 2x_2^2 - 8x_1 - 12x_2 + 34$$

s.t.

$$x_1^2 + 2x_2^2 = 5$$

15. Consider the problem

$$\text{Min} \quad 2x_1^2 - 20x_1 + 2x_1x_2 + x_2^2 - 14x_2 + 58$$

s.t.

$$x_1 + 4x_2 \leq 8$$

a. Find the minimum solution to this problem.
b. If the right-hand side of the constraint is increased from 8 to 9, how much do you expect the objective function to change?

16. Jingle Bells, Inc., has received a rush order for as many of two types of Christmas bells as can be produced and shipped during a 2-week period. Preliminary analysis by Jingle Bells indicates that the profit on this order is related to the number of each type of bell manufactured by the following function:

$$P = -x_1^2 - x_2^2 + 12x_1 + 10x_2 + 61$$

where

$$P = \text{profit in thousands of dollars}$$
$$x_1 = \text{number of units of type 1 bells in thousands}$$
$$x_2 = \text{number of units of type 2 bells in thousands}$$

Because of other commitments over the next 2 weeks, Jingle Bells has available only 60 hours in the shipping and packaging department to get the order out. It is estimated that every 1000 units of type 1 bells will require 20 hours in the shipping and packaging department and every 1000 units of type 2 bells will require 30 hours. Given the above information, how many of each type of bell should Jingle Bells produce to maximize profit?

17. Through regression analysis, a firm has learned that total profit P as a function of the number of units of two products manufactured is given by the following function:

$$P = -x_1^2 - 4x_2^2 + 6x_1 + 16x_2 + 500$$

where

$$x_1 = \text{thousands of units of product 1}$$
$$x_2 = \text{thousands of units of product 2}$$

The number of units of each product that can be produced in the next planning period is constrained by the fact that only 12,000 pounds of an ingredient used in the production of both products are available. Both products require 2 pounds of the ingredient per unit produced.

a. Develop a mathematical model that can be used to determine how many units of each product to manufacture in the next planning period.
b. Solve the mathematical model to determine how many units of x_1 and x_2 should be produced to maximize profit.
c. How much would you expect profit to increase if 1 extra pound of the scarce ingredient became available?

MANAGEMENT SCIENCE IN PRACTICE

U.S. Department of Agriculture Forest Service*
Washington, D.C.

The U.S. Department of Agriculture Forest Service is responsible for the management of the nation's forest resources. The Forest Engineering group at the Intermountain Forest and Range Experiment Station in Montana is concerned with the application of engineering and management science principles to the harvesting of timberlands. This group conducts and contracts for studies related to the utilization of harvesting equipment, the modeling of cable yarding (timber collection) systems and of helicopter or other aerial yarding systems, the design of statistically valid models for experimental forests, and the development of a variety of forest harvesting methods. Among the concerns of many of these studies are the productivity and cost of the harvesting method. Ultimately, the primary objective of all these studies is to determine the "best" methods for harvesting timber under a variety of conditions.

A Helicopter Yarding Application

Over the years, the best and most accessible timber has tended to be harvested first. As a result, much of the currently available timber lies in relatively inaccessible regions of the forests where traditional harvesting methods cannot be used. This has created a need for new harvesting techniques. One development has been to use helicopters to remove felled trees from inaccessible regions.

A major problem with using helicopters in the harvesting process is their high cost of operation. When helicopters are used, felled trees are usually marked where they lie for inclusion in a helicopter load (called a turn). This approach has proved somewhat unsatisfactory due to the added cost of helicopter time for collecting and preparing the load for removal. Also, problems with helicopter underloading (wasted capacity) and overloading (aborted loads) have occurred too often. If helicopters are to be used, it is essential that their capacity be fully utilized to maintain the highest possible levels of productivity and the lowest possible costs.

A study exploring the feasibility and cost effectiveness of harvesting methods that would prebunch felled trees into unit loads for helicopter transport was conducted. Preliminary tests indicated that unit loads could be assembled with the aid of a radio-controlled winch. In this method, the winch is anchored to a tree in the "bunching" area. To collect the felled trees for the unit loads, a cable from the winch is hooked to the felled trees. The winch then pulls the trees onto a deck where the unit loads can be assembled. Once the feasibility of this method was established, it became important to develop strategies that would provide the best productivity and cost advantages. A mathematical model was developed to identify the optimal movement and locations of the radio-controlled winch so that the total costs associated with preparing the loads in a given cutting area could be minimized.

Once a section of the forest, called a cutting unit, is identified for harvesting, the problem is to subdivide the cutting unit into smaller sections called bunching units. Figure 19.8 shows a cutting unit that has been subdivided into nine bunching units. The numerical sequence shows how the winch is moved from one bunching unit to the next.

The total time to harvest a cutting unit is dependent on specification of the bunching units. As the size of the bunching unit is increased, idle time due to winch setup time is reduced because fewer bunching units and fewer winch setups are necessary. However, as the size of the bunching unit is increased, the production time per tree increases because the average distance from the felled trees to the winch is greater. Thus, optimal sizing of the bunching units requires a balance of the setup time for the winch with the production time for the trees. The effect of larger bunching areas (greater distance between anchor trees for the winch) on setup, production, and total time is shown in Figure 19.9. Ideally, the Forest Engineering group would like to find the bunching unit configuration that minimizes the total harvesting time.

Figure 19.8
A Cutting Unit Subdivided into Nine Bunching Units

---

*The authors are indebted to Dr. William R. Taylor and Dr. Christopher B. Lofgren, consultants to the USDA Forest Service, for providing this application.

—*Continued on next page*

—Continued from previous page

Figure 19.9
Trade-off Between Setup Time and Production Time

The mathematical formulation of the problem involved two decision variables and seven constraints. The decision variables are as follows:

$$x_1 = \text{length of the bunching unit}$$
$$x_2 = \text{width of the bunching unit}$$

The objective function expresses the total production time (bunching the trees) and the total winch setup time in terms of the two decision variables. Four of the seven constraints represent upper and lower bounds on the acceptable length and width of the bunching units. A fifth constraint restricts the size of the bunching unit so that the winch cable can reach all areas of the unit. The sixth and seventh constraints place upper and lower bounds on the load weight.

Because of the complex nature of the objective function and constraints, it is not possible to simply form the Lagrangian function and take its derivatives to solve for the optimal values of x_1 and x_2. The solution procedure used is a computer algorithm that systematically identifies all the local optimal solutions to the problem. The local optimal solution that requires the minimum total time is selected as the optimal solution. The model provided excellent guidelines for increasing the productivity of the prebunching operation.

Questions
1. What factor necessitated the use of helicopters in the harvesting process?
2. What was the objective of the mathematical model developed in this application?
3. What type of solution procedure was used? Why?

Appendixes

Appendix A: Areas for the Standard Normal Distribution

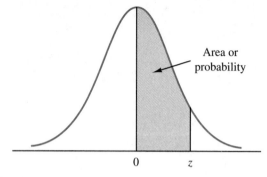

Entries in the table give the area under the curve between the mean and z standard deviations above the mean. For example, for $z = 1.25$ the area under the curve between the mean and z is 0.3944.

z	0.00	0.01	0.02	0.03	0.04	0.05	0.06	0.07	0.08	0.09
0.0	0.0000	0.0040	0.0080	0.0120	0.0160	0.0199	0.0239	0.0279	0.0319	0.0359
0.1	0.0398	0.0438	0.0478	0.0517	0.0557	0.0596	0.0636	0.0675	0.0714	0.0753
0.2	0.0793	0.0832	0.0871	0.0910	0.0948	0.0987	0.1026	0.1064	0.1103	0.1141
0.3	0.1179	0.1217	0.1255	0.1293	0.1331	0.1368	0.1406	0.1443	0.1480	0.1517
0.4	0.1554	0.1591	0.1628	0.1664	0.1700	0.1736	0.1772	0.1808	0.1844	0.1879
0.5	0.1915	0.1950	0.1985	0.2019	0.2054	0.2088	0.2123	0.2157	0.2190	0.2224
0.6	0.2257	0.2291	0.2324	0.2357	0.2389	0.2422	0.2454	0.2486	0.2518	0.2549
0.7	0.2580	0.2612	0.2642	0.2673	0.2704	0.2734	0.2764	0.2794	0.2823	0.2852
0.8	0.2881	0.2910	0.2939	0.2967	0.2995	0.3023	0.3051	0.3078	0.3106	0.3133
0.9	0.3159	0.3186	0.3212	0.3238	0.3264	0.3289	0.3315	0.3340	0.3365	0.3389
1.0	0.3413	0.3438	0.3461	0.3485	0.3508	0.3531	0.3554	0.3577	0.3599	0.3621
1.1	0.3643	0.3665	0.3686	0.3708	0.3729	0.3749	0.3770	0.3790	0.3810	0.3830
1.2	0.3849	0.3869	0.3888	0.3907	0.3925	0.3944	0.3962	0.3980	0.3997	0.4015
1.3	0.4032	0.4049	0.4066	0.4082	0.4099	0.4115	0.4131	0.4147	0.4162	0.4177
1.4	0.4192	0.4207	0.4222	0.4236	0.4251	0.4265	0.4279	0.4292	0.4306	0.4319
1.5	0.4332	0.4345	0.4357	0.4370	0.4382	0.4394	0.4406	0.4418	0.4429	0.4441
1.6	0.4452	0.4463	0.4474	0.4484	0.4495	0.4505	0.4515	0.4525	0.4535	0.4545
1.7	0.4554	0.4564	0.4573	0.4582	0.4591	0.4599	0.4608	0.4616	0.4625	0.4633
1.8	0.4641	0.4649	0.4656	0.4664	0.4671	0.4678	0.4686	0.4693	0.4699	0.4706
1.9	0.4713	0.4719	0.4726	0.4732	0.4738	0.4744	0.4750	0.4756	0.4761	0.4767
2.0	0.4772	0.4778	0.4783	0.4788	0.4793	0.4798	0.4803	0.4808	0.4812	0.4817
2.1	0.4821	0.4826	0.4830	0.4834	0.4838	0.4842	0.4846	0.4850	0.4854	0.4857
2.2	0.4861	0.4864	0.4868	0.4871	0.4875	0.4878	0.4881	0.4884	0.4887	0.4890
2.3	0.4893	0.4896	0.4898	0.4901	0.4904	0.4906	0.4909	0.4911	0.4913	0.4916
2.4	0.4918	0.4920	0.4922	0.4925	0.4927	0.4929	0.4931	0.4932	0.4934	0.4936
2.5	0.4938	0.4940	0.4941	0.4943	0.4945	0.4946	0.4948	0.4949	0.4951	0.4952
2.6	0.4953	0.4955	0.4956	0.4957	0.4959	0.4960	0.4961	0.4962	0.4963	0.4964
2.7	0.4965	0.4966	0.4967	0.4968	0.4969	0.4970	0.4971	0.4972	0.4973	0.4974
2.8	0.4974	0.4975	0.4976	0.4977	0.4977	0.4978	0.4979	0.4979	0.4980	0.4981
2.9	0.4981	0.4982	0.4982	0.4983	0.4984	0.4984	0.4985	0.4985	0.4986	0.4986
3.0	0.4986	0.4987	0.4987	0.4988	0.4988	0.4989	0.4989	0.4989	0.4990	0.4990

Appendix B: Random Digits

63271	59986	71744	51102	15141	80714	58683	93108	13554	79945
88547	09896	95436	79115	08303	01041	20030	63754	08459	28364
55957	57243	83865	09911	19761	66535	40102	26646	60147	15702
46276	87453	44790	67122	45573	84358	21625	16999	13385	22782
55363	07449	34835	15290	76616	67191	12777	21861	68689	03263
69393	92785	49902	58447	42048	30378	87618	26933	40640	16281
13186	29431	88190	04588	38733	81290	89541	70290	40113	08243
17726	28652	56836	78351	47327	18518	92222	55201	27340	10493
36520	64465	05550	30157	82242	29520	69753	72602	23756	54935
81628	36100	39254	56835	37636	02421	98063	89641	64953	99337
84649	38968	75215	75498	49539	74240	03466	49292	36401	45525
63291	11618	12613	75055	43915	26488	41116	64531	56827	30825
70502	53225	03655	05915	37140	57051	48393	91322	25653	06543
06426	24771	59935	49801	11082	66762	94477	02494	88215	27191
20711	55609	29430	70165	45406	78484	31639	52009	18873	96927
41990	70538	77191	25860	55204	73417	83920	69468	74972	38712
72452	36618	76298	26678	89334	33938	95567	29380	75906	91807
37042	40318	57099	10528	09925	89773	41335	96244	29002	46453
53766	52875	15987	46962	67342	77592	57651	95508	80033	69828
90585	58955	53122	16025	84299	53310	67380	84249	25348	04332
32001	96293	37203	64516	51530	37069	40261	61374	05815	06714
62606	64324	46354	72157	67248	20135	49804	09226	64419	29457
10078	28073	85389	50324	14500	15562	64165	06125	71353	77669
91561	46145	24177	15294	10061	98124	75732	00815	83452	97355
13091	98112	53959	79607	52244	63303	10413	63839	74762	50289
73864	83014	72457	22682	03033	61714	88173	90835	00634	85169
66668	25467	48894	51043	02365	91726	09365	63167	95264	45643
84745	41042	29493	01836	09044	51926	43630	63470	76508	14194
48068	26805	94595	47907	13357	38412	33318	26098	82782	42851
54310	96175	97594	88616	42035	38093	36745	56702	40644	83514
14877	33095	10924	58013	61439	21882	42059	24177	58739	60170
78295	23179	02771	43464	59061	71411	05697	67194	30495	21157
67524	02865	39593	54278	04237	92441	26602	63835	38032	94770
58268	57219	68124	73455	83236	08710	04284	55005	84171	42596
97158	28672	50685	01181	24262	19427	52106	34308	73685	74246
04230	16831	69085	30802	65559	09205	71829	06489	85650	38707
94879	56606	30401	02602	57658	70091	54986	41394	60437	03195
71446	15232	66715	26385	91518	70566	02888	79941	39684	54315
32886	05644	79316	09819	00813	88407	17461	73925	53037	91904
62048	33711	25290	21526	02223	75947	66466	06232	10913	75336

This table is reproduced with permission from The Rand Corporation, *A Million Random Digits,* The Free Press, New York, 1955 and 1983.

Appendix C: Values of $e^{-\lambda}$

λ	$e^{-\lambda}$	λ	$e^{-\lambda}$	λ	$e^{-\lambda}$
0.05	0.9512	2.05	0.1287	4.05	0.0174
0.10	0.9048	2.10	0.1225	4.10	0.0166
0.15	0.8607	2.15	0.1165	4.15	0.0158
0.20	0.8187	2.20	0.1108	4.20	0.0150
0.25	0.7788	2.25	0.1054	4.25	0.0143
0.30	0.7408	2.30	0.1003	4.30	0.0136
0.35	0.7047	2.35	0.0954	4.35	0.0129
0.40	0.6703	2.40	0.0907	4.40	0.0123
0.45	0.6376	2.45	0.0863	4.45	0.0117
0.50	0.6065	2.50	0.0821	4.50	0.0111
0.55	0.5769	2.55	0.0781	4.55	0.0106
0.60	0.5488	2.60	0.0743	4.60	0.0101
0.65	0.5220	2.65	0.0707	4.65	0.0096
0.70	0.4966	2.70	0.0672	4.70	0.0091
0.75	0.4724	2.75	0.0639	4.75	0.0087
0.80	0.4493	2.80	0.0608	4.80	0.0082
0.85	0.4274	2.85	0.0578	4.85	0.0078
0.90	0.4066	2.90	0.0550	4.90	0.0074
0.95	0.3867	2.95	0.0523	4.95	0.0071
1.00	0.3679	3.00	0.0498	5.00	0.0067
1.05	0.3499	3.05	0.0474	5.05	0.0064
1.10	0.3329	3.10	0.0450	5.10	0.0061
1.15	0.3166	3.15	0.0429	5.15	0.0058
1.20	0.3012	3.20	0.0408	5.20	0.0055
1.25	0.2865	3.25	0.0388	5.25	0.0052
1.30	0.2725	3.30	0.0369	5.30	0.0050
1.35	0.2592	3.35	0.0351	5.35	0.0047
1.40	0.2466	3.40	0.0334	5.40	0.0045
1.45	0.2346	3.45	0.0317	5.45	0.0043
1.50	0.2231	3.50	0.0302	5.50	0.0041
1.55	0.2122	3.55	0.0287	5.55	0.0039
1.60	0.2019	3.60	0.0273	5.60	0.0037
1.65	0.1920	3.65	0.0260	5.65	0.0035
1.70	0.1827	3.70	0.0247	5.70	0.0033
1.75	0.1738	3.75	0.0235	5.75	0.0032
1.80	0.1653	3.80	0.0224	5.80	0.0030
1.85	0.1572	3.85	0.0213	5.85	0.0029
1.90	0.1496	3.90	0.0202	5.90	0.0027
1.95	0.1423	3.95	0.0193	5.95	0.0026
2.00	0.1353	4.00	0.0183	6.00	0.0025
				7.00	0.0009
				8.00	0.000335
				9.00	0.000123
				10.00	0.000045

Appendix D: A Short Table of Derivatives

1. $\dfrac{d(c)}{dx} = 0$ (where c is a constant)

2. $\dfrac{d(x^n)}{dx} = nx^{n-1}$

3. $\dfrac{d(cu)}{dx} = c\dfrac{du}{dx}$

4. $\dfrac{d(u + v)}{dx} = \dfrac{du}{dx} + \dfrac{dv}{dx}$

5. $\dfrac{d(uv)}{dx} = u\dfrac{dv}{dx} + v\dfrac{du}{dx}$

6. $\dfrac{d(u^n)}{dx} = nu^{n-1}\dfrac{du}{dx}$

7. $\dfrac{d\left(\dfrac{u}{v}\right)}{dx} = \dfrac{v\dfrac{du}{dx} - u\dfrac{dv}{dx}}{v^2}$

8. $\dfrac{d(\ln x)}{dx} = \dfrac{1}{x}$

9. $\dfrac{d(e^x)}{dx} = e^x$

10. $\dfrac{d(\ln u)}{dx} = \left(\dfrac{1}{u}\right)\dfrac{du}{dx}$

11. $\dfrac{d(e^u)}{dx} = e^u\dfrac{du}{dx}$

Appendix E: Matrix Notation and Operations

Matrix Notation

We define a matrix to be a rectangular array of numbers. For example, the following array of numbers is a matrix D:

$$D = \begin{bmatrix} 1 & 3 & 2 \\ 0 & 4 & 5 \end{bmatrix}$$

The matrix D is said to consist of six elements, where each element of D is a number. In order to identify a particular element of a matrix, we have to specify its location. To do this, we introduce the notion of rows and columns.

All elements across some horizontal line in a matrix are said to be in a row of the matrix. For example, elements 1, 3, and 2 in the matrix D are in the first row of D, and elements 0, 4, and 5 are in the second row of D. Thus, we see that D is a matrix that has two rows. By convention, we always refer to the top row as row 1, the second row from the top as row 2, and so on.

All elements along some vertical line are said to belong to a column of the matrix. Elements 1 and 0 in the matrix D are elements in the first column of D, elements 3 and 4 are elements of the second column, and elements 2 and 5 are elements of the third column. Thus, we see that the matrix D has three columns. By convention, we always refer to the leftmost column as column 1, the next column to the right as column 2, and so on.

An easy way to identify a particular element in a matrix is to specify its row and column position. For example, the element in row 1 and column 2 of the matrix D is the number 3. This is written as

$$d_{12} = 3$$

In general, we use the following notation to refer to specific elements of the matrix D:

$$d_{ij} = \text{element located in the } i\text{th row and } j\text{th column of } D$$

We always use capital letters for the names of matrices and the corresponding lowercase versions of the same letter with two subscripts to denote the elements.

The *size* of a matrix is defined to be the number of rows and columns in the matrix and is written as the number of rows $\times$ the number of columns. Thus, the size of the matrix D above is 2×3.

Frequently we will encounter matrices that have only one row or one column. For example,

$$G = \begin{bmatrix} 6 \\ 4 \\ 2 \\ 3 \end{bmatrix}$$

is a matrix that has only one column. Whenever we have a matrix that has only one column like G, we call the matrix a column vector. In a similar manner, any matrix that has only one row is called a row vector. Using our previous notation for elements of a matrix, we could refer to specific elements in G by writing g_{ij}. However, since G has only one column, the column position is unimportant, and we need only specify the row the element of interest is in. That is, instead of referring to elements in a vector using g_{ij}, we specify only one subscript, which denotes the position of the element in the vector. For example,

$$g_1 = 6 \qquad g_2 = 4 \qquad g_3 = 2 \qquad g_4 = 3$$

Matrix Operations

Matrix Transpose   Given any matrix, we can form the transpose of the matrix by making the rows in the original matrix the columns in the transpose matrix, and by making the columns in the original matrix the rows in the transpose matrix. For example, if we take the transpose of the matrix

$$D = \begin{bmatrix} 1 & 3 & 2 \\ 0 & 4 & 5 \end{bmatrix}$$

we get

$$D^t = \begin{bmatrix} 1 & 0 \\ 3 & 4 \\ 2 & 5 \end{bmatrix}$$

Note that we use the superscript t to denote the transpose of a matrix.

Matrix Multiplication   We will demonstrate how to perform two types of matrix multiplication: (1) how to multiply two vectors, and (2) how to multiply a matrix times a matrix.

The product of a row vector of size $1 \times n$ times a column vector of size $n \times 1$ is the number obtained by multiplying the first element in the row vector times the first element in the column vector, the second element in the row vector times the second element in the column vector, and continuing on through the last element in the row vector times the last element in the column vector, and then summing the products. Suppose, for example, that we wanted to multiply the row vector H times the column vector G, where

$$H = [2 \quad 1 \quad 5 \quad 0] \text{ and } G = \begin{bmatrix} 6 \\ 4 \\ 2 \\ 3 \end{bmatrix}$$

The product HG is given by

$$HG = 2(6) + 1(4) + 5(2) + 0(3) = 26$$

The product of a matrix of size $p \times n$ and a matrix of size $n \times m$ is a new matrix of size $p \times m$. The element in the ith row and jth column of the new matrix is given by the vector product of the ith row of the $p \times n$ matrix times the jth column of the $n \times m$ matrix. Suppose, for example, that we want to multiply D times A, where

$$D = \begin{bmatrix} 1 & 3 & 2 \\ 0 & 4 & 5 \end{bmatrix} \quad A = \begin{bmatrix} 1 & 3 & 5 \\ 2 & 0 & 4 \\ 1 & 5 & 2 \end{bmatrix}$$

Let us denote by $C = DA$ the product of D times A. The element in row 1 and column 1 of C is given by the vector product of the first row of D times the first column of A. Thus we get

$$c_{11} = [1 \quad 3 \quad 2] \begin{bmatrix} 1 \\ 2 \\ 1 \end{bmatrix} = 1(1) + 3(2) + 2(1) = 9$$

The element in row 2 and column 1 of C is given by the vector product of the second row of D times the first column of A. Thus, we get

$$c_{21} = [0 \quad 4 \quad 5] \begin{bmatrix} 1 \\ 2 \\ 1 \end{bmatrix} = 0(1) + 4(2) + 5(1) = 13$$

Calculating the remaining elements of C in a similar fashion, we obtain

$$C = \begin{bmatrix} 9 & 13 & 21 \\ 13 & 25 & 26 \end{bmatrix}$$

Clearly, the product of a matrix and a vector is just a special case of multiplying a matrix times a matrix. For example, the product of a matrix of size $m \times n$ and a vector of size $n \times 1$ is a new vector of size $m \times 1$. The element in the ith position of the new vector is given by the vector product of the ith row of the $m \times n$ matrix times the $n \times 1$ column vector. Suppose, for example, that we want to multiply D times K, where

$$D = \begin{bmatrix} 1 & 3 & 2 \\ 0 & 4 & 5 \end{bmatrix} \quad K = \begin{bmatrix} 1 \\ 4 \\ 2 \end{bmatrix}$$

The first element of DK is given by the vector product of the first row of D times K. Thus, we get

$$\begin{bmatrix} 1 & 3 & 2 \end{bmatrix} \begin{bmatrix} 1 \\ 4 \\ 2 \end{bmatrix} = 1(1) + 3(4) + 2(2) = 17$$

The second element of DK is given by the vector product of the second row of D and K. Thus, we get

$$\begin{bmatrix} 0 & 4 & 5 \end{bmatrix} \begin{bmatrix} 1 \\ 4 \\ 2 \end{bmatrix} = 0(1) + 4(4) + 5(2) = 26$$

Hence, we see that the product of the matrix D times the vector K is given by

$$DK = \begin{bmatrix} 1 & 3 & 2 \\ 0 & 4 & 5 \end{bmatrix} \begin{bmatrix} 1 \\ 4 \\ 2 \end{bmatrix} = \begin{bmatrix} 17 \\ 26 \end{bmatrix}$$

Can any two matrices be multiplied? The answer is no. In order to multiply two matrices, the number of the columns in the first matrix must equal the number of rows in the second. If this property is satisfied, the matrices are said to conform for multiplication. Thus, in our example, D and K could be multiplied because D had three columns and K had three rows.

Matrix Inverse The inverse, denoted by A^{-1}, of any square matrix A consisting of two rows and two columns is computed as follows:

$$A = \begin{bmatrix} a_{11} & a_{12} \\ a_{21} & a_{22} \end{bmatrix}$$

$$A^{-1} = \begin{bmatrix} a_{22}/d & -a_{12}/d \\ -a_{21}/d & a_{11}/d \end{bmatrix}$$

where $d = a_{11}a_{22} - a_{21}a_{12}$ is the determinant of the 2×2 matrix A. For example, if

$$A = \begin{bmatrix} 0.7 & -0.3 \\ -0.3 & 0.9 \end{bmatrix}$$

then

$$d = (0.7)(0.9) - (-0.3)(-0.3) = 0.54$$

and

$$A^{-1} = \begin{bmatrix} 0.9/0.54 & 0.3/0.54 \\ 0.3/0.54 & 0.7/0.54 \end{bmatrix} = \begin{bmatrix} 1.67 & 0.56 \\ 0.56 & 1.30 \end{bmatrix}$$

Appendix F: References and Bibliography

The Role and Nature of Management Science (Chapter 1)

Churchman, C. W., R. L. Ackoff, and E. L. Arnoff, *Introduction to Operations Research.* New York: Wiley, 1957.

Forgionne, G. A., "Corporate Management Science Activities: An Update." *Interfaces*, Vol. 13, No. 3, pp. 20–23, 1983.

Gaither, N., "The Adoption of Operations Research Techniques by Manufacturing Organizations." *Decision Sciences,* Vol. 6, No. 4, 1975, pp. 797–813.

Grayson, C. J., Jr., "Management Science and Business Practice." *Harvard Business Review,* Vol. 51, 1973, pp. 41–48.

Hillier, F., and G. J. Lieberman, *Introduction to Operations Research.* 4th ed. San Francisco: Holden-Day, 1986.

Ledbetter, W. and J. Cox, "Are OR Techniques Being Used?" *Industrial Engineering,* Vol. 9, 1977, pp. 19–21.

Radnor, M., and R. D. Neal, "The Progress of Management Science Activities in Large U.S. Industrial Corporations."*Operations Research,* 21(1973): 427–450.

Shannon, R. E., S. S. Long, and B. P. Buckles, "Operations Research Methodologies in Industrial Engineering: A Survey." *AIIE Transactions,* Vol. 12, No. 4, 1980, pp. 364–367.

Thomas, G., and J. DaCosta, "A Sample Survey of Corporate Operations Research." *Interfaces,* August 1979.

Thomas G., and M. Mitchell, "OR in the U.S. Marine Corps: A Characterization." *Interfaces,* June 1983.

Linear Programming, Transportation, Assignment and Transshipment Problems (Chapters 2 to 7)

Anderson, D. R., D. J. Sweeney, and T. A. Williams, *Linear Programming for Decision Making.* St. Paul, Minn.: West, 1974.

Bazarra, M. S., J. J. Jarvis and H. D. Sherali, *Linear Programming and Network Flows.* 2nd ed. New York: Wiley, 1990.

Bradley, S. P., A. C. Hax, and T. L. Magnanti, *Applied Mathematical Programming.* Reading, Mass.: Addison-Wesley, 1977.

Charnes, A., and W. W. Cooper, *Management Models and Industrial Applications of Linear Programming.* New York: Wiley, 1961.

Charnes, A., W. W. Cooper, and E. Rhodes, "Measuring Efficiency of Decision Making Units." *European Journal of Operations Research,* Vol. 2, 1978, pp. 429–449.

Daellenbach, Hans G., and J. Bell, *User's Guide to Linear Programming.* Englewood Cliffs, N.J.: Prentice-Hall, 1970.

Dantzig, G. B., *Linear Programming and Extensions.* Princeton, N.J.: Princeton University Press, 1963.

Gass, S., *Linear Programming.* 4th ed. New York: McGraw-Hill, 1975.

Hillier, F., and G. J. Lieberman, *Introduction to Operations Research.* 4th ed. San Francisco: Holden-Day, 1986.

Hooker, J. N., "Karmarkar's Linear Programming Algorithm." *Interfaces,* Vol. 16, No. 4, pp. 75–90, 1986.

Lewin, A. Y., and R. C. Morey, "Measuring the Relative Efficiency and Output Potential of Public Sector Organizations: An Application of Data Envelopment Analysis." *International Journal of Policy Analysis and Information Systems,* Vol. 5, No. 4, 1981, pp. 267–285.

Phillips, D. T., A. Ravindran, and J. J. Solberg, *Operations Research: Principles and Practice.* 2nd ed. New York: Wiley, 1987.

Schrage, L., *LINDO: An Optimization Modeling System.* 4th ed. South San Francisco, Calif.: Scientific Press, 1986.

Schrage, L., *User's Manual for Linear, Integer, and Quadratic Programming with LINDO.* Redwood City, Calif.: Scientific Press, 1989.

Sherman, H. D., "Hospital Efficiency Measurement and Evaluation." *Medical Care,* Vol. 22, No. 10, October 1984, pp. 922–938.

Wagner, H., *Principles of Operations Research.* 2nd ed. Englewood Cliffs, N.J.: Prentice-Hall, 1975.

Integer Linear Programming (Chapter 8)

Garfinkel, R. S., and G. L. Nemhauser, *Integer Programming.* New York: Wiley, 1972.

Nemhauser, G. L., and L. A. Wolsey, *Integer and Combinatorial Optimization.* New York: Wiley, 1988.

Plane, D. R., and C. McMillan, *Discrete Optimization.* Englewood Cliffs, N.J.: Prentice-Hall, 1971.

Salkin, H. M., *Integer Programming.* Reading, Mass.: Addison-Wesley, 1975.

Zionts, Stanley, *Linear and Integer Programming.* Englewood Cliffs, N.J.: Prentice-Hall, 1974.

Network Models (Chapter 9)

Bazarra, M. S., J. J. Jarvis, and H. D. Sherali, *Linear Programming and Network Flows.* 2nd ed. New York: Wiley, 1977.

Glover, F., and D. Klingman, "Network Application in Industry and Government." *AIIE Transactions,* December 1977.

Ford, L. R., and D. R. Fulkerson, *Flows and Networks.* Princeton, N.J.: Princeton University Press, 1962.

Jensen, P., and J. W. Barnes, *Network Flow Programming.* New York: Wiley, 1980.

Minieka, Edward, and J. R. Evans, *Optimization Algorithms for Networks and Graphs.* 2nd ed. New York: Marcel Dekker, 1992.

PERT/CPM (Chapter 10)

Evarts, H. F., *Introduction to PERT.* Boston: Allyn & Bacon, 1964.

Moder, J. J., and C. R. Phillips, *Project Management with CPM and PERT.* 2nd ed. New York: Van Nostrand, 1970.

Wagner, H., *Principles of Operations Research with Applications to Managerial Decisions.* 2nd ed. Englewood Cliffs, N.J.: Prentice-Hall, 1975.

Wiest, J., and F. Levy, *Management Guide to PERT-CPM.* 2nd ed. Englewood Cliffs, N.J.: Prentice-Hall, 1977.

Inventory Models (Chapter 11)

Buffa, E. S., and W. Taubert, *Production-Inventory Systems: Planning and Control.* 3rd ed. Homewood, Ill.: Richard D. Irwin, 1979.

Davis, E. W., *Case Studies in Material Requirements Planning.* Washington, D.C.: APICS, 1978.

Greene, J. H., *Production and Inventory Control Handbook.* New York: McGraw-Hill, 1970.

Hadley, G., and T. M. Whitin, *Analysis of Inventory Systems.* Englewood Cliffs, N.J.: Prentice-Hall, 1963.

Hillier, F., and G. J. Lieberman, *Introduction to Operations Research.* 4th ed. San Francisco: Holden-Day, 1986.

Naddor, E., *Inventory Systems.* New York: Wiley, 1966.

Orlicky, J., *Material Requirements Planning.* New York: McGraw-Hill, 1975.

Plossl, G. W., *Manufacturing Control: The Last Frontier for Profits.* Reston, Va.: Reston, 1973.

Starr, M., and D. Miller, *Inventory Control: Theory and Practice.* Englewood Cliffs, N.J.: Prentice-Hall, 1962.

Stockton, R. S., *Basic Inventory Systems: Concepts and Analysis.* Boston: Allyn & Bacon, 1965.

Wagner, H., *Principles of Operations Research with Applications to Managerial Decisions.* 2nd ed. Englewood Cliffs, N.J.: Prentice-Hall, 1975.

Wight, O. W., *Production and Inventory Management in the Computer Age.* Boston: Cahners Books, 1974.

Waiting Lines (Chapter 12)

Bhat, U. N., *Elements of Applied Stochastic Processes.* New York: Wiley, 1972.

Cooper, R. B., *Introduction to Queueing Theory.* New York: Macmillan, 1972.

Cox, D. R., and W. L. Smith, *Queues.* New York: Wiley, 1965.

Gross, D., and C. M. Harris, *Fundamentals of Queueing Theory.* New York: Wiley, 1974.

Hillier, F., and G. J. Lieberman, *Introduction to Operations Research.* 4th ed. San Francisco: Holden-Day, 1986.

Newell, G. F., *Applications of Queueing Theory.* London: Chapman & Hall, Ltd., 1971.

Computer Simulation (Chapter 13)

Christy, D. P., and H. J. Watson, "The Application of Simulation: A Survey of Industry Practice." *Interfaces,* October 1983.

Emshoff, J. R., and R. L. Sisson, *Design and Use of Computer Simulation Models.* New York: Macmillan, 1970.

Fishman, George S., *Principles of Discrete Event Simulation.* New York: Wiley, 1978.

Greenberg, S., *GPSS Primer.* New York: Wiley, 1972.

Maisel, H., and G. Gnugnoli, *Simulation of Discrete Stochastic Systems.* Chicago: SRA, 1972.

Naylor, T. H., *Computer Simulation Experiments with Models of Economic Systems.* New York: Wiley, 1971.

Naylor, T. H., J. L. Balintfy, D. S. Burdick, and K. Chu, *Computer Simulation Techniques.* New York: Wiley, 1968.

Schmidt, J. W., and R. E. Taylor, *Simulation and Analysis of Industrial Systems.* Homewood, Ill.: Richard D. Irwin, 1970.

Schriber, T. J., *Simulation Using GPSS.* New York: Wiley, 1974.

Thesen, A. and L. Travis, *Simulation for Decision Making.* St Paul: West Publishing, 1992.

Decision Analysis (Chapter 14)

Behn, R. D., and J. W. Vaupel, *Quick Analysis for Busy Decision Makers.* New York: Basic Books, 1982.

Berger, J.O., *Statistical Decision Theory and Bayesian Analysis,* 2nd ed. New York: Springer-Verlag, 1985.

Bunn, D., *Applied Decision Analysis.* New York: McGraw-Hill, 1984.

Chernoff, H., and L. E. Moses, *Elementary Decision Theory.* New York: Wiley, 1959.

Fishburn, P. C., "Foundations of Decision Analysis: Along the Way." *Management Science,* Vol. 35, No. 4, April 1989, pp. 387–405.

Keeney, R. L., and H. Raiffa, *Decisions with Multiple Objectives: Preferences and Value Trade Offs.* New York: Wiley, 1976.

Raiffa, H., *Decision Analysis: Introductory Lectures on Choices Under Uncertainty.* Reading, Mass.: Addison-Wesley, 1968.

Samson, D., *Managerial Decision Analysis.* Homewood, Ill.: Irwin, 1988.

Schlaifer, R., *Analysis of Decisions under Uncertainty.* New York: McGraw-Hill, 1969.

Winkler, R. L., *An Introduction to Bayesian Inference and Decision.* New York: Holt, Rinehart & Winston, 1972.

Winkler, R. L., and W. L. Hays, *Statistics: Probability, Inference and Decision.* 2nd ed. New York: Holt, Rinehart & Winston, 1975.

Multicriteria Decision Problems (Chapter 15)

Baird, B. F., *Managerial Decisions Under Uncertainty.* New York: Wiley, 1989.

Bunn, D. W., *Analysis for Optimal Decisions.* New York: Wiley, 1982.

Dyer, J. S., "Remarks on the Analytic Hierarchy Process." *Management Science,* Vol. 36, No. 3, March 1990, pp. 249–258.

Dyer, J. S., "A Clarification of Remarks on the Analytic Hierarchy Process." *Management Science,* Vol. 36, No. 3, March 1990, pp. 274–275.

Harker, P. T., and L. G. Vargas, "The Theory of Ratio Scale Estimation: Saaty's Analytic Hierarchy Process." *Management Science,* Vol. 33, No. 11, November 1987, pp. 1383–1403.

Harker, P. T., and L. G. Vargas, "Reply to Remarks on the Analytic Hierarchy Process by J. S. Dyer." *Management Science,* Vol. 36, No. 3, March 1990, pp. 269–273.

Ignizio, J. P., *Goal Programming and Extensions.* Lexington, Mass.: D. C. Heath, 1976.

Keeney, R. L., and H. Raiffa, *Decisions with Multiple Objectives: Preferences and Value Tradeoffs.* New York: Wiley, 1976.

Lee, S. M., *Goal Programming for Decision Analysis.* Philadelphia: Auerbach, 1972.

Saaty, T. L., "Rank Generation, Preservation, and Reversal in the Analytic Hierarchy Decision Process." *Decision Sciences,* Vol. 18, 1987, pp. 157–177.

Saaty, T. L., "An Exposition of the AHP in Reply to the Paper Remarks on the Analytic Hierarchy Process." *Management Science,* Vol. 36, No. 3, March 1990, pp. 259–268.

Weiss, E. N., and V. R. Rao, "AHP Design Issues for Large-Scale Systems." *Decision Sciences,* Vol. 18, 1987, pp. 43–61.

Winkler, R. L., "Decision Modeling and Rational Choice: AHP and Utility Theory." *Management Science,* Vol. 36, No. 3, March 1990, pp. 247–248.

Zahedi, F., "Analytic Hierarchy Process—A Survey of the Method and its Applications." *Interfaces,* Vol. 16, No. 4, August 1986, pp. 96–108.

Forecasting (Chapter 16)

Bowerman, B. L., and R. T. O'Connell, *Time Series Forecasting.* 2nd ed. Boston: PWS-Kent, 1987.

Box, G. E. P., and G. M. Jenkins, *Time Series Analysis: Forecasting and Control.* Rev. ed. San Francisco: Holden-Day, 1976.

Gilchrist, W. G., *Statistical Forecasting.* New York: Wiley, 1976.

Hanke, J. E., and A. G. Reitsch, *Business Forecasting.* 2nd ed. Boston: Allyn & Bacon, 1986.

Makridakis, S., S. C. Wheelwright, and Victor E. McGee, *Forecasting: Methods and Applications.* 2nd ed. New York: Wiley, 1983.

Nelson, C. R., *Applied Time Series Analysis.* San Francisco: Holden-Day, 1973.

Thomopoulos, N. T., *Applied Forecasting Methods.* Englewood Cliffs, N.J.: Prentice-Hall, 1980.

Wheelwright, S. C., and S. Makridakis, *Forecasting Models for Management.* 4th ed. New York: Wiley, 1985.

Markov Processes (Chapter 17)

Derman, C., *Finite State Markovian Decision Processes.* New York: Academic Press, 1970.

Howard, R. A., *Dynamic Programming and Markov Processes.* Cambridge, Mass.: M.I.T. Press, 1960.

Kemeny, J. G., and J. L. Snell, *Finite Markov Chains.* Englewood Cliffs, N.J.: Prentice-Hall, 1960.

Phillips, D. T., A. Ravindran, and J. J. Solberg, *Operations Research: Principles and Practice.* New York: Wiley, 1976.

Ross, S. M., *Applied Probability Models with Optimization Applications.* San Francisco: Holden-Day, 1970.

Dynamic Programming (Chapter 18)

Bellman, R., *Dynamic Programming.* Princeton, N.J.: Princeton University Press, 1957.
Dreyfus, S., *Dynamic Programming and the Calculus of Variations.* New York: Academic Press, 1965.
Dreyfus, S., and A. M. Law, *The Art and Theory of Dynamic Programming.* New York: Academic Press, 1977.
Hillier, F., and G. J. Lieberman, *Introduction to Operations Research.* 4th ed. San Francisco: Holden-Day, 1986.
Nemhauser, G. L., *Introduction to Dynamic Programming.* New York: Wiley, 1967.

Calculus-Based Solution Procedure (Chapter 19)

Beightler, C. S., D. T. Phillips, and D. Wilde, *Foundations of Optimization.* 2nd ed. Englewood Cliffs, N.J.: Prentice-Hall, 1979.
Cooper, L., and D. Steinberg, *Introduction to Methods of Optimization.* Philadelphia: W. B. Saunders, 1970.
Gottfried, B. S., and J. Weisman, *Introduction to Optimization Theory.* Englewood Cliffs, N.J.: Prentice-Hall, 1973.
Himmelblau, D. M., *Applied Nonlinear Programming.* New York: McGraw-Hill, 1972.
Luenberger, D. G., *Introduction to Linear and Nonlinear Programming.* Reading, Mass.: Addison-Wesley, 1973.

Appendix G: Answers to Even-Numbered Problems

CHAPTER 1

2. Methodological developments based on research advances in computer technology

4. The problem is large, complex, important, new, and repetitive

6. Iconic—scale model of a new building
Analog—barometer
Mathematical—inventory cost equation

8. a. Max $10x + 5y$
s.t.
$$5x + 2y \geq 40$$
$$x \geq 0, y \geq 0$$

b. Controllable inputs: x and y
Uncontrollable inputs: profit, labor-hours per units, and total labor-hours available

d. $x = 0$, $y = 20$, profit = $100

10. If $a = 3$, $x = 13\frac{1}{3}$ and profit = $133
If $a = 4$, $x = 10$ and profit = $100
If $a = 5$, $x = 8$ and profit = $80
If $a = 6$, $x = 6\frac{2}{3}$ and profit = $67

12. A deterministic model with d = distance, m = miles per gallon, and c = cost per gallon, where total cost = $(2d/m)c$

14. Quicker to formulate, easier to solve, and/or more easily understood

16. a. Max $6x + 4y$
b. $50x + 30y \leq 80,000$
$$50x \leq 50,000$$
$$30y \leq 45,000$$

CHAPTER 2

6. $-\frac{7}{10}, -\frac{3}{2}, \frac{4}{7}$

10. $x_1 = 100$, $x_2 = 50$, $z = 750$

12. a. $x_1 = 3$, $x_2 = 1.5$, $z = 13.5$

14. a. Feasible region consists of a line segment
b. (5,1) and (2,4)
c. $x_1 = 2$, $x_2 = 4$

16. a. $x_1 = 300$, $x_2 = 420$, $z = 10,560$
b. $x_1 = 708$, $x_2 = 0$, $z = 14,160$
c. Sewing constraint is redundant; optimal solution is still $x_1 = 540$, $x_2 = 252$

20. b. $x_1 = \frac{20}{3}$, $x_2 = \frac{8}{3}$, $z = 30\frac{2}{3}$
c. $s_1 = \frac{28}{3}$, $s_2 = 0$, $s_3 = 0$

22. a. Max $\quad 5x_1 + 8x_2$
s.t.
$$1x_1 + \tfrac{3}{2}x_2 \leq 900$$
$$\tfrac{1}{2}x_1 + \tfrac{1}{3}x_2 \leq 300$$
$$\tfrac{1}{8}x_1 + \tfrac{1}{4}x_2 \leq 100$$
$$x_1, x_2 \geq 0$$

b. $x_1 = 500$, $x_2 = 150$
c. $3700
d. 725, 300, 100
e. 175, 0, 0

24. a. Max $\quad 3x_1 + 3x_2$
s.t.
$$\tfrac{3}{5}x_1 + \tfrac{3}{4}x_2 \leq 900$$
$$\tfrac{2}{5}x_1 + \tfrac{1}{4}x_2 \leq 400$$
$$1x_2 \leq 500$$
$$x_1, x_2 \geq 0$$

b. $x_1 = 687.5$, $x_2 = 500$, $z = 3562.50$
c. Yes, $x_1 = 500$, $x_2 = 800$, $z = 3900$

26. a. Max $400x_1 + 500x_2$
s.t.
$$x_1 \leq 300$$
$$x_2 \leq 150$$
$$2x_1 + 3x_2 \leq 900$$
$$x_1, x_2, \geq 0$$

c. $x_1 = 300$, $x_2 = 100$, $z = 170,000$
d. $s_1 = 0$, $s_2 = 50$, $s_3 = 0$
e. Automobile limit and dealer preparation time

28. b. $x_1 = 158\frac{1}{3}$, $x_2 = 25$, profit = 7583
c. $1x_2 \geq 1x_1$ or $-1x_1 + 1x_2 \geq 0$
d. $x_1 = 75$, $x_2 = 75$, profit = 6750

30.

Extreme Points	Objective Function Value	Surplus Demand	Surplus Total Production	Slack Processing Time
(250, 100)	800	125	—	—
(125, 225)	925	—	—	125
(125, 350)	1300	—	125	—

32. b. (4, 1), $(2\frac{1}{4}, \frac{9}{4})$
c. $x_1 = 4$, $x_2 = 1$

34. 15 ounces of Bark Bits, $\frac{5}{2}$ ounces of Canine Chow, $z = 1.025$

36. $x_1 = 6$, $x_2 = 10$, $z = 0.54$

38. $x_1 = 30$, $x_2 = 25$, cost = $55

40. Infeasibility

42. a. $x_1 = {}^{30}\!/_{16}$, $x_2 = {}^{30}\!/_{16}$, $z = {}^{60}\!/_{16}$
  b. $x_1 = 0$, $x_2 = 3$, $z = 6$
  c. Max $x_1 + {}^5\!/_3 x_2$
44. a. 180, 20
  b. Alternative optimal solutions
  c. 120, 80
46. Solution becomes infeasible
48. a. No feasible solution
  b. 1.5 additional tons of material 3
50. $20 \leq c_2 \leq 50$
52. a. $x_1 = 3$, $x_2 = 7$, $z = 27$
  b. $1 \leq c_1 \leq 3$
  c. $2 \leq c_2 \leq 6$
  d. Same solution is optimal
  e. New optimal solution has alternate optima
54. a. $x_1 = 1$, $x_2 = 3$, $z = 4$
  b. $\frac{1}{2} \leq c_1 \leq 2$
  c. $\frac{1}{2} \leq c_2 \leq 2$
  d. Same solution is optimal
  e. New optimal solution is $x_1 = 0$, $x_2 = 5$
56. a. $x_1 = 7$, $x_2 = 7$
  b. $3 \leq c_1 \leq 10.5$
  c. ${}^{10}\!/_3 \leq c_2 \leq {}^{35}\!/_3$
  d. New optimal solution is $x_1 = 0$, $x_2 = 10$; the value is 70
  e. Same solution is optimal
58. a. Optimal solution does not change
  b. $x_1 = 6$, $x_2 = 4$, $z = 26$
60. $x_1 = 65.45$, $x_2 = 261.82$, $z = \$45,818$
62. $x_1 = 384$, $x_2 = 80$

CHAPTER 3

2. a. $4 \leq c_1 \leq 12$ $3.33 \leq c_2 \leq 10$
  c. _____

Min RHS	Max RHS
725	No upper limit
133.33	400
75	135

  d. 560
4. a. More than $7.00
  b. More than $3.50
  c. None
6. a. $x_1 = 4000$, $x_2 = 10,000$; total risk = 62,000
  b. $3.75 \leq c_1 \leq$ No upper limit
    No lower limit $\leq c_2 \leq 6.4$
  c. $60,000
  d. 5%
  e. Approximately 6 cents
  f. 5.7%

8 a. $x_1 = 0$, $x_2 = 25$, $x_3 = 125$, $x_4 = 0$; $z = 525$
  b. A and C
  c. B; 425 hours
  d. Yes
10. a. $x_1 = 7.30$, $x_2 = 0$, $x_3 = 1.89$, $z = 139.73$
  b. Two and three
  c. 0, -3.41, and -4.43
  d. 0, 3.41, and 4.43
  e. Decrease the right-hand side of constraint 3 from 20 to 19
12. a. All Pro: 1000; College: 200; High School: 0
  b. Sewing and minimum All Pro production requirement
  c. 4000 minutes of unused cutting and dyeing time; all the sewing time is being used; 5200 minutes of unused inspection and packaging time; only the minimum number of All Pro models is being produced
  d. No lower limit $< c_1 \leq 5$
    $5 \leq c_2 <$ No upper limit
    No lower limit $< c_3 \leq 4$
14. a. $x_1 = 25$, $x_2 = 0$, $x_3 = 25$, profit = 1250
  b. Machine 1: 31.25, machine 2: 37.50
  c. $12.50
  d. $x_1 = 24$, $x_2 = 8$, $x_3 = 16$, profit = \$1440
16. b. $x_1 = 120,000$, $x_2 = 30,000$, $x_3 = 150,000$, value = 36,000
  c. $0.15 \leq c_1 \leq 0.60$
    No lower limit $< c_2 \leq 0.1222$
    $0.02 \leq c_3 \leq 0.20$
  d. Value of the optimal solution would increase by 4,666.67
  e. Need to resolve the problem; new optimal solution is
    $x_1 = 48,000$, $x_2 = 192,000$, $x_3 = 60,000$
18. a. $x_1 = 3$, $x_2 = 7$, $x_3 = 5$, $x_4 = 5$

CHAPTER 4

2. a. $x_1 = 77.89$, $x_2 = 63.16$, $3284.21
  b. Dept. A $15.79; dept. B $47.37
  c. $x_1 = 87.21$, $x_2 = 65.12$, $3341.34
    Dept. A 10 hours; dept. B 3.2 hours
4. a. $x_1 = 500$, $x_2 = 300$, $x_3 = 200$, $550
  b. $0.55
  c. Aroma 75; taste 84.4
  d. $0.60
6. 50 units of product 1; 0 units of product 2
  300 hours dept. A; 600 hours dept. B
8. Schedule 19 officers as follows:
  3 begin at 8:00 A.M.; 3 begin at noon; 7 begin at 4:00 P.M.; 4 begin at midnight; 2 begin at 4:00 A.M.
10. _____

Product	Modern Line	Old Line
1	500	0
2	300	400

Cost = $3850

12.

Component	Manufacture	Purchase	
Base	3750	1250	
Cartridge	5000	0	
Handle	3750	1250	Cost = $11,875

   b. Depts. A and B; add only to A

   c. Only 25 hours can be used

14. b.

Quarter	Production	Ending Inventory
1	4000	2100
2	3000	1100
3	2000	100
4	1900	500

16. x_1 = number of 10-inch rolls processed by cutting alternative i

   a. $x_1 = 0$, $x_2 = 125$, $x_3 = 500$, $x_4 = 1500$, $x_5 = 0$, $x_6 = 0$, $x_7 = 0$; 2125 rolls with waste of 750 inches

   b. 2500 rolls with no waste; however, $1\frac{1}{2}$ inch size is overproduced by 3000 units

18. a. 5 super, 2 regular, and 3 econotankers

     Total cost $583,000; monthly operating cost $4650

20. $x_1 = 48$, $x_2 = 96$, $456

     Assembler times: 480, 480, and 456

22. Investment strategy: 45.8% of A and 100% of B

     Objective function = $4340.40

     Savings/Loan Schedule

	Period			
	1	2	3	4
Savings	242.11	—	—	341.04
Funds from loan	—	200.00	127.58	—

24. a. Marginal = 0.6; average = 0.079; diminishing marginal returns have set in

   b. Relaxing the TV requirement will improve the solution

26. b. $E = 0.924$; $wa = 0.074$; $wc = 0.436$; $we = 0.489$; All other weights are zero.

   c. D is relatively inefficient; composite requires 92.4% of D's resources

   d. 34.37 patient-days (65 or older)

     41.99 patient-days (under 65)

   e. Hospitals A, C, and E

28. b. $E = 0.96$; $wb = 0.175$; $wc = 0.000$; $wj = 0.575$; $wn = 0.250$; $ws = 0.000$

   c. Clarksville is relatively inefficient; composite requires 96% of Clarksville's resources

   d. Output: $220 more profit

     Input: 4.4 less hours of operation

          2.6 less employees

          $185.61 less supplies expenses

   e. Bardstown, Jeffersonville, and New Albany

CHAPTER 5

2. $x_1 = 5$, $x_2 = 1$, $x_3 = 4$

4. a. Max $x_1 + 2x_2$

     s.t.

$$x_1 + 5x_2 + s_1 \quad\quad = 10$$
$$2x_1 + 6x_2 \quad\quad + s_2 = 16$$
$$x_1, x_2, s_1, s_2 \geq 0$$

   b. 2

   c. $x_1 = 0$, $x_2 = 0$, $s_1 = 10$, $s_2 = 16$; feasible

     $x_1 = 0$, $x_2 = 2$, $s_1 = 0$, $s_2 = 4$; feasible

     $x_1 = 0$, $x_2 = \frac{8}{3}$, $s_1 = -\frac{10}{3}$, $s_2 = 0$; not feasible

     $x_1 = 10$, $x_2 = 0$, $s_1 = 0$, $s_2 = -4$; not feasible

     $x_1 = 8$, $x_2 = 0$, $s_1 = 2$, $s_2 = 0$; feasible

     $x_1 = 5$, $x_2 = 1$, $s_1 = 0$, $s_2 = 0$; feasible

   d. $x_1 = 8$, $x_2 = 0$; value = 8

6. a. Max $60x_1 + 90x_2$

     s.t.

$$15x_1 + 45x_2 + s_1 \quad\quad = 90$$
$$5x_1 + 5x_2 \quad\quad + s_2 = 20$$
$$x_1, x_2, s_1, s_2 \geq 0$$

   b.

x_1	x_2	s_1	s_2	
60	90	0	0	
15	45	1	0	90
5	5	0	1	20

8. a.

	z_j	0	0	0	0	0	0	0
	$c_j - z_j$	5	20	25	0	0	0	

   b. Max $5x_1 + 20x_2 + 25x_3 + 0s_1 + 0s_2 + 0s_3$

     s.t.

$$2x_1 + 1x_2 \quad\quad + 1s_1 \quad\quad = 40$$
$$2x_2 + 1x_3 \quad\quad + 1s_2 \quad\quad = 30$$
$$3x_1 \quad\quad - \frac{1}{2}x_3 \quad\quad + 1s_3 = 15$$
$$x_1, x_2, x_3, s_1, s_2, s_3 \geq 0$$

   c. s_1, s_2, s_3; it is the origin

   d. 0

   e. x_3 enters, s_2 leaves

   f. 30, 750

   g. $x_1 = 10$ $s_1 = 20$

     $x_2 = 0$ $s_2 = 0$ Value = 800

     $x_3 = 30$ $s_3 = 0$

10. Slack variables have a coefficient of $+1$ in constraints

12. a. $x_1 = 540$, $x_2 = 252$

   b. $7668

   c. 630, 480, 708, 117

   d. 0, 120, 0, 18

14. $x_2 = 250$, $x_3 = 150$, $s_2 = 4000$

     Value = 4850

16. 35

18. **a.** Finds some optimal solution

 b. No, any $c_j - z_j > 0$ will work

 c. Provides largest per-unit increase

20. A = 0, B = 0, C = 33⅓; profit = 500

22. **a.** $x_1 = 0$, $x_2 = 50$, $x_3 = 75$; profit = \$210

 c. Grade B grapes and labor

24.

Max $-4x_1 - 5x_2 - 3x_3 + 0s_1 + 0s_2 + 0s_4 - Ma_1 - Ma_2 - Ma_3$

s.t.

$$
\begin{aligned}
4x_1 \quad\quad + 2x_3 - 1s_1 \quad\quad\quad\quad + 1a_1 \quad\quad\quad &= 20 \\
- 1x_2 + 1x_3 \quad\quad - 1s_2 \quad\quad\quad + 1a_2 \quad\quad &= 8 \\
-1x_1 + 2x_2 \quad\quad\quad\quad\quad\quad\quad\quad + 1a_3 &= 5 \\
2x_1 + 1x_2 + 1x_3 \quad\quad\quad\quad + 1s_4 \quad\quad\quad\quad &= 12
\end{aligned}
$$

$$x_1, x_2, x_3, s_1, s_2, s_4, a_1, a_2, a_3 \geq 0$$

26. $x_2 = 60$, $x_3 = 60$, $s_3 = 20$; value = 2040

28. 2400 boxes of 33 gallon bags

 Profit = \$480

30. $x_1 = 480$, $x_4 = 480$, $x_6 = 800$; value: 46,400

32. $x_1 = 203.478$, $x_2 = 285.2175$, $x_3 = 20$

 Profit = \$4,269,565

34. Alternative optimal solution: $x_1 = 4$, $x_2 = 4$

 $x_1 = 8$, $x_2 = 0$

36. Alternative opitmal solution: $x_1 = 4$, $x_2 = 0$, $x_3 = 0$

 $x_1 = 0$, $x_2 = 0$, $x_3 = 8$

38. Infeasible

CHAPTER 6

2. **a.** $31.25 \leq c_2 \leq 83.33$

 b. $-43.33 \leq c_{s_2} \leq 8.75$

 c. $c_{s_3} \leq {}^{26}\!/_5$

 d. Variables do not change; value = \$1920

4. **a.** $100 \leq b_1 \leq 150$

 b. $40 \leq b_2 \leq 60$

 c. $b_3 \leq 110$

6. **a.** $x_1 = 4$, $x_2 = .5$, $s_3 = 1.5$

 b. $c_1 \geq 6.25$

 c. Variables do not change; value = 47.5

 d. $c_3 \leq 11.25$

 e. Alternative optimal solution: $x_1 = 2$, $x_3 = 2$; value = 45

 or $x_3 = 3$; value = 45

8. **a.** $6.3 \leq c_1 \leq 13.5$

 b. $6\frac{2}{3} \leq c_2 \leq 14\frac{2}{7}$

 c. Variables do not change; value = \$7164

 d. Below $6\frac{2}{3}$ or above $14\frac{2}{7}$

 e. $x_1 = 300$, $x_2 = 420$; value = \$9300

10. **a.** $x_1 = 5220/11$, $x_2 = 3852/11$; value = 86,868/11

 b. No, s_1 would enter the basis

12. **a.** Increase in profit

 b. No

14. **a.** $14 \leq b_1 \leq 21\frac{1}{2}$

 b. $4 \leq b_2$

 c. $18\frac{3}{4} \leq b_3 \leq 30$

 d. Dual price = 400/9; range: $18\frac{3}{4} \leq b_3 \leq 30$

16. **a.** $400/3 \leq b_1 \leq 800$

 b. $275 \leq b_2$

 c. $275/2 \leq b_3 \leq 625$

18. Min $70u_1 + 60u_2 + 25u_3$

 s.t.

$$
\begin{aligned}
3u_1 + 5u_2 + 5u_3 &\geq 10 \\
2u_1 + 5u_2 + 6u_3 &\geq 9 \\
4u_1 + u_2 + 3u_3 &\geq 4 \\
2u_1 + 3u_2 + u_3 &\geq 6
\end{aligned}
$$

$$u_1, u_2, u_3 \geq 0$$

20. Max $5x_1 + x_2 + 3x_3$

 s.t.

$$
\begin{aligned}
-x_1 - x_2 \quad\quad &\leq -40 \\
2x_1 + 3x_2 + x_3 &\leq 50 \\
3x_1 + 2x_2 + 2x_3 &\leq 25 \\
- x_2 - x_3 &\leq -10
\end{aligned}
$$

$$x_1, x_2, x_3 \geq 0$$

22. **a.** Min $8u_1 + 12u_2$

 s.t.

$$
\begin{aligned}
u_1 + 3u_2 &\geq 2 \\
2u_1 + 2u_2 &\geq 3
\end{aligned}
$$

$$u_1, u_2 \geq 0$$

24. Max $5u_1' - 5u_1'' + 4u_2' - 4u_2'' - 7u_3 + 4u_4$

 s.t.

$$
\begin{aligned}
2u_1' - 2u_1'' + 4u_2' - 4u_2'' - 2u_3 + u_4 &\leq 3 \\
u_1' - u_1'' + u_2' - u_2'' + 2u_4 &\leq 1 \\
3u_1' - 3u_1'' + u_2' - u_2'' - u_3 &\leq 2
\end{aligned}
$$

$$u_1', u_1'', u_2', u_2'', u_3, u_4 \geq 0$$

26. **a.** Max $10x_1 + 5x_2$

 s.t.

$$
\begin{aligned}
x_1 \quad\quad &\geq 20 \\
x_2 &\geq 20 \\
x_1 \quad\quad &\leq 100 \\
x_2 &\leq 100 \\
3x_1 + x_2 &\leq 175
\end{aligned}
$$

$$x_1, x_2 \geq 0$$

 b. Min $-20u_1 - 20u_2 + 100u_3 + 100u_4 + 175u_5$

 s.t.

$$
\begin{aligned}
-u_1 \quad\quad + u_3 \quad\quad + 3u_5 &\geq 10 \\
- u_2 \quad\quad + u_4 + u_5 &\geq 5
\end{aligned}
$$

$$u_1, u_2, u_3, u_4, u_5 \geq 0$$

 Solution: $u_4 = {}^5\!/_3$, $u_5 = {}^{10}\!/_3$

 c. $x_1 = 25$, $x_2 = 100$; commission = \$750

28. a. $x_1 = 4$, $x_2 = \frac{1}{2}$; value = 75

   b. 75

   c. 1 and 2

   d. $\frac{3}{2}$ units in constraint 3

   e. $\frac{15}{2}$, 15, 0; constraint 2

   f. $12.5 \le c_1$

      $20 \le c_2 \le 60$

             $c_3 \le 22.5$

   g. $0 \le b_1 \le 6$

      $2 \le b_2 \le 6$

      $\frac{9}{2} \le b_3$

30. a. $x_1 = 4000$, $x_2 = 10{,}000$; total risk = 62,000

   b. Increase it by 2.167 per unit

   c. $48{,}000 \le b_2 \le 102{,}000$

   d. $x_1 = 5667$, $x_2 = 9167$; total risk = 72,833

   e. Variables do not change; total risk = 66,000

Chapter 7

2. a. Min $14x_{11} + 9x_{12} + 7x_{13} + 8x_{21} + 10x_{22} + 5x_{23}$

s.t.

$$
\begin{array}{rcrcrcr}
x_{11} + x_{12} + x_{13} & & & \le & 30 \\
& x_{21} + x_{22} + x_{23} & \le & 20 \\
x_{11} & + x_{21} & & = & 25 \\
x_{12} & + x_{22} & & = & 15 \\
x_{13} & + x_{23} & = & 10
\end{array}
$$

$x_{11}, x_{12}, x_{13}, x_{21}, x_{22}, x_{23} \ge 0$

   b. $x_{11} = 5$, $x_{12} = 15$, $x_{13} = 10$, $x_{21} = 20$

4. b. $x_{12} = 300$, $x_{21} = 100$, $x_{22} = 100$, $x_{23} = 300$, $x_{31} = 100$

     Cost = 10,400

6. b.

Seattle–Denver	4000;	Seattle–Los Angeles	5000;
Columbus–Mobile	4000;	New York–Pittsburgh	3000;
New York–Mobile	1000;	New York–Los Angeles	1000;
New York–Washington	3000		

   c.

Seattle–Denver	4000;	Seattle–Los Angeles	5000;
Columbus–Mobile	5000;	New York–Pittsburgh	4000;
New York–Los Angeles	1000;	New York–Washington	3000

     Cost actually decreases

8. Clifton–D_2 4000; Clifton–D_4 1000;

   Danville–D_1 2000; Danville–D_4 1000

   Customer 2 has a shortfall of 1000; customer 3's demand is not satisfied

10. 1–A 300; 1–C 1200; 2–A 1200; 3–A 500; 3–B 500

12. b. Jackson–2, Ellis–1, Smith–3

     Total completion time = 64

14. b. Bostock–Southwest, Miller–Northwest

16. b. Toy–2, auto parts–4, housewares–3

     video–1; profit = 61

18. 1–B, 2–C, 3–A, 4–D; 74 hours required

20. 1–D, 2–C, 3–B, 4–A; 505 miles traveled

22. a. Cost Matrix ($1000's):

	Supplier					
Division	*1*	*2*	*3*	*4*	*5*	*6*
1	614	660	534	680	590	630
2	603	639	702	693	693	630
3	865	830	775	850	900	930
4	532	553	511	581	595	553
5	720	648	684	693	657	747

   b. Optimal Solution:

Supplier 1–Division 2	$603
Supplier 2–Division 5	648
Supplier 3–Division 3	775
Supplier 5–Division 1	590
Supplier 6–Division 4	553
Total	$3169

24. c. $x_{14} = 320$, $x_{25} = 600$, $x_{47} = 300$, $x_{49} = 20$, $x_{56} = 300$, $x_{58} = 300$, $x_{39} = 380$

     Cost = $11,220

26. c. Optimal Solution:

Variable	Value	Variable	Value
x_{13}	50	x_{36}	0
x_{14}	250	x_{37}	150
x_{23}	100	x_{45}	150
x_{24}	0	x_{46}	100
x_{35}	0	x_{47}	0

     Objective function = 4300

28.

Optimal Solution	Units Shipped	Cost
Muncie–Cincinnati	1	6
Cincinnati–Concord	3	84
Brazil–Louisville	6	18
Louisville–Macon	2	88
Louisville–Greenwood	4	136
Xenia–Cincinnati	5	15
Cincinnati–Chatham	3	72
Total		419

Two rail cars must be held at Muncie until a buyer is found

32. a. San Jose–Los Angeles 100; Las Vegas–Los Angeles 100;

     Las Vegas–San Diego 200; Tucson–San Francisco 300

     Cost = $7800

   b. Initial solution is optimal

   c. San Jose–San Francisco 100; Las Vegas–Los Angeles 200;

     Las Vegas–San Diego 100; Tucson–San Francisco 200;

     Tucson–San Diego 100

     Cost = $7800

d. San Jose–San Francisco 100; Las Vegas–Los Angeles 200;
Las Vegas–San Francisco 100; Tucson–San Francisco 100;
Tucson–San Diego 200
Cost = \$8000

34. See Problem 4

38. See Problem 12

40. Terry 2; Carle 3; McClymonds 1; Higley usassigned
Time = 26 days

42. Toy–4; auto–1; housewares–3; video–2

CHAPTER 8

2. b. $x_1 = 1.43$, $x_2 = 4.29$; value = 41.47
Rounded: $x_1 = 1$, $x_2 = 4$; value = 37

c. $x_1 = 0$, $x_2 = 5$; value = 40
Not the same

4. a. $x_1 = 3.67$, $x_2 = 0$; value = 36.7
Rounded: $x_1 = 3$, $x_2 = 0$; value = 30
Lower bound = 30; upper bound = 36.7

b. $x_1 = 3$, $x_2 = 2$; value = 36

c. Alternative optimal solutions: $x_1 = 0$, $x_2 = 5$
$x_1 = 2$, $x_2 = 4$

6. b. $x_1 = 1.96$, $x_2 = 5.48$; value = 7.44
Rounded: $x_1 = 1.96$, $x_2 = 5$; value = 6.96
Lower bound = 6.96; upper bound = 7.44

c. $x_1 = 1.29$, $x_2 = 6$; value = 7.29

8. a. $x_3 = 1$, $x_4 = 1$, $x_6 = 1$; value = 17,500

b. Add $x_1 + x_2 \leq 1$

c. Add $x_3 - x_4 \leq 0$

10. b. Choose locations B and E

12. b. Modernize plants 1 and 3 or plants 4 and 5

d. Modernize plants 1 and 3

14. b. Use all part-time employees
Bring on as follows: 9:00 A.M.–6, 11:00 A.M.–2, 12:00 noon–6,
1:00 P.M.–1, 3:00 P.M.–6
Cost = \$672

c. Same as in part (b)

d. New solution is to bring on 1 full-time employee at 9:00 A.M., 4
more at 11:00 A.M. and part-time employees as follows:
9:00 A.M.–5, 12:00 noon–5, and 3:00 P.M.–2

16. a. New objective function: Min $25x_1 + 40x_2 + 40x_3 + 40x_4 + 25x_5$

b. $x_4 = x_5 = 1$; modernize the Ohio and California plants

c. Add the constraint $x_2 + x_3 = 1$

d. $x_1 = x_3 = 1$

18. $x_1 = 3$, $x_2 = 2$; value = 36

20. $x_1 = 0$, $x_2 = 2$, $x_3 = 20/3$; value = 32/3

CHAPTER 9

2.

Node	Shortest Route from Node 7	Distance
1	7–6–5–3–1	22
2	7–4–2	11
3	7–6–5–3	12
4	7–4	5
5	7–5–6	8
6	7–6	6

4. 1–4–5–6–8; distance = 10

6.

Node	Shortest Route from Node C	Distance
1	C–1	35
2	C–2	20
3	C–3	20
4	C–4	30
5	C–3–5	55
6	C–3–6	50
7	C–3–8–7	100
8	C–3–8	80
9	C–4–10–9	85
10	C–4–10	70

8. 1–2–8–10–11

10. 1–3, 3–4, 4–5, 5–2, 5–7, 7–8, 7–6
Total miles = 17

12. 1–2, 2–5, 5–6, 6–3, 6–8, 3–4, 8–7
Total length = 2900 feet

14. 1–4, 2–3, 3–4, 4–5, 4–6, 6–7, 7–8, 8–9, 9–11, 11–10
Minimum length = 28 miles

16. Maximal flow = 11,000 vehicles per hour

18. a. 10 hours; 10,000 gallons per hour

b. 11.1 hours; flow reduced to 9000 gallons per hour

20. Maximal flow = 23 gallons/minute
From steps 2 and 5, we see that the total flow from 3 to 5 must be
5 gallons/minute

CHAPTER 10

2. b. See Figure G10.2b

4. a. A–D–G

b. No; time = 15 months

6. a. A–D–F–H

b. 22 weeks

c. No, it is a critical activity

d. Yes, 2 weeks

e. ES = 3, LS = 4, EF = 10, LF = 11

F I G U R E G10.2b

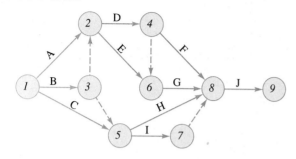

8. b. B–C–E–F–H

d. Yes, time = 49 weeks

10. a.

Activity	Time	Variance
A	5.00	0.11
B	9.00	0.11
C	8.00	0.44
D	8.83	0.25
E	7.17	0.25
F	6.00	0.11

b. 23.83, 0.47

12. a. A–D–H–I

b. 25.66 days

c. 0.2578

14. a. A–D–F–G

b. 1.5 days

c. 29.5, 2.36

d. 0.6293

16. a.

E(T)	Variance
16	3.92
13	2.03
10	1.27

b. 0.9783, approximately 1.00, approximately 1.00

18. c. A–B–D–G–H–I, 14.17 weeks

d. Yes, P(13 weeks completion) = 0.0951

20. b. Crash B(1 week), D(2 weeks), E(1 week), F(1 week), G(1 week)

Total cost = $2427

c. All activities are critical

22. b. Crash C(1 day) and E(1 day)

c. $9300

24. c. A–B–C–F, 31 weeks

d. Crash A(2 weeks), B(2 weeks), C(1 week), D(1 week), E(1 week)

e. All activities are critical

f. $112,500

26.

Activity	Cost/Week	Activity	Cost/Week
A	15	F	1
B	8	G	20
C	1	H	5
D	20	I	2
E	2	J	1

Example: at the end of 7 weeks, feasible budgets are between 92,000 and 129,000.

28. b. 6% overrun; followup on activity D

30. Corrective action desired

    Activity E—1 week behind

    Activity F—$3000 cost overrun

CHAPTER 11

2. $164.32 for each; total cost = $328.64

4. a. 1095.45

b. 240

c. 22.82 days

d. $273.86 for each; total cost = $547.72

6. a. 15.95

b. $2106

c. 15.04

d. 16.62 days

8. $Q^* = 11.73$, use 12

5 classes per year

$225,200

10. $Q^* = 1414.21$

$T = 28.28$ days

Production runs of 7.07 days

12. $Q^* = 1000$; total cost = $1200

Yes, the change saves $300 per year

14. New $Q^* = 4509$

16. 135.55; $r = dm - S$; less than

18. 64, 24.44

20. $Q^* = 100$; total cost = $3,601.50

22. $Q^* = 300$; savings = $480

24. a. 500

b. 580.4

26. a. 397

b. 0.70

c. 489, 0.35

28. a. 440

b. 0.60

c. 710

d. $c_u = $17;

30. a. 13.68 (14)

b. 17.83 (18)

c. 2, $10; 6, $30

32. a. 31.62

    b. 19.86 (20); 0.2108

    c. 5, $15

34. a. 243

    b. 93, $54.87

    c. 613

    d. 163, $96.17

    e. Yes, added cost only $41.30 per year

    f. Yes, added cost would be $4,130 per year

36. a. 40

    b. 62.25; 7.9

    c. 54

    d. 36

38. Engines   10

    Air cleaners   7

    Filter housings   2

40. Base assemblies   13

    Wheel subassemblies 9

    Tires   4

Chapter 12

2. a. 0.4512

    b. 0.6988

    c. 0.3012

4. 0.3333, 0.2222, 0.1481, 0.0988, 0.1976

6. a. 0.3333

    b. 1.3333

    c. 0.1111 hours

    d. 0.6667

8. 0.20, 3.2, 4, 3.2, 4, 0.80

    Slightly poorer service

10. a. New: 1.3333, 2, 0.6667, 1, 0.6667

        Experienced: 0.50, 1, 0.25, 0.50, 0.50

    b. New $74; experienced $50; hire experienced

12. a. 0.25, 2.25, 3, 0.15 hours, 0.20 hours, 0.75

    b. The service needs improvement

14. a. 0.1667

    b. 5

    c. 0.4167 hours

    d. 0.8333

    e. No

16. a. 0.50

    b. 0.50

    c. 0.10 hours

    d. 0.20 hours

18. a. 0.5385

    b. 0.0593

    c. 0.0099 hours

    d. 0.1099 hours

    e. 0.1384

20. a. 0.2360, 0.1771, 1.5771, 0.0127 hours, 0.1127 hours

    b. $P(\text{wait}) = 0.2023$; prefer 3-channel system

22.

Characteristic	A	B	C
P_0	0.2000	0.5000	0.4286
L_q	3.2000	0.5000	0.1524
L	4.0000	1.0000	0.9524
W_q	0.1333	0.0200	0.0063
W	0.1667	0.0417	0.0397
P_w	0.8000	0.5000	0.2286

(System C provides the best service)

24. a. 0.0466, 0.05

    b. 1.4

    c. 11:00 A.M.

26. a. 0.2668, 10 minutes, 0.6667

    b. 0.0667, 7 minutes, 0.4669

    c. $25.33; $33.34; one-channel

28. a. 10, 9.6

    b. Design A with $\mu = 10$

    c. 0.05, 0.01

    d. A: 0.5, 0.3125, 0.8125, 0.0625, 0.1625, 0.5

        B: 0.4792, 0.2857, 0.8065, 0.0571, 0.1613, 0.5208

    e. Design B is slightly better

30. a. 0.1460, 0.3066, 0.3220, 0.2254

    b. 0.2254

    c. 1.6267

    d. 4; 0.1499

32. a. 31.04%

    b. 27.58%

    c. 0.2758, 0.1092, 0.0351

    d. 3, 10.92%

34. a. 0.4790   **b.** 0.3110

    c. 0.8320   **d.** 2.9846

    e. 7.9846

    f. 95.8 minutes; 35.8 minutes

    g. Yes

Chapter 13

2. a.

Number of Arrivals	Relative Frequency
0	0.12
1	0.24
2	0.37
3	0.19
4	0.08
Total	1.00

    b. 0 + 2 + 1 = 3 customers

4. a. 0, 0, 1, 0, 1, 1

    b. Average number of arrivals = 0.5

    c. No, sample is too small

    d. 1.87

6. a.

Cars Sold	Relative Frequency
0	0.04
1	0.10
2	0.16
3	0.44
4	0.20
5	0.06
Total	1.00

8. Number served = 3, total profit = $3.75, average profit = $1.25, number lost = 0

14. Preferred order size is 200

18. Average costs: holding—190.00, order—12.50, shortage—0, total—202.50

CHAPTER 14

2. a.   Optimistic: d_1
      Conservative: d_3
      Minimax regret: d_3
   c.   Optimistic: d_1
      Conservative: d_2 or d_3
      Minimax regret: d_2

4. b.   Optimistic: large
      Conservative: small
      Minimax regret: medium

6. a. d_1 **b.** d_4

8. d_2 (medium)

10. b. Develop the software

12. $p = 0.25$

14. a. d_1 (St. Louis)
   b.

p	Best Decision(s)
$0 \leq p < 0.67$	d_1
$p = 0.67$	d_1 or d_2
$0.67 < p \leq 1.0$	d_2

16. 0.42

18. a. s_1: d_1; s_2: d_2, d_3, or d_4; s_3: d_4; s_4: d_4
   b. 12.5   **c.** 11.3   **d.** 1.2

20. 195

22. $200

24. a. d_1
   b.

p	Best Decision(s)
$0 \leq p < 0.59$	d_3
$p = 0.59$	d_1 or d_3
$0.59 < p \leq 1.0$	d_1

   c. 2
   d. d_3

26. a. $8000
   b. 13.13%
   c. Not worth doing the study

28. b. If I_1, then d_1; if I_2, then d_2
      EV(node 1) = $101.50
   c. EVSI = $1500

30. If unseasonably cold, then purchase snowplow
   If not unseasonably cold, then purchase blade

32. a. If I_1, then d_1
      If I_2, then d_1
      EV = 2000
   b. 0.57
   c. 0%

34. a. Purchase component
   b. EVPI = $9000
   c. 0.355
   d. If I_1, then manufacture
      If I_2, then purchase
      EV = 43.9
   e. EVSI = $3650
   f. 40.6%

36. a.

		Demand	
		1000	2000	3000
Amount Produced	1000	50,000	10,000	−30,000
	2000	−50,000	100,000	60,000
	3000	−150,000	0	150,000

   b. d_2 = 2000 pounds
   c. $48,000
   d. If I_1, then d_3
      If I_2, then d_2
      If I_3, then d_1
   e. $10,900
   f. 22.7%

38. a. d_3
   b. d_1

CHAPTER 15

2. a. Min $P_1(d_1^-) + P_2(d_2^+)$
      s.t.
$$
\begin{aligned}
50x_1 + 100x_2 &\leq 50{,}000 \\
3x_1 + 10x_2 - d_1^+ + d_1^- &= 4500 \\
x_2 - d_2^+ + d_2^- &= 300
\end{aligned}
$$
$$x_1, x_2, d_1^+, d_1^-, d_2^+, d_2^- \geq 0$$
   b. $x_1 = 250$, $x_2 = 375$

4. a. Min $P_1(d_1^-) + P_1(d_2^+) + P_2(d_3^-) + P_2(d_4^-) + P_5(d_5^-)$
s.t.

$$
\begin{aligned}
20x_1 + 30x_2 - d_1^+ + d_1^- &= 1800 \\
20x_1 + 30x_2 - d_2^+ + d_2^- &= 6000 \\
x_1 \qquad\quad - d_3^+ + d_3^- &= 100 \\
x_2 - d_4^+ + d_4^- &= 120 \\
x_1 + \quad x_2 - d_5^+ + d_5^- &= 300
\end{aligned}
$$

x_1, x_2, all deviation variables ≥ 0

b. $x_1 = 120, x_2 = 120$

6. a. Let x_1 = number of letters mailed to group 1 customers
x_2 = number of letters mailed to group 2 customers
Min $P_1(d_1^-) + P_1(d_2^-) + P_2(d_3^+)$
s.t.

$$
\begin{aligned}
x_1 \qquad\quad - d_1^+ + d_1^- &= 40{,}000 \\
x_2 - d_2^+ + d_2^- &= 50{,}000 \\
x_1 + x_2 - d_3^+ + d_3^- &= 70{,}000
\end{aligned}
$$

x_1, x_2, all deviation variables ≥ 0

b. $x_1 = 40{,}000, x_2 = 50{,}000$

c. Optimal solution does not change

8. a. Min $d_1^- + d_1^+ + e_1^- + e_1^+ + d_2^- + d_2^+ + e_2^- + e_2^+ + d_3^- + d_3^+ + e_3^- + e_3^+$
s.t.

$$
\begin{aligned}
x_1 \quad\; + d_1^- - d_1^+ &= 1 \\
x_2 + e_1^- - e_1^+ &= 7 \\
x_1 \quad\; + d_2^- - d_2^+ &= 5 \\
x_2 + e_2^- - e_2^+ &= 9 \\
x_1 \quad\; + d_3^- - d_3^+ &= 6 \\
x_2 + e_3^- - e_3^+ &= 2
\end{aligned}
$$

all variables ≥ 0

b. $x_1 = 5, x_2 = 7$

10. Since CR = 0.017 is less than 0.10, the degree of consistency exhibited in the pairwise comparison matrix is acceptable

12. Since CR = 0.029 is less than 0.10, the degree of consistency exhibited in the pairwise comparison matrix is acceptable

14. a. 0.723, 0.193, 0.083

b. Since CR = 0.055 is less than 0.10, the degree of consistency exhibited in the pairwise comparison matrix is acceptable

16. a. 0.503, 0.348, 0.149

b. Since CR = 0.417 is greater than 0.10, the individual's judgments are not consistent

18. a.

	D	S	N
D	1	$1/4$	$1/7$
S	4	1	$1/3$
N	7	3	1

b. 0.080, 0.265, 0.655

c. Since CR = 0.029 is less than 0.10, the manager's judgments are consistent

20. b. Criterion: 0.667, 0.333
Yield: 0.75, 0.25
Risk: 0.333, 0.667

c. CCI: 0.611; SRI: 0.389

22. b. Criterion: 0.608, 0.272, 0.120
Price: 0.557, 0.123, 0.320
Quality: 0.137, 0.240, 0.623
FM reception: 0.579, 0.187, 0.234

c. A: 0.445, B: 0.163, C: 0.392

CHAPTER 16

2. a.

Week	4-Week	5-Week
10	19.00	18.80
11	20.00	19.20
12	18.75	19.00

b. 9.65, 7.41

c. 5-week

4. Weeks 10, 11, and 12: 18.48, 18.63, 18.27
MSE = 9.25; $\alpha = 0.2$ is better

6. b. The more recent data receives the greater weight or importance in determining the forecast

8. a. Month 13: 106.4; MSE = 510.29

b. Month 13: 104.62; MSE = 540.55
Conclusion: a smoothing constant of 0.3 is better

10. Forecast for weeks 8, 9, 10, and 11: 258.64, 281.48, 283.61, and 292.71

12. 3117

14. $T_t = 20{,}746.67 - 351.429t$
Enrollment appears to be decreasing by an average of 351 students per year

16. $T_t = 28{,}800 + 421.429t$

18. a. Linear trend appears to be reasonable

b. $T_t = 19.993 + 1.774t$
Average cost increase of \$1.77 per unit per year

20. a. $T_t = 1997.6 + 397.545t$

b. 6371; 6768

22. $T_8 = 252.28; T_9 = 259.10$

24. a. A linear trend appears to exist

b. $T_t = -5 + 15_t$
Average increase in sales is 15 units per year

26. a. $T_t = 3.9041 + .0236t$
Personal income increasing at an average of 0.0236 per month

b. 4.21, 4.23, 4.26, 4.28, 4.31, 4.33

c. Actual 4.41 is above the forecast 4.33

28. 0.707, 0.777, 0.827, 0.966, 1.016, 1.305, 1.494, 1.225, 0.976, 0.986, 0.936, 0.787

30. a. Selected centered moving averages for
t = 5, 10, 15, and 20 are 11.125, 18.125, 22.875, and 27.000

b. 0.899, 1.362, 1.118, 0.621

c. Quarter 2, prior to summer boating season

32. a. $T_t = 6.329 + 1.055t$

b. 36.92, 37.98, 39.03, 40.09

c. 33.23, 51.65, 43.71, 24.86

34. a. $\hat{y} = 25.381 + 2.317x$
    b. \$43,917
36. a. $\hat{y} = 22.173 - 0.1478x$
    b. 14.783 or approximately 15 defective parts

CHAPTER 17

2. b. $\pi_1 = 0.5$, $\pi_2 = 0.5$
   c. $\pi_1 = 0.6$, $\pi_2 = 0.4$
4. a. $\pi_1 = 0.92$, $\pi_2 = 0.08$
   b. \$85
6. a.

	City	Suburbs
City	0.98	0.02
Suburbs	0.01	0.99

   b. $\pi_1 = 0.333$, $\pi_2 = 0.667$
   c. City will decrease from 40% to 33%; suburbs will increase from 60% to 67%
8. a. MDA
   b. $\pi_1 = \frac{1}{3}$, $\pi_2 = \frac{2}{3}$
10. $3 - 1 \ (0.59)$, $4 - 1 \ (0.52)$
12. 1420 will be lost
14. a. Graduate and drop out
   b. P(Drop out) = 0.15, P(Sophomore) = 0.10, P(Junior) = 0.75
   c. 0.706, 0.294
   d. Yes; P(Graduate) = 0.54
             P(Drop out) = 0.46
   e. 1479 (74%) will graduate

CHAPTER 18

2. a. 1–4–6–9–10
   b. 4–6–9–10
   c.

Route	Value	Route	Value
(1–2–5–7–10)	32	(1–3–6–8–10)	34
(1–2–5–8–10)	36	(1–3–6–9–10)	31
(1–2–5–9–10)	28	(1–4–6–8–10)	29
(1–3–5–7–10)	31	(1–4–6–9–10)	26
(1–3–5–8–10)	35		
(1–3–5–9–10)	27		

4. a. Alternative optimal solutions—value = 186
     Solution 1: A1–3, A2–2, A3–0, A4–3
     Solution 2: A1–2, A2–3, A3–0, A4–3
   b. A1–1, A2–2, A3–0, A4–3
6. a. A–G–J–M
   b. Choose H
8. a. Daily News–1, Sunday news–3, radio–1, TV–3; max exposure = 169
   b. 1, 2, 1, 2; max exposure = 139
   c. For part (a): 2, 3, 3; max exposure = 152
     For part (b): 2, 3, 1; max exposure = 127
10. Monthly production: 20, 20, 30

CHAPTER 19

2. a. $\frac{40}{9}$
   b. 4
4. 4 (\$540)
6. a. \$20
   b. $-x^2 + 20x - 20$
   c. 10
8. $x_1 = 0$, $x_2 = 2$ is a saddle point
   $x_1 = 2$, $x_2 = -2$ is a local minimum
   $x_1 = -2$, $x_2 = -2$ is a local minimum
10. $x_1 = 6$, $x_2 = 3$ (\$40,000 earnings)
12. Provides maximum solution
14. $x_1 = \dfrac{4}{\sqrt{34/5}}$, $x_2 = \dfrac{3}{\sqrt{34/5}}$ (minimum)

     $x_1 = \dfrac{-4}{\sqrt{34/5}}$, $x_2 = \dfrac{-3}{\sqrt{34/5}}$ (maximum)

16. $x_1 = \frac{36}{13}$, $x_2 = \frac{2}{13}$

Appendix H: Solutions to Self-Test Problems

CHAPTER 1

4. A quantitative approach may be considered for the following reasons:
   a. the problem is large and complex
   b. the problem is very important
   c. the problem is new and no past experience exists
   d. the problem is repetitive
8. a. Max $10x + 5y$
   s.t. $5x + 2y \leq 40$
   $x \geq 0, y \geq 0$
   b. Controllable inputs: x and y
   Uncontrollable inputs: profit (10,5), labor-hours (5,2) and labor-hour availability (40)
   c. See Figure H1.8c
   d. $x = 0, y = 20$; profit = $100
   (Solution by trial-and-error)
15. a. $TC = 1000 + 30x$
   b. $P = 40x - (1000 + 30x) = 10x - 1000$
   c. Breakeven when $P = 0$

$$Thus\ 10x - 1000 = 0$$

$$10x = 1000$$

$$x = 100$$

CHAPTER 2

1. Parts (a), (b), and (e) are acceptable linear programming relationships.
   Part (c) is not acceptable because of $-2x_2^2$.
   Part (d) is not acceptable because of $3\sqrt{x_1}$.
   Part (f) is not acceptable because of $1x_1x_2$.
   Parts (c), (d), and (f) could not be found in a linear programming model because they have the above nonlinear terms.

2. a.

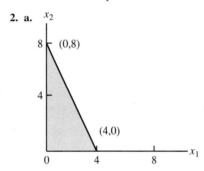

F I G U R E H1.8c

b.

c.

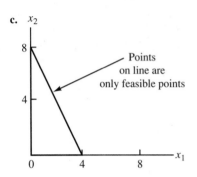

Points on line are only feasible points

5.

7.

11.

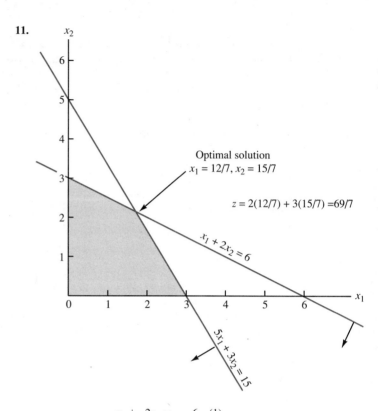

Optimal solution
$x_1 = 12/7, x_2 = 15/7$

$z = 2(12/7) + 3(15/7) = 69/7$

$x_1 + 2x_2 = 6$

$5x_1 + 3x_2 = 15$

$$\begin{array}{lrl} & x_1 + 2x_2 = & 6 \quad (1) \\ & 5x_1 + 3x_2 = & 15 \quad (2) \\ (1) \times 5 & 5x_1 + 10x_2 = & 30 \quad (3) \\ (2) - (3) & -7x_2 = & -15 \\ & x_2 = & 15/7 \end{array}$$

From (1) $\quad x_1 = 6 - 2(15/7)$

$= 6 - 30/7 = 12/7$

14. a.

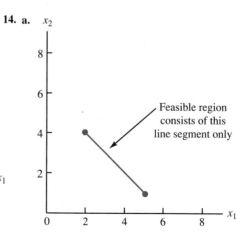

Feasible region consists of this line segment only

b. The extreme points are (5,1) and (2,4)

c.

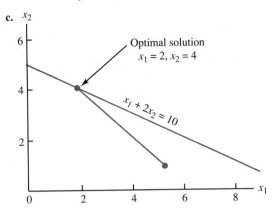

18. Max $5x_1 + 2x_2 + 8x_3 + 0s_1 + 0s_2 + 0s_3$

s.t.

$$1x_1 - 2x_2 + \tfrac{1}{2}x_3 + 1s_1 \qquad\qquad = 420$$
$$2x_1 + 3x_2 - 1x_3 \qquad + 1s_2 \qquad = 610$$
$$6x_1 - 1x_2 + 3x_3 \qquad\qquad + 1s_3 = 125$$

$$x_1, x_2, x_3, s_1, s_2, s_3 \geq 0$$

22. **a.** Let x_1 = number of units of regular model
    x_2 = number of units of catcher's model

Max $5x_1 + 8x_2$

s.t.

$$1x_1 + \tfrac{3}{2}x_2 \leq 900 \quad \text{Cutting and sewing}$$
$$\tfrac{1}{2}x_1 + \tfrac{1}{3}x_2 \leq 300 \quad \text{Finishing}$$
$$\tfrac{1}{8}x_1 + \tfrac{1}{4}x_2 \leq 100 \quad \text{Packaging and shipping}$$

$$x_1, x_2 \geq 0$$

b.

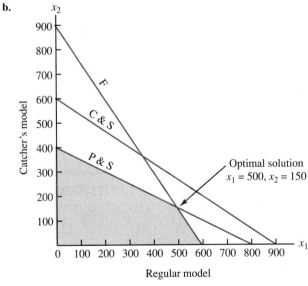

c. $5(500) + 8(150) = \$3,700$

d. C & S $1(500) + \tfrac{3}{2}(150) = 725$
    F $\tfrac{1}{2}(500) + \tfrac{1}{3}(150) = 300$
    P & S $\tfrac{1}{8}(500) + \tfrac{1}{4}(150) = 100$

e.

Department	Capacity	Usage	Slack
Cutting and sewing	900	725	175 hours
Finishing	300	300	0 hours
Packaging and shipping	100	100	0 hours

29.

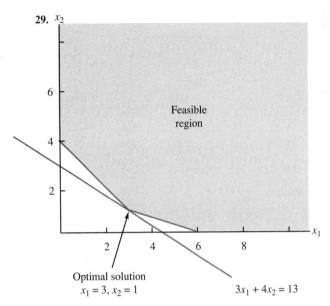

Objective function value = 13

32. **a.**

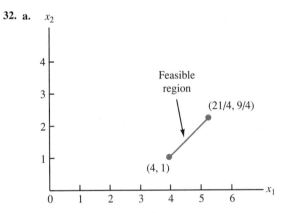

b. There are two extreme points

$$x_1 = 4 \qquad x_1 = 21/4$$
$$x_2 = 1 \qquad x_2 = 9/4$$

c. The optimal solution (see part (a)) is $x_1 = 4, x_2 = 1$

33. **a.** Min $6x_1 + 4x_2 + 0s_1 + 0s_2 + 0s_3$

s.t.

$$2x_1 + 1x_2 - s_1 \qquad\qquad = 12$$
$$1x_1 + 1x_2 \qquad - s_2 \qquad = 10$$
$$1x_2 \qquad\qquad + s_3 = 4$$

$$x_1, x_2, s_1, s_2, s_3 \geq 0$$

b. The optimal solution is $x_1 = 6, x_2 = 4$

c. $s_1 = 4, s_2 = 0, s_3 = 0$

40.

41.

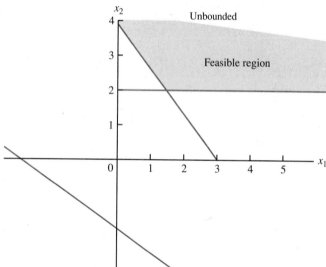

52. a. See Figure H2.52a

b. Slope of line B $= -1$
Slope of line A $= -\frac{1}{3}$

$$-1 \leq -c_1/3 \leq -1/3$$

$$1 \geq c_1/3 \quad c_1/3 \geq 1/3$$

$$c_1 \leq 3 \quad c_1 \geq 1$$

Range: $1 \leq c_1 \leq 3$

FIGURE H2.52a

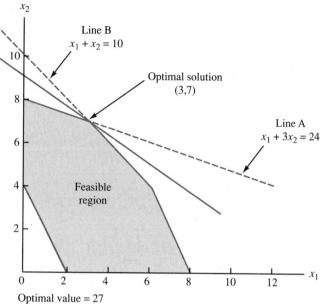

Optimal value = 27

c.

$$-1 \leq -2/c_2 \leq -1/3$$

$$1 \geq 2/c_2 \quad 2/c_2 \geq 1/3$$

$$c_2 \geq 2 \quad c_2 \leq 6$$

Range: $2 \leq c_2 \leq 6$

d. Since this change leaves c_1 in its range of optimality, the same solution ($x_1 = 3, x_2 = 7$) is optimal

e. This change moves c_2 outside its range of optimality; the new optimal solution is shown below:

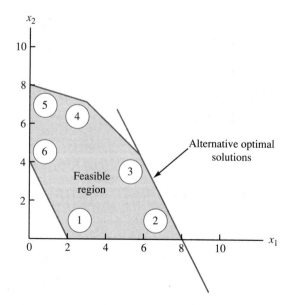

Alternative optimal solutions exist; extreme points 2 and 3 and all points on the line segment between them are optimal

53. By making a small increase in the right-hand side of constraint 1 and resolving, we find a dual price of 1.5 for the constraint; thus, the objective function will improve at the rate of 1.5 per unit increase in the right-hand side.

Since constraint 2 is not binding, its dual price is zero.

To determine the range over which these dual prices are applicable, one must obtain the range of feasibility.

CHAPTER 3

1. **a.** $x_1 = 500; x_2 = 150$; value $= 3700$
   b. The finishing, packaging, and shipping constraints are binding; there is no slack
   c. Cutting and sewing $= 0$
      Finishing $= 3$
      Packaging and shipping $= 28$
      Additional finishing time is worth $3 per unit, and additional packaging and shipping time is worth $28 per unit
   d. In the packaging and shipping department; each additional hour is worth $28

2. **a.** $4 \leq c_1 \leq 12$
      $3.33 \leq c_2 \leq 10$
   b. As long as the profit contribution for the regular glove is between $4.00 and $12.00, the current solution is optimal. As long as the profit contribution for the catcher's mitt stays between $3.33 and $10.00, the current solution is optimal. The optimal solution is not sensitive to small changes in the profit contributions for the gloves.
   c. The dual prices for the resources are applicable over the following ranges:

Constraint	Min RHS	Max RHS
Cutting and sewing	725	No upper limit
Finishing	133.33	400
Packaging and shipping	75	135

   d. Amount of increase $= (28)(20) = 560

6. **a.** $x_1 = 4000$
      $x_2 = 10,000$
      Total risk $= 62,000$
   b. $3.75 \leq c_1 <$ no upper limit
      No lower limit $< c_2 \leq 6.4$
   c. $5(4000) + 4(10,000) = $60,000$
   d. $60,000/1,200,000 = 0.05$ or 5%
   e. 0.057 or approximately 6 cents
   f. $0.057(100) = 5.7\%$

8. **a.** $x_1 = 0; x_2 = 25; x_3 = 125; x_4 = 0$
      Value of solution $= 525.0$
   b. The constraints on machine A and machine C hours are binding

c. Machine B has 425 hours of excess capacity
d. Yes, the allowable increase is only 0.05

9. **a.** No lower limit $< c_1 \leq 4.05$
      $5.923 \leq c_2 \leq 9$
      $2 \leq c_3 \leq 12$
      No lower limit $< c_4 \leq 4.5$
   b. The allowable decrease for c_1 is ∞; thus, the percentage decrease is 0%

$$\frac{1.5}{3.0} + \frac{1}{3.5} = 0.79$$

   The accumulated percentage of allowable increases and decreases is 79%; since this is less than 100%, the optimal solution will not change

   c.

Constraint	Min RHS	Max RHS
Machine A hours	133.33	800
Machine B hours	275	No upper limit
Machine C hours	137.5	825

   d. Yes, because that is outside the range of feasibility

CHAPTER 4

1. **a.** Let $x_1 =$ number of television advertisements
      $x_2 =$ number of radio advertisements
      $x_3 =$ number of newspaper advertisements

Max $100,000x_1 + 18,000x_2 + 40,000x_3$
s.t.

$2,000x_1 +$	$300x_2 +$	$600x_3 \leq$	18,200	Budget
x_1		$\leq$	10	Max TV
	x_2	$\leq$	20	Max radio
		$x_3 \leq$	10	Max news
$-0.5x_1 +$	$0.5x_2 -$	$0.5x_3 \leq$	0	Max 50% radio
$0.9x_1 -$	$0.1x_2 -$	$0.1x_3 \geq$	0	Min 10% TV

$x_1, x_2, x_3, \geq 0$

Budget $

Solution: $x_1 = 4$ $ 8,000$
      $x_2 = 14$ $4,200$
      $x_3 = 10$ $\underline{6,000}$
         $18,200$ Audience $= 1,052,000$

   b. The dual price for the budget constraint is 51.30. Thus, a $100 increase in the budget should provide an increase in audience coverage of approximately 5130. The range of feasibility for the right-hand side of the budget constraint will show this interpretation is correct.

9. Let $x_1 =$ number of shares of stock A
      $x_2 =$ number of shares of stock B
      $x_3 =$ number of shares of stock C
      $x_4 =$ number of shares of stock D

a. To get data on a per-share basis, multiply price by rate of return or risk measure value

Min $10x_1 + 3.5x_2 + 4x_3 + 3.2x_4$
s.t.

$$100x_1 + 50x_2 + 80x_3 + 40x_4 = 200,000$$
$$12x_1 + 4x_2 + 4.8x_3 + 4x_4 \geq 18,000 \text{ (9\% of 200,000)}$$
$$100x_1 \leq 100,000$$
$$50x_2 \leq 100,000$$
$$80x_3 \leq 100,000$$
$$40x_4 \leq 100,000$$

$$x_1, x_2, x_3, x_4 \geq 0$$

Solution: $x_1 = 333.3$, $x_2 = 0$, $x_3 = 833.3$, $x_4 = 2500$
Risk: 14,666.7
Return: 18,000 (9%) from constraint 2

b. Max $12x_1 + 4x_2 + 4.8x_3 + 4x_4$
s.t.

$$100x_1 + 50x_2 + 80x_3 + 40x_4 = 200,000$$
$$100x_1 \leq 100,000$$
$$50x_2 \leq 100,000$$
$$80x_3 \leq 100,000$$
$$40x_4 \leq 100,000$$

$$x_1, x_2, x_3, x_4 \geq 0$$

Solution: $x_1 = 1000$, $x_2 = 0$, $x_3 = 0$, $x_4 = 2500$
Risk: $10x_1 + 3.5x_2 + 4x_3 + 3.2x_4 = 18,000$
Return: 22,000 (11%)

c. The return in part (b) is $4000 or 2% greater, but the risk index has increased by 3333.

Obtaining a reasonable return with a lower risk is a preferred strategy in many financial firms. The more speculative, higher return investments are not always preferred because of their associated higher risk.

15. Let x_{11} = gallons of crude 1 used to produce regular
x_{12} = gallons of crude 1 used to produce high octane
x_{21} = gallons of crude 2 used to produce regular
x_{22} = gallons of crude 2 used to produce high octane

Min $0.10x_{11} + 0.10x_{12} + 0.15x_{21} + 0.15x_{22}$
s.t.

Each gallon of regular must have at least 40% A

$$x_{11} + x_{21} = \text{amount of regular produced}$$

$$0.4(x_{11} + x_{21}) = \text{amount of A required for regular}$$

$$0.2x_{11} + 0.50x_{21} = \text{amount of A in } (x_{11} + x_{21}) \text{ gallons of regular gas}$$

$$\therefore 0.2x_{11} + 0.50x_{21} \geq 0.4x_{11} + 0.40x_{21}$$

$$\therefore -0.2x_{11} + 0.10x_{21} \geq 0$$

Each gallon of high octane can have at most 50% B

$$x_{12} + x_{22} = \text{amount high octane}$$

$$0.5(x_{12} + x_{22}) = \text{amount of B required for high octane}$$

$0.60x_{12} + 0.30x_{22} = \text{amount of B in } (x_{12} + x_{22}) \text{ gallons of high octane}$

$$\therefore 0.60x_{12} + 0.30x_{22} \leq 0.5x_{12} + 0.5x_{22}$$
$$\therefore 0.1x_{12} - 0.2x_{22} \leq 0$$
$$x_{11} + x_{21} \geq 800,000$$
$$x_{12} + x_{22} \geq 500,000$$

$$x_{11}, x_{12}, x_{21}, x_{22} \geq 0$$

Optimal solution: $x_{11} = 266,667$, $x_{12} = 333,333$, $x_{21} = 533,333$, $x_{22} = 166,667$
Cost = $165,000

19. a. Let x_{11} = amount of men's model in month 1
x_{21} = amount of women's model in month 1
x_{12} = amount of men's model in month 2
x_{22} = amount of women's model in month 2
s_{11} = inventory of men's model at end of month 1
s_{21} = inventory of women's model at end of month 1
s_{12} = inventory of men's model at end of month 2
s_{22} = inventory of women's model at end of month 2

Min $120x_{11} + 90x_{21} + 120x_{12} + 90x_{22} + 2.4s_{11} + 1.8s_{21} + 2.4s_{12} + 1.8s_2$
s.t.

$$\left.\begin{array}{l} x_{11} - s_{11} = 130 \\ x_{21} - s_{21} = 95 \\ s_{11} + x_{12} - s_{12} = 200 \\ s_{21} + x_{22} - s_{22} = 150 \end{array}\right\} \text{Satisfy demand}$$

$$\left.\begin{array}{l} s_{12} \geq 25 \\ s_{22} \geq 25 \end{array}\right\} \text{Ending inventory requirement}$$

Labor-hours: Men's $2.0 + 1.5 = 3.5$
Women's $1.6 + 1.0 = 2.6$

$$\left.\begin{array}{l} 3.5x_{11} + 2.6x_{21} \geq 900 \\ 3.5x_{11} + 2.6x_{21} \leq 1100 \\ 3.5x_{11} + 2.6x_{21} - 3.5x_{21} - 2.6x_{22} \leq 100 \\ 3.5x_{11} - 2.6x_{21} + 3.5x_{21} + 2.6x_{22} \leq 100 \end{array}\right\} \text{Labor smoothing}$$

$$x_{11}, x_{12}, x_{21}, x_{22}, s_{11}, s_{12}, s_{21}, s_{22} \geq 0$$

Solution: $x_{11} = 193$; $x_{21} = 95$; $x_{12} = 162$; $x_{22} = 175$

Total cost = $67,156

Inventory levels: $s_{11} = 63$; $s_{12} = 25$; $s_{21} = 0$; $s_{22} = 25$

Labor levels: Previous   1000 hours
Month 1   922.25 hours
Month 2   1022.25 hours

b. To accommodate the new policy, the right-hand sides of the four labor-smoothing constraints must be changed to 950, 1050, 50, and 50 respectively. The new total cost is $67,175.

CHAPTER 5

3. a. With $x_1 = 0$, we have

$$x_2 = 6 \tag{1}$$

$$4x_2 + x_3 = 12 \tag{2}$$

From (1), we have $x_2 = 6$; substituting for x_2 in (2) yields

$$4(6) + x_3 = 12$$

$$x_3 = 12 - 24 = -12$$

Basic solution: $x_1 = 0, x_2 = 6, x_3 = -12$

b. With $x_2 = 0$, we have

$$3x_1 = 6 \tag{3}$$

$$2x_1 + x_3 = 12 \tag{4}$$

From (3), we find $x_1 = 2$; substituting for x_1 in (4) yields

$$2(2) + x_3 = 12$$

$$x_3 = 12 - 4 = 8$$

Basic solution: $x_1 = 2, x_2 = 0, x_3 = 8$

c. With $x_3 = 0$, we have

$$3x_1 + x_2 = 6 \tag{5}$$

$$2x_1 + 4x_2 = 12 \tag{6}$$

Multiplying (6) by $\frac{3}{2}$ and subtracting from (5) yields

$$3x_1 + x_2 = 6$$

$$\underline{-(3x_1 + 6x_2) = -18}$$

$$-5x_2 = -12$$

$$x_2 = \frac{12}{5}$$

Substituting $x_2 = \frac{12}{5}$ into (5) yields

$$3x_1 + \frac{12}{5} = 6$$

$$3x_1 = \frac{18}{5}$$

$$x_1 = \frac{6}{5}$$

Basic solution: $x_1 = \frac{6}{5}, x_2 = \frac{12}{5}, x_3 = 0$

d. The basic solutions found in parts (b) and (c) are basic feasible solutions. The one in part (a) is not because $x_3 = -12$.

6. a. Standard form:

Max $60x_1 + 90x_2$

s.t.

$$15x_1 + 45x_2 + s_1 = 90$$
$$5x_1 + 5x_2 + s_2 = 20$$
$$x_1, x_2, s_1, s_2 \geq 0$$

b. Partial initial simplex tableau:

x_1	x_2	s_1	s_2	
60	90	0	0	
15	45	1	0	**90**
5	5	0	1	**20**

7. a. Initial tableau:

Basis	c_B	x_1 5	x_2 9	s_1 0	s_2 0	
s_1	0	10	9	1	0	90
s_2	0	-5	3	0	1	15
z_j		0	0	0	0	0
$c_j - z_j$		5	9	0	0	

b. We would introduce x_2 at the first iteration

c. Max $5x_1 + 9x_2$

s.t.

$$10x_1 + 9x_2 \leq 90$$
$$-5x_1 + 3x_2 \leq 15$$
$$x_1, x_2 \geq 0$$

23.

Max $4x_1 + 2x_2 - 3x_3 + 5x_4 + 0s_1 - Ma_1 + 0s_2 - Ma_3$

s.t.

$$2x_1 - 1x_2 + 1x_3 + 2x_4 - 1s_1 + 1a_1 = 50$$
$$3x_1 - 1x_3 + 2x_4 + 1s_2 = 80$$
$$1x_1 + 1x_2 + 1x_4 + 1a_3 = 60$$

$$x_1, x_2, x_3, x_4, s_1, s_2, a_1, a_3 \geq 0$$

25. Converting to a max problem and solving using the simplex method, the final simplex tableau is

Basis	c_B	x_1 -3	x_2 -4	x_3 -8	s_1 0	s_2 0	
x_1	-3	1	0	-1	$-\frac{1}{4}$	$\frac{1}{8}$	1
x_2	-4	0	1	2	0	$-\frac{1}{4}$	4
z_j		-3	-4	-5	$\frac{3}{4}$	$\frac{5}{8}$	-19
$c_j - z_j$		0	0	-3	$-\frac{3}{4}$	$-\frac{5}{8}$	

33. Final simplex tableau:

Basis	c_B	x_1 4	x_2 8	s_1 0	s_2 0	a_2 -M	
x_2	8	1	1	$\frac{1}{2}$	0	0	5
a_2	-M	-2	0	$-\frac{1}{2}$	-1	1	3
z_j		$8 + 2M$	8	$4 + M/2$	$+M$	$-M$	$40 - 3M$
$c_j - z_j$		$-4 - 2M$	0	$-4 - M/2$	$-M$	0	

Infeasible; optimal solution condition is reached with the artificial variable a_2 still in the solution

34. Alternative optimal solutions:

Basis	c_B	x_1	x_2	s_1	s_2	s_3	
		-3	-3	0	0	0	
s_2	0	0	0	$-4/3$	1	$1/6$	**4**
x_1	-3	1	0	$-2/3$	0	$1/12$	**4**
x_2	-3	0	1	$2/3$	0	$-1/3$	**4**
z_j		-3	-3	0	0	$3/4$	**-24**
$c_j - z_j$		0	0	0	0	$-3/4$	

↑

Indicates alternative optimal solutions exist:
$x_1 = 4$, $x_2 = 4$, $z = 24$
$x_1 = 8$, $x_2 = 0$, $z = 24$

35. Unbounded solution:

Basis	c_B	x_1	x_2	s_1	s_2	s_3	
		1	1	0	0	0	
s_3	0	$8/3$	0	$-1/3$	0	1	**4**
s_2	0	4	0	-1	1	0	**36**
x_2	1	$4/3$	1	$-1/6$	0	0	**4**
z_j		$4/3$	1	$-1/6$	0	0	**4**
$c_j - z_j$		$-1/3$	0	$1/6$	0	0	

↑
Incoming
column

CHAPTER 6

1. a. Recomputing the $c_j - z_j$ values for the nonbasic variables with c_1 as the coefficient of x_1 leads to the following inequalities that must be satisfied:

For x_2, we get no inequality since there is a zero in the x_2 column for the row in which x_1 is a basic variable

For s_1, we get

$$0 + 4 - c_1 \leq 0$$

$$c_1 \geq 4$$

For s_2, we get

$$0 - 12 + 2c_1 \leq 0$$

$$2c_1 \leq 12$$

$$c_1 \leq 6$$

Range: $4 \leq c_1 \leq 6$

b. Since x_2 is nonbasic, we have

$$c_2 \leq 8$$

c. Since s_1 is nonbasic, we have

$$c_{s_1} \leq 1$$

3. a. It is the z_j value for s_1; dual price = 1
b. It is the z_j value for s_2; dual price = 2
c. It is the z_j value for s_3; dual price = 0
d.
$$s_3 = 80 + 5(-2) = 70$$
$$x_3 = 30 + 5(-1) = 25$$
$$x_1 = 20 + 5(1) = 25$$
$$\text{Value} = 220 + 5(1) = 225$$
e.
$$s_3 = 80 - 10(-2) = 100$$
$$x_3 = 30 - 10(-1) = 40$$
$$x_1 = 20 - 10(1) = 10$$
$$\text{Value} = 220 - 10(1) = 210$$

4. a. $80 + \Delta b_1(-2) \geq 0$ $\Delta b_1 \leq 40$
$30 + \Delta b_1(-1) \geq 0$ $\Delta b_1 \leq 30$
$20 + \Delta b_1(1) \geq 0$ $\Delta b_1 \geq -20$
$$-20 \leq \Delta b_1 \leq 30$$
$$100 \leq b_1 \leq 150$$
b. $80 + \Delta b_2(7) \geq 0$ $\Delta b_2 \geq -80/7$
$30 + \Delta b_2(3) \geq 0$ $\Delta b_2 \geq -10$
$20 + \Delta b_2(-2) \geq 0$ $\Delta b_2 \leq 10$
$$-10 \leq \Delta b_2 \leq 10$$
$$40 \leq b_2 \leq 60$$
c. $80 - \Delta b_3(1) \geq 0$ $\rightarrow$ $\Delta b_3 \leq 80$
$30 - \Delta b_3(0) \geq 0$
$20 - \Delta b_3(0) \geq 0$
$$\Delta b_3 \leq 80$$
$$b_3 \leq 110$$

17. a. The dual is given by:

Min $550u_1 + 700u_2 + 200u_3$
s.t.

$$1.5u_1 + 4u_2 + 2u_3 \geq 4$$
$$2u_1 + 1u_2 + 3u_3 \geq 6$$
$$4u_1 + 2u_2 + 1u_3 \geq 3$$
$$3u_1 + 1u_2 + 2u_3 \geq 1$$

$$u_1, u_2, u_3, \geq 0$$

b. Optimal solution: $u_1 = 3/10$; $u_2 = 0$, $u_3 = 54/30$
The z_j values for the four surplus variables of the dual show $x_1 = 0$, $x_2 = 25$, $x_3 = 125$, and $x_4 = 0$.
c. Since $u_1 = 3/10$, $u_2 = 0$, and $u_3 = 54/30$, machines A and C ($u_j > 0$) are operating at capacity; machine C is the priority machine since each hour is worth 54/30

19. The dual is given by

Max $5u_1 + 5u_2 + 24u_3$
s.t.

$$15u_1 + 4u_2 + 12u_3 \leq 2800$$
$$15u_1 + 8u_2 \leq 6000$$
$$u_1 + 8u_3 \leq 1200$$

$$u_1, u_2, u_3 \geq 0$$

21. The canonical form is

Max $3x_1 + x_2 + 5x_3 + 3x_4$

s.t.

$$
\begin{aligned}
3x_1 + 1x_2 + 2x_3 &\le 30 \\
-3x_1 - 1x_2 - 2x_3 &\le -30 \\
-2x_1 - 1x_2 - 3x_3 - x_4 &\le -15 \\
2x_2 \qquad\quad + 3x_4 &\le 25
\end{aligned}
$$

$$x_1, x_2, x_3, x_4 \ge 0$$

The dual is

Min $30u_1' - 30u_1'' - 15u_2 + 25u_3$

s.t.

$$
\begin{aligned}
3u_1' - 3u_1'' - 2u_2 &\ge 3 \\
u_1' - u_1'' - u_2 + 2u_3 &\ge 1 \\
2u_1' - 2u_1'' - 3u_2 &\ge 5 \\
- u_2 + 3u_3 &\ge 3
\end{aligned}
$$

$$u_1', u_1'', u_2, u_3, \ge 0$$

CHAPTER 7

1. The network model is as follows:

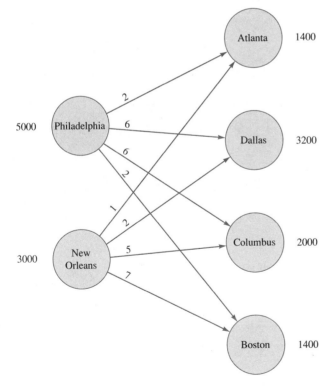

2. a. Let x_{11} = amount shipped from Jefferson City to Des Moines

x_{12} = amount shipped from Jefferson City to Kansas City

.

.

.

x_{23} = amount shipped from Omaha to St. Louis

Min $14x_{11} + 9x_{12} + 7x_{13} + 8x_{21} + 10x_{22} + 5x_{23}$

s.t.

$$
\begin{aligned}
x_{11} + x_{12} + x_{13} &\le 30 \\
x_{21} + x_{22} + x_{23} &\le 20 \\
x_{11} + x_{21} &= 25 \\
x_{12} + x_{22} &= 15 \\
x_{13} + x_{23} &= 10
\end{aligned}
$$

$$x_{11}, x_{12}, x_{13}, x_{21}, x_{22}, x_{23} \ge 0$$

b.

Optimal Solution	Amount	Cost
Jefferson City–Des Moines	5	70
Jefferson City–Kansas City	15	135
Jefferson City–St. Louis	10	70
Omaha–Des Moines	20	160
	Total	435

8. The network model, the linear programming formulation and the optimal solution are shown below. Note that the third constraint corresponds to the dummy origin. The variables $x_{31}, x_{32}, x_{33},$ and x_{34} are the amounts shipped out of the dummy origin; they do not appear in the objective function since they are given a coefficient of zero.

See Figure H7-8.

Max $32x_{11} + 34x_{12} + 32x_{13} + 40x_{14} + 34x_{21} + 30x_{22} + 28x_{23} + 38x_{24}$

s.t.

$$
\begin{aligned}
x_{11} + x_{12} + x_{13} + x_{14} &\le 5000 \\
x_{21} + x_{22} + x_{23} + x_{24} &\le 3000 \\
x_{31} + x_{32} + x_{33} + x_{34} &\le 4000 \text{ D} \\
x_{11} + x_{21} + x_{31} &= 2000 \\
x_{12} + x_{22} + x_{32} &= 5000 \\
x_{13} + x_{23} + x_{33} &= 3000 \\
x_{14} + x_{24} + x_{34} &= 2000
\end{aligned}
$$

$$x_{ij} \ge 0 \quad \text{for all } i, j$$

Optimal Solution	Units	Cost
Clifton Springs–D_2	4,000	$136,000
Clifton Springs–D_4	1,000	40,000
Danville–D_1	2,000	68,000
Danville–D_4	1,000	38,000
	Total	$282,000

Customer 2 demand has a shortfall of 1000; customer 3 demand of 3000 is not satisfied.

F I G U R E H7.8

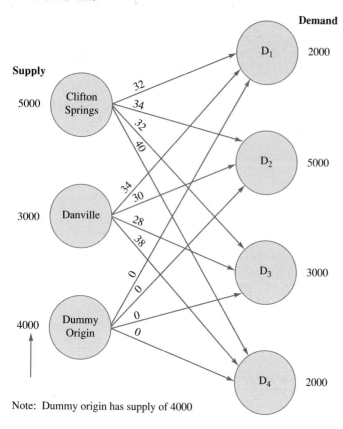

Note: Dummy origin has supply of 4000

12. a.

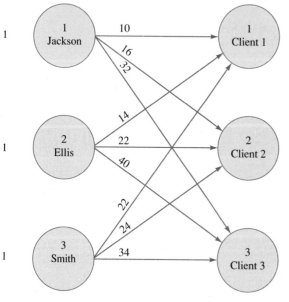

b.

$$\text{Min } 10x_{11} + 16x_{12} + 32x_{13} + 14x_{21} + 22x_{22} + 40x_{23} + 22x_{31} + 24x_{32} + 34x_{33}$$
s.t.

$$
\begin{aligned}
x_{11} + x_{12} + x_{13} &\leq 1 \\
x_{21} + x_{22} + x_{23} &\leq 1 \\
x_{31} + x_{32} + x_{33} &\leq 1 \\
x_{11} + x_{21} + x_{31} &= 1 \\
x_{12} + x_{22} + x_{32} &= 1 \\
x_{13} + x_{23} + x_{33} &= 1
\end{aligned}
$$

$$x_{ij} \geq 0 \quad \text{for all } i, j$$

Solution $x_{12} = 1$, $x_{21} = 1$, $x_{33} = 1$; total completion time = 64

23. a. Network model shown in Figure H7.23a.

   b, c. The linear programming formulation and solution as printed by The Management Scientist is shown in Figure H7.23b, c. There is excess capacity of 130 units at plant 3.

24. a. Three arcs must be added to the network model in Problem 23(a). The new network is shown in Figure H7.24a.

   b, c. The linear programming formulation and optimal solution as printed by The Management Scientist is shown in Figure H7.24b, c (page A-38).

The value of the solution here is $630 less than the value of the solution for Problem 23. The new shipping route from plant 3 to customer 4 has helped. There is now excess capacity of 130 units at plant 1.

32. a. An initial solution is given below:

	Los Angeles	San Francisco	San Diego
San Jose	4 100	10	6
Las Vegas	8 100	16	6 200
Tucson	14	18 300	10

Total cost = $7800

F I G U R E H7.23a

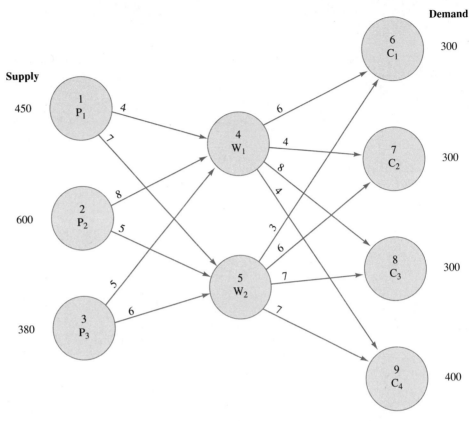

b. Note that the initial solution is degenerate. A zero is assigned to the cell in row 3 and column 1 so that the row and column indices can be computed.

u_i	v_j		
	4	8	2
0	4 100	10 ②	6 ④
4	8 100	16 ④	6 200
10	14 0	18 300	10 ⊝2

Cell in row 3 and column 3 is identified as an incoming cell.

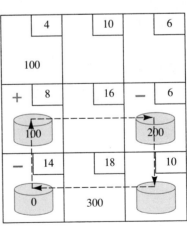

Stepping-stone path shows cycle of adjustments; outgoing cell is in row 3 and column 1.

F I G U R E H7.23b, c

LINEAR PROGRAMMING PROBLEM

MIN 4X14 + 7X15 + 8X24 + 5X25 + 5X34 + 6X35 + 6X46 + 4X47 + 8X48 + 4X49 + 3X56 + 6X57 + 7X58 + 7X59

      S.T.

        1)   X14 + X15 < 450
        2)   X24 + X25 < 600
        3)   X34 + X35 < 380
        4)   X46 + X47 + X48 + X49 − X14 − X24 − X34 = 0
        5)   X56 + X57 + X58 + X59 − X15 − X25 − X35 = 0
        6)   X46 + X56 = 300
        7)   X47 + X57 = 300
        8)   X48 + X58 = 300
        9)   X49 + X59 = 400

OPTIMAL SOLUTION

Objective Function Value =   11850.000

Variable	Value	Reduced Costs
X14	450.000	0.000
X15	0.000	3.000
X24	0.000	3.000
X25	600.000	0.000
X34	250.000	0.000
X35	0.000	1.000
X46	0.000	3.000
X47	300.000	0.000
X48	0.000	1.000
X49	400.000	0.000
X56	300.000	0.000
X57	0.000	2.000
X58	300.000	0.000
X59	0.000	3.000

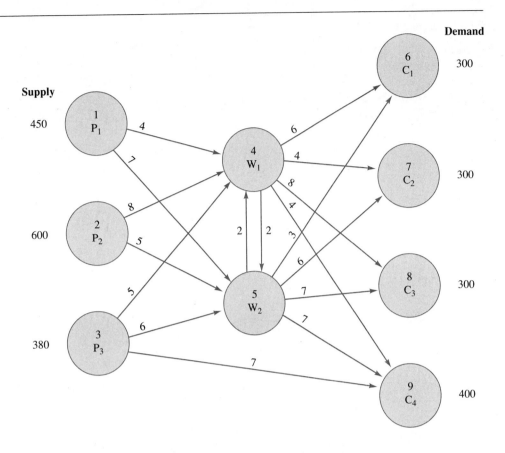

Solution is recognized as optimal; it is degenerate. Thus, the initial solution turns out to be the optimal solution; total cost = $7800.

c. To begin with, we reduce the supply at Tucson by 100 and the demand at San Diego by 100; the new solution is shown here (*continues on page A-39*):

u_i		v_j	
	4	10	2
0	4 ⟋ 100	10 ⟋ ⓪	6 ⟋ ④
4	8 ⟋ 100	16 ⟋ ②	6 ⟋ 200
8	14 ⟋ ②	18 ⟋ 300	10 ⟋ 0

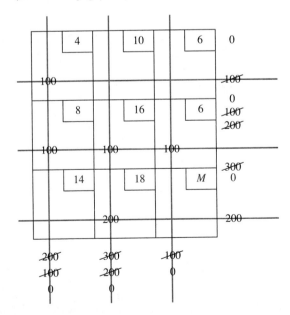

FIGURE **H7.24b, c**

LINEAR PROGRAMMING PROBLEM

MIN 4X14 + 7X15 + 8X24 + 5X25 + 5X34 + 6X35 + 6X46 + 4X47 + 8X48 + 4X49 + 3X56 +
  6X57 + 7X58 + 7X59 + 7X39 + 2X45 + 2X54

     S.T.

       1) X14 + X15 < 450
       2) X24 + X25 < 600
       3) X34 + X35 + X39 < 380
       4) X45 + X46 + X47 + X48 + X49 − X14 − X24 − X34 − X54 = 0
       5) X54 + X56 + X57 + X58 + X59 − X15 − X25 − X35 − X45 = 0
       6) X46 + X56 = 300
       7) X47 + X57 = 300
       8) X48 + X58 = 300
       9) X39 + X49 + X59 = 400

OPTIMAL SOLUTION

Objective Function Value =   11220.000

Variable	Value	Reduced Costs
X14	320.000	0.000
X15	0.000	2.000
X24	0.000	4.000
X25	600.000	0.000
X34	0.000	2.000
X35	0.000	2.000
X46	0.000	2.000
X47	300.000	0.000
X48	0.000	0.000
X49	20.000	0.000
X56	300.000	0.000
X57	0.000	3.000
X58	300.000	0.000
X59	0.000	4.000
X39	380.000	0.000
X45	0.000	1.000
X54	0.000	3.000

u_i	v_j		
	4	12	2
0	− ⟨4⟩ ②−2 ④	10	6
	100		
4	+ ⟨8⟩ − 16 6		
	100	100	100
6	14 ④	18	M (M−8)
		200	

u_i	v_j		
	2	10	2
0	4 ②	10	6 ④	100
		100	
6	8	16	M (M−8)	300
	200	100	
8	14 ④	18	10	300
		100	200
	200	300	200	700

u_i	v_j		
	2	10	0
0	4 ②	10	6 ⑥
		100	
6	8	16	6
	200	0	100
8	14 ④	18	M (M−8)
		200	

Optimal solution: Recall, however, that the 100 units shipped from Tucson to San Diego must be added to obtain the total cost:

San Jose–San Francisco:	100
Las Vegas–Los Angeles:	200
Las Vegas–San Diego:	100
Tucson–San Francisco:	200
Tucson–San Diego:	100
Total Cost = $7800	

Note that this total cost is the same as for part (a); thus, we have alternate optima.

d. The final transportation tableau is shown below. The total transportation cost is $8000, an increase of $200 over the solution to part (a).

38. Subtract 10 from row 1, 14 from row 2, and 22 from row 3 to obtain:

	1	2	3
Jackson	0	6	22
Ellis	0	8	26
Smith	0	2	12

Subtract 0 from column 1, 2 from column 2, and 12 from column 3 to obtain:

	1	2	3
Jackson	0	④	10
Ellis	0	6	14
Smith	0	0	0

Two lines cover the zeros. The minimum unlined element is 4. Step 3 yields:

	1	2	3
Jackson	0	[0]	6
Ellis	[0]	2	10
Smith	0	0	[0]

Optimal solution: Jackson   2
                   Ellis   1
                   Smith   3

Time requirement is 64 days.

41. We start with the opportunity loss matrix

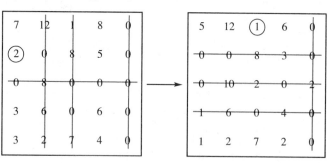

	1	2	3	4	D*
Shoe	4	11	0	5	[0]
Toy	0	[0]	8	3	1
Auto	0	10	2	[0]	3
Houseware	1	6	[0]	4	1
Video	[0]	1	6	1	0

*D = Dummy

	Optimal Solution	Profit
Toy:	2	18
Auto:	4	16
Houseware:	3	13
Video:	1	14
	Total	61

CHAPTER 8

1. a. This is a mixed-integer linear program. Its LP Relaxation is

Max $30x_1 + 25x_2$

s.t.

$$3x_1 + 1.5x_2 \le 400$$
$$1.5x_1 + 2x_2 \le 250$$
$$x_1 + x_2 \le 150$$

$$x_1, x_2 \ge 0$$

b. This is an all-integer linear program; its LP Relaxation just requires dropping the words "and integer" from the last line.

c. This is a mixed-integer linear program; its LP Relaxation is obtained by dropping the integer requirement on x_1.

d. This is an all-integer linear program; its LP Relaxation is obtained by dropping the integer requirement on all the variables.

e. This is a linear program; no variables are required to be integer.

2. a.

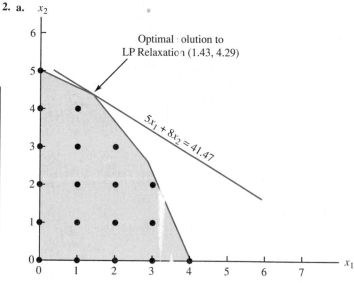

b. The optimal solution to the LP Relaxation is given by $x_1 = 1.43$, $x_2 = 4.29$ with an objective function value of 41.47. Rounding down gives the feasible integer solution $x_1 = 1$, $x_2 = 4$; its value is 37.

c.

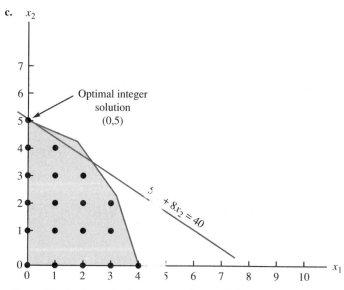

The optimal solution is given by $x_1 = 0$, $x_2 = 5$; its value is 40. This is not the same solution as that found by rounding down. It provides a 3-unit increase in the value of the objective function.

5. a. See Figure H8.5a

The feasible mixed-integer solutions are indicated by the boldface vertical lines in the graph in Figure H8.5a.

b. The optimal solution to the LP Relaxation is given by $x_1 = 3.14$, $x_2 = 2.60$; its value is 14.08.

Rounding the value of x_1 down to find a feasible mixed-integer solution yields $x_1 = 3$, $x_2 = 2.60$ with a value of 13.8. This

F I G U R E H8.5a

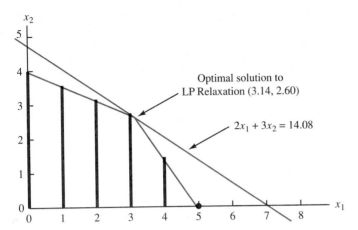

solution is clearly not optimal. With $x_1 = 3$, we can see from the graph that x_2 can be made larger without violating the constraints.

c.

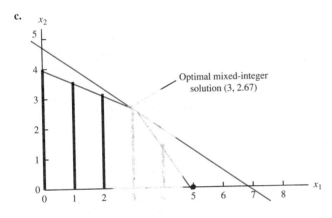

The optimal solution to the MILP is given by $x_1 = 3$, $x_2 = 2.67$; its value is 14.

7. a. $x_1 + x_3 + x_5 + x_6 = 2$
   b. $x_3 - x_5 = 0$
   c. $x_1 + x_4 = 1$
   d. $x_4 \leq x_1$
      $x_4 \leq x_3$
   e. $x_4 \leq x_1$
      $x_4 \leq x_3$
      $x_4 \geq x_1 + x_3 - 1$

11. a. See Figure H8.11a.
   Optimal solution: $y_4 = 1$, $x_{42} = 20$, $x_{43} = 20$, $x_{51} = 30$
   Value = 860

b. One just needs to add the following mutually exclusive constraint to the problem

$$y_1 + y_2 = 1$$

New optimal solution: $y_1 = 1$, $y_3 = 1$, $x_{12} = 10$, $x_{31} = 30$, $x_{52} = 10$, $x_{53} = 20$
Value = 940

c. Since one plant is already located at St. Louis, it is only necessary to add the following constraint to the model in part (a):

$$y_3 + y_4 \leq 1$$

Optimal solution: Same as part (a)

18. B & B solution:

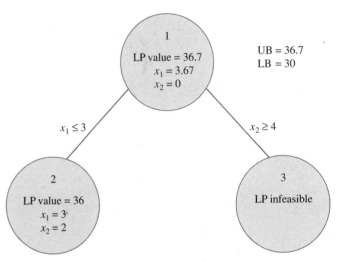

The optimal solution is given by $x_1 = 3$, $x_2 = 2$; its value is 36.

20. The LP Relaxation solved at node 1 is given below:

Max $x_1 + 2x_2 + x_3$
s.t.
$$7x_1 + 4x_2 + 3x_3 \leq 28$$
$$4x_1 + 7x_2 + 2x_3 \leq 28$$
$$x_1, x_2 \geq 0$$

Its solution is $x_1 = 0$, $x_2 = 2\,2/13$, and $x_3 = 6\,6/13$ with value $10\,10/13$. Since x_2 is the only integer variable with a fractional value, we branch on it. Rounding x_2 down to 2 yields a feasible mixed-integer solution and a lower bound of $10\,6/13$.

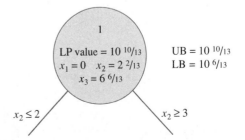

FIGURE H8.11a

Let $y_1 = \begin{cases} 1 \text{ if a plant is located at Detroit} \\ 0 \text{ otherwise} \end{cases}$ $y_2 = \begin{cases} 1 \text{ if a plant is located at Toledo} \\ 0 \text{ otherwise} \end{cases}$

$y_3 = \begin{cases} 1 \text{ if a plant is located at Denver} \\ 0 \text{ otherwise} \end{cases}$ $y_4 = \begin{cases} 1 \text{ if a plant is located at Kansas City} \\ 0 \text{ otherwise} \end{cases}$

$x_{ij} = \begin{cases} \text{thousands of units shipped from} \\ \text{plant } i \text{ to destination } j \end{cases}$ $i = 1, 2, 3, 4, 5; j = 1, 2, 3$

$$\text{Min } 5x_{11} + 2x_{12} + 3x_{13} + 4x_{21} + 3x_{22} + 4x_{23} + 9x_{31} + 7x_{32} + 5x_{33}$$
$$+ 10x_{41} + 4x_{42} + 2x_{43} + 8x_{51} + 4x_{52} + 3x_{53}$$
$$+ 175y_1 + 300y_2 + 375y_3 + 500y_4$$

s.t.

$$x_{11} + x_{12} + x_{13} \leq 10y_1$$
$$x_{21} + x_{22} + x_{23} \leq 20y_2$$
$$x_{31} + x_{32} + x_{33} \leq 30y_3$$
$$x_{41} + x_{42} + x_{43} \leq 40y_4$$
$$x_{51} + x_{52} + x_{53} \leq 30$$
$$x_{11} + x_{21} + x_{31} + x_{41} + x_{51} = 30$$
$$x_{12} + x_{22} + x_{32} + x_{42} + x_{52} = 20$$
$$x_{13} + x_{23} + x_{33} + x_{43} + x_{53} = 20$$

$$x_{ij} \geq 0 \quad i = 1, 2, 3, 4, 5$$
$$j = 1, 2, 3$$
$$y_i = 0, 1 \quad i = 1, 2, 3, 4$$

The LP problems solved at nodes 2 and 3 are given below:

Node 2:

Max $x_1 + 2x_2 + x_3$

s.t.

$$7x_1 + 4x_2 + 3x_3 \leq 28$$
$$4x_1 + 7x_2 + 2x_3 \leq 28$$
$$x_2 \leq 2$$

$$x_1, x_2, x_3 \geq 0$$

Optimal solution: $x_1 = 0, x_2 = 2, x_3 = 6\frac{2}{3}$
Value = $10\frac{2}{3}$

This is a feasible mixed-integer solution, and the lower bound can thus be increased to $10\frac{2}{3}$ at node 2.

Node 3:

Max $x_1 + 2x_2 + x_3$

s.t.

$$7x_1 + 4x_2 + 3x_3 \leq 28$$
$$4x_1 + 7x_2 + 2x_3 \leq 28$$
$$x_2 \geq 3$$

$$x_1, x_2, x_3 \geq 0$$

Optimal solution: $x_1 = 0, x_2 = 3, x_3 = 3\frac{1}{2}$
Value = $9\frac{1}{2}$

The branch-and-bound tree after solving these two linear programs is presented below:

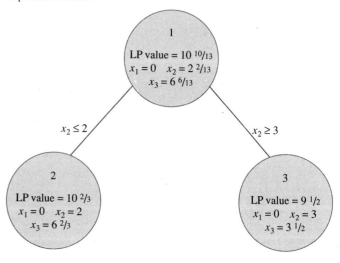

After solving the LP Relaxation at node 3, it is seen that the optimal mixed-integer solution has been found (UB = LB). It is the LP solution found at node 2; $x_1 = 0, x_2 = 2, x_3 = 6\frac{2}{3}$ with value $10\frac{2}{3}$.

CHAPTER 9

1.

Node	Shortest Route from Node 1	Distance
2	1–2	7
3	1–3	9
4	1–2–5–6–4	17
5	1–2–5	12
6	1–2–5–6	14
7	1–2–5–6–7	17

10.

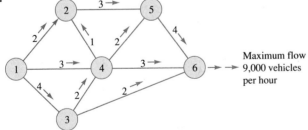

1–3	2
3–4	2
4–5	3
5–2	2
5–7	3
7–8	2
7–6	3
Total	17 miles

15.

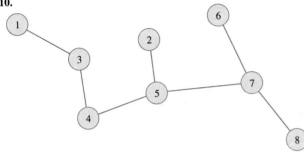

Maximum flow 9,000 vehicles per hour

CHAPTER 10

3.

6.

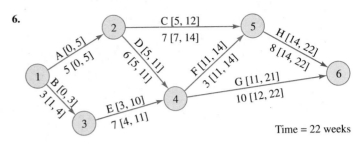

Time = 22 weeks

a. Critical path: A–D–F–H
b. 22 weeks
c. No, it is a critical activity
d. Yes, 2 weeks
d. Schedule for activity E:

Earliest start	3
Latest start	4
Earliest finish	10
Latest finish	11

10. a.

Activity	Optimistic	Most Probable	Pessimistic	Expected Times	Variance
A	4	5	6	5.00	0.11
B	8	9	10	9.00	0.11
C	7	7.5	11	8.00	0.44
D	6	9	10	8.83	0.25
E	6	7	9	7.17	0.25
F	5	6	7	6.00	0.11

b. Critical activities: B–D–F
Expected project completion time: 9.00 + 8.83 + 6.00 = 23.83.
Variance of projection completion time: 0.11 + 0.25 + 0.11 = 0.47

13.

Activity	Expected Time	Variance
A	5	0.11
B	3	0.03
C	7	0.11
D	6	0.44
E	7	0.44
F	3	0.11
G	10	0.44
H	8	1.78

From Problem 6, A–D–F–H is the critical path

$$E(T) = 5 + 6 + 3 + 8 = 22$$

$$\sigma^2 = 0.11 + 0.44 + 0.11 + 1.78 = 2.44$$

$$z = \frac{\text{Time} - E(T)}{\sigma} = \frac{\text{Time} - 22}{\sqrt{2.44}}$$

a. Time = 21 $z = -0.64$ Area 0.2389

$$P(21 \text{ weeks}) = 0.5000 - 0.2389 = 0.2611$$

b. Time = 22 $z = 0$ Area 0.0000

$$P(22 \text{ weeks}) = 0.5000$$

c. Time = 25 $z = +1.92$ Area 0.4726

$$P(22 \text{ weeks}) = 0.5000 + 0.4726 = 0.9726$$

21. a.

Activity	Earliest Start	Latest Start	Earliest Finish	Latest Finish	Slack	Critical Activity
A	0	0	3	3	0	Yes
B	0	1	2	3	1	
C	3	3	8	8	0	Yes
D	2	3	7	8	1	
E	8	8	14	14	0	Yes
F	8	10	10	12	2	
G	10	12	12	14	2	

Critical path: A–C–E

Project completion time $= t_A + t_C + t_E = 3 + 5 + 6 = 14$ days

b. Total cost = $8400

22. a.

Activity	Max Crash Days	Crash Cost/Day
A	1	600
B	1	700
C	2	400
D	2	400
E	2	500
F	1	400
G	1	500

Min $600Y_A + 700Y_B + 400Y_C + 400Y_D + 500Y_E + 400Y_F + 400Y_G$

s.t.

(event 2) $X_2 \geq 3 - Y_A$

(event 3) $X_3 \geq 2 - Y_B$

(event 4) $X_4 \geq X_2 + 5 - Y_C$

            $X_4 \geq X_3 + 5 - Y_D$

(event 5) $X_5 \geq X_4 + 2 - Y_F$

(event 6) $X_6 \geq X_4 + 6 - Y_E$

            $X_6 \geq X_5 + 2 - Y_G$

or

$$X_2 + Y_A \geq 3$$
$$X_3 + Y_B \geq 2$$
$$-X_2 + X_4 + Y_C \geq 5$$
$$-X_3 + X_4 + Y_D \geq 5$$
$$-X_4 + X_5 + Y_F \geq 2$$
$$-X_4 + X_6 + Y_E \geq 6$$
$$-X_5 + X_6 + Y_G \geq 2$$

also

$$Y_A \leq 1$$
$$Y_B \leq 1$$
$$Y_C \leq 2$$
$$Y_D \leq 2$$
$$Y_E \leq 2$$
$$Y_F \leq 1$$
$$Y_G \leq 1$$

and

$$X_6 \leq 12$$

All $X, Y \geq 0$

b. Solution of the linear programming model in part (a) will show

Activity	Crash	Crashing Cost
C	1 day	$400
E	1 day	500
	Total	$900

c. Total cost = Normal cost + Crashing cost

$$= \$8400 + \$900 = \$9300$$

26.

Activity	Cost/Week	Activity	Cost/Week
A	15	F	1
B	8	G	20
C	1	H	5
D	20	I	2
E	2	J	1

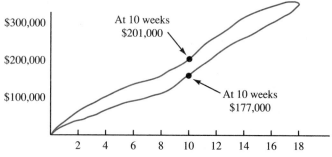

Biggest range in feasible budget occurs at 7 weeks:
($129,000 − $92,000) = $37,000

CHAPTER 11

1. a. $Q^* = \sqrt{\dfrac{2DC_0}{C_h}} = \sqrt{\dfrac{2(3600)(20)}{0.25(3)}} = 438.18$

b. $r = dm = \dfrac{3600}{250}(5) = 72$

c. $T = \dfrac{250Q^*}{D} = \dfrac{250(438.18)}{3600} = 30.43$ days

d. $TC = \dfrac{1}{2}QC_h + \dfrac{D}{Q}C_0$

$= \dfrac{1}{2}(438.18)(0.25)(3) + \dfrac{3600}{438.18}(20) = \$328.63$

13. a. $Q^* = \sqrt{\dfrac{2DC_0}{(1 - D/P)C_h}}$

$= \sqrt{\dfrac{2(7200)(150)}{(1 - 7200/25,000)(0.18)(14.50)}} = 1078.12$

b. Number of production runs $= \dfrac{D}{Q^*} = \dfrac{7200}{1078.12} = 6.68$

c. $T = \dfrac{250Q}{D} = \dfrac{250(1078.12)}{7200} = 37.43$ days

d. Production run length $= \dfrac{Q}{P/250} = \dfrac{1078.12}{25,000/250} = 10.78$ days

e. Maximum inventory $= \left(1 - \dfrac{D}{P}\right)Q$

$= \left(1 - \dfrac{7200}{25,000}\right)(1078.12) = 767.62$

f. Holding cost $= \dfrac{1}{2}\left(1 - \dfrac{D}{P}\right)QC_h$

$= \dfrac{1}{2}\left(1 - \dfrac{7200}{25,000}\right)(1078.12)(0.18)(14.50)$

$= \$1001.74$

Ordering cost $= \dfrac{D}{Q}C_0 = \dfrac{7200}{1078.12}(150) = \$1001.74$

Total cost $= \$2003.48$

g. $r = dm = \left(\dfrac{D}{250}\right)m = \dfrac{7200}{250}(15) = 432$

15. a. $Q^* = \sqrt{\dfrac{2DC_0}{C_h}\left(\dfrac{C_h + C_b}{C_b}\right)} =$

$\sqrt{\dfrac{2(12,000)(25)}{0.50}\left(\dfrac{0.50 + 5}{0.50}\right)} = 1148.91$

b. $S^* = Q^*\left(\dfrac{C_h}{C_h + C_b}\right) = 1148.91\left(\dfrac{0.50}{0.50 + 5}\right) = 104.45$

c. Max inventory $= Q^* - S^* = 1044.46$

d. $T = \dfrac{250Q^*}{D} = \dfrac{250(1148.91)}{12,000} = 23.94$

e. Holding $= \dfrac{(Q - S)^2}{2Q}C_h = \$237.38$

Ordering $= \dfrac{D}{Q}C_0 = 261.12$

Backorder $= \dfrac{S^2}{2Q}C_b = 23.74$

Total cost $= \$522.24$

The total cost for the EOQ model in Problem 4 was \$547.72; allowing backorders reduces the total cost

21.

$Q = \sqrt{\dfrac{2DC_0}{C_h}}$

$Q_1 = \sqrt{\dfrac{2(500)(40)}{0.20(10)}} = 141.42$

$Q_2 = \sqrt{\dfrac{2(500)(40)}{0.20(9.7)}} = 143.59$

Since Q_1 is over its limit of 99 units, Q_1 cannot be optimal (see Problem 23); use $Q_2 = 143.59$ as the optimal order quantity

Total cost $= \dfrac{1}{2}QC_h + \dfrac{D}{Q}C_0 + DC$

$= 139.28 + 139.28 + 4850.00 = \$5128.56$

25. a.

$c_0 = 80 - 50 = 30$

$c_u = 125 - 80 = 45$

$P(D \le Q^*) = \dfrac{c_u}{c_u + c_0} = \dfrac{45}{45 + 30} = 0.60$

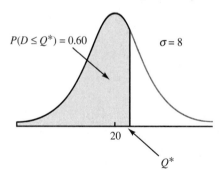

For an area of 0.60 below Q^*, $z = 0.25$

$Q^* = 20 + 0.25(8) = 22$

b. $P(\text{Sell all}) = P(D \ge Q^*) = 1 - 0.60 = 0.40$

29. a. $r = dm = (200/250)15 = 12$

b. $\dfrac{D}{Q} = \dfrac{200}{25} = 8$ orders/year

The limit of 1 stockout per year means that

$P(\text{Stockout/cycle}) = 1/8 = 0.125$

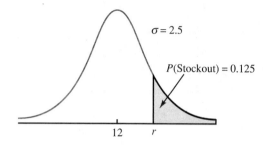

$\sigma = 2.5$

$P(\text{Stockout}) = 0.125$

12   r

For area in tail = 0.125, $z = 1.15$

$$z = \frac{r - 12}{2.5} = 1.15$$

or

$$r = 12 + 1.15(2.5) = 14.875 \approx 15$$

c. Safety stock = 3 units
   Added cost = 3($5) = $15/year

33. a. $1/52 = 0.0192$
   b. $M = \mu + z\sigma = 60 + 2.07(12) = 85$
   c. $M = 35 + (0.9808)(85 - 35) = 84$

37.

Quantity of snowblowers to be produced:	5000
Gross requirements, engines:	5000
Engines in inventory:	2000
Net requirements, engines:	3000
Gross requirements, air cleaners:	3000
Air cleaners in inventory:	1500
Net requirements, air cleaners:	1500
Gross requirements, filter housings:	1500
Filter housings in inventory:	1000
Net requirements, filter housings:	500

CHAPTER 12

5. a. $P_0 = 1 - \dfrac{\lambda}{\mu} = 1 - \dfrac{10}{12} = 0.1667$

b. $L_q = \dfrac{\lambda^2}{\mu(\mu - \lambda)} = \dfrac{10^2}{12(12 - 10)} = 4.1667$

c. $W_q = \dfrac{L_q}{\lambda} = 0.4167$ hours

d. $W = W_q + \dfrac{1}{\mu} = 0.5$ hours (30 minutes)

e. $P_w = \dfrac{\lambda}{\mu} = \dfrac{10}{12} = 0.8333$

11. a. $\lambda = 2.5$ $\mu = \dfrac{60}{10} = 6$ customers per hour

$$L_q = \frac{\lambda^2}{\mu(\mu - \lambda)} = \frac{(2.5)^2}{6(6 - 2.5)} = 0.2976$$

$$L = L_q + \frac{\lambda}{\mu} = 0.7143$$

$$W_q = \frac{L_q}{\lambda} = 0.1190 \text{ hours (7.14 minutes)}$$

$$W = W_q + \frac{1}{\mu} = 0.2857 \text{ hours}$$

$$P_w = \frac{\lambda}{\mu} = \frac{2.5}{6} = 0.4167$$

b. No; $W_q = 7.14$ minutes; firm should increase the mean service rate (μ) for the consultant or hire a second consultant

c. $\mu = \dfrac{60}{8} = 7.5$ customers per hour

$$L_q = \frac{\lambda^2}{\mu(\mu - \lambda)} = \frac{(2.5)^2}{7.5(7.5 - 2.5)} = 0.1667$$

$$W_q = \frac{L_q}{\lambda} = 0.0667 \text{ hours (4 minutes)}$$

The service goal is being met

19. a. $k = 2$ $\lambda/\mu = 14/10 = 1.4$
   From Table 12.5, $P_0 = 0.1765$

b. $L_q = \dfrac{(\lambda/\mu)^2 \lambda \mu}{1!(2\mu - \lambda)^2} P_0 = \dfrac{(1.4)^2(14)(10)}{(20 - 14)^2}(0.1765) = 1.3453$

$$L = L_q + \frac{\lambda}{\mu} = 1.3453 + \frac{14}{10} = 2.7453$$

c. $W_q = \dfrac{L_q}{\lambda} = \dfrac{1.3453}{14} = 0.961$ hours

d. $W = W_q + \dfrac{1}{\mu} = 0.0961 + \dfrac{1}{10} = 0.1961$ hours

e. $P_0 = 0.1765$

$$P_1 = \frac{(\lambda/\mu)^1}{1!} P_0 = \frac{14}{10}(0.1765) = 0.2471$$

$$P(\text{wait}) = P(n \geq 2) = 1 - P(n \leq 1)$$
$$= 1 - 0.4236 = 0.5764$$

21. From Problem 11, a service time of 8 minutes has $\mu = 60/8 = 7.5$

$$L_q = \frac{\lambda^2}{\mu(\mu - \lambda)} = \frac{(2.5)^2}{7.5(7.5 - 2.5)} = 0.1667$$

$$L = L_q + \frac{\lambda}{\mu} = 0.50$$

Total cost = $25L + $16

$$= 25(0.50) + 16 = \$28.50$$

Two channels: $\lambda = 2.5$ $\mu = 60/10 = 6$

Using equation (12.11) and $P_0 = 0.6552$

$$L_q = \frac{(\lambda/\mu)^2 \lambda \mu}{1!(2\mu - \lambda)^2} P_0 = 0.0189$$

$$L = L_q + \frac{\lambda}{\mu} = 0.4356$$

Total cost = $25(0.4356) + 2(16) = \$42.89$

Use the one consultant with an 8-minute service time

25. $\lambda = 4$, $W = 10$ minutes

  a. $\mu = \frac{1}{2} = 0.5$

  b. $W_q = W - 1/\mu = 10 - 1/0.5 = 8$ minutes

  c. $L = \lambda W = 4(10) = 40$

27. a. $\frac{2}{8}$ hours $= 0.25$ per hour

  b. $1/3.2$ hours $= 0.3125$ per hour

  c. $L_q = \dfrac{\lambda^2\sigma^2 + (\lambda/\mu)^2}{2(1 - \lambda/\mu)} = \dfrac{(0.25)^2(2)^2 + (0.25/0.3125)^2}{2(1 - 0.25/0.3125)} = 2.225$

  d. $W_q = \dfrac{L_q}{\lambda} = \dfrac{2.225}{0.25} = 8.9$ hours

  e. $W = W_q + \dfrac{1}{\mu} = 8.9 + \dfrac{1}{0.3125} = 12.1$ hours

  f. Same at $P_w = \dfrac{\lambda}{\mu} = \dfrac{0.25}{0.3125} = 0.80$

  80% of the time the welder is busy

30. a. $\lambda = 42$ $\mu = 20$

i	$(\lambda/\mu)^i/i!$
0	1.0000
1	2.1000
2	2.2050
3	1.5435
Total	6.8485

j	P_j	
0	1/6.8485	= 0.1460
1	2.1/6.8485	= 0.3066
2	2.2050/6.8485	= 0.3220
3	1.5435/6.8485	= 0.2254
		1.0000

  b. 0.2254

  c. $L = \lambda/\mu(1 - P_k) = 42/20(1 - 0.2254) = 1.6267$

  d. Four lines will be necessary; the probability of denied access is 0.1499

34. $N = 5$ $\lambda = 0.025$ $\mu = 0.20$ $\lambda/\mu = 0.125$

  a.

n	$\dfrac{N!}{(N - n)!}\left(\dfrac{\lambda}{\mu}\right)^n$
0	1.0000
1	0.6250
2	0.3125
3	0.1172
4	0.0293
5	0.0037
Total	2.0877

  $P_0 = 1/2.0877 = 0.4790$

  b. $L_q = N - \left(\dfrac{\lambda + \mu}{\lambda}\right)(1 - P_0) = 5 - \left(\dfrac{0.225}{0.025}\right)(1 - 0.4790) = 0.3110$

  c. $L = L_q + (1 - P_0) = 0.3110 + (1 - 0.4790) = 0.8320$

  d. $W_q = \dfrac{L_q}{(N - L)\lambda} = \dfrac{0.3110}{(5 - 0.8320)(0.025)} = 2.9846$ minutes

  e. $W = W_q + \dfrac{1}{\mu} = 2.9846 + \dfrac{1}{0.20} = 7.9846$ minutes

  f. Trips/day $= (8$ hours$)(60$ minutes/hour$)(\lambda)$

     $= (8)(60)(0.025) = 12$ trips

     Time at copier: $12 \times 7.9846 = 95.8$ minutes/day

     Wait time at copier: $12 \times 2.9846 = 35.8$ minutes/day

  g. Yes, five secretaries $\times$ 35.8 = 179 minutes (3 hours/day), so 3 hours per day are lost to waiting

     $(35.8/480)(100) = 7.5\%$ of each secretary's day is spent waiting for the copier

Chapter 13

1. a.

Sales	Relative Frequency
0	0.08
1	0.12
2	0.28
3	0.24
4	0.14
5	0.10
6	0.04
Total	1.00

  b. Use the following table to generate sales values:

Sales	Associated Interval of Random Numbers
0	00–07
1	08–19
2	20–47
3	48–71
4	72–85
5	86–95
6	96–99

  Using the first 10 random numbers from row 4 of Table 13.3, we obtain the following sales for 10 days of simulated operation:

Day	Random Number	Sales
1	46	2
2	27	2
3	68	3
4	74	4
5	53	3
6	44	2
7	79	4
8	06	0
9	71	3
10	22	2

c. Total sales = 25

3. a. The following table shows the relative frequencies and associated intervals of random numbers used to generate demand:

Rental Demand	Relative Frequency	Interval of Random Numbers
7	0.08	00–07
8	0.20	08–27
9	0.32	28–59
10	0.28	60–87
11	0.12	88–99
Total	1.00	

Day	Random Number	Simulated Demand
1	15	8
2	48	9
3	71	10
4	56	9
5	90	11

b. Note that no more than nine cars can be rented each day because that is all that are available

$$\text{Average rentals} = \frac{8 + 9 + 9 + 9 + 9}{5} = \frac{44}{5} = 8.8 \text{ cars}$$

c. There will be 1 lost on day 3 and 2 lost on day 5; total lost = 3

d. Average daily demand $\frac{8 + 9 + 10 + 9 + 11}{5} = \frac{47}{5} = 9.4$ cars

11. a.

Next Purchase	Probability	Interval of Random Numbers
Super Z	0.70	00–69
Devco	0.10	70–79
Floorgreen	0.20	80–99

b.

Next Purchase	Probability	Interval of Random Numbers
Super Z	0.30	00–29
Devco	0.55	30–84
Floorgreen	0.15	85–99

c.

Next Purchase	Probability	Interval of Random Numbers
Super Z	0.10	00–09
Devco	0.10	10–19
Floorgreen	0.80	20–99

d.

Random Number	Next Purchase
42	Super Z
81	Floorgreen
16	Devco
57	Devco

e.

Random Number	Next Purchase
42	Devco
81	Devco
16	Super Z
57	Super Z

f. It definitely is not. We did not see any purchases from Floorgreen for the results in part (e). Simulation for 1000 periods or more will show Floorgreen with the largest market share at approximately 48% of the purchases. Super Z has approximately 34% with Devco approximately 18%. The four-period simulation is not enough.

15. Follow the development in the text with the following modification for generating demand values.

Demand (units)	Associated Interval of Random Numbers
0	00–24
1	25–74
2	75–89
3	90–94
4	95–99

Using the same random number for demand and lead time as shown in Table 13.18, the 10-day simulation results are as follows. The column labels are the same as in Table 13.18 and are identified as follows:

A = day
B = beginning inventory for the day
C = units received from a previous order
D = random number to determine daily demand
E = daily demand
F = ending inventory for the day
G = random number to determine lead time for a new
    order
H = lead time for the new order
I = holding cost for the day
J = order cost for the day
K = shortage cost for the day

A	B	C	D	E	F	G	H	I	J	K	L
1	5	0	0.09	0	5			0.50	0.00	0.00	0.50
2	5	0	0.68	1	4			0.50	0.00	0.00	0.50
3	4	0	0.29	1	3	0.62	3	0.40	20.00	0.00	20.40
4	3	0	0.53	1	2			0.30	0.00	0.00	0.30
5	2	0	0.87	2	0			0.20	0.00	0.00	0.20
6	0	5	0.98	4	1	0.94	5	0.00	20.00	0.00	20.00
7	1	0	0.62	1	0			0.10	0.00	0.00	0.10
8	0	0	0.82	2	0			0.00	0.00	100.00	100.00
9	0	0	0.37	1	0			0.00	0.00	50.00	50.00
10	0	0	0.35	1	0			0.00	0.00	50.00	50.00
				Average Cost				0.20	4.00	20.00	24.20

CHAPTER 14

1. a.

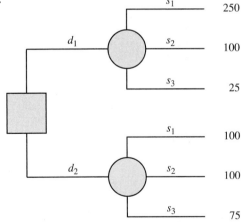

b.

Decision	Maximum Profit	Minimum Profit
d_1	250	25
d_2	100	75

Optimistic approach: Select d_1
Conservative approach: Select d_2

Regret or opportunity loss table:

Decision	s_1	s_2	s_1
d_1	0	0	50
d_2	150	0	0

Maximum regret: 50 for d_1 and 150 for d_2; select d_2

5. a.

$$EV(d_1) = 0.65(250) + 0.15(100) + 0.20(25) = 182.5$$

$$EV(d_2) = 0.65(100) + 0.15(100) + 0.20(75) = 95$$

The optimal decision is d_1

12. $EV(d_1) = p(10) + (1 - p)(1) = 9p + 1$
$EV(d_2) = p(4) + (1 - p)(3) = 1p + 3$

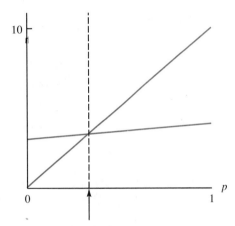

Value of p for
which EVs are equal

$9p + 1 = 1p + 3$ and hence $p = 0.25$

17. a. If s_1, then d_1; if s_2, then d_1 or d_2; if s_3, then d_2
b. EVwPI = 0.65(250) + 0.15(100) + 0.20(75) = 192.5
c. From the solution to Problem 5, we know that $EV(d_1) = 182.5$
and $EV(d_2) = 95$; thus, recommended decision is d_1; hence,
EVwoPI = 182.5
d. EVPI = EVwPI − EVwoPI = 192.5 − 182.5 = 10

23.

State of Nature	$P(s_j)$	$P(I \mid s_j)$	$P(I \cap s_j)$	$P(s_j \mid I)$
s_1	0.2	0.10	0.020	0.1905
s_2	0.5	0.05	0.025	0.2381
s_3	0.3	0.20	0.060	0.5714
	1.0		$P(I) = 0.105$	1.0000

26. a. EVSI = EVwSI − EVwoSI = 45,000 − 37,000 = $8000
b. E = EVSI/EVPI(100) = 8000/60,000(100) = 13.13%
c. Since the cost required to obtain the sample information exceeds
the expected value of the sample information, the study should
not be conducted

28. a.

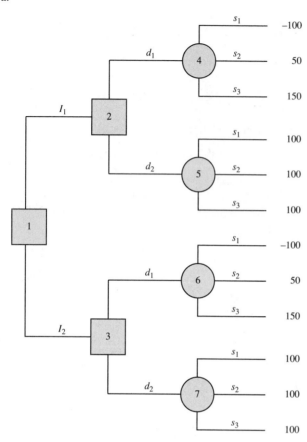

b. For I_1—Favorable:

State of Nature	$P(s_j)$	$P(I_1 \mid s_j)$	$P(I_1 \cap s_j)$	$P(s_j \mid I_1)$
s_1	0.2	0.3	0.06	0.08696
s_2	0.3	0.6	0.18	0.26087
s_3	0.5	0.9	0.45	0.65217
			$P(I_2) = 0.69$	

For I_2—Unfavorable:

State of Nature	$P(s_j)$	$P(I_2 \mid s_j)$	$P(I_2 \cap s_j)$	$P(s_j \mid I_2)$
s_1	0.2	0.7	0.14	0.45161
s_2	0.3	0.4	0.12	0.38710
s_3	0.5	0.1	0.05	0.16129
			$P(I_2) = 0.31$	

EV(node 4) = 0.087(−100) + 0.261(50) + 0.652(150) = 102.17
EV(node 5) = 100
EV(node 6) = 0.452(−100) + 0.387(50) + 0.161(150) = −1.7
EV(node 7) = 100

Decision strategy:
If I_1, then select d_1 since EV(node 4) > EV(node 5)
If I_2, then select d_2 since EV(node 7) > EV(node 6)
EV(node 1) = 0.69(102.17) + 0.31(100) = $101.50

c. Since EV(d_2) is $100, EVSI = 101.5 − 100 = 1.5, or $1500.
The consulting information is not worthwhile; the cost of $2500
is worth more than the expected gain.

CHAPTER 15

2. a. Let x_1 = number of shares of AGA Products purchased
x_2 = number of shares of Key Oil purchased
To obtain an annual return of exactly 9%:

$$0.06(50)x_1 + 0.10(100)x_2 = 0.09(50{,}000)$$

$$3x_1 + 10x_2 = 4500$$

To have exactly 60% of the total investment in Key Oil:

$$100x_2 = 0.60(50{,}000)$$

$$x_2 = 300$$

Therefore, we can write the goal programming model as
follows:

Min $P_1(d_1^-) + P_2(d_2^+)$
s.t.

$$
\begin{aligned}
50x_1 + 100x_2 &\le 50{,}000 \quad \text{funds available} \\
3x_1 + 10x_2 - d_1^+ + d_1^- &= 4{,}500 \quad P_1 \text{ goal} \\
x_2 - d_2^+ + d_2^- &= 300 \quad P_2 \text{ goal}
\end{aligned}
$$

$$x_1, x_2, d_1^+, d_1^-, d_2^+, d_2^- \ge 0$$

b. In the graphical solution shown below, $x_1 = 250$ and $x_2 = 375$

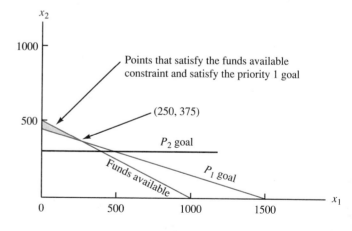

12. *Synthesization*

Step 1: Column totals are 17/4, 31/21, and 12

Step 2:

	Style		
Style	Car A	Car B	Car C
Car A	4/17	7/31	4/12
Car B	12/17	21/31	7/12
Car C	1/17	3/31	1/12

Step 3:

	Style			
Style	Car A	Car B	Car C	**Row Average**
Car A	0.235	0.226	0.333	0.265
Car B	0.706	0.677	0.583	0.655
Car C	0.059	0.097	0.083	0.080

Consistency Ratio

Step 1:

$$0.265 \begin{bmatrix} 1 \\ 3 \\ 1/4 \end{bmatrix} + 0.655 \begin{bmatrix} 1/3 \\ 1 \\ 1/7 \end{bmatrix} + 0.080 \begin{bmatrix} 4 \\ 7 \\ 1 \end{bmatrix}$$

$$\begin{bmatrix} 0.265 \\ 0.795 \\ 0.066 \end{bmatrix} + \begin{bmatrix} 0.218 \\ 0.655 \\ 0.094 \end{bmatrix} + \begin{bmatrix} 0.320 \\ 0.560 \\ 0.080 \end{bmatrix} = \overset{\text{Weighted Sum}}{\begin{bmatrix} 0.803 \\ 2.010 \\ 0.240 \end{bmatrix}}$$

Step 2: 0.803/0.265 = 3.030
2.010/0.655 = 3.069
0.240/0.080 = 3.000

Step 3: λ_{max} = (3.030 + 3.069 + 3.000)/3 = 3.033

Step 4: CI = (3.033 − 3)/2 = 0.017

Step 5: CR = 0.017/0.58 = 0.29

Since CR = 0.029 is less than 0.10, the degree of consistency exhibited in the pairwise comparison matrix for style is acceptable

16. a.

	Flavor		
Flavor	A	B	C
A	1	3	2
B	1/3	1	5
C	1/2	1/5	1

b. Step 1: Column totals are 11/6, 21/5, and 8

Step 2:

	Flavor		
Flavor	A	B	C
A	6/11	15/21	2/8
B	2/11	5/21	5/8
C	3/11	1/21	1/8

Step 3:

	Flavor			
Flavor	A	B	C	**Row Average**
A	0.545	0.714	0.250	0.503
B	0.182	0.238	0.625	0.348
C	0.273	0.048	0.125	0.149

c. Step 1:

$$0.503 \begin{bmatrix} 1 \\ 1/3 \\ 1/2 \end{bmatrix} + 0.348 \begin{bmatrix} 3 \\ 1 \\ 1/5 \end{bmatrix} + 0.149 \begin{bmatrix} 2 \\ 5 \\ 1 \end{bmatrix}$$

$$\begin{bmatrix} 0.503 \\ 0.168 \\ 0.252 \end{bmatrix} + \begin{bmatrix} 1.044 \\ 0.348 \\ 0.070 \end{bmatrix} + \begin{bmatrix} 0.298 \\ 0.745 \\ 0.149 \end{bmatrix} = \overset{\text{Weighted Sum}}{\begin{bmatrix} 1.845 \\ 1.261 \\ 0.471 \end{bmatrix}}$$

Step 2: 1.845/0.503 = 3.668
1.261/0.348 = 3.624
0.471/0.149 = 3.161

Step 3: λ_{max} = (3.668 + 3.624 + 3.161)/3 = 3.484

Step 4: CI = (3.484 − 3)/2 = 0.242

Step 5: CR = 0.242/0.58 = 0.417

Since CR = 0.417 is less than 0.10, the individual's judgments are not consistent

20. a.

b.

Criterion	Yield		Risk	
Yield: 0.667	CCI:	0.750	CCI:	0.333
Risk: 0.333	SRI:	0.250	SRI:	0.667

c.

	Criterion	
Alternative	Yield	Risk
CCI	0.750	0.333
SRI	0.250	0.667

Overall priority for CCI:

$$0.667(0.750) + 0.333(0.333) = 0.500 + 0.111 = 0.611$$

Overall priority for SRI:

$$0.667(0.250) + 0.333(0.667) = 0.167 + 0.222 = 0.389$$

CHAPTER 16

1. a.

Month	Time-Series Value	3-Month Moving Average Forecast	(Error)^2	4-Month Moving Average Forecast	(Error)^2
1	9.5				
2	9.3				
3	9.4				
4	9.6	9.40	0.04		
5	9.8	9.43	0.14	9.45	0.12
6	9.7	9.60	0.01	9.53	0.03
7	9.8	9.70	0.01	9.63	0.03
8	10.5	9.77	0.53	9.73	0.59
9	9.9	10.00	0.01	9.95	0.00
10	9.7	10.07	0.14	9.98	0.08
11	9.6	10.03	0.18	9.97	0.14
12	9.6	9.73	0.02	9.92	0.10
		Totals	1.08		1.09

$$\text{MSE(3-month)} = 1.08/9 = .12$$

$$\text{MSE(4-month)} = 1.09/8 = .14$$

Use 3-month moving averages.

b. Forecast $= (9.7 + 9.6 + 9.6)/3 = 9.63$

c. For the limited data provided, the 5-week moving average provides the smallest MSE

2. a.

Week	Time-Series Value	4-Week Moving Average Forecast	(Error)^2	5-Week Moving Average Forecast	(Error)^2
1	17				
2	21				
3	19				
4	23				
5	18	20.00	4.00		
6	16	20.25	18.06	19.60	12.96
7	20	19.00	1.00	19.40	0.36
8	18	19.25	1.56	19.20	1.44
9	22	18.00	16.00	19.00	9.00
10	20	19.00	1.00	18.80	1.44
11	15	20.00	25.00	19.20	17.64
12	22	18.75	10.56	19.00	9.00
		Totals	77.18		51.84

b. MSE(4-week) $= 77.18/8 = 9.65$
MSE(5-week) $= 51.84/7 = 7.41$

c. For the limited data provided, the 5-week moving average provides the smallest MSE

4.

Week	Time-Series Value	Forecast	Error	(Error)^2
1	17			
2	21	17.00	4.00	16.00
3	19	17.40	1.60	2.56
4	23	17.56	5.44	29.59
5	18	18.10	−0.10	0.01
6	16	18.09	−2.09	4.37
7	20	17.88	2.12	4.49
8	18	18.10	−0.10	0.01
9	22	18.09	3.91	15.29
10	20	18.48	1.52	2.31
11	15	18.63	−3.63	13.18
12	22	18.27	3.73	13.91
			Total	101.72

$$\text{MSE} = 101.72/11 = 9.25$$

$\alpha = 0.2$ provided a lower MSE; therefore $\alpha = 0.2$ is better than $\alpha = 0.1$

5. a.

Month	Y_t	3-Month Moving Averages Forecast	(Error)^2	$\alpha = 2$ Forecast	(Error)^2
1	80				
2	82			80.00	4.00
3	84			80.40	12.96
4	83	82.00	1.00	81.12	3.53
5	83	83.00	0.00	81.50	2.25
6	84	83.33	0.45	81.80	4.84
7	85	83.33	2.79	82.24	7.62
8	84	84.00	0.00	82.79	1.46
9	82	84.33	5.43	83.03	1.06
10	83	83.67	0.45	82.83	0.03
11	84	83.00	1.00	82.86	1.30
12	83	83.00	0.00	83.09	0.01
		Totals	11.12		39.06

$$\text{MSE(3-month)} = 11.12/9 = 1.24$$

$$\text{MSE}(\alpha = 0.2) = 39.06/11 = 3.55$$

Use 3-month moving averages

b. $(83 + 84 + 83)/3 = 83.3$

14. $\Sigma t = 21;\quad \Sigma t^2 = 91;\quad \Sigma Y_t = 117,100;$

$\Sigma t Y_t = 403,700;\quad n = 6$

$$b_1 = \frac{\Sigma t Y_t - (\Sigma t \Sigma Y_t)/n}{\Sigma t^2 - (\Sigma t)^2/n}$$

$$= \frac{403,700 - (21)(117,100)/6}{91 - (21)^2/6}$$

$$= \frac{-6,150}{17.5} = -351.429$$

$b_0 = \overline{Y} - b_1 \bar{t} = 19,516.667 - (-351.429)(3.5) = 20,746.67$

$T_t = 20,746.67 - 351.429t$

Conclusion: enrollment appears to be decreasing by an average of approximately 351 students per year

27. a. Four-quarter moving averages beginning with

$$(1690 + 940 + 2625 + 2500)/4 = 1938.75$$

Other moving averages are

1966.25	2002.50
1956.25	2052.50
2025.00	2060.00
1990.00	2123.75

b.

Quarter	Seasonal-Irregular Component Values		Seasonal Index	Adjusted Seasonal Index
1	0.904	0.900	0.9020	0.900
2	0.448	0.526	0.4970	0.486
3	1.344	1.453	1.3985	1.396
4	1.275	1.164	1.2195	1.217
			Total 4.0070	

Note: Adjustment for seasonal index = 4.000/4.007 = 0.9983

34.

Restaurant

(i)	x_i	y_i	$x_i y_i$	x_i^2
1	1	19	19	1
2	4	44	176	16
3	6	40	240	36
4	10	52	520	100
5	14	53	742	196
Totals	35	208	1697	349

$$\bar{x} = \frac{35}{5} = 7$$

$$\bar{y} = \frac{208}{5} = 41.6$$

$$b_1 = \frac{\Sigma x_i y_i - (\Sigma x_i \Sigma y_i)/n}{\Sigma x_i^2 - (\Sigma x_i)^2/n}$$

$$= \frac{1697 - (35)(208)/5}{349 - (35)^2/5}$$

$$= \frac{241}{104} = 2.317$$

$b_0 = \bar{y} - b_1 \bar{x} = 41.6 - 2.317(7) = 25.381$

$$\hat{y} = 25.381 + 2.317x$$

b. $\hat{y} = 25.381 + 2.317(8) = 43.917$ or \$43,917

CHAPTER 17

3. a. 0.10 as given by the transition probability

b. $\pi_1 = 0.90\pi_1 + 0.30\pi_2$ (1)

$\pi_2 = 0.10\pi_1 + 0.70\pi_2$ (2)

$\pi_1 + \pi_2 = 1$ (3)

Using (1) and (3),

$$0.10\pi_1 - 0.30\pi_2 = 0$$

$$0.10\pi_1 - 0.30(1 - \pi_1) = 0$$

$$0.10\pi_1 - 0.30 + 0.30\pi_1 = 0$$

$$0.40\pi_1 = 0.30$$

$$\pi_1 = 0.75$$

$$\pi_2 = (1 - \pi_1) = 0.25$$

7. a.

$$\pi_1 = 0.85\pi_1 + 0.20\pi_2 + 0.15\pi_3 \qquad (1)$$

$$\pi_2 = 0.10\pi_1 + 0.75\pi_2 + 0.10\pi_3 \qquad (2)$$

$$\pi_3 = 0.05\pi_1 + 0.05\pi_2 + 0.75\pi_3 \qquad (3)$$

$$\pi_1 + \pi_2 + \pi_3 = 1 \qquad (4)$$

Using (1), (2), and (4) provides three equations with three unknowns; solving provides $\pi_1 = 0.548$, $\pi_2 = 0.286$, and $\pi_3 = 0.166$

b. 16.6% as given by π_3

c. Quick Stop should take

$$667 - 0.548(1000) = 119 \text{ Murphy's customers}$$

and $333 - 0.286(1000) = \underline{\;47\;}$ Ashley's customers

Total 166 Quick Stop customers

11.

$$I = \begin{bmatrix} 1 & 0 \\ 0 & 1 \end{bmatrix} \qquad Q = \begin{bmatrix} 0.25 & 0.25 \\ 0.05 & 0.25 \end{bmatrix} \qquad (I - Q) = \begin{bmatrix} 0.75 & -0.25 \\ -0.05 & 0.75 \end{bmatrix}$$

$$N = (I - Q)^{-1} = \begin{bmatrix} 1.3636 & 0.4545 \\ 0.0909 & 1.3636 \end{bmatrix}$$

$$NR = \begin{bmatrix} 1.3636 & 0.4545 \\ 0.0909 & 1.3636 \end{bmatrix} \begin{bmatrix} 0.5 & 0.0 \\ 0.5 & 0.2 \end{bmatrix} = \begin{bmatrix} 0.909 & 0.091 \\ 0.727 & 0.273 \end{bmatrix}$$

$$BNR = [4000, 5000] \begin{bmatrix} 0.909 & 0.091 \\ 0.727 & 0.273 \end{bmatrix} = [7271, 1729]$$

Estimate $1729 in bad debts

CHAPTER 18

2. a. The numbers in the squares above each node represent the shortest route from that node to node 10

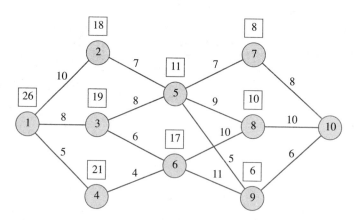

The shortest route is given by the sequence of nodes (1−4−6−9−10)

b. The shortest route from node 4 to node 10 is given by (4−6−9−10)

c.

Route	Value	Route	Value
(1−2−5−7−10)	32	(1−3−6−8−10)	34
(1−2−5−8−10)	36	(1−3−6−9−10)	31
(1−2−5−9−10)	28	(1−4−6−8−10)	29
(1−3−5−7−10)	31	(1−4−6−9−10)	26
(1−3−5−8−10)	35		
(1−3−5−9−10)	27		

3. Use four stages; one for each type of cargo. Let the state variable represent the amount of cargo space remaining.

a. In hundreds of pounds, we have up to 20 units of capacity available.

Stage 1 (Cargo Type 1):

x_1	0	1	2	d_1^*	$f_1(x_1)$	x_0
0−7	0	—	—	0	0	0−7
8−15	0	22	—	1	22	0−7
16−20	0	22	44	2	44	0−4

Stage 2 (Cargo Type 2):

x_2	0	1	2	d_2^*	$f_2(x_2)$	x_1
0−4	0	—	—	0	0	0−4
5−7	0	12	—	1	12	0−2
8−9	22	12	—	0	22	8−9
10−12	22	12	24	2	24	0−2
13−15	22	34	24	1	34	8−10
16−17	44	34	24	0	44	16−17
18−20	44	34	46	2	46	8−10

Stage 3 (Cargo Type 3):

x_3	0	1	2	3	4	d_3^*	$f_3(x_3)$	x_2
0–2	0	—	—	—	—	0	0	0–2
3–4	0	7	—	—	—	1	7	0–1
5	12	7	—	—	—	0	12	5
6–7	12	7	14	—	—	2	14	0–1
8	22	19	14	—	—	0	22	8
9	22	19	14	21	—	0	22	9
10	24	19	14	21	—	0	24	10
11	24	29	26	21	—	1	29	8
12	24	29	26	21	28	1	29	9
13	34	31	26	21	28	0	34	13
14–15	34	31	36	33	28	2	36	8–9
16	44	41	38	33	28	0	44	16
17	44	41	38	43	40	0	44	17
18	46	41	38	43	40	0	46	18
19	46	51	48	45	40	1	51	16
20	46	51	48	45	50	1	51	17

Stage 4 (Cargo Type 4):

x_4	0	1	2	3	d_4^*	$f_4(x_4)$	x_3
20	51	49	50	45	0	51	20

Tracing back through the tables, we find

Stage	State Variable Entering	Optimal Decision	State Variable Leaving
4	20	0	20
3	20	1	17
2	17	0	17
1	17	2	1

Load 1 unit of cargo type 3 and 2 units of cargo type 1 for a total return of $5100

b. Only the calculations for stage 4 need to be repeated; the entering value for the state variable is 18

x_4	0	1	2	3	d_4^*	$f_4(x_4)$	x_3
18	46	47	42	38	1	47	16

Optimal solution: $d_4 = 1$, $d_3 = 0$, $d_2 = 0$, $d_1 = 2$
Value = 47

10. The optimal production schedule is given below:

Month	Beginning Inventory	Production	Ending Inventory
1	10	20	10
2	10	20	0
3	0	30	0

CHAPTER 19

1. a.

$$\frac{df(x)}{dx} = 12 - 12x = 0$$

$$x = 1$$

$$\frac{d^2f(x)}{dx^2} = -12 < 0$$

Therefore $x = 1$ yields the maximum for the function; the value of the function at this maximum is

$$f(1) = 12(1) - 6(1)^2 - 30 = -24$$

b. Same solution as part (a)

c.
$$f(2) = 12(2) - 6(2)^2 - 30 = -30$$

$$f(10) = 12(10) - 6(10)^2 - 30 = -510$$

The maximum is at $x = 2$

2. a.
$$\frac{df(x)}{dx} = 9x^2 - 40x = 0$$

Solving, we get $x(9x - 40) = 0$; thus, $x = 0$ or $40/9$

$$\frac{d^2f(x)}{dx^2} = 18x - 40$$

At $x = 0$, we get $\frac{d^2f(0)}{dx^2} = -40 < 0$; thus, $x = 0$ yields a maximum

At $x = 40/9$, we get $\frac{d^2f(40/9)}{dx} = 40$; thus, $x = 40/9$ yields the minimum for the function

b.
$$f(0) = 60$$

$$f(4) = 3(4)^3 - 20(4)^2 + 60 = -68$$

Therefore, the minimum is at $x = 4$

7.
$$\frac{\partial f}{\partial x_1} = 8x_1 + 4x_2 - 8 = 0$$

$$\frac{\partial f}{\partial x_2} = 4x_2 + 4x_1 - 6 = 0$$

Solving these equations simultaneously, we obtain $x_1 = 1/2$ and $x_2 = 1$

$$\frac{\partial^2 f}{\partial x_1^2} = 8 \qquad \frac{\partial^2 f}{\partial x_1 \partial x_2} = 4$$

$$\frac{\partial^2 f}{\partial x_2 \partial x_1} = 4 \qquad \frac{\partial^2 f}{\partial x_2^2} = 4$$

$$\frac{\partial^2 f}{\partial x_1^2} = 8 > 0$$

$$\left(\frac{\partial^2 f}{\partial x_1^2}\right)\left(\frac{\partial^2 f}{\partial x_2^2}\right) - \left(\frac{\partial^2 f}{\partial x_1 \partial x_2}\right)^2 = (8)(4) - (4)^2 = 16 > 0$$

Therefore, $x_1 = 1/2$ and $x_2 = 1$ is a minimum solution for the problem

11. a. Setting up the Lagrangian function, we get

$$L(x_1, x_2, \lambda) = x_1^2 - 14x_1 + x_2^2 - 16x_2 + 113 + \lambda(2x_1 + 3x_2 - 12)$$

$$\frac{\partial L}{\partial x_1} = 2x_1 - 14 + 2\lambda = 0$$

$$\frac{\partial L}{\partial x_2} = 2x_2 - 16 + 3\lambda = 0$$

$$\frac{\partial L}{\partial \lambda} = 2x_1 + 3x_2 - 12 = 0$$

Solving these simultaneously yields

$$x_1^* = 3$$

$$x_2^* = 2$$

$$\lambda^* = 4$$

$$\frac{\partial^2 L(3, 2, 4)}{\partial x_1^2} = 2 \qquad \frac{\partial^2 L(3, 2, 4)}{\partial x_1 \partial x_2} = 0$$

$$\frac{\partial_2 L(3, 2, 4)}{\partial x_2 \partial x_1} = 0 \qquad \frac{\partial^2 L(3, 2, 4)}{\partial x_2^2} = 2$$

$$\frac{\partial^2 L(3, 2, 4)}{\partial x_1^2} = 2 > 0$$

$$\left(\frac{\partial^2 L(3, 2, 4)}{\partial x_1^2}\right)\left(\frac{\partial^2 L(3, 2, 4)}{\partial x_2^2}\right)$$

$$- \left[\frac{\partial^2 L(3, 2, 4)}{\partial x_1 \partial x_2}\right]^2 = (2)(2) - (0)^2 = 4 > 0$$

Therefore, we have found the minimum solution to the problem

b. Since $\lambda = 4$, we would expect the value of the solution to decrease by 4

Index

Numbers that are followed by an *f* are references to a figure. Numbers that are followed by a *t* are references to a table.